The Concise Blackwell Encyclopedia of Management

This encyclopedia is dedicated to my mentor and close friend,
Professor Sir Roland Smith, for his invaluable help, guidance
and friendship throughout my career. And to his wife,
Lady Joan Smith, for her unstinting support to myself and
my family.

Cary L. Cooper

The Concise Blackwell Encyclopedia of Management

Edited by Cary L. Cooper and Chris Argyris
Manchester School of Management and Harvard University

Consulting editors

Derek F. Channon
Imperial College, University of London

Gordon B. Davis
University of Minnesota

Barbara R. Lewis and Dale Littler
University of Manchester, Institute of Science and Technology

Robert E. McAuliffe
Babson College

Nigel Nicholson
London Business School

John O'Connell
American Graduate School of International Management (Thunderbird)

Dean Paxson and Douglas Wood
Manchester Business School

Lawrence H. Peters, Charles R. Greer, Stuart A. Youngblood
Texas Christian University

A. Rashad Abdel-khalik
University of Florida

Nigel Slack
Warwick University

Patricia H. Werhane and R. Edward Freeman
University of Virginia

Copyright© Blackwell Publishers Ltd, 1998
Editorial Organization© Cary L. Cooper, 1998

First published 1998

2 4 6 8 10 9 7 5 3 1

Blackwell Publishers Inc.
350 Main Street
Malden, Massachusetts 02148, USA

Blackwell Publishers Ltd
108 Cowley Road
Oxford OX4 1JF
UK

Library of Congress Cataloging-in-Publication Data

The concise Blackwell encyclopedia of management /
   edited by Cary L. Cooper and Chris Argyris; consulting editors, Lawrence H. Peters
. . . [et al.].
        p.   cm.
   Includes index.
   ISBN 0-631-20885-2. — ISBN 0-631-20911-5 (pbk.)
   1. Management–Encyclopedias.   I. Cooper, Cary L.   II. Argyris,
Chris, 1923–   .
   HD30.15.C66   1998   98-9489
   658'.003—dc21   CIP

British Library Cataloguing in Publication Data
A CIP catalogue record for this book is available from the British Library.

Typeset in 9 on 10pt Ehrhardt by Page Brothers, Norwich
Printed in Great Britain by T. J. International Ltd, Padstow, Cornwall

This book is printed on acid-free paper

—— Contents ——

—— Thematic Contents ——

International Management

Business Ethics

Human Resource Management

Managerial Economics

Management Information Systems

Contributors

A. Rashad Abdel-khalik, *University of Florida*
Chris Adams, *Andersen Consulting*
Seymour Adler, *Stevens Institute of Technology*
Reena Aggarwal, *Georgetown University*
George M. Alliger, *SUNY at Albany*
Teresa M. Amabile, *Harvard Business School*
Chris Argyris, *Harvard University*
Richard D. Arvey, *University of Minnesota*
James T. Austin, *Ohio State University*
Stephanos Avgeropoulos, *The Management School, Imperial College*
Kostas Axarloglou, *Babson College*
Frances L. Ayres, *University of Oklahoma*

Vickie Bajtelsmit, *Colorado State University*
Kashi R. Balachandran, *New York University*
Timothy T. Baldwin, *Indiana University*
David B. Balkin, *University of Colorado*
Paul Barnes, *Rutgers University*
William P. Barnett, *Stanford University*
Steve H. Barr, *North Carolina State University*
Jan Barton, *University of Alabama*
Bernard Bass, *SUNY, Binghamton*
Gilbert Becker, *St Anselms College*
David Bennett, *Aston Business School, Aston University*
H. John Bernardin, *Florida Atlantic University*
John Bessant, *University of Brighton*
Leonard Bierman, *Texas A&M University*
John Bigelow, *Boise State University*
Richard S. Blackburn, *University of North Carolina*
R. Ivan Blanco, *Barry University, Florida*
Matt Bloom, *Cornell University*
John Board, *London School of Economics*
John R. Boatright, *School of Business Administration, Loyola University*
Roberto Bonifaz, *Babson College*
Walter Borman, *University of South Florida*
John W. Boudreau, *Cornell University*
Norman E. Bowie, *Curtis L. Carson School of Management, University of Minnesota*

Bryan Boyd, *Arizona State University*
David Bracken, *University of South Florida*
Michael T. Brannick, *University of South Florida*
James A. Breaugh, *University of Missouri, St Louis*
William Breslin, *Harvard University*
Bob Bretz, *University of Iowa*
Michael Brocklehurst, *The Management School, Imperial College*
L. David Brown, *Boston University*
Susan A. Brown, *Indiana University*
Margaret Bruce, *Manchester School of Management*
Robert Bruner, *Darden Graduate School of Business, University of Virginia*
Allen Buchanan, *University of Wisconsin-Madison*
Elmer Burack, *University of Illinois, Chicago*
Peter Burcher, *Aston Business School, Aston University*
John G. Burgoyne, *Lancaster University*
Michael J. Burke, *Tulane University*
W. Warner Burke, *Teachers College, Columbia University*
Richard Butler, *University of Bradford*

Jeffrey L. Callen, *New York University*
Kim Cameron, *University of Michigan*
David Camino, *Universidad Carlos III de Madrid*
Robert L. Cardy, *Arizona State University*
Thomas Carson, *Loyola University, Chicago*
Wayne F. Cascio, *University of Colorado at Denver*
Philip Chang, *University of Calgary*
Derek F. Channon, *The Management School, Imperial College*
Julia Channon, *Price Waterhouse*
Georgia T. Chao, *Michigan State University*
C.S. Agnes Cheng, *University of Houston*
Norman L. Chervany, *University of Minnesota*
Frederick D.S. Choi, *New York University*
Andrew Clarkson, *Boston University*
Chris W. Clegg, *University of Sheffield*
Jeanette N. Cleveland, *Colorado State University*

Gwen Coats, *State University of New York, Albany*

Philip L. Cochran, *Penn State University*

Adrienne Colella, *Rutgers University*

Mary Ann Collins, *Brandeis University*

Rosann Collins, *University of South Florida*

John Cordery, *University of Western Australia*

Benita Cox, *The Management School, Imperial College*

James A. Craft, *University of Pittsburgh*

David Cravens, *Texas Christian University*

Thomas G. Cummings, *University of Southern California*

Joel E. Cutcher-Gershenfeld, *Michigan State University*

Amit Das, *Nanyang Technological University*

Gordon B. Davis, *University of Minnesota*

Dale L. Davison, *Thunderbird American Graduate School of International Management*

David L. Deephouse, *Louisiana State University*

J. Gregory Dees, *Graduate School of Business Administration, Harvard University*

John Delaney, *University of Iowa*

Suresh Deman, *University of Bradford and Mayo-Deman Consultants*

Peter Dempsey, *Rossmore Dempsey & Co*

Angelo S. DeNisi, *Rutgers University School of Management and Labor Relations*

Gerardine DeSanctis, *Duke University*

Gary W. Dickson, *North Carolina State University*

Robert Dipboye, *Rice University*

Greg Dobbins, *University of Tennessee*

Thomas Donaldson, *Wharton School, University of Pennsylvania*

George Dreher, *Indiana University*

Thomas W. Dunfee, *Wharton School, University of Pennsylvania*

Randall B. Dunham, *University of Wisconsin-Madison*

Ronald Duska, *American College*

James Dworkin, *Purdue University*

William Dyer, *Brigham Young University*

John Edmunds, *Babson College*

Miriam Erez, *Technion-Israel Institute of Technology*

Vihang R. Errunza, *McGill University*

Paul Evans, *INSEAD*

Gordon C. Everest, *University of Minnesota*

Ellen A. Fagenson-Eland, *George Mason University*

M. Ali Fekrat, *Georgetown University*

Daniel C. Feldman, *University of South Carolina*

Mark Fenton-O'Creevy, *London Business School*

Gerald R. Ferris, *University of Illinois*

Peter Feuille, *University of Illinois, Urbana-Champaign*

Stephen Fineman, *University of Bath*

Jack Fiorito, *Florida State University*

Cynthia D. Fisher, *Bond University*

Robert Folger, *Tulane University*

John A. Fossum, *University of Minnesota*

Colette A. Frayne, *California Polytechnic State University*

William C. Frederick, *Joseph M. Katz Graduate School of Business, University of Pittsburgh*

Dwight Frink, *University of Mississippi*

Daniel G. Gallagher, *James Madison University*

Robert D. Gatewood, *University of Georgia*

David Gefen, *Georgia State University*

Gordon Gemmill, *City University Business School*

Jennifer M. George, *Texas A&M University*

Barry Gerhart, *Cornell University*

J. Michael Geringer, *California Polytechnic State University*

Connie Gersick, *University of California, Los Angeles*

Robert A. Giacolone, *University of Richmond*

James Godfrey, *James Madison University*

Jayne M. Godfrey, *University of Tasmania*

Alan H. Goldman, *University of Miami*

Luis R. Gomez-Mejia, *Universidad Carlos III de Madrid*

Kenneth E. Goodpaster, *University of St Thomas*

Michael E. Gordon, *Rutgers University*

Linda S. Gottfredson, *University of Delaware*

Severin V. Grabski, *Michigan State University*

David A. Gray, *University of Texas, Arlington*

Michael Greatorex, *Manchester School of Management*

Jerald Greenberg, *Ohio State University*

Jeffrey Greenhaus, *Drexel University*

Steve Greenland, *Manchester School of Management*

Charles R. Greer, *Texas Christian University*

Martin Greller, *University of Wyoming*
Ricky W. Griffin, *Texas A&M University*
Dorothy Griffiths, *The Management School, Imperial College*
David Guest, *Birkbeck College, London*
Barbara A. Gutek, *University of Arizona*

J. Richard Hackman, *Harvard University*
Christian Haefke, *Institute for Advanced Studies, Vienna*
Jerald Hage, *University of Maryland*
Teoh Hai Yap, *Nanyang Technological University, Singapore*
Colin L. Hales, *University of Surrey*
Donald C. Hambrick, *Columbia University*
Christine Harland, *University of Bath*
Alan Harrison, *Cranfield School of Management, Cranfield University*
Edwin Hartman, *Rutgers University*
John Heap, *Leeds Metropolitan University*
Christian Helmstein, *Institute for Advanced Studies, Vienna*
Robert L. Heneman, *Ohio State University*
Peter Herriot, *Sundridge Park Management Centre*
Nigel Holden, *Manchester School of Management*
Edwin P. Hollander, *Bernard M. Baruch College, CUNY*
William Holley, *Auburn University*
Robert House, *Wharton School*
William Howell, *American Psychological Association*
Mark A. Huselid, *Rutgers University School of Management and Labor Relations*

Daniel Ilgen, *Michigan State University*
Blake Ives, *Southern Methodist University*
Ivailo Izvorski, *University of Yale*

Ellen Jackofsky, *Southern Methodist University*
Susan E. Jackson, *New York University*
Rick Jacobs, *Penn State University*
Kevin Jagiello, *Manchester Business School*
Brian D. Janz, *University of Memphis*
Paul Jarley, *Louisiana State University*
Donald Jarrell, *Drexel University*
Alicja A. Jaruga, *University of Lodz, Poland*
Cynthia Jeffrey, *Iowa State University*
Mariann Jelinek, *College of William and Mary*
Gary Johns, *Concordia University*

Nancy Brown Johnson, *University of Kentucky*
David Johnston, *Andersen Consulting*
Kent A. Jones, *Babson College*

Steven J. Kachelmeier, *University of Texas, Austin*
Aldona Kamela-Sowinska, *Poznan School of Economics, Poland*
Ruth Kanfer, *University of Minnesota*
John D. Keiser, *University of Massachusetts*
John Kelly, *London School of Economics and Political Science*
Ian Kessler, *Templeton College, Oxford*
William R. King, *University of Pittsburgh*
Richard Klimoski, *Ohio State University*
Debra Kolb, *Simmons College*
P.L. Koopman, *Free University, Amsterdam*
Ellen Ernst Kossek, *Michigan State University*
Kathy E. Kram, *Boston University*
Roderick Kramer, *Stanford University*

M. Ameziane Lasfer, *City University Business School*
Bill Lattimer, *Andersen Consulting*
Mark Laycock, *Bank of England*
Ricardo Leal, *University of Nevada, Reno*
Carrie Leana, *University of Pittsburgh*
Terry L. Leap, *Clemson University*
Gerald E. Ledford, Jr, *University of Southern California*
Barbara A. Lee, *Rutgers University*
David Lei, *Southern Methodist University*
Fiona Leverick, *Aberdeen Business School*
Joakim Levin, *Stockholm School of Economics*
Edward L. Levine, *University of South Florida*
Barbara Lewis, *Manchester School of Management*
Wei Li, *Fuqua School of Business*
Dale Littler, *Manchester School of Management*
Oliver London, *London and Associates*
Clinton O. Longenecker, *University of Toledo*
Joan Luft, *Michigan State University*

Robert McAuliffe, *Babson College*
Robert M. McCaffrey, *Cornell University*
James C. McKeown, *Pennsylvania State University*
Christopher McMahon, *University of California, Santa Barbara*

Thomas F. McMahon, *Loyola University, Chicago*
Lisa Mainiero, *Fairfield School of Business*
Gordon Mandry, *Manchester Business School*
Steven V. Mann, *University of South Carolina*
James Martin, *Wayne State University*
Mark J. Martinko, *Florida State University*
Richard O. Mason, *Southern Methodist University*
Marick Masters, *University of Pittsburgh*
Nicholas J. Mathys, *DePaul University*
Thomas C. Mawhinney
Larry M. May, *Washington University, St Louis*
Sumon C. Mazumdar
Bruce M. Meglino, *University of South Carolina*
Mark E. Mendenhall, *University of Tennessee*
Yaw M. Mensah, *Rutgers University, New Brunswick*
Marshall W. Mcyer, *University of Pennsylvania*
Susan Miller, *Durham University*
Vincent-Wayne Mitchell, *Manchester School of Management*
Michael H. Moffett, *Thunderbird American Graduate School of International Management*
Susan Albers Mohrman, *University of South Carolina*
Kevin W. Mossholder, *Louisana State University*
J. Keith Murnighan, *University of British Columbia*
Kevin R. Murphy, *Colorado State University*

Debra L. Nelson, *Oklahoma State University*
R. Ryan Nelson, *University of Virginia*
Jeffry Netter, *University of Georgia*
Jerry M. Newman, *SUNY, Buffalo*
David P. Newton, *Manchester Business School*
Nigel Nicholson, *London Business School*
Fred Niederman, *University of Baltimore*
Stella M. Nkomo, *University of North Carolina, Charlotteville*
David Norburn, *The Management School, Imperial College*

John O'Connell, *Thunderbird American Graduate School of International Management*
Greg Oldham, *University of Illinois*
Judy Olian, *University of Maryland*
Per Olsson, *Stockholm School of Economics*
Colleen O'Malley, *Transition Works*
Daniel Ortiz, *University of Virginia*

J. Douglas Orton, *Hautes Études Commerciales, Paris*
Paul Osterman, *Massachusetts Institute of Technology*
Catherine A. Ouellette, *American Institute for Managing Diversity*
Ben Oviatt, *Georgia State University*

Ramona L. Paetzold, *Texas A&M University*
Lynn Sharp Paine, *Graduate School of Business Administration, Harvard University*
Laurie Pant, *School of Management, Suffolk University*
Roy L. Payne, *University of Sheffield*
Jose Azevedo Pereira, *Manchester Business School*
Richard Peterson, *University of Washington*
Jon L. Pierce, *University of Minnesota, Duluth*
Lidija Polutnik, *Babson College*
Jeffrey T. Polzer, *Northwestern University*
Marshall Scott Poole, *University of Minnesota*
Sunil Poshakwale, *Manchester Business School*
Walter W. Powell, *University of Arizona*
Laura Power, *Treasury Department, Washington D.C.*
Elaine Pulakos, *Personnel Decisions Research Institute*
Vesa Puttonen, *Helsinki School of Economics and Business Administration*

James Campbell Quick, *University of Texas, Arlington*

Robert J. Rafalko, *Webster University*
David Ralston, *University of Connecticut*
Elizabeth C. Ravlin, *University of South Carolina*
Sangkyu Rho, *Seoul National University*
Djenan Ridjanovic, *Université Laval*
Peter Smith Ring, *Loyola Marymount University*
Catherine A. Riordan, *University of Missouri-Rolla*
David Rogers, *New York University*
Michelle A. Romero, *Georgia Institute of Technology*
Paul Rosenfeld
Joseph Rosse, *University of Colorado, Boulder*
Hannah R. Rothstein, *Baruch College*
Richard L. Rowan, *University of Pennsylvania*
Jill Rubery, *Manchester School of Managememt, UMIST*

Br. Leo V. Ryan, *DePaul University*

Paul Sackett, *University of Minnesota*

Marcus Sandver, *Ohio State University*

Edgar H. Schein, *Massachusetts Institute of Technology*

Frank Schmidt, *University of Iowa*

Neal Schmitt, *Michigan State University*

Herbert P. Schoch, *Nanyang Technological University, Singapore*

Richard J. Schoenberg, *The Management School, Imperial College*

Randall S. Schuler, *New York University*

Paul Seguin, *University of Michigan*

Manuel Serapio, *University of Colorado, Denver*

David Sharp, *University of Western Ontario*

James B. Shaw, *Bond University*

John C. Shearer, *Oklahoma State University*

Mark Sherman, *University of Houston, Clear Lake*

Caren Siehl, *Thunderbird American Graduate School of International Management*

Thomas F. Siems, *Federal Reserve Bank of Dallas*

John K. Simmons, *University of Florida*

Henry P. Sims, Jr, *University of Maryland, College Park*

Joseph F. Sinkey, Jr., *University of Georgia*

Nigel Slack, *Warwick Business School, University of Warwick*

Sandra Slaughter, *Carnegie Mellon University*

H. Jeff Smith, *Georgetown University*

Scott Snell, *Pennsylvania State University*

Paul E. Spector, *University of South Florida*

Gregory K. Stephens, *Texas Christian University*

Dianna Stone, *SUNY, Albany*

Mary Stone, *University of Alabama*

Thomas H. Stone, *Oklahoma State University*

Eugene Stone-Romero, *SUNY, Albany*

John Storey, *Open University*

Detmar W. Straub, *Georgia State University*

Linda Stroh, *Loyola University, Chicago*

Norman C. Strong, *University of Manchester*

Stephen Stumpf, *University of Tampa*

Charles Sutcliffe, *Southampton University*

Amadou N.R. Sy, *McGill University*

Stephen J. Taylor, *Lancaster University*

R. Roosevelt Thomas, *American Institute for Managing Diversity*

Joe Tidd, *The Management School, Imperial College*

Linda Klebe Trevino, *Smeal College of Business Administration, Pennsylvania State University*

Leo Troy, *Rutgers University*

Theofanis Tsoulouhas, *North Carolina State University*

Roger Tutterow, *Kennesaw State University*

David Twomey, *Boston University*

Andrew Van de Ven, *University of Minnesota*

Chris Veld, *Tilburg University*

Marc J. Ventresca, *Northwestern University*

Anil Verma, *University of Toronto*

Nicholas Vettas, *Fuqua School of Business*

Peter Villanova, *Appalachian State University*

Premal Vora, *King's College*

Toby D. Wall, *University of Sheffield*

John P. Wanous, *Ohio State University*

Hugh Watson, *University of Georgia*

Gary R. Weaver, *University of Delaware*

Ron Weber, *University of Queensland*

Theresa M. Welbourne, *Cornell University*

Ivo Welch, *Anderson Graduate School of Management, UCLA*

Patricia H. Werhane, *Darden Graduate School of Business Administration, University of Virginia*

Michael A. West, *University of Sheffield*

James C. Wetherbe, *University of Minnesota*

Hoyt Wheeler, *University of South Carolina*

David A. Whetten, *Brigham Young University*

Marleen Willekens, *Catholic University of Leuven*

Kevin Williams, *SUNY, Albany*

Dominic Wilson, *Manchester School of Management*

Douglas Wood, *Manchester Business School*

Richard W. Woodman, *Texas A&M University*

Steve Worrall, *Manchester School of Management*

Mo Yamin, *Manchester School of Management*

Chee Sing Yap, *National University of Singapore*

Arthur Yeung, *University of Michigan*

David Yorke, *Manchester School of Management*

William Youngdahl, *Arizona State University*

A

absenteeism The term can be defined as the failure to report for scheduled work. Absenteeism is distinguished from lateness or tardiness, which indicates a failure to show up for scheduled work on *time* and from turnover, which indicates a permanent break in the employment relationship. Traditionally, managers have been interested in absenteeism because of its cost to organizations, while academic researchers have been interested in absenteeism on the assumption that it indicates something about employees' social or psychological attachment to the organization (*see* COMMITMENT; PSYCHOLOGICAL CONTRACT).

The Measurement of Absenteeism

Many organizations are notoriously lax when it comes to recording systematically instances of absence. When they do so, they often codify absence instances with attributions as to cause which are of suspect accuracy (*see* ATTRIBUTION). Consequently, contemporary researchers most often simply divide absenteeism into *time lost*, the number of days missed over some period, and *frequency*, the number of inceptions or spells of absence over some period irrespective of the duration of each incident. To permit comparisons of employees with a different number of scheduled days or to characterize absenteeism at the group level these figures can also be expressed as rates. Following the logic that absence is missing *scheduled* work, not reporting due to jury duty, vacation, or maternity leave is not generally counted as absence.

Absence is a low base rate behavior, in that most employees exhibit relatively low absence levels while a few exhibit higher levels. Thus, a frequency distribution for absenteeism is truncated on the low end and positively skewed. Because it is a low base rate behavior, absence measures for individuals must be aggregated over a reasonably long period of time (3 to 12 months) to achieve adequate reliability of measurement. Even then, the reliability of absence measures (indexed by interperiod stability or internal consistency) is tenuous and varies across samples. Some validity evidence suggests that frequency of absence is more likely than time lost to reflect a voluntary component (Chadwick-Jones, Nicholson, & Brown, 1982; Hackett & Guion, 1985). Because of its nonnormal distribution, researchers should give serious consideration to transforming absence data or using alternative statistical procedures (e.g., tobit) in its analysis. Managers should be aware that a few extreme absentees can have a disproportionate effect on means calculated from absence distributions, especially for small samples.

The Correlates and Causes of Absenteeism

A longstanding tradition concerns the correlation between demographic variables and absenteeism. This research reveals reliable associations between AGE and absence among men (younger workers exhibit more absence

(Hackett, 1990)) and gender and absence (women are absent more than men) (*see* WOMEN AT WORK). However, little theory has emerged to explain these associations, and they tend to be confounded by differences in occupation and job STATUS.

Johns (1987) presents several "models" of absenteeism that correspond to both popular explanations and research-based explanations for absenteeism. Concerning the *medical model*, there is very little evidence regarding the association between verified illness and absence. However, self-reported health status is correlated with absence, and people tend to attribute the majority of their own absence to minor medical problems. The ultimate accuracy of such attributions is questionable, since "sickness" absence has motivational correlates, medical diagnoses often reflect prevailing community standards, and people sometimes adopt sick roles that manifest themselves in absence.

The *withdrawal model* suggests that absenteeism is an attempt to remove oneself temporarily from aversive working conditions. The voluminous literature on the relationship between JOB SATISFACTION and absenteeism reveals a very modest relationship, with dissatisfaction with the work itself being the facet most associated with absenteeism (Hackett & Guion, 1985). The progression-of-withdrawal hypothesis posits a movement from temporary absence to permanent turnover. In fact, there is a positive relationship between these variables at the individual level, a condition that is necessary but not sufficient to prove such a progression.

The *deviance model* derives from the negative consequences of absence for organizations. In its more elaborate form, it suggests that absentees harbor negative dispositional traits that render them unreliable (*see* PERSONALITY). People tend to make negative attributions about the causes of others' absenteeism, and absenteeism is a frequent cause of employee/management conflict. People also have a tendency to under-report their own absenteeism and to see their own behavior as exemplary compared to that of their coworkers and occupational peers (Johns, 1994). Evidence for an actual connection between negative traits and absenteeism is sparse and indirect. A necessary condition would be cross-situational consistency in absenteeism, and there is some evidence for that. More rigorous proof would be an association between absenteeism and other negative behaviors. Bycio's (1992) review indicates that more frequent absentees tend to be poorer performers and notes that "a disposition for delinquency" is one possible explanation.

The *economic model* of absence suggests that attendance behavior is influenced by economic and quasi-economic constraints and opportunities. Those who value highly their nonwork time are more likely to be absent, and looser contractual provisions regarding attendance result in more absence (*see* NONWORK/WORK). Absence tends to increase when unemployment falls and when lucrative overtime pay is available. Some INDUSTRIAL RELATIONS scholars have argued that absence is a form of unorganized conflict that substitutes for some of the functions of collective action.

The *cultural model* of absence begins with the observation that there is often more variance between aggregates of individuals (such as work groups, departments, organizations, occupations, industries, and nations) than within these aggregates. Mechanisms of social influence and control subsumed under the label absence culture have been advanced to account in part for these differences between groups (Chadwick-Jones et al., 1982; Johns & Nicholson, 1982). Some rich case studies of absence cultures exist, and work unit absence has been shown to account for individual absence over and above individual-level predictors. What is needed currently is more rigorous evidence on the formation and content of absence cultures (*see* ORGANIZATIONAL CULTURE).

In addition to the research subsumed under the above models, other eclectic themes can be seen in contemporary research. These include investigations of mood and absence (*see* EMOTIONS IN ORGANIZATIONS), the self-regulatory and coping functions of absence, and the prediction of absence using within-person rather than between-person models.

Managing Absenteeism

The deviance model has tended to dominate management approaches to absence. As a result, surveys show that punishment and discipline systems are the most common methods of controlling absence. Used alone, they are not especially effective because of negative side effects and because few employees are actually punished. More effective are mixed consequence systems that punish extreme offenders but reward good attenders with money, time off, and so on (Rhodes & Steers, 1990) (*see* REWARDS). JOB ENRICHMENT and flexitime have both been associated with reduced absence, as have SELF-MANAGEMENT programs that teach employees to regulate their own attendance behavior. Badly needed are theories that translate the likely causes of absenteeism into credible interventions and organizations with the foresight to experiment with these interventions. Obsession with extreme offenders has distracted managers from giving attention to the attendance behavior of *all* employees.

see also **Job characteristics; Motivation; Personality, Person–job fit; Performance; Stress**

Bibliography

Bycio, P. (1992). Job performance and absenteeism: A review and meta-analysis *Human Relations.*, 45, 193–220.

Chadwick-Jones, J. K., Nicholson, N. & Brown, C. (1982). Social psychology of absenteeism. New York: Praeger.

Goodman, P. S. & Atkin, R. S. (Eds), (1984). Absenteeism. San Francisco: Jossey-Bass.

Hackett, R. D. (1990). Age, tenure, and employee absenteeism *Human Relations.*, 43, 601–619.

Hackett, R. D. & Guion, R. M. (1985). A reevaluation of the absenteeism–job satisfaction relationship *Organizational Behavior and Human Decision Processes.*, 35, 340–381.

Johns, G. (1987). Understanding and managing absence from work In S. L. Dolan & R. S. Schuler (Eds), Canadian readings in personnel and human resources management. 324–335. St. Paul, MN: West.

Johns, G. (1994). Absenteeism estimates by employees and managers: Divergent perspectives and self-serving perceptions *Journal of Applied Psychology*, 79, 229–239.

Johns, G. & Nicholson, N. (1982). The meanings of absence: New strategies for theory and research *Research in Organizational Behavior.*, 4, 127–173.

Martocchio, J. J. & Harrison, D. A. (1993). To be there or not to be there? Questions, theories, and methods in absenteeism research *Research in Personnel and Human Resources Management.*, 11, 259–329.

Rhodes, S. R. & Steers, R. M. (1990). Managing employee absenteeism. Reading, MA: Addison-Wesley.

GARY JOHNS

accounting exposure   The risk of foreign exchange (currency) appreciation or depreciation which may alter the monetary values of accounting entries. Accounting exposure includes both translation risk and transaction risk. As an example, translation risk occurs when a parent organization must produce consolidated balance sheets for their multinational operations. In so doing, the parent company must translate the assets, liabilities, revenues, expenses, and income of their foreign operations into domestic currency terms. Transaction risk, occurs, on the other hand, when an organization is forced to pay for goods and services produced in another country. For example, a US computer manufacturer located in California would be required to pay a Japanese semiconductor manufacturer in Japanese yen, not in US dollars. The transaction, however, will need to be reported in US dollars on the US computer manufacturer's balance sheet. Changes in the value of foreign currency will affect the value of assets (translation) or the amount of foreign currency required to meet foreign obligations (transaction).

see also **Translation exposure**

Bibliography

Eiteman, D. K., Stonehill, A. J. & Moffett, M. H. (1992). *Multinational business finance.* 6th edn, Reading, MA: Addison-Wesley Publishing.

JOHN O'CONNELL

accounting income concepts   Economic gain is and has been a significant motivating factor underlying activities of both individuals and business entities, although the nature of the specific activities varies across different cultures and over the centuries. While the concept of economic gain remains a constant motivating factor underlying human behavior, its measurement varies considerably. In some cultures economic gain might be measured by the number of cows, horses, or camels one owns or the number of households one can maintain. In other cultures it might be measured by the quantity of some monetary unit that can be exchanged for desired possessions. Even where the measurement unit is universal, the measurement process is subject to the exercise of extensive judgment and even debate.

"Income" is a term commonly used in modern society to describe economic gain. But there is no universal agreement on a single definition of income, partly due to the need to measure income over short and somewhat arbitrary time periods. Lifetime income is a reasonably simple concept. One can compare an accepted basic measure of wealth commanded by an individual or other economic entity at the end of its life to the same measurement at the beginning of its life with the difference being income. One measurement of lifetime income is the quantity of cash commanded by an individual or other entity at the end minus the quantity of cash commanded at the beginning of its life. This assumes that all net assets are converted to cash. In other words, lifetime income is the net cash flow over the life of an entity. Net cash flow could be used to measure income over shorter interim time periods but most would argue that the ability to command future positive net cash flows is a better measure of economic gain than past cash flows for a short period of time. This opens the path for considerable judgment and debate on the measurement of economic gain or income.

A complication to the clarification of the concept of income is created by the existence of other closely related terms. Terms such as "profit" and "earnings" have often been used interchangeably with "income." There is also sometimes confusion about whether one is referring to a gross or a net measurement. In Statement of Financial Accounting Concepts No. 5 (1984) (SFAC 5), "Recognition and Measurement in Financial Statements of Business Enterprises," the US Financial Accounting Standards Board (FASB) chooses to use the term "earnings" rather than "income" and also introduces a concept described as "comprehensive income" (paras 33 to 42). Here we will consider the concept of income as a net measurement, more precisely described as the net change in economic position for an individual or other economic entity from specified sources. Economic position can be defined and measured in various ways and is sometimes referred to as "net wealth."

In discussing various concepts of income one might begin with current accounting practice. However, significant difficulties arise from this approach due to differences in the concept of income as well as the specific measurements across countries. Furthermore, income is commonly defined and measured according to specified rules rather than by the application of a clearly defined concept. In the USA the measurement of income is primarily governed by the application of rules relating to the measurement of revenue and expense. Thus, income is not clearly defined as a concept in accounting practice. Rather it is the result of the application of revenue recognition and expense matching concepts. In addition to articulation of the concepts of revenue recognition and expense matching, many rules have been promulgated by the FASB and other standard setting bodies to guide the measurement of revenues and expenses in specific situations, including specialized industries. Gains and losses are distinguished from revenues and expenses and are also included in the computation of income according to specific rules.

Although current accounting practice does not offer a clear concept of income, several concepts exist in the accounting and economic literature. The writings of the economist J. R. Hicks offer a good starting point. In his book *Value and Capital* he states that "it would seem that we ought to be able to define a man's income as the maximum value which he can consume during a week, and still be as well off at the end of the week as he was at the beginning" (p. 172). In order to apply this definition some measurement rules must also be specified. In a world of certainty, the measurement of all relevant future net cash flows discounted to the present by an appropriate discount rate would receive strong support among accounting theorists as the best measure of "well off." The change in

this measure during a period becomes the basis for determining income. (For a more complete discussion of the determination of income under certainty see R. K. Jaedicke & R. T. Sprouse, 1965.)

There is much disagreement on the measurement of income in the real world – the world of uncertainty. The discounting of estimated future cash flows offers one possibility. But the subjectivity inherent in this measurement process and the notion that such estimations may fall beyond the scope and responsibility of accounting drives one quickly to consider other measurement processes. As one evaluates other measurement processes and, therefore, alternative income concepts, it becomes paramount to consider the purpose of income measurement.

The conceptual framework articulated by the FASB offers one source of arguments concerning the purpose of income measurement. Statement of Financial Accounting Concepts No. 1 (1978) (SFAC 1), "Objectives of Financial Reporting by Business Enterprises," indicates that the basic purpose of financial reporting is to provide information that will assist in the prediction of future net cash flows (para. 37). The measurement and reporting of income is considered important in fulfilling this objective. It is often described as a measure of enterprise "performance." The FASB indicates that the primary focus of financial reporting is information about an enterprise's performance provided by measures of earnings and its components (SFAC 1, para. 43).

In Statement of Financial Accounting Concepts No. 2 (1980) (SFAC 2), "Qualitative Characteristics of Accounting Information," relevant information is described as information that is capable of making a difference in decisions. This occurs by improving decision-makers' capacities to predict or by confirming or changing earlier expectations. "Relevance" includes the characteristics of predictive value, feedback value, and timeliness (SFAC 2, paras 51 to 57). One might focus on the notion of feedback value and conclude that an income concept that focuses solely on completed or past events is sufficiently relevant. However, when considered in the context of the objectives of financial reporting, with the emphasis on providing information to assist in the assessment of future cash flows especially for investment decisions, predictive value seems to assume a higher degree of relevance. The theoretically preferred concept of income that discounts future cash flows under conditions of certainty adds further weight to the importance of predictability. In other words, income should measure economic gain in such a way that the prediction of future economic gains is enhanced.

Income and Capital Maintenance

Income concepts are best described through various definitions of capital maintenance. Although not identical in concept, capital maintenance can be related to notions of economic position, net wealth, and "as well off as" that are commonly used. The US Financial Accounting Standards Board (FASB) recognized the importance of explaining income concepts through reference to capital maintenance and attempted to describe the earnings (income) concept used in current accounting practice with reference to the maintenance of financial capital. But this is a nebulous concept that did little to clarify the nature of income.

Although not often described as a capital maintenance concept, one could argue that the strongest definition of capital maintenance is the maintenance of the ability to generate future net cash inflows. The direct measurement of this concept through the discounting of estimated future net cash flows is generally believed to be impractical under conditions of uncertainty and perhaps beyond the scope of current accounting responsibility.

A capital maintenance concept that has been discussed widely in the literature is the maintenance of physical capital. This is also sometimes referred to as the maintenance of productive or operating capacity. The underlying theory behind this concept is that an entity must provide for the replacement of all income-generating factors that have been consumed during a period before income occurs. The measurement process in the application of this theory focuses on the determination of replacement costs for consumed income-generating factors (expired assets). A potential problem inherent in this measurement process is that there are several replacement cost figures that may be available for a particular item. For example, the current and estimated future replacement costs of an item may differ. Also, an item may no longer be available or available only with improved technology. Conventional wisdom tends to favor using a replacement cost that best reflects the current cost of replacing a similar asset even if the asset is not available. This is commonly referred to as the "current cost." In periods of rising prices the use of replacement costs to measure expenses, as compared to the alternative of actual past prices paid, tends to reduce the computed income.

There are several potential variations in the suggested use of replacement costs in the measurement of income that do not strictly conform to the concept of physical capital maintenance. One variation is to subtract estimated replacement costs for expired assets from revenues to obtain an operating income and then adjust for the difference between estimated replacement and actual past costs of the expired assets to obtain net income. This results in a final income figure that is equal to the income obtained under current FASB guidelines and rules. This procedure yields income figures for both the physical and financial capital maintenance concepts. The operating income is the income figure according to the physical capital maintenance concept, while the final income figure is the income according to the FASB notion of financial capital maintenance.

A second variation is to consider any price changes during the period on assets still held at the end of the period as holding gains and losses. Those who support this approach argue that a gain or loss occurs due to the acquisition of an item at a price that differs from the current acquisition price. Thus, an item held during a period of changing prices creates a holding gain or loss. A price increase or holding gain would be added in arriving at income while a price decrease or holding loss would be deducted. Some have suggested disclosing this figure separately after income rather than adding or subtracting it directly in arriving at income.

Recognizing a distinction between general price level and specific price changes is another important issue for income measurement. Specific price changes are derived from the replacement costs for specific items. General price level changes are measured by an average of all price changes for a broad cross-section of items in the total economy through an index relating to some base year. This is often described as reflecting the changes in purchasing power of the basic monetary unit in a country, such as the dollar in the USA. In capital maintenance terms, computing income using general price indices is described conceptually as the maintenance of invested purchasing power. There are several problems and complexities associated with the recognition of general price level changes in computing income. Business entities, even very large entities, operate only in segments of the total economy. General price movements as determined by a large cross-section of items in the economy may not reflect the price changes experienced by a particular business entity. Another issue raised by consideration of general price level changes is the potential divergent impact of the changes on monetary versus nonmonetary items. Since general price level changes reflect a change in the purchasing power of the basic monetary unit, it is argued that a purchasing power gain or loss occurs on monetary items as they are held through periods of changing prices. For example, in a period of rising prices (decline in purchasing power) a loss occurs on monetary assets while a gain occurs on monetary liabilities. This potential gain or loss is further complicated by interest rates that often are attached to financial instruments considered as monetary items. If an interest rate attached to a monetary item such as a bond includes a charge for "inflation expectations," the theoretical purchasing power gain or loss is reduced.

Under the invested purchasing power concept of capital maintenance, nonmonetary items are restated by adjusting for the changes in the monetary unit that have been experienced since the acquisition of the item. The historical acquisition price of the item is typically restated by multiplying by the current general price level index over the index at the time of acquisition. Although the restatement does not result in a gain or loss on the item, the restatement does affect the measurement of income as adjusted expenses are related to adjusted revenues.

A business entity may experience general and specific prices moving in opposite directions. For example, the computer industry has recently experienced falling specific prices while general prices have increased mildly. The potential divergence between the general price level movement and the change in specific prices experienced by a particular entity during a period may affect the predictive quality of income computed for that entity when adjusting for general price level changes while items are replaced at specific prices. But the use of the specific price or replacement cost framework in computing income has potential predictive weaknesses as well. Actual replacement cost when an item is replaced may differ from the replacement cost estimated at the time the item was utilized and expensed. Also, a particular item may not be replaced by the same or even by a similar item. Changing technology, modification of product lines, and other changes can cause replacement costs to vary and muddle the predictive characteristics of income computed under a replacement costing framework. The use of the "current cost" system may improve the matching of revenues and expenses but may not necessarily be highly predictive of actual future replacement costs and/or future operating margins.

Adjustments for general price level changes may affect the measurement of lifetime income since general price level changes reflect the underlying fluctuations in the purchasing power of the monetary measuring unit. Cash remaining upon liquidation may not have the equivalent purchasing power as the beginning cash. A change in the purchasing power would cause the measured income to be different from the total difference in cash. Adjustment for specific price changes only, in the current or replacement cost framework, will not change lifetime income since fluctuations in the purchasing power of the monetary unit are not considered. Changes in specific replacement prices affect the measurement of income only while items are being held and replacement is anticipated. Therefore, the lifetime cash difference remaining after liquidation will be equal to the lifetime measured income.

There is some support for the use of exit market prices in measuring income. Accounting practice in the USA requires this for some items such as certain marketable securities held for sale. Agricultural products and precious metals are some other examples where this may occur. In these cases income is recognized before the item is sold. There are advocates who favor an increase in the use of exit market prices for items held and readily salable in the measurement of income. This would tend to advance the measurement of income to earlier periods in most cases but would not change total lifetime income.

To summarize, the measurement of income is a difficult task in the complex real world of economic uncertainties. Measurement is especially difficult in periods of changing prices. Both the concept of income and its measurement are subject to variations. Yet, income measurement is arguably the most important dimension of financial reporting and essential in meeting the basic objectives and purposes of accounting. Current accounting practice has generally relied on measurement rules for revenues, expenses, gains and losses in determining income. Prior debate and research have not resulted in agreement on a concept of income for accounting practice. Furthermore, clarification and agreement on a single concept of income is difficult in a world of changing prices and technology with potentially differing capital maintenance objectives.

Bibliography

Bedford, N. M. (1965). *Income Determination Theory: An Accounting Framework*. Reading: Addison Wesley.

Hicks, J. R. (1946). *Value and Capital*. Oxford: Clarendon Press. Second Edition.

Jaedicke, R. K. & Sprouse, R. T. (1965). *Accounting Flows: Income, Funds and Cash*. New Jersey: Prentice-Hall.

Johnson, L. T. & Storey, R. K. (1982). Recognition in Financial Statements: Underlying Concepts, and Practical Conventions. Stamford, CN.

Report of the Committee on Corporate Financial Reporting (1972). *Supplement to the Accounting Review*, 47.

Revsine, L. (1973). *Replacement Cost Accounting*. New Jersey: Prentice-Hall.

Solomons, David (1961). Economic and Accounting Concept of Income. *The Accounting Review* July.

JOHN K. SIMMONS

accounting profit Accounting profit is defined as total revenues from output sold in a given period minus those costs incurred during that period (including depreciation expenses). The difference between the accounting definition of profits and economic profits lies in how costs and depreciation are calculated (*see* ECONOMIC PROFIT). Under generally accepted accounting practices, all costs incurred by the firm in a given period are expensed in that period (except expenditures on tangible assets, which are depreciated over several periods). This means that expenditures on research and development, training, trademarks, goodwill, and patents (i.e. all sources of intangible capital) are expensed in the current period, even though they may yield benefits well into the future. As a result, accounting profits will overstate economic profits whenever current period profits were generated in part by previous investments in intangible assets because there are no accounting costs applied in the current period for those intangible assets and those assets are not often included in calculations of the firm's total value. In addition, the depreciation expense for tangible assets allowed under accounting rules is not the same as the ECONOMIC DEPRECIATION for those assets.

These problems with accounting measures of economic profits have led some economists to argue that there is no relationship between accounting profits and economic profits (Fisher and McGowan, 1983). This strong assertion has been challenged by several economists and remains controversial; see Long and Ravenscraft (1984) and Martin (1984). Salamon (1985) and Edwards, Kay and Mayer (1987) provide recommendations regarding proper adjustments of accounting profits and those circumstances where they will more reliably approximate economic profits. Salamon suggests using conditional internal rate of return (IRR) estimates from financial statements as a proxy for the economic rate of return which can be used to infer the measurement errors from using accounting profits. He found that accounting rates of return, while strongly correlated with the estimated IRR, nevertheless showed considerable variation that the IRR could not explain. The measurement error from using accounting rates of return was systematically related to firm size and therefore cast doubts on cross-section studies of the relationship between concentration and profitability.

Bibliography

Edwards, J., Kay, J. & Mayer, C. (1987). *The Economic Analysis of Accounting Profitability*. Oxford: OUP.

Fisher, F. M. & McGowan, J. J. (1983). On the misuse of accounting rates of return to infer monopoly profits. *American Economic Review*, 73, 82–97.

Long, W. F. & Ravenscraft, D. J. (1984). The misuse of accounting rates of return: comment. *American Economic Review*, 74, 494–500.

Martin, S. (1984). The misuse of accounting rates of return: comment. *American Economic Review*, 74, 501–506.

Salamon, G. L. (1985). Accounting rates of return. *American Economic Review*, 75, 495–504.

ROBERT E. MCAULIFFE

acculturation Acculturation is the process one goes through to become as comfortable as possible in another culture. Probably the most common method of acculturation is that of assimilating portions of the new culture to go along with those you already have. This does not involve giving up your own culture, but instead, adding those features of the new culture which allow you to function more effectively. There are also those people who attempt to avoid acculturation by separating themselves as much as possible from the local culture. They associate only with those persons of their own culture. This approach builds walls between cultures and is not suggested as an approach if intercultural understanding and dealings are intended.

Bibliography

Bird, A. & Dunbar, R. (1991). Getting the job done over there: Improving expatriate productivity. *National Productivity Review* Spring, 145–56.

Mendenhall, M. & Oddou, G. (1985). The dimensions of expatriate acculturation: A review. *Academy of Management Review*, **10 (1)**, 39–47.

JOHN O'CONNELL

acquisition strategy Acquisition provides a rapid means of gaining an established product market position. Compared to the alternate routes for achieving growth or diversification, acquisitions overcome the relatively long timescales and potential resource constraints of internal development and do not involve the dilution of control inherent within STRATEGIC ALLIANCES.

Acquisitions may be a particularly attractive means of corporate development under certain strategic and financial conditions. In mature industries containing a number of established players, entry via acquisition can avoid the competitive reaction that can accompany attempts to enter the industry by internal development: rather than intensifying the rivalry by adding a further player, the potential competition is purchased. In other industries in which competitive advantage is held in assets built up over considerable periods of time, for example the back-catalogs in the record or film industries, acquisitions can immediately achieve a market position that would be virtually impossible to develop internally. The Japanese electronics company Sony, for example, has achieved this with its acquisition of CBS Records and Columbia Pictures.

Financially, acquisitive growth may be particularly attractive to a quoted company if its price: earnings ratio is relatively high compared to that of potential target companies. Under such circumstances an acquisition funded by shares may provide an immediate earnings per share enhancement to the acquiring firm. A further stimulus to the acquisition boom of the late 1980s in Britain was the existence of accounting standards that permitted acquirers to offset the goodwill element of an acquisition's cost against reserves rather than treating it as an asset that had to be depreciated over time, reducing future stated profits.

The importance of acquisitions is evidenced by the volume of activity. In 1994, US companies spent in excess of $222 billion on domestic acquisitions and a further $24 billion on cross-border transactions. Comparative figures for companies within the European Union are $67 billion and $60 billion respectively (data source: *Acquisitions Monthly*). However, acquisitions are not without their risks: empirical studies have consistently shown failure rates approaching 50 per cent, regardless of the criteria used.

A recent study by McKinsey and Company revealed that 43 per cent of a sample of international acquisitions failed to produce a financial return that met or exceeded the acquirer's cost of capital (Bleeke & Ernst, 1993). Non-financial studies show little improvement over John Kitching's (1974) early finding that between 45 per cent and 50 per cent of acquisitions are considered failures or not worth repeating by the managements involved. Further support comes from Michael Porter's (1987) examination of the diversification record of large US firms over the period 1950–86. He found that 53 per cent of all acquisitions were subsequently divested, rising to 74 per cent for unrelated acquisitions.

As one would expect given this performance record, a significant amount of research has been conducted to examine the factors determining acquisition success or failure (see Haspeslagh & Jemison (1991, pp. 292–309) for a concise review of the research literature). Two key success criteria emerge. First, there must be clear opportunities to create value through the acquisition and, second, the acquired company must be effectively integrated into the new parent in a way that takes account of both strategic and human considerations. Each is discussed in turn below.

The purchase price of an acquisition typically includes a bid-premium of 30–40 per cent over the previous market value of the target company. Premiums of that order in general make it difficult for acquisitions to be a financial success for the acquiring company. Many acquisitions fail because the perceived benefits of increased market share and technological, manufacturing, or market synergies fail to increase profit margins or raise turnover by the amount necessary to justify the price paid to conclude the deal. Acquisitions can only be justified in cases in which the post-merger benefits have been solidly defined. In order to successfully create value through acquisition, the future cashflow stream of the acquired company has to be improved by an amount equal to the bid-premium, plus the often overlooked costs incurred in integrating the acquisition, and the costs incurred in making the bid itself. Four basic value-creation mechanisms are available to achieve this:

1. *Resource sharing*, in which certain operating assets of the two merging companies are combined and rationalized, leading to cost reductions through economies of scale or scope. (The British pharmaceutical company Glaxo planned to save $600 million annually following its acquisition of Wellcome by combining headquarters operations, and rationalizing duplicated R&D facilities onto selected sites.)

2. *Skills transfer*, in which value-adding skills such as production technology, distribution knowledge, or financial control skills are transferred from the acquiring firm to the acquired, or vice versa. Additional value is created through the resulting reduction in costs or improvement in market position. The effective transfer of functional skills involves both a process of teaching and learning across the two organizations, and therefore tends to be a longer-term process than resource sharing. Nevertheless, it is often the primary value-creating mechanism available in *cross-border* acquisitions, in which the opportunities to share operational resources may be limited by geographic distance. For example, in its acquisition of the Spanish brewer Cruz del Campo, the drinks company Guinness planned to recoup the acquisition premium by using its marketing expertise to establish

Cruz as a major national brand in the fragmented Spanish market.

3. *Combination benefits.* These are size-related benefits such as increased market power, purchasing power, or the transfer of financial resources. A company making a large acquisition within its existing industry, or a series of smaller ones, may succeed in raising profit margins by effecting a transformation of the industry structure. The emergence of a dominant player within the industry should reduce the extent of competitive rivalry, as well as providing increased bargaining power over both suppliers and customers for the acquiring company. The European food processing industry, for example, has consolidated rapidly through acquisitions, driven both by a desire to reduce competitive rivalry and a belief that larger brand portfolios will help to maintain margins in the face of increasing retailer concentration. Financially based combination benefits may be available. The superior credit rating of an acquirer may be used to add value by refinancing the debt within an acquired company at a lower interest rate. In other instances in which the acquired company has been a loss-maker prior to acquisition, the associated tax credits can be consolidated to the new parent, thereby reducing the latter's tax charge.

4. *Restructuring* is applicable when the acquired company contains undervalued or underutilized assets. Here, acquisition costs are recouped by divesting certain assets at their true market value, and by raising the productivity of remaining assets. The latter may be accomplished by closing down surplus capacity, reducing head office staff, or rationalizing unprofitable product lines. Very often the two elements are combined: for example, the closure of surplus capacity may lead to a vacant factory site which can then be sold off at a premium for redevelopment. A further form of restructuring is the concept of "unbundling." This involves acquiring an existing conglomerate (or other portfolio of businesses) the market value of which is less than the sum of the individual constituent businesses. The businesses are then sold off piecemeal, creating a surplus over the acquisition cost. Restructuring is essentially financially based, in that it does not require any strategic capability transfer between the two firms. Rather, the skill of the acquirer is in recognizing and being able to realize the true value of the targets' assets. A classic illustration of value-creation through restructur-

ing is Hanson plc's acquisition of the diversified tobacco company, Imperial. Hanson paid $5 billion for Imperial and within a year had sold off its food and brewing interests, along with its London head office, for $3 billion, leaving it with the core tobacco business that generated 60 per cent of Imperial's previous profits for only 40 per cent of the acquisition cost.

The presence of value-creating opportunities does not in itself guarantee a successful acquisition. Plans have to be effectively implemented before the benefits can be realized in practice. This is the second area in which acquisitions frequently fail. In many instances organizational issues block the ability of the acquirer to create the planned value. Key personnel may depart following the acquisition, clashes of organizational culture may lead to mistrust and lack of communication, or inappropriate control systems may hinder the efficiency of the newly acquired firm.

Haspeslagh & Jemison's (1991) comprehensive study of the acquisition process has highlighted the fact that the appropriate form of post-acquisition integration will depend on two principal characteristics of the acquisition. First, the value-creation mechanism(s) will determine the degree of *strategic interdependence* that needs to be established between the two companies. Resource sharing and skills transfer imply high to moderate strategic interdependence respectively, while combination benefits and restructuring imply little or no interdependence. Second, the extent to which it is necessary to maintain the autonomy of the acquired company in order to preserve its distinctive skills will determine the need for *organizational autonomy*. Where critical employees are loyal to a distinctive corporate culture, as in many service businesses, it may be important to preserve that culture post-acquisition. Consideration of these characteristics suggests the appropriate form of post-acquisition strategy, as illustrated in figure 1.

Effective implementation also depends on creating an atmosphere of mutual cooperation following the acquisition. Resource sharing, skills transfer and, to a lesser extent, combination benefits all create value through the transfer of strategic capabilities between the acquiring and acquired firms. Because of the high degree of change often involved, and the uncertainty likely to be felt by employees on both sides following the acquisition, it is critical that the acquirer works to create an overall atmosphere that is conducive to the required capability transfer. Haspeslagh & Jemison

Need For Strategic Interdependence

		Low	High
Need for Organisational Autonomy	High	Preservation	Symbiosis
	Low	Holding	Absorption

Figure 1 Types of acquisition integration approach.
Source: Haspeslagh & Jemison (1991).

(1991) argue that there are five key ingredients to such an atmosphere:

1. *Reciprocal organizational understanding.* In order to work together effectively, both companies need to understand each other's history, culture, and management style. This two-way learning process is particularly important in the context of skills transfer, as the acquirer must ensure that the source and origins of the sought-after skills are not inadvertently destroyed during the integration process.

2. *Willingness to work together.* Employees of both companies may have a natural reluctance to cooperate together post-acquisition. Fears over job security, changes in management style, or simple distrust of the new organization may all hinder the willingness to work together. Research suggests that the negotiation stage of an acquisition can play an important role in creating an atmosphere of cooperation. Successful implementation is more likely where there is a clear vision of the future, assurances are maintained, and concern is shown for the people involved. Post-acquisition, reward and evaluation systems also can be used to encourage cooperation.

3. *Capacity to transfer and receive the capability.* In order for skills transfer to occur, it has to be possible to accurately identify and define the skills and to actually effect their transfer. In some smaller acquisitions, for instance, it may prove difficult to transfer the acquirer's control and reporting systems, as the receiving management does not have the time both to collect substantial amounts of additional data and continue to run its business as before.

4. *Discretionary resources.* Managements need to keep in mind that acquisitions frequently take up more managerial resource than was planned initially. Once a fuller understanding of the newly acquired company is developed post-acquisition, new opportunities and problems will often emerge that require managerial time and attention.

5. *Cause–effect understanding of benefits.* Finally, the correct atmosphere for implementation can only be generated when there is a clear understanding of how value will be created through the acquisition. Those involved in the value-creation process must understand the benefits sought and the costs involved in achieving them. The detailed knowledge about these two elements may be held at different organizational levels. Executive management will have conceptualized the benefits of acquisition, but operating management who will conduct the day-to-day implementation frequently hold the knowledge about the associated costs. Open communication between those charged with planning and implementing the acquisition becomes critical. Value can only be created when the acquisition benefits outweigh the implementation costs.

Bibliography

Bleeke, J. & Ernst, D. (eds), (1993). *Collaborating to compete: using strategic alliances and acquisitions in the global marketplace.* New York: John Wiley.
Cartwright, S. & Cooper, C. (1992) *Mergers and acquisitions: the human factor Oxford4 Butterworth–Heinemann.*
Haspeslagh, P. & Jemison, D. (1991). *Managing acquisitions: creating value through corporate renewal.* New York: Free Press.
Kitching, J. (1967). Why do mergers miscarry? *Harvard Business Review*, 45, 84–101.
Kitching, J. (1964). Winning and losing with European acquisitions. *Harvard Business Review*, 52, 124–36.
Norburn, D. & Schoenberg, R. (1994). European cross-border acquisition: how was it for you? *Long Range Planning*, 27 (4) 25–34.
Porter, M. (1987). From competitive advantage to corporate strategy. *Harvard Business Review* (May–June), 43–59.

RICHARD SCHOENBERG

adaptability screening   The process of determining one's ability to deal with overseas assignments. Screening takes the form of testing (among other skills) the ability to deal with change; handle stress; make decisions without full knowledge; and be at ease in cultures which are entirely different than that of the person being tested. Screening can be an essential part of planning for the success of an expatriate.

Bibliography

Brown, R. (1987). How to choose the best expatriates. *Personnel Management* June, 67.
Naumann, E. (1993). Organizational predictors of expatriate job satisfaction. *Journal of International Business Studies* 61–4.

JOHN O'CONNELL

adoption process   The consumer adoption process is a micro process and focuses on the "mental process through which an individual consumer passes from first hearing about an innovation, to final adoption," i.e., the consumer goes through a series of stages of acceptance in the process of adopting a new idea.

Rogers (1983) defines these stages as the following: Awareness: the consumer is exposed to a product innovation, is cognizant of it, but lacks information about it. Interest: the consumer is stimulated to seek information about an innovation. Evaluation: the consumer considers whether or not it would make sense to try the innovation, a "mental trial." Trial: the consumer tries the innovation on a small scale, if possible, to improve his/her estimate of the product's utility. Adoption/rejection: the consumer decides to make full/regular use of the product.

An alternative model, offered by Robertson (1971), the "acceptance process," has stages of problem recognition, awareness, comprehension, attitude formation, legitimation/conviction, trial, and adoption. This model focuses on the use of particular information sources at the various stages. Typically, impersonal sources (e.g., MASS MEDIA) have most value in creating initial product awareness, and INTERPERSONAL COMMUNICATIONS have most value at the later, evaluative, stages.

Time pervades the adoption process in relation to: the time from awareness of a new product to purchase (for an individual consumer or household); the identification of adopter categories; and rate of adoption. With respect to adopter categories, Rogers (1983) assumed a normally distributed adopter pattern of: innovators, early adopters, early majority, late majority, and laggards. Rate of adoption refers to how quickly a product innovation is accepted by those who will adopt it; for example mobile telephones and video recorders have been adopted much more quickly than dishwashers and electric toothbrushes.

The adoption process is affected by product characteristics (*see* DIFFUSION PROCESS) and by consumer variables. With respect to consumer variables, a number of researchers have tried to profile early adopters and consumer innovators in relation to: demographic and socioeconomic factors, personality traits, perceptions of risk, product interest, consumption characteristics, media habits, and opinion leadership, but have found varying conclusions.

Bibliography

Engel, J. F., Blackwell, R. D. & Miniard, P. W. (1990). *Consumer behaviour* 6th edn, Orlando, FL: The Dryden Press. Chapter 23.

Robertson, T. R. (1971). *Innovative behaviour and communication.* New York: Holt, Rinehart & Winston.

Rogers, E. M. (1976). New product adoption and diffusion. *Journal of Consumer Research,* **2**, March.

Rogers, E. M. (1983). *Diffusion of innovations* 3rd edn, New York: Free Press.

Rogers, E. M & Shoemaker, F. L. (1971). *Communication of innovations* 2nd edn, New York: Free Press.

Schiffman, L. G. & Kanuk, L. Z. (1991). *Consumer behaviour* 4th edn, Prentice-Hall. Chapter 18.

BARBARA LEWIS

advanced manufacturing technology Advanced manufacturing technology (AMT) is an umbrella term used to describe a wide range of automation and related technologies which have emerged during the past two decades as a consequence of developments in information technology (IT). The label "advanced" derives from the perception in the 1970s that IT applied in manufacturing would open up radically different ways of doing things and would require a different approach to its management. It was widely expected that such a "revolution" in manufacturing technology would have an equally powerful impact on productivity and performance – and as a result there was strong pressure on firms to adopt this new generation of technology.

Underpinning this was the growing recognition that the emergence of IT would accelerate developments along three important paths in manufacturing:

- It would open up dramatic new possibilities in the automation of manual tasks.
- It would facilitate the integration of such automation.
- It would be applicable across a wide range of manufacturing sectors.

Originally mechanization was aimed at substituting manual labor with mechanical equipment; as the pace of industrialization grew so did the attempt to take this one stage further and replace the monitoring and control activities in manufacturing by some form of automatic device. This trend was limited by the availability of suitable technology until the emergence of electronics. Experiments during the Second World War gave a considerable boost to automation, and the development of digital computers in the 1960s enabled a new generation of automatic control. These systems were originally applied only in large, capital-intensive industries, but diffused more widely as computing power became more easily available. With the development of the microprocessor it became feasible to automate individual machines and functions. Diffusion of such automation accelerated rapidly during the 1980s, and spread across from large capital-intensive firms through to very small and specialized applications and sectors. For some, microelectronics-based automation became something of a solution looking for a problem.

From the late 1970s the trend towards integration began to accelerate. There were distinct limits to what could be integrated mechanically, but the potential of IT to communicate in a common language of electronic signals enabled the emergence of integrated systems for monitoring and controlling industrial applications. At first this was confined to simple integration of functions within a particular item of equipment; then it spread to linked applications within a sphere of activity, after which it began to open up integration between functional areas and beyond. Significantly this moved the emphasis from what might be termed "substitution innovation" (doing what had always been done but a little better, for example faster or more accurately), towards doing completely new things or doing old things in radically new ways. This opened up the possibilities for using AMT strategically, for example, in making the business more flexible, faster, or more customer responsive.

IT offers radical improvements in the processing, storage, retrieval, and communication of information. Because much of manufacturing involves information activity there is considerable scope for improvement through IT. Recognition of the huge possibilities in applying IT led to its being seen as heralding a new Industrial Revolution, with electronics playing the role which steam power had done in the eighteenth century.

Nature of AMT

AMT is not simply the application of IT but its combination with several other technologies to enable a

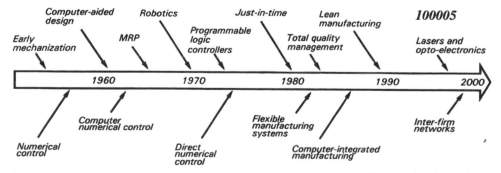

Figure 1 Convergent streams in AMT

particular set of applications. It can be usefully represented as a convergent stream which continues to develop, as shown in figure 1. Characteristic of these component technologies is a three-stage process, moving from discrete automation of individual tasks, through increasing integration of functions to a final stage in which the basic configuration is adapted and extended to suit widely different applications.

The emergence of AMT can be seen through considering some particular elements which illustrate these trends. FLEXIBLE MANUFACTURING SYSTEMS (FMS) are the archetypal manifestation of AMT, at least in engineering-based manufacture, although their component parts are themselves applied much more widely in other industries. robotics are used to manipulate parts, tools and materials, automated guided vehicles (AGVs) are used to transport materials or assemblies, and programmable logic controllers (PLCs) are used to monitor and control most types of process. All can be integrated to different levels of sophistication. Other applications of AMT, which demonstrate the same pattern of evolution from discrete automation and "substitution" innovation towards integrated and more strategic innovations, include computer-aided design (CAD) and computer-aided production management systems, based on versions of material requirements planning. Other elements in the AMT convergent stream include "mechatronics" (the convergence of mechanical and electronic systems), laser and other optical technologies, and the increasing use of new materials and forming processes.

Managing AMT

AMT appeared to represent a perfect marriage between technological potential and the manufacturing challenges of the late twentieth century. Industrial experience in a variety of applications confirmed the powerful advantages which could be used technically and also strategically. But in the late 1980s evidence began to accumulate about problems with achieving these advantages. In a few extreme cases the considerable investment made in AMT failed completely; but in most cases what was reported was a general feeling of expectations not being fully met. It became clear that unlocking the full potential offered by AMT involved more than simply adopting the technology.

Several studies showed that two key features are associated with successful implementation of AMT. The first is that the investment needs to be made within the context of a clear strategic framework. Rather than selecting and investing in CIM because it is fashionable, successful firms have a clear understanding of their business, knowing where they want to be in the marketplace and how they plan to compete, and the implications this has for manufacturing. They also know their present strengths and weaknesses within their manufacturing operations (in terms of equipment, facilities, experience, and skills) and can plan a step-by-step strategy which builds up to highly integrated automation in a series of stages rather than in a single step. This underlines the importance of manufacturing strategy as a precursor to investment in AMT.

The second key point is that successful firms recognize that they need to make significant and far-reaching changes to the way production is organized and managed. Using a "revolutionary" technology such as CIM requires a similarly radical degree of organizational change along a number of dimensions, including the skills profile, the functional and hierarchical structure, the philosophy of management and control, and the underlying culture of the organization. The nature of the organizational changes required depends on the scale of technological shift (small changes can often be absorbed with only slight variations on the existing pattern, whereas larger shifts require a fundamental rethink of the way the organization operates). Equally, technologies which span more than one functional boundary are likely to pose problems of organizational integration; for example, one of the major requirements in effective CAD/CAM utilization is the organization of the multidisciplinary, multifunctional design process to enable close co-operation and integration.

The dimensions of such change vary with each application but there is a general trend towards a new model for manufacturing organization. This includes elements such as more emphasis on skills and on training, more team working, more decentralized autonomy, flatter structures, and closer integration between different functional areas. AMT provides a catalyst for moving towards this kind of model since it is unlikely to deliver its full benefits without such changes.

The lists below indicate typical dimensions of change in organization design (Bessant et al., 1992).

Work organization:
(1) from single skill to multiskill developments;
(2) from high division of labor to integrated tasks;
(3) from long skill lifecycle to short skill lifecycle;
(4) from skill life = employee life to skill life & employee life;
(5) from individual work/accountability to team work/accountability;
(6) from payment by results to alternative payment systems;
(7) from supervisor-controlled to supervisor-supported;
(8) from low work discretion to increased flexibility/autonomy.

Changes in management organization:
(9) from sharp line staff boundary to blurred boundaries;
(10) from steep pyramid to flat structure;
(11) from vertical communication to network communication;
(12) from formal control to "holographic adjustment";
(13) from functional structures to product-/project-/customer-based;
(14) from differentiated status to single status
(15) from rigid and non-participative to flexible-participative.

Inter-organization relationships:
(16) from tight boundaries between firms to blurred boundaries;
(17) from "arm's length dealing" to co-operative relations
(18) from short-term to long-term relationships;
(19) from confrontational to co-operative relationships/partnerships;
(20) lack of customer involvement to "customer is king."

Significantly, much of the evolution of this alternative model for manufacturing organization took place in parallel with the emergence of AMT. Concepts like just-in-time, total quality management, and cellular manufacturing were applied with increasing frequency and it became clear that many of the benefits offered by AMT could also be realized (at lower cost and with less organizational disruption) through the adoption of new organizational forms. A key theme in lean manufacturing is that many of the differences between "best practice" plants and others lie in work organization and production management, rather than in levels of AMT being deployed.

The emerging prescription for successful AMT implementation is one which combines the two themes of technological and organizational change, and employs AMT to augment rather than supplant a skilled workforce organized around high quality, customer-focused, flexible teams. There is no conflict but rather a complementarity; the nature and direction of organizational change (new LAYOUT patterns, new work organization, new organization structures, etc.) are precisely those which are needed to support more advanced and capital-intensive applications of AMT. This model should be seen not simply as the extension of technical integration but rather as the convergence of two streams (new IT based equipment and systems and new approaches like just-in-time and total quality management). Rather than simply computer-integrated manufacturing, perhaps a better term would be "total integrated manufacturing."

Bibliography

Bessant, J. (1991). *Managing advanced manufacturing technology: The challenge of the fifth wave.* Oxford/Manchester: NCC-Blackwell.

Bessant, J., Smith, S., Tranfield, D. & Levy, P. (1992). *Factory 2000: organisation design for the factory of the future. International Studies of Management and Organisation,* **22**.

Diebold, J. (1964). *Beyond automation: Managerial problems of an exploding technology.* New York: McGraw-Hill.

Ettlie, J. (1988). *Taking charge of manufacturing.* San Francisco: Jossey-Bass.

Jacobsson, S. & Edquist, C. (1986). *Flexible automation.* Oxford: Basil Blackwell.

Jaikumar, R. (1986). Post-industrial manufacturing. *Harvard Business Review,* **64**, 6.

Majchrzak, A. (1988). *The human side of factory automation.* San Francisco: Jossey-Bass.

JOHN BESSANT

advantage matrix   During the 1970s, the Boston Consulting Group recognized that the GROWTH SHARE MATRIX had a number of limitations, in that an underlying experience effect (*see* EXPERIENCE AND LEARNING EFFECTS) was not always present and that differentiated products need not be as price-sensitive as undifferentiated or commodity products. As a result, the Advantage Matrix was developed, as shown in figure 1. In this system four generic environments were identified on the basis of the potential size of competitive advantage that could be generated, and the number of ways in which a competitor could establish a leadership position within an industry.

Volume businesses, stalemate businesses, fragmented businesses, and specialized businesses are identified within this system. As shown in figure 1, only in volume businesses does the historic experience effect (*see* EXPERIENCE AND LEARNING EFFECTS) analysis tend to hold. In specialized businesses a relationship also exists between size and profitability within specific but different segments. In stalemate and fragmented businesses, size *per se* does not necessarily determine relative cost. Despite the BCG's modification of the Growth Share Matrix for portfolio planning, the revised matrix is much less well known and, regrettably, the deficiencies of the original concept remain insufficiently discussed.

Bibliography

Boston Consulting Group (1974). *Segmentation and strategy.* Boston, MA: Boston Consulting Group.

Boston Consulting Group (1974). *Specialization.* Boston, MA: Boston Consulting Group.

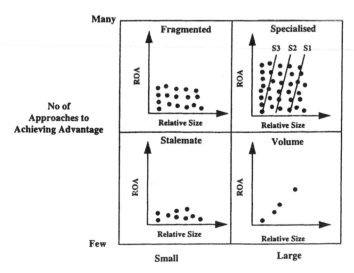

Figure 1 The BCG Advantage Matrix.
Source: Boston Consulting Group.

Rowe, A.J., Mason, R. O., Dickel, K. E., Mann, R. B. & Mockler, R. J. (1994). *Strategic management* 4th edn, Reading, MA: Addison-Wesley. See pp. 119–22.

DEREK F. CHANNON

advertising   Advertising is a paid form of non-personal presentation and communication about an organization and/or its goods and services, by an identified sponsor, that is transmitted to a target audience through a mass medium.

Advertising is a one-way communication from an organization to a customer and is subject to the consumer selective processes of: exposure, perception, selection, distortion, and retention, i.e., the audience is not obligated to be attentive or respond, which in turn depends on: consumer attributes, needs and values, predispositions, characteristics of the company and its messages, and channels of communications. Key features of advertising are: its public presentation, which confers a legitimacy; its persuasive nature, which is possible through repetition; and its expressive nature in so far as it dramatizes a company and its products or services.

Advertising is an integral element of an organization's MARKETING COMMUNICATIONS. It may be planned and executed within an organization or handed over to specialists, i.e., advertising agencies. Advertising is an industry in its own right although it employs relatively few people, the major expenditures being for media time and space.

The major stages in the development of an organization's advertising are: setting advertising objectives; deciding on the budget; planning messages; selecting the media; and evaluating advertising effectiveness.

Advertising objectives flow from prior decisions on an organization's target MARKET (or segments; (*see* MARKET SEGMENTATION), market POSITIONING and MARKETING MIX and are various (e.g., Colley (1961) lists 52 possible objectives). They are concerned with informing, persuading and reminding current and potential buyers/customers/consumers, including other organizations in the distribution chain, with respect to products, and organizations/institutions. Product and brand advertising is typically focused on generating or defending sales whereas institutional advertising is usually concerned with promoting an organization's image or reputation, developing goodwill, or improving a company's relationships with various groups to include customers, channels (of distribution) members, suppliers, shareholders, employees, and the general public.

In setting the advertising budget, organizations may take account of factors such as stage in the PRODUCT LIFE CYCLE, MARKET SHARE and customer base, competition, advertising frequency, and product substitutability. These and other variables are built into advertising expenditure models which, as a result of developing computer technology, are becoming increasingly complex. The advertising budget can be established on the basis of what is affordable, as a percentage of sales, on the basis of competitors' expenditures, on the basis of objectives and tasks.

Advertising messages represent the creative aspect of advertising and organizations are concerned with developing messages, evaluating and selecting among them, and executing them effectively.

In deciding on advertising media, it is necessary to take account of the desired reach, frequency, and impact; choose among the major media types and vehicles; and decide on media timing.

The choice of media types is influenced by considerations such as the product/service being advertised, target audience media habits, the advantages and limitations of the media, and their costs. Advertising media comprise: television, radio, newspapers, magazines, trade journals, posters (billboards), and DIRECT MAIL. They are distinguished from other forms of communication (*see* MARKETING COMMUNICATIONS and COMMUNICATIONS MIX), e.g., PUBLICITY, because the time and/or space has to be paid for.

Developing of advertising messages and choice of media is influenced, in part, by product sensitivity and advertising controls. For example, companies need to be aware of the sensitive nature of advertising alcohol and tobacco, the misuse of which may contribute to health and social problems. Advertising controls embrace government (legal) regulations and self-regulation. Various legal statutes impinge on advertising, e.g., the Trades Descriptions Act, the Medicines Act, food and drug labeling requirements, consumer credit regulations, together with restrictions with respect to the advertising of alcohol, tobacco, medicines, professional services, etc. Examples of industry self-regulation may be seen in various codes of practice, the Advertising Standards Authority, and the television advertising standards authorities.

The effectiveness of advertisements may be assessed in two major ways: pre-testing adverts (e.g., copy testing) and post-evaluating their effectiveness (e.g., recall and recognition tests). Advertisers also try to measure the communications effects on awareness, knowledge, preferences, and sales, although it is accepted that relationships between advertising and sales are not necessarily causal due to: the influence of other variables in the marketing mix; competitors' activities; and sales effects over time, e.g., adverts may not be seen immediately, impact may be later, there may be carry-over effects, or sales may be brought forward at the expense of future sales.

Bibliography
Colley, R. H. (1961). *Defining advertising goals for measured advertising results.* New York: Association of National Advertisers.
Dibb, S., Simkin, L., Pride, W. M. & Ferrell, O. C. (1994). *Marketing concepts and strategies* European edn, London: Houghton Mifflin Co. Chapter 15.
Kotler, P. (1994). *Marketing management: Analysis, planning, implementation and control* 8th edn, Englewood Cliffs, NJ: Prentice-Hall. Chapter 23.

BARBARA LEWIS

affirmative action   Affirmative action is the practice of giving explicit consideration to race, gender, national origin, or some other protected characteristic in making an employment decision. It is designed to counter the lingering effects of prior discrimination, whether intentional or not, by employers individually and collectively, as well as to provide a workforce more representative of the gender and ethnic makeup of the qualified labor market for the positions within an organization.

Affirmative action is required by federal law for recipients of federal contracts, may be ordered by a court as part of the settlement or remedy in a lawsuit charging an employer with discrimination, or may be voluntary.

Required Affirmative Action

Executive Orders 11246 and 11375 require federal contractors and subcontractors to practice affirmative action in hiring and in other employment decisions (such as promotions, job assignments). The Office of Federal Contract Compliance Programs, part of the US Department of Labor, may conduct compliance reviews, either before or after the contract is awarded, may receive and investigate complaints from current employees or from applicants, and may commence administrative proceedings or judicial action. Remedies for violations of the Executive Orders include termination of the contract, debarment from future federal contracts, or injunctions.

Affirmative Action as a Remedy

Federal courts have ordered employers or trade unions to engage in race- or gender-conscious affirmative action as a remedy for prior intentional discrimination. For example, in *Local 28 of the Sheet Metal Workers' International Assn* v. *EEOC*, 478 US 421 (1986), the Supreme Court approved explicit quotas for admission to union membership to remedy prior intentional race discrimination that was "persistent" and "egregious." A similar outcome for gender discrimination occurred in *EEOC* v. *AT&T*, 365 F. Supp. 1105 (E.D. Pa. 1973) (see Kirp et al., 1986, pp. 161–6 for a critical analysis of this case and other court-ordered affirmative action settlements related to gender).

Voluntary Affirmative Action

Voluntary affirmative action differs from court-ordered affirmative action in that the employer need not admit to prior discriminatory employment practices. The employer must first develop an affirmative action plan that meets the criteria listed in *United Steelworkers of America* v. *Weber*, 443 US 193 (1979): (a) the plan cannot "unnecessarily trammel" the interests of majority employees by requiring their discharge; (b) the plan cannot create an absolute bar to the advancement of majority employees, but a delay in advancement, in order to give minority employees an earlier opportunity at advancement, is permissible; and (c) the plan must be temporary in that it must be designed to eliminate a "manifest racial imbalance," but not operate to maintain that balance once it is attained. Preferences must cease when balance is attained.

The Court approved a voluntary affirmative action plan in *Johnson* v. *Transportation Agency*, 480 US 616 (1987), in which the agency used gender as one criterion among several to select a woman for promotion to the position of road dispatcher. When, however, a layoff or other job loss is at stake, the outcome has been quite different. In *Wygant* v. *Jackson Board of Education*, 476 US 267 (1986), the Supreme Court ruled that a layoff plan that sought to maintain the same proportion of minority teachers after the layoff as previously violated the US Constitution's Equal Protection Clause. The Court denied that affirmative action could be a remedy for "societal discrimination" if there was no evidence of past intentional discrimination by the School Board.

Bibliography
Kirp, D. L., Yudof, M. G. & Franks, M. S. (1986). *Gender Justice*, Chicago: University of Chicago Press.

BARBARA LEE

agency theory When human interaction is viewed through the lens of the economist, it is presupposed that all individuals act in accordance with their self-interest. Moreover, individuals are assumed to be cognizant of the self-interest motivations of others and can form unbiased expectations about how these motivations will guide their behavior. Conflicts of interest naturally arise. These conflicts are apparent when two individuals form an agency relationship, i.e. one individual (principal) engages another individual (agent) to perform some service on his/her behalf. A fundamental feature of this contract is the delegation of some decision-making authority to the agent. Agency theory is an economic framework employed to analyze these contracting relationships. Jensen and Meckling (1976) present the first unified treatment of agency theory.

Unless incentives are provided to do otherwise or unless they are constrained in some other manner, agents will take actions that are in their self-interest. These actions are not necessarily consistent with the principal's interests. Accordingly, a principal will expend resources in two ways to limit the agent's diverging behavior: (1) structure the contract so as to give the agent appropriate incentives to take actions that are consistent with the principal's interests and (2) monitor the agent's behavior over the contract's life. Conversely, agents may also find it optimal to expend resources to guarantee they will not take actions detrimental to the principal's interests (i.e. bonding costs). These expenditures by principal and/or agent may be pecuniary/non-pecuniary and are the costs of the agency relationship.

Given costly contracting, it is infeasible to structure a contract so that the interests of both the principal and agent are perfectly aligned. Both parties incur monitoring costs and bonding costs up to the point where the marginal benefits equal the marginal costs. Even so, there will be some divergence between the agent's actions and the principal's interests. The reduction in the principal's welfare arising from this divergence is an additional cost of an agency relationship (i.e. "residual loss"). Therefore, Jensen and Meckling (1976) define agency costs as the sum of: (1) the principal's monitoring expenditures; (2) the agent's bonding expenditures; and (3) the residual loss.

Barnea et al. (1985) divide agency theory into two parts according to the type of contractual relationship examined – the economic theory of agency and the financial theory of agency. The economic theory of agency examines the relationship between a single principal who provides capital and an agent (manager) whose efforts are required to produce some good or service. The principal receives a claim on the firm's end-of-period value. Agents are compensated for their efforts by a dollar wage, a claim on the end-of-period firm value, or some combination of the two.

Two significant agency problems arise from this relationship. First, agents will not put forward their best efforts unless provided the proper incentives to do so (i.e.

the incentive problem). Second, both the principal and agent share in the end-of-period firm value and since this value is unknown at the time the contract is negotiated, there is a risk sharing between the two parties (i.e. the risk-sharing problem). For example, a contract that provides a constant dollar compensation for the agent (principal) implies that all the risk is borne by the principal (agent).

Contracts that simultaneously solve the incentive problem and the risk-sharing problem are referred to as "first-best." First-best contracts provide agents with incentives to expend an optimal amount of effort while producing an optimal distribution of risk between principal and agent. A vast literature examines these issues (see e.g. Ross, 1973; Shavell, 1979; Holmstrom, 1979).

The financial theory of agency examines contractual relationships that arise in financial markets. Three classes appear in the finance literature: (1) partial ownership of the firm by an owner-manager; (2) debt financing with limited liability; and (3) information asymmetry. A corporation is considered to be a nexus for a set of contracting relationships (Jensen and Meckling, 1976). Not surprisingly, conflicts arise among the various contracting parties (manager, shareholder, bondholders, etc.).

When the firm manager does not own 100 percent of the equity, conflicts may develop between managers and shareholders. Managers make decisions that maximize their own utility. Consequently, a partial owner-manager's decisions may differ from those of a manager who owns 100 percent of the equity. For example, Jensen (1986) argues that there are agency costs associated with free cash flow. Free cash flow is discretionary cash available to managers in excess of funds required to invest in all positive net present value projects. If there are funds remaining after investing in all positive net present value projects, managers have incentives to misuse free cash flow by investing in projects that will increase their own utility at the expense of shareholders (see Mann and Sicherman, 1991).

Conflicts also arise between stockholders and bondholders when debt financing is combined with limited liability. For example, using an analogy between a call option and equity in a levered firm (Black and Scholes, 1973; Galai and Masulis, 1976), one can argue that increasing the variance of the return on the firm's assets will increase equity value (due to the call option feature) and reduce debt value (by increasing the default probability). Simply put, high variance capital investment projects increase shareholder wealth through expropriation from the bondholders. Obviously, bondholders are cognizant of these incentives and place restrictions on shareholder behavior (e.g. debt covenants).

The asymmetric information problem manifests itself when a firm's management seeks to finance an investment project by selling securities (Myers and Majluf, 1984). Managers may possess some private information about the firm's investment project that cannot be credibly conveyed (without cost) to the market due to a moral hazard problem. A firm's securities will command a lower price than if all participants possessed the same information. The information asymmetry can be resolved in principle with various signaling mechanisms. Ross (1977) demonstrates how a manager compensated by a known incentive schedule can use the firm's financial structure to convey private information to the market.

Bibliography

Barnea, A., Haugen, R. & Senbet, L. (1985). *Agency problems and financial contracting.* Englewood Cliffs, NJ: Prentice Hall.
Black, F. & Scholes, M. (1973). The pricing of options and corporate liabilities. *Journal of Political Economy*, 81, 637–54.
Galai, D. & Masulis, R. (1976). The option pricing model and the risk factor of stock. *Journal of Financial Economics*, 3, 53–82.
Holmstrom, B. (1979). Moral hazard and observability. *Bell Journal of Economics*, 10, 74–91.
Jensen, M. (1986). Agency costs of free cash flow. *American Economic Review*, 76, 323–29.
Jensen, M. & Meckling, W. (1976). Theory of the firm: managerial behavior, agency costs, and ownership structure. *Journal of Financial Economics*, 3, 306–60.
Mann, S. & Sicherman, N. (1991). The agency costs of free cash flow: acquisition activity and equity issues. *Journal of Business*, 64, 213–24.
Myers, S. & Majluf, M. (1984). Corporate financing and investment decisions when firms have information that investors do not have. *Journal of Financial Economics*, 13, 187–221.
Ross, S. (1973). The economic theory of agency: the principal's problem. *American Economic Review*, 62, 134–39.
Ross, S. (1977). The determination of financial structure: the incentive signalling approach. *Bell Journal of Economics*, 8, 23–40.
Shavell, S. (1979). Risk-sharing and incentives in the principal–agent relationship. *Bell Journal of Economics*, 10, 55–73.

STEVEN V. MANN

aggregate capacity management   Aggregate capacity management is the activity of setting the capacity levels of an organization in the medium term. The important characteristic of capacity management here is that it is concerned with capacity measured in aggregated terms. Thus aggregate plans may assume that the mix of different products and services will remain relatively constant during the planning period.

Typically, in aggregate capacity management, operations managers are faced with a forecast of demand which is unlikely to be either certain or constant. They will also have some idea of their own ability to meet this demand. Nevertheless, before any further decisions are taken they must have quantitative data on both capacity and demand. So step one will be to measure the aggregate demand and capacity levels for the planning period. The second step will be to identify the alternative capacity plans which could be adopted in response to the demand fluctuations. The third step will be to choose the most appropriate capacity plan for their circumstances.

Measuring Demand and Capacity

Demand forecasting is a major input into the capacity management decision. As far as capacity management is concerned there are three requirements from a demand forecast. The first is that it is expressed in terms which are useful for capacity management, which means it should give an indication of the demands that will be placed on an operation's capacity, and expressed in the same units. The second is that it is as accurate as possible, and the third that it should give an indication of relative uncertainty, so that operations managers can make a judgment between plans that would, at one extreme, virtually guarantee the operation's ability to meet actual demand, and, at the other, plans that minimize costs.

In many organizations aggregate capacity management is concerned largely with coping with seasonal demand fluctuations. Almost all products and services have some seasonality of demand and some also have seasonality of supply.

The Alternative Capacity Plans

There are three "pure" options for coping with supply or demand variation:

- Ignore the fluctuations and keep activity levels constant (level capacity plan).
- Adjust capacity to reflect the fluctuations in demand (chase demand plan).
- Attempt to change demand to fit capacity availability (demand management).

In practice most organizations will use a mixture of all of these "pure" plans, although often one plan may dominate.

In a level capacity plan, the processing capacity is set at a uniform level throughout the planning period, regardless of the fluctuations in forecast demand. This means that the same number of staff operate the same processes and should therefore be capable of producing the same aggregate output in each period. Where non-perishable materials are processed, but not immediately sold, they can be transferred to finished goods inventory in anticipation of sales at a later time period. This can provide stable employment patterns, high process utilization, and usually also high productivity with low unit costs. Unfortunately, it can also create considerable inventory. Nor are such plans suitable for "perishable" products, products which are tailor-made against specific customer requirements, or products susceptible to obsolescence.

Very high underutilization levels can make level capacity plans prohibitively expensive in many service operations, but may be considered appropriate where the opportunity costs of individual lost sales are very high, for example, in high-margin retailing. It is also possible to set the capacity somewhat below the forecast peak demand level in order to reduce the degree of underutilization. However, in the periods where demand is expected to exceed planned capacity, customer service may deteriorate.

The opposite of a level capacity plan is one which attempts to match capacity closely to the varying levels of forecast demand. Such pure "chase" demand plans may not appeal to operations which manufacture standard, non-perishable products. A pure chase demand plan is more usually adopted by operations which cannot store their output such as service operations or manufacturers of perishable products. Where output can be stored the chase demand policy might be adopted in order to minimize or eliminate finished goods inventory.

The chase demand approach requires that capacity is adjusted by some means. There are a number of different methods of achieving this, although all may not be feasible for all types of operation.

Overtime and idle time.   Often the quickest and most convenient method of adjusting capacity is by varying the number of productive hours worked by the staff in the operation. The costs associated with this method are overtime, or in the case of idle time, the costs of paying staff who are not engaged in direct productive work.

Varying the size of the workforce.   If capacity is largely governed by workforce size, one way to adjust capacity is to adjust the size of the workforce. This is done by hiring extra staff during periods of high demand and laying them off as demand falls. However, there are cost, and possibly also, ethical implications to be taken into account before adopting such a method. The costs of hiring extra staff include those associated with recruitment as well as the costs of low productivity while new staff go through the LEARNING CURVES. The costs of lay-off may include possible severance payments, but might also include the loss of morale in the operation and loss of goodwill in the local labor market.

Using part-time staff.   A variation on the previous strategy is to recruit staff on a part-time basis, that is for less than the normal working day. This method is extensively used in service operations such as supermarkets and fast food restaurants, but it is also used by some manufacturers to staff an evening shift after the normal working day. However, if the fixed costs of employment for each employee, irrespective of how long he or she works, are high, then using this method may not be worthwhile.

Subcontracting.   In periods of high demand an operation might buy capacity from other organizations. Again, though, there are costs associated with this method. The most obvious one is that subcontracting can be expensive because of the subcontractor's margin. Nor may a subcontractor be as motivated to deliver on time or to the desired levels of quality.

Many organizations have recognized the benefits of attempting to manage demand in various ways. The objective is to transfer customer demand from peak periods to quiet periods. This is usually beyond the immediate responsibility of operations managers, whose primary role is to identify and evaluate the benefits of demand management, and to ensure that the resulting changes in demand can be satisfactorily met by the operations system. One method of managing demand is to change demand by altering part of the "marketing mix," for example by changing prices or promotional activities to make them more attractive in off-peak periods. A more radical policy may be to create alternative products or services to fill capacity in quiet periods.

Choosing an Aggregate Capacity Management Approach

An operation must be aware of the consequences of adopting each plan. For example, a manufacturer, given an idea of current capacity and given a demand forecast, must calculate the effect of setting an output rate at a particular level. A method which is frequently cited as helping to assess the consequences of adopting capacity plans is the use of cumulative representations of demand and capacity. The most useful consequence of this is that, by plotting capacity on a cumulative graph, the feasibility and consequences of a capacity plan can be assessed. Some impression of the inventory implications can also be gained from a cumulative representation by judging the area between the cumulative production and demand curves. This represents the amount of inventory carried over the period.

The cumulative representation approach succeeds in indicating where operations managers can plan to provide the appropriate level of capacity required at points of time in the future. However, in practice, the management of capacity is a far more dynamic process which involves controlling and reacting to actual demand and actual capacity as it occurs. This aggregate capacity control process can be seen as a sequence of partially reactive capacity decision processes.

see also **Capacity strategy; Inventory management**

Bibliography

Vollmann, T. E., Berry, W. L. & Whybark, D. C. (1992). *Manufacturing planning and control systems.* 3rd edn, Boston, MA: Irwin.

NIGEL SLACK

Aida model This is one of a number of models of MARKETING COMMUNICATIONS which show how a targeted buyer or customer progresses from a state of unawareness of a product or service to purchase of it. The Aida model is an acronym for: Attention → Interest → Desire → Action.

The first term relates to the cognitive stage of the process, indicating a need for the marketing communicator to gain the receiver's attention before attempting to do anything else. Developing interest and desire (to purchase) are elements in the affective stage, i.e., where positive attitudes toward and preference for the product or service are sought. Action is the conative stage (the purchase).

Measures taken before and after a form of communication is used will enable objective(s) to be set and the success of it to be analyzed. Progression logically through the stages is not always possible – indeed much depends on the product or service being offered and the target groups of receivers.

see also **Communications objectives**

Bibliography

Cox, K. K. & Enis, B. M. (1972). *The marketing research process.* Pacific Palisades, CA: Goodyear Publishing Co., Inc.
Kotler, P. (1994). *Marketing management: Analysis, planning, implementation and control* 8th edn, Englewood Cliffs, NJ: Prentice-Hall. Chapter 22.
Strong, E. K. (1925). *The psychology of selling.* New York: McGraw-Hill.

DAVID YORKE

AIDS awareness training Acquired Immune Deficiency Syndrome (AIDS) awareness training entails educating members of an organization about Human Immunodeficiency Virus (HIV) infection, how it is spread, and new developments in HIV/AIDS research and treatment. Training also focuses on ensuring that HIV-positive employees are treated appropriately by their supervisors, coworkers, and the organization as a whole, have their rights to privacy respected, and are able to remain productive as long as they can. Dispelling myths about HIV and AIDS, educating employees in prevention, and communicating an organization's policies are important elements. Training can include the use of videos, group discussions, seminars, workshops, forums, and presentations as well as materials.

Bibliography

Esposito, M. D. & Myers, J. E. (1993). Managing AIDS in the workplace. *Employee Relations*, 19, 53–75.

Pincus, L. B. & Trivedi, S. M. (1994). A time for action: responding to AIDS. *Training & Development*, **January**, 45–51.
Stodghill, R. II, Mitchell, R., Thruston, K. & Del Valle, C. (1993). Why AIDS policy must be a special policy. *Business Week*, **February 1**, 53–4.

JENNIFER M. GEORGE

allowances Expatriates often receive, as part of their compensation, additional funds for specific purposes to allow them to live more comfortably or to compensate them for inconveniences. Allowances could include: relocation costs; the expenses of home leave for the expatriate and his/her family; cost-of-living adjustments; educational costs for children; and other costs deemed important by the expatriate and agreed to by the employer. Allowances can add a great deal to the cost of sending an employee on an overseas assignment.

see also **Compensation package**

Bibliography

Mendenhall, M., Punnett, B. & Ricks, D. (1995). *Global management.* Cambridge, MA: Blackwell Publishers.

JOHN O'CONNELL

antitrust policy Antitrust policy in the US and Europe (EU) is based on several statutes which identify various forms of business behavior which are deemed to be anticompetitive and therefore illegal. The three main antitrust statutes in the US are the 1890 Sherman Act, the 1914 Clayton Act and the 1914 Federal Trade Commission Act. Their counterparts concerning competition policy in the EU lie in Articles 85 and 86 of the 1957 Treaty of Rome. Each of these laws has several sections which are written in language which is open to interpretation. As a result, the implementation of policy is dependent (in part) on the philosophies of the members of the governmental agencies and judiciary who are empowered, at any given point in history, to enforce the law.

Debate in the US has continued for decades as to the original intent of the framers of the Sherman and Clayton Acts. Bork (1966) believes that Senator Sherman was concerned with the reduction of output and DEADWEIGHT LOSS inefficiency resulting from monopoly. Martin (1994) and others believe that their original intent was also to protect consumers from unfair prices yielding excess economic profits (*see* ECONOMIC PROFIT) and in some instances to protect small businesses from unfair practices of their larger rivals. Still others, including Katzman (1984), argue that the original intent, in part, grew out of the concern that economic power, from both large absolute size and large relative size of firms, may translate into political power, to the detriment of democracy and the country's social structure. The interpretation of these statutes and the rigor with which they are enforced has varied over time and likely will continue to do so. In a historical analysis of the first century of antitrust in the US, Schwartz (1990) details cycles of approximately 25 years between peak periods of aggressive antitrust enforcement.

There is also controversy concerning the economic theory supporting these statutes. Kovaleff (1990) has compiled the works of numerous current antitrust scholars who provide an array of studies on the merits of US antitrust law at the conclusion of its first century. Much of this work continues to focus on the perceived tradeoff between abuses of economic power and the benefits of economic efficiency resulting from large firm size.

EU policy in some respects parallels that of the US in that it prohibits artificial restrictions on competition and proscribes abuses of market power. As Martin (1994) points out though, EU policy also has the goal of fostering the economic integration of the Community. Moreover, EU policy more forcefully and directly allows efficiency, *when ultimately used to benefit consumers*, as an exempting factor against charges of violations of the law. Finally, EU policy specifically allows for small and medium sized firms to fix prices, share markets, and otherwise follow cartel-like activities (*see* CARTELS), in order to better compete with a dominant firm, while under US law these activities have been declared illegal in all circumstances. Moreover, the promotion of smaller firms as an end in and of itself appears to be a more prominent goal in the EU than in the US.

Bibliography

Bork, R. (1966). Legislative intent and the policy of the Sherman Act. *Journal of Law and Economics*, 9, 7–48.

Greer, D. (1992). *Industrial Organization and Public Policy*. 3rd edn, New York: Macmillan.

Howard, M. (1983). *Antitrust and Trade Regulation*. Englewood Cliffs, NJ: Prentice-Hall.

Katzman, R. (1984). The attenuation of antitrust. *The Brookings Review*, 2, 23–7.

Kovaleff, T. (1990). A symposium on the 100th anniversary of the Sherman Act. *Antitrust Bulletin*, 35.

Martin, S. (1994). *Industrial Economics*. 2nd edn, New York: Macmillan.

Neale, A. (1977). *The Antitrust Laws of the U.S.A.* 2nd edn, Cambridge: CUP.

Schwartz, L. (1990). Cycles of antitrust zeal: predictability? *Antitrust Bulletin*, 35, 771–800.

GILBERT BECKER

360 degree appraisals The central idea of a 360 degree appraisal system is to obtain performance evaluations on individual employees from multiple perspectives or sources. Typically, ratings are gathered from supervisors, peers, and subordinates, or some combination of these sources (e.g. Bracken, 1994). Self-ratings and customer ratings may also be elicited. Other terms used to describe 360 degree appraisals include multi-rater systems, upward feedback, and full-circle feedback.

The purpose of 360 degree appraisals is usually to provide feedback to individuals on how their performance is viewed by a number of organizational constituencies (e.g. Edwards et al., 1985). The appraisal done for this purpose will be part of a feedback process that encourages an honest self-diagnosis of strong and weak performance areas, and sets in motion developmental efforts to improve effectiveness in the relatively weak areas. These evaluations have also been used as administrative performance appraisals that feed into personnel decisions, such as promotions and succession planning.

There are a number of issues associated with administering a 360 degree appraisal program. Best practice thinking at this point (e.g. Bracken, 1994) suggests, first, that behavioral rather than trait rating scales should be employed. Second, selection of raters should be managed

carefully to avoid, for example, ratees nominating only "friendly raters" to provide them with feedback. Third, ratings should be made anonymously to encourage honest appraisals. Finally, raters should be trained to use the rating form properly to help them make accurate appraisals.

Bibliography

Bracken, D. W. (1994). Straight talk about multi-rater feedback. *Training and Development*, 48, 44–51.

Edwards, M. R., Borman, W. C. & Sproul, J. R. (1985). Solving the double-bind in performance appraisal: a saga of solves, sloths, and eagles. *Business Horizons*, 85, 59–68.

WALTER C. BORMAN
and DAVID W. BRACKEN

appropriate technology The term used to describe which type of technology is suitable for a country. One of the major concerns of international organizations today is whether or not current technological advances – methods of doing business, up-to-date communications systems, robotics production, and others – can be used in developing nations. The use of advanced technologies requires an infrastructure which many nations do not possess. Also troubling is the cultural impact technological advancement sometimes carries with it. For example, will agribusiness approaches destroy the self-worth of farmers in developing nations leading to problems in the society? Is the appropriate technology for some countries one of a past era? If so, is that older technology still compatible with the technology presently used by multinationals? Answers to questions involving appropriate technology have implications both economically and socially for developing nations as well as the companies introducing the technology.

Bibliography

Dawson, L. M. (1987). Transferring industrial technologies to less developed countries. *Industrial Marketing and Management*, 16, 265–71.

Deans, P. C. & Kane, M. J. (1992). *International dimensions of information systems and technology*. 2nd edn, Boston, MA: PWS-Kent Publishing Company.

JOHN O'CONNELL

arbitration Arbitration is one of the most common methods of alternate dispute resolution. Alternate dispute resolution is a method of settling legal questions without having to file lawsuits or otherwise use the litigation system of any given country. Arbitration is commonly called for in international contracts to avoid the cost and time commitment which is demanded by litigation. Litigation in a foreign country exposes an organization to a legal system which may favor local citizens. The legal system may also be totally unfamiliar to a foreign businessperson, thereby placing this person at a distinct disadvantage when compared to local business people who have grown up with the system.

Arbitration involves a hearing before an impartial arbitrator. The arbitrator may be selected by the parties at odds or may have been agreed to in the original contract bringing the parties together. Depending upon the system under which the proceedings are heard, the arbitrator may be allowed to impose a compromise settlement or select between the positions presented by the parties in dispute. Decisions of the arbitrator are confidential and do not set precedent. Thus, a business desiring to settle a dispute in private and quickly would probably desire to use an alternate dispute resolution method such as arbitration. The United Nations convention on Arbitration established a number of rules and procedures which apply to the arbitration of international matters.

Bibliography
Litka, M. (1991). *International dimensions of the legal environment of business.* 2nd edn, Boston, MA: PWS-Kent Publishing Company.

JOHN O'CONNELL

arbitration agreements   An arbitration agreement specifies that if parties to a contract are in conflict, the arbitration process will be used to settle the dispute. Such agreements are common in international business contracts in order to avoid many of the problems associated with litigation. It is important that arbitration agreements specify the exact nature of the process to be used, the number of arbitrators, the country whose rules of arbitration are to be followed, and the language of the proceeding. If details of the arbitration process are not included in the contract then an arbitration organization should be specified. The International Chamber of Commerce has such a facility, as do many individual countries.

see also **Arbitration**

JOHN O'CONNELL

area-based divisional structure   Several variants of this form of organizational structure occur. They are especially to be found in multinational corporations; but they may exist in relatively undiversified national concerns, and particularly in service industries such as retailers, banks, railroads, utilities, insurance, and restaurants. The advantages of such a structure include the ability to tailor strategy to the needs of each geographic market; that it takes advantage of local market, fiscal, and tax opportunities on a local basis; and that it produces a cadre of multifunctional general managers. Disadvantages include problems of coordination with product divisions and functions; problems of maintaining a common corporate image/reputation

from area to area; problems of standardizing marketing, and especially pricing policies; and potentially additional costs due to an extra tier of management.

Area-functional Structure
This variant of area structure is commonly found under conditions where there are:
● low levels of product diversification
● high levels of regional market differentiation
● economies of scale in production, transportation, and/or distribution that occur on a regional basis
● low levels of interregional trading

This structure is illustrated in figure 1. Such firms tend to organize their global interests on a highly integrated basis in any region of the world, and to link individual national manufacturing and marketing activities within a region into integrated, interdependent operations. In some cases regional product design may be undertaken, while pricing, distribution, promotion, and production within a region tend to be centralized and determined at the regional divisional headquarters. This structure is often found where regional influences are more important than global influences, while production ECONOMIES OF SCALE are limited. Such industries include specialist foods, products subject to climatic variation (e.g., tropical versus arctic); and products meeting specific ethnic and cultural requirements. However, an increasing number of traditionally regional markets are globalizing, and as this tendency increases the regional structure becomes potentially unstable. For example, the Ford Motor Corporation, which for many years operated an area-based divisional structure, was undergoing a fundamental change toward a global product-based structure in the mid-1990s.

Area Product Divisional Structure
This structure is illustrated in figure 2. It tends to be found where:
● there are large MNCs involving a network of product and geographic interests, and where there is no home market dominance
● there is a need to provide significant coordination on an area basis between local activities

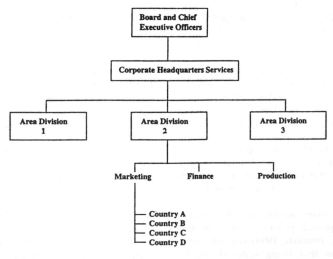

Figure 1 Area-functional organizational structure.

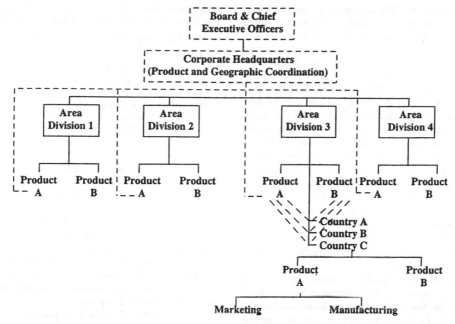

Figure 2 Area product organizational structure.

- product flow is high between national subsidiaries within a region, but is relatively low between regions

This type of organization is an extension of the local umbrella HOLDING COMPANY STRUCTURE and is widely used in diversified companies as a means of coordinating and controlling operations for a variety of product areas within a specific geographic region. This type of organization is also close to a MATRIX STRUCTURE requiring multilevel product and geographic coordination and integration, and also usually involving multiple executive reporting relationships. The area division becomes in many respects a regional headquarters and is often seen as a localized extension of the corporate headquarters. As MNC overseas operations become an increasingly important component of corporate strategy, there is a need to closely supervise these activities to prevent serious potential losses of control. Such organizations may also act as localized cash centers which, because of their time zone differences, may require localized inputs in addition to central cash, leads and lags, foreign exchange, transfer pricing, and tax management.

A regional headquarters, therefore, performs this type of role, as well as reducing local frictions and local legal and fiscal conformity. Moreover, it is still possible to use expatriate managers to fill key positions in regional offices, to ensure that close linkages with the headquarters culture are maintained and that the corporation can generate general managers with a global perspective.

Such structures have tended to be introduced first in particular areas. Thus many US corporations have initially established European and/or Latin American headquarters, before extending the principle on a global scale, the ultimate move being the treatment of North America as similar to other regions. Regional headquarters tend to be located in favorable tax environments such as Switzerland, but many companies may use such operations as booking centers, while main personnel locations have favored cities or countries with central location, transportation, and communication facilities, together with proximity to business information, governments, and supranational authorities. As a result, major centers in Europe would include Brussels, London, and (to a lesser extent) Paris.

Bibliography

Channon, D. F. & Jalland, M. (1979). *Multinational strategic planning*. New York. Amacom.
Prahalad, C. K. & Doz, Y. L. (1987). *The multinational mission*. New York: Free Press.

DEREK F. CHANNON

arms-length pricing Arms-length pricing refers to situations in which market forces establish the price of goods (i.e., no special relationship exists between buyer and seller). Thus, an organization purchasing under arms-length pricing would receive the best price negotiable. The price would tend to be similar for all buyers of similar nature. Arms-length concepts become a bit more important when one is dealing with "transfer prices" or "reinvoicing" activities. Transfer pricing or reinvoicing involve the buying and selling of goods between a parent company and its subsidiary. Such transactions many times come under the scrutiny of tax authorities. If other than arms-length pricing is used between parent and subsidiary it could have serious future income tax implications.

see also **Reinvoicing; Transfer price**

Bibliography

Eiteman, D. K., Stonehill, A. J. & Moffett, M. H. (1992). *Multinational business finance*. 6th edn, Reading, MA: Addison-Wesley Publishing.

JOHN O'CONNELL

artificial intelligence The attempt to program computers to perform tasks that require intelligence when performed by humans is known as *artificial intelligence*. Examples of such tasks are visual perception, understanding natural language, game-playing, theorem-proving, medical diagnosis, and engineering design.

Beginning in the late 1950s, AI researchers have modeled a variety of problems (such as playing checkers or proving theorems in mathematics) in terms of state space search. A *state* denotes a particular configuration of the components of a problem. The position of pieces on a chess board and the structure of terms in a mathematical expression are examples of states (for the problems of chess-playing and theorem-proving, respectively). The application of a permissible operator (such as a legal move in the game of chess or an expansion of terms in a mathematical expression) alters the state of a problem. The set of all possible states, together with the operators that enable transitions among them, constitutes the *state space* representation of a problem.

The solution of an AI problem consists of a search through the state space, i.e. the successive application of operators until the final state of the problem matches the desired goal state (a checkmate in chess or the simplest expression of a theorem). Unless the problem is very limited in scope (e.g. playing tic-tac-toe), the state space is hopelessly large for an exhaustive search (the game of chess has more than 10^{120} states). Additional knowledge (beyond the rules of the game) is required to guide the state space search in promising directions. This search control knowledge is commonly called *heuristic knowledge*. The process of problem-solving in AI described above is called *heuristic search* (Newell & Simon, 1976).

Chess-playing and theorem-proving are examples of tasks where the careful application of logic has to be supplemented by heuristic knowledge to produce an efficient solution. As AI research progressed, it was discovered that specialized tasks, such as diagnosis, design, and planning, require even more knowledge to formulate (in state space terms) and solve (through heuristic search). In order for knowledge to facilitate the solution of an otherwise intractable problem, the knowledge must be represented in a suitable form for use by a computer program. Methods of reasoning about the knowledge to apply it to a particular situation must also be specified. The representation of domain knowledge and efficient methods of reasoning with it have become central concerns of AI since the 1970s (Feigenbaum & McCorduck, 1983). Certain formalisms, including if–then rules, semantic networks, frames, and predicate logic, have been developed to represent and utilize knowledge efficiently in problem-solving.

AI methods have been successfully applied to problems in computer vision, robotics, knowledge-based systems (*see* EXPERT SYSTEMS), understanding natural language and machine learning (the extraction of patterns from large volumes of data). AI-based computer systems have been successfully deployed in manufacturing to support the design and diagnosis of products and processes. In services, AI has been applied to a variety of tasks, including medical diagnosis, financial statement analysis, and logistics management. In addition to dedicated AI systems, AI techniques have also been used to improve the user interfaces of conventional information systems.

see also **Information systems, strategic use of**

Bibliography

Newell, A. & Simon, H. A. (1976). Computer science as empirical inquiry: symbols and search. *Communications of the ACM*, **19** (3), 113–26.

Feigenbaum, E. A. & McCorduck, P. (1983). *The Fifth Generation: Artificial Intelligence and Japan's Computer Challenge to the World*. Reading, MA: Addison-Wesley.

AMIT DAS

assessment centers Assessment centers (also referred to as the assessment center method) represent a structured and comprehensive approach to the measurement of individual differences regarding knowledge, skills, abilities, and other dispositions (*see also* KSAOs) that have been found to be relevant to the work environment. Traditionally, assessment centers were designed to assess the potential of people for managerial assignments in large organizations (Thornton and Byham, 1982). More recently, they are seen as useful whenever the need for extensive individual assessments can justify the effort and expense.

The noteworthy features of an assessment center include job-related assessment dimensions, groups of ratees assessed by multiple raters, multiple and complementary methods for assessment, the separation of observations and evaluations, and flexibility of purpose.

In the assessment center literature, the word dimension is used to denote a set of job-relevant tasks, BEHAVIORs, performance domains, or specific abilities needed to perform well on a job (Zedeck, 1986; Klimoski, 1993). Examples of assessment dimensions are "delegation," "interpersonal skills," and "organizing and planning." The number of actual dimensions used has varied from 10 to 25 (Zedeck, 1986) and would depend on such things as the purpose of the center, the nature of the job to which the center is linked and the need for comprehensiveness.

Candidates are assessed in cohorts of from 10 to 15, and many of the assessments themselves are based on observations of individuals performing as a member of a six- to eight-person group. Further, teams of assessors, rather than one individual, are used to observe and produce written evaluations of candidates.

The staff of a center are usually trained human resource professionals, but occasionally psychologists and line managers are involved in assessments. The assessments themselves can be based on paper-and-pencil tests (including INTELLIGENCE TESTS, personality tests, and interest measures), work task simulations (e.g. the in-basket test), individual interviews, and situational exercises with groups of candidates. Such exercises can be leaderless group discussions or role playing in job areas like budget planning, negotiations, or personnel decision-making. In their review of the reports of 50 centers, Gaugler et al. (1987) found that the number of assessment devices used ranged from one to eleven (mean of seven), with observations of candidates taken over a one to three day period. To accomplish this, most centers had a two to one ratio of candidates to staff.

Procedurally, each candidate follows a schedule designed to insure that all tests and exercises can be administered given the time and staff available. For example, while some individuals are completing a test or an interview, others would be participating in group exercises. In the group exercises staff are trained to observe and record candidate behaviors and make preliminary evaluations. However, final assessments are formulated in an "integration session." This occurs at the end of the assessment phase and serves as the vehicle for discussing and integrating what has been learned and for generating reports.

The behavior and performance of each candidate is reviewed and summarized at the integration session. Depending on the purpose of the center, the staff will discuss and reach consensus on each candidate's performance on one or more of the following: the assessment tasks or exercises, behavioral and/or performance dimensions, and the assessment exercises as a whole (Harris et al., 1993). In some instances, the staff might also be asked to make a rating or recommendation (for hiring or promotions) or a prediction of the candidate's likely future success in the company (Zedeck, 1986).

As of the time of their review, Gaugler et al. (1987, p. 493) estimated that over 2000 organizations were using assessment centers and doing so for a wide variety of purposes. These include personnel selection, placement, the early identification of management potential, promotion, management development, and training. For some of these purposes, staff members not only prepare reports, but provide personal (even face-to-face) feedback to the candidates themselves. And although assessment centers are most frequently used to get at management potential, they have also been used to assess college students, engineers, salespeople, military personnel, rehabilitation counselors, school administrators, and others (Gaugler et al., 1987).

There is now fairly convincing evidence that assessment center judgements or ratings are statistically related to important job outcomes. The meta-analysis of Gaugler et al. (1987) revealed a corrected correlation of 0.37 against a set of criteria. The highest correlations were obtained, however, when center data were used to predict advancement criteria; somewhat lower validities are usually found in attempts to predict future JOB PERFORMANCE.

Current writing and research on assessment centers has gone beyond questioning the potential usefulness of such centers. Instead the emphasis is now on why and how they work, when they should be used (relative to alternatives) and with whom (Klimoski and Brickand practitioners seem less interested in concerns over predictive validity and are trying to address issues of assessment center construct validity, e.g. Russell and Domm, 1995).

Bibliography

Gaugler, B. B., Rosenthal, D. B., Thornton, G. C. & Bentson, C. (1987). Meta-analysis of assessment center validity. *Journal of Applied Psychology Monograph*, **72**, 493–511.

Harris, M. M., Becker, A. S. & Smith, D. E. (1993). Does the assessment center scoring method affect the cross-situational consistency of ratings? *Journal of Applied Psychology*, **78**, 675–78.

Klimoski, R. (1993). Predictor constructs and their measurement. *Personnel Selection in Organizations*, Schmitt, N. & Borman, W. San Francisco: Jossey-Bass.

Klimoski, R. J. & Brickner, M. (1987). Why do assessment centers work? The puzzle of assessment center validity. *Personnel Psychology*, **40**, 243–60.

Russell, C. J. & Domm, D. R. (1995). Two field tests of an explanation for assessment centre validity. *Journal of Occupational and Organizational Psychology*, **68**, 25–47.

Thornton, G. C. & Byham, W. C. (1982). *Assessment Centers and Managerial Performance*, San Diego, CA: Academic Press.

Zedeck, S. A. (1986). A process analysis of the assessment center method. *Research in Organization*, **8**, 259–96.

RICHARD KLIMOSKI

assessment of management information system   In order to evaluate the resources being spent on information management and whether or not it is meeting organizational needs, assessment of the MANAGEMENT INFORMATION SYSTEM function can be performed periodically. The evaluation should be carried out within the context of the organization and its strategies and plans.

There are two persistent questions relative to the information systems of an organization:

1 How much should be spent on information systems? (allocation of organizational resources to information systems).

2 How good are the information systems and the function that supports them? (evaluation of organization, management, and services of the information systems function).

Within industries, spending levels on information systems differ substantially among successful companies. Within the constraints of resource availability, how much should be spent depends on two factors: (1) what the organization wants to achieve with information technology; and (2) how much it must spend to be competitive. Companies differ in culture, capabilities, and the way they use information technology, so what organizations wish to achieve will differ; industries differ in their use of information technology, so what organizations must spend to be competitive will differ by industry. This suggests that information systems can only be evaluated within their organizational and environmental context.

An in-context approach to information system assessment provides the framework for investigating these key management questions. The in-context assessment framework is presented as a complete assessment approach. A company may wish to perform a complete, comprehensive assessment, but it is more likely that the assessment will be targeted at a high-level evaluation or at a specific problem area. The value of the in-context assessment framework is in identifying factors to be included in assessment and in defining the overall context for targeted assessments.

The Context for Information Systems

The information architecture of a company serves an organization which: (1) exists in an industry with a competitive environment; (2) has a specific organizational structure, management style, and culture; and (3) has specific information requirements. These define the overall context for assessment of the information management function and the portfolio of information system applications.

The existing *industry context and competitive environment* define what is expected of information systems at the current time. This can change as new applications and new information products (and other innovations) are used to change the industry structure and basis of competitive advantage. The relevant assessment questions should do more than merely determine whether information systems meet industry and environmental norms. Since information technology can help achieve competitive advantage by changing the way the organization or the industry operates, the MIS function and information systems should also be assessed on participation in competitive innovation and change.

Organizations differ in the way they approach problems and the way they respond to competitive pressures. These differences are reflected in the *organizational structure, culture, and management style* of the organization. This context is important in an assessment of how well the information systems fit the organization as it currently exists. The assessment can also identify changes in information systems that are necessary to support strategic changes in culture and organization.

Overview of the Process

A complete, comprehensive assessment of information systems can be divided into four stages, each of which is subdivided into a series of assessment activities that focus on the major areas of interest. The four stages represent a logical order of assessment in that there is a sequential dependency between the various stages. This suggests that assessment should proceed in a systematic fashion, since the activities within each stage build upon knowledge gained in prior stages. However, within each stage there is only a limited dependency between the individual activities, so the sequence of these may be determined by specific priorities or by convenience factors.

In general, it may be possible to postpone or even omit a particular activity within a given stage, although it is probably inadvisable to omit a stage altogether. When an assessment is targeted or limited in scope, the stages provide a framework for doing enough investigation to establish an appropriate context for the area of assessment interest. For example, a targeted assessment of END–USER COMPUTING should first establish some context consisting of relevant organizational context and infrastructure context. For a limited assessment with a wide scope, the framework identifies the range of things to be considered, even though the depth of analysis may be limited. The framework of four stages and the areas of assessment are as follows:

Stage I: Analysis of the organizational context for information systems
 1 Analysis of the industry and competitive environment of the organization
 2 Analysis of the historical development, culture, structure, and activities of the organization
 3 Analysis of the organization's requirements for information and technology support

Stage II: Assessment of the information system infrastructure
 4 Assessment of information systems architecture of applications and databases
 5 Assessment of the technical architecture for information systems
 6 Assessment of organization and management structure for information systems
 7 Assessment of the investment in information systems

Stage III: Assessment of the organizational interface for information systems
 8 Assessment of information system planning and control
 9 Assessment of information system use
 10 Assessment of end-user computing

Stage IV: Assessment of information system activities
 11 Assessment of application development and maintenance
 12 Assessment of information system operations
 13 Assessment of capacity planning and technology acquisition
 14 Assessment of information system support functions
 15 Assessment of information system safeguards
 16 Assessment of information system personnel management

The steps in the assessment framework are organized in a top–down fashion. They proceed from the most general topic of competitive environment and company structure to the overall structure of information systems and the service level being provided to the management interface between information system and organization and then to the specific activities within the information system function. The evaluation of the information management function is an organizational evaluation; it deals with processes more than outcomes.

1 *Stage I: Analysis of the organizational context for information systems.* At the conclusion of this stage of analysis, there should be a clear definition of competitive forces, major competitors, and key success factors in the market. There should be an understanding of the way the organization has responded to the competitive environment through its organization, policies, culture, etc. There should be an appreciation at a general level of the organization's requirements for information and support services and how these relate to the context of the organization and its environment.

2 *Stage II: Assessment of the information system infrastructure.* After establishing the organizational context in stage I, stage II of the assessment analyzes the various components of the information system's infrastructure, i.e. the institutional structures and established processes that define the organization's information system's capability. The infrastructure is viewed in four dimensions: an *information dimension* (the application systems and databases that provide information support); a *technical dimension* (the architecture of computer equipment, system or non-application software, and telecommunications facilities); an *organizational dimension* (the organization and management structure of the information systems function); and an *economic dimension* (the organization's investment in information systems).

3 *Stage III: Assessment of the organizational interface for information systems.* Having assessed the institutional structures that represent the established information system's capability, the next stage is to evaluate the management processes that act as the essential interface between these structures and the rest of the organization. There is an assessment of information system planning and control to evaluate the existence of these processes and their quality. Assessment of information

system use examines how effectively the organization uses its information system and meets the real needs of its users.

4 *Stage IV: Assessment of information system activities.* The last stage covers assessment of activities and management within the information system function. There are six activities that encompass the assessment of individual functions contained within the information system. Assessment of *application development and maintenance* is an evaluation of the methods and procedures for systems developed by professional programmers. The use of standard methods, methodologies, and development tools are included. Assessment of *information system operations* looks at the organization and management of operations. It includes an evaluation of facilities, use of operations software, and scheduling of work. Assessment of *capacity planning and technology acquisition* examines the processes by which the information management function tracks utilization, forecasts needs, employs performance measurement tools, and evaluates alternatives. The step also evaluates the processes by which new technologies are identified and considered for use. Assessment of *information system support functions* is an evaluation of the way that the function deals with its customers, the users of applications, and end users who need support. Assessment of *information system safeguards* is a study of the security measures and backup and recovery provisions. It may focus on how well the organization has done in studying security issues and in providing for backup and recovery. Assessment of *information system personnel management* considers the current personnel policies and procedures and evaluates how they are working in terms of recruitment, upgrading, and retention.

The assessment framework guides the assessment team in organizing its work, collecting data, and structuring its analysis and reporting. All activities performed by the MIS function are assessed within the organizational context of competitive environment and organizational strategy. Targeted evaluations, such as an assessment of MIS personnel management, are performed within the overall context.

GORDON B. DAVIS

asset pricing The modern theory of asset prices has its foundations in the portfolio selection theory initiated by Markowitz (1952). In a one-period framework Markowitz assumed that agents' utilities, and hence the price they will pay, depend only on the means and variances of returns. This mean-variance model can be justified either on the grounds of quadratic utility (for arbitrary distributions of the asset returns) or on the grounds of multivariate normal (or, more generally, elliptic) distribution of asset returns (for arbitrary preferences). Although quadratic utility has the unappealing properties of satiation and increasing absolute risk aversion in the sense of Arrow–Pratt and multivariate normality violates the limited liability properties of assets, the mean-variance model has had a pervasive influence on financial economics.

The portfolio frontier obtained within the mean-variance framework can be generated by any two frontier portfolios, a property called two-fund separation. Lintner (1965), Sharpe (1964), and Mossin (1966) combined the two-fund separa-

tion with the assumptions that agents have homogeneous beliefs, that markets clear in equilibrium, and that there is unlimited lending and borrowing at the riskless rate. The resulting model, the capital asset pricing model (CAPM), has been the major framework of thinking about the trade-off between risk and return. The (unconditional) CAPM states that the excess return on each asset (return less the risk-free rate) is proportional to the asset's market beta:

$$E(R_i - R_f) = \beta_{im} E(R_m - R_f)$$

where R_m is the return on the market portfolio and $\beta_{im} = \text{cov}(R_i, R_m)/\text{var}(R_m)$, the asset's market beta, measures the covariance of the asset's return with the market return. Black (1972) derived the CAPM for an economy without a riskless asset (the zero-beta CAPM).

The CAPM has been extensively tested. Black et al. (1972) and Fama and MacBeth (1973) originated the two frameworks in which most of the tests were done. However, the unsatisfactory empirical performance of the CAPM, as well as the problems identified by Roll (1977) related to the unobserved nature of the market portfolio are the reasons why the single-period, single-beta relation had to be relaxed. Historically, the first direction was to place the individual decision making in an intertemporal set-up in which agents maximized utility, thus leading to the intertemporal CAPM (ICAPM) of Merton (1973). The other is the arbitrage pricing theory (APT) of Ross (1976).

Merton, working in continuous time under the assumptions of many identical agents with homogeneous expectations and market clearing, derived the ICAPM. The asset prices in Merton's model follow a diffusion process. If the investment opportunity set, namely the drift and diffusion parameters, and the instantaneous correlations between the returns of the different assets, do not change over time, then a continuous time version of the static CAPM holds: one obtains a single-beta security–market-line relationship. If the investment opportunity set is stochastic, however, a multi-beta relationship emerges:

$$E(R_i - R_f) = \beta_{im} E(R_m - R_f)$$
$$+ \sum \beta_{is} E(R_s - R_f)$$

where β_{is} measures the covariance of the return of the ith asset with the sth state variable. Thus, with a stochastically changing investment opportunities set agents need to hedge the future changes in their consumption for a given level of wealth. Given the interpretation of the S state variables as portfolios, the S portfolios are often referred to as hedge portfolios.

To derive the arbitrage pricing theory (APT) Ross (1976) assumes that asset returns are generated by a linear factor model:

$$R_i = E(R_i) + \sum \beta_{ik} f_k + \epsilon_i$$

where each factor f_k (without loss of generality) and the error ϵ_i are zero-mean. In well-diversified portfolios the excess expected return on each asset will be given by a linear combination of the βs above:

$$E(R_i) = R_f + \sum \beta_{ik} \lambda_k$$

where the βs are referred to as factor loadings while the λs are the risk premiums.

Huberman (1982) offers an alternative derivation of the APT. Connor (1984) was the first to use equilibrium arguments in relation to the APT. Connor and Korajczyk (1986, 1988) extend his arguments. Dybvig and Ross (1983) and Ingersoll (1984) contain useful extensions and refinements of the APT.

There has been substantial empirical work on the APT. Roll and Ross (1980) use factor analysis to test the APT while Connor and Korajczyk (1988) use "asymptotic" principal components analysis to uncover the factors. On the other hand, Chen et al. (1986) explicitly specify five macroeconomic variables (unexpected change in the term structure, unexpected change in the risk premium, change in expected inflation, the unexpected inflation rate, and the unexpected change in industrial production) that proxy for the economy-wide factors. Shanken (1982, 1985) questions the possibility of testing the APT; Dybvig and Ross (1983) present the counter-argument.

The works of Ross (1976), Cox and Ross (1976), Harrison and Kreps (1979), and Ross (1978) contain what has come to be known as the fundamental theorem of asset pricing: the absence of arbitrage is equivalent to the existence of a positive linear pricing rule and still further equivalent to the existence of an optimal demand for some agent with increasing preferences. From this theorem it follows that the absence of arbitrage implies the existence of a strictly positive stochastic process called a stochastic discount factor μ_t such that:

$$1 = E_t(\mu_{t+1} R_{i,t+1})$$

For the CAPM (an equilibrium model):

$$\mu_t = \frac{1}{R_f} + \frac{E_t(R_m - R_f)}{(R_m)} \cdot \frac{E(R_m) - R_m}{R_f}$$

while for the consumption CAPM (CCAPM) $\mu_t = U'(C_{t+1})/U'(C_t)$. The theoretical work on both the ICAPM and APT preceded much of the empirical work which found that price–earnings ratios (Basu, 1977), dividend yields (Fama and French, 1988), and size (Banz, 1981; Reiganum, 1981; Schwert, 1983; Chan et al., 1985) improve the fit of the single-beta CAPM. Some of these papers, together with the weekend effect (French, 1980) and the January effect (Keim, 1983) have been interpreted as evidence of market inefficiency. However, as Fama (1970) has noted, a test of market efficiency, being performed within the framework of a specific model, is a test of that particular model as well. Much research has been done on whether any of these statistics are proxies for others. Reiganum (1981) has shown that the price–earnings effect disappears when controlling for size. Recently, Fama and French (1992, 1993) have shown that size and book-to-market equity (portfolios proxying for factors related to size and book-to-market equity) have high explanatory power for the cross-section (variance) of expected returns.

Considerable work has also been done on testing the conditional CAPM (Sharpe, 1964; Constantinides, 1982). Keim and Stambaugh (1986), among others, have shown that in a CAPM context the risk premium is time varying. Harvey (1989) and Ferson and Harvey (1991) show that the betas are also time varying. These authors have argued that failing to recognize the time variability may lead to a premature rejection of the model.

Historically, the difficulties in identifying the relevant state variables to be used in Merton's ICAPM have led Breeden (1979) to reduce the multi-beta model to a single-beta, CCAPM model:

$$E(R_i - R_f) = \beta_{ic} E(R_c - R_f)$$

where R_c is the return on a security which is perfectly correlated with aggregate consumption and $\beta_{ic} = \text{cov}(R_i, d \ln C)/\text{var}(d \ln C)$.

Lucas (1978) independently derives this asset pricing model in discrete time for a pure exchange economy in which aggregate consumption equals the aggregate dividend in equilibrium. For that model the price of asset i is a properly discounted sum of next period's payoff:

$$P_{it} = E_t \left[\frac{U'(C_{t+1})}{U'(C_t)} (P_{i,t+1} + D_{i,t+1}) \right]$$

where the representative consumer is assumed to maximize a time- and state-separable utility function with periodic utility $U(C_t)$. Cox et al. (1985a, 1985b) present a full-fledged general equilibrium model (with production) in continuous time along these lines and apply it to a study of the term structure of interest rates. Brock (1982) also derives asset prices in a production economy.

The consumption-based CAPM has not been very successful empirically. The Euler equations have been rejected by Grossman and Shiller (1981), Hansen and Singleton (1982), and Grossman et al. (1987). Moreover, the simple separable utility representative agent model gives rise to various asset pricing puzzles such as the equity premium puzzle of Mehra and Prescott (1985) and the risk-free rate puzzle of Weil (1989).

Recent work on the consumption-based asset pricing model has focused on the calibration of preferences and investment opportunities to include various market frictions (borrowing and short-sales constraints, transactions costs (Bewley, 1992; Heaton and Lucas, 1992)), time non-separable preferences (Constantinides, 1982), recursive preferences allowing for a partial separation between the coefficient of relative risk aversion and the coefficient of intertemporal substitution (Epstein and Zin, 1989, 1991) and various forms of agent heterogeneity (following the work of Constantinides, 1982; Mankiw, 1986; Heaton and Lucas, 1992; Telmer, 1993).

Bibliography

Banz, R. (1981). The relationship between return and market value of common stocks. *Journal of Financial Economics*, **9**, 3–18.

Basu, S. (1977). Investment performance of common stocks in relation to their price–earnings ratios: a test of the efficient market hypothesis. *Journal of Finance*, **3**, 663–82.

Bewley, T. (1992). Some thoughts on the testing of the intertemporal asset pricing model. Manuscript, Cowles Foundation, Yale University.

Black, F. (1972). Capital market equilibrium with restricted borrowing. *Journal of Business*, **45**, 444–55.

Black, F., Jensen, M. & Scholes, M. (1972). The capital asset pricing model: some empirical tests. *Studies in the theory of capital markets*. Ed. Jensen, Michael, New York: Praeger, 79–121.

Breeden, D. (1979). An intertemporal asset pricing model with stochastic consumption and investment opportunities. *Journal of Financial Economics*, **7**, 265–96.

Brock, W. (1982). Asset prices in a production economy. *The economics of information and uncertainty*, Ed. McCall, J. Chicago, IL: University of Chicago Press.

Chan, K. C., Chen, N. & Hsieh, D. (1985). An exploratory investigation of the firm size effect. *Journal of Financial Economics*, 14, 451–71.

Chen, N., Roll, R. & Ross, S. (1986). Economic forces and the stock market. *Journal of Business*, 59, 383–403.

Connor, G. (1984). A unified beta pricing theory. *Journal of Economic Theory*, 34, 13–31.

Connor, G. & Korajczyk, R. (1986). Performance measurement with the arbitrage pricing theory. *Journal of Financial Economics*, 15, 373–94.

Connor, G. & Korajczyk, R. (1988). Risk and return in an equilibrium APT. *Journal of Financial Economics*, 21, 255–89.

Constantinides, G. (1982). Intertemporal asset pricing with heterogeneous agents and without demand aggregation. *Journal of Business*, 55, 253–67.

Cox, J., Ingersoll, J. & Ross, S. (1985a). An intertemporal general equilibrium model of asset prices. *Econometrica*, 53, 363–84.

Cox, J., Ingersoll, J. & Ross, S. (1985b). A theory of the term structure of interest rates. *Econometrica*, 53, 385–407.

Cox, J. & Ross, S. (1976). The valuation of options for alternative stochastic processes. *Journal of Financial Economics*, 3, 145–66.

Dybvig, P. & Ross, S. (1983). Yes, the APT is testable. *Journal of Financial Economics*, 40, 1173–88.

Epstein, L. & Zin, S. (1989). Substitution, risk aversion, and the temporal behavior of consumption and asset returns: a theoretical framework. *Econometrica*, 57, 937–69.

Epstein, L. & Zin, S. (1991). Substitution, risk aversion, and the temporal behavior of consumption and asset returns: an empirical analysis. *Journal of Political Economy*, 99, 263–86.

Fama, E. (1970). Efficient capital markets: A review of theory and empirical work. *Journal of Finance*, 25, 383–417.

Fama, E. & French, K. (1988). Dividend yields and expected stock returns. *Journal of Financial Economics*, 22, 3–25.

Fama, E. & French, K. (1992). The cross-section of expected stock returns. *Journal of Finance*, 47, 427–66.

Fama, E. & French, K. (1993). The economic fundamentals of size and book-to-market equity. *Journal of Financial Economics*, 33, 3–56.

Fama, E. & MacBeth, J. (1973). Risk, return, and equilibrium. *Journal of Political Economy*, 81, 607–36.

Ferson, W. & Harvey, C. (1991). The variation of economic risk premiums. *Journal of Political Economy*, 99, 385–415.

French, K. (1980). Stock return and the weekend effect. *Journal of Financial Economics*, 8, 55–69.

Grossman, S. & Shiller, R. (1981). The determinants of the variability of stock market prices. *American Economic Review*, 71, 222–27.

Grossman, S., Melino, A. & Shiller, R. (1987). Estimating the continuous time consumption-based asset pricing model. *Journal of Business and Economic Statistics*, 5, 315–28.

Hansen, L. P. & Singleton, K. (1982). Generalized instrumental variables estimation in nonlinear models. *Econometrica*, 50, 1269–86.

Harrison, M. & Kreps, D. (1979). Martingales and arbitrage in multiperiod securities markets. *Journal of Economic Theory*, 20, 381–408.

Harvey, C. (1989). Time-varying conditional covariances in tests of asset pricing models. *Journal of Financial Economics*, 24, 289–318.

Heaton, J. & Lucas, D. (1992). The effect of incomplete insurance markets and trading costs in a consumption–based asset pricing model. *Journal of Economic Dynamics and Control*, 16, 601–20.

Huberman, G. (1982). A simple approach to arbitrage pricing. *Journal of Economic Theory*, 28, 183–91.

Ingersoll, J. (1984). Some results in the theory of arbitrage pricing. *Journal of Finance*, 39, 1021–39.

Keim, D. (1983). Size-related anomalies and stock return seasonality. *Journal of Financial Economics*, 12, 13–32.

Keim, D. & Stambaugh, R. (1986). Predicting returns in the stock and bond markets. *Journal of Financial Economics*, 17, 357–90.

Lintner, J. (1965). The valuation of risky assets and the selection of risky investments in stock portfolios and capital budgets. *Review of Economics and Statistics*, 47, 13–37.

Lucas, R. (1978). Asset prices in an exchange economy. *Econometrica*, 46, 1426–45.

Mankiw, N. G. (1986). The equity premium and the concentration of aggregate shocks. *Journal of Financial Economics*, 17, 211–19.

Markowitz, H. (1952). Portfolio section. *Journal of Finance*, 7, 77–91.

Mehra, R. & Prescott, E. (1985). The equity premium: a puzzle. *Journal of Monetary Economics*, 15, 145–61.

Merton, R. (1973). An intertemporal capital asset pricing model. *Econometrica*, 41, 867–87.

Mossin, J. (1966). Equilibrium in a capital asset market. *Econometrica*, 35, 768–83.

Reiganum, M. (1981). Misspecification of capital asset pricing. *Journal of Financial Economics*, 9, 19–46.

Roll, R. (1977). A critique of the asset pricing theory's tests. Part I: On past and potential testability of the theory. *Journal of Financial Economics*, 4, 129–76.

Roll, R. (1980). An empirical investigation of the arbitrage pricing theory. *Journal of Finance*, 35, 1073–1103.

Roll, R. (1981). A possible explanation of the small firm effect. *Journal of Finance*, 36, 879–88.

Ross, S. (1976). The arbitrage theory of capital asset pricing. *Journal of Economic Theory*, 13, 341–60.

Ross, S. (1978). A simple approach to the valuation of risky streams. *Journal of Business*, 51, 341–60.

Schwert, W. (1983). Size and stock returns and other empirical regularities. *Journal of Financial Economics*, 12, 3–12.

Shanken, J. (1982). The arbitrage pricing theory: is it testable? *Journal of Finance*, 37, 1129–40.

Shanken, J. (1985). Multi-beta CAPM or equilibrium-APT? A reply. *Journal of Finance*, 40, 1189–96.

Sharpe, W. (1964). Capital asset prices: a theory of market equilibrium under conditions of risk. *Journal of Finance*, 19, 425–42.

Telmer, C. (1993). Asset pricing puzzles and incomplete markets. *Journal of Finance*, 48, 1803–32.

Weil, P. (1989). The equity premium puzzle and the risk-free rate puzzle. *Journal of Monetary Economics*, 24, 401–21.

IVAILO IZVORSKI

asymmetric information

Asymmetric information exists when one party in the market or transaction has more or better information than the other party. Furthermore, the party with less information cannot rely on the other for the necessary information and cannot easily acquire it. For example, Akerlof (1970) noted that sellers of used cars have more information about the quality of the used car than buyers. This asymmetry can place the party with less information at a disadvantage and can interfere with market exchange to the point where market transactions break down. Akerlof showed that if buyers in the used car market considered all cars to be "average" in quality, no sellers of above-average quality cars would want to sell. This would reduce the average quality of the cars remaining in the market until only the worst cars (lemons) were traded; (*see* LEMONS MARKET; IMPERFECT INFORMATION). There is a tendency in these markets for quality levels to fall if consumers cannot discriminate between high-quality and low-quality products. The problem of asymmetric information also arises in employment decisions, insurance markets and credit markets where the person who is applying for a job, insurance or credit knows more about his or her abilities, health or risk than the employer, insurer or creditor. Firms have incentives to acquire more information in these situations while job applicants and consumers have incentives to provide more information, perhaps through SIGNALING.

High-quality producers have incentives for signaling in these markets to convince consumers that their products are better than average. Guarantees or warranties can be provided to assure consumers that a product will perform above the average. Firms also have incentives to invest in their reputation and in brand names to indicate that the product is a high-quality product. The product's price itself may convey information about quality in the appropriate circumstances. For example, Milgrom and Roberts (1986) found that both price and ADVERTISING could provide signals to consumers for new, experience goods that are frequently purchased. High-quality firms have incentives to set a low price because they will benefit more from future repeat purchases than low-quality producers. However, Bagwell and Riordan (1991) suggest that, for a new durable product, the initial price should be high to signal that it is a high-quality product to uninformed consumers. As sales occur and more of the market becomes informed that this is a high-quality product, the firm should decrease price to maximize profits.

Bibliography

Akerlof, G. A. (1970). The market for lemons: quality uncertainty and the market mechanism. *Quarterly Journal of Economics*, 84, 488–500.
Bagwell, K. & Riordan, M. K. (1991). High and declining prices signal product quality. *American Economic Review*, 81, 224–39.
Milgrom, P. & Roberts, J. (1986). Price and advertising signals of product quality. *Journal of Political Economy*, 94, 796–821.
Shughart, W. F., Chappell, W. F. & Cottle, R. L. (1994). *Modern Managerial Economics*. Cincinatti, OH: South-Western Publishing.
Stiglitz, J. E. (1987). The causes and consequences of the dependence of quality on price. *Journal of Economic Literature*, 25, 1–48.

ROBERT E. MCAULIFFE

at-risk pay At-risk pay is compensation that is not guaranteed, such as VARIABLE COMPENSATION. Schuster and Zingheim (1992) distinguish three types. "Add-on pay" is in addition to normal base pay. "Potential base pay at risk" funds a variable pay plan by deferring part of the market-based increases that otherwise would flow into base pay. Pure "at-risk pay" reduces base pay, providing an employee an "ante" for variable pay opportunities. Lawler (1990) argues that at least 5 percent of cash compensation must be at risk to motivate employee performance through variable pay. Variables affecting the motivational effectiveness of at-risk pay include percentage at risk, individual preferences, the employee's organizational level, and organizational culture.

Bibliography

Lawler, E. E. III (1990). *Strategic Pay: Aligning Organizational Strategies and Pay Systems*, San Francisco: Jossey-Bass.

Schuster, J. R. & Zingheim, P. K. (1992). *The New Pay: Linking Employee and Organizational Performance*, New York: Lexington Books/Macmillan.

GERALD E. LEDFORD

attitudinal structuring Attitudinal structuring refers to efforts by negotiators to shape their opponents' perceptions about the nature of the issues to be negotiated. Attitudinal structuring is one of four bargaining subprocesses identified by Walton and McKersie (1965). (For the others, *see* DISTRIBUTIVE BARGAINING; INTEGRATIVE BARGAINING.)

The Nature of Attitudinal Structuring

Attitudinal structuring is typically viewed as the result of a conscious, carefully planned effort by negotiators to influence their opponents' perceptions about the nature of bargaining issues and the character of bargaining team members. However, perceptions of the entire negotiation process may also be influenced by the largely spontaneous actions and deeds of parties. Because labor–management negotiation occurs at regular intervals and agreements must be administered on a daily basis, the past actions of the parties both at and away from the bargaining table can influence how each party approaches the next bargaining round.

The Importance of Attitudinal Structuring

Because bargaining issues have both distributive and integrative elements, perceptions play a large role in determining how the parties approach negotiations. By cultivating an atmosphere of friendliness, mutual respect, trust, and cooperation, negotiators can encourage their opponents to view issues largely in integrative terms and participate in joint problem-solving. In contrast, hostile language, shouting, threats, deception, and refusal to acknowledge a party's legitimate interests encourages the opponent to take a more distributive approach to negotiations. Such words and deeds can have long-term effects, hampering subsequent efforts to switch from distributive to integrative bargaining.

Bibliography

Fisher, R. & Ury, W. (1981). *Getting to Yes: Negotiating Agreement without Giving in*, New York: Penguin Books.
Lewicki, R. J. & Litterer, J. A. (1985). *Negotiation*, Homewood, IL: Richard D. Irwin.
Walton, R. E. & McKersie, R. B. (1965). *A Behavioral Theory of Labor Negotiations: an Analysis of a Social Interaction System*, New York: McGraw-Hill.

PAUL JARLEY

attribution An attribution is a causal explanation. Attribution theory is concerned with the cognitive processes and consequences of the processes by which individuals explain the behavior and outcomes of others as well as their own behavior and outcomes (Martinko, 1994).

Heider (1958) is most often credited as the founder of attribution theory. His basic thesis was that people are motivated to predict and control their environments. An essential prerequisite for control is an understanding of the basic causal mechanisms operating in the environment. Thus, average people can be viewed as "naive psychologists" attempting to understand and explain cause and effect relationships so that they can attain mastery in their environments.

Although there are many variations of attribution theory, Kelley and Michela (1980) note that research on attributions has focused on two primary areas:

(1) the achievement motivation model which emphasizes how individuals explain their own successes and failures (see the work of Weiner (1986) and his colleagues); and
(2) the process by which observers account for and explain the outcomes of others (see Kelley (1973); Green & Mitchell, 1979; Martinko & Gardner, 1987).

Attribution theories have been applied to a wide range of phenomena including stereotyping, LEADERSHIP, performance evaluation processes, interpersonal CONFLICT, IMPRESSION MANAGEMENT, and accounts of organizational responsibility.

Several models of attributional processes have been developed to describe the role and function of attributions in motivating individual behavior. The achievement motivation models of Weiner (1986) and his colleagues as well as the learned helplessness models suggested by Abramson, Seligman, and Teasdale (1978) and Martinko and Gardner (1982) all show the role of attributions with regard to individual behavior. While the achievement motivation models focus on the role of attributions regarding individual success and failure, the learned helplessness models focus specifically on passive and maladaptive reactions to failure. Thus, learned helpless individuals often display passive behavior and fail to exert effort even when success may be possible because they believe that prior failures were due to stable and internal characteristics such as lack of ability (see LOCUS OF CONTROL). The learned helplessness models are most helpful in understanding and explaining the behavior of poor performers whereas the achievement-oriented models address the more general process of explaining and predicting reactions to success and failure.

In both the learned helplessness and achievement motivation models, individuals process information about prior outcomes to arrive at causal attributions. These attributions are believed to affect most directly subjects' expectancies, which, in turn, influence individuals' affective states (e.g., depression and anxiety) and affect the probabilities of target behaviors and the consequences (outcomes) generated. A basic assumption of both these models is that attributions can be classified within a limited number of underlying cognitive dimensions. The models almost always include the dimensions of internal/external and stable/unstable. The internal/external dimension is concerned with whether the locus of causality is inside the person or in the environment. The stability dimension is concerned with whether or not the cause is likely to remain constant or change over time. Combining the polar opposites of these two dimensions, attributions can be classified as: stable/internal (e.g., ability); stable/external (e.g., task); unstable/internal (e.g., effort); and unstable/external (e.g., chance/luck). In addition, other dimensions such as intentionality, controllability, and globality have also been proposed (Abramson et al. 1978; Weiner, 1986) but have less research support.

Research has generally supported attributional models of learned helplessness and achievement motivation. In particular, there appears to be reasonably clear relationships between attributions and expectations. It has also been found that certain types of attributions are related to particular affective states. Thus, for example, attributing failure to an internal and stable characteristic such as lack of ability has been associated with depression. On the other hand, the linkage between attributions and behaviors is not as clear. Attributions affect behaviors primarily through the influence that they have on expectations.

Several models have also been developed to describe how individuals make attributions for the behavior of others. The majority of these responsibility assignment models (e.g., Green & Mitchell, 1979) generally use the three factors described by Kelley's cube to explain the attribution process. Essentially, these models indicate that observers evaluate the environment and the target person to determine which of three causal factors is responsible for the outcome. The belief about causation then drives the observer's response (behavior) toward the actor. The three types of causal factors that are believed to be responsible for the outcome are: the person, the stimuli, and the specific occasion. To make a determination of the causal factor that is primarily responsible, observers are posited to evaluate the behavior of the target along the dimensions of:

(1) the distinctiveness of the response – performance on this versus other tasks;
(2) consistency – over time and occasions; and
(3) consensus – comparison to others.

The final assignment of responsibility is made according to the principle of covariation which attempts to determine whether or not changes in causes are related to different outcomes. Thus, there must be multiple observations and causes must vary for analysis to occur. As Kelley (1967) indicated: "The effect is attributed to that condition which is present when the effect is present and which is absent when the effect is absent." Thus a leader is most likely to blame a subordinate for poor performance if he observes that the subordinate typically performs poorly on other tasks, has consistently performed this task poorly on other occasions, and that everyone else performs this same task well. In general, the research has documented that information regarding the dimensions described by Kelly's cube is related to the nature and severity of leaders' reactions to poor subordinate performance.

Two issues appear to recur in the attributional literature and research regarding organizational behavior. First is the effect of attributional processes on LEADERSHIP behavior and leader–subordinate interactions. Particular attention has been devoted to the impact of attributional biases such as the fundamental attribution error on leader evaluations of employee performance. Another key issue has been the validity of descriptions of attributional processes within organizational contexts. Lord and Maher (1990) have suggested that the rational process depicted by attributional models may not always provide a realistic description of the processes by which people assign causality in specific organizational situations. Thus, for example, as a result of experience, leaders may develop cybernetic short-cuts or schemata in assigning causality regarding the outcomes associated with a particular job and set of workers, thereby bypassing the more thorough causal analyses suggested by attribution theory. In addition, some researchers have questioned whether or not other cultures have the same need for causal analysis and suggest that other dimensions or depictions of the process of responsibility assignment and achievement motivation may be appropriate for other cultures (*see* CULTURE).

see also **Motivation**

Bibliography

Abramson, L. Y., Seligman, M. E. P. & Teasdale, J. D. (1978). Learned helplessness in humans: Critique and reformulation. Journal of Abnormal Psychology, 87 (1), 49–74.

Green, S. & Mitchell, T. (1979). Attributional processes of leaders in leader–member interactions. Organizational Behavior and Human Performance., 23, 429–458.

Heider, F. (1958). The psychology of interperelations. New York: Wiley.

Kelley, H. H. (1967). Attribution theory in social psychology In D. Levine (Ed.), Nebraska symposium on motivation, 1967. Lincoln: University of Nebraska Press.

Kelley, H. H. (1973). The process of causal attribution American Psychologist, 28, 107–128.

Kelley, H. H. & Michela, J. L. (1980). Attribution theory and research. Annual Review of Psychology., 31, 457–501.

Lord, R. G. & Maher, K. J. (1990). Alternative information processing models and their implications for theory, research, and practice. Academy of Management Review, 15 (1), 9–28.

Martinko, M. J. (Ed.), (1995). Attribution theory: An organizational perspective. Delray Beach, FL: St. Lucie Press.

Martinko, M. J. & Gardner, W. L. (1982). Learned helplessness: An alternative explanation for performance deficits. Academy of Management Review, 7 (2), 195–204.

Martinko, M. J. & Gardner, W. L. (1987). The leader member attribution process. Academy of Management Review., 12 (2), 235–249.

Mitchell, T. R. & Wood, R. E. (1980). Supervisor's responses to subordinate poor performance: A test of an attributional model. Organizational Behavior and Human Performance, 25, 123–138.

Weiner, B. (1986). An attribution theory of motivation and emotion. New York: Springer-Verlag.

MARK J. MARTINKO

audit risk In forming an opinion on the financial statements, the auditor faces various audit-related risks and risk components. Two types of audit-related risk can be distinguished: *audit risk* and *business risk*. Audit risk can generally be defined as the *probability* of incorrectly reporting on the financial statements, and is a function of a number of auditor- and auditee-related risk components. Business risk relates to the adverse consequences to the audit firm arising from any litigation or criticism concerning the auditor's work or the client's audited financial statements. Some major elements of business risk (*see*, for example, Brumfield et al., 1983) are litigation, sanctions imposed by public or private regulatory bodies, and impaired professional reputation.

Two distinct approaches have evolved in the literature (*see*, for example, Cushing & Loebbecke, 1983): the *risk analysis approach* and the *audit modeling approach*. The former approach focuses only on risk related to audit tasks, thereby ignoring business risk. *Audit risk analysis* has been the result of a movement toward the idea of basing audit scope and timing decisions on a more explicit analysis of audit risk. The major purpose of audit risk models is to help the auditor to obtain a *given* degree of confidence that the financial statements do not contain a material error. Economic considerations are not explicitly taken into account, and the focus is rather on effective audit risk control. In the second approach, *audit decision models* are more comprehensive in nature as compared to audit risk models: a broader set of factors are taken into account (such as, audit risk, audit costs, etc.). This type of model may serve as an aid for auditors to identify an efficient and cost-effective way by which a *suitable level* (i.e., cost minimizing) of confidence can be achieved.

The most general definition of audit risk is the risk or probability of incorrectly reporting on the financial statements. This embodies both the risk of incorrect rejection or *α-risk* (also type I error risk) and the risk of incorrect acceptance or *β-risk* (also type II error risk). The distinction between α and β risk types is used both in the context of a single reported book value and at the aggregated level of the financial statements as a whole. The difference between α and β risk is clarified in the article by Elliott & Rogers (1972). It stems from the application of the statistical hypothesis testing approach to the audit setting, which permits the auditor to measure and control both types of risk.

Along another dimension that is directly related to the use of statistical sampling methods in audit testing, audit risk can also be viewed to entail two other types of risk: *sampling* and *nonsampling risk*. Roberts (1978) defined sampling risk as "the portion of audit risk of not detecting a material error that exists because the auditor examined a sample of the account balances or transactions instead of every one." Nonsampling risk then is "the portion of audit risk of not detecting a material error that exists because of inherent limitations of the procedures used, the timing of the procedures, the system being examined, and the skill and care of the auditor." Although both types of risk are defined here in the light of β-risk, a distinction between sampling and nonsampling risk equally applies to α-risk. Roberts further defines another concept, the Δ-risk, as the sampling risk of unwarranted reliance in statistical compliance tests.

Finally, there exist three distinct forms of (total) audit risk (*see*, for example, Arens & Loebbecke, 1994; Senetti, 1990). First, there is the *planned level of acceptable audit risk* (or, desired audit risk), specified before the substantive audit procedures are performed; second, there is the *true ex post level of audit risk* (a synonym for ex post audit risk is *achieved audit risk*), which is unknown to the auditor; and third there is the *estimate of ex post audit risk* as made by the auditor.

"Multiplicative" Audit Risk Model
The use of an audit risk model for financial statement auditing has been established in various auditing standards. General statements about risk consideration have evolved into detailed guidance on quantitative risk assessment. An understanding of the importance of risk evaluation was already shown in professional standards in the USA as early as 1963 (*see* AU Section 150.05 of The American Institute of Certified Public Accountants (AICPA) professional standards):

> The degree of risk involved also has an important bearing on the nature of the examination. . . . The effect of internal control on the scope of the examination is an outstanding example of the

influence on auditing procedures of a greater or lesser degree of risk of error; i.e., the stronger the internal control, the less the degree of risk.

The first explicit incorporation of a formula in the standards occurred only in 1972, when the AICPA published Statement of Auditing Procedure No. 54 (which was later incorporated as Section 320 of the Codification of Statements of Auditing Standards (SAS 1)). At that stage of development, the problem was modeled as one of setting the "reliability" level of substantive test of details (S) so that its combination with the subjective reliance on internal accounting control and other relevant factors (C) would provide a combined reliability level (R) sufficient to meet the auditor's overall objectives for the audit. Or:

$$S = 1 - \frac{(1 - R)}{(1 - C)}$$

The relationship with risk was described as follows:

> The combined reliability is the complement of the combined risk that none of the procedures would accomplish the particular audit purpose, and the combined risk is the product of such risks for the respective individual procedures . . . (SAS 1 section 320B.31)

The audit risk model was given further authoritative support by the publication of Statement of Auditing Standard (SAS) 39 (1981) and SAS 47 (1983). SAS 39 proposes the following multiplicative model for audit *planning* purposes:

$$AR = IR \times CR \times AP \times TD$$

Where:

AR = allowable audit risk level that financial statements are materially misstated;

IR = inherent risk of material misstatement; i.e. susceptibility of an assertion to a material misstatement assuming that there are no related internal control structures or procedures;

CR = control risk, or the risk of a material misstatement given that it has occurred and has not been detected by the system of internal control;

AP = risk that analytical review procedures will fail to detect a material misstatement;

TD = risk that substantive tests of detail fail to detect a material misstatement, given that it has occurred and has not been detected by the system of internal control.

The SAS 39 model is specified in terms of risk factors instead of reliance factors, and includes a factor for analytical review procedures and other relevant substantive tests. SAS 39 also raises the issue of inherent risk, but asserts that this risk is potentially costly to quantify and that for this reason it is implicitly and conservatively set at unity. It further suggests that the proposed model might be used in *planning* a statistical sample by selecting an acceptable ultimate risk, subjectively assessing inherent (IR), control (CR) and analytical review risk (AR) and then solving for tests of detail risk (TD) as follows: TD = AR / (IR * CR* AR). SAS 39 does *not* contemplate the use of the

formula to conditionally revise an audit plan or to *evaluate* audit results.

SAS 47 updated the concepts and terminology of SAS 39 to provide further guidance in considering audit risk both at the financial statement level and at the level of individual account balances or classes of transactions. The basic approach remains the same although certain terms have been redefined. SAS 47 explicitly incorporates a factor for inherent risk and combines analytical review risk (AR) and test of details risk (TD) in one risk factor, namely, detection risk (DR). Unlike SAS 39, SAS 47 emphasizes the need of audit risk and materiality "to be considered together in determining the nature, timing, and extent of auditing procedures and in *evaluating* the results of these procedures" (para. 1) (*italics added*). The suggestion to use the ARM for risk evaluation has been heavily criticized in subsequent audit risk literature, as the model is clearly not fit to correctly measure achieved (ex post) audit risk.

An interesting discussion of the assumptions and limitations of ARM has been provided by Cushing & Loebbecke (1983). The major points of their criticism are the following: first, it is assumed that the individual risk components of the ARM are *independent* of each other, whilst there exist interdependencies between these factors. Inherent risk, analytical review risk, and substantive test of detail risk all depend on control risk. Failure to consider these interdependencies when internal control is weak tends to understate the risk factor being assessed. As a result the use of the model might expose the auditor to a higher level of ultimate risk than he or she would consider acceptable. Second, the model does not provide any guidance for *aggregating* the risk assessments made at the disaggregated level of accounts or transactions to the risk for the financial statements as a whole. Third, the model only considers sampling risk (and β-risk) and assumes that the nonsampling risk component is negligible. Fourth, the ARM is ill-equiped to explicitly consider other economic factors such as the audit cost or the effect of potential misstatement. Fifth, the ARM should only be used as a *planning* tool, namely, to determine the appropriate level of sampling risk for substantive tests of details, and not as a risk evaluation model.

Although the audit risk model as defined by SAS 39/47 has been accepted by several auditing firms as a planning aid for their audits, there appear to be wide differences in the way in which audit firms in different countries implement the audit risk model. This is not surprising in itself, since little guidance is provided in audit standards about the underlying determinants of the risk components in the model (in particular w.r.t. inherent risk and control risk), which might result in differences in their conceptual interpretations. A number of empirical studies (*see*, for example, Jiambalvo & Waller, 1984; Daniel, 1988; Strawser, 1990, 1991; Waller, 1993) have investigated some behavioral aspects related to the use of the ARM in practice. From the evidence there seems to be reason to believe that the audit risk model might not be descriptive of risk judgment in practice.

Bayesian Approaches to Modeling Audit Risk

Given the limitations of the "multiplicative" audit risk model for evaluation of (ex post) audit risk, several authors have discussed an alternative approach for the combination of risk components into an overall ex post audit risk measure, which is derived from the application of Bayesian theory of *conditional dependence* to the audit judgment process. The approach is fundamentally different from the US Statement on Auditing Standard (SAS) 39/47 model that is a *joint* (multiplicative) ad hoc risk model. From a theoretical perspective the Bayesian approach to risk modeling is superior as it is based on the laws of subjective probability theory.

Several versions of Bayesian audit risk models have been proposed in the literature, based on alternative assumptions about the conditional nature of the various steps in the audit process. Two major categories of models can be distinguished. A first category views inherent risk as the prior probability of material error in the financial statements, but does not recognize the sequential and conditional nature of various audit procedures. The audit risk model introduced in 1980 by the Canadian Institute of Chartered Accountants (CICA, 1980) is an example of such a model. In a second category of models (*see*, for example, Kinney, 1989; Sennetti, 1990) the conditional and sequential nature of various audit procedures is explicitly recognized.

Bibliography

Arens, A. A. & Loebbecke, J. K. (1994). *Auditing: An integrated approach*. Englewood Cliffs, NJ: Prentice-Hall.

Brumfield, C. A., Elliott, R. K. & Jacobson, P. D. (1983). Business risk and the audit process. *Journal of Accountancy* Apr., 60–8.

CICA (1980). *Extent of audit testing: A research study*. Canadian Institute of Chartered Accountants.

Cushing, B. E. & Loebbecke, J. K. (1983). Analytical approaches to audit risk: A survey and analysis. *Auditing: A Journal of Practice and Theory*, 2, Fall, 23–41.

Daniel, S. J. (1988). Some empirical evidence about the assessment of audit risk in practice. *Auditing: A Journal of Practice and Theory*, 7, Spring, 174–81.

Elliott, R. K. & Rogers, J. R. (1972.). Relating statistical sampling to audit objectives. *Journal of Accountancy* July, 46–55.

Jiambalvo, J. & Waller, W. (1984). Decomposition of audit risk. *Auditing: A Journal of Practice and Theory*, 3, Spring, 80–8.

Kinney, Jr, W. R. (1989). Achieved audit risk and the outcome space. *Auditing: A Journal of Practice and Theory*, 8, Supplement, 867–84.

Roberts, D. M. (1978). *Statistical sampling*. American Institute of Certified Public Accountants.

Sennetti, J. T. (1990). Toward a more consistent model for audit risk. *Auditing: A Journal of Practice and Theory*, 9, Spring, 103–12.

Strawser, J. R. (1990). Human information processing and the consistency of audit risk judgments. *Accounting and Business Research*, 21, Winter, 67–75.

Strawser, J. R. (1991). Examination of the effect of risk model components on perceived audit risk. *Auditing: A Journal of Practice and Theory*, 10, Spring, 126–35.

Waller, W. S. (1993). Auditors' assessment of inherent and control risk in field setting. *The Accounting Review*, 68, Oct., 783–803.

MARLEEN WILLEKENS

autonomous work groups   These are groups of employees with overlapping skills who collectively perform a relatively whole task (e.g., manufacturing a complete product), whilst exercising a high level of discretion over the conduct of work. Sometimes called "self-regulating," "self-managing," "semiautonomous," or "internally led" work groups (*see* SELF-MANAGEMENT), they are the most common structural outcome associated with sociotechnical systems interventions. According to this perspective such work designs enhance productivity by encouraging the control of key variances at source and locating intertask coordination requirements within a single work unit. They are held to be more performance effective than individual JOB DESIGNS when technically required cooperation is high and when there is a high level of uncertainty or variability associated with boundary transactions or work processes. A positive effect on employee MOTIVATION and attitudes is also predicted, since such structural arrangements yield jobs which are congruent with psychologically significant human VALUES, such as the needs for variety, autonomy, meaningful work, opportunities to learn, and social support (Pasmore, 1988). Autonomous work groups often feature as part of an overall HUMAN RESOURCES STRATEGY oriented toward labour flexibility and employee COMMITMENT.

In practice, the degree of autonomy exercised by these work groups varies, but typically involves three categories of workplace DECISION MAKING (Susman, 1979). First, there are decisions associated with regulating the immediate production or work process. These concern the coordination of task performance or the allocation of resources within the group. Second, there are decisions which affect the work group's overall level of independence within the organization, such as determining the order of production. Finally, there are decisions concerning the internal governance of the group, such as the process whereby collective decisions are reached.

The capacity of an autonomous work group to operate effectively depends on the degree of:

(1) *task differentiation* – the extent to which the group's task is independent of others within the organization;
(2) *boundary control* – the degree to which employees can influence transactions with their work environment and protect work boundaries from external intrusions; and
(3) *task control* – the extent to which employees are free to regulate their own behavior to convert inputs (e.g., information, raw materials) into a completed product or service, such as by varying the pace of work.

Therefore, autonomous work groups require first-level management practices which clearly define and protect the boundaries of the group's discretion, avoid close direct supervision, and ensure that members possess the necessary information, knowledge, and skill to exercise control effectively (Manz & Sims, 1987). Group-based performance feedback and REWARD systems are also common, whilst skill-based pay is often used as a means of encouraging the development of multiskilling.

Studies confirm that appropriately designed autonomous work groups positively affect productivity and some specific work attitudes (e.g., intrinsic JOB SATISFACTION). However, they have not consistently given rise to improvements in performance motivation, ABSENTEEISM, or labor turnover (Goodman, Devadas, & Hughson, 1988), leading some researchers (e.g., Wall, Kemp, Jackson, & Clegg, 1986) to question motivational explanations of their effects.

see also **Group decision making; Organizational design; Team building**

Bibliography

Goodman, P. S., Devadas, R. & Hughson, T. G. (1988). Groups and productivity: Analyzing the effectiveness of self-managing teams. In J. P. Campbell, R. J. Campbell & Associates (Eds), Productivity in organizations. San Francisco: Jossey-Bass.

Manz, C. C. & Sims, H. P. (1987). Leading workers to lead themselves: The external leadership of self-managing teams. Administrative Science Quarterly, **32**, 106–128.

Pasmore, W. A. (1988). Designing effective organizations: The sociotechnical systems perspective. New York: Wiley.

Susman, G. I. (1979). Autonomy at work: A sociotechnical analysis of participative management. New York: Praeger.

Wall, T. D., Kemp, N. J., Jackson, P. R. & Clegg, C. W. (1986). Outcomes of autonomous work groups: A long-term field experiment. Academy of Management Journal, **29**, 280–304.

JOHN CORDERY

average total cost   This measures the total economic costs of production per unit produced in the short run and is also referred to as short run average cost. Average total costs include the opportunity cost of capital employed (i.e. the normal risk-adjusted rate of return on capital), so a firm operating on its average total cost curve is earning zero ECONOMIC PROFIT. Since economic profits are the signal for entry and exit from the industry, the average total cost curve represents a benchmark curve in the short run for predicting whether entry or exit will occur (*see* LONG RUN COST CURVES).

Average total costs in the short run consist of average fixed costs and average variable costs. FIXED COSTS are those costs of production which do not vary with the level of output and are fixed in the short run. Therefore average fixed costs (fixed costs per unit produced) decrease as the quantity produced increases. Variable costs are those costs which vary with the level of output produced such as labor, material inputs, etc. Average variable costs are the variable costs per unit produced and will decrease initially but will eventually increase because of DIMINISHING RETURNS to the variable inputs. Thus the "typical" average total cost curve is U-shaped, representing decreasing per unit costs initially as more units are produced, but reaching a minimum and then rising as output rises per period.

see also **Average variable costs; Short run cost curves; Fixed costs**

Bibliography

Carlton, D. W. & Perloff, J. M. (1994). *Modern Industrial Organization*. 2nd edn, New York: HarperCollins.

Douglas, E. J. (1992). *Managerial Economics*. 4th edn, Englewood Cliffs, NJ: Prentice-Hall.

ROBERT E. MCAULIFFE

average variable costs   Variable costs are those costs which vary with the level of output produced by the firm in the short run and average variable costs are total variable costs per unit produced. If the firm did not produce output in a given period, these costs would not be incurred. The variable costs of production will be affected by the per unit cost of each variable input in production (e.g. hourly wage rates for workers), the productivity of the inputs in production, and the production technology available to the firm.

The average variable cost curve is important for short run decisions when the price received for producing output is so low that the firm may choose not to produce. A firm should shutdown its operations when, in the short run, it cannot earn revenues sufficient to pay its average variable costs. The firm has no choice regarding its FIXED COSTS in the short run since these costs must be paid whether or not the firm shuts down. Therefore, fixed costs should have *no* effect on the firm's short run decisions. However, the firm does not have to pay the variable costs of production in the short run, so if operating the plant costs more than the revenues earned, the firm should shutdown and simply pay its fixed costs. For a perfectly competitive firm, the shutdown point occurs where marginal cost equals average variable cost (i.e. when average variable cost is at a minimum). At any price below this point, revenues earned from operations will fail to cover the costs of operations. The firm will have greater losses if it operates and should shutdown.

Bibliography

Carlton, D. W. & Perloff, J. M. (1994). *Modern Industrial Organization*. 2nd edn, New York: HarperCollins.

Douglas, E. J. (1992). *Managerial Economics*. 4th edn, Englewood Cliffs, NJ: Prentice-Hall.

ROBERT E. MCAULIFFE

—— B ——

back translation   When a document or communication is translated into another language, a back translation is often a good idea to assure that the original translation was correct. For example, a British manager was instructed to write a contract for a foreign partner's signature but the contract had to be in Japanese. The manager would normally write the contract in English and then have it translated to Japanese. In order to check on the validity of the initial translation, the Japanese contract should be "back translated" to English before being sent for signature. Problems associated with changed meanings or misinterpretation of intent will be minimized by such actions.

JOHN O'CONNELL

balanced score card   A critical element in successful strategy implementation is an appropriate management control system. Many systems do not provide the critical information required by management to assess the corporations progress to achieving its strategic vision and objectives. The balanced score card is a performance measurement system developed by Kaplan and Norton which, although including financial measures of performance, also contains operational measures of customer satisfaction, internal processes, and the corporation's innovation and improvement activities, which are seen as the key drivers of future financial performance. The approach provides a mechanism for management to examine a business from the four important perspectives of:

- How do customers see the firm? (*customer perspective*)

Table 1   The balanced scorecard

Goals	Measures	Goals	Measures
Financial perspective		*Customer perspective*	
Survival	Operating cashflow	New product	Percentage of sales from new products
Success	Quarterly sales growth and operating income by SBU	Speed of response	Customer measure of on-time delivery
Future prosperity	Increase market share; increase productivity; reduce capital intensity	Preferred supplier	Customer ranking survey; customer satisfaction index
			Market share
Internal business perspective		*Innovation and learning perspective*	
Higher productivity	Value added per employee	Technology leadership	New product design time; patent rate versus completion
	Waste as % output		No employee suggestions
	Capital intensity; machine utilization rate	Product focus efficiency	Percentage of products equal to 80% of sales; revenue per employee
Design productivity; new product introduction	Engineering efficiency – actual versus scheduled; time to market	Employee motivation	Staff attitude survey

Source: Kaplan & Norton (1990, 1993)

- What does the firm excel at? (*internal perspective*)
- Can the firm continue to improve and create value? (*innovation and learning perspective*)
- How does the firm look to shareholders (*financial perspective*)

The system also avoids information overload by restricting the number of measures used so as to focus only on those seen to be essential. The balanced score card presents this information in a single management report and brings together often disparately reported elements of the firm's strategic position such as short-term customer response times, product quality, teamwork capability, new product launch times and the like. Second, the approach guards against suboptimization by forcing management to examine operation measures comprehensively.

The system requires management to translate their general mission statements for each perspective into a series of specific measures which reflect the factors of critical strategic concern. A typical scoreboard is illustrated in table 1.

The precise score card design should reflect the vision and strategic objectives of the individual corporation. The key point is that the scorecard approach puts strategy and corporate vision rather than control as the key element of design and is consistent with the development of corporate transformation techniques, cross functional organizations, and customer–supplier interrelationships.

Building the Balanced Score Card

While each organization is unique, to improve acceptance and commitment to the revised measurement system, a number of companies have sought to involve teams of managers in the design of their scorecards. This also insures that line management create a system which reflects their needs, rather than with traditional systems which tend to be control driven by finance and accounting specialists. A typical score card design project might involve the following stages:

(1) *Preparation*. SBU's should be selected for which a score card measurement system is appropriate. These should have clearly identifiable customers, production facilities, and financial performance measures.

(2) *Interviews: first round*. Each senior SBU manager is briefed on the approach and provided with documents on the corporate vision, mission, and strategy. A facilitator interviews the senior managers to obtain their views and suggestions, as well as a number of key customers to learn about their performance expectations.

(3) *Executive workshop*. The top management team is brought together to begin the development of an appropriate score card which links measurements to strategy.

(4) *Interviews: second round*. The output of the workshop is reviewed and consolidated and views are sought about the process of implementation.

(5) *Executive workshop: second round*. A second workshop is then held with senior managers together with their direct subordinates and a larger group of middle managers to design them to any change programs under way, and to develop an implementation plan. Stretch targets should also be developed for each measure, together with preliminary action programs for their achievement. The team must also agree on an implementation program,

including communication to employees, integrating the score card in management philosophy, and developing an appropriate information system.

(6) *Implementation*. A newly formed team develops an implementation plan for the score card, including linking the measures to databases and information systems, communicating the system through the organization, and facilitating its introduction.

(7) *Periodic review*. The score card should be constantly reviewed to insure that it meets the needs of management.

Bibliography

Gouillard, F. J. & Kelly, J. N. (1995). Transforming the Corporation. New York: McGraw-Hill. See chapter 6.

Kaplan, R. S. & Norton, D. P. (1990). The balanced scorecard – measures that drive performance. *Harvard Business Review*, **January–February**, 71–9.

Kaplan, R. S. & Norton, D. P. (1993). Putting the balanced scorecard to work. *Harvard Business Review*, **Sept.–Oct.**, 134–47.

Kaplan, R. S. & Norton, D. P. (1996). *The Balanced Scorecard*. Boston, MA: Harvard School Press.

DEREK F. CHANNON

bankruptcy A central tenet in economics is that competition drives markets toward a state of long-run equilibrium in which inefficient firms are eliminated and those remaining in existence produce at a minimum average cost. Consumers benefit from this state of affairs because goods and services are produced and sold at the lowest possible prices. A legal mechanism through which most firms exit the market is generally known as insolvency and/or bankruptcy.

Bankruptcy occurs when the assets of a firm are insufficient to meet the fixed obligations to debtholders and it can be defined in an accounting or legal framework. The legal approach relates outstanding financial obligations to "the fair market value" of the firm's assets while an accounting bankruptcy would simply be a negative net worth in a conventional balance sheet (Weston and Copeland, 1992). Under bankruptcy laws the firm has the option of either being reorganized as a recapitalized going concern (known as Chapter 11 in the USA or administration in the UK) or being liquidated (Chapter 7 in the USA or liquidation in the UK).

Reorganization means the firm continues in existence and the most informal arrangement is simply to postpone the payment required (known as extension) or an agreement for creditors to take some fraction of what is owed as full settlement (composition). Liquidation, however, occurs as a result of economic distress in the event that liquidation value exceeds the going concern value. Although bankruptcy and liquidation are often confounded in the literature, liquidation (dismantling the assets of the firm and selling them) and bankruptcy (a transfer of ownership from stockholders to bondholders) are really independent events.

The efficient outcome of a good bankruptcy procedure, according to Aghion (1992), should either:

1. Close the company down and sell the assets for cash or as a going concern, if the present value of expected cash flows is less than outstanding obligations; or

2. Reorganize and restructure the company, either through a merger or scaling down or modifying creditors' claims.

Each country has its own insolvency laws, but bankruptcy remedies are very similar in most industrialized nations, incorporating in various ways the economic rationale for:

- fairness among creditors;
- preservation of enterprise value;
- providing a fresh start to debtors; and
- the minimization of economic costs.

There is, however, a widespread dissatisfaction with the existing procedures, as laws have been developed haphazardly with little or almost no economic analysis about how regulations work in practice. Governments and legal structures have not kept pace with the globalization of business and internationalization of financial markets and they have particularly not kept pace in the area of resolving the financial problems of insolvent corporations. For both bankruptcy and insolvency procedures, the key economic issue should be to determine the legal and economic screening processes they provide, and to eliminate only those companies that are economically inefficient and whose resources could be better used in another activity.

Company insolvencies have increased very sharply in the last few years, and currently stand at record levels in many countries. Several factors may severely affect corporate default, and although the combination of recession and high interest rates is likely to have been the main cause of this rise in defaults, the more moderate increases in company failures, which have accompanied more severe downturns in the past, suggest that other factors may also have been important. One important common determinant in companies' failures is the general economic conditions for business; the other is the level of debt. Both capital leverage (debt as a proportion of assets) and income gearing (interest payments as a proportion of income), together with high levels of indebtedness in the economy, may lead to companies' insolvencies.

Recent developments in the theory of finance have considerably advanced our understanding of the nature and role of debt. Debt, unlike any other "commodity," entails a "promise" to pay an amount and the fulfillment of this promise is, by its nature, uncertain. Many of its features, however, can be understood as means of overcoming uncertainty, transaction costs, and incomplete contracts, arising from asymmetric information between the parties concerned.

The risk of bankruptcy and financial distress, however, highlights the fact that conflicts of interest between stockholders and various fixed payment claimants do still exist. These conflicts arise because the firm's fixed claims bear default risk while stockholders have limited-liability residual claims and influence the managerial decision process. Bankruptcy procedures often do not work well, because incomplete (private) contracts cannot be reconciled so laws have to step in. Bankruptcy, as such, does not create wealth transfers to shareholders or undermine the provisions of debt finance but it creates, due to asymmetric information, a conflict of interest between creditors and shareholders, which harms companies' prospects.

The implications of these conflicts of interest have been explored by a number of researchers, including Jensen and Meckling (1976), Myers (1977), and Masulis (1988). One consistent message in these papers is that these conflicts create incentives for stockholders to take actions that benefly maximize firm value.

Jensen and Meckling (1976) argue that rational investors are aware of these conflicts and the possible actions firms can take against creditors. Thus when loans are made they are discounted immediately for the expected losses these anticipated actions would induce. This discounting means that, on average, stockholders do not gain from these actions, but firms consistently suffer by making suboptimal decisions. If the firm is confronted with a choice between investment and debt reduction, it will continue to invest past the efficient point. Then creditors will prefer a debt reduction to investment and, since there are no efficiencies, stockholders must prefer investment.

However, if the actions of the owners (managers or shareholders) are unobservable several complications arise. First, there is asset substitution. Since the owner only benefits from returns in non-default states, risky investments of given mean return will be chosen in preference to safer investments (moral hazard). Owners benefit from the upside gains from high risk investments but do not bear the costs of downside losses. Those inflicted on creditors rather than shareholders. This is the standard consequence that debt can cause firms to take on uneconomic projects simply to increase risk and shift wealth from creditors to stockholders.

Second, there is underinvestment. Owners do not benefit from the effort that they apply to improve returns in insolvency states. Those accrue for creditors not owners. Since some of the returns to investments accrue to bondholders in bankrupt states, firms may be discouraged from carrying out what would otherwise be profitable investments (Myers, 1977).

Third, there is claim dilution, that is an incentive for owners to issue debt that is senior to existing debt. Senior debt has priority over existing debt in the event of bankruptcy; it can therefore be issued on more favorable terms than existing debt, which leaves existing creditors' claims intact in the event of bankruptcy.

The literature suggests, therefore, that bankruptcy impediments to pure market solutions are concerned with the free rider and holdout problems caused by the inconsistent incentives arising in a business contract specifying a fixed value payment between debtor and creditor, particularly given limited liability. Limited liability implies "moral hazard" and "adverse selection" due to asymmetric information problems. Consequently, the prospect of corporate insolvency may result in increased borrowing costs and, simultaneously, a reduction in the amount of funds available.

Bibliography

Aghion, P. (1992). The economics of bankruptcy reform. Working paper 0 7530 1103 4. London: London School of Economics.

Akerlof, G. A. (1970). The market for lemons: quality uncertainty and the market mechanism. *Quarterly Journal of Economics*, 84, 488–500.

Altman, E. I. (1993). *Corporate financial distress and bankruptcy*. New York: John Wiley.

Davis, E. P. (1992). *Debt, financial fragility, and systemic risk.* Oxford: Clarendon Press.

Jensen, M. & Meckling, W. (1976). Theory of the firm: managerial behavior, agency costs and ownership structure. *Journal of Financial Economics*, 3, 305–60.

Masulis, R. W. (1988). *The debt/equity choice.* New York: Ballinger Publishing Company.

Myers, S. C. (1977). Determinants of corporate borrowing. *Journal of Financial Economics*, 4, 147–75.

Webb, D. (1991). An economic evaluation of insolvency procedures in the United Kingdom: does the 1986 Insolvency Act satisfy the creditors' bargain? *Oxford Economic Papers*, 42, 139–57.

Weston, J. F. & Copeland, T. E. (1992). *Managerial finance.* Orlando, FL: The Dryden Press.

White, M. J. (1988). The corporate bankruptcy decision. *Journal of Economic Perspectives*, 3, 129–51.

DAVID CAMINO

bargaining The practice of negotiating the price of goods with shop owners. Generally this custom is carried out in small retail stores and is quite common in many countries. The intent of bargaining is to obtain a lower purchase price than is offered by the seller. Many shops in Mexico and India accept bargaining as a way of life. Be careful, however, because not all store owners may accept bargaining even if the practice is common in their country.

JOHN O'CONNELL

bargaining unit A bargaining unit is a group of employees, union and non-union, who are designated (by election outcome or by employer voluntary recognition) as appropriate for union representation. If a union representation election is held, these employees are eligible voters. Following a union election victory, these employees become the unit for which a collective bargaining agreement is negotiated. Most bargaining units are relatively small (200 employees or fewer), but some are very large, including several thousand workers employed at different locations of the same employer. One employer may also negotiate with several different unions, each representing a different group of employees in a different bargaining unit, at the same location.

DAVID A. GRAY

barriers Barriers are limitations on free trade which are usually imposed by governments. Barriers may also take the form of consumer demands or the nature of the economic development of a particular country. The nature of the barrier and its impact on a particular importer or exporter must be considered when selecting countries in which to conduct business operations. The following is a list of common types of barriers to free trade or other international business activities. The list is not exhaustive but does provide a feel for the types of barriers which exist.

1 Buy local campaigns – Many governments or other interest groups within a country attempt to use the patriotic feelings of consumers to encourage them to buy local items instead of imports. In some cases, rebates or tax incentives may be offered for local products which are not available to imports. Buy local campaigns by unions or others have been very successful in increasing the demand for domestically-produced goods.

2 Custom's requirements – Time delays for custom's inspections, detailed paperwork, strict adherence to detailed standards for foreign products, quarantine requirements for certain goods or property, slow administrative processing, and other problems discourage exporters and importers. Delays and other requirements also add cost to the trade transaction, which is probably the most significant barrier to trade.

3 Discriminatory taxation – Foreign products may be taxed at higher rates than domestic products. The effect is to drive the price of imports higher than those of local products.

4 Domestic content requirements (DCR) – One method of increasing the domestic presence of foreign manufacturers is to require that goods produced in a country have a certain percentage of their value provided domestically. For example, assume a country or common market required at least 60% of the value of autos sold within its borders to be produced locally. Manufacturers would have to prove that for every $20,000 auto, local labor and locally produced parts made up at least $12,000 of that value. DCRs effectively prohibit a foreign auto manufacturer from establishing an assembly facility in another country and then importing all of the parts to construct an auto.

5 Duties – Taxes assessed against the value or numbers of products being imported into a country. (A duty could also apply to exports in some cases.) A duty raises the selling price of the products in the host country. Higher prices means fewer buyers and protection for local industry which may produce the same or similar products. There are a number of types of duties which may be used to achieve different outcomes.

6 Export quotas – Restrictions on the amount of specific goods which may be exported are common. If a country believes a specific product should remain in the domestic market (energy resources, for example) quotas on export may be established.

7 Infrastructure limitations – Lack of financial, transportation, or communication facilities is a barrier to modern trade activities. Although insufficient infrastructure levels are probably not a result of a government determined to discourage trade, insufficient infrastructure development may make efficient foreign operations impossible.

8 Import quotas – Restrictions on the amount of specific goods which can be imported into a country. In order to protect local industry government may institute controls to limit the numbers or values of goods imported. This allows local industry to develop and compete with imported items.

9 Labor laws – Labor laws which provide for large payments to employees upon dismissal or make it difficult to dismiss employees are also a barrier to the entry of a foreign company. Strict labor laws generally favor the employee and increase the costs to the employer.

10 Licensing requirements – In order to conduct import/export activities an import/export license must be secured from the appropriate governmental authority. Some countries make the task of securing a license quite

simple while others have more arduous procedures to follow. Any additional paperwork, and regulations for special permits for special products or countries of origin, makes trade more difficult.

11 Local ownership requirements – These require a foreign company to be partially owned by local interests (many times a controlling interest of more than 50%). It discourages many investors because of the loss of control over the company's operations.

12 Past political risks – Prior government expropriation or confiscation of foreign company assets acts to increase the risk for investors thereby forming a barrier to their entering local markets.

13 Staffing restrictions – Foreign organizations may be required to limit the number of non-host country employees. The inability to bring expatriates into a country may affect the ability to properly manage a firm or to achieve the necessary level of skills to effectively operate the organization.

Barriers to free trade or other international business activity must be taken into consideration before the decision is made to enter a particular country. Barriers are not only those produced by government but also by unions, consumers, and the general level of economic development of a country.

see also **Duty**

Bibliography

Ashegian, P. & Ebrahimi, B. (1990). *International business.* Philadelphia, PA: HarperCollins.

Ball, D. A. & McCulloch, Jr., W. H. (1990). *International business: Introduction and essentials.* Homewood, IL: Irwin.

Bowker, R. R. (1994). *Report on U.S. trade and investment barriers (1993): Problems of doing business with the U.S.* Chester, PA: Diane Publishing Company.

Buchholz, R. A. (1991). Corporate responsibility and the good society: From economics to ecology. *Business Horizons,* **34,** 19–31.

Czinkota, M. R., Rivoli, P. & Ronkainen, I. A. (1989). *International business.* Chicago, IL: The Dryden Press.

Korth, C. (1985). *Barriers to international business.* Englewood Cliffs, NJ: Prentice-Hall.

Vernon, R. & Well, L. T. (1981). *Economic environment of international business.* 3rd edn, Englewood Cliffs, NJ: Prentice-Hall.

JOHN O'CONNELL

barriers to entry and exit   One of Porter's Five Forces (*see* FIVE FORCES MODEL), barriers to entry are strategies or circumstances that protect a firm from competition by making new entry difficult, or by putting potential entrants at a disadvantage. Viewed another way, barriers to entry can be considered to be the additional costs which a potential entrant must incur before gaining entry to a market. Bain (1956, pp. 3–5) argues that entry barriers should be defined in terms of any advantage that existing firms hold over potential competitors, while Stigler (1968, pp. 67–70) contends that, for any given rate of output, only those costs that must be borne by the new entrants but that are not borne by firms already in the industry should be considered in assessing entry barriers. The main effect of barriers to entry is that they may keep the number of companies competing in an industry small, and allow incumbents to earn supernormal profits in the long term. For them to be effective, they must, in principle, increase costs for the challenger more than they do for the incumbent.

Viewed from their function as entry deterrent conditions, there are three broad categories of activities that lower the threat of entry; namely, structural obstacles to entry, risks of entry, and reduction of the incentive for entry. Seen from another dimension, barriers to entry can exist naturally (e.g., natural monopolies), or they can be the result of specific action by the companies concerned (although this latter distinction is sometimes misleading, as competing in a naturally monopolistic industry may well be the result of strategic decision). Finally, barriers can generally be classified as either dependent on or independent of size.

Size-independent Structural Barriers

Size-independent cost conditions include: government subsidies, tariffs, and international trade restrictions (anti-dumping rules, local content requirements, and quotas); regulatory policies; licensing; special tax treatment; restrictions on price competition; favorable locations; proprietary information; proprietary access to financial resources, raw materials, and other inputs; proprietary technologies, know-how, or proprietary low-cost product design; EXPERIENCE AND LEARNING EFFECTS and proprietary access to distribution channels and markets.

To constitute credible barriers, the above need to be defensible and to continue holding in the long term. They can be obtained by encouraging government policies that raise barriers by means of trade protection, economic regulation, safety regulation (product standards and testing, plant safety, or professional body membership or accreditation requirements), or pollution control. Barriers can also be set up: by limiting access to raw materials; by exclusive ownership of the relevant assets or sources; by, for example, purchasing assets at pre-inflation prices; by tying up suppliers (by means of contracts, for example, and also by convincing them that it is risky to take on products which lack consumer recognition); by raising competitors' input costs (for example, by avoiding passing on scale economies through suppliers and bidding up the cost of labor if they are more labor-intensive); by foreclosing alternate technologies (and obliging challengers to take defenders head-on); by investing in the protection of proprietary know-how (by means of patents, secrecy, etc.); by blocking channel access; by raising buyer switching costs and the costs of gaining trial (e.g., by targeting the groups most likely to try other products with discounts); or, finally, by molding of customer preferences and loyalty (through, for example, advertising and promotional activities that increase the costs that the new entrant will have to incur to attract customers), by filling product or positioning gaps, and by brand proliferation (which reduces the market share that will become available to the new entrant).

Size-dependent Structural Barriers

In addition, depending on the size of the firm, other barriers may become available. ECONOMIES OF SCALE and minimum efficient scale effects, for example, force the aspiring entrant to come in on a large scale (with all the risks and costs this entails, particularly if incumbents are unable to accommodate the new entrant, and are thus expected to retaliate), or accept a cost disadvantage. In addition, the absolute size of the required investment in certain industries and the fact that such investment may have to be made up front, and can be unrecoverable, limits the pool of potential entrants and may act as a deterrent for smaller potential entrants.

To make use of these barriers, scale economies can be pursued in production, if feasible. They can also be pursued in marketing and R&D, and it is in those areas where they are likely to be a more readily available tool as, there, scale thresholds are largely determined competitively. Similarly, although the amount of capital necessary to compete in an industry is not controled by the firm, it is possible to increase it by methods such as raising the amount of financing available to dealers or buyers, or employing more investment–intensive technologies.

Bibliography

Bain, J. S. (1956). *Barriers to new competition*. Cambridge, MA: Harvard University Press.

Harrigan, K. R. (1981). Barriers to entry and competitive strategies. *Strategic Management Journal*, 2, 395–412.

Porter, M. E. (1979). How competitive forces shape strategy. *Harvard Business Review*, **57** (2), (March–April). Reprinted, with deletions, in H. Mintzberg & J. B. Quinn, *The strategy process: concepts, contexts, cases*. 2nd edn, Englewood Cliffs, NJ: Prentice-Hall. See pp. 61–70.

Porter, M. E. (1980). *Competitive strategy: techniques for analyzing industries and competitors*. New York: The Free Press.

Porter, M. E. (1985). *Competitive advantage: creating and sustaining superior performance*. New York: The Free Press.

STEPHANOS AVGEROPOULOS

base currency   This is the currency in which a currency exchange rate is quoted. For example, if the US dollar is trading at 0.56 British pounds, the British pound is the base currency.

JOHN O'CONNELL

basic market structures   The basic product market structures in economics are perfect competition, MONOPOLISTIC COMPETITION, oligopoly, and MONOPOLY. Perfect competition represents the benchmark for welfare analysis where there are numerous buyers and sellers, none of whom is large enough to affect the market price if they leave the market. Any firm that wishes to enter the industry or exit may do so at little cost. The product is homogeneous (no PRODUCT DIFFERENTIATION) and consumers and producers are completely informed. These conditions discipline producers and consumers so that neither has any influence over price. The firm facing a perfectly competitive market sells as much as it can at the market price and cannot compete for consumers other than on price. If the firm were to charge a higher price, consumers would immediately switch to other suppliers whose identical products are perfect substitutes. Thus the demand curve facing a perfectly competitive firm is perfectly (or infinitely) elastic and perfectly competitive firms, unable to affect the market price, are said to be *price takers* (*see* ELASTICITY). In addition, since each firm is so small relative to the market and has so many rivals, there is no advantage from efforts to anticipate competitors' reactions or engage in strategic behavior.

When products are differentiated, information is imperfect, entry or exit is costly, or the number of sellers or buyers is small, markets are imperfectly competitive. Firms in these markets generally have some control over price and therefore face downward sloping demand curves. Prices in these markets may exceed the MARGINAL COST of production and the market may not be efficient in allocating output. Producers may also fail to be technically efficient since they face less pressure to keep costs as low as possible (*see* IMPERFECT INFORMATION). Under imperfect competition firms may compete for customers on other dimensions than simply price. Firms may compete through product differentiation, ADVERTISING, strategic behavior and other means.

When firms compete in monopolistic competition, each produces a unique, differentiated product. Entry into the market is free, and firms advertise and pursue research and development to further differentiate their products. Free entry may drive profits down to zero, but recent research in spatial models indicates that long-run economic profits are possible if existing firms can choose their locations and deter entry (Eaton and Lipsey, 1978). Excess capacity may exist in monopolistically competitive markets since firms will produce less output than required for minimum average cost. These markets may generate too much or too little product differentiation depending on the strengths of two opposing effects. When a new firm enters the market with a new brand, it cannot acquire all of the consumer surplus from the new product. Since it is socially optimal to introduce a new product if the social benefits outweigh the social costs, there may be too little product differentiation when each firm cannot appropriate all of the CONSUMER SURPLUS generated by its brand. The opposing effect is that any new product is likely to steal consumers away from existing firms. Since these consumers were already served and stealing them represents a negative externality to the other firms that the entrant does not consider, there may be a tendency for too much product differentiation. The net effect depends on which of these two forces is stronger; see Dixit and Stiglitz (1977).

In markets where producers are oligopolists, each firm reacts to its rivals' strategies and so strategic behavior becomes important. Profit-maximizing firms must consider how their competitors will respond when determining their best strategy (*see* GAME THEORY). Since each firm's expectations about the reaction of rivals can be modelled in a variety of ways, predictions about the behavior and performance of oligopolists will depend upon the model. If the oligopolists were to collude on prices, a cartel would exist and the firms could collectively act as a monopoly. If there is no collusion between the firms, a noncooperative oligopoly exists. In models of noncooperative oligopoly, there may be COURNOT COMPETITION where each firm believes its rivals will keep their production levels (quantities) constant whatever its choice of output, or firms could compete through research and development expenditures, advertising, prices, product differentiation, or other means with varying expectations about competitors' responses in each case; see Lambin (1976).

When there is a single producer of a product, that firm has a monopoly in the market. The monopolist maximizes profits by restricting output and raising prices until marginal revenue equals marginal cost. This normally enables the firm to earn ECONOMIC PROFIT and to maintain monopoly to prevent other firms from entering the market.

These entry barriers may be granted by the government through licensing or patents, they may exist because of ECONOMIES OF SCALE (i.e. the firm is a natural monopoly), or they may be created by the firm itself through strategic behavior. Even a natural monopoly may not be sustainable if it can be profitable for entry at some price and cost combinations; see Sharkey (1982).

Bibliography

Carlton, D. W. & Perloff, J. M. (1994). *Modern Industrial Organization*. 2nd edn, New York: HarperCollins.
Dixit, A. & Stiglitz, J. (1977). Monopolistic competition and optimum product diversity. *American Economic Review*, 67, 297–308.
Douglas, E. J. (1992). *Managerial Economics*. 4th edn, Englewood Cliffs, NJ: Prentice-Hall.
Eaton, B. C. & Lipsey, R. G. (1978). Freedom of entry and the existence of pure profit. *Economic Journal*, 88, 455–69.
Lambin, J. J. (1976). *Advertising, competition, and market conduct in oligopoly over time*. Amsterdam: North-Holland.
Sharkey, W. W. (1982). *The Theory of Natural Monopoly*. Cambridge: CUP.

ROBERT E. McAULIFFE

basket of currencies   A group of currencies used as the basis for valuing a single monetary unit. Groups of countries in many parts of the world are cooperating to promote their mutual economic interests. In some cases this results in the harmonizing and/or centralizing of monetary transactions between the countries. A standardized monetary unit is essential in order to achieve true economic integration. One of the problems associated with a centralized monetary system is: "Which of the countries' currency should be used as the standard for the group?" In order to avoid problems associated with nationalist sentiment toward one currency or another, some country groups have opted to develop a new currency unit. For example, the European Community developed the European Currency Unit or ECU. The ECU is valued by combining the weighted average of each member country's existing currency value. The member's currencies are referred to as a "basket of currencies." The basket of currencies which establish the value of the ECU is comprised of the national currency of each European Community member.

JOHN O'CONNELL

BCG matrix   The BCG matrix, as its name implies, is the eponymous technique developed by the Boston Consultancy Group, that gained popularity in the 1970s. It was advanced as a technique for assisting companies to analyze their diverse business portfolios. It is based on two major premises. The first relates to what the BCG terms the experience curve effect by which the total costs involved in manufacturing, distributing, and selling a product decline with increased experience in production. The experience is a composite of economies of scale and specialization; the modifications to or redesign of products to obtain lower costs; productivity improvements from technological change and/or learning effects leading to the adoption of new production methods; and the displacement of less efficient factors of production. The effects of experience can be depicted by plotting real unit cost against cumulative production volume as a measure of accumulated experience. If logarithmic scales are used then a straight line is normally

obtained. In fact, the Boston Consultancy Group argued that real unit costs fall by 20 to 30 percent for each doubling of cumulative experience. The implication, then, is that businesses should focus on securing high volume, and therefore high MARKET SHARE, through aggressive pricing. The second premise is that the consumption of resources, in particular cash, is a direct function of market growth. BCG developed a four-box matrix (see figure 1) with market growth and market share relative to that of the next largest competitor (since this is the true indicator of COMPETITIVE ADVANTAGE) as the two parameters. Each is measured as "high" or "low." Businesses can then be categorized according to whether or not they are "stars" (high market growth, low relative market share); "cash cows" (low growth, high share); "problem children" (high growth, low share); or "dogs" (low growth, low share). The cash cows should have lower costs than their rivals and demand comparatively lower investment. They therefore generate cash which can be employed to convert some of the "question marks" into "stars" which are essentially cash neutral. The stars of today should become the cash cows of the future. Generally, it is argued that the deletion of the "dogs" should be seriously considered.

Relative market share

Market Growth	High	Low
High	Stars	Problem Children
Low	Cash cows	Dogs

Figure 1   The BCG Matrix

The technique has been extensively reviewed and apparently accepted, probably because of its simplicity and easy comprehensibility. However, there have been many criticisms. There may be problems in defining "market" and hence "market share"; the measures of "high" and "low" are subjective and easily manipulatable; the possibilities of external financing are excluded from the analysis; and the influence of non-price factors on demand tends to be ignored. Moreover, the approach is overly deterministic and the acceptance of its prescriptions could lead to suboptimum and even significantly inappropriate decisions. For example, so-called "dog" businesses might have cost and demand interrelationships with other businesses, and to delete these, as the analysis implies, could have adverse consequences for businesses at present in more attractive quadrants.

In general, the analysis rests on the assumption that businesses' products have a life cycle (*see* PRODUCT LIFE CYCLE), of which, in particular, the "mature" stage is of sufficient duration to enable the company to reap the benefits of its previous investments in current "cash cows." The industry might, however, witness the introduction of a new technology which might give a "groin kick" to the technology of the future cash cow, thereby undermining its future market position. The emphasis on market share can blinker decision-makers to such a possibility and perhaps further the dependence on a vulnerable industry, while rivals may leapfrog the firm by acquiring experience through the purchase of plant and equipment which embody state-of-the-art technology. Finally, cash cows may require considerable investment in order to protect their competitiveness, a fact which the analysis seems to overlook somewhat.

Bibliography

Hedley, B. (1976a). A fundamental approach to strategy development. *Long Range Planning*, **9** (6), 2–11.
Hedley, B. (1976b). Strategy and the "business portfolio". *Long Range Planning*, **10** (1), 9–15.
Wensley, R. (1981). Strategic marketing: Betas, boxes or basics. *Journal of Marketing*, **45**, 173–182.

DALE LITTLER

behavior A behavior is any observable act by an individual (e.g. talking, walking). Clusters of similarly related behaviors are often referred to as habits or trait. Behavior represents the lowest observable level of this hierarchy; work behaviors might include either purposeful or reflexive acts. Purposeful behaviors are goal-directed. They are usually directed toward achieving some performance outcome. Job behavior is believed to be a function of ability, motivation, and the opportunity afforded in a specific organizational setting (Campbell et al., 1970). Abilities include intelligence, skills and aptitudes, interests, and temperament factors (*see* KSAOs). Motivational factors include individual incentives, as well as temperament and preference predispositions to exert effort in performing one's job. Opportunity variables refer to situational and organizational factors, including nature of work, organizational climate, and group influences (see Campbell et al., 1970; Peters and O'Connor, 1980).

Bibliography

Campbell, J. P., Dunnette, M. D., Lawler, E. E. & Weick, K. E. (1970). *Managerial Behavior, Performance, and Effectiveness*, New York: McGraw-Hill.
Mischel, W. & Peake, P. K. (1982). Beyond deja vu in the search for cross-situational consistency. *Psychological Review*, **89**, 730–55.
Peters, L. H. & O'Connor, E. J. (1980). Situational constraints and work outcomes: the influences of a frequently overlooked construct. *Academy of Management Review*, **5**, 391–7.

JEANETTE N. CLEVELAND

behavior modeling Behavior modeling is one key aspect of social cognitive theory (Bandura, 1986) that has been investigated extensively in organizational settings. Through the process of observing others, an individual learns how behaviors are performed and the consequences they produce. As a result, observational learning enables individuals to reduce time-consuming trial-and-error behaviors. A meta-analysis of seventy studies on the effectiveness of management training showed that behavior modeling was effective in a variety of training situations (Burke and Day, 1986).

Behavior modeling training is a process in which a live or videotaped model demonstrates the behavior(s) required for performance. Individuals then imitate the model's behavior in simulated (e.g. role plays) or actual work situations. Typically, learning points are generated by the trainers and are used as a basis for providing feedback to the trainees regarding what was done effectively and what should be done differently.

Bibliography

Bandura, A. (1986). *Social Foundations of Thought and Action*, Englewood Cliffs, NJ: Prentice-Hall.
Burke, M. J. & Day, R. R. (1986). A cumulative study of the effectiveness of managerial training. *Journal of Applied Psychology*, **71**, 232–46.

COLETTE A. FRAYNE

behavioral observation scales Behavioral observation scales (BOS) are summated rating scales, one of the oldest and most popular formats for the appraisal of performance (Kirchner and Dunnette, 1957; Latham and Wexley, 1977, 1994). This popularity may be at least partially a result of the relatively simple process required for developing and using the scales.

The first step in the development of summated scales is to generate declarative statements that are related to work behavior and are either desirable or undesirable in nature. Latham et al. (1979) first gathered reports of CRITICAL INCIDENTS TECHNIQUE from persons familiar with the job of foreman and then wrote declarative statements based on those incidents. For example, all incidents that concerned a foreman rewarding an employee for doing a good job served as the basis for the declarative statement, "Praise and/or reward subordinates for specific things they do well." The same procedure was followed for all critical incidents. In this initial step of scale development, the idea is to err on the side of collecting too many items. Statistical analysis of the responses through an item analysis procedure can reduce the set of statements to a manageable number for practical use. However, the set of declarative statements should represent the entire domain of job performance.

Next, a format for scoring rater responses is selected. Numerous options are available, the most common of which are words of frequency (e.g. a continuum from "always" to "never") and of intensity (e.g. a continuum from "strongly agree" to "strongly disagree"). Although the response format is often arbitrarily selected, some studies indicate that there may be an optimal type and number of response categories for summated scales. Bass et al. (1974), for example, derived statistically optimal 4–9 point scales with adverbs for frequency and amount, while Spector (1976) identified optimal categories of agreement, evaluation, and frequency. In terms of the optimal number of scale points for summated scales, the research results are mixed (e.g. Komorita and Graham, 1965; Matell and Jacoby, 1971). Lissitz and Green (1975), however, found that reliability increases only up to 5 scale points, and levels off thereafter.

Once the declarative statements have been written and the response format and number of scale points selected, the next step is to organize the sequence of declarative statements on the rating format. Most summated scales are set up with a series of items, each followed by a format such as "strongly agree, agree, undecided, disagree, and strongly disagree." It is, however, advisable to change the order for the response format so that the responses are not always in the same position. This procedure is designed to preclude a response-set bias whereby the rater merely checks all responses on the far left (e.g. "strongly agree") or far right ("strongly disagree") without even reading the items. If the sequence of the response format is varied, the rater may have to pay greater attention to what and how to rate (*see* RATING ERRORS).

There should be a number of declarative statements representing each dimension. It is advisable to randomize all items on the appraisal instrument across dimensions. With the completion of these procedures, the summated scale is ready for an initial run. It is important to conduct an item analysis on the summated responses, but the item analysis can be done on data that are administratively useful. Thus, after the summated scales have been adjusted to reflect the item-analysis information, the resultant scores can be used for personnel decisions.

Research with BOS compared to other rating formats such as BEHAVIORALLY ANCHORED RATING SCALES shows little difference in psychometric characteristics, but raters prefer BOS to most other formats. There is no evidence of less (or more) bias as a function of this format (Bernardin et al., 1995).

Bibliography

Bass, B. M., Cascio, W. F. & O'Connor, E. J. (1974). Magnitude estimations of expressions of frequency and amount. *Journal of Applied Psychology*, **59**, 313–20.

Bernardin, H. J., Hennessey, H. W. & Peyrefitte, J. (1995). Age, racial, and gender bias as a function of criterion specificity: a test of expert testimony. *Human Resource Management Review*, **5**, 63–77.

Kirchner, W. K. & Dunnette, M. D. (1957). Identifying the critical factors in successful salesmanship. *Personnel*, **34**, 54–9.

Komorita, S. S. & Graham, W. K. (1965). Number of scale points and the reliability of scales. *Educational and Psychological Measurement*, **4**, 987–95.

Latham, G. P., Fay, C. H. & Saari, L. M. (1979). The development of behavioral observation scales for appraising the performance of foremen. *Personnel Psychology*, **32**, 299–311.

Latham, G. P. & Wexley, K. N. (1977). Behavioral observation scales for performance appraisal purposes. *Personnel Psychology*, **30**, 255–68.

Latham, G. P. & Wexley, K. N. (1994). *Increasing Productivity through Performance Appraisal*, **2nd edn**, Reading, MA: Addison-Wesley.

Lissitz, R. W. & Green, S. B. (1975). Effect of the number of scale points on reliability: a Monte Carlo approach. *Journal of Applied Psychology*, **60**, 10–13.

Matell, M. S. & Jacoby, J. (1971). Is there an optimal number of alternatives for Likert scale items? Study I: reliability and validity. *Educational and Psychological Measurement*, **31**, 657–74.

Spector, P. E. (1976). Choosing response categories for summated rating scales. *Journal of Applied Psychology*, **61**, 374–5.

H. JOHN BERNARDIN

---

behaviorally anchored rating scales   Behaviorally anchored rating scales (BARS) are graphic performance rating scales with specific behavioral descriptions defining various points along each scale (Smith and Kendall, 1963). Each scale represents a dimension, factor, or work function considered important for work performance. Typically, both raters and ratees are involved in the development of the dimensions and the generation of behavioral descriptions.

The original BARS procedure was basically an iterative process whereby a sample from the rater population began development of the scales. Their work was then scrutinized by additional samples of raters. In the original conceptualization of the BARS method, raters were instructed to record the behaviors observed on each applicable job dimension throughout the appraisal period. They were then to decide to which dimension each behavior belonged, and to indicate, on the rating scale, the date of and details associated with each incident. Each entry was to be made on the rating scale at the effectiveness level that was considered most appropriate for that incident. The scaling of the effectiveness level of the observation (that is, the place on the page at which the observer recorded the incident) was to be guided by a comparison with the series of illustrative "behavioral anchors" and generic performance level descriptors. The illustrative behaviors would have been identified from prior research as belonging to a particular job dimension and as representing a specific effectiveness level for that dimension.

It was not necessary that the notation of observed behavior be made at the exact point on the graphic scale at which some illustrative behavior had been previously scaled. Rather, the observer was to *infer* the behavioral dimension involved and to decide what had been observed in relation to the specific behavioral and more generic examples. The rater, thus, would interpolate between the illustrative examples when recording a brief notation of the behavior that had been observed.

The behavioral anchoring illustrations were to be concrete and specific, and located at irregular intervals along the relevant scale according to effectiveness. The dimensions themselves would have been chosen only after considerable discussion of organizational goals and objectives. After a period of observation and incident-recording, the rater could, if necessary, make a summary rating. This summary, plus the notes, could serve as a basis for discussion with the ratee and/or as a criterion measure.

Numerous variants of the BARS procedure have been introduced since the approach was first proposed. A complete discussion of the various appraisal formats that have been introduced under the guise of BARS can be found in Bernardin and Smith (1981). Several comparisons of the BARS approach to other rating methods, such as BEHAVIORAL OBSERVATION SCALES, have found no reliable advantage to any rating method, including BARS.

Bibliography

Bernardin H. J. & Smith, P. C. (1981). A clarification of some issues regarding the development and use of behaviorally anchored rating scales. *Journal of Applied Psychology*, **66**, 458–63.

Smith, P. C. & Kendall, L. M. (1963). Retranslation of expectations: an approach to the construction of unambiguous anchors for rating scales. *Journal of Applied Psychology*, **47**, 149–55.

H. JOHN BERNARDIN

---

benchmarking   In the late 1970s, the Xerox Corporation woke up to the fact their Japanese competitors were selling copiers at prices at which Xerox could sometimes not manufacture. After realizing this, Xerox set out to understand why and to learn, from their competitors, concepts such as value engineering and tear down. Xerox also began to learn from competitors about other best practice techniques. This has developed into the now widely

Table 1 The Xerox 12-Step Benchmarking Process.

Step	Description
Phase 1 – planning	
1	Identify what to benchmark
2	Identify comparative companies
3	Determine data collection method and collect data
Phase 2 - analysis	
4	Determine current performance gap
5	Project future performance levels
Phase 3	
6	Communicate findings and gain acceptance
7	Establish functional goals
Phase 4 - action	
8	Develop action plans
9	Implement specific actions and monitor progress
10	Recalibrate benchmarks
Phase 5 - maturity	
11	Attain leadership position
12	Fully integrate practices into processes

Source: Bogan & English (1994, p. 82).

practised methodology of benchmarking, and has been extended to all elements of a business.

There are usually around ten generic categories for designing benchmarking architecture:

- customer service performance
- product/service performance
- core business process performance
- support processes and services performance
- employee performance
- supplier performance
- technology performance
- new product/service development and innovation performance

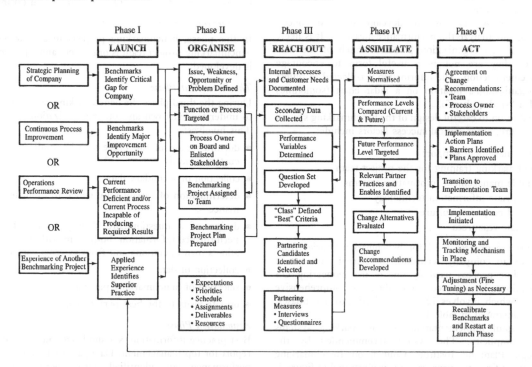

Figure 1 The benchmarking process.

Table 2   Integrating benchmarking and re-engineering

Seven-step re-engineering process	*Tools applied*
Step 1. Identify the value-added, strategic processes from a customer's perspective.	Performance benchmark analysis (cost, quality, cycle time, and the like). Customer satisfaction benchmark analysis. Value analysis.
Step 2. Map and measure the existing process to develop improvement opportunities.	Flowcharting and process management tools. Performance measurement tools.
Step 3. Act on improvement opportunities that are easy to implement and are of immediate benefit.	Informal benchmarking for short-term solutions. Implementation planning tools.
Step 4. Benchmark for best practices to develop solutions, new approaches, new process designs, and innovative alternatives to the existing system.	Best practice benchmarking among processes and performance systems.
Step 5. Adapt breakthrough approaches to fit your organization, culture, and capabilities.	Process redesign tools. Implementation planning tools.
Step 6. Pilot and test the recommended process redesign.	Training, and pilot test techniques. Apply lessons learned from past successful pilots.

- cost performance
- financial performance

In designing a benchmark architecture, the first step is to design a system that enables management to achieve the organization's strategic objectives.

Second, it is necessary to create a common language for measuring performance. This should be consistent with the corporate culture.

Third, it is necessary to develop plans to collect, process, and analyze the performance measures. It is likely that while the organization possesses much of the data needed, they are not in a useful form to encourage management action. The information is collected to reflect the organization's position on a radar chart (sometimes called a "spider chart").

In addition to careful design of the benchmarking system architecture, other critical success factors include:

- top management support
- benchmarking training for the project team
- suitable management information systems
- appropriate information technology
- internal corporate culture
- adequate resources

The precise process used for benchmarking varies from company to company according to internal culture and needs. The process used by one of the pioneering US corporations, Xerox, used one of the more comprehensive systems which involves 12 steps divided into five phases, and is illustrated in table 1.

Successful implementation of benchmarking systems favors simplicity. The system recommended by the Strategic Planning Institute Council on Benchmarking advocates a five-step process. This is illustrated in figure 1. These phases are explained in the following subsections.

Launch

The launch phase requires management to decide which improvement areas have the greatest impact or potential for the corporation. These usually flow from the STRATEGIC PLANNING process, from an analysis of the corporation's internal and external best practices. Continuous monitoring should also be undertaken to identify opportunities for improvement in CORE PROCESS functions and businesses.

The Organize Phase

In this phase, benchmarking projects to a clear focus, a benchmarking project team is organized, and a project plan is developed.

The Reach Out Phase

During the third phase the benchmarking team reaches out to understand its own and other organizations' processes. This involves:

- documentation of the process to be studied, based on customer needs
- collection of secondary data
- determination of variables by which to evaluate performance
- design of a questionnaire through which to solicit performance information, both from within the corporation's own operations and from external corporations
- collection of data
- selection of benchmarking partners
- on-site visits to the best performing partners

Assimilation Phase

Best practice information is assimilated and prepared for a report for top management. Data gathered are normalized, performance gaps identified, future performance goals targeted, and implementation for changes recommended.

Act Phase

In this final phase the benchmarking team works with senior management and core process owners to develop an agreed implementation program. This leads to the development of formalized action plans, implementation schedules measurement and monitoring systems, and benchmark recalibration plans. Once this has been done, responsibility passes to an implementation benchmarking team.

Benchmarking is not only a tool in its own right but also forms an essential component in re-engineering projects (*see* VALUE-DRIVEN RE-ENGINEERING). The integration between these two activities is illustrated in table 2.

Bibliography

Anonymous (1987). *Leadership through quality: implementing competitive benchmarking.* Xerox Corporation Booklet, Part 1.

Anonymous (1992). *Benchmarking: focus on world class practices.* AT&T.

Anonymous (1993). *Benchmarking. PIMS Letter on Business Strategy No. 54.* PIMS Europe Ltd.

Bogan, C. E. & English, M. J. (1994). *Benchmarking for best practices, winning through innovative adaptation.* New York: McGraw-Hill. (This is one of the best books to date on the benchmarking process and this entry has drawn heavily on this work.)

Garvin, D. (1993). Building a learning organization. *Harvard Business Review,* 71, 78–91.

McNair, C. J. & Leibfried, K. H. J. (1992). *Benchmarking.* New York: HarperCollins.

Walleck, S. A., O'Halloran, D. & Leader, C. A. (1991). Benchmarking. *McKinsey Quarterly* no. 1, 3–24.

DEREK F. CHANNON

benefit allowance An employee may receive additional payments from the employer with which to purchase insurance or other types of benefits. Expatriates also receive such payment although the benefits purchased may be different from those normally purchased in the home country. For example, education expenses for private schooling for children may seem appropriate benefit overseas, but left unfunded by the employer while in the home country.

see also **Compensation package**

JOHN O'CONNELL

benefits communication Compared with pay (direct compensation), the communication of benefits (indirect compensation) is a much greater challenge for employers. Although benefits typically comprise at least a third of total compensation costs, many benefit plans are not clearly apparent to employees. For example, vacations, holidays, and other forms of paid time off are part of employees' paychecks and not always recognized as benefits even though they represent an expense to employers. Also some benefits (e.g. pension plans and flexible benefit programs) can be especially difficult for employees to understand.

To ensure that employees receive essential information about pension and other benefit plans the Employee Retirement Income Security Act (ERISA) mandates certain written communication. These include requirements that participants receive the following documents, written in clear and appropriate language: (a) a summary plan description (SPD) for all applicable plans with information about eligibility and ERISA rights with plan identification information and an explanation of inquiry and appeal processes; and (c) a summary annual report (SAR) containing relevant financial information for all applicable plans.

Beyond meeting mandatory requirements, most employers now realize that a proactive communications program is needed to build awareness, understanding, and appreciation among employees with respect to benefits.

An increasingly popular method of communication is the personalized annual benefit report, which combines computer-produced individual information with standard text. Other techniques now utilized by employers to achieve communications goals include: (a) paycheck inserts; (b) articles in company publications; (c) contests; (d) interactive computer programs; (e) video cassettes; (f) employee meetings and focus groups; or (g) letters to the home and internal memoranda.

Bibliography

Kumata, H. (1979). *Communication Dynamics for Employee Benefit Programs,* Brookfield, WI: International Foundation of Employee Benefit Plans.

McCaffery, R. M. (1992). *Employee Benefit Programs: a Total Compensation Perspective,* Boston: PWS-Kent.

ROBERT M. MCCAFFERY

Berne Convention for the Protection of Literary and Artistic Works (1886) The Berne Convention is one of the oldest agreements dealing with copyright protection. Under the Berne Convention member countries offer each other the same protections as they would provide for their own citizen's copyrights. This is referred to as "national treatment." Copyrights protected by this agreement include those for the written word, music, and visual arts. Copyrights are afforded protection for the life of the author plus fifty years. Although the United States is not a signatory to the Berne Convention, US copyright laws also allow protection for the author's life plus fifty years.

Bibliography

Schultz, J. S. & Windsor, S. (1994). *International intellectual property protection for computer software: A research guide and annotated bibliography.* Littleton, CO: Fred B. Rothman & Company.

Seminsky, M. & Bryer, L. G. (eds) (1994). *The new role of intellectual property in commercial transactions.* New York: John Wiley & Sons.

JOHN O'CONNELL

best practices This was a related activity which formed part of the work out process in the US General Electric company. Historic success had led to a degree of complacency in the company and, as part of his radical campaign to modify the culture of GE, Jack Welch instituted a program of effectively BENCHMARKING GE against a carefully selected group of companies that were also seen as excellent in terms of management practices. Nine companies, including seven major US corporations and two leading Japanese multinationals, participated in a year-long study to identify these concerns' best practices. The main findings of the study were that these highly productive concerns exhibited the following characteristics:

- They managed processes rather than people.

- They used process mapping and benchmarking to identify opportunities for improvement. This involved writing down every single step, no matter how small, in a particular task.
- They emphasized continuous improvement and praised incremental gains.
- They relied on customer satisfaction as the main measure of performance, so overcoming the tendency to focus on internal goals at the customer's expense.
- They stimulated productivity by introducing a constant stream of high-quality new products for efficient manufacturing.
- They treated suppliers as partners.

Bibliography
Tichy, N. M. & Sherman, S. (1993). *Control your own destiny or someone else will.* London: HarperCollins. See p. 205.

DEREK F. CHANNON

beta coefficient   In portfolio theory, a company's beta coefficient measures the variability of that company's returns relative to the variability of the returns in the market and it helps determine the company's cost of capital within the capital asset pricing model. An investor who can always receive the risk-free rate of return, r_f, will want to be compensated for additional risk from holding any stock. This is the risk premium for that stock and represents the additional return required by investors over the risk-free rate. If investors have diversified their portfolios, the additional risk incurred by investing in stock j is not the variance of that company's returns (since diversification will reduce some of the risk), but rather how that company's returns relate to the rest of the portfolio. The beta coefficient measures the additional risk a given stock adds to a portfolio and for stock j it is defined as:

$$B_j = ((r_j - r_f, r_m - r_f))(r_m - r_f)$$

where cov() is the covariance of the risk premium of stock j with the risk premium of the market portfolio, var() is the variance of the risk premium of the market, r_f is the risk-free rate of return, r_j is the return to stock j and r_m is the return to the market portfolio. The beta coefficient is simply the estimated coefficient from a linear regression of the risk premium for stock j against the risk premium for the market as a whole.

A company can determine its cost of equity capital by determining the risk premium diversified investors will require to add stock j to their portfolios. This is given by:

$$\text{cost of equity capital} = r_f + \beta_j(r_m - r_f)$$

where β_j is the beta coefficient for company j. Since an average stock will move with the market, an average stock should have a beta coefficient of one. This means that the cost of equity capital for such a company equals the market return: if the market rises or falls by one percent, the company's stock will also rise or fall by one percent. If a company's beta coefficient is 2.5, the stock will rise or fall two and a half times more than any rise or fall in the market. This would be a more risky stock to add to the portfolio and a portfolio comprised of such stocks would be considered aggressive.

Bibliography
Berndt, E. R. (1991). *The Practice of Econometrics.* Reading, MA: Addison-Wesley.
Brigham, E. F. & Gapenski, L. C. (1993). Intermediate Financial Management. New York: Dryden.
Shughart, W. F., Chappell, W. F. & Cottle, R. L. (1994). *Modern Managerial Economics.* Cincinatti, OH: South-Western Publishing.

ROBERT E. MCAULIFFE

bill of materials   The bill of materials (BOM) is a file or set of files which contains the "recipe" for each finished product assembly in a material requirements planning system. It consists of information regarding which materials, components and sub-assemblies go together to make up each finished product, held on what is often known as a product structure file. Associated data about each item, such as part number, description, unit of measure and lead time for manufacturing or procurement are held on a part or item master file.

For each finished product, a bill of materials is originally created from design and process planning information. The designs might be developed internally or be supplied by the customer. They will initially be in the form of drawings and material lists. The process planning information may be in the form of assembly charts. Together with information on the relevant lead times, these form the basis of the inputs to the BOM.

While most MRP systems can cope with part numbers allocated at random, it is necessary for all items within the organization to be given a unique part number. Clearly the information on the BOM needs to be accurate, since inaccuracies can lead to incorrect items or incorrect quantities of items being ordered. This accuracy needs to be audited. However, in many operating environments, there are continual changes to the BOM in the form of product modifications. These modifications may originate from many sources, such as safety legislation, production process changes, improvements for marketing purposes or value analysis exercises. The control of the implementation of modifications can be a time-consuming task, especially since factors such as the depletion of unmodified stocks and the timing of combined modifications have also to be considered.

There is an accepted numbering system for BOM levels which allocates level 0 to the finished product and increases the level number as the raw material stage is approached. Items that appear at several levels in a BOM, for example in the final assembly as well as in sub-assemblies, are usually assigned the lowest level code at which the item occurs. This ensures that when MRP processing proceeds from one level code down to the next, all gross requirements for the item are accumulated before continuing any further (*see* NETTING PROCESS IN MRP).

The number of levels of assembly breakdown is determined by the complexity of the product; however some BOMs are unnecessarily complicated by including too many sub-assembly stages, and many companies have made determined efforts to flatten their BOM structures.

Bills of materials for hypothetical products are sometimes created to help in the forecasting and master production schedule of products which could have an extremely wide variety of saleable end items. These are referred to as planning BOMs, and may take the form of modular BOMs or BOMs which separate out common items from optional items and features. For example, in car production, there may be thousands of items common to each model; there may also be optional items such as air conditioning assemblies and features such as an automatic gearbox or a manual gearbox. If forecast ratios of the take-up of these optional and feature sub-assemblies can be determined, then a planning BOM can be created using these ratios as the "quantity per" parent hypothetical finished product. It is these planning BOMs that are then used for master production scheduling in this environment.

see also **Manufacturing resources planning**

Bibliography

Clement, J., Coldrick, A. & Sari, J. (1992). *Manufacturing data structures: Building foundations for excellence with bills of material and process information.* Essex Junction, VT: Oliver Wight.
Vollmann, T. E., Berry, W. L. & Whybark, D. C. (1992). *Manufacturing planning and control systems.* New York: Irwin.

PETER BURCHER

Black–Scholes   This is a famous equation for determining the price of an option, first discovered in 1972 by Fischer Black of Goldman Sachs and Myron Scholes of the University of Chicago and published in Black and Scholes (1973). The unique insight of this research was to use arbitrage in solving the option-pricing problem. Black and Scholes reasoned that a position which involved selling a call option and buying some of the underlying asset could be made risk-free. It would be a hedged position and, as such, should pay the risk free rate on the net investment. Using continuous-time mathematics they were able to solve for the call price from the equation for the hedged position. This resulted in an equation for the value of a European option (i.e. one which cannot be exercised before maturity) which did not need to take account of the attitude to risk of either the buyer or seller.

The equation (expressed for a call option) is:

$$c = SN(d_1) - Ee^{-rt}N(d_2)$$

where c is the call price, S is the asset price, $N(x)$ is a normal-distribution probability, E is the exercise price, r is the interest rate in continuous form and t is years to maturity.

The $N(d_1)$ and $N(d_2)$ values, which are probabilities from the normal-distribution, have values for d_1 and d_2 calculated as follows:

$$d_1 = \frac{log(S/E) + rt + 0.5\sigma^2 t}{\sigma\sqrt{t}}$$

and

$$d_2 = d_1 - \sigma\sqrt{t}$$

where σ is the standard deviation of returns on the asset per annum.

In the equation, the value of a call option depends on five variables: the asset price (S), the exercise price (E), the continuous interest rate (r), the time to maturity (t), and the standard deviation of returns on the asset (σ) (which is usually known as the volatility). Of these five variables, only the volatility is unknown and needs to be forecasted to the maturity of the option. The call price in the equation is a weighted function of the asset price (S) and the present value of the exercise price (Ee^{-rt}). The weights are respectively $N(d_1)$, which is the hedge ratio or "delta" of the option, and $N(d_2)$, which is the probability that the option matures in the money.

Many academic papers have proposed more complicated models, only to conclude that the simple Black–Scholes model can be modified to give almost equally good results. Several assumptions are necessary to derive the model, but it is surprisingly robust to small changes in them. The first assumption is that the asset price follows a random walk with drift. This means that the asset price is lognormally distributed and so returns on the asset are normally distributed. This assumption is widely used in financial models. The second assumption is that the distribution of returns on the asset has a constant volatility. This assumption is clearly wrong and use of the model depends crucially on forecasting volatility for the period to maturity of the option. The third assumption is that there are no transaction costs, so that the proportions of the asset and option in the hedged portfolio may be continuously adjusted without incurring huge costs. This assumption sounds critical, but it is relatively unimportant in liquid markets. The fourth assumption is that interest rates are constant, which is not correct but is of little importance since option prices are not very sensitive to interest rates. The fifth assumption is that there are no dividends on the asset, which once again is unrealistic, but modification of the model to accommodate them is relatively simple (e.g. Black, 1975).

While most of the theoretical results in finance have not had any impact on practitioners, the Black–Scholes model is universally known and used. The existence of the equation has facilitated the development of markets in options, both on-exchange (beginning with the Chicago Board Options Exchange in 1973) and over the counter. Without the equation, there could not have been such rapid growth in the use of derivative assets over the last twenty years. Many derivative assets might even not exist.

Bibliography

Black, F. & Scholes, M. (1973). The pricing of options and corporate liabilities. *Journal of Political Economy*, 81, 637–59.
Black, F. (1975). Fact and fantasy in the use of options. *Financial Analysts Journal*, 31, 36–41, 61–72.

GORDON GEMMILL

bluffing and deception   Deception can be defined as causing someone to have false beliefs (or intentionally causing someone to have false beliefs). To bluff in a negotiation is to attempt to deceive the other party about one's intentions or negotiating position. Another kind of deception that is common in both negotiations and sales is deception about the features of the good or service being sold.

Bluffing

It is generally contrary to one's own self-interest to reveal one's intentions while negotiating. A seller who is negotiating with a potential customer usually has a minimum price below which she is unwilling to sell. Generally, it would be contrary to her own self-interest for her to reveal her minimum price, for, if she does, the buyer will be unwilling to offer anything more than that minimum. It can be to one's advantage to make false claims about one's negotiating position, e.g., a seller stating a minimum acceptable price that is higher than her actual minimum or a buyer misstating the maximum price she is willing to pay. Such claims can enable one to reach a more favorable settlement than one would have otherwise obtained. But, if (as in most cases) the parties to the negotiation don't know the negotiating position of the other party, misstating one's intentions in this way risks losing an opportunity to reach a mutually acceptable agreement. (One might state a position unacceptable to the other party when, in fact, one's actual position is acceptable to him.)

Is it morally wrong for negotiators to make deliberate false claims about their intentions or negotiating positions? For example, would it be wrong for me to tell you that $90,000 is absolutely the lowest price that I will accept for my house, when I know that I would be willing to accept as little as $80,000? Such statements count as lies according to most dictionary definitions of lying; they are intentional false statements that are intended to deceive others. However, Carr argues that such statements are not lies since people do not expect to be told the truth about such matters in negotiations. On Carr's account, nothing said by a notoriously dishonest person could constitute a lie, because others do not expect her to speak truthfully. (See Carson 1993 for a detailed discussion of the question of whether bluffing constitutes lying.)

According to Carr, it is morally permissible for people to misstate their intentions in negotiations, because "it is normal business practice" and is "within the accepted rules of the business game." Carr claims that actions which conform to normal and generally accepted business practices are *ipso facto* morally permissible. This principle seems highly implausible in light of reflection on such things as slavery and child labor, which were once normal and "generally accepted" business practices. Carson, Wokutch, and Murrmann (1982) argue that the morality of misstating one's negotiating position depends on the actions of the other parties to the negotiation: there is a strong presumption against misstating one's negotiating position if the other party is not misstating her position, but little presumption against doing this if the other person is misstating her position. Carson (1993) develops a "generalized principle of self-defense." This principle implies that the moral presumption against lying and deception does not hold when one is dealing with people who are, themselves, engaged in lying and deception and thereby harming one.

Deception about the Nature of the Products being Sold

In negotiations sellers often provide prospective buyers information about the goods or services being sold. What are the obligations of sellers in such cases? This question is central to ethics of sales. We need to distinguish between deception, lying, withholding information, and concealing information. Roughly, deception is causing someone to have false beliefs. Lying arguably requires the intent to deceive others, but lies that don't succeed in causing others to have false beliefs are not instances of deception. A further difference between lying and deception is that, while all lies are false statements, deceiving someone needn't involve making false statements; true statements can be deceptive and some forms of deception don't involve making any statements. Withholding information does not constitute deception. It is not a case of *causing* someone to have false beliefs; it is merely a case of failing to correct false beliefs or incomplete information. On the other hand, actively concealing information usually constitutes deception. Both negotiators and salespeople make factual representations about goods and services they are selling. Deceptive statements about what is being sold (whether or not they are lies) raise serious ethical questions. There is, on the face of it, a strong moral presumption against such statements due to the harm they are likely to cause potential buyers.

Discussions of the ethics of sales often focus on the ethics of withholding information. The legal doctrine of *caveat emptor* ("buyer beware") says that sellers are not obligated to inform prospective buyers about the properties of the goods they sell. Buyers, themselves, are responsible for determining the quality of the goods they purchase. *Caveat emptor* permits sellers to withhold information about the things they sell, but it doesn't permit lying or (active) deception about such matters. Many take this legal principle to be an acceptable moral principle and hold that sellers have no moral duty to provide buyers with information about the goods they are selling. David Holley argues that *caveat emptor* is no longer an acceptable standard. Given the complexity of many modern goods, it is impossible for most people to judge their quality with any accuracy. Holley claims that salespeople are obligated to reveal all information they would want to know if they were considering buying the product. This seems too strong; it implies that a sales clerk in a store is obligated to inform customers if he knows that the product they are looking at can be purchased at a lower price elsewhere.

see also **Negotiation; Negotiation tactics**

Bibliography

Carr, A. (1968). Is business bluffing ethical? *Harvard Business Review*, **46**, 143–53.

Carson, T. (1993). Second thoughts about bluffing. *Business Ethics Quarterly*, **3**, 317–41.

Carson, T., Wokutch, R., & Murrmann, K. (1982). Bluffing in labor negotiations: Legal and ethical issues. *of Business Ethics*, 1, 13–22.

Dees, J. & Crampton, P. (1991). Shrewd bargaining on the moral frontier: Towards a theory of morality in practice. *Business Ethics Quarterly*, 1, 135–67.

Ebejer, J. & Morden, M. (1988). Paternalism in the marketplace: Should a salesman be his buyer's keeper? *Journal of Business Ethics*, 7, 337–9. (This paper criticizes both *caveat emptor* and Holley's views.)

Holley, D. (1986). A moral evaluation of sales practices. *Business and Professional Ethics Journal*, 5, 3–22.

Kavka, G. (1983). When two "wrongs" make a right: An essay in business ethics. *Journal of Business Ethics*, 2, 61–6.

THOMAS L. CARSON

bonuses Bonuses are cash payments for employees who achieve a goal or level of performance that is desired by management. Bonuses are a type of VARIABLE COMPENSATION that is given out on a one-time only basis and is not built into the salary (Belcher and Atchison, 1989). Bonuses are very flexible and can be used to reward employees for achieving goals that represent individual, team, unit, or organization performance (Gomez-Mejia and Balkin, 1992). For example, GAINSHARING plans will provide a bonus to all employees in a work unit if they are able to exceed expected unit performance standards within a specified period of time.

Bibliography

Belcher, D. W. & Atchison, T. J. (1989). *Compensation Administration*, 2nd edn, Englewood Cliffs, NJ: Prentice-Hall.

Gomez-Mejia, L. R. & Balkin, D. B. (1992). *Compensation Organizational Strategy and Firm Performance*, Cincinnati, OH: South-Western.

DAVID B. BALKIN

brand   The original thinking behind branding was to take a commodity and to endow it with special characteristics through imaginative use of name, PACKAGING, and ADVERTISING. Aaker (1991) defines a brand as: "a distinguishing name and/or symbol (such as a logo, trademark, or package design) intended to identify the goods or services of either a seller or a group of sellers and to differentiate those goods or services from those of its competitors." Central to the value or equity of the brand is a set of assets, including: BRAND LOYALTY; brand awareness; perceived quality; and brand associations. A manufacturer brand is initiated by a producer, such as Coca Cola, and a private or "own-label" brand is initiated by a retailer, such as Tesco's "Value" product line (*see also* PRODUCT).

Bibliography

Aaker, D. A. (1991). *Managing brand equity – Capitalizing on the value of a brand name*. New York: Free Press. Chapter 1.

Macrae, C. (1991). *World class brands*. Reading, MA: Addison Wesley.

MARGARET BRUCE

brand equity   There has been increasing contemporary consideration of brand value or equity. This can be regarded as "the incremental cash flow resulting from a product with the brand name vs the cash flow which would result without the brand name" (Schoker & Weitz, 1988). Successful brands generally have a set of powerful associations attributed to them by customers that act to differentiate them clearly from competing products. These qualities embrace intangible factors which collectively form the image of the brand, as well as other aspects of the product, such as performance, which generally reinforce this general brand image.

It is generally argued that there has to be continued investment in the brand through advertising and product development to project and support the brand's values. The returns are in the form of higher margins that customers are prepared to pay for the particular benefits attributed to the brand and BRAND LOYALTY, the latter being especially important given the costs of replacing lost customers, and the additional revenues that can be obtained over the lifetime of existing customers through, for example, cross-selling of other products.

Some companies have attempted to value their brands but to date there has been no agreed methodology for including these values in companies' balance sheets. Firms often seem prepared to pay significant amounts to acquire brands, as the Nestle takeover of Rowntree seemed to indicate. However, in the acquisition of brands, the additional value paid for the perceived value of a brand is, under existing UK accounting practice, written off as "goodwill." Nevertheless, the value of the brand is being challenged. Friday April 2, 1993, which has gone down in history as "Marlboro Friday," appeared to be apocalyptic for the brand. Under pressure from cheaper "generic" cigarettes, Philip Morris reduced the price of Marlboro cigarettes by a fifth. In hindsight, the strategy appears to have been successful since Marlboro's market share and revenues have subsequently recovered. Commentators have argued that in this case, at least, Philip Morris had allowed the price differential between Marlboro and its competitors to increase beyond a level that consumers regarded as reasonable for the image that Marlboro had. Nevertheless, many retailers market products under their own name which benefit from the perceived values associated with the retailer and which are generally offered at a lower price than manufacturers' brands. The power of manufacturers to influence the channel of distribution through their own brands which have influential customer franchises is being eroded and more manufacturers, in order to ensure continued volume of output, are being compelled to supply retailer branded merchandise.

Bibliography

Peters, T. (1988). *Thriving on chaos*. New York: Macmillan, as quoted in P. Doyle (1994). Branding. In M. J. Baker (Ed.), *The marketing book* 3rd edn, (pp. 471–483). Oxford: Butterworth Heinemann.

Schoker, A. & Weitz, B. (1988). A perspective on brand equity – principles and issues. In L. Leuthesser (Ed.), *Defining, measuring and managing brand equity: a conference summary* (pp. 88–104). Cambridge, MA: Marketing Science Institute.

D. LITTLER

brand loyalty   Consideration of consumer buying behavior over a period of time involves an understanding of brand loyalty which follows from the formation of brand images and brand preferences.

Brand image is a set of associations or perceptions that consumers have for a brand; it is awareness or recognition. It also implies attitudes toward a brand, either positive or negative, which are learned over time.

Brand preference is a definite expression of positive attitude. One would normally expect people to buy a preferred brand or brands, assuming that they are in the market for the product. However, there are occasions when the product may not be needed or the consumer cannot afford the preferred brand, or the preferred brand may not be available.

Brand loyalty implies purchasing the same brand more than once, again assuming that this is the preferred brand, although this may not necessarily be the case. Brand preference and brand loyalty may exist in relation to manufacturers' brands (e.g., Heinz) and distributors' brands (e.g., Safeway), and loyalty may prevail with respect to stores.

Definitions of brand loyalty have evolved and are typically concerned with a degree of consistency in the preference for each brand by a consumer, over a specified period of time. Some definitions also refer to "biased choice behavior" with respect to branded merchandise, or "consistent" purchasing of one brand, or the proportion of purchases a consumer (or household) devotes to the brand most often bought. There are inherent dangers in looking at sequences of purchases to define and measure loyalty as individuals and households may be buying more than one brand on a regular basis (e.g., toothpaste, breakfast cereals).

Further, Day (1970) offers a two-dimensional concept of brand loyalty, bringing together attitudes and behavior. He asks "Can behavior patterns be equated with preferences to infer loyalty?," and distinguishes between spurious and intentional loyalty. Spurious loyalty may just be habit or consistent purchase of one brand due to non-availability of others, continuous price deals, better shelf space, etc. Intentional loyalty occurs when consumers buy a preferred brand, as would be evidenced by some attitude measurement. When a consumer is intentionally loyal and insists on a particular brand, he or she will be prepared to shop around for this brand, or defer purchase if the brand is unavailable – rather than accept a substitute.

Research has been unable to pinpoint particular determinants of brand loyalty, though a number of empirical investigations have suggested and looked for relationships between brand loyalty and: personal attributes, e.g., socioeconomic variables; group influence; levels of demand; sensitivity to promotion; and store factors.

Nevertheless, manufacturers and distributors are concerned to encourage loyalty to their brands and switching away from other brands. Consumers switch brands for reasons of: curiosity with respect to new/different brands; disappointment with present brand; reassurance with respect to a favored brand; chance; inducement; and availability. Additionally, consumers may be multi-brand buyers for reasons of: indifference; perception that brands are perfect substitutes; for variety's sake; several preferences within a household; and as a response to availability and promotions.

Bibliography

Carmen, J. M. (1970). Correlates of brand loyalty: Some positive results. *Journal of Marketing Research*, 7, Feb., 67–76.

Day, G. S. (1970). *Buyer attitudes and brand choice behavior*. Chicago: Free Press.

Jacoby, J. & Chestnut R. (1978). *Brand loyalty: Measurement and management*. New York: Ronald/John Wiley.

BARBARA LEWIS

brand piracy This is the unauthorized and therefore illegal use of a brand name or product which has trademark, patent, or copyright protection. It is a form of property right theft which is common in many countries of the world. "Rolex" watches may be purchased in many parts of Southeast Asia for $29.95 or in New York City for $50.00. Louis Vuitton handbags are sold in many parts of the world for 10% of their cost in Louis Vuitton stores. Of course these watches and handbags are copies of the original with pirated brand names and designs. Copies of original designs using well-known brand names are often referred to as knock-offs. Knock-offs of well-known brands of watches, clothing, handbags, and other products account for billions of dollars in lost revenues each year for the legal producers of the products. International producers of items subject to brand pirating must carefully research protections provided by countries in which they trade.

see also **Intellectual property**

Bibliography

Cateora, P. R. (1993). *International marketing*. 5th edn, Homewood, IL: Irwin.

International Intellectual Property Alliance Staff (1992). *Copyright piracy in Latin America: Trade losses due to piracy and the adequacy of copyright protection in 16 Central and South American countries*. Washington, DC: International Intellectual Property Alliance.

JOHN O'CONNELL

bribery The seeking to influence a decision (most commonly of a public official) through the giving of favors, gifts, or money directly to the official or to others on his/her behalf. Bribery of a public official is illegal in virtually all countries. Both the official and the person presenting the bribe are subject to criminal action if found guilty of the act. A problem exists, however, as to what the exact nature of bribery is and when (if ever) it is legal to make payments to officials or others to obtain preferential treatment. Some countries have attempted to outline legal versus illegal activities in their antibribery legislation (*see* FOREIGN CORRUPT PRACTICES ACT for the United States' approach). Generally, if a payment or gift is given in order to influence the decision of a public official, the payment is a bribe and is illegal.

Bribery or questionable payments are known by many names throughout the world. The following is a partial list of terms used in various languages. Note that the terms used below are not all illegal activities in their home country:

Language	term	meaning
Arabic:	baksheesh	"gratuity"
French:	pot-de-vin	"jug of wine"
	or pourboire	"tip"
German:	nutzliche abgabe	"useful contribution"
	or Schmiergeld	"grease money"
Italian:	bustarella	"little envelope"
	or baccone	"little bite"
Japanese:	kuroi kiri	"black mist"
Persian:	bakshish	"tip"
Spanish:	el soborno	"payoff"
	or la Mordida	"the bite" (Mexico)
Yiddish:	schmir	"smear" or "grease"

English: Bribery, pay offs, payola, lure, bait, compensation, lubrication, grease payments, and others.

Bibliography

Bowie, N. E. (1990). "Business ethics and cultural relativism" in P. Madsen and J. M. Shafritz (eds) *Essentials of Business Ethics*. New York: Meridian.

Coye, R. (1986). Individual values and business ethics. *Journal of Business Ethics*, 5 (1), 45–9.

D'Andrale, K. (1985). Bribery. *Journal of Business Ethics*, 4, 239–48.

Johnson, H. L. (1985). Bribery in international markets: Diagnosis, clarification, and remedy. *Journal of Business Ethics* May, 447–55.

Lane, W. H. & Simpson, D. G. (1984). Bribery in international business: Whose problem is it? *Journal of Business Ethics* February, 35–42.

Tong, H. (1982). What American business managers should know and do about international bribery. *Baylor Business Studies* November, 7–18.

JOHN O'CONNELL

broadbanding   Broadbanding is a pay innovation that collapses a pay structure with many pay grades into a structure with a few larger pay ranges called bands (Caudron, 1993). Each band covers a pay range that formerly represented several pay grades. Broadbanding gives managers greater flexibility to encourage employees to move in a horizontal direction in their careers by broadening their skills and competencies. Firms that have delayered their hierarchies and reduced the number of job titles and promotion opportunities for employees may benefit from the increased flexibility in the pay structure that can be provided by broadbanding (Abosch, 1995). Broadbanding places a decreased emphasis on remuneration based on job evaluation and use of control points such as a midpoint or a maximum of pay range. It places an increased emphasis on encouraging employees to develop new skills and paying for the skills according to their market value.

Broadbanding can be used to reinforce teamwork and collaboration since it reduces hierarchy and status differences between employees in the pay structure. Firms that use the pay and promotion systems to recognize status and hierarchial differences between employees may not have a culture that is supportive of a broadbanding pay policy (Hofrichter, 1993).

Bibliography
Abosch, K. S (1995). The promise of broadbanding. *Compensation and Benefits Review*, **27**, 54–8.
Caudron, S. (1993). Master the compensation maze. *Personnel Journal*, **72**, 64B–64O.
Hofrichter, D. (1993). Broadbanding: a "second generation" approach. *Compensation and Benefits Review*, **25**, 53–8.

DAVID B. BALKIN

budget constraint   When choosing the products which will give the consumer the most satisfaction, a consumer's expenditures cannot exceed his or her budget. In practice, this constraint may include the resources available through borrowing and selling assets, but, in most textbook examples, the consumer is limited to this period's income. For example, to illustrate a consumer's decision to buy two products, X and Y, where the consumer's entire income will be exhausted on these two goods, the budget constraint would be:

$$I = P_x^* X + P_y^* Y$$

where I is the consumer's income, P_x is the price of good X, X is the quantity of X consumed. If the consumer spent all of her income on good X, then Y would be zero and the maximum amount of X which could be consumed is $X = (I/P_X)$. The budget constraint shows the combinations of the products the consumer could feasibly buy given market prices and the consumer's income and shows the rate at which a consumer is *able* to substitute purchases of X for Y. Utility maximization requires that the rate at which consumers are able to substitute products just equals the rate that they *desire* to do so given their tastes. The consumer's desired rate of substitution is his or her marginal rate of substitution and utility is maximized when the consumer's indifference curves are just tangent (equal) to the budget constraint.

When the budget constraint is plotted with good Y on the vertical axis and good X on the horizontal axis, the vertical intercept of the budget constraint will be (I/P_Y) (where the consumer spends all of her income on good Y) and the slope of the budget line will be $-P_X/P_Y$. An increase in P_Y will make the budget constraint flatter, reducing the height of the vertical intercept (since less of Y can be purchased) while an increase in P_X will make the budget line steeper and will reduce the horizontal intercept.

Bibliography
Douglas, E. J. (1992). *Managerial Economics*. 4th edn, Englewood Cliffs, NJ: Prentice-Hall.
Shughart, W. F., Chappell, W. F. & Cottle, R. L. (1994). *Modern Managerial Economics*. Cincinatti, OH: South-Western Publishing.

ROBERT E. MCAULIFFE

budgeting   Budgeting is the process by which the goals of an organization, and the resources to attain those goals, are quantified and communicated. Specifically, budgets are used to plan and control operations and to make long-term investments. Planning entails coordination, marshalling and allocating resources, and control involves performance evaluation.

In not-for-profit organizations like government agencies and charities, the focus of budgeting has been to balance revenues from taxes or donations with expenditures. Recently governments world-wide have been facing pressures to raise efficiency while maintaining balanced budgets. These pressures may change the focus of budgeting to stress efficiency and prioritization of expenditures. The US Government Performance and Results Act of 1993 is an example of this change.

Financial Planning

Planning is achieved through a series of interrelated budgets known as the master budget. The master budget is a coordinated business plan, which summarizes the planned operating, investing, and financing activities of the business for the budget period.

Figure 1: Amount of $500,000 budget allocated to Manager A (in $1000s). Bargaining zone is noted by x's

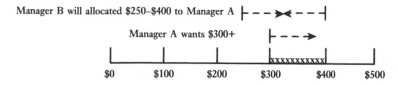

The master budget, portrayed in figure 1, comprises two sets of budgets: (1) operating budgets, and (2) financial budgets. Within these two broad categories of operating and financial budgets, there can be an unlimited number and variety of budgets and sub-budgets, depending on the level of detail desired. Operating budgets summarize the expected operating activities – sales, purchases, labor, overhead, and discretionary expenses – culminating in the income statement. The income statement is sometimes grouped with financial budgets. Here it is included with operating budgets on the premise that it is a summary display of operating results during the budget period. Financial budgets summarize the investing activities, cash flows, and the pro forma balance sheet. These budgets articulate in that they feed into each other and form part of an interdependent whole. But the impetus clearly flows from operations.

At the epicenter of budgeting is the projected sales. Forecasting sales is critical because all other budgeted activities depend on it. Organizations develop demand forecasts in different ways. Some use highly sophisticated models and market surveys, while others rely on simple extrapolations of past year's sales. Many use multiple sources of information including the views of line managers and field sales force. Forecasts from these separate sources are consolidated into the final sales budget.

The sales forecast is used to develop budgets for operating, investing, and financing activities. For operations, the forecast is used to budget for the acquisition of inputs and for discretionary spending. Operating budgets vary by industry and by company. Manufacturing firms develop a production budget showing the product units to be manufactured, ending inventories for work-in-process and finished goods, direct labor, direct materials, and overhead. A budget for selling and administrative expenses is also prepared. Merchandising firms, on the other hand, develop budgets for merchandise purchases together with budgets for labor, inventories, and selling and administrative expenses. Service firms develop a set of budgets that show how the demand for their services will be met.

The sales forecast is also used to prepare the financial budgets. The capital budget summarizes the investing activities – resources that require medium- and long-term advance commitment. The advance commitments ensure that capacity is on hand when expected sales materialize. But they also entail considerable risk, because, once committed, they cannot be altered easily in the short run. These commitments inject rigidity into the cost structure of the firm, magnifying the impact of small variations in sales on profits – a condition known as the operating leverage effect.

The cash budget reflects the cash flows associated with planned operating, investing, and financing activities. The importance of the cash budget stems from its strategic role in cash management – investing surpluses and financing deficits. For global enterprises, these "treasury functions" can become highly complex, not only because of the burgeoning supply of derivatives (futures, options, swaps, caps, floors, collars, etc.), but also because different financing strategies entail different risk profiles. Reliance on debt to leverage the return to shareholders entails additional constraints and higher fixed financing costs. These fixed costs further magnify the impact of demand variability on profits – a condition known as the financial leverage effect.

The pro forma balance sheet incorporates the cumulative results of all the budgeted activities to display the financial position of the firm at the conclusion of the budget period. It shows the projected configuration of assets, liabilities, and shareholders' equity. If desired or mandated configurations are not obtained, then budgets are revised to reconfigure the balance sheet.

When budgets are approved, resources are allocated to implement the planned activities. As implementation proceeds, results are monitored for control and evaluation.

Management Control

Control often centers on operating activities, i.e., profits. To this end, two budgets are used: one for the forecasted level of activity – the master budget – and the other for the level of activity actually attained – the flexible budget. The latter is based on the same input – output ratios for variable inputs as in the master budget. These two budgets together with actual results are used to disaggregate the profit variance between profits under the master budget and actual profits into two components: (1) profits missed or earned because of failing to reach or exceeding the forecasted level, and (2) profits missed or earned because of efficiency and price variances. These aggregate differences are decomposed further into specific volume and price variances. An alternative but less customary formulation is to divide the differences between actual profits and profits under the master budget into (1) a profit-linked productivity measure derived by comparing actual profits with profits based on a flexible budget using budgeted input-output ratios but actual prices, and (2) another component lumping the effects on profits of volume and price differences between the master budget and the flexible budget. But to have confidence in any of these measures, it is imperative not only to have truthful budgets, but also to have knowledge about how different costs behave in response to changes in the level of activities.

Cost Behavior

Accountants have traditionally relied on the economist's short-run cost curves to understand the behavior of costs. They have, therefore, assumed that costs either change with output (variable) or remain constant (fixed). Although this dichotomy has the advantage of providing a quick perspective of the behavior of costs as a function of volume, it is flawed because it suppresses valuable detail about the behavior of costs.

Two momentous events have combined to heighten the need for a better knowledge of costs and to provide the wherewithal to meet that need. One is the growing intensity of global competition; the other is the unrelenting wave of information technology. The former has raised the cost of relying on distorted cost information, while the latter has lowered the cost of getting the needed information. Consequently, the focus on cost behavior has shifted from volume as the cost driver to activities as cost drivers. Under this so-called activity-based costing (ABC), activities drive costs, and products, markets, and customers drive activities. In diversified firms operating in competitive markets, a detailed knowledge of cost drivers can provide a strategic advantage.

Focus on activities undertaken to attain the organization goals raises three types of questions. First, which activities are indispensable for the attainment of organization goals and how can they be done with fewer resources? Second, which activities are dispensable for the attainment of organization goals and how can they be eliminated? Third, which activities can be supplied with and without acquiring a capability in advance? The first two lead to a distinction between value-added and non-value-added activities. For value-added activities, budgets aim at getting *more* output with *fewer* resources. Performance evaluation is driven by the input – output efficiency or productivity. However, the simple model of volume-driven costs is substituted by activity-driven costs. For non-value-added activities, budgets aim at getting *less* output with *fewer* resources, i.e., use less of the non-value-added activities with even lower costs. Performance evaluation is driven by the progress made toward the eventual elimination of these activities.

The third question has strategic implications. Resources are either acquired on demand or in fixed quantities in advance before actual demand is realized. For resources acquired on demand, costs are flexible. Productivity enhancements immediately translate into profits. For resources acquired in advance, costs are independent of the amount used – at least in the short run. Productivity enhancements do not translate into profits instantaneously. Profits will not improve unless released capacity from one activity is redeployed in another value-added activity or until spending is reduced.

Managerial Behavior

Organizational theorists have posited a positive relationship between subordinate performance and participation in budgeting. Two sets of behavioral issues arise when such budgets are used for performance evaluation: impact of budgeting on behavior and truthful budgeting and reporting. Both fall under the concept of goal congruence – the alignment of individual and organizational goals.

Budgets that emphasize specific rather than firm-wide outcomes may induce myopia and window dressing. Emphasis on cost-cutting may motivate managers to resort to myopic actions like purchasing large quantities of materials to get price discounts and producing large quantities of finished products to avail themselves of economies of scale. But both these actions increase inventories *and* costs. When budgets stress a single measure, managers resort to gaming behavior – window dressing – to manipulate that measure regardless of its side-effects.

A system-wide, integrated control and evaluation system using multiple performance measures alleviates the problem (Kaplan, 1990; Campi, 1992; Atkinson et al., 1995). This approach admits that maximizing the efficiency of sub-units is not equivalent to maximizing the efficiency of the whole firm (Turney, 1991). But multiple performance measures do not necessarily influence the direction and intensity of a manager's effort in the same way. A perfectly congruent and noiseless performance measure will induce optimum results – maximum intensity in the best direction. A performance measure is noisy when events other than the manager's efforts influence the measure. Recent research cautions that if the basic measure is perfectly congruent but noisy, then the primary role for additional performance measures is to reduce noise (Feltham & Xie, 1994). The use of noncongruent performance measures would produce results that differ from the optimum in both direction and intensity. Similarly, if a performance measure is noiseless but noncongruent, then the role for additional measures will be to improve congruence. However, if the additional measures are noisy, then results will again differ from the optimum in both direction and intensity.

Truthful budgeting and reporting are the domain of the agency theory (Jensen & Meckling, 1976). Contemporary literature asserts that misrepresentation of information occurs because of two conditions: (1) the subordinate manager has *private* information that top management needs for budgeting, and (2) the information is used for both budgeting and performance evaluation. These two conditions give rise to what is known as moral hazard, where the subordinate is motivated to misrepresent private information because of the very nature of the evaluation system. The existence of moral hazard creates another phenomenon called information impactedness. This arises when subordinates have valuable private information, but do not communicate it truthfully because of fear of jeopardizing their self-interest.

Internal managerial reporting falls into two categories: managerial reporting as part of contracting process and managerial reporting outside the context of a contracting setting (Baiman & Evans, 1983; Conroy & Hughes, 1987). Under the first category, a common difficulty is devising an appropriate incentive structure to induce truth in budgeting and maximum intensity of effort in execution (Weitzman, 1976). By providing penalties for understating budgets and bonuses for achieving and even larger bonuses for exceeding the budget, managers are induced to avoid slack and shirking. Empirical evidence suggests that risk-averse subordinates create more slack than risk-neutral ones, and that truth-inducing schemes reduce slack for the latter group, not for the former (Young, 1985; Waller, 1988). The implication is to induce subordinates into risky behavior to reduce slack (Kim, 1992). Nevertheless, the link between participation and slack remains equivocal. In fact, there is old and new evidence that participation reduces slack through better communication, even when budgets are used for evaluation and there is information asymmetry (Dunk, 1993; Cammann, 1976; Merchant, 1985; Onsi, 1973).

The second category involves information impactedness in capital budgeting (Sridhar, 1994). It is shown that truthful reporting depends on the manager's talent. A more talented manager always reports his or her assessment of a project truthfully, while a less talented manager may report truthfully or untruthfully when the magnitude of the difference between the productivities of the more and the less talented managers is small. Otherwise, the less talented manager understates the benefits of a project to discourage investment and guard his or her reputation. Either way, the firm's investment decisions are bound to be distorted.

Bibliography

Atkinson, A. A. et al. (1995). *Management Accounting*. Chapter 14, Englewood Cliffs: Prentice-Hall.

Baiman, S. & Evans III, J. H. (1983). "Predecision Information and Participative Managerial Control Systems." *Journal of Accounting Research*, Autumn, 371–95.

Cammann, C. (1976). "Effects of the use of Control Systems." *Accounting, Organizations and Society*, 301–13.

Campi, J. P. (1992). "It's Not as Easy as ABC." Journal of Cost Management, Summer, 5–12.

Conroy, R. & Hughes, J. (1987). "Delegating Information Gathering Decisions." *The Accounting Review*, Jan., 50–66.

Dunk, A. S. (1993). "The Effect of Budget Emphasis and Information Asymmetry on the Relation Between Budgetary Participation and Slack." *The Accounting Review*, April, 400–10.

Feltham, G. A. & Xie, J. (1994). "Performance Measure Congruity and Diversity in Multi-Task Principal/Agent Relations." *The Accounting Review*, July, 429–53.

Jensen, M. C. & Meckling, W. H. (1976). "The Theory of the Firm, Managerial Behavior, Agency Costs, and Capital Structure." *Journal of Financial Economics*, Oct., 305–60.

Kaplan, R. S. (ed.) (1990). *Measures for Manufacturing Excellence*. Boston: Harvard Business School Press.

Kim, D. C. (1992). "Risk Preferences in Participative Budgeting." *The Accounting Review*, April, 303–18.

Merchant, K. A. (1985). "Budgeting and the Propensity to Create Budgetary Slack." *Accounting, Organizations and Society*, 201–10.

Onsi, M. (1973). "Factor Analysis of Behavioral Variables Affecting Budgetary Slack." *The Accounting Review*, July, 535–48.

Sridhar, S. S. (1994). "Managerial Reputation and Internal Reporting." *The Accounting Review*, April, 343–63.

Turney, P. B. B. (1991). "How Activity-Based Costing Helps Reduce Cost." *Journal of Cost Management*, Winter, 29–35.

Waller, W. (1988). "Slack in Participative Budgeting: The Joint Effect of a Truth-Inducing Pay Scheme and Risk Preference." *Accounting, Organizations and Society*, Feb., 87–98.

Weitzman, M. L. (1976). "The New Soviet Incentive Model." *Bell Journal of Economics*, Spring, 251–57.

Young, M. (1985). "Participative Budgeting: The Effects of Risk Aversion and Asymmetric Information on Budgetary Slack." *Journal of Accounting Research*, Autumn, 829–42.

M. ALI FEKRAT

bureaucracy　This widely used concept has a variety of meanings, some positive, some less so. The sociologist Weber (1946) thought bureaucracy synonymous with rational organization: bureaucracies embodied the ideals of rational–legal Authority such that all but policy decisions are based on rules, which themselves are internally consistent and stable over time (*see* DECISION MAKING). Political scientists tend to think of bureaucracy as governance by bureaus having the following characteristics: they are large, they are staffed by full-time employees who have careers within the organization, and they rely on budget allocations rather than revenues from sales since their outputs cannot be priced in voluntary *quid pro quo* (Downs, 1967; Wilson, 1989). There is a third definition of bureaucracy, which is far less flattering; bureaucracy is inefficient organization, is inherently antidemocratic, cannot adapt to change, and, worse, exacerbates its own errors (Crozier, 1964). Discussion of bureaucracy tends to be ideologically tinged. The political left emphasizes the rationality and neutrality of government while downplaying the power of bureaucracy itself, while the right uses bureaucracy as an epithet or shibboleth and focuses on bureaucracy's antidemocratic tendencies and inefficiencies.

Properties of Bureaucracy

The properties of bureaucracy are best understood in comparison with other forms of organization. Weber, for example, focuses on comparisons between bureaucracy and traditional forms of administration. Compared to traditional organizations, the structure of bureaucracy exhibits much greater differentiation and integration. With respect to differentiation, there is intensive division of labor, a hierarchy of authority, and, perhaps most importantly, a clear separation of official duties from personal interests and obligations, what Weber calls separation of home from office. With respect to integration, bureaucracies have written rules and regulations, codified procedures for selection and advancement of officials, and a specialized administrative staff charged with maintaining these rules and procedures. And compared to traditional organizations, bureaucracies constrain the conduct of officials while offering powerful incentives for compliance. The constraints lie in strict super- and subordination requiring all actions to be justified in terms of the larger purposes of the organization, the norm of impersonality that requires detachment and objectivity, and advancement contingent on both seniority and performance (*see* CONTROL). The incentives consist of the prospect of a lifetime career, salaries paid in cash rather than in kind, and (in Europe if not the United States) a modicum of social esteem attached to the status of official or *fonctionnaire*. The elements of differentiation, integration, constraints, and incentives render bureaucratic organizations both more powerful and more responsive to central authority than traditional administration. The power of bureaucracies results from their capacity for coordinated action. Their responsiveness to centralized authority arises from the dependence of individual bureaucrats on their salaries and other emoluments of office. These four elements, according to Weber, also render bureaucracy more efficient than traditional forms of organization. "Precision, speed, unambiguity, knowledge of the files, continuity, discretion, unity, strict subordination, reduction of friction and of material and personal costs – these are raised to the optimum point in the strictly bureaucratic administration . . ." (Weber, 1946, p. 214).

Compared to modern business organizations, bureaucracies have somewhat different and in some respects less attractive properties. One must ask, to begin, whether comparison of business and bureaucracy is warranted given Weber's insistence that the bureaucratic model describes both private and public administration. Public and private administration were remarkably similar at the time Weber was writing. Indeed, much of the United States public sector was modeled explicitly after the private sector at the beginning of the twentieth century. It is not accidental that the reform movement in the United States, which called for administration devoid of politics, coincided with the emergence of scientific management, which called for active management of firms. Nor is it accidental that in the 1940s the same theory of organization was believed to apply to public- and private-sector enterprises. Public and private organizations have diverged in the last 50 years, however. Divergences have occurred in several domains, most notably organizational design, accounting practices, and performance measurement. With respect to organizational design, virtually all large firms have moved from functional to divisionalized organizational structures, that is, from designs in which the principal units are responsible for different activities (such as purchasing, manufacturing, and sales) to designs in which the principal units are self-contained businesses responsible for profit as well as for other objectives (*see* DECENTRALIZATION). To be certain, patterns of divisionalization have changed over time – firms typically have fewer and somewhat larger business units as a result of several waves of DOWNSIZING – but until very recent times there have been no comparable innovations in the public sector (*see* ORGANIZATIONAL DESIGN). For the most part, public agencies have retained the same organizing principles – organization by function – they used 90 years ago. With respect to accounting, public-sector agencies have departed substantially from private-sector practices. At the beginning of this century, public entities issues consolidated financial reports and maintained capital accounts just like private businesses. Consolidated accounting gave way to much more complicated fund accounting during the 1920s, when it was believed necessary to segregate revenues and expenditures intended for different purposes into separate funds. Capital accounting has all but disappeared from the public sector, though accounting for long-term indebtedness remains out of necessity. With respect to performance measurement, the public sector lags substantially behind private businesses (*see* ORGANIZATIONAL CHANGE). In business operations, not only is financial analysis necessary and universal, but firms' internal operations are often typically gauged against industry benchmarks assembled by consultants and trade associations. By contrast, very little comparative performance assessment exists for government. In the United States, at least, performance comparisons across governmental units are strongly resisted. Just as at the beginning of the twentieth century, some efforts to make government more businesslike are now underway. Some services have been privatized altogether. Others have been placed in public corporations, which are held responsible for breaking even if not making a profit. And some government agencies now measure customer satisfaction, just as businesses do.

Liabilities of Bureaucracy

If public-sector bureaucracies suffer in comparison with private-sector management, one must ask whether these liabilities arise from systematic causes, that is, the structure of bureaucracies themselves, or from other causes. Both sociologists and economists have argued that at least some of the liabilities of bureaucracy are systematic, although for different reasons. Sociologists have focused on bureaucratic dysfunctions of various kinds, including displacement of goals, so-called vicious cycles in which different dysfunctions feed on one another, and spiraling bureaucratic growth. Economists, by contrast, have emphasized the efficiency disadvantages of bureaucracies compared to firms, asking whether, in general, nonmarket transactions are inefficient compared to market transactions and, specifically, the funding of bureaucracies through budgets rather than market transactions is conducive to over-production of bureaucratic services. These potential liabilities of bureaucracy should be reviewed seriatim.

Displacement of goals. Bureaucracies are known for rigid adherence to rules and procedures, even when rules and procedures appear to impede the objectives of the organization. The notion of goal displacement provides both a description and an explanation for this seemingly nonrational conduct. Goal displacement, following Merton (1958), describes the process whereby means become ends in themselves, or "an instrumental value becomes a terminal value." The displacement of goals is especially acute in settings, such as bureaucracies, where the following conditions obtain: the technical competence of officials consists of knowledge of the rules, advancement is contingent on adherence to the rules, and peer pressure reinforces the norm of impersonality, which requires rules and procedures to be applied with equal force in all cases. What is important is goal displacement, at least as originally conceived, argues that bureaucracies are efficient in general – under conditions anticipated by their rules and procedures – but inefficient in circumstances that cannot be anticipated. The implications of goal displacement for INNOVATION and new product development have been realized only gradually: bureaucracy can be antithetical to innovation.

Vicious cycles. A more thoroughgoing critique of bureaucracy argues that dysfunctions are normal rather than exceptional and, moreover, that dysfunctions accumulate over time such that organizational stasis is the expected outcome. The elements of the vicious cycle of bureaucratic dysfunctions are impersonal rules that seek to limit the discretion of individual workers, centralization of remaining decisions, isolation of workers from their immediate supervisors as a consequence of limited DECISION-MAKING authority, and the exercise of unofficial power in arenas where uncertainty remains. Thus, as Crozier (1964) observes, maintenance people exercise undue influence in state-owned factories because their work is inherently unpredictable and cannot be governed by rules. The logic of vicious cycles, it should be pointed out, yields several consequences. To begin, new rules will arise to eliminate whatever islands of POWER remain in the organization, but these rules will trigger further centralization, isolation, and power plays as new sources of UNCERTAINTY arise. Second, to the arising externally, line managers have the opportunity to reassert power that would otherwise erode through the dynamics of vicious cycles. External crisis, in other words, may be an antidote to bureaucracies' tendency toward rigidity over time.

Spiraling growth. Bureaucratic systems also tend toward growth other things being equal (Meyer, 1985). Until recently, growth of government and of administrative staff in private firms was endemic. The causes of growth lie in several factors, but chief among them are people's motives for constructing organizations in the first place. People construct formal organizations in order to rationalize or make sense of otherwise uncertain environments; organizations, in fact, succeed at making the world more sensible; as a consequence, there is continuous construction of bureaucracy and hence bureaucratic growth as people attempt to perfect their rationalization of an inherently uncertain world (*see* ORGANIZATION AND ENVIRONMENT). Two comments are in order. First, the logic of bureaucratic growth is built into administrative theory as developed by Simon (1976) and others. Irreducible uncertainty in the environment in conjunction with the belief that administrative organization can rationalize uncertainty will result in continuous growth in administration. Second, the growth imperative is so strong that deliberate campaigns to "downsize" or "restructure" organizations must be launched in order to achieve meaningful reductions in staff (*see* RESTRUCTURING). Downsizing continues to occur at record rates in United States' firms but may have reached a limit now that modest industrial expansion is underway.

Inefficiency. Economists have asked persistently without resolution whether public sector bureaucracies are inherently less efficient than private-sector enterprises. Several answers have been proffered, none fully satisfactory. From the 1940s to the present time, the Austrian school of economics, von Mises (1944) and others, have argued that any departure from market principles yields both inefficient transactions and antidemocratic tendencies. This position has proved difficult to reconcile with contemporary transaction–cost theories, which argue that hierarchies may be more efficient than markets under some circumstances. In the 1970s, the efficiency question was cast somewhat differently: might bureaus, which depend on budgets for their sustenance, overproduce compared to firms subject to the discipline of the market (Niskanen, 1971)? Here too the answer was equivocal, as analysis showed that rent-maximizing monopolists would have similar incentives to overproduce whether they were located in public bureaucracies or private firms. Despite the absence of strong analytic underpinnings for the belief that bureaucracies are more apt to harbor inefficiencies than private-sector organizations, PRIVATIZATION of governmental functions is occurring rapidly and with positive results in many countries. It is unclear whether the liabilities of public bureaucracies are simply the liabilities of established organizations that have been shielded from extinction for too long, or whether bureaucracies suffer disadvantages in comparison with private organizations regardless of their age.

Research on Bureaucracy

Organizational research and research on bureaucracy were once synonymous or nearly so, as the bureaucratic model was believed descriptive of all organizations, for-profit and non-profit, and governmental (*see* NOT-FOR-PROFIT MARKETING). Case studies of bureaucracy written during the 1950s and 1960s encompassed government agencies and industrial firms alike as evidenced by titles like Gouldner's (1954) *Patterns of Industrial Bureaucracy*. Early quantitative research on organizations, such as the work of the Aston group and the studies emanating from the Comparative Organization Research Program in the United States, focused mainly on relations among elements of organizational structure (size, hierarchy, administrative ratio, formalization, centralization, etc.) that flowed from the bureaucratic model implicitly if not explicitly (Blau & Scheonherr, 1971). As attention shifted to external causes of organizational outcomes, the bureaucratic model lost some of its relevance to research. Thus, for example, the key causal variable in resource dependence models of organizations is control of strategic resources, which is more germane to businesses than to government bureaus. The key dependent variables in organizational POPULATION ECOLOGY are births and deaths of organizations, which are infrequent in the public sector. And institutional organizational theory has very much downplayed Weber's notion of bureaucracy as rational administration and has

substituted for it the notion that all organizations, bureaucratic and nonbureaucratic alike but especially the former, seek social approval or legitimation rather than efficiency outcomes (*see* LEGITIMACY).

Some research on bureaucracy remains. Development economists continue to study the role of national bureaucracies in promoting or retarding economic growth. Others, again mainly economists, pursue the comparative efficiency of private- versus public-sector service delivery and possible advantages of creating competition among public agencies. And the study of public administration remains a viable although by no means a growing field. But research on bureaucracy is no longer at the core of organizational theory even though most of the public sector and much of the administrative component of the private sector continues to be organized along bureaucratic lines.

Bibliography

Blau, P. M. & Schoenherr, R. (1971). The structure of organizations. New York: Basic Books.

Crozier, M. (1964). The bureaucratic phenomenon. Chicago: University of Chicago Press.

Downs, A. (1967). Inside bureaucracy. Boston: Little-Brown.

Gouldner, A. W. (1954). Patterns of industrial bureaucracy. Glencoe: Free Press.

Merton, R. K. (1958). Bureaucratic structure and personality In Social theory and social structure, (2nd edn, pp. 195–206). Glencoe: Free Press.

Meyer, M. W. (1985). Limits to bureaucratic growth. Berlin and New York: de Gruyter.

Niskanen, W. (1971). Bureaucracy and representative government. Chicago: Aldine.

Simon, H. A. (1976). Administrative behavior, (3rd edn) New York: Free Press.

Weber, M. (1946). Bureaucracy In H. Gerth and C. Wright Mills (Eds), From Max Weber: Essays in sociology, (pp. 196–244). Glencoe: Free Press.

von Mises, L. (1944). Bureaucracy. New Haven: Yale University Press.

Wilson, J. Q. (1989). Bureaucracy. New York: Basic Books.

MARSHALL W. MEYER

business and society Business and Society has two meanings. (1) It refers to the relationships that business firms have with society's institutions and nature's ecosystems. (2) The term also refers to the field of management study that describes, analyzes, and evaluates these complex societal and ecological linkages.

Business and Society Relationships

Business, while recognized as an economic activity, is strongly affected by the surrounding social and ecological environment. A society's legal system, its politics and government regulations, community attitudes and public opinion, concepts of morality and ethics, and the forces of social change including science, technology, and rivalry among nations, can exert both negative and positive influences upon a business firm's costs, prices, and profits. Global business firms particularly must learn to deal effectively with demographic diversity, religious and ethnic movements, and public concerns about ecological impacts of business operations.

Business exerts a reciprocal influence upon society through its economic decisions and policies, such as providing jobs, creating income, producing goods and services, and investing capital in plant, equipment, and new product development. These beneficial economic impacts are frequently accompanied by negative social impacts, such as environmental pollution, hazardous working conditions, unsafe or unreliable consumer products, various forms of discriminatory practices, illegal and unethical actions, and excessive political influence on a society's political and governmental systems. A positive social influence may be felt when business firms provide social services not otherwise available, such as health care and retirement plans for employees; when they design and build attractive and environmentally sensitive plants and offices, or lend executives to local governments or nonprofit institutions, or support local community initiatives through philanthropic contributions to educational, cultural, and charitable organizations.

Quite clearly, in these and other ways, business and society influence one another, sometimes negatively and sometimes with positive results for both (Paul, 1987; Sethi and Falbe, 1987).

Business and Society as a Field of Management Study
In the United States, the two central questions that led to the formation of a new field of management study, variously called "Business and Society," "Business and Its Environment," and "Social Issues in Management," were rooted in the reciprocal ties that bind business and society to one another. The questions were: (1) Should a business firm deliberately and voluntarily try to promote social goals and purposes other than those involved in the pursuit of profits? (2) If so, what criteria should determine the content, scope, and limits of business's social responsibilities?

Two schools of thought developed. One asserted that corporations should voluntarily act in socially responsible ways, even if doing so lowered profits. Howard Bowen's 1953 book, *Social Responsibilities of the Businessman*, was the first comprehensive statement of this doctrine. Earlier in the century, however, a few corporate leaders had acknowledged the need for business firms to look beyond profit goals by accepting a measure of social responsibility for their actions (Heald, 1970). The Committee for Economic Development (1971) affirmed this position by proposing a social contract between business and society that broadened business's social responsibilities.

Others (Friedman, 1970) opposed these views, saying that business makes its main contribution to society by producing goods and services at a profit under competitive market conditions. Nothing should be allowed to interfere with this economic function, as long as business operations are conducted legally and ethically. Voluntarily seeking social goals would be economically diversionary, would penalize socially responsible firms by imposing extra costs not experienced by their less responsible competitors, would substitute private corporate judgments for public policy, and would reintroduce a corporate paternalism hostile to free choice. A related view (Chamberlain, 1973) expressed doubt that even the most well-intentioned social initiatives undertaken by corporations could have a significant impact due to their interference with deeply ingrained profit motives, economic growth, and the public's preference for high levels of consumer goods and services.

This basic philosophical argument was gradually replaced by three further theoretical developments, each of which became a conceptual pillar of this new field of study. Some scholars (Preston & Post, 1975; Buchholz, 1992) argue that corporate social performance is best monitored through the instruments of public policy and government regulatory agencies such as the Environmental Protection Agency, the Consumer Product Safety Commission, the Equal Employment Opportunity Commission, the Occupational Safety and Health Commission, etc. Companies could take their cues for publicly desired social actions by adhering to the nation's laws, public policies, and government regulations, rather than relying on the social conscience of the firm's executive managers.

Other scholars (Freeman, 1984) believe that corporations can best attain their overall strategic objectives, both economic and social, by responding positively to stakeholder demands, thus substituting corporate social performance for the more philosophical principle of SOCIAL RESPONSIBILITY (Ackerman, 1975; Frederick, 1994; Miles, 1987). A closely related view is that specific social issues affecting a given company can be identified, tracked, and managed to the firm's advantage (Wartick & Cochran, 1985). Theories incorporating the public policy/stakeholder responsiveness/issues management approaches had become the field's dominant conceptual paradigm by the early 1990s.

During the 1980s, BUSINESS ETHICS also became a significant component of Business and Society studies. Introduced into the field by business ethics philosophers, it represents an effort to apply moral principles to ethical issues that arise in the workplace (Beauchamp and Bowie, 1988; Donaldson, 1989).

To summarize, the Business and Society field of management study attempts to clarify business's multiform relations with society and thereby to improve the ability of firms to plan and manage their interactions with this broad social and ecological environment. Because economic, social, political, ecological, and ethical interests are affected by these linkages, many of the questions studied are controversial and ultimately philosophical in nature, while nevertheless bearing on the effective management of the firm (Preston, 1986; Wood, 1991).

In the United States, four professional academic organizations promote Business and Society teaching and research: the Social Issues in Management division of the Academy of Management, founded in 1971; the Society for Business Ethics, founded in 1978; the Society for the Advancement of Socio-Economics, founded in 1989; and the International Association for Business and Society, founded in 1989–90.

see also **Economics and ethics; Social responsibility; Stakeholder theory**

Bibliography

Ackerman, R. W. (1975). *The Social Challenge to Business*. Cambridge, Mass: Harvard University Press.

Beauchamp, T. & Bowie, N. E. (1988). *Ethical Theory and Business* 3rd edn, Englewood Cliffs, NJ: Prentice-Hall.

Bowen, H. R. (1953). *Social Responsibilities of the Businessman*. New York: Harper.

Buchholz, R. A. (1992). *Business Environment and Public Policy: Implications for Management and Strategy* 4th edn, Englewood Cliffs, NJ: Prentice-Hall.

Chamberlain, N. W. (1973). *The Limits of Corporate Responsibility*. New York: Free Press.

Committee for Economic Development. (1971). *Social Responsibilities of Business Corporations*. New York: Committee for Economic Development.

Donaldson, T. (1989). *The Ethics of International Business*. New York: Oxford University Press.

Frederick, W. C. (1994). From CSR₁ to CSR₂: The maturing of Business and Society thought. *Business and Society*, 33, 150–64.

Freeman, R. E. (1984). *Strategic Management: A Stakeholder Approach*. Boston: Pitman.

Friedman, M. (1970). The social responsibility of business is to increase its profits. *New York Times Magazine* 13 Sept.,122–6.

Heald, M. (1970). *The Social Responsibilities of Business: Company and Community, 1900–1960*. Cleveland, Ohio: Case-Western Reserve Press.

Miles, R. H. (1987). Environment: A Grounded Theory. Englewood Cliffs, NJ: Prentice-Hall.

Paul, K. (Ed.) (1987). *Business Environment and Business Ethics: The Social, Moral, and Political Dimensions of Management*. Cambridge, Mass: Ballinger.

Preston, L. E. (1986). Social issues in management: An evolutionary perspective. In D. A. Wren & J. A. Pearce (eds), *Papers Dedicated to the Development of Modern Management*. Ada, Ohio: Academy of Management.

Preston, L. E. & Post, J. E. (1975). *Private Management and Public Policy: The Principle of Public Responsibility*. Englewood Cliffs, NJ: Prentice-Hall.

Sethi, S. P. & Falbe, C. M. (eds), (1987). *Business and Society: Dimensions of Conflict and Cooperation*. Lexington, Mass: Lexington Books.

Wartick, S. L. & Cochran, P. (1985). The evolution of the corporate social performance model. *Academy of Management Review*, 10, 758–69.

Wood, D. J. (1991). Corporate social responsiveness revisited. *Academy of Management Review*, 16, 691–718.

WILLIAM C. FREDERICK

business ethics   The study of ethics is the study of human action and its moral adequacy. Business ethics, then, is the study of business action – individual or corporate – with special attention to its moral adequacy. Business persons confront ethical issues, whatever their position in the corporate structure and whatever the size and complexity of the organization. Sometimes responsible judgment and action are clear, but not always. Consider the problems surrounding whistleblowing and loyalty, sexual harrassment in the workplace, intellectual property, the limits of product safety, and ethical differences across cultural borders. What managers often need is an orderly way to think through the moral implications of a policy decision – a perspective and a language for appraising the alternatives available from an ethical point of view. For many, this is the most operational definition of business ethics.

The field of business ethics is at least as old as commerce itself, but in the modern period we can date it from the industrial revolution. Individuals, corporate forms of organization, and even capitalism as a socio-economic system have come under moral scrutiny from proponents and critics alike. In the second half of the twentieth century, there has been a renaissance of interest in the subject, spurred by events and by disciplinary realignments. The events included political and social movements for civil rights, women's equality, and environmental awareness. Also deserving of mention in relation to ethical reflection in the US are

Watergate, the Wall Street Insider Trading scandal, the Savings & Loan crisis, and the collapse of the Soviet Union. In terms of disciplinary focus, business education has expanded beyond psychology and the social sciences in search of a more humanistic outlook, so that recent efforts in the field are philosophical, theological, and literary.

The modern corporation is a microcosm of the community in which it operates and also a macrocosm of the individual citizen living and working in that wider community. Insofar as the corporation resembles the wider community, issues arise that are similar to those in classical political philosophy: the legitimacy of authority; the rights and responsibilities associated with entry, exit, membership, promotion, and succession; civil liberties; moral climate. Insofar as the corporation resembles an individual person in the community, issues arise that are similar to those in classical moral philosophy: responsibility, integrity, conscience, virtue; duties to avoid harm and injustice; respect for the law; provision for the needs of the least advantaged. There are differences in each realm, of course, since the respective analogies are imperfect, but the similarities are strong enough to help organize the normative issues that present themselves to business management (*see* MORAL STATUS OF CORPORATIONS).

Modes of Ethical Inquiry

It has often been observed that ethical inquiry can take three forms: descriptive, normative, and analytical. Descriptive ethics is not, strictly speaking, philosophical. It is better classified among the social sciences, since it is aimed at empirically neutral descriptions of the values of individuals and groups. To say, for example, that a business executive or an organization disapproves of workplace discrimination or approves of bribery is to make a descriptive ethical observation, one that can presumably be supported or refuted by pointing to factual evidence.

Normative ethics, by contrast, is not aimed at neutral factual claims, but at judgments of right and wrong, good and bad, virtue and vice. To say that a business executive or an organization disapproves of workplace discrimination or approves of bribery and is right or wrong in doing so is to add a normative ethical claim to a descriptive one. If it is to be supported or refuted, of course, some criteria of "rightness" or "wrongness" must be provided.

Analytical ethics (sometimes called metaethics) is neither a matter of describing moral values nor advancing criteria for right and wrong. Instead, it steps back from both of these activities in order to pose questions about the meaning and objectivity of ethical judgments. At this remove, the aim is to explore differences among scientific, religious, and ethical outlooks; the relation of law to morality; the implications of cultural differences for ethical judgment, and so forth.

The Dynamics of Normative Ethics

Within normative ethics, there are two interacting levels of reasoning that need to be distinguished. First, and most familiar, is reasoning from moral common sense. In our personal lives and in our professional lives, most of us operate with a more or less well-defined set of ethical convictions, principles, or rules of thumb that guide decision-making. Seldom are such values or rules spelled out explicitly in a list, but if they were, the list would

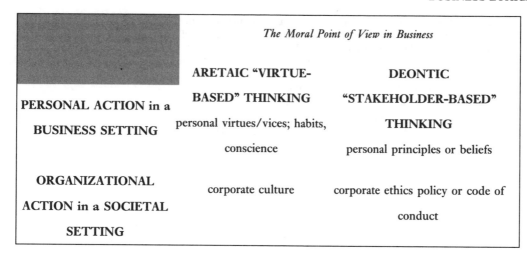

The Moral Point of View in Business

	ARETAIC "VIRTUE-BASED" THINKING	DEONTIC "STAKEHOLDER-BASED" THINKING
PERSONAL ACTION in a BUSINESS SETTING	personal virtues/vices; habits, conscience	personal principles or beliefs
ORGANIZATIONAL ACTION in a SOCIETAL SETTING	corporate culture	corporate ethics policy or code of conduct

Figure 1   Two units of analysis and two aspects of action

probably include such items as:

- Avoid harming others
- Respect others' rights (Be fair, just)
- Do not lie or cheat (Be honest)
- Keep promises and contracts (Be faithful)
- Obey the law

Such a repertoire of common-sense moral judgments is often sufficient. It functions as an informal checklist that we are prepared to live by both for the sake of others and for our own inner well-being. In the context of business behavior, the toleration of toxic workplace conditions, racial discrimination, and false advertising are as clearly contrary to moral common sense as honoring agreements with suppliers and obeying tax laws are in accord with it.

Unfortunately, problems arise with common sense both hypothetically and in practice. And when they do, we seem forced into another kind of normative thinking. The problems come from two main sources: (1) internal conflicts or unclarities about items on personal or corporate checklists, and (2) external conflicts in which others' lists (persons or corporations) differ, e.g., are longer, shorter, or display alternative priorities. How can we keep this promise to that supplier while avoiding risk to those customers? What does it mean to be fair to employees? When, if ever, does "affirmative action" become "reverse discrimination"? If competitors don't value honesty, why should we? Such questions drive us beyond moral common sense to what is called critical thinking. Here the search is for principles or criteria that will justify the inclusion or exclusion of common-sense norms, clarify them, and help resolve conflicts among them. It is the dynamic interaction between moral common sense and our attempts at critical thinking that lead to what some call "reflective equilibrium" (Rawls, 1971, p. 20ff).

Aspects of the Moral Point of View

The history of ethics reveals a widely shared conviction that ethics can and should be rooted in what has been termed the moral point of view. For many, the moral point of view is understood in religious terms, a perspective that reflects God's will for humanity. For others, it is under-

stood in secular terms and is not dependent for its authority on religious faith. But setting aside differences about its ultimate source, there is significant consensus regarding its general character. The moral point of view is a mental and emotional standpoint from which all persons are seen as having a special dignity or worth, from which the Golden Rule gets its force, from which words like "ought," "duty," and "virtue" derive their meaning. It is our principal guide for action. Two basic features of action deserve special notice. Any action or decision has:

(i) an aretaic aspect, highlighting the expressive nature of our choices. When a person acts, she or he is revealing and reinforcing certain traits or "habits of the heart" which are called virtues (and vices). The same may be true of groups of persons in organizations. Sometimes we refer in the latter cases to the culture or mindset or value system of the organization. The key to the aretaic aspect of action is its attention to actions as manifestations of an inner outlook, character, set of values or priorities. Four classical virtues that have often been the focus of ethical analysis and reflection in the past are: prudence, justice, temperance, and courage. Others include honesty, compassion, fidelity (to promises), and dedication to community (the common good). Vices of individuals or groups include greed, cruelty, indifference, and cowardice.

(ii) a deontic aspect, highlighting the effective nature of our choices – the way in which our actions influence our relationships with others and change the world around us. Actions have stakeholders and consequences when viewed from this perspective that affect the freedom and well-being of others (see STAKEHOLDER THEORY). The deontic aspect of actions relates to their effects on the world, in particular, their effects on living creatures whose interests or rights might be at stake. Management and the board are bound legally and ethically to a fiduciary role in relation to the shareholders of the enterprise, but they must also be attentive to other stakeholders. This kind of extended moral awareness, despite the ambitions of some of the great thinkers of the past, is no more reducible to a mechanical decision procedure than is balanced judgment in education, art, politics, or even sports. Ethics need not be unscientific, but it is not a science. It may be more akin to staying healthy. Acknowledging our limitations regarding knowledge and certainty in ethics is not the same as embracing the motto "There's no disputing tastes." Sometimes stakeholder interests and rights, as well as the needs of the wider community are in tension with one another, making ethical judgment very difficult for individuals and for managers of organizations.

This "bifocal" perspective on action (expressive and effective) signals a duality in what we referred to as the moral point of view. Through one set of lenses, moral judgment concentrates on the expressive meaning of actions and policies – what they reveal about those who initiate them. Through another set of lenses, the focus shifts to the effective or transactional significance of what we do. If our inquiry concentrates on an individual's or an organization's habits or culture (content, genesis, need for maintenance or change, etc.) it is aretaic. If the focus is on the interests and rights of stakeholders of personal or corporate decisions, it is deontic.

While a comprehensive review of the many ways in which philosophers, past and present, have organized critical thinking is not possible here, we can sketch several of the more important normative views that have been proposed. These views provide avenues for ethical analysis

in the sense that discussions of cases or pending decisions often can be illuminated (and even resolved) by one or more of them. Three of these avenues fall under the heading of "Stakeholder-based" thinking (figure 1), while the fourth maps onto "Virtue-Based" thinking. (See figure 2.)

Stakeholder-based Thinking

Stakeholder thinking is the most highly developed approach to ethical analysis, and displays three distinctive avenues: interest-based, rights-based, and duty-based.

Interest-based avenues. One of the more influential avenues of ethical analysis, at least in the modern period, is what we can call interest-based. The fundamental idea behind interest-based analysis is that the moral assessment of actions and policies depends solely on consequences, and that the only consequences that really matter are the interests of the parties affected (usually human beings). On this view, ethics is all about harms and benefits to identifiable parties. Moral common sense is thus disciplined by a single dominant objective: maximizing net expectable utility (happiness, satisfaction, well-being, pleasure). Critical thinking, on this view, amounts to testing our ethical instincts and rules of thumb against the yardstick of social costs and benefits.

There is variation among interest-based analysts, depending on the relevant beneficiary class. For some (called egoists) the class is the actor alone – the short- and long-term interests of the self. For others, it is some favored group – Greeks or Englishmen or Americans – where others are either ignored or discounted in the ethical

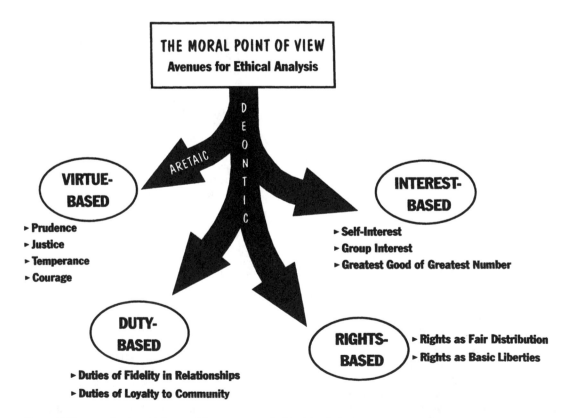

Figure 2 The moral point of view and four avenues of ethical analysis.

calculation of interests. The most common variation (called utilitarianism) enlarges the universe of moral consideration to include all human beings, if not all sentient (feeling) beings. In business management, interest-based reasoning often manifests itself as a commitment to the social value of market forces, competitive decision-making, and (sometimes) regulation in the public interest. Problems and questions regarding interest-based avenues of ethical analysis are several: How does one measure utility or interest satisfaction? For whom does one measure it (self, group, humankind, beyond)? What about the tyranny of the majority in the calculation?

Rights-based avenues. A second influential avenue is rights-based analysis. Its central idea is that moral common sense is to be governed not by interest satisfaction, but by rights protection. And the relevant rights are of two broad kinds: rights to fair distribution of opportunities and wealth (contractarianism), and rights to basic freedoms or liberties. Fair distribution is often explained as a condition that obtains when all individuals are accorded equal respect and equal voice in social arrangements. Basic liberties are often explained in terms of individuals' opportunities for self-development, property, work's rewards, and freedoms including religion and speech.

In management practice, rights-based reasoning is evident in concerns about stakeholder rights (consumers, employees, suppliers) as well as stockholder (property) rights. Questions regarding this avenue include: Is there not a trade-off between equality and liberty when it comes to rights? Does rights-based thinking lead to tyrannies of minorities that are as bad as tyrannies of majorities? Is this avenue too focused on individuals and their entitlements with insufficient attention to larger communities and the responsibilities of individuals to such larger wholes?

Duty-based avenues. The third avenue of ethical analysis is duty based. While this avenue is perhaps the least unified and well-defined, its governing ethical idea is duty or responsibility not so much to other individuals as to communities of individuals. In the duty-based outlook, critical thinking turns ultimately on individuals conforming to the legitimate norms of a healthy community. According to the duty-based thinker, ethics is not finally about interests and rights, since those are too individualistic. Ethics is about playing one's role in a larger enterprise – a set of relationships (like the family) or a community (communitarianism). The best summary of this line of thinking was echoed in John F. Kennedy's inaugural speech: "Ask not what America can do for you, ask what you can do for America."

In practice, duty-based thinking underlies appeals to principles of fiduciary obligation, public trust, and corporate community involvement (*see* FIDUCIARY DUTY). Problems and questions regarding this avenue include the fear that individualism might get swallowed up in a kind of collectivism (under the communitarian banner) and that priorities among conflicting duties are hard to set.

Virtue-based Thinking

Virtue-based thinking lies on the expressive side of the distinction made earlier between deontic and aretaic outlooks on human action. The focus of virtue-based thinking is on developing habits of the heart, character traits, and acting on them. Actions and policies are subjected to ethical scrutiny not on the basis of their effects or their consequences (for individuals or for communities), but on the basis of their genesis – the degree to which they flow from or reinforce a virtue or positive trait of character. *Newsweek* magazine devoted its June 13, 1994 issue to the theme of virtue-based ethics in American culture. In an article entitled "What is Virtue?," Kenneth L. Woodward observed that "[T]he cultivation of virtue makes individuals happy, wise, courageous, competent. The result is a good person, a responsible citizen and parent, a trusted leader, possibly even a saint. Without virtuous people, according to this tradition, society cannot function well. And without a virtuous society, individuals cannot realize either their own or the common good" (pp. 38–9).

There is an emphasis in virtue-based analysis on cultivating the traits and habits that give rise to actions and policies, on the belief that too often "the right thing to do" cannot be identified or described in advance using one of the other avenues. The most traditional short list of basic (or "cardinal") virtues includes prudence, temperance, courage, and justice. Some of the most popular management books in recent years have suggested virtue-based thinking in their titles: *The Art of Japanese Management* (Pascale and Athos, 1981), *In Search of Excellence* (Peters and Waterman, 1982), *The Seven Habits of Highly Effective People* (Covey, 1989). In the wider philosophical and cultural literature, *After Virtue* (MacIntyre, 1981), and *A Book of Virtues* (W. Bennett, 1993), have extended the rediscovery of virtue-based thinking.

In management contexts, the language of virtue is frequently encountered in executive hiring situations as well as in management development training. Another management context that may prove to be more amenable to virtue-based thinking than to stakeholder-based thinking is environmental awareness. Often debates over the impacts of business behavior on the environment have focused on the economic inclusion of "special" stakeholders (like future generations or animals or living creatures generally). While this approach is, logically speaking, an option, it may be less practically compelling than an approach which interprets management ethics in this arena, alongside community involvement, as a virtue akin to temperance.

Questions associated with virtue-based thinking include: How are we to understand the central virtues and their relative priorities in a secular world that does not appear to agree on such matters? Are there timeless character traits that are not so culture-bound that we can recommend them to anyone, particularly those in leadership roles? And can virtue(s) be taught?

Each of the four avenues (figure 2) represents a concentration of critical thinking in ethics which might be addressed, if not resolved. All have in common a sustained effort to give practical voice to the moral point of view in business life.

Bibliography

Beauchamp, T., & Bowie, N. (eds). (1993). *Ethical Theory and Business*, 4th edn. Englewood Cliffs, NJ: Prentice-Hall.

De George, R. T. (1993). *Competing with Integrity in International Business*. New York: Oxford University Press.

Donaldson, T. (1989). *The Ethics of International Business*. New York: Oxford University Press.

Donaldson, T. & Werhane, P. H. (1993). *Ethical Issues in Business: A Philosophical Approach.* 4th edn. Englewood Cliffs, NJ: Prentice-Hall.

Freeman, R. E., and Gilbert, D. R. (1988). *Corporate Strategy and the Search for Ethics.* Englewood Cliffs, NJ: Prentice-Hall.

Matthews, J., Goodpaster, K. & Nash, L. (eds) (1991). *Policies and Persons: A Casebook in Business Ethics,* 2nd edn. New York: McGraw-Hill.

Novak, M. (1993). *The Catholic Ethic and the Spirit of Capitalism.* New York: Free Press.

Rawls, J. (1971). *A Theory of Justice.* Cambridge, Mass.: Harvard University Press.

Regan, T. (1984). *Just Business: New Introductory Essays in Business Ethics.* New York: Random House.

Stone, C. (1975). *Where the Law Ends: The Social Control of Corporate Behavior.* New York: Harper & Row.

Velasquez, M. (1992). *Business Ethics: Concepts and Cases.* 3rd edn Englewood Cliffs, NJ: Prentice-Hall.

Walton, C. (1988). *The Moral Manager.* Cambridge, Mass: Ballinger.

Werhane, P. (1991). *Adam Smith and His Legacy for Modern Capitalism.* New York: Oxford University Press.

KENNETH E. GOODPASTER

business-to-business marketing Business-to-business marketing refers to the marketing of products and services to organizations rather than to households or ultimate consumers. The implied alternative is CONSUMER MARKETING, although the distinction between the two areas is not entirely clear-cut (*see* CONSUMER MARKETING). Business-to-business marketing has also been termed variously: industrial marketing, commercial marketing, institutional marketing.

Although many of the same products will be bought by both business and consumers, it is possible to identify a number of ways in which the emphasis of business-to-business marketing differs from that of consumer marketing and this is reflected in the large volume of literature and research programs devoted exclusively to the business-to-business marketing area (Chisnall, 1989; Gross et al., 1993; Reeder et al., 1991; Webster, 1991). These differences are seen to have considerable implications for the manner in which business-to-business marketing is undertaken.

Market structure is the first of these, with business markets tending to have a greater concentration of both buyers and sellers in comparison to consumer markets. Derived demand is another feature, with the demand for business products and services said to be dependent to an extent on the level of activity the buying organization generates in its own markets, although this will clearly not always be the case. The scale of business purchases is often seen as greater than that for consumers and products are generally held to be more technologically complex although both of these factors are relative and something of broad generalizations (Chisnall, 1989).

The manner in which purchase decisions are made is another area in which businesses are said to differ from consumers. Many organizations employ professional purchasers, or have a purchasing department, although it has been noted that the purchasing department is often not the most powerful influence on supplier choice (Webster & Wind, 1972). Purchases are generally made not for self-gratification but to achieve organizational objectives and are therefore often held to be based more on "rational,"

"economic," or "task" considerations, such as price, quality, and delivery criteria, than the purchases of individual consumers. Some authors assert that the "rational" nature of business buying behavior has been overemphasized. Chisnall (1989), for instance, refers to the influence of "non-task" factors such as motivation, personal values, or political, social, and cultural influences, as important in business purchase decisions. However, it is widely recognized that business buying is more likely than consumer buying to be guided, at least, by formalized rules, evaluation criteria, or procedures.

Business purchase decisions are also typically seen as a more complex process than those of consumers, involving several people, frequently from different departments. A pioneer study in 1958, for example, showed that in 106 industrial firms three or more persons influenced buying processes in over 75 percent of companies studied (*see* Alexander et al., 1961). A number of researchers have studied the concept of the BUYING CENTER, i.e., all organizational members involved in the buying decision, and have noted that this is likely to vary considerably according to the purchasing situation (*see* for instance, Robinson et al., 1967; Johnston & Bonoma, 1981). Various different organizational purchasing roles have been identified by Webster & Wind (1972), some or all of which may be played by individuals in the buying center. These include "users" of the product or service in question; "gatekeepers," who control information to be received by other members of the buying center; "deciders," who actually make the purchase decision, whether or not they have the formal authority to do so; and "buyers," those who do have formal authority for supplier selection, but whose influence is often usurped by more powerful members of the buying center (*see also* ORGANIZATIONAL BUYING BEHAVIOR).

Finally, and perhaps most importantly, the importance of long-term, relatively stable relationships between buyers and sellers has been emphasized, with extensive work conducted by researchers involved in the International Marketing and Purchasing (IMP) Group (Håkansson, 1982 & 1987; Ford, 1990). This recognition has led to the development of the interaction and NETWORK approaches to business-to-business marketing, where the role of MARKETING MANAGEMENT is seen in terms of the management of a range of individual buyer–seller relationships in the context of a broader network of interconnected supplier, buyer, and competitor organizations.

The various differences in emphasis between business-to-business marketing and consumer marketing have led to attempts to develop the scope of the MARKETING CONCEPT and to reappraise such marketing tools as the MARKETING MIX, which is seen as inappropriate in its traditional form.

see also **Marketing; Marketing concept; Marketing management; Marketing mix; Relationship marketing**

Bibliography

Alexander, R. S., Cross, J. S. & Cunningham, R. M. (1961). *Industrial marketing.* Homewood, IL: Irwin.

Chisnall, P. M. (1989). *Strategic industrial marketing* 2nd edn, Prentice-Hall.

Ford, D. (Ed.) (1990). *Understanding business markets: Interaction, relationships, networks.* London: Academic Press.

Gross, A. C., Banting, P. M., Meredith, L. N. & Ford, I. D. (1993). *Business marketing*. Boston: Houghton Mifflin Co.

Håkansson, H. (Ed.) (1982). *International marketing and purchasing of industrial goods: An interaction approach*. Chichester: John Wiley.

Håkansson, H. (Ed.) (1987). *Industrial technological development: A network approach*. London: Croom Helm.

Johnston, W. J. & Bonoma, T. V. (1981). The buying center: Structure and interaction patterns. *Journal of Marketing*, **45**, Summer, 143–156.

Reeder, R. R., Brierty, E. G. & Reeder, B. H. (1991). *Industrial marketing*, 2nd edn, Englewood Cliffs, NJ: Prentice-Hall.

Robinson, P. J., Faris, C. W. & Wind, Y. (1967). *Industrial buying and creative marketing*. Boston: Allyn & Bacon Inc.

Webster, F. E. (1991). *Industrial marketing strategy* 3rd edn, New York: John Wiley.

Webster, F. E. Jr & Wind, Y. (1972). *Organizational buying behavior*. Englewood Cliffs, NJ: Prentice-Hall.

FIONA LEVERICK

buyer behavior models Parallel to the development of thought about the variables that are important in understanding CONSUMER BUYER BEHAVIOR have been attempts to organize the variables into models of the buying process and consumer behavior. The purpose of such models is to try to understand the buying process and aid market research. Models serve to simplify, organize, and formalize the range of influences which affect purchase decisions, and try to show the extent of interaction between influencing variables. Some models are descriptive and others decision models.

Descriptive models are designed to communicate, explain, and predict. They may postulate at a macro level some variables and the relationships between them (e.g., sales, income, price, advertising); or, at a micro-level, consider more detailed links between a variable and its determinants (e.g., the effect of advertising on sales). In addition, a model at a micro-behavioral level may create hypothetical consumers and dealers who interact – with resulting behavior patterns being investigated. The well-known, available, models of consumer buyer behavior are descriptive and include those of Howard & Sheth (1969), Nicosia (1966), Andreasen (1965), Engel, Kollat & Blackwell (*see* Engel et al., 1993).

The Howard and Sheth model is concerned with individual decision-making and has its roots in stimulus-response learning theory. The focus is on repeat buying, and therefore the model incorporates the dynamics of purchase behavior over time. The model has four central parts: inputs or stimulus variables to include products and social factors; perceptual and learning constructs; output response variables; and exogenous variables to include environment, financial status, and culture. From these elements, it is possible to consider the impact of decision mediators in consumer motivations and brand choice decisions.

Nicosia's model is also focused on individual consumers' decision-making and considers the relation between a firm and its potential customers with respect to a new product. He used computer simulation techniques to explain the structure of consumer decision-making. The consumer starts off with no experience of the product, and from exposure to the environment and the company's marketing effort forms predispositions, attitudes, and motivations which lead, via information search and evaluation, to purchase.

Andreasen's model is a general one based on specific conceptions about attitude formation and change; the key to change being exposure to information, either voluntary or involuntary.

Engel, Kollat & Blackwell focus on motivation, perception, and learning in the buying decision process and their model has elements such as a central control unit, information processing, decision process, and environmental influences.

In addition to these descriptive models are others which are also predictive, e.g., stochastic learning models and queuing models. Stochastic learning models contain probabilistic elements and consider buying over time, usually purchases of brands in a product category. The basic approach is that an individual consumer learns from past behavior and the degree of satisfaction will influence future purchases. Also, more recent buying experiences with a particular brand/product will have greater effect than those which took place at a more distant time. These models analyze the relative purchase frequencies of brands in a product category and estimate the probabilities of switching brands on the next purchase. If such probabilities are assumed to be constant then market shares, for the future, can be computed.

Finally, with regard to decision models: these have been designed to evaluate the outcomes from different decisions, and they include optimization models to find a best solution, and heuristic ones which use rules of thumb to find reasonably good solutions. They incorporate differential calculus, mathematical programing, statistical decision theory, and game theory.

Bibliography

Andreasen, A. R. (1965). Attitudes and consumer behavior: A decision model. In L. Preston (Ed.), *New research in marketing* (pp. 1–16). Berkeley: Institute for Business and Economic Research, University of California.

Bettman, J. R. (1979). *An information processing theory of consumer choice*. Reading, MA: Addison Wesley.

Engel, J. F., Blackwell, R. D. & Miniard, P. W. (1993). *Consumer behavior*, 7th edn, New York: The Dryden Press.

Howard, J. A. & Sheth J. N. (1969). *The theory of buyer behavior*. New York: John Wiley.

Loudon, D. L. & Della Bitta, A. J. (1993). *Consumer behavior*, 4th edn, McGraw-Hill Int. Chapter 19.

Nicosia, F. M. (1966). *Consumer decision processes*. Englewood Cliffs, NJ: Prentice-Hall.

Schiffman, L. G. & Kanuk, L. Z. (1991). *Consumer behavior*, 4th edn, Prentice-Hall. Chapter 20.

Sheth, J. N. (Ed.) (1974). *Models of consumer behavior*. New York: Harper & Row.

BARBARA LEWIS

buyer behavior theories As the discipline of consumer behavior has developed, various theories have contributed to understanding behavior. These include economic theory. Economists were the first professional group to offer a theory of buyer behavior. The Marshallian theory holds that consumer purchasing decisions are largely the result of "rational" and conscious economic calculations, i.e., the individual seeks to spend his or her income on goods that will deliver the most likely utility (satisfaction) according to his or her tastes and relative prices.

This model assumes that consumers derive satisfaction from consumption (probably not the case with expenditure on insurances, dental treatment, etc.) and seek to maximize satisfaction within the limits of income. The model also assumes that consumers have complete information with respect to supply, demand, and prices; complete mobility, i.e., can reach any market offer at any time; and that there is pure competition. In practice, consumers typically are not aware of and cannot judge all product offerings and may have restricted access. Consequently, consumers may well be "satisficing" rather than "maximizing" their utility.

Economic theory does have a role to play in understanding consumer behavior, in so far as people may be "problem solvers," trying to make rational and efficient spending decisions. However, it is also necessary to consider and understand the marketing and other stimuli that impact on buyer behavior (*see* CONSUMER BUYER BEHAVIOR), together with buyers' individual characteristics, i.e., to take account of various social and psychological influences on buying behavior.

Bibliography

Katona, G. (1953). Rational behaviour and economic behaviour. *Psychological Review*, Sept., 307–318.

Kotler, P. (1965). Behavioural models for analysing buyers. *Journal of Marketing*, **29**, Nov., 37–45.

Loudon, D. L. & Della Bitta, A. J. (1993). *Consumer behavior*, 4th edn, McGraw-Hill Int. Chapter 19.

Schewe, C. D. (1973). Selected social psychological models for analysing buyers. *Journal of Marketing*, **37**, July, 31–39.

BARBARA LEWIS

buying center   In the 1960s and 1970s several surveys of industry purchasing practices in the UK and the USA established, inter alia, that industrial PURCHASING decisions involved many individuals from different functions within an organization in what is now generally referred to as a buying center or decision-making unit (DMU). Webster & Wind identified five buying "roles" within the context of this buying center: users, influencers, buyers, deciders, and GATEKEEPERS (Webster & Wind, 1972). This classification is now widely accepted as a general model though additional roles may be identifiable on closer examination of specific instances. The various roles discernible within the buying center may sometimes be fulfilled by only one or two individuals, while on other occasions these roles may be allocated to different individuals, departments and levels of seniority, according to the circumstances of each purchase. With the development of more collaborative approaches to inter-organizational marketing, such as partnership sourcing, it seems reasonable to extend the membership of the buying center, on occasion, to include representatives of suppliers.

Further studies have suggested that the composition of the buying center and the influence of these departments and functions on any particular purchase occasion may vary according to such variables as: buy class (a NEW TASK generally requires a broader membership of the buying center than does a MODIFIED or straight RE-BUY); the specific purchase criteria and their relative importance (e.g., an emphasis on technical specifications may require additional technical representation in the buying center); phase of the buying cycle; the complexity of the product/service under consideration; the competitive and strategic significance of the purchase; the cost of the purchase over its useful life; the relevance of the purchase to different departments within the organization; and the cultural attitude of the organization to PERCEIVED RISK. It has also been suggested that the political and cultural "pecking order" of departments and individuals within an organization can be an important variable, allowing some individuals to have considerable influence over purchasing decisions outside their functional areas of responsibility (Pettigrew, 1975; Strauss, 1964).

Bibliography

Pettigrew, A. M. (1975). The industrial purchasing decision as a political process. *European Journal of Marketing*, **5**, Feb., 4–19.

Strauss, G. (1964). Work-flow frictions, inter-functional rivalry and professionalism: A case study of purchasing agents. *Human Organisations*, **23** (1), 137–149.

Webster, F. E. Jr & Wind, Y. (1972). *Organizational buying behavior*. Englewood Cliffs, NJ: Prentice-Hall.

DOMINIC WILSON

——— C ———

capital adequacy Capital adequacy affects all corporate entities, but as a term it is most often used in discussing the position of firms in the financial sectors of the economy, and in particular whether firms have adequate capital to guard against the risks that they face. A balance needs to be struck between the often conflicting perspectives of the various stakeholders; lenders require capital to ensure that there is a cushion against possible losses at the borrowing firm, while shareholders often focus upon return on capital. For firms operating in the financial sector, the general public also has a stake in the firm as failure may have implications for the financial stability of the system as a whole.

The focus of financial stability is primarily upon banks because of the functions that they perform. Banks not only provide a significant proportion of the financing required by the economy, but they also act as a conduit for payments. Further, the financial sector is used by central banks as a mechanism for transmitting changes in monetary policy througto the real economy. The focus of financial stability is the financial system itself, rather than an individual institution, but the means by which financial stability is achieved is through the review of individual institutions. (See George (1994) for a policy speech on supervision and financial stability.)

Users of the financial sector of the economy benefit from the competition within this sector, and in response banks, and other firms, seek to optimize their business mix. In order to allow competition within the financial sector those agents responsible for monitoring capital adequacy need to give firms the freedom to take risks. On occasions, this means that firms in the financial sector will fail. If this never happened either the costs to the users of banking services would be prohibitive (and/or the range of services themselves extremely limited) or the lender of last resort would effectively be taking all of the risks, but have no influence over which risks it acquired.

Permitting banks to fail indicates a possible conflict between capital adequacy, deposit protection (see Stone and Zissu, 1994a), and the perspective of other stakeholders such as shareholders. Deposit protection schemes are operational in many countries, but most do not protect the full value of every depositor's claim. The intention is usually to ensure that depositors bear some responsibility for their actions when a bank is liquidated. If the deposits were entirely risk free then a significant group of stakeholders would have no interest in the risks being taken and banks might be tempted into acquiring inappropriate types and levels of risk.

Capital adequacy is intended to aid financial stability and, as a result, the role of an individual institution in the system is the overriding concern, rather than individual institutions *per se*. As the relationship between banking activities and other parts of the financial sector is increasing in breadth and depth, there is the possibility of financial stability being disrupted by non-banking activities. It is also the case that some sources of disruption could originate from international activities. These developments have encouraged greater discussion among supervisors of different financial sectors, both domestically and internationally.

Risk and Capital Adequacy

Banks, by virtue of their role in the economy, transform risks. The commonest risks transformed are those of credit and liquidity, which are also the risks that banks have been assuming for the longest periods of time. Hall (1993) provides a list of statutes relating to the financial sector of the economy for Japan, UK, and USA, including some legislation still in place from the 1930s. Many banks have extended their financial intermediation role and risk taking from traditional activities to include many forms of market risk; this is an indication of the continuing evolution of banks and their role in the economy.

Risks are often described as "qualitative" when it is difficult to provide an accurate value as to their impact. This is in contrast to those risks seen as quantitative. An example of a qualitative risk is settlement risk where, although the amounts at risk can be measured, the probability of loss is difficult to assess. An illustration of settlement risk was provided by the demise of the Herstatt Bank in Germany during 1974. In order to alleviate this particular risk there has been a concerted effort to promote real-time payment settlement systems and a general reduction in settlement times. In this case the interested parties have not only been the supervisors, but also industry bodies and individual firms in the financial sector. Another example of a qualitative risk is reputational risk, affecting either one particular bank or an entire sector of the banking community. Other risks in this category involve various management and systems issues, including valuation methods and risk management for complex products, as well as acts that are potentially criminal.

Some commentators would suggest that there are no new risks in the system, but it would appear that certain types of products and activities amplify the impact of a given risk; an example would be some forms of derivative contracts. While derivatives may be a relatively recent tool by which banks intermediate risk, capital adequacy standards have also evolved to reflect their development. Some of the standards are based upon holding given quantities of capital for a given risk, while other standards may be qualitative. The Basle Supervisors Committee issues statements on qualitative standards, such as the paper on risk management guidelines for derivatives, as well as minimum quantitative standards, such as the Basle Accord.

Banks and securities firms are required to hold capital against their quantitative and qualitative risks. Until recently the main capital requirements, for banks, have addressed credit and counterparty risk. For securities firms the focus has been upon market risk. However, with the implementation of the Capital Adequacy Directive (which applies to banks and securities firms in the EU) and proposed amendments to the Basle Accord, banks will be required to hold capital against some of their market risks (see Stone and Zissu, 1994a). Both the Basle Accord and the Capital Adequacy Directive represent minimum standards and local supervisors have the ability to impose higher requirements. For example, the Basle Accord has 8 percent as the minimum ratio between capital- and risk-weighted assets, but some supervisors impose higher ratios which typically reflect qualitative risks at individual banks.

Capital may be in the form of equity, tier 1 capital, and various forms of subordinated debt, upper and lower tier 2 capital, and must be capable of absorbing losses either on a continuing basis or at least in the event of a bank's liquidation. Supervisors normally impose limits on the contribution that different forms of capital can make to the composition of the capital base.

It should be noted that the quantitative capital standards are based upon the values of the positions held by the firms in the financial sector. Often national bodies produce guidelines and recommendations on the application of accounting principles to banks and financial firms, such as the British Bankers' Association statements of recommended practice. Differences can occur between countries, in the capital required for an exposure, or position, due to different accounting standards. This is a feature of on- and off-balance sheet items; however, the International Accounting Standards Committee is in the process of producing international guidance.

Capital Adequacy Agents

Agents and agencies responsible for monitoring capital adequacy vary from country to country, and on occasions within countries; Hall (1993) describes the banking regulation and supervisory framework for Japan, the UK, and the USA. In some countries a single agency is responsible for capital adequacy of all participants in the financial sector of the economy; in other countries several agencies may be responsible for a given constituency. The lender of last resort is not necessarily the same as the agency responsible for the monitoring of the capital adequacy of banks or other parts of the financial sector.

Although capital adequacy frameworks operate in, and are shaped by, the national environment, they may also be influenced by international fora. The Basle Supervisors Committee, with representatives from the G10 countries plus Luxembourg and Switzerland, has been meeting at the Bank of International Settlements since 1975 to address international banking issues. Some countries that are not members of the Basle Committee nevertheless adopt their standards. The European Union (EU) also has an interest in developments in capital adequacy standards, setting common minimum standards to enable the free flow of services and capital within the Community (the Single Market initiative). However, while the standards issued by the Basle Supervisors Committee may be considered as "guidance," the EU initiatives are in the form of directives which are legal in nature and as a result influence the balance between supervision and regulation. The International Organization of Securities Commissions (IOSCO) through its technical committee, which has been meeting since 1987, also has convergence of capital standards as one of its aims.

Both the Basle Committee and the EU have significantly altered the capital adequacy standards that apply to banks in the past fifteen years. The Basle Committee issued the Basle Accord in July 1988 and this was followed by the EU Directive on the Solvency Ratio for Credit Institutions (89/647/EEC) in 1989. These two comparable initiatives led to an 8 percent minimum capital requirement to support credit risk at banks being adopted by the members of G10, the EU and more widely. The list of EU directives (below) provides a perspective of the range of quantitative and qualitative issues that comprise current capital adequacy standards for banks; some also apply to securities firms, while others describe the roles and responsibilities among the supervisors of a global banking or securities group. Broader descriptions of some of these issues are contained in Maisel (1981), and Stone and Zissu (1994b).

Modernizing capital adequacy standards tends to create step changes in requirements. Very often the changes in capital requirements are derived or generated in international fora, such as Basle or the EU, and negotiations and consensus building take time and resources. When the Basle Accord was released in July 1988, it was recognized that market risk also needed to be addressed; it is likely that the Accord will be amended to encompass market risk during 1996.

The process of updating capital adequacy standards is made more complex as the techniques used by banks to manage particular risks may evolve during the discussion of the requirements to address that particular risk. The step changes in capital adequacy standards often arise due to the time taken to build the necessary consensus not just among the supervisors, but also between the banks and the supervisors. The occasionally abrupt changes are in contrast to the more evenly paced evolution within individual banks and the financial sector as a whole. Although capital standards may lag behind market developments and the activities of banks, it does not necessarily mean that the supervisors are unaware of developments, or have not devised interim treatments until the developments are formally addressed in revised standards.

While the revisions to capital adequacy standards may not always be at the cutting edge, in contrast to the position of some individual banks, the standards apply to a diverse range of banks. As a result they need to be capable of being applied to the majority of banks, even if they are less technically advanced than methods used by a small minority of banks.

As the purpose of capital adequacy is not necessarily to protect a bank from failure, but to promote financial stability in the system, supervisors consider losses in that context. Significant losses published by firms in the financial sector serve to remind everybody that risks need to be actively managed and the response to these losses by the marketplace often reinforces the qualitative aspects of capital adequacy standards.

As a generalization there is probably a trend towards the greater use of qualitative standards for capital adequacy. This brings with it the ability to adjust the demands and expectations of those responsible for monitoring capital adequacy to the activity and needs of individual banks. No two banks are exactly the same. These qualitative standards are underpinned by the quantitative standards which require specific amounts of capital to support a given volume of a particular form of risk, or provide outright limits on certain activities and exposures.

European Union Directives Influencing Capital Adequacy Standards

77/780/EEC First Banking Coordination Directive
89/646/EEC Second Banking Coordination Directive (home versus host supervisors, branching within the EU and who is the lead supervisor for a banking group)
86/635/EEC Bank Accounts Directive (accounting standards for banks)
87/62/EEC Monitoring and Controlling Large Exposures of Credit Institutions
89/647/EEC Solvency Ratio for Credit Institutions
91/31/EEC Amendments to the Solvency Ratio for Credit Institutions (credit risk oriented capital requirements)
89/299/EEC Own Funds of Credit Institutions
91/633/EEC Amendments to the Own Funds of Credit Institutions
92/16/EEC Amendments to the Own Funds of Credit Institutions (forms and volumes of capital)
92/30/EEC Consolidated Supervision Directive
93/6/EEC Capital Adequacy of Investment Firms and Credit Institutions (market risk based capital requirements)
93/22/EEC Investment Services Directive

Bibliography

George, E. A. J. (1994). The pursuit of financial stability. *Bank of England Quarterly Bulletin*, 34, 60–6.
Hall, M. J. B. (1993). *Banking regulation and supervision: A comparative study of the UK, USA and Japan.* 1st edn, Brookfield, VT: Edward Elgar.
Maisel, S. J. (1981). *Risk and capital adequacy in commercial banks.* 1st edn, Chicago, IL: University of Chicago Press
Quinn, B. (1993). The Bank of England's role in prudential supervision. *Bank of England Quarterly Bulletin*, 33, 260–4.
Richardson, G. W. H. (1974). Speech to the Institute of Bankers. *Bank of England Quarterly Bulletin*, 14, 54 5.
Stone, C. A. & Zissu, A. (1994a). *Global risk based capital regulations. Vol. I: Capital adequacy.* 1st edn, New York: Irwin Professional Publishing.
Stone, C. A. & Zissu, A. (1994b). *Global risk based capital regulations. Vol. II: Management and funding strategies.* 1st edn, New York: Irwin Professional Publishing.
The Basle Committee on Banking Regulations and Supervisory Practices (1988). *International convergence of capital measurement and capital standards.* Basle.
The Basle Committee on Banking Regulations and Supervisory Practices (1994). *Risk management guidelines for derivatives.* Basle.

MARK LAYCOCK

capital budgeting Capital budgeting involves decisions on resource allocation, particularly for the production of future goods and services. Capital budgeting process comprises four phases: **identification, evaluation, selection,** and **control.**

Identification of Capital Budgeting Projects

Identification of capital budgeting projects can be initiated by top management or come about as a result of an opportunity seen by lower management. Through communication between various management levels, projects should be identified in accordance with company goals and strategies.

Projects can be identified by types based on functional purposes: replacement; expansion; foreign operations; abandonment; general and administrative; research and developing or advertising and promoting; social expenditures and high technology. In addition, capital budgeting projects can be classified as mandatory projects, cost-saving projects, and revenue-generating projects. Mandatory projects are must-do investments (e.g., pollution control) whose identification begins with regulation and industrial trends. Identification of cost-saving projects begins by examining on-going firm activities, and identification of revenue-generating projects starts with either existing activities or newly created activities. Information required for identifying different types of projects can be external or internal, financial or nonfinancial, firm-specific or market-based.

Evaluation and Selection of Capital Projects

Objective means should be developed to quantify capital budgeting projects to form a reasonable base for evaluation. The quantitative parameters of a project typically include the economic life, the future cash flows, the initial cash outlay, and the cost of capital. Table 1 provides examples of different appraisal methods.

Discounted Cash Flow (DCF) Methods

Net present value (NPV): All future cash inflows and outflows are discounted using a selected cost of capital. The NPV is then calculated as the difference between the total present value of net cash inflows and the initial cash outflow. A positive NPV implies that the project is profitable. The cost of capital is based on the financing cost (i.e., the market interest rate of borrowing or lending) and perceived project risk.

Internal rate-of-return (IRR): The IRR is the interest rate that equates the present value of cash outflows and cash inflows. The calculation of IRR is not affected by the cost of capital. A trial-and-error method using different interest rates is applied to find the IRR. If IRR is greater than the selected cost of capital, then the project is considered profitable.

A comparison of NPV and IRR: NPV is expressed explicitly as the effect of an investment on the firm's wealth position and is considered a theoretically preferred method. IRR is only implicitly associated with wealth. In cases where it is necessary to evaluate the additive wealth effect, IRR is not applicable. Moreover, the IRR cannot handle periodical variations of rate of return and is problematic when cash flows have alternative signs. One advantage of IRR, especially as a medium of communication, is that it does not require cost of capital in the initial calculation stage; the cost of capital matters only during the final project selection stage.

While NPV and IRR can reach the same conclusion regarding the profitability for a single project, they may lead to inconsistent decisions when evaluating multiple projects as, for example, is shown in Table 1. The IRR method tends to favor projects with shorter lives, smaller sizes, and earlier cash inflows. The differences between IRR and NPV result from the reinvestment rate assumption. When project lives differ in length, the NPV assumes that the reinvestment rate for future projects equals the cost of capital while the IRR assumes that it equals the IRR. The superiority between these two methods depends on

Table 1   Comparison of capital budgeting appraisal methods for mutually exclusive projects

Year	Mutually exclusive projects						
	A	B	C	D	E	F	G

Cash flows in nominal dollars

Year	A	B	C	D	E	F	G
0	(100,000)	(50,000)	(100,000)	(200,000)	(200,000)	(30,000)	(250,000)
1	40,000	20,000	30,000	0	0	22,000	0
2	40,000	20,000	30,000	0	0	22,000	0
3	40,000	20,000	30,000	0	300,000	3,000	0
4	40,000	20,000	30,000	0			0
5			30,000	0			0
6			30,000	430,000			0
7							600,000

Discounted cash flows based on 10% interest rate

Year	A	B	C	D	E	F	G
0	(100,000)	(50,000)	(100,000)	(200,000)	(200,000)	(30,000)	(250,000)
1	36,364	18,182	27,273	0	0	20,000	0
2	33,058	16,529	24,793	0	0	18,182	0
3	30,053	15,026	22,539	0	225,394	2,254	0
4	27,321	13,660	20,490	0			0
5			18,628	0			0
6			16,934	242,724			0
7							307,895

Appraisal methods

	A	B	C	D	E	F	G
NPV	26,795	13,397	30,658	42,724	25,394	10,436	57,895
IRR	21.86%	21.86%	19.91%	13.61%	14.47%	33.75%	13.32%
PI	1.27	1.27	1.31	1.21	1.13	1.35	1.23
PB	2.5	2.5	3.33	5.47	2.50	1.36	6.42
PB-DCF	3.02	3.02	4.26	5.82	2.89	1.55	6.81
ARR	15.00%	15.00%	13.33%	19.17%	16.67%	18.89%	23.33%

NPV: Net present value
IRR: Internal rate of return
PI: profitability index (the NPV divided by initial outlay)
PB: Payback period based on nominal dollars
PB-DCF: Payback period based on discounted cash flows
ARR: Accounting rate of return

the proximity of the cost of capital or the IRR to the real reinvestment rate.

Payback Period

The payback period is the number of periods needed to break even on an investment and it is compared to a threshold payback period to determine the project acceptability. This method provides a measure for project liquidity which affects the project's risk. For a project that has uniform cash flows and an unlimited economic life, the payback period equals the inverse of the IRR. Payback method has two disadvantages: it ignores the time value of money, and it does not measure a project's profitability. The payback method does not consider cash flows beyond

the payback period – accordingly, it favors earlier cash flows. A common practice in capital budgeting is to use the payback period as a yardstick to delineate undesirable projects, then the profitability based on the DCF methods can be used to select the best project.

Accounting Rate of Return (ARR)

ARR is calculated as the average annual income divided by the initial or average investment. A target ARR is needed in selecting the project, which may depend on the cost of capital, the project risk, and the division's past performance. Instead of net cash flows, the accounting income (after the deduction of depreciation) is used as the numerator. One important aspect of ARR is that the ex post performance measure is often based on the actual ARR. Many studies show that the stock market employs a firm's overall ARR to evaluate its performance. Moreover, management compensation plans are often based on data which either directly use or relate to ARR. Although ARR has serious theoretical drawbacks in that it does not consider time value of money, it remains to be an important method as an ex post performance measure.

Variation of the Basic Methods

Profitability index (PI): The profitability index measured as the total present value of future net cash inflows divided by the initial investment is a modification of the NPV method. It is consistent with the reinvestment rate assumption employed by the NPV but with a tendency of not favoring large projects. With reference to table 1, the top four projects that PI favors are small projects: A, B, F, and C. While A and B (shorter lives) have higher rankings than C using the IRR, they have lower rankings than C using the PI. For firms with limited fund and high financing costs, the PI may work better than the NPV method.

Payback method based on discounted cash flows (PB–DCF) or break-even time (BET): An alternative way of calculating the payback period is first converting all the cash flows into the present value and then calculating the payback period based on the discounted future cash flows. The payback period represents the break-even time after the basic financing costs are covered. This method is also known as the break-even time (BET). For firms that concern time-to-market as a critical strategy, the BET has the advantage of identifying new projects that will cover at least the financing costs in a relatively short time and still improve the firm's competitive position.

The bailout payback method: This method measures the time that a project will take for the cumulative cash flows from operations plus the disposal value of the equipment in a particular period to equal the initial investment. Projects using general-purpose equipment should be less risky than that using special purpose equipment because the former frequently have disposal values far exceeding that of the latter. The bailout payback considers the differences in the behavior of the disposal values of project investments and is a useful risk indicator.

Depreciation Method and Tax Effect

The choice of depreciation method has no impact on project evaluation for tax-exempt organizations. However, this is not the case when taxes do need to be considered. In evaluating tax effects, aspects that need to be considered include the nature of the institutions (individual, partnership, or corporation), differences in financial and tax accounting treatments, tax rules for allowable depreciation amount, useful lives and allowable depreciation methods, and the resulting marginal tax rate applicable to individual projects. If capital projects involve activities in different countries, the tax benefit in one country often can be a driving force in determining profitability.

Methods for Including Risk Consideration

Simple risk-adjustment methods: Subjective assessment is first conducted based on project characteristics and types. For example, projects with small initial investments, earlier cash flows, and shorter payback times, projects on

replacement or expansion of the existing operations, and projects involving domestic instead of foreign operations may be considered less risky projects. For riskier projects, either the selection criterion is raised or the estimated future cash flows are decreased (the *certainty equivalent approach*). Once the cash flows are adjusted for risk, the regular selection criteria can be applied.

Probabilistic risk analysis techniques: Commonly employed techniques include sensitivity analysis, simple probability analysis, decision-tree analysis, and Monte Carlo simulation. Sensitivity analysis examines the consequences of changing key assumptions; it helps to identify the range of change in the assumptions within which the project remains profitable. Simple profitability analysis assigns probability to future cash flows; their expected values are used to assess the level of cash flows and their variance is used to assess the risk. Decision-tree analysis and Monte Carlo simulation apply complicated probability analyses.

Company Practices and Trends

Based on survey studies, the discounted cash flow method is the most popular method and the payback method the second most popular method for countries such as the USA, Australia, Canada, Ireland, South Korea and the UK. The only exception is Japan which uses the payback method as the primary method and the ARR as the secondary method. Studies find that the preference of the simple methods over the complicated methods is affected by firm size, industry, and project type. Most studies have found that the IRR is preferred to the NPV and the preference is affected by the capital budget size and project type. Studies also show that more companies are using sophisticated capital budgeting techniques. While the IRR is still a method preferred to the NPV, the NPV is gaining popularity in practice.

Control: Post-Completion Audit of Projects

This serves three functions: a control mechanism; an implementation mechanism to overcome the psychological and political problems associated with proposing and terminating projects; and a learning mechanism that compares the actual performance with the past estimates to gain insight into improving future investment decisions. To successfully operate the post-completion auditing process, it is important to let the operating managers know that the purpose of the post-completion audit is not to penalize managers for making wrong estimations during the past budgeting stage, but to learn from past experiences.

While the post-completion audit is costly, it should be conducted regularly as long as it is cost-effective. The basis used to select projects should be applied to both the actual and the budgeted data. Empirical studies indicate that many firms select projects based on discounted cash flow (DCF) techniques, but monitor them using reported accounting ratios. This flawed method will lead managers erroneously to the use of simple accounting measures (e.g., the accounting rate of return (ARR)) to select projects. Studies also show that the post-completion audit can play an important role in improving firm performance and an increasing number of managers have implemented this procedure.

C. S. AGNES CHENG

capital structure   Capital structure is the mixture of securities issued by a company to finance its operations. Companies need real assets in order to operate. These can be tangible assets, such as buildings and machinery, or intangible assets, such as brand names and expertise. To pay for the assets, companies raise cash not only via their trading activities but also by selling financial assets, called securities, financial instruments or contingent claims. These securities may be classified broadly as either equity or debt (though it is possible to create securities with elements of both). Equity is held as shares of stock in the company, whereby the company's stock holders are its owners. If the company's trading activities are sufficiently successful, the value of its owners' equity increases. Debt may be arranged such that repayments are made only to the original holder of the debt, or a "bond" may be created which can be sold on, thus transferring ownership of future repayments to new bondholders.

Capital structure can be changed by issuing more debt and using the proceeds to buy back shares, or by issuing more equity and using the proceeds to buy back debt. The question then arises: is there an optimal capital structure for a company? The solution to this question, for the restricted case of "perfect markets," was given by Franco Modigliani and Merton Miller (1958), whose fame is now such that they are referred to in finance textbooks simply as "MM!" A perfect market is one in which there are neither taxes nor brokerage fees and the numbers of buyers and sellers are sufficiently large, and all participants are financially sufficiently small relative to the size of the market that trading by a single participant cannot affect the market prices of securities. MM's "first proposition" states that the market value of any firm is independent of its capital structure. This may be considered as a law of conservation of value: the value of a company's assets is unchanged by the claims against them. It means that in a perfect and rational market a company would not be able to gain value simply by recombining claims against its assets and offering them in different forms. Modigliani and Miller (1961) likewise deduced that whether or not cash was disbursed as dividends was irrelevant in a perfect market.

MM's first proposition relies on investors being able to borrow at the same interest rate as companies; if they cannot, then companies can increase their values by borrowing. If they can, then there is no advantage to investors if a company borrows more money, since the investors could, if they wished, borrow money themselves and use the money to buy extra shares of stock in the company. The investors would then have to pay interest on the cash borrowed, as would the company, but will benefit from holding more equity in the company, resulting in the same overall benefit to the investor.

An analogy which has been used for this proposition is the sale of milk and its derivative products (see Ross et al., 1988). Milk can be sold whole or it can be split into cream and low cream milk. Suppose that splitting (or recombining) the milk costs virtually nothing and that you buy and sell all three products through a broker at no cost. Cream can be sold at a high price in the market and so by splitting off the cream from your milk you might appear to be able to gain wealth. However, the low cream milk remaining will be less valuable than the original, full cream milk – a buyer has a choice in the market between full cream milk and milk with its cream removed; offered both at the same price, he would do best to buy full cream milk, remove its cream and sell it himself. Trading in the perfect market would act so as to make the combined price of cream and low cream milk in the perfect market the same as the price of full cream milk (conservation of value). If, for example, the combined price dropped below the full cream price then traders could recombine the derivative products and sell them at a profit as full cream milk.

What was considered perplexing, before Modigliani and Miller, is now replaced by a strong and simple statement about capital structure. This is very convenient because any supposed deviations can be considered in terms of the weakening of the assumptions behind the proposition. Obvious topics for consideration are the payment of brokers' fees, taxes, the costs of financial distress and new financial instruments (which may stimulate or benefit from a temporarily imperfect market). New financial instruments may create value if they offer a service not previously available but required by investors. This is becoming progressively harder to achieve; but even if successful, the product will soon be copied and the advantage in the market will be removed. Charging of brokers' fees simply removes a portion of the value and (as long as the portion is small!) this is not a major consideration, since we are concerned with the merits of different capital structures rather than the costs of conversion. Taxes, however, can change the result significantly: interest payments reduce the amount of corporation tax paid and so there is a tax advantage, or "shield," given to debt compared with equity. When modified to include corporate taxes, MM's proposition shows the value of a company increasing linearly as the amount of debt is increased (Brealey and Myers, 1991). This would suggest that companies should try to operate with as much debt as possible. The fact that very many companies do not do this motivates further modifications to theory: inclusion of the effect of personal tax on shareholders and inclusion of the costs of financial distress. Modigliani and Miller suggested that the increase in value caused by the corporate tax shield is reduced by the effect of personal taxes on investors. In addition, the costs of financial distress increase with added debt, so that the value of the company is represented by the following equation, in which PV denotes present value:

$$\text{value of company} = \text{value if all equity-financed}$$
$$+ PV, (\text{tax shield}) - PV, (\text{costs of financial distress})$$

As debt is increased, the corporate tax shield increases in value but the probability of financial distress increases, thus increasing the present value of the costs of financial distress. The value of the company is maximized when the present value of tax savings on additional borrowing only just compensates for increases in the present value of the costs of financial distress.

One element of financial distress can be bankruptcy. It is generally the case throughout the world's democracies that shareholders have limited liability. Although shareholders may seem to fare badly by receiving nothing when a company is declared bankrupt, their right simply to walk away from the company with nothing is actually valuable, since they are not liable personally for the company's unpaid debts. Short of bankruptcy there are other costs, including those caused by unwillingness to invest and shifts in value engineered between bondholders and shareholders, which increase with the level of debt. Holders of corporate debt, as bonds, stand to receive a maximum of the repayments owed; shareholders have limited liability, suffer nothing if the bondholders are not repaid and benefit from all gains in value above the amount owed to bondholders. Therefore, if a company has a large amount of outstanding debt it can be to the shareholders' advantage to take on risky projects which may give large returns, since this is essentially a gamble using bondholders' money! Conversely, shareholders may be unwilling to provide extra equity capital, even for sound projects. Thus a company in financial distress may suffer from a lack of capital expenditure to renew its machinery and underinvestment in research and development. Even if a company is not in financial distress, it can be put into that position by management issuing large amounts of debt. This devalues the debt already outstanding, thus transferring value from bondholders to shareholders. Interesting examples of this are to be found in leveraged buyouts (LBOs), perhaps the most famous being the attempted management buyout of R. J. R. Nabisco in the 1980s (Burrough and Helyar, 1990). Top management in R. J. R. Nabisco were, of course, trying to become richer by their actions – an extreme example of so-called agency costs, whereby managers do not act in the shareholders' interest but seek extra benefits for themselves.

There is, finally, no simple formula for the optimum capital structure of a company. A balance has to be struck between the tax advantages of corporate borrowing (adjusted for the effect of personal taxation on investors) and the costs of financial distress. This suggests that companies with strong, taxable profits and valuable tangible assets should look towards high debt levels, but that currently unprofitable companies with intangible and risky assets should prefer equity financing. This approach is compatible with differences in debt levels between different industries but fails to explain why the most successful companies within a particular industry are often those with low debt. An attempt at an explanation for this is a "pecking order" theory (Myers, 1984). Profitable companies generate sufficient cash to finance the best projects available to management. These internal funds are preferred to external financing since issue costs are thus avoided, financial slack is created, in the form of cash, marketable securities, and unused debt capacity, which gives valuable options on future investment, and the possibly adverse signal of an equity issue is avoided.

Bibliography

Brealey, R. A. & Myers, S. C. (1991). *Principles of corporate finance.* 4th edn, New York: McGraw-Hill.

Burrough, B. & Helyar, J. (1990). *Barbarians at the gate: The fall of R. J. R. Nabisco.* London: Arrow Books.

Miller, M. (1977). Debt and taxes. *Journal of Finance*, 32, 261–76.

Modigliani, F. & Miller, M. (1958). The cost of capital, corporation finance and the theory of investment. *American Economic Review*, 48, 261–97.

Modigliani, F. & Miller, M. (1961). Dividend policy, growth and the valuation of shares. *Journal of Business*, 34, 411–33.

Myers, S. C. (1984). The capital structure puzzle. *Journal of Finance*, 39, 575–92.

Ross, S. A., Westerfield, R. W. & Jaffe, J. F. (1988). *Corporate finance.* 3rd edn, Chicago, IL: G. S. B. Chicago, University of Chicago. 434–35.

DAVID P. NEWTON

career Career refers to the series of occupations and jobs which individuals hold over their work lives. The study of careers in organizations has focused on six issues in particular: (a) how individuals' aptitudes, interests, and skills change over the course of their working lives; (b) how individuals make decisions about which jobs to pursue and which organizational positions to accept (or leave); (c) how individuals adjust to new job situations; (d) how organizations plan for and manage these transition processes; (e) the impact of short-run career decisions on longer-term career options, and (f) the integration (or conflict) between career demands and personal life demands (Feldman, 1988).

While the term career generally applies to all occupations and jobs, over time the term has also developed some frequently used connotations. In some cases, the term career has been used to connote an occupation or profession requiring high levels of education and training. For example, it is not uncommon for law and medicine to be labeled as careers, but plumbing and construction not to be so labeled. In other cases, the term career has been used to connote either long-term commitment to or heavy psychological investment in an occupation or an organization. For instance, the term career diplomat refers to an individual who has made a long-term commitment to public service, while the term career employee refers to an individual who has spent most of his or her life working for one company.

Bibliography

Feldman, D. C. (1988). *Managing Careers in Organizations*, Glenview, IL: Scott Foresman.

DANIEL FELDMAN

career anchors Career anchors are the self-perceived sources of stability in the individual's internal career. When people enter a field or occupation they typically are anchored only in the externally defined criteria of progress: grades in school, encouragement from counselors, test scores on talents or interests, and feedback if they are in an apprenticeship or other kind of work situation. As the individual progresses through school and early occupational experiences, he or she begins to form a self-image based on the matching of external feedback and internal feelings of accomplishment and satisfaction. In other words, individuals begins to define themselves in terms of a matching of what they feel they are good at and enjoy doing with external feedback that they are good at it and that their efforts are considered worthwhile by others. If mismatches occur, because either they find they do not have the talent for a certain kind of work or they discover that they do not like a certain kind of work, they seek a change in CAREER until there is some matching of talents and motives with external rewards and feedback.

As we progress into our careers we also find that our values have to match those of our chosen occupation or organization. The emerging self-image, what I am defining as the career anchor, then consists of three components: (a) my self-perceived talents; (b) my motivation toward certain kinds of work; and (c) my values as they are articulated in my work. The career anchor is a product of work experience and is therefore not likely to be very firm until we are at least five to ten years into our career. But once we have stabilized our self-image we tend to want to hold on to that image even if our external work situation begins not to match it. The career anchor, then, can be defined as that element of ourselves that we would not give up if forced to make a choice. What we do in our occupations is not necessarily correlated with our anchors and most occupations have in them people with different career anchors.

Research has so far revealed at least eight kinds of career anchors.

(1) Technical or functional competence: the person defines him or herself by competence in a certain craft and continues to look for ever more challenge in that area of competence. This kind of person wants to become the world's best salesperson, engineer, auto mechanic, surgeon, or whatever.

(2) Managerial competence: the person defines him or herself by the ability to manage others and measures progress by climbing to ever higher positions of responsibility in organizations. This person wants to be able to attribute the success of an organization or project to his or her own managerial capabilities based on analytical skills, interpersonal and group skills, and the emotional capacity to deal with high levels of responsibility.

(3) Security or stability: the person defines himself or herself by having achieved a position of career success and stability that allows him or her to relax and to have a feeling of having made it. This sort of person is less concerned with type of work and more concerned with a feeling of security.

(4) Autonomy or independence: people define themselves by being free and on their own in what they do in their career. Freelance consultants, teachers, some independent businesspeople, field salespersons, and so forth would exemplify this anchor.

(5) Entrepreneurial creativity: people define themselves by their ability to create their own enterprise. They measure themselves by the size of the enterprise and its success.

(6) Service or dedication to a cause: people define themselves by their commitment to some deep value that the occupation permits them to express, e.g. teaching, environmentalism, human resource management, some aspects of medicine and the ministry.

(7) Pure challenge: people define themselves less by the type of work they do and more by the sheer joy of competing or winning out over impossible obstacles.

(8) Lifestyle: people define themselves by the ability to integrate the demands of work, family, and self-oriented growth concerns. The career is not perceived as the dominant element, but only one element to be integrated into the whole of life.

Career anchors serve to stabilize and give meaning to the internal career and thus must be identified by the career occupant at those points when career or life choices have to be made, so that those choices maximize the opportunities

to match the needs of the individual with the requirements of the organization or occupation.

Bibliography

Schein, E. H. (1978). *Career Dynamics*, Reading, MA: Addison-Wesley.
Schein, E. H. (1987). Individuals and careers. *Handbook of Organizational Behavior*, Lorsch, J. Englewood Cliffs, NJ: Prentice-Hall.
Schein, E. H. (1993). *Career Anchors*, **rev. edn**, San Diego, CA: Pfeiffer & Co.
Schein, E. H. (1995). *Career Survival: Strategic Job/role Planning*, San Diego, CA: Pfeiffer & Co.

EDGAR H. SCHEIN

career choice   Career choice, defined as a decision about which career to pursue, is one of many work–leisure decisions made by people throughout their lives. Related, but somewhat more focused, decisions are OCCUPATIONAL CHOICE and job choice. A career is "a sequence of work-related positions occupied throughout a person's life" (London and Stumpf, 1982, p. 4). Career choice encompasses those CAREER STAGES and transitions over time that reflect personal needs, motives, and aspirations, as well as societal and organizational expectations and constraints.

In practice, career choice is not a singular decision. People make many choices within their broader, often unarticulated, decisions about their work life. Decisions to change positions within an organization, change jobs, change organizations, change work locations, or change occupations are all part of a broader choice regarding one's career. As such, each of these decisions is a career decision, or at least part of the collection of activities that is viewed as one's career choice.

Bibliography

London, M. & Stumpf, S. A. (1982). *Managing Careers*, Reading, MA: Addison-Wesley.

STEPHEN A. STUMPF

career pathing   Career pathing (CP) is a basic planning tool linked to career planning and career development. It is used by both individuals and organizations, although for substantially different purposes. The essence of CP is a coherent series of steps to achieve a particular job or career objective. It combines developmental goals, activities to achieve these goals, and timing. The format of CP varies widely; common forms range from listings of steps to sophisticated charts and diagrams generated by computers. Since its introduction in the 1970s and fast growth subsequently, the basic concepts and applications of CP have undergone remarkable transformation.

The rationalization of career planning and development methods, mostly in large or high tech organizations, led to the design of sophisticated CP tools (Burack and Mathys, 1996). A number of factors nurtured this growth and included: relatively stable economic and competitive conditions; rapid advances in software packages and computer technology, including the personal computer; the need for more powerful succession and management development tools; and rapid access to career planning information. The process of planning the organization's future staffing defines future human resource needs, timing, positional capabilities, and the availability of current personnel to meet these requirements. CP became the road map that translated general staffing planning into individualized time-activity paths. Where job structures were relatively stable, general CP documents and matrices were generated which defined standard "career ladders" and job relationships. Thus, within organizations, two quite different forms of CP emerged. One was driven primarily by internal organization needs and the other by individual enterprise members interested in internal opportunities.

CP for people outside organizations was driven by both short- and long-range individual needs (Burack and Mathys, 1996). This CP reflected work-family matters, focused on formal and informal learning, and emphasized individual growth. It was driven by personal and job-related needs, values, and goals. This CP model encouraged broad, flexible, and contingent thinking.

Recent economic and competitive developments, however, greatly changed the focus of CP for the organization, its members, and individuals generally. The reinvention of organizations, driven by turbulent economic and global competitive conditions, transformed CP for individuals and organizations alike. Change drivers included: global competition; the replacement of job security by job or skill mobility; newly emerging technologies, job families, and work procedures; shifts to process flow from a hierarchical orientation; dual careers; and workforce diversity.

New models of CP are emerging that are developmental for the person and organization. They combine a long-term view with short-term needs for flexibility and possible career changes for individuals. CP also includes spiritual and emotional dimensions (Otte and Kahnweiler, 1995). Job, positional, and employer changes, along with concurrent learning and reflective processes, are to nurture an inner voice or vision of future possibilities and valued directions and goals. New career planning approaches include analyzing past and future needed competencies, exploring and executing plans, and learning from these experiences to guide "next steps." CP provides the specific steps and experiences to achieve the plans. Short-term survival dictates the development of contingency CP models, much flexibility, and frequent reviews for possible changes.

The new organizational CP models *consciously* link enterprise staffing needs and learning strategies with people's career plans (Burack and Mathys, 1996; Gutteridge et al., 1993; Stewart, 1995) and are often enacted on a global stage. Short- and long-term strategic business needs drive individual development while CP structures incorporate self-development and optional paths based on individual progress and needs and shifting competitive circumstances. Ford's Leadership and Development Program, Motorola's Globally Oriented Development Programs, and Nationwide Insurance's Technical Excellence Program for Information Service Employees provide examples of CP models.

Bibliography

Burack, E. H. & Mathys, N. (1980). *Career Management in Organizations*, Lake Forest, IL: Brace-Park Press.
Burack, E. H. & Mathys, N. (1996). *Human Resource Planning*, 3rd edn, Northbrook, IL: Brace-Park Press.
Gutteridge, T. G., Leibowitz, Z. B. & Shore, J. E. (1993). *Organizational Career Development*, San Francisco: Jossey-Bass.
Otte, F. L. & Kahnweiler, W. M. (1995). Long-range career planning during turbulent times. *Business Horizons*, January–February, 2–7.
Stewart, T. A. (1995). Planning a career in a world without managers. *Fortune*, March 20, 72–80.

ELMER H. BURACK

career plateau The phenomenon of career plateauing in organizations presents an important and perplexing challenge to human resources management (HRM) and an array of conceptual and empirical problems to organizational behavior scholars. The first problem is definitional. How do we decide when an employee is plateaued? Three types of criteria can be found applied in the literature. First, many researchers have taken time in current position as a measurable and objective benchmark. Employees in post for more than five years would typically be counted as immobile or "plateaued" by this standard, though this or alternative cutoffs have the drawback of looking worryingly arbitrary, and, at the same time, liable to mischaracterize the experience and career positions of many groups, such as professionals. A second alternative is to use a subjective criterion – individuals' expectations of future advancement – defining as plateaued those who expect no or minimal further status increase. The problem with this approach is the questionable accuracy of people's reading of future opportunities and their own capabilities. A less common third alternative, of increasing interest, is the concept of implicit age-grade timetables. These may be assessed subjectively – whether employees believe themselves to be on track relative to peers, or ahead of or behind schedule. Individuals' positions relative to company norms may also be assessed objectively.

Plateauing by any of these definitions is an organizational problem to the degree that the people to whom it applies have desires or expectations which have not been or are not being fulfilled. This is regarded as especially problematic for managerial ranks, whose career expectations are more deeply socialized and hierarchical than other workers', and whose motivation and commitment organizations are most concerned to maintain.

Research has shed light on several aspects of the phenomenon. First, career success is often foretold by rapid early upward movements in a person's history, and conversely, people who get off-track early typically fail to recover momentum. Second, it is mistaken to assume that plateauing is necessarily associated with loss of motivation and effectiveness. The distinction needs to be drawn between mere immobility and frustrated feelings of being "stuck." Some people are contentedly plateaued, often called "solid citizens," as distinct from "high fliers" and "deadwood." Third, people's aspirations and interests change over the career cycle. Early career ambition may, as the realities of limited horizons sink in, become deflected into other life spheres. Not all forms of this displacement need detract from the individual's organizational contribution, though in some cases "insurgent" and "alienated" orientations may develop if there is resentment and frustration at perceived unfairness of career opportunities.

Finally, the phenomenon of plateauing is becoming more common as organizations restructure towards "delayered" or "flattened" structures. One recent survey estimated that 25 percent of the US workforce was plateaued. Plateauing presents a challenge to HRM to the degree that employees maintain hierarchical views of career fulfillment – the view that "up is the only way." One solution is increased lateral mobility, sabbaticals, and alternative developmental paths. To date, organizations have been slow to seek these remedies, often being more aware of the short-term costs than of the long-term benefits to the organizational culture.

Bibliography

Chao, G. T. (1990). Exploration of the conceptualization and measurement of career plateau: a comparative analysis. *Journal of Management*, 16, 181–93.

Feldman, D. C. & Weitz, B. A. (1988). Career plateaus reconsidered. *Journal of Management*, 14, 69–90.

Lawrence, B. S. (1988). New wrinkles in the theory of age: demography, norms, and performance ratings. *Academy of Management Journal*, 31, 309–37.

Nicholson, N. (1993). Purgatory or place of safety? The managerial career plateau and organizational age grading. *Human Relations*, 46, 1369–89.

Veiga, J. F. (1981). Plateaued versus nonplateaued managers: career patterns, attitudes, and path potential. *Academy of Management Journal*, 24, 566–78.

NIGEL NICHOLSON

career stages   The word CAREER has both an internal and an external meaning. From an external, societal point of view the concept of career refers to the sequence of formal roles that are associated with a given occupation. In academia, for example, the external career consists of being a graduate student, instructor, assistant professor, and associate professor, the granting of tenure, and then being made full professor. Most occupations have formal or informal status progressions of this sort. From an internal point of view, the concept of career refers to the sequence of life roles that an individual envisions as he or she progresses through one or more external careers. Thus, in the internal career of an academic there may be a progression from student to graduate student in a specific field of interest, to researcher, teacher, scholar, and ultimately revered and successful scholar, measured by peer acceptance, publications, references, and so forth. There will usually be some correspondence between the formal occupationally designated sequence of roles and the internal experienced sequence, but not necessarily. In defining career *stages*, therefore, it is necessary to specify whether we mean in the internal or in the external career.

Externally defined career stages are usually well defined by formal occupational criteria, and by organizations if the career is embedded in an organization. Thus a young engineer can pretty well see his or her external career in terms of the amount of schooling necessary, entry into an organization as a technical person or management trainee, followed by that organization's specification of how it defines career development. Most organizations have some career paths that are based on historical data of what previous entrants have experienced and can tell the young engineer or manager-to-be what steps to expect.

When one analyzes a large number of occupations certain generic career stages seem to characterize most of them: (a) a period of pre-career choosing of a field and educational preparation for entry into that field; (b) formal training in the chosen field or occupation; (c) entry into the occupation or organization; (d) a period of learning, apprenticeship, and socialization; (e) a period of full use of one's talent, leading to some form of granting of tenure through being given permanent membership, a professional license, or some other form of certification; (f) a period of productive employment; (g) a branching into administrative, managerial, and other forms of becoming a leader; and (h) gradual disengagement, part-time work, and eventual retirement.

At any point in the external career the person may discover that his or her internal career and CAREER ANCHORS are out of line with what the external career offers in terms of challenge, opportunities, and rewards. At that point the person may switch to another career and start going through the stages over again, but usually in a more truncated form because the experience acquired in one career is often transferable to another career. The engineer employed in a technical organization may discover a talent and desire for entrepreneurial work or for management, and may decide to start a company or switch to an organization that provides more managerial opportunities. Some training in management may then be required and the person may have to start at the bottom of the new career ladder.

Career stages in the external career can be thought of as a series of movements along three different dimensions: (a) *moving up* in the hierarchical structure of the occupation or organization; (b) *moving laterally* across the various subfields of an occupation or functional groups of an organization; and (c) *moving in* toward the centers of influence and leadership in the occupation or organization. Depending on what the person is looking for in his or her internal career, movement along each of these dimensions will have different meanings. For some, like managers, it is moving up that is important; for some, like the technical person, it is job challenge and lateral movement to new and challenging work that is most important; and for some, like the power or socially motivated person, it is moving toward the inner circle and positions of influence that is most important.

Each dimension has its own stages associated with it, but these are usually idiosyncratic in particular occupations or organizations. In summary, career stages in the externally defined career are the sequence of roles and statuses defined by a particular occupation or organization as the way to progress through the career. They may or may not correspond to the individual's own sense of his or her internal career stages.

Bibliography

Schein, E. H. (1978). *Career Dynamics*, Reading, MA: Addison-Wesley.

Schein, E. H. (1987). Individuals and careers. *Handbook of Organizational Behavior*, Lorsch, J. Englewood Cliffs, NJ: Prentice-Hall.

Schein, E. H. (1993). *Career Anchors*, rev. edn, San Diego, CA: Pfeiffer & Co.

Schein, E. H. (1995). *Career Survival: Strategic Job/role Planning*, San Diego, CA: Pfeiffer & Co.

EDGAR H. SCHEIN

carnet   When goods enter a country all duties and taxes must normally be paid. There are, however, situations in which duties do not have to be paid. One such situation exists when goods are brought into a country to serve as sales samples, for professional purposes, or if the goods are on the way to another country. In these situations, temporary entry to the country is usually under the "carnet" system. A carnet is a set of vouchers issued by International Chambers of Commerce or other business associations which are accepted by customs officials as proof that the goods are not for resale in the country. Carnets are usually good for one year. If the goods have not been transported out of the country by that time, duties will be payable. There are three major types of carnets:

1 ATA carnet – ATA stands for Admission Temporaire or temporary admission. An ATA carnet allows certain types of property to be imported into and temporarily held in a country without payment of import duties. Property allowable under the ATA carnet includes product samples, advertising materials, professional equipment (for presentations, etc.), and promotional literature and items. An ATA carnet is valid for a one-year period. If property brought into a country under an ATA carnet is still in the country after a year, it becomes subject to duty payment.

2 ECS carnet – This is a very specific use of carnet. ECS stands for Echantillon Carnet Sample. The ECS carnet is used specifically for trade samples or other commercial samples (not imports, just samples). Under the ECS carnet literally all entry requirements are nullified. Thus no duties are payable on commercial or sales samples. The ECS carnet is usually good for up to one year.

3 TIR carnet – TIR refers to the French words, Transport International Routier, which translates into International Road Transport. This type of carnet is used for goods which are passing through a country on the way to another country. As long as the goods are not unloaded and reloaded in the country the carnet allows goods to pass without customs duties or customs inspection (of course when the goods reach the final country destination all customs inspections and duties for the final country apply).

Bibliography

Johnson, T. E. (1994). *Export–Import procedures and documentation.* New York: Amacom.

Zodl, J. A. (1992). *Export–Import: Everything you and your company need to know to compete in world markets.* Cincinnati, OH: Betterway Books.

JOHN O'CONNELL

cash management One of the most important tasks of international finance associated with a multinational enterprise (MNE) is cash management. Cash management is essentially knowing what the cash needs are throughout the MNE; what the sources of cash are (parent and subsidiary operations, investment returns, borrowing, etc.), how to effectively access cash when needed, and how to most effectively use available cash when not needed in company operations. One of the problems with multinational operations is that delays or restrictions are often encountered when attempting to move cash out of certain countries. Also the cost of moving cash between countries will normally involve fees and/or expenses not encountered with domestic cash movements. One of the challenges of international cash management is to get cash to where it is

needed, when it is needed, with the fewest movements (therefore, the lowest transfer costs).

see also **Coordination center; Multilateral netting**

Bibliography

Celi, L. J. & Rutizer, B. (1991). *Global cash management.* 1st edn, New York: (HarperCollins).

Eiteman, D. K., Stonehill, A. J. & Moffett, M. H. (1992). *Multinational business finance.* 6th edn, Reading, MA: Addison-Wesley Publishing.

Kuhlmann, A. R., Mathis, F. J. & Mills, J. (1991). *First steps in treasury management: Prime cash.* 2nd edn, Toronto, Canada: Treasury Management Association of Canada.

JOHN O'CONNELL

ceteris paribus In economic analysis, many factors can affect a given variable. As an analytical device, economists employ the "ceteris paribus" assumption (Latin for "all else equal") to isolate the effect of one of the independent variables on the dependent variable. For example, the demand for a product will be affected by the price of that product, the prices of products which are substitutes, COMPLEMENTS, and consumers' income among other possible variables. To find the effect of a change in the product's own price on the quantity demanded, the assumption "ceteris paribus" is used to derive a theoretical conclusion. This makes the statement about the relation between the quantity demanded and price a *conditional* statement: *if* no other factors affecting demand are changed, *then* a rise in the product's price should cause the quantity demanded to fall. Clearly, if the conditions are changed (e.g. incomes increase and this is a normal good), then we may not expect to see a decrease in the quantity demanded even if the price is higher because all else was not equal (constant).

ROBERT E. MCAULIFFE

chaebol structure The Korean chaebol is that country's near equivalent of the Japanese KEIRETSU STRUCTURE. Unlike the keiretsu, however, it is usually still managed at the top level by members of the founding family, and strategy is still set centrally, as in the prewar Japanese ZAIBATSU STRUCTURE. Furthermore, these concerns do not contain banking institutions within their structures; and although trading companies exist, these act mainly as exporting agencies rather than as in the soga shosha.

The main reason for these differences is the late development of the Korean economy, in which industrialization took place mainly after the Korean War of the early 1950s. The industrial base left after the World War II period of Japanese colonialization was largely destroyed in the war, which also led to the division of the peninsular into North and South Korea.

After the War the South Korean economy was almost solely dependent upon the USA for military and economic aid. Some import substitution projects were undertaken, but the then President, Mr Sygman Rhee, was not especially interested in heavy governmental intervention.

Nevertheless, the late 1950s saw the rapid development of the early chaebol, fueled by favorable import license concessions, access to scarce foreign exchange, and governmental properties seized from the Japanese. However, in 1960 the Rhee government was overthrown and the emerging chaebol were coerced to accept government guidance from the Ministry of Trade and Industry, in a similar manner to MITI in Japan. The position of the Korean government was also strengthened by their control over the banking industry. As a result, a partnership was developed between the chaebol and government, yielding a dramatic growth in the Korean economy from the 1960s to the present day.

In the 1970s, government concern at the rising economic dominance of the chaebol led to the introduction of laws to curb their growth. Some firms were pushed to reduce the level of family ownership by issuing their stocks on the capital market; tax payments and access to bank credits were also closely controled. Some real estate disposals and divestments of subsidiaries by the leading 20 chaebol were also introduced by government. Nevertheless, industrial concentration by the top ten chaebol increased, and by the early 1980s these concerns held around a 25 per cent share of Korea's manufacturing industry.

By the mid-1980s the Korean economy was heavily dependent upon the chaebol, and to restrict their activity would have been to enforce a slowdown in the nation's economic growth. There was, however, an increase in competition between the leading chaebol, as they came to compete for market share both at home and overseas. Moreover, after initially copying the evolution of Japanese industry in the postwar period, the companies began to develop their own competence in R&D, technology, marketing, and management skills. Development in industries similar to those behind the Japanese economic miracle, such as shipbuilding, heavy engineering, consumer electronics and, more recently, automobiles, formed the backbone of the emerging Korean economy. The changing nature of the chaebol also led to a reduction in government intervention and greater corporate independence. Nevertheless, the chaebol were not given control of the banking industry, as was the case with the keiretsu. By the late 1980s the top 30 chaebol groups held around 40 per cent of the Korean market.

The Korean chaebol were much younger than their Japanese counterparts which, prior to World War II, had developed as family-dominated zaibatsu groups following the Meiji Restoration and the subsequent industrialization of Japan. The oldest of the "big four" groups, Samsung, was created in 1938, while the remainder were mainly established in the 1950s. As a result, many were still owned by the families of their founders, with on average some 30 per cent of listed company stock in their hands. This figure was relatively higher for the larger chaebol groups.

The family ownership patterns of the Korean chaebol have been classified into three types, as shown in figure 1. In the first of these types, ownership is direct and complete, with the founder and his family owning all the chaebol affiliated companies. In the second form, the family own a holding company which, in turn, owns affiliated subsidiaries: the Daewoo group is an example of this form. The third type enjoys interlocking mutual ownership, with the founding family owning the group holding company and/or some form of foundation which, in turn, owns the affiliated companies: this form is typified by the Samsung group. As the chaebol evolve, the trend has been to move progressively from the first structure to the third.

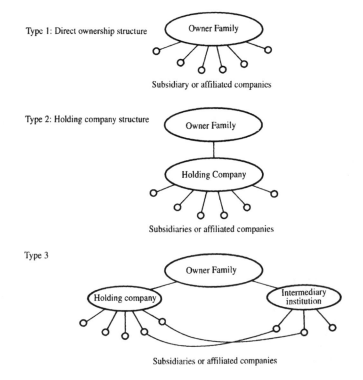

Figure 1 The organizational structure of Korean chaebols.
Source: Hattori (1989, p. 88).

While family ownership of keiretsu groups is generally very low, or presently nonexistent, it has been shown that more than 30 per cent of the executives of the top 20 chaebol groups are members of the founding family. Family members thus play significant roles in the direction of the chaebol and, in particular, the eldest of the founder's sons is usually groomed to succeed the father when he retires. Fathers-in-law, sons-in-law, brothers, uncles, and nephews are also recruited into management.

The four leading chaebol are all dominated by family executives. The Samsung group has one of the highest rates of non family member executive management, but family members still dominate the most important positions. In Hyundai the founder had seven sons, five of whom manage ten major group operations: a sixth is being groomed to succeed his father, while the founder's brother heads Hyundai Motors. In the LG group, the founder has six sons and five brothers, many of whom occupy senior positions. Daewoo, created only in 1967, is still led by its founder and, apart from his wife, no other members of the family are actively involved in management, although the future position of the founder's children is still unclear.

While family ownership is a critical factor in the management of chaebol, it is also important to understand that Korean tradition allows the unequal distribution of family wealth clearly in favor of the eldest son. Moreover, the Korean concept of the family is defined strictly on the basis of blood ties, whereas in Japan zaibatsu families could absorb non-blood tie related managers by adoption, marriage, or appointment. Thus, in Korea, chaebol successors are generally confined to family members related by blood.

In chaebol structures, the central office still maintains strict control over strategy and monitoring the performance of operating units. By contrast, after the elimination of the zaibatsu holding companies, Japanese keiretsu groups have a much looser system of influence over the strategies of member corporations via their presidents' councils and other integrating mechanisms.

Unlike the keiretsu groups, the Korean chaebol contain neither powerful trading companies nor significant internal financial service institutions. General trading companies within the chaebol only began to develop from the mid-1970s, as a result of discussions with government on how to stimulate exports. By the mid-1980s each of the major groups had created general trading companies, but the focus of these concerns was exports rather than the much wider role undertaken by the soga shosha. Nevertheless, by the early 1990s, the nine largest general trading companies were responsible for over 50 per cent of Korean exports.

The lack of financial service institutions within the chaebol structure has meant that they have been forced to rely heavily on external finance to fuel their growth. In particular, they have been dependent upon government funds, which has provided the state with a major mechanism for influencing chaebol strategies, especially with regard to focus and diversification. Major groups have, however, been actively attempting to build their positions in the financial services sector, but these efforts are still weak by comparison with the position of the keiretsu.

In terms of management style, the Korean chaebol are more influenced by Japanese systems than by those of the West, despite the heavy US influence in the period after the Korean War and until relations with Japan were restored in the mid-1960s.

From the influences of the USA and Japan, coupled with Korea's own history and traditions, Korean companies have evolved their own system of management, sometimes referred to as K-Style management. This includes top down decision making, paternalistic leadership, clan management, *intival* (or harmony-oriented cultural values), flexible lifetime employment, personal loyalty, seniority and merit-based compensation, and conglomerate diversification strategies.

Bibliography

Chen, M. (1995). *Asian management systems*. London: Routledge. See chapters 12 and 15.

Chang, C. S. (1988). Chaebol: the South Korean conglomerates. *Business Horizons*, 51–7.

Hattori, T. (1989). Japanese zaibatsu and Korean chaebol. In Kae H. Chung, Hak Chong Lee (eds), *Korean managerial dynamics*. New York: Praeger. See pp. 79–98.

Korean Development Institute (1982). *Ownership structure of Korean Chaebols*. Seoul, Korea: KDI.

Lee, S. M. & Yoo, S. J. (1987). Management style and practice of Korean Chaebols. *California Management Review*, 95, 95–110.

Lee, S. M. & Yoo, S. J. (1987). The K-type management: a driving force of Korean prosperity. *Management International Review*, 27 (4), 68–77.

DEREK F. CHANNON

change, methods Specific methods used to change organizations are often referred to as *interventions*. Interventions are the planned change activities designed to increase an organization's effectiveness (Cummings & Worley, 1993, p. 163). In the ORGANIZATION DEVELOPMENT paradigm, effectiveness includes both productivity and quality of work life.

Antecedents and Conditions for Effective Change
Effective change depends in large measure on valid diagnosis of organizational functioning and problems (Woodman, 1990). A valid identification and exploration of what the organization does well and poorly is a natural precursor to change. Argyris (1970), for example, has argued that effective ORGANIZATIONAL CHANGE depends upon three things:

(1) valid and useful information about the organization and its problems;
(2) free and informed choice on the part of organizational members with regard to courses of action that they might take; and
(3) internal commitment by participants in the change effort to the actions chosen.

Absent these antecedents, effective change is seen as quite problematic.

In a similar vein, Cummings and Worley (1993) see effective change management as based on the following antecedents:

(1) motivating change by creating a readiness for change among employees and attempting to overcome resistance to the change (*see* RESISTANCE TO CHANGE);
(2) creating a shared vision of the desired future state of the organization; and

(3) developing political support for the needed changes.

Porras and Robertson (1992) have reviewed the literature dealing with change methodology in order to identify conditions that would seem to be related to effective interventions. In brief, these conditions include:

(1) The organization's members must be the key source of energy for the change, not some external consultant or change agent.
(2) Key members of the organization must recognize the need for change and be attracted by the potential positive outcomes from the change program.
(3) A willingness to change norms and procedures, in order to become more effective, must exist.

Key members of the organization must exhibit both attitudes and behaviors that support new norms and procedures.

Finally, recent meta-analyses (see VALIDITY GENERALIZATION) of systematically evaluated organizational change programs have provided strong support for the notion that organizational change efforts are most effective when they are systemwide and "multifaceted" (Macy & Izumi, 1993; Robertson, Roberts, & Porras, 1993). Multifaceted interventions are those that take place in multiple subsystems of the organization, seek change in multiple variables of interest, and/or employ multiple change methods.

Focus of Change Efforts

Managers and change agents must have some means to link the conclusions from the diagnosis with effective action. Such attempts at identifying linkages have often taken the form of a model or typology that would categorize interventions by their focus or change targets. The "classic" forerunner of such categorization schemes is the dichotomy of human processual and technostructural interventions developed by Friedlander and Brown (1974). Human processual interventions focus on processes, such as COMMUNICATION, problem solving, and decision making, through which individuals accomplish the organization's work. Technostructural interventions are targeted on changing the organization's technology (e.g., task methods and processes, work design) and structure. A more recent example of such a categorization scheme is that used by McMahan and Woodman (1992) in a survey of *Fortune* 500 industrial firms. McMahan and Woodman were able to identify the change methods used by these organizations as falling into one of the four following categories:

Human Processual. Emphasis on human relationships, TEAM BUILDING, work team interaction, process consulting, or conflict resolution.
Technostructural. Emphasis on sociotechnical systems, task and technology work designs, or organization and group structure (see JOB DESIGN).
Strategic Planning. Emphasis on strategic business planning processes, strategic change or visioning; primarily top management involvement (see TOP MANAGEMENT TEAMS; MISSION STATEMENTS).
Systemwide. Emphasis on organization-wide improvement activities; LEADERSHIP, culture, quality improvement,

and transformation-type organizational change projects (see TOTAL QUALITY MANAGEMENT).

Implementation Theory

The applied theories that can serve to guide change methods are called implementation theories (Porras & Robertson, 1992). (For a discussion of the theory domains involved in organizational change, see ORGANIZATION DEVELOPMENT). Implementation theories can be further broken down into three categories, each corresponding to a different level of specificity in terms of prescribing change actions. At the most general level of specification are *strategy theories*, which describe broad strategies that can be used to change human systems. *Procedure theories*, at a higher level of specificity, include descriptions of major steps to be taken in order to complete a process of change. The most specific category of implementation theories, called *technique theories*, focuses tightly on, say, a single "step" identified in a procedure theory.

Weisbord's (1988) "practice theory" of OD provides an example of an implementation theory. Weisbord proposes four guidelines for effective organizational change:

(1) assess the potential for action;
(2) get the whole system in the room;
(3) focus on the future; and
(4) structure systems tasks people can do for themselves.

The ideas and concepts in Weisbord's implementation theory are themselves theoretically grounded, being drawn from the theory and practice of Fred Emery, Kurt Lewin, Douglas McGregor, and Eric Trist, among others.

Many years ago, Kurt Lewin stated that there was a good THEORY. Implementation theories provide the field with a means for identifying important antecedents and conditions necessary for effective organizational change. Further, implementation theories provide guidance that can link the problems identified during organizational diagnosis with the solutions or action steps needed to address them. In sum, implementation theory summarizes what the field knows about change methods, why they work, and how they might be successfully used.

see also **Politics**

Bibliography

Argyris, C. (1970). Intervention theory and method: A behavioral science view. Reading, MA: Addison-Wesley.

Cummings, T. G. & Worley, C. G. (1993). Organization development and change, (5th edn) St. Paul, MN: West.

Friedlander, F. & Brown, L. D. (1974). Organization development Annual Review of Psychology, 25, 313–341.

Macy, B. A. & Izumi, H. (1993). Organizational change, design, and work innovation: A meta-analysis of 131 North American field studies, 1961–1991. In R. W. Woodman & W. A. Pasmore (Eds), Research in organizational change and development, (Vol. 7, pp. 235–313). Greenwich, CT: JAI Press.

McMahan, G. C. & Woodman, R. W. (1992). The current practice of organization development within the firm. Group & Organization Management, 17, 117–134.

Porras, J. I. & Robertson, P. J. (1992). Organizational development: Theory, practice, and research. In M. D. Dunnette & L. M. Hough (Eds), Handbook of industrial and organizational psychology, (2nd edn, vol. 3, pp. 719–822). Palo Alto, CA: Consulting Psychologists Press.

Robertson, P. J., Roberts, D. R. & Porras, J. I. (1993). An evaluation of a model of planned organizational change: Evidence from a meta-analysis In R. W. Woodman & W. A.

Pasmore (Eds), Research in organizational change and development, (vol. 7, pp. 1–39). Greenwich, CT: JAI Press.

Weisbord, M. R. (1988). Towards a new practice theory of OD: Notes on snapshooting and moviemaking. In W. A. Pasmore & R. W. Woodman (Eds), Research in organizational change and development, (vol. 2, pp. 59–96). Greenwich, CT: JAI Press.

Woodman, R. W. (1990). Issues and concerns in organizational diagnosis. In C. N. Jackson & M. R. Manning (Eds), Organizational development annual, Vol. 3: Diagnosing client organizations. Alexandria, VA: American Society for Training and Development.

RICHARD W. WOODMAN

channels of distribution Products and services are moved from their source of production to the customer by means of a channel of distribution. The channel may be simple when the producer sells direct to customers (through, for example, DIRECT MAIL) or it can consist of one or more intermediaries, such as agents, WHOLESALERS, and retailers. The form, and complexity, of the distribution channel employed depends on the product (its perishability, bulk, frequency of purchase, whether or not it is an industrial or consumer product), the customers for the product, and their geographical dispersion.

A producer may employ an intermediary because it is the traditional practice of the industry, although often significant competitive advantages can be gained from innovating. Selling direct can be employed by firms selling particular categories of industrial products, such as expensive capital goods or bulk raw materials. Such sales involve high-value dispatches, relatively infrequent purchases, and special pre-sale NEGOTIATION on price and technical specifications. However, direct selling (*see* DIRECT MARKETING) is employed widely in consumer markets, and is gaining more widespread appeal, partly because of the often considerably lower costs.

Where independent intermediaries are used, a distinction can be drawn between those who act merely on behalf of the manufacturer (e.g., selling and distributing the product) without purchasing the product (i.e., they do not take title), and those who take title and undertake all further responsibility for distribution and perhaps other aspects of marketing. Intermediaries who do not take title include brokers and manufacturers' sales agents. A broker will attempt to find possible purchasers of the product and bring the manufacturer and these potential customers together. Manufacturers' sales agents fulfill similar functions, although they will often employ their own sales staff, carry stock on consignment, and provide ancillary services such as financing, installation, and so on. Both brokers and agents receive a commission on any sales.

Intermediaries who do take title include wholesalers and retailers. These both buy and sell. Wholesalers will collect a range of goods from various manufacturers and usually sell them to other intermediaries (e.g., small retailers). Wholesalers are used when, for example, the amount sold per customer is relatively small, or when customers are widely scattered geographically. Generally, wholesalers sell to other companies or to retailers. Retailers, which carry out a similar function, mostly sell to the final customer. Large retailers will generally take deliverers.

There are various transfers between the different elements of the distribution chain. Five types of transfer can be identified: *physical goods transfers* – the movement of goods, ranging from the initial raw materials, through components and subassemblies, to the final product; *ownership transfer* – as the product passes through the chain, the ownership of the physical goods can change; *payment transfer* – the movement of money for the payment of goods and services; *information transfer* – the flow of information between different stages in the chain; and *influence transfer* – the way in which different elements in the chain attempt to promote themselves and thereby influence other elements in the chain.

Bibliography

Dibb, S., Simkin, L., Pride, W. M. & Ferrell, O. C. (1994). *Marketing: Concepts and strategies*, European edn, London: Houghton Mifflin Co. Chapters 10, 11, 12.

McCarthy, E. J. & Perreault, W. D. (1993). *Basic marketing*, 11th edn, Homewood, IL: Irwin. Chapters 13, 14.

DALE LITTLER

character Character is revealed in a person's typical behavior in important matters, including moral ones. Your character may be good or bad according to whether you are virtuous or vicious, and strong or weak according to whether you can be relied on to act on your VALUES even under pressure. Ethicists and psychologists, particularly personality theorists, study character and the causal and conceptual links among traits.

To identify your self with your character is misleading in this sense: a significant character change would not by itself mean that you have ceased to exist and have been replaced by someone else. Yet an extreme change in character may justify saying, meaningfully but with some exaggeration, that Jones is a different man, or not the man I married. Strong character does have to do with consistency of thought, value, and action over time. One who is consistent in this way, especially one who acts according to the values one espouses, is a person of INTEGRITY.

Aristotle famously claims that ethics is primarily about the virtues of character rather than about principles, though he grants principles a role in ethics. His view is no longer quaint: in recent years the notions of virtue and character have gained respectability among business ethicists.

This is not to say that character and virtue have obviated principles. We cannot assume that any single sort of ethical theory will address all issues equally well, but principle-based theories seem particularly ill-suited to certain practical moral issues with which managers and others must often deal. Faced with a moral problem that requires action, a manager will likely find that (for example) Kantian ethics and utilitarianism yield no determinate results, but instead create subsidiary arguments about the right sort of preference, or the precise maxim of the act in question. If those arguments could be settled, there would be a further one about which of the general approaches is right. If that problem could be solved, moreover, there would still be the practical issue of whether people will actually do the right thing, as those of good character do. Depending in part on the nature, size, and environment of an organization, a manager may be able to bring about morally good behavior most effectively by populating the organization with employees of good and strong character rather than by enforcing moral rules.

If the virtues of character were simply dispositions to act according to certain principles, then virtue and character ethics would not differ from principle-based ethics; but virtue and character ethicists deny that there are algorithms linking virtues to action-guiding principles. On the contrary, a person of good character does not merely act according to principles, but in cases in which principles give little guidance is sensitive to all significant aspects of the situation, including possible indirect and long-term consequences. This practical wisdom resembles the ability of a consistently successful businessperson to assess opportunities and act effectively; it is not a matter of simply knowing textbook rules, important as these may be.

A person of good and strong character is one whose interests are such that being moral makes him or her happy and fulfilled. For such a person the question, why is it in my best interests to be moral? can hardly arise. A life anchored by a set of clear and coherent values will likely be preferable to one in which happiness is based on ephemera. But couldn't a bad person of strong character be equally well off? Probably not: such people arouse opposition and lose the benefits of cooperation.

A person of bad character is capable of good acts where these serve that person's interests or fit enforced norms comfortably, much as a person who lacks knowledge may make true statements. But just as education is a matter of imparting actual knowledge, so training in morality should build good character. Acting morally need not be painful – for the person of good character it is not – but it cannot be based on self-interest alone.

To understand how your virtues are related and why you have them requires understanding your character, of which virtues are its iceberg's tip. Teachers, parents, and managers who would affect character must consider psychological relations, which are not relations merely among virtues. Here is another reason why a character is not simply a disposition to act in a certain way: a character trait has no less ontological status than does a psychological state, which is not a mere disposition. A description of a character trait may explain a whole set of virtues. In fact, a particular trait (firmness, for example) may be the psychological basis of both a virtue (courage) and a vice (obstinacy), especially in one who is not perfectly rational.

A pervasive ORGANIZATIONAL CULTURE can make people of weak character act against their values, though it may occasionally support good character. There is no obligation for managers to improve their employees' character, but they should maintain an organization in which good character does not put one at a disadvantage.

Can character be taught, by BUSINESS ETHICS professors or anyone else? If, as Aristotle claims, habituation creates character, there is a problem: how can character be related to the rationality definitive of humans, whereby the agent controls ephemeral desires in aid of an appropriate long-term conception of happiness? If building character is just a matter of forming habits, then moral education should proceed not by appeals to the intellect but by positive and negative reinforcement, and business ethics courses taught in the usual way are a waste of time, and too late.

Yet a business ethics course may indeed help build character. The case study method, or case method, can assist students in developing practical wisdom, including the sensitivity to details, consequences, and nuances that we attribute to a person of character. Insofar as it deals with issues of character, moreover, a course in business ethics can show the moral importance of corporate culture and of a human resources policy that takes character into account.

Bibliography
Aristotle. (1985). *Nicomachean Ethics* trans. T. Irwin. Indianapolis: Hackett. (Includes a glossary of key terms.)
French, P., Uehling, T. & Wettstein, H. (eds). (1988). *Ethical Theory: Character and Virtue* Midwest Studies in Philosophy 13. Minneapolis: University of Minnesota. (Includes several essays on character.)
Hartman, E. M. (1996). *Organizational Ethics and the Good Life.* New York: Oxford University Press.
Kupperman, J. (1991). *Character.* New York: Oxford University Press.
Schoeman, F. (Ed.) (1987). *Responsibility, Character, and the Emotions.* New York: Cambridge University Press. (Includes several essays on character.)
Solomon, R. C. (1992). *Ethics and Excellence: Cooperation and Integrity in Business.* New York: Oxford University Press. (An important analysis of business ethics from an Aristotelian point of view).

EDWIN M. HARTMAN

chief information officer   The chief information officer (CIO) is the highest-ranking manager responsible for the management of information resources and information technology within an organization. Although the position of CIO varies from organization to organization, the CIO often reports to the president and chief executive officer. The position usually has two broad responsibilities: (a) the management of information technology (e.g. hardware, software, and networks); and (b) the management of the information resources (applications, databases, and personnel) used by the organization.

As the most senior information technology officer, it is the CIO's responsibility to understand the organization's mission and objectives and the potential benefits of using information technology. The CIO's challenge is to seek out opportunities where information technology can be deployed to achieve organization objectives as well as to find ways in which information technology can be used to gain competitive advantage.

The aggressive use of information technology and the growth in the creation, need, and use of information has focused the CIO on corporate information as a manageable resource. In this role, the CIO must understand how information is used by the organization in accomplishing its objectives and how to best manage this information as a critical and valuable corporate asset.

BRIAN D. JANZ

child care benefit   Child care, defined as assisting employees with caring for children is a type of dependent care benefit and family supportive policy. Child care benefits can reduce employees' financial burden and level of WORK–FAMILY CONFLICT. Work–family conflict can negatively influence employee behaviors, including tardiness, intention to turnover (Youngblood and Chambers-Cook, 1984), performance, absenteeism, job satisfaction, recruitment

(Kossek and Nichol, 1992), and organizational commitment (Grover and Crocker, 1995).

Although large employers (over 100 employees) are more likely to offer at least several types of child care benefits, under the Family and Medical Leave Act of 1993 (FMLA), all employers with 50 or more employees located within a 75-mile radius must provide an unpaid leave of absence of up to 3 months for the birth or adoption of a child, and/or to take care of serious health problems for a child and other family members (including oneself). Beside leaves, the most popular forms of assistance relate to: (a) time (flextime, job sharing, part-time work, and flexplace); (b) information (resource and referral, work–family seminars); (c) financial (flexible benefits or spending accounts, discounts, vouchers, adoption); and (d) direct services (on or near site care center, sick care, consortiums, and summer camps) (Galinsky et al., 1991). As employers become more experienced with child care, they usually develop policies to manage broader issues of work–family and work–life integration. Such policies include those related to elder care, organizational culture change (training supervisors to be aware of work-family issues, assessment of cultural barriers impeding policy use); work–family stress management (seminars and coordination with employee assistance plans (EAPS)), and corporate giving (both financial and through donation of employee time) to community and national work–family initiatives (Galinsky et al., 1991).

Bibliography

Galinsky, E., Friedman, D. E. & Hernandez, C. A. (1991). *The Corporate Reference Guide to Work–Family Programs*, New York: Families and Work Institute.

Grover, S. L. & Crocker, K. (1995). Who appreciates family-responsive human resource policies? The impact of family-friendly policies on the organizational attachment of parents and non-parents. *Personnel Psychology*, 48, 271–88.

Kossek, E. E. & Nichol, V. (1992). The effects of on-site child care on employee attitudes and performance. *Personnel Psychology*, 45, 485–509.

Youngblood, S. A. & Chambers-Cook, K. (1984). Child care assistance can improve employee attitudes and behavior. *Personnel Administrator*, 29, 45–7.

ELLEN ERNST KOSSEK

Civil Rights Act of 1964 Title VII of the Civil Rights Act of 1964, as amended by the Equal Employment Opportunities Act of 1972 and the CIVIL RIGHTS ACT of 1991, forbids employer and union discrimination based on race, color, religion, sex, or national origin. Title VII specifically forbids any employer to fail to hire, to discharge, to classify employees, or to discriminate with respect to compensation, terms, conditions, or privileges of employment opportunity due to race, color, religion, sex, or national origin. Title VII also prohibits retaliation against persons who file charges or participate in EQUAL EMPLOYMENT OPPORTUNITY COMMISSION (EEOC) investigations.

Title VII covers private employers, state and local governments, and educational institutions that have 15 or more employees. The federal government, private and public employment agencies, labor organizations, and joint labor–management committees for apprenticeship and training must also abide by the law.

Theories of Discrimination

There are two legal theories under which a plaintiff may prove a case of unlawful discrimination: disparate treatment and disparate impact. A disparate treatment claim exists where an employer treats some individuals less favorably than others because of their race, color, religion, sex, or national origin. Proof of the employer's discriminatory motive is critical in a disparate treatment case.

A disparate impact claims exists where an employer's facially neutral employment practices, such as hiring or promotion examinations, though neutrally applied and making no adverse reference to race, color, religion, sex, or national origin, have a significantly adverse disparate impact on a protected group, and the employment practice in question is not shown to be job-related and consistent with business necessity by the employer.

Filing Procedures

The EEOC is a five-member commission appointed by the President to establish equal employment opportunity policy under the law it administers. The EEOC supervises the conciliation and enforcement efforts of the agency.

The time limitation for filing charges with the EEOC is 180 days after the occurrence of the discriminatory act. After the conclusion of the proceedings before the EEOC, an individual claiming a violation of Title VII has 90 days after receipt of a right-to-sue letter from the EEOC to file a civil lawsuit in a federal district court. If an aggrieved individual does not meet the time limit of Title VII, the individual may well lose the right to seek relief under the Act.

Protected Classes

The legislative history of Title VII of the Civil Rights Act demonstrates that a primary purpose of the Act is to provide fair employment opportunities for black Americans. The protections of the Act are applied to blacks based on race or color. The word race, as used in the Act, applied to all members of the four major racial groupings: white, black, native American, and Asian-Pacific. Native Americans can file charges and receive the protection of the Act on the basis of national origin, race, or in some instances color. Individuals of Asian-Pacific origin may file discrimination charges based on race, color, or in some instances national origin. Whites are also protected against discrimination because of race and color.

Title VII requires employees to accommodate their employees' or prospective employees' religious practices. Most cases involving allegations of religious discrimination revolve around the determination of whether an employer has made reasonable efforts to accommodate religious beliefs (see *Trans World Airlines* v. *Hardison*, 432 US 63, 1977).

Title VII permits religious societies to grant hiring preferences in favor of members of their religion. It also provides an exemption for educational institutions to hire employees of a particular religion if the institution is owned, controlled, or managed by a particular religious society. The exemption is a broad one and is not restricted to the religious activities of the institution.

Employers that discriminate against female or male employees because of their sex are held to be in violation of Title VII. The EEOC and the courts have determined that the word sex, as used in Title VII, means a person's gender and not the person's sexual orientation. State and local legislation, however, may provide specific protection against discrimination based on sexual orientation. An employer must be able to show that criteria used to make an employment decision that has a disparate impact on women, such as minimum height and weight requirements, are in fact job-related. All candidates for a position requiring physical strength must be given an opportunity to demonstrate their capability to perform the work. Title VII was amended by the Pregnancy Discrimination Act (PDA) in 1978 (Section 701 (k)). The amendment prevents employers from treating pregnancy, childbirth, or other related medical conditions in a manner different than the treatment of other disabilities. Thus, women disabled due to pregnancy, childbirth, or other related medical conditions must be provided with the same benefits as other disabled workers. An employer who does not provide disability benefits or paid sick leave to other employees is not required to provide them for pregnant workers.

Quid pro quo sexual harassment involves supervisors seeking sexual favors from their subordinates in return for job benefits such as continued employment, promotion, a raise, or a favorable performance evaluation. In such a case, where a supervisor's actions affect job benefits, the employer is liable to the employee for the loss of benefits plus punitive damages because of the supervisor's misconduct. A second form of sexual harassment is hostile working environment harassment. With this type of harassment, an employee's economic benefits have not been affected by the supervisor's misconduct, but the supervisor's sexually harassing conduct has nevertheless caused anxiety and "poisoned" the work environment. An injunction against such conduct can be obtained and attorneys' fees awarded. Moreover, if such conduct drives the employee to quit the job, the employer may be responsible for all economic losses caused the employee plus punitive damages (see *Meritor Savings Bank* v. *Vinson*, 477 US 57, 1986; *Harris* v. *Forklift Systems, Inc.*, 114 S Ct 367, 1993).

Title VII protects members of all nationalities from discrimination. The judicial principles that have emerged from cases involving race, color, and gender employment discrimination are generally applicable to cases involving allegations of national origin discrimination. Thus, physical standards such as minimum height requirements, which tend to exclude persons of a particular national origin because of the physical stature of the group, have been unlawful when these standards cannot be justified by business necessity.

Adverse employment based on an individual's lack of English language skills violates Title VII when the language requirement bears no demonstrable relationship to the successful performance of the job to which it is applied.

Title VII Exceptions

Section 703 of Title VII exempts several key practices from the scope of Title VII enforcement. It is not an unlawful employment practice for an employer to hire employees on the basis of religion, sex, or national origin in those certain instances where religion, sex, or national origin is a bona fide occupational qualification (BFOQ) reasonably necessary to the normal operation of a particular enterprise. Section 703 (h) of the act authorizes the use of "any

professionally-developed ability test [that is not] designed, intended, or used to discriminate."

Employment testing and educational requirements must be "job-related;" that is, the employers must prove that the tests and educational requirements bear a relationship to job performance.

Section 703 (h) provides that differences in employment terms based on a bona fide seniority system are sanctioned as long as the differences do not stem from an intention to discriminate.

Affirmative Action

Employers, under affirmative action plans (AAPs), may undertake special recruiting and other efforts to hire and train minorities and women and help them advance within the company. Such plans have resulted in numerous lawsuits contending that Title VII, the Fourteenth Amendment, or COLLECTIVE BARGAINING contracts have been violated.

A permissible AAP should conform to the following criteria: (a) the affirmative action must be in connection with a "plan;" (b) there must be a showing that affirmative action is justified as a remedial measure, and the plan must then be remedial to open opportunities in occupations closed to protected classes under Title VII or designed to break down old patterns of racial segregation and hierarchy; (c) the plan must be voluntary; (d) the plan must not unnecessarily trammel the interests of whites; and (e) the plan must be temporary (see *Steelworkers* v. *Weber*, 443 US 193, 1979).

When an employer's AAP is not shown to be justified, or "unnecessarily trammels" the interest of nonminority employees, it is often called reverse discrimination. For example, a city's decision to rescore police promotional tests in order to achieve specific racial and gender percentages unnecessarily trammeled the interests of nonminority police officers (see *San Francisco Police Officers' Association* v. *San Francisco*, 812 F2d 1125, CA 9, 1987).

DAVID P. TWOMEY

Civil Rights Act of 1991   Between 1989 and 1991 the US Supreme Court reoriented Title VII jurisprudence to favor employers. The Civil Rights Act of 1991 (CRA 1991) modified or reversed these decisions, augmented the types of damages available to plaintiffs, and provided for jury trials in cases of intentional discrimination.

In a disparate treatment (intentional discrimination) case, the plaintiff must prove discriminatory intent. Section 105 of CRA 1991 set forth the burden of proof for disparate impact (facially neutral employment practices that have an adverse impact on a protected group) cases, codifying the concepts of business necessity and job relatedness enunciated in *Griggs* v. *Duke Power Co.*, 401 US 424, 1971. A new shifting burden of proof scheme resulted: (a) the plaintiff must demonstrate through relevant statistical comparisons that a particular employment practice used in selecting or promoting employees causes a disparate impact; (b) the defending employer may then proceed to demonstrate that a particular employment practice does not cause the disparate impact; or (c) the defending employer must demonstrate (with the burden of persuasion, not just production of evidence) that the challenged practice is job-related for the position in question and consistent with business necessity.

Victims of discrimination are entitled to remedies, including back pay and benefits, less their interim earnings. In addition to these remedies, under the Civil Rights Act of 1991, victims of intentional discrimination can now receive compensatory and punitive damages capped for sex and religious discrimination, depending on the size of the employer.

The Civil Rights Act of 1991 makes it an unlawful employment practice for an employer to adjust scores, use different cut-off scores, or otherwise alter the results of employment tests on the basis of race, color, religion, sex, or national origin. This provision addresses the so-called "race norming" issues, whereby the results of hiring and promotion tests are adjusted to assure that a minimum number of minorities are included in application pools.

DAVID P. TWOMEY

coalition formation   This state occurs when some but not all members of a group organize themselves to push their perspective on an issue (see POLITICS). Thompson (1967, p. 126) wrote that "coalition behavior is undoubtedly of major importance to our understanding of complex organizations." But even though the concepts of coalitions and coalition formation have been used to describe organizations and organizational action (e.g., Cyert & March, 1963; Pfeffer & Salancik, 1978); organizational behavior has paid little attention to the literature on coalitions in social psychology, GAME THEORY, or political science (Murnighan, 1978; 1994).

Early results found that the least endowed tended to coalesce and exclude the most endowed. These "strength is weakness" findings, which suggested the supremacy of the underdog, were soon debunked. New research showed that when power bases vary, strength is weakness only when parties with different resources are effectively interchangeable. Partners with just sufficient resources to do the job appear optimal: fewer resources may imply smaller outcome demands, and greater attractiveness. When parties are not interchangeable, however, strength is extremely valuable, and no longer the harbinger of exclusion (i.e., weakness). The political and the social psychological literature also suggest that small but sufficient coalitions are most frequent.

Founders tend to possess a diverse network of weak ties, rather than strong links to only a few others (see NETWORKING). Thus, a coalition's strength may rest on infrequent, nonrepetitive interaction with many others, rather than on frequent, well-established interactions with a few close contacts. Political models also suggest that coalitions form incrementally, as interconnected sets of interacting dyads. Put simply, *coalitions form one person at a time* (Murnighan & Brass, 1991). Once a coalition is successful at achieving a critical mass, continued growth becomes considerably easier.

Being surreptitious may be critical in the success of many organizational coalitions: keeping quiet helps blunt the formation of an organized opposition, i.e., counter-coalitions, which von Neumann and Morgenstern's (1947) classic, original model assumed would be excluded parties'

natural reaction to a coalition forming. Successful coalitions tend to be fluid, forming quickly, expanding and bursting at decision time, and quickly disappearing (Murnighan & Brass, 1991).

Political models suggest that founders add similar members to ensure their own centrality in the final coalition. New parties are invited to balance each other's ideology, on either side of the founder's position. The coalition can grow until it is just large enough, keeping the range of its ideologies at a minimum and increasing the likelihood that its final policy positions will most closely resemble the founder's. This kind of political strategy, which may be well understood by astute organizational tacticians, has not found its way into the organizational literature.

Within an organization, executives who are involved in many productive projects (i.e., organizational coalitions) are viewed as politically powerful (see POWER). A few organization members may be in several dominant coalitions: They represent Thompson's (1967) concept of *the inner circle*, a select few whose interconnectedness provides them with considerable influence. These are the people who wield considerable coalitional and political influence in organizations (see INFLUENCE; LEADERSHIP).

see also Intergroup relations; Interorganizational relations; Joint venture strategy

Bibliography

Cyert, R. & March, J. G. (1963). A behavioral theory of the firm. Englewood Cliffs, NJ: Prentice-Hall.

Murnighan, J. K. (1978). Models of coalition formation: Game theoretic, social psychological, and political perspectives. Psychological Bulletin, **85**, 1130–1153.

Murnighan, J. K. (1994). Game theory and organizational behavior. In B. M. Staw & L. L. Cummings (Eds), Research in organizational behavior. Greenwich, CT: JAI Press.

Murnighan, J. K. & Brass, D. J. (1991). Intraorganizational coalitions. In Bazerman, M. H., Lewicki, R. J. & Sheppard, B. H. (Eds), Research on negotiation in organizations. Greenwich, CT: JAI Press.

Pfeffer, J. & Salancik, G. (1978). The external control of organizations. New York: Harper & Row.

Thompson, J. D. (1967). Organizations in action. New York: McGraw-Hill.

von Neumann, J. & Morgenstern, O. (1947). The theory of games and economic behavior. Princeton, NJ: Princeton University Press.

J. KEITH MURNIGHAN

Cobb–Douglas production function   The Cobb–Douglas production function is frequently employed in the economic analysis of production and costs. This production function relates output produced to the inputs of production. If labor hours, L, and capital, K, are the only inputs in production, the Cobb–Douglas production function is:

$$q = AL^{\alpha}K^{\beta}$$

where A is a coefficient that represents the level of technology and α and β are coefficients indicating how output responds to changes in each of these inputs (additional inputs can be added to the function above in a similar fashion). A convenient feature of the Cobb–Douglas production function above is that ECONOMIES OF SCALE in production can be determined by examining the coefficients *alpha* and *beta*. When there are economies of scale in production, doubling all inputs will cause output to increase by more than double. In the case above, if we double the labor and capital inputs, we would have:

$$q = A(2L)^\alpha (2K)^\beta = 2^{(\alpha+\beta)} AL^\alpha K^\beta$$

Doubling the inputs used in production will cause output to rise by $2^{(alpha+beta)}$, so the returns to scale in production can be determined by summing the coefficients of the Cobb–Douglas production function. If the sum of (*alpha* + *beta*) equals one, then there are CONSTANT RETURNS TO SCALE.

Estimates of the Cobb–Douglas production by a linear regression of the logarithm of output against the logarithm of the relevant inputs in production; see Berndt (1991) and Maddala (1992).

Bibliography

Berndt, E. R. (1991). *The Practice of Econometrics*. Reading, MA: Addison-Wesley.
Cobb, C. & Douglas, P. H. (1928). A theory of production. *American Economic Review*, 18,139–65.
Maddala, G. S. (1992). *Introduction to Econometrics*. 2nd edn, New York: Macmillan.

ROBERT E. MCAULIFFE

codes of ethics (also called codes of conduct or professional codes): statements of behavioral ideals, exhortations, or prohibitions, common to a culture, religion, traditional professions, fraternal organizations, corporations, and trade associations. Codes combine philosophical statements and high ideals with admonitions to avoid specific illegal actions and to espouse certain moral principles, especially those that elevate personal behavior or improve interpersonal relationships.

Codes have been considered the primary means of institutionalizing ethics into the culture, religion, professions, learned societies, or corporations. Historically, the Code of Hammurabi contains paragraphs of rules governing business, moral, and social life reaching back into the third millennium BC to the earlier Codes of UrNammu (ca. 2060–2043 BC), the Code of Lipit-Ishtar (ca. 1983–1733 BC), and the Code of Eshnunnia (ca. 1950 BC). These codes were compilations of customs, laws, and rules of ancient Mesopotamia, going back to Sumerian times. The UN Universal Declaration on Human Rights (1948) is our most contemporary counterpart.

Among Hebrew Laws there are two that are truly codes, containing casuistic laws and moral principles: The Book of the Covenant and the Book of Deuteronomy. The Ten Commandments represent a code of conduct taught by all Christian denominations. The Koran offers similar guidance for Muslims.

A Code of Conduct is one mark of a profession, as in the Hippocratic Oath sworn by medical doctors. Professions are characterized by both the promulgation and enforcement of their codes. For example, the legal profession can disbar lawyers for unethical conduct. Ethics is a qualifying component for the CPA examination. Fraternal organizations and learned societies have increasingly adopted codes or standards of professional conduct. The Academy of Management has adopted a Code of Ethical Conduct. Public-sector codes exist for civil servants (US Code for Federal Civil Servants), for city managers, and for public administration professionals.

De George proposes that:

> codes should be regulative; should protect the public interest and the interests of those served; should not be self-serving; should be specific and honest, and should be both policeable and policed. (1982, p. 229)

During the 1970s and 1980s, codes gained widespread acceptance in business. Codes vary according to their intended function. Codes are sometimes called Corporate Directives, Administrative Practices, Standards of Business Conduct, or a Code of Best Practice. The preface or preamble usually defines the basic philosophy of the corporation and the scope of the codes.

Scholars have examined the varied contents of corporate codes. The most comprehensive listings of contents has been published in the Hammaker, Horniman, and Rader study of *Standards of Conduct in Business* (1977, pp. 55–8). Their listing contains 17 categories of topics covered in the codes of *Fortune* 500 firms, along with specific prohibitions within each category ranging from 3 to 38 examples each.

Codes are developed to highlight company philosophy or policy, to define employee rights and obligations, and to specify environmental responsibilities. Most codes speak to the purpose, administration and authority of the code, the nature of the company, employee issues, legal requirements, and civic responsibilities (Weaver, 1993, pp. 49, 55–6).

Surveys conducted by the Conference Board, Bentley, and Touche Ross all reveal significant numbers of corporate codes. Berenbeim (1992) reported that 83 percent of US firms have codes. In 1993 Bentley College reported that 93 percent of the responding *Fortune* 1,000 indicated codes as "the best means to achieve their goals" (Weaver, 1993, p. 46). A Touche Ross National Survey revealed their correspondents believed codes are the "most effective measure for encouraging ethical behavior" (1988, p. 3).

Attempts to develop universal business codes have been undertaken by various international governmental bodies with minimal success. Conflicts in ideology and special interests defeated the multiyear effort to introduce a UN Code of Conduct for Transnational Corporations. Some specialized UN agencies have achieved success on industry-specific issues, for example, WHO Code on Pharmaceuticals and Tobacco. The International Monetary Fund (IMF) and World Bank have codified specific industry practices between nations.

More success toward international codes appears to have been achieved in the non-governmental area. The International Chamber of Commerce (ICC) "Business Charter for Sustainable Development" or the Sullivan Principles Governing Business in South Africa are examples of non-governmental codes.

Regional efforts to develop codes for business include new European Community (EU) legislation, for example, the European Convention on Human Rights (1950), or Organization for Economic Cooperation and Development (OECD) Guidelines for Multinational Enterprises (1976).

Corporations themselves develop codes according to their geography. Caterpillar and Levi Strauss and Co. have worldwide codes of ethics; Johnson and Johnson, a worldwide credo; and McDonald's, worldwide standards of best practice. Most firms operate in the domestic market and their codes reflect prevailing domestic corporate and public concerns.

Enforcement of codes presumes promulgation, implementation, and incorporation into the system to insure compliance. Advocates and critics agree that code enforcement often fails because of inadequate communication, inconsistent implementation, and weak systems of enforcement. Compliance with the "spirit of the code" is often too general and sporadic; compliance with the "letter of the law" too legalistic and stultifying. Because codes mix ideals, rules, protocol, laws, and etiquette, enforcement often admits to varied interpretations, and suffers the risk of unequal application sometimes resulting in discrimination and injustice. Internal compliance includes supervision, ethics training, personal integration, ethics officers or ombudsmen, and review panels. External compliance involves audits, government regulation and enforcement, and the courts.

Only cooperatively developed, carefully articulated, clearly understood, widely promulgated, and sympathetically enforced codes preserve the individual conscience, promote the ethical environment, and permit the code to be efficacious – whether in the corporate or public sector.

Future codes will continue to address company authority, employee rights, and obligations, and introduce more specific stakeholder references, with increasing emphasis on accountability, self-development, globalization, the environment, and new public-interest areas. Codes must be recognized as only one aspect of a larger system of institutional efforts directed to developing and promoting an ethical environment.

Bibliography

Berenbeim, R. (1992). *Corporate Ethics Practices*. New York: The Conference Board.
De George, R. T. (1982). *Business Ethics*. New York: Macmillan.
Hammaker, P. M., Horniman, A. B. & Rader, L. T. (1977). *Standards of Conduct in Business*. Charlottesville, Va.: Olson Center for the Study of Applied Ethics.
Touche Ross. (1988). *Ethics in American Business*. Detroit: Touche Ross.
Weaver, G. R. (1993). Corporate codes of ethics: Purpose, process, and content issues. *Business and Society*, 32, (1), 44–58.

LEO V. RYAN

cognitive dissonance   Individual consumers' cognitions for products which are expressed in terms of values, beliefs, opinions, and attitudes (*see* CONSUMER ATTITUDES) tend to exist in clusters that are generally both internally consistent, and consistent with behavior; and an individual strives for consistency within his or her self.

However, any two cognitive elements or attitudes may or may not be consonant with each other. If such an inconsistency exists in a pre-purchase situation, a consumer has a state of conflict which makes it difficult to make a choice. If after a purchase there is inconsistency between cognitive elements then cognitive dissonance is said to exist, i.e., it is a post-purchase state of mind.

When making choices between alternatives, consumers invariably experience cognitive dissonance as on few occasions do they make a completely "right" decision; consumers may remain aware of positive features of rejected alternatives and negative features of a selected alternative – which are inconsistent/dissonant with the action taken.

Cognitive dissonance will be high when: the buying decision is important, either psychologically or in terms of financial outlay; when a number of desirable alternatives are available; when the alternatives are dissimilar with little cognitive overlap, e.g., the choice between a television or a washing machine; and when decision choice is a result of freewill with no help or applied pressure from others.

The existence of cognitive dissonance is psychologically uncomfortable and so consumers develop strategies to reduce/eliminate it to re-achieve consistency or consonance. These include: eliminating responsibility for the decision, e.g., return the product; change attitudes towards the product to increase cognitive overlap; deny, distort or forget information (e.g., cigarette smokers and health warnings); seek new information to confirm one's choice; or reduce the importance of the decision.

Bibliography

Cummings, W. H. & Venkatesan, M. (1976). Cognitive dissonance and consumer behavior: A review of the evidence. *Journal of Marketing Research*, Aug., 303–308.
Festinger, L. (1957). *A theory of cognitive dissonance*. Stanford University Press.
Loudon, D. L. & Della Bitta, A. J. (1993). *Consumer behavior*, 4th edn, McGraw-Hill Int. Chapter 18.
Schiffman, L. G. & Kanuk, L. Z. (1991). *Consumer behavior*, 4th edn, Prentice-Hall. Chapter 9.

BARBARA LEWIS

collective bargaining   Collective bargaining is a term used to describe the process that unions and employers follow to jointly establish the terms and conditions of employment for workers represented by unions. Although nonunion employees cannot engage in collective bargaining, some individuals who do not belong to unions are covered by collective bargaining agreements because their coworkers are unionized. To accomplish the process of bargaining, representatives of labor and management must meet and confer about mandatory bargaining issues, such as wages, hours, grievance procedures, and other terms and conditions of employment. Bargaining legislation determines the issues over which unions and employers must bargain, and differences in the scope of bargaining exist across nations and the private and public sectors. For example, in the USA, public sector bargaining laws have created different mandatory bargaining issues across states.

There is no legal requirement that collective bargaining end in an agreement. If the negotiating parties reach an agreement, a contract or collective bargaining agreement covering a specific period of time is signed and the terms and conditions of employment are set out in that agreement. If the parties fail to reach agreement, a bargaining impasse occurs and several things can happen. The workers may continue to work without an agreement.

The employer may impose its final bargaining offer as the new agreement (unions may strike in response to this). The parties may jointly agree to submit the dispute to a neutral third party, though this occurs rarely. Finally, the workers may decide to engage in a work stoppage or the employer may lock the workers out (which prevents them from working during the impasse). Although private sector workers are permitted to conduct a STRIKE, US public sector employees are generally forbidden by law from striking. Accordingly, public sector bargaining impasses are resolved by a variety of procedures (as determined by state law), including mandatory INTEREST ARBITRATION, fact-finding, mediation/parties (for a review of public sector bargaining, see Lewin et al., 1988).

The extent of collective bargaining varies considerably across industries, occupations, and nations (see Curme et al., 1990; Freeman and Rogers, 1993). In general, although employers have never completely approved of collective bargaining, it has been argued that firms have bargained more aggressively in recent years to obtain union concessions or break the union (see Freeman and Rogers, 1993). This is partly responsible for the decline in union coverage in the USA from about 35 percent of the private, non-agricultural workforce in 1955 to about 10 percent in 1994.

Research has indicated that workers who are covered by collective bargaining agreements typically earn higher wages (by about 15 percent) and have better employment conditions than similar workers who are not unionized. Research also indicates that firms bargaining with their workers are somewhat less profitable than comparable non-bargaining firms. There is substantial debate in the academic literature regarding differences in the productivity rates of unionized and nonunion workers (for a review, see Freeman and Medoff, 1984).

Bibliography

Curme, M. A., Hirsch, B. T. & Macpherson, D. A. (1990). Union membership and contract coverage in the United States, 1983–1988. *Industrial and Labor Relations Review*, **44**, 5–33.

Freeman, R. B. & Medoff, J. (1984). *What Do Unions Do?*, New York: Basic Books.

Freeman, R. B. & Rogers, J. (1993). Who speaks for us? Employee representation in a nonunion labor market. *Employee Representation: Alternatives and Future Directions*, Kaufman, B. E. & Kleiner, M. M. 13–79. Madison, WI: Industrial Relations Research Association.

Lewin, D., Feuille, P., Kochan, T. A. & Delaney, J. T. (1988). *Public Sector Labor Relations: Analysis and Readings*, 3rd edn, Lexington, MA: D. C. Heath.

JOHN T. DELANEY

commitment This is concerned with the level of attachment and loyalty to an organization among its employees. Organizations increasingly compete to attract and retain the most able staff and those committed to the organization might be expected to have longer tenure. Demands to compete through high quality require a workforce willing to display the motivation, flexibility, and belief in product or service that produces high performance, and commitment should help to ensure this. Indeed, Walton (1985) has contrasted a traditional relationship between employer and employee based on control with one based on commitment, arguing that all organizations need to pursue a high commitment approach if they are to survive. This has been one of the factors behind advocacy of human resource management.

Despite its intuitive appeal, commitment is a complex phenomenon. Interest has focused on four main issues. These are: the focus or target of commitment; the definition and measurement of commitment; the causes of variations in levels of commitment; and the consequences of commitment. The picture is made more complex by the presence of two rather different strands of scholarship, one concerned with commitment as an attitude, the other with commitment as behavior.

Attitudinal or Organizational Commitment

Interest in commitment as an attitude has been mainly concerned with commitment to an organization. It is equally plausible to consider commitment to a job, a work team, a profession, to one's family, or to a range of other foci. Indeed, the possibility of multiple and potentially competing commitments has led to a strand of research on dual commitment.

In their influential work on organizational commitment, Mowday, Porter, and Steers (1982) define it as "the relative strength of an individual's identification with and involvement in an organization." They elaborate this to incorporate: belief in the VALUES and goals of the organization, willingness to exert effort on behalf of the organization, and desire to be a member of the organization. They have developed a widely used scale, the Organizational Commitment Questionnaire (OCQ) to measure these elements. Both the definition and the measure have been criticized for conflating commitment with outcomes such as effort and propensity to stay.

Meyer and Allen (1991) have proposed alternative definitions and measures, distinguishing affective and continuance commitment. Affective commitment emphasizes identification with the organization and is predicted to impact on job performance. Continuance commitment borrows from the work of Becker (1960) and others who have given emphasis to the exchange component inherent in the concept of commitment. Individuals will wish to stay with an organization as long as they gain a positive exchange. This exchange may be financial but over time "side bets" such as pensions, career prospects, and friendship develop. For both financial and nonfinancial reasons, staff cannot then "afford" to leave. Continuance commitment therefore predicts tenure. There is some support for the distinction between continuance and affective commitment, and this approach holds out promise for the future.

Much research has sought to identify antecedents of organizational commitment (Mathieu & Zajac, 1990). The evidence is inconsistent but supports the importance for high commitment of providing jobs with some autonomy and scope for self-expression and policies which ensure fairness of treatment and, particularly for newcomers to the organization, confirmation of expectations about working in the organization.

The general theory of organizational commitment predicts that high commitment should result in greater motivation and performance, lower ABSENTEEISM and lower labor turnover. Despite the more specific predictions of Meyer and Allen and evidence from at least one study linking organizational commitment and performance (Meyer, Paunonen, Gellatly, Goffin, & Jackson, 1989), most research shows that organizational commitment has little impact on performance or on absenteeism but does have some ability to predict labor turnover. In general, the impact of organizational commitment on a range of outcomes has been less than theory would predict.

Behavioral Commitment

The second main strand of research is concerned with the process whereby individuals become bound or committed to their actions. Drawing on cognitive dissonance theory, Salancik (1977) proposed that the propensity to act will be greater when an individual volunteers to act, when the action to be taken is explicit, when it is done in the presence of other people, and when the decision is hard to revoke. This approach underpins organizations such as Weightwatchers and Alcoholics Anonymous but can equally well be applied to decisions to join an organization or to decisions taken in work groups and committees. A commitment to act is expected to increase the probability of subsequent action and of attitudes moving in line with behavior. This approach has been successful in predicting tenure based on analysis of the circumstances surrounding the process of CAREER CHOICE (Kline & Peters, 1991). Indeed, insofar as comparisons are possible, behavioral commitment appears to have more impact on performance than organizational commitment.

After two decades of research on organizational commitment, evidence about the causes remains blurred and evidence on the effects of organizational commitment remains disappointing. One reason for the initial interest of some researchers was disillusion at the failure of JOB SATISFACTION to predict behavior. Yet in many studies where the two have been compared, commitment has fared no better than job satisfaction as a predictor of performance and tenure. It appears that the concept may need further unbundling to build on the work of Meyer and Allen in separating out the various components and to clarify the focus of commitment. More attention also needs to be paid to the dynamics of commitment and the processes through which levels of organizational commitment can be changed among long-tenure workers. Ethical questions associated with commitment should not be ignored; the "exchange" may become very one-sided and the temptation to enhance quit rates through policies to reduce commitment may appeal to some managers irrespective of its impact on worker well being. Finally, current trend job insecurity (see JOB LOSS) and rapid RESTRUCTURING and delayering of organizations presents a growing challenge to the viability of organizational commitment, increasing the possibility of a shift in the focus of individual commitment to their profession, their work-group, or even to themselves.

see also Psychological contract; Employee involvement

Bibliography

Becker, H. (1960). Notes on the concept of commitment. American Journal of Sociology, 66, 32–42.

Kline, C. J. & Peters, L. H. (1991). Behavioral commitment and tenure of new employees: A replication and extension. Academy of Management Journal, 34, (1), 194–204.

Mathieu, J. & Zajac, D. (1990). A review and meta-analysis of the antecedents, correlates, and consequences of organizational commitment. Psychological Bulletin, 108, (2), 171–194.

Meyer, J. & Allen, N. (1991). A three-component conceptualization of organizational commitment. Human Resource Management Review, 1, 61–89.

Meyer, J., Allen, N. & Gellatly, I. (1990). Affective and continuance commitment to the organization: Analysis of measures and analysis of concurrent and time-lagged relations. Journal of Applied Psychology, 75, 710–720.

Meyer, J., Paunonen, S., Gellatly, I., Goffin, R. & Jackson, D. (1989). Organizational commitment and job performance: It's the nature of the commitment that counts. Journal of Applied Psychology, 74, 152–156.

Mowday, R., Porter, L. & Steers, R. (1982). Employee–organizational linkages. New York: Academic Press.

Salancik, G. (1977). Commitment and the control of organizational behavior and belief. In B. M. Staw & G. R. Salancik (Eds), New directions in organizational behavior. Chicago: St Clair Press.

Walton, R. (1985). From control to commitment in the workplace. Harvard Business Review, 63, 76–84.

DAVID GUEST

communication Through communication, organizations and their members exchange information, form understandings, coordinate activities, exercise influence, socialize, and generate and maintain systems of beliefs, symbols, and VALUES. Communication has been called the "'nervous system' of any organized group" and the "glue" which holds organizations together.

Claude Shannon's classic mathematical theory of communication defined seven basic elements of communication (Ritchie, 1991): a source which encodes a message and transmits it through some channel to a receiver, which decodes the message and may give the sender some feedback. The sender and receiver may be individuals, machines, or collectives such as organizations or teams. The channel is subject to a degree of noise which may interfere with or distort the transmission of the message. Other distortions may come during encoding or decoding, if errors are introduced or if the source and receiver have different codes. The process of communication occurs through a series of transmissions among parties, so Shannon's single message is only the basic building block of larger interchanges among a system of two to N entities. This system may be represented as a communication network in which communicators are nodes and the various types of communication relationships links. Distortion may also be introduced as the message passes through multiple links, with small changes at each node. Communication is dependent on its context; many scholars argue that the interpretation of messages is only possible because the receiver has contextual cues to supplement message cues.

Due to the complexity of the organizational communication process and the many levels at which communication occurs, there is no generally agreed theory of organizational communication. Different positions have been advanced on several issues.

A major controversy concerns what is communicated, i.e., the substance of communication. One position assumes that messages transmit information, defined as anything which reduces the receiver's uncertainty (Ritchie, 1991). This stance, first advanced in Shannon's theory, portrays communication as something amenable to precise analysis. The amount of information in a given message can, in theory, be measured, and messages compared on metrics of uncertainty reduction. This view has been adopted metaphorically by a wide range of analysts who view organizations as information processing systems or focus on uncertainty reduction. The information perspective has been criticized for reducing ideas, feelings, and symbols to a set of discrete bits pumped through a conduit from sender to receiver (Axley, 1984). An alternative position is that the essence of communication is *meaning*, encompassing ideas, emotions, VALUES, and skills which are conveyed via symbolization and demonstration. Meaning cannot be reduced to information, because it depends on associations among symbols grounded in the surrounding culture and the communicators' experience. The meaning of a message or interaction is grasped through a process of interpretation which requires communicators to read individual signs in light of the whole message and its context, but simul-taneously understand the whole by what its constituent signs signify. This *hermeneutic circle* implies that meaning can never be established finally or unequivocally. Interpretation is a continuing process, always subject to revision or qualification. The information-centered and meaning-centered conceptions of communication represent two quite different approaches, the former being favored by empirical social scientists and the latter by ORGANIZATIONAL CULTURE and critical researchers.

There are also at least two positions on the role of communication in organizations. One regards communication as a *subprocess* which plays an important role in other organizational processes. For example, communication serves as a channel for the exercise of LEADERSHIP or for the maintenance of interorganizational linkages. The other position argues that communication is the process which *constitutes* the organization and its activities. Rather than being subsidiary to key phenomena such as leadership, communication is regarded as the medium through which these phenomena and, more generally, organizations are created and maintained. This viewpoint is reflected in a wide range of organizational research, including Herbert Simon's *Administrative Behavior*, analyses of leadership as a language game, and most studies of organizational culture. The two positions have quite different implications for practice. For example, in the case of leadership communication the subprocess view implies that a leader should make sure that leadership functions are conveyed effectively, while the constitutive view implies that the leader should try to use communication to create and maintain leader–follower relationships and to generate a shared vision.

Another way of describing the role of communication is to delineate the functions it plays for organizations and their members. While the list is potentially endless, at least seven critical functions can be distinguished. Communication serves a *command and control* function in that it is the medium by which directives are given, problems identified, MOTIVATION encouraged, and performance monitored (*see* UPWARD COMMUNICATION). The Weberian BUREAUCRACY emphasizes this function of communication, and the first wave of formal information systems for accounting attempted to automate it, with mixed results. The *linking* function of communication promotes a flow of information between different parts of the organization, enabling the organization to achieve a degree of coherency among disparate units and personnel. The linking function plays a key role in INNOVATION and in the diffusion of innovations

within organizations. Important to linking are upward and lateral communication flows. A third function of communication is *enculturation*, which refers to the creation and maintenance of organizational cultures and to the assimilation of members into the organization. Rituals, myths, metaphors, MISSION STATEMENTS, and other symbolic genres contribute to this function.

In addition to the three intraorganizational functions, communication also serves two additional interorganizational functions. The fourth function is *interorganizational linking*, which serves to create and maintain interorganizational fields. This linking function is accomplished via boundary spanning personnel and units and through shared information systems used to monitor interorganizational ventures. The fifth is *organizational presentation*, which defines the organization to key audiences, such as potential customers, other organizations, the state, and the public at large. This function contributes to the maintenance of an organization's institutional legitimacy. It is carried out through such diverse activities as public information campaigns, corporate advocacy advertisement. Two functions of communication apply to both intra- and interorganizational situations. The *ideational* function of communication refers to its role in the generation and use of ideas and knowledge in the organization (*see* GATEKEEPERS). Simon's description of decision premises and their circulation through the organization is one example of the ideational function. This function is critical to the processes of social reasoning and organizational learning which contribute to ORGANIZATIONAL EFFECTIVENESS. There is also an *ideological* function of communication: it is the vehicle for the development and promulgation of ideologies, systems of thought which normalize and justify relations of POWER and CONTROL. Postmodern analysis of organizations asserts that the reigning discourse in organizations defines what is correct and incorrect and who is able to decide matters of truth and falsehood. This arbitrary allocation of power leaves some groups with unquestioned control and omits others from consideration. Such processes are hard to uncover and change, because they occur in the course of normal, everyday communication and thus seem natural and nonproblematic.

Organizations have two distinct communication systems, formal and informal. The *formal communication system* is a part of the organizational structure and includes supervisory relationships, work groups, permanent and ad hoc committees, and management information systems. In traditional organizations the major design concern was vertical communication, focusing on command and control; more contemporary forms such as matrix or networked organizations also focus on formal lateral communication (*see* MATRIX ORGANIZATION). Formal channels, especially vertical ones, are subject to a number of communication problems. These include unintentional distortion and omission of information as it is passed up the hierarchy, delays in message routing, and intentional distortions by subordinates attempting to manipulate superiors or protect themselves.

The *informal communication system* emerges from day-to-day interaction among organizational members. Ties in the informal network are based on proximity, friendship, common interests, and political benefits more than on formal job duties (*see* POLITICS). The informal system includes the "grapevine" and the "rumor mill." The informal communication network is usually more complex and less organized than the formal network. Messages pass through the informal network more rapidly, and members often regard them as more accurate and trustworthy than those from the formal system. An organization's informal communication system is important for several reasons. First, it often compensates for problems in formal communication. Members can use informal channels to respond to crises and exceptional cases rapidly. They can use informal contacts to make sense of uncertain, ambiguous, or threatening situations. Second, use of informal networks may improve organizational decision making, because it allows members to talk "off the record" and "think aloud," hence avoiding the negative consequences of taking a public position. This is especially valuable when problems are ill defined or solutions unclear. Third, informal networks foster innovation, because they are more open and rapid, and because they often connect people from different departments or professions.

The nature of *communication channels* exerts an important influence on its functions and effectiveness. The archetypal communication situations occur in face-to-face interactions or in public speeches to large audiences. However, communication occurs through many other MEDIA, including written formats, telephone, fax, electronic mail, teleconferencing, computer conferencing, and broadcast technologies. Information technologies such as electronic mail and computer networks vastly increase the connections among members and may stimulate a greater flow of ideas and innovations and change power relations. Studies have shown that the nature of the medium used affects the communication process; for example, NEGOTIATION generally is more effective through face-to-face and (to a lesser extent) audio media than through video or written media. In order to guide communicator's media choices, researchers have attempted to rank order these media in terms of their *social presence*, the degree to which they convey a sense of direct personal contact with another, and in terms of *media richness*, the degree to which a medium allows immediate feedback, multiple channels, variety of language, and personal cues. Generally, face-to-face communication is classified as the richest and highest social presence medium, followed by meetings, videoconferencing, telephone and teleconferencing, e-mail, written memos, and, finally, numerical information. Achieving the correct match between media richness and the communication situation is an important determinant of effectiveness. Variables governing media choice include a degree of equivocality and uncertainty in the situation (the more uncertain, the richer the medium needed), sender and receiver characteristics, and organizational norms. Also important in media choice is what the medium symbolizes; a personal meeting might signal the importance the convener attaches to an issue, whereas an electronic mail message might suggest the same issue is less critical. While social presence, richness, and symbolism are important to consider, studies have shown variations in the ranking of media on these dimensions; so, media choice is also dependent on the nature of the organization.

Numerous prescriptions and recommendations have been offered to improve organizational communication. Perhaps the most common is that the organization's communication system should be as open as possible. However, more communication is not necessarily better communication. At the personal level open communication can be threatening and exhausting to those who have to deal with difficult issues and personal problems they might otherwise avoid. At the organizational level open communication can result in communication overload and in CONFLICT. Another common prescription emphasizes the importance of clarity and uncertainty reduction, but this too may be somewhat overrated. Eisenberg (1984) discusses the value of purposefully ambiguous communication. Its uses include the downplaying of differences in order to build consensus and masking negative consequences of ORGANIZATIONAL CHANGE in order to promote acceptance of innovations. A final common admonition is to promote rational argumentation and discussion. While this certainly is good currency, overemphasis can blind us to the creative potential of inconsistency and logical jumps and to the importance of the emotions. Like many things that seem simple and straightforward, communication conceals considerable complexity.

Bibliography

Axley, S. (1984). Managerial and organizational communication in terms of the conduit metaphor. Academy of Management Review, 9, 428–437.

Conrad, C. (1990). Strategic organizational communication. (2nd edn) Fort Worth, TX: Holt, Rinehart, & Winston.

Eisenberg, E. M. (1984). Ambiguity as strategy in organizational communication. Communication Monographs, 51, 227–242.

Jablin, F. M., Putnam, L. L., Roberts, K. H. & Porter, L. W. (1987). Handbook of organizational communication. Newbury Park, CA: Sage.

Ritchie, L. D. (1991). Information. Newbury Park, CA: Sage.

Sitkin, S. B., Sutcliffe, J. M. & Barrios-Choplin, J. R. (1992). A dual-capacity model of communication media choice in organizations. Human Communication Research, 18, 563–598.

Weick, K. (1979). The social psychology of organizing. Reading, MA: Addison-Wesley.

MARSHALL SCOTT POOLE

communications mix The marketing communications mix is a subset of the MARKETING MIX and includes all the techniques available to the marketer, and which may be "mixed," in order to deliver a message to the target group of buyers, customers, or consumers.

Techniques, broadly, may be classified using two dimensions – first, whether they are delivered personally (e.g., PERSONAL SELLING, telemarketing) or whether the medium used is impersonal (e.g., ADVERTISING, PACKAGING, SALES PROMOTION, PUBLIC RELATIONS); and secondly, whether or not the technique involves a payment by the sponsor. All of the first group are thus "commercial." Examples of "non-commercial" techniques are PUBLICITY and opinion leaders (*see* INTERPERSONAL COMMUNICATIONS).

Different techniques have different strengths (and conversely, weaknesses). There is a need for the marketer to define the target groups, to set objectives for each, and to evaluate the most cost-effective means of reaching the target(s) and attaining the objectives. A different mix, for example, would be employed at different stages of the PRODUCT LIFE CYCLE. A similar situation exists for products or services of high or low value (where the degree of PERCEIVED RISK in the target's mind will vary) and depending on whether the target group is concentrated or dispersed.

see also **Marketing communications**

Bibliography

Crosier, K. (1994). In M. J. Baker, *The marketing book*, 3rd edn, Oxford: Butterworth Heinemann.

Kotler, P. (1994). *Marketing management: Analysis, planning, implementation and control*, 8th edn, Englewood Cliffs, NJ: Prentice-Hall. Chapter 22.

McCarthy, E. J. & Perreault, W. D. (1993). *Basic marketing*. Homewood, IL: Irwin. Chapter 15.

Semenik, R. J. & Bamossy, G. J. (1994). *Principles of marketing*. Cincinnati, OH: South-Western Publishing Co. Chapter 10.

DAVID YORKE

communications objectives   The objectives of MAR-KETING COMMUNICATIONS are concerned, primarily, with information and education about companies and their products and services and, ultimately, with consumer purchase and satisfaction, together with achievement of corporate goals such as profits, return-on-investment, growth, and market shares.

However, "purchase" behavior is typically the end result of the CONSUMER DECISION-MAKING PROCESS and the marketing communicator wishes to move the target audience (e.g., buyer/consumer) through several stages of readiness to buy, i.e., moving them through the cognitive, the affective, and the conative (or behavioral response) stage.

Thus, specific objectives might be to: provide information about a new product/brand and create awareness of the product/brand; generate interest in the product or brand from a target market (or segment – *see* MARKET SEGMENTATION); encourage sales from new customers; increase sales among existing customers; increase MARKET SHARE; introduce price concessions; provide information on product changes and availability; and educate customers or the general public about features/benefits of the product. Communication objectives might also be concerned with providing information and generating attitudes and responses from other organizations in the distribution chain, e.g., encouraging new distributors or improving dealer relationships; or relate to consumers' attitudes and responses toward organizations, e.g., generating goodwill and creating a corporate image.

Marketing communications objectives which are concerned with consumers' responses to products/brands are reflected in various response hierarchy models which have been offered, e.g., AIDA MODEL DAGMAR MODEL, HIERARCHY OF EFFECTS MODEL, and innovation-adoption model. These models assume that a buyer moves through the cognitive, affective and behavioral stages in that order, i.e., the "learn-feel-buy" sequence alternative sequences, depending on the product category and consumer involvement, are buy-feel-learn and feel-buy-learn.

As a consequence, communications objectives may be set depending on the product, consumer involvement, and stage in the consumer decision-making process.

Bibliography

Colley, R. H. (1961). *Defining advertising goals for measured advertising results*. New York: Association of National Advertisers.

Kotler, P. (1994). *Marketing management: Analysis, planning, implementation and control*, 8th edn, Englewood Cliffs, NJ: Prentice-Hall, p. 602.

Lavidge, R. J. & Steiner, G. A. (1961). A model for predictive measurements of advertising effectiveness. *Journal of Marketing*, 25, Oct., 61.

McCarthy, E. J. & Perreault, W. D. Jr (1993). *Basic marketing*, 11th edn, Homewood, IL: Irwin. Chapter 15.

Rogers, E. M. (1962). *Diffusion of innovation*. New York: The Free Press, pp. 79–86.

Semenik, R. J. & Bamossy, G. J. (1994). *Principles of marketing*. Cincinnati, OH: South-Western Publishing Co. Chapter 10.

BARBARA LEWIS

communications research   Communications research is aimed at optimizing the effectiveness of communications through *ex ante* and communications mix. ADVERTISING effectiveness tends to receive more emphasis because it usually commands much higher expenditures than other elements of the communications mix. Pre-testing (before the communication is used on the public at large) may be employed to assess reactions to different forms of the communication in order to identify the version which is likely to yield the most favorable response. A variety of research techniques may be employed, ranging from the gathering and analysis of attitudes to laboratory tests using equipment to measure physiological responses, such as pupil dilation, heartbeat, and blood pressure. Post-testing can include evaluating consumers' ability to recall or to recognize communications (generally advertisements).

The relationship between sales and expenditure on communications is much more difficult to ascertain. However, by the use of carefully designed experiments (*see* EXPERIMENTATION) it may be possible to measure the sales effect of, say, advertising. For example, Du Pont's Paint Division divided its 56 sales areas into high, average, and low MARKET SHARE territories. In one third, Du Pont allocated the normal amount to advertising; in another third, it allocated two and a half times the amount; and in the final third, four times the normal amount. The experiment suggested that an increased spend on advertising increased sales at a diminishing rate, and that the sales increase was weaker in Du Pont's high market share territories (Buzzell, 1964). Other research on effectiveness has attempted to identify an historical relationship between sales and, for example, the expenditure on advertising using advanced statistical techniques.

Generally, though, there are significant difficulties in assessing the impact of communications on sales. First, without carefully controlled experimentation, one cannot conclude that there is any direct link between the communication and the sales/profits secured; there are too many other variables involved. Even if all the extraneous variables are controlled, there might still be some external influence, unthought of by the experimenters, that may affect the results.

Secondly, the full impact of the communication may be spread over time. Taking the case of advertising, some people who are acquainted with the advertising in the early stages of the campaign may react quickly; others may, for various reasons, delay a response. A further group of people may not learn of the advertising for some time after it starts. In the same way, the full effects of reducing or stopping advertising may not become apparent for some time; there may well be a "carry over" effect. Thus, when considering the impact of advertising at any given time, it is possible to have a distorted picture of its general effectiveness. It may well be that there is a steep rise in sales stemming from the advertising, but this may be because the advertising has *brought forward* sales that, in its absence, would have been made some time in the future; so the total sales may be unaffected. Of course, this may well be what the advertiser desired as he or she will have the advantage of obtaining, perhaps, a higher market share (and earlier); in addition, there will be resulting higher sales revenue in the early stages of the PRODUCT LIFE CYCLE concerned.

Thirdly, the creativity of the communication can be expected to influence its effectiveness. Thus, spending large amounts of money on advertising will not lead inevitably to substantial sales if the campaign itself leads to resentment, fails to stimulate interest, or lacks credibility. Similarly, of course, any communication will be ineffective, in the medium term, if the product is unreliable, of poor quality, or has undesirable side-effects. Because of the specificity of most of the marketing variables (i.e., the development of a specific campaign for a specific product), it becomes difficult to make general conclusions about the effectiveness of an additional dollar spent on advertising.

Bibliography

Buzzell, R. D. (1964). E. I. Du Pont de Nemours and Co.: Measurement of effects of advertising. *Mathematical models and marketing management* (pp. 157–79). In Boston: Division of Research, Graduate School of Business Administration, Harvard University.

DALE LITTLER

comparable worth   Comparable worth is the notion that pay should be based on the relative value of jobs within employing organizations without regard to gender-based differences in labor supply behavior and/or job segregation. Comparable worth was developed to address situations in which jobs held predominantly by women requiring substantial education and responsibility (e.g. registered nurses) are often paid less within employing organizations than jobs held predominantly by men that do not (e.g. carpenters and painters).

The Equal Pay Act requires men and women working in the *same* job or one with *substantially similar* requirements be paid the same (unless there are bona fide differences in performance, experience, merit, and so forth). The act lists factors to be compared in measuring similarity, including skill, effort, responsibility, and working conditions. Comparable worth argues that pay for *dissimilar* jobs should be equal if the relative requirements across the factors are similar (or comparable).

Comparability is determined by applying job evaluation to measure levels of skill, effort, responsibility, and working conditions (or other similar factors) across a set of jobs. Each job's point total is the sum of the measures across these factors. Jobs with equal points are considered of comparable worth and would be expected to be paid equally. The evaluation would also be used to establish pay differences between jobs of different worth.

Comparable worth has been implemented in some US state and local public employment jurisdictions and across all employers in the Province of Ontario.

JOHN A. FOSSUM

comparative cost advantage   When a country is able to supply one or more of the resources to produce a product at lower prices than other countries, it has a comparative cost advantage. Mexico, for example, has a comparative cost advantage in terms of labor expense when compared to its northern neighbors and the rest of the industrialized nations of the world. Many of the industrialized nations are capitalizing on Mexico's low wages by building and operating plants on the Mexican border. This helps both the Mexican people and the companies seeking lower costs. The cost advantage could be in any of the resources necessary for production: labor, energy, raw materials, or other areas. One of the problems with comparative cost advantages is that they are transient. That is, as Mexico's economy develops and more companies seek low labor costs, demand will push costs higher. It is also possible that as citizens of Mexico see the money being made by foreign companies, demands will be made to make their wage system equal to that of the home countries of the visiting organizations.

There is another aspect of comparative cost advantage that carries with it a great deal of concern. Comparative cost advantage is also present when the cost of complying with regulations governing an organization's actions are extremely high in the home country whereas those regulations do not exist (or the cost of compliance is far less) in a host country (*see* REGULATORY COST ADVANTAGE). Current examples of regulatory cost advantage give rise to some serious ethical and/or legal questions. For example: "Do companies locate in countries because laws are less stringent than in the company's home country?;" "Does evidence indicate that companies have left countries because of what they consider an oppressive legal system (for example from the United States because of its high cost of litigation; uncertainty; and high liability insurance costs)?;" "Do companies locate in developing countries to avoid strict pollution liability regulations and responsibility?;" or "Are high levels of taxation for social insurance and pension plans driving companies to other countries?" Questions such as these are common. The answer to each is probably "yes." One must remember, though, that monetary rewards for taking advantage of regulatory cost advantages are probably only temporary as environmental legislation sweeps the globe and countries realize the long-term effects of their legal systems. Whether to take advantage of cost advantages may actually be more of an ethical decision on the part of a company instead of a financial one.

Bibliography

Davis, K. & Blomstrom, R. L. (1975). *Business and society: Environment and responsibility*. 3rd edn, New York: McGraw-Hill.

JOHN O'CONNELL

compensable factor   Compensable factors are job attributes that reflect the relative worth of jobs inside an organization and are chosen to reflect its values and strategic plan. A company concerned with costs might evaluate jobs for their accountability, defined in terms of fiscal responsibility. Jobs lower in accountability would receive lower ratings on this compensable factor. Jobs lower across all compensable factors would be of relatively less value than other jobs. A compensable factor must be work-related, business-related, and acceptable to the parties involved.

JERRY M. NEWMAN

compensation package (expatriate) The total of various types of compensation which are paid to an expatriate. The package can include the employee's base salary, plus differentials for housing; home leave; children's education; auto allowance; and other benefits. The package compensates the expatriate for work performed as well as the inconvenience of moving and working overseas. Compensation packages may include a number of different categories of payments or benefits. A list of common categories of pay or other compensation provides an idea of the variety of costs or expenses which may be incurred by an expatriate as well as the immense cost frequently associated with sending an employee overseas. The following list is arranged alphabetically with the terms commonly used in international human relations management. Some terms are narrowly defined, while others are quite broad and overlap with others on the list.

1 Base salary – An expatriate's base salary is the comparable salary for the same work and position as would be paid in the expatriate's home country. Adjustments are made to the base salary for expenses, inconveniences, and hardships encountered in the host country.
2 Benefit allowance – An employee may receive additional payments from the employer with which to purchase insurance or other types of benefits. Expatriates also receive such payment although the benefits purchased may be different from those normally obtained in the home country. For example, education expenses for private schooling for children may seem appropriate benefit overseas, but left unfunded by the employer while in the home country.
3 Completion allowance – Sometimes referred to as a completion bonus, this payment is offered an employee as incentive to stay the full time period of the assignment. An employee may encounter situations of such inconvenience, hardship or danger, that employers have difficulty with employees requesting early departure from assignments. The completion allowance is a reward which is offered to the employee, but is actually paid at the end of the normal assignment period (or at other times if agreed upon between employer and employee).
4 Cost of living allowance – An additional amount of compensation paid to an employee on foreign assignment. The allowance permits the employee to maintain the same standard of living in the host country as was normal in the home country. The allowance includes funds for increased costs of food, transportation, housing, and other goods and services. The problem which arises many times, however, is that the quality or quantity of goods and services normally available is not the same as in the home country. For example, the cost of housing in Japan is far greater than in the United States. A housing allowance would be given to make up for the cost difference, but housing in Japan is normally quite small when compared to the United States and can be quite inconvenient for US citizens.
5 Danger pay – Employees may be placed in danger when they are transferred to certain countries because of political unrest, actions of terrorists, active war or insurrection, or public reaction to citizens of specific foreign countries. Some companies will compensate their employees at higher levels when the job places them in extraordinarily high danger. "Danger" pay is given to employees from the time they enter the dangerous country or region until the time they leave. Danger pay may also be referred to as hazardous duty pay.
6 Education allowance – When a person is accompanied by family members on an overseas assignment special arrangements can be made for the children's education. Differences exist in educational facilities and programs throughout the world. To exactly match the needs of a child in two different countries may be difficult. An education allowance provides funds which may be used to provide special education opportunities or enroll a student in private school. In this way the child's educational progress will be affected as little as possible by the move to a foreign country.
7 Enroute expenses – Travel expenses between the home country and the assignment location are referred to as "enroute" expenses. Enroute expenses include: airfare and other transportation expense; meals; hotel costs; tips and other incidental expenses. Enroute expenses can be very high and should be reimbursed (or better yet, paid in advance) by the employer.
8 Expatriate differential – Companies many times pay (or make available as a benefit) an extra amount of compensation to expatriates to make up for the inconvenience and extra problems associated with living outside of one's own country. The differential makes up for higher housing costs; education for children; leasing an automobile or other costs. The differential ceases to be paid when the expatriate returns to the home country. Sometimes this causes problems with living standards because often the same amount of money purchases so much more overseas than in the employee's home country. The expatriate literally suffers a reduced standard of living when returning to the home country.
9 Fringe benefits – Items of indirect compensation provided to employees. Fringe benefits include: insurance (life, health, disability, dental, legal services, and others are available); company-sponsored education programs; scholarship programs for employee's children; vacation time; employer paid or subsidized lunches; company car; sick leave; retirement programs; and many others depending upon the country of employment and the agreement with the employer. Fringe benefits are provided for a number of reasons including the following: (a) incentives for persons to begin and continue employment, (b) to increase morale, (c) due to local customs, (d) union agreements. Many fringe benefits also receive favored tax treatment for both the employer and the employee. For example, in

the United States employer paid insurance premiums are generally not taxed as income (subject to some specific exceptions) to employees and are deducted as a business expense by the employer. Fringe benefits which are not taxable or taxable at a lower rate for employees (e.g., employer paid life insurance in the United States) are referred to by some people as "perqs" or "perquisite."

10 Furnishing allowance – An amount of money made available to an expatriate to furnish the apartment or home selected in the host country.

11 Hardship allowance – An organization sending employees overseas may offer additional pay for the inconvenience or because the location of overseas employment is considered less than desirable. Such pay is often referred to as a "hardship allowance."

12 Home leave – An expatriate (including family) is often given paid leave each year to return to his/her home country. Normally all expenses of the trip home are paid by the company. Home leaves were developed to allow expatriates and their families to maintain ties with relatives, friends, and others. This eases problems commonly associated with the transition to and from the foreign location.

13 Housing allowance – A common benefit provided to expatriates. Housing allowances are provided in several forms: additional salary to help pay housing costs; provision of employer-owned housing in the foreign country; and reimbursement (or paid directly to the landlord) of the actual cost of housing incurred by the expatriate.

14 Living allowance – A compensation to account for additional costs of living in an expatriate's host country versus the home country. Examples of costs of living which are commonly higher in other countries are: food, housing, transportation, and services. If the expatriate would normally take advantage of goods and services while in the home country, a living allowance is normally provided for those same goods and services in a host country. This is an important consideration for an employee considering an overseas assignment. It is also important to recognize that the degree or quality of goods or services may also vary and must be taken into consideration as well.

15 Overbase compensation – Base salaries between the home country and the host country are usually equalized for an expatriate. That is the pay in the host country would be the same for the same job in the home country. Adjustments in the form of higher pay to offset inconveniences, dangers not occurring in the home country, or longer periods of work (as are expected in some countries) are referred to as "overbase" compensation.

16 Relocation allowance – A payment given to employees to cover the cost of moving themselves, family, and personal possessions to the site of a foreign assignment. The costs of relocating employees may be quite high depending upon the assignment location.

17 Rest and relaxation leave (R&R) – When an expatriate employee is assigned to a location which is exceptionally inconvenient compared to the employee's home country (some Middle Eastern oil-field locations, for example) companies often pay for a week or two-week excursion away from the location to rest and relax. R&R allows employees to reacclimatize themselves in order to avoid burnout.

18 Settling-in allowance – Moving to another country normally takes a considerable amount of time and effort before all of one's personal property and family is settled in a new home. It is common for expatriates to take a minimal amount of personal property when first assigned and live in temporary quarters until suitable permanent accommodation is found. An expatriate does not always know the nature of the accommodation and cannot make rational decisions about what property to bring, what amount is appropriate, and what will fit into the new living situation. A settling-in-allowance is an amount of money given to an expatriate for temporary quarters, storage expenses in the new country, and other expenses (known and unknown) likely to be associated with the initial move to a new country.

19 Travel time – As part of the compensation package, most companies allow an expatriate a specified number of days to travel to their assignment country. Full pay and specified expenses are paid during this period of time.

It is also very important when comparing average housing, food, or transportation costs between the home and host countries, to not only consider the cost differential but also the qualitative differences. For example, the average middle manager in the United States may have housing costs of $2,000 per month, whereas the Japan assignment will have average housing costs of $5,000 per month. What is often overlooked is that the United States housing is a detached home having 3,000 square feet of area, whereas the Japanese home is an apartment having 1,200 feet of living space. Qualitative differences are important and cannot be made up for with additional compensation alone.

Bibliography

Bird, A. & Dunbar, R. (1991). Getting the job done over there: Improving expatriate productivity. *National Productivity Review* Spring, 145–56.

Black, J. S. & Gregerson, H. B. (1991). When Yankee comes home: Factors relating to expatriate and spouse repatriation adjustment. *Journal of International Business Studies*, **22** (4), 471–94.

Business International Corporation (1982). *World executive compensation and human resource planning*. New York: Business International Corporation.

Feldman, D. C. & Thomas, D. C. (1992). Career management issues facing expatriates. *Journal of International Business Studies*, **23** (2), 271–94.

Feldman, D. C. & Thompson, H. B. (1993). Expropriation, repatriation, and domestic geographical relocation: An empirical investigation of adjustment to new job assignments. *Journal of International Business Studies*, **24** (3), 507–30.

Harris, J. E. (1989). Moving managers internationally: The care and feeding of expatriates. *Human Resources Planning*, **12**, 49–53.

Harvey, M. (1985). The executive family: An overlooked variable in international assignments. *Journal of International Business Studies*. Columbia Journal of World Business, 785–800.

Pulatie, D. (1985). How do you ensure success of managers going abroad? *Training and Development Journal* December, 22–4.

Reynolds, C. (1986). "Compensation of overseas personnel" in *Handbook of Human Resource Administration*. 2nd edn, New York: McGraw-Hill.

Toyne, B. & Kuhne, R. J. (1983). The management of the international executive compensation and benefits process. *Journal of International Business Studies*, 14 (32), 37–50.

JOHN O'CONNELL

compensation strategy Compensation strategy is the deliberate utilization of the pay system as an essential integrating mechanism through which the efforts of various subunits and individuals are directed toward the achievement of an organization's strategic objectives, subject to internal and external constraints. Consistent with this definition, each firm faces a repertoire of pay choices. The degree of success associated with each of these depends on two factors. The first is how well the alternative(s) selected enable the organization to cope better with contingencies affecting it at a given point in time. The second is the extent to which the pay choices made are synchronized with the firm's overall strategic direction.

Bibliography

Gomez-Mejia (1992). Structure and process of diversification, compensation strategy, and firm performance. *Strategic Management Journal*, 13, 381–97.

Gomez-Mejia, L. R. & Balkin, D. B. (1992). *Compensation, Organisation Strategy, and Firm performance*, Cincinnati, OH: South-Western.

LUIS R. GOMEZ-MEJIA

competitive advantage Competitive advantage may be secured through differentiation of the organization and/or its products and services in some way in order to gain preference by all or part of the market over its rivals. This may result in higher MARKET SHARE and/or margins than competitors. In general, competitive advantage will be obtained through offering higher customer value. Day & Wensley (1988) argue that there is no common meaning of "competitive advantage," it being used interchangeably with "distinctive competence" to mean relative superiority in skills and resources, or with "positional superiority in the market," as providing greater customer value yields high market share.

Resource-based theories argue that there are two related sources of competitive advantage: assets, i.e., the resource endowments the business has accumulated (e.g., investments in the scale, scope and efficiency of facilities and systems, brand equity, etc.), and capabilities, defined as "the glue that brings these assets together and enables them to be deployed advantageously" (Dierickx & Cool, 1989). Capabilities differ from assets in that they cannot be given a monetary value. They are, according to Dierickx & Cool, "so deeply embedded in the organisational routines and practices that they cannot be traded or imitated." They include skills and processes, and are often tacit. They have some similarity to the core competencies described by Prahalad & Hamel (1990) except that these are seen as the capabilities which support multiple businesses within an organization.

Day (1994) suggests that two capabilities are particularly critical to competitive advantage, namely, market sensing capability, which is the ability to detect changes in the market and to anticipate the possible responses to market-ing actions that may be taken; and customer linking capability, which embraces the "skills, abilities and processes needed to achieve collaborative customer relationships so that individual customer needs are quickly apparent to all functions and well-defined procedures are in place for responding to them."

As Porter (1980) argues, it is important to establish a competitive advantage which is *sustainable*, i.e., not easily eroded by environmental changes, or imitated by existing or potential competitors.

Bibliography

Day, G. S. (1994). The capabilities of market-driven organisations. *Journal of Marketing*, 58, Oct., 37–52.

Day, G. S. & Wensley, R. (1988). Assessing advantage: A framework for diagnosing competitive superiority. *Journal of Marketing*, 52, 1–20.

Dierickx, I. & Cool, K. (1989). Asset stock and accumulation and sustainability of competitive advantage. *Management Science*, 35, 1504–1511.

Porter, M. E. (1980). *Competitive strategy: Techniques for analyzing industries and competitors*. New York: Free Press.

Prahalad, C. K. & Hamel, G. (1990). The core competence of the corporation. *Harvard Business Review*, 68, (3), May–June, 79–91.

DALE LITTLER

competitive position – market attractiveness matrix During the 1970s, the US General Electric company (GE) developed a portfolio model measuring the relative attractiveness of its multiple businesses for investment purposes. In conjunction with McKinsey and Company, GE developed a portfolio model which differed from that of the Boston Consulting Group's GROWTH SHARE MATRIX in that it examined those variables assessed by management to be the critical success factors affecting a business. These factors were then used to identify the position of a business in a three by three matrix, each cell of which indicated a recommended investment strategy. A number of factors, the identification of which is found useful, and the matrix itself, are illustrated in figure 1.

The process of positioning a business is similar to that of the Shell directional policy matrix. The position of each business on the two composite dimensions is determined by a qualitative scoring system described in the measurement of "market attractiveness" and "competitive position." Businesses are plotted on the matrix, with their relative size indicated by the area of the circle representing each one. An alternate method of weighting each variable has been used in some companies, the values of the main PIMS (*see* PIMS STRUCTURAL DETERMINANTS OF PERFORMANCE) variables being subdivided to determine the two composite variables and then used to calculate the relative matrix position of a business.

Each cell in the matrix suggests an alternate investment strategy for the businesses contained in it, as shown. Businesses in the top left-hand corner are high in market attractiveness and enjoy a strong competitive position: such businesses enjoy high growth and should receive priority for any investment support needed. Businesses in the grow/penetrate cell are also primary candidates for investment, in an effort to improve competitive position while growth prospects remain high. Defend/invest position businesses are in less attractive markets, but

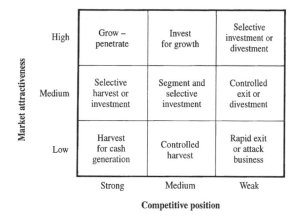

Figure 1 The market attractiveness – competitive position matrix.
Sources: Channon, D. F. (1993), *Australia Pacific Bank Case*; and Stratpack Limited.

investment should be maintained as needed to defend the strong competitive position established. Businesses in the bottom left-hand corner are candidates for harvesting: the market attractiveness is low, probably indicating that growth is low but the relative competitive position remains high. Such businesses are therefore usually producing good profits which cannot justifiably be reinvested. Surplus cash is therefore extracted for use in investing in businesses that are short of funds, or to be used to provide other types of resource.

Businesses in the center are candidates for selective investment, usually on the basis of careful market segmentation. Businesses at the bottom center and right center are candidates for withdrawal/divestment or for the pursuit of niche strategies. Businesses in the bottom right cell are both in unattractive markets and have a weak competitive position. Such businesses may well be making losses and are not likely to produce a strong positive cashflow. As a result they are clear candidates for divestment or closure. A more sophisticated but difficult alternative is to deploy them as attack businesses against a competitor's harvest businesses, to depress their cash-generating capability. Note that each strategy also implies different objectives, and the company's management information systems and reward systems need to be tuned to reflect this.

The Competitive Position – Market Attractiveness Matrix and the directional policy matrix provide more sophisticated methodologies for assessing the strategic position of a business, and can allow management to incorporate due consideration of critical variables that influence individual businesses.

Competitive Position

In assessing the competitive position of an individual business, a number of variables are usually taken into consideration. The calculation of relative competitive position can be operationalized by scoring a company's position along a series of appropriate dimensions. The precise dimensions can be selected by management on the basis of their detailed knowledge of the business, and weighted according to their assessment of the relative importance of each dimension. This is illustrated in table 1. A number of such factors based on the critical variables

identified in the PIMS program are used in one such system as follows.

Competitive position measures:
- Absolute market share: measured as a company's market share of its defined served market.
- Relative share: using the PIMS definition, this is defined as a percentage of the company's share divided by the sum of the largest competitors.
- Trend in market share: the trend in the company's share over the past three years.
- Relative profitability: the relative profitability of the company's product as the percentage of the average of that of the three largest competitors.
- Relative product quality: an assessment of the relative level of the quality of a company's product compared with those of its three largest competitors, from the customer's perspective.
- Relative price: the relative price of a company's product as a percentage of the average of those of its three largest competitors.
- Customer concentration: the number of customers making up 80 per cent of the company's business; the fewer the number of buyers, the greater the buyer power.
- Rate of product innovation: the percentage of sales from products introduced in the past three years, which indicates the degree of maturity of a business.
- Relative capital intensity: the capital intensity of a company's business, as a percentage of that of its three largest competitors: high relative capital intensity is usually a weakness.

Each of these factors, which may or may not be weighted, can be scored from 1 to 5, with the high score representing a very strong position and the low score a weak one. Summarizing the score for each dimension and dividing this by the total possible score provides a coordinate for competitive position on the matrix.

Market Attractiveness

This is assessed from data on the market/industry characteristics of a business. While the factors that

Table 1 An example of the business strength competitive position assessment with the weighted score approach

Critical success factors	Weight*	Rating†	Weighted score
Market share	0.10	5	0.5
SBU growth rate	x	3	—
Breadth of product line	0.05	4	0.2
Sales distribution effectiveness	0.2	4	0.8
Proprietary and key account advantages	x	3	—
Price competitiveness	x	4	—
Advertising and promotion effectiveness	0.05	4	0.2
Facilities location and newness	0.05	5	0.25
Capacity and productivity	x	3	—
Experience curve effects	0.15	4	0.6
Raw materials costs	0.05	4	0.2
Value added	x	4	—
Relative product quality	0.15	4	0.6
R&D advantages/position	0.05	4	0.2
Cash throw-off	0.1	5	0.5
Calibre of personnel	x	4	—
General image	0.05	5	0.25
TOTAL	1.00		4.3

Key: * x means that the factor does not affect the relative competitive position of the firms in that industry;
  † 1 = very weak competitive position, 5 = very strong competitive position.
Source: Hofer & Schendel (1978)

determine attractiveness may vary, managerial input can be used to assess these and the relative importance of each variable by weighting them. An example is shown in table 2.

The following variables have also been found to be useful:

- Size: the size of a market is obviously important. However, in assessing size careful market definition is imperative and eventually needs to be conducted on a segment-by-segment basis. The size should also be sufficiently large for the firm to make it worthwhile to provide products or services.
- Historic growth rate: this is useful as a guide for predicting future trends.
- Projected growth rate: this needs to be carefully assessed and overoptimism avoided. Sensitivity analysis can be used to assess the impact of different growth rates.
- Number of competitors: the larger the number of competitors, the greater is the level of rivalry that may be expected.
- Competitor concentration: more concentrated markets are generally more attractive, whereas fragmented markets are usually more price competitive.
- Market profitability: more profitable markets are obviously more attractive.
- Barriers to entry: markets with high barriers to entry are more attractive than those in which the entry of new competitors is easy.
- Barriers to exit: high barriers to exit tend to increase competition, especially in high capital intensity industries, as competitors erode away margins in order to maintain capacity utilization.

- Supplier power: a small number of suppliers of critical raw materials and the like reduces market attractiveness.
- Buyer power: a small number of large customers enhances buyer power, especially in fragmented industries, and reduces market attractiveness.
- Degree of product differentiation: the higher the level of differentiation, the more attractive the market is, as high differentiation tends to reduce price competition.
- Market fit: markets that are truly synergistic with other corporate activities enhance attractiveness.

Having measured the position of a business along these and any other relevant dimensions, market attractiveness is assessed by assigning a value between 1 and 5 to a business according to its relative position. If the variables are weighted, this weight should also be applied and the scores summed to arrive at an overall total. This is divided by the maximum possible score to generate the value of the market attractiveness coordinate in order to plot a business's position on the matrix.

Criticisms of the system are that it requires accurate identification of the multiplicity of variables required to position a business correctly. The weighting and numerical scoring system can deceive with its pseudo-scientific approach. There is also a desire on the part of managers to attempt to avoid the disinvest cells. Data are often not available to provide an accurate assessment of the position of a business and therefore, as a consequence, there is a tendency to drift toward the moderate score. Furthermore, it is difficult to ensure consistency between the businesses. Finally, when markets change, very misleading positionings can occur in terms of market attractiveness. Thus, in GE when the electronics industry was globalizing in the 1980s,

Table 2 An example of the industry/market attractiveness assessment with the weighted score approach

Attractiveness criterion	Weight*	Rating†	Weighted score
Size	0.15	4	0.6
Growth	0.12	3	0.36
Pricing	0.05	3	0.15
Market diversity	0.05	2	0.1
Competitive structure	0.05	3	0.15
Industry profitability	0.2	3	0.6
Technical role	0.05	4	0.2
Inflation vulnerability	0.05	2	0.1
Cyclicality	0.05	2	0.10
Customer financials	0.1	5	0.5
Energy impact	0.08	4	0.32
Social	GO	4	—
Environmental	GO	4	—
Legal	GO	4	—
Human	0.05	4	0.2
TOTAL	1.00		3.38

Key: * Some criteria may be of the GO/NO GO type; † 1= very unattractive. 5 = highly attractive
Source: Hofer & Schendel (1978)

the company was often measuring its position on the basis of the US market. During the 1980s, therefore, under the leadership of Jack Welch, positioning shifted to the concept of being either number one or number two in the world or that businesses should be sold, closed, or fixed. As a result the portfolio of GE was dramatically changed. Nevertheless, when used well, the multivariate approach offers management a more realistic tool than the simplistic approach of the original BCG bivariate model. Moreover, in the 1990s, such a tool can be coupled with VALUE-BASED PLANNING to provide a very sophisticated portfolio planning tool.

Bibliography

Hax, A. & Majluf, N. T. (1984). *Strategic management: an integrative perspective.* Englewood Cliffs, NJ: Prentice-Hall.
Channon, D. F. (1993). *Australia Pacific Bank Case.* The Management School, Imperial College, University of London.
Hofer, C. W. & Schendel, D. (1978). *Strategy formulation: analytical concepts.* St. Paul, MN: West.

DEREK F. CHANNON

competitive strategy Widely popularized by Michael Porter (e.g., 1980) during the 1980s, "competitive strategy" tended to be accepted as a new approach to organizational strategy. Its roots are within the traditional area of industrial economics, and particularly the structure-conduct-performance paradigm. Porter argues that there are five major forces which affect the attractiveness of an industry. These are: intra-industry rivalry; the threat of new entrants; the existence, or potential development, of substitutes; the power of customers; and the power of suppliers. New entrants pose a threat as they augment existing capacity and may be disruptive because they will have to secure a market position in order to justify the costs of entry. Substitutes place a ceiling on the price that can be charged. Supplier

power can lead to higher input costs and is increased where suppliers are highly concentrated relative to the customer industries; and they have a unique product and there are switching costs. The power of customers, which can result in downward pressure on margins, is enhanced where they purchase in large volume, the product they purchase is standard or undifferentiated, and the product accounts for a significant proportion of the buyer's cost and, therefore, profits. Rivalry is likely to be intense where there are many firms of equal size, growth is slow, the product is undifferentiated, and there are high fixed costs presenting significant barriers to exit. Porter argues that it is these specific industry factors that are important since macro-economic and other factors (see ENVIRONMENTAL ANALYSIS) will affect all industries equally. The major objective is then for organizations to position themselves favorably with regard to each of these five forces. Thus, they may strive to establish or reinforce barriers to entry; or build in switching costs to reduce the power of customers; or develop alternative sources of supply through collaborative product development with other possible suppliers.

Porter assumes that industries evolve, with distinct phases to their life cycle (nascent, growth, maturity, decline), and he applies the five forces framework to each of these stages. He develops the concept of strategic groups based on the view that industries can be disaggregated into clusters of firms with each cluster pursuing different strategies. There may be mobility barriers inhibiting the movement of firms from one cluster to another. However, the approach is essentially descriptive and, it can be argued, always depending on the criteria employed to define the clusters.

Porter argues that the major focus of competitive strategy is to provide customer value. This can be perceived in terms of lowering customer costs and/or allowing the customer to secure higher quality, etc. Firms can follow one of four generic competitive strategies (*see* GENERIC STRATEGIES). They can aim at the lowest cost position or differentiation within the market as a whole; or they can strive for one of these positions aimed at a particular segment/or segments of the market (*see* FOCUS STRATEGY). Firms which neither aim at the lowest cost position nor the differentiated position become, according to Porter, "stuck in the middle" with suboptimum returns. However, there is little empirical evidence to substantiate his thesis; indeed, there has been increasing evidence that high performers can follow high levels of efficiency as well as having a significantly differentiated market position (e.g., Hall,1980; Cronshaw et al., 1994).

Porter's work and that of his followers makes at least three important contributions: first, it provides a coherent framework for analyzing industries; second, it emphasizes the importance of exit barriers as an influence on corporate behavior; and third, it focuses on the means of providing customer value. In later work, Porter has noted the need to adopt a more dynamic approach to competitive strategy formation (Porter, 1991).

Commentators such as Ohmae (1988) believe that the focus on "competitive strategy" can lead to an emphasis on competitors per se rather than on the changing values and requirements of customers, and that this may lead to tit-for-tat competitive rivalry, perhaps at the expense of providing adequately satisfactory offerings to customers, thereby opening up opportunities to those, including new entrants, which do.

Bibliography

Cronshaw, M., Davis, E. & Kay, J. (1994). On being stuck in the middle or Good Food Costs Less at Sainsbury. *British Journal of Management*, **5**, 19–32.

Hall, W. K. (1980). Survival strategies in a hostile environment. *Harvard Business Review*, **58**, (5), Sept.–Oct., 75–85.

Ohmae, K. (1988). Getting back to strategy. *Harvard Business Review*, **66**, (6), Nov.–Dec., 149–156.

Porter, M. E. (1980). *Competitive strategy: Techniques for analyzing industries and competitors*. New York: Free Press.

Porter, M. E. (1991). Towards a dynamic theory of strategy. *Strategic Management Journal*, **12**, special issue, "Fundamental Research Issues in Strategy and Economics", 95–117.

DALE LITTLER

competitor analysis In conducting competitor analysis, it is necessary to examine those key competitors that presently and/or in the future may have a significant impact on the strategy of the firm. Usually this means the inclusion of a wider group of organizations than the existing immediately direct competitors. In many cases, it is the failure of firms to identify the competitors that may emerge in the future that leads to blind spots. Competitors for evaluation therefore include the following.

Existing Direct Competitors

The firm should concentrate upon major direct competitors, especially those growing as rapidly as or faster than itself. Care should be taken to uncover the sources of any apparent competitive advantage. Some competitors will not appear in every segment but rather in specific niches. Different competitors will therefore need to be evaluated at different levels of depth. Those which already do, or could

have an ability to, substantially impact on CORE BUSINESSES need the closest attention.

New and Potential Entrants

Major competitive threats do not necessarily come from direct competitors, who may have much to lose by breaking up established market structures. New competitors include the following:

- firms with low barriers to entry (*see* BARRIERS TO ENTRY AND EXIT)
- firms with a clear experience effect (*see* EXPERIENCE AND LEARNING EFFECTS) or SYNERGY gain
- forward or backward integrators
- unrelated product acquirers, for whom entry offers financial synergy
- firms offering a potential technology bypass to gain competitive advantage

Competitor Intelligence Sources

Collecting legal detailed information on actual and potential competitors is surprisingly easy if the task is approached systematically and continuously. Moreover, the level of resource needed for the task is not extensive. It is therefore, perhaps, surprising how few firms actually undertake the task, and set out their strategies while being almost oblivious to the behavior of competitors. Key sources of competitive information include the following:

- Annual reports and 10 K's and, where available, the annual reports or returns of subsidiaries/business units.

- Competitive product literature.

- Competitor product analysis and evaluation by techniques such as tear down.

- Internal newspapers and magazines. These are useful in that they usually give details of all major appointments, staff background profiles, business unit descriptions, statements of philosophy and mission, new products and services, and major strategic moves.

- Competitor company histories. These are useful to gain an understanding of competitor corporate culture, the rationale for the existing strategic position, and details of the internal systems and policies.

- Advertising. This illustrates and identifies themes, choice of media, spend level, and the timing of specific strategies.

- Competitor directories. These are an excellent source for identifying the organization's structure and strength, mode of customer service, depth of specialist segment coverage, attitudes to specific activities, and relative power positions.

- Financial and industry press. These sources are useful for financial and strategic announcements, product data, and the like.

- Papers and speeches of corporate executives. These are useful for details of internal procedures, the organization's senior management philosophy and strategic intentions.

- Sales force reports. Although they are often biased, intelligence reports from field officers provide front line intelligence on competitors, customers, prices, products, service, quality, delivery, and the like.

- Customers. Reports from customers can be actively solicited internally or via external market research specialists.
- Suppliers. Reports from suppliers are especially useful in assessing competitor investment plans, activity levels, efficiency, and the like.
- Professional advisers. Many companies use external consultants to evaluate and change their strategies and/or structures.
- Stockbroker reports. These often provide useful operational details obtained from competitor briefings. Similarly, industry studies may provide useful information about specific competitors within a particular country or region.
- Recruited competitor personnel. The systematic debriefing of recruited personnel provides intimate internal details of competitive activity.
- Recruited executive consultants. Retired executives from competitors can often be hired as consultants, and information about their former employers can be effectively determined by requesting their assistance in specific job areas.

Competitor Analysis Database
In order to evaluate competitor strengths and weaknesses, systematic data collection on each actual and potential competitor is necessary. The most important competitors need to be comprehensively and continuously monitored. Competitors that pose a less immediate threat can be monitored on a periodic basis. The data to be collected should include the following:
- name of competitor or potential competitor
- numbers and locations of operating sites
- numbers and nature of the personnel attached to each unit
- details of competitor organization and business unit structure
- financial analysis of parent and subsidiaries, stock market assessment, and details of share register; potential acquirers/acquisitions
- corporate and business unit growth rate/profitability
- details of product and service range, including relative quality and price
- details of served market share by customer segment and by geographic area
- details of communication strategy, spending levels, timing, media choice, promotions, and advertising support
- details of sales and service organization, including numbers, organization, responsibilities, special procedures for key accounts, any team selling capabilities, and the method of the sales force segmentation approach
- details of served markets (including identification and servicing of key accounts), estimates of customer loyalty, and market image
- details of niche markets served, key accounts, estimates of customer loyalty, and relative market image
- details of specialist markets served
- details of R&D spending, facilities, development themes, special skills and attributes, and geographic coverage
- details of operations and system facilities, capacity, size, scale, age, utilization, assessment of output efficiency, capital intensity, and replacement policies
- details of key customers and suppliers
- details of personnel numbers, personnel relations record, relative efficiency and productivity, salary rates, rewards and sanctions policies, degree of trade unionization
- details of key individuals within the competitor organization
- details of control, information, and planning systems

From such a database, the strategy of a competitor can be analyzed and assessed as to future strategic actions and suggestions can be made as to how the firm can gain and sustain competitive advantage.

Analyzing Competitor Strategy
The strategy of key competitors should be analyzed and evaluated with a view to assessing their relative strengths and weaknesses, in order to identify strategic alternatives for the firm. Most large firms are multibusiness and competitor strategy needs to be evaluated at several levels:
- by function – marketing, production, and R&D
- by business unit
- by corporation as a whole

From this analysis likely competitor moves and responses to external moves can be assessed.

Function Analysis
For each competitor business, the main functional strategies should be identified and evaluated. While all of the desirable details may not be immediately available, continuous competitor monitoring will usually permit a comprehensive picture to be built up over time. The objective is not merely to gain competitive details but to evaluate the relative position of the evaluating firms to assess competitive position, BENCHMARKING opportunities, and the like.

Marketing Strategy
- What product/service strategy is adopted by each competitor relative to yours? What is the market size by product market/customer segment? What is the market share for each competitor by served market segment?
- What is the growth rate for each product/service market segment? What is the growth rate of each competitor by segment? What are the degree and trend in market segment concentration?
- What is the product/service line strategy of each competitor? Is it full line or specialist niche?
- What is the policy toward new services adopted by each competitor? What has been the rate of new product introduction?
- What is the relative service/product quality of each competitor?
- What pricing strategy does each competitor adopt by product/service line/consumer segment?
- What are the relative advertising and promotion strategies of each competitor?
- How do competitors service each product market segment?

- What are the apparent marketing objectives of each competitor?
- How quickly do competitors respond to market changes?
- How does marketing fit in competitor cultures? Has the function been the source of key executives in the past?

Production / Operations Strategy

- What are the number, size, and location of each competitor's production/operations complexes? How do these compare with each other? What product range does each produce? What is their estimated capacity? What is capacity utilization?
- What is the level of each competitor's capital employed in depreciable assets? Is it owned property?
- What working capital intensity is employed in debtors, stocks, and creditors?
- How many people are employed at each unit? What salaries are paid? What is the relative productivity?
- What is the degree of trade unionization? What is the labor relations record?
- What sales are made to other internal business units? What supplies are received from other internal business units?
- What incentive/reward systems are used?
- What services are subject to OUTSOURCING? Is this increasing or decreasing?
- How does production fit into each competitor's organization? Has production/operations been a source of key executives?
- How flexible is each competitor to changes in market conditions? How fast has each competitor been able to respond to changes?

Research and Development Strategy

- Where are new services developed?
- What is the estimated expenditure level on R&D compare? How has this changed?
- How many people are employed in research, and how many in development?
- What is the recent record for each competitor in new product introductions and patents?
- Are there identifiable technological thrusts for individual competitors?
- How rapidly can each competitor respond to innovations? What sort of reaction has typically been evoked?

Financial Strategy

- What is the financial performance of each competitor by business in terms of return on assets, return on equity, cashflow, and return on sales?
- What dividend payout policy appears to be in place? How are cashflows in and out controled?
- What is the calculated SUSTAINABLE GROWTH RATE on the existing equity base?
- How does the competitor's growth rate compare with the industry average? Is adequate cash available to sustain the business and allow for expansion? Do other businesses have priority for corporate funds?
- How well are cash and working capital managed?

Business Unit Strategy

Each competitor also needs to be evaluated at the business unit level to see where the business fits within the overall competitor strategy. Such questions should address the role of the business unit, its objectives, organizational structure, control and incentive systems, strategic position, environmental constraints and opportunities, position of SBU head, and performance.

Group Business Objectives

The position of each business within a competitor's total portfolio also needs to be evaluated. Questions that may influence behavior at the business unit level include: an evaluation of overall group financial objectives, growth capability and shareholder expectations, key strengths and weaknesses, ability to change, and the nature of the overall portfolio; GENERIC STRATEGIES adopted, values and aspirations of key decision makers, and especially the CEO; historic reactions to earlier competitive moves; and beliefs and expectations about competitors.

From this analysis, the objective is to assess likely competitor future strategies and responses to competitive moves. In most industries success is dependent on gaining an edge on competitors, and this type of evaluation is therefore as important as basic market or customer analysis.

Bibliography

Ansoff, I. (1987). *Corporate strategy.* Harmondsworth, UK: Penguin. See chapter 8.
Channon, D. F. (1986). *Bank strategic management and marketing.* Chichester: John Wiley. See chapter 4.
Garner, J. R., Rachlin, R. & Sweeny, H. W. A. (1986). *Handbook of strategic planning.* New York: John Wiley.
Sammon, W. L. (1986). Assessing the competition: business intelligence for strategic management. In J. R. Gardner, R. Rachlin, & H. W. A. Sweeny (eds), *Handbook of strategic planning.* New York: John Wiley.

DEREK F. CHANNON

complements Complements are those products which are consumed together with another product, such as tires or gasoline and an automobile. The services of the automobile cannot be rendered without gasoline, so a consumer's willingness to pay for an automobile will be affected by the cost of gasoline. The prices of complementary goods have a negative effect on the quantity demanded for a product because if the price of a complement (gasoline) rises, the total cost of driving an automobile is now higher and this may reduce the demand for automobiles.

The negative effect of the price of complementary goods on the demand for a product would be observed as a negative cross elasticity of demand. This means that a given percentage increase (decrease) in the price of a complementary good will cause the demand for the related product to fall (rise) by "Y" percent.

Bibliography

Douglas, E. J. (1992). *Managerial Economics.* 4th edn, Englewood Cliffs, NJ: Prentice-Hall.
Hirschey, M. & Pappas, J. L. (1995). *Fundamentals of Managerial Economics.* 5th edn, New York: Dryden.

ROBERT E. MCAULIFFE

computer-supported cooperative work Advances in technologies, such as networks, telecommunication, file-sharing systems, and multimedia devices, have led to the development of computer-supported cooperative work or collaborative computing systems. Computer-supported cooperative work (CSCW) is the use of computer-based technology to facilitate work tasks involving multiple parties. CSCW refers to software applications and their use, and not to the more rudimentary technologies (such as networks, databases, videoconferencing, etc.) that make CSCW possible. In this sense, CSCW is not a type of technology, but a technology application. CSCW designers take component technologies, integrate them, and develop functionality that will service the needs of a work group. Common examples of CSCW include electronic messaging, joint authoring, discussion databases, workflow management, and electronic meetings.

CSCW can be described in terms of collaboration concepts, computer systems design, application types, and impact on work groups.

Collaboration Concepts

Because most, if not all, work involves some degree of interface between two or more parties, many organizational tasks can be conceived in terms of a cooperative work process. The unique focus of CSCW is on the interface between co-working parties, that is, on their collaboration. Those aspects of work which are done independently are of less concern in CSCW, except in so far as the inputs or outputs of one work process affect those of another work process. Tasks which are done entirely in a joint manner are of particular concern to CSCW designers. Business meetings and classroom learning represent extreme examples of CSCW, because all parties are present and actively working together in those contexts. Other collaborative work settings include systems development, business planning, project design, report development, forms passing, and joint decision-making. CSCW is concerned with the design of systems to support these kinds of collaborative work activities.

The parties involved in a cooperative work process are not restricted to people. They can be documents, machines, or transactions. Shared work among computer processors, for example, can fall within the domain of CSCW, as can the flow of paperwork through an office environment. Central to cooperative work processes is the concept of *coordination*. Coordination is the synchronous aspect of a cooperative work process, the juncture of dependency between two otherwise independent work tasks. Once the coordination required for a cooperative work task has been fully specified, a system can be designed to support coordination. Typically, a cooperative work task has many coordination processes within it, some of which are performed by people and some of which are computerized. CSCW is concerned with augmenting the computer-based coordination within cooperative work tasks.

Computer Systems Design

Whereas the development of user-friendly software for individual work has been driven by the principle of WYSIWYG, or "what you see is what you get," the development of collaborative systems has been driven by the principle of WYSIWIS, or "what you see is what I see." Collaborative design involves the creation of *shared workspaces* in which multiple parties access common computer files. Computer bulletin boards exemplify this principle, as many people can post articles and share the bulletin board space. Similarly, collaborative word-processing applications allow multiple authors to develop a common document.

Major issues in CSCW design include data management, media selection, and multi-user interfaces. Data management involves specification of private versus shared information, determining which information will be exchanged and in what format, and specifying information security and ownership procedures, such as which party involved in the collaboration is able to change common information and under what conditions. Issues of file updating and concurrency control are critical in CSCW design, since more than one party may have the capability to update a common data file at the same time. Maintaining accurate, current, and nonredundant data can be a complicated process in a CSCW system that is simultaneously utilized by many parties. Designers are increasingly interested in creating *group memories*, or a shared KNOWLEDGE BASE, whereby uses of CSCW applications result in historical repositories that can serve as resources for future coordination needs. Advances in group memory management may lead to further automation of coordination activities and the embedding of intelligence into CSCW applications.

Media for CSCW include text, sound, graphics, and/or video. Since so much of cooperative work involves interpersonal conversation, many CSCW designs include either a voice component or the ability to exchange text-based messages in real time (instantaneously). CSCW systems are increasingly multimedia, as in computer conferencing and electronic meeting systems. The CSCW designer must understand human communication processes and the relative impact of various communication media on the ability of people to work together effectively.

CSCW systems require multi-user interfaces, that is, simultaneous access to system components by more than one party. The CSCW interface must accommodate different people, different input and display preferences, and different learning styles. As an example, consider a large electronic whiteboard used in a conference room setting. Some meeting participants may wish to draw freehand on the board, while others prefer to display documents typed within a word processor. More than one participant may want to use the board during the meeting; and everyone may want to leave the meeting with copies of material placed on the board so that they can work on it privately at a later time. The CSCW designer must assure flexibility for multiple forms of input, manipulation, and output of system data. Further, any one user may require the ability to track information as it stops or flows between various parties involved in the cooperative activity. The use of *threading* in electronic bulletin boards illustrates this latter capability; bulletin board postings are arranged to indicate the content, timing, and party involved in the posting:

The corporate plan is being developed
    (M. Jones), 6/9/95
Suggested item for the corporate plan
    (K. Finch), 6/9/95
Comment on Finch's suggestion
    (M. Blar), 6/10/95
Comment on Finch's suggestion
    (E. Wharch), 6/12/95
Comment on Wharch's comment
    (M. Jones), 6/16/95

Another suggested item for the corporate plan
    (G. Parch), 6/23/95

Application Types

CSCW applications are often referred to as *groupware*. The term "groupware" usually refers to a software system, whereas the broader CSCW term refers to the application of that software in a collaborative work task. Nevertheless, groupware and CSCW are sometimes used interchangeably.

CSCW applications can be distinguished along a number of dimensions, the most important being the *time* and *place* of the coordination involved. Four general types of CSCW settings are possible (*see* figure 1):

1 *Same time, same place.* All parties are co-located when the coordination takes place, such as in a group meeting.
2 *Same time, different place.* Parties coordinate at the same time but work in different physical locations, such as in a teleconference.
3 *Different time, same place.* Parties move through the same location but at different points in time, such as in shared office spaces or meeting rooms.
4 *Different time, different place.* Coordination is entirely asynchronous and physically dispersed, as in electronic bulletin board discussions. Coordination becomes more difficult, and the opportunities for computer support therefore greater, as coordination moves beyond the same time, same place setting to more dispersed, asynchronous work settings.

Some CSCW applications are commercially available as "off-the-shelf" software, whereas others are custom built to suit specialized coordination needs. Most commercial software vendors today offer some types of CSCW applications. In addition to the coordination settings which they support, CSCW applications can also be differentiated in terms of their various features, the numbers of parties they accommodate, and the type of work or task which they support. Some of the more widely available CSCW applications today are as follows:

- electronic mail
- calendaring
- computer conferencing
- conversation management
- electronic bulletin boards
- electronic discussion groups
- electronic meeting systems
- group decision support
- project management systems
- group writing and editing
- document sharing
- joint authoring/editing
- workflow management

Electronic meeting systems (EMS) are a special type of CSCW system designed specifically for group meetings. To the extent that an EMS contains facilities to support decision-making, it is a GROUP DECISION SUPPORT SYSTEM (GDSS). An EMS provides such facilities as

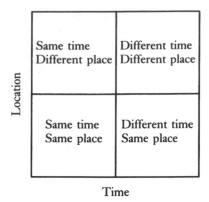

Figure 1   Four major settings for CSCW applications

electronic agendas, electronic whiteboards, shared notepads, and group writing programs. A GDSS may include these facilities as well but also includes group decision models, such as risk analysis, forecasting, and choice algorithms.

Impact on Work Groups

CSCW systems aim to smooth the linkages among the activities in a coordination task, resulting in tighter integration among otherwise independent or loosely coupled tasks. CSCW systems also aim to enhance the overall quality of the coordination endeavor.

Efficiency gains can be realized as CSCW systems automate systems that previously were done through manual means. For example, phone calls or typed memos can be replaced with electronic mail. Documents can be exchanged electronically instead of through traditional mail systems, and manual whiteboards in meeting rooms can be replaced with computerized boards. Automation can reduce costs, decrease the time required to complete a work task, and/or make the coordination process easier and less stressful for those involved.

CSCW systems also can create new possibilities for coordination, linking work processes that otherwise were not connected. For example, a CSCW system may allow participants in a project, who would otherwise work independently, to access each others' materials, even if project participants are not in the same location. Similarly, CSCW systems can enable strangers to discuss common problems and solutions via bulletin boards; popular Usenets on the internet illustrate this CSCW application. CSCW systems which pool the knowledge of multiple parties to solve complex problems bring a level of sophistication to the work setting that inevitably will have a significant impact on the business or organizational setting in which that work is conducted.

CSCW systems are having a major impact on business process re-engineering, on the support of mobile, dispersed workers, and on the creation of the "virtual organization." Business process re-engineering requires that work be redesigned to yield a "leaner" organization, with a minimal number of business processes and rapid workflow. CSCW contributes to re-engineering as it supports specific, multiparty coordination tasks. Electronic communication systems, workflow systems, and project management software have been particularly helpful in re-engineering efforts. Similarly, CSCW is facilitating the trend toward a more mobile, dispersed workforce. Work-at-home, the ability to communicate with co-workers while traveling, and the use of contract workers who electronically link to work facilities, are all made possible due to CSCW developments such as electronic mail, scheduling software, computer conferencing, and electronic meeting systems.

The effectiveness of a CSCW system depends on the design of the technology, the task(s) for which it is used, and how it is used. Users may compare one CSCW system to another to see which is the most effective for a given work task. But equally significant in determining CSCW effectiveness is the way in which the CSCW system is managed. For example, researchers have found that the same electronic conferencing system brought many benefits to one group or organization but brought no advantages at all in other groups or settings. Solid understanding of how work is to change with a new system, adequate training of all parties involved, and a commitment to an efficient, participative management style are among the factors thought to be critical to successful CSCW adoption.

At the extreme, a geographically dispersed workforce makes possible an organization without physical facilities, that is, a virtual organization. Collaboration occurs across time and space, with workers located in homes or office sites of their choice. Work occurs in shared computerized spaces connected via electronic networks; and there is little formal management structure, as workers operate with a high amount of professional independence. Research societies, consulting agencies, and brokerage firms illustrate the kinds of work suited to virtual forms of organizing. Many forecasters anticipate proliferation of virtual organizations in the future, with CSCW systems facilitating this trend.

The development of CSCW systems blends perspectives from the disciplines of economics, computer science, communication, social psychology, and management. Since CSCW is a rather new area of management information systems, techniques for systems design and methods for assessing CSCW impacts are still in their early stages.

Bibliography

Galegher, J., Kraut, R. E. & Egido, C. (eds) (1990). *Intellectual Teamwork: The Social and Technological Bases of Cooperative Work*. Hillsdale, NJ: Lawrence Erlbaum.

Greenberg, S. (Ed.) (1991). *Computer Supported Cooperative Work and Groupware*. New York: Academic Press.

Malone, T. W. & Crowston, K. (1994). Toward an interdisciplinary theory of coordination. *Computing Surveys*, 261.

GERARDINE DeSANCTIS

concept testing Concept testing is concerned with the evaluation of a new PRODUCT CONCEPT to: determine ways to improve the concept; ascertain the best target markets; and gauge potential customer acceptance to warrant further product development (*see* NEW PRODUCT DEVELOPMENT).

A product concept is "a printed or filmed representation of a product or service. It is simply a device to communicate the subject's benefits, strengths and reasons for being" (Schwartz, 1987). The concept is a description of the product that also includes the benefits it offers.

Concept tests identify: whether or not there is sufficient consumer appeal to warrant further development; the appropriate target market; and ways to improve the concept. They also provide an estimate of the percentage of people who may try the new product (Moore & Pressemier, 1993). Concept testing can also be used to help assess ADVERTISING or POSITIONING approaches by identifying which benefits should be offered.

A variety of techniques are available for concept testing, e.g., qualitative discussions with potential customers to assess their reaction to possible new product ideas, postal questionnaire surveys, telephone interviews, and personal interviews (*see* SURVEY RESEARCH). Monadic tests are where the respondents evaluate one concept. Competitive tests involve presenting the new concept alongside the old concept(s). Monadic tests have yielded successful applications; others argue that competitive tests are more realistic. Cooper (1993) argues that the most reliable results arise from a full-proposition concept test, i.e., a test designed to convey to the final customer what the final product will be and do. Information objectives for the concept test include: a measure of the customer's interest in the proposed product, a measure of the liking of the product, a comparative measure with competing products/brands currently in use, and an indication of the intention to purchase.

It is important to note that concept tests are likely to overstate the market acceptance, so that a result of "30 would definitely buy" is not likely to translate into a MARKET SHARE of 30 percent. The respondent may well continue to buy competing products, the potential buyers may lack information on the product because they may not be reached by advertising and promotion, and people may tend to respond positively to concept tests where money and commitment is not involved. Typical problems with concept tests include asking the 'wrong' respondents and promising more than the product will actually deliver. Product adoption (*see* ADOPTION PROCESS) can be longer than could be predicted in a concept test, e.g., automotive bank teller machines took years to become fully accepted.

A single exposure may not be a good predictor of eventual reaction to a product. Concept tests can only estimate the number of people who will try the product. The concept can change between the test and the market introduction (*see* TEST MARKETING), CONSUMER ATTITUDES can change, and other new products may be introduced between the test and the market introduction. All of this can affect the accuracy of the predictions from concept tests.

Bibliography

Cooper, R. G. (1993). *Winning at new products: Accelerating the process from idea to launch*, 2nd edn, Reading, MA: Addison Wesley. Chapter 6, pp. 153–161.

Moore, W. L. & Pressemier, E. A. (1993). *Product planning and management: Designing and delivering value*. New York: McGraw-Hill. Chapter 8, pp. 253–265.

Schwartz, D. (1987). *Concept testing: How to test new product ideas before you go to market*. New York: American Management Association.

MARGARET BRUCE

concurrent auditing techniques   Concurrent auditing techniques are tools that auditors use to collect evidence on the reliability of a computer-based application system at the same time as the application system carries out live operational processing of transaction data. They are implemented via program instructions that are embedded within the application software or within the system software, such as the database management system, that supports the application system (Clark et al., Groomer & Murthy, 1989). In sensitive, high-materiality application systems, concurrent auditing techniques may be executed continuously. Alternatively, they may be executed periodically – e.g. during random intervals or during high-risk intervals. The evidence they collect can be reported immediately to the auditor, which is likely to be the case if high-risk errors or irregularities are identified during application system processing. Alternatively, the evidence they collect can be stored and reported periodically, which is likely to be the case when the expected losses associated with the exceptions identified are low.

Development

Concurrent auditing techniques are not new. They were developed in the late 1960s and early 1970s to address certain problems that were emerging in conducting audits of computer systems. These problems were as follows:

Disappearing paper-based audit trail.   Historically, auditors have placed substantial reliance on the paper trail used to document the events that occur in accounting systems. They have referenced this paper trail to determine whether errors or irregularities have occurred within a system. With the emergence of computer systems, much of the paper-based audit trail has disappeared. Without purposeful design, adequate recording of events may not occur in a computer system. Concurrent auditing techniques provide a means for auditors to ensure that a system records the events in which they are interested.

Difficulty of performing transaction walkthroughs. One way in which auditors have sought to understand an application system is to trace material transaction types through the various processing steps in the system. In most manual systems, this technique is fairly straightforward to use. With increasing use of computer systems, however, the range of functions that could be provided on a cost-effective basis within application systems has expanded. As a result, application systems have become more complex, and transaction walkthroughs have become more difficult to undertake. Auditors have used concurrent auditing techniques to collect evidence on a transaction as it passes through an application system and to assemble and report this evidence in a way that can be easily understood.

The need for timely identification of errors and irregularities.   Because of the speed with which computers operate, errors or irregularities have not always been identified on a timely basis. In some cases, organizations have suffered substantial losses as a result. Traditional *ex post* or retrospective auditing has sometimes been inadequate as a means of identifying errors or irregularities on a timely basis. Auditors have used concurrent auditing techniques to identify errors or irregularities immediately they have occurred.

The above reasons for using concurrent auditing techniques remain valid today. Several recent other factors, however, have emerged that motivate more extensive use of concurrent auditing techniques. These factors include the following:

Increased integration of information systems.   Information systems are becoming increasingly integrated, both within an organization and externally via links to systems in other organizations. As a result, the complexity of information systems is increasing. Concurrent auditing techniques help auditors to understand how the reliability of different components of an information system impacts on the reliability of other components.

Increased incidence of distributed information systems.   The locations where information systems functions are performed are becoming increasingly dispersed. The infrastructure that now supports many information systems comprises physically remote, heterogeneous hardware and software platforms. Auditors may be unable to visit all sites where information processing is conducted. Concurrent auditing techniques can be installed at remote sites to collect evidence on their behalf.

Increased exposures when errors and irregularities occur.   As systems become increasingly integrated and perform a greater range of functions (sometimes safety-critical functions), the expected losses from errors and irregularities increase. For example, a computer virus that is introduced into one system can propagate quickly to other systems via communication networks. As a result, timely identification of errors becomes more important. Concurrent auditing techniques permit errors and irregularities to be identified as they occur.

Presence of Entropy in Systems

All systems suffer entropy – i.e., the tendency toward disorder and eventual collapse. Information systems experience entropy for a variety of reasons. For example, system design errors or programing errors may exist such that they would slowly undermine the effectiveness and efficiency of the system. User information requirements can also change and, as a result, an information system may no longer meet its users' needs. Concurrent auditing techniques provide a means of detecting entropy as it occurs. For example, they can be used to detect increasing error rates during data capture and input.

The need for more effective and efficient audits.   During the 1980s and 1990s, auditors have been placed under substantial pressure to improve the effectiveness and efficiency of their audits. Many of their clients have suffered from prolonged periods of economic recession. Moreover, institutional and regulatory changes have occurred that have substantially increased competition in the market-place for audit services. Concurrent auditing techniques sometimes provide a more cost-effective way of performing some types of audit functions, thereby allowing auditors to better cope with client and market place pressures.

Types of Techniques

Over the years, a large number of different types of concurrent auditing techniques have been proposed. Nevertheless, Mohrweis (1988) argues that they all fall into three general categories: (1) those that can be used to test an application system with test data during normal processing; (2) those that can be used to select transactions during normal processing for audit review; and (3) those that can be used to trace, map, or document the state of a system during normal processing.

The subsections below provide a brief description of five concurrent auditing techniques (see further, Weber, 1988). The first, "Integrated Test Facility," is an example of a concurrent auditing technique that is used to collect test data during normal processing. The second and third, "System Control Audit Review Files" and "Continuous and Intermittent Simulation," are examples of concurrent auditing techniques that are used to select transactions during normal processing for subsequent audit review. The fourth and fifth, "Snapshots" and "Extended Records," are examples of concurrent auditing techniques that trace, map, or document the state of a system during normal processing.

Integrated Test Facility

The integrated test facility technique (ITF) involves auditors establishing a minicompany or dummy company on the live files processed by an application system. For example, in a payroll system, auditors might establish a master-file record for a fictitious employee. Auditors then submit test data to the application system as part of the normal transaction data entered into the system. They monitor the effects of their test data on the dummy entity they have established.

Two major design decisions must be made when auditors use ITF. First, auditors must determine what method will be used to enter test data. One approach is to select and tag live transactions. The tagged transactions then update not only their target records but also the dummy entity that has been established. An alternative approach is to design and create test transactions specifically for the application. These test update only the dummy entity. Second, auditors must determine how the effects of test transactions will be masked within the application system being tested. One approach is to submit transactions that have immaterial amounts and which, therefore, are unlikely to be noticed by application system users. A second approach is to submit reversal entries so that the net effect of the test transactions is zero. A third approach is to modify the application system so the test transactions are not counted in the application system's control totals. This third approach is the most expensive, but it is often the most effective.

System Control Audit Review File. With a system control audit review file (SCARF), auditors embed audit routines into an application system and collect data on events that are of interest to them. These data are then written to a file (hence the name of the technique) for subsequent review or subsequent use in other tests that auditors may wish to conduct.

Leinicke et al. (1990) describe an example of how SCARF might be used within an insurance company to detect unauthorized changes to policyholder master records followed by subsequent fund withdrawals. When a name-and-address change is made to a policyholder record, the change can be recorded via SCARF. Any subsequent withdrawal of funds above a material amount can then be monitored by SCARF and reported for audit scrutiny. In this way a fraudulent withdrawal of funds can be detected.

For example, without authorization, an insurance company employee may change a policyholder's name and address to their own name and address. The employee then may fraudulently borrow money against the policy or withdraw funds against the policy.

Continuous and Intermittent Simulation. Continuous and intermittent simulation (CIS) has been proposed by Koch (1981) as a means of collecting audit evidence concurrently with application system processing when the application system uses a database management system to support updating and querying of application files.

CIS has two major components. First, like SCARF, the database management system must be able to trap transactions that are of interest to the auditor. Koch initially proposed that the database management system be modified to capture transactions. Some current database management systems, however, provide facilities that allow auditors to write their own software routines that the database management system will execute on their behalf. Second, auditors must write software modules that will replicate the application system processing that is of interest. The database management system then passes the transactions it captures across to these modules. These modules in turn determine the results that should be produced as a result of the transaction. The results produced by the audit modules are then compared with the results produced by the application system. Deviations are written to a file for scrutiny by the auditor.

To illustrate the use of CIS, consider a financial application where auditors are concerned about the accuracy of the calculations relating to the payout value when a customer of the financial institution pays out a loan early. The database management system would identify a payout transaction as being one of the transactions that interest the auditor. It would capture the payout transaction and pass the transaction across to the audit modules. The modules would then calculate the payout value. In the meantime, the application system also would have calculated the payout value. The payout value calculated by the audit modules would then be compared with the payout value calculated by the application system. If a discrepancy existed between the two values, an exception would be written to an audit file.

Snapshot. The snapshot technique is straightforward. As the name implies, it involves taking "snapshots" or "pictures" of a transaction as it winds its way through an application system. In essence, it is an automated version of a manual transaction walkthrough. Snapshots are taken at material processing points in the application system. Auditors must first identify these points and then embed audit modules within the application system at these points. At each of these points, the audit modules typically take a snapshot of the transaction just prior to processing and a snapshot just after processing. The auditor then has the before-image of the transaction and the after-image of the transaction as a basis for evaluating the authenticity, accuracy, and completeness of the application processing carried out. These snapshots are written away to an audit file for subsequent scrutiny by the auditor.

To illustrate use of snapshot, consider an order that is input to a manufacturer's order entry system. The order may pass through a number of processing points that are of audit significance. For example: the customer has to be an authorized customer; the amount of the purchase must be within certain credit limits; a discount might be given depending upon the status of the customer and the type of product that the customer is wanting to purchase; the order might be "exploded" via a bill-of-materials to determine the parts required to make the product ordered; shortages of parts may invoke a purchase order being placed on a supplier. At some or all of these points, snapshots might be taken so the auditor can examine the veracity of processing at each point.

Extended Records. Extended records are a simple extension of the snapshot technique. Using conventional snapshot, individual snapshots are simply written to an audit file. Auditors then must assemble all the snapshots that pertain to a particular transaction and a particular stream of processing that the transaction undergoes. If a large number of snapshots are taken, assembling related snapshots can be onerous.

The extended records technique collects all related snapshots together in a single record. As a transaction passes through the various snapshot points, the snapshots are appended to a record that is eventually written to a file for audit scrutiny. Auditors then do not bear the overheads of sorting related snapshots together. More timely scrutiny of veracity of the transaction and the application processing stream is possible.

Users of the Techniques

In spite of the apparent benefits of concurrent auditing techniques, they have had a checkered history. Table 1 reports the results of a number of surveys taken periodically since 1978 (see also Reeve, 1984). A common definition for the different types of concurrent auditing techniques has not been used in the surveys. Moreover, in some cases, data were not collected on a particular technique, and different types of auditors were surveyed.

Nevertheless, a common theme emerges – namely, concurrent auditing techniques are not in widespread use, and usage has not increased over the years.

The results of the surveys also indicate that several factors seem to affect usage of concurrent auditing techniques. First, internal auditors are more likely to use concurrent auditing techniques than external auditors. Concurrent auditing techniques can require substantial resources to establish and maintain them, and internal auditors are better placed to support and use concurrent auditing techniques. Second, concurrent auditing techniques are more likely to be used if auditors are involved in the development work associated with a new system. It is easier to install concurrent techniques from the outset rather than to retrofit an application system with a concurrent auditing technique. Third, concurrent auditing techniques are more likely to be used if other types of computer-based audit techniques are also in use. Auditors are more likely to have the knowledge to employ concurrent auditing techniques if they use a portfolio of computer-based audit techniques. Fourth, concurrent auditing techniques are more likely to be used as the incidence of automatically-generated transactions increases. The audit trail is less visible for these types of transactions, and there can be high exposures if an error or irregularity occurs.

Limitations

Use of concurrent auditing techniques often is not straightforward. A number of drawbacks exist:

(1) Auditors must have a reasonable level of knowledge about computer systems if they are to design and implement concurrent auditing techniques effectively. In addition, they must have a good knowledge of the application system.
(2) Stakeholders in the application system must support the use of concurrent auditing techniques. For example: management must provide the resources needed to design, implement, and use concurrent auditing techniques; information systems personnel must keep auditors abreast of changes to the application system that might impact any concurrent auditing techniques that have been implemented; application system users must be prepared to bear the costs sometimes associated with the disruption that occurs when concurrent auditing techniques are used.
(3) Concurrent auditing techniques are unlikely to be effective unless they are implemented in application systems that are stable. If application systems are subject to frequent change, the costs of maintaining concurrent auditing techniques are likely to be prohibitive.

Bibliography

Clark, R., Dillon, R. & Farrell T. (1989). Continuous auditing. *Internal Auditor*, 46, Spring, 3–10.

Table 1: Survey of usage of concurrent auditing techniques

Study	Technique		
	Integrated text facility	Embedded audit modules/SCARF	Snapshot/extended records
IIA (1977)	5.0%	15.8%	18.4%
Perry & Adams (1978)	15.0%	20.0%	20.0%
Tobinson & Davis (1981)	13.3%	13.3%	4.4%
Langfield-Smith (1987)	22.7%	2.1%	–
Mohrweis (1988)	12.2%	11.9%	9.9%
IIA (1991)	11.0%	11.0%	–

Groomer, S. M. & Murthy, U. S. (1989). Continuous auditing of database applications: An embedded audit module approach. *Journal of Information Systems*, 3, Spring, 53–69.

Institute of Internal Auditors (IIA) (1977). *Systems auditability and control study: Data processing audit practices report*. Altamonte Springs, Fl.: The Institute of Internal Auditors Research Foundation.

Institute of Internal Auditors (IIA) (1991). *Systems auditability and control: Module 2: Audit and control environment*. Orlando, Fl.: The Institute of Internal Auditors Research Foundation.

Koch, H. S. (1981). Online computer auditing through continuous and intermittent simulation. *MIS Quarterly*, 5, 29–41.

Langfield-Smith, K. (1987). The use of computer-assisted audit techniques in Australian Internal Audit Departments. *The EDP Auditor Journal*, 11, 28–40.

Leinicke, L. M., Rexroad, W. M. & Ward, J. D. (1990). Computer fraud auditing: It works. *Internal Auditor*, 47, Aug., 26–33.

Mohrweis, L. C. (1988). Usage of concurrent EDP audit tools. *The EDP Auditor Journal*, 111, 49–54.

Perry, W. E. & Adams, D. R. (1978). Use of computer audit practices. *EDPACS*, 6, Nov., 3–18.

Reeve, R. C. (1984). Trends in the use of EDP audit techniques. *The Australian Computer Journal*, 16, May, 42–7.

Tobinson, G. & Davis, G. B. (1981). Actual use and perceived utility of EDP auditing techniques. *The EDP Auditor Journal* Spring, 1–22.

Weber, R. (1988). *EDP auditing: Conceptual foundations and practice* 2nd edn, New York: McGraw-Hill Book Company.

RON A. WEBER

conflict Conflict is a common phenomenon in virtually all societies and organizations. Many definitions have been proposed. Some emphasize differences in perceptions or interests of the parties. Kolb and Putnam (1992), for example, argue that conflict exists "when there are real or perceived differences that arise in specific organizational circumstances and that engender emotion as a consequence" (1992: p. 312) (*see* EMOTIONS IN ORGANIZATIONS). Others define conflict in terms of actual behavior where parties interfere with each other's aims: Deutsch (1973) defines conflict as a phenomenon that "exists whenever incompatible activities occur" (1993: p. 10). There are many other definitions relating to the concerns and circumstances surrounding conflict.

Some definitions include both interest and behavior differences, as in the definition proposed here: "Conflict is incompatible behavior among parties whose interests differ" (Brown, 1983, p. 4). Incompatible behavior refers to intentional, purposeful behavior opposing the interests of the other party rather than accidental actions. Interests refer to stakes affected by an interaction between parties.

This definition focuses attention on conflicts experienced both behaviorally and psychologically. What of situations when one but not both elements are present? Sometimes the parties have different interests but do not display incompatible behavior. Potential conflicts may remain latent or covert when parties are unaware of or unable to express their differences in interest directly. Such hidden conflicts are quite common, for example, when large POWER differences between the parties hinder open expression of differences. It is common for subordinates to remain silent about disagreements with organizational superiors, even when it would be beneficial for the organization as a whole for those differences to be explicitly discussed.

In other situations, the parties may engage in incompatible behavior when their interests are not in conflict. Such mistaken conflicts are often grounded in misperceptions of the various interests involved by one or more of the parties (*see* ATTRIBUTION). It is quite common for parties with a history of conflict to assume that their interests conflict even when their interests are in fact similar. Union and management representatives, for example, may "assume the worst" and negotiate to impasse even when both parties have stronger interests in cooperation than in conflict (*see* COLLECTIVE BARGAINING).

Paying attention to both interests and behavior in defining conflict clarifies the potential for future interaction. Hidden conflict may easily evolve into overt conflict if the parties come to understand their interests more clearly. Mistaken conflict may evaporate for the same reason.

The sources of conflict are legion. Among the most important are resource scarcities that lead to conflict among rival claimants, task differences that generate conflict over coordination and priorities, power inequalities that catalyze struggles over CONTROL and authority, and culture and value differences that produce struggles over identity and respect. For organizational purposes the most explicit attention is often paid to resources, tasks, and power, though differences in less visible cultural factors may sometimes produce the most explosive results. Conflicts that combine multiple sources, such as tensions between individuals or groups that differ in power and cultural identity, may be extremely hard to resolve (Brown, 1983). Organizations often have difficulty in coping with differences among ethnic groups that are unequal in social and organizational power.

Is conflict a problem? Much of the early research on organizational conflict assumed that conflict was basically dysfunctional (see Pondy, 1967). It is clear that conflict sometimes fosters suppression or distortion of important information, strong feelings of hostility and antagonism, and behavior that is destructive to the purposes of organizations and their members. Regulating extremes of conflict escalation is important for ORGANIZATIONAL EFFECTIVENESS.

On the other hand, many investigators have suggested that conflict in some situations can be constructive (e.g., Coser, 1956). In organizations, moderate levels of conflict encourage wide exchanges of information, energetic PARTICIPATION in problem-solving, and generation of creative alternatives for problem solving (*see* CREATIVITY; INNOVATION). Lack of conflict may in itself be a problem, as in groupthink, for example.

Whether conflict is desirable or problematic depends on the situation. Finding new ways to resolve differences among organizational subunits, such as maintenance and production units of a manufacturing firm, may be vital to improving organizational performance. Such solutions may be difficult to find if disagreements cannot be voiced. At the same time, managing conflict may require regulating such disagreements so they do not escalate. Conflict management may require encouraging the expression of differences in some situations, and regulating that expression in others.

Conflict as a *process* is shaped by the perceptions of the parties, the group cohesiveness within parties, the COMMUNICATIONS between parties, and their behavior in response to each other. When conflict is well managed, the parties regularly question their own assumptions to avoid stereotyping and groupthink. They communicate freely, and act as joint problem solvers instead of adversaries. Too often, however, parties tend to develop stereotypes that favor themselves and denigrate other parties, mobilize strong LEADERSHIP and group conformity within parties, restrict their communications with others, and take pre-emptive action to counter expected aggression. This combination of tendencies can easily lead to self-reinforcing patterns of conflict escalation, in which parties can point to the other's behavior as justifying their own escalation. Thus initially constructive conflict can easily escalate into excessive conflict. A similar pattern can produce too little conflict: positive stereotypes that overemphasize common interests, high levels of cohesion across parties, reduced communication about differences, and actions to avoid or suppress conflict can combine in a self-reinforcing pattern.

Organizational conflict has been examined from several levels of analysis. Sheppard (1992) has argued that much of the confusion of present conflict theory can be understood in terms of the different levels of analysis and the perspectives associated with those levels. Much research has focused at the level of specific disputes, and examined the behavior, tactics, and consequences of conflict episodes. Analysis at this level produces ideas about the dynamics and tactics by which individuals deal with specific problems (see NEGOTIATION). Other researchers have examined conflicts at the level of the institutional context, and focused on the norms, rules, structures, and organizational interdependencies against which conflicts are evoked or controlled (see INDUSTRIAL RELATIONS; INTERORGANIZA-TIONAL RELATIONS). These investigations produce ideas about institutions and policies within which conflicts can be controlled. Between the levels of the specific dispute and the institutional context is the relationship level of analysis, which addresses the ongoing relations between parties over a series of conflicts. Relationship analysis also deals with systems and strategies that enable the management of conflict in an ongoing relationship. This level of analysis is affected by both institutional contexts and events of specific conflict episodes – but it has received less attention than the other two levels.

The study of conflict in organizations has evolved significantly over recent decades. Much research in the 1960s focused on the growing functional specialization in organizations and the conflicts inherent in the performance of organizational tasks carried out by diverse subunits. As organizations have reconfigured themselves to deal with increasing environmental UNCERTAINTY and competition, the importance of conflict among departments or project teams or interorganizational networks has focused increas-ing attention on conflict handling as a critical capacity.

Struggles over the allocation of organizational resources has also been the basis for increasing concern with conflict rooted in political differences (see POLITICS). In part these struggles reflect tensions over class differences in the larger society. They also reflect increased awareness of the dependence of organizations on external resources and the demands from external constituencies. Conflict over power differences often generate more communication difficulties, asymmetrical mobilization, and more unpre-

dicted explosions than conflicts over task differences (Brown, 1983).

More recently still, organizations have become con-cerned with conflicts produced by differences in cultural background or roles. Conflicts between "identity groups" that define the self-concepts of their members have become increasingly relevant to organizations that are recruiting a workforce diverse in cultural and ethnic identities (Alderfer, Alderfer, Tucker, & Tucker, 1980). Cultural differences are often value-laden and poorly understood, and so may be the basis for rapid and difficult-to-control conflict escalation, especially when they are closely correlated with power differences (Kanter, 1977). Tensions across gender and ethnic differences have produced serious misunderstandings and explosive conflicts in many orga-nizations.

Cultural differences also illustrate limitations to our existing understanding of conflict in organizations. Orga-nizational conflict has been studied in some depth in Western industrialized countries, but much less is known about how it is experienced in other cultures. With increased interaction across national and cultural bound-aries within and between organizations, there is more scope for conflicts across cultural divides. In cultures valuing competition and individualism, like the United States (where much of the conflict research has been done), differences may produce overt conflict and distributive processes. In cultures that place a higher value on community welfare and cooperation, such as Japan, other ways of expressing differences and integrating diversity may be more common.

The changing demographics of the workforce in some industrialized countries are giving new impetus to the study of conflicts across gender and ethnic differences within societies. Attention to such conflicts is an urgent need, especially where it is linked to gross discrepancies in wealth and power.

More attention is also needed for understanding conflicts that involve values, ideologies and emotional commitments that are not easily susceptible to "rational" analysis and resolution (Carnevale & Pruitt, 1992). Many of the most costly and intransigent organizational conflicts have roots in incompatible values and ideologies which have been resistant to resolution. Such conflicts may not be resolvable – but they may be transformed to make their outcomes less destructive (Vayrynen, 1991).

Conflict theorists have infrequently spanned the levels of analysis necessary to integrate institutional and episodic perspectives to understand ongoing conflict that is rooted in systemic organizational relations. Often they have also failed to account for the variety of interests at stake in important conflicts. Many conflict theorists operate on the assumption that conflict is best understood in bilateral rather than multilateral terms, so their theories provide little help for understanding conflicts that involve many stakeholders, multiple interests, and complex forces operating at several levels of analysis. Learning more about such conflicts and their management is increasingly urgent as global interdependence expands. The most serious shortcoming of this definition is the restricted range of global experience represented in currently available theory and research about conflict and its organizational implications.

see also **Intergroup relations; Interorganizational relations; Commitment, Organizational culture; Organizational effectiveness**

Bibliography

Alderfer, C. P., Alderfer, C. J., Tucker, L. & Tucker, R. (1980). Diagnosing race relations in management. Journal of Applied Behavioral Science, **16**, 135–166.

Brown, L. D. (1983). Managing conflict at organizational interfaces. Reading, MA: Addison–Wesley.

Carnevale, P. J. and Pruitt, D. G. (1992). Negotiation and mediation. Annual Review of Psychology, **43**, 531–582.

Coser, L. (1956). The functions of social conflict. New York: Free Press.

Deutsch, M. (1973). The resolution of conflict. New Haven: Yale University Press.

Kanter, R. M. (1977). Men and women of the corporation. New York: Colophon.

Kolb, D. & Putnam, L. (1992). The multiple faces of conflict in organizations. Journal of Organizational Behavior, **13**, 311–324.

Pondy, L. R. (1967). Organizational conflict: Concepts and models. Administrative Science Quarterly, **12**, 296–320.

Sheppard, B. H. (1992). Conflict research as schizophrenia: The many faces of organizational conflict. Journal of Organizational Behavior, **13**, 205–207.

Vayrynen, R. (1991). To settle or to transform: Perspectives on the resolution of national and international conflict. In R. Vayrynen (Ed.), New directions in conflict theory: Conflict resolution and conflict transformation. (pp. 1–25). London: Sage.

L. DAVID BROWN and ANDREW E. CLARKSON

constant returns to scale This describes a specific technology of production for the firm. When constant returns in production exist, a firm that doubled all inputs in production would see a doubling of its output. In the case of the COBB–DOUGLAS PRODUCTION FUNCTION, constant returns to scale occur when the of the exponents for the inputs in production sum to one. Since with constant returns to scale there are no penalties to the firm whether it expands or contracts, there is no theoretically unique optimal size plant that minimizes the costs of production. With no theoretical limit on the size of firms in the industry, the theoretical number of firms in the industry is also indeterminate.

see also **Economics of scale**

ROBERT E. MCAULIFFE

consumer attitudes Attitudes may be considered as a mental state of readiness, organized through experience, exerting a directive or dynamic influence upon an individual's response to all objects and situations with which he/she is related.

Attitudes structure the way consumers perceive their environment and guide the ways in which they respond to it, i.e., attitudes are characterized by a pre-disposition or state-of-readiness to act or re-act in a particular way to certain stimuli. They are relatively enduring and are useful guidelines as to what buyers may do in certain circumstances.

Attitudes have three components. The cognitive component refers to beliefs, i.e., the knowledge or descriptive thoughts one has, for example, about a product or brand, which is a function of available information. The affective component refers to the emotional content of attitudes and arouses either like or dislike; such feelings derive from personality, motives, social norms, and previous experience. The conative component, or action tendency, concerns the disposition to take action of some kind, e.g., a purchase; a consumer may have favorable attitudes without making purchases or even intending to purchase.

A number of sources of influence are important in the formation of attitudes. These include: information exposure – the cognitive content of attitudes is largely built up from information from other people and from the media; group membership – the attitudes and opinions of people one interacts with have an impact on the individual; environment, to include economic factors; and present levels of need satisfaction.

Attitudes are held toward many aspects of buying and consuming, e.g., toward products and services, brands, companies, stores, product appearance and packaging, promotion and price, and levels of service. Attitudes vary along various dimensions: direction, e.g., positive or negative, favorable or unfavorable; intensity, i.e., how positive or negative; complexity, i.e., toward one or more aspects of a product or brand; and fixity, i.e., will they change. With regard to complexity, one can refer to overall or general attitudes, e.g., toward a model of car; and to particular or specific attitudes, e.g., the individual features of a car such as its design, performance, or service provided. Further, one can consider "determinant" buying attitudes (see Alpert, 1971; Myers & Alpert, 1968) which refer to the features/aspects of a product that are critical in the decision to purchase a specific item or brand/model, e.g., cars and safety.

A major question for marketers is the extent to which attitudes predict subsequent purchase behavior. This has been considered by Fishbein (1967), and others (Sheth, 1974; Ajzen & Fishbein, 1980; Fishbein & Ajzen, 1975; Wells, 1985), who present a framework in which a consumer moves from beliefs to attitudes to purchase intention to purchase. Fishbein's suggestion is that purchase intention may be a better predictor of behavior than merely having favorable attitudes. Even so, one has to take account of "intervening" variables which may prevail between the stages of intention to buy and purchase: these include economic factors, availability, price, and promotional activities.

Attitude change also needs to be taken into account. This includes changes in direction, intensity, and complexity. Factors which affect attitude change are: the attitudes themselves, e.g., extreme attitudes are harder to change; individual factors, e.g., personality and product needs; marketing communications, both the MASS MEDIA and INTERPERSONAL COMMUNICATIONS; and the MARKETING ENVIRONMENT, in particular economic variables and financial considerations.

Bibliography

Ajzen, J. & Fishbein, M. (1980). *Understanding attitudes and predicting social behavior.* Englewood Cliffs, NJ: Prentice-Hall.

Alpert, M. I. (1971). Identification of determinant attributes: A comparison of methods. *Journal of Marketing Research*, **8**, May, 184–191.

Engel, J. F., Blackwell, R. D. & Miniard, P. W. (1990). *Consumer behavior*, 6th edn, Orlando, FL: The Dryden Press. Chapter 11.

Fishbein, M. (1967). Attitudes and prediction of behavior. In M. Fishbein (Ed.), *Readings in attitude theory and measurement* (pp. 477–492). New York: John Wiley.

Fishbein, M. & Ajzen, I. (1975). *Belief, attitude, intentions and behavior*. Reading, MA: Addison Wesley.

Foxall, G. R. & Goldsmith, R. E. (1994). *Consumer psychology for marketing*. London: Routledge. Chapter 5.

Hawkins, D. I., Best, R. J. & Coney, K. A. (1992). *Consumer behavior: Implications for marketing strategy*, 5th edn, Homewood, IL: Irwin. Chapter 12.

Loudon, D. L. & Della Bitta, A. J. (1993). *Consumer behavior*, 4th edn, McGraw-Hill Int. Chapters 12, 13.

Myers, J. H. & Alpert, M. I. (1968). Determinant buying attitudes: Meaning and measurement. *Journal of Marketing*, 32, Oct., 14.

Schiffman, L. G. & Kanuk, L. Z. (1991). *Consumer behavior*, 4th edn, Prentice-Hall: Chapter 8.

Sheth, J. N. (1974). An investigation of relationships among evaluative beliefs, affect, behavioral intention and behavior. In J. U. Farley, J. A. Howard & L. W. Ring (Eds), *Consumer behavior, theory and application* (pp. 89–114). Boston: Allyn & Bacon.

Solomon, M. R. (1992). *Consumer behavior*. Needham Heights, MA: Allyn & Bacon. Chapter 5.

Wells, W. D. (1985). Attitudes and behavior. *Journal of Advertising Research* March, 40–44.

BARBARA LEWIS

consumer buyer behavior Consumer buyer behavior has developed, since the 1960s, as a separate discipline within marketing, for a number of reasons. The impact of the MARKETING CONCEPT throughout all industries, in both the public and private sectors, and on an international basis, has led to increasing consumer awareness and sophistication. Consumers are better educated and informed and thus more discriminating in their selection of goods and services. Hence, it behoves manufacturers and distributors to research and understand their needs and preferences and to respond accordingly. With the fast pace of product introductions, spurred by technological development, companies need to search for better information about what people are willing to buy. Product life cycles are shorter and so it is necessary to anticipate consumer lifestyles and to develop products to satisfy future needs. The growth of segmentation as a MARKETING STRATEGY enables companies to better cater for the needs of specific, homogeneous groups of consumers. Further, there is: increased interest in consumer protection and the growth of private consumer groups; the setting of public policy to protect the interests and well-being of consumers; and increasing environmental concerns. Additionally, computer and statistical developments provide the tools and techni-

ques to facilitate research into consumer behavior and develop customer databases.

In consumer markets (*see* MARKETS), various market exchanges take place between companies and "consumers" who may be described as "consumers," "buyers," "customers," "purchasers," etc., as a function of their involvement in buying and consuming. This is better understood in terms of buying roles within a household or family. These roles are typically: *initiator* – someone who first suggests the idea of buying a particular good or service; *influencer(s)* – those who have implicit or explicit influence from within or outside the household; *decider(s)* – a person who decides on any component of a buying decision in relation to whether to buy, what to buy, where from, when, and how to pay; *purchaser* – to mean the purchasing agent who goes into a shop; and *user(s)* – those who use or consume the product/service. In addition, one can consider who pays for/funds the purchase. Also, the extent to which joint decision-making is evident, i.e., where two or more people fulfil buying role(s) (see e.g., Davis, 1976; Davis & Rigaux, 1974; Filiatrault & Brent–Ritchie, 1980); this in turn may depend on stages in the CONSUMER DECISION-MAKING PROCESS.

Consumer buyer behavior is concerned with the process of buying and consuming goods and services. One can also consider consumer shopping behavior, i.e., visiting the retail shopping environment, which is characterized by various personal and social motives (see Tauber, 1972). Personal motives include: role playing, diversion, self-gratification, learning about new trends, physical activity, and sensory stimulation. Social motives include social experience outside the home, communication with others having a similar interest, peer group attraction, status and authority, and pleasure of bargaining.

Consumer buyer behavior is partly explained and understood in terms of economic theory (*see* BUYER BEHAVIOR THEORIES). However, it is also necessary to consider social and psychological explanations, together with other influences on consumers (see figure 1), to include marketing and other stimuli and buyer characteristics.

Marketing stimuli relate to the activities and inputs of manufacturers and distributors, in particular the components of their MARKETING MIX, namely, product, price, place, and promotion. Other stimuli include economic, political, and technological elements in the MARKETING

Consumer buyer behavior

Marketing Stimuli	Other Stimuli		Buyer's Characteristics	Buyer's Decision Process		Buyer's Decision
Product Price Place Promotion	Economic Technological Political Cultural	→	Culture Social Personal Psychological	Problem recognition Information search Evaluation Decisions Post-purchase behavior	→	Product choice Brand choice Dealer choice Purchase timing Purchase amount

Figure 1   Influences on Consumers
Source: Kotler, 1994, p. 174

ENVIRONMENT. These impact on buyers whose social and cultural background (*see* CULTURE; SOCIAL CLASS), LIFE-STYLES, and group memberships (*see* INTERPERSONAL COMMUNICATIONS) influence their buying behavior.

In addition, one needs to consider the make-up of consumer psychological characteristics (e.g., PERSONALITY; consumer needs and motives; consumer perceptions; consumer learning), together with an understanding of the ways in which consumer attitudes are formed and developed (*see* CONSUMER ATTITUDES; COGNITIVE DISSONANCE), and the ways in which consumers perceive and handle risk in buying situations (*see* PERCEIVED RISK).

In most buying situations, consumers progress through a decision-making process (*see* CONSUMER DECISION-MAKING PROCESS), which results in various buying decisions in relation to product and brand choice, store/dealer choice, purchase time, methods of payment, etc. Buying decisions of special interest to researchers and practitioners include those which involve a time dimension, e.g., BRAND LOYALTY and the ADOPTION PROCESS for product innovations.

Bibliography

Davis, H. L. (1976). Decision-making within the household. *Journal of Consumer Research*, **2**, March, 241–260.

Davis, H. L. & Rigaux, B. P. (1974). Perceptions of marital roles in decision process. *Journal of Consumer Research*, **1**, 51–62.

Filiatrault, P. & Brent-Ritchie, J. R. (1980). Joint purchase decisions: A comparison of influence structure in family and couple decision-making units. *Journal of Consumer Research*, **6**, Sept., 131–140.

Katona, G. (1960). *The powerful consumer*. New York: McGraw-Hill.

Kotler, P. (1991). *Marketing management: Analysis, planning, implementation and control*, 8th edn, Prentice-Hall Int., p. 174.

Tauber, E. M. (1972). Why do people shop? *Journal of Marketing*, **36**, Oct., 46–49.

BARBARA LEWIS

consumer decision-making process The consumer decision-making process is concerned with buying operations and the stages that a buyer (individual or household) may be involved in when making purchases. These are usually referred to as stages of: problem recognition, information search, information evaluation, purchase decisions, and post-purchase evaluations.

Problem recognition occurs when a consumer recognizes a buying problem or goal, an unsatisfied or unfilled need. Sources of problems are various and include: assortment deficiency (e.g., the coffee jar is empty), exposure to new information, expanded desires for more or better products and services, expanded means (i.e., finance available), and changing expectations and needs. Buying needs may relate to products, brands, stores, service, etc., and a variety of needs will prevail at any one time which have to be prioritized (for an individual or household) as a function of time, money, urgency, role involvement, etc. A readiness to buy thus emerges.

Information search is the stage at which consumers attempt to match needs with market offerings, to identify purchase alternatives and find out more about them. Information may come from: personal sources, such as friends, family, neighbors; commercial sources, e.g., advertising and promotion, displays and salespeople; public sources, e.g., mass media and consumer organizations; and experience/use.

The amount of information sought will be a function of both product and individual factors. Product factors include frequency of purchase, price, social conspicuousness, essentiality of the product, and intensity of need. Individual factors, or search styles, include values and aspirations, degree of involvement with the purchase, risk perceptions and risk handling styles (*see* PERCEIVED RISK), availability of information without search, previous experience and knowledge of the product, time available, perceptions of the costs and value of information search, and satisfaction to be gained from searching.

Information Evaluation (see Bettman, 1979)

When considering consumers' evaluation of information with respect to product and brand alternatives, formal or informal organization of information may occur. Formal organization might include detailed financial analysis, e.g., with respect to house or car purchase. Further, alternatives are evaluated with respect to various decision criteria. These are related to: costs, e.g., price, operating costs, repairs, service, extras; performance, e.g., durability, economy, efficiency, dependability; suitability – of brand, style, store image, appearance, etc.; and convenience – of store location, atmosphere, service, etc.

Alternatives which are evaluated will be part of an awareness set as the consumer does not necessarily have information with respect to all the alternatives available. Those which meet initial buying criteria fall into a consideration set, which leads to a choice set.

At this point one can refer to consumer purchase intentions, i.e., those products/brands or other aspects of buying and consuming that a consumer (or household) is intending to carry out in the form of purchase decisions. However, one has to be aware that intervening variables may come into play between purchase intention and purchase decision. These include attitudes of other consumers, availability, and unexpected situational factors (e.g., with respect to income and employment), and may delay purchase decisions or cause them not to take place at all. For example, plans for a holiday may be cancelled due to unforeseen financial circumstances or ill health, and intention to purchase satellite television may be postponed because a washing machine suddenly breaks down and has to be replaced.

Purchase decisions are made with respect to products and services, stores, and methods of payment. Product decisions include choice of brands (including distributors' *versus* manufacturers' brands), reaction to price deals, and impulse purchase decisions. Decisions also relate to choice of store (to include location, personnel, atmosphere, car parking, services, credit availability), home shopping, mail order, and frequency of shopping.

Post-purchase Evaluation

After purchasing, consumers experience some level of satisfaction or dissatisfaction with each of their decisions. With respect to product/brand choice, if perceived product performance meets consumer expectations then he/she is satisfied; if performance does not meet expectations (i.e., disconfirmed expectations) then dissatisfaction occurs. Dissatisfaction leads to one of several post-purchase activities to include: returning the product, seeking information to confirm the choice made (*see* COGNITIVE DISSONANCE), or complaining (see Gilly & Hansen, 1985).

Further, results of purchasing activities can be evaluated either informally, among family and friends, or more formally, e.g., with respect to car performance and costs, comparison with others. Post-purchase evaluations provide the consumer with an idea of how well he/she is doing in the market and add to his/her state of experience, knowledge, and information to be used in future purchasing decisions.

When considering models of the consumer decision-making process it is important to note that not all the stages may be relevant, timing between stages varies, and feedback loops exist. Further, the extent to which a formal process does happen will depend on the extent of consumer involvement. One can consider a continuum of low–high involvement consumer decision-making. Products which are expensive, risky, reflect self-image, or have positive reference group influence (*see* INTERPERSONAL COMMUNICATIONS) may be referred to to extensive problem solving, i.e., active information search and evaluation. At the other end of a continuum are routine, low involvement (often re-purchase) situations with no motivated search for information (the costs are likely to outweigh the benefits), and the consumer proceeds on the basis of what he/she already knows. This is further developed by Assael (1987) who identified four types of consumer buying behavior based on the degree of buyer involvement and the degree of difference among brands. These are: *complex buying behavior*, when consumers are highly involved and there are significant differences between brands (e.g., personal computers); *dissonance-reducing buying behavior*, when consumers are highly involved in a purchase but see little difference between brands (e.g., carpets); *habitual buying behavior*, characterized by low consumer involvement and little difference between brands (e.g., petrol and commodities); and *variety seeking buying behavior*, with low involvement but significant differences between brands (e.g., biscuits, soap powders).

Bibliography

Assael, H. (1987). *Consumer behavior and marketing action*. Boston: Kent Publishing Co.
Bettman, J. R. (1979). *Information processing theory of consumer behavior*. Reading, MA: Addison Wesley.
Engel, J. F., Blackwell, R. D. & Miniard, P. W. (1990). *Consumer behavior* 6th edn, Orlando, FL: The Dryden Press. Chapters 17, 18, 19.
Gilly, M. C. & Hansen, R. W. (1985). Consumer complaint handling as a strategic marketing tool. *Journal of Consumer Marketing* Fall, 5–16.
Hawkins, D. I., Best, R. J. & Coney, K. A. (1992). Consumer behavior: Implications for marketing strategy, 5th edn, Homewood, IL: Irwin. Chapters 14, 15, 16, 17, 18.
Kotler, P. (1994). *Marketing management: Analysis, planning, implementation and control*, 8th edn, Prentice-Hall, pp. 193–201.
Loudon, D. L. & Della Bitta, A. J. (1993). *Consumer behavior*, 4th edn, McGraw-Hill Int., Chapters 15, 16, 17, 18.
Solomon, M. R. (1992). *Consumer behavior*. Needham Heights, MA: Allyn & Bacon. Chapter 8.
Wilkie, W. L. (1994). *Consumer behavior*, 3rd edn, New York: John Wiley. Chapters 17, 18, 19.

BARBARA LEWIS

consumer marketing   Consumer marketing refers to the buying of products and services for personal or household use, as opposed to buying by organizations. The implied alternative is BUSINESS-TO-BUSINESS MARKETING, although the distinction between the two areas is not entirely clear-cut (*see* BUSINESS-TO-BUSINESS MARKETING). The techniques of consumer marketing management dominate most standard marketing textbooks, with the result that specialized textbooks tend not to be exclusively devoted to consumer marketing in the same way as for business-to-business marketing. Indeed, the view of MARKETING MANAGEMENT presented in standard texts such as Kotler (1994) or McCarthy & Perreault (1993) is often seen as essentially synonymous with *consumer*, as opposed to business-to-business, marketing management (*see* MARKETING MANAGEMENT). More recently, however, consumer marketing, especially for services, has developed somewhat in nature and scope to include, in particular, some of the techniques more traditionally found in BUSINESS-TO-BUSINESS MARKETING, for example (*see* RELATIONSHIP MARKETING).

Consumer purchase decision-making is also generally held to be subject to the influence of "non-task" or "irrational" factors to a far greater extent than business-to-business marketing. CONSUMER BUYER BEHAVIOR is a major area for research in marketing and has involved the investigation of such areas as: individual decision-making influences (such as personality, perceptions, and attitudes); group decision-making influences (such as opinion leadership, reference groups, or lifestyle influences); and cultural influences on consumer behavior (*see* CONSUMER BUYER BEHAVIOR).

Bibliography

Kotler, P. (1994). *Marketing management: Analysis, planning, implementation and control*, 8th edn, Englewood Cliffs, NJ: Prentice-Hall.
McCarthy, E. J. & Perreault, R. (1993). *Basic marketing*, 11th edn, Homewood, IL: Irwin.

FIONA LEVERICK

consumer surplus   The difference between the maximum amount a consumer is willing to pay to buy a product (also called the consumer's reservation price) and the price actually paid is called the consumer's surplus. This measures how much consumers value a product beyond what they paid for it. In a market, consumer surplus is the area under the demand curve and above the price charged. This measures the benefit to consumers of having this product available and hence the benefits to society from the production of this good if there are no externalities in production or consumption.

When a firm raises its price above the MARGINAL COST OF PRODUCTION, those consumers who continue to buy the product pay a higher price and this represents a reduction in their consumer surplus. Since these consumers still purchase the product, it represents a transfer from the consumers to the firm. However, some consumers will not continue to buy the good at the higher price because the new price exceeds their reservation price. Since these consumers were willing to pay the cost to society of producing the good (the marginal cost) and do not receive it, they have lost consumer surplus. Moreover, the firm does not capture any of this lost surplus as profit because these consumers have left the market. Conceptually, the firm should be willing to produce this good and sell it for the marginal cost of production once the firm has earned its profits in the market. Since this makes the consumers who have left the market better off and the firm no worse off, it is a Pareto optimal allocation and so allocative efficiency would be improved. Because this exchange does not occur, the consumer surplus of those consumers who have left the market is lost and this is called DEAD-WEIGHT LOSS since no one in society recovers those lost benefits.

In a similar vein, when a firm considers introducing a new product, it is concerned about whether it can cover the costs of production, including the opportunity costs. If the firm is unable to cover these costs, the product will not be produced. Yet, it is possible that the benefits to society from producing the good (as measured by consumers' surplus) exceed the costs. The problem is that the firm cannot capture all the benefits to consumers when it cannot practice PRICE DISCRIMINATION and this can lead to less PRODUCT VARIETY than would be socially optimal.

Bibliography

Dixit, A. K. & Stiglitz J. E. (1977). Monopolistic competition and optimum product diversity. *American Economic Review*, **67**, 240–59.

Waterson, M. (1984). *Economic Theory of the Industry*. Cambridge: CUP.

Willig, R. D. (1976). Consumers' surplus without apology. *American Economic Review*, **66**, 589–97.

ROBERT E. MCAULIFFE

consumerism Consumerism involves those activities of government, business, independent organizations, and consumers themselves which help protect consumers against unfair or unethical business practices.

The main era of development for the consumerist movement was in the USA in the early 1960s when President John F. Kennedy presented his consumers' Bill of Rights to Congress in 1962. This Bill established the basic principles of consumerism, namely, the *right to safety*, to be protected against dangerous and unsafe products; the *right to be informed* and protected against fraudulent, deceitful, and misleading statements, advertisements, labels, etc. and to be educated on how to use financial resources wisely; the *right to choose* and be assured access to a variety of products and services at competitive prices – although when competition is not possible government regulation should be substituted; and the *right to be heard* by government and business regarding unsatisfactory or disappointing practices.

In addition, one of the most successful consumer groups was founded around this time. Ralph Nader's Public Citizen group lifted consumerism into a major social force, following publication of his book *Unsafe at Any Speed* (1965), which was a detailed examination of the automobile industry. Following similar investigations into meat processing and money lending, several laws were passed which established fairer practices. Consumer organizations have won battles for consumers in many other countries, e.g., in Scandinavia, Netherlands, France, Germany, Japan, and the UK, in a number of areas of business activity. For example, the practice of inertia selling which involved the sending of unsolicited goods to people was curbed in the

UK by laws passed in 1971 and 1975; and organizations such as the Better Business Bureau in the USA and the Consumers' Association in the UK have fought for truth in advertising, adequate food labeling of nutrition and ingredients, and the use of "sell-by" and "open-by" dates.

Consumerism can be seen as the ultimate expression of the MARKETING CONCEPT since it compels companies to think from the consumer's perspective. For example, environmental groups have raised consumer awareness of green issues and companies have responded to the opportunity by creating "green" products. One UK group, the Campaign for Real Ale (CAMRA), successfully ensured the existence of naturally-fermented beers which were in danger of being phased out by the major breweries. Several reasons have been given for the growth of consumerism in Western economies, such as a more impersonal marketplace, increased product complexity, more intrusive advertising, increasing two-earner families, mass media which are quick to publicize unethical questionable practices by marketers, and the emergence of less materialistic values in consumers (Hawkins & Best, 1995).

In one sense, there is a philosophical conflict between the existence of consumerism and the marketing concept, because if the marketing concept were operating properly, there should be no need for consumerism. However, the diversity of consumer needs means that it is virtually impossible to produce products which satisfy every individual's needs. Secondly, organizations must produce goods within certain cost parameters to ensure profit. Thirdly, not all organizations have embraced or implemented the marketing concept fully. In practice, these three considerations explain the existence of both consumerism and the marketing concept.

Bibliography

Bloom, P. N. & Greyser, G. A. (1981). The maturity of consumerism. *Harvard Business Review*, Nov.–Dec., **59**, 130–139.

Hawkins, D. I., Best, R. J. & Coney, K. A. (1995). *Consumer behavior, implications for marketing strategy*, 6th edn, Boston, MA: Irwin. Chapter 21.

Nader, R. (1965). *Unsafe at any speed*. Public Citizen group.

VINCE MITCHELL

contestable markets As originally presented by Baumol, Panzar and Willig (1982), perfectly contestable markets represented an alternative and more general benchmark for evaluating MARKET STRUCTURE than PERFECT COMPETITION. In perfectly contestable markets, new firms can enter and exit an industry costlessly and at no disadvantage relative to existing firms, and this potential competition severely limits the pricing options of existing firms. Costless entry and exit at no disadvantage imply that factors such as ASYMMETRIC INFORMATION, SUNK COSTS, FIRST-MOVER ADVANTAGES and STRATEGIC BEHAVIOR by existing firms have no effect on the entrant's decision to enter the industry. Since entrants are at no disadvantage relative to incumbent firms, whenever existing firms charge a price sufficient to generate economic profits, entry will occur driving economic profits to zero (*see* ECONOMIC PROFIT). Costless exit and entry also mean that the entrant can enter the market, earn economic profits, and exit before the incumbent firm can retaliate, sometimes referred to as "hit and run" entry. For hit and run entry to succeed, entrants must be able to enter the market and earn profits before the existing firm retaliates. This means that prices must adjust more slowly than output in the market.

According to Baumol, Panzar and Willig, perfectly contestable markets result in efficient production even in those cases where perfect competition might fail, as in a natural monopoly. A natural monopoly faces ECONOMIES OF SCALE where the average cost of production is falling in the range of output demanded by the market. Since average cost is declining, the marginal cost curve must lie below it and this means that the marginal cost pricing required by perfect competition would not allow the firm to cover its total costs. Perfect contestability requires that the existing firm(s) be able to cover total costs without attracting entry and so a natural monopoly would be forced by potential competition to set its price at its lowest average cost of production.

Perfect competition requires large numbers of small firms producing homogeneous products, among other conditions, to achieve efficiency. Perfectly contestable markets emphasize the importance of *potential* competitors rather than existing competitors and do not require DIMINISHING RETURNS in production. Another important point Baumol, Panzar and Willig raise is that existing firms must produce efficiently or they will be vulnerable to "hit and run" entry by potential entrants. This means that certain inefficiencies attributable to monopoly or oligopoly such as X-efficiency or inefficient organization cannot occur in perfectly contestable markets since entry will force these firms to become efficient or drive them out of business.

Some researchers have argued that few markets are perfectly contestable and that this analytical approach is less general than might at first appear. For example, Shepherd (1984) observed that perfect contestability requires *ultra* free entry and no exit barriers (no sunk costs). He asserted this was more restrictive than the requirements of perfect competition because in a sufficiently small interval of time, firms always have sunk costs; see Weitzman (1983). Furthermore, for potential entry to discipline existing firms to the extent Baumol, Panzar and Willig claim, entry must not only be ultra free but *total* in that entrants could replace the existing firms. Yet if entrants can replace existing firms, the assumption employed by Baumol, Panzar and Willig that existing firms do not react to entry is very restrictive and if entrants are small, they cannot discipline existing firms to the extent the theory suggests. For Shepherd, these and other concerns lead him to believe that the traditional industry analysis of industrial organization with its focus on the internal market rivalry and interactions between firms is more appropriate.

Bibliography

Baumol, W. J., Panzar, J. C. & Willig, R. D. (1982). *Contestable Markets and the Theory of Industry Structure*. San Diego: Harcourt Brace Jovanovich.
Baumol, W. J. (1982). Contestable markets: an uprising in the theory of industry structure. *American Economic Review*, 72, 1–15.
Schwartz, M. & Reynolds, R. J. (1983). Contestable markets: an uprising in the theory of industry structure: comment. *American Economic Review*, 73, 488–90.
Shepherd, W. G. (1984). 'Contestability' vs. competition. *American Economic Review*, 74, 572–87.
Weitzman, M. L. (1983). Contestable markets: an uprising in the theory of industry structure: comment. *American Economic Review*, 73, 486–7.

ROBERT E. MCAULIFFE

contingent claims In layman's language, a contingent-claims market can be understood by comparing it with betting in a horse race. The state of the world corresponds to how the various horses will place, and a claim corresponds to a bet that a horse will win. If your horse comes in, you get paid in proportion to the number of tickets you purchased. But *ex ante* you do not know which state of the world will occur. The only way to guarantee payment in all states of the world is to bet on all the horses.

The state-preference model is an alternative way of modeling decision under uncertainty. Consumers trade contingent claims, which are rights to consumption, if and only if a particular state of the world occurs. In the insurance case, in one state of the world the consumer suffers a loss and in the other, she or he does not; however, *ex ante* he does not know which state will occur, but wants to be sure to have consumption goods available in each state.

In a corporate context Deman (1994) identified basically two theories of takeovers: (1) agency theory, and (2) incomplete contingent-claims market. The latter theory hypothesizes that takeovers result from the lack of a complete state-contingent claims market. The main argument can be summarized briefly. If complete state-contingent claims markets exist, then shareholders' valuations of any state distribution of returns are identical (because of one price for every state-contingent claim) and hence, they agree on a value-maximizing production plan. However, in the absence of complete-state contingent claims markets, any change in technologies (i.e. a change in the state distribution of payoffs) is not, in general, valued identically by all shareholders. Thus, majority support for such a change in plan may be lacking. Takeover is a contingent contract which enables a simultaneous change in technologies and portfolio holdings.

Merton (1990) describes some commercial examples of contingent claims which include: futures and options contracts based on commodities, stock indices, interest rates, and exchange rates, etc. Other examples are Arrow–Debreu (AW) securities, which play a crucial role in general equilibrium theory (GE), and options. Under AW conditions, the pricing of contingent claims is closely related to the optimal solutions to portfolio planning problems. Thus, contingent claims analysis (CCA) plays a central role in achieving its results by integrating the option-pricing theory with the optimal portfolio planning problem of agents under uncertainty.

One of the salient features of CCA is that many of its valuation formulae are by and large or completely independent of agents' preferences and expected returns, which are some times referred to as risk neutral valuation relationships. Contributions to CCA have adopted both continuous and multiperiod discrete time models. However, most of them are dominated by continuous time, using a wide range of sophisticated mathematical techniques of stochastic calculus and martingale theory. There are several other facets of contingent claims, such as the option price theory of Black and Scholes (1973), and Merton (1977), general equilibrium and pricing by arbitrage illustrated in Cox et al. (1981), and transaction costs in Harrison and Kreps (1979). CCA, from its origin in option pricing and valuation of corporate liabilities, has become one of the most powerful analysis tools of intertemporal GE theory under uncertainty.

Bibliography

Black, F. & Scholes, M. S. (1973). The pricing of options and corporate liabilities. *Journal of Political Economy*, 81, 637–59.

Cox, J. C., Ingersoll, J. E. & Ross, S. A. (1981). The relationship between forward prices and future prices. *Journal of Financial Economics*, 9, 321–46.

Deman, S. (1994). The theory of corporate takeover bids: a subgame perfect approach. *Managerial Decision Economics*. Special Issue on Aspects of Corporate Governance, 15, 383–97.

Harrison, J. M. & Kreps, D. M. (1979). Martingale and arbitrage in multi-period securities markets. *Journal of Economic Theory*, 20, 381–408.

Merton, R. C. (1977). On the pricing of contingent claims and the Modigliani–Miller theorem. *Journal of Financial Economics*, 5, 241–49.

Merton, R. C. (1990). *Continuous-time finance*. Cambridge, MA: Basil Blackwell.

SURESH DEMAN

contract manufacturing   A method of entering a foreign market in which a company uses manufacturers in foreign countries to make (or assemble) their product and distribute it through the foreign manufacturer's existing marketing channels. Thus, entry to the country is achieved with the assistance of local companies using proven marketing channels. Although the cost of this type of method is usually a substantial portion of the product revenues, it allows a company to test the market for its goods and become more familiar with doing business overseas.

see also **Market entry strategies**

Bibliography

Deresky, Helen (1994). *International management*. 1st edn, New York: HarperCollins.

JOHN O'CONNELL

control   The concept of control is of such wideranging significance and usage in almost all fields of inquiry, that it almost defies definition. The core of the concept is represented by the study of cybernetics as the application of an operator to effect an activity in relation to a standard. Note that this does not need to imply conformance to a standard – control can be effected to depart from as well as to maintain a standard. The essential notion is that some desired criterion exists or can be conceived, and that an agent or operator can effect an activity (behavior, mechanism, strategy, etc.) with reference to it.

In psychology, the basic cybernetic model was influentially employed by Miller, Galanter, and Pribram (1960) as a goal-oriented alternative to behaviorist models of human action. In everyday tasks, it was argued, cognition and intent effect behaviors through TOTE cycles: Test-Operate-Test-Exit. The control sequence is exited when the results of behavior meet the test standard via feedback (e.g., perception). This model has been widely adopted and elaborated to explain a variety of human functions, including learning, task behaviors, intention, and self-regulation. Control theory typically conceives of nested cycles from the most basic, and largely unconscious, perceptual–motor operations up to the most strategic or conceptual levels (Lord & Levy, 1994). Applications of control theory are used to diagnose and correct dysfunctions in various contexts, such as errors and skill acquisition.

Within organizational behavior the concept of control has wide relevance. Feedback processes and feedback seeking are of particular importance (Ashford & Cummings, 1983), since both feedback and standards are required by organizational control systems. These concepts are especially important in the field of MOTIVATION, since goals and intentions mobilize control attempts. Of particular interest here are individual differences in control-related motivation, such as achievement, power (*see* POWER) (Heckhausen, 1991), and LOCUS OF CONTROL. Although the strength of need for control varies across individuals (*see* PERSONALITY) it has long been recognized that a drive for competence is a normal human characteristic. Indeed, so pervasive is this motive, coupled with the cognitive disposition to make causal attributions in chance situations, that it is commonplace for people to believe they have more scope for control than is actually feasible: the so-called "control illusion" (Langer, 1983). This is responsible for many typical errors of management and LEADERSHIP (*see* ATTRIBUTION).

At the more general level of business operations, control theory can be of great practical value in understanding system failures and how to enhance management effectiveness (*see* ORGANIZATIONAL EFFECTIVENESS; SYSTEMS THEORY). The notion of a control loop (see figure 1) can be applied to system performance at any level to inquire whether standards are appropriate, whether operations affect behavior, whether results meet standards, whether sensors are tuned to detect variances and whether they are positioned at appropriate positions in the system. The results of this analysis can be used to reform any of the elements, e.g., DECISION MAKING, environmental scanning, stategic goals, operating standards, measurement methods, REWARDS and disincentives, resourcing and sources of disturbance, or to question the constitution and focus of the control system overall. The model is thus a powerful aid to managerial control at various levels – from the analysis and regulation of individual motivation to the STRATEGIC MANAGEMENT of the firm. The field has a potentially rich future, in which one can expect to see increasingly sophisticated computer modeling of control systems as an aid to their analysis, design, and reform.

Bibliography

Ashford, S. J. & Cummings, L. L. (1983). Feedback as an individual resource: Personal strategies of creating information. Organizational Behavior and Human Performance, 32, 370–398.

Heckhausen, H. (1991). Motivation and action. New York: Springer-Verlag.

Langer, E. J. (1983). The psychology of control. Beverly Hills, CA: Sage.

Lord, R. G. & Levy, P. E. (1994). Moving from cognition to action: A control theory perspective Applied Psychology: An International Review, 43, 335–398.

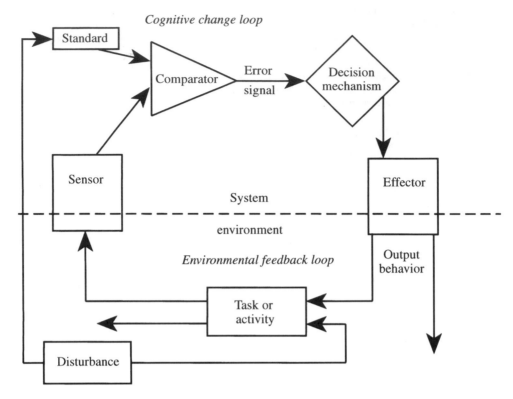

Figure 1 Basic negative feedback loop in a control system
Source: R. G. Lord and P. E. Levy (1994). Reprinted by permission of Lawrence Erlbaum Associates Ltd., Hove, UK.

Miller, G. A., Galanter, E. & Pribram, K. H. (1960). Plans and the structure of behavior. New York: Holt, Rinehart & Winston.

NIGEL NICHOLSON

control issues in foreign holdings As a result of disparate and changing competitive, market and regulatory circumstances, many organizations have been pressured to adapt their resources and objectives. Such organizations have internationalized some or all of the activities comprising their value chains, often through full or partial ownership of foreign operations. Efforts to effectively manage foreign holdings may be complicated, however, by the increased strategic and operational complexity associated with coordinating and controlling activities across multiple national and competitive environments (Bartlett and Ghoshal, 1995).

Control is the process by which one entity uses mechanisms of a formal nature (e.g. ownership, organizational structure) or informal nature to influence the behavior and output of another entity (Geringer and Hebert, 1989). Control plays a critical role in determining an organization's capacity for achieving its strategic objectives, since it affects the organization's ability to monitor, coordinate and integrate the activities of its various business operations in a manner consistent with critical organizational and environmental variables. To fully achieve their objectives, organizations must therefore design and implement appropriate and effective control systems within and among their foreign holdings.

Three complementary and interdependent dimensions comprise the foundation of an effective control system: (a) the *focus* of control (i.e. the scope of activities over which the organization seeks to exercise control); (b) the *extent* or degree of control sought over these focal activities; and (c) the *mechanisms* used to exercise control (Geringer and Hebert, 1989). An organization must simultaneously consider all three of these dimensions in order to design and implement an effective control system; otherwise the organization's competitiveness and prospects for attainment of its objectives may be compromised.

Bibliography

Bartlett, C. A. & Ghoshal, S. (Eds) (1995). *Transnational Management: Text, Cases, and Readings*, **2nd edn**, Burr Ridge, IL: Richard D. Irwin.

Geringer, J. M. & Hebert, L. (1989). Control and performance of international joint ventures. *Journal of International Business Studies*, **20**, 234–54.

J. MICHAEL GERINGER

convertibles A convertible is a bond with an option to exchange the bond into "new" shares of common stock of the issuing company under specified terms and conditions. These include the conversion period and the conversion ratio. The conversion period is the period during which the bond may be converted into shares. The conversion ratio is the number of shares received per convertible. The conversion price, which is the effective price paid for the common stock, is the ratio of the face value of the convertible and the conversion ratio. Convertibles almost always have a call provision built in. Special types of convertibles are mandatory convertible bonds, exchangeable bonds, and LYONS.

A convertible is much like a bond with a warrant attached. However, this concept is not very useful for valuation purposes. An important problem is that the exercise price of the warrant (the conversion price) is paid by surrendering the accompanying bond. Therefore the exercise price changes through time. The fact that most convertibles are callable creates another valuation problem. Brennan and Schwartz (1980) have developed a model which takes all these factors into account.

Motives for the issuance of convertibles can be divided into traditional and modern motives. Traditional motives are that convertibles are (1) a deferred sale of stock at an attractive price and (2) a cheap form of capital (Brigham, 1966). These motives are criticized by Brennan and Schwartz (1988). The first motive is based on the fact that normally the conversion price is above the market price of the underlying stock at the issuance date. However, the conversion price should in fact be compared to the underlying stock price at the exercise date. If the underlying stock price is higher than the conversion price, the company suffers an opportunity loss. If it is lower than the conversion price, the conversion right will not be exercised. The second motive is based on the fact that the coupon rate of a convertible is lower than the coupon rate of an ordinary bond. However, if the cost of the conversion right is taken into account it can be demonstrated that the cost of convertibles is relatively high (see Veld (1992) for a numerical example). The cost of convertibles is neither a reason to issue, nor a reason to refrain from issuing convertibles. Its cost is just an adequate compensation for the risk involved in its investment.

Modigliani and Miller have demonstrated that in perfect markets the financing decision of the firm is irrelevant for its market value. Therefore, modern motives for the issuance of convertibles are based on market imperfections. Brennan and Schwartz (1988) argue that convertibles are relatively insensitive to the risk of the issuing company. If the risk increases, the value of the bond part decreases, but the value of the warrant part increases, because the value of a warrant is an increasing function of the volatility. This makes it easier for bond issuers and purchasers to come to terms when they disagree about the riskiness of the firm. Because of the insensitivity towards risk, convertibles may result in lower agency costs between share and bondholders. Bondholders are less concerned about the possibility that shareholders attract risky projects. Because of their conversion right they also participate in the value created if risky projects are undertaken (Green, 1984). Other motives, based on imperfections, include the reduction of flotation costs compared to the case where the firm raises debt now and equity later, and the possibility to "polish" the company's financial accounts by recording the convertible as debt on the balance sheet (Veld, 1992).

With regard to the optimal moment to call convertibles, Ingersoll (1977) has demonstrated that this moment occurs when the conversion value, this is the value of the common stock to be received in the conversion exchange, equals the call price. However, in an empirical study he finds that in practice the calls show a delay. On average the conversion value of the bonds was 43.9 percent above the call price.

Exchangeable Bonds

An exchangeable bond may be converted into existing shares of the same or an alternative company. It is much like a convertible, except that in a convertible, the bond may be converted into "new" shares. Analogously, the conversion right of an exchangeable bond is equivalent to a covered warrant. An example of a large issue of exchangeable debt is the IBM US$300 million offering in January 1986, which is convertible into the common stock of Intel Corporation. An analysis of exchangeable debt is made by Ghosh et al. (1990).

LYONS

Liquid yield option notes (LYONS) are zero–coupon, callable, puttable convertibles. This security was created by Merrill Lynch in 1985. It was first issued by Waste Management Inc. in spring 1985. A number of subsequent issues were made in the United States. McConnell and Schwartz (1986) have developed a valuation model, which takes all the above mentioned characteristics of LYONS into account.

Mandatory Convertible Bonds

Mandatory convertible bonds are convertibles which may be converted during the conversion period and which are automatically converted at the end of the conversion period.

Bibliography

Brennan, M. J. & Schwartz, E. S. (1980). Analyzing convertible bonds. *Journal of Financial and Quantitative Analysis*, 4, 907–29.

Brennan, M. J. & Schwartz, F. S. (1988). The case for convertibles. *Journal of Applied Corporate Finance* Summer, 55–64.

Brigham, E. F. (1966). An analysis of convertible debentures: theory and some empirical evidence. *The Journal of Finance*, 21, 35–54.

Ghosh, C., Varma, R. & Woolridge, J. R. (1990). An analysis of exchangeable debt offers. *Journal of Financial Economics*, 19, 251–63.

Green, R. C. (1984). Investment incentives, debt, and warrants. *Journal of Financial Economics*, 13, 115–36.

Ingersoll, J. (1977). An examination of corporate call policies on convertible securities. *The Journal of Finance*, 32, 463–78.

McConnell, J. J. & Schwartz, E. S. (1986). LYON taming. *The Journal of Finance*, 41, 561–76.

Veld, C. (1992). *Analysis of equity warrants as investment and finance instruments*. Tilburg, Netherlands: Tilburg University Press.

CHRIS VELD

cooperation agreement When there is a need in one country for resources in order to produce products and the availability of those resources in another country a cooperation agreement may be in order. For example, country A needs electrical power to produce clothing and country B has excess electrical power but needs clothing. An agreement is made for country B to supply power in return for future payment in clothing that country A is then able to produce.

JOHN O'CONNELL

coordination center A financial clearing house to handle the needs of an organization. A coordination center is usually located in a tax haven or other site which offers low operating costs and favorable tax regulations. The center is a centralized finance and planning unit with responsibility for handling financial transactions of a region or worldwide operations of the company; providing a central location for all administrative processes of the company (accounting, information systems, insurance and self-insurance administration, and other administrative activities); and the planning function related to all of its activities.

Bibliography

Celi, L. J. & Rutizer, B. (1991). *Global cash management.* 1st edn, New York: Harper Business (HarperCollins).

JOHN O'CONNELL

copyright Protection for written or artistic work given by a government for a specific period of time. Items subject to copyright are literary works, works of art, musical scores, stories or words to a song; labels; and other written works. It is very common for citizens of some countries to use copyrighted works without authorization from the copyright holder. The unauthorized use is commonly referred to as pirating or copying and is illegal in most countries of the world. Pirating of copyrighted works costs copyright holders billions of dollars in lost revenues each year. Any holder of a copyright should strongly consider protecting that right in as many countries as possible. Several international agreements have been reached which protect copyrights and other intellectual property rights (this term also includes patents and other rights as well).

see also **Berne Convention for the Protection of Literary and Artistic Works; Universal copyright convention**

JOHN O'CONNELL

core businesses Made popular as a theme in the late 1980s, many Western companies, especially in the USA, found that their strategies of DIVERSIFICATION had not achieved the improvement in profit performance that was expected. Successful corporations were identified as usually having developed a "core" business around which related activities had been developed. In companies that had adopted a RELATED DIVERSIFIED STRATEGY new activities had been added, usually as a result of common technology or skill, mode of marketing and distribution, and the like. Financial SYNERGY was not significantly recognized, although in practice it was an integral component, in the strategic development of some conglomerates. Many such diversification moves occurred by acquisition.

During the 1980s the initial impact of the research on corporate excellence was to indicate that successful firms were those in which some logic occurred in diversification moves. As a result of unsuccessful acquisitions (*see* ACQUISITION STRATEGY), these were either sold or floated off and the proceeds returned to shareholders to avoid predatory attacks on the parent.

In addition, the significant take-up of VALUE-BASED PLANNING focusing on shareholder value encouraged the divestment of businesses contributing negative value. Interestingly, these short-term pressures from the stock market, which only influenced Western companies, were largely absent in Japan, where the KEIRETSU STRUCTURE provided a stability which could actually permit firms to redefine their core business on a regular basis. As a result, Japanese firms and their Keiretsu groups have increased their degree of diversification. Similar patterns of corporate development can also be observed amongst the Korean chaebol (*see* CHAEBOL STRUCTURE) and large businesses owned and/or managed by Chinese in the Pacific Rim.

Bibliography

Peters, T. & Waterman, R. (1982). *In search of excellence.* New York: Harper & Row.

DEREK F. CHANNON

core competences Core competences are " . . .a set of differentiated skills, complementary assets, and routines that provide the basis for a firm's competitive capacities and sustainable advantage in a particular business" (Teece et al., 1990). They are " . . .the specific tangible and intangible assets of the firm assembled into integrated clusters, which span individuals and groups to enable distinctive activities to be performed" (Winterschied, 1994).

The concept of core competences is associated with the resource-based view of the firm. Rather than emphasizing (as in traditional approaches to strategy) products and markets, and focusing competitive analysis on product portfolios, the resource-based approach regards firms as bundles of resources which can be configured to provide firm-specific advantages. Prahalad & Hamel (1990) characterize the difference of approach as between a "portfolio of competences versus a portfolio of businesses". The resource-based model is able to address a number of issues which mainstream strategic analysis has found difficult. Amongst these issues are diversification (see Mahoney & Pandian, 1992), and the changes in competitive environment that most firms are experiencing (globalization, deregulation, technological change, and quality), which mean that traditional sources of competitive advantage are being eroded (Hamel & Prahalad, 1994).

The term "core competences" is most closely associated with the work of Hamel & Prahalad. Other terms which are used include intangible resources (Hall, 1992), strategic capabilities (Stalk & Shulman, 1992), strategic assets (Dierickx & Cool, 1989; Amit & Schoemaker, 1993), firm resources (Barney, 1991), core capabilities (Leonard-Barton, 1992), and distinctive competences (Andrews, 1971).

Core competences are typically characterized as:

- unique to the firm
- sustainable because they are hard to imitate or to substitute
- conferring some kind of functionality to the customer (in the case of products and some services) or to the provider (in the case of other services)
- partly the product of learning and, hence, as incorporating tacit as well as explicit knowledge
- generic because they are incorporated into a number of products and/or processes

Recognition of the potential significance of core competences for competitive advantage was stimulated by research such as that by Rumelt (1974), which showed that of nine potential diversification strategies, the two which were most successful were those which were built on an existing skill or resource base within the firm.

Hamel & Prahalad have distinguished between three types of competences: market access, integrity-related, and functionally related. Market access competences bring the firm into contact with its customers; integrity-related competences enable the firm to do things to a higher quality, better and/or faster than its competitors; and functionally related competences confer distinctive customer benefits.

Within the literature and debate on the subject, there is a division between what Klavans (1994) has characterized as technological and institutional views of competences. The former focuses on "objective" capabilities, such as Honda's knowledge of engine design; while the latter focus on, for example, managerial processes for organizational learning. Leonard-Barton (1992) goes further than this. She defines what she describes as a core capability, as a knowledge set which has four dimensions: employees' knowledge and skills; knowledge and skills embodied into technical systems; managerial systems which enable the creation of knowledge; and the values and norms associated with the knowledge and its creation. She argues that this fourth dimension is often ignored. In so arguing, she shares the view of, amongst others, Child (1972), that the identification of core competences is, at some level, a political process.

The concept has proved to be attractive both to industrialists and to business strategists. At a time when companies are increasingly homogeneous in terms of technologies, regulatory environments, and location, the suggestion that competitive advantage can be won through the configuration and application of corporate level resources has great appeal. Writing in 1992, the *Economist Intelligence Unit* identified the following uses for the concept:

- to guide diversification through the identification of basic strengths
- to drive revitalization through the identification of core business areas
- to guard competitiveness through an earlier recognition of key skills (many firms realize what they have lost through outsourcing or divestment only when it is too late)
- to provide a focus and justification for R&D in the development and maintenance of core competences
- to inform the selection of strategic alliances which build on complementary core competences
- to balance Strategic Business Unit (SBU) objectives with company objectives

This relationship between the center and SBUs is a critical issue in the management of core competences. By definition, core competences exist beyond individual SBUs. They are underlying strengths which inform, support, and differentiate the firm's business across its SBUs. Since they are not the only source of competitive advantage, there is the potential for conflict and tension between SBU objectives and corporate objectives. To deploy core competences effectively requires, at some level, cross-SBU consensus on objectives and practice. For many firms who have followed the path of increasing SBU autonomy, achieving such consensus is a major challenge in the management and/or exploitation of core competences. Yet without such a consensus firms cannot exploit, maintain, and protect their competences.

Other challenges relate to the identification, development, and maintenance of core competences. There are significant difficulties involved in the identification of core competences. At one level, firms all too easily proclaim one or more core competences. This proclamation is usually the result of internal reflection rather than external comparisons, and can lead to firms attempting to protect an advantage which they subsequently find that all their competitors share. A second difficulty is the scope of core competences. One of the most widely cited examples of a competence is Honda's expertise in engines. But, what exactly does this expertise consist of? The issue in identification is the level of specificity which should be employed. Is it sufficient to say Honda has a core competence in engine design, or should the identification of a core competence try to delve deeper into what it is about Honda's engine design that provides them with advantage; or, perhaps more significantly, what it is about the way in which they manage their engine design expertise that provides the advantage? This issue of scope is an obstacle for many firms in the identification of their competences. Prahalad & Hamel (1990) recommend three tests to help identify core competences. A core competence should: first, provide potential access to a wide range of markets; second, make a significant contribution to the perceived customer benefits of the end product; and, third, be difficult for competitors to imitate.

This leads to the challenges of development. Acquisitions, alliances, and licensing may all play a critical role. In turn, this raises issues about the capacity of the organization to learn, but the process of learning is one of the least discussed elements of core competence management. Competences take time to develop (Dierickx & Cool, 1989) which necessitates a longer-term and committed approach to strategic direction-setting. Such an approach is often difficult in the current turbulent environment. Firms need to engage in long-term visioning about where they might want to be in 10–20 years' time, and about the competences which they will need to deliver this vision (Hamel & Prahalad, 1994).

The key issue in the maintenance of core competences is who "owns" them within the firm. Given that they cross SBUs, who is responsible for their continued development and use? They are all too easily lost through being taken for granted, outsourced, or starved of development resources. A related issue is their longevity: core competences do not last for ever. Firms need to review their competency portfolio on an ongoing basis in order to maintain and retain only those which continue to provide advantage.

see also **Strategic core competences**

Bibliography

Amit, R. & Schoemaker, P. J. H. (1993). Strategic assets and organisational rent. *Strategic Management Journal*, 14, 33–46.

Andrews, K. R. (1971). *The concept of corporate strategy*. Homewood, IL: Irwin.

Barney, J. B. (1991). Firm resources and sustained competitive advantage. *Journal of Management*, 17, 99–120.

Child, J. L. (1972). Organisational structure, environment and performance: the role of strategic choice. *Sociology*, 6, 1–22.

Dierickx, I. & Cool, K. (1989). Asset stock accumulation and sustainability of competitive advantage. *Management Science*, 35, 1504–14.

Economist Intelligence Unit (1992). *Building core competences in a global economy*. Research report no. 1-12. New York: *Economist* Intelligence Unit.

Hall, R. (1992). The strategic analysis of intangible resources. *Strategic Management Journal*, 13, 135–44.

Hamel, G. & Prahalad, C. K. (1994). *Competing for the future*. Cambridge, MA: Harvard Business School Press.

Klavans, R. (1994). The measurement of a competitor's core competence. In G. Hamel & A. Heene (eds), *Competence-based competition*. Chichester: John Wiley.

Leonard-Barton, D. (1992). Core capabilities and core rigidities: a paradox in managing new product development. *Strategic Management Journal*, 13.

Mahoney, J. T. & Pandian, J. R. (1992). The resource-based view within the conversation of strategic management. *Strategic Management Journal*, 13, 363–80.

Prahalad, C. K. & Hamel, G. (1990). The core competence of the corporation. *Harvard Business Review*, 68, 79–91.

Rumelt, R. P. (1974). *Strategy, structure and economic performance*. Cambridge, MA: Harvard University Press.

Stalk, G., Evans, P. & Shulman, L. (1992). Competing on capabilities: the new rules of corporate strategy. *Harvard Business Review*, 70, 57–69.

Teece, D. J., Pisano, G. & Shuen, A. (1990). *Firm capabilities, resources and the concept of strategy*. Consortium on Competitiveness and Co-operation Working Party no. 90-9. Berkeley, CA: Center for Research in Management, University of California, Berkeley.

Winterschied, B. C. (1994). Building capability from within: the insiders' view of core competence. In G. Hamel & A. Heene (eds), *Competence-based competition*. Chichester: John Wiley.

DOROTHY GRIFFITHS

core process Such a process is defined as a set of linked activities that take an input and transform it to create an output which is of value to the customers of the process. The concept of horizontal activity flows forms the basis for business process re-engineering. Traditional business was organized by functional departments that might include production, procurement, logistics, sales, marketing, accounts, and technology. Each department undertook elements of work which was then passed on to another department, often with responsibilities passing upwards within each department before responsibility was passed to the next, and then coming down into the lower levels of the business for operational action. This upward *and* downward activity led to inefficiencies, slow speed, and possibly poor levels of customer satisfaction. The contrast between the business system and the core process business method is illustrated in figure 1.

To eliminate the inefficiencies of this vertical up and down movement, to reduce time within the corporation, and to reduce costs by removing unnecessary organizational layers, the concept of viewing the corporation as a series of horizontal flows has been conceived in the West. It has become exceptionally fashionable in recent years, in the guise of re-engineering, business process re-design, transformation, and core process re-design and has led companies to adopt the cross-functional form of organization. In many cases, adopting the concept has led to dramatic breakthroughs in cost, time, and quality. There are also high levels of failure for a variety of reasons.

The concept of core processes is the key to the introduction of re-engineering. There are many processes within the corporation, but only a small number will be critical or "core." These may vary somewhat between organizations but, usually, in re-engineering projects the corporation reorganizes around three to five critical processes. Those selected within the individual corporation will be focused on one or more of the critical strategic

CORE PROCESS

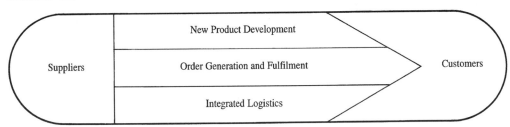

BUSINESS SYSTEM

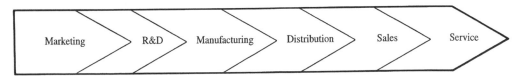

Figure 1 The core process versus business system approach.
Source: McKinsey & Co. (1991).

factors that determine competitive success. Stated in terms of time, quality of product and/or service, and cost, they should become faster in time-to-market, and yield improved on-time delivery and reduced administrative costs. For manufacturing companies, core processes will often include:

- product design and development
- procurement
- logistics
- manufacture
- despatch and shipment

Each core process will usually involve a number of key activities which cut across the traditional functional vertical activities of the corporation. For example, the integrated logistics core process for a consumer goods company includes forecasting, purchasing, manufacturing, and distribution to the wholesaler through the retailer to the ultimate consumer. Some may be similar across industries, such as new product development where time-to-market might be critical. Others may be industry-specific.

The achievement of breakthrough performance gains requires the introduction of a disciplined and phased approach. McKinsey and Company advocates a five-phase approach, as set out below.

Phase 1: Identifying Processes

Core process redesign requires corporations to re-think their value chains and re-evaluate their organizational structures. The identification and definition of core processes is therefore an initial and critical activity, requiring creativity and effort. McKinsey have identified a number of principles that are useful in defining core processes:

- A core process should address major strategic directions and problems in terms of competitive position, and should be readily recognizable to customers and suppliers.
- All major processes and information flows affecting throughput time, total cost, and quality should be included. This involves capturing major interdependencies and identifying any unnecessary functions and systems that can be eliminated.
- The focus should be defined at high enough levels such that re-design can yield "breakthrough" improvements.
- The core process view of the corporation seeks to optimize the interdependent activities and functions within a core process. Some functions such as manufacturing may form part of more than one core process.
- The same core processes may not be core for every company.

Phase 2: Defining Performance Requirements

Each core process should address one or two objectives of competitive success which should be defined in terms of key performance requirements. These will usually be strategic rather than merely financial, covering areas such as time, quality, service, and new product success rates. These key performance indicators also need to be projected forward and any gap between current and required

performance clearly identified. This requires evaluating these gaps by BENCHMARKING against the best.

Phase 3: Pinpointing Problems

When performance gaps have been identified, a detailed diagnostic study needs to be undertaken to seek out the causes and so identify opportunities for change. This involves a detailed PROCESS MAPPING and information flows, and an analysis of the existing information and technical systems architecture. An understanding of the existing systems architecture is essential, since improvements in core processes almost invariably involve heavy investment in information technology. However, few corporations can consider changing their key information processing in one go; nor would this be practicable. Prioritization of any changes is therefore essential.

The detailed mapping will identify a large number of process and systems problems, the causes of which contribute to performance gaps. These problems, too, need to be prioritized and addressed. Many of these problems may seem small, but cumulatively they add up.

Phase 4: Developing a Vision

This phase has the twin objectives of developing a long-term re-design vision and a set of specific change initiatives. It begins by identifying options and creating a master plan. After the options have been reviewed, a set of specific long-term and short-term initiatives are selected that address all the key elements of work processes information systems and organization design.

Phase 5: Making It Happen

Once specific initiatives have been defined, a detailed roll-out needs to be developed to ensure that improvement opportunities are achieved. Many initiatives are usually involved in this process. To minimize risk many of these will need to be tested by experimentation. This will involve many individuals throughout the business or corporation. To reduce fears and to encourage change, it is essential to adequately communicate about the initiatives and to achieve a number of "quick wins." These both stimulate longer-term initiatives and also provide the performance gains to pay for the change process. The sequencing of change is essential. Launching initiatives in waves helps to reduce risk and allows the organization to add skills and capabilities. Further progress against key initiatives can be monitored against planned time frames, costs, and estimated benefits.

Bibliography

Kaplan, R. B. & Murdock, L. (1991). Core process redesign. *McKinsey Quarterly* no. 2, 27–43.

Johansson, H. J., McHugh, P., Pendlebury, A. J. & Wheeler, W. A. III (1993). *Business process reengineering*. Chichester: John Wiley.

McManus, J. J. (1994). *An implementation guide on how to reengineer your business*. Cheltenham, UK: Stanley Thornes.

DEREK F. CHANNON

corporate governance   In the *broad sense* "corporate governance" is concerned with those decisions made by the senior executives of a firm and the impacts of their decisions on various stakeholder groups. Normally these executives are the officers in charge of specific functional areas (finance, marketing, etc.) and, depending on the corporate structure, could also include officers in charge of geographic areas or major product lines. In the *narrow sense* "corporate governance" refers only to the activities of the actual board of directors. In this sense the term refers to the relationship between the board and the firm.

The ethical issues in corporate governance are more subtle than in many of the other areas of firm/stakeholder relations. The reason for this is that, following a strict interpretation of neoclassical economics, it is possible to make an argument that would *favor* the "exploitation" of various stakeholder groups such as customers or employees if the shareholders would thus benefit. Many products entail a certain degree of risk to the consumer. For example, it is all but impossible to manufacture an automobile that is 100 percent safe. From a neoclassical perspective the firm should increase the safety of a product until the marginal costs of more safety equals the marginal benefits of more safety. Thus, from the neoclassical perspective the level of safety built into a product should be a function of the costs (such as bad public relations, lost sales, costs of lawsuits and regulations, and so on) and benefits (generally higher profits) to shareholders.

According to a strict reading of neoclassical economics the one and only responsibility of senior management is to the firm's shareholders. In the case of corporate governance the principal stakeholders are the shareholders. The senior management team and the board are in both theory and law the agents of the shareholders. Their goal, according to the theory, should be to maximize the utility of the shareholders.

Even from a neoconservative perspective no argument can be made that senior management should "exploit" the firm's shareholders. Miles Mace has noted that a major finding of his pathbreaking work "was that directors of large- and medium-sized companies did not do much to represent their principal constituency, the stockholders" (1986, p. vii). Whom then do they represent? In general they appear to represent the interests of senior management. Excessive executive pay, lavish perquisites, and insider trading, are all cases where senior management can and often does exploit the shareholders. Thus even if it is possible to weave an argument that would defend exploitation of customers, workers, and other stakeholders it is not possible to make such an argument with respect to shareholders.

The structure of boards of directors is a key area of study in corporate governance. In the United States, Canada, and Great Britain most corporations have boards of directors that are composed of a mix of "inside" and "outside" directors. Inside directors are corporate employees (such as the CEO, executive vice-presidents of functional areas, and general counsel).

Historically, boards were dominated by outside directors. However, earlier in this century as professional managers began to replace founder-owners the composition of boards began to shift in the direction of more insiders. Some have argued that this could be a serious problem. An inside director is "in a very precarious position at a board meeting. Unwilling to say anything in disagreement with his boss, he usually sits quietly and waits until he is called upon to speak" (Nader, Green, & Seligman, 1976, p. 98). As a result some reformers such as Harold Williams, US Securities and Exchange Commission Chair 1977–81,

suggested that boards should have only one inside director – the CEO. Others, such as retired ITT chair Harold Geneen, have suggested that boards should have no inside directors (Braiotta & Sommers, 1987, p. 10). In part as a result of this pressure there has been a trend over the last several decades away from insider-dominated boards and back toward outsider-dominated boards.

Pay differentials and executive compensation are other major issues in corporate governance. One company that is often regarded as one of the more socially responsible firms in the world, Ben and Jerry's Homemade, Inc., until recently capped the CEO's salary at seven times that of the entry-level employees. However, in the United States today the average CEO of a major firm earns more than 150 times the salary of an average employee (Monks & Minow, 1995, p. 157). This is considerably higher than the differentials in any other major industrialized country.

Ethical issues in corporate governance are a particularly interesting subset of issues encountered in the field of business ethics because of the distinctive roles of the board and senior management in the modern corporation. Theoretically, no argument can be made that would justify the "exploitation" of the firm or its stockholders by the senior management team. Nonetheless, in the "real world" there are innumerable examples of such behavior.

Bibliography

Braiotta, L. Jr. & Sommers, A. A. Jr. (1987). *The Essential Guide to Effective Corporate Board Committees*. Englewood Cliffs, NJ: Prentice-Hall.

Crystal, G. (1991). *In Search of Excess*. New York: W. W. Norton.

Cochran, P. L. & Wartick, S. L. (1988). *Corporate Governance: A Review of the Literature*. Morristown, NJ: Financial Executives Research Foundation.

Conference Directorship Practices. (1967). Joint report from National Industrial Conference Board and American Society of Corporate Secretaries (Studies in Business Policy no. 125), New York.

Demb, A. & Neubauer, F.-F. (1992). *The Corporate Board: Confronting the Paradoxes*. New York: Oxford University Press.

Lorsch, J. W., with MacIver, E. (1989). *Pawns or Potentates: The Reality of America's Corporate Boards*. Boston: Harvard Business School Press.

Mace, M. L. (1986). *Directors: Myth and Reality*. Boston: Harvard University Press.

Monks, R. A. G. & Minow, N. (1995). *Corporate Governance*. Cambridge, Mass: Blackwell Publishers.

Mueller, R. K. (1982). *Board Score: How to Judge Boardworthiness*. Lexington, Mass.: Lexington Books.

Nader, R., Green, M., & Seligman, J. (1976). *Taming the Giant Corporation*. New York: W. W. Norton.

PHILIP L. COCHRAN

corporate punishment   The question of whether some form of punishment is appropriate and warranted for corporations that break the law centers around two chief issues. The first issue is the metaphysical status of the corporation: is "corporate punishment" a *meaningful* pairing of terms? – in other words, is the corporation the sort of entity that can be punished? The second issue concerns the justice and effectiveness of punishment, assuming we answer the previous questions in the affirmative.

Another way of phrasing the first issue is to ask whether the corporation is a moral agent. Only moral agents are punishable. For example, a person who is judged criminally insane will not be punished: rather his activities will be curtailed or monitored, or he will be separated from society at large or confined and treated. This may be done to protect the person so judged, or to protect the public from that person.

One school of thought regarding the metaphysical status of the corporation is what Thomas Donaldson refers to as the Structural Restraint View (Donaldson, 1982). This point of view holds that the corporation is tightly bound to its charter and as such lacks the basic moral prerequisite of freedom to act morally or immorally. If this view is correct, then the concept of punishment is irrelevant, and we must treat the offending corporation in much the same way that we treat the criminally insane: by way of regulations and restrictions.

Another school of thought holds that corporations are best thought of as "artificial and invisible" persons. According to this view, advanced first by the philosopher Peter French, corporations are sufficiently like persons to be held morally accountable for their actions. Like persons, corporations display intentional behavior because they have in place central decision-making units such as boards of directors, which "direct" the conduct of the corporation. Thus, the problem of assigning moral responsibility to corporations vanishes because corporations are *collective* persons and all persons are morally accountable for their actions.

These considerations about the metaphysical status of the corporation are important for the application of the kinds of theories of punishment that are found in the study of ethics. Such theories conceive of justifiable punishment along grounds of retribution, rectification, rehabilitation, deterrence, and others. Aristotle defines retribution as "suffering in return for one's action." He defines rectification as "taking away the gain restoring the equilibrium" for wrongs done by one and inflicted on another. Rehabilitation is the theory which holds that just punishment should show the offender the error of his ways, allowing him one day to return to society as a respectable citizen. Punishment as deterrence holds that justice is served if the nature of the punishment is so fearful that it discourages the offender or others from committing crimes.

Notice that justice as retribution seems to have little application to the punishment of corporations unless the corporation is sufficiently like a person that it can be "made to suffer" – an intentional notion that seems to have little relevance to the nature of corporations. However, the other notions of punishment – rectification, rehabilitation, and deterrence – do seem to have meaningful applications where corporate lawbreaking takes place, so we do not need to be driven to the other extreme, the Structural Restraint View. Corporations may be moral agents in the way that nation-states are conceived of as moral agents – and nations can be and are punished by way of reparations, and such punishments can set an example to that nation and others as deterrents for similar conduct in the future.

Thus, it is clear that in order to decide whether a corporation is the sort of entity that can be punished, we must decide the appropriateness of referring to this institution within a framework of a close family of moral terms: responsibility, liability, moral blame and censure, moral freedom, and agency. The fact that corporations are best defined as "liability-limiting mechanisms" makes the ascription of moral responsibility (and the assignment of punishment) especially problematic.

The second issue concerns the balance between justice and effectiveness of punishment of corporations which have broken the law. Corporations, unlike persons, cannot be incarcerated, so we are left to the recourse of imposing fines on them. Unfortunately, the levying of fines by judges on lawbreaking corporations can have unintended and unwanted effects. If the fines are truly weighty, they can easily harm innocent people. For example, a large fine imposed on a chemical corporation for illegal disposal of toxic wastes can have the unintended and undesirable effect of causing layoffs in the company, thus harming employees who had no part in the decision to dump wastes illegally and no part in the activity of illegal dumping. Such fines can also result in a company's decision to close down a less profitable plant in a small community, possibly depriving that community of its largest tax base and source of employment. Ponderous fines can also cause higher prices for the company's product, thus making the product less competitive and narrowing the range of consumer choice. If the fine is very large, it may even have the effect of putting the company out of business altogether.

Because of these considerations, judges have been understandably reluctant to impose large fines on lawbreaking corporations. The US Sentencing Commission learned that between 1984 and 1987, the average federal fine imposed on corporations for violations of the law was $48,000, and 67 percent of those fines amounted to $10,000 or less. Thus, it is understandable that many corporate executives began to reason that it was often cheaper to break the law and pay the fine than it was to treat hazardous chemicals or eliminate smokestack emissions – the fines became part of the "cost of doing business." In November of 1991, the US Sentencing Commission, after years of deliberation, issued a new set of guidelines for federal judges sentencing individuals and especially organizations convicted of breaking the law. In part, these sentencing guidelines were inspired by the success of the Defense Industry Initiatives (DII) – a voluntary agreement signed by 46 defense contractors in 1986 designed to prevent fraud and overcharging on government contracts. The DII mandated the creation of codes of conduct, designated officers of the corporation whose responsibility it was to oversee ethics of compliance, required internal reporting systems made up of telephone "hotlines" and ethics "ombudsmen" to allow reporting of legal and ethical violations without fear of retribution, and provided for compulsory ethics training for each of the company's employees and agents.

The 1991 US Sentencing Guidelines likewise mandated the creation of such an ethics compliance program but broadened the requirement to include *all* organizations, defense or otherwise, profit or nonprofit. Under the new guidelines, fines are to be assessed against lawbreaking organizations on a multiple of three to four times the cost of harm or damage done by the violating corporation. However, these fines could be reduced to less than 1 percent of that total provided that the offending organization fully and sincerely took part in the investigation of the wrongdoing (which can lead to mandatory jail sentences for individuals responsible for the crime), and provided that the company or organization had already in place a seven-step ethics and legal-compliance program similar to the one developed for the DII.

How extensive the ethics-training and compliance program must be in order to be granted leniency under these guidelines depends on three factors: the size of the organization, the ethically sensitive nature of its business, and the organization's prior history of enforcement actions taken against it.

Bibliography

Donaldson, T. (1982). *Corporations and Morality*. Englewood Cliffs, NJ: Prentice-Hall.

Ewing, A. C. (1970). *The Morality of Punishment*. Montclair, NJ: Patterson Smith.

French, P. (1979). The corporation as a moral person. *American Philosophical Quarterly*, **16**, 207ff.

Rafalko, R. (1989). Corporate punishment: A proposal. *Journal of Business Ethics*, **8**, 917–28.

Rafalko, R. (1994). Remaking the corporation: The 1991 US Sentencing Guidelines. *Journal of Business Ethics*, **13**, 625–36.

Werhane, P. (1985). *Persons, Rights and Corporations*. Englewood Cliffs, NJ: Prentice-Hall.

ROBERT J. RAFALKO

corporate strategy   Corporate strategy is regarded as encompassing the aims and objectives of the organization together with the means of how these are to be achieved. It is, by definition, holistic, i.e., it embraces all of the company's different businesses and functions. Andrews (1971) defined corporate strategy as: "the pattern of major objectives, purposes or goals and essential policies or plans for achieving those goals, stated in such a way as to define what business the company is in or is to be in and the kind of company it is or is to be" (28). Chandler (1962) believed that it should also be concerned with "the allocation of resources necessary for carrying out these goals" (13).

In defining its corporate strategy, the firm has to satisfy the sometimes contradictory expectations of several differing constituencies including, obviously, customers as well as suppliers, shareholders, and employees. It has been suggested that in countries such as the UK the short-term requirements of institutional shareholders prevent longer term investments, often to the detriment of sustainable competitiveness (*see* COMPETITIVE STRATEGY).

It is widely believed that corporate strategy should address the essentials of the organization, namely, the "what," "why," "how," and "when," of the organization. It is concerned with "what businesses is the company in or would like to be in?" Secondly, it embraces "why the company is in business," i.e., the specific sales, profit, rate of return, and growth targets it has or should have. Thirdly, the company needs to define "how" it aims to achieve those targets, such as the technologies it will use, the markets it is or should be operating in, and the products it markets or should market in order to achieve those objectives. Finally, the company needs to decide "when" it aims to achieve those goals and the period over which it defines its strategy.

Often, companies engage in formal STRATEGIC PLANNING as a means of developing a coherent corporate strategy, and the corporate strategy may be embodied in written strategic plans. In recent years, there has been much emphasis on COMPETITIVE STRATEGY with the focus on identifying the various structural determinants of performance and positioning the company to exploit these advantageously. However, it has been convincingly argued that a sound corporate strategy will be informed by a close monitoring of the evolving requirements of the various constituencies that the organization has to satisfy, and in particular of its existing and potential customer targets.

Bibliography

Andrews, K. (1971). *The concept of corporate strategy*. Homewood, IL: Irwin.

Chandler, A. D. (1962). *Strategy and structure*. Cambridge, MA: MIT Press.

DALE LITTLER

corrective discipline   The prevalence of the EMPLOYMENT-AT-WILL doctrine in the United States has, until recently, resulted in only minimal emphasis on appropriate approaches to discipline for employees who were not covered by labor agreements. At-will employees could legally be discharged for any number of unfair reasons, so there was little practical or scholarly interest in the procedural and substantive fairness of their treatment. On the other hand, roughly half of all grievance arbitration in this country has traditionally involved determining whether management issued discipline for "just cause." As a consequence, the earliest PROGRESSIVE discipline is found in the texts of ARBITRATION decisions.

In his early decision in the *International Harvester* case (Elkouri and Elkouri, 1985) Arbitrator Seward explained corrective discipline in the following manner: "corrective rather than retributive discipline . . . involves more than the mere matching of penalties with offenses . . . its purpose is not to 'get even' with the employee but to influence his future conduct." From these humble beginnings in the realm of arbitral jurisprudence, corrective discipline has since become a fundamental principle of human resource management. This is largely because it is consistent with the concept of employees as human resources who can be developed and enhanced like any other resources. While the corrective approach to discipline recognizes that most types of misconduct at work do not disqualify an employee from continued employment, it acknowledges that certain extreme types of misconduct render employees unworthy of corrective efforts. Typically these types of gross misconduct include assault, theft, and other types of criminal activity taking place on the employer's time or premises.

Bibliography

Elkouri, F. & Elkouri, E (1985). *How Arbitration Works*, **4th edn**, Washington, DC: BNA.

Fairweather, O. (1984). *Practice and Procedure in Labor Arbitration*, **2nd edn**, Washington, DC: BNA.

Redeker, J. R. (1989). *Employee Discipline*, Washington, DC: BNA.

MARK R. SHERMAN

cost leadership strategy   This is one of the GENERIC STRATEGIES proposed by Porter (1980) (*see* COMPETITIVE STRATEGY). Companies having the lowest costs should be in a strong position with regard to: *competitors*, because they will always be able to undercut them, while taking advantage of a higher margin to invest in increasing market share, new product development, and other corporate development policies; *suppliers*, because they can more easily absorb increases in costs; *customers*, because they are able to respond to demands for lower prices; and *substitutes*, because they will be better able to react to them in terms of cost. In order to be a cost leader, the company must have low overheads, be highly efficient, and generally not direct resources to activities which are seen as being extraneous to achieving continued lowest cost. Companies may follow a focused cost leadership strategy aimed at particular customers or market segments (*see* MARKET SEGMENTATION), or a broad market cost leadership strategy. There are risks to the emphasis on cost leadership, in particular the bases of customer choice may move toward non-price factors and technological change may shift the COMPETITIVE ADVANTAGE to rivals, including late entrants.

Bibliography

Porter M. E. (1980). *Competitive strategy: Techniques for analyzing industries and competitors*. New York: Free Press. Chapter 2.

DALE LITTLER

cost of capital   The cost of capital is the rate of return that investors in the market require in order to participate in the financing of an investment. The cost of capital is the rate used by managers of value-maximizing firms to discount the expected cash flows in capital budgeting. The investment projects which offer expected returns greater than the cost of capital are accepted because they generate positive net present values (NPV) while projects with expected returns lower than the cost of capital should be rejected. Thus, the cost of capital is the hurdle rate used to evaluate proposed investment projects.

When the project is marginal and does not significantly shift the risk profile of the firm, the cost of capital can be computed as the weighted average costs of the various sources of finance. In the case where the firm is financed by debt and equity, the weighted average cost of capital (WACC) is computed as follows:

$$WACC = r_D(1 - \tau_c)\frac{D}{V} + r_E\frac{E}{V} \qquad (1)$$

where r_D is the cost of debt finance, τ_c is the marginal corporation tax rate, r_E is the cost of equity finance, D is the market value of debt, E is the market value of equity and V is the market value of the firm, i.e. $E + D$. In principle each project should be valued at its own cost of capital to reflect its level of risk. However, in practice, it is difficult to estimate project-by-project cost of capital. Instead, the firm's overall weighted average cost of capital is used as a benchmark and then adjusted for the degree of the specific risk of the project.

The cost of capital can also be regarded as the rate of return that a business could earn if it chooses another investment with equivalent risk. The cost of capital is, in this case, the opportunity cost of the funds employed as the result of an investment decision. For value-maximizing firms, the cost of capital is the opportunity cost borne by various investors who choose to invest in the proposed project and not in other securities and, thus, it is estimated as the expected rates of return in the securities market. For regulated companies the cost of capital can be used as a target fair rate of return.

Modigliani and Miller (markets and no taxes (i.e. τ_c in equation (1) is zero), the cost of capital of a firm is independent of the type of securities used to finance the project or the capital structure of the firm. The main argument advocated is that as debt is substituted for equity, the cost of the remaining equity increases but the overall cost of capital, r_0, is kept constant:

$$r_g = r_0 + (1 - r_D)\frac{D}{E} \qquad (2)$$

When taxes are introduced, Modigliani and Miller (1963) show that firms will prefer debt to equity finance because of the tax shields associated with the company's borrowing plans. However, Miller (1977) demonstrated that the value of corporate interest tax shields can be completely offset by the favorable treatment of equity income to investors and, as result, the firm's cost of capital is independent of its financing method.

The current main problems associated with the cost of capital relate to the estimation of the components of the WACC. While r_D can be proxied by the average interest rate paid by the firm on its loans, τ_c should be the marginal not the standard corporation tax rate. Lasfer (1995) showed that in the UK the effective corporation tax rates vary significantly from one firm to another and that a large number of companies are tax exhausted and do have lower debt in their capital structure compared to tax-paying firms. Thus the net tax advantages to corporate borrowing are unknown unless one computes the effective tax rate for each individual company.

The cost of equity, r_E can be based on the capital asset pricing model (CAPM) and computed as:

$$r_E = r_f + \beta(r_m - r_f) \qquad (3)$$

where β is the risk measure and $(r_m - r_f)$ is the risk premium on the overall stock market, r_m, relative to the risk-free rate of return, r_f. However, the validity of this formulation has, recently, been the subject of severe empirical criticisms (Fama and French, 1992). Stulz (1995a) argues that the cost of equity capital should be estimated using the global rather than the local CAPM because capital markets are integrated. This method involves an estimation of a global market portfolio and for countries that are only partially integrated in international capital markets, the computation of the cost of capital may not be possible.

The traditional formulation of the WACC assumes that managers are value maximizers. Recent evidence provides a challenge to this assumption and argues that managers do not act to maximize shareholder wealth but, instead, maximize their own utility. In this case the WACC should be modified to account for the agency costs of managerial discretion. Stulz (1995b) defined the agency cost adjusted cost of capital by incorporating into the discount rate the impact of agency costs in the same way that the WACC approach incorporates in the cost of capital the tax shield of debt. However, it is not clear whether, in investment decisions, managers should adjust the discount rate or the expected cash flows. Moreover, the agency costs of managerial discretion depend on a firm's capital structure, dividend policy, and other firm-specific factors which might be difficult to value. Furthermore, the above measurements can be difficult because they involve measuring expectations by market participants which are not directly measurable. In practice, the "true" cost of capital is likely to be unobservable.

Bibliography

Fama, E. F. & French K. R. (1992). The cross-section of expected stock returns. *Journal of Finance*, 47, 427–66.

Lasfer, M. A. (1995). Agency costs, taxes and debt: the UK evidence. *European Financial Management*, 1, 265–85.

Miller, M. H. (1977). Debt and taxes. *Journal of Finance*, 32, 261–76.

Modigliani, F. & Miller, M. H. (1958). The cost of capital, corporate finance, and the theory of investment. *American Economic Review*, 48, 261–97.

Modigliani, F. & Miller, M. H. (1963). The cost of capital, corporate finance, and the theory of investment: a correction. *American Economic Review*, 53, 433–43.

Stulz, R. (1995a). The cost of capital in internationally integrated markets. *European Financial Management*, 1, 11–22.

Stulz, R. (1995b). Does the cost of capital differ across countries? An agency perspective. Keynote address prepared for the fourth meeting of the European Financial Management Association, London, June 1995.

M. AMEZIANE LASFER

cost-pricing relationship   Marketing activity makes up the bulk of total activity of most businesses. Marketing with its focus on product, price, promotion and place (the traditional marketing mix), drives all the other activities. Price is the most elusive among these marketing mix variables in terms of making pricing decisions. Controversy is frequently engendered by disagreement between accountants and marketing personnel when deciding the appropriate price for a product or service.

In the long run the price established must be viable to remain competitive, and at a level which covers all costs, including marketing costs. Since marketing costs account for 40 to 50 percent of total costs and since pricing is a major marketing decision, understanding the cost–pricing relationship and its application to market profitability analysis is vitally important in any business situation.

Pricing: Concepts and Issues

Many different labels are subsumed under price: rent, fees, fares, etc. It is the amount of money paid in exchange for a product or service. From a marketing perspective, price must reflect the perceived value of a firm's product to a customer. If set above perceived value, the firm risks pricing its product out of the market. If below, it may not be viable to offer this product line. Price is thus a major determinant of buying behavior, as well as the source of revenue for the firm.

Different philosophies underpin the different approaches to price determination. Market-based pricing has an external focus, with a pricing strategy that is particularly responsive to customers' demand function, competitors' prices, threats from new product entries, in addition to the firm's cost structure. Understanding the impact of long-run costs is important for assessing profitability in competitive markets, but market factors are key considerations for this market-based pricing approach.

In contrast, cost-based pricing is essentially cost driven and is more prevalent in a production-oriented environment than in the more marketing-oriented environment today. Production cost sets the stage for price determina-tion, usually a simple exercise of applying a markup on cost to yield a required gross margin or target return on investment. Hence, the term "markup pricing" is widely used to describe this approach. As Kjaer-Hansen (1967) pointed out, in the post-War marketing environment, this "old fashioned pricing system, based on a summation of ascertained costs, will not be capable of satisfying the requirements introduced by the modern trend of demand conditions" (p. 216, *Financial Dimensions of Marketing*, 1981, where he is quoted). Yet, the legal implication of the cost base used for pricing is important for marketers when there are charges of predatory pricing practices with the effect of adversely affecting competition. Committe & Grinnell (1992) and Ursic & Helgeson (1994) point out that after 1975 the courts explicitly began to apply cost-based standards to predatory pricing cases. Various cost concepts were applied by the courts, including average-total cost and marginal cost, with one interpretation of the latter being short-run variable cost. To assist companies in answering pricing practice queries in court, Ursic & Helgeson (1994) suggest that prices be set, if possible, above marginal cost or average variable costs or even above average-total cost.

The marketing literature is replete with descriptions of pricing techniques which are usually variants of the two basic types just explained. Examples are Kotler's (1991) markup pricing, target-return pricing, perceived-value pricing, going-rate pricing, and sealed-bid pricing; price adaptations such as geographic pricing; and other pricing categories such as loss-leader pricing, image pricing, and two-part-pricing. Pricing policy is imperative for a firm with the price established at a competitive, yet reasonable, level to the customer, and which also provides an adequate return to the firm.

The pricing decision therefore is among the most important considerations in marketing, yet formulating a successful pricing strategy can prevent marketers from becoming too preoccupied with the market place, and accountants with margins, costs, and turnover ratios. The importance of a marketing–accounting interface is described in a later section.

Cost: Concepts and Issues

Costs, as perceived in conventional accounting, are monetary units paid in return for goods and services. Behind this seemingly easy definition lies a gamut of cost concepts, each delineating possibly different cost elements.

(1) Costs identified by behavior in relation to volume of activity, into variable costs, semi-variable costs, and fixed costs. An understanding of cost behavior is necessary in cost–volume–profit analysis, which is a useful accounting tool for marketing analysis. For example, in segment profitability analysis, cost–volume–profit relationships are invoked to determine the volume at which segment revenue just covers its specific costs. Moreover, useful information is generated about the sensitivity of segment contribution to volume fluctuations.

Another area where marketing cost analysis is based on cost behavior patterns is flexible budgeting. Flexible budgets are prepared to show costs at the different levels of sales activity, which can be used for performance evaluation purposes. Comparing the actual costs with static budgets would be misleading.

(2) Costs identified to cost objects (e.g., products, departments) such as direct costs and indirect costs. Direct costs traceable to marketing departments or sub-units of marketing departments provide reliable input for performance analysis of these departments and of their respective managers.

(3) Costs identified by differences in time horizon into short-run and long-run, and by their relevance to short-run pricing and other decisions, like using differential costs in decisions concerning acceptance of one-off orders and product abandonment.

(4) Costs identified by controllability into controllable and noncontrollable costs for a marketing department. Uncontrollable costs will be the allocated costs including those of corporate headquarters, frequently described as common costs. This classification has particular application to performance measurement of marketing departments.

These classifications of costs are not mutually exclusive. For example, depending on the situation, relevant costs can be variable and fixed, or direct and indirect.

Two principal costing methods emerge based on these cost concepts, which are relevant to marketing analysis. Direct variable costing which treats only variable costs as production costs is of significance to marketing mainly because of its emphasis on the contribution margin approach. Contribution margin represents the excess of sales over variable costs, including variable marketing costs. This contribution approach has been recommended for market segment profitability analysis (American Accounting Association, 1972) and for making marketing decisions such as product introduction, product abandonment, and pricing.

Variable costing has been specifically recommended for consideration by companies with international business activities. Since such companies are removed, both politically and geographically, from the domestic markets, and since they are likely to have different objectives in different countries, with different demand and competition, the charging of different prices in different countries is seen as having more applicability internationally than domestically. Variable costing could facilitate such differential pricing (Weekly, 1992).

In absorption (full) fixed manufacturing costs are also part of the costs of production or inventoriable costs. This method is invoked if both direct and indirect costs are assigned to the market segments.

Horngren et al. (1994) also found strong support for full product costs for pricing decisions in various cross-country studies. Mills's (1988) conclusion, therefore, that "the dysfunctional effects of full/absorption costing reliant on arbitrary allocation methods may be of less importance in practice than in theory" is probably valid.

More Recent Costing Approaches

Activity-based costing. Marketing costs can make up to 50 percent of total costs for some products (Stevenson et al., 1993). The accounting system, however, is oriented to the needs of external users, and secondarily to the needs of marketing decision-makers. Stevenson et al. (1993) discussed how activity-based costing (ABC) can be applied-context. This new costing approach more appropriately identifies cost drivers related to marketing activities, such as advertising, selling, and marketing research time, so as to better allocate marketing costs to products.

Lewis (1991) also addressed the need to use ABC techniques for marketing functions, with emphasis on physical distribution: selling, warehousing, packing and shipping, and general office. Physical distribution costs "are a major factor in worldwide competition and should not be ignored in discussions of performance measurements and integrated cost systems" (Lewis, p. 34). ABC is advocated to identify, classify, and allocate the physical distribution costs using appropriately identified cost drivers.

Another application of ABC to marketing was cited by Yong et al. (1993) in the banking industry, specifically in relation to the impact on future product pricing of the allocation of mortgage department customer telephone center costs. By incorporating capacity utilization into ABC, to obtain a close approximation of long-run costs, strategic advantage in the market place could be assessed to enable decisions in relation to pricing and product entry/exit to be made more easily.

Since "developments in ABC show great promise in delivering more reliable measures of long-run incremental costs" (Committe & Grinell, 1992, p. 58), this costing technique has been recommended as a worthwhile tool for predatory pricing cases for the measurement of long-run incremental costs. This application of ABC arose from several influential court opinions which indicated the need to rely on a "causation approach to cost measurement" (Committe & Grinell, 1992, p. 58).

Target costing. In target costing cost is not used to set the price which is mainly determined by market conditions, but cost will affect a firm's decision whether to market the product at all. The procedure involves assessing the market's willingness to pay for a product which then establishes its target price. Working backwards, by subtracting the target profit, gives the target cost which the firm must hold down to through cost reduction efforts, or, if a new product, through improved product design. Drucker would call this approach "price-driven costing," as opposed to "cost-driven pricing."

Product life cycle costing. Product life cycle costing tracks and accumulates costs attributable to each product from initial research and development to final customer service and support in the market place (Horngren et al., 1994). Since marketing costs represent a major component in a product's life cycle costs, this costing technique has a useful marketing application. This is to undertake to better manage marketing costs through separate identification of costs, not on an annual product-by-product basis, but over each product's life cycle. This allows a comparison of the level of marketing costs incurred by different products, and assessment of the likely impact of the interrelationships among cost components. In relation to the latter, for example, significant reductions in the research and development and product design cost categories can lead to major increases in customer-service-related costs in later periods.

Marketing-Accounting Interface

Any discussion of costs and pricing underscores the importance of the cost–pricing relationship in marketing, already recognized by the American Accounting Association in 1972, but which still holds true today. Cost represents the "floor for price" (Kotler, 1991) and a knowledge of costs is essential for pricing decisions which, of course, are also based on other market considerations.

Market segment profitability analysis is essentially an attempt to analyse post hoc how costs and pricing decisions have resulted in specific profit outcomes. Profitability data for this purpose are normally generated by the accounting function. This emphasizes the importance of a constructive marketing–accounting interface between these two functions.

Overall, it does seem that much more needs to be done to improve the marketing–accounting interface, especially in today's global competitive environment. The view expressed by Trebuss (1978, p. 525) on the "limited attention this topic has received in business research and literature" still rings true today.

Bibliography

American Accounting Association (1972). Report of the Committee on Cost and Profitability Analyses for Marketing. *The Accounting Review*, 7, supplement, 577–615.

Committe, B. E. & Grinnell, D. J. (1992). Predatory pricing, the price–cost test, and activity-based costing. *Cost Management* Fall, 52–8.

Horngren, C. T., Foster, G. & Datar, S. (1994). *Cost accounting*. Englewood Cliffs, NJ: Prentice-Hall.

Kjaer-Hansen, M. (1967). Marketing costs and their importance in pricing. In *Financial Dimensions of Marketing*, Richard M. S. Wilson (ed.), 1981, 214–23.

Kotler P. (1991). *Marketing Management*. Englewood Cliffs, NJ: Prentice-Hall.

Lewis, R. J. (1991). Activity-based costing for marketing. *Management Accounting* US, Nov., 33–8.

Mills, R. W. (1988). Pricing decisions in UK manufacturing and service companies. *Management Accounting* Nov., 38–9.

Stevenson, T. H., Barnes, F. C. & Stevenson, S. A. (1993). Activity-based costing: An emerging tool for industrial marketing decision-makers. *Journal of Business & Industrial Marketing*, 8, 2, 40–52.

Trebuss, A. S. (1978). Improving corporate effectiveness: Managing the marketing finance interface. In *Marketing Effectiveness*, S. S. Shapiro & V. H. Kirpalani, 525–36.

Ursic, M. L. & Helgeson, J. G. (1994). Using price as a weapon. *Industrial Marketing Management*, 23, 125–31.

Weekly, J. K. (1992). Pricing in foreign markets: Pitfalls and opportunities. *Industrial Marketing Management*, 21, 173–9.

Yong, G. Y. & Wu, R. C. (1993). Strategic Costing + ABC. *Management Accounting* US, Nov., p. 33.

HERBERT P. SCHOCH and TEOH HAI YAP

cost variances and investigation   Management control in organizations involves three primary phases: planning, coordination (during plan implementation), and control. An important part of the control phase is performance feedback and evaluation that may involve both financial and nonfinancial measures. The most common financial control measure, budgetary control, involves the ex post comparison of actual financial results with the ex ante budgetary expectations. The term "cost variance" is used in accounting to denote the deviation of an actual or observed cost from the expected cost level. As such, the analysis of cost variances is a subset of budgetary control techniques used to ensure compliance of individual behavior with organizational goals. The expected cost level can be budgeted cost, standard cost, or the cost estimated from a frontier cost function.

The primary objective of cost variance analysis is to permit organizational managers to detect and correct inefficiencies wherever they exist in operations involving expenditures. Three kinds of decisions are generally necessary: (1) what kinds of variances to compute, (2) the level of disaggregation required, and (3) whether or not to investigate a particular variance once computed.

Types of Variances Computed

The types of variances computed depend on the responsibility centers and the level of management for which the review is performed. Since the objective is to determine the degree of corrective action needed, the variances computed, mostly quantitative, must relate to key performance indicators considered critical to the success of the responsibility center.

At the highest levels of the organization, the key performance indicators may consist of general concepts like product leadership, growth in market share, product innovation, cost competitiveness, and so forth. At the lower levels of the organization, at the cost centers where cost variances are usually of primary interest, key performance indicators usually pertain to the usage and cost of materials, labor (if a key component of costs), and overhead. At revenue centers (where revenue generation is of primary interest), key performance indicators may consist of sales price variances, product mix variances, market share variances, and industry volume variances.

Recently, in manufacturing contexts, increasing interest is focusing on product cycle time. Essentially, product cycle time refers to the time it takes raw materials to be processed to the completed product stage. Holding other factors constant, the shorter the product cycle time, the lower the product unit cost.

Level of Disaggregation of Cost Variances

Budgets are established in part to provide a benchmark for evaluating performance. For cost centers, these budgets typically seek to achieve efficiency and control by specifying the expected cost levels. In discretionary and administrative cost centers, these cost budgets are typically not related to output levels (since output may be difficult to measure); instead the budgets represent the spending levels authorized for the budget period. Budget variances refer to deviations of actual spending levels from the budget. Unfavorable budget variances (i.e., spending levels above expected) would typically call for investigation from the cost center manager, while favorable variances may not require any explanation unless they are material.

The more interesting issue involving cost variances, however, arises in the case of engineered cost centers where inputs and outputs are directly measurable and can be related to each other. In such centers, the budget specification for spending levels must be a function of output levels.

In conventional accounting practice, labor standards were developed for repetitive manufacturing processes using time and motion studies, denoting the best way of performing a given operation. From these standards emerged standard costing that establishes a standard cost for each product cost element. The implementation of standard costing meant that the standards established for manufacturing operations provided the basis for establishing the budget.

Typically, standards were established for direct materials, direct labor, and manufacturing overhead. The standards specified the quantities of materials expected per unit of output and the expected price. For labor, the standards specified the number of labor hours required and the budgeted labor rates. For manufacturing overhead, the aggregate behavior of the overhead costs would be identified as a linear function of some input measures of activity such as total direct labor hours or machine hours. The budgeted overhead costs would then reflect the expected level of the input measure of activity in which budgeted overhead costs could be also related to the budgeted output level.

The ex post analysis of cost variances in such a system consists of two primary components: the flexible budget variance (FVB) and the budget adjustment variance (BAV). Algebraically, letting FBV represent the flexible budget variance and BAV the budget adjustment variance, the computations can be represented as follows:

$$FBV = AQ*AP - SQ*SP \quad (1a)$$

$$= AQ*AP - (sq*AY)*SP \quad (1b)$$

$$BAV = SQ*SP - BQ*SP \quad (2a)$$

$$= (sq*AY)*SP - (sq*BY)*SP \quad (2b)$$

where:

AQ = actual quantity of inputs used;

AP = actual price of inputs;

SP = standard price of materials;

AY = actual volume of output;

BY = budgeted volume of output;

BQ = budgeted quantity of inputs;

SQ = standard quantity of input that should have been used given the actual output level;

sq = standard quantity of input per unit of output.

Further, in a manufacturing context, the flexible budget variance is decomposed into price and efficiency or quantity variances. These variances are computed (using terms defined earlier) as follows:

For materials:

Purchase price variance
$$= AQ*AP - AQ*SP \quad (3)$$

Quantity or efficiency variance
$$= AQ*SP - SQ*SP \quad (4)$$

For labor:

Labor rate variance
$$= AH*AR - AH*SR \quad (5)$$

Labor efficiency variance
$$= AH*SR - SH*SR \quad (6)$$

where:

AQ = actual quantity of materials purchased;

AQ = actual quantity of materials used;

AH = actual hours used to produce the output of the period;

$SH = sh*AY$
= standard hours allowed for the output of the period;

sh = standard hours required per unit of output;

AY = actual output of the period;

and all other terms are as defined earlier.

For manufacturing overhead, the most commonly applied three-variance approach involves the identification of a manufacturing overhead spending variance and a manufacturing overhead efficiency variance (which together make up the flexible budget variance for overhead), and a denominator volume variance. Algebraically, this decomposition of the variances can be represented as:

Overhead spending variance:
$$= \text{actual MOH} - (\text{budgeted FMOH} + v*AX) \quad (7)$$

Overhead efficiency variance
$$= (\text{budgeted FMOH} + v*AX)$$
$$- (\text{budgeted FMOH} + v*SX) \quad (8a)$$

$$= (AX-SX)*v \quad (8b)$$

Overhead denominator variance
$$= (\text{budgeted FMOH} + v*SX)$$
$$- ([f+v]*SX) \quad (9a)$$

$$= \text{budgeted FMOH} - f*SX \quad (9b)$$

where:

MOH = total manufacturing overhead costs (i.e., fixed plus variable manufacturing overhead);

$FMOH$ = fixed manufacturing overhead costs;

v = variable manufacturing overhead costs per unit of the cost driver (X);

AX = Actual volume of the overhead cost driver (e.g., total labor hours)

SX = standard volume of the overhead cost driver expected given the actual volume of output ($SX = sx*AY$, where sx is the amount of cost driver per output unit);

f = budgeted FMOH/DX
= fixed manufacturing overhead rate per unit of the cost driver;

DX = denominator volume of the cost driver used to unitize the fixed manufacturing overhead costs.

In contexts where multiple inputs of the same type can be substituted for each other, the input efficiency variance can be further decomposed into an input mix variance and an input yield variance. The input mix variance represents the effect of the choice of mix of inputs on total costs, while the yield variance reflects the difference between the total quantities of inputs used (regardless of the type) and the total quantities expected given the output of the process.

Algebraically, this can be represented as follows:

$$\text{Mix variance} = \Sigma \ (AQ \ * \ SP) - \Sigma \ [(\Sigma; \ AQ) \ * (SM) \ * \ SP] \ (10a)$$

$$= \Sigma \ (AM - SM) \ * \ SP \ * \ (\Sigma \ AQ) \ (10b)$$

$$\text{Yield variance} = \Sigma \ [(\Sigma \ AQ) \ * \ (SM) \ * \ SP] - \Sigma(SQ \ * \ SP) \ (11a)$$

$$= \Sigma \ [(\Sigma \ AQ - \Sigma \ SQ) \ * \ SM \ * \ SP] \ (11b)$$

where:

$$AM = AQ \ / \ \Sigma \ AQ$$

= actual proportion of input j relative to the total actual input quantities used;

$$SM = SQ \ / \Sigma \ SQ$$

= standard proportion of input j relative to the total standard input quantities;

and all other terms are as defined earlier.

Variance Investigation

The degree to which variances are disaggregated depends on the underlying factors of causation. Material price variances, for example, are likely to be due to price forecasting errors, deficient purchasing practices, purchases of materials of a quality slightly different from original specification, or a combination of all three factors. Labor rate variances, on the other hand, may be caused by unexpected changes in the average labor mix (given different wage rates), unexpected changes in the average wage rate paid to labor of a given grade, or a combination of such factors. Similarly, input efficiency variances may be caused by significant changes in the productivity of the input factor, errors in the forecasted rate of productivity, or a combination of factors.

Under these conditions, it is apparent that nonzero variances can be caused by random errors with no control significance, or by problems in the control environment that require correction. Since there are likely to be non-zero costs of investigating the cause of any variance observed, decision rules have to be formulated on what variances should be investigated, and which ones should not be investigated. Among the decision rules used in practice are the following:

(1) Investigate all negative (unfavorable) variances.
(2) Investigate all variances exceeding budgeted (or standard) costs by a fixed percentage (e.g., 10).
(3) Investigate all variances exceeding budgeted (or standard) costs by more than a given standard deviation (e.g., one standard deviation). This rule is known as the control chart rule.

Of these decision rules, the most sophisticated is the use of control charts. Essentially, the control chart rules take the following form: "Investigate if actual costs exceed X; otherwise do not investigate." The level of X is then set so that the combined costs of investigating and of not investigating are minimized when the system is out of control.

Summary of Research

Derivation of Variances. The conventional accounting method of computing variances relates manufacturing overhead costs to the volume of activity as a linear function, with some of the overhead costs fixed and others variable. This approach has not changed much. Instead, researchers have focused on refinements of direct cost variances, or on the identification of generic cost functions.

Hasseldine (1967) and Wolk & Hillman (1972) proposed refinements to the traditional approach of deriving the mix and yield variances. They pointed out an inaccuracy that stemmed from computing the conventional mix and yield variances, given changes in input prices. Using linear programing, Demski (1967) proposed a sweeping overhaul of the traditional approach. He demonstrated the feasibility of his approach with an actual application in an oil refinery. Mensah (1982) proposed that neoclassical cost functions such as the Cobb-Douglas (or linear programing, if appropriate) should be incorporated into the conventional analysis, and proposed a method of computing the yield and mix variances that linked them to the parallel concepts of allocative and technical inefficiencies so well known in the economics literature. He related these to the more commonly used Farrell (1957) approach (which relies on proportionality of the inefficiency in the use of the inputs), although the Russell measure (which assumes non substitution technology) might be more appropriate in some circumstances (Marcinko & Petri, 1984; Callen, 1988).

One difficulty in adopting these suggestions is the identification of the efficient production frontier. In the conventional setting, it is assumed that the efficient frontier can be identified through a combination of efficient processes and using regression to identify the best linear function for overhead.

Some researchers (Callen, 1988; Darrough, 1988) have focused on the problem of identifying the best functional form for the production possibility set. Others such as Mensah & Li (1993) have focused on identifying the production frontier by using parametric approaches, such as the translog function, as well as nonparametric approaches, such as data envelopment analysis (DEA). DEA is particularly interesting as a potential tool for evaluating performance because it does not assume any particular functional form. It is important to note, however, that these subsequent researchers are concerned with more than just the problem of identifying inefficiency for a single period. The estimation of the neoclassical production function (or the related DEA) is commonly based on cross-sectional data because time-series data are rarely available for a given cost center (and would be subject to nonstationarity even if available). Consequently, the functions identified are long-run functions, involving the identification of economies of scale present in the data, etc. In contrast, conventional standard cost systems assume short-run Leontief fixed-proportion production functions. Thus, it is an empirical question whether some of the more generalized functions can be applied in a meaningful way to identify and correct inefficiencies in practice.

Activity-based Costing. Conventional standard cost systems assume that overhead costs can be always directly related to output volume. Researchers who have re-examined that issue have concluded that the assumption is generally invalid. This has led to the emergence of activity-based costing (ABC). Essentially, ABC identifies activities as the cost drivers of overhead costs, rather than output. As a result, the diversity of output, batch size, the number of parts used in manufacturing a product, the number of setups, the number of times parts are ordered, and the number of times products are shipped can all affect the level of overhead costs incurred. Specifically, Robin Cooper, Robert Kaplan, and Peter Turney (among others) have led the cost accounting revolution that has resulted in a re-examination of the traditional unit-based allocation of overhead (see, for example, Cooper, 1988a; 1988b; 1989a; 1989b; Cooper & Kaplan, 1988; Kaplan, 1984; and Johnson & Kaplan, 1991).

One important contribution of the ABC proponents has been the recognition that the traditional distinction between fixed and variable costs may be incorrect. That is, while some costs may be fixed from the perspective of the volume of output, they are not fixed from the perspective of the activities that drive those costs. Thus, ABC proponents advocate the segregation of costs (and associated activities) into (1) unit-level costs, (2) batch-level costs, (3) product-level costs, and (4) facility-level costs. Unit-level costs are costs directly related to the volume of output for a given product (e.g., quantity of direct materials and direct labor used). Batch-level costs are incurred each time a batch of output is produced because of the related batch activities (e.g., machine setup, ordering costs for a batch of components, scheduling costs for a batch of output). Product-level costs are costs incurred at the product level relating to the product type (e.g., engineering change orders and new vendors for new components). Finally, facility-level costs are costs that relate to the entire facility (e.g., depreciation on factory buildings and non-dedicated equipment).

Finally, it must be noted that ABC does not directly address the issue of variance analysis. However, it can be argued that ABC makes possible a far more sophisticated type of variance analysis for overhead than is possible under the conventional system. Since overhead costs are now better related to the cost driver activities, ex post analysis of performance can focus on two things:

(1) Given the actual volume of output, are the batch-level and product-level activities consistent with the budget?
(2) Given the actual level of the batch-level and product-level activities, are the actual costs consistent with the budgeted unit costs?

Unfortunately, much of the work to date on ABC has focused on identifying the actual costs of production as opposed to the budgetary control implications for the more refined costing system.

Cost Variance Investigation

The identification of cost variances is designed to alert management to possible control problems in operations. However, deciding whether or not to investigate the variance is complicated. The complexity of the decision stems from the fact the variance could have been caused by a random factor, just as it could signal some problems in the environment requiring correction.

Several approaches to the cost variance investigation decision have been suggested in the literature (see Kaplan (1975) and Magee (1976) for relevant literature reviews). Among them are the Markovian approach (Dittman & Prakash, 1978), the mathematical programing approach (Kaplan, 1978; Magee, 1977), the information theory approach (LEV, 1969), and the decision theory approach (Dittman & Prakash, 1979).

Lev's (1969) information theory approach may be regarded as a sophisticated version of the basic approach which focuses on analyzing all variances above a given percentage of budgeted costs. His approach essentially requires the arrangement of all variances within the budget control system in order to compute the variances as fractions of total sales (or output). Using information theory, those variances that show the largest variance are reflected by the expected information measures.

The most widely-used of these sophisticated variance investigation techniques is the control chart approach. Essentially, the control chart approach involves comparing the value of the observed cost variance (X) against some pre-specified upper and lower limits. In the basic control chart approach, the upper and lower limits are established as a fixed standard deviation based on the past observations of the variance in the process. But how does one know what is the appropriate number of standard deviations to use? The approach proposed by Dittman and Prakash (1979) seeks to minimize the total expected costs of investigation by considering the distributions of both the "in control" and "out of control" states. Since there are costs to carrying out the investigation and even higher costs in letting an "out of control" process continue unchecked, the objective is to determine what critical value of the cost variance should trigger an investigation.

Because of the uncertainties associated with estimating the probabilities of the "in control" and "out of control" states, it is conceivable that parameters estimation errors compromise the theoretical benefits of the sophisticated techniques such as Dittman and Prakash's. Magee's (1986, p. 213) suggestion that simulation may be a useful technique to try out in this context deserves serious consideration. Findings from a simulation study by Magee (1976) suggest that simple rules like "Investigate all variances exceeding 10 percent of budgeted costs" may be preferable in practice. On the other hand, statistical process control (which uses the same underlying principle) has long been used in industry and has generally been found to be useful.

Further Development

The traditional standard cost paradigm which dates back to Taylor's initial studies into scientific management and the idea that there are optimal methods of performing specific tasks which can be uncovered through time can be referred to broadly as the cost management paradigm. In its broad essence, cost management proponents hold to the view that continuous improvements in production operations are possible through the continual search for and elimination of non value-added activities. Thus, instead of identifying a cost frontier (or a set of standard costs) good for an indefinite period of time, efforts are directed at constantly redefining the cost frontier.

As a result, cost variances in the traditional sense are perceived to be limited in their usefulness. Instead, a series of ideas have been advanced, many of which draw from innovations first developed among Japanese world-class manufacturers. Principal among these ideas are benchmarking, total quality control/just-in-time (TQC/JIT) philosophy, and target costing. In the benchmarking approach, the ratio of costs of performing specific functions relative to a base (such as total revenue) is computed for a given decision-making unit and compared to other units (or companies). The idea is to ensure that this ratio can be reduced to that of the most efficient unit in the industry. While this approach is frequently applied to costs incurred for overhead functions like administration, accounting, and personnel, there is no particular reason why it cannot be extended to the evaluation of functions in both upstream (basic research and product development) and manufacturing operations.

Under the total quality control/just-in-time (TQC/JIT) philosophy, conventional standard costing (where standards are established once a year or so) is regarded as obsolete. Instead, a kind of dynamic standard costing system is instituted in which the standards are continually ratcheted upwards as they are achieved. The idea is to strive for continual improvements in operations through the elimination of defects in output and the streamlining of operations such that output proceeds smoothly on a consistent basis. This objective can be related to target costing. In target costing, a company establishes a target cost for the design and manufacturing of a product and then strives to achieve that target through the continual refinement of operations.

Bibliography

Callen, J. (1988). An index number theory of accounting cost variances. *Journal of Accounting Research (new series)*, **3**, 2, 87–108.

Darrough, M. N. (1988). Variance analysis: A unifying cost function approach. *Contemporary Accounting Research*, **5**, Fall, 199–221.

Demski, J. (1967). An accounting system structured on a linear programing model. *Accounting Review*, Oct., 701–12.

Dittman, D. & Prakash, P. (1978). Cost variance investigation: Markovian control of Markov processes. *Journal of Accounting Research*, **16**, Spring, 14–25.

Dittman, D. & Prakash, P. (1979). Cost variance investigation: Markovian versus optimal control. *Accounting Review*, Apr., 358–73.

Farrell, M. J. (1957). The measurement of productive efficiency. *Journal of the Royal Statistical Society*, Series A, **120**, 3, 253–81.

Hasseldine, C. R. (1967). Mix and yield variances. *The Accounting Review*, July, 497–515.

Kaplan, R. S. (1975). The significance and investigation of cost variances: Survey and extensions. *Journal of Accounting Research*, Autumn, 311–37.

Kaplan, R. S. (1978). Optimal investigation strategies with imperfect information. *Journal of Accounting Research*, Spring, 32–43.

Lev, B. (1969). An information theory analysis of budget variances. *The Accounting Review*, Oct., 704–10.

Magee, R. P. (1976). A simulation analysis of alternative cost variance investigation models. *Accounting Review*, July, 529–44.

Magee, R. P. (1977). Cost control with imperfect parameter knowledge. *Accounting Review*, Jan., 190–9.

Magee, R. P. (1986). *Advanced management accounting*. New York: Harper & Row.

Marcinko, D. & Petri, E. (1984). Use of the production function in calculations of standard cost variances – An extension. *The Accounting Review*, July, 488–95.

Mensah, Y. M. (1982). A dynamic approach to the evaluation of input variable cost center performance. *The Accounting Review*, Oct., 681–700.

Mensah, Y. M. & Li, S-H. (1993). Measuring production efficiency in a not-for-profit setting: An extension. *The Accounting Review*, Jan., 66–88.

Wolk, H. I. & Hillman, A. D. (1972). Materials mix and yield variances: A suggested improvement. *The Accounting Review*, July, 549–55.

YAW M. MENSAH

countercyclical hiring Countercyclical hiring is a staffing strategy that is pursued to a limited extent by companies seeking to obtain bargains in key managerial and professional personnel by hiring during economic downturns. With conventional hiring, which occurs on a procyclical basis, companies hire during economic upturns. As such they attempt to hire employees at times when other companies are also competing for labor. Thus, there is higher demand for labor during economic upturns and it should be more difficult to obtain highly qualified key employees (Bright, 1976). As a result, companies that do not practice countercyclical hiring should find it more difficult to obtain the human resources needed to develop an advantage *vis-à-vis* their competitors.

The contrarian strategy of countercyclical hiring is based on the rationale that companies can invest in their stock of human resources by hiring key managerial and professional employees before there is a realized need, based on the knowledge that the services of such highly qualified individuals will be needed in the future. Thus companies that pursue countercyclical hiring strategies stockpile human resources for the future (Greer, 1984; Greer and Stedham, 1989; Greer and Ireland, 1992).

To date there have been two empirical studies of countercyclical hiring. The first found that companies that practice countercyclical hiring do so because of the quality of employees that can be hired. Unsurprisingly, organizations that conduct human resource forecasting (to avoid personnel shortages) are more likely to hire on a countercyclical basis (Greer and Stedham, 1989). A more recent study found the financial performance of companies to be positively related to countercyclical hiring, along with human resource planning (to avoid personnel shortages), the importance of having a regular managerial age distribution, emphasis on employee development and career development, and the perceived quality of applicants (Greer and Ireland, 1992). Because there are obvious economic costs and potential risks of creating perceptions of unfairness when new employees are hired concurrently with layoffs of present employees, countercyclical hiring strategies are envisioned to be implemented on only a limited basis. Nonetheless, countercyclical hiring can be an important contributor to the development of competencies which allow companies to differentiate themselves from their competitors.

Bibliography

Bright, W. E. (1976). How one company manages its human resources. *Harvard Business Review*, **54**, 81–93.

Greer, C. R. (1984). Countercyclical hiring as a staffing strategy for managerial and professional personnel: some considerations and issues. *Academy of Management Review*, 9, 324–30.

Greer, C. R. & Ireland, T. C. (1992). Organizational and financial correlates of a contrarian human resource investment strategy. *Academy of Management Journal*, 35, 956–84.

Greer, C. R. & Stedham, Y. (1989). Countercyclical hiring as a staffing strategy for managerial and professional personnel: an empirical investigation. *Journal of Management*, 15, 425–40.

CHARLES R. GREER

counterpurchase agreements   Two purchase contracts are agreed to by buyer and seller. Buyer agrees to purchase goods or services at a specified price (contract number one). Seller agrees to purchase a certain value of goods from buyer over a given period of time (contract number two). Contract number one is not valid unless contract number two is accepted and signed. Thus all or part of the sales price of the original goods or services is paid for with other goods or services.

see also **Countertrade**

JOHN O'CONNELL

countertrade   An arrangement in which partial or total payment for imports is made in the form of goods or services rather than money. Countertrade is also sometimes referred to as Compensatory Trade. There are a large ranging from informal barter between willing buyers and sellers to a number of different types of contractual agreements between governments or business organizations.

Countertrade takes place for a number of reasons. There may be little or no currency available, unstable governments make currency difficult to exchange, or currency restrictions may be in effect. In these situations a number of countertrade scenarios may be appropriate. The following is a list of some of the more common types of countertrade.

1 Buy back – An agreement between an exporter of capital goods (for example, processing equipment to be used by the buyer to produce a finished product) to accept future payment for those goods in the form of the finished product of the buyer.

2 Compensation trade – When an importer and an exporter agree to exchange specified goods as payment to each other for those goods. The exchange does not have to occur at the same time.

3 Cooperation agreements – When there is a need in one country for certain resources in order to produce products and there is availability of those resources in another country a cooperation agreement may be in order. For example, country A needs electrical power to produce clothing and country B has excess electrical power but needs clothing. An agreement is made for country B to supply power in return for future payment in clothing that country A is then able to produce.

4 Counterpurchase agreements – Two purchase contracts are agreed to by buyer and seller. The buyer agrees to purchase goods or services at a specified price (contract number one). The seller agrees to purchase a certain value of goods from the buyer over a certain period of time (contract number two). Contract number one is not valid unless contract number two is accepted and signed. Thus all or part of the sales price of the original

goods or services is paid for with other goods or services.

5 Offset trade – When an importer pays an exporter with goods or services.

6 Switch trade – A situation in which an importer is contractually bound to complete the purchase of goods from an exporter. The importer for some reason cannot fulfill its contract and instead "switches" the contract to another importer who then fulfills the remaining portion of the contract. Switching many times involves several importers who may pay in currency or in goods. Exporters allow switching to occur in order to complete the countertrade transaction.

The above are all examples of trade in which countertrade plays a role in an international trade transaction. Countertrade is an important facet of world commerce and should be considered by companies seeking to do business with organizations or governments of countries in which appropriate currency is blocked or in short supply. Countertrade may also be a way of turning what otherwise may be a bad loan or unpaid transaction into something of potential value.

Bibliography

Czinkota, M. R., Rivoli, P. & Ronkainen, I. A. (1989). *International business*. Chicago, IL: The Dryden Press.

Eiteman, D. K., Stonehill, A. J. & Moffett, M. H. (1992). *Multinational business finance*. 6th edn, Reading, MA: Addison-Wesley Publishing.

Grosse, R. & Kujawa, D. (1995). *International business: Theory and managerial applications*. 3rd edn, Boston, MA: Richard D. Irwin Inc.

Rugman, A. M. & Hodgetts, R. M. (1995). *International management: A strategic management approach*. New York: McGraw-Hill Inc.

JOHN O'CONNELL

country risk assessment   An attempt to evaluate the extensiveness of economic, political, and social risks associated with a particular country or region of the world. Risk assessment allows management to estimate the potential impact of country risk on their activities in the country. The greater the country risk, the greater the return that should be expected from an investment or loan. The factors associated with country risk are very similar to those associated with what is referred to as "political risk." This is because many of the contributing factors to country risk result in government action to resolve problems. Political risk is the impact of government action on an organization's assets and its ability to continue operations. A detailed discussion of risk assessment is under the heading of "Political risk assessment."

Bibliography

Coplin, W. D. & O'Leary, M. K. (1994). *The handbook of country and political risk analysis*. New York: Political Risk Services.

Cosset, J. & Roy, J. (1991). The determinants of country risk ratings. *Journal of International Business Studies*, 22 (1), 135–42.

Howell, L. D. (1994). The political sociology of foreign investment and trade: Testing risk models for adequacy of protection. *AGSIM Faculty Publication*, No. 94–05.

JOHN O'CONNELL

country similarity theory   The conduct of trade is dependent upon there being a supply of goods and services and a corresponding demand for those (or similar) goods and services. The country similarity theory states that countries having the most similarities with one another (degree of industrialization; per capita incomes; savings habits; communications and transportation systems; degree of technology; language; etc.) will be the most likely to trade with one another. This rather logical theory is based upon the premise that similar countries will be interested in similar goods and services. Not a devastatingly scientific theory, but one which at least points to specific countries as being good candidates for a company's first foray into international trade.

JOHN O'CONNELL

Cournot competition   The term Cournot competition refers to a model of OLIGOPOLY which was introduced by the French mathematician and economist Antoine Augustin Cournot in 1838 and is widely used in Industrial Organization economics. The model considers a fixed number of firms which choose their output levels trying to maximize their profits. Given the total output produced, the market demand curve determines the price and the profit for each firm. In the Cournot equilibrium each firm does not want to change its output level given the output of its competitors. The firms have Cournot conjectures, i.e. they take the output level of their competitors as given. It is important to recognize that the Cournot equilibrium is just the Nash equilibrium of the corresponding simultaneous-move game. In a Cournot equilibrium, the prices are higher (respectively, lower), the total output is lower (higher), and the per firm profit is higher (lower) than in PERFECT COMPETITION (MONOPOLY). In fact, as the number of firms increases, the Cournot equilibrium approaches the perfectly competitive outcome.

The Cournot model has to be distinguished from other models of oligopoly competition such as Stackelberg competition (with FIRST-MOVER ADVANTAGES instead of simultaneous moves), Bertrand competition (where firms compete with prices instead of quantities as the strategic variable) and Edgeworth competition (with capacity constraints).

Bibliography

Cournot, A. A. (1927). *Researches into the Mathematical Principles of the Theory of Wealth* (English translation; originally *"Recherches sur les principes mathématiques de la théorie des richesses"*, 1838). 2nd edn, New York: Macmillan.
Daughety, A. F. (ed.) (1988). *Cournot Oligopoly*. Cambridge: CUP.
Vives, X. (1989). Cournot and the oligopoly problem. *European Economic Review*, 33, 503–14.

NIKOLAOS VETTAS

craft unions   A craft union represents workers who possess a specialized skill or perform a particular function. Examples include bricklayers, masons, plasterers, and electricians. Employees enter the craft as an apprentice and work their way up to the role of journeyman and through several years of on-the-job training. The union represents these employees in COLLECTIVE BARGAINING and also determines which individuals will have the opportunity to enter the trade. By restricting entry into the skilled trades, craft unions are able to keep wages high. Craft unions also control the hiring process through the mechanism of the hiring hall.

Bibliography

Kochan, T. A., Katz, H. C. & McKersie, R. B. (1986). *The Transformation of American Industrial Relations*, New York: Basic Books.
Slichter, S. H., Healy, J. J. & Livenash, E. R. (1960). *The Impact of Collective Bargaining on Management*, Washington, DC: Brookings Institution.

JAMES B. DWORKIN

creativity   Organizational researchers and high-level managers in organizations have displayed growing interest in creativity in recent years, perhaps because individual and team creativity is seen as the primary means by which organizations can maintain competitive advantage. Creativity is generally defined as the generation of ideas or products that are both novel and appropriate (correct, useful, valuable, or meaningful). However, theorists and researchers have a long history of disagreement over the definition of creativity. Gestalt psychologists and, more recently, cognitive psychologists have focused on the creative process (the thought processes and stages involved in creative activity). Other theorists have argued that creativity is best conceptualized in terms of the person (the distinguishing characteristics of creative individuals).

Although many contemporary theorists think of creativity as a process and look for evidence of it in persons, current definitions most frequently use characteristics of the product as the distinguishing signs of creativity. Most product definitions stipulate that a creative product or response must be both novel and appropriate. An additional criterion used by some researchers is that the task should be heuristic (open-ended) rather than algorithmic (having a clear path to solution). Although many researchers operationally define creativity as performance on creativity tests, most consider consensual product assessment by experts as more appropriate; a product or idea is deemed creative to the extent that appropriate observers agree it is creative. Similarly, in identifying particularly creative individuals in work organizations, most researchers rely on the consensual assessment of managers and peers.

Prior to about 1980, the field of creativity research was dominated by a personality trait approach that sought to identify reliable individual differences between persons who consistently produce highly creative work and persons who do not. As a result, some areas of inquiry that are potentially important for organizational studies were virtually ignored. There was a concentration on the creative person to the neglect of creative situations; there was a narrow focus on intrapersonal determinants of creativity to the neglect of external determinants; and, within studies of intrapersonal determinants, there was an implicit concern with genetic influences to the neglect of contributions from learning and the social environment. Contemporary theorists have begun to argue that creativity is best conceptualized not as a personality trait or a general ability but as a behavior resulting from particular constellations of personal characteristics, cognitive abilities, and environmental factors (e.g., Amabile, 1988).

Personal Characteristics

A cluster of personal characteristics has been repeatedly identified as important to high-level creative behavior:

(a) self-discipline in matters concerning work;
(b) an ability to delay gratification;
(c) perseverance in the face of frustration;
(d) independence of judgment;
(e) a tolerance for ambiguity;
(f) a high degree of autonomy;
(g) an absence of sex-role stereotyping;
(h) an internal LOCUS OF CONTROL;
(i) an orientation toward Risk-taking; and
(j) a high level of self-initiated, task-oriented striving for excellence.

Recently, creativity theorists and researchers have also shown an interest in the role of MOTIVATION in creativity. Research suggests that intrinsic motivation (engaging in an activity because of interest, involvement, or personal challenge) is more conducive to creativity than extrinsic motivation (engaging in an activity to achieve some external goal).

Although it is important for creative individuals to be skilled in their particular domain, several domain-independent features of cognitive style appear to be relevant to creativity:

(a) perceptual flexibility;
(b) cognitive flexibility;
(c) understanding complexities;
(d) keeping response options open as long as possible;
(e) suspending judgment;
(f) using "wide" categories;
(g) remembering accurately;
(h) breaking out of performance scripts; and
(i) perceiving creatively.

Research on entrepreneurship has begun to examine the impact of the personality traits, motivational orientations, and cognitive style of entrepreneurs on their creative activity.

Work Environment Influences

Social–psychological experiments on the effect of particular factors on the creativity of adults and children have demonstrated that evaluative pressures, surveillance, contracted-for reward, competition, and restricted choice can undermine intrinsic motivation and creativity by focusing the individual on external reasons for doing the task (Amabile, 1988). Expanding beyond these experimental methods, research in work organizations has utilized the observational methods of interviews and questionnaires to examine the complex effects of work environment on individual and team creativity. Work environments most conducive to the fulfillment of creative potential appear to be characterized by: a high level of worker autonomy in carrying out the work, encouragement to take risks from administrative superiors, work groups that are both diversely skilled and cooperative; COMMUNICATION and collaboration across work groups, and a substantial degree of challenge in the work. There appear to be four "balance factors" handled effectively by managers who promote creativity: goals that are set clearly at the overall strategic level (see GOAL-SETTING), but left loose at the operational level; REWARDS that are neither ignored nor overly emphasized; performance appraisal systems that provide constructive, frequent feedback on work without generat-

ing threatening negative criticism; and pressure arising from the challenging, urgent nature of the work rather than from arbitrary time pressure or intraorganizational competitive pressure.

Current research on work environments is directed toward identifying the links between individual or team creativity and overall organizational INNOVATION.

Creativity Enhancement in Organizations

Since the 1950s, a growing number of creativity-enhancement training programs have been offered to organizations. The oldest and most widely used program, and the source from which most such programs have been developed, is the Creative Problem Solving process. This process, developed during the 1950s and 1960s from the brainstorming technique, involves the use of checklists and forced relationships in addition to the brainstorming principles of deferred judgment and quantity of idea generation.

Synectics, a somewhat similar process, relies more heavily on the use of metaphor and analogy in the generation of novel ideas. The guiding principle of synectics is to "make the familiar strange and strange familiar" – to use cognitive techniques for distancing oneself from habitual thought patterns, and to also attempt to see connections between something new and something that is already understood. The prescribed cognitive techniques include personal analogy, direct analogy, symbolic analogy, and fantasy analogy.

Although research on the long-term effectiveness of creativity-training programs is limited, many managers and human resource management professionals utilize such programs for employee development.

In order to gain a more comprehensive understanding of creativity in organizational contexts, contemporary theorists are attempting to integrate personality, cognitive, and work environment factors.

Bibliography

Amabile, T. M. (1988). A model of creativity and innovation in organizations In B. M. Staw & L. L. Cummings (Eds), Research in organizational behavior, (vol. 10) Greenwich, CT: JAI Press.
Isaksen, S. (Ed.), (1987). Frontiers in creativity research: Beyond the basics. Buffalo, NY: Bearly.
Runco, M. A. & Albert, R. S. (Eds), (1990). Theories of creativity. Newbury Park, CA: Sage.
Sternberg, R. J. (Ed.), (1988). The nature of creativity. New York: Cambridge University Press.

TERESA M. AMABILE and MARY ANN COLLINS

critical incidents technique   The Critical Incidents Technique (CIT) was developed by Flanagan (1954) for assembling lists of behaviors that are critical to effective job performance. The procedure consists of four steps.

(1) A panel of subject matter experts (SMEs), e.g. supervisors, job incumbents, or other knowledgeable persons, provides written examples of effective or ineffective job behaviors. These are called critical incidents. These examples indicate what led up to the behavior, what the employee actually did, the consequences of the behavior, and whether the consequences were under the control of the employee.

(2) All the examples are put on index cards and then sorted into categories of similar behaviors (e.g. all cards that describe examples of how one would handle an emergency situation are grouped together).

(3) The categories of behaviors identified in step 2 are given a name descriptive of the behaviors that comprise them (e.g. handling emergency situations).

(4) These categories are then rated according to how critical or important they are for effective job performance.

A refinement of the original CIT approach is to use two groups of SMEs. The second group is used to verify the work of the first group. Once the incidents have been developed and categorized by the first group of SMEs, the second group is given the names and definitions of all categories and a separate listing of all incidents. The second group attempts to place each incident into one of the predefined categories. If a sufficient percentage of the second group of SMEs place an incident in its appropriate category, the incident is retained. If not, the incident is dropped. Another refinement has been to ask SMEs for examples of "routine" behaviors, in addition to examples of particularly effective and ineffective behaviors. This provides a broader overall view of job activities. The CIT is well suited for developing PERFORMANCE APPRAISAL systems and for determining the training needs of employees.

Bibliography

Flanagan, J. C. (1954). The critical incidents technique. *Psychological Bulletin*, **51**, 327–58.

JAMES B. SHAW

cross-cultural communication Communication between cultures is one of the greatest challenges facing an international manager. Not only does the manager face the normal problems of creating a concise and clear communication, but the communication must be accomplished in the context of another culture. The following discussion reviews a number of areas which must be considered in order to conduct successful cross-cultural communication.

1 The medium of communication – The "medium" is the method by which a message is sent. Mediums of communication include writing (notes, E-mail, annual statements, letters, etc.), speaking (telephone, videotape, public address system, face-to-face conversation, etc.), body language (eye contact, motions of the hands and arms, head down or looking straight ahead, etc.), tone of voice (high anxious tone, soft, aggressive and loud), depicting a message in pictures (directions for use, signs, etc.), or any combination of mediums. A very important aspect of cross-cultural communications is knowledge of which medium is acceptable for different situations. For example, is a note sufficient to convey a message or do the formalities of a culture require a face-to-face meeting. Sending a note may be taken as a rude approach from someone who does not want to face the person receiving the message. On the other hand, a face-to-face meeting when a simple note would convey the same message may place more importance on the communication than intended by the sender. The medium used depends on a number of factors including: large or small audience; how quickly the message must be sent; distance of communication (across the room or to another country); intent of message (good news or downsizing of the organization); legal considerations (contracts, hiring/firing); simple or complex message; message content needed in future; and the availability of various communications media.

2 The information intended versus the information received – People normally feel that communication is successful when the person receiving the message does not have any questions or does not express any concern over the message's content. If the sender delved further into the reasons that no questions were asked or concerns expressed he/she may find one or more of the following had occurred: the receiver did not understand the message sufficiently to respond in any manner; the receiver felt the message content was irrelevant and chose to ignore it; the message was unimportant, or there could have been any number of other misinterpretations which occur during the process we call "communication." When developing information to be included in a communication the sender must take into consideration the audience (education level, cultural values, need for direction as well as acceptance of direction from superiors, etc.). The challenge in cross-cultural communication is to make certain that the message is received in the way intended. This requires a great deal of understanding on the part of the sender of the receiver's cultural background and current situation. Failure to have knowledge of the parties who receive messages will virtually assure miscommunication. The message will be either too intricate, too simple, or irrelevant to some or all of those to whom it is transmitted. The result will be that the message is not understood (too intricate), people feel talked down to (too simple), or the message is not taken seriously (felt to be irrelevant).

3 Timing of communications – Determining the appropriate time for communicating certain ideas is extremely important for successful cross-cultural communications. Some cultures desire to discuss work only at work and leave the rest of the time for family and friends. Japanese managers may allow themselves to have fun after work but rarely on the job. Social occasions are just that in many countries, whereas in the United States social occasions are commonly the site of business contacts. The first time one meets a Middle Eastern business person is not the time to get right to business discussions, relationship-building and trust are important precursors to business activity. Even important communications must be relayed at the appropriate time or their import may be overshadowed by the ill timing of the message.

4 Who communicates – One of the problems international managers have is that they are unfamiliar with

communication patterns in different cultures. Cultures in which relationship building is important may not allow a business discussion to take place between the company president and an unknown representative from another company. Instead a lower level manager or representative will act as a go–between. The importance of a message will often dictate who the communicator will be. For example, when Johnson and Johnson had a problem with Tylenol which had been tampered with, the head of the company appeared on television. This showed the importance of the message to the consuming public. If a middle manager had made the recall announcement its impact would not have been as great.

When communicating across cultures it is important to know the expectations of all parties to the communication. Expectations as to the proper wording, timing, place of communication, sender of the message, and appropriate medium of communication. If the timing, wording, sender or receiver, medium, or any of a number of other important considerations is inappropriate, the communication has a good chance of failing.

Bibliography

Black, J. S. & Mendenhall, M. (1993). Resolving conflicts with Japanese: Mission impossible? *Sloan Management Review* Spring, 83.
Brislin, R. W. (1981). *Cross-cultural encounters*. New York: Pergamon Press.
Evans, W. A., Sculli, D. & Yau, W. S. L. (1987). Cross-cultural factors in the identification of managerial potential. *Journal of General Management*, 13 (1), 52–7.
Francis, J. N. (1991). When in Rome? The affects of cultural adaptations on the intercultural business negotiations. *Journal of International Business Studies*, 22 (3), 403–28.
Hayes, J. & Allison, C. W. (1988). Cultural differences in the learning styles of managers. *Management International Review*, 28 (3), 75–80.
Moran, R. (1988). *Venturing abroad in Asia: Complete business traveller's guide to cultural differences in eleven Asian countries*. New York: McGraw-Hill Book Co.
Moran, R. T. (1994). *NAFTA: Managing the cultural differences*. Houston, TX: Gulf Publishing Company.
Terpstra, V. & David, K. (1985). *The cultural environment of international business*. Dallas, TX: South Western Publishing.

JOHN O'CONNELL

cross-cultural training Cross-cultural training is designed to help people become more aware of the differences between cultures throughout the world. An understanding of the differences makes employees more sensitive to the values, wants, and needs of others. Such an awareness can make management more effective and employees more productive in jobs located either in other countries or involving contacts with other countries. Friction associated with work force diversity may also be reduced through cross-cultural training.

Cross-cultural training is commonly carried out in the following ways: (1) lectures by persons familiar with different cultures; (2) awareness training in which employees are exposed to the values and behaviors found in a particular culture; (3) experiential training through field trips, role playing, or country visits; (4) attribution training to assist in developing an understanding of why people act or do things in the way they do; (5) behavior modification

training to allow employees to understand the reward and punishment systems in another country.

see also **Expatriate training**

Bibliography

Alkhafaji, A. F. (1990). *International management challenge*. Acton, MA: Copley.
Evans, W. A., Sculli, D. & Yau, W. S. L. (1987). Cross-cultural factors in the identification of managerial potential. *Journal of General Management*, 13 (1), 52–7.
Ferraro, G. P. (1990). *The cultural dimension of international business*. Englewood Cliffs, NJ: Prentice-Hall.
Kuroda, Y. & Suzuki, T. (1991). A comparative analysis of the Arab culture: Arabic, English, and Japanese language and values. *International Association of Middle Eastern Studies*
Landis, D. & Brislin, R. (1983). *Handbook on intercultural training*. New York: Pergamon Press.
Mendenhall, M. E., Dunbar, E. & Oddou, Gary (1987). Expatriate selection, training, and career pathing: A review and critique. *Human Resource Management*, 26, 331–45.
Pulatie, D. (1985). How do you ensure success of managers going abroad. *Training and Development Journal*, December, 22–4.
Ronen, S. & Tung, R. L. (1981). Selection and training of personnel for overseas assignments. *Columbia Journal of World Business*, Spring, 68–78.

JOHN O'CONNELL

cross-functional management structure Many Japanese companies introduced cross-functional management structures during the 1960s when they recognized, first, that interdepartmental communication and cooperation were poor and departmental group dynamics were not aligned toward corporate strategy and, second, for a specific function such as quality management, departmental responsibilities were usually unclear and the department lacked the authorization to act. In 1962, therefore, Toyota recognized that it was necessary to introduce a cross-functional management structure as part of its TQC (Total Quality Control) program.

The first step in cross-functional management is to select a method of analyzing cross-functions that is consistent with overall strategy. At Toyota Motor, functions were divided into four groups; overall planning, objective functions, means functions, and service functions. By contrast, Toyota Auto Body, a related concern, recognized two functions; primary functions and step-by-step management. Other Japanese concerns adopted similar concepts, as shown in table 1, while the term "cross-functional management" became widespread in Japan during the 1980s. Most companies viewed quality assurance, cost (or profit) management, delivery control, and personnel management as primary functions, while new product development was seen as an auxiliary function. However, not all functions were given the same priority and significance. Normally, primary functions did not change; while auxiliary functions, which also often included sales management and occasionally purchasing and safety, might change according to conditions and corporate needs.

Top management identified the organizational structure clearly and specifically in order to promote cross-functional management. Groups of functions by implementation format were used to categorize cross-functional forms into four categories (type O to type III) according to the size and structural complexity of the concerns involved. The existence of departments having primary responsibility for

Table 1   Organization and administration of cross-functional management committee meetings.

Items	Kacru Ishikawa	Toyota Motor Corporation	Komatsu Ltd
Organization	Cross-functional committee	Quality function and cost function committees	Quality assurance function committee (as example)
Reporting role	Report to board of executive committee	Report to board of executive committee	Report to TQC promotion committee
Responsibilities	Responsible for dealing with cross-functional matters in all departments, assigning responsibilities, and establishing system rules and audits	Same level of responsibility as board of directors or board of managing directors; serves as a practical decision-making body	Responsible for improvement of the quality assurance system – which includes all processes from product planning to sales and service – and for upgrading the level of quality assurance
Areas of work		Planning, auditing, coordinating, and recommending	
Composition	Committee chairman: executive with the rank of senior vice president or executive vice president who is in charge of functions	Chairman: generally a senior vice president of a department to which a particular function is closely linked	Committee: quality assurance managing executives
	Committee members: about five executives with the rank of director or higher, one or two executives from other areas, and a facilitator	Members: executives of functionally related departments	Committee members: about five related executives
	Staff support office: each department concerned	Facilitators: about ten executives with the rank of vice president or senior vice president who report directly to the chairman	Staff support office: quality assurance department
Additional items	[Example] quality assurance 1 Monthly status of quality assurance and investigation of claims status 2 Establishment and revision of departmental assignments concerning areas of cross-function responsibilities	(1) Establishment of objectives; (2) plans and policies to achieve targeted objectives; (3) plans concerning new products, equipment, manufacturing, and sales; (4) important bottom-up items; (5) measures to eliminate barriers to implementation; (6) action necessary as a result of checking; (7) checking performance results of corporate policy and the plan for subsequent year; (8) other necessary items for cross-functional management	In order to carry out its objectives, the committee reviews and makes recommendations to the TQC committee on the following: 1 Plan concerning corporate quality assurance 2 Concerning quality assurance a. Improvement plan for the system and the improvement programme b. System improment items and departments responsible
Meeting frequency	Regular and monthly	Once a month, as a rule	Once every other month, as a rule

Source: Kozo Koura (1993).

each and every function was a prerequisite. A slightly less complex methodology has grouped the structures of corporations receiving the Deming prize into three classes; simple, general, and advanced.

A simple structure is illustrated in figure 1. In it, the TQC promotion committee promotes cross-functional management. This structure is found in smaller concerns with up to around ten executives and a limited labor force, with the TQC committee operating through a series of smaller focused subcommittees.

The general structure is found in larger corporations and is shown in figure 2. The structure of a leading construction company, Hazama-Gumi, is illustrated. The main office and branch office each have their own TQC committee which, in turn, has three subordinate functional committees covering quality assurance, awarded contract management, and profit management. The central office also has two additional committees covering subcontracting management and technology development. In many companies a variant of this structure involves the TQC

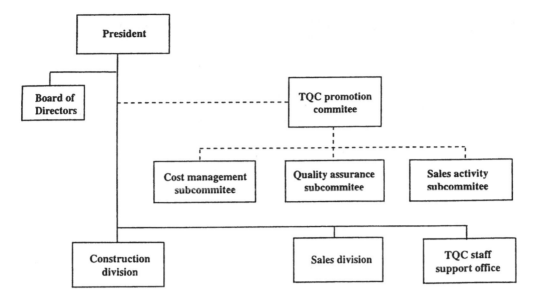

Uchino Construction

Company receiving 1985 Deming Prize, small medium sizes company category

Figure 1 A simple cross-functional structure.
Source: Kozo Koura (1993).

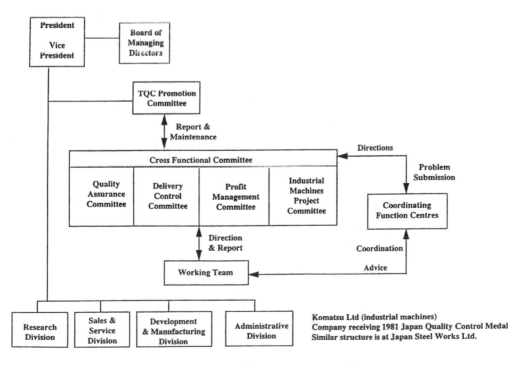

Komatsu Ltd (industrial machines)
Company receiving 1981 Japan Quality Control Medal
Similar structure is at Japan Steel Works Ltd.

Figure 2 A general cross-functional organization.
Source: Kozo Koura (1993).

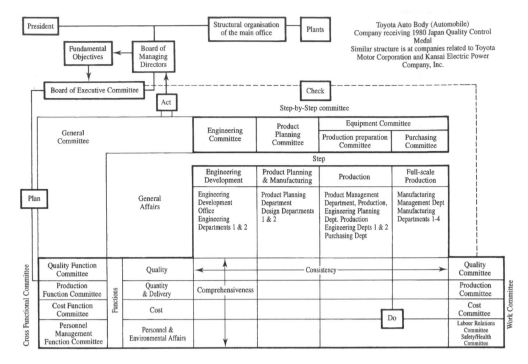

Figure 3 An advanced cross-functional structure.
Source: Kozo Koura (1993).

promotion committee operating with a series of substructure cross-functional committees. For example, in Komatsu these consist of quality assurance, delivery control, profit management, and industrial machines project committees.

The advanced structure was first established by the Toyota Motor Corporation and has been widely adopted by other companies within the Toyota Group. In an assembly business without other divisions, each and every function of quality, cost delivery, and personnel management is applied horizontally to each step of the process; product planning design, test production, production preparation, full scale production, sales, and service. (See figure 3.)

In this example, the general committee and the cross-functional committee service the company executive committees. Each functional committee is composed of the executives concerned and responsible primarily for the "plan" stage of the PDCA cycle. Each department in charge of each step is responsible for implementation ("do"). Major issues emerging between the "plan" and "do" stages are reviewed by the cross-functional committee. The "step-by-step" committee is composed of executives in charge of each step, and also includes executives and senior managers of the departments concerned. This group also coordinates targeted items for each function with action items, and checks the assurance status of the development process. The work committee for senior managers is convened by an executive who is responsible for a given function. This committee is in charge of deploying corporate functional policy and is responsible for coordination and checking during the deployment stages.

The cross-functional committee within Japanese corporations is primarily responsible for the establishment, maintenance, and improvement of cross-functional management in the areas of quality, cost, profit, and delivery. It also has other responsibilities concerned with improvement. These include cross-functional management in other functions; creating and promoting long-term and annual cross-functional management plans; company-wide horizontal deployment of the results of cross-functional management; and planning and implementation of cross-functional audits.

The serious way in which Japanese companies address the issue of cross-functional coordination compares with conventional Western structures that emphasize vertical, hierarchical arrangements. The use of the HORIZONTAL STRUCTURE is a relatively very recent phenomenon in the West and is usually implemented as an element in the introduction of corporate re-engineering projects.

The effects of cross-functional management structures include the following:

- accelerated decision making and implementation of quality assurance, cost/profit management, and delivery control policies

- greater awareness of cross-functional management issues at all levels of the organization and improved departmental cooperation and relationships

- that as a result of cross-functional treatment of issues, no extra departments or sections are required

- that employee suggestions are implemented more easily

- that departmental executives adopt a perspective more tuned to corporate needs, rather than to narrow departmental interests

Bibliography

Kozo Koura (1993). Administrative aspects and key points of cross-functional management.

Kenji Kurogane *Cross functional management*. Tokyo: Asian Productivity Organisation.

Masao Kogure (1986). Cross-functional management. *Quality Control*, 37 special issue, 253–9.

Shiggeru Aoki (1981). Cross functional management for top management. *Quality Control*, **32** (2), 92–8; **32** (3), 66–71; **32** (4), 65–9.

DEREK F. CHANNON

cross licensing Situations exist in which different companies are working on similar research and development projects at the same time. One company makes advances in one area and the other in a second area. By joining effort and sharing discoveries and technology, both companies could move forward more quickly than either could alone. This synergistic approach (resulting in mutual benefit) could be accomplished by a cross-licensing arrangement. Under cross-licensing each company gives the other permission to use patented or copyrighted technology, processes, or inventions. Cross-licensing achieves two things: (1) gains for both companies are increased through the dual use of intellectual property rights; and (2) both companies still protect their property rights because the only party able to use them is the company designated in the cross-licensing agreement.

Bibliography

Deresky, Helen (1994). *International management*. 1st edn, New York: HarperCollins.

Seminsky, M. & Bryer, L. G. (eds) (1994). *The new role of intellectual property in commercial transactions*. New York: John Wiley & Sons.

JOHN O'CONNELL

cross-training Cross-training refers to teaching employees the knowledge, skills, and abilities (see KSAOs) necessary to successfully perform the work duties of other members of their work group. As distinguished from training, cross-training refers to the instruction of employees in knowledge, skills, and abilities outside those required by the positions for which they were explicitly or initially hired (Schneider, 1976; Cascio, 1986).

From the organization's perspective, cross-training is implemented to increase flexibility in staffing positions, to prevent workers' obsolescence or CAREER PLATEAU, and to make work teams more autonomous and self-sufficient. From the individual's perspective, cross-training is undertaken to acquire additional skills and abilities necessary for promotions or pay raises, to enhance his or her contributions to current work groups, and to increase external marketability. Increasingly, cross-training is being utilized to create and sustain semi-autonomous or SELF-MANAGING TEAMS (Hackman and Oldham, 1980).

The introduction of cross-training usually takes place in three stages: (a) analysis of the job demands required by other positions and employees' current levels of abilities; (b) implementation of the training itself through a variety of methods (e.g. lectures, demonstrations, and vestibule training); and (c) evaluation of the effectiveness of the training (as measured by employee reactions to the training

and measures of employee learning and performance) (Wexley and Latham, 1981).

Bibliography

Cascio, W. F. (1986). *Managing Human Resources*, New York: McGraw-Hill.

Hackman, J. R. & Oldham, G. R. (1980). *Work Redesign*, Reading, MA: Addison-Wesley.

Schneider, B. (1976). *Staffing Organizations*, Pacific Palisades, CA: Goodyear.

Wexley, K. & Latham, G. P. (1981). *Developing and Training Human Resources in Organizations*, Glenview, IL: Scott Foresman.

DANIEL C. FELDMAN

cultural adaptation The process through which a person becomes able to function successfully in another culture. Failure to adapt is the major reason expatriates find themselves unable to complete overseas assignments. Generally people are chosen for overseas assignment for their technical ability or other skills related to the tasks required of them by the employer. Thus, it is typically not the inability to do a task which causes failure, it is the inability to adapt to the new cultural environment.

Bibliography

Briody, E. K. & Chrisman, J. B. (1991). Cultural adaptation on overseas assignments. *Human Organization*, **50** (3), 264–82.

David, K. (1991). *"Field research" in the cultural environment of international business*. Cincinnati, OH: South-Western.

Francis, J. N. (1991). When in Rome? The affects of cultural adaptations on the intercultural business negotiations. *Journal of International Business Studies*, **22** (3), 403–28.

Howard, C. G. (1982). How best to integrate expatriate managers into the domestic organization. *Personnel Administrator* July, 27–33.

Johnson, M. (1992). *Cultural guide to doing business in Europe*. 2nd edn, Boston, MA: Butterworth-Heinemann.

Watson, W. E., Kumar, K., Subramanian, R. & Nonis, S. A. (1990). Differences in decision making regarding risk between culturally diverse and culturally homogeneous groups. *IAMM Proceeding*, 1, 130–2.

JOHN O'CONNELL

cultural assimilation This is the process through which a person not only is aware of the differences and nuances of a new culture, but also is able to incorporate these differences into daily work and private lives. This does not mean the employee gives up home country values or attitudes, but instead takes the position that both cultures can coexist with one another. A simple home country example will show how this works in a diverse work force. An employee works his way up in the organization from yard worker to middle management. The employee is able to easily converse with yard workers and top management on their terms. Two separate cultures exist between workers and top management, but this manager has learned to coexist in each without making judgments about which is better or worse or good or bad. Cultural assimilation does much the same thing for expatriates.

Bibliography

Glover, M. K. (1990). Do's and taboos: Cultural aspects of international business. *Business America*, **August**, 2–6.

JOHN O'CONNELL

cultural diversity The existence of different cultures between countries; in different parts of the same country; or within a single organization. Multinational organizations as well as many purely domestic organizations are faced with cultural diversity every day. Diversity may be displayed in the variety of social and ethnic backgrounds of workers or the variety of customers one serves. Learning to live and work in a culturally diverse world requires education and the ability to accept others as they are.

see also **Cultural variables**

Bibliography

Ajiferuke, M. & Boddewyn, J. (1970). Culture and other explanatory variables in comparative management studies. *Academy of Management Journal*, **13**, 153–63.

Anderson, L. R. (1983). Management of the mixed-cultural work group. *Organizational Behavior and Human Performance*, **31**, 303–30.

Cox, T., Lobel, S. A. & McLeod, P. L. (1991). Effects of ethnic group cultural differences on cooperative and competitive behavior on a group task. *Academy of Management*, **4**, 827–47.

Evans, W. A., Sculli, D. & Yau, W. S. L. (1987). Cross-cultural factors in the identification of managerial potential. *Journal of General Management*, **13** (1), 52–7.

Hofstede, G. (1980). *Culture's consequences: International differences in work-related values.* Beverly Hills, CA: Sage Publications.

JOHN O'CONNELL

cultural literacy Cultural literacy is the expert knowledge of both surface and core cultural values, norms, mores, traditions, and operating procedures of a culture. Empirical research in the field shows that expatriates serving in an expatriate assignment must increase their cultural literacy in order to be successful in these assignments.

Cultural literacy involves more than knowing, for example, when and how to bow in Japan when greeting a client. An expatriate who is culturally literate understands why that tradition exists, and understands the deeper core cultural values to which that tradition is linked. When expatriates do not possess high levels of cultural literacy they naturally operate from their personal views regarding what is and what is not appropriate behavior across various life situations in the foreign culture. One's personal views are obviously only workable as guides to behavior in one's culture of birth. Thus, applying personal views as guides to one's behavior while overseas invariably leads expatriates into troubling, embarrassing, and sometimes dangerous incidents in the foreign culture.

Cultural literacy enables an expatriate to understand the reasons behind the behavior he or she encounters overseas, and this understanding enables the expatriate to avoid stereotyping, racial prejudice, and other forms of inappropriate behavior while living and working in a foreign culture. Living and working in a foreign culture requires the expatriate to learn a new mental framework, one that can guide the expatriate in choosing culturally correct behaviors in the foreign culture. The acquisition of cultural literacy requires significant amounts of effort by the expatriate. Companies often try to assist in this task by offering cross-cultural training programs and other types of training.

Bibliography

Black, J. S., Gregersen, H. B. & Mendenhall, M. (1992). *Global Assignments: Successfully Expatriating and Repatriating International Managers* San Francisco: Jossey-Bass.

Black, J. S. & Mendenhall, M. (1990). A practical but theory-based framework for selecting cross-cultural training methods. *Human Resource Management*, **28**, 511–39.

Black, J. S., Mendenhall, M. & Oddou, G. (1991). Toward a comprehensive model of international adjustment: an integration of multiple theoretical perspectives. *Academy of Management Review*, **16**, 291–317.

Mendenhall, M. & Oddou, G. (1985). The dimensions of expatriate acculturation: a review. *Academy of Management Review*, **10**, 39–47.

Oddou, G. & Mendenhall, M. (1984). Person perception in cross-cultural settings: a review of cross-cultural and related literature. *International Journal of Intercultural Relations*, **8**, 77–96.

MARK E. MENDENHALL

cultural maps A cultural map groups countries (cultures) based upon their similarity to one another. Cultural maps were developed by Geert Hofstede as a method of comparing cultures along what he referred to as value dimensions. A cultural map essentially shows how cultures of different countries are similar and how they are different along four dimensions: (1) Individualism – the tendency to look out for yourself first and the employer and society next. (2) Masculinity – aggressiveness, assertiveness, and inability to think of the good of others. (3) Power distance – the acceptance of an unequal distribution of power between employees of an organization; the acceptance of the right of others to command. (4) Uncertainty avoidance – the degree of acceptance of uncertain situations; the willingness to make decisions; to be flexible. Charts (cultural maps) are developed by showing the degree to which a country exhibits each of the dimensions. Countries tend to cluster when their value dimensions are similar.

The implications of cultural maps in the international business setting are very important. If one agrees with the precept that interactions between parties (trade agreements, contracts, etc.) who are similar are more likely to be successful than if the parties are dissimilar, cultural maps may allow an organization to better choose international partners based upon similar cultural attributes. Maps can also be of assistance even if countries are not close together on various attributes. Training and other preparation can take place to deal with those differences more successfully. The idea of a cultural map is not the source of all answers, but it is a valuable tool for use by international organizations.

Bibliography

Elashmawi, F. & Harris, P. R. (1993). *Multicultural management: New skills for global success.* Houston, Texas: Gulf Publishing Company.

Ferraro, G. P. (1990). *The cultural dimension of international business.* Englewood Cliffs, NJ: Prentice-Hall.

Hofstede, G. (1980). *Culture's consequences: International differences in work-related values.* Beverly Hills, CA: Sage Publications.

JOHN O'CONNELL

cultural noise Cultural noise refers to impediments to successful communication between people of different cultures. Sources of cultural noise include differences in: language (e.g., same words have different meanings); values (e.g., importance of being on time or setting work schedule times in a culture); nonverbal cues (e.g., interpretation of body language); and many others. Persons involved in international communication (or domestic, if communication involves other cultures) should be aware of any barriers which may affect the message from being interpreted in the way the sender intended. This requires special understanding of the communication process and the various sources of cultural noise which may impede that process.

see also **Communication; Cross-cultural communication**

Bibliography

Moran, R. (1988). *Venturing abroad in Asia: Complete business traveller's guide to cultural differences in eleven Asian countries.* New York: McGraw-Hill Book Co.

JOHN O'CONNELL

cultural norms   Cultural norms are standards of conduct or acceptable behavior in any given culture. The way people communicate (adding gestures versus just speaking); the way they eat (fork in right hand if from United States and left hand if from Europe); how close one stands when communicating to another (distant in the United States, close in Latin America); equality of men and women (strive for equality in many countries; not an issue in other countries); the work ethic (commitment to employer versus individual creativity); and many other situations are influenced by the norms of a society or culture. An expatriate or other person living overseas should be aware of the normative behaviors of the host country prior to taking up residence.

see also **Cultural variables; Expatriate training**

Bibliography

Howard, C. G. (1982). How best to integrate expatriate managers into the domestic organization. *Personnel Administrator*, July, 27–33.

JOHN O'CONNELL

cultural profiles   A description of a country (culture) based upon its acceptance or adherence to specific cultural variables. Cultural profiles are used to compare countries and cultures based upon preselected dimensions.

see also **Cultural variables**

JOHN O'CONNELL

cultural relativism   Cultural relativism refers to the proposition that what is right or wrong, good or bad, justifiable or not, depends upon the culture in which it occurs. Two examples illustrate cultural relativism: drinking alcoholic beverages is not bad or wrong in Great Britain or Ireland but is wrong (and punishable by authorities) in Middle Eastern countries; bribery is illegal under the laws of the United States, but is an accepted business practice in many countries.

It is difficult to dispute the above part of the cultural relativism proposition (that major differences exist between cultures/countries between what is considered good/bad; moral/immoral; etc). However, problems of ethics and even law may occur if one takes cultural relativism to its extreme and believes the following; "Therefore, in order to get along in another country/

culture, it is acceptable to act in the same manner as those from that country/culture." As an example of potential problems, such a feeling would allow a United States organization (when in another country which lacked strict antibribery laws) to bribe public officials, even though bribery is illegal under the US Foreign Corrupt Practices Act. Cultural relativism may be an appropriate part of the decision-making process in some instances, but its application must be tempered by common sense and a respect for the laws of both the host and home country.

Bibliography

Bowie, N. E. (1990). "Business ethics and cultural relativism" in P. Madsen and J. M. Shafritz (eds) *Essentials of Business Ethics.* New York: Meridian.

JOHN O'CONNELL

cultural sensitivity   An awareness of the differences between cultures and how these differences affect ways in which others work and live. It is the acceptance of differences, rather than a feeling that one way of doing things is either right or wrong. A culturally sensitive person is open to other ways of doing things and cares about adapting to differences rather than changing others to fit a model of "how one is supposed to act or believe."

see also **Cultural insensitivity; Expatriate training**

Bibliography

Black, J. S. & Mendenhall, M. (1993). Resolving conflicts with Japanese: Mission impossible? *Sloan Management Review* Spring, 83.
Glover, M. K. (1990). Do's and taboos: Cultural aspects of international business. *Business America* August, 2–6.
Ricks, D. A. (1983). *Big business blunders: Mistakes in multinational marketing.* Homewood, IL: Dow Jones-Irwin.

JOHN O'CONNELL

cultural variables   The factors which are evaluated in determining the extent and nature of cultural differences. The following set of variables were described by Harris and Moran in their interesting book *Managing Cultural Differences.* Each variable is important to an international manager because it may be the source of a particular work behavior or attitude with which the manager is unfamiliar.

Harris and Moran's cultural variables are presented below (in alphabetical order, not order of importance):

1 Associations – This variable addresses the various groups with which an individual may be associated. Groups are of many types: fraternal, religious, business, professional, trade, union, advocacy (e.g., environmental), political, and many others. Each group may have an impact on an employee in terms of ethical issues, work habits, priorities, loyalties, and other important factors which may affect job performance. The exact nature of the impact depends upon the employee, the group, and the country/culture being reviewed.

2 Economy – General economic factors also contribute to the way people conduct themselves on the job. The type of economy (capitalist, high government control, low government control, public versus private ownership, etc.) affects areas such as incentive systems, availability of goods and services, a worker's feelings about achievement, and loyalty to an employer.

3 Education – The types and amounts of educational opportunities offered in a country provide a reasonable measure of the availability of trained employees as well as the needs for further training to meet the needs of employers. Educational levels may dictate hiring practices (host country nationals versus expatriates) as well as the types and levels of company training programs to be offered.

4 Health – Of growing importance is the general health of people in a country. Healthy employees tend to be more productive and happier then those suffering ill health. The quality and availability of the health-care system in a country will affect the services, etc. which may have to be provided by a company. Social health-care versus private health-care has great implications for employee expectations about what the company should provide in benefits. In some countries employers are actively involved in promoting the good health of employees and their families, while in other countries employers do not become involved.

5 Kinship – The family and its importance in the life of an employee is another cultural variable which may affect employees. The trend toward family unit size is decreasing in some countries and holding stable in others. Large families are common in some countries, while smaller ones seem more acceptable in others. Family units consisting of only immediate family (parents and children) exist in many parts of the world whereas extended family units (grandparents, parents, children, and other family members) are common elsewhere. The responsibilities placed upon a family in terms of time commitments and income needs have real implications for employers.

6 Politics – The political system found in a particular country impacts both employees and the employer. If the system is democratic, employees will probably be more democratic and flexible in their attitudes. Controlled political systems (communistic, dictatorial) may decrease creativity, company loyalty, and the work ethic as well as other characteristics normally thought to be important to managers. Politics may dictate the sources of raw materials for a company, the sources of labor, the type of distribution system used, and the general activities related to commerce.

7 Recreation – This variable describes the role of leisure time in the life of a worker and his/her family. In some countries leisure time is an important and sought-after goal. Company benefits in these countries include long vacations, personal days off, provision of company-sponsored recreation activities, and on site workout and sports facilities. None of these benefits exist in some countries. In other countries, the employer is a part of the employee's leisure time as well and the employee's family literally becomes a part of the bigger company family. A country's/culture's need for leisure or free time and what the employee normally does with this time has important implications for a manager.

8 Religion – In certain countries religion is the most important cultural variable related not only to the workplace but also to the daily lives of the people (Middle Eastern countries). In other countries the impact is much more difficult to perceive or measure (United States, Australia). Religious teachings guide the everyday work and other activities of many workers around the world. These must be taken into consideration by managers when dealing with many factors such as the employee's workweek, hours of work, religious holidays, values of the company.

Bibliography

Deresky, Helen (1994). *International management.* 1st edn, New York: HarperCollins.

England, G. E. (1978). Managers and their values systems: A five-country comparative study. *Columbia Journal of Business* Summer, 35–44.

Graham, J. L. (1985). The influence of culture on business negotiations. *Journal of International Business Studies,* **16 (1),** 81–96.

Harris, P. R. & Moran, R. T. (1987). *Managing cultural differences.* 2nd edn, Houston, Texas: Gulf Publishing.

Kelley, L., Whatley, A. & Worthley, R. (1987). Assessing the affects of culture on managerial attitudes: A three-culture test. *Journal of International Business Studies* Summer, 17–31.

Mead, Richard (1994). *International management: Cross cultural dimensions.* Cambridge, MA: Blackwell Publishers.

Webber, R. (1969). *Culture and management, text and readings in comparative management.* Homewood, IL: Irwin.

JOHN O'CONNELL

culture shock Frustration, confusion, fear, apprehension, and even disorientation because of differences between a person's own culture and the culture in which he/she is currently working or living. Expatriates many times suffer from culture shock. A person who does not know how to behave in personal or business activities in another culture may feel (and actually be) left out of activities and discussions. The expatriate may be perceived as being uncaring about the concerns and values of others.

Culture shock can lead to dissatisfaction and anxiety on the part of the employee. An employee (and family members as well) must be properly oriented to the new culture to reduce the impact of culture shock. Without this cultural integration the chances of expatriate failure are dramatically increased.

see also **Expatriate training**

Bibliography

Briody, E. K. & Chrisman, J. B. (1991). Cultural adaptation on overseas assignments. *Human Organization,* **50 (3),** 264–82.

Hofstede, G. (1980). *Culture's consequences: International differences in work-related values.* Beverly Hills, CA: Sage Publications.

Moran, R. T. (1989). Coping with re-entry shock. *AGSIM Faculty Publication,* No. 89–05,

Oberg, K. (1960). Culture shocks: Adjusting to new cultural environments. *Practical Anthropology,* July–Aug 1960, 177–82.

JOHN O'CONNELL

current value accounting This discussion will concentrate on those measurement bases that are currently feasible – historical cost (HC), historical cost adjusted for general price level change (GPL), current replacement cost (CRC), and current exit value (EV). The HC and GPL bases are needed for understanding the relationship of the current value accounting. The feasibility of CRC and EV is generally not considered high, but available research and experience demonstrate that certain versions of these systems are feasible today. This is in contrast to another possible valuation basis – discounted cash flow.

The discounted cash flow valuation method (also called economic value or direct valuation) consists of projecting future cash flows related to an asset, then discounting those flows to the present using an appropriate discount rate. However, the process of predicting future cash flows must be subjective, which reduces the feasibility of this choice. Further, the assumptions made and the choice of discount rate are likely to vary materially between users.

Although current value accounting discussions may appear to emphasize asset valuation, the choice of systems to be used has important effects on the values at which liabilities and owners' equity will be reported as well as the form and content of the income statement.

The USA has had one short period (1979–1983) where large companies were required to release GPL and CRC information, but no such requirements are in effect today. Other countries have current standards requiring various types of current value or GPL disclosure. And the International Accounting Standards Committee has adopted International Accounting Standard 29 requiring GPL restatement in hyper-inflationary economies (those having three-year total inflation rates over 100 percent). In essence, standard setters seem to avoid the problem of changing prices until it becomes too big to ignore.

In summary, the two systems of MC and GPL fail to provide relevant information for statement users and both suffer from the allocation problem. CRC provides somewhat more useful information, but the most commonly applied version still suffers from the allocation problem. In addition CRC may overstate the actual value of assets and the income dichotomy involved is difficult to apply and is somewhat artificial. The EV system provides information that answers important user questions and resolves the changing dollar and allocation problems. Unfortunately it suffers from the purchase loss and market saturation problems. Thus there is no perfect system, but a combination of CRC and EV seems most promising to provide information useful to decision-makers.

Historical Cost Accounting
The historical cost accounting system (HC) (without adjustment for change in general price level) is the system most often used in practice in the USA today. Since we report depreciated historical cost, the real question answered by HC would be: "How many dollars were spent to get to the current position after deducting the dollars which were assumed related to past operations?" The corresponding question answered by the income statement is: "How many dollars were received by (or promised to) the firm minus the number of dollars spent (or to be spent) to obtain those goods and services used to obtain the revenue?"

There are problems inherent in generating and interpreting the answers given by HC statements to the above questions. First, we have very little, if any, basis for choosing depreciation methods and parameters to apply to fixed assets, which has led to some accountants calling it arbitrary. Thus, all accounting figures that depend on allocations – primarily inventory and fixed assets – must be viewed as the product of arbitrary allocations over periods. The book values of these assets, therefore, cannot be considered any more appropriate or "correct" than many other possible figures. It is *extremely* important to be aware of this allocation problem and of its potential effects on the meaning and reliability of accounting statements, especially since the statements prepared nowadays are generally based on HC. Perhaps it is equally important to recognize that alternative bases too suffer from some variation of this problem. In principle, however, the current replacement cost system does not have to be subject to the allocation problem, but its implementation does.

HC statement totals and subtotals lack meaning (because they add incompatible units), and many items lack relevance to current decisions, except for taxation. Most managerial decisions are based on some form of current value (exit value, entry value, or subjective economic value), and only at the time of acquisition does the historical cost represent the current value of an asset. Since the firm continues to hold the asset, the total benefit from the asset will be the past benefits plus estimated future benefits. Even if the past benefits can be determined based on historical cost, future benefits cannot. In summary then, a decision-maker is unlikely to consider either the original historical cost or the depreciated historical cost as relevant information.

The lack of meaning of statement totals is sometimes referred to as the "apples and oranges problem" since different book values are the net outcome of numerous judgments and assumptions. An additional serious issue is the decline in the purchasing power of money over the years. The assets might include cash measured in end-of-1995 dollars, marketable securities in 1980 dollars, accounts receivable in 1996 dollars, inventory in 1995 and earlier dollars (including some depreciation from the distant past), land in 1950 dollars, depreciable assets in 1950 to 1995 dollars, and notes receivable in 1997 or later dollars.

This is similar to saying I have 1 yard, 2 unidentified units of length, 3.5 meters, 6 groups of units of undetermined length (inventory), 4 feet (too old to identify), 3 inches, and 1/2 future centimeters. They cannot be added together *without adjustment*. Similarly in the accounting situation, we can choose an appropriate standard of measurement and convert all of our "mixed" dollars to some common scale and then add.

General-Price-Level-Adjusted Historical Cost
The general-price-level-adjusted historical cost system (GPL) is based upon the idea of adjusting HC statements for the changing amount of goods and services that can be purchased with a dollar at different points in time. Assume that we choose the purchasing power of a December 31, 1994 dollar as our measurement unit. We can then convert all of our past dollar figures to this scale by computing the ratio of purchasing power of the December 31, 1994 dollar to the purchasing power of the dollar at the time of purchase (e.g., 1958) and multiplying this ratio times the number of dollars spent at that time to get the cost in terms of purchasing power of the asset. This explicitly recognizes that the economic meaning of a dollar changes over time. Note particularly that it is still a historical cost system. The measurement of cost is based on purchasing power given up rather than number of dollars given up.

Thus, the GPL system would provide answers to user questions such as: "How much purchasing power was given up to get to the position the firm holds today?" Again we must modify the question slightly, due to depreciation, to:

"How much purchasing power was given up to get to the current position after deducting the purchasing power assumed related to past operations?" The corresponding income statement question is: "How much purchasing power was received by (or promised to) the firm minus the purchasing power given up to obtain those goods and services necessary to generate the revenue?"

With inflation, GPL statements are more satisfying in answering those questions than unadjusted historical cost statements. The GPL approach also provides for the recognition of the gains and losses experienced by companies as they hold liabilities and assets through changes in the general price level. To illustrate, assume $1,000,000 from Creditor Company when the price index is 120 ($_{120}$1,000,000). If the loan is repaid at a time when the price index is 150, the Debtor Company will have made a GPL "gain" because it borrowed more valuable (price index 120) dollars than it repaid. In terms of purchasing power, Debtor Company repaid only the equivalent of $800,000 price index 120 dollars ($_{150}$1,000,000 x 120/150), thereby gaining $_{120}$200,000 of purchasing power. We could view the situation as a repayment of $_{150}$1,000,000 on a loan of $_{150}$1,250,000 (= $_{120}$1,000,000) for a gain of $_{150}$250,000 (= $_{120}$200,000). (Actually GPL accounting would recognize this gain at the time the price index moved from 120 to 150 whether the loan had been repaid or not.)

There are two sides to every transaction and if the Debtor Company has a GPL gain on its liability, the Creditor Company has suffered an equal GPL loss on its long-term receivable. The general result is that a creditor loses and a debtor gains during periods of inflation. Of course, no company is solely a debtor or solely a creditor so that every company has some gain and some loss during inflationary periods. The net of these gains and losses, however, will be determined by the company's *net monetary position*. The net monetary position is the balance between the company's monetary assets (primarily cash and receivables fixed in dollar terms) and monetary liabilities. The company is called a net debtor if its monetary liabilities exceed its monetary assets and it will have a net GPL gain in a period of inflation. Conversely if the company's monetary assets exceed its liabilities, it is a net creditor and will suffer a net GPL loss during inflation.

One problem with computing GPL loss (gain) in this manner and disclosing it separately is that this procedure may lead statement readers to believe that the GPL loss is a nonoperating item, which may not be the case. Also the interest rates being paid will have been set after taking expected inflation into account. So the debtor's GPL gain may be offset by having to pay a higher interest rate on borrowed money.

It is important to emphasize that the adjustments from dollars of one time to dollars current at another time are just that: adjustments. They do not represent a gain any more than a conversion of 100 yards to 300 feet would mean a gain in distance. The adjustment is done only to state all items in the statements in common units so that they may be added, subtracted, etc., with each other to produce totals which are of a known "dimension" – purchasing power expressed in dollars current to a given time – rather than totals composed of dollars of indeterminate origin (and meaning).

Unfortunately the GPL system does not solve the problems of allocation and lack of relevance; knowledge of the purchasing-power-adjusted historical cost of an asset is unlikely to be much more useful in a current decision than the unadjusted dollar cost itself.

Current Replacement Cost Accounting

The current replacement cost (CRC) system measures assets at the amounts it would cost to replace them today. Thus, the CRC system would question "How much revenue was received minus the cost *at the date of sale* necessary to generate the revenue?" (the net of which is called *current operating profit*), and "How much did the replacement cost of assets increase during the period?" (called *holding gain*). There are, unfortunately, conceptual as well as practical problems with the CRC system.

The first problem relates to the choice between measuring the replacement cost of a particular asset held by the firm in its current condition and measuring the replacement cost of the services equivalent to what the firm expects to benefit from using the asset. This is sometimes referred to as the identical asset versus equivalent services controversy. The methods of estimating CRC of the identical asset involve either estimating directly the cost of purchasing the asset in its current condition from the secondary (used) asset market or estimating the current cost of purchasing the asset new then applying some "appropriate" depreciation method to arrive at a figure that must really be defined as the "depreciated book value based on current cost of replacing the asset new" rather than the current replacement cost of the asset held. The estimation of the current cost in new condition can be accomplished by locating the same asset for sale in the primary market if it is still being sold new, applying a specific price index for the type of asset involved to the HC, or using engineering estimates to compute a best estimate of the cost new if it were still available new. However, many assets currently held by firms are not available new. When one considers that one is choosing a depreciation method, which also involves all of the allocation problem, and that the result may bear little relationship to the CRC of the asset held by the firm, it may be that direct estimation of the cost in the used asset market is seen to be preferable when available.

Furthermore, an asset is not typically replaced by the same asset. Replacement is more often done by purchasing other assets that will provide equivalent services for the least cost. This method requires that the company estimates: (1) the type of services expected; (2) the number of units of this service remaining in the old asset; (3) the assets available for equivalent services; and (4) the cost of each alternative means of acquiring the equivalent services. Determining the CRC of equivalent services becomes much more difficult as we consider assets with various capacities, service lives, and operating costs.

The two primary US authoritative pronouncements on CRC information (Securities and Exchange Commission in its Accounting Series Release 190 and Statement of Financial Accounting Standard No. 33) required disclosure of the current cost of the asset in new condition as well as its depreciated value. This position has the practical effect of eliminating the direct reference to the used asset market method which is the only variation of the CRC system that avoids the allocation problem. However, neither requirement is currently in effect.

Another problem with CRC relates to the dichotomization of accounting income into current operating profit (COP) and holding gain (HG). COP provides a good estimate of the firm's continuing ability to earn profits because COP is revenues net of cost at current dollars. However, the assumption that best estimates of future prices are the current prices is not quite valid when related to commodity prices (even specific commodity prices). Further, the majority of sales and cost of sales are typically incurred well before the end of the period.

HG is intended to measure the gain from increase (decrease) in CRC of assets (liabilities). This calculation can get somewhat complex since the asset's CRC may be depreciating through normal use throughout the period. Unfortunately, holding gains and losses are occurring continuously, which makes the calculation difficult, especially when it is coupled with the allocation problem. It seems more reasonable to skip the disaggregation of HG and COP and consider the depreciation expense as the decrease in CRC during the period, which avoids all need to choose a depreciation method.

Drake & Dopuch (1965) point out another conceptual difficulty with the COP–HG dichotomy. They note that certain types of assets are necessary to operate a given type of business and that COP should be affected by those assets' holding gains, but that the CRC system would not allow for this adjustment. Drake & Dopuch also point out that certain costs of speculative activity (e.g., inventory carrying costs) may be charged to operations. The proper identification of COP and HG is so difficult as to reduce the usefulness of this dichotomy. However, an important feature of the CRC system is that it can include all necessary adjustments to take account of the changing purchasing power of the dollar.

In summary, the CRC system is conceptually more relevant to current decisions than historical cost and can be adjusted for changes in the purchasing power of the dollar, but in its most common implementations it still suffers from the allocation problem and computational difficulties.

Exit (Realizable) Value

The exit value (EV) accounting system reports assets at the net amount for which they *could be* sold to a willing buyer within a short period of time. A short period of time is defined as long enough to allow an orderly sale, but not long enough to allow disposal of fixed assets through ordinary use of services. Net amount is defined as the selling price less disposition costs including tax effects all discounted to the point of measurement.

The EV system generates statements that would help users to answer questions like: "What amount could be realized from the orderly disposal of the firm's assets less the amount required for the liabilities?;" and "How much has that amount increased over the accounting period?" The EV system does this by measuring assets at EV (as defined above) and liabilities at the amount for which they could be settled at the measurement date, with the net being the residual equity. No attempt is made to subdivide residual equity. Depreciation expense is typically computed as the decline in EV during the period, thereby avoiding the allocation problem.

The most prevalent misconception about the exit value system is the confusion between orderly sale and liquidation. Other misconceptions hold that EV measurements are not additive or that EV statement preparation is not feasible. In a technical sense EV measurements are not additive, but a logical criterion exists for deciding which unique sum of exit values to use (the highest sum).

Contentions that either current replacement cost (CRC) or EV statement preparation is not feasible can best be answered by referring to earlier studies. These show that a surprising number of assets can be measured by direct reference to used asset markets. Further these measurements are frequently more reliable and verifiable than similar historical cost (HC) measurements. It is also clear that EV is at least as feasible as the common versions of CRC.

Having discussed the erroneous criticisms of the EV system, it is only fair to turn to the valid criticism: EV provides a very low measurement of asset value (which causes a "loss" to be recognized at the time of purchase of an asset) and market saturation (unique asset or relatively large stock of the asset, which can in some circumstances cause difficulty in determining EV).

It is frequently true that EV is a low value for an asset, a relationship that allows use of EV statements to evaluate management decisions. If a firm is holding an asset, we can assume that the management believes that asset is worth *at least* its EV. If the asset was not expected to yield at least its EV within the firm, the management should sell it for its EV. There is no comparable presumption available relative to CRC. The fact that a firm holds an asset does *not* imply that the management believes that asset is worth its CRC because the management knows the asset cannot be sold for the CRC. Instead the CRC can be viewed as the maximum amount the firm would lose if it lost that particular asset.

This view was best outlined by James Bonbright (1937) when he referred to "value to the owner." Very simply, value to the owner was defined as the amount of loss a firm would suffer if deprived of a particular asset. This value would be a minimum of the EV since at worst the firm could have sold the asset. The maximum value lost would be the CRC since the firm could simply replace the asset for its CRC if the firm's management believed the economic value was between the EV and the CRC, the value to the owner would be economic value. This approach to asset valuation appeals to many accountants. It is logical. It is understandable. Unfortunately it is *not* feasible since subjective economic value must be known. The value to the owner concept does, however, clearly outline the limits of asset valuation.

Bibliography

Drake, D. & Dopuch N. (1965). On the case for dichotomizing income. *Journal of Accounting Research*, Autumn, 192 205.

Bonbright, J. C. (1937). *The Valuation of Property*. New York: McGraw Hill.

JAMES C. McKEOWN

cutoff score Cutoff (or "critical" or "passing") scores represent minimum acceptable standards on employment, licensing, certification, or academic tests. Scores below the cutoff indicate unacceptable performance, except in the case of multiple cutoffs, when each cutoff represents a distinct level of performance.

Cutoff scores are typically calculated from both empirical data and some form of judgment. The fact that subjectivity plays a role does not represent a legal problem as long as the method used is rational, systematic, and documented (Society for Industrial and Organizational Psychology, 1987). While adverse impact for different gender, ethnic, and age groups generated by cutoff scores is a concern (Cascio et al., 1988), court rulings indicate that the standard to be met is equal treatment, not equal results. The setting of separate cutoffs by race, color, religion, sex, or national origin is prohibited by the CIVIL RIGHTS ACT of 1991.

Types

After Berk (1986), the procedures used to develop cutoff scores can be classified into three major categories: judgmental, judgmental-empirical, and empirical-judgmental. There are many variants within each category. Unfortunately, different methods may yield different cutoff scores. Recent research, however, has demonstrated some convergence among methods (see Woehr et al., 1991).

Judgmental. Included here are the Angoff, the Nedelsky, and the Ebel methods and variants of these (see Cascio et al., 1988). In the Angoff method, subject matter experts (SMEs) are asked to rate each test item in terms of the probability that a minimally competent (but nonetheless competent) individual could answer the item correctly. The mean for all judges is computed for each item, and the cutoff score is then simply the mean of all item means. The other SME methods are more complicated, for the judges are also asked to either rate item importance (Nedelsky method) or identify incorrect item alternatives prior to providing probability ratings (Ebel method). These methods are popular and relatively easy, and can be completed prior to the collection of any test data. However, they are sensitive to method of implementation (e.g. whether test answers as well as questions are provided to SMEs; Hudson and Campion, 1994).

Judgmental-empirical. Here, expert judgments are augmented by empirical data. Very often some kind of iterative rating is used (e.g. experts rate item probabilities, are shown actual item difficulties computed from pilot data, and are permitted to revise probability estimates). Under this heading we can also place norm-referenced models, where cutoff scores are based on an examination of the test score distribution alone or including other information. One may simply establish a cutoff score deemed to be appropriate given the distribution (e.g. one standard deviation above the mean). Thorndike's method of predictive yield also integrates projected personnel needs, proportion of offers accepted, and distribution of test scores to establish a cutoff score which will make available the required number of new hires. Or issues like adverse impact, selection ratio, and recruiting cost information can be combined to set a cutoff score which optimizes utility (Martin and Raju, 1992).

Empirical-judgmental. These methods include the contrasting groups method, where high and low performers are identified on some criterion (e.g. job ratings). Members in both groups take the test, and the score that best discriminates between the two groups becomes the cutoff score (unless either false positives or false negatives are undesirable, in which case the cutoff score is set to achieve one of these ends). The borderline method also fits under this category. In this method, minimally competent job performers are identified, and the mean or median score of these individuals on the test in question is the cutoff score. The judgmental element in these and similar methods lies in how the relevant individuals or groups are initially identified.

Selection Above the Cutoff: Ranking versus Banding

The selection of individuals above a cutoff score can occur in a variety of ways. It may be a simple pass–fail decision. Individuals may also be rank ordered by their score on the examination with selection taking place in some form of top–down procedure. In band scoring, multiple cutoff scores are set and individuals within each band (bounded by the cutoff scores) can be selected at random. After all the candidates in the highest scoring band have been selected, the process then shifts to the next lowest band, so that all individuals in that band are eligible.

Bibliography

Berk, R. A. (1986). A consumer's guide to setting performance standards on criterion-referenced tests. *Review of Educational Research*, 56, 137–72.

Cascio, W. F., Alexander, R. A. & Barrett, G. V. (1988). Setting cutoff scores: Legal, psychometric, and professional issues and guidelines. *Personnel Psychology*, 41, 1–24.

Hudson, J. P. & Campion, J. E. (1994). Hindsight bias in an application of the Angoff method for setting cutoff scores. *Journal of Applied Psychology*, 79, 860–5.

Martin, S. L. & Raju, N. S. (1992). Determining cutoff scores that optimize utility: a recognition of recruiting costs. *Journal of Applied Psychology*, 77, 15–23.

Society for Industrial and Organizational Psychology (1987). *Principles for the Validation and Use of Personnel Selection Procedures*, 3rd College Park, MD: Society for Industrial and Organizational Psychology.

Woehr, D. J., Arthur, W. & Fehrmann, M. L. (1991). An empirical comparison of cutoff score methods for content-related and criterion-related validity settings. *Educational and Psychological Measurement*, 51, 1029–39.

GEORGE M. ALLIGER and GWEN COATS

D

DAGMAR model The DAGMAR model (Defining Advertising Goals for Measured Advertising Results) is a model of MARKETING COMMUNICATIONS and was developed by Colley (1961) specifically for the measurement of ADVERTISING effectiveness. It postulates that the customer/buyer moves from a state of unawareness through awareness of the product or service, comprehension (an understanding of what the product or service will do), conviction that it will meet requirements, to action (a purchase). A benchmark measure is first taken of the position along the spectrum to which members of the target group(s) have progressed. Objectives are then established, advertising is produced, and a further measure is taken to discover whether or not any effective shift has occurred (i.e., whether or not the objectives have been met). Precise measurement is impossible as so many other variables are present. Furthermore, such variables become more numerous the further one moves toward action.

see also **Communications objectives**

Bibliography

Colley, R. H. (1961). *Defining advertising goals for measured advertising results.* New York: Association of National Advertisers.

Kotler, P. (1994). *Marketing management: Analysis, planning, implementation and control*, 8th edn, Englewood Cliffs, NJ: Prentice-Hall. Chapter 22.

DAVID YORKE

data warehousing W H Inmon, a pioneer in the field of data warehousing, offers the following definition: "A data warehouse is a subject-oriented, integrated, time-variant, non-volatile collection of data in support of management's decision-making process" (Inmon, 1992, p. 29). A subject-oriented view allows users to easily locate and access the data they need. Because the warehouse is nonvolatile and time-variant, users can perform historical or trend analysis. Because the data in the warehouse are integrated, users can examine and join together data generated from many different applications.

In an operational view, a data warehouse is a collection of data from multiple applications, files, databases, found throughout the organization in operational systems and stored in a consistent, structured format. The data stored in the warehouse are a copy and a summary of data from these multiple sources reorganized for easy and efficient retrieval. This combination of content, structure, and access provides the availability benefits to data-warehouse users.

The data warehouse provides a foundation for analytical processing by separating operational and decisional data processing. There are fundamental differences between these kinds of processing. Operational processing involves the detailed, day-to-day procedures in which data are accessed and updated with short response times. Decisional processing refers to the analytical activities involved in looking across the organization for information to use in management analysis and decision-making. Because data in the data warehouse are integrated, have historical perspective and are stored at both summary and detail levels, a company can perform more substantive, accurate, and consistent analyses using the data warehouse as a foundation for DECISION SUPPORT SYSTEMS, EXECUTIVE INFORMATION SYSTEMS, and access tools. In theory, there is no reason why both operational and decision support systems cannot be based on the same data. In practice, there are many organizational advantages in having two parallel systems. One major advantage is eliminating the immediate need to migrate legacy information systems to an integrated architecture.

Most large organizations are constrained by existing system designs. Typically, information systems are large, old, written in COBOL, and file based. They are essential to the organization's business and must be operational at all times. Today, they pose one of the most serious problems for large organizations. Problems of failures, maintenance, inappropriate functionality, lack of design documentation, and poor performance can be very costly.

Many organizations are working to re-engineer legacy information systems. It requires a major change in almost every aspect of information system design, development, and management. Building a data warehouse architecture, without major changes to existing systems, may be the first step an organization should take to respond to the problems of legacy systems. By reducing the volume of data in the legacy systems environment, the data warehouse architecture streamlines systems so that both operational and decision processing can be done more efficiently. In addition, it reduces the amount of maintenance typically done in legacy systems.

Operational systems are separated from decision support systems by introducing redundant but better quality data to support business needs. As with any redundant data, they have to be properly managed to be up to date. Redundant data stored in a data warehouse are derived from data sources found in legacy systems. With respect to legacy data, warehouse data are the derivation target. However, with respect to user views of data, warehouse data are the derivation source. This derivation link between legacy data, warehouse data, and user views represents the essence of data warehousing.

The link between legacy systems and a data warehouse is supported by extraction and transformation tools. Besides extracting data, they map the source data to the target database. They also automatically generate the program instructions for data transformations. Next, the tools integrate and transform the data before moving it to the warehouse. This step can include converting fields and values and summarizing, condensing, and converting data from one platform or database to another.

The second category of tools consists of DATABASE MANAGEMENT SYSTEMS (DBMS). A DBMS is used to house a data warehouse. This category is dominated by well-known DBMSs, although there are specialized systems designed and developed specifically for data warehousing. Making up the third category are the data access and view tools for the end user. The primary objective of a data warehouse is to provide data for user summary or other data views. Users are interested more in analytical than operational data, since different types of business analyses are only possible from summary data (total, average, minimal, maximal, number of sales, variance, standard deviation) are basic indicators of how a company is doing. They are often done within a specific time frame (time dimension), in a specific geographical area (space dimension), for a specific product or a type of products (form dimension). Hence, indicators and dimensions are two major characteristics of user data requirements supported by this category of data warehousing tool.

In summary, a data warehouse is a permanent, integral part of an organization's portfolio of information systems. In a global and highly competitive environment data are managed, and exploited for management decision-making.

Bibliography

Inmon, W. H. (1992). *Building the Data Warehouse*. New York: Wiley–QED.

DJENAN RIDJANOVIC

database   A database is a collection of related information which is capable of being organized and accessed by a computer. Depending on the software being used, information can be entered in numeric or word form. Common numerical database systems such as spreadsheets allow a high degree of querying, analysis, sorting, and extraction of information. The most common usage of databases in marketing is to develop a customer database. Typically, customer information such as purchase history, value and timing of orders, responses to previous offers, name, address, and demographic characteristics will be gathered as well as additional information from salespersons' reports and external sources such as geodemographic profiles (*see* GEODEMOGRAPHICS). Database marketing allows closer monitoring of profitable/least profitable customers, allow cross-selling of goods, identify possible customer segments, and help in communicating individually with customers. Database marketing has developed hand in hand with a more tailored approach to marketing goods and services, since more is known about customers as individuals and they can be reached through DIRECT MAIL campaigns.

Database can also be useful for bibliographic searches, site location, media planning, market forecasting, market potential studies, and MARKET SEGMENTATION studies. Many commercial numeric databases exist which contain information on sales, population characteristics, the business environment, economic forecasts, specialized bibliographies, and other material. For example, ABI/Inform contains abstracts of articles in approximately 1,300 business publications worldwide. Predicasts (PTS) provides numerous on-line databases on products, markets, competitors, demand forecasts, annual reports, etc. is an ongoing program of research conducted by the Strategic Planning Institute (Cambridge, MA, USA) into the impact of MARKETING STRATEGIES: over 250 companies provide data on over 2,000 businesses for at least four years' trading. Given the huge diversity of databases available,

several networks have been established to allow users easier access to each. One of the largest of these host networks is DIALOG which contains over 200 different databases. NEXIS is another large system.

Bibliography

Fletcher, K. (1994). The evolution and use of information technology in marketing. In M. J. Baker (Ed.), *The marketing book*, 3rd edn (pp. 333–357). Oxford: Butterworth Heinemann.
Rapp, S. & Collins, T. L. (1987). *Maximarketing*. New York: McGraw-Hill.

VINCE MITCHELL

database management system   A computerized system for creating and maintaining databases. A minimal database management system (DBMS) performs the following functions:

- defines a database
- stores and accesses data
- retrieves and displays or prints data in response to a request
- maintains data in the database (insert, modify, delete)
- maintains the integrity of the stored data according to its defined structure and constraint rules

The request for data may come directly and interactively from human users, or from programs or stored procedures through some application programming interface (API). A DBMS may be designed to operate in a variety of environments: multi-user, client/server, host-based, etc. in which case additional functionality and interfaces are required.

DBMSs can be classified on various bases. Perhaps the most common is on the underlying data structure: hierarchical, network, and relational (which is not a complete taxonomy since it leaves out the single flat file, and the object-role data model). Another basis for classifying DBMSs is on their purpose or role within the platform of an information system. Client DBMSs are primarily intended for the *ad hoc*, interactive end user. They usually have simplified data structuring capabilities and rich, easy-to-use, data access, query, reporting, and manipulation capabilities. They may or may not offer the ability for a user-written program to access the database, either from a standard programming language, such as COBOL or C, or using a built-in programming language.

Development DBMSs provide capabilities for the system developer to build application systems. They provide an interface to one or more programming languages (which may include their own built-in language). They generally provide facilities to define menus, screens, queries, reports, and user views, which can all be combined to build an application information system. DBMSs primarily intended for system developers may also include facilities for the interactive end user.

Many DBMSs run mainly on a personal computer platform. The next tier of DBMS primarily runs on mini- or mainframe computers or in a network environment (though most also run on PCs) and generally offer higher levels of functionality. Most include facilities for both the interactive end user and the system developer. They are generally distinguished by offering a richer programming language interface, triggers and stored procedures, enhanced backup and recovery, greater access and quality control, concurrent update control, synchronization and replication management, etc. Another class of DBMS is the database server, intended primarily to run in a network and provide services to a set of clients. A database server does not normally interface directly with human users (although such facilities could be provided by the same vendor).

In the evolution of DBMSs and data languages, there are different generations. The third generation of programming languages, such as COBOL and PASCAL, gave rise to the first generation of DBMSs. They read and write records one at a time from a single file. Fourth-generation languages (4GL) are specifically designed to process and retrieve sets of records, even from multiple files or tables, in a single statement. The dominant 4GL is SQL (pronounced 'sequel') for which there is now an ANSI and ISO standard. A second-generation DBMS incorporates a fourth-generation language. Most DBMSs today provide some flavor of SQL, whether directly to the end user, to the application programmer (perhaps as extensions to a conventional programming language), underneath an easy-to-use prompting interface, or at the interface between the client DBMS and the database server.

The next or third generation of DBMS is an object-oriented DBMS or simply an object management system. An OODBMS incorporates the principles of object-orientation in its programming language and its user interface(s), while still providing all the functionality of a second-generation DBMS. The third generation of DBMS is marked by some of the following:

- higher level of semantics in the definition of the database (or object base)
- handling heterogeneous, multimedia forms of information
- explicitly representing the temporal and spatial dimensions of information
- offering a natural language user interface
- employing rules of inference (as in EXPERT SYSTEMS)
- operating in a distributed or client/server environment.

GORDON C. EVEREST

deadweight loss The term "deadweight loss" refers to the welfare loss due to inefficient allocation of resources caused by deviations between market prices and marginal costs. Inefficient allocations of resources can occur in a variety of situations including, for example, the situation where a market is not perfectly competitive or the situation where a sales tax is imposed on a perfectly competitive industry.

When resources are allocated inefficiently (e.g. as a result of a sales tax), there are typically two effects:

(1) welfare transfers that simply redistribute CONSUMER SURPLUS and producer surplus among consumers, producers and the government; and
(2) net reductions of consumer surplus and/or producer surplus that represent welfare loss.

For example, a higher market price due to a tax will cause some consumers to leave the market and reduce their consumer surplus. However, this reduction in consumer surplus is not captured by producers or by the government.

It is pure welfare loss, otherwise known as "deadweight loss."

Bibliography

Bergson, A. (1973). On monopoly welfare losses. *American Economic Review*, 63, 853–70.

Harberger, A. (1964). Taxation, resource allocation and welfare. Due, J. *The Role of Direct and Indirect Taxes in the Federal Revenue System*. Princeton, NJ: Princeton University Press.

WEI LI

decentralization For both organizational sociologists and management specialists, the distribution of POWER is probably the single most important structural attribute. If most members of the organization participate in its decisions, then the organization can be considered to be decentralized. In contrast, if most of the decisions and especially the most important ones are made by one person, then the organization is categorized as centralized.

Essentially, the problem of decentralization is a problem of power or of CONTROL. And there are a variety of ways in which the organizational literature, this has been addressed including the topics of hierarchy of authority, closeness of supervision and of control.

There is much less agreement on how best to measure this concept and the field has basically three different approaches. Tannenbaum (1968) pioneered in the structural study of power as distinct from the study of power bases with what he called the control graph. This measure, a general survey of the members of the organization, reports how much influence, which he called control, each level in the hierarchy has over the others. He found generally there are about four or five levels. With particular shaped slopes, Tannenbaum could then define specific distributions of power as democratic. In contrast, the research of the Aston group (Pugh, Hickson, Hinings, & Turner, 1968) measured the level to which a decision was delegated (see DELEGATION) in a large battery of decisions based on information from five or six informants. Likewise, the Blau measures (Blau & Schoenherr, 1971) are essentially ones of delegation, although they did not include as many decision areas. A third way of measuring the distribution of power is by asking individual members of the organization how often they participate in decision-making, again where a number of different kinds of decisions are listed. This approach has not been prominent in the research of Hage and Aiken (1967).

All of the above research studies have tended to use averages either across decisions and informants or individuals who have been surveyed. This methodological procedure assumes that participation, influence, or delegation is approximately the same in all areas of decision-making and in addition assumes that as one moves from the top of the hierarchy to the bottom, there is a steady increase in the amount of centralization. The one exception has been the work of Tannenbaum, which did allow for nonlinear arrangements but his approach has been little employed in the field. There are three distinctive kinds of discontinuity that can be discerned.

First, work decisions might be delegated, providing workers with a considerable amount of autonomy while strategic decisions are concentrated at the top. This is very common in traditional organizations where crafts people or semiprofessionals work. These organizations are small and there is a strong sense of self-control (*see* SELF-MANAGEMENT).

Second, strategic decisions and work decisions might be decentralized in some parts of the organization and not in others. Most typically, research and development might be given considerable autonomy while production, marketing, and finance/accounting might be much more centralized. These organizations are sometimes called mixed mechanistic/organic.

Third, strategic decisions might be decentralized to divisions heads within the same organization as in the famous studies of Chandler (1962) but then each of the divisions might be quite centralized. More recently there has been a further step in this same process, namely the decentralization of strategic decisions to what are called profit centers, that is subunits within divisions.

As yet, there has been little research on the patterns of decentralization across the levels of the hierarchy and particularly between headquarters and the various divisions or profit centers and its consequences for the performance of the organization. However, all of the evidence points to a steady movement toward greater autonomy being given to smaller and smaller units, first as cost centers then as profit centers. Another critical issue in this debate is the question of which functions if any are maintained at the central headquarters beyond investment decisions, and what consequences does this have. Again, there is wide variety of patterns, with marketing, research, and other functions in some large companies being maintained at the corporate headquarters. Again, there has been a tendency to gradually decentralize. It is quite another question whether or not decentralization really means effective sharing of power. There are two lines of attack on this assumption in the literature. First, some such as Blau and Schoenherr (1971) have argued that if the organization is highly formalized, then decisions can be easily delegated, giving people the sense of participating without the reality. This work has not, however, made much distinction between strategic decisions and work decisions. Second, others such as Pfeffer (1981) argue that if the top executive or power elite control the agenda and the criteria by which people are rewarded, then there may be the appearance of decentralization and participation but, in fact, the power elite effectively controls the organization (*see* TOP MANAGEMENT TEAMS).

Finally, we must conclude with a special comment about decentralization in Japanese organizations. Considerable job autonomy is provided for the worker. Furthermore, there is extended discussion of major decisions up and down the hierarchy. This pattern might be called a combination of centralization and decentralization. What distinguishes it from the American or European discussions is the heavy emphasis on delegation rather than a joint decision-making within the entire hierarchy (*see* INTERNATIONAL MANAGEMENT).

see also **Decision making; Differentiation; Organizational design**

Bibliography

Blau, P. & Schoenherr, R. (1971). The structure of organizations. New York: Basic.

Chandler, A. D. (1962). Strategy and structure: Chapters in the history of industrial enterprise. Cambridge, MA: MIT Press.

Hage, J. (1980). Theories of organizations. New York: Wiley–Interscience.

Hage, J. & Aiken, M. (1967). Relationship of centralization to other structural properties. Administrative Science Quarterly, 12, 72–91.

Hall, R. H. (1992). Organizations: Structures, processes, and outcomes. (5th edn) Englewood Cliffs, NJ: Prentice-Hall.

Mintzberg, H. (1979). The structuring of organizations. Englewood Cliffs, NJ: Prentice-Hall.

Pfeffer, J. (1981). Power in organizations. London: Pitman Press.

Pugh, D. S., Hickson, D. J., Hinings, C. R. & Turner, C. (1968). Dimensions of organization structure. Administrative Science Quarterly, 13, 65–105.

Tannenbaum, A. S. (1968). Control in organizations. New York: McGraw-Hill.

JERALD HAGE

decision making   Because the quality and the acceptance of organizational decisions is vital to a company's functioning, this topic has traditionally been a focus of attention in the management literature. Alongside these sources, with their often normative and typically rational approach, are more recent studies which tend to take a more descriptive, analytic viewpoint. These studies clearly show that organizational decisions generally take an entirely different course from the one recommended by the classical literature.

Depending on:

(1) various context factors;
(2) the topic of decision making; and
(3) the policy of management, organizational decision-making processes can assume very different shapes (Koopman & Pool, 1990).

Decision making can show much or little centralization, and much or little formalization. Sometimes information plays an important role in the decision preparation, sometimes POWER processes determine the contents of the decision and information primarily serves the purpose of legitimating after the fact (*see* LEGITIMACY). On the whole, research results in this field show that decision-making processes can vary primarily on four dimensions:

1. Centralization. The amount of centralization is one of the most important parameters of decision making. Much research has been done of the manner in which decentralization and participation take place in decision making and of the question of how effective participation is.

2. Formalization. A second important dimension is the extent to which the decision making is formalized. Decisions can take place according to an established procedure set down in advance, or they can proceed more flexibly, according to informal considerations of what is required or desirable.

3. Information. The way in which the substance of a decision comes about is important. On the basis of what information is a decision made? What alternatives are developed or sought, and from where do they come? Have important possibilities or consequences been overlooked?

4. Confrontation. The extent to which there is confrontation and CONFLICT in the decision making process. This last dimension comes from models of decision making as a political process, in which parties try to achieve their own interests on the basis of their power positions (*see* POLITICS).

Theoretically, classification based on the four dimensions would yield sixteen different models. Koopman and Pool argued that, in practice, combination of these dimensions leads to a typology of four basic models of decision making which can reasonably accommodate most literature in this field (Koopman & Pool, 1990; see figure 1). They distinguish in this order: the neo-rational model, the bureaucratic model, the arena model, and the open-end model, in order to encompass as much empirical research as possible, and models based upon it. For example, Hickson, Butler, Cray, Mallory, & Wilson (1986) distinguished sporadic, fluid, and limited processes. Schwenk (1988) discussed the rational choice perspective, the organizational perspective and the political perspective. Thompson and Tuden (1959) distinguished decisions through computation, majority judgment, compromise, and inspiration. Fahey (1981) reduced reality to two contrasting types of decision making: rational–analytical versus behavioral–political. McCall and Kaplan (1985) spoke of quick versus convoluted action. Shrivastava and Grant (1985) distinguished the managerial autocracy model, the systematic bureaucratic model, the political expediency model, and the adaptive planning model.

There is often a clear relationship between the various models and the context (organizational structure and culture, environment) in which the decision making takes place. These relations are summarized in table 1.

The *neo-rational model* is characterized by strong centralization, combined with low formalization and confrontation, when fairly simple decision making processes are guided and controlled from one point: the top

management. There is little power distribution in the organization. This is termed the *neo*-rational model because it takes account of some fundamental characteristics relating to human cognitions and emotions. Because of this the behavior of decision makers is characterized by "bounded rationality" and "SATISFICING" (as opposed to maximal) goal achievement.

This type of decision-making process may primarily be expected in the organizational type that Mintzberg (1979) termed a "simple structure" or "autocracy." In terms of ORGANIZATIONAL CULTURE, Harrison's (1972) "power culture" would be most conducive to this type of decision-making process.

The model is rational in the sense that decision-making aims to maximize the goals of top management. Intuition and quick decisions are more typical of this model than extensive analysis and study of alternatives. A dynamic and/or threatening environment can lead decision-making processes to follow the neo-rational model: they demand quick reaction.

Characteristic of the *bureaucratic model* is that decision making is "constricted" by rules and regulations. They may be rules of the organization itself, such as JOB DESCRIPTIONS, tasks and competences, meeting rules, etc., but also rules that are laid down outside the organization, as by legislation or by directives from the head office. Different actors or groups are expected to make their contribution at various stages, even if it merely means initialing a document. Various alternatives are explored and officially documented. The selection of the best solution is conducted by way of existing procedures. In contrast to the neo-rational model, the bureaucratic model usually involves fairly complex decision-making processes. Its counterpart in Mintzberg's structural typology is the "machine BUREAUCRACY" and in Harrison's culture typology the "ROLE culture." The environment is characterized by stability and predictability. When time

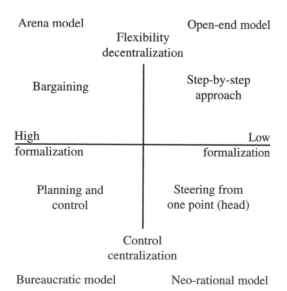

Figure 1 Four models of decision making
Source: P. L. Koopman and J. Pool (1990). Reprinted by permission of John Wiley & Sons, Ltd.

Table 1   The four decision-making models and their hypothetical relationships with various context factors.

	Neo-rational model	Bureaucratic model	Arena model	Open-end model
Context factors				
Environment:				
Complexity	low	low	high	high
dynamics	high	low	low	high
hostility	high	low	high	low/high
Organization:				
power distribution	low	low	high	high
type or org. (Mintzberg)	autocracy	machine bureaucracy	professional bureaucracy	adhocracy
type of culture (Harrison)	power culture	role culture	person culture	task culture
Characteristics of decision maker	proactive, intuitive	reactive, analytic	autonomous, intrapreneur	innovative, willing to take risks
Type of subject:				
complexity	low	high	low/high	high
dynamics	high/low	low	high	high

pressure or external threats increase, decision making increasingly leans to the neo-rational model (temporary centralization). If innovation requirements are central, then characteristics of the open-end model gain the upper hand.

Power in the organization is distributed; power differences are small. There is no central machinery that can easily impose its will. Although there is a certain degree of coordination (primarily through professional training), the organization must constantly contend with the problem of acquiring sufficient consensus and acceptance for decisions. Mutual contention and lack of cooperation threaten the quality of the decision making. This type of decision making, over controversial topics, is primarily found in organizations composed of relatively independent units, such as universities or other "conglomerates." Decision making sometimes takes place at two levels: at the first level a small group of insiders arrives at the critical choices, which are subsequently legitimized for the constituency by the official bodies and by means of arguments which are accepted by these bodies. The natural counterpart in the structural typology of Mintzberg is the professional bureaucracy; in the culture typology of Harrison we should think of the "person culture."

Decision making in the *open-end model* is characterized by a limited view of the goals or of the means by which to achieve them. Chance circumstances and unpredictable events cross the path of this approach. Again and again, people must adapt to new demands and possibilities. This forces them to take a step-by-step approach (Quinn, 1980). Best known in this connection are the publications on the garbage can model, which were preceded by studies of the "Carnegie School" (Cyert & March, 1963).

A characteristic of the open-end model is that, depending on the problem in question, expertise of various types and locations must be gathered on a temporary basis (project management). The message here is: organize flexibly (*see* FLEXIBILITY). Gradually, by way of iterations and recycling, the end product comes into view. Complex innovative decisions (e.g., automation) often take place in this way (*see* INNOVATION). Mintzberg's adhocracy forms the organizational structure conducive to this type of decision making. The environment is complex and dynamic. Such an organization generally has a "task culture" (Harrison, 1972).

Context and "Strategic Choice"

Decision making does not take place in a vacuum, but in a certain context, which can be described at various levels. From low to high aggregation levels, one can distinguish the decision maker(s), the group, the organization, and the environment. Each of these context levels makes up part of decision making and influences it. Furthermore, decision making is not a neutral exercise, but it is about something. Subjects of decision making can differ in complexity, in controversiality, in political import. Both of these factors (i.e., context and subject) are of importance for the manner in which the decision-making processes can be structured and controlled and for the course that they ultimately take.

In particular, the organization as the context in which decisions are made influences the manner in which decisions take place. The organizational context is, as Hickson et al. (1986) put it, "the rules of the game." Decision-making processes are largely determined by

structural characteristics of the organization in which they take place (*see* ORGANISATIONAL DESIGN). Several researchers found a relationship between the type of organization and the dominant types of decision-making processes.

However, a decision-making process does not only come about as the result of interaction of several forces. Often one or more central actors (usually termed the "dominant coalition"), manage to give a strong personal accent to the decision-making process. This does not take place in complete freedom. A number of factors escape the control of management. No single party has complete control of the steering wheels, even if a coalition is dominant. Other actors or parties will also try to influence the direction the process takes. Nevertheless, a certain amount of leeway remains to give intentional form to decision-making processes, within the contingencies formed by the topic and the context.

A similar line of thought is used in the discussion of organizational structure as in Child's (1972) concept of "strategic choice." The presence of leeway for strategic choices implies that, in addition to the determining effects of environmental factors and technology, opportunities still remain for personal accents. As opposed to a complete determinism, it is stated, there are opportunities for the management of a company to choose, without altering the determining influence of the contingency factors mentioned.

The same can be said of decision-making processes: although they are partly determined by their substance and the context in which they take place, the decision makers still have some discretion. The amount of discretion can vary by case and by organization, but how it is used largely determines how effective and efficient the decision-making process will be.

see also **Strategic management; Institutional theory; Organization and environment; Top management teams; Group decision making**

Bibliography

Child, J. (1972). Organization structure and strategies of control: A replication of the Aston study. Administrative Science Quarterly, **17**, 163–177.

Cyert, R. M. & March, J. G. (1963). A behavioral theory of the firm. Englewood Cliffs, NJ: Prentice-Hall.

Fahey, L. (1981). On strategic management decision processes. Strategic Management Journal, **2**, 43–60.

Harrison, R. (1972). Understanding your organizations character. Harvard Business Review, **50**, 119–128.

Hickson, D. J., Butler, R. J., Cray, D., Mallory, G. R. & Wilson, D. C. (1986). Top decisions: Strategic decision-making in organizations. Oxford, UK: Basil Blackwell.

Koopman, P. L. & Pool, J. (1990). Decision making in organizations. In C. L. Cooper & I. T. Robertson (Eds), International review of industrial psychology, (vol. 5), pp. 101–148. New York: Wiley.

McCall, M. W. & Kaplan, R. E. (1985). Whatever it takes: Decision-makers at work. Englewood Cliffs, NJ: Prentice-Hall.

Mintzberg, H. (1979). The structuring of organizations: A synthesis of the research. Englewood Cliffs, NJ: Prentice-Hall.

Pool, J. & Koopman, P. L. (1992). Strategic decision making in organizations: A research model and some initial findings In D. Hosking & N. Anderson (Eds), Organizational change and innovation: Psychological perspectives and practices in Europe. (pp. 71–98). London: Routledge.

J. B. (1980). Strategies for change: Logical incrementalism. Homewood, IL: Irwin.

k, C. R. (1988). The essence of strategic decision making. Lexington, MA: Lexington Books.

Shrivastava, P. & Grant, J. H. (1985). Empirically derived models of strategic decision-making processes. Strategic Management Journal, **6**, 97–113.

Thompson, J. D. & Tuden, A. (1959). Strategies, structures and processes of organizational decision. In J. D. Thompson, P. B. Hammond, R. W. Hawkes, B. H. Junker & A. Tuden (Eds), Comparative studies in administration. Pittsburgh: Pittsburgh University Press.

PAUL KOOPMAN

decision support systems Decision support systems (DSS) process, store, and present information to support managerial decision-making. The task of decision-making can vary greatly between functions within an organization, between individual decision-makers who have different styles of taking action, between different tasks or types of decisions, and between organizations. Therefore, decision support systems take different forms. The DSS supports decision-makers in understanding the nature of the environment and in assessing probable consequences of various alternative actions, but does not "make the decision."

DSSs consist of applications built from tools with a user interface appropriate to decision-makers. The applications access data and employ models to support managerial decision-making. Data may be gathered from a single process from within an organization (such as customer transactions), from multiple processes (these often provide links between separate processes for receiving revenue and for disbursing funds), and/or from outside data sources such as online databases or customer help (or complaint) lines. Data-oriented DSS can be used, for example, to search a sales transaction database looking for subsets of clients that share particular characteristics and define a segment. Models are frequently financial or statistical in nature but may also include optimization or other mathematical tools. They are used to refine, shape, and organize the data. Financial models can be used for "what if" analysis in projecting the effect of changing policies or macroeconomic conditions on the probable effectiveness of various actions.

The DSS user interface allows the user to directly manipulate data and/or models and to format the output as desired. For example, a typical DSS will allow the user to examine timeline data as either tables or graphs. DSS with Windows-style features may allow shifting from one format to another with a keystroke or mouse action. Similarly, a DSS can draw data from organizational transaction processing systems and deposit them within a spreadsheet or database package on the user's desk for their further manipulation. As an example, a DSS application for a hospital might be constructed to support bidding on a contract with a health maintenance organization. Such an application would be built from data for clinical costs, patient revenue, and physician preferences gathered from various departments based on historical data derived from operational processes. Where such bidding on contracts might be a recurring task, the application would be built to be updated with current data.

The DSS may be designed to support one or more of Herbert Simon's phases of decision-making: intelligence, design, and choice. Intelligence is the gathering of information about the nature of the problem; design is formulating alternative action plans or solutions to the problem; and choice is selecting among the alternatives. In the hospital scenario, the DSS may support the intelligence activity by periodically drawing information from clinical and financial transactions, by integrating internal data with information drawn from external sources that provide baselines of activity or a basis for forecasting. The DSS can support alternative designs by comparing proposed contracts for profitability, given varying demand and cost scenarios. It can support choice by comparing alternative scenarios on various criteria selected by senior managers. It will present ranking of alternatives and the relative sensitivity to changes for particular criteria.

A DSS may be designed for top, middle, and lower management levels. In the hospital scenario, for example, a comprehensive DSS can provide information for high-level executives formulating major contracts; for middle managers ensuring that medical resources are available for implementing the contract; and for operational managers selecting the most cost-effective techniques for providing direct care.

The purpose of a DSS is to provide relevant data as a mechanism for managers to make decisions based on an understanding of the environment and an examination of relevant alternatives. As a by-product, managers tend to have more confidence in their decision, knowing that their investigation has been thorough. They have more effective means to communicate their decision to peers and to persuade others to implement the decision. A successful DSS will provide some combination of better decisions (where the link between decisions and outcomes can be demonstrated), more efficient use of time in decision-making and more satisfaction or confidence with the decision-making process.

DSSs can be built in a number of ways. For a particular decision or problem, the DSS may be built using a prototype model. Prototyping emphasizes quick development of an approximation of the final system. The user observes the prototype and provides feedback on how to improve it. Development and feedback proceed in an iterative fashion until the user is satisfied. Where the DSS aims to provide a wide array of corporate data for repetitive use over many decisions, a repository for data is built with interfaces to draw or receive data from other corporate systems. Such a system is likely to have both structured reports that are regularly updated and a more complex interface that specialists can use to generate detailed *ad hoc* reports. The term DSS has generally been applied to corporate or department-wide decision-making systems; however, personal computing tools, such as spreadsheets and database packages, allow knowledge workers to develop DSS procedures to support individual decision-making.

Expanding on the original concept of DSS are EXECUTIVE INFORMATION SYSTEMS (EIS) and GROUP DECISION SUPPORT SYSTEMS (GDSS). The EIS supports senior managers in terms of specific decision-making and in monitoring key indicators of progress for their organization. The GDSS supports decision-making by groups or teams rather than by single individuals. In addition to tools for supporting data and modeling, the GDSS generally will have meeting support tools that automate brainstorming and voting functions.

Bibliography

Alter, S. L. (1980). *Decision Support Systems: Current Practice and Continuing Challenges*. Reading, MA: Addison-Wesley.

DeSanctis, G. & Gallupe, B. (1987). Group decision support systems: a new frontier. *Management Science*, 33 (5), 43–59.

Gorry, G. M. & Scott-Morton, M. S. (1971). A framework for management information systems. *Sloan Management Review*, 13 (1), 55–70.

Houdeshel, G. & Watson, H. J. (1987). The management information and decision support (MIDS) system at Lockheed-Georgia. *MIS Quarterly*, 11 (2), 127–40.

Silver, M. S. (1991). Decisional guidance for computer-based decision support. *MIS Quarterly*, 15 (1) 105–22.

Simon, H. (1977). *The New Science of Management Decision*. Englewood Cliffs, NJ: Prentice-Hall.

Sprague, R. H. Jr (1980). A framework for the development of decision support systems. *MIS Quarterly*, 4 (4), 1–26.

Sprague, R. H. Jr & Carlson, E. D. (1982). *Building Effective Decision Support Systems*. Englewood Cliffs, NJ: Prentice-Hall.

Watson, H. J. et al. (eds) (1992). *Executive Support Systems*. New York: Wiley.

FRED NIEDERMAN

declining industry This is a mature industry whose sales are decreasing. Such an industry is in the final stage of its life cycle, although industry sales may revive at some point (*see* PRODUCT LIFE CYCLE; Jacquemin (1987) and Porter (1980)). When an industry's sales are declining, net rates of exit by firms will increase either through failure or through acquisition by other firms. The industry structure may consolidate and industry concentration may rise. In this stage of the industry life cycle, surviving firms often must compete on the basis of costs since many substitutes are available to consumers.

If there are exit barriers or if firms are unwilling to leave the industry, competition between the firms that remain in a declining industry may intensify. In the extreme case, firms may engage in a "war of attrition" where no firm wants to be the first to leave the industry since the remaining firm or firms will be able to earn economic profits. Porter (1980) identifies several sources of exit barriers including specialized assets, fixed costs of exit (such as settling labor and other contracts) and strategic barriers where presence in the declining market may confer advantages for the firm in other markets in which it sells. Whinston (1988) theoretically evaluated the social welfare consequences of exit and observed that firm exits from a declining industry may not be optimal since the "wrong" (lower cost) firm may exit before the higher cost firm. Furthermore, multiplant firms may reduce their capacity when the efficient outcome would require that small firms exit the industry. These welfare effects are similar to the biases from free entry but in reverse; see also Tirole (1988).

Bibliography

Jacquemin, A. (1987). *The New Industrial Organization: Market Forces and Strategic Behavior*. Cambridge, MA: MIT.

Porter, M. E. (1980). *Competitive Strategy*. New York: Free Press.

Tirole, J. (1988). *The Theory of Industrial Organization*. Cambridge, MA: MIT.

Whinston, M. D. (1988). Exit with multiplant firms. *The Rand Journal of Economics*, 19, 568–88.

ROBERT E. MCAULIFFE

decreasing cost industry A decreasing cost industry is one where costs decrease as the industry expands. In this case, the industry's long run supply curve slopes downward; as the industry produces more output, the minimum average cost of production for each firm decreases with the decrease in costs. Firms in a decreasing cost industry do not necessarily have ECONOMIES OF SCALE in production; the decrease in costs may reflect lower input costs which reduce the minimum point of the AVERAGE TOTAL COST curve as the industry grows.

Input costs may decline as the industry expands if there are economies of scale in the production of an important input. For example, economies of scale in the production of computer chips allow personal computer manufacturers to produce more computers at lower cost as chip prices fall. An industry may also experience decreasing cost if there are "economies of agglomeration." These economies can occur when a number of firms produce in a specific geographic area and as their number grows, supporting services such as transportation can be provided to all firms at lower cost. Again, this lowers each firm's costs as the industry grows and so the minimum point on the average cost curve where there are zero economic profits is lower (*see* ECONOMIC PROFIT). Managers in decreasing cost industries can use this knowledge to anticipate price changes. When the industry expands prices and costs may initially rise, but they will decrease below their original levels in the long run as entry and industry output increase. Decreasing cost industries have long run supply curves which are negatively sloped.

ROBERT E. MCAULIFFE

delegation When a manager must depend on others to accomplish an objective, the notion of *delegation of authority* comes into play. Delegation means conferring of authority from an executive to another to accomplish a particular assignment. Delegation gets the DECISION MAKING closer to the locus of where the decision is actually implemented. Typically, delegation refers to granting authority in a downward direction, although delegation can also be directed laterally or even upward. The idea of delegation has been well established in the historical management literature, and was a prominent part of the early principles of management (*see* Terry, 1972).

Delegation is closely associated with the term participation, and *participative leadership*. Participation implies that the leader invites followers to participate actively in discussions, problem solving, and decision making, but retaining final decision-making authority. Delegation is somewhat stronger, implying the locus of decision making is in the hands of the follower.

Participation and delegation are points on a continuum, rather than discrete modes of leader behavior. But whatever the degree, delegation does not mean that a leader abdicates responsibility. A manager who delegates retains the overall responsibility, and must follow up to assure that the delegated task has been carried out.

One of the more widely known prescriptive models of delegation is the Vroom–Yetton (1974) model. The model attempts to answer the question of the conditions under which a leader should be directive versus participative. Vroom and Yetton propose a direction-participation continuum ranging from extreme leader decision making, through increasingly involving forms of participation, to pure delegation. The situational characteristics that define the conditions include such factors as: quality requirement, sufficiency of information, problem structure, and importance of subordinate acceptance (*see* GOAL-SETTING). Depending on the combination of these situational variables, the degree of decision-making participation and/or delegation is recommended.

Delegation is also related to the more contemporary concept of superleadership (Manz & Sims, 1989) which means "leading others to lead themselves." A Super Leader is one who develops followers to the point where they are capable of accepting a high degree of responsibility and decision-making discretion. Manz and Sims would describe a follower to whom a leader would delegate as empowered self-leaders. SuperLeadership is a more fine-grained and contemporary form of delegation. Also, today, one is more likely to find the popular use of the term "EMPOWER-MENT" (rather than delegation) to represent a broad philosophy and practice of participation and delegation (*see* EMPLOYEE INVOLVEMENT).

Perhaps the most important contemporary form of real delegation are self-managing or self-directed teams (Manz & Sims, 1993) (*see* SELF-MANAGED TEAMS). After development and experimentation in the 1970s and 1980s, self-managing teams have become considerably more diffused in the early 1990s. Self-managing teams are a form of delegation where the work group becomes empowered with a very high degree of decision-making discretion. In an important meta-analysis (*see* VALIDITY GENERALIZATION), Macy, Bliese and Norton (1991) have empirically shown the bottom line contribution of self-managing teams to organizational productivity. Also, at the professional or middle level of organizations, empowered professional or KNOWLEDGE WORKER teams are becoming more important. These include teams such as concurrent engineering teams, product improvement teams, office worker teams, and new venture teams.

see also **Self-management; Leadership; Power**

Bibliography

Macy, B. M., Bliese, P. D. & Norton, J. J. (1991). Organizational change and work innovation: A meta-analysis of 131 North American field experiments—1961–1990. Working paper, Texas Technical University.

Manz, C. C. & Sims, H. P. Jr. (1989). SuperLeadership. New York: Berkley.

Manz, C. C. & Sims, H. P. Jr. (1993). Business without bosses: How self-managing teams are producing high-performing companies. New York: Wiley.

Terry, G. R. (1972). Principles of management. (6th edn) Homewood, IL: Irwin.

Vroom, V. H. & Yetton, P. W. (1974). Leadership and decision-making. New York: Wiley.

HENRY P. SIMS JR.

delivery dependability   Delivery dependability is one of the commonly quoted operations objectives which define the performance of the operations function. Delivery dependability is generally taken to mean keeping delivery promises. It can be viewed as the other half of delivery performance along with delivery speed.

Although speed and dependability are the two halves of delivery performance they are fundamentally different in as much as speed is usually quoted and defined as part of the specification for the order. Customers may make some attempt to specify dependability also (by the use of penalty clauses for late delivery, for example), but this remains a performance objective which becomes important when a history of performance, good or bad, is established.

Dependability has a number of attributes in common with quality. It is a "conformance" measure, but conformance to time rather than specification. It is also an attribute which influences customer satisfaction over the longer term rather than one which necessarily ensures an immediate sale.

Measuring Delivery Dependability

In principle dependability is a straightforward concept, where

$$\text{Dependability} = \text{due delivery date} - \text{actual delivery date}$$

When delivery is on time the equation will equal zero; a positive measure means delivery is early and negative means delivery is late.

However, measurement is not always so straightforward. For example, the "due date" can mean the date originally requested by the customer or the date quoted by the operation. Also there can be a difference between the delivery date scheduled by the operation and that which is promised to the customer. Nor are delivery dates immutable; they can be changed, sometimes by customers but more often by the operation. If the customer requests a new delivery date this may be used to calculate delivery performance.

The Benefits of Delivery Dependability

It is worth distinguishing between the external benefits of delivery dependability (how the outside customer views dependability), and its internal benefits (what internal customers gain), and how it benefits the whole operation.

Delivery dependability is often seen as a "qualifying" (*see* ORDER-WINNERS AND QUALIFIERS) performance objective. However, this may not be the case. Although it is an attribute judged over the longer term by customers, that is not the same as being a qualifier. The key questions is, "Can an operation win more business directly by being more dependable?" Partly this is a consequence of customers becoming more sophisticated in their purchasing behavior.

The most significant internal benefit of dependability is the stability it gives. In a highly dependable operation relatively little is wasted on coping with unexpected events. Perhaps more significant is the reduction in the fragmenting effects of continuing interruptions to routine operations and the absence of a lack of trust in the internal working of the operation. Operations managers can "keep their eye on the ball."

From this stability can come other benefits, most notably less inventory. Part of the reason for the build up of inventory between stages in an operation is that it buffers each stage from the output variation of its neighbors. In-process inventory is often justified on the basis that internal deliveries might not be on time and therefore inventory is required to protect the operation. However, with increased dependability there is no need for the "insurance" of buffer inventory.

Improving Delivery Dependability

A number of prescriptions have been advocated as to how the external and internal dimensions of delivery dependability may be improved. Most commonly a link is drawn between dependable delivery and dependable technology. The effectiveness of any operations MAINTENANCE practices will clearly affect internal, and therefore external, dependability. Other prescriptions include the following.

- *Plan ahead*: often when a delivery is late the root cause will be some occurrence which was unexpected by the operation. Frequently the unexpected event could have been predicted with some internal mechanism which looks forward for indications of possible trouble.

- *Do not overload capacity*: loading an operation above its operational capacity often results in missed internal delivery dates. The consequences of excess load may be a lack of control and overlooked due dates.

- *Flexibility can localize disruptions*: certain types of flexibility can service to localize disruptions when they do occur, by providing alternative processing capability. However, flexibility does not prevent disruption; although it can limit its effects.

- *Monitor progress closely*: a common cause of lateness seems to be overlooked internal delivery dates. Every day that internal lateness is not recognized is a day less in which to do something about it. An internal monitoring system may become self-reinforcing because when internal dependability increases and flow becomes more predictable, it is easier for internal customers to signal late deliveries.

- *Emphasize internal supplier development*: initially the role of internal customers may be to monitor the delivery performance of their suppliers. Later it may be a matter of improving communications, for example, holding joint improvement team meetings and so on.

Bibliography

Ferdows, S. K. & De Mayer, A. (1990). Lasting improvement in manufacturing performance: In search of a new theory. INSEAD Working Paper. Fontainebleau: INSEAD.

New, C. C. & Sweeney, M. T. (1984). Delivery performance and throughput efficiency in UK manufacturing industry. *International Journal of Physical Distribution Management*, 14, 7.

NIGEL SLACK

delivery risk   Risk associated with fears of a buyer that parts or repairs will not be available for machinery or equipment purchased overseas. Delivery risk is the uncertainty concerning delays in delivery of parts, lack of guarantees that parts will be available in the future, or interference with deliveries because of labor unrest or government action in a foreign country.

JOHN O'CONNELL

demand   The assessment of demand is crucial to responsible pricing analysis and decision-making, yet demand can often be an unknowable and even a mercurial factor. At one extreme, analysis of demand can be little more than a statistical extrapolation of historic demand data, regardless of the validity of the data, the methodology used for their collection, or the assumptions underlying their use (as with the Ford Edsell motor-car). At another extreme, assessment of demand can be no more than intuitive guesswork propped up by selective data (as with the Sinclair C5 electric mini-car).

The demand for a product or service can be seen as historic, existing, latent, or potential. Historic demand describes customers (individuals and organizations) who have purchased a particular product or service in the past, whereas existing demand describes customers who are currently purchasing the product or service, and potential demand describes those customers who might purchase the product or service in the foreseeable future given various changes in marketing strategy or environmental circumstances (e.g., protectionism). Some authorities also use the term latent demand to refer, in effect, to demand which could be developed reasonably quickly (so distinguishing latent demand from potential demand) with appropriate marketing strategies but which meanwhile remains dormant. The most easily adapted aspect of marketing strategies is PRICING and this is usually the quickest way to translate latent demand or potential demand into existing demand. Yet too much demand can be just as problematic for a supplier as too little demand and a responsible pricing policy will therefore depend crucially on careful assessment of demand.

Clearly there will often be similarities between these forms of demand but there can also be important differences. For example, the product or service in question may well have changed significantly over time to the extent that historic demand is no longer a useful indication of potential demand. The characteristics of demand can also change over time (e.g., in disposable income, customer sophistication, sensitivity to particular product aspects). And there is usually sufficient environmental change and uncertainty about the data to mean that demand should generally be assessed cautiously. Demand is even more difficult to assess where a product or service is innovative, making historic reference points even more problematic. This caution is captured in the concept of realizable demand which refers to that fraction of potential demand which an organization considers it can realistically achieve with its MARKETING STRATEGY and PRICING decisions.

DOMINIC WILSON

demand curves   For individuals or markets, demand curves show the relationship between the quantity demanded and the price of the good (holding everything else constant). Given the LAW OF DEMAND, the quantity demanded will be inversely related to the relative price of the good. The demand curve will shift whenever any other variables in the DEMAND FUNCTION change (except the price of the product itself). Since total revenue is equal to price, P, times quantity, Q, and the demand curve expresses quantity demanded as a function of price alone, the demand curve is also the average revenue curve. In other words, dividing total revenues (sales) by the number of units sold yields the average revenue (price) per unit sold.

Bibliography

Douglas, E. J. (1992). *Managerial Economics.* 4th edn, Englewood Cliffs, NJ: Prentice-Hall.

Shughart. W.F., Chappell, W. F. & Cottle, R. L. (1994). *Modern Managerial Economics*. Cincinatti, OH: South-Western Publishing.

ROBERT E. MCAULIFFE

demand function   The demand function shows the relationship between the quantity demanded and *all* variables or factors which affect demand. These variables include the price of the product itself, the prices of related goods (*see* COMPLEMENTS), consumer income levels, consumer preferences, the information available to consumers, the product's quality, consumer expectations and the advertising and promotional efforts for the product and for competing products. Additional variables may include the population in the market, the weather and other factors specific to a product's market.

Of the variables listed above, firm managers can only control a few. A firm can exert some control over the price it charges, its own advertising outlays, and the quality of its product (including the services offered before and after the sale). Douglas (1992) refers to these variables as strategic variables which the firm can use to enhance its market position.

The specific form the demand function will take depends on the relationship between the quantity demanded and these variables in a given market and time period. For example, the Cobb–Douglas form of the demand function allows the variables to affect demand multiplicatively. In the simplest case where only three variables affect the demand for the product, the Cobb–Douglas demand function is:

$$Q_x^d = P_x^\alpha A_x^\beta I_x^\gamma$$

where Px is the price of product x, Ax is the level of advertising for the product and Ix is the real income of consumers in the market. In this example, the coefficients α, β and γ would measure the ELASTICITY of demand with respect to its own price, advertising and income respectively. Other functional relationships for demand can be specified and estimated; (see Berndt (1991) and linear regression).

Bibliography

Berndt, E. R. (1991). *The Practice of Econometrics*. Reading, MA: Addison-Wesley.

Douglas, E. J. (1992). *Managerial Economics*. 4th edn, Englewood Cliffs, NJ: Prentice-Hall.

Shughart, W. F., Chappell, W. F. & Cottle, R. L. (1994). *Modern Managerial Economics*. Cincinatti, OH: South-Western Publishing.

ROBERT E. MCAULIFFE

demographics   Demographics comprise probably the most important variable in the MARKETING ENVIRONMENT of any organization. Demographics describe, and provide a statistical study of, a human population in terms of its size, structure, and distribution. Size is the number of individuals in a population, and is determined by: fertility and birth rates; life expectancy and death rates; and migration between and within countries. Structure describes the population in terms of age, gender, education, and occupation, and distribution refers to the location of individuals in terms of geographic region or rural, urban, or suburban location.

Demographic data are developed, primarily, from population censuses and the study of demographics is concerned with understanding trends to include forecasts of future demographic size, structure, and distribution.

Demographics impact on the behavior of consumers and contribute to the overall demand for goods and services. They are changing in a number of ways, influenced by social and cultural variables (*see also* CULTURE). Such trends, in developed economies, include:

- increased life expectancy and an aging population
- a slowing down of the birth rate and population growth
- growing per capita income and discretionary income
- changing mix of household expenditure
- increasing participation of women in the work force and their changing roles at home and at work
- increasing proportion of white collar workers
- trends in literacy and education
- geographical shifts in population, e.g., urban to rural and city to suburbs and new towns
- changing ethnic and racial mixes
- changing family and household structure, to take account of age profiles, later marriage and age of child-bearing, fewer children in a family, divorce and single-parent families, increasing numbers of single-person households, and total number of households
- increased home ownership and increased ownership of consumer durables
- widespread availability of credit
- fewer traditional shoppers and more home shopping
- increased leisure time and participation in leisure activities
- changing media habits
- increases in crime and social problems.

These changes/trends are of key interest to marketing organizations. For example, they may see opportunities arising as particular age groups increase, or threats occurring as some age groups decline. Demographic trends have implications for: product and service development; identification of target MARKETS and market segments (*see* MARKET SEGMENTATION) and other elements in the MARKETING MIX. These impact not only on manufacturers and distributors but also on those organizations which supply consumer good manufacturers, e.g., producers of commodities and capital equipment.

see also **Lifestyles**

Bibliography

Central Statistical Office. *Annual abstract of statistics*. London: HMSO.

Hawkins, D. I., Best, R. J. & Coney, K. A. (1995). *Consumer behavior: Implications for marketing strategy*, 6th edn, International student edition. Chicago: Irwin. Chapter 3, pp. 78–88.

Kotler, P. (1994). *Marketing management: Analysis, planning, implementation and control*, 8th edn, Englewood Cliffs, NJ: Prentice-Hall. Chapter 6.

McCarthy, E. J. & Perreault, W. D. Jr (1993). *Basic marketing*. Homewood, IL: Irwin. Chapter 6.

Palmer, A. & Worthington, I. (1992). *The business and marketing environment*. Maidenhead: McGraw-Hill. Chapters 9 & 10.

Pol, L. G. (1986). Marketing and demographic perspective. *Journal of Consumer Marketing* Winter, 56–64.

United States Bureau of the Census. *Statistical abstract of the United States.* Austin: Reference Press.

Wilkie, W. L. (1994). *Consumer behavior,* 3rd edn, New York: John Wiley, pp. 54–83.

BARBARA LEWIS

denationalization The process of transferring ownership and operational control from government to private ownership.

see also **Privatization**

JOHN O'CONNELL

derailing Derailing occurs when employees or managers are thrown off their expected CAREER PATHING by either their own behaviors or external events. Derailment may take the form of plateauing early. Derailment does not refer to: persons who, having reached their CAREER potential ("topping out"), "drop or opt out;" promotable employees with no place to go; or those who fail to win a promotion every time one is available. Persons who are derailed have typically experienced at least moderate career success prior to derailment. McCall et al. (1988, pp. 168–9) have identified ten factors associated with derailing of successful executives: (a) insensitivity to others (abrasive or bullying style), the most frequent cause for derailment; (b) failing to meet organizational performance problems; (c) cold, aloof, and arrogant interpersonal style; (d) betrayal of trust; (e) overmanaging and failing to build a team; (f) too ambitious and playing politics; (g) failing to staff effectively, picking people who fail; (h) inability to think strategically; (i) failure to adapt to a boss with a different style; and (j) overdependence on a mentor or advocate.

Bibliography

McCall, M. W., Lombardo, M. M. & Morrison, A. M. (1988). *The Lessons of Experience,* Lexington, MA: Lexington.

THOMAS H. STONE

deregulation This is the abolishment or considerable weakening of an existing regulatory regime to increase the responsiveness of a previously regulated industry to its input and/or output markets and lead to more competition.

Deregulation can take place within any one country or part thereof (such as the deregulation of the US airline industry or of London buses), across larger geographic areas (such as the telecommunications industry in Europe), or on a global basis.

Causes and Timing

Deregulation can be the result of two main developments. First, it may become desirable because of the growing inefficiencies that regulation can impose by artificially isolating markets that the growth of multinationals and the GLOBALIZATION of the marketplace tend to integrate. Second, it may become desirable when technological innovations make regulatory limitations obsolete; for instance, by means of fundamentally transforming cost structures or, again, redefining the boundaries of industries.

The need for deregulation, therefore, typically emerges as a result of largely external influences, although government action is usually required to permit and enact the required changes. As far as the incentives for government itself are concerned, this not only has to take into account social and efficiency considerations and the interests of consumers, but also the interests of producers, who may well have developed close political ties while regulated. According to the balance between these factors, government involvement can either be responsive (in which case it acts upon requests by powerful interest groups adversely affected by regulation, such as innovative producers or overcharged consumers), or proactive (in which case it acts before any powerful interest group expresses any desire for deregulation, this sometimes being observed in cases in which deregulation forms part of a larger government initiative, such as PRIVATIZATION). Historically, banking is one of the industries that has been deregulated as a result of innovations, whereas public utilities have been deregulated as a result of political initiative.

The Impact of Deregulation

Impact on market structure and level of competition. Deregulation has a profound impact on a firm's competitive environment. Because it reduces barriers to entry (*see* BARRIERS TO ENTRY AND EXIT), allows firms to go into related fields, and encourages new firms to develop, it increases the number of firms in the previously regulated market, and enhances competition in that market. The new firms may well bring with them cost cutting technologies, additional capacity, and hence the ability to cut prices. At the same time, unbundling gives customers greater flexibility to make product/service and price/performance tradeoffs, so their level of knowledge increases and they become more price sensitive.

An additional factor which makes the environment more competitive is that, in their effort to match new entrants, established competitors often imitate new offerings without full knowledge of their own costs, thereby leading to deep price cuts.

A McKinsey study on the post-deregulation US airline, financial services, telephone, trucking, and railroad industries made some detailed observations as to the implications of these changes (Bleeke, 1991). According to the study, therefore, an industry changes immediately after deregulation when a number of new companies enter the market. Prices and profitability fall rapidly, the most attractive segments often become the least profitable, the variation in profitability between the best and worst performers widens, and many entrants go out of business or merge with stronger competitors. Waves of mergers and acquisitions initially consolidate weak competitors and subsequently combine the strong, and many companies are forced to abandon many areas of activity, largely because of the increasing cost of competing in any single one of them. During this period, the overall market grows, despite any failures, and flexibility is key to survival, particularly with respect to pricing, so that all potential sources of profit can be exploited. Similarly, the organization's resources need to be conserved, and large expenditures need to be considered twice, even if they are intended to lead to the introduction of cost cutting technology.

Some five years after deregulation, the industry stabilizes and the competitive environment changes again.

The weakest competitors have all gone, larger companies have learned how to compete with new rivals, and the price gap between new entrants and existing companies diminishes as the latter's cost cutting efforts have taken effect. At this stage, the deregulated market can be assumed to have completed the phase of post-deregulation re-organization and should be considered just like any competitive industry.

Impact on the use of technology and the variety of output.   Regulated industries face little competition, and they find it relatively easy to pass on increased costs to customers. This means that they need not worry so much about cost cutting, although some recently developed regulatory regimes have shown the capability to success-fully control costs. The use of technology in regulated industries, therefore, is predominantly applied to providing higher levels of service. As deregulation puts heavy emphasis on cost cutting, however, cost cutting technol-ogies are brought into the industry.

Similarly, unbundling and the removal of constraints on price and product competition lead to a broader range of offerings and affords the customer a full range of product/service and price/performance tradeoffs. Lower quality at lower prices becomes an option, therefore, but when deregulation is not complete and some monopolistic elements remain (e.g., because of natural monopolies), the danger of lower quality for higher profits remains or even increases as the oversight of the regulatory authority ceases to exist.

Impact on culture, skills, and the strategic process.   Turning to the organizations themselves, culture is one of the predominant variables that need to change with deregulation. The traditional attitude of regulated organi-zations is to accept the guidance of the regulatory authorities and so to be reactive rather than proactive. By contrast, many of the new competitors entering a deregulated industry deliberately seek to gain competitive advantage by circumventing existing regulatory barriers (as these are weakened during the process of deregulation), and this makes proactive strategy development advisable for the incumbent companies as well. This typically demands a complete and time-consuming change in organizational culture.

In addition, while regulation requires an emphasis on political and negotiation skills to deal with the regulator, the post-deregulation market environment requires heavier emphasis on planning, marketing, and financial skills.

As a result, therefore, previously regulated companies typically go through a transitory period of weakness upon deregulation, during which the new skills are developed or brought in and assimilated.

Impact on strategic outcome

Diversification.   Turning to the strategy innovations of the deregulated firms, these are often influenced by the kind of relationship that the firm previously enjoyed with its regulator. If this was cosy, and if the firm had focused all its activities around the regulator, diversification will follow into other markets with equal or better profit potential (the reason why the firm would have avoided such diversifica-tion while regulated is that the regulator would have been unable to act to the firm's advantage in unrelated

industries). Similarly, if deregulation implies that the regulator adopts a change agent role, to reduce the amount of help that it used to provide to the regulated firms, then the increasing divergence between the interests of the regulator and the regulated industry would again be expected to lead the firm into markets over which the regulator has no control.

In addition to product market diversification, geographic diversification also takes place with deregulation, for the same reasons. Moreover, this can be due to the fact that the regulated firm is now free to go abroad (and has the incentives to do so), or it may be that a particular deregulation is coordinated internationally (e.g., the European deregulation in telecommunications).

Alliances and acquisitions.   Where deregulation opens up new markets, either by means of the combination of technologies or by allowing companies to enter foreign markets, alliances, joint ventures, and acquisitions are often pursued as a means of acquiring missing skills or rapidly building market share.

Impact on structure.   Turning to organizational structure, diversification and a newly competitive environment both result in a strong trend toward organizational restructuring, this mainly involving divisionalization and the setting up of a series of customer-oriented marketing units to deal with the increased range of services and products offered.

In addition, particularly where deregulation takes place in conjunction with privatization and involves the setting up of a competitive market starting from a single organization, the incumbent organization may have to be split into a number of competing enterprises, horizontally or vertically; or, alternately, third parties may be given the right to establish new companies and compete.

Overall impact on performance.   Having already discussed the effect that deregulation has on prices (and the ways in which this can be moderated), the impact on performance should follow. Overall, however, it is not possible to evaluate the likely impact of deregulation on any particular firm without consideration of the actions which any such firm takes to prepare for and react to deregulation. In the long term, performance may either increase or fall, because while regulation is expected to assure a reasonable stream of profits for all, deregulation opens the way to both very low and much higher levels of profits.

In the short term, the profits of established competitors are very often under threat, and profitable national monopolies are likely to face a difficult time adjusting to their new environment, particularly if all regulatory protection is removed at once. Initially, profits tend to fall, until reorganization and change of culture for competition are complete. At this point, a longer-term danger exists if the organization overlooks important environmental changes, and this may well determine whether it survives in the competitive environment. If it adjusts, a whole new range of opportunities for consider-ably higher turnover are open to it, both nationally and internationally. Otherwise, if it remains largely unchanged in its culture and organization, it is likely to perish. A third possibility that is sometimes observed is that an organiza-tion appears to be adjusting well but, for a number of reasons, makes the wrong choices in the product market.

Bibliography
Bleeke, J. A. (1983). Deregulation: riding the rapids. *McKinsey Quarterly* (Summer), 26–44.
Bleeke, J. A. (1990). Strategic choices for newly open markets. *Harvard Business Review*, **68** (5), September–October, 158–66. Reprinted in *McKinsey Quarterly* (1991), no. 1, 75–89.
Channon, D. F. (1986). *Global banking strategy*. Chichester: John Wiley. See chapter 9.
Mahimi, A. & Turcq, D. (1993). The three faces of European deregulation. *McKinsey Quarterly*, no. 3, 35–50.
Mahon, J. F. & Murray, E. A. Jr. (1981). Deregulation and strategic transformation. *Journal of Contemporary Business*, **9** (2), 123–38.

STEPHANOS AVGEROPOULOS

differentiation strategy This is the alternative generic strategy to the COST LEADERSHIP STRATEGY, as suggested by Porter (1980). Organizations strive to secure a sustainable COMPETITIVE ADVANTAGE by distinguishing themselves from their competitors using such means as design, customer service, image, packaging, and additional functionality in ways which are perceived by customers as adding value. The differentiation strategy can be focused on particular customers or market segment(s) or devised for the general market.

see also **Competitive strategy**

Bibliography
Porter, M. E. (1980). *Competitive strategy: Techniques for analyzing industries and competitors*. New York: Free Press. Chapter 2.

DALE LITTLER

diffusion process The diffusion process is concerned with how product innovations are spread or assimilated within a market or industry. It is a macro process and may be defined as the process by which the acceptance of an innovation (product, service, or idea) is spread by communications (impersonal and interpersonal) to members of a social system (e.g., market or target segment) over a period of time. In other words, it is the spread of a new idea from its source of invention or creation to its ultimate users or adopters.

A number of product characteristics influence the diffusion of innovation and the rate of adoption by users (*see* ADOPTION PROCESS), i.e., some products may be an overnight success (e.g., video recorder), and some may be very slow to diffuse (e.g., dishwasher). These characteristics are:

- relative advantage with respect to ease of operations and reliability, i.e., the degree to which a new product appears superior to the buyer than previous products, and existing substitutes;
- compatibility: i.e., the degree to which a potential customer feels that a new product is consistent with present needs, values, and behavior, i.e., with experiences in the social system, or complementary processes in the case of industrial innovations;
- complexity: the degree to which a new product is difficult to comprehend and use – more complex innovations take longer to diffuse;
- divisibility: the degree to which a new product may be tried on a limited basis – the more opportunity to try, the easier it is for a consumer or user to evaluate; and

- communicability: the degree to which results from product use and ownership are observable and describable to others, i.e., the ease of seeing a product's benefits and attributes – so that products with a high degree of social visibility (e.g., fashion) are more easily diffused.

see also **Adoption process**

Bibliography
Robertson, T. S. (1967). The process of innovation and the diffusion of innovation. *Journal of Marketing* Jan., 14–19.
Rogers, E. M. (1962). *Diffusion of innovations*. New York: Free Press.
Schiffman, L. G. & Kanuk, L. Z. (1991). *Consumer behavior*, 4th edn, Prentice-Hall. Chapter 18.

BARBARA LEWIS

diminishing returns When additional units of a factor of production are added to fixed amounts of other inputs in production, at some point the increase in output which results will decrease. Holding other inputs constant means that the level of technology used to combine inputs in production is also held constant. There may be diminishing total returns where total output actually falls from additional units of an input – as when too many workers in a plant reduce the total output produced by interfering with each other, in which case the total product of labor would be declining. Or there may be diminishing average returns where the average output decreases from additional units of an input. If the input which is increased is labor, the average product of labor would be decreasing in this case.

Diminishing *marginal* returns occur when additional units of an input result in a smaller increase in output or, equivalently, the MARGINAL PRODUCT of that input will decline. Since diminishing returns applies when at least one input in production is held constant, it represents a short run phenomenon. When all inputs in production are varied, the question is one of returns to scale.

see also **Economies of scale; Law of variable proportions**

Bibliography
Douglas, E. J. (1992). *Managerial Economics*. 4th edn, Englewood Cliffs, NJ: Prentice-Hall.
Stigler, G. J. (1966). *The Theory of Price*. 3rd edn, New York: Macmillan.

ROBERT E. McAULIFFE

direct importing Direct importing exists when the only parties to the transaction are the importer who arranges the purchase of goods from an exporter and the exporter who sells the goods. No intermediaries (freight forwarders, customhouse brokers, etc.) are involved with the transaction. Direct importing requires a great deal of knowledge of the import transaction and its various requirements as well as a good deal of faith in the exporter.

Bibliography
United States Customs Service (1994). *A basic guide to importing*. Lincolnwood, IL: NTC Publishing Group.

JOHN O'CONNELL

direct mail Direct mail is a part of DIRECT MARKETING and, specifically, is ADVERTISING that is sent directly to the mailing address of a target customer. Thus, it offers the advertiser the opportunity for high audience selectivity and targeting, and wide-ranging geographic flexibility. It can be personalized (via individual letters) but much direct marketing is either lacking in personalization or is personalized with computer fill-ins, leading to a "junk mail" appearance.

Evidence of the growth of direct mail is seen in the: generation and sale/purchase of computer-based mailing lists, i.e., databases (*see* DATABASE), so that direct mail messages may be carefully targeted to create consumer awareness and/or to generate action; the growth of specialized direct mail agencies; and the increasing marketing orientation of the postal services with various incentive discounts.

Bibliography

Dibb, S., Simkin, L., Pride, W. M. & Ferrell, O. C. (1994). *Marketing: Concepts and strategies*, European edn, Boston, MA: Houghton Mifflin Co. Chapter 16.

DAVID YORKE

direct marketing Direct marketing is sometimes confused with DIRECT MAIL. It is not a medium but a marketing technique, comprising an interactive system of marketing, which uses one or more communications media (direct mail, print, telephone, i.e., telemarketing, broadcast) for the purpose of soliciting a direct and measurable consumer response. Its objective is to make a sale or obtain a sales lead enquiry.

Computers are an indispensable tool in direct marketing, in particular in generating personalized direct mail sources. Indeed, the success of direct marketing depends on the acquisition and maintenance of a DATABASE of customers or potential customers.

The growth of direct marketing has been stimulated by socio–economic changes (e.g., an aging population, single-person or single-parent households, and working women with less shopping time), the increasing use of credit, a consumer convenience orientation, rising discretionary income, and developing computer technology and communications media.

Bibliography

Dibb, S., Simkin, L., Pride, W. M. & Ferrell, O. C. (1994). *Marketing: Concepts and strategies*, European edn, Boston, MA: Houghton Mifflin Co. Chapter 16.
Kotler, P. (1994). *Marketing management: Analysis, planning, implementation and control*, 8th edn, Englewood Cliffs, NJ: Prentice-Hall. Chapter 24, pp. 653–683.
Roberts, M. L. & Berger, P. D. (1989). *Direct marketing management*. Englewood Cliffs, NJ: Prentice-Hall.
Schiffman, L. G. & Kanuk, L. L. (1991). *Consumer behavior*, 4th edn, pp. 292-294. Prentice-Hall.

DAVID YORKE

directional matrix This summarizes the major growth strategies. As defined by Ansoff (1965), it consists of two parameters: markets and technologies, subdivided according to whether or not they are "new" or "existing." The quadrants are: *market penetration (existing markets and technologies)* with the aim being to increase volume sales through, for instance, higher market share or greater per capita consumption from, for example, new uses for the product; NEW PRODUCT DEVELOPMENT, involving the introduction of products based on new technologies into existing markets; *market development*, which involves extending the geographical reach of existing products; and DIVERSIFICATION, the introduction of products based on new technology into new markets. It is obvious that the last strategy is the most risky option. Although overly simplistic and general, the framework may be useful for practitioners when formulating specific development strategies. It does not draw the distinction between organic, or internal, development, and external development through mergers and acquisitions.

see also **Corporate strategy**

Bibliography

Ansoff, H. I. (1965). *Corporate strategy: An analytic approach to business policy for growth and expansion*. New York: McGraw-Hill. Chapter 6.

DALE LITTLER

discounted cash flow models Discounted cash flow (DCF) models are used to determine the present value (PV) of an asset by discounting all future incremental cash flows, C_t, pertaining to the asset at the appropriate discount rate r_t:

$$PV = \sum_{t=1}^{T} \frac{C_t}{(1 + r_t)^t}$$

Present value analysis (originating from Irving Fisher, 1930) using DCF models is widely used in the process of deciding how the company's resources should be committed across its lines of businesses, i.e. in the appraisal of projects. The typical application of a DCF model is the calculation of an investment's net present value (NPV), obtained by deducting the initial cash outflow from the present value. An investment with positive NPV is considered profitable. The NPV rule is often heralded as the superior investment decision criterion (see Brealey and Myers, 1991). Since present values are additive, the DCF methodology is quite general and can be used to value complex assets as well. Miller and Modigliani, in their highly influential 1961 article, note that the DCF approach can "be applied to the firm as a whole which may be thought of in this context as simply a large, composite machine." They continue by using different DCF models for valuation of shares in order to show the irrelevance of dividend policy. The DCF approach is also the standard way of valuing fixed income securities, e.g. bonds and preferred stocks (Myers, 1984).

Option-pricing models can in a sense be viewed as another subfamily of DCF models, since the option value may be interpreted as the present value of the estimated future cash flows generated by the option. Since the estimation procedures for options' future cash flows are derived from a specific and mathematically more advanced theory (introduced for finance purposes by Black and Scholes (1973)), option-pricing theory is usually treated separately from other types of DCF modeling.

Myers (1984) identifies four basic problems in applying a DCF model to a project: (1) estimating the discount rate; (2) estimating the project's future cash flows; (3) estimating the project's impact on the firm's other assets' cash flows; and (4) estimating the project's impact on the firm's future investment opportunities.

When estimating the discount rate one must bear in mind that any future cash flow, be it from a firm, from an investment project or from any asset, is more or less uncertain and hence always involves risk. It is often recommended to adjust for this by choosing a discount rate that reflects the risk and discounting the expected future cash flows. A popular model for estimating the appropriate risk-adjusted discount rate, i.e. the cost of capital, is the capital asset pricing model (CAPM) by Sharpe (1964), where the discount rate is determined by adding a risk premium to the risk-free interest rate. The risk premium is calculated by multiplying the asset's sensitivity to general market movements (its beta) to the market risk premium. However, the empirical validity of CAPM is a matter of debate. Proposed alternatives to the single-factor CAPM include different multifactor approaches based on Ross's arbitrage pricing model (Ross, 1977). Fama and French (1993) identify five common risk factors in returns on stocks and bonds that can be used for estimating the cost of capital.

Different procedures for estimating future cash flows are normally required, depending on which type of asset is being valued. The Copeland et al. (1994) DCF model for equity valuation provides a practical way of determining the relevant cash flows in company valuation. By forecasting a number of financial ratios and economic variables, the company's future balance sheets and income statements are predicted. From these predictions, the expected free cash flows (i.e. cash not retained and reinvested in the business) for future years are calculated. The sum of the discounted free cash flows for all coming years is the company's asset value, from which the present market value of debts is deducted to arrive at a valuation of the equity.

Irrespective of asset type, cash flows should normally be calculated on an after-tax basis and with a treatment of inflation that is consistent with the discount rate, i.e. a nominal discount rate requires cash flows in nominal terms (Brealey and Myers, 1991). It is also important to ensure that all cash flow effects are brought into the model – including effects on cash flows from other assets influenced by the investment.

An intelligent application of DCF should also include an estimation of the impact of today's investments on future investment opportunities. One example is valuation of equity in companies with significant growth opportunities. The growth opportunities can be viewed as a portfolio of options for the company to invest in second-stage, and even later stage projects. Also research and development and other intangible assets can, to a large part, be viewed as options (Myers, 1984). Another example concerns the irreversible character of many capital investments. When the investment itself can be postponed, there is an option to wait for more (and better) information. Ideas such as these are exploited in Dixit and Pindyck (1994), where it is shown how the complete asset value, including the value from these different types of opportunities, can be calculated using option-pricing techniques or dynamic programming.

Bibliography

Black, F. & Scholes, M. (1973). The pricing of options and corporate liabilities. *Journal of Political Economy*, **81**, 637–59.

Brealey, R. A. & Myers, S. C. (1991). *Principles of corporate finance.* 4th edn, New York: McGraw-Hill.

Copeland, T., Koller, T. & Murrin, J. (1994). *Valuation: Measuring and managing the value of companies.* 2nd edn, New York: John Wiley.

Dixit, A. K. & Pindyck, R. S. (1994). *Investment under uncertainty.* Princeton, NJ: Princeton University Press.

Fama, E. F. & French, K. R. (1993). Common risk factors in stock and bond returns. *Journal of Financial Economics*, **33**, 3–56.

Fisher, I. (1930). (repr. 1965). *The theory of interest.* New York: Augustus M. Kelley.

Miller, M. H. & Modigliani, F. (1961). Dividend policy, growth, and the valuation of shares. *Journal of Business*, **34**, 411–33.

Myers, S. C. (1984). Finance theory and financial strategy. *Interfaces*, **14**, 126–37.

Ross, S. A. (1977). Return, risk and arbitrage. (eds) Friend, I. & Bicksler, J. L. *Risk and return in finance.* Cambridge, MA: Ballinger.

Sharpe, W. (1964). Capital asset prices: a theory of market equilibrium under conditions of risk. *Journal of Finance*, **19**, 425–42.

PER OLSSON and JOAKIM LEVIN

discrimination in employment is treating some employees, job applicants, or other job applicants less favorably than others on the basis of characteristics that have little or no relationship to the person's abilities to perform a particular job. Most such behavior is unregulated. Under the traditional EMPLOYMENT AT WILL doctrine, unless bound by contract or law, an employer may make whatever employment decisions it wishes for any reason whatsoever or, indeed, for no reason at all.

The United States Constitution and various federal and state statutes abrogate the traditional "at will" rule in many respects. The Fourteenth Amendment's equal protection clause, for example, prevents public employers from intentionally discriminating on the basis of race, sex, national origin, religion, illegitimacy, or, in some cases, even citizenship absent a persuasive justification. Section 1981, a Civil War era statutory provision, prohibits racial discrimination in the making, enforcing, and performance of employment contracts by private employers.

Four modern federal statutes fill out the picture. The Age Discrimination in Employment Act prohibits both private and public employers of 20 or more employees from discriminating against workers 40 years old or older. The Rehabilitation Act and the Americans with Disabilities Act prohibit public and private employers with at least 15 employees from discriminating against the disabled. Title VII of the Civil Rights Act of 1964 prohibits public and private employers with 15 employees or more from discriminating on the basis of race, color, religion, sex, national origin, and citizenship. Of these statutes, Title VII is the most important. It provides the widest coverage and, in many respects, serves as the model for the others.

Title VII covers discrimination in all aspects of employment. It makes it unlawful for an employer

> to fail or refuse to hire or to discharge any individual, or otherwise to discriminate against any individual with respect to his compensation, terms, conditions, or privileges of employment, . . . [or] to limit, segregate, or classify his employees or applicants for employment in any way which would deprive or tend to deprive any individual

of employment opportunities or otherwise adversely affect his status as an employee, because of such individual's race, color, religion, sex, or national origin. (Title VII, §2000e-2(a)(1)–(2))

It also prohibits labor unions and employment agencies from engaging in similar activities.

There are two primary restrictions on Title VII's reach. It covers discrimination on the basis of only a few specified characteristics and it requires that the challenged practice concern the employment relationship. Thus, Title VII does not prohibit employment discrimination on the basis of sexual orientation, although some state statutes and local ordinances do, and it does not prohibit an employer from discriminating against minority-owned vendors, although other federal and state civil rights provisions may.

Title VII prohibits practices whose aim is to discriminate and practices pursued for other, perhaps legitimate, reasons that have a discriminatory effect. The first type of practice is called disparate treatment. To prove such intentional discrimination, the employee or applicant must show that a prohibited characteristic, such as race or sex, was a motivating factor in an employment decision adverse to her. She can prove this in many different ways. One way is to prove that she is a member of a protected class and possesses the minimal qualifications for the job, that she applied for it and was rejected, and that the employer continued to seek applications from people with the same qualifications. If she shows all that, then the employer must provide a legitimate business reason for its action, which the employee bears the burden of disproving.

The second type of practice may be challenged under a theory of disparate impact. If an employee or applicant can show that an otherwise valid practice has an adverse, disproportionate impact on individuals in a protected group, the burden of proof switches to the employer to show that the challenged practice is "job related . . . and consistent with business necessity" (Title VII, §2000e-2(k)(1)(A)(i)). If an employer fails to carry this burden, the practice is declared unlawful and liability follows. Although disparate treatment actions can challenge employment practices affecting individuals or whole groups, disparate impact actions can challenge only practices affecting groups of employees or applicants. By its nature, a disparate impact action requires statistical evidence of how a disputed employment practice affects various groups differently.

In addition, Title VII requires employers to make reasonable accommodations for employees whose religious beliefs make it difficult, if not impossible, for them to fulfill standard employment requirements. An employer must, for example, ask other employees whether they would be willing to substitute for an employee whose religion forbids her from working on a day the employer requires her services. Whether an accommodation is reasonable depends on the burden it would place on the employer and other employees. Similarly, the American with Disabilities Act requires covered employers to make reasonable accommodations for employees' and applicants' disabilities if they are otherwise qualified for a particular job. Thus, for example, an employer would have to make training materials available in large print or otherwise accessible to a sight-impaired employee who would otherwise be able to fulfill a particular job's requirements.

Strictly speaking, accommodation requirements embody a different theory of anti-discrimination than do ordinary anti-discrimination provisions. Whereas ordinary provisions prohibit an employer from taking some characteristic into account on the grounds that the characteristic should make no difference, accommodation requirements place an affirmative duty on the employer to recognize and alleviate certain differences. Accommodation provisions, in other words, require the employer to take into account characteristics that ordinary anti-discrimination provisions would insist that it be blind to.

see also **Civil Rights Act of 1964; Civil Rights Act of 1991**

Bibliography

Brest, P. (1976). Foreword: In defense of the antidiscrimination principle. *Harvard Law Review*, **90**, 1–54.

Epstein, R. (1992). *Forbidden Grounds: The Case Against Employment Discrimination Laws*. Cambridge, Mass.: Harvard University Press.

Rutherglen, G. (1987). Disparate impact under Title VII: An objective theory of discrimination. *Virginia Law Review*, **73**, 1297–345.

Sunstein, C. (1991). Why markets don't stop discrimination. *Social Philosophy and Policy*, **8**, 22–37.

Title VII of the Civil Rights Act of 1964. *United States Code*, **42**, §§2000e–2000e-17.

DANIEL R. ORTIZ

discriminatory taxation   Charging higher tax rates to foreign companies than for domestic companies. This type of protectionist action is not as common as it has been in the past but it still exists in many countries. The system of taxation in a foreign country must be considered when determining the method by which a company will enter that country. For example, if a local company is charged lower tax rates than a foreign-owned company, a local joint venture may be in order.

see also **Barriers; Political risk**

JOHN O'CONNELL

diseconomies of scale   Diseconomies of scale are said to exist when long run average total costs increase because a firm is too large. These diseconomies may arise because of technological factors but are usually attributed to decreasing returns to management. As the size of the firm increases, the firm's planning and coordinating activities become more unwieldy and, as more bureaucratic layers are added to the organization, managers are separated from the market and their customers. If consumer preferences change rapidly or if new products are frequently introduced by rivals, larger firms may be disadvantaged by their lack of flexibility and slow adjustment to the market.

An interesting recent example has been the reorganization of IBM. In the early years of the computer industry, there were no independent suppliers of computer chips and peripheral devices and computer manufacturers had to be vertically integrated to produce those inputs. But, as the industry grew, so did independent suppliers who could specialize and produce components very efficiently. As this occurred, changes in technology and factor costs decreased the MINIMUM EFFICIENT SCALE (MES) for computer manufacturing. Even if IBM's separate divisions were as efficient as their competitors, the internal pricing and cost information did not reflect this efficiency. The organization has been restructured so that the divisions operate as separate companies to be closer to the market.

Bibliography

Carlton, D. W. & Perloff, J. M. (1994). *Modern Industrial Organization*. 2nd edn, New York: HarperCollins.
Hirschey, M. & Pappas, J. L. (1995). *Fundamentals of Managerial Economics*. 5th edn, New York: Dryden.

ROBERT E. McAULIFFE

distributed systems Organizational information requirements have traditionally been met either by a large mainframe computer (i.e. a centralized system) or by a collection of small independent computers (i.e. a decentralized system). However, neither system can completely satisfy the rapidly changing needs of the users. In a centralized system, users can share information, but typically rely on an information systems department to provide access to it. In a decentralized system, users can typically access information themselves, but cannot easily share it across the organization. By connecting decentralized computer systems, users can not only access information themselves but also share it across the organization. A distributed system is a collection of computer systems that are interconnected by a communication network; it provides users and applications transparent access to data, computational power, and other computing resources.

What is a Distributed System?

The term *distributed system* has been applied to systems with widely different structures and characteristics (e.g. computer network, multiprocessor system). Rather than trying to precisely define it, a distributed system can be described by answering the following questions: (a) what is being distributed?; (b) what are the characteristics of a distributed system?; and (c) what is and is not an example of a distributed system?

What is being distributed? The definition of a distributed system assumes that multiple computers or *processing units* are connected via some communication network. A processing unit is an autonomous computer system including CPU, storage, and operating system. In addition to processing units, both process and data could be distributed. Processes of applications may be divided into subsets and distributed to a number of processing units. Data used by applications may be distributed to a number of processing units.

Characteristics of a distributed system. A distributed system in general has the following characteristics:

- multiple, possibly heterogeneous, processing units
- electronic connections via a communication network
- single system image providing transparent access to at least some of its resources (e.g. file, application)
- significant interaction among processing units

As processes and data are distributed to multiple processing units, coordination is required to provide adequate services. If the services can be provided to users without much interaction between processing units (i.e. communication and coordination between units), it would be difficult to call such a system "distributed."

Such coordination should be transparent to users. Transparency is the key to a distributed system. Ideally, users should not see a distributed system at all. They should see a single system which provides a number of services and resources. They should not have to know where the resources are in order to accomplish their tasks. In reality, this ideal situation is not typically achieved and users are aware that they are using a distributed system.

Examples of distributed systems. Consider the system shown in figure 1. It represents a geographically distributed

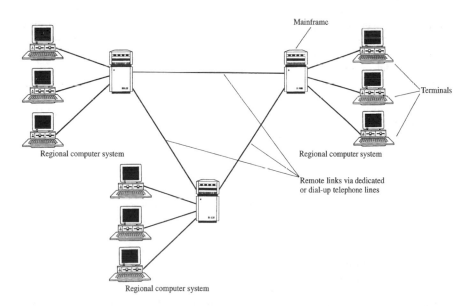

Figure 1   Regional computers connected via remote links

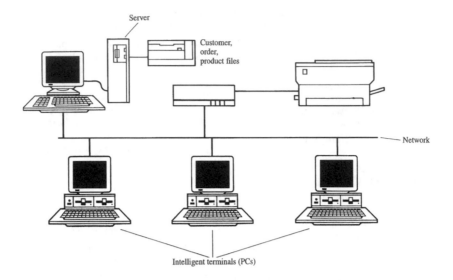

Figure 2   LAN-based database system

organization where each region has its own computer (i.e. processing unit). All computers are interconnected via dedicated or dial-up telephone lines. Most of a region's work is done on its own computer. Users, however, can submit jobs to a remote computer via communication lines. Is this a distributed system? It has multiple processing units interconnected by a communication network. It may or may not provide some form of single system image, depending on the methods by which remote jobs can be submitted. Most likely, however, the user would need to be aware that he/she is submitting a remote job. Furthermore, there is minimal interaction among processing units in providing services. Therefore, this would not be considered to be a distributed system.

Figure 2 shows a system where intelligent terminals (e.g. workstations) are connected to a general purpose computer (e.g. database server). Is this a distributed system? This system also has multiple processing units interconnected via a network. It has a single system view. There are interactions between the server and workstations. However, this cannot be considered to be a distributed system. This is because intelligent terminals are not autonomous processing units. The interaction between the server and the terminal is a master/slave relationship and there are no interactions between terminals. This system is rather a centralized system.

Figure 3 shows a distributed database system where the database is stored at several computers (i.e. database servers). In this system, users can write a query against the database as if it were stored at a single computer. In order to satisfy a user request, the system performs the following steps:

1 Determining where the needed data are located.
2 Determining an access strategy that specifies which copy of the data to access (and when), where the data will be processed, and how they will be routed.
3 Accessing and processing data at each of these servers.

4 Routing the response to the requesting server for final processing.

If (a copy of) all the data required by a retrieval request is located at the requesting node, then only local accessing and processing are needed (step 4). However, if some needed data are not located at the requesting server, then data must be accessed from, and possibly processed at, other servers. Is this a distributed system? There are multiple processing units and they are interconnected via a communication network. Users see only one database. If the user's query requires data that are stored at more than one server, the servers must cooperate to answer the query. This is clearly a distributed system.

Components of a Distributed System
A distributed system consists of several components. The essential components to provide transparency are: network, directory service, and file system.

Network
A network provides the mechanism for processing units to communicate with each other. A computer network consists of a set of computer systems, termed *nodes*, interconnected via communication *links*. It allows multiple computers to exchange data and share resources (e.g. printer).

Given a set of nodes, the network topology defines how these nodes are connected. Examples of network topologies are meshed, star, bus, and ring topologies. The links in a network can utilize different technologies and have varying speeds and channel capacities.

Distributed directory service
In addition to being connected, a distributed system must know where resources are located. Finding resources (e.g. data and application) in a distributed system is the task of the directory service. It must map a large number of system objects (e.g. files, functions, printers, etc.) to user-oriented names. A distributed directory service makes distribution

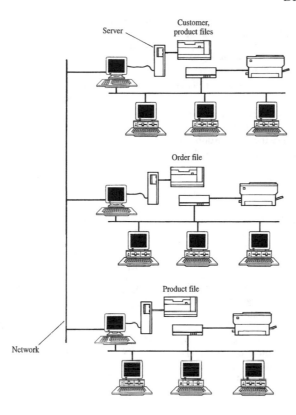

Figure 3   Distributed database system

transparent to users. Users do not have to know the location of a remote file, application, or printer.

Distributed file system

A distributed file system provides transparent access to any files on the network. It utilizes a directory service to locate files. To enhance retrieval efficiency, files can be redundantly stored at multiple nodes. Such redundancy increases the complexity of a file system. If there are multiple copies of the same file, the file system first locates its copies using the directory service and must determine how and where read-only access will be performed. Furthermore, consistency among multiple copies of data must be maintained by the file system as the files are updated. Concurrency control/recovery mechanisms are responsible for maintaining consistency among multiple copies of the same file.

Why Distribute?

Distributed systems can yield significant cost and performance advantages over centralized systems for organizations. These advantages include improved system performance (i.e. response time), reduced system costs, improved reliability/availability, and scalability.

System performance (i.e. response time) can be improved if regularly used applications and data are close to their users. If requests can be processed locally, communication delays due to remote access can be avoided. Furthermore, since each node handles only a portion of the requests, contention for CPU and disk input/output

services is reduced. System performance can be further improved by exploiting the parallelism inherent in distributed systems.

System costs can be reduced. A system of smaller computers is less expensive than a single central computer with equivalent computing power. Further, communication costs can be reduced if the regularly used applications and data are local to their users. Reliability/availability is improved since system crashes or link failures do not cause a total system failure. Even though some of the resources may be inaccessible, distributed systems can still provide limited service. If the same resources are provided by more than one node, reliability/availability is further improved, since only one of the nodes providing the resources needs to be available. Scalability is also improved. In a distributed environment, it is much easier to accommodate increases in system capacity. Major system overhauls are seldom necessary. Expansion can usually be handled by adding processing and storage power to the network.

However, there are several disadvantages. Distributed systems are much more complex than a centralized system. First of all, there are many more components in distributed systems (software as well as hardware). Therefore, distributed systems can be quite difficult to implement and manage. Maintaining adequate security can be a serious problem. Since users as well as resources are distributed, maintaining security over the network is much more difficult than in a centralized environment.

Bibliography

Ozsu, M. & Valduriez, P. (1991). *Principles of Distributed Database Systems.* Englewood Cliffs, NJ: Prentice-Hall.

Stallings, W. & Van Slyke, R. (1994). *Business Data Communications,* 2nd edn. London: Macmillan.

SANGKYU RHO

distributional effects in performance appraisal
Distributional effects in performance appraisal have traditionally referred to effects that influence the distribution of a set of ratings. Specifically, these effects, which include leniency effects and central tendency effects, were viewed as causing distributions of ratings to deviate from a "true" underlying normal distribution. Distributional effects were often seen as proxies for RATING ACCURACY, and were the focus of various interventions over the years, including the development of alternative ratings scale formats and RATER TRAINING programs, though there was not even total agreement on how these effects should be assessed (see Saal et al., 1980).

It has become clear, however, that there is no basis for assuming that the true distribution of ratings in a group is normal, and so there is no basis for assuming that any deviations from a normal distribution reflect rating inaccuracy or even RATING ERRORS. This has led some scholars to suggest that we simply abandon any consideration of these indices as criterion variables in performance appraisal research since they are not reasonable proxies for rating accuracy. Others, while agreeing that these indices are not good proxies for accuracy, and should not, therefore, be considered as errors, have instead proposed a different use of distributional effects as criterion measures in appraisal research conducted in field settings.

Specifically, DeNisi and Peters (1991, 1992) have suggested that indices of these effects, as well as indices of HALO EFFECTS, all provide important information about the distribution of ratings, both within and between ratees. Although they should not be considered errors or proxies of accuracy, DeNisi and Peters argue that they can provide important information in field settings where measures of rating accuracy are usually not available. As such, they have suggested renaming these indices "elevation indices" (which would be similar to leniency effects), "within-ratee discriminability indices" (which would be similar to halo effects) and "between-ratee discriminability indices" (which would include information about central tendency as well the overall distribution of ratings). These indices would then provide information about the extent to which raters could provide information about relative strengths and weaknesses for ratees (see Murphy, 1991, for a discussion of behavioral accuracy), as well as the extent to which raters could differentiate among ratees for allocating merit pay and other rewards (see Kane et al., 1995).

Thus, distributional indices may provide information about the limitations to the usefulness of a set of ratings obtained in the field. Furthermore, these authors, and others (see Dickinson, 1993), have suggested that indices of rating distribution might be related to ratees' perceptions of the fairness of the appraisal system and the ability of the raters to defend their ratings and decisions. Such reactions may well be more important to organizations interested in using appraisals to improve performance on the job than

are measures of rating accuracy (Ilgen, 1993), and information about distributions of ratings (and halo) may be quite important as determinants of these reactions. Although further research is clearly needed before this proposed role can be considered seriously, this does represent a new direction for research on distributional effects in performance appraisal.

Bibliography

DeNisi, A. S. & Peters, L. H. (1991). Memory reorganization and performance appraisal: a field experiment (paper presented at the Annual Meeting of the Academy of Management, Miami, FL).

DeNisi, A. S. & Peters, L. H. (1992). Diary keeping and the organization of information in memory: a field extension (paper presented at the Conference of the Society for Industrial and Organizational Psychology, Montreal).

Dickinson, T. L. (1993). Attitudes about performance appraisal. *Personnel selection and assessment,* Eds. Schuler, H., Farr, J. & Smith, M. Hillsdale, NJ: Erlbaum.

Kane, J. S., Bernardin, H. J., Vilanova, P. & Peyrefitte, J. (1995). The stability of rater leniency: three studies. *Academy of Management Journal,* 38, 1036–51.

Ilgen, D. R. (1993). *Performance appraisal accuracy: An illusive or sometimes misguided goal? Personnel selection and assessment,* Eds. Schuler, H., Farr, J. & Smith, M. Hillsdale, NJ: Erlbaum.

Murphy, K. R. (1991). Criterion issues in performance appraisal: behavioral accuracy versus classification accuracy. *Organizational Behavior and Human Decision Processes,* 50, 45–50.

Saal, F. E., Downey, R. G. & Lahey, M. A. (1980). Rating the ratings: assessing the quality of ratings data. *Psychological Bulletin,* 88, 413–28.

ANGELO S. DeNISI

distributive bargaining   Distributive bargaining refers to situations where the parties view their interests as irreconcilable and see little opportunity for a settlement that will yield joint gain. Distributive bargaining is often contrasted with INTEGRATIVE BARGAINING, but elements of both may be present in any negotiation.

The Character of Distributive Bargaining
Distributive bargaining emphasizes bargaining positions, is adversarial, and creates winners and losers. Central to distributive bargaining is the notion of a contract zone. The size of the contract zone is defined by the parties' resistance points. A resistance point is the least desirable position a party is willing to accept to achieve an agreement. Where the parties' resistance points overlap, settlement is possible since each party can make an offer that exceeds the other's minimum acceptable position. The greater the overlap in the parties' resistance points, the greater the range of potential settlements. Agreement is achieved through a series of offers and counter offers that lead to convergence in the parties' positions. The winner is the party that achieves a settlement that is closer to the opponent's resistance point than its own.

Distributive Bargaining Strategies
Negotiators attempt to discover their opponent's resistance point while concealing their own. Each negotiator applies a combination of persuasive and coercive tactics to induce movement in the opponent's position. Concessions must be made in a manner that gives the impression that the party's new position reflects its true resistance point. Common

tactics include commitment, deception, information manipulation, and threats (*see* NEGOTIATION TACTICS).

Bibliography

Lax, D. A. & Sebenius, J. K. (1986). *The Manager as Negotiator: Bargaining for Cooperation and Competitive Gain*, New York: The Free Press.

Lewicki, R. J. & Litterer, J. A. (1985). *Negotiation*, Homewood, IL: Richard D. Irwin.

Walton, R. E. & McKersie, R. B. (1965). *A Behavioral Theory of Labor Negotiations: an Analysis of a Social Interaction System*, New York: McGraw-Hill.

PAUL JARLEY

distributive justice Distributive justice refers to the *perceived fairness* of amounts received from resource allocation decisions (e.g. whether employees' salary increases are considered fair). Judgments of fairness vary depending on which norm of distributive justice is applied: equity, equality, need, or others.

Equity theory (Adams, 1965) applies readily to distributive justice in the workplace. Equity calls for correspondence between outcomes (e.g. wages) and the performance-related inputs of employees (e.g. productivity). With equivalent outcome–input ratios across workers, pay, for example, would be considered equitable. Equity, however, is "in the eye of the beholder" – perceptions determine the assumed sizes of outcomes and inputs, which outcomes and inputs seem relevant, and the choice of which outcome–input ratio to use for comparison (e.g. one coworker versus another, or a national industry-wide average versus the average in all local businesses). The equality norm says that each person should be treated the same; therefore, each person would receive the same outcome. The need norm argues that each person is treated differently depending on need. Those with greater needs would receive greater outcomes.

Lack of distributive justice (e.g. perceived underpay) can provoke a number of responses, including poor work quantity or quality, absenteeism, turnover, employee theft, and sabotage. In general, reactions to undesirable events, such as distributive injustice, produce numerous unpredictable coping responses. People can rationalize being underpaid, for example, by exaggerating (cognitively distorting) perceived intrinsic benefits such as fun in performing a task (i.e. task-enhancement effects). These "bad pay, but enjoyable work!" effects tend to result from PROCEDURAL JUSTICE – that is, when outcomes come from fair decision-making methods. When unfair outcomes come from *unfair* procedures, employees more often show resentment, retaliation, and lower quantity and/or quality of performance (see Folger et al., 1978).

Bibliography

Adams, J. S. (1965). Inequity in social exchange. *Advances in Experimental Social Psychology*, Berkowitz, L. (ed.), **2**, New York: Academic Press.

Cropanzano, R. & Folger, R. (1989). Referent cognitions and task decision autonomy: beyond equity theory. *Journal of Applied Psychology*, **74**, 293–9.

Folger, R. & Cropanzano, R. (1996). *Organizational Justice and Human Resources Management*, San Francisco: Jossey-Bass.

Folger, R., Rosenfield, D. & Hays, R. P. (1978). Equity and intrinsic motivation: the role of choice. *Journal of Personality and Social Psychology*, **37**, 2243–61.

Greenberg, J. (1987). A taxonomy of organizational justice theories. *Academy of Management Review*, **12**, 9–22.

ROBERT FOLGER

diversification Most companies begin as single business concerns serving a local regional market. In the early years of corporate development, most companies operate with a limited product range. While the initial market offers scope, expansion may still come from market and/or geographic growth. The great majority of companies either choose, or are forced, to limit their growth aspirations.

Those corporations which choose, or are presented with opportunities, to develop tend to do so by diversification as and when their original strategies mature. The evolution of strategic development has led to the development of a number of models, based especially on the work of Chandler. On the basis of his observations, Scott produced an early model of corporate growth, shown in figure 1. In this model, companies evolved from the single business phase to an integrated structure and finally to a related, or unrelated, diversified strategy which, as indicated by Chandler, was managed by a multidivisional structure. In refinements of this stages of corporate growth model, the product market/geographic diversification strategies amongst large corporations, initially in the USA, and in manufacturing industry were examined. This was later extended to cover other major developed country economies and to embrace service industries and, more recently, combinations of service and manufacturing concerns, as these developed from the 1970s onward. This research indicated that there were some industries which had difficulty in diversifying substantially, because of their cashflow generating characteristics and the need to invest in all aspects of the business in order to maintain an integrated flow of product. These were concerns that had adopted a dominant business strategy, which corresponded trauma, such as the first oil-price shock for oil companies or the impact of PRIVATIZATION for utilities concerns, was necessary for such firms to have the funds or the will to move to a fully diversified mode, by adopting either a RELATED DIVERSIFIED STRATEGY or a conglomerate strategy. The definition of each of these categories is dealt with at length elsewhere; however, financial relatedness tends to be neglected, and moves which embrace this variable tend to be classified as unrelated. Nevertheless, it can be argued that the combination of a cash-generating business such as gambling with investment in hotels represents a clear way to achieve financial SYNERGY.

The strategic evolution of the top 200 British corporations is shown in figure 2. In this sample no differentiation has been made between service and manufacturing concerns; state-owned enterprises have been included, as have service industries without "turnover" measures. Historically, most such research has used classifications such as "Fortune 500," which was traditionally biased toward manufacturing, to identify the sample for evaluation.

The evolutionary trend has clearly been from undiversified strategies to more diversified concerns. Until 1980 the number of single business companies declined steadily, from 34 per cent in 1950 to only 2 per cent in 1980. This attrition occurred as a result of companies diversifying or

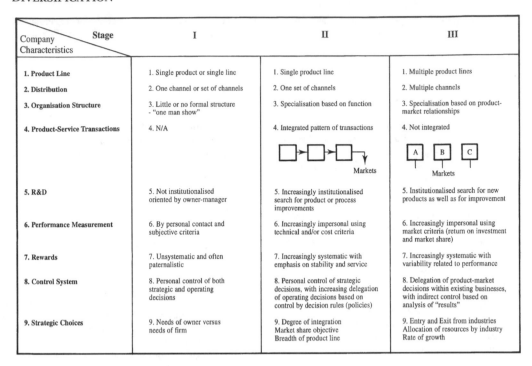

Figure 1   Three stages of organizational development.
Source: Scott (1971, p. 7).

being acquired by more diversified corporations. Those enterprises remaining in the category were those involved in highly successful industries, such as high-share food retailers, or those protected from stock market pressures by enjoying mutual ownership, such as some building societies and life insurance concerns. During the late 1980s, the number of single business concerns increased. This was a function of the process of privatization, which created a number of large new firms in the utilities industry, particularly in water and electricity supply. Interestingly, these newly created public companies were, in most cases, seeking to diversify by geography and partially by vertical integration.

Many firms diversify initially by limited moves through an ACQUISITION STRATEGY into new activities to become dominant business concerns. For most, this is a transitory step toward full diversification. There remains, however, a stable core of dominant business concerns which lack either the financial resources or the product market/technological skills to break out from the position. Such firms tend to be involved in high capital intensity, low differentiation businesses, in which free cashflows are inadequate to provide the funds to move into new markets.

Most firms that diversify do so by acquisition, by purchasing businesses in areas which appear to be related to the original CORE COMPETENCES of the firm. However, this strategy is often flawed by the failure to clearly identify relatedness, by inexperience in acquisition (and in particular post-acquisition) procedures, and by a lack of attention by top management, as reflected in the board structure, to achieving the expected synergy. Nevertheless,

by 1990 the number of related diversified corporations amongst the top 200 British firms had increased from 20 per cent in 1950 to a level of 53 per cent.

The number of large British firms which could be classified as conglomerates in 1990 showed a reduction from the 19 per cent identified in 1980. The number of unrelated diversified concerns had grown to this level consistently from 1950 onward. Although the trend observed in the UK was not as marked as in the USA, the pattern was similar. During the 1980s, the reduction in the number of conglomerate strategies came about because some companies reduced their product market scope, there were acquisitions and break-ups of highly diversified concerns, and the make-up of the top 200 companies was influenced by the addition of the substantial number of newly privatized concerns.

Overall, based on the UK experience, and supported by research in other developed economies (albeit over a lesser period of time, and less concerned with service businesses), there is clear evidence that enterprises grow, at least in part, by diversification by product and/or geography.

The process of diversification has largely occurred through acquisition, especially in the West. In recent times, stock market and external pressures have led some companies to reduce their product market scope by divestment, although others have continued to diversify. In the absence of similar pressures, Asian corporations seem to have successfully continued to diversify. Despite the evolutionary trend toward diversification, there is strong evidence that many of those using such moves are unsuccessful. The reasons for this include the following:

- *Lack of integration capacity.* Many diversifiers do not possess the managerial skills to successfully integrate new activities.
- *Lack of board attention.* In many companies, especially those breaking out from dominant business positions, little attention is paid at board level to new business ventures.
- *Misunderstandings about relatedness.* Many moves into apparently related industries turn out not to be; for example, brewing companies might have diversified into hotels as a way of selling more beer, without recognizing that sales of alcohol were a small component in successful hotel operation.
- *Inexperience with acquisitions.* Most diversifications occur as a result of acquisitions. Unfortunately, the majority of companies available for purchase tend to suffer from some weakness, which usually needs correction. This is turn requires a skillful post-acquisition TURNAROUND STRATEGY, which companies diversifying themselves out of relative weakness rarely possess. As a result, acquisitions may well not generate the performance that was expected.
- *Clash of corporate cultures.* Each organization has a unique culture. It is imperative that the disparate cultures of organizations attempting to merge are sufficiently compatible to avoid dysfunctional organization side-effects.
- *Incorrect market identification.* Not necessarily the same as problems with relatedness, this error may occur in particular with unrelated diversification moves in which apparently attractive entries are made into markets that turn out to be much less attractive. For example, many manufacturing firms in mature markets attempted to enter the financial services market, often with disastrous consequences.

- *Difficulties of synergy release.* It has been shown that while synergy is relatively easy to identify in theory, it is extremely difficult to release in practice, with the possible exception of financial synergy.
- *Move too small.* Many firms embarking on diversification moves for the first time tend to adopt a timid approach, making only a relatively small move. Apart from not achieving competitive advantage in the industry sector into which the firm diversifies, small moves also suffer from a lack of board attention, and difficulties of integration.
- *Inadequate functional skills.* These can be related to several of the other reasons for failure. If the diversifying firm lacks the critical success factor core skills, these must be rapidly imported or the move may well fail.
- *Imposition of wrong style of management.* Diversification often involves entry into a new industry, in which the style of management may be quite different from that of CORE BUSINESSES. Top management often fails to recognize such differences, and endeavors to introduce a culture, values, and control systems which, while relevant to the core business, are wholly inappropriate to the diversification.

Overall, diversification by product and by geography seems to be a natural process of evolution. The parameters that define the boundaries are not yet clearly delineated. Interestingly, while Chandler puts forward the proposition that structure follows strategy, the ultimate degree of diversification which can be achieved by the firm may be driven by structure. Is the KEIRETSU STRUCTURE espoused by major Japanese and Korean entities superior to the SBU structure used by Western corporations, in which failing units are candidates for divestment, superior or not? Time may tell.

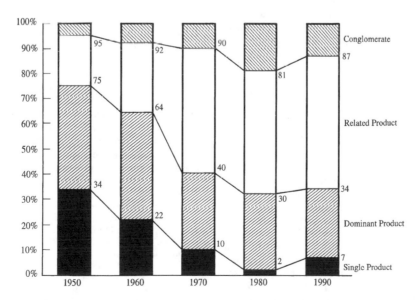

Figure 2 Diversification in the top 200 UK companies, 1950–1990.
Sources: Channon (1973), Times 1000, and Annual Reports 1980–1990.

Bibliography

Chandler, A. D. (1962). *Strategy and structure.* Cambridge, MA: MIT Press.

Channon, D. F. (1973). *Strategy and structure of British enterprise.* Cambridge, MA: Harvard Division of Research.

Channon, D. F. (1978). *The service industries: strategy, structure and financial performance.* London: Macmillan.

Rumelt, R. (1974). *Strategy structure and financial performance.* Cambridge, MA: Harvard Division of Research.

Scott, B. R. (1971). Stages of corporate development. Unpublished paper, Harvard Business School.

Wrigley, L. (1971). Divisional autonomy and diversification. Unpublished doctoral dissertation, Harvard Business School.

DEREK F. CHANNON

diversity   The term diversity is used to recognize the fact that any organization's workforce includes people from many different backgrounds. "Diversity" does not exist at the individual level; differences among the people who comprise a team, department, or organization create diversity (see Jackson et al., 1995, for an extended discussion).

Types of Diversity

Gender diversity is increasingly apparent throughout the world. Not only are more women working, but gender-based occupational segregation is declining in many countries, so within corporations men and women are more likely to be found working side-by-side. Age diversity is increasing too. Many industrialized countries are experiencing declining rates of population growth, which push employers to hire both more youth and more older employees. Furthermore, as organizations allow the higher education of younger employees to substitute for the job experiences that previous cohorts of employees had to accrue in order to be promoted, relatively young employees are found more often in higher level jobs. Consequently, age diversity is replacing the homogeneity associated with traditional age-based stratification.

Throughout much of the world, ethnic and cultural diversity are increasingly important to businesses. For example, as the 1980s grew to a close, the US Department of Labor projected that 22 percent of new entrants into the labor force would be immigrants and that an additional 20 percent would be ethnic minorities (Johnston and Packer, 1987). In many European countries, ethnic and cultural diversity is increasing owing in part to the consolidation of economic markets and related changes in immigration and employment policies. Finally, the need to manage cultural diversity effectively becomes apparent to corporations as they expand their operations into foreign countries.

Managing Diversity

The phrase managing diversity is used as a broad umbrella term to refer to management practices intended to improve the effectiveness with which organizations utilize the diverse range of available human resources. Programs designed to actively manage diversity recognize that diversity can have many consequences, including some that are positive and some that are negative. For example, knowledge-based diversity can improve the quality and creativity of a group's decision-making processes. On the other hand, demographic diversity appears to increase the amount of turnover that occurs among employees – presumably because it causes interpersonal conflict and

interferes with communications (for reviews, see Cox, 1993; Triandis et al., 1994; Jackson and Ruderman, 1996). The challenge is to manage diversity in ways that maximize the positive consequences and minimize the negative consequences.

Because there are many types of diversity and many possible consequences of diversity, no single program or set of practices can be used to manage diversity effectively. Reaping the benefits of diversity often requires investing substantial time and effort to create large-scale organizational change. The components of such a change effort can affect many aspects of human resource management, but the activities most likely to be affected are training and development, career planning, performance measurement, compensation, and benefits (for detailed descriptions of what US organizations are doing, see Morrison, 1992; Cox, 1993; Jackson, 1993; Cross et al., 1994).

Education and training may be offered in an effort to increase cultural sensitivity, reduce stereotyping, and develop interpersonal skills for working in multicultural environments. Among the many possible career planning activities that may be changed, the introduction of MENTORING PROGRAMS, which can help to insure that employees from all backgrounds have access to informal networks, may be one of the most beneficial. Sound performance measurement practices can improve an organization's ability to fully utilize a diverse workforce by reducing bias, insuring that all employees receive feedback and coaching, regardless of their personal backgrounds. In addition, 360 DEGREE APPRAISALS can be used to identify whether employees are perceived as equally effective, regardless of whether they are similar or different to the raters. To communicate how serious they are about the importance of managing diversity effectively, some organizations link pay raises and bonuses to a manager's demonstrated effectiveness in this area. Regarding benefits, the area most affected is family-centered benefits, which may be expanded in recognition of the diversity of family situations faced by employees. Finally, non-traditional work arrangements such as FLEXIBLE WORKPLACE/TELE-COMMUTING are additional practices that organizations use in their effort to effectively manage diversity.

Ultimately, the best approach to managing diversity will depend on the specific types of diversity present in an organization and the types of outcomes of most concern to the organization. Therefore, those who wish to improve the ability of an organization to manage diversity effectively must be willing to develop a comprehensive understanding of the issue, design interventions that fit the situation, carefully monitor the many potential consequences, and learn throughout the process.

Bibliography

Cox, T. Jr (1993). *Cultural Diversity in Organizations: Theory, Research, and Practice,* San Francisco: Berrett-Koehler.

Cross, E., Katz, J. H., Miller, F. A. & Seashore, E. (1994). *The Promise of Diversity,* Burr Ridge, IL: Irwin Professional Publishing.

Jackson, S. E. (ed.) (1993). *Diversity in the Workplace: Human Resources Initiatives,* New York: Guilford.

Jackson, S. E., May, K. A. & Whitney, K. (1995). Understanding the dynamics of diversity in decision making teams. *Team Decision Making Effectiveness in Organizations,* Eds. Guzzo, R. A. & Salas, E. San Francisco: Jossey-Bass.

Jackson, S. E. & Ruderman, M. N. (1996). *Diversity in Work Teams: Research Paradigms for a Changing Workplace*, Washington, DC: American Psychological Association.

Johnston, W. B. & Packer, A. E. (1987). *Workforce 2000: Work and Workers for the 21st Century*, Washington, DC: US Department of Labor.

Morrison, A. M. (1992). *The New Leaders: Guidelines on Leadership Diversity in America*, San Francisco: Jossey-Bass.

Triandis, H. C., Kurowski, L. & Gelfand, M. (1994). Workplace diversity. *Handbook of Industrial and Organizational Psychology*, Eds. Triandis, H. C., Dunnette, M. & Hough, L.4, Palo Alto, CA: Consulting Psychologists Press.

SUSAN E. JACKSON

dividend growth model   One of the simplest stock valuation models is the dividend growth model, often attributed to Gordon (1962). For instance, suppose that a firm pays dividends once a year and that after one year, when that dividend is paid, the stockholder plans to sell the investment. The value of the stock, P_0, at the beginning of the year will be

$$P_0 = \frac{E(d_1) + E(P_1)}{1 + k} \qquad (1)$$

where $E(P_1)$ is the estimate of the value of the stock at the end of the year and $E(d_1)$ is the estimate of the dividend per stock paid then and k is the discount rate for that firm based upon its level of risk. This model may be extended to take into account the permanent nature of the firm and the fact that the stock owner is uncertain as to when he intends to sell the stock. Thus

$$P_0 = \frac{E(d_1)}{1 + k} + ., ., ., ., . + \frac{E(d_n)}{(1 + k)^n} \qquad (2)$$

where $E(d_n)$ is the dividend expected at the end of year n. Now, if it is assumed that the dividend per stock is constant

$$P_0 = d_1 \left(\frac{1}{1 + k} + ., ., ., . + \frac{1}{(1 + k)^n} \right) \qquad (3)$$

If equation (3) is multiplied by $(1 + k)$ and this is subtracted from equation (3) then

$$P_0 \times k = d_1 - \frac{1}{(1 + k)^n} \qquad (4)$$

As n approaches infinity then the last term on the right-hand side of equation (4) approaches zero. Therefore

$$P_0 = \frac{d_1}{k} \qquad (5)$$

It should not be thought that this model assumes that the investor holds the stock for an infinite period of time! After whatever period the stock is held for, it will be purchased by another whose valuation is based upon holding it for another finite period who in turn will sell it on to another who will similarly hold it, and so on. The effect of this is that the stock is held by a series of owners for a period approaching infinity and the price at which it passes between them reflects the infinite time horizon of that dividend stream. Thus this model is not sensitive to how long the present stockholder intends to hold the stock.

The main problems with this simple dividend model are the assumption of constant d and k over an infinite time horizon, and their estimation. An assumption of a constant growth in dividends may easily be incorporated into the model. Let the annual growth in dividends grow at a compound rate, g. Thus

$$P_0 = \frac{D_0(1 + g)}{1 + k} + ., ., ., ., . + \frac{D_0(1 + g)^n}{(1 + k)^n} \qquad (6)$$

Multiplying equation (6) by $(1 + k)/(1 + g)$ and subtracting equation (6) from it gives

$$\frac{P_0(1 + k)}{(1 + g)} - P_0 = D_0 \left(1 - \frac{(1 + g)^n}{(1 + k)^n} \right) \qquad (7)$$

If $k > g$ and as $D_1 = D_0(1 + g)$ the right-hand side of equation (7) simplifies to D_1. Thus

$$P_0 = \frac{D_1}{k - g} \qquad (8)$$

Models have been developed to vary some of the above assumptions. For example, Fuller and Hsia (1984) have developed a three-step dividend growth rate model which assumes that the "middle step" growth rate g_2 is exactly half way between the other two. This is

$$P_0 = [D_0/(k - g_3)][(1 + g_3) + H(g_1 - g_3)] \qquad (9)$$

where D_0 is the current dividend per share, g_1 is the growth rate in phase 1, g_2 is the growth rate in phase 2, g_3 is the long-run growth rate in the final phase, and $H = (A + B)/2$ where A is the number of years in phase 1 and B is the end of phase 2.

Say the present dividend is 1.00, and that its growth is 12 percent but declining in a linear fashion until it reaches 8 percent at the end of ten years. Because the total above-normal growth is ten years, H is five years. Thus

$$\begin{aligned} P_0 &= [1/(0.14 - 0.08)] \\ &\quad [(1.08 + 5(0.12 - 0.08)] = 21.33 \end{aligned} \qquad (10)$$

A surprising variable to be included in these models is the dividend per share. This may be adjusted to include the firm's reported earnings per share. Consider the firm's sources and application of funds statement:

$$y_t + e_t + r_t = d_t + i_t \qquad (11)$$

where y_t is the firm's reported earnings, e_t is the firm's new external funds received during the period, r_t is the depreciation charged for the period, d_t is the dividend paid during the period, and i_t is the amount of new investment made during the period. It will be seen that the firm's economic (or Hicksian) income also equals its dividend, that is

$$y_t + e_t + r_t - i_t = d_t \qquad (12)$$

It should not be thought that the results of these models will necessarily coincide with market values. The user may have quite different expectations. They may be useful, therefore, to quantify the effect of different forecasts. They may also be used to compute forecasts and expectations built into existing stock prices.

Bibliography

Gordon, M. J. (1962). *The investment, financing and valuation of the corporation*. Homewood, IL: Irwin.

Fuller, R. J. & Hsia, C. (1984). A simplified common stock valuation model. *Financial Analysts Journal*, **40**, 49–56.

PAUL BARNES

divisional structure In his classic study of the evolution of large-scale US corporate enterprise, Chandler (1962) observed that as large corporations evolved they became more complex. He reported, for example, that the natural development of the railroads made it impossible to centralize all decision making. Decentralization was essential because communication systems were inadequate for information to be passed in time for the center to influence or make decisions.

Control diversify: he explored in depth the evolution of four major US corporations, The Du Pont Corporation, Standard Oil (later Exxon), General Motors, and Sears Roebuck, and observed how in the late 1920s a new organizational form developed in these concerns. Led by the Du Pont Company, these firms all found that the growing complexity of the organization made a FUNCTIONAL STRUCTURE inefficient and unwieldy. As a result, these firms developed a divisional form of organization in which operations were subdivided into a series of multifunctional units. The role of the central office changed to one of supervision and coordination of the organizational units, which were operationally autonomous, and the establishment of overall strategy. While this structure, shown in figure 1, became the key organizational form for diversified companies and was spread around the world by US corporations, and especially by US consultants McKinsey and Company, the Mitsubishi ZAIBATSU

STRUCTURE in Japan had developed in a very similar fashion some 15 years earlier.

The new structure broke the organization up in a way which provided divisional management with all the ingredients to operate as a complete business which could be measured in terms of profit performance. It made it easier for central management to establish investment policy, apply rewards and sanctions based on performance, and establish alternative strategies for different divisions; perhaps most of all, it helped to develop a cadre of general managers, which facilitated the strategy of further diversification. Functionally organized companies seriously lacked in their capability to diversify because, apart from the CEO, they did not develop such general managers. The central office could also develop a sophisticated service function, especially in finance and planning.

In the postwar period the divisional structure spread rapidly throughout US industry, and as many of these firms began to move overseas, particularly into the developed countries of Europe, it gave them a dramatic advantage by comparison to the functional or holding company structures more normal in Europe. Servan Schreiber (1969) described this as the "American challenge" and noted that it was the divisional form of organization that was the secret of the success of American corporations in penetrating European markets.

Throughout the 1970s in manufacturing industry around the world, the divisional form of organization became widely accepted in diversified corporations. As observed by Chandler (1962), in related product diversified and geographically diversified corporations the divisions were supported by a large central office, with sophisticated staff units charged with insuring interdivisional coordina-

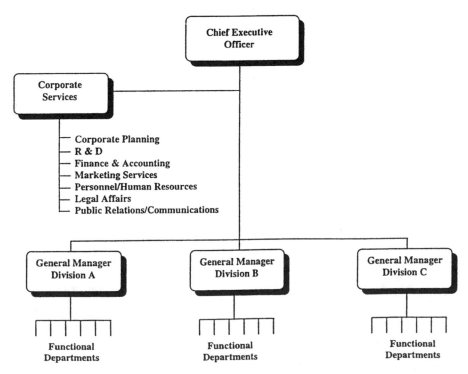

Figure 1 The multidivisional form of organizational structure.

tion where necessary; for example, insuring efficient management of interdependency for products such as feedstocks and the like, coordinating corporation-wide services in specialist areas such as computing, and providing an overall perspective via strategic planning and finance. Some central management of human resources and legal and external affairs was also normal.

The role of the board in the divisional organization was to set and monitor strategy, to measure and evaluate the performance of the divisions, to assign resources, to establish management information and control systems, to design and implement reward and sanction systems, and to make key appointments. The constitution of the board consisted usually of the chairman and chief executive, together with executives concerned with finance, often planning and human resources management, plus non-executive directors. In many, but not all, divisional structures, the general managers of major divisions were also included as members of the board.

In the late 1960s, the development of conglomerate businesses challenged the concept of the large central office. The new conglomerates operated a wide range of unrelated businesses, organized as product divisions, but the central office of such corporations was very small. The primary functions of the central office in these corporations were the establishment of overall strategy, acquisition search and purchase, post acquisition rationalization, and tight financial monitoring of divisional performance. Some also had a number of general operating managers attached to the center who were capable of evaluating the operating activities of divisions placed under their control. The rationale for this small central office system was that there was deliberately no SYNERGY, other than financial, between the operating divisions; hence there was no need for central interdivisional coordination, R&D, and the like. This system appeared to be very successful for many years, especially when the overall technology requirements of the corporation were limited. However, failure occurred at Litton Industries when a number of major technological projects went out of control simultaneously. This caused a serious loss of stock market confidence in conglomerates, although in reality the financial performance of the group, when well managed, remained superior to that of related diversified businesses.

In the 1980s and 1990s, superior information technology and the trend toward delayering has extended the concept of the small central office to most forms of diversified corporations while, despite some moves back to CORE BUSINESSES, many conglomerates remain.

The choice as to whether a geographic or product division system was adopted was a function of the degree of product complexity. As product diversity increased there was a clear move toward the adoption of a product division system. Industries such as food, where strong local needs made the establishment of uniform product and marketing strategies difficult, were somewhat of an exception. Geographic divisions were common in such cases: production and products themselves were therefore localized and the need to establish centralized product divisional management had less value. By the late 1970s, most large diversified firms in the USA and UK had found and adopted the multidivisional form, and a substantial number were endeavoring to operate this in conjunction with a portfolio system of management, the most commonly used of which was the GROWTH SHARE MATRIX. The same trend was found amongst the major corporations of other leading European countries; however, the degree of penetration of the divisional form was less developed and holding companies were still common, in part due to the complex shareholding patterns found in many European groups. These made it difficult to establish a common central office to set strategy for quasi-independent subsidiaries, in which minority shareholdings might hold considerable influence.

In the late 1970s, it also became recognized that the make-up of a division itself might be suboptimal. For example, in large divisions some activities might be growing rapidly while the main activities might be in decline. Since the corporate strategic resource allocation objectives and performance measurement tended to be established at the divisional level, such a growth business might be treated as a Cinderella business. At the US General Electric Company, therefore, it became recognized that the division did not necessarily represent the appropriate breakdown of the corporation. Hence, from the development of the PIMS program, and in conjunction with McKinsey and Company, the SBU STRUCTURE was developed. The SBU then became the lowest level planning unit in General Electric. A large division could therefore consist of several SBUs, each of which might be assigned a different strategic objective, performance measure, and dedicated resources, irrespective of the overall expected performance of the division itself. With this structure it was also possible to transfer some of the historic central staff functions to the divisional level and so reduce the size of the central office.

The divisional form was also important in the development of international strategy. As well as increasing the degree of product diversity, many corporations had developed international operations. The early multinationals tended to emerge from the European colonial powers, who established overseas operations in their colonies. British companies, for example, set up operations in the old Empire, French, and Dutch companies similarly. These concerns operated essentially as stand-alone units, since communications were inadequate to permit any central office control over operations. There was also no coordinated R&D, and the industries concerned tended to be either low-technology, such as food, or to involve the gathering of raw materials such as oil. The HOLDING COMPANY STRUCTURE was therefore the norm for such corporations, with central office control usually being exercised by the annual visit of a senior main board director.

After World War II, by contrast, major US corporations began to develop their overseas activities. Unlike the early Europeans, the US corporations moved to penetrate the developed economies, and especially Western Europe. Moreover, it was the technology-led concerns in computing, chemicals, and the like which decided to go multinational. These firms were amongst the earliest to adopt the divisional form of organization.

In the early stages of internationalization, such firms normally established a separate international division. Exports from all domestic product divisions passed through such an export division. As international activities

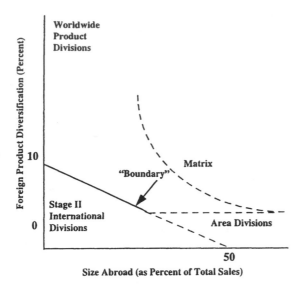

Figure 2 Activities overseas and structure.
Source: J. Stopford (1980), p. 108.

developed, however, it became normal not only to establish overseas sales organizations but also to set up production facilities. In the early phases of this process the establishment of geographic divisions tended to be common. Further development of overseas production facilities, coupled with growing product complexity, caused tension between overseas geographic divisions and domestic product-based divisions. As a result, there was pressure to ensure coordination between all similar product activities and to develop worldwide product research facilities. The possibility of interplant cross-border product and feed stock interchange therefore led to the movement toward the creation of worldwide product divisions. The boundaries between these three divisional variants were mapped by Stopford & Wells (1972) and are shown in figure 2.

From the early 1970s, there was also a growing trend in some industries to move to truly global rather than regionally oriented strategies. Products and components could be produced in one region and shipped around the world for assembly before being sold in a third region. This trend to complexity in both product and geography led to the development of an even more complex organizational form, the MATRIX STRUCTURE which usually divided the corporation into a combination of both geographic and product divisions. In this structure, multiple reporting relationships were common, in which country executives reported to both area and product divisions.

The divisional organizational form has been an extremely important structural development in the management of the modern corporation. While the structure has continued to evolve, the basic premise remains, and its widespread adoption around the world has been a major element in the development of the strategy and structure of the diversified enterprise.

Bibliography

Chandler, A. D. (1962). *Strategy and structure.* Cambridge, MA: MIT Press.

Channon, D. F. (1973). *The strategy and structure of British enterprise.* Cambridge, MA: Harvard Division of Research.
Dyas, G. P. & Thanheiser, H. T. (1976). *The emerging European enterprise.* London: Macmillan.
Rumelt, R. P. (1974). *Strategy, structure and economic performance.* Cambridge, MA: Harvard University Press.
Schreiber, J. J. S. (1969). *The American challenge.* New York: Aran Books.
Stopford, J. (1980). *Growth and organisational change in the multinational firm.* Arno Press.
Stopford, J. & Wells, L. T. (1972). *Management and the multinational enterprise.* London: Longman.
Williamson, O. E. (1985). *The economic institutions of capitalism.* New York: The Free Press.

DEREK F. CHANNON

double taxation One of the problems sometimes encountered by employees sent on overseas assignments is the income tax implications of working in one country, but being a citizen of another country. Since most tax systems base their assessment on the total income of a person, it is possible that the expatriate will be requested to pay taxes in the host country and in the home country "based upon the same income." Countries which commonly have foreign workers employed within their borders often have tax agreements with other countries to assure that taxes are only paid once. Persons employed overseas must carefully determine their tax status in each country in which they work or live. If tax laws do assess more taxes than would have been collected in the home country, the compensation package for the overseas worker is often adjusted to reduce the burden.

see also **Compensation package**

Bibliography

Nexia International Staff (1994). *International handbook of corporate and personal taxes.* New York: Chapman & Hall.

JOHN O'CONNELL

downsizing (historical) This refers to a set of voluntary activities, undertaken on the part of the management of an organization, designed to reduce expenses. This is usually, but not exclusively, accomplished by shrinking the size of the workforce. However, downsizing is a term used to encompass a whole range of activities from personnel layoffs and hiring freezes to consolidations and mergers of organization units.

In the early 1980s organizational downsizing came into prominence as a topic of both practical and scholarly concern. Practically, this is because between one-third and one-half of all medium and large size firms in North America and Western Europe downsized during the 1980s and early 1990s. Two-thirds of the companies that engaged in downsizing did so more than once. The popularity of downsizing has brought into question the common assumptions that increased size, complexity, and resources are inherently associated with ORGANIZATIONAL EFFECTIVENESS. Smaller and leaner have become associated with success, not largesse and over-abundance.

The concept of organizational downsizing has arisen out of popular usage, not precise theoretical construction. In fact, identifying the definition and conceptual boundaries of downsizing is more relevant for theoretical purposes than for practical ones. Cameron, Freeman, and Mishra

(1993) found that the terminology used to describe downsizing strategies was quite unimportant to practicing managers, except for the negative connotations associated with decline (i.e., no manager wants to implement a decline). A wide array of terms were found by Cameron et al. to be used interchangably, even though each may have a different connotation.

For scholarly purposes, precise conceptual meaning is required in order for cumulative and comparative research to occur. For example, on the surface, downsizing can be interpreted as a mere reduction in organizational size. When this is the case, downsizing is often confused with the concept of organizational decline, which also can be interpreted as mere reduction in organizational size. Yet important differences exist that make downsizing and decline separate phenomenon conceptually and empirically. Several important attributes of downsizing also make it distinct from other related concepts such as lay-offs, nonadaptation, or growth-in-reverse. These attributes of downsizing are; (1) *intent*; (2) *personnel*; (3) *efficiency*; and (4) *work processes*.

Intent. Downsizing is not something that happens *to* an organization, but it is something that managers and organization members undertake purposively as an *intentional* set of activities. This differentiates downsizing from loss of marketshare, loss of revenues, or the unwitting loss of human resources that are associated with organizational decline. Downsizing is distinct from mere encroachment by the environment on performance or resources because it implies organizational action.

Personnel. Second, downsizing usually involves *reductions in personnel*, although it is not limited solely to personnel reductions. A variety of personnel reduction strategies are associated with downsizing such as transfers, outplacement, retirement incentives, buyout packages, layoffs, attrition, and so on. These reductions in personnel may occur in one part of an organization but not in others, but can still be labeled organizational downsizing. Downsizing does not always involve reductions in personnel, however, because some instances occur in which new products are added, new sources of revenue opened up, or additional work acquired without a commensurate number of employees being added. Fewer numbers of workers are then employed per unit of output compared to some previous level of employment.

Efficiency. A third characteristic of downsizing, is that it is focused on improving the *efficiency* of the organization. Downsizing occurs either proactively or reactively in order to contain costs, to enhance revenue, or to bolster competitiveness. That is, downsizing may be implemented as a defensive reaction to decline or as a proactive strategy to enhance organizational performance. By and large, downsizing in most firms has been implemented as a defensive reaction to financial crisis, loss of competitiveness, or inefficiency. Proactive and anticipatory downsizing has been rare.

Work Processes. Finally, downsizing affects *work processes*, wittingly or unwittingly. When the workforce contracts, for example, fewer employees are left to do the same amount of work, and this has an impact on what work gets done and how it gets done. Overload, burnout, inefficiency, CONFLICT, and low morale are possible consequences, or more positive outcomes may occur such as improved productiv-

ity or speed (Cameron, 1994) (*see* ROLE). Moreover, some downsizing activities may include restructuring and eliminating work (such as discontinuing functions, abolishing hierarchical levels, merging units, or redesigning tasks) which lead, of course, to some kind of work redesign (*see* JOB DESIGN). Regardless of whether the work is the focus of downsizing activities or not, work processes are always influenced one way or another by downsizing.

Note that the level of analysis is the organization itself, not the individual or the industry. For example, a substantial literature exists on the psychological reactions individuals have to layoffs and job loss. Impacts on financial well-being, health, personal attitudes, family relationships, and other personal factors have been investigated by a number of researchers (Kozlowski, Chao, Smith, & Hedlund, 1993). However, whereas laying off workers is by far the most common action taken in organizations engaging in downsizing, it entails a much broader set of actions and connotations. At the industry level of analysis, a large literature also exists on divestitures and organizational mergers. Market segmentation, divesting unrelated businesses, reinforcing CORE COMPETENCES, and consolidating industry structures are among the topics addressed. The definition of organizational downsizing being described here, however, may or may not involve selling off, transferring out, merging businesses, or altering the industry structure. Much less research has investigated the organization level of analysis than the individual and industry levels of analysis. That is, strategies for approaching downsizing, processes for implementing downsizing, and impacts on organizational performance have been under-investigated in the scholarly literature.

To summarize, organizational downsizing refers to an intentionally instituted set of activities designed to improve organizational efficiency and performance which affects the size of the organization's workforce, costs, and work processes. It is implied that downsizing is usually undertaken in order to improve organizational performance. Downsizing, therefore, may be reactive and defensive or it may be proactive and anticipatory. Ineffectiveness or impending failure are the most common motivations for downsizing, but they are not prerequisites to downsizing. Downsizing may be undertaken when no threat or financial crisis exists at all.

Most research to date indicates that the impact of downsizing on organizational performance is negative. Cameron (1995) reported that two-thirds of companies that downsize end up doing it again a year later, and the stock prices of firms that downsized during the 1980s actually lagged the industry average at the beginning of the 1990s. More than 70 percent of senior managers in downsized companies said that morale, TRUST, and productivity suffered after downsizing, and half of the 1,468 firms in another survey indicated that productivity deteriorated after downsizing. A majority of organizations that downsized in a third survey failed to achieved the desired results, with only 9 percent reporting an improvement in quality. These outcomes are not universal, of course, but organizations whose performance improves as a result of downsizing have managed the process as a renewal, revitalization, and culture change effort, not just as a strategy to reduce expenses or organization size.

see also **Organizational design**

Bibliography

Cameron, K. S. (1994). Strategies for successful organizational downsizing. *Human Resource Management Journal*, 33, 189–212.

Cameron, K. S. (1995). Strategic downsizing: The case of a U.S. Army Command Working Paper, University of Michigan Business School.

Cameron, K. S., Freeman, S. J. & Mishra, A. K. (1993). Downsizing and redesigning organizations. In G. P. Huber & W. H. Glick (Eds), *Organizational change and redesign.* (pp. 19–63). New York: Oxford University Press.

Kozlowski, S. W. J., Chao, G. T., Smith, E. M. & Hedlund, J. (1993). Organizational downsizing: Strategies, interventions, and research implications. In C. L. Cooper I. T. Robertson (eds) *International Review of Industrial and Organizational Psychology*, **Volume 8**, New York: Wiley.

KIM S. CAMERON

downsizing Downsizing refers to the planned elimination of positions or jobs. While there are as many positions as there are employees, jobs are groups of positions that are significant in their significant duties – such as nurses, computer programmers, or financial analysts. Downsizing may occur by the reduction of work (not just employees), as well as the elimination of functions, hierarchical levels, or units of an organization. It may also occur by the implementation of cost-containment strategies that streamline activities such as transaction processing, information systems, or authorization procedures.

Downsizing does not include the discharge of individuals for cause, or individual departures via normal retirement or resignations. The word "normal" is important in this context. Voluntary severance and early retirement packages are commonly used to reduce the size of the workforce, especially among firms with traditional "no layoff" policies. Even if targeted workers are considered "redundant," "excessed," or "transitioned," the result is the same – employees are shown the door – but it is called something else (Cascio, 1993).

Downsizing is often a reactive response to organizational decline (Cameron et al., 1988), although it may also be a proactive measure taken by organizations that perceive future competitive threats. For example, many banks are downsizing proactively because they perceive threats to their competitive position in the market place as a result of further deregulation of their industry and resulting competition from a host of other providers of financial services, including insurance companies and brokerage firms. Regardless of cause, however, downsizing is less an analytical concept than a descriptive term that lacks a body of theory associated with it. It has been examined in hundreds of articles from a number of perspectives in academic journals, books, and the popular press. Some of these perspectives are: organizational symptoms and consequences (e.g. Touby, 1993); strategic management of downsizing processes (e.g. Kozlowski et al., 1993); impact of downsizing on organizational survivors (e.g. Noer, 1994), as well as on those who leave (e.g. Cappelli, 1992); legal issues in downsizing; downsizing issues in countries other than the United States (e.g. Vollmann and Brazas, 1993); and the financial and economic consequences of downsizing (e.g. Worrell et al., 1991).

Conditions that precipitate downsizing, or related types of organizational changes, may be internal (excessive overhead costs, labor-displacing new technology) or external (economic recession, global competition, deregulation, industry consolidation). One or more of these conditions leads to a strategic decision to change the organization (for example, by downsizing, delayering, restructuring, or reengineering).

To implement the strategy, decision-makers initiate a set of processes. Depending on the strategy in question, such processes may include one or a combination of the following: reducing the number of employees, flattening the hierarchy of the organization, selling off assets, or eliminating activities that do not add value. Such actions lead to a series of outcomes: organizational, psychological, and financial. Organizational outcomes include, for example, changing spans of control, outsourcing activities or functions, redesigning management jobs, empowering lower-level employees (often forming self-managed work teams), and changing reward systems. Psychological outcomes include alterations in the PSYCHOLOGICAL CONTRACT that binds workers to their employers (Filipczak 1995) and changes in commitment, motivation, and career orientation. Finally, financial outcomes include changes in the financial performance of the organization. Financial performance includes variables such as changes in cost structure, changes in sales, profits, earnings, and returns on common stock.

The Lure of Downsizing

To achieve the organizational and financial outcomes described above, many executives see downsizing as a compelling strategy. It is compelling because only two ways exist for companies to become more profitable: either increase revenues or cut costs. Further, most observers would agree that future costs are more predictable than future revenues. Human resources represent costs, so logically to become more profitable, costs are lowered by decreasing the number of employees.

Consequences of Downsizing

Many myths surround the practice of downsizing, but facts show a different picture. Mounting evidence suggests that, when it is used as a "quick fix" to reduce the costs of doing business, the cutting of large numbers of employees over a relatively short period of time will produce little long-term reduction. In fact, it may even *increase* costs. Here are some facts about downsizing practices (Cascio, 1995): (a) profitability does not necessarily follow downsizing; (b) productivity results after downsizing are mixed; (c) for many companies, downsizing is a first resort, not a last resort; (d) downsizing continues long after economic recession is over; (e) financially sound companies, some with record profits, are downsizing; (f) the best predictor of whether a company will downsize in a given year is whether it has downsized in the previous year; (g) middle managers continue to lose jobs out of proportion to their presence in the workplace; (h) for the majority of companies, downsizing has had adverse effects on work load, morale, and employee commitment; (i) for those who lose their jobs, downward mobility is the rule rather than the exception; and (j) in the United States, the courts have sharply limited the ability of plaintiffs to prevail in all but the most blatant cases of age discrimination.

In light of these findings, a number of organizations are rethinking the basic philosophy of downsizing. Instead of asking, "What is the irreducible core number of people we need to run our business?" (a downsizing philosophy), some are raising a different question, namely "How can we change the way we do business, so that we can use the people we do have most effectively?" This is a philosophy of responsible restructuring in which companies rely on their workers to provide sustained competitive advantage.

Bibliography

Cameron, K. S., Sutton, R. I. & Whetten, D. A. (1988). Issues in organizational decline. *Readings in Organizational Decline*, Eds. Cameron, K. S., Sutton, R. I. & Whetten, D. A. Cambridge, MA: Ballinger.

Cappelli, P. (1992). Examining managerial displacement. *Academy of Management Journal*, 35, 302–17.

Cascio, W. F. (1993). Downsizing. What do we know? What have we learned? *Academy of Management Executive*, 7, 95–104.

Cascio, W. F. (1995). *Guide to Responsible Restructuring*, Washington, DC: US Department of Labor, Office of the American Workplace.

Filipczak, B. (1995). You're on your own: training, employability, and the new employment contract. *Training*, January, 29–36.

Kozlowski et al. (1993). Organizational downsizing: strategies, interventions, and research implications. *International Review of Industrial and Organizational Psychology*, 8, 263–332.

Noer, D. (1994). *Healing the Wounds: Overcoming the Trauma of Layoffs and Revitalizing Downsized Organizations*, San Francisco: Jossey-Bass.

Touby, L. (1993). The business of America is jobs. *Journal of Business Strategies*, 14, 21–31.

Vollmann, T. & Brazas, M. (1993). Downsizing. *European Management Journal*, 11, 18–29.

Worrell, D. L., Davidson, W. N. III & Sharma, V. M. (1991). Layoff announcements and stockholder wealth. *Academy of Management Journal*, 34, 662–78.

WAYNE F. CASCIO

drug testing Drug testing refers to a variety of techniques used to determine if employees or job applicants are likely to use drugs. Drug tests may be used to decide who is hired, terminated, or referred to employee assistance programs.

Types of Drug Testing Procedures

Drugs are metabolized into by-products that can be detected for a period of days to weeks, depending on the drug and the extent of its use. These metabolites form the basis for the most common type of drug test, a biochemical assay of urine (or, much less frequently, of blood or hair). Thin-layer chromatography and enzyme immunoassay or radioimmunoassay are inexpensive tests that can be used to quickly screen for metabolites from a number of drugs. However, because of their high error rates, these techniques should be confirmed by more expensive gas chromatography or mass spectrometry tests (Frings et al., 1989).

A less common approach involves screening employees on the basis of their likelihood of *future* drug use. Many integrity tests (see INTEGRITY TESTING) include an assessment of substance use based on self-reports of attitudes toward, and prior involvement with, drugs or drug users. Personality tests can be used to assess more general tendencies toward drug use and other counterproductive behavior.

A third approach uses either psychomotor or cognitive tasks – usually presented via computer – to directly assess performance impairment. By testing employees daily and comparing their responses to baseline levels of performance, this approach has the potential to detect impairment caused by a number of factors in addition to drug use, while also reducing complaints of invasion of privacy.

Basis for Testing

In addition to screening job applicants, drug testing programs may also target current employees. *Random* testing programs are designed to detect drug users who are not eliminated by pre-employment drug testing. Firms can also test "*for cause,*" such as following an accident or when there is some other reason to suspect drug use. Employees who have undergone drug rehabilitation may be required to undergo periodic *fitness-for-duty* testing to ensure they remain drug-free. Finally, some organizations test employees prior to their performing safety-sensitive tasks.

The different reasons for testing may call for different types of drug tests. Pre-employment screening can be based either on a history of drug use (the justification for biochemical methods) or a prediction of future drug or alcohol use (the justification for integrity-type tests). Biochemical drug tests are generally the best option in testing based on suspicion of drug use because they offer evidence of actual drug use. Their major limitation is that the presence of metabolites only establishes that drugs were used at some time in the past; they cannot determine if they were used at work or home or if they affected job performance. Only analyses of actual levels of drugs or alcohol can determine if an employee is currently under the influence of drugs. Impairment testing may be a suitable alternative for screening incumbents' readiness to perform.

Effectiveness

As Crown and Rosse (1991) note, most research on the validity of drug testing has been concerned with validity of measurement (e.g. whether urinalysis accurately detects drug use), rather than validity of prediction (e.g. whether drug test results predict relevant job outcomes). Urinalysis, with appropriate confirmatory testing, appears to have adequate validity of measurement, if proper procedures and a certified laboratory are used. Existing research evidence suggests that urinalysis testing is modestly related to subsequent absenteeism, accidents, and turnover, but not necessarily to job performance (Normand et al., 1990). Reviews suggest that integrity tests are related to a variety of counterproductive behavior, as well as to job performance (Ones et al., 1993). Too few data regarding impairment testing exist to allow generalizations about its validity.

The type of testing and the manner in which drug testing is conducted can substantially affect perceptions of PROCEDURAL JUSTICE, which can, in turn, affect employees' loyalty and motivation (Konovsky and Cropanzano, 1993). Testing programs are most likely to be seen as fair if they are not punitive, provide advance notice, or are based on credible suspicion of drug use. Employers need to weigh the benefits of drug testing against the potential costs of alienating applicants and employees who perceive such testing as unfair and invasive of privacy.

Bibliography

Crown, D. F. & Rosse, J. G. (1991). Critical issues in drug testing. *Applying Psychology in Business: the Handbook for Managers and Human Resource Professionals*, Eds. Jones, J., Steffy, B. & Bray, D. Lexington, MA: Lexington Books.

Frings, C. S., Battaglia, D. J. & White, R. M. (1989). Status of drugs-of-abuse testing in urine under blind conditions: an AACC study. *Clinical Chemistry*, 35, 891–4.

Konovsky, M. & Cropanzano, R. (1993). Justice considerations in employee drug testing. Workplace: Approaching Fairness in Human Resource Management, Cropanzano, R. Hillsdale, NJ: Erlbaum. 171–92.

Lehman, W. E. K. & Simpson, D. D. (1992). Employee substance use and on-the-job behaviors. *Journal of Applied Psychology*, 77, 309–21.

Normand, J., Salyards, S. D. & Mahoney, J. J. (1990). An evaluation of preemployment drug testing. *Journal of Applied Psychology*, 78, 629–39.

Ones, D. S., Viswesvaran, C. & Schmidt, F. L. (1993). Comprehensive meta-analysis of integrity test validities: findings and implications for personnel selection and theories of job performance. *Journal of Applied Psychology*, 78, 679–703.

Rosse, J., Miller, J. & Ringer, R. (1996). The deterrent effect of drug and integrity testing. *Journal of Business and Psychology* in the press.

Zwerling, C., Ryan, J. & Orav, E. J. (1990). The efficacy of preemployment drug screening for marijuana and cocaine in predicting employee outcomes. *Journal of the American Medical Association*, **264**, 2639–43.

JOSEPH G. ROSSE

dual-career couples Rapoport and Rapoport (1969) were the first to use the term dual-career couple to describe couples where both partners were committed to their careers, supported one another's CAREER pursuits, and shared family responsibilities. Today, dual-career couples are more broadly defined as couples living together in a committed relationship, where both work outside of the home. Dual-career couples are also called dual-earner couples, two-income couples, and dual-wage earners.

Dual-career Couples and Well-being
There are many intellectual, emotional, and psychological benefits associated with a dual-career life-style (see Gilbert, 1994). When compared to traditional couples (i.e. employed husband, unemployed wife), women in dual-career couples experience greater self-esteem, better physical and mental health, and greater economic independence. Men in dual-career families report increased emotional involvement with children, improved health, and lowered pressure to be financial providers.

While dual-career couples report many advantages to their lifestyle, they also experience stress while balancing work and family roles. WORK–FAMILY CONFLICT, defined as conflict arising from competition between job and home responsibilities, is related to decreased marital satisfaction (Greenhaus et al., 1987), lower JOB SATISFACTION and family satisfaction, and increased stress (Parasuraman et al., 1992). However, social support, particularly from supervisors and spouses, reduces perceived stress and directly improves well-being (Rudd and McKenry, 1986; Parasuraman et al., 1992; Gilbert, 1994).

Gender Differences
The term dual-career couple conjures up images of partners who have achieved true equality through support-

ing each other's career interests and equitably sharing home and family duties. Men's participation in the home has increased since 1970, primarily due to their increased involvement in childcare rather than in household work (Gilbert, 1994). However, studies consistently find that women in dual-career couples still shoulder most of the home and family responsibilities, experience greater role overload, and have less leisure time than dual-career men (see Duxbury and Higgins, 1994).

Both gender role and societal expectations contribute to differences between women and men in dual-career couples. For example, Duxbury and Higgins (1991) examined the sources of stress in dual-career couples when balancing work and family demands. They found that women who were highly dedicated to their jobs were more likely to experience stress at work than men who were similarly involved and committed to their jobs. Duxbury and Higgins suggested that this occurs because employers see women, and women see themselves, as being primarily responsible for family and household tasks. Hence, these women may experience strain at work because they are behaving in non-traditional ways and are perceived as not attending to their family responsibilities.

Conversely, men who were highly committed and involved in their family roles were found to be more likely to experience stress at work than women who were similarly committed to their families. Duxbury and Higgins suggested that this occurs because men themselves and their employers see men's core role as that of breadwinner. Family-involved men may experience stress from work because they are seen by their employers as uncommitted to their jobs.

Organization and Government Support of Working Couples
Although the number of dual-career couples in the United States has increased dramatically since the 1960s, organization and government policies are lagging behind in their support of their unique needs. Many organizations still operate under the paradigm that employees are in traditional families with a working husband, homemaker wife, and children. More employers, however, are supporting dual-career families with programs and benefits such as alternative career paths, job sharing, flexible work schedules, FLEXIBLE WORKPLACE/TELECOMMUTING, PART-TIME EMPLOYMENT, and CHILD CARE BENEFITS and elder care benefits. Unfortunately, even when the organization's policies and programs are supportive of dual-career couples, the organizational culture, norms, and values often reinforce long hours and job commitment as the way to succeed and sanction employees who strive for more balance in their lives (Kofodimos, 1993).

The Family and Medical Leave Act of 1993 has made it easier for couples to juggle home, career, and family responsibilities in times of critical need or illness; however, much debate exists between government decision-makers over how far the government should go to support working couples. The dual-career family will continue to be a major political and social issue throughout the 1990s.

Bibliography

Duxbury, L. E. & Higgins, C. A. (1991). Gender differences in work-family conflict. *Journal of Applied Psychology*, **76**, 60–74.

Duxbury, L. & Higgins, C. (1994). Interference between work and family: a status report on dual-career and dual-earner mothers and fathers. *Employee Assistance Quarterly*, **9**, 55–80.

Gilbert, L. A. (1994). Current perspectives on dual-career families. *Current Directions in Psychological Science*, **3**, 101–5.

Greenhaus, J. H., Bedian, A. G. & Mossholder, K. W. (1987). Work experiences, job performance, and feelings of personal and family well-being. *Journal of Vocational Behavior*, **31**, 200–15.

Gutek, B. A., Searle, S. & Klepa, L. (1991). Rational versus gender role explanations for work–family conflict. *Journal of Applied Psychology*, **76**, 560–8.

Hochschild, A. (1989). *The Second Shift*, New York: Viking Press.

Kofodimos, J. (1993). *Balancing Act: How Managers Can Integrate Successful Careers and Fulfilling Personal Lives*, San Francisco: Jossey-Bass.

Parasuraman, S., et al. (1992). Role stressors, social support, and well-being among two-career couples. *Journal of Organizational Behavior*, **13**, 339–56.

Rapoport, R. & Rapoport, R. N. (1969). The dual career family: a variant pattern and social change. *Human Relations*, **22**, 3–30.

Rudd, N. M. & McKenry, P. C. (1986). Family influences on the job satisfaction of employed mothers. *Psychology of Women Quarterly*, **10**, 363–71.

Sekaran, U. (1986). *Dual-career Families*, San Francisco: Jossey-Bass.

ELLEN A. FAGENSON-ELAND
and COLLEEN E. O'MALLEY

duty A tax on goods imported into (or exported from) a country. The purpose of a duty is to increase the price of goods to make domestic goods more competitive or to raise tax revenues for a government. Duties may also be used to punish exporters or countries for unfair trade practices. There are a number of different types of duties which may be applied to imports or exports. A list of different types of duties follows

1 Ad valorem duty – Ad valorem duties are taxes which are paid on imported items. The duty is expressed as a percentage amount of the value of goods which clear customs. Thus, if a 10% ad valorem duty was due on $50,000 worth of goods, the duty would amount to $5,000.

2 Anti-dumping duty – From time to time, products imported into a country have sales prices which are far below the exporter's local market for such goods. This means the goods are sold for less in other countries than their market price in the exporter's home country. When this occurs production and distribution of similar domestic products of the importing country may be harmed. In order to protect local industry, taxes may be imposed on specific imports to drive their prices up, thereby allowing local industry to compete. This tax is sometimes referred to as an anti-dumping duty.

3 Autonomous duty – Autonomous duties are levied as penalties against persons who attempt to circumvent customs restrictions or quotas. It is also applied to protect domestic industry against an unexpected increase in imports of specific types of products.

4 Compensatory duty – A reduction in tax for one commodity in exchange for increased taxes on others. A country may reduce duties on some imports from a particular country to offset higher duties being paid on other commodities. It is possible that higher duty items are more subject to public scrutiny and thus require the duty to remain high. To provide some break to a country's trading partner duties on other items may be relaxed.

5 Concessional duty – A duty between trading partners which is very low. Concessional duties are also applied by industrialized nations to developing nations in order to promote developing country economic growth.

6 Countervailing duty (CVD) – When a foreign government provides subsidies for the production of goods, those goods can be exported at low sales prices. In an attempt to offset the impact of exporting country subsidies, importing countries often attach a special duty to counter the low import price (thus, the name countervailing duty). The CVD raises the price of the import thereby reducing the competitive effects of the export country's original government subsidy.

7 Differential duty – A duty based upon the status of trading partners. Those countries seen as the most advantageous partners generally receive lower duties then partners whose trade status is not as high.

8 Exclusionary duty – This duty is aimed directly at stopping the importation of certain items or punishing a country for unfair trade practices. The suggested US 100% duty on Japanese luxury automobiles in 1995 is an example of an exclusionary duty imposed to punish Japan for what the US felt were unfair trade practices.

9 Marking duty – "Marking" is the indication of imports as to the country of origin. If improper marking occurs an additional duty is applied as a penalty.

10 Penalty duty – Any duty which is additional to regular duties. Penalty duties are imposed to add additional costs on an exporter/importer for not complying with fair trade practices or the customs laws of a country. Penalty duties include "marking" duties, "exclusionary" duties, "anti-dumping" duties, and "retaliatory" duties.

11 Preferential duty – When a country offers favored treatment to another country it often does so by reducing duties on products imported from that country. Such duties are referred to as preferential duties.

12 Prohibitive duty – A duty designed to stop the flow of imports of specific goods. Prohibitive duties may be arranged so as to apply at a low rate for a specified number or value of goods and then at a much higher or prohibitive rate for additional numbers of imports.

13 Protective duty – A tax placed on imported goods to carry out protectionist activities of a government. Taxes increase the cost of imports to consumers thereby reducing their demand. Properly applied duties will increase the development of local industry, as well as protect it from foreign competition.

14 Retaliatory duty – A penalty duty (in addition to other duties) imposed by a country to punish another country for unfair trade practices. President Clinton's 1995 threat to increase United States duties to 100% on imported Japanese luxury cars is in retaliation for Japan's closed markets with respect to most imports.

15 Specific duty – A tax levied on imports. The amount of duty is specified as an amount per unit of weight or unit of other measurement. For example, $1.00 per item imported or $1.00 per pound or hundred weight.

16 Unilateral duty – A duty imposed by executive order to punish a country for unfair trade practices. It may also be used to reduce the flow of specific types of imports. Unilateral duties are temporary, lasting until the trade problem has been resolved.

Bibliography

Albaum, Gerald, Strandskov, Jesper, Duerr, Edwin & Dowd, Lawrence (1994). *International marketing and export management*. 2nd edn, Wokingham: Addison-Wesley.

Czinkota, M. R., Rivoli, P. & Ronkainen, I. A. (1989). *International Business*. Chicago, IL: The Dryden Press.

Daniels, J. D. & Radebaugh, L. E. (1994). *International business: Environments and operations*. 7th edn, Reading, MA: Addison-Wesley Publishing.

Grosse, R. & Kujawa, D. (1995). *International business: Theory and managerial applications*. 3rd edn, Boston, MA: Richard D. Irwin Inc.

Johnson, T. E. (1994). *Export–Import procedures and documentation*. New York: Amacom.

Rugman, A. M. & Hodgetts, R. M. (1995). *International management: A strategic management approach*. New York: McGraw-Hill Inc.

Taoka, G. M. & Beeman, D. R. (1991). *International business*. New York: Harper Collins.

Toyne, B & Walters, Peter, G. P. (1993). *Global marketing management*. Boston: Allyn and Bacon.

Zodl, J. A. (1992). *Export–Import: Everything you and your company need to know to compete in world markets*. Cincinnati, OH: Betterway Books.

JOHN O'CONNELL

dysfunctional performance appraisals A dysfunctional appraisal is the result of any intentional or unintentional rater, ratee or organizational action that undermines the intended purpose of an organization's PERFORMANCE APPRAISAL process. Organizations typically develop, implement, and operate performance appraisal systems with the underlying assumption that the process provides the organization with a host of *potential benefits*. These benefits can include: (a) effective performance planning and goal setting; (b) a systematic basis for evaluating and documenting employee contributions to the organization; (c) increased emphasis on employee development and performance improvement; and (d) a systematic basis for making critical human resource management decisions, including those such as compensation, promotion, discharge, and training (Cardy and Dobbins, 1994). Appraisals become dysfunctional when the potential benefits of the appraisal process fail to be realized.

Causes and Outcomes of Dysfunctional Appraisals

Dysfunctional performance appraisals are caused by organizational, managerial, and/or employee factors that reduce or diminish the overall effectiveness of the process (Murphy and Cleveland, 1991). Organizational factors include poorly designed rating formats and procedures, lack of top management support, lack of effective rater training, insufficient resources to effectively reward performance, and a non-supportive organizational culture (Mohrman et al., 1989).

Managers, in their role as raters, are frequently viewed as the primary cause of dysfunctional appraisals when they lack the ability and/or motivation to conduct effective appraisals (Longenecker et al., 1987). When managers (raters) fail to establish unambiguous performance standards, fail to provide ongoing performance measurement and feedback, fail to take sufficient time to prepare and conduct the appraisal, and fail to interact with candor and honesty in their review of an employee's performance, the process can easily become dysfunctional (Longenecker and Goff, 1992). Employees (ratees) can cause the appraisal process to become dysfunctional when they possess unrealistic expectations, are defensive in responding to performance feedback, are cynical or contemptuous of the process, or take a passive role in reviewing and responding to their performance review.

The outcomes of dysfunctional appraisals are numerous. When appraisals are dysfunctional, organizations lose a valuable human resource management tool, managers fail to utilize a potentially useful process for improving employee performance, and employee JOB SATISFACTION, motivation, commitment, and development typically suffer.

Bibliography

Cardy, P. L. & Dobbins, G. H. (1994). *Performance Appraisal: an Alternative Perspective*, Cincinnati, OH: South-Western Publishing Company.

Longenecker, C. O., Gioia, D. A. & Sims, H. P. (1987). Behind the mask: the politics of employee appraisal. *Academy of Management Executive*, 1, 183–93.

Longenecker, C. O. & Goff, S. (1992). Performance appraisal effectiveness: a matter of perspective. *SAM-Advanced Management Journal*, 57, 17–23.

Mohrman, A. M. Jr, Resnick-West, S. M. & Lawler, E. E. (1989). *Designing Performance Appraisal Systems*, San Francisco: Jossey-Bass.

Murphy, K. R. & Cleveland, J. N. (1991). *Performance Appraisal: an Organizational Perspective*, Boston: Allyn and Bacon.

CLINTON O. LONGENECKER

E

early retirement policy Retirement has traditionally been defined as withdrawal from the workforce altogether or at the end of a person's active life. Feldman (1994) provides a modified definition of retirement as the exit from an organizational position or career path of considerable duration, taken by individuals after middle age, and taken with the intention of reduced psychological commitment to work thereafter. The concept of early retirement, however, is ambiguous and there is no precise reference point which is considered early. Generally, the normal age for retirement in most Western countries is around age 65. Hence age 65 is generally considered both as a legal and as a labor-force or behavioral reference point (Kohli and Rein, 1991). Job changes in a person's twenties and career changes in a person's thirties are transitions but these are not thought of as retirement (Feldman, 1994).

There are several factors influencing an individual's decision to retire early. These include individual differences (especially demographic), opportunity structures in career paths, organizational variables, and macroeconomic and external environment variables (Feldman, 1994).

There are two reasons why employers and sometimes employees support early retirement. One is centered on productivity. There is literature suggesting that the wages of some older workers exceed their marginal productivity. Second, due to reputational concerns, both employers and employees prefer early retirement to dismissal (Casey, 1992).

In many Western economies, early retirement has been utilized to facilitate the elimination of redundancies and organizational downsizing (Casey, 1992). In addition, early retirement can help a company restructure its workforce and provide new career opportunities to younger workers.

Bibliography

Casey, B. (1992). Redundancy and early retirement: the interaction of public and private policy in Britain, Germany and the USA. *British Journal of Industrial Relations,* 30, 426–43.

Feldman, D. C. (1994). The decision to retire early: a review and conceptualization. *Academy of Management Review,* 19, 285–311.

Kohli, M. & Rein, M. (1991). The changing balance of work and retirement. *Time for Retirement: Comparative Studies of Early Exit from the Labor Force,* Eds. Kohli, M., Rein, M., Guillemard, A. & Gunsteren, H. V. Cambridge: Cambridge University Press.

CARRIE R. LEANA

economic depreciation This is sometimes referred to as "Hotelling" depreciation; see Fisher and McGowan (1983) and Edwards, Kay and Mayer (1987). Economic depreciation reflects the change in the value of an asset during a period; this includes physical depreciation and any changes in the market value of the asset. If the PRESENT VALUE of an asset's remaining cash flows (discounted at the asset's INTERNAL RATE OF RETURN) has changed from the beginning of the period to the end, that change represents the economic depreciation. Since accounting standards apply somewhat arbitrary depreciation schedules to physical assets (such as straight line depreciation, sum-of-year's digits and double declining balance), it is unlikely that reported depreciation will be equal to economic depreciation. As a result of this problem and others, accounting profits will not equal economic profits and the accounting rate of return will not equal the economic rate of return (*see* ACCOUNTING PROFIT; ECONOMIC PROFIT).

Bibliography

Edwards, J., Kay, J. & Mayer, C. (1987). *The Economic Analysis of Accounting Profitability.* Oxford: OUP.

Fisher, F. M. & McGowan, J. J. (1983). On the misuse of accounting rates of return to infer monopoly profits. *American Economic Review,* 73, 82–97.

Shughart, W. F., Chappell, W. F. & Cottle, R. L. (1994). *Modern Managerial Economics.* Cincinatti, OH: South-Western Publishing.

ROBERT E. MCAULIFFE

economic environment The economic environment is one of the elements in the MARKETING ENVIRONMENT in which a supplier organization is operating. A national government, after taking account of international factors such as capital and currency movements, is responsible for creating and maintaining a favorable macroeconomic environment (*see* MACRO ENVIRONMENT). It achieves this by the use of monetary and fiscal policies aimed at manipulating the levels of inflation and employment and, hence, the levels of disposable and discretionary income among various segments of the population. Thus, the level of economic activity will govern the possible success of all organizations. At any one time, the economic environment for different countries will vary widely. Thus, the ability to forecast changes from current base levels will be a major factor in the decision to invest or not.

Bibliography

Dibb, S., Simkin, L., Pride, W. M. & Ferrell, O. C. (1994). *Marketing, concepts and strategies* European edn, Boston, MA: Houghton Mifflin Co. Chapter 2.

Palmer, A. & Worthington, I. (1992). *The business and marketing environment.* Maidenhead: McGraw-Hill. Chapter 6.

Semenik, R. M. & Bamossy, G. J. (1993). *Principles of marketing.* Cincinnati, OH: South-Western Publishing Co. Chapter 2.

DAVID YORKE

economic exposure The foreign exchange risk associated with doing business in other countries. The total economic exposure is the extent to which the overall present value of an organization may be impacted by fluctuating exchange rates. The selling of products, obtaining of raw materials or subproducts, and other activities expose a business to economic exposure. The value of currency may rise or fall before, during, or after a transaction takes place. Parties to import/export transactions or businesses doing business in other countries are therefore exposed to losses related to deteriorating currency values while awaiting payment for goods already delivered or those currently being delivered.

Bibliography

Miletello, F. C. & Davis, H. A. (1994). *Foreign exchange management*. Morristown, NJ: Financial Executives Research Foundation.

Weigand, R. (1983). International investments: Weighing the incentives. *Harvard Business Review* July–August, 146–52.

JOHN O'CONNELL

economic profit   Economic profits are defined as total revenues in a given period minus *all* costs of production in that period, including the economic costs of tangible and intangible assets and the opportunity cost of those assets employed (*see* OPPORTUNITY COSTS). For example, any costs incurred for training, research and development, and other intangible assets would be depreciated over their expected economic lifetime rather than expensed in the current period. The normal, risk-adjusted rate of return to capital would be included in the calculation of economic costs, so that firms which earned the normal rate of return would have zero economic profits (although they would show positive accounting profits) (*see* ACCOUNTING PROFITS). When economic profits are positive, they serve as a signal for entry into the industry, while negative economic profits indicate that firms should exit the industry. In the long run, economic profits in competitive markets should be driven to zero by the forces of entry and exit unless there are barriers to entry or barriers to exit (*see* BARRIERS TO ENTRY). In fact, Bain (1941) suggested using the accounting profit rate above the competitive return as a measure of the height of entry barriers in an industry. However, this is an appropriate measure only when the accounting rate of return equals the economic rate of return.

Fisher and McGowan (1983) argued that the appropriate theoretical measure of the economic rate of return is the internal rate of return (IRR) and they asserted there was little relation between the accounting rate of return and the economic rate of return (*see* INTERNAL RATE OF RETURN). The accounting rate of return is calculated as accounting profits divided by either total assets or owners equity. But accounting statements report assets at their historic costs and not at their current (or replacement) cost, so inflation and the failure to capitalize intangible asset values will cause accounting rates of return to deviate from the economic rate of return. Fisher and McGowan showed that the accounting rate of return will not equal the economic rate of return because: (i) the depreciation methods used by accountants do not reflect economic depreciation, (ii) the investments made by a firm in any given period will not generally have the same "time shape" (stream of future cash flows), and (iii) the accounting rate of return will vary with the rate of growth of the firm. From their simulations using the same stream of cash flows from a hypothetical investment but different methods of depreciation, Fisher and McGowan found that the accounting rate of return was a misleading measure and concluded it may provide no information about the economic rate of return (*see* ECONOMIC DEPRECIATION).

Not surprisingly, these results generated considerable controversy in the literature. Long and Ravenscraft (1984) and Martin (1984) suggested that other measures of profitability, such as the Lerner index, may serve as better measures of market power for economic analysis. Long and Ravenscraft also argued that in practice, the correlation between accounting profits and economic profits was very high and the examples used by Fisher and McGowan were not representative of industry. Salamon (1985) also found that there was a strong correlation between the accounting rate of return and the estimated *conditional* internal rate of return (IRR) which can be obtained from firms' financial statements. However, he also found systematic errors occurred when the accounting rate of return was employed, so the accounting measure could not simply be treated as a randomly "noisy" proxy for the economic rate of return.

Fisher (1984) noted in his reply that the fundamental problem of accounting rate of return data is that profits in the numerator are measured as an average of *past* investments while total assets in the denominator are based on historic costs and may include recent capital that has been added in the expectation of future profits. The economic rate of return is forward-looking and relates the stream of benefits from an investment to the specific asset that generated them. Because of averaging and a backward-looking perspective, accounting rates of return cannot equal the economic rate of return.

Edwards, Kay and Mayer (1987) evaluated several possible adjustments to accounting procedures that might improve the content of accounting information. They suggested that accountants should report several measures of a firm's profits and asset value since there is no single, unambiguous measure of the "true" values and different sources of information are required for different purposes. For example, when an asset or activity has a very long life (such as a going concern) the internal rate of return does not necessarily provide useful information because the IRR is a single value defined for the lifetime of an asset and cannot be used to evaluate performance for a fraction of that asset's life. Other measures of profitability from accounting data may provide investors, economists and others with better information. Among other suggestions they recommend that value-to-the-owner rules should be used by accountants to value company assets and liabilities where assets are valued (in most cases) at replacement cost, all changes in book values should have entries in the profit and loss statement and profits and asset values should be adjusted for inflation.

Bibliography

Bain, J. S. (1941). The profit rate as a measure of monopoly power. *Quarterly Journal of Economics*, **55**, 271–93.

Edwards, J., Kay, J. & Mayer, C. (1987). *The Economic Analysis of Accounting Profitability*. Oxford: OUP.

Fisher, F. M. (1984). The misuse of accounting rates of return: reply. *American Economic Review*, **74**, 509–17.

Fisher, F. M. & McGowan, J. J. (1983). On the misuse of accounting rates of return to infer monopoly profits. *American Economic Review*, **73**, 82–97.

Long, W. F. & Ravenscraft, D. J. (1984). The misuse of accounting rates of return: comment. *American Economic Review*, **74**, 494–500.

Martin, S. (1984). The misuse of accounting rates of return: comment. *American Economic Review*, **74**, 501–6.

Salamon, G. L. (1985). Accounting rates of return. *American Economic Review*, **75**, 495–504.

ROBERT E. MCAULIFFE

economics and ethics

I. Economics

"Economics" is frequently defined as the science of choice, where choice is understood to be the selection of one course of action (or policy) from among a set of options, on the basis of weighing costs and benefits. Essential to the economic conception of choice is the recognition that every choice involves costs – at the very least, the cost of the most valued forgone alternative that could have been chosen. Economics attempts to explain particular choices of individuals by applying a model of rationality. Large-scale social phenomena, such as the behavior of markets, are then explained by showing how they emerge from the interactions of large numbers of individual choices.

The model of rationality that mainstream economics employs is that of *individual utility-maximization*. The rational individual is understood to be an agent who attempts to maximize his expected utility. In contemporary economics, utility is identified with the satisfaction of preferences.

As a *positive* (that is, explanatory and predictive) theory, economics purports to be able to account for human behavior so far as individuals act rationally (in the defined sense). However, to the extent that human beings care about being rational, to describe an action as rational is to commend it, while to characterize an action as irrational is usually taken to be a criticism. For this reason, the model of rationality with which economics operates is viewed as *normative* as well as positive. In other words, economics purports not only to explain and predict behavior (so far as it is rational), but also to guide behavior by determining how agents, including policy-makers, should act if they wish to act rationally.

II. Ethics

"Ethics" is sometimes understood to refer to a code of conduct, but in the literature of contemporary ethics generally and of business ethics in particular it is more often understood to be a *practical activity* – a reflective and self-critical process of making decisions about which acts (or policies) are right, wrong, or permissible. As a practical activity, ethics is also understood to include the process of making judgments about the praiseworthiness or blame-worthiness of particular agents. Furthermore, ethics is a *rational* practical activity at least in the sense that both in ethical theorizing and in everyday ethical discourse, *reasons* are given to support or to criticize the moral judgments individuals make.

It is therefore appropriate to request that one who advances a moral judgment be prepared to support it, and to support it with relevant considerations. Generally speaking, only certain sorts of considerations are widely recognized to be relevant in moral discourse – only certain types of reasons count as reasons to support or criticize moral judgments. Among the most important are appeals to basic and widely shared values – fairness, human welfare, and individual autonomy being among the most common. One distinctive feature of moral reasons is their *impersonal* character. If A declares that abortion is wrong, it is appropriate for B to ask "And why is it wrong?" Moreover, if A were to answer "Because it makes me ill" he would not have given the right sort of reason to support his judgment, because a statement of personal distaste does not qualify as the sort of consideration that can support a moral judgment.

Many ethical theorists have also observed that moral judgments themselves have an equally important characteristic: They are made from a point of view which purports to be impartial. Thus if a person sincerely makes a moral judgment (for example, about the rightness of a certain act) then he is understood to be committed to universalizing the judgment – that is, to judging that the same type of act, in the same circumstances, would be right if another person performed it.

III. The Apparent Conflict Between Economics and Ethics

Economics appears to recognize only one reason for acting – namely, that doing this rather than that will maximize one's expected utility. Ethics, in contrast, not only offers a variety of considerations (human welfare, individual autonomy, fairness, etc.), but also requires that individuals sometimes act contrary to their own interests. On the surface at least, then, ethics and economics advance opposing conceptions of how one ought to choose. Moreover, if the model of economic rationality is accepted as a positive theory, an account of how human beings do in fact invariably behave, it seems to rule out the possibility of ethical conduct. If all people actually do – and all they can do because of the laws of human psychology – is to seek to maximize their expected utility, then it is futile to exhort them to act ethically. To the extent that economic thinking dominates the methodology of the sorts of courses that are taught in business schools and pervades the characteristic patterns of decision-making of business people, the very idea of business ethics becomes problematic.

IV. The Theory of the Market as the Reconciliation of Ethics and Economics

Some of the most eloquent advocates of the extensive market systems of social interaction that emerged in Western Europe in the seventeenth and eighteenth centuries proposed a way of reconciling economics and ethics. DeMandeville (1714) argued that in a market system "private vices" make "public virtues": purely self-interested conduct that fits the traditional description of moral vices, if it occurs within the context of market institutions, produces public benefits. Similarly, Adam Smith (1776) extolled the market as a system that harnesses self-interested action for the common good. DeMandeville and Smith presaged the First Fundamental Theory of Welfare Economics: In a perfectly competitive market, free exchanges among individual utility maximizers will result in an equilibrium that is efficient in the Paretian sense of efficiency – there will be no redistribution of goods that will make anyone better off without making someone worse off.

According to this simple conception of the relation between ethics and economics, the realm of market exchanges is an area of human life in which ethics is not needed for the production of morally admirable results. Human welfare emerges, in the aggregate, as a fortunate by-product of amoral or even immoral behavior.

This simple view of the relationship between economics and ethics is itself subject to ethical criticism, however. One obvious difficulty, of course, is that markets in the real world are not perfectly competitive and lack other features, such as perfect information, which the ideal market of the First Fundamental Theorem possesses. Thus the justification for reliance upon market systems, and for tolerating unethical behavior within them, cannot be that market systems are necessarily efficient.

More importantly, however, a number of ethical theories, as well as much common-sense moral thinking, challenge the assumption that efficiency is a sufficient standard for evaluation. The main difficulty is that outcomes can be efficient (in the technical economic sense explained above) and yet grossly unfair. For example, a system in which a minority of masters owned everything and a majority of slaves owned nothing would be efficient in the Paretian sense if it were not possible to improve the lot of the slaves without worsening that of the masters.

The basic point can be put in a different way, without recourse to such an extreme example. Economic theory only tells us that in perfect markets efficient outcomes will emerge from free exchanges for gain, but market processes cannot be expected to correct for inequities in the initial distribution of assets which individuals bring to the market. Some individuals, through no fault of their own, simply have fewer assets to bargain with. Ethical reasoning is needed to determine whether, or under what conditions, undeserved differences in initial endowments are unjust; and if so, what means of correcting or preventing them are permissible.

A second major area in which economic thinking by itself is inadequate and in which reliance upon ethical reasoning is unavoidable is the problem of *externalities*. In all real-world markets there are externalities or "spill–over" effects, costs or benefits that arise from exchanges but that accrue to others than (or in addition to) the exchangers themselves. A familiar example is pollution. When a manufacturer and a supplier of raw materials make an exchange which allows the manufacture of a chemical, they each calculate the costs and the benefits of the exchange to themselves. However, if, as a result of the exchange, toxic fumes are discharged into the air, costs will be imposed on others and these costs will not be fully taken into account in the exchange. In some cases economics can offer suggestions as to how to "internalize external costs" (for example, by a policy in which the government issues exchangeable permits to spill certain amounts of pollution into the air), but economics cannot by itself tell us whether such a policy is fair or even whether the harm which the externality represents is important enough to require such remedies.

Two more examples will illustrate the dependence upon ethics of economics, as a discipline which purports to provide guidance for policy. First, consider the pervasive policy question of which sorts of goods or services ought to be offered for sale in markets. Should not only cars and legal services but recreational drugs, sex, or babies for adoption be marketable? Positive economics can tell us under what conditions marketing an item will contribute to efficient outcomes, but it cannot tell us whether it ought to be marketed if it is admitted that there are other considerations that are relevant besides efficiency. To assume that efficiency is the only thing that matters is to endorse a particular moral theory – namely utilitarianism – not to avoid moral theory, and economics by itself cannot tell us which moral theory to endorse.

Second, consider a basic tool of economic analysis for government bureaucracies and business cost–benefit analysis is often presented as if it were a value-neutral,

scientific procedure for making decisions about the use of scarce resources, in fact a number of difficult ethical questions must be answered before it can be employed. The first of these, of course, is "Whose costs and benefits are to count?" The second is "Whose judgments about costs and benefits are to be used?" (For example, in deciding whether to commit public funds for abortion, do we count costs to fetuses?) A third question is a variant of a complaint noted above concerning the use of efficiency as the sole or overriding standard for evaluation: "Why should we be concerned only with maximizing the ratio of benefits to costs rather than with how costs and benefits are distributed among people who will be affected?" (For example, if we think that one element of a just health-care system is the fair distribution of the costs of providing access to care for all, then we are denying that distribution of costs and benefits is irrelevant.) In addition, the standard ways of measuring costs and benefits are themselves ethical issues. For example, when cost–benefit analysts assign a value to lives they typically either equate the value of a life with total expected life-time earnings or with how much the individual would be willing to pay to avoid some specified probability of death. The former measure systematically disadvantages women and minorities who have lower expected life-time earnings, due to historical patterns of educational and employment discrimination. The latter, if taken literally, automatically assigns higher value to the lives of the wealthy, since how much an individual is willing to pay is a function of how much resources he or she has access to.

None of this is to deny, of course, that ethics does not also depend upon economics, as well. Any ethical theory in which a consideration of the consequences of actions and policies for human welfare or freedom is understood to be relevant will require some way of estimating costs and benefits. Similarly, any acceptable view of the ethically responsible use of resources will have to be concerned with efficiency to some extent.

V. The New Economics: Making Room for Ethics

One of the most striking and fruitful developments in economics in recent years has been a growing awareness that peoples' ethical commitments do in fact influence their behavior in all areas of human life, even the life of "economic man" in the market. As a consequence, economists are rethinking the very foundations of their discipline, as well as their conception of its subject matter. Instead of assuming that all behavior is self-interested and in consequence proposing far-fetched egoistic explanations of what certainly seems to be non–self-interested behavior, more and more economists are attempting to see how the standard tools of economic analysis can be adapted to model moral behavior. Thus far, four main areas of research have been especially prominent: (1) the role of moral commitments in solving or avoiding problems in the supply of public goods; (2) the function of moral commitments in fostering successful cooperation within organizations; (3) the necessity of moral commitments for the well-functioning of markets; and (4) the contribution which moral commitments make to the welfare of the individuals who have them.

(1) *Morality and public goods*. Standard economic analyses which assume that most agents act in purely

self-interested ways in all circumstances predict that public goods will not be supplied or will be undersupplied if contribution to them is left voluntary. The prediction is that if he can expect to enjoy the good if it is produced through the contributions of others, each self-interested individual will refrain from contributing because he will regard his own contribution as an available cost. Unfortunately for the analysis, there are many cases in which public goods are supplied at higher levels than the analysis predicts, even without resorting to coercion to ensure contributions. Substantial voter turn-out is one example among many: if voters behaved as standard economic theory predicts no one would vote in elections in which the chance that his vote would determine the outcome are negligible, yet many people do vote in these circumstances. Once we allow the possibility that significant numbers of people may vote because they believe it is their *duty* to do so and that their sense of duty overrides or suspends a purely self-interested calculation of the expected costs and benefits of contributing to the public good of substantial voter turn-out, we have the beginnings of a more satisfactory analysis of voting behavior.

(2) *The contribution of morality to successful cooperation in organizations.* A number of empirical studies (e.g. Guth et al., 1982) have revealed the role that moral values play in fostering successful and sustained cooperation in organizations, including business firms. In particular, there is considerable evidence that commitment to moral norms concerning fairness is often crucial in avoiding or resolving conflicts between labor and management and that recognition of workers' rights to participate in decision-making can increase productivity.

(3) *The moral underpinnings of markets.* Unless most participants in market exchanges have a modicum of trust and honesty, for example, transaction costs and enforcement costs for commercial contracts would be prohibitively high. Moreover, since the efficiency of markets depends upon competitiveness, moral inhibitions against engaging in anti-competitive practices (including sabotaging one's rivals) play an important role even if they are viewed only as supplementing the fear of prosecution for violations of antitrust law. For these reasons what may be called the morality of the market is sometimes described as a public good for all who seek to benefit from markets: it is in everyone's interest that there be sufficient moral commitments among others so that markets can function well, even though from a purely self-interested point of view, being moral is a cost to the individual and he has reason to attempt to take a free ride on the moral restraint of others.

(4) *The contribution of an individual's moral commitments to his own self-interest.* The final area of economic research on ethics challenges the preceding assumption that individual self-interest only speaks in favor of encouraging moral commitments in *others*, as opposed to oneself. To take only one example that has been studied in some detail (Frank, 1988), the fact that an individual who is a potential cooperator is known to be honest can make it possible to overcome "commitment problems" that otherwise might block mutually advantageous cooperation. Commitment problems are ubiquitous in business and wherever there are principal/agent relationships with significant agency risks. An agency risk exists whenever there is a divergence between the interests of an agent to whom a principal entrusts some activity and the interests of the principal which he engaged the agent to further. Often, close monitoring of the agent's activity is not feasible or would be too costly to the principal. Under such circumstances the ability of the agent to make a credible commitment to serve the principal's interest even when not doing so would further his own interests is a valuable economic asset for the agent. Moreover, for a number of reasons, the least costly way for an agent to be able to convince others that he has certain moral qualities (such as honesty) may be to actually cultivate those qualities, not merely to try to feign them.

In all of these areas of research, economists are expanding what has traditionally been regarded as the proper subject matter of economics to include moral behavior, not just self-interested behavior. In doing so, they are recognizing a more complex and mutually enriching relationship between economics and ethics.

Bibliography

Bowie, N. (1991). Challenging the egoistic paradigm. *Business Ethics Quarterly*, 1, 1–21.

Buchanan, A. (1985). *Ethics, Efficiency and the Market*. Totowa, NJ: Rowman & Allanheld.

Collard, D. (1978). *Altruism and Economy: A Study in Non-selfish Economics*. New York: Oxford University Press.

DeMandeville, B. (1714). *The Fable of the Bees* ed. P. Harth. Harmondsworth: Penguin.

Etzioni, A. (1988). *The Moral Dimension: Toward a New Economics*. New York: Macmillan.

Fox, A. (1974). *Beyond Contract: Work, Power and Trust Relations*. London: Faber.

Frank, R. (1988). *Passions within Reason: The Strategic Role of the Emotions*. New York: W. W. Norton.

Guth, W., Schmittberger, R., & Schwarze, B. (1982). An experimental analysis of ultimate bargaining. *Journal of Economic Behavior and Organization*, 3, 367–88.

Hausman, D. & McPherson, M. (1993). Taking ethics seriously: Economics and contemporary moral philosophy. *Journal of Economic Literature*, 31, 671–731.

Isaac, R. M., Mathieu, D., & Zajac, E. E. (1991). Institutional framing and perceptions of fairness. *Constitutional Political Economy*, 2, 329–70.

Smith, A. (1776, 1976). *An Enquiry into the Nature and Causes of the Wealth of Nations* (eds) R. H. Campbell & A. S. Skinner. Oxford: Clarendon Press.

ALLEN BUCHANAN

economies of scale Economics of scale exist when increasing all inputs in production causes output to rise by more than the percentage change in inputs. Therefore, if all inputs were doubled (that is, the scale of the firm's operations doubled) output would more than double. Typically firms vary in terms of *size* and not scale: large firms do not use all inputs in the same proportion as smaller firms. Expressed in terms of costs for a single product firm, the AVERAGE TOTAL COST of production declines as output increases when there are economies of scale. These economies of scale may occur at the plant level or the firm level of operations. A firm may operate several plants and there may be economies in the management of the firm or in the consolidation of its financial activities. Economies of scale and ECONOMIES OF SCOPE combined with the level of demand in the market have an important effect on the feasible number of firms in an industry (see Panzar (1989), MINIMUM EFFICIENT SCALE, and MARKET STRUCTURE).

The sources of economies of scale at the firm level are not well understood although Sharkey (1982) offers several possibilities. At the level of the plant, economies of scale reflect the technological or engineering aspects of production. For example, if there are fixed setup costs to produce a specific model on an assembly line, then the per unit setup costs will be lower the greater the number of units produced. Another possibility is based on the law of large numbers, when unit sales double firms do not have to double their inventories to achieve a given probability of having supplies available to consumers. Firms can also achieve gains from specialization from their labor and capital inputs at higher output levels. In addition, there may be advantages when a firm can purchase inputs at lower cost with volume discounts.

For a single product firm, there are economies of scale when average cost per unit is declining. When average costs are declining, then MARGINAL COSTS OF PRODUCTION must be less than average costs. Therefore one measure of economies of scale is the ratio of average costs to marginal costs:

$$s = AC/MC = \frac{TC}{Q} \times \frac{\Delta Q}{\Delta TC} \qquad (1)$$

where TC is the total cost of production, Q is the quantity of output produced, ΔTC is the change in total costs and ΔQ is the change in output produced. There are economies of scale when $s > 1$ and DISECONOMIES OF SCALE when $s < 1$. Another measure of economies of scale is the cost ELASTICITY which measures the percentage change in total costs for a given percentage change in output. It can be expressed as:

$$\varepsilon_{TC} = \frac{\frac{\Delta TC}{TC}}{\frac{\Delta Q}{Q}} = \frac{\Delta TC}{\Delta Q} \times \frac{Q}{TC} \qquad (2)$$

which is simply the inverse of the scale economy measure in (1) above. There are economies of scale when $\varepsilon_{TC} < 1$ since costs will increase by less than the increase in output and diseconomies of scale exist when $\varepsilon_{TC} > 1$.

A classic empirical study of economies of scale is due to Nerlove (1963) who examined economies in electricity generation. He found that economies of scale existed in the industry but were exhausted by the largest firms. Sharkey (1982), and Panzar (1989) provide surveys of both theoretical and empirical issues regarding economies of scale for single product and multiproduct firms. The measurement and estimation of economies of scale for multiproduct firms is much more complicated than for single product firms because firms may vary their output mix among the different products they produce and therefore will have different costs depending on their output mix (see Baumol et al. (1982) and Panzar (1989)). Bailey and Friedlaender (1982) suggest that mergers in the trucking industry may be motivated by economies of scale and scope once the multiproduct nature of trucking services is recognized

Bibliography

Bailey, E. E. & Friedlaender, A. F. (1982). Market structure and multiproduct industries. *Journal of Economic Literature*, **20**, 1024–48.

Baumol, W. J., Panzar, J. C. & Willig, R. D. (1982). *Contestable Markets and the Theory of Industry Structure*. San Diego: Harcourt Brace Jovanovich.

Nerlove, M. (1963). Returns to scale in electricity supply. Christ, C. *Measurement in Economics: Studies in Mathematical Economics and Econometrics*. Stanford: Stanford University Press.

Panzar, J. C. (1989). Technological determinants of firm and industry structure. Schmalensee, R. & Willig, R. D. *Handbook of Industrial Organization*. New York: North-Holland.

Sharkey, W. W. (1982). *The Theory of Natural Monopoly*. Cambridge: CUP.

ROBERT E. MCAULIFFE

economies of scope   Economies of scope occur when two or more products can be produced together at lower cost than by producing them separately. Rather than increasing the *scale* of the firm's operations (ECONOMIES OF SCALE), costs are changing with changes in the *scope* of the firm's operations (the number of products produced). Economies of scope may arise when two or more products share a common, "public good" input in joint production, where once that common input is acquired it is available to produce other products at no cost; see Bailey and Friedlaender (1982) and Panzar (1989). There may be economies from shared inputs which give rise to economies of scope when costs are reduced in acquiring those inputs in volume or in sharing them (such as sharing overhead, reputation or management). Often knowledge is an important input in production that, once acquired, makes it less costly to produce or sell closely related products. Economies of scale and scope may therefore interact to create advantages for large firms and increase the MINIMUM EFFICIENT SCALE (MES) of operation.

If a firm produces two products ($q1$ and $q2$), the degree of economies of scope can be measured as the difference between the total costs of producing both products separately and the total costs of producing the two products jointly, divided by the total costs of producing the two products jointly. Defining the total costs of producing both q_1 and q_2 jointly as $C(q1,q2)$, this is calculated as:

$$Sc = \frac{C(q_1,0) + C(0,q_2) - C(q_1,q_2)}{C(q_1,q_2)}$$

and economies of scope exist when S_c is greater than zero; see Bailey and Friedlaender (1982) and Baumol, Panzar and Willig (1982).

Friedlaender, Winston and Wang (1983) found there were both economies of scale and economies of scope in US automobile manufacturing for large cars, small cars, and trucks. US producers could share common parts and designs between these products and could exploit pecuniary economies of scale through volume purchases of common parts and materials from suppliers. When the US Department of Justice sought to break up the regional Bell companies from AT&T long distance operations, AT&T initially suggested there were economies of scope in long distance and local phone service and that economic efficiency would be reduced if the natural monopoly in communications were ended. Using Bell system data, Evans and Heckman (1984) tested to determine whether one firm could produce communications output in the US at lower cost than two firms over the period 1958–77. They found that for qualifying data points, costs would be lower if *two* firms produced that output. In other words, the Bell System did not satisfy the necessary cost requirements to be classified as a natural monopoly.

Bibliography

Bailey, E. E. & Friedlaender, A. F. (1982). Market structure and multiproduct industries. *Journal of Economic Literature*, 20, 1024–48.

Baumol, W. J., Panzar, J. C. & Willig, R. D. (1982). *Contestable Markets and the Theory of Industry Structure*. San Diego: Harcourt Brace Jovanovich.

Evans, D. S. & Heckman, J. J. (1984). A test for subadditivity of the cost function with application to the Bell system. *American Economic Review*, 74, 615–23.

Friedlaender, A. F., Winston, C. & Wang, K. (1983). Costs, technology and productivity in the U.S. automobile industry. *Bell Journal of Economics*, 14, 1–20.

Panzar, J. C. (1989). Technological determinants of firm and industry structure. Schmalensee, R. & Willig, R. D. *Handbook of Industrial Organization*. New York: North-Holland.

Sharkey, W. W. (1982). *The Theory of Natural Monopoly*. Cambridge: CUP.

ROBERT E. MCAULIFFE

EFTPOS   EFTPOS or electronic funds transfer at point of sale, refers to debit or "plastic" card payment at the point of sale by direct funds transfer from the customer's account to the retailer's account. It evolved in the early to mid 1980s. It is an area of continuing development and is fast becoming a leading payment system for retailers.

Bibliography

McGoldrick, P. J. (1990). *Retail marketing*. Maidenhead: McGraw-Hill.

Penn, V. (1990). Retail EFTPOS 90: Paper holds out against plastic. *International Journal of Retail and Distribution*, 19, (1), 10–12.

STEVE GREENLAND

elasticity   This measure indicates the responsiveness of a buyer or seller to a change in the value of an economic variable. Perhaps the most important type is price elasticity of demand which measures the size of the reaction by consumers of a product to a change in the price of that product. Additional measures including price elasticity of supply, cross elasticity, income elasticity, and cross-advertising elasticity are also important in determining the strategic behavior of firms and outcomes in markets. Price elasticity of demand (ϵ_p) is calculated as the percentage change in quantity demanded resulting from a small percentage change in price. Written in the form of a fraction this becomes

$$\epsilon_p = \frac{\%\Delta Q}{\%\Delta P}$$

where the symbol Δ indicates a change in quantity (Q) or price (P). Where the exact demand curve is already known, an infinitesimally small change in price can be used to calculate what is known as the point elasticity. More commonly, when a manager makes discrete changes in price, the estimation of elasticity involves a range of prices and quantities. Calculating elasticity using the average price and quantity over these ranges yields a useful approximation.

As the LAW OF DEMAND indicates that price and quantity demanded are inversely related, the value of ϵ_p should always be negative. Since the negative sign adds no information about the size of the reaction, by convention it is typically dropped. Three levels of responsiveness are observable. When a large reaction by consumers occurs (the percentage change in quantity demanded exceeds that of price), ϵ_p has a value greater than 1 and demand is said to be elastic with respect to price. The small reaction case, $\epsilon_p < 1$, is that of inelastic demand, while the case where price and quantity reactions exactly offset each other, $\epsilon_p = 1$, is identified as unit elastic demand.

The degree of consumer sensitivity to a price change is influenced by several factors. Switching to alternative products is common when one product's price is changed. Demand for a product thus tends to become more elastic where the number and closeness of available substitutes rises as this switching of products more readily and easily occurs. Nelson (1974) in his study of advertising cautions that elasticity actually depends on the number of alternatives of which the consumer is aware. Managers need to consider this and the appropriate market boundaries (see MARKET DEFINITION) in determining their business strategy. In perfect competition, where large numbers of produce identical products, demand for any one firm's product is perfectly elastic and all firms become price takers. Where a strategy of product differentiation is possible, it can be used to create a more inelastic demand for a product. One well known example is that of 7UP being marketed as the "UNCOLA" in an effort to distinguish itself from its rivals.

Similarly, a product requiring a greater portion of the consumer's budget will tend to have a more elastic demand as a result of the stronger income effect from a price change. Perhaps most apparent is that the greater the extent to which a product is perceived as being a necessity, the more inelastic its demand tends to be with respect to price. Finally, demand tends to become more elastic over longer time periods. This results from the fact that typically a wider array of substitutes become available over time. Also, a consumer simply has more time to react to the price change.

Price elasticity of demand is central to a firm's sales revenues. As a firm's total revenues are dependent on the product's price and the number of units sold, the impact of a price change on revenues depends singularly on the product's elasticity of demand. As the law of demand indicates that price and quantity demanded move in opposite directions, a change in price creates two opposing forces on revenues. The elasticity of demand indicates which force is stronger. A price cut in the face of an elastic demand for the product will increase the total receipts from its sales because of the large and more than offsetting rise in unit sales. Similarly, a price rise where demand is elastic will reduce total revenues.

Price elasticity of demand also plays a vital role in determining optimal prices. For profit maximization, a firm should produce until the MARGINAL REVENUE (MR) equals the MARGINAL COST (MC) of production. For linear demand curves it has been demonstrated that marginal revenue is related to price (P) and elasticity by the equation

$$MR = P \times [1 - (1/\epsilon_p)].$$

As such, if a firm maximizes profits, marginal revenue in the equation above equals marginal cost, and this relation can be used to show that the best price to charge is dependent on both elasticity and cost. Douglas (1992) shows that this relationship can be written as

$$P = MC + [-1/(\epsilon_p + 1)]x \ MC$$

which yields a markup pricing strategy. The profit maximizing markup of price is a percentage of cost and is inversely related to the product's demand elasticity. That is, the more elastic is the demand for the product, the lower will be its profit maximizing markup price.

Bibliography

Douglas, E. (1992). *Managerial Economics: Analysis & Strategy.* 4th edn, Englewood Cliffs: Prentice-Hall.

Mansfield, E. (1993). *Managerial Economics: Theory, Applications, and Cases.* 2nd edn, New York: W.W. Norton.

Nelson, P. (1974). Advertising as Information. *Journal of Political Economy*, **82**, 729–54.

GILBERT BECKER

electronic commerce Electronic commerce is the application of computer and communications technology so as to enhance or redefine business transactions between firms and their customers, suppliers, or other business partners. Prior to the era of information technology, the customer–supplier relationship usually involved a person-to-person exchange of cash or its equivalent for a product or service. Today's business transactions have usually been enhanced by a variety of electronic and communication devices. Some have made transactions more efficient, such as the use of scanning equipment at the point of purchase, or terminals to authorize credit. Automated teller machines (ATM) provide cost efficiencies to the bank while giving customers 24 hour access to banking services. Enhanced service and lower costs are also shared characteristics of self-service fueling stations, automated highway toll systems, debit cards, and so on. Time, as in the ATM example, can be stretched via innovative use of technology; but while time expands, distances can be collapsed. For instance, online reservation systems give customers and travel agents access to a worldwide assortment of travel products. Similarly, order entry systems, coupled with televised home shopping networks, provide customers in their home with the ability to order a product and ensure its availability.

Although the above examples are all targeted at transactions involving consumers, similar systems have evolved to make the business relationship between corporate buyers and suppliers more efficient and effective. By adopting standardized formats for common transactions, commerce between organizations can be largely automated. Such electronic data interchange (EDI) systems, for instance, permit a large retailer to electronically place orders with its major suppliers. Some retailers now routinely provide their suppliers with online access to the detailed store sales information generated by their check-out scanners. With these data the supplier can help decrease inventory carrying costs while better serving customers. Similar electronic linkages let retailers instantly interact with freight carriers, warehouses, distributors, banks, government agencies, and other business partners.

The Future of Electronic Commerce

The next generation of electronic commerce appears likely to transform rather than just enhance the relationship between customer and supplier. It will lead to new products, new formats for old products, and new marketing and distribution channels. Emerging global data highways such as the internet give individual customers the opportunity to electronically shop for products or services throughout the world. Suppliers, big or small, now have inexpensive access to a worldwide marketplace. Start-up airlines use reservation systems to reach a worldwide market relatively inexpensively; similarly, a small producer of golf clubs in California or of cowboy hats in Arizona can, without benefit of distributors or retail stores, sell merchandise in England or Australia by use of the Internet's world wide web. Services and information-based products, such as music recordings or commercial art, are even more likely to benefit from these highways. The spouse of a professor in Montana can establish an Internet-based business providing copy-editing or transla-tion service to journals throughout the world and employ TELECOMMUTING copy-editors and translators from Ire-land, India, or Peru. A fashion advertiser in New York can employ a design team consisting of independent contrac-tors, perhaps including a photographer and model in Paris, a graphic artist in Hawaii, a fashion reporter in Milan, and layout specialists in New York and Melbourne. In such examples of computer-supported cooperative work, as the work day ends in one part of the world, a time-constrained project can be handed off to others many time zones away.

Enhancing Customer Service

Although many people think that electronic ordering and payment are essential elements of electronic commerce, they are among the riskier transactions and are usually not necessary for significant improvement in customer service. The emerging examples of electronic commerce enhance the purchasing process in a wide variety of ways, often by providing the customer with better access to information about the product and its uses. For instance, a number of firms in high-technology industries are providing inter-ested prospective customers with solicited announcements of new products via electronic mail notification. Additional marketing and technical information can then be retrieved by the customer from an online data repository accessible via the Internet or a proprietary network.

Similar marketing repositories can identify retail outlets where the product can be purchased, prospective custo-mers can listen to segments of recorded music, or test out software prior to purchase. In some instances, such as in the semiconductor industry, customers can design or help to design the products. Customers with access to the World Wide Web are being given the ability to design simple made-to-order products such as T-shirts, business cards, flower arrangements, and so on, thus providing us with a small taste of the opportunities in electronic commerce that should soon follow.

After the sale, there are continued opportunities to enhance the customer's use of the product. For instance, Federal Express uses the World Wide Web to let customers track the process of package deliveries. Similarly, Millipore, a manufacturer of filtration equipment and chemicals, gives its customers access to a database showing how their various chemical products react with other chemicals. Software developers are providing updates online, and computer manufacturers provide access to their internal help desk support DATABASES. In a similar manner, car companies might provide customers with maintenance histories of particular cars or mortgage companies details on escrow accounts and the like.

Products Appropriate for Electronic Distribution
Eventually, however, many products will be ordered, paid for, and even delivered electronically. It is still not obvious what products will be the best candidates to move to an electronic distribution system, but among the likely attributes are those that are information-based, are time sensitive in their value, and are expensive to distribute by current means. Prospective customers who are already connected to electronic networks would also seem to be necessary and, fortunately, this pool is rapidly expanding. Software, information databases, and CD-music are examples of likely candidates, and electronic marketing and distribution channels have recently emerged for many products within these product classes. As the price of computers and communication decreases, the quality of the customer interface will increase. Computers will also become more and more portable as they are increasingly connected to cellular communication networks. With these improvements, more and more aspects of electronic commerce will become possible (including realistic face-to-face videoconferencing) and more products will be sold and distributed electronically.

New Business Rules
Although inevitable and rapidly approaching, the future of electronic commerce is difficult to predict based on today's business rules. The new technologies will create new business rules. One new rule has been mentioned already: that firms will inexpensively, although perhaps unintentionally, market to an audience throughout the world. A second emerging rule is that customers will increasingly have to be motivated to pull marketing information from the network rather than having it pushed at them as in traditional advertising. Firms will need to find creative ways to ensure that customers find their product descriptions. A variety of new mechanisms will have to be pursued. For instance, in the past a professor requiring a new textbook for a course might have looked at the publisher's catalogs, the list of free examination copies distributed by the publishers, or spoken to a publisher's representative (all marketing channels designed and controlled by publishers). In the future that instructor might be more likely to go and look on the network to see what book an admired professor had listed in his course syllabus, seek guidance from a discussion list of peers teaching the same course, or query a professional association's edited information repository of resource information for the particular course. None of these marketing channels is directly controlled by the publisher and each provides a worldwide channel for an independent producer, say a textbook-writing professor, to take advantage of.

The example of the professor assumes that there will be a future requirement for textbooks. A third business rule likely to change is the form of products, particularly information-based products (e.g. books, magazines, music, theater, movies, education), which potentially can be electronically distributed. A heritage of paper-driven commerce has left us with product packages such as books, journals, music recordings, catalogs, yellow page directories, and so on. These packages are often tied to the economics of paper-based production. In the distant future, for instance, the publisher of a scholarly journal should be less likely to wait three months and then publish a largely unrelated set of articles (a heritage traceable to the economics of the printing process). A more likely model is for individual scholarly works to be published electronically as they are accepted by their peers. So, too, perhaps for the works of performing artists, which might be released one title at a time and carefully targeted, perhaps by using the World Wide Web to reach members of a performer's fan club located throughout the world.

The ability to target a relatively small group for high margin returns is likely to be a fourth rule of the new electronic commerce. Textbooks are likely to fall victim to such personalization. They may be replaced by loose modules of knowledge woven together by an individual faculty. Already we are seeing versions of this with tailored textbooks now being offered by some publishers. These permit an individual faculty member to select from among a set of candidate chapters, cases, articles, and perhaps his or her own publications.

Market targeting and personalization can be as narrow as a single customer. For instance, an electronic newspaper might be individually tailored to the interests of a particular subscriber. Similarly, yellow page-like searches of electronic *databases* can generate not only indexes but advertisements based on the search criteria.

Barriers to Innovations in Electronic Commerce
Electronic commerce still faces many barriers. As electronic commerce moves away from proprietary networks and toward the open and largely unregulated Internet, there will be increased opportunities for fraud. SECURITY OF INFORMATION SYSTEM procedures are being devised to authenticate the identity of both the buyer and seller and to permit the transfer of payments in a secure manner. The issue of fraud and security is not unique to the Internet, however, and some level of loss will probably be acceptable. Nevertheless, the current publicity surrounding the weaknesses of the Internet have delayed the involvement of many firms. Technological problems beyond security must be overcome. At present the Internet is a relatively slow and unreliable delivery mechanism that can make even the most professional market presence appear poorly conceived. For instance, using electronic networks to display graphic images or transfer sound gives a prospective customer a richer view of the product, but they take a long time to transfer, particularly for users from countries remote from the computer providing the data.

There are also operational problems to overcome. The availability of a worldwide distribution system, though convenient, can often extend a firm's marketing reach beyond its ability to distribute or support. Further, products and brands that are tailored to particular cultures or countries may be difficult to differentiate or even inappropriate on a global marketing platform. Dealing with multiple languages is another operational concern as is providing 24 hours a day manned support systems.

A variety of public policy issues must also be addressed, and from an international context. One is the issue of PRIVACY IN INFORMATION SYSTEMS; customers worry that their purchase behavior will be available without their permission or that they will be the targets of unsolicited mailings. The technical solutions related to the security of financial transactions, particularly data encryption, raise other public policy issues such as whether a government will let its citizens use a security scheme that cannot be broken by government security specialists. To condone the use of these programs may leave society open to threats from criminals and other governments, as well as from tax avoiders. The protection of intellectual property issues is another concern. The client/server architecture of the Internet makes it very easy to appropriate and modify images, sounds, text, and the general look and feel of the productions of others. Variations in the protection of intellectual property from one country to another further complicate the problem. Some areas of electronic commerce also are perceived as socially unacceptable in a particular culture. Pornography, gambling, or information on the making of nuclear weapons are uses of the Internet that could lead to attempts to create and enforce regulations. Such regulations, though probably difficult to enforce for illegitimate businesses, could nevertheless have negative consequences for legitimate businesses. But, because of the ability to quickly relocate electronic businesses anywhere in the world, the regulatory issues are complicated and not readily solved by regulation within any one country.

The magnitude of change that electronic commerce will mean for many industries suggests that there will be institutional resistance to protect the status quo and past investments. Such resistance, coupled with the relatively low costs of entry for early participants, will produce many new start-up firms, some of which are likely to be very successful. Industry boundaries are likely to shift and new forms of business evolve. On the other hand, these same factors will lead to an increase in the amount of economic disruption experienced by many currently successful firms and industries. Such disruptions are likely to be widespread and painful for many sectors of societies and their economies.

BLAKE IVES

embargo To embargo is to prohibit or forbid the movement of certain or all goods to a certain country or countries. One of the most recent embargoes was that placed against Iraq after its invasion of Kuwait in the early 1990s. As of the writing of this book (mid-1995) much of that embargo is still in place. As with the United Nations' sanctioned embargo of Iraq, most embargoes are implemented in times of war or to attempt to force political change other than by military force. Embargoes are difficult to implement and even more difficult to enforce over long periods of time. Embargoes not only harm the country to which they are imposed, but also all of the international exporters and support organizations who were involved with export of goods and services to that country.

Bibliography
Korth, C. (1985). *Barriers to international business.* Englewood Cliffs, NJ: Prentice-Hall.

JOHN O'CONNELL

emergent strategy Emergent strategy, as termed by Mintzberg (1987), is a strategy that is not carefully pre-planned; it is realized in the absence of intentions, or despite unrealized intentions. As Mintzberg notes: "strategies can form as well as be *formulated.* A realized strategy can emerge in response to an evolving situation, or it can be brought

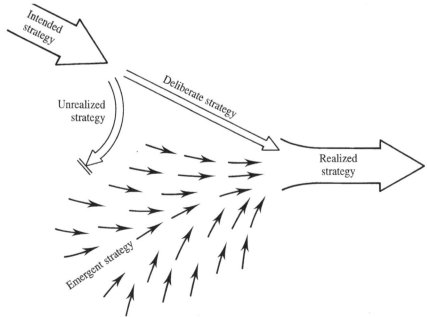

Figure 1   Emergent Strategy
Source: Mintzberg, 1987.

about deliberately, through a process of formulation followed by implementation." Such a view is in contrast to traditional STRATEGIC PLANNING which is founded on the premise that it is possible to analyze the MARKETING ENVIRONMENT, forecast possible outcomes, select strategic alternatives based on an evaluation of the returns each is likely to yield, and devise plans to implement the chosen strategic options in order to ensure that they come about. However, it is increasingly recognized that UNCERTAINTY considerably clouds the ability to predict all the possible influences and therefore possibilities that might arise. Consequently, there may be unforeseen opportunities and difficulties. Even carefully planned strategies might lead to different outcomes to those sought. (See figure 1.)

Bibliography

Mintzberg, H. (1987). Five Ps for strategy. *California Management Review*, **30**, (1), Fall.

DALE LITTLER

emotions in organizations   The study of emotions in organizations stems from the acknowledgment that our experience of work is often essentially about feelings, such as of hate, joy, tedium, jealousy, pride, anger. While this might seem an obvious point, research in organizational behavior has been slow to grasp the emotional complexity of work life, focusing more on attitudes toward work, such as JOB SATISFACTION, or extreme negative states relating to impaired performance, such as STRESS.

Although there is no strong consensus on the definitions of feelings and emotions, some useful distinctions can be drawn. A feeling is essentially a subjective experience, a personal awareness of some bodily state, perturbation or more diffuse psychological change. Some writers argue that certain feelings of working have a special status, a flow-related experience where the self is absorbed – such as getting "lost" in one's work of writing, painting, repairing, or negotiating. This form of acquaintance-knowledge is as yet unexplored in social science (Sandelands, 1988).

Emotion episodes and private feeling do not always correspond – one can "be" angry without feeling angry. With dramatic skill, emotion display can be used strategically or politically in organizations to attract attention or influence decisions or relationships (*see* IMPRESSION MANAGEMENT). Emotions are also situation-ally/normatively defined – the "correct" emotions for an office party, boardroom, meeting a client, job interview, or redundancy announcement. The social constitution and construction of emotions suggests that people tacitly "negotiate" the form and boundaries of appropriate emotional display, and that feelings can change on personal reflection, telling, and through argument.

Traditionally, emotional processes have been separated from cognitive, thinking, ones. It has been claimed that rationality in organizations is achievable if interfering emotions can be controlled or obliterated. For example, psychoanalytic theorists contend that personal anxieties, often stemming from primitive, unconscious, vulnerabilities, are enacted in work life, and they hinder effective LEADERSHIP and group processes. People cope with these anxieties by producing protective individual and social defenses – which prevent rational thought and action. The task of the psychoanalytic consultant is to treat the organ-ization like a diseased patient, and bring it to healthy rationality (Kets de Vries, 1991).

Other writers suggest optimal rationality is unattainable. Hunches, acts of faith, and feelings will unlock a problem or change the course of events. Feelings will steer us down some paths and guide us away from others. Processes of emotions and rationality are still relatively distinct, but the former serve the latter (Frank, 1993). A more radical approach goes a step further in insisting that emotions and rationality are in fact inseparable, as is thinking and feeling. We have feelings about what we want and what we want is infused with feelings; feelings are intrinsic, not residual to individual, interpersonal, and group functioning (Kemper, 1993).

Given that self-regulation is a very large part of what makes organization possible, emotions may be considered intrinsic to organizational order. They will influence a range of behaviors, from loyalty and honesty to COMMIT-MENT and care. In a sense, ORGANIZATIONAL CULTURE is the emotional order of the organization, features of which can be openly exploited, or engineered. Where a "strong" culture is desired, an atmosphere of excitement, enthusiasm, or passion for the task or company is orchestrated through social events, bonding rituals, and scripts reinforcing the company's "way" (Van Maanen and Kunda, 1989).

Company control of emotional performance can be seen to be relatively benign, even fun, "all about good acting." The enthusiasm, smiles, and "have a nice day," common to many corporate office encounters and service transactions, can be split off from private feeling – in order to sustain the organizational act or social game. But some writers have argued that this is not always the case. The "emotional labor" (i.e., being employed to smile, enthuse, be sincere, etc.) can be an onerous, identity-disturbing, form of role taking (Hochschild, 1983; Wouters, 1989).

Emotional labor is, to a degree, built into many professional jobs, where presented image or demeanor has to be learned and sustained to maintain a proper role – such as nurse, doctor, lawyer, or banker. If the emotional mask slips, the professional encounter is threatened. Emotional labor tends to be most onerous in jobs with low autonomy, where one group can impose their valuation of emotionality on another group (especially men on women) and where people represent their companies to outsiders.

see also **Personality**

Bibliography

Fineman, S. (Ed.) (1993). Emotion in organizations. London: Sage.

Frank, R. H. (1993). The strategic role of the emotions. Rationality and Society, **5**, (3), 160–194.

Hochschild, A. (1983). The managed heart. Berkeley: University of California.

Kemper, T. D. (1993). Reasons in emotions or emotions in reason. Rationality and Society, **5**, (3), 275–282.

Kets de Vries, M. F. R. (Ed.) (1991). Organizations on the Couch: Clinical perspectives on organizational behavior and change. San Francisco: Jossey Bass.

Pekrun, R. & Frese, M. (1992). Emotions in work and achievement. In C. L. Cooper & I. T. Robertson (Eds), International review of industrial and organizational psychology. (Vol. 7) Chichester, UK: Wiley.

Sandelands, L. E. (1988). The concept of work feeling. Journal for the Theory of Social Behavior, 18, (4), 437–457.

Van Maanen, J. & Kunda, G. (1989). 'Real feelings': Emotional expression and organizational culture. Research in Organizational Behavior, 11, 43–103.

Wouters, C. (1989). The sociology of emotions and flight attendants: Hochschild's 'Managed Heart' Theory, Culture and Society, 6, (1), 95–123.

STEPHEN FINEMAN

employability Employability, as opposed to employment security, is a new form of PSYCHOLOGICAL CONTRACT between employers and employees. It implies three elements in the employment relationship: (a) the employee is responsible for developing the right skills to be employable inside and outside the company; (b) the employer is responsible for providing employees information, time, resources, and opportunities to assess and develop skills that are needed; and (c) the employment relationship can be dissolved if the employee's contribution or aspiration does not match the employer's needs.

Employability emerged in the late 1980s because of two contributing forces. First, many companies like IBM cannot afford their traditional commitment to employment security in the midst of DOWNSIZING and restructuring. Second, new business realities mandate companies to be flexible to capture changing business opportunities. For example, one of Intel's strategic capabilities is to shift its resources (especially people) swiftly from declining businesses to emerging businesses.

Employability requires a supportive infrastructure in four areas (Waterman et al., 1994): (a) a change in attitudes and values – shifting loyalty from company to individual career; (b) open sharing of information – future business direction and required competencies; (c) resource allocation to offer employees self-assessment and continuous learning; and (d) clear and fair procedures to transfer and redeploy employees.

Researchers have different views on employability. While some believe that it may improve organizational productivity and flexibility (Waterman et al., 1994), others are concerned about its impact on employee commitment and contribution to companies (Pfeffer, 1994).

Bibliography

Pfeffer, J. (1994). *Competitive Advantage through People*, Boston: Harvard Business School Press.

Waterman, R. H., Waterman, J. A. & Collard, B. A. (1994). Toward a career resilient workforce. *Harvard Business Review*, **July–August**, 87–95.

ARTHUR K. YEUNG

employee involvement Employee involvement refers to the process of engaging employees in their work and increasing their participation in decision-making. In particular, employee involvement ensures that employees who are closest to the work have the power to control work methods, and are able to use their knowledge and skills to improve work processes (Lawler, 1992). This approach also attempts to move information and power downward in the organization, so that employees can work autonomously and regulate their own behavior (Cummings and Worley, 1993). As a consequence, organizations that use this approach typically experience a flattening of the organizational hierarchy.

Although there is no one theoretical basis for employee involvement, it is derived from a number of key human relations assumptions (see, for example, Argyris, 1957). Specifically, it is assumed that when employees are given challenging work, and allowed to participate in decision-making, they will (a) become more motivated and willing to control their own behavior, (b) become more involved in their work, (c) increase their commitment to organizational goals, and (d) use their skills and abilities to make valuable contributions to organizational goals.

Employee involvement has been used as the foundation for a wide array of management programs, including: quality circles, JOB INVOLVEMENT, quality of work life programs, EMPLOYEE EMPOWERMENT, and total quality management.

Bibliography

Argyris, C. (1957). *Personality and Organization*, New York: Harper Collins.

Cummings, T. & Worley, C. (1993). *Organizational Development and Change*, **5th edn**, Minneapolis: West.

Lawler, E. E. (1992). *The Ultimate Advantage: Creating the High Involvement Organization*, San Francisco: Jossey-Bass.

DIANNA L. STONE

employer unfair labor practices Sections 8(a)(1) through 8(a)(5) of the National Labor Relations Act (Wagner Act of 1935) contain five employer unfair labor practices. Unfair labor practice charges are filed with the NATIONAL LABOR RELATIONS BOARD (NLRB) and may be appealed to a US Circuit Court. Section 8(a)(1) forbids an employer from interfering with, restraining, or coercing employees who join, form, or assist a labor organization (union). Section 8(a)(2) makes it unlawful for an employer to dominate or interfere with a labor organization. This section was originally used to eliminate company unions and sweetheart arrangements between employers and labor organizations. EMPLOYEE INVOLVEMENT programs, work teams, and action committees have recently been the subject of litigation under this section of the Act. Section 8(a)(3) makes it illegal for an employer to discriminate against employees because of their union affiliation or sympathies. Threatening to fire employees, giving pay raises during a union organizing campaign, closing or relocating a plant that becomes unionized, or spying on union meetings are all potential violations of section 8(a)(3). Section 8(a)(4) prohibits an employer from retaliating against a person who testifies in a NLRB hearing. Section 8(a)(5) requires employers to bargain in good faith with a certified bargaining representative. Good faith bargaining requires that employers meet at a reasonable time and place with union negotiators, supply them with relevant information, avoid delays or evasive bargaining tactics, and refrain from taking unilateral action on existing contract terms (e.g. changing the pay scale in the collective bargaining agreement without consulting union officials) (Norris and Shershin, 1992; Leap, 1995).

Bibliography

Leap, T. L. (1995). *Collective Bargaining and Labor Relations*, **2nd edn**, Englewood Cliffs, NJ: Prentice-Hall.

Norris, J. A. & Shershin, M. J. (1992). *How to Take a Case Before the NLRB*, **6th edn**, Washington, DC.

TERRY L. LEAP

employment at will   The principle of Employment at Will (EAW) is a common-law doctrine stating that, in the absence of law or contract, employers have the right to hire, promote, demote, and fire whomever and whenever they please. The principle was stated explicitly in 1887 by H. G. Wood (Wood, 1887).

In the United States EAW has been interpreted as the rule that when employees are not specifically covered by union agreement, legal statute, public policy, or contract, an employer "may dismiss their employees at will . . . for good cause, for no cause, *or even for causes morally wrong*, without being thereby guilty of legal wrong" (Blades, 1967, p. 1405). Today at least 60 percent of all employees in the private sector of the economy, from part-time or temporary workers to corporate presidents, are "at will" employees.

EAW has been widely interpreted as allowing employees to be demoted, transferred, or dismissed without having a hearing and without requirement of good reasons or "cause" for the employment decision. This is not to say that employers do not have reasons, usually good reasons, for their decisions. But there is no legal obligation to state or defend their decisions. Thus EAW sidesteps the requirement of due process or grievance procedures in the workplace, although it does not preclude the institution of such procedures.

As a recognized common-law principle, traditionally EAW has been upheld in the US state and federal courts. However, in the last 15 years legal statutes have increased the number of employees who are protected from EAW, including those protected by equal opportunity and age discrimination legislation. Moreover, what is meant by "public policy" has been expanded. For example, cases in which an employee has been asked to break a law or to violate a stated public policy, cases where employees are not allowed to exercise certain constitutional rights such as the right to vote, serve on a jury, or collect worker compensation are all considered wrongful discharges. Employees won 67 percent of their suits on wrongful discharge during a recent three-year period. These suits were won, not on the basis of a rejection of the principle of EAW, but rather because of breach of contract, lack of just cause for dismissal when a company grievance policy was in place, or violations of public policy (Geyelin, 1989, B1).

EAW is often justified for one or more of the following reasons:

1 The proprietary rights of employers guarantee that they may employ or dismiss whomever and whenever they wish.
2 EAW defends employee, managerial, and employer rights equally, in particular the right to freedom of contract, because an employee voluntarily contracts to be hired and can quit at any time.
3 In choosing to take a job, an employee voluntarily commits herself to certain responsibilities and company loyalty, including the knowledge that she is an "at will" employee.
4 Extending due-process rights and other employee protections in the workplace often interferes with the efficiency and productivity of the business organization.
5 Legislation and/or regulation of employment relationships further undermine an already over-regulated economy.

On the other side, there are a number of criticisms of EAW. Perhaps the most serious is that while EAW is defended as preserving employer and employee rights equally, it is sometimes interpreted as justifying arbitrary treatment of employees. This is analogous to considering an employee as a piece of property at the disposal of the employer or corporation. When I "fire" a robot, I do not have to give reasons, because a robot is not a rational being; it has no use for reasons. On the other hand, if I fire a person arbitrarily I am making the assumption that she does not need reasons for the decision, a questionable logic. If I have hired persons, then I should treat them as such, with respect throughout the employment process. This does not preclude firing, but it does ask employers to give reasons for their actions, for reasons are appropriate when one is dealing with persons.

There are other grounds for not abusing EAW as part of recognizing equal obligations implied by freedom of contract. Arbitrariness, although not prohibited by EAW, violates the managerial model of rationality and consistency. This ideal is implied by a consistent application of this common-law principle, that EAW protects employees, managers, and employers equally and fairly. We expect managers, in their roles as employers, to act reasonably and consistently in their decision-making. Not giving reasons for employment decisions belies that expectation. Thus even if EAW itself is justifiable, the practice of EAW, when interpreted as condoning arbitrary employment decisions, is not.

Looking ahead, the signs are clear that the doctrine of EAW will continue to be refined and challenged. Within the corporation new approaches to work and organizational activity are bringing new modes of employee participation that encourage greater employee expression. The challenge for management and employees is to find creative ways to minimize burdensome litigation while at the same time balancing employer and employee rights.

Bibliography

Arvanites, D. & Ward, B. T. (1990). Employment at will: A social concept in decline. In J. J. Desjardins & J. J. McCall (eds), *Contemporary Issues in Business Ethics*, 2nd edn, Belmont, Calif.: Wadsworth Publishing, 147–54.

Blades, L. E. (1967). Employment at will versus individual freedom: On limiting the abusive exercise of employer power. *Columbia Law Review*, 67.

Ewing, D. (1983). *Do It My Way or You're Fired!* New York: John Wiley.

Feinman, J. M. (1991). The development of the employment at will rule revisited. *Arizona State Law Journal*, 23, 733–40.

Geyelin, M. (1989). Fired managers winning more lawsuits. *Wall Street Journal*, 7 Sept., B1.

Hutton v Watters. (1915). 132 Tenn. 527, S.W. 134.

Payne v. *Western*. (1884). 81 Tenn. 507.

Summers, C. B. (1980). Protecting *all* employees against unjust dismissal. *Harvard Business Review*, Jan./Feb.

Werhane, P. H. (1985). *Persons, Rights, and Corporations*. Englewood Cliffs, NJ: Prentice-Hall.

Wood, H. G. (1887). *A Treatise on the Law of Master and Servant*. Albany, NY: John D. Parsons.

PATRICIA H. WERHANE

employment interview   The employment interview is defined as a dialogue initiated by one or more persons to gather and evaluate information on the qualifications of a job applicant (Dipboye, 1992). With the possible exception of reference checks and application blanks, this is the most frequently used technique of personnel selection. Even when other selection procedures are used, information often influences the final decision only after it has been filtered through interviewer judgments.

Structured and Unstructured Interviews

An important basis for distinguishing among types of interviews is the degree to which they are structured. Most interviews tend to be unstructured in that few constraints are placed on how they go about gathering information and evaluating applicants. At the other end of the continuum are the highly structured interviews in which interviewers are required to ask the same questions in the same way of all applicants, with no follow-up questions or other deviations allowed (Campion et al., 1988). An example is the SITUATIONAL INTERVIEW. The questions are usually focused on specific requirements of the job and the answers of all applicants are quantitatively scored relative to a common set of predetermined standards. The "patterned interview" falls somewhere between these two extremes. One example is the Patterned Behavior Description Interview (Janz et al., 1986). Similar to the highly structured interview, the patterned interview is focused on specific requirements of the job and the questioning and evaluation of applicants is standardized. However, interviewers in a patterned interview are allowed more discretion in gathering information and can ask follow-up questions.

The Validity and Reliability of Interviews

Similar to other selection techniques, employment interviews are evaluated on their reliability and validity. Typically, reliability has been assessed by examining the extent to which interviewers agree in evaluating the same applicants. Validity is usually assessed by examining the relationship of interviewer judgments at the time of application to the applicants' later performance on the job.

Several recent meta-analyses have provided insight into the features of interviews that can enhance their reliability and validity (Wiesner and Cronshaw, 1988; Marchese and Muchinsky, 1993; Huffcut and Arthur, 1994; McDaniel et al., 1994). The findings suggest that the questions and rating dimensions used in interviews should be based on formal JOB ANALYSIS and interviewers should not have access to applicants' test scores prior to the interview. On the other hand, the findings do not provide strong support for using "board interviews." The most consistent finding across these meta-analyses is that structured interviews are more valid than those that are unstructured. Indeed, the levels of validity that have been found for structured interviews approach the validities that have been found for mental abilities tests, which are considered to be among the best techniques for employee selection. Exactly how much structure is needed is still open for debate. There is some evidence that interviews with high levels of structure are no more valid than more moderately structured interviews (Huffcut and Arthur, 1994). Another issue that remains unresolved is whether the level of prediction achieved with a highly structured interview can exceed the level of prediction achieved with well-constructed objective procedures such as mental abilities tests, biographical application blanks, or weighted application blanks. Some structured

interviews may measure attributes that can be more cheaply measured with paper-and-pencil measures at no loss of validity (Dipboye, 1989).

Why Structured Inteviews Are More Reliable and Valid

The research on interview processes suggests that the subjectivity of the typical interview can lead to a variety of interviewer errors. Structuring the interview may improve the validity and reliability of interviewer judgments because it helps to eliminate these errors. One likely source of advantage is that structured interviewing procedures are based on formal job analyses and are consequently more job-related than unstructured procedures. A second potential advantage of the various structured formats is the manner in which they handle ancillary data. Interviewers usually have other sources of information on applicants, such as test scores, biographical data, reference checks, and school transcripts, and their final impressions also can be influenced, to some extent, by these data (Dipboye, 1989). Structured interviews either do not allow interviewers to preview such ancillary information, or provide for a more structured preview of this information than found in the typical unstructured interview. Finally, structured interviews incorporate a variety of procedures in the judgment phase of the process that have been shown in previous research to enhance the accuracy and reliability of judgment. Interviewers are encouraged to delay their evaluation of the applicant until after the session, thus separating information gathering from the final integration and evaluation of information. Also, well-defined rating scales, such as the BEHAVIORALLY ANCHORED RATING SCALES, are often provided. This is in contrast to the use of graphic rating scales that are so often found in unstructured interviews.

In the formation of a final judgment of the applicant's qualifications, structured procedures statistically combine the information gathered on the applicant, usually through simple averaging or summation of ratings. In contrast, the global evaluations formed with unstructured procedures allow interviewers to combine their impressions of applicants using intuitive and idiosyncratic combinations.

The use of interviews is pervasive in the selection of employees. It should be noted, however, that they serve a variety of other functions in addition to selection. The most notable of these alternative functions is RECRUITING. The research suggests, however, that if the objective is selection then the interview should be focused solely on the assessment of applicants' job qualifications. To fulfill other functions, such as recruitment, separate interview sessions should be arranged that are kept independent from assessment of the applicant. Moreover, the interview should be structured. Although some individual interviewers may be quite effective in assessing applicants even in the context of an unstructured interview, most interviewers fall far short of what is considered to be acceptable levels of validity and reliability when allowed to follow their intuitions.

Bibliography

Campion, M. A., Pursell, E. D. & Brown, B. K. (1988). Structured interviewing: raising the psychometric properties of the employment interview. *Personnel Psychology*, 41, 25–42.
Dipboye, R. L. (1989). Threats to the incremental validity of interviewer judgments. *The Employment Interview: Theory,*

Research, and Practice, Eds. Eder, R. W. & Ferris, G. R. Newbury Park, CA: Sage Publications.

Dipboye, R. L. (1992). *Selection Interviews: Process Perspectives*, Cincinnati, OH: South-Western.

Huffcutt, A. I. & Arthur, W. Jr (1994). Hunter and Hunter (1984) revisited: interview validity for entry-level jobs. *Journal of Applied Psychology*, 79, 184–90.

Janz, T., Hellervik, L. & Gilmore, D. (1986). *Behavior Description Interviewing: New, Accurate, Cost-effective*, Boston: Allyn and Bacon.

McDaniel, M. A., Whetzel, D. L., Schmidt, F. L. & Maurer, S. (1994). The validity of employment interviews: a comprehensive review and meta-analysis. *Journal of Applied Psychology*, 79, 599–616.

Marchese, M. C. & Muchinsky, P. M. (1993). The validity of the employment interview: a meta-analysis. *International Journal of Selection and Assessment*, 1, 18–26.

Wiesner, W. H. & Cronshaw, S. R. (1988). The moderating impact of interview format and degree of structure on interview validity. *Journal of Occupational Psychology*, 61, 275–90.

ROBERT L. DIPBOYE

empowerment   Prior to its adoption as a management term, the word empowerment was most often used, in fields such as politics, social work, feminist theory, and Third World aid. Writers in these fields have taken it to mean providing individuals (usually disadvantaged) with the tools and resources to further their own interests, *as they see them*. Within the field of management, empowerment is commonly used with a different meaning: providing employees with tools, resources, and discretion to further the interests of the organization (as seen by senior management).

Conger and Kanungo (1988) define empowerment as a psychological construct. They suggest that empowerment is the process of fostering self efficacy beliefs among employees. This implies both removing sources of powerlessness and providing employees with positive feedback and support.

Empowerment, in this sense of a psychological construct, is a principal goal of most forms of EMPLOYEE INVOLVEMENT.

see also **Decision making; Power; Influence**

Bibliography

Conger, J. A. & Kanungo, R. N. (1988). The empowerment process: Integrating theory and practice. Academy of Management Review., 13, 471–482.

MARK FENTON-O'CREEVY

end-user computing   Prior to the 1980s, the information systems (IS) function maintained a virtual monopoly over the acquisition, deployment, and operation of information technology resources. Many of these responsibilities have been transferred to those who use the information. These are termed "end users." Three major forces explain the transformation process:

1 *Hardware and software improvements* have increased the availability, affordability, and usability of information technologies. Microcomputers, personal productivity software (e.g. spreadsheets, database management systems, and word processing), fourth-generation languages, personal peripheral devices (e.g. mice, pen-based interfaces, and laser printers), tele-communications and net-

works support widespread individual use of information technology.

2 Enhanced *computer-related knowledge and skills* within the end-use community have motivated and enabled end users to use IS products and technologies.

3 An *organizational environment* conducive toward end-user computing (EUC) has fostered the employment of EUC products and technologies as productivity enhancement tools.

Types of End Users

End-user computing is a diverse phenomenon. End users can be categorized based on variables such as computer skill, method of use, application focus, education and training requirements, and need for ongoing support. Four categories represent end users:

1 *Non-programming end users*. These users access computerized data through a limited menu or graphical user interface (GUI)-based environment. They follow a well-defined set of procedures. Software is provided by others.

2 *Command-level users*. Users perform inquiries and simple calculations such as summation and generate unique reports for their own purposes. They understand the availability database(s) and are able to specify, access, and manipulate information.

3 *End-user programmers*. These users utilize both command and procedural languages directly for their individual information needs. They develop their own applications, some of which are used by others. Use by others is a by-product of what is essentially analytic programming performed on a "personal basis" by quantitatively oriented managers and professionals.

4 *Functional support personnel*. They support other end users within their particular functional area. By virtue of their skill with information technology, they have become informal centers of systems design and development expertise. In spite of the time spent supporting other end users, these individuals do not view themselves as programmers or IS professionals. Rather they are market researchers, financial analysts, and so forth, whose primary task within their function is to provide tools and processes to access and analyze data.

Benefits and Risks

There are a number of significant advantages to end-user development applications. First, EUC provides some relief from the shortage of development personnel. A common complaint by users is that they cannot get the IS solutions they need when they need them. There are not enough analysts and programmers to keep up with the demand.

Secondly, EUC eliminates the problem of REQUIREMENTS DETERMINATION FOR INFORMATION SYSTEMS by IS personnel. One of the major problems in information systems is the eliciting of a complete and correct set of requirements. Various techniques and methodologies have been proposed, but it still remains a difficult process. The problem is made more difficult because the analyst is an outsider who must be able to communicate with a user in eliciting the requirements that the user may not fully understand him or herself. While having users develop their own system may not eliminate the problem of obtaining requirements, it does place an "insider" in the role of requirements problem-solver.

Thirdly, EUC transfers the IS implementation process to end users. This transfer effectively eliminates the potential conflict from technical system experts and non-technical users, one of the major reasons why systems are not utilized. Users may develop less sophisticated systems when they do the design and development themselves, but they will use them.

EUC also poses a number of serious risks to the organization. First, elimination of the role of systems analyst also results in the elimination of an external reviewer throughout the development process. The systems analyst provides an organizational mechanism for enforcing standards, supplying technical expertise, and providing an independent review of requirements.

Secondly, there are limits to a user's ability to identify correct and complete requirements for an application. For example, human cognitive limits stem from behavior based on anchoring and adjustment, concreteness, recency, intuitive statistical analysis, and the structure of the problem space. In addition, errors in decision-making relative to requirements result from over-analysis and inefficient search, solving the wrong problem and applying a wrong analysis or model. Thirdly, there is often a lack of user knowledge and acceptance of application quality assurance procedures for development and operation. This risk is evidenced in testing, documentation, validation procedures, audit trails, and operating controls.

Management of EUC
The challenge for organizations is to find ways to manage EUC to maximize the benefits of EUC while minimizing the risks. Though management may be perceived as encompassing many different attributes, the three most critical attributes relating to EUC are the following:

1 *Policy setting and planning.* Policy setting identifies appropriate EUC practices and clarifies the acceptable form of outcomes concerning EUC activities. Planning efforts are aimed at identifying goals/objectives and establishing the framework for coordination and allocation of resources to EUC activities.
2 *Support.* EUC support refers to activities such as provision of tools and training opportunities that enhance the development and growth of EUC in organizations.
3 *Control.* Control processes ensure that planned activities are performed effectively/efficiently and in compliance with policies and plans.

End-user computing is expected to be a permanent phenomenon. It requires resources that must be managed carefully to ensure proper diffusion and use within the organization. Technical and managerial infrastructures need to be created to support EUC at all levels of the organization (i.e. individual, departmental/work group, and organizational).

R. RYAN NELSON

entry documents   When goods are imported into a country they first must pass through customs for inspection, application of duties, and formal review of documents required for entry. If entry documents are not made available or are incomplete, goods will not normally be allowed to enter. Entry documents which may be required include:

1 Commercial invoice – A commercial invoice is a document which is used to provide details of an international trade transaction. Information normally required includes: buyer and seller's names, types of property, value of goods, origin and destination points, and parties accepting delivery of goods.
2 Pro forma invoice – Sometimes the commercial invoice associated with an export/import transaction is not available when goods are ready to enter a country. The US customs authorities allow the importer to substitute a pro forma invoice until the original commercial invoice can be presented.
3 Customs invoice – Some countries require a customs invoice. A customs invoice must be completed on the form specified by the country. The invoice includes information which the country desires to know but which is not found on the ordinary commercial invoice.
4 Entry manifest or customs manifest – Some countries require that a specific form, referred to as an entry or customs manifest be provided. The manifest acts as documentation of the release of the goods.
5 Proof of right of entry (bill of lading or evidence of title or possession) – Documents used to prove ownership or legal possession of goods are needed in order to allow their entry. In other words, proof that the goods are being brought to a country by a party who has the legal right to seek entry for those goods.
6 Packing list – Generally a shipper will prepare a form that lists the types and quantities of goods being shipped. The list is used by the shipper and the receiver of goods to verify receipt of goods. This list may also be required by some customs authorities.
7 Certificate of origin – Some countries impose tariffs on certain goods from certain countries. In order to determine which imported goods are subject to tariffs, a country may require a document certifying the country of origin of the goods. The certificate allows a country to properly assess applicable tariffs or to release goods in a shorter period of time if no duties are payable.
8 Certificate of health – When exporting goods which are meant for human consumption or for use in medical care of humans, all countries require that certification of the product's purity be provided. The document is generally required to be certified by appropriate officials of the exporting country. The intent of health certification is to reduce the chances of importing contaminated goods which may cause disease or introduce pests into a country.
9 Surety bond – Customs authorities often require importers to post a bond to guarantee payment of duties or other assessments. If duties and costs are not paid the customs authority may apply to the surety for payment under the bond.
10 Phytosanitary inspection certificate – A phytosanitary inspection certificate is an official government statement from the exporting country that exports of plants, animals, meat, and other commodities have been inspected and are free from disease or insects which

might damage the health or agriculture of the importing country.

11 Miscellaneous documents – Customs authorities also may request special documents associated with certain types of property or for imports from certain countries.

Importers and exporters should seek assistance from the customs authorities of each country before entering into import/export contracts. This will allow the identification of documents required to complete the transaction.

Bibliography

Albaum, Gerald, Strandskov, Jesper, Duerr, Edwin & Dowd, Lawrence (1994). *International marketing and export management.* 2nd edn, Wokingham: Addison-Wesley.

Deresky, Helen (1994). *International management.* 1st edn, New York: HarperCollins.

International Chamber of Commerce (ICC) (1990). *Incoterms 1990.* New York, NY: ICC Publishing Corp.

Johnson, T. E. (1994). *Export–Import procedures and documentation.* New York: Amacom.

United States Customs Service (1994). *A basic guide to importing.* Lincolnwood, IL: NTC Publishing Group.

Zodl, J. A. (1992). *Export–Import: Everything you and your company need to know to compete in world markets.* Cincinnati, OH: Betterway Books.

JOHN O'CONNELL

environmental analysis   Organizations exist within a complex and dynamic environment which can be described as the MARKETING ENVIRONMENT. Understanding this environment is one of the most important and difficult aspects of management and has traditionally been regarded as a marketing responsibility (*see* MARKETING AUDIT). Obviously, the number of variables influencing this marketing environment are many, so environmental analysis attempts to identify the most influential factors and trends affecting the organization and its offerings.

Kotler (1994) has suggested that it may be helpful to group these variables into two interdependent but distinguishable categories: the MICRO ENVIRONMENT and the MACRO ENVIRONMENT, together comprising the MARKETING ENVIRONMENT. Analysis of the macro environment – sometimes referred to as the external marketing audit – can usefully be considered under six headings: the demographic environment; the ECONOMIC ENVIRONMENT; the natural environment; the technological environment; the political environment; and the cultural environment. Whereas all six of these aspects of the environment will be relevant to all markets, some aspects will, of course, be more applicable than others in specific markets. There can also be a danger of compartmentalization using this approach – for example, important issues of ecology or consumerism might seem less significant when split up between six headings. Perhaps the most notable limitation of this approach to environmental analysis is that it seems to give little priority to competitors *per se* and it may therefore be appropriate to add a "competitive environment" to Kotler's six categories.

The level of effort and resources which any organization will invest in environmental analysis will depend on many factors including: the availability and reliability of SECONDARY DATA (e.g., census data, government statistics, published market analyses); the cost of PRIMARY DATA (e.g., commissioned market research, in-house surveys);

the volatility of the environment (where analysis can be out of date even before it is finished); the competitiveness of markets (why should organizations invest in analysis when there is little threat of losing customers?); and what priority managers give to environmental analysis, in the context of other demands on their time.

It is often suggested that the environment is becoming increasingly complex and fast-moving. This observation has, of course, been made of many earlier centuries also, but it does seem particularly true of the late 20th century and this emphasizes the importance of environmental analysis, while also highlighting the problems of analyzing such volatile dynamics. These problems have encouraged the development of different analytical techniques, such as scenario development (Schoemaker, 1993), delphi methods (Linstone & Turoff, 1975), and even the use of chaos theory (Stacey, 1975), in order to understand the marketing environment surrounding an organization.

see also **Marketing environment**

Bibliography

Day, G. S. & Wensley, R. (1988). Assessing advantage: A framework for diagnosing competitive superiority. *Journal of Marketing,* **52**, April, 1–20.

Kotler, P. (1994). *Marketing management: Analysis, planning, implementation and control* 8th edn, Englewood Cliffs, NJ: Prentice-Hall. Chapter 6, pp. 150–171.

Linstone, H. A. & Turoff, M. (1975). *The delphi method: Techniques and application.* Reading, MA: Addison Wesley.

Porter, M. E. (1979). How competitive forces shape strategy. *Harvard Business Review,* **57**, Mar.–Apr., 137–145.

Sanderson, S. M. & Luffman, G. A. (1988). Strategic planning and environmental analysis. *European Journal of Marketing,* **22**, 14 27.

Schoemaker, P. J. H. (1993). Multiple scenario development: Its conceptual and behavioral foundation. *Strategic Management Journal,* **14**, 193–213.

Shapiro, B. P. (1988). What the hell oriented. *Harvard Business Review,* **66**, 119–25.

Stacey, R. D. (1995). The science of complexity: An alternative perspective for strategic change processes. *Strategic Management Journal,* **16**, 477–495.

DOMINIC WILSON

environmental orientation   This is part of the training process for employees who expect to be assigned to overseas locations. In addition to the cultural aspects of the new country, employees must also be familiar with the political scene, language, monetary system, transportation and communications systems, and other aspects of the living "environment." Knowledge of these items will decrease inconvenience and stress for the new expatriate.

see also **Expatriate training**

JOHN O'CONNELL

environmental scanning   Change and the constant need for adaptation, renewal and updating will become more prevalent than ever before between now and our entrance into the twenty-first century (Schuler, 1989). While retaining flexibility and a willingness to adapt are critical in successfully dealing with change, it is also important to be able to anticipate change. Anticipating change enables an organization to set in motion the processes to change the procedures and the practices necessary to address the changes. Correct anticipation enables an organization to bring the necessary procedures and practices on line just at the time the changes are having their impact (Schrenk, 1989).

To ensure that correct practices and procedures are on line for effective human resource management, human resource managers and planners are scanning the events occurring and expected to occur in demographics, international affairs, technology, and organization and economics. Changes in these areas have major implications for the practice of human resource management.

Because meeting these changes is more important than ever, organizations need to ensure that they have the capability to do so. A major way to attain this capability is through environmental scanning. Environmental scanning is a process of systematic surveillance and interpretation designed to identify events, elements and conditions of the environment that have potential relevance for and impact on an organization (Coates, 1986).

The Context of Environmental Scanning

The main context of environmental scanning lies in the business environment, which is increasingly global and fast moving. Fundamental changes are occurring and creating new business challenges and opportunities. A business, or a human resource function, that lacks sensitivity to these changes is likely to suddenly discover that it faces serious difficulties (Schrenk, 1989).

A second context of environmental scanning is an organization's business planning process and the business strategies that emerge from this process. To succeed, an environmental scanning activity must be consistent with both the method and timing of the relevant business planning activity. In addition, business strategies determine which trends and implications are of concern to an organization. For example, a growing software company might be greatly troubled by an anticipated shortage of programmers, while a similar company that is phasing out of business would not care about such a development (Schrenk, 1989). In this way, environmental scanning is closely linked with STRATEGIC HUMAN RESOURCE PLANNING.

Components of Environmental Scanning

Environmental scanning is composed of several components, including forecasting future conditions, selecting forecasting techniques, identifying and prioritizing major issues that impact human resource management, developing plans that anticipate those issues, and then preparing the organization for successfully dealing with them. Companies regularly monitor the major aspects of the environment for their relevance to and implications for human resource management (Jackson and Schuler, 1995). These aspects include (a) workforce demographics, (b) international conditions, (c) economic and organizational trends, and (d) technological trends and developments. While there are many other aspects of the environment, these have major implications for human resource management and organizations. Reference to the external environment includes characteristics of the organization itself. While this may not seem to be the external environment to the organization, it is a very important external environment to human resource management (Coates, 1987). In description and discussion of these aspects of the external environment the thrusts are to (a) reveal the current and future (predicted) conditions and characteristics of each component, and (b) suggest some implications of this information for human resource management and organizations.

Steps in Environmental Scanning

The first step in an environmental scanning process is to decide which topic areas to select for analysis. Topic areas are broad categories of trends, such as demographics or economics, that are largely defined by conventional technical disciplines. This step facilitates data gathering, analysis, and reporting (Schrenk, 1989).

The second step in the environmental scanning process is to gather data. There are an enormous number and variety of possible data sources. The primary problem at this step is deciding what information to use and what to ignore or discard.

The third step is to define trends from the data that have been gathered. Trend definition abstracts and simplifies the data. It facilitates further analysis and communication, but the data invariably lose detail. Thus, it can conceal as well as reveal.

Once good data have been obtained and trends established, significant implications or likely consequences must be defined. This fourth step is where experience, creativity, and multiple views can all play a role. While some trends may have general implications and consequences, the real key is to specify the important implications for the organization involved. Implications for a particular organization will vary as a function of geographic location, business conditions, STRATEGY, work force characteristics, and a host of other factors.

Once significant implications have been defined, the fifth step is to prioritize them. It often is easy to create long lists of possible consequences, but unless such lists are pruned, they will bury the process in excessive detail. Eliminating relatively unimportant implications basically is a matter of judgment.

The sixth step in environmental scanning is to define issues. An issue may arise from a single implication or a combination of them. Here again, judgment is a key ingredient. The question at this point is, "How does one select the most important issues and develop issue statements?" This is a critical step, since it forms the foundation for much of what occurs in strategic human resource planning (Jackson and Schuler, 1995).

Human resource environmental scanning has already demonstrated that environmental scans are both feasible and practical. A great deal of valuable information is available, along with effective ways of evaluating it to identify significant trends and human resource implications. Properly used, environmental scans can add significant value to the strategic human resource planning process. The real challenge at this point is to make environmental scanning accepted and effective within the realities of a specific organization and its planning processes.

Bibliography

Coates, J. F. (1986). *Issues Management*, Mt Airy, MD: Lomond Publications.

Coates, J. F. (1987). An environmental scan: Projecting future human resource trends. *Human Resource Planning*, 10, 219–89.

Jackson, S. E. & Schuler, R. L. (1995). Understanding human resource management in the context of organizations and their environments. *Annual Review of Psychology*, **46**, 237–64.

Schrenk, L. P. (1989). Environmental scanning. Dyer, L. *Human Resource Management Evolves Roles and Responsibilities*, Washington, DC: ASPA/BNA.

Schuler, R. S. (1989). Scanning the environment: Planning for human resource management and organizational change. *Human Resources Planning*, **12**, 258–76.

RANDALL SCHULER

environmental scanning (marketing)

Environmental scanning is the process of examining the MARKETING ENVIRONMENT, usually with the intention of identifying trends and developments in the environment which may require MARKETING STRATEGIES or tactics to be adjusted. The complexity, volatility, and potential strategic significance of environmental developments are becoming more apparent to many organizations and there is increasing attention to using information and communication technologies to cope with the rapidly growing volume of data concerning environmental developments. For example, there are now many commercially available MARKETING INFORMATION SYSTEMS (MkIS) and executive information systems (EIS) which claim to offer environmental scanning services. On closer examination, however, these systems often only scan those aspects of the environment at which they are "directed" (through programming) by the systems designers and managers involved and so they risk perpetuating and legitimizing the very perceptual prejudices which they are meant to correct. Computer systems do, of course, provide a valuable aid to coping with the sheer diversity and volume of environmental data, both in terms of scanning and in terms of analysis and manipulation, but there is no substitute for the human characteristics of alertness, curiosity, and openness-to-innovation which are essential in turning environmental "scanning" into environmental "understanding."

Bibliography

Brownlie, D. (1994). Environmental scanning. In M. J. Baker (Ed.), *The marketing book* 3rd edn, London: Heinemann. pp. 139–192.

Calori, R. (1989). Designing a business scanning system. *Long Range Planning*, **22**, (113), Feb., 69–82.

DOMINIC WILSON

EPOS

EPOS or electronic point of sale systems record data, concerning goods sold, via highly efficient electronic scanning equipment reading product bar-codes at the retailer checkout. Their introduction has radically improved distribution and merchandise management in the retail sector by providing detailed and accessible information concerning product movement through stores and purchasing behavior, dramatically reducing the paperwork associated with inventory control.

Bibliography

Harris, D. & Walters, E. (1992). *Retail operations management*. Prentice-Hall.

McGoldrick, P. J. (1990). *Retail marketing*. Maidenhead: McGraw-Hill.

Rosenbloom, B. (1991). *Marketing channels*. Chicago: The Dryden Press.

STEVE GREENLAND

Equal Employment Opportunity Commission

The Equal Employment Opportunity Commission (EEOC) is the federal agency in charge of administering Title VII of the Civil Rights Act, the Equal Pay Act, the Pregnancy Discrimination Act, the Age Discrimination in Employment Act, and the Americans with Disabilities Act. The major activity of the agency is to process charges of discrimination related to these laws, with the resolution of said charges via conciliation and/or legal action. The agency, run by five presidentially appointed commissioners, processes over 90,000 discrimination charges per year.

LEONARD BIERMAN

equity theory

Introduced by Adams (1965) as an extension of the distributive justice concept (*see* DISTRIBUTIVE JUSTICE), equity theory proposes that people's attitudes and behavior are affected by their assessment of their work contributions (referred to as *inputs*) and the REWARDS they receive (referred to as *outcomes*). Inputs may include such contributions as effort, SKILL, and seniority. Outcomes may include such rewards as pay, STATUS, and recognition.

People are said to compare the ratios of their own perceived outcomes/inputs to the corresponding ratios of other people or groups. Reference comparisons may be made to such others as: coworkers on the job, industry standards, or oneself at an earlier point in time. The theory focuses on individuals' perceptions of their own and others' outcomes and inputs rather than actual states. When one's own outcome/input ratio is believed to be greater than another's, the individual is theorized to experience a state of *overpayment inequity*, causing feelings of guilt. In contrast, when one's own outcome/input ratio is believed to be less than another's, the individual is theorized to experience a state of *underpayment inequity*, causing feelings of anger. When one's own outcome/input ratio is believed to match that of other persons or groups, a state of *equitable payment* is said to exist, resulting in feelings of satisfaction (*see* JOB SATISFACTION).

The negative emotions associated with inequitable states are undesirable, motivating people to alter either behaviorally or cognitively – their own or the other's outcomes or inputs (if possible) so as to achieve an equitable state. For example, workers who feel underpaid may be motivated to lower their own outcomes (a behavioral reaction), or to convince themselves that their work contributions are not as great as another who is believed to receive higher outcomes (a cognitive reaction). Likewise, people may respond to overpayment by raising their own inputs, or by convincing themselves that relative to the comparison other, their own contributions are sufficiently great to merit the higher reward received. Research has generally supported these claims (for a review, see Greenberg, 1982). Researchers have used equity theory to explain a wide variety of work-pay cuts, and layoffs. Although early tests of equity theory were conducted in the laboratory, more recent research has been successful in finding support for equity theory in a wide variety of work settings.

Attempting to refine equity theory and extend it to a wide variety of social situations (beyond the work context used by Adams), Walster, Walster, and Berscheid (1978) proposed equity theory as a general theory of social behavior. For example, they used equity theory to explain behavior in marriage and romantic relationships as well as parent–child relationships.

Equity theory has been criticized on several grounds, including the necessity of distress as a motivator of attempts to redress inequities, uncertainties regarding the choice of a comparison other, vagueness regarding the choice of a mode of inequity redress, and difficulties in quantifying inequities (see Adams & Freedman, 1976).

see also **Motivation**

Bibliography

Adams, J. S. (1965). Inequity in social exchange. In L. Berkowitz (Ed.), Advances in experimental social psychology. (Vol. 2, pp. 267–299). New York: Academic Press.

Adams, J. S. & Freedman, S. (1976). Equity theory revisited: Comments and annotated bibliography In L. Berkowitz & E. Walster (Eds), Advances in experimental social psychology. (Vol. 9, pp. 43–90). New York: Academic Press.

Greenberg, J. (1982). Approaching equity and avoiding inequity in groups and organizations. In J. Greenberg & R. L. Cohen (Eds), Equity and justice in social behavior, (pp. 389–435). New York: Academic Press.

Walster, E., Walster, G. W. & Berscheid, E. (1978). Equity: Theory and research. Boston, MA: Allyn & Bacon.

JERALD GREENBERG

equivalent treatment   When two countries agree to treat goods imported from each other as if they were local goods (i.e., the same laws and regulations which apply to local goods are applied to imported goods). Thus, imported items from countries which are part of the agreement are treated as if they were local goods when applying taxes, product standards, etc. This type of agreement is also referred to as national treatment, a reciprocal agreement, or reciprocity.

see also **Reciprocity**

JOHN O'CONNELL

ethics of computer use   Ethics is the study and evaluation of human conduct in the light of moral principles. In an information society, human conduct is greatly influenced by the use of computers, communication devices, and other forms of information technology. Using information technology inevitably creates ethical issues: situations in which an agent's acts, which were undertaken in order to achieve his or her own goals, materially affect one or more stakeholders' ability to achieve their goals. The affected parties may either be helped or harmed (ethics work for the good as well as for bad or evil).

A moral agent can be an individual, a profession, an organization, or an entire society. Agents must address several central questions when facing an ethical issue: "What action should I take?," "How should I live my life?," or "What kind of person or organization do I want to be?" These questions are eternal; they deal with the good, the right or the just. The context in which they must be answered, however, changes with every major change in technology and social organization. The transition from ancient Egyptian and Greek societies to the *polis* of fifth-century BC Athens, required the reflections of a Socrates, a

Plato and an Aristotle to redefine the meaning of "the good" and of virtue in the newly emerged social system. Similarly, in the modern day, there has been a transition from an industrial society, rooted in machines that augment physical energy and the organizational values of Taylor and Ford, to a knowledge- or information-based society. The new society is founded on computers and communication technologies and tends toward flatter, more highly networked, organizational units with intensive external relationships. All of this change requires a fundamental re-examination of ethics and morality.

Ethics requires the examination of an issue from several crucial points of view. What is the agent's duty (deontology)? What are the results of the act (consequentialism)? What does it say about the agent's character (virtue)? And is the outcome fair (justice)? The questions are universal, but their application is shaped fundamentally by the nature of an information society. In the contemporary information society, at least seven crucial issues face moral agents at the individual, professional, organizational, and societal levels.

(1) *Technologically induced social change*   Technology is generally implemented in order to secure economic and social gains. In the process, however, the flow and the balance of benefits and burdens to the stakeholders in the social system are changed. Some people win; others lose, physically, psychologically, economically, or socially. Resulting from this redistribution of social status is a set of ethical issues that managers and MIS professionals must resolve, such as worker displacement, under-employment or "dumbing down" of jobs, depersonalization, new health hazards, over-reliance on technology, spatial reallocation (e.g. TELECOMMUTING), technological illiteracy, and the need for education and training.

(2) *Privacy*   Modern information technology makes the acquisition and integration of information about people and their behavior and its storage, processing, dissemination, and use feasible and economical. On the one hand, some of this information is wanted and needed by decision-makers in business, government, and other organizations; on the other hand, some of it is gathered at the ethical cost of invading individual privacy. Sensitive, sometimes quite intimate, information about people is revealed to those who do not have a legitimate need to know it or who are not authorized by the subject party to know it. Managers must balance their temptation to acquire these data against their obligation to respect the privacy and autonomy of others. This ethical issue has led to the adoption of principles of fair information practices based on the concept of informed consent: no personal information should be acquired on a secret basis; an individual should be able to discover personal information that is being kept about him or her; the individual should be able to correct the record; the individual who gives consent for the collection of information for one purpose should be able to prohibit its collection for use for any other purpose; and any party collecting and handling personal information must assure its accuracy and reliability (see also below) and take reasonable

precautions to prevent its misuse. Relevant US legislation includes the Freedom of Information Act of 1966, the Fair Credit Reporting Act of 1970, the Privacy Act of 1974, and the Privacy Protection Act of 1980 (*see* PRIVACY IN INFORMATION SYSTEMS).

(3) *Property* Property is something that can be possessed, controlled, or owned while excluding others from these privileges. As John Locke argued in the seventeenth century, people earn the right to make something their property by virtue of their physical and intellectual labor. Because information is intangible and mental, however, and it is symbolic, readily reproducible, facility transmittable, easily shared, and highly "leakable," it is difficult to exercise this right effectively with intellectual property. One's intellectual property is a source of wealth and value; consequently, other people are motivated, tempted and, frequently, able to take it without compensating its owner. Managers must steward and safeguard their organization's intellectual property and ensure that their organizations and employees respect the property of others. This leads to issues such as software piracy, fraud, and theft in electronic funds transfers and accounts, and copyright infringements of all types. A related class of issues is program damage such as is caused by software viruses, worms, logic bombs and Trojan horses. Relevant US legislation includes the Copyright Act of 1976, the Electronic Funds Transfer Act of 1980, the Semiconductor Chip Protection Act of 1984, the Computer Fraud and Abuse Act of 1986, and proposed computer virus legislation (*see* SECURITY OF INFORMATION SYSTEMS).

One's intellectual capability and know-how is also property. Initiatives in the name of ARTIFICIAL INTELLIGENCE and EXPERT SYSTEMS to delve into a worker's mind, to capture the principles of his or her reasoning, and to program them into computer systems, may also violate or compromise the property rights of that individual.

(4) *Accuracy and reliability* In an information society most people rely on information to make decisions that materially affect their lives and the lives of others. They depend on computers, communication devices, and other technologies to provide this information. Errors in information can result in bad decisions, personal trauma, and significant harm to other, often innocent, parties. Users are entitled to receive information that is accurate, reliable, valid, and of high quality (at least, adequate for the purposes to which they intend to put it). But this also entails a significant opportunity cost. Error-free, high-quality information can be approximated only if substantial resources are allocated to the processes by which it is pry, managers must make an ethical tradeoff between conserving the resources and competencies under their control and allocating them to produce higher-quality information. In any case, a certain minimal, socially acceptable, level of accuracy is required of all information and information systems.

(5) *Burden* The cost of providing information at any level of accuracy or quality is borne, usually, by a limited class of people. For managers, this raises a question of fairness: are the providers unduly burdened and adequately compensated for their contributions? At the governmental level, the Federal Paperwork Reduction Act of 1980 represents an attempt to relieve US citizens of some of the burdens involved in filling out forms.

(6) *Access* Information is the primary currency in an information society and in information-intensive organizations. Managers are responsible for its just and equitable allocation. In order to participate effectively in a democratic society, people must have access to information concerning things that affect their work and their lives; and, therefore, they must have access to a minimal level of technology for handling information and they must receive an adequate level of general and technological education.

(7) *Power* Power is the ability to influence or control other individuals or organizations. Its acquisition and use engenders responsibility. Information, including the capability to produce and handle it, is a fundamental source of power and a generator of responsibility. The principal intent of the strategic and marketing use of information technology, for example, is to enhance this power base. Wielding this power, however, must result in considerable help or harm to others. In industry, for example, capturing vital information sources can result in monopolistic power, which, in a free market economy, raises serious questions for managers and for government as to how this power is to be channeled, allocated, and used responsibly.

The combined forces of technological "push" and demand "pull" will only serve to exacerbate these ethical issues for managers in the future as the increased use of information technology results in more information being made generally available. The availability of information creates its own demand due to its perceived benefits; and, consequently, more parties hasten to use the information in order to secure its benefits for themselves.

Bibliography

Johnson, D. G. (1985). *Computer Ethics.* Englewood Cliffs, NJ: Prentice-Hall.

Johnson, D. G. & Snapper, J. W. (1985). *Ethical Issues in the Use of Computers.* Belmont, CA: Wadsworth.

Mason, R. O., Mason, F. M. & Culnan, M. J. (1995). *Ethics of Information Management.* Thousand Oaks, CA: Sage Publications Inc.

Oz, E. (1994). *Ethics for the Information Age.* Dubuque, IA: Wm. C. Brown Communications Inc.

RICHARD O. MASON

event studies The term "event study" describes an empirical research design widely used in finance and accounting. Event studies employ a common general methodology aimed at studying the impact of specified economic or financial events on security market behavior. The occurrence of an event is used as the sampling criterion and the objective of the research is to identify information flows and market behavior both before and after the event. Although some event studies have examined the volatility of returns and patterns of trading volume surrounding events (for a review see Yadav, 1992), most studies have focused on an event and its impact on the market prices of securities. Price-based event studies were originally designed to test the semi-strong form of the efficient market hypothesis (Fama et al., 1969) with the expectation that efficiency would be reflected in a full and immediate response to the new information conveyed by the event. In the mid-1970s a new type of price-based approach was developed (Mandelker, 1974; Dodd and Ruback, 1977) called value event studies; their main aim was not to study market efficiency but to examine the impact of events on the market value of specific companies (or groups of companies).

The scope of events studied ranges from firm-specific incidents (e.g. announcements of stock splits, or changes in dividend policy) to more general phenomena such as regulatory changes or economic shocks. Analysis occurs over "event windows" or test periods when evidence of abnormal behavior in the market is sought. Such abnormality occurs relative to behavior during an estimation or benchmark period, which is used to estimate the benchmark for the expected behavior of a parameter around the event. Abnormality can occur in the form of abnormal returns, abnormal trading volumes or changes in the levels of the volatility of returns. The research methodologies used in each case are similar, differing only in respect of evaluating criterion. Accordingly, the brief description that follows will take into account only the general price-based event studies.

Formally, abnormal return is the difference between the actual and expected return during the test period:

$$AR_{it} = R_{it} - R_{it}^a st$$

where AR_{it} is the abnormal return on security i during period t, R_{it} the actual return during period t, and $R_{it}^a st$ is the expected return on security i during period t. Several alternatives exist to determine the expected return. The market model approach uses a regression analysis (usually OLS) to estimate the security returns as a function of the market index during the estimation period and then uses this model in conjunction with the actual market return during the test period to calculate the expected return. In this case, the classic configuration of the expected return generating model is the following (Fama et al., 1969):

$$R_{it}^* = \alpha_i + \beta_i R_{mt} + u_{it} \text{ for } t = 1, 2, l, T$$

where R_{mt} is the return on the market index for period t (systematic component of return), α_i is the intercept coefficient and β_i is the slope coefficient for security i, u_{it} is the zero mean disturbance term for the return on security i during period t (unsystematic component of return) and T is the number of (sub-)periods during the benchmark period.

The model does not imply the acceptance of any explicit assumptions about equilibrium prices. This fact, and the specific design characteristics, which allow for an easy and powerful statistical treatment, constitute the main reasons for its wide popularity. The alternative mean adjusted method assumes that the best predictor for a security's return is given by historic performance. This assumption implies that each security's expected return is a constant given by its average return during the estimation period:

$$R_{it}^* = \frac{1}{T} \sum_{t=1}^{T} R_{it}$$

where R_{it} is the return on security i over the T (sub-)periods of the estimation interval.

The market-adjusted return method assumes that the expected market return constitutes the best predictor for each security's market performance. The market return on the index during the test period is then the predicted return for each security:

$$R_{it}^* = R_{mt}$$

Finally, CAPM based benchmarks define the expected return of each security as a function of its systematic risk or β and of the market price of risk, effectively the difference between the return on the market index and the return on the risk-free security:

$$R_{it}^* = R_{ft} + \beta_i(R_{mt} - R_{ft})$$

where R_{ft} is the risk-free rate of return during period t and β_i is the systematic risk of the security i (previously estimated with reference to the market index).

A variant of this approach uses a control portfolio benchmark, under which the expected return of a specific security or group of securities is given by the expected return of a portfolio with the same β.

The estimation of expected returns is usually considered the main source of variations in event study methodology. Other aspects of the methodology are: (1) the reference basis used to calculate the returns (logarithmic or discrete); (2) the measurement interval (the more common are monthly, weekly or daily returns); (3) treatment of disturbancies during the event window; (4) the duration of the event window; and (5) the choice of market index (where used).

To reflect the uncertain holding period pre- and post-event, it is usual to present the abnormal return in both periodic return form and as cumulative abnormal returns (CAR). The hypothesis normally tested then becomes whether CARs during the test period are significantly different from zero.

Some of the recent developments in event studies are: (1) the application of the methodology to the market for debt securities (Crabbe and Post, 1994); (2) the study of the likely implications of non-constant volatility on abnormal return estimates (Boehmer et al., 1991); (3) the employment of non-parametric tests of abnormal returns when the usual assumption of normally distributed returns seems problematic (Corrado, 1989); (4) and the implementation of multiple regression approaches based on the application of joint generalized least squares (GLS) techniques (Bernard, 1987).

The volume of event study literature has grown significantly in recent years and shows every sign of continued expansion. At the theoretical level, two topics for continuing research are the control for extra market effects in the securities return generating processes; and the handling of statistical problems caused by samples of thinly traded securities. At the empirical level, the great challenge is accounting for the observed abnormal returns.

Bibliography

Bernard, V. L. (1987). Cross-sectional dependence and problems in inference in market-based accounting research. *Journal of Accounting Research*, **25**, 1–48.

Boehmer, E., Musumeci, J. & Poulsen, A. B. (1991). Event-study methodology under conditions of event-induced variance. *Journal of Financial Economics*, **30**, 253–72.

Brown, S. J. & Warner, J. B. (1980). Measuring security price performance. *Journal of Financial Economics*, **8**, 205–58.

Brown, S. J. & Warner, J. B. (1985). Using daily stock returns: the case of event studies. *Journal of Financial Economics*, **14**, 3–32.

Corrado, C. J. (1989). A nonparametric test for abnormal security-price performance in event studies. *Journal of Financial Economics*, **23**, 385–95.

Crabbe, L. & Post, M. A. (1994). The effect of a rating downgrade on outstanding commercial paper. *Journal of Finance*, **49**, 39–56.

Dodd, P. & Ruback, R. (1977). Tender offers and stockholder returns: an empirical analysis. *Journal of Financial Economics*, **5**, 351–73.

Fama, E. F., Fisher, L., Jensen, M. & Roll, R. (1969). The adjustment of stock prices to new information. *International Economic Review*, **10**, 1–21.

Mandelker, G. (1974). Risk and return: the case of merging firms. *Journal of Financial Economics*, **1**, 303–36.

Strong, N. (1992). Modelling abnormal returns: a review article. *Journal of Business Finance and Accounting*, **19**, 533–53.

Salinger, M. (1992). Value event studies. *The Review of Economics and Statistics*, **74**, 671–7.

Yadav, P. K. (1992). Event studies based on volatility of returns and trading volume: a review. *British Accounting Review*, **24**, 157–85.

J. AZEVEDO PEREIRA

exchange   While it is often seen as the central concept underpinning marketing, there is some debate over exactly what constitutes exchange. At the simplest level, exchange might be seen as the action of voluntarily transferring ownership of a product or service to another in return for another object deemed to be equivalent in value. Wider definitions of the scope of exchange might not see payment as a necessary condition or indeed might not restrict the scope of exchange to two parties or to products and services. The debate is paralleled by that on the nature and scope of marketing itself and is well summarized in Bagozzi (1975).

Bibliography

Bagozzi, R. P. (1975). Marketing as exchange. *Journal of Marketing*, **39**, 4 Oct., 32–39.

FIONA LEVERICK

exchange exposures   Exchange exposures are the ways an organization can suffer losses due to changes in the rates of exchange between currencies. The exposure essentially is due to the fact that payables, receivables, or investments denominated in other currencies may change in value over time. There are two categories of business activity that expose a business to losses due to fluctuations in exchange rates.

1 Transaction exposure – This exposure arises when a business enters into transactions in which foreign currency payments are expected to be made "to" the business at some time in the future or in which foreign currency payments are to be made "by" the business at some time in the future. As time passes currency values may change. If foreign currency values fall, the business will be paid in lower value currency. If foreign currency values increase, the company will have to use more of its domestic currency to purchase foreign currency with which to pay debt.

2 Translation exposure – Translation exposure is an accounting measure. If an organization has assets valued in a foreign currency, it faces the possibility that the currency will fall in value. If this occurs, the decrease in value "translates" into reduced value of business assets.

Bibliography

Eiteman, D. K., Stonehill, A. J. & Moffett, M. H. (1992). *Multinational business finance*. 6th edn, Reading, MA: Addison-Wesley Publishing.

JOHN O'CONNELL

exclusive agent   This term describes the relationship between a principal (e.g., a manufacturing company) and an agent (e.g., a manufacturer's representative) in which the principal grants the agent exclusive rights (e.g., to sell a particular product in a particular country or region). Thus, the exclusive agent is the only party who can represent the manufacturer in selling products in a specific geographic region. Anyone seeking the product will have to work through the exclusive agent. In return for the grant of exclusivity, the agent usually agrees to some minimum level of representation and performance.

Bibliography

Clark, J. B. (1990). *Marketing today*. Englewood Cliffs, NJ: Prentice-Hall.

JOHN O'CONNELL

executive compensation   Because senior managers are responsible for creating and implementing the firm's strategy, most companies recognize the need to develop special pay packages for these individuals. Thus, executive compensation addresses the reward systems used for chief executive officers (CEOs) and members of the top management team (e.g. vice presidents and other officers of the firm). Executive compensation is significant because of its visibility and symbolism, and its ramifications for pay systems at lower levels of the organization.

Executive salaries have shown limited correlation with firm size or performance, have grown at a much faster rate than the salaries for production workers or middle managers, and are substantially higher in the USA than overseas. Since 1992, numerous groups have expressed concern with executive pay, including politicians, the Securities and Exchange Commission, institutional investors, boards of directors, and individual shareholder groups (Boyd, 1994). Still, despite such criticism, a properly designed executive compensation system can help a firm to significantly boost its effectiveness. Key elements to the understanding of executive compensation include its components and implications for design of reward systems.

Components

The elements of an executive's pay package include base salary, BONUSES, long-term compensation, and benefits. Many chief executives also have golden parachutes, which are severance agreements triggered by a change in firm ownership or control. Base salary is considered a fixed form of compensation, and accounts for one-half to tof total cash compensation (Gomez-Mejia and Balkin, 1992; Boyd, 1995). Because this is a base, annual salary is generally of little motivational value, and difficult to reduce in the face of poor CEO performance or weak economic conditions. Executive pay surveys (Conference Board, 1994; *The Wall Street Journal*, 1995) indicate that base salary varies widely both across and within industries.

The sum of annual salary and bonus is called total cash compensation. Bonuses are short-term awards, and are used by a vast majority of firms in compensating key executives (Conference Board, 1994). Experts recommend that both objective (e.g. stock price, return on investment (ROI), or market share) and subjective (e.g. the quality of CEO strategic decision making, as evaluated by the board of directors) criteria be developed for bonus awards. Because bonuses are a form of contingent compensation, they are a source of personal risk. The uncertainty associated with this risk can be a powerful motivational tool, and pay packages which emphasize bonus pay have been linked with higher levels of firm performance. However, excessive emphasis on bonus pay can be ineffective or encourage inappropriate behaviors. Use of either bonus pay or long-term compensation can be considered forms of PAY FOR PERFORMANCE.

The third element of executive pay is long-term compensation. One danger of bonus pay is that it may encourage executives to sacrifice long-term strategic goals in exchange for short-term profit gains. Long-term compensation plans help to balance the emphasis on long- and short-term goals, and can also help to align the interests of senior managers with those of shareholders. Long-term compensation plans are used by a minority of firms, but are gradually gaining in popularity (Conference Board, 1994). Awards for long-term compensation are generally some combination of company stock (in the form of stock options) and cash. The present value of such compensation is complex to calculate, and option losses do not translate to a real loss for executives. So there is still debate about the motivational value of these awards. Additionally, there are many issues associated with the effective administration of long-term compensation programs.

The last element of executive pay is benefits. While some firms offer identical benefits to all employees, most companies provide far more extensive benefits for senior executives. Aside from the ubiquitous company car, common executive perks include financial and tax planning, low-interest loans, and membership in country clubs, health clubs, and other social organizations.

Design Implications

The growing emphasis on STRATEGIC HUMAN RESOURCE MANAGEMENT has prompted many firms to re-evaluate their executive pay practices. Increasingly, these firms recognize that the characteristics of an effective executive compensation system will differ substantially across industries, and may even differ for two firms competing in the same industry. Ideally, there will be a strong link between the firm's strategy, key goals, relevant context, and the composition of the executive pay package. To develop a truly strategic system, Hambrick and Snow (1989) recommended that firms begin with a thorough analysis of their situation, including their strategy, pay at competing firms, job mobility of key staff, and so forth. This information should then guide the following steps: (a) selecting the type and amount of incentives (e.g. base versus bonus pay, cash versus stock); (b) setting criteria for receiving incentives (e.g. subjective versus objective criteria, short-term versus long-term goals, difficulty of goals); and (c) administering incentives (e.g. degree of customization for different staff or divisions, levels of visibility and stability of pay packages).

Bibliography

Boyd, B. K. (1994). Board control and CEO compensation. *Strategic Management Journal*, **15**, 335–44.

Boyd, B. K. (1995). Board control, compensation mix, and firm performance (paper presented at the Academy of Management Annual Conference, Vancouver).

Conference Board (1994). *Top Executive Compensation*, New York: Conference Board.

Gomez-Mejia, L. R. (1994). Executive compensation: a reassessment and a future research agenda. *Research in Personnel and Human Resources Management*, **12**, 161–222.

Gomez-Mejia, L. M. & Balkin, D. B. (1992). *Compensation, Organizational Strategy, and Firm Performance*, Cincinnati, OH: South-Western.

Hambrick, D. C. & Snow, C. C. (1989). Strategic reward systems. Snow, C. C. *Strategy, Organization Design, and Human Resource Management*, Greenwich, CT: JAI Press.

The Wall Street Journal (1995). Special section on executive pay. *The Wall Street Journal*, **April 12**, R1–R16.

BRIAN K. BOYD

executive information systems   An executive information system (EIS) is a computerized system that provides executives with internal and external information relevant to their strategic management. Characteristics typical of an EIS include:

- custom-tailored to individual executives
- extracts, filters, compresses, and tracks critical data
- provides current status information, trend analysis, exception reports, and drill down
- accesses and integrates a broad range of internal and external data
- user friendly
- used directly by executives without intermediaries
- presents graphical, tabular, and textual information
- provides support for electronic communications
- provides data analysis capabilities
- provides organizing tools

Development of an EIS

Organizations develop an EIS for a variety of reasons. Some are to achieve more timely, relevant, concise, complete, or better information. Other reasons are to be more responsive to changing market conditions, to support a total quality management program, or to facilitate downsizing of the organization. Critical to the success of an EIS is a strong high-level executive sponsor (such as the CEO). The sponsor initiates the project, allocates the needed resources, participates in the system's design, uses the system, and handles political resistance. Usually an EIS is developed by executive mandate rather than a comprehensive cost–benefit analysis. Executive sponsors also appoint operating sponsors to oversee the day-to-day development of the system. The operating sponsor may be selected from information systems or a functional area. This sponsor selects the EIS staff, draws up plans for the system's development, and helps resolve routine issues and problems.

The EIS staff is responsible for building, operating, and enhancing the system. The group must combine solid technical, business, and interpersonal skills. This staff performs tasks such as determining information requirements, evaluating hardware and software, designing screens, installing local area networks, and accessing needed data. An EIS includes a variety of internal and external and hard and soft information. Organizational databases and analyst spreadsheets are major sources of internal data. External data may come from marketing intelligence and electronic news and stock price databases. Soft information in the form of explanations, assessments, and predictions are sometimes included as annotations to screens in order to enhance the user understanding of the harder information displayed.

Evolution of EISs
Most systems are developed using special-purpose EIS software. A strong current trend is the use of client/server rather than mainframe-oriented software. EISs are developed using a prototype/evolutionary development methodology. There is seldom a final product; they evolve in response to new or changing information requirements, the need to add new applications and capabilities (e.g. decision support systems), and to satisfy the needs of additional users.

While a firm's executives are the primary audience for an EIS, successful systems frequently spread to additional users. Powerful push/pull forces are at work. The executives want to "push" the systems down to lower-level organizational personnel so that they can benefit from the system, while this same personnel want to "pull" the system down in order to see the information that higher-level executives are using. This process tends to extend the EIS to a broader audience than the top executives.

HUGH WATSON

executive orders A variety of executive orders have been issued in the past 60 years to help to eliminate employment discrimination by the federal government and by private employers who have contracts with the federal government. In general, executive orders are orders issued by the president having the same force or effect as a statute or other law. A few of the pertinent executive orders are described below.

Order 10925
This executive order, issued by President Kennedy in 1961, required federal contractors to take affirmative action to insure that applicants were employed, and employees treated, without regard to race, creed, color, or national origin. This was the first executive order to contain an affirmative action provision as part of its nondiscrimination prohibitions.

Order 10988
This executive order, issued in 1962, provided collective bargaining rights for federal employees.

Order 11141
This order, issued by President Johnson in 1964, prohibited federal contractors and their subcontractors from discriminating on the basis of age. This executive order was the first to extend nondiscrimination to federally assisted construction contracts. The overlap of the Age Discrimination in Employment Act of 1967 with this order has attenuated its effect.

Order 11246
This executive order, issued in 1965, provided the basis for the federal government contract compliance program. It required compulsory language to be included in nonexempt federal contracts and in secondary contracts resulting from them (e.g. subcontracts), indicating that contractors did not discriminate on the basis of race, color, religion, or national origin. Additionally, the language provided notification that the contractors would take affirmative action to insure that employees would be hired and treated without regard to their race, color, religion, or national origin. Much of the language of this order was taken from earlier executive orders. The order authorized individual federal agencies to impose sanctions and penalties under the order, which strengthened the enforcement of the order relative to earlier orders.

Order 11375
This 1967 amendment to executive order 11246 added prohibitions against discrimination on the basis of sex.

Order 11478
This order, issued in 1969 by President Nixon to amend order 11246, stated a federal policy of prohibiting employment discrimination on the basis of race, color, religion, sex, national origin, handicap, or age in each of the executive departments and agencies (and in contractors holding at least $10,000 worth of federal contracts). It established "affirmative program(s) of equal employment opportunity" in all such departments and agencies. It also authorized the EQUAL EMPLOYMENT OPPORTUNITY COMMISSION to issue rules and regulations necessary to implementation of the order. Finally, the order mandated merit as the basis for federal personnel policies.

Order 12086
This executive order, issued by President Carter in 1978 as part of the Reorganization Plan, eliminated the enforcement powers of the independent federal agencies and concentrated the enforcement power for executive order 11246 in the Secretary of Labor. The Office of Federal Contract Compliance Programs (OFCCP), under the secretary's direction, has issued an extensive set of regulations to implement the requirements of order 11246. In particular, all contracts and subcontracts exceeding $10,000 must contain an equal opportunity clause (see orders 11246 and 11478). Contractors and subcontractors (nonconstruction) employing 50 or more persons and having a federal contract worth at least $50,000 must also develop a written affirmative action plan. Construction contractors and subcontractors holding federal contracts in excess of $10,000 must engage in affirmative action.

RAMONA L. PAETZOLD

expatriate An expatriate is a person who was transferred to a foreign country by his/her employer. It is common for multinational companies to send home country nationals to represent the company overseas. While in the host country and away from their home country, these employees are referred to as expatriates. Expatriates also include employees from outside of the home country who are transferred to a third country.

see also **Expatriate training; Selection of expatriates**

Bibliography

Bird, A. & Dunbar, R. (1991). Getting the job done over there: Improving expatriate productivity. *National Productivity Review* Spring, 145–56.

Howard, C. G. (1991). "Expatriate managers," in *Proceedings of the International Academy of: Management and Marketing*. Washington, DC: Howard Publication – International Academy of Management.

Kobrin, S. J. (1988). Expatriate reduction and strategic control in American multinational corporations. *Human Resource Management*, **27** (1), 63–75.

Mendenhall, M. & Oddou, G. (1985). The dimensions of expatriate acculturation: A review. *Academy of Management Review*, **10** (1), 39–47.

Napier, N. K. & Peterson, R. B. (1990). Expatriate reentry: What do repatriates have to say? *Human Resource Planning*, **14**, 19–28.

JOHN O'CONNELL

expatriate assignment   An expatriate assignment is a job transfer that takes the employee to a workplace that is outside the country in which he or she is a citizen. There are differences between an expatriate assignment and other job assignments of an international nature. Expatriate assignments are longer in duration than other types of international assignments (e.g. business trips), and require the employee to move his or her entire household to the foreign location. Thus, in an expatriate assignment, the employee's home base of business operations is in the foreign country.

Expatriate assignments offer unique challenges to expatriate employees. Virtually all expatriates run into situations where the home office wants them to do one thing, while local situations dictate that another thing should be done instead.

The expatriate assignment requires expatriate managers to face a number of complex issues that their domestic counterparts either do not face, or face with less intensity. Examples of such issues are the integration of large international acquisitions, understanding the meaning of performance and accountability in a globally integrated system of product flows, building and managing a worldwide logistics capability, developing multiple country-specific corporate strategies, managing products and services around the world with differing competitive dynamics in each market, forming and managing collaborative agreements (OEM contracts, licensing, joint ventures), balancing the need for global integration while simultaneously responding to local demands, and managing a multicultural workforce within foreign environments.

Expatriates usually find an expatriate assignment to be one of the biggest challenges of their entire CAREER. Increasingly, firms are investing in cross-cultural training programs to prepare expatriates to operate successfully in their expatriate assignment. Additionally, most companies offer a variety of support systems to employees as part of the expatriate assignment. One of the principal barriers to

cross-cultural adjustment is the lack of a way for expatriates –especially non-working spouses of employees – to become members of a social network. Many firms offer programs of one sort or another that are geared to helping expatriates to develop friendships with other expatriates and host-nationals, and to provide support with the day-to-day realities of living in a foreign culture (housing, schooling, transportation, shopping, and so forth) (*see* EXPATRIATE SUPPORT SYSTEM).

Expatriate assignments are much more costly than simply hiring local nationals to work in a foreign subsidiary; however, there are advantages to using expatriates over local nationals. Expatriates know how the parent company operates and can pass on this knowledge to local employees. By working overseas they learn how foreign markets operate, and how foreign consumers and clients react to the products or services the company offers. Also, they gain skills in cross-cultural management and develop a global perspective. Expatriate assignments, then, can be a powerful strategic tool in developing global business skills within the senior ranks of a firm's management.

Bibliography

Black, J. S., Gregersen, H. B. & Mendenhall, M. (1992). *Global Assignments: Successfully Expatriating and Repatriating International Managers*, San Francisco: Jossey-Bass.

Black, J. S., Mendenhall, M. & Oddou, G. (1991). Toward a comprehensive model of international adjustment: an integration of multiple theoretical perspectives. *Academy of Management Review*, **16**, 291–317.

Mendenhall, M., Punnett, B. J. & Ricks, D. (1995). *Global Management*, Cambridge, MA: Blackwell Publishers.

Prahalad, C. K. (1990). Globalization: the intellectual and managerial challenges. *Human Resource Management*, **29**, 27–37.

MARK E. MENDENHALL

expatriate support system   The expatriate support system (ESS) is a set of programs developed by a company to develop and promote multicultural skills among employees who must travel abroad on long-term assignments. The system's effectiveness is measured by its ability to ease an employee's transition from the USA (or any other country) to a different country's cultural environment. The system may not eliminate all the pains created by this cultural transition, but it should reduce them to a minimum. The most effective ESS is that which allows employees to become open-minded, to learn how to adapt to a new environment, and even to enjoy the cultural transition as a valuable learning experience. The support system should also address the needs of the employee's spouse and children traveling with him or her.

An ESS includes all or any combination of the following: educational programs to develop employees' multicultural skills; a mentorship or buddy program in the foreign country to help employees during the first weeks abroad; short travel programs to the country of destination prior to the actual assignment to help the employee get acquainted with the country; information supplied to employees about schools, churches, recreational activities, native meals, transportation systems, driver's license, health care, and many other aspects of the new country. It must include programs to ease employees' re-entry to the USA (or home country), to help them cope with the fact that they are now different and that being different is fine. This component should also involve other employees who must interact with a returning colleague. As employees accept the new cultural diversity paradigm and learn how to cope with it, the ESS should be deactivated.

R. IVAN BLANCO

expatriate training   Providing employees going on foreign assignment with the knowledge and techniques necessary to be successful on their assignments. Training may take place both prior to and after the actual assignment transfer has been made. The types and extensiveness of training should be based upon both the duration and the importance of the foreign assignment. It is logical that an employee sent overseas for 60 days would need different types of training than an employee sent overseas for three years. An employee sent to do a specific job within an organization facility in another country needs different training than the employee sent to develop new markets or to negotiate contracts with foreign partners or governments. Differences in what is expected of employees must be factored into the duration and type of training offered to each employee. Failure to properly train expatriates will almost assure their failure to either complete the foreign assignment or to meet employer expectations in cases where the full assignment period has been achieved.

Training an expatriate's family members to recognize the problems and inconveniences of foreign assignment is also extremely important. Family members face the same problems as the expatriate in terms of language differences; cultural adaptation; living condition changes; and other possible sources of problems. What many people do not realize, however, is that the expatriate still has the organization as a base from which to work (fellow employees, familiar products, communication with home office, etc.) whereas family members may be virtually uprooted with few if any ties with their former home. A sound expatriate training program includes the training of family members as well as the employee.

Expatriate training is commonly divided into three approaches:

1 Information giving approach – This is the most widespread of all of the approaches. Unfortunately, many companies offer only this approach. Included in this approach is information about the new country's culture, geography, living conditions, life-styles, and language. Commonly used methods to provide this type of training include: seminars, films, audio tapes, books and brochures. This approach offers information only, without the chance to apply the new information or to test its assimilation by the students.
2 Affective approach – This approach attempts to apply training in a more experiential manner. Real examples of problems are set forth for discussion: role-playing activities take place; stress reduction and change management techniques are taught. This type of training prepares the expatriate on a more realistic and practical level. Affective approaches seek to allow the individual to become more self-confident; what is being taught will actually increase his/her ability to carry out the assignment more effectively.
3 Immersion approach – This approach seeks to place the employee in as similar a condition as the activity actually taking place in the foreign country. Immersion may include visits to the new country to allow the employee to explore and learn on a first-hand basis. Immersion training involves extensive simulation of common problem situations in which the employee can learn without being exposed to failure while actually on the overseas assignment. The approach seeks to teach the employee to be sensitive to other cultures and act accordingly. This approach is normally very time consuming and expensive. It relies on a low student to instructor ratio and a substantial commitment of resources by the organization.

All of the approaches are focused upon allowing the employee to overcome problems associated with overseas assignments. It may even be necessary to use one or more of these approaches when sending an employee to a different part of the same country.

Bibliography

Hays, R. D. (1974). Expatriate selection: Insuring success and avoiding failure. *Journal of International Business Studies*, 5, 25–37.

Mendenhall, M. E., Dunbar, E. & Oddou, Gary (1987). Expatriate selection, training, and career pathing: A review and critique. *Human Resource Management*, 26, 331–45.

Ronen, S. & Tung, R. L. (1981). Selection and training of personnel for overseas assignments. *Columbia Journal of World Business* Spring, 68–78.

Torbiorn, J. (1982). *Living abroad.* New York: John Wiley.

JOHN O'CONNELL

expected present value   Future cash flows are sometimes known with certainty, for example if they are coming from a portfolio of government bonds. More often, however, there is some uncertainty around exactly what the future cash flows will be. The future cash flows from an investment during the next three years might be $100 each year, but could be lower or higher, depending on how future events develop. The uncertainty can be described in terms of probability distributions, which could be discrete or continuous. For example, there might be a probability of 0.8 that the cash flow for year one will fall between $90 and $110. The probabilities might be symmetric around the most likely outcome, or they might be skewed. Whether the probabilities are symmetric or skewed, the expected value of each year's cash flow can be computed. This is done by assigning a probability to each possible amount of cash flow that might occur, then proceeding to multiply each outcome by its probability of occurring and adding the products together.

In mathematical terms for the discrete case:

$$\text{Expected Cash Flow} = \sum_j x_i p(x_i)$$

where x_i represents each possible cash flow outcome, $p(x_i)$ is the density function associated with the outcomes and the summation is over all i outcomes.

In the continuous case, the expected cash flow is expressed as:

$$\text{Expected Cash Flow} = \int xf(x)dx$$

where x is the random variable describing future cash flows and $f(x)$ is the corresponding density function.

With the expected future cash flows computed, it is possible to compute expected present value. Each expected future cash flow is discounted, giving its present value. The present values of all the expected future cash flows are summed, yielding the total expected present value. If the initial investment is subtracted from the total expected present value, the resulting number is called expected net present value.

In mathematical terms, for the discrete case:

$$\text{Expected Present Value} =$$

$$\sum_{j} \left(\sum_{i} x_i p(x_i) \right) (i + r),^{-j}$$

where j are the time periods and the summation is over all outcomes, i.

In the continuous case:

$$\text{Expected Present Value} =$$

$$\int \int e^{-rt} xf(x) dx dt$$

where t represents the continuous passage of time.

The naive decision rule is that a firm should approve every investment project that offers a positive expected net present value. This rule ignores risk aversion (Friedman and Savage, 1948), and it also excludes the necessity of scrutinizing the distribution of the expected cash flows. An investment with a positive expected net present value has a measurable probability of giving a negative return. It is an essential part of the analysis to compute the probability that the return on investment will be negative. Business managers also calculate the probability that the return on investment will be lower than some minimum acceptable amount. They express this as a rate of return and call it the *hurdle rate*. If each of the annual cash flows comes out in the lower tail of its probability distribution, the final outcome of the investment will be worse than its expected present value.

Bibliography

Brigham, E. F. & Gapenski, L. C. (1993). *Intermediate Financial Management*.
Friedman, M. & Savage L. J. (1948). The utility analysis of choices involving risk. *Journal of Political Economy*, 56, 279–304.

JOHN EDMUNDS AND ROBERTO BONIFAZ

$$E(X) = \int_x xf(x)dx \tag{1}$$

where *int* is the integral over the complete range of *possible* values for X; see Greene (1993) or Kmenta (1986). When the random variable X is discrete, the expected value is calculated as

$$E(X) = \sum_x xf(x) \tag{2}$$

where $\sum_x$ indicates the summation is over all possible values of x.

In business analysis, managers work with observed sample data and not necessarily with formal probability distributions. The sample mean, denoted $\overline{X}$ can then be calculated for the observed values of the variable of interest. For example, a firm may want to calculate its average weekly sales in the last quarter from weekly data. In this case, there are twelve weekly observations and the sample mean would be calculated by simply summing the weekly sales figures and dividing by twelve. If a manager randomly selected any single week from the twelve, any single week's sales would be equally likely, so the probability of any specific week's sales being selected would be one-twelfth and this is the value $f(x)$ would take in the summation in equation (2) above. The summation in equation (2) would then be:

$$\overline{S} = \sum_{i=1}^{12} S_i \times \frac{1}{12} = \frac{1}{12} \sum_{i=1}^{12} S_i \tag{2}$$

where S is the level of sales in each week. It should be noted that the sample mean of sales calculated above may not equal any of the sales figures which occurred but rather it represents the likely value for weekly sales if the company were to have several quarters like the last. Suppose, for example, that sales were 1 million units for the first six weeks of the quarter and 2 million units for the second six weeks. The mean value of sales would then be 1.5 million units, a value which did not occur during the sample period.

For forecasting, a manager will need to assign probabilities based on her best estimate of the likely outcomes since past data will not be available or may not apply. In these cases, it is crucial to perform sensitivity analysis to determine how sensitive the conclusions or forecasts are to changes in the underlying assumptions (or probabilities).

Bibliography

Douglas, E. J. (1992). *Managerial Economics*. 4th edn, Englewood Cliffs, NJ: Prentice-Hall.
Greene, W. H. (1993). *Econometric Analysis*. 2nd edn, New York: Macmillan.
Kmenta, J. (1986). *Elements of Econometrics*. 2nd edn, New York: Macmillan.

ROBERT E. MCAULIFFE

expected value The mean, or expected value, is a measure of central tendency for a random variable and it is one of the characteristics of probability distributions; the variance is another common characteristic. If the random variable, X is continuous and has specific values denoted by x, and the probability distribution of the values of X is given by $f(x)$, then the expected value of X, $E(X)$, is calculated as

experience and learning effects Costs per unit of output may be reduced for technological and organizational reasons as a result of producing a large output rather than a small one. If such cost reduction is linked to the level of cumulative output, then the firm is said to be enjoying the experience, or learning, effect (sometimes also referred to as

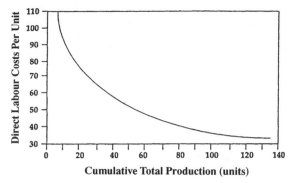

Figure 1 Typical experience curve (linear scales).

the labor portion of manufacturing costs, but also to costs incurred at every stage of what is today called the value chain (*see* VALUE CHAIN ANALYSIS), including marketing and R&D costs, and overhead. Bruce Henderson, together with the Boston Consulting Group (BCG), studied the concept in detail, and ways were found in which to utilize it for strategic decision making.

The experience curve specifies that, for every doubling in cumulative output, unit costs of value added net of inflation will fall by a fixed percentage α, typically 20 per cent. This means that the concept can be used to predict costs further down in time. If C_t and C_0 are the costs at times t and 0, respectively, and P_t and P_0 are accumulated volume of production at times t and 0, the following relationship holds:

$$C_t = C_0 \left(\frac{P_t}{P_0}\right)^{-\alpha}$$

The curve is plotted using a grid, with inflation adjusted cost per unit on the vertical axis, and accumulated volume of production, measured in units produced, on the horizontal axis (see figure 1). Plotted on logarithmic scales, the experience curve becomes a straight line, as shown in figure 2.

It is worth observing here that the curve can be drawn on a marginal as well as an average basis, as the two only differ by a constant proportion in a straight line. This is convenient, as unit costs are typically measured over a small portion of total production. More importantly, price and profit are concepts best examined marginally.

For the curve to be meaningful, it is important to define products accurately and consistently. The BCG recommends that these are defined in terms of perceived value to the customer, which implies that the same experience curve would continue to apply for product innovations which continue to serve the same customer requirements.

learning by doing (Arrow, 1962), the progress curve, or the improvement curve. If the cost reduction is linked to the number of units produced per unit of time, then ECONOMIES OF SCALE are involved. ECONOMIES OF SCOPE refer to cost reduction which is the effect of production in a large organization that administers many lines of production. These effects are interlinked in practice, but merit individual treatment for analytic purposes.

The Learning Effect

Cost reduction as a result of growth in cumulative output has been documented at least as early as in 1925, when it was observed in relation to the direct labor costs of aircraft manufacturing. When discussed in the context of direct labor costs, this cost reduction is referred to as the learning effect. Put simply, learning improves labor productivity; that is, the more units employees will produce, the more ways they will find to produce them faster and cheaper. This may be because repetition allows workers to discover improvements and short cuts which increase their efficiency.

The Experience Effect

During the mid-1960s, such cost reductions were also explicitly observed by Bruce Henderson at the Westinghouse Corporation, where he was a consultant. A consensus then emerged that such cost reductions applied not only to

Bibliography

Allan, G. B. & Hammond, J. S. (1975). *Note on the use of experience curves in competitive decision making.* Case no. 175-174, Harvard Business School. Boston, MA: Intercollegiate Case Clearing House/Cranfield, UK: Case Clearing House.

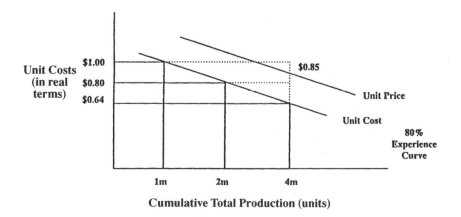

Figure 2 Typical experience curve drawn on logarithmic scales. As cumulative volume grows there is a real decline in product cost – this can lead to cost leadership pricing strategies.

Arrow, K. J. (1962). The economic implications of learning by doing. *Review of Economic Studies*, **29** (3), Reprinted 1970 in Perspectives Series. Boston, MA: Boston Consulting Group Inc.

Boston Consulting Group (1982). *Perspectives on experience*. Boston, MA: Boston Consulting Group Inc.

Buzzell, R. D., Gale, B. T. & Sultan, R. G. (1975). Market share – a key to profitability. *Harvard Business Review*, **53** (1), 97–107.

Hax, A. C. & Magiluf, N. S. (1984). *Strategic Management: An Integrative Perspective*. New Jersey: Englewood Cliffs. See pp. 108–26.

Henderson, B. D. (1980). *The experience curve revisited*. Perspectives Series. Boston, MA: Boston Consulting Group Inc.

Henderson, B. D. (1984). The application and misapplication of the experience curve. *Journal of Business Strategy*, **4** (3), 3–9.

Hirschman, W. B. (1964). Profit from the learning curve. *Harvard Business Review*, **42** (1), 125–39.

STEPHANOS AVGEROPOULOS

experimentation   Experimentation is a type of primary marketing research (*see* PRIMARY RESEARCH) in which the experimenter systematically manipulates the values of one or more variables (the independent variables), while controlling the values of other variables, to measure the effect of the changes in the independent variables on one or more other variables (the dependent variables).

Experimentation is often used to infer causal relationships. Causation cannot be inferred unless there is evidence that (1) the change in the independent variable(s) occurs before or simultaneously with the change in the dependent variable(s), (2) the effects of other extraneous variables are measured or controlled, and (3) there is a strong association between the changes in independent and dependent variables in the way predicted by hypotheses. Unfortunately, the scientific process is such that, even if these conditions are satisfied, one can never prove causation, only infer that a causal relationship may exist.

The need to rule out other causal factors in order to infer that the changes in the experimental variables cause the changes in the dependent variables is the reason behind the control of other possible causal factors. Control is obtained by devices such as (1) use of a control group which receives no treatment, (2) randomization, where test units are assigned to different experimental and control groups at random, (3) matching, where test units are matched on background variables before being assigned to groups, (4) use of a laboratory where conditions are controllable, (5) use of specific experimental designs that control extraneous variables, and (6) measuring and accounting for the effect of extraneous variables using statistical techniques such as multiple regression or analysis of covariance.

There are many types of experimental design. The simplest, the "after-only" design, involves changing the independent variable (the treatment) and following this with measurement of the dependent variable. Obvious weaknesses include the lack of a benchmark for comparison purposes and failure to control for the effect of extraneous variables. The "before-after" design which takes measurements of the dependent variable both before and after the treatment does allow effect of the treatment to be measured by the difference between the before and after measurement. This design suffers from a lack of control of intervening variables.

The "before-after with control group" design (with cases assigned to groups at random) can help to overcome the problem of intervening variables in that changes to many intervening variables will affect both groups and so the effect of the treatment can be measured when the before-after differences for the treatment group and the control group are compared.

Statistical designs permit the effect of changes to more than one independent variable to be measured. They allow the researcher to control for specific extraneous variables and an efficient design will allow several effects to be measured using as small a number of observations as possible. A randomized block design is useful when there is one major extraneous variable in addition to the dependent variable and treatment variable. The units being tested are assigned to groups or blocks defined by the extraneous variable, the experiment is carried out on the test units and the results analyzed to see if the treatment has an effect and to see if the effect is different in the various blocks. A Latin square design is similar to a randomized block design except that it allows the experimenter to specify blocks using two non-interacting external variables thus allowing the experimenter to control for two extraneous variables. A Graeco-Latin square allows the experimenter to control for a third non-interacting extraneous variable.

A factorial design is used to measure the effects of two or more independent variables. Factorial designs allow interaction effects to be measured.

Data obtained from such experimental designs are analyzed using statistical methods such as analysis of variance (*see* STATISTICAL QUALITY TECHNIQUES).

Experiments can take place in the field or in the laboratory. The advantage of field experiments is the high degree of realism that can be generated. Unfortunately, there is a lack of control, especially over intervening variables such as the weather, competitors, and the economy at large. What is worse is that the researcher may not be aware of changes to these variables. Field research is harder to conceal from competitors who have an opportunity of early discovery of possible new developments. Field research often turns out to be time-consuming and costly. However, for TEST MARKETING of new products or for measuring the effects of advertising, field experiments in actual market conditions may be necessary.

Laboratory experiments allow the researcher more control over not only the possible extraneous variables but also the measurement of the dependent variables and the changes to the independent variables. It is easier to use electronic/mechanical devices to measure dependent variables in the laboratory and the changes to the independent variables can be speeded up to reduce the time needed to conduct the experiment. However, because the experiment is conducted in an artificial environment, the generalizability of the results of laboratory experiments to the real world is reduced. Copy testing of TV (or press) commercials is an example of experimentation often carried out in the laboratory.

Bibliography
Aaker, D. A., Kumar, V. & Day, G. S. (1995). *Marketing research*, 5th edn, New York: John Wiley. Chapter 12.

MICHAEL GREATOREX

expert systems   Computer programs designed to mimic the problem-solving activity of human experts in specialized domains are known as expert systems. Human expertise is characterized by extensive knowledge of the problem domain (Chi et al., 1988). For a computer program to attain a comparable level of performance, the domain knowledge of human experts must be captured and represented in the program. Because of the centrality of domain knowledge in problem-solving, expert systems are also known as knowledge-based systems.

The Structure of Expert Systems

The development of an expert system begins with the acquisition of knowledge from a human expert. A systems professional (known as a knowledge engineer) works closely with a domain expert to accumulate and organize a body of explicit knowledge relevant to the problem being solved. Since expert knowledge is often tacit (difficult to articulate), a variety of methods is used in the knowledge acquisition process. These methods include interviewing, analysis of past records of expert decisions, and observation of experts engaged in their natural activity.

Once a body of domain knowledge has been acquired, the knowledge must be represented in a form suitable for use in a computer program. A number of knowledge representation formalisms have been developed over the years. The most common of these are if–then rules (also called condition–action rules or production rules), though other formalisms such as frames and predicate logic have also been implemented in some commercial systems.

If–then rules, as their name suggests, have two parts: a set of conditions necessary for the rule to "fire" (the *if* part), and a set of actions or consequences resulting from the application of the rule (the *then* part). Two hypothetical rules from the field of automobile repair may be:

> *Rule 1*: if (CAR DOES NOT START) then (CHECK BATTERY), and

> *Rule 2*: if (BATTERY OK) then (CHECK FUEL SUB-SYSTEM)

A rule-based expert system contains a large number of such if–then rules. The set of rules in an expert system is collectively called the *knowledge base* of the expert system.

Problems are solved by the expert system by composing the individual stored rules into sequences that connect the initial state to the goal state. The composition of individual rules into sequences is called *chaining*; both backward and forward chaining systems are possible. In *backward chaining*, reasoning proceeds from the goal state to identify the prior states leading to the observed outcome. Diagnostic expert systems often employ backward chaining to identify fault hypotheses which would account for the observed malfunction. In *forward chaining*, reasoning starts at the initial state and progresses through successive states until an acceptable goal state is found. A design expert system may use forward chaining to generate a configuration of components that satisfies certain constraints. Certain problems are better suited to backward chaining, while others are better solved by forward chaining. It is also possible to combine the use of both forms of reasoning in a single expert system. The part of the expert system program that performs reasoning on the knowledge base is called the inference engine.

While each if–then rule has a simple structure, the programming of rule-based expert systems becomes complex as the number of rules in the system increases (commercial systems may have thousands of rules). Clever pattern-matching algorithms have been devised to identify all the rules whose *if* conditions are satisfied in each state of problem-solving. Selecting one of the applicable rules as the most promising one to fire (called *conflict resolution*) is also a non-trivial programming task.

The knowledge in an expert system may not be completely deterministic, i.e. there may be uncertainty in the relation between the *if* and the *then* parts of a rule. For instance, finding a chemical pattern in a sample from a drilling site does not guarantee the presence of oil, it only provides probabilistic evidence. To represent such uncertainty in rules and propagate it through the reasoning process, a variety of methods (certainty factors, Bayesian networks, Dempster–Shafer theory, and fuzzy sets) have been developed. Because of their capacity to process uncertain information, expert systems are not restricted to choosing single alternatives; instead, they can rank a set of alternatives in order of their likelihood, given the information available.

Though the reasoning processes of expert systems are based on formal logic, human reasoning does not always closely follow the tenets of formal logic. One such characteristic of human reasoning is non-monotonicity – the possibility that conclusions, once accepted, may be revised in view of new information. Implementing non-monotonic reasoning enables an expert system to mimic the human expert's reasoning more closely, but implementing such a capability is a formidable programming task.

In addition to a knowledge base and an inference engine, some expert systems also have rudimentary capabilities for explaining the reasoning behind the system's conclusions or requests for information. In most cases, the explanation facility is little more than a trace of the rules fired to produce the conclusion, but even such a minimalist explanation is better than having none at all, and provides some insight into the operation of the system.

Some expert systems also attempt to automate the knowledge acquisition process by conducting a dialog with the user. An analysis of the knowledge base identifies the items of knowledge that can be used to generate hypotheses or choose among them. The user is then requested for these items of information through a structured question-and-answer dialog, and his/her responses are incorporated into the knowledge base. Automated knowledge acquisition opens up the possibility of improving system performance with usage.

Commercial Applications of Expert Systems

Significant commercial interest in expert systems was generated by the pioneering systems of the early 1980s: MYCIN (Buchanan & Shortliffe, 1984) in medical diagnosis; R1 (McDermott, 1982) in computer system configuration; and PROSPECTOR in mineral exploration. These programs amply demonstrated the power of knowledge-intensive approaches in solving otherwise intractable problems. The early programs were all hand-crafted in the LISP programming language, took multiple man-years of effort (from domain experts as well as software designers), and ran on special-purpose hardware. Though some high-technology companies invested in similar hand-crafted expert systems for their own applications, the popularity of expert systems technology in the business world spread mainly after inexpensive expert system "shells" became available.

An *expert system shell* is a commercially available programming environment that allows the entry of domain knowledge in the form of rules. An inference engine (usually capable of forward as well as backward cthe entry of rules and the observation of system performance. Many commercial shells also include interfaces to other software such as databases and programming languages. The availability of inexpensive shells running on desktop computers enabled individuals and organizations to create their own expert systems with minimal effort, and a large number of such systems appeared in organizations. With domain experts increasingly able to enter rules by themselves, the difficulties of knowledge acquisition were significantly reduced. In some ways, expert system shells became vehicles for END-USER COMPUTING, by which means skilled professionals, such as engineers and scientists, could institutionalize their personal expertise.

Today, expert systems are widely used in businesses to perform tasks ranging from diagnosis of manufacturing processes to credit approval by credit card companies. By encapsulating human expertise in computer programs, expert systems make such expertise durable, portable, and affordable. Numerous organizational scholars have also written about the organizational impacts of formalizing knowledge into expert systems.

Current Directions in Expert Systems Research

The first generation of expert systems, though commercially successful, had several shortcomings. They did not differentiate clearly between the knowledge used to construct the state space formulation of a problem and the knowledge used to guide heuristic search. This gave the knowledge acquisition process a somewhat haphazard character, making it prone to cost and time overruns. First-generation expert systems were made up entirely of an undifferentiated set of if–then associations. While this simplified the control structure of the programs, maintenance of the expert system in the face of rule additions became a problem (since the newly added rule could conflict with any of the existing rules). First-generation systems were also remarkably brittle, in the sense that any question even slightly outside the precisely defined scope of the system would evoke a "don't know" response.

Research into the second generation of expert systems (mid-1980s to the present) has sought to reframe the expert system development process as a modeling activity. Attempts are now made to create and use explicit models of the domain to which the expert system will be applied. The use of explicit models in expert systems overcomes many of the difficulties of the earlier-generation systems. Models provide a hierarchical organization for the knowledge in a system: the structure of the underlying model is clearly differentiated from associational if–then rules about the behavior of the model. The focus on a model also provides guidance to the knowledge acquisition process through the separation of domain knowledge from search control knowledge. Hopes have been expressed about the potential reusability of models across tasks and systems,

thus simplifying maintenance. Finally, a model-based approach also has the potential to deal with novelty, hence it may produce less brittle expert systems.

Traditionally, knowledge acquisition has been a frequent bottleneck in the development of expert systems. An active area of current research is the attempt to bypass the knowledge acquisition bottleneck through machine learning. Machine learning programs take as input a set of past cases (containing observed symptoms as well as expert judgments) and attempt to detect regularities in the relation between the symptoms of a case and the judgment of the expert in that case. Given sufficient data, it is possible to approximate the heuristics used by the expert in making his/her judgments, alleviating the need for the first-hand acquisition of this knowledge. The machine-generated heuristic knowledge can be programmed easily into an expert system.

see also **Artificial intelligence**

Bibliography

Chi, M. T. H., Glaser, R. & Farr, M. (eds) (1988). *The Nature of Expertise*. Hillsdale, NJ: Lawrence Erlbaum.

Buchanan, B. G. & Shortliffe, E. H. (1984). *Rule-based Expert Programs: the MYCIN Experiments of the Stanford Heuristic Programming Project*. Reading, MA: Addison-Wesley.

McDermott, J. (1982). R1: a rule-based configurer of computer systems. *Artificial Intelligence*, **19** (1), 39–88.

AMIT DAS

export agent   A party who assists in moving goods between buyers and sellers, but never takes title to the goods himself. This is an extremely important function in international trade. It is carried out by a large number of specialists in a variety of areas. Agents locate and bring together products, manufacturers, markets, buyers, and sellers of goods. The agent could work on behalf of either the seller (exporter) or buyer (importer). The following list consists of agents with a variety of responsibilities. A particular type of agent listed may be just another name for one of the other categories. They are still listed and briefly identified because the alternate name may not be known by the international businessperson. Common types of export agents include:

1 Broker – A broker is a person who brings together a buyer and a seller. An export broker brings together exporters and importers for a fee. A broker generally does not have any further involvement in the trade transaction (although some brokers can and do provide additional services).

2 Buying agent – When a company does not have employees stationed overseas to purchase goods, a buying agent may be employed to represent the company. Buying agents know the foreign market for goods and how to negotiate in foreign markets. They can be of great assistance in completing foreign transactions. The authority of the agent should be carefully spelled out in the contract between the agent and the company to make certain the company's interests are appropriately represented.

3 Cargo broker – A person who acts as a middle-man between cargo owners and shipowners. By locating ships for hire, the cargo broker earns a commission. The commission is often referred to as an "address

commission." Cargo brokers play an important role in international trade, especially when one considers the inexperience of many cargo owners in terms of transporting goods overseas.

4 Combination export manager (CEM) – Combination export managers are in the business of purchasing goods from a number of companies and then combining those goods to meet existing orders or to place on the export market. Often manufacturers of goods do not produce sufficient quantities to take advantage of the most efficient modes of transportation or discounts for shipment of large lots. A CEM can take advantage of such efficiencies and/or discounts by combining the production of many companies. Although CEMs do occasionally work on a commission basis for manufacturers, they more commonly buy and sell as a separate entity involved in the export business. It is very common for CEMs to specialize in particular goods or industries. In this way they become familiar to both producers and buyers of particular goods.

5 Commission agent – It is common for companies involved in foreign trade to work through representatives or agents who sell goods on behalf of the companies. These agents usually work for a percentage of the goods sold (a commission). In many countries these people are referred to as manufacturers' representatives. Commission agents usually specialize in certain types of products or industrial output in order to build their relationships with both buyers and sellers. In order to monitor their activities, commission agents are required by many countries to be registered and bonded.

6 Confirming house – A United Kingdom trade intermediary who performs financing and other functions for exporters. The confirming house, unlike other export agents, actually finances exports by allowing the exporter to be paid from its funds when the exports are shipped. The confirming house also usually handles the contracts for both the seller and buyer and may arrange transportation if necessary.

7 Customhouse broker – Importers often feel that their tasks are complete when arrangements have been made to pay for and take delivery of imported items. However, another obstacle may lie in the path of the successful completion of the transaction: the customs authority of a country. Obtaining custom's approval to bring goods into a country (clearing customs) is not always a simple task. Appropriate papers must accompany imports and all requirements of the importing country must be met. Privately-owned and operated consultants called customhouse brokers are ready to assist importers in clearing goods through customs. All necessary papers will be obtained, clearances, certificates (country of origin, health, etc.) and the documents will be checked by the broker in order to speed the customs clearing process. For this service they charge a fee. Customhouse brokers are licensed by the appropriate government agency. These people generally know how to get goods cleared quickly and are usually worth the expenditure.

8 Distributor – A distributor is an intermediary who acts on behalf of others to distribute goods. Distributors are very common in international trade. Instead of attempting to directly enter foreign markets (normally a very time-consuming and expensive proposition) an exporter may instead enter into a relationship with an importer to become a "distributor" for the exporter. A distributor does more than just import goods. A distributor also packages or repackages if necessary, advertises the goods, distributes them, and may even provide service after the sale. For all of this activity the distributor usually retains a portion of the sales and is commonly granted exclusive rights to distribute the product in a specified region. Hiring a distributor to handle goods in a foreign country is one of the simpler methods of entering a foreign market.

9 Exclusive agent – This term describes the relationship between a principal (e.g., a manufacturing company) and an agent (e.g., a manufacturer's representative) in which the principal grants the agent exclusive rights (e.g., to sell a particular product in a particular country or region). Thus, the exclusive agent is the only party who can represent the manufacturer in selling products in a specific geographic region. Anyone seeking the product will have to work through the exclusive agent. In return for the grant of exclusivity, the agent usually agrees to some minimum level of representation and performance.

10 Export broker – A broker is a person who brings together a buyer and a seller. An export broker brings together exporters and importers for a fee. A broker generally does not have any further involvement in the trade transaction.

11 Export commission house – An export commission house is an agent of the buyer of goods. Export commission houses are located in the country which produces the exports. As an agent for the export buyer, the export commission house seeks out manufacturers of products requested by importers. The commission house handles the majority of the transaction thereby relieving both the exporter and the importer from a great deal of work. Commission houses are compensated through commissions paid by the buyer of goods.

12 Export trading company (ETC) – An export trading company is an organization established for the purpose of facilitating the export of goods and services. The company's ownership may be domestic, foreign, or any combination of the two. Its clients are producers of goods, importers of all types, governments of different countries, all of whom are interested in exporting or importing items.

13 Freight forwarder – A freight forwarder is a trade intermediary who arranges for the transportation of goods. Freight forwarders can also offer additional services to exporters and importers because of the expertise they gain in dealing with the trade transaction.

14 Import broker – Many persons who are involved in exporting activities do not have the knowledge or contacts to successfully conduct trade activities. An import broker is hired by exporters to locate buyers (importers) for the exporter's goods. Typically, the import broker receives a commission for services rendered.

15 Intermerchant – An intermerchant works for exporters and importers to solve problems with converting soft currencies to hard currencies. Some currencies are

more readily convertible than others. The so called "hard" currencies are regularly traded and generally pose no problems in the exchange process. "Soft" currencies, however, are often difficult to exchange. An intermerchant is a person specializing in solving problems associated with hard and soft currency exchange. The intermerchant makes necessary arrangements for paying for goods sold between countries with hard currencies and those with soft currencies.

16 Manufacturer's export agent – This trade intermediary acts on behalf of producers who desire to offer goods for export. The agent, who finds buyers for the producer's goods, does not purchase for his own account and is paid strictly on a commission basis.

17 Resident buyer – This intermediary represents foreign buyers of locally produced goods. Most resident buyers are employees of the foreign firms they represent. Resident buyers look to establish long-term relationships with producers of goods by handling all of the details of purchase, shipping, and delivery to the foreign buyer.

18 Resident buying agents – Most organizations conducting international trade do not use their own employees to either buy or sell goods in various countries. The differences between business practices, language, and cultural problems usually make employee arrangements difficult at best. Instead of using employees, organizations may turn to intermediaries in each country to secure goods needed by the organization in its home country (or other country of production). Intermediaries who purchase goods for a foreign company (to be shipped to that foreign company) are referred to as "resident buying agents."

19 Resident selling agents – Most international enterprises do not have actual production taking place in each of the countries. They also normally do not have their own employees in each country because the costs would be prohibitive for all but the largest of organizations. It is very common under these circumstances to use the services of an intermediary to sell a company's goods in overseas markets. Intermediaries who act on behalf of an organization to sell its products in a given country are referred selling agents.

20 Wholesaler/distributor – Wholesalers/distributors purchase large quantities of goods from suppliers and resell them on international markets. Often individual importers do not have the ability to secure certain products from overseas suppliers or they find that suppliers will sell only in container lots or other large bulk quantities. The inability to secure small amounts of goods at fair prices has led to the development of wholesale international traders and distributors. Wholesale international traders purchase large quantities of goods from suppliers, break them into smaller lots, and resell the goods to others. By working through the international wholesaler/distributor the smaller business may have access to a larger number of goods than would otherwise be (economically) available.

Bibliography

Czinkota, M. R., Rivoli, P. & Ronkainen, I. A. (1989). *International Business*. Chicago, IL: The Dryden Press.
Grosse, C. U. & Grosse, R. E. (1988). *Case studies in international business*. Englewood Cliffs, NJ: Prentice Hall.
Johnson, T. E. (1994). *Export–Import procedures and documentation*. New York: Amacom.
Maruca, R. F. (1994). The right way to go global: An interview with whirlpool. CEO David Whitman. *Harvard Business Review* March–April, 134–45.
Zodl, J. A. (1992). *Export–Import: Everything you and your company need to know to compete in world markets*. Cincinnati, OH: Betterway Books.

JOHN O'CONNELL

export financing   There are a number of methods of paying for goods and services imported from other countries. The methods are relatively common and are much the same as those used in the financing of other goods and services. Eight common methods are reviewed below.

1 Acceptance financing – A method of financing imports and exports through a short-term line of credit. The lending bank may include specific documentation requirements to show evidence of title to the merchandise. The required documentation normally consists of either a warehouse receipt or a bill of lading.

2 Collection – Collection involves the payment by an importer for goods sold by an exporter. Collection papers are the documents specified in the sales contract which must be provided to the buyer (or the buyer's bank) in order for payment to be made.

3 Consignment – Consignment is a process through which an owner of goods (consignor) transfers them to an agent (consignee) who is then responsible for selling the goods to others. In international trade, consignment is actually a method of financing import transactions. The exporter of goods (consignor) transfers goods to an importer (consignee) who then sells the goods. When the goods are sold the proceeds are divided between the agent (a commission for selling the goods) and the exporter (the balance of the amount paid).

4 Documentary credit – This is the formal name for a letter of credit. A seller under a letter of credit is paid by a bank upon presentation of the shipping papers and other documents specified in the letter of credit. Unless it is irrevocable, a letter of credit does not guarantee that the credit might not be revoked by the bank prior to presentation of the documents. Specific types of letters of credit are available to provide additional assurances to the seller that payment will be made upon presentation of the proper documents.

5 Factoring foreign accounts receivable – With regard to financing a company's operations, factoring refers to the use of accounts receivable as a source of borrowed funds or as an asset to be sold to others. Banks will often grant credit based upon the value of the accounts receivable of a company. As the receivables are collected the bank is repaid.

6 Foreign accounts receivable purchases – Factoring is also accomplished by parties who purchase the foreign receivables of an exporter at a discount. The company receives immediate payment and the factor receives payments from the debtors.

7 Open account – A method of arranging payment for exports which provides a stated number of days in which the importer must make payment. Open accounts are normally used only when the importer is well known to the exporter.

8 Payment in advance – When an exporter has no dealings with an importer or those dealings were less than satisfactory, payment in advance may be required. Payment in advance may also be required when the order is for specially designed or custom-made goods which no other importer could use.

Bibliography

Bowker, R. R. (1993). *International handbook of financial reporting.* London: Chapman & Hall.

Johnson, T. E. (1994). *Export–Import procedures and documentation.* New York: Amacom.

United States Customs Service (1994). *A basic guide to importing.* Lincolnwood, IL: NTC Publishing Group.

Zodl, J. A. (1992). *Export–Import: Everything you and your company need to know to compete in world markets.* OH: Betterway Books.

JOHN O'CONNELL

export management company (EMC)   Export management companies provide services to local companies seeking to export goods. Services vary from acting as the agent of the exporter, to arranging sales, to purchasing the goods in the name of the EMC for reselling. More commonly, however, an EMC acts as an external export department for companies who are new to exporting and do not have the in-house expertise to carry out the entire export transaction. Hiring a specialized company to perform export related activities is often the least time-consuming way to enter the export market. EMCs may be compensated on a commission, fee, or other basis as agreed under contract with the exporter.

JOHN O'CONNELL

export trading company (ETC)   There are two distinct definitions of this term: (1) An export trading company is an organization established for the purpose of facilitating the export of goods and services. The company's ownership may be domestic, foreign, or any combination of the two. Its clients are producers of goods, importers of all types, governments of different countries, all of whom are interested in exporting or importing items. (2) A specially recognized (Under the Export Trading Act of 1982) company organized for the purpose of exporting United States goods and services. ETCs are eligible for special business and financial assistance through government and private sources and are exempt from many of the provisions of US antitrust laws (because their operations involve mainly foreign transfer of goods).

JOHN O'CONNELL

exporting   It is not easy to make a clear-cut distinction between exporting and INTERNATIONAL MARKETING, either for conceptual purposes or in terms of operational practices. However, it could be argued that, whereas exporting entails some elements of international marketing, international marketing can be understood as a business function quite independent of exporting. In international marketing, the emphasis is on: firms' strategy development; the management of marketing functions pertaining to firms' overall international position; and the degree and complexity of their involvements in foreign markets. Exporting may be seen, therefore, as one of the minimal stages of firms' involvements with foreign markets. The characterization of exporting as "selling in foreign markets" is only of limited value, implying that exporting is somewhat hit-and-miss or unfocused.

The point not to be overlooked is that a majority of all international firms, no matter how globally known and dominant today, were at one time small or at least substantially smaller international players. Exporting can then be seen to be a element of the growth path or learning curve of international business operations. In the 1970s and 1980s a substantial number of academic studies examined exporting firms with the center of interest being how they became exporters. There were two dimensions of interest. The first dimension was concerned with the motives that stimulated non-exporters to become exporters: the second with the stages of internationalization, in other words forms or degrees of dependence on foreign business. With respect to the first dimension, the motives would be classified in terms of internal and external impulses, on the one hand, and proactive and reactive factors, on the other, as exemplified in table 1.

The second dimension, which attracted considerable scholarly attention, posited stages of internationalization of the firm through the increasing extension of its exporting activities and their sophistication. The 1970s and 1980s produced a number of models in Europe and the USA, based on industry samples. The Swedish scholars Johanson & Vahlne (1977) proposed a four-stage model, according to which firms: export sporadically; export using an agent; export via a sales subsidiary; and manufacture in a foreign

Table 1   Motives for non-exporters to become exporters

	Internal stimuli	*External stimuli*
Proactive factors	● management decision ● economies of scale ● unique product or competence ● perceived profitability ● marketing competence	● identified foreign business opportunities ● stimulation/incentives from government, chambers of commerce
Reactive factors	● risk diversification ● excess capacity ● retrenchment	● unsolicited foreign orders ● small or shrinking home market

subsidiary. Other models have attempted to demonstrate a "natural" progression from passive or occasional exporting to a stage of making no distinction between home and foreign markets. But these characterizations have been criticized by subsequent scholars who, with some justification, find them "too logical" and therefore not consistent with actual experience. This has developed, in the USA, to a keen interest in the managerial influences, including competencies, on export development; in Europe, studies of internationalization have led to extensive investigations of firms' international networking (*see* NETWORK) behavior.

The problem with these preoccupations with export motivations and stages of internationalization is that they deflect attention from exporting as an everyday business activity. It is in the exporters' task that we find a clear distinction between exporting and international marketing. First of all, exporting is a form of foreign market entry (*see* INTERNATIONAL MARKET ENTRY AND DEVELOPMENT STRATEGIES), the essential characteristic of which is that it involves direct selling to foreign customers. The selling can be completely direct in the sense that, even if the firm makes use of the services of an export house or a locally appointed agent or sets up an export department, the direct investment in the foreign market is small. In other words, exporting is selling into foreign markets with a permanent and (more or less) exclusive representation by a *stockholding* market intermediary such as a distributor.

With respect to export departments, it should be emphasized that their prime purpose, generally, is not to support the foreign sales effort through undertaking market studies or assisting with export development plans, but to process the paperwork associated with the physical transfer of products into foreign markets. Such activity can include: the issuing and processing of invoices; the arranging of payments inward and outward in foreign currencies; the preparation of company brochures in foreign languages; and the supervision of transportation arrangements taking account of special requirements concerning customs procedures and goods certification in the target market.

As for the job of export managers, one of their main tasks is to forecast demand in given foreign markets and to prepare the company accordingly to meet it. Evidence suggests that forecasts of demand are based on personal relationships (*see* RELATIONSHIP MARKETING) with customers which are particularly close. The export manager is unlikely to engage in the more sophisticated and expensive forms of international marketing research, which seek to create coherent and systematic methodologies for identifying foreign customers and developing specific, culture-sensitive, business approaches. It would, however, be mistaken to assume that the export manager is perforce less adroit than the international marketing manager. The point to emphasize is that they represent different approaches to business development in foreign markets, the crucial difference residing in the scale of investment that the firm is willing to commit to foreign markets. In relative terms, selling industrial refrigerators to Saudi Arabia may be equally demanding as developing a marketing strategy for the same products in China.

Bibliography

Johanson, J. & Vahlne, J.-E. (1977). The internationalisation process of the firm – a model of knowledge development and increasing foreign market commitments. *Journal of International Business Studies*, 8, (1), Spring/Summer 23–32.

NIGEL HOLDEN

exposure Exposure describes the extent to which an organization's financial condition is affected by various factors. Factors include: fluctuations in exchange rates, market price changes during the export transaction, government action causing political risk, and others.

JOHN O'CONNELL

expropriation This form of political risk involves a government seizing a foreign organization's property. Compensation is not guaranteed. If forthcoming, compensation after expropriation may be delayed and be in amounts far less than the actual value of the assets taken. Expropriation in one form or another has taken place in most industrialized and developing nations.

see also **Political risk**

Bibliography

Morgan, L. L. (1977). *The case for the multinational corporation.* New York: Praeger.

JOHN O'CONNELL

external equity/external competitiveness External equity is one of two organizing concepts (along with INTERNAL EQUITY/INTERNAL CONSISTENCY) used to define the structure and form of a traditional JOB-BASED PAY system. External competitiveness refers to the pay rates of an organization's jobs in relation to its competitors' pay rates. Thus, unlike the concept of internal equity, external equity is concerned with relative pay rates among (not within) organizations (Milkovich and Newman, 1993, p. 190). The conventional view is that the lower bound of a job-specific pay rate is set by the labor market (this is the point below which it is not possible to attract newcomers to the organization) and the upper bound reflects product market competition. Management sets pay rates within these limits based upon such things as the concern for internal equity, the need to control labor costs, and the organization's ability to pay.

A highly competitive pay rate (a rate that exceeds or leads the market) would be set in an attempt to increase such things as the number and quality of applicants and the likelihood that qualified individuals will accept job offers, and to control voluntary turnover (Williams and Dreher, 1992). Firms that lag the market rate would, in principle, find it difficult to attract and retain talent but might maintain a labor cost advantage over the competition.

The principle means of establishing external equity is to conduct WAGE AND SALARY SURVEYS to estimate the pay ranges set at competing firms. While the goal is to estimate the market wage for a particular job, the process of collecting relevant data requires considerable judgment – leading some to conclude that the market wage is an illusive concept (Rynes and Milkovich, 1986).

Bibliography

Milkovich, G. T. & Newman, J. M. (1993). *Compensation,* Homewood, IL: Richard D. Irwin.

Rynes, S. L. & Milkovich, G. T. (1986). Wage surveys: dispelling some myths about the "market wage." *Personnel Psychology*, **39**, 71–90.

Williams, M. L. & Dreher, G. F. (1992). Compensation system attributes and applicant pool characteristics. *Academy of Management Journal*, **35**, 571–95.

GEORGE F. DREHER

extra-territorial application of employment law
The application of equal employment opportunity (EEO) laws such as Title VII of the 1964 Civil Rights Act, the Age Discrimination in Employment Act (ADEA), and the Americans with Disabilities Act (ADA) in multinational enterprises (MNEs) has generated a degree of uncertainty. Foreign employers doing business in the United States must generally abide by US EEO law (*Sumitomo Shoji America* v. *Avigliano*, 28 FEP Cases 1753, 1982; *MacNamara* v. *Korean Airlines*, 48 FEP Cases 980, 1988). The US Supreme Court ruled in *Boureslan* v. *Aramco*, 55 FEP Cases 449 (1991) that Title VII did not apply to American citizens working abroad for American employers. This ruling was overturned by the CIVIL RIGHTS ACT OF 1991. Section 701 of Title VII now provides language similar to that contained in the ADEA and the ADA. Thus, US citizens working in foreign countries for US companies are protected from various types of employment discrimination based on race, sex, religion, national origin, color, age, and disability status. There is an exemption if compliance with Title VII or the ADA would cause the employer to violate the law of a foreign country where the employee is working. Section 702 of Title VII also states that the law "shall not apply to an employer with respect to aliens outside of any State" (Bureau of National Affairs, 1991).

Bibliography
Bureau of National Affairs (1991). *Fair Employment Practices*, Washington, DC: Bureau of National Affairs.

TERRY L. LEAP

F

factor-comparison job evaluation method Under the factor-comparison method, jobs are evaluated using two standards: a set of COMPENSABLE FACTORS and the wages for a group of benchmark jobs (Milkovich and Newman, 1996). These two standards are combined to form a job comparison scale which is then used to arrange non-benchmark jobs into the final job hierarchy. The set of benchmark jobs must cover the entire range of each compensable factor. First, each benchmark job is ranked on all the compensable factors, resulting in a matrix which arrays rankings for each benchmark job on each compensable factor. Second, these rankings are translated into dollar amounts by determining how much of the total wage for a benchmark job is associated with each compensable factor. The sum of these dollar values must add up to the total wage for that job. Third, for each compensable factor, two sets of rank orders are created: one arranging the factor's rankings for all benchmark jobs from high to low and another similarly arranging the dollar values. These two rank orders are adjusted until the hierarchy of benchmark jobs is the same for both. (Large discrepancies in rankings usually indicate a benchmark job that should not be used for job evaluation purposes.) This sequential process creates the job comparison scale where the level of each compensable factor has a dollar value assigned to it plus an array of benchmark jobs to serve as anchors. Non-benchmark jobs can then be slotted into each compensable factor using the benchmark jobs as a standard of comparison. The total wage for each job is simply the sum of its dollar-valued rankings on each compensable factor.

Bibliography

Milkovich, G. T. & Newman, J. M. (1996). *Compensation*, **5th edn**, Homewood, IL: Richard D. Irwin.

MATTHEW C. BLOOM

fail-safing The concept of fail-safing has emerged since the introduction of Japanese methods of operations improvement. Called *poka-yoke* in Japan (from *yokeru*, to prevent, and *poka*, inadvertent errors) the idea is based on the principle that human mistakes are, to some extent, inevitable. The important issue, therefore, is to prevent them becoming defects. *Poka-yokes* are simple and preferably inexpensive devices or systems which are incorporated into a process to prevent inadvertent operator mistakes resulting in a defect.

Typical *poka-yokes* are such devices as limit switches on machines which allow the machine to operate only if the part is positioned correctly, gauges placed on machines through which a part has to pass in order to be loaded onto, or taken off, the machine, incorrect size or orientation stopping the process, digital counters on machines to insure that the correct number of cuts, passes, or holes have been machined, checklists which have to be filled in, either in preparation for, or on completion of, an activity, and light beams which activate an alarm if a part is positioned incorrectly.

More recently, the principle of fail-safing has been applied to service operations. Service *poka-yokes* have been classified as those which "fail-safe the server" (the creator of the service) and those which "fail-safe the customer" (the receiver of the service).

Examples of fail-safing the server include color coding cash register keys to prevent incorrect entry in retail operations, the McDonalds french fry scoop which picks up the right quantity of fries in the right orientation to be placed in the pack, trays used in hospitals with indentations shaped to each item needed for a surgical procedure – any item not back in place at the end of the procedure might have been left in the patient – and paper strips placed round clean towels in hotels (the removal of which helps housekeepers to tell whether a towel has been used and therefore needs replacing).

Examples of fail-safing the customer include the locks on aircraft lavatory doors, which must be turned to switch the light on, beepers on ATMs to ensure that customers remove their cards, height bars on amusement rides to insure that customers do not exceed size limitations, outlines drawn on the walls of a child care center to indicate where toys should be replaced at the end of the play period, and tray stands strategically placed in fast-food restaurants to remind customers to clear their tables.

see also **Maintenance; Service recovery; Failure analysis**

Bibliography

Chase, R. B. & Stewart, D. M. (1994). Make your service fail-safe. *Sloan Management Review*, Spring, 35–44.

NIGEL SLACK

failure rates (expatriates) Although not a pleasant task, determining the rate of failure of employees assigned to overseas positions is important to an organization. Records can show the trends over time as well as offering comparisons with other companies. If the human relations department keeps such records along with the reasons for failure, programs may be instituted to increase expatriate success. For example, if a common reason for failure is language unfamiliarity, intensive language education could be instituted for all future expatriates.

see also **Expatriate; Expatriate training**

Bibliography

Black, J. S. (1988). Work role transitions: A study of American expatriate managers in Japan. *Journal of International Business Studies*, **19** (2), 277–94.

JOHN O'CONNELL

Federal Mediation and Conciliation Service The Federal Mediation and Conciliation Service (FMCS) was established by the Labor Management Relations Act of 1947 as an independent agency. It took over all mediation and conciliation functions of the federal government, replacing the former United States Conciliation Service, which was in the Department of Labor. The FMCS is headed by a director appointed by the President with Senate approval.

The FMCS is required by statute to offer its services to help to settle labor disputes affecting interstate commerce through the offices of its commissioners located throughout the country. It may act either upon request by one of the parties or on its own initiative.

A party desiring to terminate or modify an existing COLLECTIVE BARGAINING agreement must notify the FMCS of the dispute. When the FMCS has intervened in a dispute, both the union and the employer must participate fully in any meetings called by the service. If mediation or conciliation does not result in a settlement, the service must urge the parties to voluntarily seek other means of settlement, including ARBITRATION. Either party may reject the FMCS suggestion without violating any obligation imposed by the Act. The FMCS also provides arbitration and fact-finding services to parties requesting them. It makes available panels of qualified potential arbitrators or fact-finders for the parties' selection. It publishes annual data on the locations (by states) and nature of the services it has provided. The FMCS also provides and participates in educational programs for the parties and for arbitrators.

JOHN C. SHEARER

fiduciary duty   is a duty of a person in a position of trust to act in the interest of another person without gaining any material benefit, except with the knowledge and consent of that other person.

The term describes the legal duty of trustees, guardians, executors, agents, and others who are in an explicit fiduciary relation, but a fiduciary relation may exist in law whenever one person has superior power or influence over another person and the other person places confidence in or relies on that person. Although it is primarily a legal term, *fiduciary duty* is also used to describe the purely ethical duty of a person in a position of trust. Thus, some breaches of fiduciary duty by lawyers (who are in a fiduciary relation with clients) constitute ethical but not legal misconduct.

In business, officers and directors of corporations are fiduciaries with a duty to act in the interest of the corporation and, to some extent, the stockholders. Members of partnerships and joint enterprises are fiduciaries with respect to each other's interest; majority stockholders are considered in law to have a fiduciary duty similar to that of officers and directors; and minority stockholders in closely held corporations are fiduciaries under certain conditions. Corporations and their members may have a fiduciary duty toward employees, customers, and other constituencies in such matters as employee pension plans and client investment accounts, and the duty of loyalty that employees have to a firm is sometimes regarded as fiduciary in character.

The concept of fiduciary duty originated in common law for cases in which one person entrusts property to the care of another, and it remains a central concept in the law of trusts. Use of the concept has been extended over time to other trust-like situations in order to prevent abuse when one person has superior power over another. Historically, fiduciary duty belongs to the law of equity, in which courts decide cases on the basis of justice or fairness instead of strictly formulated rules, and the concept developed as a means for imposing duties where precise rules cannot be easily formulated. Fiduciary duties are further unlike the specific duties created by contracts in that they are imposed on all persons in fiduciary relations and cannot be easily altered by the affected parties.

Among the features of fiduciary duty, the most prominent are:

(1) *An open-ended duty to act in the interest of another.* The acts that a person in a fiduciary relation are required to perform are generally not specified in advance, so that a fiduciary has wide latitude in the means used to advance the interests of another. The standards for evaluating the performance of a fiduciary are commonly those of due care, good faith, and, in business, the business judgment rule, all of which can be satisfied by many different acts.

(2) *A closed-in duty to avoid acting in self-interest.* Generally, the acts in a fiduciary's self interest that violate a fiduciary duty are clearly stated in the law. Among such specific legal prohibitions are self-dealing, acceptance of bribes, direct competition, and use of confidential information.

(3) *Strongly mandatory, moralistic character.* Whereas much of corporate law can be altered by agreement or contract between the affected parties, fiduciary duties are relatively unalterable. An agent can engage in self-dealing, for example, with the knowledge and consent of the principal, but courts hold such departures from fiduciary duty to very stringent standards.

The importance of fiduciary duty for business ethics lies principally in the question, to whom do officers and directors owe a fiduciary duty? The standard answer is that management has a fiduciary duty to stockholders and to stockholders alone, so that corporations ought to be run solely in their interest, which is to say that managers should seek to maximize stockholder wealth. This stockholder view of the corporation has been challenged on two different grounds. Some critics argue that the ethical basis of a fiduciary duty to serve the interests of stockholders has been undermined by the changed nature of corporate property, caused in part by the separation of ownership and control noted by Berle and Means. Stockholders, according to these critics, do not entrust their property to the managers of corporations but are merely investors who can be said to own only their stock, not the corporation. Thus, Dodd (1932) argued that corporate managers no longer had a strict fiduciary duty to serve the interests of stockholders but were free to operate the corporation for the benefit of diverse constituencies. In the famous Berle–Dodd debate, Berle (1932) agreed that the traditional ethical basis of management's fiduciary duty to stockholders had been undermined but argued against freeing managers to serve other interests because of the danger of unbridled management discretion.

Other critics of the stockholder view of the corporation contend that the same conditions which create a fiduciary duty to serve the interests of stockholders also apply to other constituencies, with the result that a fiduciary duty is owed to these other constituencies as well. Thus, officers and directors may have a fiduciary duty to other investors, such as bondholders, to protect their investments; to employees to maintain remunerative employment; to consumers to meet their needs and to protect them against harm from defective products; and so on. Such arguments lend support to STAKEHOLDER THEORY as an alternative to the stockholder view.

Recent developments in corporate law reflect both of these grounds of criticism, and shifting understandings of the fiduciary duty of management remain central to the ongoing debate over the purpose of corporations and the interests that they ought to serve.

Bibliography

Bayne, D. C. (1958). The Fiduciary Duty of Management: The Concept in the Courts. *University of Detroit Law Review*, 25, 561–94.

Berle, A. A. (1932). For Whom Corporate Managers Are Trustees: A Note *Harvard Law Review*, 45, 1365–72.

Bratton, W. W. (1992). Public Values and Corporate Fiduciary Law. *Rutgers Law Review*, 44, 675–98.

Clark, R. C. (1985). Agency Costs versus Fiduciary Duties. In J. W. Pratt & R. J. Zeckhauser (eds), *Principals and Agents: The Structure of Business*. (pp. 55–79). Boston: Harvard Business School Press.

Dodd, E. M. (1932). For Whom Are Corporate Managers Trustees? *Harvard Law Review*, 45, 1145–63.

Frankel, T. (1983). Fiduciary Law. *California Law Review*, 71, 795–836.

Scott, A. W. (1949). The Fiduciary Principle, *California Law Review*, 37, 539–55.

Sealy, L. S. (1962). Fiduciary Relationships. *Cambridge Law Journal*, 69–81.

JOHN R. BOATRIGHT

final offer arbitration Final offer arbitration (FOA) is a type of INTEREST ARBITRATION used to resolve contract negotiation disputes. In contrast to conventional interest arbitration, where an arbitrator has wide discretion to fashion an award, FOA places severe limits on the arbitrator's decision authority. The arbitrator is required to select the final arbitration offer submitted by the employer or by the union; a compromise outcome is prohibited. In FOA by package, the arbitrator selects one party's entire package of offers on all the disputed issues. In FOA by issue, the arbitrator selects one party's final offer separately on each disputed issue. The underlying rationale for FOA is that its all or nothing nature will give each party a strong incentive to submit reasonable offers.

PETER FEUILLE

financial repatriation and multinational firms The return on any investment, whether a stock, bond, or construction of a manufacturing facility, is determined by the cash flows returned over time. Multinational firms must, in order to pursue the maximization of stockholder wealth, return cash flows from foreign affiliates to the parent in order to ultimately justify the investment. The way in which cash flows are repatriated to the parent firm will have, however, a significant impact on the profitability of the foreign affiliate, the parent, and the tax liabilities of both. A number of recent cases of multinational firms earning substantial returns on their foreign affiliates, but not via dividend distributions, has raised the level of concern of host- and home-country governments over the repatriation policies and decisions of their multinationals. This article provides some preliminary evidence on a national basis of the methods employed by US-based firms in the repatriation of earnings from foreign affiliates.

Repatriation of Earnings Versus Foreign Income
The *repatriation of earnings* is distinctly different from what is often termed *foreign income*. The US Department of Commerce (the primary source of data for this analysis) defines *foreign income* as the total of distributed earnings (dividends paid to the US-based firm), reinvested earnings (retained earnings of the foreign affiliate of the US-based firm), and net interest income from the foreign affiliate. (The use of the terms *parent* and *affiliate* is a little troublesome in the following analysis, given the data collected by the US Department of Commerce). The cash flows reported to the Department of Commerce are for foreign firms which a US-based firm (incorporated within the United States) holds a 10 percent or greater voting equity interest. The US firm, therefore, may not be a true *parent* (holding controlling or exclusive interest), but simply a major equity holder.) Both distributed earnings and net interest are net of withholding taxes by the host-country government. *Repatriated earnings*, which we wish to distinctly differentiate from *foreign income*, occur in four major forms:

1. *Distributed earnings or dividends*. Dividends, or distributed earnings, are profits from foreign affiliate operations arising from either current period or prior period earnings, including capital gains/losses, which are paid to the owners of the affiliate (either foreign or domestic). (Unless otherwise noted, we refer here to the *net payment* resulting from the series of cash flows between affiliate and parent. It is not unusual for payments to be made both to the parent from the affiliate, and to the affiliate from the parent – interest payments, for example.)

2. *Royalties and license fees*. Fees paid for the use, sale, or purchase of intangible property, such as technological techniques, patents, brand names, and so forth.

3. *Net interest*. Interest paid by the foreign affiliate resulting from credit extended by the parent to the foreign affiliate for its capitalization and on-going funding needs, as well as interest payments on capital leases.

4. *Distributed charges*. Charges imposed by the parent on the foreign affiliate for services provided. This category includes allocated expenses (allocated expenses or reimbursements for management, professional, technical, or other services that normally would be included in "other income" in the income statement of the provider of the service), rentals for the use of tangible property (rentals for operating leases of one year or less and net rent on operating leases of more than one year; net rent is equivalent to the total lease payment less the return of capital (depreciation) component), and film and television tape rentals.

Table 1 Comparison of foreign income and repatriation of earnings: foreign affiliates of US-based firms, 1993 (millions of US dollars)

Income of foreign affiliate	Net receipt ($)	With tax	Net remittance ($)	Repatriation of earnings from foreign affiliate
Gross earnings including capital gains				
Less royalties and license fees	14,926	(746)	14,179	(1) Royalties and license fees from affiliate
Less distributed charges	4,908	(-0-)	4,908	(2) Distributed charges from affiliate
Earnings before interest and taxes				
Less interest	1,398	(169)	1,229	(3) Interest earnings from affiliate
Earnings before taxes				
Less corporate taxes				
Earnings after tax	56,117			
Reinvested	29,565			
Distributed (dividends)	26,552	(947)	25,605	(4) Net distributed earnings from affiliate (dividends)
Income = earnings before capital gains plus capital gains income plus net interest after withholding taxes less withholding taxes on distributed earnings = 56,117 + 1,398 − 169 − 947 = $56,399				Sum of four = total repatriated earnings = 14,179 + 4,908 + 1,229 + 25,605 = $45,921

Notes

1. Data abstracted from "US direct investment abroad: reconciliation with international transactions accounts," Table 2, US direct investment abroad: detail for historical-cost position and balance of payments flows, *Survey of Current Business*, US Department of Commerce, August 1994, p. 128.
2. All values are net cash inflows received by US-based firms; receipts from foreign affiliates less payments to foreign affiliates.
3. All cash flows repatriated to the United States are net of withholding taxes. Withholding tax rates for royalties, interest, and dividends are normally determined by bilateral tax treaty. Currently, there are no withholding taxes on charges to foreign affiliates by host country governments.
4. A foreign affiliate may owe interest, royalties, and other payments to un-affiliated firms (other than the US-based firm which may or may not be its parent). This analysis focuses on those cash flows due the US-based firm alone.

A potential fifth method of repatriating earnings is in the form of *intra-firm debt*. Whereas net interest payments implicitly measure the return on intra-firm debt, the ability to restructure the repayment schedule on principal does allow the individual multinational firm significant discretion. However, the US Department of Commerce data does not consider this a repatriation of earnings, and we will omit this potential form of repatriation for the purposes of this article. (The subject is an important one. Many US-based multinational firms have in the past made loans from their foreign affiliates to the US parent with no interest charges and no debt maturity stated. The US tax authorities have subsequently re-classified these financial structures as dividends for all intents and tax purposes.)

The distinction between *foreign income* and *repatriation of earnings* recognizes that distributed earnings (dividends) represent a distribution of part of foreign income, whereas the other three primary conduits of cash flow are charges or rents for services or technologies or capital used by foreign affiliates and are deducted on determining foreign income. All of these cash flows are separate from the business risk of the foreign affiliate – i.e., determined and fixed by contract – whereas dividend distributions are normally a function of foreign income available to be distributed.

Recent Repatriation Amounts and Trends

Table 1 provides a methodological comparison of *foreign income* and *repatriation of earnings* to US-based firms from foreign affiliates, as well as empirical estimates of total net cash flows for US-based firms in 1993. As shown, the relationship between income and repatriation is a loose one, with three of the four cash flows of repatriation – royalties, charges, and net interest – acting as costs within the income statement of the foreign affiliate. The value of foreign income itself includes both reinvested earnings and distributed earnings, whereas repatriation's total value is

Table 2 Repatriated earnings of US-based firms from all foreign affiliates, 1989–1993 (millions of US dollars, percentage of total repatriation)

Cash flow	1989	1990	1991	1992	1993
Royalties and license fees	$9,158	$12,381	$12,970	$14,284	$14,179
	(18%)	(22%)	(25%)	(27%)	(31%)
Charges for services	4,341	4,460	4,434	4,880	4,908
	(8%)	(8%)	(9%)	(9%)	(11%)
Net interest received	57	1,663	1,045	1,004	1,229
	(0%)	(3%)	(2%)	(2%)	(3%)
Distributions (dividends)	37,793	37,123	32,716	33,081	25,605
	(74%)	(67%)	(64%)	(62%)	(56%)
Total repatriation	$51,349	$55,632	$51,165	$53,249	$45,921
Foreign income	$52,628	$57,150	$50,687	$48,561	$56,399

Source: Data abstracted from "US direct investment abroad: reconciliation with international transaction accounts," *Survey of Current Business*, US Department of Commerce, annually.

largely determined by the dividend distribut decision by/ for the foreign affiliate.

Table 2 provides an overview of repatriation from foreign affiliates for the 1989–93 period. The first and foremost observation is the relative growth of royalties as a proportion of total repatriated funds, rising from 18 percent to 31 percent, while dividends dropped precipitously from 74 percent in 1989 to about 56 percent in 1993. A second point is that total repatriated cash flows – in nominal dollars – remained relatively constant over this period, approximately $50 billion per year. It is fairly clear, however, that dividends are in recent periods increasingly less dominant as the method employed for the repatriation of cash flows from the foreign affiliates of US-based firms.

Dividends – the distributed profits of foreign affiliates – are, of course, the most obvious and historically the largest in terms of repatriation. Dividends are, however, an increasingly smaller proportion of total earnings repatriated to US-resident firms. Although total repatriated earnings and total foreign income are of a very similar magnitude over this period, the distinction is significant. For example, in both 1991 and 1992, total repatriated earnings exceeded the total amount of foreign income for that year by all foreign affiliates of US-based multinational firms. It appears that, even in this most recent period, there are changing patterns of earnings remittance by US multinationals.

Summary
Multinational firms must continually balance the needs of their shareholders for current income, and the needs of their foreign affiliates for profitability and reinvestment, with the complexities of international taxation, currency risk, and country risk. The method by which US-based multinational firms repatriate their profits has been changing in recent years. It appears that for the present, a number of alternative repatriation methods such as royalties and license fees may continue to grow as conduits for the repatriation of foreign earnings.

MICHAEL H. MOFFETT
and DALE L. DAVISON

finite and infinite loading Loading is the process of allocating tasks and activities to work centers. There are two main approaches to loading operations, finite and infinite loading.

Finite loading is an approach which only allocates work to a work center up to a set limit. This limit is the estimate of capacity for the work center (based on the times available for loading). Work over and above this capacity is not accepted and so the work center is not allowed to exceed the capacity limit. Finite loading is particularly relevant for operations where it is possible to limit the load, and it is necessary to limit the load, and the cost of limiting the load is not prohibitive.

Infinite loading is an approach to loading which does not limit accepting work, but instead tries to cope with it. The load on each work center may therefore exceed its theoretical capacity constraints. Infinite loading is relevant for operations where it is not possible to limit the load, or it is not necessary to limit the load, or the cost of limiting the load is prohibitive.

In complex planning and control activities where there are multiple stages, each with different capacities and with varying mix arriving at the facilities, such as a machine shop in an engineering company, the constraints imposed by finite loading may make loading calculations complex and not worth the considerable computational power which would be needed.

see also **Scheduling**

Bibliography

Vollman, T. E., Berry, W. L. & Whybark, D. C. (1992). *Manufacturing planning and control systems.* 3rd edn, Burr Ridge, IL: Irwin.

NIGEL SLACK

first mover advantage   The timing of strategic moves may be critical for success as a result of the positive advantages accruing to first movers. Being first has a significant payoff when: (i) it enhances the firm's image and reputation with buyers; (ii) early entry can tie up key raw material sources, new technologies, distribution channels, and the like, so as to shift the cost boundaries of a business or industry; (iii) first time operators build customer loyalty which is hard to dislodge; (iv) it constitutes a pre-emptive of IT has been a major mechanism for achieving long-term first mover advantages, which have been very difficult to overcome by follower competitors. Examples would include American Hospital Supply's ordering systems for hospitals, the American Airlines flight booking system, Merrill Lynch's Cash Management Account, and Direct Line Insurance's motor insurance operation.

For such success it is necessary to:

- redefine the business to use IT to fundamentally transform the existing way of operating, usually to provide a superior quality of service at a significantly reduced cost
- be first to introduce new systems, including the necessary investment to achieve rapid growth to pre-empt the position of any followers
- exploit first mover advantage to achieve customer loyalty to a brand position, which will remain after competitors attempt to follow

However, being first is no guarantee of success. Indeed, it may involve much greater risk than being an early follower. First mover disadvantages occur when: pioneering is expensive and experience effects are low; technological change is so rapid that early investments rapidly become obsolete; copying is easy and customer loyalty is fickle; and the skills and know-how of first movers are easy to replicate. It is, therefore, extremely important to assess the critical timing for market entry and to insure that adequate resources are available and are deployed to pre-empt early competitive moves.

Bibliography

Porter, M. (1980). *Competitive strategy.* New York: The Free Press. See pp. 232-3.
Thompson, A. J. Jr. & Strickland, A. J. (1993). *Strategic management.* Homewood, IL: Irwin.

DEREK F. CHANNON

five forces model   This concept originates in the work of Michael Porter. It is designed to help the analysis of the basic posture of competition in any industry, by taking a broader look at the forces of competition than is usually considered, and bringing together a number of different factors in a convenient model. In essence, the five forces model specifies five main sources of competition; namely, the bargaining power of suppliers and buyers, the threat of potential entry from outside the industry, the threat posed by industries producing substitute goods or services, and, finally, competition from companies currently in the same industry.

The development of a viable strategy, therefore, should first involve the identification and evaluation of all five forces, the nature and importance of which vary from industry to industry and from company to company, and then aim to protect the firm from the resultant dangers. An outline of the model is depicted in figure 1. Subsequently, each of the forces is discussed, in turn.

The Bargaining Power of Suppliers

The main ways in which suppliers can influence combatants in an industry are by raising prices (thereby squeezing buyers' profitability), by reducing the quality of the product or service supplied, including delivery schedules etc. (thereby damaging a company's reputation), or even by reducing output to any given company or to the industry as a whole.

Therefore, suppliers may have considerable bargaining power. Whether they constitute a strong or a weak competitive force depends on a number of factors. A supplier group is powerful: (i) if its concentration is high, and more so than the industry it supplies; (ii) if its product is not a standard commodity that is available on the open market from a variety of suppliers, but is unique, or at least differentiated; (iii) if the supplier's product makes up a sizeable fraction of the costs of an industry's product; (iv) if the supplier's product is crucial to the industry's production process; (v) if the supplier can supply the industry more cheaply than the industry can make the input itself; (vi) if the supplier's product significantly affects the quality of the industry's product; (vii) if there are no substitute products; (viii) if there are switching costs that are high enough to prevent the industry from making use of any available substitutes; (ix) if there is a credible threat of the supplier integrating forward into the industry's business; or (x) if the industry is not an important customer of the supplier group (if the industry is an important customer, the supplier's fortunes will be closely tied to the industry, so there will be an incentive to protect it by means of reasonable pricing and quality, and assistance in other activities, such as R&D).

In general, suppliers are more likely to exercise their leverage when market conditions in their own industry are weak.

In addition to controling the above factors, the firm can limit the power of the supplier: (i) by buying from several sources to insure competition – though not too many, so as to remain significant to each buyer; (ii) by dividing orders between suppliers that are themselves in competition; (iii) by occasionally seeking proposals from other suppliers, to collect information and test the market; (iv) by raising the quantities demanded by means of aggregating purchases with sister business units or companies – or by making longer-term agreements, with phased deliveries; or (v) by attempting to understand the supplier's costs.

The Bargaining Power of Buyers

As with suppliers, buyers can become a threat to profitability. They can force prices down, or demand higher quality or more service. To do this, they may decide to play

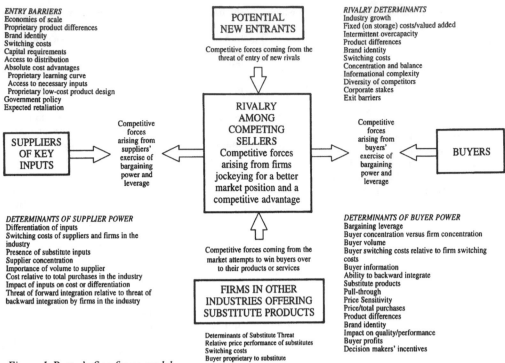

Figure 1 Porter's five forces model.
Source: derived from Porter (1980) and Porter (1979), reprinted in Mintzberg & Quinn (1991).

producers against each other, or refuse to buy from any single producer.

Buyers can generally be classified as commercial buyers or consumers. In broad terms, however, their buying behavior is independent of this classification, except that where the commercial buyer is a retailer who can influence consumers' purchasing decisions, his bargaining power is significantly enhanced.

As with suppliers, the extent to which an industry is threatened by its buyer groups is influenced by a number of factors. In principle, a buyer group is powerful: (i) if it is concentrated; (ii) if the products that it purchases from the industry are standard and undifferentiated (enabling the buyers to compare suppliers and sometimes play one against another); (iii) if the quality of the product is not particularly important; (iv) if there are readily available substitutes; (v) if the industry's product does not save the buyer money; (vi) if buyers purchase in large volumes (in which case they are likely to be more skilled in negotiation) and/or purchase a sizeable part of the industry's output (in which case they pose a greater threat if they change to another supplier), particularly if heavy fixed costs characterize the industry; (vii) if the products purchased represent a significant fraction of the buyers' cost, turnover, or income, or form a significant component of their own product (in which case buyers are likely to be more selective); or (viii) if buyers pose a credible threat of integrating backward.

Buyers are more likely to exercise their bargaining power if they earn low profits, as this will create an incentive to lower purchasing costs or otherwise squeeze the industry,

or to attempt to share its profits; for example, by backward integration.

In addition to controling the above factors, the firm can limit the power of buyers by targeting and selling to buyers who possess the least power to influence it adversely. In general, a company can only sell profitably in the long term to powerful buyers if it is a low-cost producer or if its product is sufficiently differentiated. If the company lacks both, each sale to a powerful buyer makes the company more vulnerable, and targeting and selling to the weaker buyers only becomes very important.

The Threat of New Entrants

New entrants to an industry often bring with them substantial resources and additional capacity, and they require market share. In all but the most perfectly competitive markets, this can be destabilizing. This is particularly true where organic entry is involved, but the acquisition of a weaker company within the industry by a strong company from outside it may well have the same effect.

The seriousness of this threat depends on how likely it is for a new firm to enter the industry, the difficulty aspiring entrants would face in entering the industry, and the response that they would expect to encounter once they started to compete in that industry. The first of these is largely a function of how promising the industry appears. High industry growth rates indicate future profitability, and high current profits are also inducive. The factors that affect the obstacles to entry are discussed in more detail in the section devoted to BARRIERS TO ENTRY AND EXIT.

The Threat of Substitute Products

The availability of substitute products influences the actions of the firm's customers. The fewer the substitutes, and the greater the difficulty of switching to them, the more secure the firm's revenue is.

Rivalry Among Competing Sellers in an Industry

All of the above forces constitute threats that must be dealt with by more or less every company in an industry. In addition, companies have to face each other's competitive initiatives, typically implemented using the traditional tools of product introduction and innovation, pricing, quality, features, services, marketing campaigns, the use of distribution, and the like.

Intense rivalry is related to a number of factors, including: (i) the existence of a large number of competitors that are comparable in size and power, making it more difficult for a winner to emerge and for stability to be reached; (ii) slow industry growth, and hence insufficient business for everyone, which implies that whenever any competitor has expansionary views, fights for market share are likely; (iii) the acquisition of a (weak) existing firm by a strong firm outside the industry, making aggressive share building moves likely; (iv) a lack of product differentiation or high switching costs, obliging all companies to fight for exactly the same market; (v) perishable products, as these put more pressure on firms to achieve rapid sales; (vi) high fixed costs, also creating a strong temptation to cut prices, to increase capacity utilization; (vii) capacity indivisibilities; (viii) high exit barriers (see BARRIERS TO ENTRY AND EXIT); (ix) the speed with which competitors can respond to any given initiative; as the faster they can do so, the smaller the reward is from any such initiative; (x) competitors dissatisfied with their current standing and eager to improve it by launchg offensive attacks; and (xi) competitors diverse in terms of resources, styles, strategies, priorities, and personalities, with different ideas of how to compete.

Except where a head-on collision is deemed necessary and beneficial, such as where a large market share is required, companies can defend themselves by building barriers to entry, including differentiation and switching costs. When they choose to venture into new markets, they can avoid being fiercely resisted by selecting fast growing sectors with low fixed costs and by staying clear from markets that cannot accommodate them or those where incumbents have high exit barriers.

When a company's strengths and weaknesses have been identified (see also SWOT ANALYSIS), the company must be positioned so that it can exploit, rather than be damaged by, any changes anticipated in environmental factors, such as the product life cycle, industry growth rates, and the like, and then also protected and ready to effectively respond to any initiatives from other companies. Pursuing offensive strategies without taking these factors into account is risky, and unlikely to remain successful in the long run.

Bibliography

Cowley, P. (1986). Margins and buyer/seller power in capital intensive businesses. PIMS Asso. Ltr no. 40. Cambridge, MA: Strategic Planning Institute (PIMS Associates).
Porter, M. E. (1979). How competitive forces shape strategy. Harvard Business Review, 57 (2), 137–45. Reprinted, with deletions, in H. Mintzberg & J. B. Quinn (1991). The strategy process: concepts, contexts, cases. (2nd edn), Englewood Cliffs, NJ: Prentice-Hall. See pp. 61–70.
Porter, M. E. (1980). Competitive strategy: techniques for analyzing industries and competitors. New York: The Free Press.
Thompson, A. Jr. (1980). Competition as a strategic process. Antitrust Bulletin, 25 (4), 777–803.
Thompson, A. J. Jr & Strickland, A. J. (1993). Strategic Management. Homewood, IL: Irwin. See pp. 66–75.
Yip, G. (1979). Entry of new competitors: How safe is your industry? PIMS Asso. Ltr no. 17. Cambridge, MA: Strategic Planning Institute (PIMS Associates).

STEPHANOS AVGEROPOULOS

fixed costs Fixed costs are defined to be those costs which are independent of the level of output in the short run. As such, these costs often are incurred prior to the actual production of the good in question. Fixed costs include, but are not limited to, the following:

(1) the cost of capital goods (e.g. buildings, machinery),
(2) the cost of land,
(3) property taxes, and
(4) the cost of various types of insurance.

The total dollar expenditures for any or all of the above costs may change over time, but nonetheless do not vary with the number of units produced on a daily or monthly basis. As such, each of these costs is classified as fixed. Some payments to employees, notably workers or managers who receive a fixed salary which is not tied to production levels, are also fixed costs. In contrast, hourly wages, energy costs and materials costs vary directly with the level of production and are classified as variable costs. The term overhead costs is often used by managers, but this term holds varying meanings for different managers who sometimes mix fixed and variable costs under this heading.

The importance to managers of the distinction between fixed costs and those which are variable is that the former costs should not be included in the decision as to the proper level of production which a firm should establish in the short run. The rule for PROFIT MAXIMIZATION requires that the firm equate its marginal revenue and marginal cost of production in order to find an ideal output. Since the extra cost of producing additional units of output is not influenced by the firm's fixed costs, these fixed costs should not be considered in this decision. Of course, since fixed costs are part of the firm's total costs they will help to determine the overall level of profits which the firm achieves.

The level of fixed costs may also play a role in determining entry into and exit from an industry. Very high fixed costs may deter entry (see BARRIERS TO ENTRY). In addition, some fixed costs may not be recoverable by a firm which fails prior to the depreciation of its fixed assets. These fixed costs, classified as SUNK COSTS, may also influence entry and exit as they affect the level of risk facing the owners of the firm.

Bibliography

Hyman, D. (1993). Modern Microeconomics Analysis and Application. 3rd edn, Boston: Irwin.

GILBERT BECKER

flexible workplace/telecommuting Flex-place involves working at home or other locations away from and without computer links to the traditional office. Telecommuting involves work conducted while away from the traditional office but electronically linked to it. Although many of the advantages and disadvantages discussed in this entry apply to both activities, the trend is to bring the distant worker to the workplace electronically.

As technology advances, working at home becomes more feasible, more affordable, and more commonplace. Today's telecommuters embrace telephones, computers, faxes, e-mail, and online groupware, and are beginning to use desktop video conferencing. With 7.6 million people telecommuting in the USA in 1994 and the number growing at 15 percent per year (Hequet, 1994), visible examples are easy to find. Oldsmobile is creating five telecommuting virtual zone offices (Laabs, 1995). The US General Services Administration has set up four telework centers near Washington, DC (Maynard, 1994). Bell Atlantic is offering at least partial telecommuting options to 16,000 management employees (Smith, 1994), while 12 percent of AT&T's work force has telecommuting options (Sears, 1995).

The effective implementation of telecommuting requires technical as well as organizational support. The technical end appears to be developing more quickly. Ameritech and Bell Atlantic, for example, are both providing commercially available telework services. Whether the managers of telecommuting (employers) will do their part of the work remains to be seen. Most employees report that they like the idea of telecommuting but are skeptical about their bosses providing adequate support (Betts, 1995).

Telecommuting is being used to attract and retain skilled employees. It can significantly reduce real estate costs. With fewer cars on the road, air quality can be improved and traffic congestion alleviated. It also has been argued that telecommuting can increase productivity and heighten morale.

The cost of the infrastructure to support telecommuting can be quite high. Employees may lose some of the social aspects that make their jobs enjoyable at the workplace. Organizations are less skilled at managing telecommuters than they are workers in their facilities, and may be ineffective at employee selection, training, and communication. There is concern among some managers that workers will not work all of the hours for which they are paid, although it might be beneficial to shift the focus to work accomplished rather than number of hours worked. In addition, existing supervisory and management models must be modified to deal with distant workers.

It is clear that telecommuting exists today and is rapidly expanding. It presents technical, social, and managerial challenges but promises payoffs for organizations and their members. Effectively utilized telecommuting will likely give tomorrow's organizations a competitive edge.

Bibliography

Barnes, K. (1994). Tips for managing telecommuters. *HR Focus*, **71**, 9–10.

Betts, M. (1995). Workers slow to accept telecommuting. *Computerworld*, **29**, 97.

Buckle, T. (1995). Companies keep making the same telecommuting mistakes. *Communications News*, **32**, 72.

Connelly, J. (1995). Let's hear it for the office. *Fortune*, **131**, 221–2.

Currid, C. (1995). Tips for telecommuting. *Information Week*, **January 23**, 64.

Greengard, S. (1994). Making the virtual office a reality. *Personnel Journal*, **73**, 66–70.

Greengard, S. (1994). Workers go virtual. *Personnel Journal*, **73**, 71.

Hequet, M. (1994). How telecommuting transforms work. *Training*, **31**, 56–61.

Kirrane, D. E. (1994). Wanted: flexible work arrangements. *Association Management*, **46**, 38–45.

Korzeniowski, P. (1995). Telecommuting – a driving concern. *Business Communciations Review*, **25**, 45–8.

Laabs, J. J. (1995). Oldsmobile replaces zone offices with virtual offices. *Personnel Journal*, **74**, 12.

Maynard, R. (1994). The growing appeal of telecommuting. *Nation's Business*, **82**, 61–2.

Rockwell, M. (1995). Bell Atlantic to offer package of telecommuting services. *Communications Week*, **March 20**, 90.

Rockwell, M. (1995). Ameritech focuses on telecommuting. *Communications Week*, **March 27**, 49.

Sears, S. B. (1995). The telecommuting connection. *Credit World*, **83**, 6–8.

Smith, R. (1994). Bell Atlantic's virtual work force. *Futurist*, **28**, 13.

Stanko, B. B. & Matchette, R. J. (1994). Telecommuting: the future is now. *Business and Economic Review*, **41**, 8–11.

RANDALL B. DUNHAM and JON L. PIERCE

focus groups A focus group interview, a form of depth interview, is conducted by a trained moderator with a small group of respondents. Focus group interviews are often referred to as a type of qualitative marketing research (*see* QUALITATIVE RESEARCH). They are used mainly as alternatives to structured interviews using questionnaires, in complex situations where direct questioning may not provide satisfactory information due to respondents being unwilling or unable to give answers to questions that they find embarrassing or feel are invasions of privacy. Also, focus groups are used in preliminary research to help in clarifying the research issues, in new product research and concept testing, in advertising and communications research, in studying attitudes and behavior, and in designing questionnaires for use in subsequent research.

Groups of about ten individuals are selected and often each group is chosen to represent a particular market segment (*see* MARKET SEGMENTATION). The discussion is usually taped or videoed. Although the interview is relatively unstructured, the moderator leads the group to provoke an in-depth and interactive discussion of the relevant topics.

The advantages of focus groups include the stimulation from interaction within the group which allows each individual to refine and expand his/her views in the light of contributions from other members of the group. Furthermore, the ability to show the video tape of the discussion to executives provides them with almost direct contact with customers. The disadvantages include the possibility of respondents "lying" in order to conform to group pressures or, conversely, disagreeing with fellow participants to whom they take a dislike. The moderator can introduce biases. Interpreting and reporting the results of the discussions is subjective. Because the number of groups is usually small and the selected samples not random, generalizing the results to the population is hazardous.

Bibliography

Malhotra, N. K. (1993). *Marketing research: An applied orientation.* Englewood Cliffs, NJ: Prentice-Hall. Chapter 6.

MICHAEL GREATOREX

focus strategy The focus strategy is one of Porter's (1980) generic strategies (*see* GENERIC STRATEGIES) and involves concentrating on one or more niches or segments (*see* MARKET SEGMENTATION), as against aiming at broad market appeal. Companies adopting a focus strategy aim to secure a sustainable COMPETITIVE ADVANTAGE by being able to differentiate more effectively, or have lower costs, than their rivals for the particular customer clusters which they have targeted. However, there is the risk that competitors may adopt a narrower focus or that the costs of the focus strategy make those adopting it uncompetitive compared to those firms aiming at the broad market. Moreover, if such a niche strategy is highly profitable it will attract rivals which, in turn, will diminish profits.

see also **Competitive strategy; Cost leadership strategy; Differentiation strategy**

Bibliography

Porter, M. E. (1980). *Competitive strategy: Techniques for analyzing industries and competitors.* New York: Free Press. Chapter 2.

DALE LITTLER

forced distribution method of performance evaluation The forced distribution method of PERFORMANCE APPRAISAL derives its name from the fact that those responsible for providing evaluations, the raters, are "forced" to distribute ratings for the individuals being evaluated into a "prespecified" performance distribution. Typically the performance distribution is chosen to reflect the normal curve, so that a relatively small percentage of ratees are required to be placed in the extremes (best and worst performers) and larger percentages of ratees are placed in the categories toward the middle of the performance distribution.

For example, an evaluator rating 25 individuals might be instructed to place three individuals in the category labeled "outstanding" and three individuals in the category labeled "poor." The evaluator might further be asked to place five individuals in the category described as "above average" and five more individuals in the category described as "below average." Finally, the evaluator would place nine individuals in the category labeled "average." In this way the evaluator has forced the distribution of ratee performance into a predetermined set of ratings.

In this simple example several issues emerge. First, the criterion on which the performance judgment is based must be decided, to ask raters to make their judgments based on the "overall performance" or on each of a series of performance dimensions (e.g. long-range planning, employee development, business development, or communications). Next, the designer of the system must decide the number of performance categories to be used and the definitions for each of these categories. In the example above, five categories were specified with simple labels defining distinct levels of effectiveness. In most applications of forced distribution ratings, the number of categories will range from five to eleven. Definitions of

categories can be as brief as a simple word or more elaborate descriptions of performance. Finally, the specification of the number of ratees to be placed in each category must be given as an instruction to the raters. Here the most frequently used strategy is to have the final distribution of ratees reflect an approximation to the normal curve. While this strategy tends to be the "norm," other less statistically oriented distributions can be and are used.

Forced distributions have several advantages for the conducting of performance appraisals. Among these advantages are: (a) the ratings require relatively simple comparative judgments by the rater; (b) the prespecified distribution rules out leniency errors and central tendency errors; and (c) raters know, directly, the outcome of the ratings. Forced distribution ratings also have disadvantages. These include: (a) there is no real evaluation of *absolute* performance levels; (b) there is no ability to compare ratings across groups; (c) when multiple criteria are used, raters must separately sort all ratees for each criterion; and (d) this method does not provide specific information for the purpose of appraisal feedback and performance coaching.

Bibliography

Cascio, W. F. (1991). *Applied Psychology in Personnel Management,,* Englewood Cliffs, NJ: Prentice-Hall.

Muchinsky, P. M. (1995). *Psychology Applied to Work,* Pacific Grove, CA: Brooks/Cole.

Saal, F. E. & Knight, P. A. (1995). *Industrial/Organizational Psychology: Science and Practice,* Pacific Grove, CA: Brooks/Cole.

RICK JACOBS

Foreign Corrupt Practices Act (FCPA) A United States law (1977) which prohibits a US company from making payments to foreign government officials to influence those officials to make decisions beneficial to the company. The FCPA is essentially a United States law against bribing foreign officials to act on behalf of a US company. Under the act, no bribe, contribution, transfer of funds, or other payment can be made to or on behalf of a foreign government official for the purpose of benefiting a US company. US firms doing business overseas are required to keep detailed records of expenditures related to overseas activities and make those records available to the Securities and Exchange Commission and/or The United States Department of Justice.

Bibliography

Cash, M. M. (1988). *Strategic intervention in organizations: Resolving ethical dilemmas in corporations.* Newbury Park, CA: Sage.

Gillespie, K. (1987). Middle East response to the U.S. Foreign Corrupt Practices Act. *California Management Review* Summer, 9–30.

US Congress Act of 1977. *The United States Code of Congressional and Administrative News.* 95th Congress, First Session 1977, Vol. 1, 91 stat., Public Law, 95–213, 1494–500.

Wood, D. J. (1994). *Business and society.* 2nd edn, New York: HarperCollins.

JOHN O'CONNELL

foreign currency Accounting regulations for foreign currency vary internationally. Foreign currency accounting regulations are contained in Statement of Financial Accounting Standard No. 52, "Foreign Currency Translation," (1981) (SFAS 52) in the USA; Statement of Standard Accounting Practice No. 20 (SSAP 20) in the UK; CICA 1650, "Foreign Currency Translation," in Canada; AASB 1012 and AAS 20, "Foreign Currency Translation" in Australia; International Accounting Standard IAS 21, "The Effects of Changes in Foreign Exchange Rates;" standards issued by the Business Accounting Deliberation Council in Japan; recommendations issued by Sweden's Authorized Accountant Association; the Plan Comptable Général in France, and other forms of regulation in various countries. Not all countries' regulations regulate all foreign currency accounting issues; nor do all countries' regulations concur. It is noteworthy that the European Community's (EC's) Fourth and Seventh Directives are both silent concerning foreign currency accounting, requiring merely the disclosure of exchange rates used to translate foreign currency balances.

Offshore Investments

To incorporate a firm's equity investment in operations with foreign-currency denominated accounts into the firm's own group accounts, it is necessary to translate the foreign operation's accounts into the investor's reporting currency. Of the following translation methods the current rate and temporal methods are those most frequently adopted.

The *current rate method* was used by British accountants in the 19th century and has been followed by UK, European, Asian, Australian, and New Zealand firms. It is currently permitted for self-sustaining operations under international, US, Canadian, UK, European, Australian, and Asian accounting standards. All the foreign operation's assets and liabilities are translated at the exchange rate ruling on balance date. Profit and loss statement items are translated using exchange rates ruling at the times of the transactions or approximations thereto. Because a self-sustaining operation operates independently of the investor, the investor's currency risk is limited to its "net investment." Most international standards therefore require that the net investment in self-sustaining operations, i.e., assets less liabilities, be translated using the current rate method.

A claimed advantage of the current rate method is that it preserves the relativity of measures in the foreign operation's accounts. A claimed disadvantage is that when assets valued at other than current values are translated using a current exchange rate, the resultant measure is devoid of economic meaning.

The *temporal method* is sometimes required by international, US, Canadian, UK, European, and Australasian countries' accounting standards, and generally is to be applied only where the foreign investment is "integrated," i.e., where the overseas firm frequently exposes the reporting firm to currency risk because of financial and/ or operating interdependencies. Under the temporal method, assets and liabilities are translated using exchange rates corresponding to their valuation: historical-cost-valued items are translated using historical exchange rates; items at current or revalued amounts are translated using exchange rates ruling at their (re)valuation. Revenues and expenses are translated using exchange rates at the time of the transactions.

The current rate and temporal methods often produce translation differences of the opposite sign. Because all assets and liabilities are translated at current rates under the current rate method, and assets generally exceed liabilities, the accounting exchange rate exposure arises from net assets. In contrast, the temporal method generally yields an exposure from net liabilities since liabilities are more frequently measured at current values than are assets. While the temporal method retains the subsidiary's measurement system, the current rate method yields exchange rate gains or losses consistent with the parent entity's economic currency exposure from the subsidiary's net assets and does not distort the relationships of items in the offshore operation's accounts.

The *monetary–non-monetary method* translates monetary items using balance-date exchange rates and non-monetary items using historic exchange rates, yielding effects similar to the temporal method if assets are not revalued. Where revaluations are common, as in some European and most Australasian countries, the differences can be material.

The *current–non current method* entails translating current assets and liabilities at balance-date exchange rates; non current items are translated at historic rates. The method was common when rates moved gently, as within a stabilization system like the European Monetary System. It was advocated on the grounds that current items were likely to be settled at rates approximating the current rate. In contrast, exchange rates might have returned to prior levels by the time long-term items were settled.

Translation Policies under Hyperinflation

For subsidiaries in countries with high inflation, a particular problem arises due to two economic relationships:

(1) Purchasing power parity, whereby an inverse relation between currency strength and inflation rates ensures that asset values in countries with different exchange rates remain relatively constant in terms of either currency.
(2) The "Fisher effect," where there is an inverse relation between interest rates and currency movements so that as a currency strengthens relative to another, the interest rate weakens.

Over extended periods, both effects tend to operate. Translating the accounts of an operation in a hyperinflationary country can therefore distort the accounts relative to the parent's. US and UK standards respond differently to the problem: US Statement of Financial Accounting Standard (SFAS) 52 requires temporal translation if prices more than double in three years; while Statement of Standard Accounting Practice (UK) (SSAP) 20 requires inflation adjustments to the foreign operation's accounts before using the current rate method. International Accounting Standard (IAS) 21 permits either method.

Treatment of Translation Gains and Losses

Translation gains or losses (differences) can pass through earnings or go directly to reserves such as a foreign currency translation reserve. Internationally, regulations require different practices for different translation methods. In turn, the extent of integration of the investor and investee operations determines the translation method. The current rate method is required for self-sustaining operations and combines with taking translation gains and losses to reserves; the temporal method combines with taking translation differences to earnings for integrated operations.

Foreign Currency Transactions of the Reporting Firm

Foreign currency transactions are recorded at exchange rates ruling when the transactions occur. When resultant debts or receivables are settled before balance date, realized gains or losses are recorded in earnings: there appears to be no international or national accounting regulation requiring that they be taken directly to reserves.

At balance date, any unsettled monetary assets or liabilities are translated using the balance-date exchange rate. Most countries' accounting standards require the unrealized gains or losses to be taken to earnings if the item is short term (current). For long-term monetary items there has been greater diversity. IAS 21 and US, UK, Australian, and New Zealand standards require unrealized gains or losses on long-term monetary items that are not hedges to be recognized as income or expenses of the period when the exchange rate moves. The Canadian accounting standard recently adopted this practice. Previously, it required them to be deferred to a balance sheet account and amortized the related items' lives. Deferral and amortization policy was once required under Australian regulations also.

Foreign Currency Hedges

Countries vary considerably in their treatment of foreign currency hedges, and many countries' standards do not cover hedge accounting. International Accounting Standard (IAS) 21 does not deal with hedge accounting except to require equity classification of exchange differences from monetary items forming part of an enterprise's net investment in a foreign subsidiary or hedging a net investment until the investment is disposed. Then, these differences are recognized as income or expenses (IAS 21, para. 17). US Statement of Financial Accounting Standard (SFAS) 52, requires identical treatment, as do UK Statement of Standard Accounting Practice (SSAP) 20, paras 51, 57, AASB 1012, para. 31 (Australia) in AASB 1012, para. 31 and CICA 1650.50 (Canada).

Where foreign currency transactions such as forward contracts hedge an identifiable, specific foreign currency commitment such as a purchase or sale commitment, Australian, New Zealand, and US accounting standards require the unrealized gains or losses on the hedge transaction to be deferred and included in measuring the hedged commitment (AASB 1012 (XXV); as in New Zealand; SFAS 52, para. 21). The Canadian approach defers the gain or loss until monetary item settlement (CICA 1650.54).

The treatment of premiums or discounts on forward contracts can depend upon the purpose of the contracts. Under Australian, New Zealand, and US regulations, if the purpose is not to hedge a specific identifiable foreign currency commitment, the premiums or discounts are deferred to the balance sheet and amortized over the lives of the contracts. If a contract hedges a specific identifiable commitment, the portion related to the commitment may be included in measuring (AASB 1012, Commentary; SSAP 21, para. 5.5; SFAS 52, para. 19). International, UK, and Canadian standards are silent on the treatment.

Disclosure

Almost all countries with foreign currency accounting standards require disclosure of the amount of exchange rate differences included in the period's net profit or loss; net exchange differences classified as a separate component of equity; and a reconciliation of amounts at the start and end of the period. Additional disclosures sometimes required include details of changes in the classification of significant foreign operations and the financial impact of the changes (IAS 21, para. 44); and the amounts and currencies of payables and receivables (AASB 1012, para. 60).

Reactions to Proposed and Actual Accounting Standards

Most research investigating reactions to proposed and actual foreign currency accounting standards emanates from the USA. Research indicates that firms increased foreign exchange risk management to reduce exposure to earnings variability subsequent to the introduction of Statement of Financial Accounting Standard, the predecessor to SFAS 52 (SFAS) 8. Further studies of lobbying and changes in financing or operating activities in response to SFAS 8 indicate managerial risk aversion to increased reported income variability and that managers adopted the new standard when it had the potential to most reduce their contracting and political costs.

While their results have been mixed, researchers have generally found negative stock price responses to SFAS 52 and that the share price effects are associated with the extent to which the SFAS-induced earnings variability affected firms' earnings-based contracts and political vulnerability.

Foreign Currency Accounting Policy Choices

In one of the few publications to examine firms' voluntary foreign currency accounting policies, Taylor, Tress & Johnson (1990) note that most Australian firms prefer current rate translation. They investigate why firms varied in taking the consequential translation differences to reserves, operating earnings, or extraordinary earnings and find that the selected policies facilitated risk sharing between shareholders and managers. Godfrey (1992) finds evidence that voluntary policies were optimal in sharing risk between Australian lenders, shareholders, and managers. She finds that Australian companies' policies for translating accounts of overseas subsidiaries and for foreign currency long-term debt combined to yield an accounting hedge if the firm hedged its economic exchange rate risk, and did not give an accounting hedge if the firm did not hedge the economic risk.

Godfrey (1994) investigates whether, prior to regulation of accounting for foreign currency long-term debt, Australian managers used accounting policies to reflect firms' underlying exchange rate risk exposure, or whether the policies were used opportunistically to influence reported earnings levels. Policies included taking all currency differences to current earnings; deferring and amortizing them over the life of the debt; or recognizing them in earnings only when the debt was repaid. She finds that managers chose methods that reflected the firms' underlying economic exposures to currency risk. In particular, when foreign debt hedged currency exposure for foreign currency-export-earning assets, managers selected the method that best reflected the results of the hedging objective.

Generally, research indicates that Australian firms' voluntary reporting practices reflected the underlying nature of the firms' foreign currency exposures and that alternative practices imposed costs on the firms and their shareholders.

Bibliography

Financial Accounting Standards Board (1995). *Original Pronouncements–Accounting Standards as of June 1995*, Vol. 1. New York: John Wiley & Sons, Inc.

Godfrey, J. M. (1992). Foreign Currency Accounting Policies: Reporting the exchange rate/asset value correlation. *Accounting and Finance*.

Godfrey, J. M. (1994). Foreign currency accounting policies: The impact of asset specificity. *Contemporary Accounting Research*, Spring.

Taylor, S., Tress, R. B. & Johnson, L. W. (1990). Explaining intraperiod accounting choices: The reporting of currency translation gains and losses. *Accounting and Finance*.

JAYNE M. GODFREY

foreign currency accounting

Introduction

In the USA, accounting for foreign currency transactions and translation of foreign denominated financial statements is covered in Financial Accounting Standards Board (FASB) Statement of Financial Accounting Standards No. 52 (1981) (SFAS 52). Foreign currency accounting issues affect the financial reporting for companies that operate in foreign countries.

Transaction gains and losses occur when a transaction is denominated in a currency other than the functional currency of the business entity. As an example, a US company may purchase merchandise from a Swiss company and incur a payable or liability denominated in Swiss francs. Transaction gains and losses occur due to changes in exchange rates between the time the transaction occurs and the time payment is made. These transaction gains and losses are usually included in the income of the US company because they represent a real economic gain or loss. Exceptions include (1) foreign currency transactions intended to hedge specific purchase commitments, and (2) transactions that are part of a long-term investment in a foreign country.

Reporting Issues

Translation gains and losses occur as a result of companies acquiring subsidiaries based in foreign countries. Such subsidiaries may maintain a set of books denominated in the foreign currency. However, when companies prepare periodic financial statements of a consolidated entity it is necessary that all financial statements are denominated in the same currency (for US based multinationals this would be the dollar). SFAS 52 seeks to report the effect of translation gains and losses in a way that assures that the reported gains and losses which flow through the income statement correspond to the underlying economic reality of the transaction. SFAS 52 is based on the concept of an entity's functional currency. The functional currency is defined in SFAS 52 (5) as "the currency of the primary economic environment in which the entity operates; normally that is the currency of the environment in which an entity primarily generates and expends cash."

To illustrate, suppose a US clothing manufacturer establishes a foreign subsidiary. The subsidiary operates a manufacturing plant to manufacture clothing that is shipped primarily to US markets for resale. The employees of the company are located in the foreign country, but the operation is financed using US debt and the raw materials used are shipped from the USA. Sales prices for the final products are determined primarily based on current prices for competitive goods in US markets. Here the functional currency would be the US dollar. Translation gains and losses that occur because of translating from the subsidiary's financial statements (expressed in foreign currency) to the parent's (expressed in dollars) are recognized in the parent's income statement each year. This is because the expectation is that when the functional currency is the dollar, any gains and losses are real gains and losses to the parent entity and should be recognized as such. In contrast, consider the same situation but assume the clothing manufactured uses textiles from the foreign country and is primarily resold in that country. The foreign subsidiary's debt is financed at a bank in that country and the employees are almost entirely from the foreign country. The foreign subsidiary essentially operates as a self-contained entity. Here the functional currency would be the local currency and any gains and losses occurring from translating from the foreign currency to the US dollar would not be recognized in earnings but would instead be carried to a separate stockholders' equity account, "Cumulative Translation Adjustments." The rationale here is that any gains and losses accruing as a result of translation from the subsidiary to the parent are not expected to be realized and as a result forcing such translation gains and losses to flow through the parent company's earnings is misleading.

Accounting Requirements

Statement of Financial Accounting Standards No. 52 replaced Statement of Financial Accounting Standards No. 8 (1975) that required that all gains and losses from transactions and translation flow through earnings. This was viewed by management and many analysts as misleading and causing excessive earnings volatility or costly hedging designed to protect the appearance of the income statement, without being necessarily based on sound management practice.

The effectiveness of Statement of Financial Accounting Standards No. 52 (SFAS 52) hinges on the extent to which it leads to reporting which reflects the underlying cash flows of the consolidated entity, which is critically dependent on the selection of the functional currency. Table 1 summarizes the major determinants of functional currency as stipulated by SFAS 52. It is important that the financial statement user and corporate management realize that the functional currency choice reflects a significant degree of management interpretation of the SFAS 52 guidelines and that alternative interpretations may lead to significantly different reported earnings. Another important point to note is that for tax purposes foreign currency gains and losses are recognized on a transactions basis (as dividends are transmitted from the foreign subsidiary to the

Table 1   Functional currency selection criteria

Functional currency = parent currency (translation gains and losses flow through earnings)	*Functional currency = local currency* (translation gains and losses are reflected in equity and bypass earnings)
1. Cash flows related to the foreign entity directly impact parent's cash flows on a current basis.	1. Cash flows related to the foreign entity do not impact parent's current cash flows.
2. Sales prices for foreign entity's products are determined by worldwide competition and vary with changes in exchange rates.	2. Sales prices are locally determined.
3. The sales market is the parent company market.	3. The sales market is primarily the local market.
4. Labor, material, and other expenses are obtained from the parent entity.	4. Labor, material, and other expenses are locally incurred.
5. Financing depends on the parent company or is denominated in the currency of the parent.	5. Financing is in local currency.
6. There is a high volume of intercompany transactions.	6. The volume of intercompany transactions is low.

Source: SFAS 52 ¶ 42 (1981)

parent). Thus, managements' choice for financial reporting purposes is independent of any direct cash flow effects.

Research on the Effects

Research in foreign currency accounting has focused on three primary areas: (1) theoretical analyses of the role of translation in valuation and interpretation of financial statements; (2) empirical tests of the impact of foreign currency reporting methods on analysts' forecasting ability; and (3) managements' incentives to manage earnings through foreign currency reporting.

Theoretical analyses of translation methods. Beaver & Wolfson (1982) identify two desirable properties for financial statement translation. These are "economic interpretability" and "symmetry." Economic interpretability implies that book values on the balance sheet equal market values. Symmetry requires that economically equivalent investments result in the same financial statement numbers upon translation into a common currency. Beaver & Wolfson demonstrate that under certain conditions market value accounting with translation at market value is necessary to achieve both economic interpretability and symmetry. Goldberg & Godwin (1994) extend this analysis to isolated economies and reach a similar conclusion.

The impact of foreign currency on analysts' forecasts. Griffin & Castanias (1987) and Ayres & Rodgers (1994) report that

analysts' forecast errors decreased following Statement of Financial Accounting Standards No. 52 (SFAS 52) adoption. This finding is consistent with the contention of analysts that SFAS 8 made forecasting earnings more difficult due to the volatility in earnings induced by exchange rate fluctuations.

Management's incentives to manage earnings. Several studies report findings consistent with the hypothesis that management uses foreign currency reporting to "manage" earnings. Ayres (1986) reported that early adopters of SFAS 52 had lower earnings prior to SFAS 52 adoption and were closer to debt and dividend constraints than were firms that deferred adoption. The impact of SFAS 52 adoption on earnings was generally positive (about 11 percent of earnings), allowing management to use SFAS 52 to boost earnings in a poor performance year. In addition Elliott & Philbrick (1990) and Ayres & Rodgers (1994) both find evidence consistent with managers adopting SFAS 52 with an income – smoothing motivation.

Bibliography

Ayres, F. L. (1986). Characteristics of firms electing early adoption of SFAS 52. *Journal of Accounting and Economics*, 8, June, 143–58.

Ayres, F. L. & Rodgers, J. (1994). Further evidence on the impact of SFAS 52 on analysts' earnings forecasts. *Journal of International Financial Management and Accounting*, June, 120–41.

Beaver, W. & Wolfson, M. (1982). Foreign currency translation and changing prices in perfect and complete markets. *Journal of Accounting Research*, Autumn, 528–50.

Elliott, J. A. & Philbrick, D. R. (1990). Accounting changes and earnings predictability. *The Accounting Review*, Jan., 157–74.

Goldberg, S. R. & Godwin, J. H. (1994). Foreign currency translation under two cases – integrated and isolated economies. *Journal of International Financial Management and Accounting*, June, 97–119.

Griffin, P. A. & Castanias, R. P. (1987). *Accounting for the translation of foreign currencies: The effects of Statement 52 on equity analysts.* Research Report Stamford, CT: Financial Accounting Standards Board.

FRANCES L. AYRES

foreign exchange Foreign exchange is the currency of one country located in a second country. A country generally uses the foreign currency it has on hand to pay debts owed in the issuing country. Foreign exchange may also refer to the actual process of exchanging one currency for another. Foreign exchange markets have been established throughout the world for such exchanges to take place.

Bibliography

Agenor, P. R. (1992). *Parallel currency markets in developing markets: Theory, evidence, and policy implications.* Princeton, NJ: Princeton University.

Miletello, F. C. & Davis, H. A. (1994). *Foreign exchange management.* Morristown, NJ: Financial Executives Research Foundation.

Peters, C. C. & Gitlin, A. W. (eds) (1993). *Strategic currency investing: Trading and investing in the foreign exchange markets.* Hinsdale, IL: Probus Publishing Company Inc.

JOHN O'CONNELL

foreign exchange management The value of a firm can be thought as the net present value of all expected cash flows. If the firm's future cash flows are largely affected by changes in exchange rates the firm is said to have large foreign exchange exposure. Traditionally the foreign exchange exposure is divided into three elements (Eiteman et al., 1995):

1. Transaction exposure: the effect of possible changes in exchange rates on identifiable obligations of the company. The risk arises from the imbalance of net currency cash flows based on commercial, financial or any other committed cash flows in a given currency.

2. Accounting exposure: arises from consolidation of assets, liabilities and profits denominated in foreign currency when preparing financial statements (also called translation exposure).

3. Economic exposure: extends the exchange exposure beyond the current accounting period. Arises from the fact that changes in future exchange rates may affect the international competitiveness of a firm and therefore, the present value of future operating cash flows generated by firm's activities (also called operating or competitive exposure).

Increased economic uncertainty translates into higher levels of financial market volatility. This, in turn, subjects any given exposure to a greater degree of risk. This risk is the subject of foreign exchange management whose importance has increased in the turbulent financial environment in recent decades.

Reducing a firm's exposure to exchange rate fluctuations is called hedging. The goal of hedging is to reduce the volatility of a firm's pre-tax cash flows and hence to reduce the volatility of the value of the firm.

The relevance of risk management is an interesting topic itself. Traditional finance theory suggests that, given well-diversified portfolios of investors, hedging would not benefit shareholders. The usual reasoning is that investors can diversify their portfolios to manage the exchange risk in a way that matches their preferences. Some argue, however, that managers have better information concerning the current exposure of the firm than investors. Also, hedging reduces the probability that the firm goes bankrupt and reduces agency costs between shareholders and bondholders (Smith et al., 1995).

The findings of Nance et al. (1993) suggest that firms which hedge have more complex tax schedules, have less coverage of fixed claims (the probability of the firm encountering financial distress increases with lower coverage, the coverage of fixed claims being measured as the earnings before interest and taxes divided by total interest expense), are larger, have more growth options in the investment opportunity set and employ fewer "substitutes for hedging." Firms with fewer substitutes have fewer liquid assets and higher dividends. The explanation is based on the idea that firms have, in addition to hedging, alternative methods to reduce the conflict of interest between shareholders and bondholders.

Many techniques and instruments have been developed for controlling financial risk. This is called financial engineering. Due to increasingly important international operations of companies and high volatility in exchange rates, financial engineering has become an industry of enormous growth in recent years. However, the basic tools of financial engineering were developed many years ago. The basic hedging tools to control foreign exchange risk are:

1. Currency forwards are binding agreements between a buyer and a seller calling for the trade of a certain amount of currency at a fixed rate in a certain date in the future. The buyer benefits if prices increase by the settlement date. Correspondingly, the seller benefits from a price decrease.

2. Currency futures are similar to forward contracts with a few exceptions. First, gains and losses are realized each day, not only at the settlement date. The process is called marking to market. Second, futures are traded at organized exchanges while trading in forwards occurs between banks and firms mainly by telecommunication linkages.

3. Currency options are contracts that give the option buyer the right, but not the obligation, to buy (call option) or sell (put option) a certain amount of currency at a fixed price for a prespecified time period.

4. Currency swaps are transactions in which two parties agree to exchange an equivalent amount of two different currencies for a specified period of time.

Empirical studies suggest that swaps and forwards are the most frequently used external (or, off-balance sheet) hedging instruments. Beside these instruments, firms use internal possibilities for managing exchange risk, i.e. matching, exchange rate clauses, leading and lagging, etc. There are numerous ways of hedging and financial engineering actively produces new complex instruments for firms' use. Now it becomes extremely important for managers to have clear goals for risk management. Without a clear set of risk management goals, using derivatives can produce problems. Therefore, a firm's risk management strategy must be integrated with its overall corporate strategy (Froot et al., 1994).

While most of hedging instruments are suitable for controlling both the transaction and accounting exposures their benefit is limited when managing economic exposure. Because economic exposure is rooted in long-term international fundamental forces, it is much more difficult to hedge on a permanent basis. At the same time, its significance as a prerequisite of long-term profitability of a firm has increased in recent decades. Yet, many multinational companies have been reluctant to consider economic exposure as an important strategic risk.

Bibliography

Eiteman, D. K., Stonehill, A. I. & Moffet, M. H. (1995). *Multinational business finance.* 7th edn, Reading, MA: Addison-Wesley.

Froot, K. A., Scharfstein, D. S. & Stein, J. C. (1994). A framework for risk management. *Harvard Business Review,* 72, 91–102.

Nance, D., Smith, C. W., Jr. & Smithson, C. (1993). On the determinants of corporate hedging. *Journal of Finance,* 48, 267–84.

Smith, C. W., Jr., Smithson, C. W. & Wilford, D. S (1995). *Managing financial risk.* 2nd edn, Illinois/New York: Irwin.

VESA PUTTONEN

foreign exchange markets   Foreign exchange markets are the institutional frameworks within which currencies are bought and sold by individuals, corporations, banks and governments. Trading in currencies no longer occurs in a physical marketplace or in any one country. London, New York, and Tokyo, the major international banking centers in the world, have the largest share of the market, accounting for nearly 60 percent of all transactions. The next four important centers are Singapore, Switzerland, Hong Kong, and Germany. Over half of transactions in the foreign exchange markets are cross-border, that is between parties in different countries. Trading is performed using the telephone network and electronic screens, like Reuters and Telerate. More and more, however, trading is conducted through automated dealing systems which are electronic systems that enable users to quote prices, and to deal and exchange settlement details with other users on screen, rather than by telex machine or telephone. Counterparties in foreign exchange markets do not exchange physical coins and notes, but effectively exchange the ownership of bank deposits denominated in different currencies. In principle, a tourist who makes a physical exchange of local currency for foreign currency is also a participant in the foreign exchange market and indeed for some currencies seasonal flows of tourist spending may alter exchange rates, though in most markets rates are driven by institutional trading. Other currencies may not be officially converted except for officially approved purposes and the currency rate is then determined by a parallel market which is more indicative of market trends than officially posted rates by the central bank or by the commercial bankers (Kamin, 1993).

According to the Bank for International Settlement's latest triennial survey of the global foreign exchange market, around US$880 billion worth of currencies are bought and sold daily. This represents a 42 percent growth in size compared to the previous survey of 1989 and makes the foreign exchange market the world's biggest and most liquid market. The time zone positions of major international financial markets make the foreign exchange market a 24-hour global market. Unlike the different stock exchanges and securities markets around the world, the foreign exchange market is virtually continuously active with the same basic assets being traded in several different locations. Throughout the day, the center of trading rotates from London to New York and then to Tokyo. Less than 10 percent of the daily turnover in foreign exchange transaction is between banks and their customers in response to tangible international payments. The remaining transactions are mostly between financial institutions themselves and are driven by international financial investment and hedging activities that are stimulated by the increasing deregulation of financial markets and the relaxation of exchange controls. Trading activity in foreign exchange markets shows few abnormalities and with the exception of late Friday and weekends, day of the week distortions are minimal. Trading activity in most centers is characterized by a bimodal distribution around the lunch hour. New York, however, has a unimodal distribution of activity, peaking at the lunch hour which coincides roughly with high activity in London and Frankfurt at the end of the business day in those locations (Foster and Viswanathan, 1990).

Currencies

Although its share is a declining trend, the US dollar remains predominant in foreign exchange turnover. About 83 percent of all foreign exchange transactions involve the US dollar with main turnover between the US dollar and the deutsche mark, Japanese yen, British pound, and the Swiss franc. This small group of currencies accounts for the bulk of interbank trading. Significant amounts of trading occur in other European currencies and in the Canadian dollar, but these can be considered second-tier currencies in that they are not of worldwide interest mostly because of the limited amount of trade and financial transactions denominated in those currencies. In the third tier would be the currencies of smaller countries whose banks are active in the markets and in which there are significant local markets and some international scale trading. The Hong Kong dollar, the Singapore dollar, the Scandinavian currencies, the Saudi rial, and Kuwait dinar are such currencies. Finally, the fourth tier would consist of what are called the exotic currencies, those for which there are no active international markets and in which transactions are generally arranged on a correspondent-bank basis between banks abroad and local banks in those centers to meet the specific trade requirements of individual clients. This group includes the majority of the Latin American currencies, the African currencies, and the remaining Asian currencies. A currency needs to be fully convertible to be traded in international foreign exchange markets. If there are legal restrictions on dealings in a currency, that currency is said to be inconvertible or not fully convertible and sales or purchases can only be made through the central bank often at different rates for investment and foreign transactions.

Transactions

A spot transaction in the currency market is an agreement between two parties to deliver within two business days a fixed amount of currency in return for payment in another at an agreed upon rate of exchange. In forward transactions the delivery of the currencies, the settlement date, occurs more than two business days after the agreement. In forward contracts short maturities, primarily up to and including seven days, are dominant. There are two types of forward transactions: outright forwards and swaps. Outright forwards involve single sales or purchases of foreign currency for value more than two business days after dealing. Swaps are spot purchases against matching outright forward sales or vice versa. Swap transactions between two forward dates rather than between spot and forward dates are called "forward/forwards." Spot transactions have the largest share in total foreign exchange transactions, accounting for just under half of the daily turnover. However, forward transactions have increased in volume faster and now nearly match the share of spot transactions. Activity in currency futures and options, which approximately represents 6 percent of the market, accounts for the rest of the turnover.

Market Efficiency

Market efficiency is of special interest to both academics and market participants with respect to the foreign exchange markets. Modern finance theory implies that prices in the foreign exchange markets should move over time in a manner that leaves no unexploited profit opportunities for the traders. Consequently, no foreign exchange trader should be able to develop trading rules that consistently deliver profits. This assertion seems to be supported by the traders' performance in real life. However, published research results, so far, show evidence of *ex post* unexploited profit opportunities in the currency markets. Dooley and Shafer (1983) also reported that a number of filter rules beat the market even in the *ex ante* sense. Some authors have argued that the filter profits found in exchange markets are explicable in the light of the speculative risk involved in earning them and may perhaps not be excessive or indicative of inefficiency.

A filter rule refers to a trading strategy where a speculator aims to profit from a trend by buying a currency whenever the exchange rate rises by a certain percentage from a trough and selling it whenever it falls by a certain percentage from a peak. If foreign exchange markets were efficient, the forward rate today would be an optimal predictor of future spot rate and by implication would be the best forecaster. The empirical evidence suggests that the forward rate is not an optimal predictor of the future spot rate, i.e. it is a biased predictor. The rejection of forward market efficiency may be attributable to the irrationality of market participants, to the existence of time-varying risk premiums, or to some combination of both of these phenomena (Cavaglia et al., 1994). Crowder (1994) is one of the examples which argues that once allowance is made for fluctuations in the risk premium, efficiency is preserved. Currently there is no consensus among the researchers on the existence of market inefficiency or on the explanations for the inefficiency.

Participants

The major participants in the foreign exchange markets are banks, central banks, multinational corporations, and foreign exchange brokers. Banks deal with each other either directly or through brokers. Banks are the most prominent institutions in terms of turnover and in the provision of market-maker services. The interbank market accounts for about 70 percent of transactions in the foreign exchange markets. Banks deal in the foreign exchange market for three reasons. First, banks sell and buy foreign currency against customer orders. Second, banks operate in the market in order to meet their own internal requirements for current transactions or for hedging future transactions. Finally, banks trade in currencies for profit, engaging in riskless arbitrage as well as speculative transactions. In carrying out these transactions the banks both maintain the informational efficiency of the foreign exchange market and generate the high level of liquidity that helps them to provide effective service to their commercial customers. According to the BIS survey in April 1992 in London, the top 20 banks out of 352, acting as foreign exchange market makers, account for 63 percent of total market turnover. In all international markets there is a continuing trend towards a declining number of market-making banks as a result of both mergers among banks and of the withdrawal of some smaller banks who have inadequate capital to trade at the level needed for profitability in such a highly competitive business.

Non-financial corporations use the foreign exchange market both for trade finance and to cover investment/ disinvestment transactions in foreign assets. In both activities the objective of the corporation is to maximize its profits by obtaining the most advantageous price of foreign exchange possible. Although small in scale, the corporations' involvement in foreign exchange markets extends to management of their foreign exchange exposure through derivative products and, in the case of larger corporate entities, to actively seeking profit opportunities that may exist in the market through speculative transactions.

In their role of regulating monetary policies, central banks of sovereign states are often in the position of both buying and selling foreign exchange. The objective of central banks' involvement in the foreign exchange markets is to influence the market-determined rate of their currencies in accordance with their monetary policy. Central banks often enter into agreements with one central bank lending the other the foreign exchange needed to finance the purchase of a weak currency in the market to maintain the value of their currencies within a mutually agreed narrow band of fluctuations. Stabilization is intended to prevent wild fluctuations and speculations in the foreign exchange market, but central banks are increasingly cautious about signaling a commitment to a fixed intervention rate. Even the Exchange Rate Mechanism (ERM) of the European Union, in which currencies were contained within narrow bands of their central rate, was unable, in spite of the committed support of all European central banks, to prevent a concerted market adjustment. In September 1992 the Bank of England lost many millions of foreign currency reserves in a short and unsuccessful defense of sterling. Both sterling and the Italian lira were on that occasion forced out of the ERM bands.

Risks

Counterparty credit risk, settlement risk, and trading risk are the three major risks that are faced by market participants in the foreign exchange markets. Credit risk relates to the possibility that a counterparty is unable to meet its obligation. Settlement risk arises when the counterparty is able and willing but fails to deliver the currency on settlement day. The settlement of a foreign exchange contract is not simultaneous; therefore, counterparties are usually not in a position to insure that they have received the countervalue before irreversibly paying away the currency amount. In the foreign exchange markets there are unequal settlement periods across countries. Different time zones may expose the party making the first payment to default by the party making the later payment. In 1974 US banks paid out dollars in the morning to a German bank, Bankhaus Herstatt, but did not receive German marks through the German payment system when German banking authorities closed at 10.30 a.m. New York time. Herstatt received the dollars in the account of its US correspondent but did not pay out the marks. Market risk refers to the risk of adverse movements in the rate of foreign exchange. A market participant in the foreign exchange market risks loss when rates decline and it has a long position (owns the asset) or when rates rise and it has a short position (has promised to supply the asset without currently owning it).

Quotation and Transaction Costs

The exchange rate quoted for a spot transaction is called the spot rate and the rate that applies in a forward transaction is called the forward rate. If a currency is trading at a lower price against another currency on the forward market than on the spot market, it is said to be at a discount. If, however, the currency is more expensive forward than spot, it is said to be at a premium. What determines whether a currency trades at a premium or discount is the interest rate differential in money markets. The currency with higher/lower interest rate will sell at a discount/premium in the forward market against the currency with the lower/higher interest rate. However, some research has shown a small bias in the forward rate explained by a time-varying risk premium.

Traders in the foreign exchange markets always make two-way prices, that is they quote two figures: the rate at which they are prepared to sell a currency (offer) and the rate at which they are willing to buy a currency (bid). The difference is called the spread and represents the market maker's profit margin. The spread is conventionally very narrow in stable currencies with a high volume of trading. Liquidity is usually extremely good for major currencies and continuous two-way quotations can be obtained. However, in unstable, infrequently traded currencies, it can become a good deal wider. It widens with uncertainty – spreads on internationally traded currencies such as British pound, US dollar, or deutsche mark will widen if the international financial markets are in turmoil. The evidence from foreign exchange markets, however, does not support an unequivocal relationship between the market liquidity and the transaction costs. Bid–ask (offer) spreads are not necessarily lowest when the liquidity is high. More trading by informed risk averse participants brings about higher costs. Bollerslev and Domowitz (1993) report that small traders (banks) in foreign exchange markets tend to increase both the quoted spread and market activity at the beginning and at the end of their regional trading day, because they are more sensitive with respect to their inventory positions at the close than larger banks and have less information based on retail order flow at the beginning than larger banks that operate continuously. Another factor which may effect the transaction cost in foreign exchange markets is unobservable news. News events which change traders' desired inventory positions result in order imbalances, changing the relative demand and supply for the currency, with the potential of changing the spreads (Bollerslev and Domowitz, 1993).

Exchange Rate Systems

From the end of World War II until 1971 the leading industrialized countries under the hegemony of the US economy committed themselves to a fixed exchange rate system. This period in the international monetary system is known as the Bretton Woods system and aimed to preserve a fixed exchange rate between currencies until fundamental disequilibrium appeared, at which point through devaluation or revaluation a new fixed parity was established. The Bretton Woods system was based on the strength of the US economy whereby the US government pledged to exchange gold for US dollars on demand at an irrevocably fixed rate (US$35 per ounce of gold). All other participating countries fixed the value of their currencies in terms of gold, but were not required to exchange their currencies into gold. Fixing the price of gold against each currency was similar to fixing the price of each currency against each other.

With the increasing competitiveness of the continental European economies and the Japanese economy against the US economy, the USA had become unable to meet its obligations under the Bretton Woods system and the fixed exchange rate system gave way to the floating exchange rate system in 1973. Under the floating exchange rate system currencies are allowed to fluctuate in accordance with market forces in the foreign exchange markets. However, even in systems of floating exchange rates where the going rate is determined by supply and demand, the central banks still feel compelled to intervene at particular stages in order to help maintain stable markets. The Group of Seven (G7) council of economic ministers has in the past attempted coordinated interventions in the foreign exchange markets with a view to stabilizing exchange rates. The exchange rate system that exists today for some currencies lies somewhere between fixed and freely floating. It resembles the freely floating system in that exchange rates are allowed to fluctuate on a daily basis and official boundaries do not exist. Yet it is similar to the fixed system in that governments can and sometimes do intervene to prevent their currencies from moving too much in a certain direction. This type of system is known as a managed float. Economists are not in agreement as to which of the exchange rate systems, fixed or floating, can create stability in currency markets and is a better means for adjustments to the balance of payments positions (Friedman, 1953;

Dunn, 1983). A fixed exchange rate system is unlikely to work in a world where the participating countries have incompatible macroeconomic policies and the economic burden of adjustments to the exchange rates usually fall on the deficit countries. The floating exchange rate system, on the other hand, has not delivered the benefits that its advocates put forward. The exchange rate volatility during the floating rate period is severe and is not consistent with underlying economic equilibria due to the activities of short-term speculators. The European Union's aim is not to create a fixed exchange rate system, but to create a monetary union where the exchange rate fluctuations are eliminated with adoption of a single currency by the member countries. However, to reach this goal a transitional period where a stability in exchange rates through conversion of member countries' macroeconomic performances to a specified desirable level is necessary. Since the Maastricht Treaty of 1989 the European Union countries have not been successful in achieving these macroeconomic targets, thus raising serious concerns about the monetary union.

Bibliography

Bollerslev, T. & Domowitz, I. (1993). Trading patterns and prices in the interbank foreign exchange market. *The Journal of Finance*, 48, 1421–1443.

Cavaglia, S. M., Verschoor, W. F. & Wolff, C. C. (1994). On the biasedness of forward foreign exchange rates: irrationality or risk premia? *Journal of Business*, 67, 321–343.

Committeri, M., Rossi, S. & Santorelli, A. (1993). Tests of covered interest parity on the Euromarket with high quality data. *Applied Financial Economics*, 3, 89–93.

Copeland, L. S. (1994). *Exchange rates and international finance.* 2nd edn, Wokingham: Addison-Wesley.

Crowder, W. J. (1994). Foreign exchange market efficiency and common stochastic trends. *Journal of International Money and Finance*, 13, 551–564.

Dooley, M. P. & Shafer, J. R. (1983). Analysis of short run exchange rate behaviour: March 1973 to November 1981. *Exchange rate and trade instability*. Bigman, D. & Taya, T., Cambridge, MA: Ballinger, 187–209.

Dunn, R. M. (1983). *The many disappointments of flexible exchange rates*. Princeton Essays in International Finance. Princeton: University of Princeton Press..

Eichengreen, B., Tobin, J. & Wyplosz, C. (1995). Two cases for sand in the wheels of international finance. *The Economic Journal*, 105, 162–172.

Foster, D. & Viswanathan, S. (1990). A theory of intraday variations in volumes, variances and trading costs. *Review of Financial Studies*, 3, 593–624.

Friedman, M. (1953). The case for flexible rates. *Essays in positive economics*. Chicago, IL: University of Chicago Press.

Group of Ten Deputies (1993). *International capital movements and foreign exchange markets*. Rome: Bank of Italy.

Kamin, S. B. (1993). Devaluation, exchange controls, and black markets for foreign exchange in developing countries. *Journal of Development Economics*, 40, 151–169.

Krugman, P. (1991). Target zones and exchange rate dynamics. *Quarterly Journal of Economics*, 51, 669–682.

The Bank of England (1992). The foreign exchange market in London. *Bank of England Quarterly Bulletin*, November 408–417.

Tucker, A. L., Madura, J. & Chiang, T. C. (1991). *International financial markets*. St Paul, MN: West Publishing Company.

ISMAIL ERTURK

foreign national   An employee of an organization who comes from another country. When hiring takes place on a geocentric basis (from employees throughout the world) it is very common to have employees of several countries in a company's home or regional offices. Foreign nationals are citizens of countries other than the one to which they are assigned.

see also **Staffing**

JOHN O'CONNELL

foreign source income   When a person receives income from a source outside of his/her own country it is considered "foreign source income." Depending upon the countries involved and the duration of stay (if any) in another country taxes may have to be paid in either or both of the countries involved. It is very important to determine the consequences of receiving income from foreign sources before entering into contracts or other relationships overseas.

Bibliography

Langar, M. (1992). *Tax exile report: How to escape confiscatory taxes in the U.S. and other high tax countries*. Rolands Castle, Hants: Scope International.

JOHN O'CONNELL

franchising   Franchising has become, increasingly, a significant business format in recent years. For example, about one third of retail sales in the USA are now estimated to come from franchise arrangements, and more than a quarter of all British foreign retail investments are in the form of franchises. Burger-King, the major hamburger restaurant chain, has 7,500 outlets in 56 countries. Benetton, the Italian retailer, has some 6,000 outlets in over 80 countries. The popularity of franchising as a form of market entry (*see* INTERNATIONAL MARKET ENTRY AND DEVELOPMENT STRATEGIES) is due to the fact that it entails less risk and makes less demands on capital than other options such as international joint ventures or acquisitions. Advantages to the franchisee also include a rapid international awareness of brands and trademarks and sales growth, witness McDonalds, Benetton, and Body Shop who have been particularly successful at "exporting" their business concepts to franchisees worldwide.

There is evidence to suggest that franchises which are set up to test a business idea without prior MARKETING RESEARCH are prone to failure, and that successful franchises are those in which a close relationship exists between franchisor and franchisee to the extent that their complementary companies become vertically integrated business organizations.

Bibliography

Daniels, J. D. & Radebaugh, L. H. (1994). *International business: Environments and operations*. Reading, MA: Addison Wesley.

McGoldrick, P. & Davies, G. (1995). *International retailing: Trends and strategies*. London: Pitman Publishing.

NIGEL HOLDEN

freedom of contract   The view that competent individuals should be at liberty to enter into private, consensual exchange agreements of their choosing, without interference from third parties, including governments. To the extent that government has an active role in economic life, it is to protect this freedom and to help enforce the contracts made under it. Belief in freedom of contract is generally accompanied by an endorsement of extensive individual property rights.

This belief in individual liberty grew out of the major Western political and social transformations of the seventeenth and eighteenth centuries. The transformations were driven by doubts about external moral authority, increasing faith in individual rationality, and a new appreciation of the potential of freely functioning markets. Consent became the preferred ground for obligation in political and private life.

Freedom of contract is supported by two distinct, but often intertwined traditions: classical liberalism and free-market economics. Classical liberalism has its intellectual roots in John Locke's writing on civil government and John Stuart Mill's work on liberty. It has received recent expression in the libertarianism of Robert Nozick. Classical liberalism emphasizes the inherent moral value of individual autonomy and private property rights. The core idea is that people should be free to govern their lives and their property, so long as they do not obstruct the rights of others to do the same. Free-market economics, on the other hand, derives the value of contractual freedom from a theory of social welfare. Often associated with Adam Smith, this line of reasoning has found more recent champions in Friedrich Hayek and Milton Friedman. They argue that prosperity (or, more precisely, economic efficiency) is a social good of overriding importance, and that it is best achieved when people are free to seek their own gain. Just as liberals are skeptical about external moral authority, these economists are skeptical about centrally controlled social engineering.

Though few would deny that contractual freedom has some value, critics have raised a number of questions about its legitimate extent. Even the proponents of freedom of contract recognize a need for limits. All but the most radical add two qualifications. The first is that private contractual agreements should not unjustly harm third parties. The second is that neither party to an agreement should use force or fraud. Breach of either condition could provide a rationale for societal intervention. For most proponents, these are the only conditions that justify interference with private contracts and they are to be interpreted very narrowly. Critics, however, support more extensive grounds for intervention. These may be simplified into three areas: remedying defects in voluntariness, protecting community interests, and preventing self-destructive behavior.

Defects in Voluntariness. Both the liberal and economic defenses of freedom of contract seem to rest on the idea that individuals make informed, rational, and free choices. The value of freedom is questionable when people make uninformed, irrational, or impaired choices. Critics argue that the prohibition against force and fraud does not go far enough. Even mentally competent adults who are not subject to force or fraud may lack crucial information and may not know they lack it; the costs of personally gathering missing information (search costs) may be very high; even if provided with the information, they may not have the education or capacity to understand it, especially with complex products; they may be pressed to make a decision without enough time to think it through; they may be in a state of mind that temporarily impairs their reasoning; they may be acting under some form of duress; they may be subtly manipulated in some way; or, they may have very little relative bargaining power. Some critics go so far as to suggest that the very idea of a free choice that is not corrupted by social conditioning and constrained by external circumstances is a chimera.

More moderate critics use common defects in voluntariness to assert that societies have an obligation to create favorable decision-making conditions and to protect people when these conditions do not obtain. They argue for a wide array of regulations and legal protections, from information disclosure requirements to "cooling off" periods in which parties have a right to rescind a contract. Proponents respond that individuals can and should learn to protect themselves from unfavorable conditions. *Caveat emptor* is a common corollary to freedom of contract.

Community Interests. Some critics go further to argue that communities have a legitimate interest in many private contracts. Proponents open the door to community interests by acknowledging that unjust harm to third parties may justify social intervention. Though it is not what proponents had in mind, interpreted broadly, harm to third parties could include intangible harms to the community, its social fabric, and its shared values. In this regard, communities often attempt to limit the kinds of things subject to market exchange (or "commodified"). Economic exchanges that have been outlawed include the sale, for example, of sexual services (prostitution and surrogacy), votes in an election, public offices, human organs, oneself into slavery, and babies. In many early societies, even land was not treated as a commodity to be owned or traded. Beyond blocking exchanges, communities might want to regulate them to preserve shared values and objectives. Examples of social values potentially threatened by private contracts include DISTRIBUTIVE JUSTICE, preservation of human dignity, community aesthetics, and the absence of discrimination against religious, ethnic, or gender groups. Social values of this sort have been used to argue for rent control, minimum wage laws, health and safety regulations, zoning restrictions, limits on the production and sale of pornography.

Communitarian critics of freedom of contract argue that harm to community values can justify social interference with private contracts. Proponents of contractual freedom counter this argument by pointing out the potentially oppressive results of allowing this type of restraint. Community values about the appropriate role and worth of women and minority groups have been used to justify discrimination. Proponents also point out the costs of these constraints. They argue, for instance, that minimum wage laws increase unemployment, and the absence of a market in human kidneys for transplants limits the supply and results in more deaths from kidney disease.

Self-Destructive Behavior. A few critics of freedom of contract go further. Even when conditions of informed voluntary choice are met, people may choose to engage in economic exchanges that are not judged to be in their own long-term interest. This judgment may be made by the individuals themselves in more reflective moments, by elders who have more life experience, or by some collective social assessment. Even if such contracts are isolated and do not negatively impact others in the community, some would argue that society should play the role of protecting people from themselves. Examples in this area are difficult to identify because they often raise issues of voluntariness and community values as well. Common candidates, however, are drug laws, laws against assisted suicide, and laws against gambling. Liberal proponents tend to respond to paternalistic criticisms by arguing that it is none of society's business if individuals choose self-destructive paths that do not directly harm others. This is an objectionable form of *paternalism*. Economic proponents stress the fact that mentally competent adults are in a better position than anyone else to determine what is in their own best interest, even if their judgment is not perfect and even if it changes over time.

Courts and legislatures have been sympathetic to many of these criticisms, leading some observers to claim that freedom of contract is dead. However, others see this freedom expanding, as societies experiment with new commodities (such as sexual surrogacy and organ sales) and as former communist countries embrace free markets. What is certain is that the extent and limits of freedom of contract will continue to be a contentious and rich issue of debate for the foreseeable future.

see also **Economics and ethics**

Bibliography

Andre, J. (1992). Blocked exchanges: A taxonomy. *Ethics*, **103**, 29–47. (An extensive survey with references to the literature.)

Atiyah, P. S. *The Rise and Fall of Freedom of Contract*. Oxford: Oxford University Press.

Friedman, M. (1962). *Capitalism and Freedom*. Chicago: University of Chicago Press.

Hayek, F. (1960). *The Constitution of Liberty*. Chicago: University of Chicago Press.

Nozick, R. (1974). *Anarchy, State, and Utopia*. New York: Basic Books.

Paul, E. F., Miller F. D. Jr., & Paul, J. (1985) (eds), *Ethics and Economics*. Oxford: Blackwell. (Particularly the essays by Amartya Sen and Allan Gibbard.)

Trebilcock, M. J. (1993). *The Limits of Freedom of Contract*. Boston: Harvard University Press. (A comprehensive treatment.)

J. GREGORY DEES

functional currency   A multinational company (MNC) may have earnings and disbursements in a large number of currencies. When it comes to reporting the results of its transactions in various accounting reports, the currency unit used in the reports is the currency of its country of incorporation. Thus, a firm whose home country is in Australia may do business in 40 countries, but when its accounting reports are issued all values are expressed in Australian dollars. The Australian dollar is the company's functional currency.

JOHN O'CONNELL

functional intermediary   A functional intermediary is a person, or firm, who has actual physical involvement in a trade transaction. Examples of functional intermediaries are freight consolidation firms, ocean shipping companies, railroad carriers, and lighter firms which offload cargo from larger ships.

JOHN O'CONNELL

functional structure   In the single-business firm, the natural way to divide up the various activities is to organize by specialist function, as shown in figure 1, in which is illustrated a typical functional structure for a small to medium manufacturing business. At the top is a board, usually composed of the senior managers of the specialist functions together with a chairman and chief executive. In many companies the personnel and R&D function heads are not included on the board, and operate predominantly in line support roles. Human resources management and R&D are thus often excluded from the formulation of strategy. The board may or may not contain nonexecutive directors. As a result of investor and political pressure, the presence of nonexecutive directors is becoming the norm in public companies. However, in many smaller concerns and those that are privately owned, nonexecutives may still be excluded.

Depending upon the size of the business, the marketing and finance functions may be fully developed or the company may essentially operate a sales function and an accounting function. In smaller concerns, the accounting function may also be responsible for the company secretary and for legal aspects of the preparation of budgets and plans. Medium-term corporate plans, which tend to be financial in orientation, may also be developed.

As such firms grow larger, the functions become more fully developed. Research and development, which in smaller companies often tends to be subordinate to the production function, develops into a full blown function. Finance and accounting tend to become separated. Marketing is introduced and tends to become superordinate to the sales function. A separate company secretary position is often established and a specialist corporate planner is introduced. While such companies may still be essentially single-business, it is common that multisite operations may

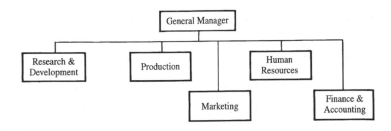

Figure 1 Functional organizational structures.

commence, and the production function may therefore develop to involve several site managers, with an overall production manager located at the primary central site. Similarly, the sales function is often changed by the effort to open new markets, and especially export markets overseas. The introduction of an additional export sales manager is thus also likely as overseas sales expand and distribution is established, usually via the use of agents or distributors in the early stages.

The functional structure is also very effective in managing the single business in the service industry sector. In retailing, for example, a similar structure would be found; although "production" as a function is not normally present, being replaced by a function usually known as "operations." This essentially refers to distribution system management and the management of stores. These are usually grouped geographically and handled by regional managers. Merchandising and buying are other critical functions which essentially replace marketing.

The functional structure is the logical pattern for dividing up the activities of the business, provided that it is not too complex, either by product or geography. Even when a single-business firm expands geographically, it is possible to retain a form of functional structure in many cases, provided that production is not distributed but remains centralized.

Major problems arise with the functional structure as the firm diversifies by product and/or geography, where the latter also contains production facilities. When these new strategic moves occur, a number of structural variants tend to be invoked, including the introduction of the functional holding company, the holding company (*see* HOLDING COMPANY STRUCTURE), the area division and the product division (*see* DIVISIONAL STRUCTURE). It is extremely unusual that firms move from a functional to a MATRIX STRUCTURE, an SBU STRUCTURE, or a customer-based structure, these usually being found in large complex organizations.

Apart from problems of handling diversification, problems associated with the functional form include: a failure to develop general management skills; difficulties in functional coordination; potential over-specialization; that profit responsibility is forced to the top; that it may lead to functional empire building; and that there may be a tendency to prevent entrepreneurship and reconfiguration of the value chain.

Bibliography

Chandler, A. D. (1962). *Strategy and structure*. Cambridge, MA: MIT Press.

Channon, D. F. (1973). *The strategy and structure of British enterprise*. Cambridge, MA: Harvard Division of Research.

Thompson, A. A. & Strickland, A. J. J. (1993). *Strategic management: concepts and cases*, (7th edn), Homewood, IL: Irwin. See pp. 223–5.

DEREK F. CHANNON

G

gainsharing Gainsharing is a term used to describe a set of group-based incentive programs that provide employees in a designated work group (usually a business unit, smaller organization, or department) with a share of the financial gains realized due to increases in productivity, improvements in processes, or reductions in costs. The philosophy supporting these plans is that employees will improve productivity if provided with (a) an incentive that shares the gains with employees, and (b) a mechanism for voicing their suggestions. Most gainsharing plans consist of two components to assure these goals are met. The first is a bonus plan, and the second is a form of employee participation.

Although historically one of three plans were used (i.e. SCANLON PLAN, Rucker Plan, or Improshare), today's programs include customized bonus formulas and participation systems. However, all gainsharing plans share the goal of including *only* criteria that employees can change (cost of production, sales value of production, customer service, quality, and so forth). An additional factor differentiating gainsharing from other forms of organizational-based rewards (such as PROFIT SHARING) is that the bonus is paid out more frequently, usually quarterly, although some pay weekly.

The second component of gainsharing is an employee involvement program. Not all gainsharing programs implement the involvement system, but, when used, they are designed to provide employees with a mechanism for communicating ways to improve the production process. More sophisticated involvement plans consist of layers of suggestion committees that are staffed by peers who are empowered with budget authority to approve suggestions.

THERESA M. WELBOURNE

game theory The theory of games is the study of the strategic behavior of rational agents in multiagent decision problems. The term "game" is used in reference to the interactions between a number of decision makers or "players," each one having a set of possible actions or strategies available, with outcomes or payoffs to each player depending on the actions of the other players. Because the payoff to each player depends on the actions of the rest of the players, each player behaves strategically in adopting an action. Formalization of game theory is considered to have begun with the publication of the *Theory of Games and Economic Behavior* (Von Neumann and Morgenstern, 1944) and since then, game theory has become an important analytical tool in economics and other fields.

Games can be either cooperative or noncooperative. In cooperative games, players pursue strategies aimed at maximizing joint payoffs, presuming that the players can negotiate agreements with COMMITMENT to playing these strategies. By contrast, in noncooperative games, agents act in their own self-interest. The difference between non-cooperation and cooperation is demonstrated by the PRISONER'S DILEMMA, and the Cournot solution, as opposed to the cartel solution, in oligopoly. The "core" is another example of a cooperative solution.

Noncooperative games can be classified as static games of complete or incomplete information, and dynamic games of complete or incomplete information. Information is complete when every player knows the payoffs of the rest of the players from the possible combinations of actions that can be chosen by the players. An example of a game with incomplete information is an auction where each agent knows the utility he will receive from obtaining the good that is being sold, however the payoff that other bidders will receive from obtaining it and their willingness to pay for it may be unknown.

In static games, for example in a Cournot model, players choose their strategies once and for all, and when choosing strategies they are not informed about the strategy choices of other players. In dynamic games, players may move sequentially, or select strategies in repeated play. For instance, in the Stackelberg duopoly model, one leading firm moves first by selecting an output level, and the second firm makes an output choice having observed the leader's output. Primary equilibrium solution concepts include *Nash equilibrium* in static games of complete information, Bayes–Nash equilibrium in static games of incomplete information, subgame-perfect equilibrium in dynamic games of complete information and perfect Bayesian equilibrium in dynamic games of incomplete information.

The Nash equilibrium was proposed by the mathematician and economist John Nash in 1950. According to this concept, a strategy profile for all players is a Nash equilibrium if no player benefits by deviating from his strategy given the strategy choice of the other players. As an example, consider the "battle of the sexes" game, where a man and a woman would like to spend the evening together, however, the woman would prefer to go to the opera and the man would prefer to go to a wrestling match. Relevant utility payoffs are given by the following matrix (the first number is the woman's payoff, the second number is the man's payoff):

		Man	
		Opera	Wrestling
	Opera	2,1	0,0
Woman			
	Wrestling	0,0	1,2

This game has two Nash equilibria, (Opera, Opera) and (Wrestling, Wrestling), because neither one of the players benefits by deviating from his strategy, given the strategy choice of the other player. For instance, starting from the (Opera, Opera) equilibrium where the payoff is (2,1), the man would not unilaterally deviate to a wrestling match because he would then receive a zero payoff. An application of the Nash equilibrium is in the Cournot model.

The Bayes–Nash equilibrium concept expands Nash equilibrium to Bayesian games. Bayesian games analyze the strategic behavior of agents in the presence of incomplete information, and were defined and analyzed by the economist Harsanyi (1967). Harsanyi proposed a way for transforming games of incomplete information (which cannot be analyzed) to games of complete but IMPERFECT INFORMATION (which can be analyzed). The "Harsanyi transformation" amounts to the observation that although some players may be incompletely informed about the payoffs to other players from the possible strategy profiles (i.e. some player's may not know the "types" of other players), it is reasonable to assume that they have beliefs about the presence of possible types. A Bayes–Nash equilibrium is a strategy for each type of every player such that each player maximizes his expected payoff by playing this strategy, given the specified strategies for all types of the rest of the players and the player's beliefs about the types of the rest of the players. As an example, the Bayes–Nash equilibrium concept can be used to determine the equilibrium in a market with Cournot quantity competition and imperfect information, in the sense that firms do not know the precise cost structure of other firms but have beliefs about these costs.

In dynamic games of complete information, consider the Stackelberg model presented above as an example. The equilibrium in the Stackelberg model can be obtained by "backward induction." A standard Cournot *reaction function* can be obtained by starting from the follower's problem that determines the optimal response to each possible output choice of the leader. The leader's problem is then to choose an output level that maximizes his profit, taking the reaction of the follower into account. The equilibrium obtained in this way is the unique credible Nash outcome. This outcome has the property of yielding a profit to the leader that is higher than the profit to the follower, and higher than the Cournot-profit the leader would make if the players moved simultaneously in a Cournot fashion (*see* FIRST-MOVER ADVANTAGES). There is one more candidate outcome. The follower could threaten to produce the Cournot output regardless of the leader's choice, thus forcing the leader to produce the Cournot output as well. This threat, however, is not a credible threat, for if the leader chooses the Stackelberg outcome after all, the follower cannot maximize profits unless it participates. Credibility and backward induction were extended to games where players move simultaneously in several periods by Selten (1965) with his concept of a subgame perfect Nash equilibrium, necessitating strategies which are Nash equilibria for the entire game and every subgame of the entire game. The perfect Bayesian equilibrium concept incorporates the intuition behind subgame perfection, and extends the concept of Bayes–Nash equilibrium to dynamic games of incomplete information. For example, the perfect Bayesian equilibrium concept can be used to characterize the equilibria in a model where an incumbent firm engages in limit pricing to deter the entry of other firms that are incompletely informed about the incumbent firm's MARGINAL COST of production.

Bibliography

Friedman, J. W. (1986). *Game Theory with Applications to Economics*. New York: OUP.

Fudenberg, D. & Tirole, J. (1991). *Game Theory*. Cambridge, MA: MIT.

Gibbons, R. (1992). *Game Theory for Applied Economists*. Princeton, NJ: Princeton University Press.

Harsanyi, J. (1967). Games with incomplete information played by Bayesian players Parts I, II, and III. *Management Science*, 14, 159–82, 320–34, 486–502.

Nash, J. (1950). Equilibrium points in n-person games. *Proceedings of the National Academy of Sciences*, 36, 48–9.

Rasmusen, E. (1990). *Games and Information: An Introduction to Game Theory*. Cambridge, MA: Blackwell.

Selten, R. (1965). Spieltheoretische behandlung eines oligopolmodells mit nachfrageträgheit. *Zeitschrift für Gesamte Staatswissenschaft*, 121, 301–24, 667–89.

Shubik, M. (1982). *Game Theory in the Social Sciences*. Cambridge, MA: MIT.

Von Neumann, J. & Morgenstern, O. (1944). *Theory of Games and Economic Behavior*. Princeton, NJ: Princeton University Press.

THEOFANIS TSOULOUHAS

gap analysis   The first step in strategic analysis is the establishment of the corporate mission, which can then be translated into a series of quantifiable objectives. These will normally be at least partially financial, but a number are likely to be strategic. The corporate objectives can then be compared with an extrapolated performance for the corporation, generated from the sum of the expectations of the business units.

A comparison of the objectives and the expected business outcomes will usually lead to a performance gap between the two. Gap analysis is concerned with why the gap occurs and the development of measures for reducing or eliminating it. This might be achieved by changing the objectives, or by changing strategy at the level of the businesses.

1. The corporation's portfolio of businesses remains unchanged.
2. Competitive success strategies in the firm's products and markets will continue to evolve as in the past.
3. The demand and profitability opportunities in the firm's marketplaces will follow historic trends.
4. The corporation's own strategies in the respective businesses will follow their historic pattern of evolution.

The first step in gap analysis is to consider revising the corporate objectives. Should expected outcomes from the businesses exceed aspirations, the objectives can be revised upward. When aspirations substantially exceed possible performance, it may be necessary to revise the objectives downward.

When, after such adjustments, a significant gap still remains, new strategies need to be developed to eliminate the gap. To forecast sales increases likely to result from the introduction of alternative growth strategies for each business, managers can estimate the following measures of market structure:

• industry market potential (IMP)
• relevant industry sales (RIS)
• real market share (RMS)

The IMP is estimated as shown in figure 1. It is assumed, first, that all customers who might reasonably use the product will do so, second, that the product will be

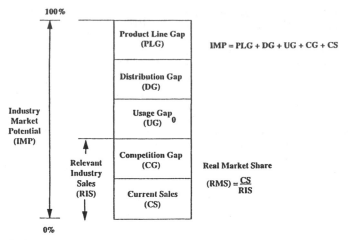

Figure 1 Gap analysis.
Source: Rowe et al. (1994, p. 245).

used as often as possible and, third, that the product will be used to the fullest extent. The IMP therefore represents the maximum possible unit sales for a particular product. The difference between this value and current sales represents the growth opportunity for each product. The RIS equals the firm's current sales plus competitive gaps, and the RMS equals sales divided by the RIS.

Four components then contribute to the gap between the firm's sales potential and its actual performance, as follows:

- *Product line gap.* Closing this gap involves completing a product line, in either width or depth, and introducing new or improved products.
- *Distribution gap.* This gap can be closed by expanding distribution coverage, intensity, and exposure.
- *Change gap.* Using this strategy, the firm endeavors to encourage nonusers to try the product and to encourage existing users to consume more.
- *Competitive gap.* This gap can be closed by improving the firm's position through taking extra market share from existing competitors.

If the expected gap cannot be closed by decreasing industry market potential or gaining additional market share, attention may be shifted to assessing the firm's portfolio of businesses with a view to modifying it to add higher-growth activities and/or divesting low-growth businesses.

Bibliography

Ansoff, I. (1987). *Corporate strategy.* Harmondsworth, UK: Penguin.

Drucker, P. (1989). *The new realities.* London: Mandarin. See pp. 202–3.

Rowe, A. J., Mason, R. O., Dickel, K. E., Mann, R. B. & Mockler, R. J. (1994). *Strategic management* 4th edn. Reading, MA: Addison-Wesley. See pp. 240–6.

Weber, J. A. (1977). Market structure profile and strategic growth opportunities. *California Management Review*, **20** (1).

DEREK F. CHANNON

gatekeepers   Gatekeepers can have an important (if often unnoticed) informal influence on organizational purchasing (*see* ORGANIZATIONAL BUYING BEHAVIOR; PURCHASING PROCESS), although they are not members of the decision-making unit (DMU) in a formal sense. The term refers to those individuals who control access to an organization (such as receptionists, telephone operators, security staff, personal assistants, secretaries, and aides) and so may influence the flow of information into an organization. As information is a crucial aspect of the process of marketing between organizations, the influence of gatekeepers can be appreciated.

DOMINIC WILSON

gender effects in recruiting   Recruiting is crucial for an organization because it ultimately affects the composition of the workforce (*see* RECRUITING). Special consideration must be given to the effects of gender in recruiting because of the potential legal and organizational impacts.

Gender must be considered in all steps of the recruitment process. Planning for recruitment must take into account the current, future, and desired gender characteristics of the organization's workforce, and must be designed to support the desired or mandated gender balance within the organization. The current gender balance within the organization must also be considered in the choice of internal or external recruiting (*see* RECRUITING SOURCES). If a gender imbalance already exists within an organization, internal recruiting may act to perpetuate, rather than solve, such a situation. The organization's internal structure, particularly in the area of career movement, must be considered. For example, in some organizations, formalized structures such as job ladders not only create but also help to maintain gender segregation (Perry et al., 1994).

Whether posted internally or externally, recruiting messages must be framed so that one gender is not favored (inadvertently or otherwise). For example, general terms such as "manager" may evoke gender-based schema in a recruiter's mind. A description of actual job duties may avoid this problem (Kulik, 1989). It is a generally accepted practice (and legally mandated in many cases) for advertisements to indicate whether the company has an equal opportunity policy.

The choice of the target group for recruiting is also important in the identification of potential gender effects. If the target group is mostly populated by one gender (e.g. women in nursing), the recruiter must balance that reality against the demands of the organization, as well as any legal or internal mandates, for gender balance in the workplace. However, the gender indentification of the job (a "male" or "female" occupation) and the gender of current job occupants must be noted as a potential source of discrimination in the recruiting process. The continuation of existing gender patterns of hiring may result in continued sex segregation in the workplace (Heilman, 1983).

Gender effects can be particularly influential in the selection process. Recruiters generally have limited time and information on which to base their selection decisions and, thus, stereotypes tend to have a strong effect. Gender-based stereotypes (e.g. about one gender's particular talents or aptitudes for a job) may, thus, result in a biased hiring decision (Powell, 1987). Beliefs about appropriate appearance, age, or level of attractiveness for the ideal candidate may also receive more attention in selection than actual job-relevant credentials.

Appropriate training for those screening or interviewing candidates is one method of alerting those involved in the recruitment process to possible biases.

Bibliography

Heilman, M. E. (1983). Sex bias in work settings: the lack of fit mode. *Research in Organizational Behaviour*. Eds. Cummings, L. L. & Staw, B. M. 5, Greenwich, CT: JAI Press.
Kulik, C. T. (1989). The effects of job categorization on judgments of the motivating potential of jobs. *Administrative Science Quarterly*, 34, 68–90.
Perry, E. L., Davis–Blake, A. & Kulik, C. T. (1994). Explaining gender-based selection decisions: a synthesis of contextual and cognitive approaches. *Academy of Management Review*, 19, 786–820.
Powell, G. N. (1987). The effects of sex and gender on recruitment. *Academy of Management Review*, 12, 731–43.

FIONA A. E. MCQUARRIE

gender issues in international assignments   Gender issues in international assignments generally focus on the selection and performance of women who work in foreign environments. Globally, most organizations recognize an international assignment as a critical prerequisite for career advancement to executive management. However, the vast majority of managers and expatriates in multinational companies are male (Rossman, 1990).

Three common reasons are often cited by organizations in their reluctance to assign women to international assignments: (a) women are less interested in international assignments than men; (b) foreigners, especially those in male-dominated cultures, are less likely to accept women professionals; and (c) for safety reasons, organizations prefer to send men to remote locations, developing countries, or isolated work assignments. Research by Adler (1990) and her colleagues has concluded that these reasons are largely without merit.

Advantages and disadvantages have been identified for women in international assignments (Adler and Izraeli, 1988). Advantages include: higher visibility in the organization due to the rareness of a female expatriate; the general assumption that a female expatriate must be highly qualified since she passed the selection hurdle; and affordable resources available to help (e.g. maids, cooks, childcare). Disadvantages include: barriers in selection; limited opportunities for a woman when the home office seeks to protect her by restricting her travel and exposure to outsiders; and dual-career concerns (*see* DUAL-CAREER COUPLES) are more likely to be problematic for married women. More research is needed to determine the extent to which international assignments can be managed to maximize the success for women expatriates.

Bibliography

Adler, N. J. (1990). *International Dimensions of Organizational Behavior*, 2nd edn, Boston: PWS–Adler, N. J. & Izraeli, D. N. (Eds) (1988). *Women in Management Worldwide*, Armonk, NY: M. E. Sharpe.
Rossman, M. L. (1990). *The International Businesswoman of the 1990s*, New York: Praeger.

GEORGIA T. CHAO

generic strategies   Several efforts to classify strategy have been made at various times. One of the earliest was Ansoff's (1965) PRODUCT MARKET DIVERSIFICATION

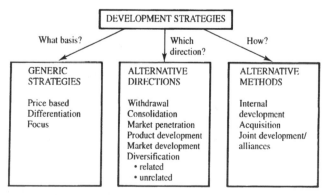

Figure 1 Development strategies.
Source: Johnson & Scholes (1993).

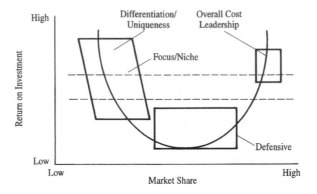

Figure 2 The Porter curve: profitability versus market share of the four generic competitive strategies.
Source: Rowe et al. (1994).

MATRIX. This specifies an appropriate strategy for the marketing of new or existing products to new or existing markets, and is described in more detail in the appropriate section. A weakness was that the sustainability of the strategies involved was not addressed.

Porter made this point and, viewing strategy as basically aimed at securing a long-term market developed another classification of what he called generic strategies.

He suggested that there are three generic strategies to choose from, and each business unit can have its own strategy. According to Porter, a business can strive to supply a product or service more cost-effectively than its competitors (cost leadership), it can strive to add value to the product or service through differentiation and command higher prices (differentiation), or it can narrow its focus to a special product market segment which it can monopolize (focus). Not following any of these strategies characterizes a firm as being "stuck in the middle."

The place of generic strategies in the overall strategy of a firm is indicated in figure 1, which also shows the relationship between Porter's and Ansoff's strategies.

The rationale for the three strategies, and their completeness as an option set, are depicted in figures 2 and 3, respectively. The isoquants, lines of equal return, make it explicit that the same return on investment can be achieved with two different market shares depending on the generic strategy chosen.

Bibliography

Cronshaw, M. J., Davis, E. & Kay, J. (1990). On being stuck in the middle – good food costs less at Sainsbury's. *Proceedings of the British Academy of Management Annual Conference, Glasgow.*

Gilbert, X. & Strebel, P. (1991). Developing competitive advantage. In H. Mintzberg & J. B. Quinn (eds), *The strategy process: concepts, contexts, cases* (2nd edn), Englewood Cliffs, NJ: Prentice-Hall. See pp. 82–93.

Johnson, G. & Scholes, K. (1993). *Exploring corporate strategy* (3rd edn). Englewood Cliffs, NJ: Prentice-Hall.

Mathur, S. S. (1986). Strategy: framing business intentions. *Journal of General Management*, **12** (1), 77–97.

Mathur, S. S. (1988). How firms compete: a new classification of generic strategies. *Journal of General Management*, **14** (1), 30–57.

Mintzberg, H. (1988). Generic strategies: toward a comprehensive framework. In *Advances in strategic management*, **5**, 1–67. Greenwich, CT: JAI Press. Reprinted, in abbreviated form, in H. Mintzberg & J. B. Quinn (eds) (1991), *The strategy process: concepts, contexts, cases* (2nd edn). Englewood Cliffs, NJ: Prentice-Hall. See pp. 70–82.

Porter, M. E. (1980). *Competitive strategy: techniques for analyzing industries and competitors*. New York: The Free Press.

Porter, M. E. (1985). *Competitive advantage: creating and sustaining superior performance*. New York: The Free Press. See pp. 11–26.

Rowe, A. J., Mason, R. O., Dickel, K. E., Mann, R. B. & Mockler, R. J. (1994). *Strategic management: a methodological approach.* 4th edn. Reading, MA: Addison-Wesley. See pp. 134–44.

STEPHANOS AVGEROPOULOS

COMPETITIVE ADVANTAGE

	Lower cost	Differentiation
Broad target	1 Cost leadership	2 Differentiation
Narrow target	3A Cost focus	3B Differentiation focus

(COMPETITIVE SCOPE)

Figure 3 Three generic strategies.
Source: Porter (1980).

genetic screening   Genetic screening for employment purposes is the practice of predicting work-relevant behaviors or dispositions based on genetic marker information. Although this staffing practice is still virtually nonexistent among US corporations (see Office of Technology Assessment, 1990), rapidly accelerating advances in genetic research are leading to (a) the identification of "genetic markers" for a vast range of diseases and dispositions, and (b) the development of cost-effective and accurate genetic screening tests for genetic counseling purposes as well as for potential employment applications. The types of work-related behaviors that are potentially predictable from genetic information include interpersonal orientation (based on a marker for extraversion–introversion), cognitive processing (based on a marker for field dependence-independence), and aggression. Susceptibility to disease is also predictable from genetic information. Examples include disposition toward cancer and heart disease, or vulnerability to exposure from chemicals (e.g. oxidizing agents) used in production processes that could increase the probability of pulmonary disease (see Olian, 1984; Rothstein, 1989). This type of predictor information has obvious implications for employer health care costs.

Genetic screening has potential utility for staffing purposes to the extent that traditional scientific standards of validity are attained for such tests. For certain diseases or susceptibilities, the low base rate in the population and the complex pattern of interactions among genetic markers in predicting actual disease impose upper limits on the validity of the tests in traditional populations of applicants. More critically, however, the practice of genetic screening introduces profound ethical and public policy challenges (Olian, 1984; Greenfield et al., 1989). These stem primarily from the immutable nature of genetic markers as the basis for employment and allocation decisions, and the fact that many genetic markers are distributed unequally across racial, ethnic and gender groups. For these and other reasons, various commentators have cautioned against premature adoption of these practices (see Draper, 1991; Strudler, 1994).

Bibliography

Draper, E. (1991). *Risky Business*, Cambridge: Cambridge University Press.

Greenfield, P. A., Karren, R. J. & Zacharias, L. S. (1989). Screening workers: an examination and analysis of practice and public policy. *Employee Relations*, 11 (5), 1–47.

Office of Technology Assessment (1990). *Genetics in the Workplace*, Washington, DC: US Government Printing Office.

Olian, J. D. (1984). Genetic screening for employment purposes. *Personnel Psychology*, 37, 423–38.

Rothstein, M. (1989). *Medical Screening and the Employee Health Cost Crisis*, Washington, DC: Bureau of National Affairs.

Strudler, A. (1994). The social construction of genetic abnormality: ethical implications for managerial decisions in the work place. *Journal of Business Ethics*, 13, 839–48.

JUDY D. OLIAN

geodemographics Geodemographic groups of consumers (i.e., identified by geographic and demographic variables), referred to as geodemographic classifications, are built on the premise that people who live in similar neighborhoods are likely to have similar purchasing and lifestyle habits (*see also* LIFESTYLES). Most classifications are built by using data from the Census of Population such as employment type, age, marital status, family size, property type, etc. Other variables can be used and some classifications have adopted this approach, e.g., Mosaic, Finpin. Sometimes, a preliminary process called principal component analysis is used on the raw variables to identify commonalities in the data. Either the raw variables or the principal components are then subject to cluster analysis to identify similar types of geographical areas. (For details of the classifications and methods, *see Journal of Market Research Society*, 1989.)

Some of the major classifications in the UK are: ACORN (A Classification Of Residential Neighbourhoods); PIN (Pinpoint Identification Neighbourhoods); Mosaic; and

Superprofiles (see table 1 for details). As an example, ACORN classifications have been divided into six major categories, i.e., Thriving, Expanding, Rising, Settling, Aspiring, and Striving. These are further desegregated into 17 groups and 54 types. For example, the ACORN category Thriving includes groups of Wealthy Achievers in Suburban Areas, Affluent Greys in Rural Communities, and Prosperous Pensioners in Retirement Areas, and thus provides a means of locating where these types of individuals are likely to reside.

One question which has been raised in the literature is: does it really make sense to use one standard segmentation tool across all sorts of industry sectors, markets, products, and organizations? The answer appears to be that each general classification product does discriminate, but the degree of discrimination varies according to market sector and there is no single best standard geodemographic product for all situations from those available. Two of the first market-specific applications to be devised were Financial Mosaic and Finpin, which were designed specifically to segment the market for financial services. Sources of data used for Financial Mosaic include: the number of company directors, the level and value of share ownership, the level of application for various financial services, the proportion of mortgages and outright home owners, and the frequency and value of County Court Judgements. This has resulted in a classification of 36 Financial Mosaic types; for example, Young Entrepreneurs, Wealthy Businessmen, and Captains of Industry are three types which are grouped under Capital Accumulators. The demand for, and supply of, tailored or bespoke segmentation classifications has risen recently, e.g., Investor ACORN incorporates data from the Investor's Register, a database of over 1 million investors, and Art ACORN combines demographic data with information from the box offices of arts venues throughout Great Britain. The extension of these more targeted classifications is to have a bespoke classification for each particular market. If organizations have sufficient information on their customers, this can be used to create bespoke classifications for any product market, e.g., cars, food, hi-fis, etc.

CCN has made major inroads into building classifications within many European countries. Euromosaic identifies ten major pan-European types which are consistent across the European countries of: Great Britain; the Netherlands; Germany; Spain; Ireland; Sweden; and Belgium. An example of a Euromosaic type is Elite suburbs. These are well-established suburban neighborhoods in large and medium-sized cities, consisting of residential properties in large grounds. These people are wealthy, but live in restrained luxury.

The major advantages of geodemographics are: their multi-faceted nature, i.e., they do not rely on unidimensional classification variables; their ease of use and actionability, being linked to the postcode system and covering all consumer addresses within the UK; their ability to link with different data sets which have been geodemographically coded for above-the-line and below-the-line marketing activities, e.g., TV audience rating data and regional press; and their ability to describe the types of houses people live in which can help the marketer to understand his/her target segment. They are now an essential part of retail site analysis and branch/store

Table 1 The Main 1991 Census-based geodemographic classifications in the UK

Classification system	No. of input variables	No. of clusters	Non-census data used?
ACORN	79	(a) 6 (b) 17 (c) 54	No
PIN	49	(a) 4 (b) 16 (c) 42	No
FINPIN	58	(a) 4 (b) 10 (c) 40	FRS data
MOSAIC	87	(a) 11 (b) 52	Credit data; Electoral Roll; PAF data; CCJs; Retail access; Age model; prop'n. director
SuperProfiles	120	(a)10 (b) 40 (c) 160	TGI; electoral roll; credit data; CCJs
DEFINE	146	(a) 10 (b) 50 (c) 1050	Credit data; Electoral Roll; Unemployment statistics; Insurance rating
Neighbors & Prospects	48	(a) 9 (b) 44	No

Source: Sleight, 1995.
(a) (b) and (c) identify different levels of aggregation.
FRS = Financial Research Survey; CCJ = County Court Judgement; PAF = Postal Address File; TGI = Target Group Index.

assessment. For example, by knowing how many of a certain type of customer are within a branch/store catchment area, a more accurate assessment of alternative branch locations and of market and sales targets can be undertaken. They are useful in media planning, since media data sources such as the National Readership Survey and Target Group Index are geodemographically coded. Advertising and promotional messages can also be communicated to the target audience using DIRECT MAIL and door-to-door leaflet campaigns which can be geodemographically targeted. Finally, they are extensively used in customer profiling which involves geodemographically analyzing existing customers.

Geodemographic systems do have several weaknesses. First, because the Census information is released at an aggregated level of about 150 households (Enumeration District), classifications are not particularly good at targeting certain differences, e.g., age, at the household or postcode level. However, several products have been designed to overcome this problem. 'Monica' from CACI

attempts to use the Christian names of household dwellers to indicate their likely age band, e.g., Ethel and Arthur are names which have an older age profile than Simon and Amanda.

A second problem, known as the "ecological fallacy," refers to the assumption that the behavior of all individuals will be the same within a given geodemographic type. Since geodemographic classifications describe neighborhoods rather than people, it is fallacious to assume that all the people within a given neighborhood will purchase in the same way. Mosaic is one system which has attempted to address both the age and the aggregated data problem by incorporating many variables which are measured at the postcode, rather than at the Enumeration District, level. This allows more precise targeting, since there are typically only 15 households per postcode. In addition, Persona from CCN, is one of the first behavioral targeting systems. If in geodemographic terms "you are where you live," with Persona, "you are what you do." Developed from the National Shopping Survey, it divides UK households into distinctive behavioral types. These types range from so-called "Bonviveurs" to "New Teachers" and "Craftsmen" and "Home Makers." Such data counter another of the weaknesses of traditional Census-based classifications in that they give more information about people's income, assets, leisure activities, and purchasing behavior, which is not available from the Census.

A final problem with Census-based classifications is the age of the data: classification is conducted only once every ten years in most countries including the UK. Fifty-six percent of the data contained within Mosaic is non-Census information and is updated regularly; although the Mosaic types themselves are only updated every two years.

see also **Market segmentation; Segmentation variables**

Bibliography

Journal of Market Research Society. (1989), **31**, (N4), January, Special issue on geodemographics.

Sleight, P. (1995). Explaining geodemographics. *APMAP*, January, No. 347, 48.

VINCE MITCHELL

global alliance   *see* STRATEGIC ALLIANCE

global branding   The use of the same brand name for products everywhere they are sold in the world. Global branding has the advantages of building name identification, new products take on the good name of established products, and there are economies in developing packaging, advertising, trademarks, etc. It is also simpler to move into new markets when the name of your product is well known in surrounding markets. Coca Cola is probably the best known product that uses global branding. Global branding, however, may cause some problems as well. A product which suffers problems because of, for example, consumer injuries from its use, may put the company's entire product line in question throughout the world. There are also potential problems related to words having different meanings in different countries. Advertising print, product names, and distribution materials must be carefully reviewed for words, colors, or even numbers which may be offensive in certain cultures. Global brands may also infer support for a particular political view (British Airlines, American Express, etc.) which may be unacceptable in some countries.

Bibliography

Pradeep, A. R. & Preble, J. F. (1987). Standardization of marketing strategy by multinationals. *International Marketing Review*, Autumn, 18–28.

JOHN O'CONNELL

global leadership   In a recent article (Handy, 1996), it was noted that a German senior manager described organizations in Germany as "organizations largely run by engineers. Such people think of the organization as a machine, something that can be designed, measured, and controlled – managed in other words." Today, our metaphors for organizations are changing from a machine image to more organic images such as organizations as networks, communities, or knowledge systems. With such change has come a renewed focus on leadership being critical to organizations.

In the past, most studies of leadership have been based on the assumption that leadership derives from position: leaders became leaders by virtue of their roles in the organization. As companies change from hierarchy-based management structures to more delayered, empowered systems, our conceptions of leadership also need to change (Hesselbein *et al.*, 1996). The more widely distributed knowledge becomes, the more that leadership needs to be distributed amongst a variety of individuals in the organization. For example, employees in customer-interface roles must be leaders in their interactions with customers and in disseminating the knowledge which they gain in these interactions to other parts of the organization.

In addition to the challenge of distributing leadership due to the shift to distributed knowledge, organizations today are facing the challenge of developing leaders who will be effective in global organizations that span numerous cultures. Companies are focusing on developing the set of leadership competences. Although there may be some born global leaders, this set is too small to meet the needs of today's global organizations. For the most part, global leadership must, and can, be learned (Ashkenas *et al.*, 1995).

What does this leadership look like? Leaders of knowledge-based, global organizations will behave and lead in a variety of ways, but they share a focus on several key issues (Drucker, 1996):

- They begin with the question "What needs to be done?"
- They follow with "What can and should I do to make a difference?"
- They focus on performance and results.
- They are supportive of diversity in people and do not seek to reinforce mirror images of themselves.
- Relatedly, they develop their followers and are not fearful of strong, competent followers (Kouzes & Posner, 1995).
- They test themselves against high standards of leadership and role model the behaviors and qualities which they wish to see in others. They are doers.

In summary, global leaders share a common focus on articulating a vision which leads to measurable results and by leading through action, notably personal action.

Much of the research on leadership has focused on transformational leadership, or leadership which leads to changes in followers of organizations and in the leader himor herself (Kouzes & Posner, 1995). Change and global leadership are inextricably linked. The key change challenges which face global leaders are linked to the changes that are occurring as organizations move from being bureaucratic machines to being knowledge-based networks. Specifically, leaders must guide their organizations to produce results today, even as they push for transformation which will positively impact the future.

Finally, the work of Ulrich (1996) generates some useful thoughts about the importance of credibility and capability. Ulrich argues that successful leaders must be both personally credible and must be able to create organizational capability. Credible leaders engender trust and commitment from those who follow their vision. Organizational capability results from a leader who shapes a stronger organization through development, systems, and processes.

To conclude, organizations are changing rapidly. Global leaders are faced with the challenge of leading this transformation even as the role of leadership is being transformed. Often, leaders are finding that they, themselves, need to change personally and to develop new abilities. The future promises to be a time of exciting, rapid change, with the effective leaders being those individuals who can transform and be transformed in the midst of this change.

Bibliography

Ashkenas, R., Ulrich, D., Jick, T. & Kerr, S. (1995). *The boundaryless organization*. San Francisco, CA: Jossey-Bass.

Drucker, P. (1996). Leading the organizations of the future. In Hesselbein, F., Goldsmith, M., & Beckhard, R. (eds), *The leader of the future*. San Francisco, CA: Jossey-Bass.

Handy, C. (1996). The new language of organizing and its implications for leaders. In Hesselbein, F., Goldsmith, M., & Beckhard, R. (eds) *The leader of the future*. San Francisco, CA: Jossey-Bass

Hesselbein, F., Goldsmith, M. & Beckhard, R. (Eds), (1996). *The leader of the future*. San Francisco, CA Jossey-Bass.

Kouzes, J. & Posner, B. (1995). *The leadership challenge*. San Francisco, CA: Jossey-Bass.

CAREN SIEHL

global sourcing   Sourcing is the acquiring of goods, labor, and materials necessary to produce a product. An origination that seeks the resources to produce its goods from any place that may have an availability of resources is said to employ a global sourcing strategy. Global sourcing has come about because of differences in supply and price of various resources. When sufficient supplies are not available locally or the cost of any resource is very high locally, firms begin to seek resources elsewhere. Global sourcing is not without its problems: increased transportation costs, increased possibilities of interruption of supplies (natural disaster, political problems, etc.), delays in shipment (weather, strikes, etc.) (*see* SOURCING), and becoming too reliant on foreign sources of supply, all add to the risks of doing business through foreign sourcing.

Bibliography

Swan, A. C. & Murphy, J. F. (1991). *Cases & materials on the regulation of international business and economic relations*. New York: Mathew Bender & Co.

JOHN O'CONNELL

global strategy   A global strategy can be considered as a coherent overarching strategy for the parts of the world in which an organization operates. Yip (1989) suggests that it emerges as part of a three-stage process. First, the development of a core strategy or a distinct COMPETITIVE ADVANTAGE, generally in the firm's domestic market. Second, the extension of the firm's geographical reach of the core strategy, which will be adapted to match local features. Third, globalization, viewed as the international marketing of standard offerings (Levitt, 1983), through the integration of these adapted strategies into a global strategy. This is an obvious simplification of the international development of organizations which may not involve this sequence of stages.

A global strategy tends to be seen as synonymous with a standard strategy across international markets. Such a strategic approach can be regarded as yielding distinct advantages through, in particular, economies of scale. However, as several commentators have noted, there are many barriers toward such a standard global strategy, including differences in the physical environment and culture, and they question the feasibility of a global standardized branding strategy, arguing that the differences, from language alone, far outweigh any similarities. Adaptability and variation in MARKETING STRATEGIES across geographical markets are likely to be the norm. As Bradley (1991) notes, it may be an essential requirement to acknowledge dissimilarities between countries and adjust marketing strategies to suit specific regional requirements. Quelch & Hoff (1986) suggest that there is a spectrum of strategic possibilities with different elements (such as product features, advertising message content) having greater or smaller degrees of homogeneity across markets.

It has been suggested (e.g., Littler & Schlieper, 1995) that many markets may be converging under the influences of more widespread communications, the market DIVERSIFICATION strategies of manufacturers and retailers and the development of free trade areas, such as the European Union, leading to more standardization across markets.

Bibliography

Bradley, F. (1991). *International marketing strategy*. Prentice-Hall.

Levitt, T. (1983). The globalization of markets. *Harvard Business Review*, **61**, May–June, 92–102.

Littler, D. & Schlieper, K. (1995). The development of the Eurobrand. *International Marketing Review*, **12**, 22–37.

Quelch, J. A. & Hoff, E. J. (1986). Customizing global markets. *Harvard Business Review*, **64**, May–June, 59–68.

Yip, G. S. (1989). Global strategy in a world of nations? *Sloan Management Review*, **30**, Fall, 29–41.

DALE LITTLER

globalization   The development of international strategy forms a natural part in the evolution of many corporations, as does product market diversification. The main reasons tend to be to exploit perceived market opportunities, superior competitive positions as the result of lower costs, investment incentives, market access and the like, and access to raw materials or other critical resources. In addition, overseas development may occur as a result of fluctuation in exchange rates, lower overseas cost structures, host country government policies, and the pattern of international competition. For some industries – such as automobiles, aerospace, personal computers, and pharmaceuticals – this has led to radical transformations of the industries on a global basis.

The early development of international strategy tends to begin with the establishment of export organizations using local agents or dedicated sales teams. With success may come the establishment of assembly operations and overseas production complexes. Such activities tend to be managed by the creation of an export division. Further overseas development by multi product line businesses normally results in the creation of worldwide product division systems in which geographic responsibility may be most concerned with local integration, legal, and tax considerations, rather than operational management. Ultimately, matrix structures may develop, incorporating product and geographic responsibilities.

International patterns of competition can thus be categorized in a number of different ways:

(1) Licensing foreign corporations to use the corporation's technology and/or distribute products and services.
(2) Operating as a domestic-based corporation and exporting overseas via agents/distributors or dedicated organizations.
(3) Adopting a multi-country strategy whereby strategy varies from country to country to fit local specific needs and where economies of scale are less important. Such industries have tended to include food, breweries and retailing, although in some cases global strategies have developed or are emerging for brands such as McDonalds, Coca Cola, Fosters Lager, and Marks and Spencer.
(4) Operating a global low cost strategy by attempting to become a key low cost supplier to buyers around the world. Such industries might include oil, chemicals, automobiles, and computer chips.
(5) Adopting a global differentiation strategy to create products differentiated from competitors but with a consistent image. Such strategies can be found in Citibank in global electronic funds transfer, Sony in consumer electronics, and General Electric in industrial diamonds.
(6) Adopting a global focus strategy by attempting to service a specific niche in many strategically important countries, such as Citibank in global retail banking, Caterpillar in earth moving equipment, and Boeing in aerospace.

The choice as to which strategy to adopt is dependent upon the characteristics of the specific industry that the firm is engaged in, and has been changing over time as a result of:

- increasing similarities between national markets as a result of greater international travel, greater information exchange, more similarities in lifestyles, media coverage and the internationalization of corporate strategies
- the emergence of substantial economies of scale and the effect on unit costs in manufacturing, marketing, and R&D
- economic policies which permit worldwide presence, with the creation of trading blocs such as the European Union

McKinsey and Company has identified a number of factors favouring globalization, therefore, which can be classified as follows:

- demand factors: homogeneous requirements for customers operating worldwide (such as machine tools and plant construction); uniform technical standards (for instance, chemicals and metals); homogeneous demand from consumers (as in consumer electronics, automobiles, and cameras).
- supply factors: significant economies of scale, purchasing, manufacturing, distribution, and R&D; advantages in access to strategic resources; opportunities for clear product/service differentiation.

- economic factors: low/no customs barriers; free movement of capital; favorable fiscal regimes.

Bibliography
Henzler, H. & Hall, W. (1986), *McKinsey Quarterly*, Winter, 52-68.
Thomson, A. A. Jnr & Strickland, A, J. (1995), *Strategic Management Concepts and Cases.* 8th edition, 158-169. Irwin, Homewood, Illinois.
Porter, M. E. (1990), The Competitive Advantage of Nations. 53-57. Free Press. New York.
Bolt, J. F. (1988), Global Competitors: Some Criteria for Success. 34-41. *Business Horizons*, **31**, No. 1 Jan-Feb.

DEREK F. CHANNON

goal setting This theory of MOTIVATION was originally developed by Locke (1968) to explain human action in specific work situations. The underlying assumptions of the theory are that goals and intentions are cognitive and volitional, and that they serve as the immediate regulators of human action. The two major findings of the theory are that specific goals lead to higher performance levels than general goals, and that difficult goals are positively and linearly related to performance. These effects are subject to two conditions – feedback, and the acceptance of goals by the performers. Goals regulate behavior through three mechanisms: choice/direction, intensity/effort/resource allocation, and duration/persistence. The effect of goal-setting in complex tasks is regulated by a fourth mechanism of strategy development, which is necessary for reaching the goal. The two unique characteristics of the goal-setting theory that make it more effective than any other theory of motivation to date are its strong empirical basis, and its continuous process of development.

The original goal-setting model (Locke, 1968) consisted of a sequential process of five steps: Environmental Stimuli → Cognition → Evaluation → Intentions/Goal-Setting → Performance. Goal-setting theory was developed by starting with goals and intentions as the two conscious motivational factors closest to the action. It then worked backward progressively to the preceding stages of evaluation, and cognition. The term *goal* refers to attaining a specific standard of proficiency on a given task, usually within a specified time limit. Goals have two main attributes: content and intensity. *Goal content* refers to the object or result being sought (e.g., producing 10 percent more units, reaching an executive position within 10 years). Goal difficulty specifies a certain level of standard of task proficiency. *Goal intensity* refers to the amount of physical and mental resources that goes into formulating the goal or a plan of action to realize it (Locke & Latham, 1990). It is expressed by goal COMMITMENT, effort, and attention. The parsimony of the early research paradigm which focused on the relationship between goals and performance allowed us to establish the strong empirical support to the effect of goal specificity and difficulty on performance. Once these basic relationships were established, the focus shifted backward to the *evaluation phase*, and the next step of theory development began. Four important variables that are evaluative by nature, serve to explain mediating and moderating effects on the goal–performance relationship: feedback Knowledge-of-results, expectancies, self-efficacy, and goal commitment. *Feedback* pertains to performance evaluation relative to the goal, and it was identified as a necessary condition for goals to affect performance (Erez, 1977). Feedback may have negative effects on performance when it shifts resources to off-task processes of self-regulation, in particular, for individuals with low levels of self-efficacy (Kanfer, 1990). *Self-efficacy* is a judgment of one's capability to accomplish a certain level of performance (Bandura, 1986). Goal difficulty positively affects perceptions of self-efficacy, which further affect intentions, personal goals, and performance. In a cyclical process past performance affects self-efficacy, which further affects self-set goals and performance. *Expectancies* reflect the evaluations people make of their chance to obtain goals. For a given level of goal difficulty, individuals with high rather than low expectancies are more likely to attain their goals. Perceptions of self-efficacy, and expectancies determine the level of goal attractiveness which influences goal acceptance. *Goal acceptance* refers to initial agreement with the goal, whereas *goal commitment* refers to adherence to the goal, and resistance to changing the goal at a later point in time. Goal commitment both mediates and moderates the effect of goal difficulty on performance. A significant drop-off in performance is observed if and when goal commitment declines in response to increasingly difficult goals. Feedback and goal commitment were identified as the two necessary conditions for goals to affect performance. Participation in goal setting was found to be one effective method for enhancing goal commitment (Latham, Erez, & Locke, 1988). Goal evaluation is guided by *values*, which determine what people consciously consider beneficial to their welfare. VALUES mediate between needs and goals which can be viewed as applications of values to specific situations (Locke, 1991). In parallel to the continuous research on the evaluation phase there is a growing interest in cognition which precedes evaluation. *Cognition* draws attention to paradigms of complex tasks, and multiple goals. The magnitude of goal effects on performance decreases as task complexity increases. Goals of complex tasks affect performance to the extent that they lead to the development of effective plans and strategies. However, very often, goals generate pressure for immediate results and they become counter-productive when planning and strategy development is required. The negative effect of goals on the performance of complex tasks is mainly observed at initial stages of skill acquisition (Kanfer, 1990). The multiple goal paradigm is guided by the assumption that the human organism has a pool of limited resources. As a result, there is a trade-off relationship in the performance of multiple goals. More resources are shifted toward specific and difficult goals than general or easy goals, and to the attainment of performance goals which are supported by feedback.

It seems that the most recent phase of theory development is that of examining goals in different contextual levels – individual goals, group goals (Weldon & Gargano, 1988), visionary goals of leaders, and the effect of cultural values on goal choice and goal commitment (Erez & Earley, 1993). Monetary rewards is another situational factor which mediates, as well as moderates the effect of goals on performance. REWARDS increase goal commitment, but at the same time they inhibit the attainment of complementary goals which are not compensated for (Wright, George, Farnsworth, & McMahan,

1993). To summarize, the continuous development of the goal-setting theory integrates different motivational theories into one coherent model which contributes to our understanding of how goals affect the performance of multiple tasks, including performance quantity and quality, and at multiple levels of analysis – individuals, groups, organizations, and cultures. In its present development, the goal-setting theory is identified as a meta-cognitive theory of self-regulation, with a growing emphasis on the underlying cognitive resource allocation processes (Kanfer, 1990).

see also **Management by objectives**

Bibliography

Bandura, A. (1986). Social foundations of thought and action: A social cognitive theory. Englewood Cliffs, NJ: Prentice-Hall.

Erez, M. (1977). Feedback: A necessary condition for the goal setting-performance relationship. Journal of Applied Psychology, **62**, 624–627.

Erez, M. & Earley, P. C. (1993). Culture, self-identity, and work. New York: Oxford University Press.

Kanfer, R. (1990). Motivation theory and industrial and organizational psychology. In M. D. Dunnette & L. M. Hough (Eds), Handbook of industrial and organizational psychology. (Vol. 1, pp. 75–170). Palo Alto, CA: Consulting Psychology Press.

Latham, G. P., Erez, M. & Locke, E. A. (1988). Resolving scientific disputes by the joint design of crucial experiments: Application to the Erez–Latham dispute regarding participation in goal setting. Journal of Applied Psychology (Monograph), **73**, 753–77.

Locke, E. A. (1968). Toward a theory of task motivation and incentives. Organizational Behavior and Performance, **3**, 157–189.

Locke, E. A. (1991). The motivation sequence, the motivation hub, and the motivation core. Organizational Behavior and Human Decision Processes, **50**, 288–299.

Locke, E. A. & Latham, G. P. (1990). A theory of goal setting and task motivation. Englewood Cliffs, NJ: Prentice-Hall.

Weldon, E. & Gargano, G. M. (1988). On cognitive effort. Personality & Social Psychology Bulletin, **14**, 159–171.

Wright, P. M., George, J. M. Farnsworth S. R. & McMahan, G. C. (1993). Productivity and extra-role behavior: The effects of goals and incentives on spontaneous helping. Journal of Applied Psychology, **78**, 374–381.

MIRIAM EREZ

goodwill accounting   Goodwill accounting is a complex and controversial reporting issue. Being an intangible asset, the degree of uncertainty associated with its measurable benefits tends to be higher than for tangibles. Goodwill has a value only in relation to a given firm. Unlike patents or brand names that could be sold or exchanged individually in the market place, goodwill is inseparable from the business as a whole. It is often described as the most "intangible" of intangibles.

Goodwill can be thought of as the ability of a firm to generate "above-average" earnings. Box 1 highlights additional factors that are thought to generate goodwill.

A characteristic of these factors, however, is that they give rise to goodwill as a result of their interaction with other assets of the firm. Thus high-quality products (inventory) coupled with a favorable location enables the firm to achieve a higher volume of sales than would be possible had the firm's location been less accessible to the consuming public. However, location is not an asset that can be valued separately. This interaction or dependence gives rise to a significant measurement problem.

Box 1: Factors generating goodwill

- Superior management team
- Weakness in a competitor's management
- Effective advertising
- Secret manufacturing process
- Good labor relations
- Excellent credit rating
- Top-flight training program for employees
- Favorable association with another company
- Favorable tax conditions
- Favorable government relations
- Production economies
- Low-cost funds
- Cash reserves
- Assurance of supply
- Good public relations
- Unfavorable developments in a competitor's operations
- Access to technology

Source: Catlett & Olsen (1968)

Goodwill can be developed internally and/or externally. As an example of the former, expenditures on advertising, employee training, or patent development incurred to benefit current operations often generate goodwill (i.e., increased future earning power) as a byproduct. Assume that a company acquires another company and pays more for the target company than the sum of the fair market values of the target's net assets. In this instance, the premium paid acknowledges the existence of goodwill; i.e., above-average future earnings expectations on the part of the acquirer.

Measurement issues associated with goodwill are:

(1) Should goodwill, whether internally- or externally-developed, be recognized (i.e., measured and recorded) in the accounts?
(2) If goodwill is recognized, how should it affect shareholders' equity? Should it be treated as a permanent asset and written down only when there is evidence that its value has been impaired? Or, should it be amortized to income in some systematic fashion?

Goodwill Recognition

An asset may be defined as a probable future economic benefit that is obtained or controlled by a particular entity as a result of a past transaction or event. Since goodwill is associated with a stream of above-average earnings, most would agree that it is an asset. The question is whether it should be recognized as such in the accounts.

Internally developed goodwill is often a byproduct of transactions such as advertising and employee development activities. In these instances it is extremely difficult, if not impossible, to determine which portion of the actual expenditure is associated with normal operating benefits and which is associated with producing a future stream of above-average earnings. Since these expenditures work in concert in generating goodwill, it is impossible to reliably identify the transactions that give rise to this intangible asset. Owing to difficulties of measurement, expensing or non-recognition of internally-developed goodwill is common.

External-developed goodwill, in contrast, is more amenable to measurement albeit with differing degrees of reliability, especially using the *excess earnings* approach. This measure draws on the theory that an asset's value is equal to the discounted present value of the future earnings stream that it generates. Since goodwill generates above-average or excess earnings (i.e., earnings in excess of the industry average), the present value of this excess earnings stream is a measure of the value of this intangible asset.

This measurement approach is not without its drawbacks, however. Issues relate to (1) determining what constitutes a representative rate of return as a measure of normal earnings, (2) choosing an appropriate discount rate, (3) obtaining reliable estimates of excess earnings, and (4) determining the relevant time horizon for discounting purposes.

A measurement approach that is considered to be more objective is the *excess cost* approach. Under this measurement scheme, goodwill is recognized when a business is acquired. The difference between the purchase price and the fair market value of the identifiable net assets acquired represents the value of goodwill. *Negative goodwill* is said to arise whenever the purchase price is less than the fair market value of net assets acquired.

Of the two measurement approaches described above, the excess cost approach is most popular in practice because it is based on a past transaction. It is also relatively more objective.

Asset versus Expense

Should goodwill, once recognized, be treated as a permanent asset and written off only when there is evidence that its value has been impaired? Should it be amortized instead to income on a periodic basis? Or, should goodwill immediately be charged to shareholders' equity without taking it through the income statement?

Treating goodwill as a permanent asset is rationalized on several grounds. First, as purchased goodwill is being used up, some would argue that it is constantly being replaced by internally-developed goodwill. Thus, goodwill in total does not deteriorate. Periodic goodwill amortization under these circumstances understates asset values. Moreover, being an arbitrary process, goodwill amortization adds a random element to reported earnings, destroying the usefulness of past earnings as a predictive device.

Those favoring periodic amortization of capitalized goodwill argue that goodwill has a finite life. Favorable circumstances that make possible an above-average earnings stream, such as a unique product design or a conscientious sales team, do not last forever. Hence, keeping goodwill on the books indefinitely causes assets to be overstated. Amortization of purchased goodwill is also consistent with the treatment accorded internally-developed goodwill. All funds expended to generate future earnings are therefore charged to earnings. Also, amortization is consistent with the matching principle as expenditures for goodwill are made with the intention of generating future benefits.

Periodic amortization, however, raises yet another issue; namely, over what time period should goodwill be amortized? While a logical tack would be to amortize goodwill "over the periods expected to be benefited," the latter has proven difficult to operationalize in practice. Factors which need to be considered in determining a relevant amortization horizon include:

(1) Legal, regulatory or contractual provisions that may limit the maximum useful life.
(2) Effects of obsolescence, demand, competition, and other economic factors that may reduce useful life.
(3) The service life expectations of individuals or groups of employees.
(4) Expected actions of competitors and others that may restrict present competitive advantages.
(5) The fact that goodwill may be a composite of many individual factors with varying effective lives.

The effects of goodwill amortization on accounting rates of return and profitability statistics have led some to conclude that amortization periods are likely to be chosen more for pragmatic reasons than pure matching considerations.

The immediate write-off of acquired goodwill is yet another reporting option for purchased goodwill. Proponents of this alternative argue that immediate write-off treats both internally- and externally-developed goodwill in similar fashion. Since internally-generated goodwill is expensed, so too should purchased goodwill be, especially since goodwill is an integral part of the business as a whole. As such there is no predictable relationship to the costs paid on acquisition to justify its continued existence.

Concomitantly, determining the future periods likely to benefit from goodwill is so difficult that immediate write-off to shareholders' equity is justified.

Diversity in National Practice Treatments

In the USA, goodwill accounting is prescribed by two authoritative accounting pronouncements, Accounting Principles Board (APB) Opinions Nos. 16 and 17. APB Opinion No. 16 states that an acquisition by purchase is the only objective means of measuring goodwill. Accordingly, it requires that the excess of purchase price over the sum of the amount assigned to identifiable net assets acquired be recorded as goodwill. Negative goodwill must first be allocated proportionately to reduce the carrying values assigned to noncurrent assets to their fair market values with any remaining negative goodwill classified as a deferred credit (a liability). The latter would be amortized over a period similar to that for positive goodwill. APB Opinion No. 17, in turn, requires that goodwill be amortized to income over its estimated useful life, but not over a period to exceed 40 years.

Table 1 illustrates the wide diversity of international practice.

In this discussion of goodwill accounting differences, the differences in national tax treatments for goodwill have not been addressed. Thus, the reporting differences under discussion relate primarily to financial reporting differences. On this score numerous studies have shown that the securities markets are not misled by differences in accounting rules. Despite the academic evidence, however, business concern over the differential impact of national goodwill accounting treatments has failed to die. In a recent survey of US chief financial officers, one of the most frequently voiced complaints was that differences in accounting for purchased goodwill give non-US companies a competitive advantage in acquiring foreign target companies.

Differences in accounting treatments for purchased goodwill are perhaps most pronounced between the UK and the USA. Unlike the US practice, the accounting treatment preferred by UK managers is to write-off

Table 1: International comparison of goodwill accounting

	Aus	Can	Fra	Ger	HK	Jpn	Itl	Ndl	Swz	US	UK	EC	IASC
Purchased goodwill													
Permanent asset recognition	U	U	U	A	A	U	U	U	U	U	U	U	U
Asset recognition & amortized	R	R	R	A	A	A	A	A	A	R	R	A	R
Charged to equity	U	U	A	A	A	U	A	A	U	U	A	A	A
Internally-developed goodwill													
Asset recognition	U	U	U	U	U	U	U	U	U	U	U	U	U
Max. amortization period	20	40	20	15	NS	5	10	10	NS	40	20	5	20

Country/institutional codes:
Aus: Australia; Can: Canada; Fra: France; Ger: Germany; HK: Hong Kong; Jpn: Japan; Itl: Italy; Ndl: Netherlands; Swz: Switzerland; US: United State; UK: United Kingdom; EC: European Community; IASC: International Accounting Standards Committee;
Table entries:
U: Unauthorized treatment; R: Required treatment; A: Allowed treatment

goodwill immediately against reserves. While goodwill is not deductible for taxes in either the USA or the UK, differences in accounting treatment for goodwill provide an incentive for UK companies to offer more than US acquirers for common acquisition targets, in the knowledge that their future earnings need not be penalized by the higher price paid. To ascertain whether this is indeed the case, Choi & Lee (1991) found merger premiums associated with UK acquisitions to be consistently higher than those for US acquisitions. Moreover, higher premiums offered by UK acquirers were in part associated with not having to amortize goodwill against earnings. A follow-up study including German and Japanese acquirers again finds higher merger premiums offered by firms that enjoy favorable accounting treatments relative to US acquirers. Tax considerations were even more important, however, owing to the tax deductibility of goodwill charges in these countries. This evidence suggests that diversity in goodwill accounting does impact market behavior.

Bibliography

Catlett, G. R. & Olsen, N. O. (1968). Accounting for goodwill. *AICPA Accounting Research Study No. 10*. New York.

Choi, F. D. S. & Lee, C. (1991). Merger premia and national differences in accounting for goodwill. *Journal of International Financial Management and Accounting*, Autumn, 219–40.

Choi, F. D. S. & Mueller, G. G. (1993). *Globalization of Financial Accounting and Reporting*. New Jersey: Financial Executives Research Foundation.

Duvall, L et al. (1992). Can investors unravel the effects of goodwill accounting? *Accounting Horizons*, June, 1–14.

Lee, C. & Choi, F. D. S. Effects of alternative goodwill treatments on merger premia: Further empirical evidence. *Journal of International Financial Management and Accounting*.

Riley, Jr. V. J. (1988). The U.S. on sale. *Chief Executive* Nov.–Dec., 46–51.

Russell, A., et al. (1989). *Accounting for Goodwill*. London: Chartered Association.

Weetman, P. & Gray, S. (1990). International financial analysis and comparative corporate performance: The impact of UK versus US accounting principles on earnings. *Journal of International Financial Management and Accounting*, Summer & Autumn, 111–30.

FREDERICK D. S. CHOI

governing law International contracts will often specify the country whose laws will be used to deal with any disputed areas of the contract. The law specified is referred to as governing law. Problems may arise when governing law is not the same as that which is stated to be jurisdictional (i.e., the country in which the dispute is lodged is different than the governing law country in the contract). Countries tend to allow governing specifications of a contract to stand when a contract has been properly drawn. There are no guarantees, however, that contract governing law statements will be upheld by the courts.

JOHN O'CONNELL

graphic rating scale method of performance evaluation A graphic rating scale, defined as any rating scale consisting of points on a continuum, is a generic label given to a broad category of rating formats (Cascio, 1991). Raters are presented with a description of a dimension on which the ratees are to be evaluated, and a continuum with anchor points that demarcate levels of effectiveness along that continuum. The rater is asked to judge the level of effectiveness for each ratee, using that rating continuum. The number of points on the rating scale can vary from three upward. Research has indicated that five to nine scale points result in the highest quality of ratings (Finn, 1972).

Graphic rating scales are probably the most common rating format. One reason for this popularity is that the graphic rating scale category can be adapted to a wide variety of specific formats. Other reasons for their popularity include: (a) they are fairly easy to construct; (b) they have a fairly high level of user acceptability; and (c) they have face validity (Cardy and Dobbins, 1994).

Graphic rating scales can be differentiated based on the type and amount of information presented in the anchors. The most common format uses ambiguous adjectives (e.g. "marginal," "average," or "outstanding") as anchors. A more sophisticated format would use specific *behavioral descriptions* for each anchor point. Where research is used to help to define the level of effectiveness represented by these specific behavioral statements, the format would be considered a BEHAVIORALLY ANCHORED RATING SCALES or BEHAVIORAL OBSERVATION SCALES.

Graphic rating scales can also be classified based on whether the judgments asked for are of an absolute or relative nature. Graphic scales of an absolute type ask raters to indicate a ratee's specific level on a dimension. In contrast, relative rating scales ask raters to judge a ratee's level on a dimension *relative* to the level exhibited by other ratees. For example, a relative graphic scale might have scale anchors such as "one of the worst," "about on an average with his or her peers," and "one of the best." With an absolute graphic rating scale, everyone could be rated at a high level. With the relative scale format, some ratees must be rated average and low. While absolute judgments theoretically do not include comparisons with other ratees, research has demonstrated that relative comparisons do influence the absolute judgment (Laming, 1985). Research has also identified a number of specific RATING ERRORS and methods for minimizing these effects (*see* RATER TRAINING).

Bibliography

Cardy, R. L. & Dobbins, G. H. (1994). *Performance Appraisal: Alternative Perspectives*, Cincinnati, OH: South-Western.

Cascio, W. F. (1991). *Applied Psychology in Personnel Management*, Reston, VA: Reston Press.

Finn, R. H. (1972). Effects of some variations in rating scale characteristics on the means and reliabilities of ratings. *Educational and Psychological Measurement*, 32, 255–65.

Laming, D. (1985). The relativity of "absolute" judgments. *British Journal of Mathematical and Statistical Psychology*, 37, 152–83.

ROBERT L. CARDY

graphology Graphology, or handwriting analysis, is an increasingly used, yet scientifically unsupported, technique for selecting and promoting workers and for retaining managers after mergers or acquisitions. The use of graphology as a personnel staffing tool assumes that (a) the writer's personality will reveal itself in his or her handwriting, and (b) personality traits are predictive of success on the job (*see* INTEGRITY TESTING).

Scientific research on graphology shows that reliable differences in handwriting are associated with such phenomena as adolescence and psychosis, but not with temporary situational stressors. Furthermore, personality profiles developed by some graphologists on the basis of handwriting samples can be matched to the person whose handwriting was analyzed by friends and relatives of that person. Thus, there is some evidence to link personal characteristics with graphological markers (Nevo, 1987). On the other hand, there is very little to link these analyses with predictions of employee success at work.

Graphological findings are not reliable. In other words, analyses of the same handwriting sample by different graphologists can produce inconsistent or contradictory results (McCarthy, 1988, p. 19). Furthermore, research suggests that accurate graphological analyses are dependent on the *content* they extract from the handwriting samples, rather than from the writing itself (Ben-Shakhar et al., 1986). Any job-related information that a graphological analysis uncovers can be obtained more directly and less expensively from other devices, such as personality tests, biographical history inventories, and structured interviews. These devices will also gather additional job-related information that is not attainable from handwriting analysis.

Although graphology is very popular in Europe and Israel, and increasingly popular in the United States, there is little basis for recommending its use. Finally, United States users should be aware that analysis of handwriting without the writer's knowledge (a common practice) may be an illegal invasion of privacy under United States employment law.

Bibliography

Ben-Shakhar, G., Bar-Hillel, M., Bilu, Y., Ben-Abba, E. & Flug, A. (1986). Can graphology predict occupational success? Two empirical studies and some methodological ruminations. *Journal of Applied Psychology*, **71**, 645–53.

McCarthy, M. (1988). Handwriting analysis as a personnel tool. *The Wall Street Journal*, **August 25**, 19.

Nevo, B. (Ed.) (1987). *The Scientific Aspects of Graphology*, Springfield, IL: Charles C. Thomas.

HANNAH R. ROTHSTEIN

green issues *see* CONSUMERISM

grievance determinants Conjecture abounds about what causes individuals to file GRIEVANCES, but research is quite scarce that clearly identifies particular factors as determinants of grievance-filing behavior. Not only is the volume of research small, but published findings typically are associated with methodological problems that limit their internal and external validity.

Environmental Determinants

Several facets of the work environment are related to the grievance rate in an organization, defined as the number of grievances filed per 100 workers over a given period, usually one year (Gordon and Fryxell, 1993). Low grievance rates are encountered in relatively stable organizations that are largely free of technological change. Further, the greater the conflict apparent during the union organizing process, the higher is the grievance rate following certification of the union.

Individual Determinants

Although a few demographic and personality characteristics of individual workers have been found to be related to their propensity to file a grievance, none of these findings has been replicated in an independent sample (Gordon and Miller, 1984). Further, research results are inconclusive with regard to whether the tendency to file a grievance is related to the level of a worker's job performance.

Supervisory Style

Supervisors who are considerate toward subordinates tend to have lower grievance rates. Gordon and Bowlby (1989) reported that union members are more likely to file a grievance when they perceive greater threat to contractual rights inherent in a supervisor's actions and when management's actions are judged to be motivated by personal animus toward the worker.

Bibliography

Gordon, M. E. & Bowlby, R. L. (1989). Reactance and intentionality attributions as determinants of the intent to file a grievance. *Personnel Psychology*, **42**, 309–29.

Gordon, M. E. & Fryxell, G. E. (1993). The role of interpersonal justice in organizational grievance systems. *Justice in the Workplace: Approaching Fairness in Human Resource Management*, Eds. Cropanzano, R. Hillsdale, NJ: Lawrence Erlbaum Associates.

Gordon, M. E. & Miller, S. J. (1984). Grievances: a review of research and practice. *Personnel Psychology*, **37**, 117–46.

MICHAEL E. GORDON

grievance procedure A grievance procedure is a sequence of steps, negotiated by the union and company, written in their collective bargaining agreement for the purpose of resolving grievances during the life of the agreement without a strike or lockout. A grievance procedure is included in 99 percent of the collective bargaining agreements in the United States and typically includes three to five steps. As an example, step 1 consists of the aggrieved employee contacting his or her shop steward (or departmental representative) about the alleged violation of a provision of the collective bargaining agreement. A meeting is then held with the first line supervisor within a defined period of time, such as within ten days after the occurrence of the event which caused the grievance, e.g. a denial of promotion. Most grievances are resolved at this step and a resolution at this step helps to build a better relationship between the shop steward and the first line supervisor. If the grievance is not resolved, the first line supervisor then provides a written answer in a defined period, e.g. five working days.

The grievant and/or the union has the option of appealing the grievance to step 2 within a certain number of days. If appealed, the grievance is usually reduced to writing and presented to management. A step 2 meeting is held and this meeting includes higher level officials of the union and the company. The union will probably add members of the grievance committee, which includes officers of the local union and interested shop stewards; the company will add a representative, such as a labor relations specialist who has plant-wide responsibility for handling employee grievances. A resolution of the grievance at this level will have plant-wide application and may have an effect on the resolution of grievances in other departments. However, the parties may negotiate a settlement and agree that the settlement of the grievance at this step will not set a precedent in future grievances; for example, returning a discharged employee to work on a last chance agreement but without backpay. In fact, these types of settlements may be reached at any step in the processing of the grievance.

If the grievance is not resolved at step 2, management will provide a written answer in a specified number of days in which to appeal the grievance to step 3, which will include a union representative who represents the local union in grievance administration, negotiations, and arbitration. The company will add the corporate labor relations manager to represent the company position on the grievance. Any resolution of the grievance at this step will have company-wide implications and may affect the resolution of grievances at other company facilities and plants. If the grievance is not resolved at step 3, the management will provide a written answer within a specified period of time.

The union then must determine whether to appeal the grievance to the final step in the grievance procedure, which is arbitration. This action usually must be taken within 30 days after the receipt of the company's step 3 answer. This time period allows the local union members to discuss the grievance at a local meeting and determine whether to advance the grievance to arbitration.

The characteristics of a grievance procedure include: (a) three to five steps; (b) time limits for taking each action; (c) additional higher level officials at each step in the procedure; and (d) arbitration as the last step to bring finality to the grievance.

Grievance procedures are also provided in nonunion settings. These grievance procedures are included in the employees' handbook or policy manual. Although there has been an increase in employer-promulgated arbitration, most grievance procedures in the nonunion sector do not provide for arbitration as the last step for resolving the grievance.

Bibliography

Bureau of National Affairs (1992). *Basic Patterns in Union Contracts*, Washington, DC: Bureau of National Affairs.

Gordon, M. E. & Miller, S. J. (1994). Grievances: a review of research and practice. *Personnel Psychology*, 37, 117–46.

Lewin, D. & Peterson, R. B. (1988). *The Modern Grievance Procedure in the United States*, New York: Quorum Books.

WILLIAM H. HOLLEY JR

grievances Grievances are formal allegations by a party to a COLLECTIVE BARGAINING agreement that relate to the proper interpretation and/or application of the agreement. Some agreements, however, permit the parties to file grievances about issues pertaining to matters not specified in the contract such as company rules and past practice. Contract administration is the process used to resolve grievances.

Types of Grievances

Grievances may be filed by individual employees or by the union on its own behalf. In the service industries, collective bargaining agreements even permit management to file grievances (Bureau of National Affairs, 1989), although it seldom initiates such action.

Subject Matter of Grievances

Management typically seeks to restrict grievances to alleged violations of specific contract provisions, whereas unions prefer to define grievances more broadly as "any complaint arising out of the workplace, regardless of whether the specific issue in dispute is included in the contract" (Repas, 1984, p. 41). Most grievances pertain to company disciplinary actions (e.g. demotions, suspensions, or discharges). Other subjects of grievances are work rules (e.g. use of profane language, horseplay, and excessive absenteeism or tardiness), work assignments (e.g. which job classification is entitled to perform certain work), personnel assignments (e.g. shift or overtime assignments, layoffs, or transfers), supervision (e.g. supervisors doing bargaining unit work), administration of wage or seniority benefits, and general working conditions.

Bibliography

Bureau of National Affairs (1989). *Basic Patterns in Union Contracts*, **12th edn**, Washington, DC: Bureau of National Affairs.

Repas, B. (1984). *Contract Administration: a Guide for Stewards and Local Officers*, Washington, DC: Bureau of National Affairs.

MICHAEL E. GORDON

group decision making A principal assumption behind the structuring of organizational functioning into work groups is that better decisions will be made than by group members working alone. However, a good deal of research has shown that groups are subject to social processes which undermine their DECISION MAKING effectiveness. While they make better decisions than the average of decisions made by individual members, work groups consistently fall short of the quality of decisions made by the best individual member (Brown, 1988). The implications of this for the functioning of boards and TOP MANAGEMENT TEAMS are considerable. Organizational behaviorists and social psychologists have therefore devoted considerable effort to identifying the processes which give rise to deficiencies in group decision making:

1 PERSONALITY factors can affect social behavior such as shyness of individual members, who may be hesitant to offer their opinions and knowledge assertively, thereby failing to contribute fully to the group's store of knowledge.

2 Group members are subject to social conformity effects causing them to withhold opinions and information contrary to the majority view – especially an organizationally dominant view.

3 Group members may lack communication skills and so be unable to present their views and knowledge successfully. The person who has mastered IMPRESSION MANAGEMENT within the organization may disproportionately influence group decisions even in the absence of expertise (*see* INTERPERSONAL SKILLS).

4 The group may be dominated by particular individuals who take up disproportionate "air time" and argue so vigorously with the opinion of others, that their own views prevail. It is noteworthy that "air time" and expertise are correlated in high performing groups and uncorrelated in groups that perform poorly.

5 Particular group members may be egocentric (such as senior organizational members whose egocentricity may have carried them to the top) and consequently unwilling to consider opinions and knowledge contrary to their own, offered by other group members.

6 STATUS and hierarchy effects can cause some members' contributions to be valued and attended to disproportionately. When a senior executive is present in a meeting his or her views are likely to have an undue influence on the outcome.

7 Risky shift is the tendency of work groups to make more extreme decisions than the average of members' decisions. Group decisions tend to be either more risky or more conservative than the average of individual members' opinions or decisions. Thus shifts in the extremity of decisions affecting the competitive strategy of an organization can occur simply as a result of group processes rather than for rational or well-judged reasons.

8 Janis (1982), in his study of policy decisions and fiascoes, identified the phenomenon of groupthink, whereby tightly knit groups may err in their decision making, as a result of being more concerned with achieving agreement than with the quality of group decision making. This can be especially threatening to organizational functioning where different departments see themselves as competing with one another, promoting "in-group" favoritism and groupthink.

9 The social loafing effect is the tendency of individuals in group situations to work less hard than they do when individual contributions can be identified and evaluated. In organizations, individuals may put less effort into achieving quality decisions in meetings, as a result of the perception that their contribution is hidden in overall group performance.

10 Diffusion of responsibility can inhibit individuals from taking responsibility for action when in the presence of others. People seem to assume that responsibility will be shouldered by others who are present in a situation requiring action. In organizational settings, individuals may fail to act in a crisis involving the functioning of expensive technology, assessing that others in their team are taking responsibility for making the necessary decisions. Consequently, the overall quality of group decisions is threatened.

11 The study of brainstorming groups shows that quantity and often quality of ideas produced by individuals working separately, consistently exceed quality and quantity of ideas produced by a group working together. This is due to a "production-blocking" effect. Individuals are inhibited from both thinking of new ideas and offering them aloud to the group by the competing verbalizations of others.

12 Another difficulty besetting group decision making is the tendency of groups to "satisfice" or make *minimally acceptable decisions*. Observations of group decision-making processes repeatedly show that groups tend to identify the first minimally acceptable solution or decision in a particular situation, and then spend time searching for reasons to accept that decision and reject other possible options. Groups tend not to generate a range of alternatives before selecting, on a rational basis, the most suitable option.

This catalogue of deficiencies in relation to group decision making indicates that the process is more complex and potentially more disastrous than is commonly understood within organizational settings. Recently researchers have begun to identify ways in which some of these deficiencies may be overcome. For example, research on groupthink suggests both that the phenomenon is most likely to occur in groups where a supervisor is particularly dominant, and that cohesiveness per se is not the crucial factor. Supervisors can therefore be trained to be facilitative, seeking the contributions of individual members before offering their own perceptions.

Rogelberg, Barnes-Farrell, & Lowe (1992), have offered a structured technique for overcoming some of these deficiencies called "the stepladder technique." In this procedure each group member has thinking time before proposing any decisions. Then pairs of group members present their ideas to each other and discuss their respective opinions before making any decisions. The process continues with each subgroup's presentation being followed by time for the group to discuss the problem and ideas proposed. A final decision is put off until the entire group has presented.

Initial evidence suggests that such procedures can enable groups to make decisions of a quality at least as good as those of their best individual members. This is consistent with the finding that fostering disagreement in a structured way in organizations leads to better decisions (Tjosvold & Deemer, 1980). Techniques such as this offer one solution to the problem that unless the most accurate group member is assertive and confident, he or she does not influence the ratings of quality of group decisions. Finally, there is some evidence that work groups which take time out to reflect upon and appropriately modify their decision-making processes are more effective than those which do not (Maier, 1970).

While organizational behaviorists have contributed a great deal to the understanding of how individual performance may be facilitated, research on the processes by which group decision making can be optimized is still in its infancy. The potential pay-off for organizations in improving decision-making quality throughout organizations is enormous.

Bibliography

Brown, R. (1988). Group processes: Dynamics within and between groups. Oxford, UK: Blackwell.

Janis, I. L. (1982). Groupthink: Psychological studies of policy decisions and fiascoes. Boston, MA: Houghton-Mifflin.

Maier, N. R. F. (1970). Problem solving and creativity in individuals and groups. Belmont, CA: Brooks Cole.

Rogelberg, S. G., Barnes-Farrell, J. L. & Lowe, C. A. (1992). The stepladder technique: An alternative group structure facilitating effective group decision making. Journal of Applied Psychology, 77, 730–737.

Stasser, G., Kerr, N. L. & Davies, J. H. (1989). Influence processes and consensus models in decision-making groups. In P. B. Paulus (Ed.), Psychology of group influence, (pp. 279–326). Hillsdale, NJ: Erlbaum.

Tjosvold, D. & Effects of controversy within a cooperative or competitive context on organizational decision-making. Journal of Applied Psychology, 65, 590–595.

MICHAEL A. WEST

group decision support systems A class of computer-supported cooperative work system intended for use in group problem-solving, planning, choice, and other decision tasks. A GDSS specifically targets group decision-making, whereas CSCW systems support a broader range of multiparty work activities. A GDSS may be created simply by applying a single-user DECISION SUPPORT SYSTEM (DSS) to a problem confronting a group. For example, a board of directors may use a forecasting model to project sales and expenses for a new business; a project team may apply risk analysis to compare possible courses of action; or an engineering group may use computerized optimization techniques to evaluate approaches to producing chemical compounds. These are very rudimentary forms of GDSS. More sophisticated GDSSs bring facilities that are specially designed for use by groups. In this sense, a GDSS means more than simply applying a DSS to a group context.

Particular implementations vary, but most GDSSs include two types of facilities to support group decision-making: (a) discussion management; and (b) decision modeling. These are two general approaches to group problem-solving that have been used in organizations for many years, and a GDSS adds computerization to each of these longstanding approaches.

The *discussion* approach to group problem-solving involves bringing various experts and/or stakeholders together to identify issues and provide an environment for resolution. The strength of the discussion approach is that talking about a problem in a group setting can lead to divergent perspectives on the problem's causes and creative thinking about how to solve it. Group discussion provides broad input on a problem, which can facilitate rapid idea generation and commitment to implementation of solutions. Decision *modeling* involves formulation of a mathematical representation of the problem and solution tradeoffs. Once modeled, the problem is "solved" by using one or more algorithms deemed appropriate for the model. In some cases the models are spatial as well as mathematical, using graphical techniques to display variables and relationships to the group. The strengths of the group modeling approach are that it allows consideration of many variables and relationships simultaneously, and multiple parties can provide inputs to the model specification and analysis. Mathematical models facilitate rational analysis of complex problems and help to overcome the cognitive limitations of a decision-making group. Inputs to the model can be objective or opinion-based. A GDSS contains facilities to support group discussion and modeling.

GDSS Functionality

Discussion support.   To support group discussion, GDSSs include facilities for group note-taking, idea organization (clustering), voting and opinion polling, candid commenting, and storage and retrieval of meeting minutes. Additional facilities might include anonymous recording of individual inputs and step-by-step procedures for using the features within the system. Groups might create their own step-by-step procedures, piecing together features according to the particular needs of their meeting. Alternatively, they might use pre-established discussion procedures, such as Robert Rules of Order or a meeting protocol, to guide their discussion.

Decision Modeling

To support decision analysis, GDSSs take decision models developed for individual use, such as multi-criteria modeling, forecasting, and risk analysis, and explode their

components to accommodate input from multiple parties. For example, a multi-attribute utility model might be exploded to allow several $(2-n)$ people to (a) generate criteria; (b) weight criteria; (c) identify alternatives; (d) rate alternatives against criteria; and (e) calculate a relative score for each alternative. The model may generate various types of outputs for the group, such as lists of criteria, the average weight given by group members to each criterion, lists of alternatives, and average ratings given to each alternative on each criterion. More sophisticated GDSSs may provide extensive statistics on the model outputs, graphical display of group opinions, and the opportunity to change the parameters of the model and perform dynamic "what-if" analyses. Expansion of individual decision models to accommodate multi-party input, processing, and output requires extensive computer programming and numerous design decisions regarding how data should be entered, processed, and displayed.

GDSS Operation

Typically, groups do not rely upon a GDSS for their entire problem-solving process but rather use a subset of available features at various points during their deliberations. Verbal discussion in a meeting, or electronic messaging in the case of dispersed groups, supplements use of the GDSS. The typical setting for GDSS use today is the face-to-face meeting (rather than dispersed conferences) (see figure 1). In a GDSS-supported meeting, each participant has a workstation through which ideas, votes, comments, and so on can be entered. Usually, such information is entered anonymously. Simultaneous and anonymous entry of information speeds up the data-gathering process and encourages group members to be creative and uninhibited in self-expression. Once entered, information then can be publicly shared on a common viewing screen or software window, which provides a focal point for the group discussion. In a face-to-face meeting the common screen is physically located in the front of the room. If group members are dispersed across a network, public information is viewed in a designated window or screen at the individual's private workstation. A network is needed to connect all of the workstations together into a common workstation, or server, where the heart of the GDSS software resides.

Design Rationale

GDSS design is based on a systems view of group decision-making in which the group's size, styles of interacting and other characteristics are *inputs* along with the task at hand to the group decision *process*. The group's decision process occurs as members exchange information with one another and work to solve the problem that they confront. Certain *outcomes* will result. Group decision outcomes can be described in terms of their quality, the time required for the group to reach the solution, the total number of ideas generated, the degree of consensus among members about the final solution, and members' willingness to implement the solution. *Feedback* in the system occurs as decision outcomes serve as inputs to future interactions that group members undertake. The entire group decision process takes place within a broader social context, such as a particular organization, institution, or society, which has a dynamic relationship with the group's decision system,

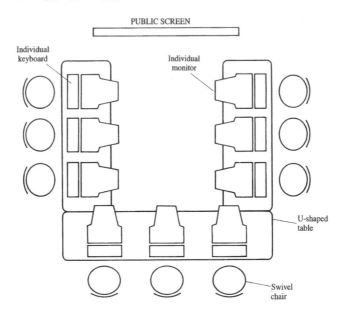

Figure 1   Typical GDSS configuration for a face-to-face meeting

affecting how inputs to interaction are defined and how the group decision process is conducted.

GDSS designers treat the inputs to the decision process as givens and proceed to consider how the group interaction process might be improved. That is, given a particular problem, a set of people responsible for resolving it, and a specific social context, then how might technology be designed to facilitate analysis and resolution of the problem? GDSS designers have relied heavily on a large body of research which documents the difficulties that groups experience during decision-making and methods for overcoming these difficulties. The literature indicates that groups are more creative, engage in more thorough analysis, reach higher-quality decisions, and gain higher commitment to solution implementation when there is full and even participation in the decision process, rather than low participation or dominance by a few members. Unfortunately, groups often have difficulty achieving full and even participation in their deliberations due to the *process losses* associated with interpersonal communication. In other words, when one person faces a decision, energy focuses solely on problem analysis and solution, but in a group setting, tremendous energy is expended in regulating interpersonal communication and dealing with socioemotional issues, such as conflict, influence, and the like.

Group researchers argue that process losses can be overcome and decision-making improved if groups are supplied with process interventions that promote more even participation, appreciation of multiple viewpoints, and systematic reasoning. Group discussion techniques and decision models provide these kinds of interventions, and GDSS designers often begin by automating techniques that originally were designed to be implemented manually or with minimal computer support. For example, computer files and view screens can be used instead of flipcharts or electronic blackboards; keyboards can be used instead of index cards or round-robin voice voting; and inputs to

decision models can be made via electronic files or by members themselves, rather than by a special facilitator or modeling expert. A key aspect of the GDSS design is separate, but linked, facilities for managing individual (private) versus group (public) work.

GDSS Design Alternatives

GDSS design is centered around providing discussion and modeling support to a group's decision process. Table 1 shows how GDSS designers map system functionality to group process needs. Systems vary, of course, in their specific features and implementation, and there are several useful dimensions for distinguishing among GDSS designs.

Comprehensiveness

The degree to which the GDSS offers a full range of functionality. The more extensive the system's functionality, the more comprehensive it is. More comprehensive GDSSs can be applied to a variety of decisions, whereas less comprehensive systems target particular aspects of the group problem-solving process (e.g. idea generation, impact assessment) or particular types of decisions (e.g. transportation, agriculture). More comprehensive systems also may be more complex and may require training or other forms of guidance to facilitate their operation.

Restrictiveness

The degree to which the GDSS limits the decision-making process to a particular sequence of operation or problem-solving procedure. Whereas comprehensiveness concerns *what* functions are available, restrictiveness governs *how* the functional options are used. More restrictive GDSSs attempt to guide the group through a structured method of applying the available options. Less restrictive GDSSs offer no prespecified decision path, so the group is free to choose among the options and use them in any order.

Table 1   Examples of GDSS functionality to support group processes

Group process	Possible GDSS functionality
Discussion	
Participation	Anonymous, simultaneous entry of ideas followed by display of idea lists on a common viewing screen
Influence	Weighting ideas (weights of all ideas sum to 1000 points); ranking, or ordering, ideas; rating, or scaling ideas (such as on a 1–7 scale); voting yes/no on each idea
Leadership	Combining weights either equally or according to a scheme that favors influence by certain members, such as the leader or experts Providing the leader with functions that are not accessible to other users
Emotional expression	Candid commenting, opinion polling
Conflict management	Issue identification and analysis, stakeholder analysis; statement of positions and graphics to illustrate shifts in positions over time
Memory	Group note-taking, storage and retrieval of meeting minutes, clustering ideas into common categories or themes
Decision analysis	
Problem structuring	Agenda management, outlining, problem formulation techniques, cognitive mapping
Idea generation	Electronic brainstorming, nominal group technique, creativity techniques
Alternatives evaluation	Multi-criteria decision models, risk analysis, stakeholder analysis, contingency analysis
Impact assessment	Forecasting models, scenario analysis
Implementation planning	Planning techniques, budget models

Decisional Guidance

The degree to which the GDSS enlightens or persuades users as they choose among the system options. Decisional guidance may be *informative* (providing pertinent information that enlightens the selection or use of options but without suggesting how to proceed) or *suggestive* (providing judgmental recommendations on what procedures or data to apply and how to apply them). The guidance may be *predefined*, with a fixed set of guidelines that are available to all groups that use the system) or *dynamic*, applying intelligence so that the system can "learn" in response to the progress of the particular user group.

Interface

The GDSS software interface might be described along a number of dimensions, but a key dimension is the *representation* that members work with as they interact with the software. Representations may be *process-oriented*, emphasizing actions that the group can undertake, such as defining the problem, evaluating alternative solutions, or formulating future strategies. The process-oriented interface presents the group with procedures for formulating or solving the problem, and data (usually in the form of member opinions or comments) are created as the procedures are applied. Alternatively, *data-oriented* representations emphasize information associated with the particular problem, such as health information, soil data, or public opinion surveys. The interface then allows the

group to apply processes (such as decision models) to the available data. To date, most GDSSs favor the use of process representations as the dominant interface, with data representations being secondary.

Information Exchange

Some GDSSs support creation and sharing of only *task-related* information (such as problems, alternatives, criteria, or strategies), whereas others support exchange of *socio-emotional* information as well (such as expressions of frustration or praise, joking, or the overall mood of the group). The *pattern* of information exchange supported by the GDSS also can vary across system implementations. Information exchange patterns in GDSSs may include:

1 *One-to-all communication*: all information entered into the system becomes public, or available to all members of the group.
2 *One-to-one communication*: individual members can selectively communicate with other members as part of the group decision process.
3 *Subgroup communication*: group members are divided into subgroups, and models or messages operate based on these subgroups.

Finally, the *storage* of information in the GDSS can affect information exchange in the group. Alternative storage designs include:

1 *Complete histories*: comments, votes, model outputs, or other information created during the problem-solving process are stored as a continuing history with new information added as the group process unfolds.

2 *Dynamic replacement*: only the most recently generated data are presented to the group; historical information is either deleted or stored outside of the group's active workspace.

3 *Keyed storage*: data are organized according to some meaningful scheme, such as by date, by topic, or by group member.

The content, pattern, and storage of information exchange supported by the GDSS are critical design decisions that potentially can affect the decision process the group experiences as it attempts to understand and resolve the problem at hand.

Control Over Functionality

Who determines what functions are made available to the group, the sequencing of those functions, and when or how they are applied? Alternative designs include:

1 *User controlled*: each group member has access to all system functions, and the members select and apply the functions as they see fit.

2 *Leader controlled*: a group leader or facilitator, who has access to full system functionality, determines the subset of functionality that is presented to members.

3 *Shared control*: system operation is divided among various parties, such as between the leader and members. The shared control mode can be implemented in a variety of ways. For example, to support negotiations, operations may be divided between members representing different sides of an issue. An alternative design is to share control among a leader, group members, and a technician, with the technician performing functions that are too complex for group members, such as file retrieval or complex data manipulations.

Private versus Public Work

To support *private work*, the GDSS facilitates individual recording of ideas, comments, votes, and the like, and responds to whatever commands the individual enters at his or her workstation. *Public work* represents an aggregation of individual work and is located in the shared workspace. In some implementations, only a group leader or representative can control operation of the shared workspace. In other systems, each group member has direct access to the shared workspace and is free to control its operation. Usually, at least some of the public GDSS functions operate automatically. Determining the content and configuration of private and public workspaces is an important issue in GDSS design.

Bibliography

Bostrom, R. P., Watson, R. T. & Kinney, S. T. (1992). *Computer Augmented Teamwork: A Guided Tour*. New York: Van Nostrand Reinhold.

Jessup, L. M. & Valacich, J. (eds) (1993). *Group Support Systems: New Perspectives*. New York: Macmillan.

Nunamaker Jr, J. F., Dennis, A. R., Valacich, J. S., Vogel, D. R. & George, J. F. (1991). Electronic meeting systems to support group work: theory and practice at Arizona. *Communications of the ACM*, 34 (7), 30–39.

GERARDINE DESANCTIS and
GARY W. DICKSON

group development This term expresses the assumption that group behavior changes systematically over time. That means a management committee will function differently after working together for a year than when first convened; a project group will face different challenges near its deadline than mid-way through a task. More importantly, it means that these changes can be understood and predicted through general theoretical concepts. Most group development research has sought to identify characteristic sequences of change, but efforts have also been made to understand how, why, and when developmental changes occur. Such knowledge helps us interpret team behavior accurately, and manage teams in ways that fit their needs.

Group development can be viewed in two ways. First, development can mean the path a group takes over its lifespan toward the accomplishment of its main tasks. This is important for understanding how temporary groups, with specific purposes to accomplish within time limits, progress from start to finish (*see* PROJECT MANAGEMENT). Such research traditionally examined either short-term problem-solving groups in the laboratory, or longer-term therapy or sensitivity training groups. Most of these studies portray group development as a gradual forward evolution through a universal series of stages. For example, in their seminal work, Bales and Strodtbeck (1951) characterized group problem-solving as a progression from orientation (problem definition), to evaluation (assessment of alternatives), to control (solution construction). Tuckman's (1965) synthesis of group development literature is representative of subsequently proposed sequences: In the "forming" stage, this model suggests members explore and test task and social boundaries; in "storming," they battle over interpersonal and task issues; in the "norming" stage, groups resolve differences and establish social and work norms; finally "performing," members use the roles and norms they have built to carry out work.

Some recent research on task groups has questioned the paradigm of group development as a universal stage progression, and explored aspects of development other than those covered in traditional stage models. Poole (1983) showed there are many sequences through which decisions can develop in groups, not just one. Gersick (1988) found that project teams in organizations did not progress gradually, through uniform stages, but in punctuated equilibrium – alternating periods of momentum and disjunctive change. Soon after convening, each team formed a unique set of behavior patterns and assumptions (largely implicit) about task, teammates, and outside stakeholders. Teams worked within these patterns for long portions of their time, and made major changes in compact bursts, at temporal milestones – e.g., half way toward their deadlines. Groups' attention to time, pacing, and deadlines, not the completion of given stages of work, regulated their progress.

A second way to view group development is different from, but compatible with, the first. It concerns groups which last for significant periods of time, whether their life spans are temporary (as above) or open-ended. Here, group development concerns change over time in groups' abilities to work effectively. For example, research on therapy and Sensitivity Training groups examined the maturation of groups' capacities for productive work, as moderated by their developing abilities to deal with TRUST (openness and honesty of communication), CONTROL (competition for power), and dependency (seeking direction from authority figures versus making decisions within the group) (*see* GROUP DECISION MAKING).

Longitudinal studies of work groups in organizations are unfortunately rare. The potential value of longitudinal research shows in such work as Katz' (1982) finding, based on cross-sectional study, that research-and-development team effectiveness rises, then declines over the years as intrateam COMMUNICATION waxes and wanes; or Hackman and Walton's (1986) observations on long-term changes in SELF-MANAGING TEAMS' needs for coaching versus independence.

see also **Socialization; Culture, Group decision making**

Bibliography

Bales, R. F. & Strodtbeck, F. L. (1951). Phases in group problem solving. *Journal of Abnormal and Social Psychology, 46,* 485–495.

Gersick, C. J. G. (1988). Time and transition in work teams: Toward a new model of group development. *Academy of Management Journal, 31,* 9–41.

Hackman, J. R. & Walton, R. E. (1986). Leading groups in organizations. In P. S. Goodman (Ed.), *Designing effective work groups.* San Francisco: Jossey-Bass.

Katz, R. (1982). The effects of group longevity on project communication and performance. *Administrative Science Quarterly, 27,* 81–104.

Poole, M. S. (1983). Decision development in small groups II: A study of multiple sequences of decision making. *Communication Monographs, 48,* 1–24.

Tuckman, B. (1965). Developmental sequence in small groups. *Psychological Bulletin, 63,* 384–399.

CONNIE J. G. GERSICK

growth share matrix   Derived from the early work of the Boston Consulting Group in the 1960s on experience curves, the growth share matrix became, and remains, the most widely used portfolio model for influencing investment and cash management policy in diversified corporations. The matrix is illustrated in figure 1. The horizontal axis is drawn to a logarithmic scale and identifies the relative market share of each of the businesses within the company's portfolio. In this system relative market share is defined as that of the company's business divided by that of its largest single competitor. By definition, therefore, only one company within a defined market can have a relative share greater than one. The vertical axis depicts the industry growth rate in real terms, with the impact of inflation removed.

Businesses are mapped on to the matrix, with the size of each business being reflected by the area of the circle used to depict it. The relative position of each business within the four quadrants indicates the expected cashflow to be generated and suggests an investment strategy. The cut line on the vertical axis is set at 10 per cent real growth, while the relative share cut line is set usually at the 1.0x level.

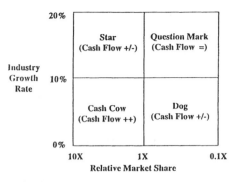

Figure 1 The Boston Consulting Group growth share matrix.

A business in the bottom left quadrant is a cash cow. A high market share coupled with slow real growth is expected to generate surplus cash as a result of high profitability due to lower cost. Moreover, future investment needs of such businesses are limited as growth has declined.

Those in the top left quadrant are star businesses with high relative share and high growth. While such businesses are profitable, they are largely cash neutral, since profits need to be continuously reinvested while the growth rate remains high in order to maintain market position.

Businesses in the top right quadrant enjoy high growth but low relative share. The objective for a few such question mark businesses is to take the surplus cashflow from the cash cows in order to invest heavily while the growth rate is high, to convert them into future stars.

Those in the bottom right quadrant are said to be dog businesses. These concerns have low relative share and low growth. They are expected to suffer a cost disadvantage as a result of their low share. However, it is anticipated that to convert such businesses into cash cows would take disproportionate effort in a mature market, where share gain would have to be obtained from established high share rivals. Such businesses are therefore candidates for harvesting, exit, or disposal.

The underlying concept that, for the average business, there is an 80 per cent experience effect (*see* EXPERIENCE AND LEARNING EFFECTS) and that relative market share can be used as a relatively easily measured surrogate for cumulative production volume.

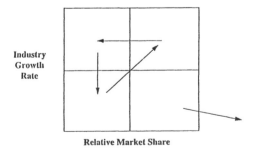

Figure 2 The growth share matrix cashflow sequence for success.

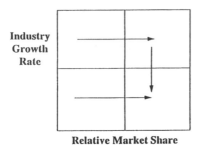

Figure 3 The growth share matrix sequence for disaster.

Businesses with a high relative market share should therefore enjoy a significant cost advantage compared with competitors:

relative market share	4x	2x	1x	0.5x	0.25x
relative cost	64%	80%	100%	120%	165%

Similarly, real growth rate is seen as a surrogate for market attractiveness, with high and low real growth equating to high and low attractiveness, respectively. The rationale for this stems from the concept of the product life cycle.

The growth share model can be used in a variety of different ways. First, it permits the company to map its businesses in a way that enables management to rapidly visualize the position of its total portfolio. As a result the strategic dynamics for the total corporation can be planned for its future development. The ideal sequence for development is depicted in figure 2. Surplus cash is syphoned off from cash cows and redeployed, first to any star businesses requiring it, and then to a carefully selected number of question marks with a view to building these into the stars of the future. Dog businesses, unless strong in cash generation, should be divested or closed. Good cash generating dog businesses are due to low capital intensity and are candidates for harvesting rather than divestment.

By contrast, the sequence for disaster, illustrated in figure 3, indicates a failure to invest in star businesses due to a lack of positive cashflow businesses. As a result, stars lose share to become question marks which, in turn, are converted into dogs as markets mature.

It can be argued that the graphic presentation of the matrix represents a static snapshot of the business portfolio. This criticism has been addressed by the development of the share momentum graph illustrated in figure 4.

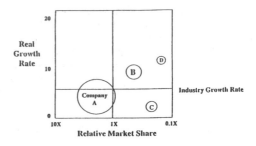

Figure 5 The industry growth share matrix.

This graph is developed over a relevant time period (say, five years) and, by plotting the position of each business unit in terms of the two dimensions of total market growth versus growth in sales for the business, the businesses that have been gaining or losing share can be readily observed. Those businesses falling below the diagonal have been losing share, while those above it have been gaining share. The chart is a useful quick indication to management as to which businesses are succeeding or failing relative to the market; it also offers a useful correction in situations in which management may believe that it is performing well in achieving growth in a business, whereas in reality it may be losing share.

The growth share matrix can also be a useful tool in evaluating competitive dynamics. This is illustrated in figures 5 and 6.

The relative market position of major competitors is illustrated in figure 5. The vertical cut line is in this case set at the industry overall growth rate level. Those competitors above the cut line are growing faster than the market average, while those below it are losing share. A consequence of this analysis is that different competitors may classify businesses in different ways. Competitor A, with the largest market share, is clearly operating as a cash cow, but is also trading market share for cash by growing at less than the market, allowing competitors B and D to see their businesses as question marks and therefore investment opportunities. Only competitor C recognizes that its business is a dog.

Taking the same industry over time, as shown in figure 6, clearly indicates that competitor B has been growing

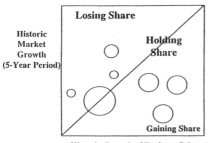

Figure 4 The share momentum graph.

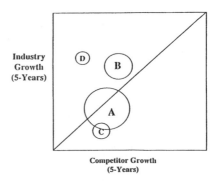

Figure 6 The industry share momentum matrix.

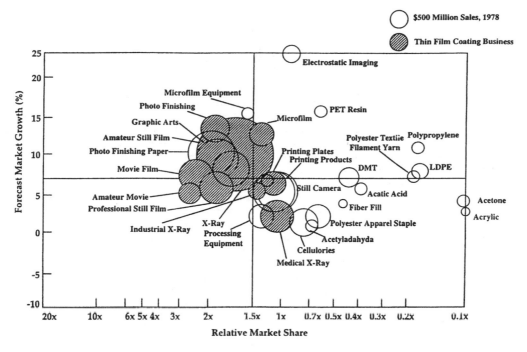

Figure 7 The growth/share matrix for Eastman Kodak, 1978.
Source: Bogue & Buffa (1986).

faster than competitor A, as well as faster than the market as a whole.

In addition to analysis at the level of the industry as a whole, further refinements of growth share analysis are to analyze businesses by product and by technology. For example, the 1978 product portfolio of Eastman Kodak is illustrated in figure 7. The figure shows that many of the company's activities are concerned with thin film coatings, yielding ECONOMIES OF SCOPE and shared experience in this area of technology. As a result, product groups that might otherwise have been classified as dogs may well make a contribution to Kodak's overall position in a core technology. A similar analysis might well have been concerned with activities rather than technology. Share momentum charts can also be developed that reflect product-based portfolios over time.

The growth share matrix has therefore provided an extremely useful multifunctional management tool for both diagnosing the position of the multibusiness and multi-product firm and for understanding industrial and competitive dynamics.

However, the technique is also subject to a number of criticisms, which include the following:

1. Growth share matrix positioning implies that relative market share can be used as a surrogate for cost. There is therefore a fundamental assumption that, on average, an 80 per cent experience effect underlies market share. Evidence from the PIMS program suggests that the actual cost advantage derived from higher and lower relative shares is substantially less than this.

2. Detailed experience analysis is rarely undertaken, due to the cost and the lack of appropriate data. Moreover, the impact of shared experience from technology, activities, and the like may not be adequately incorporated.

3. The model assumes that only the two variables of relative market share and industry growth rate are necessary to establish the strategic position of a business. Evidence from the PIMS program and actual practice clearly indicates that these variables alone, while important, can be readily outweighed by other factors such as relative investment intensity, productivity, and the like.

4. In calculating relative market share it is assumed that "market" has been accurately defined. This need not be the case, especially in situations in which market boundaries are in a state of flux as a result of geographic, product, or customer segment changes.

Bibliography

Bogue, M. C. & Buffa, E. S. (1986). *Corporate strategic analysis.* New York: The Free Press. See chapters 2 and 5.

Hax, A. L. & Majluf, N. S. (1984). *Strategic management.* Englewood Cliffs, NJ: Prentice-Hall. See chapter 7.

Henderson, B. D. (1973). *The experience curve reviewed, IV. The growth share matrix of the product portfolio.* Perspectives no. 135. Boston, MA: Boston Consulting Group.

Lewis, W. W. (1977). *Planning by exception.* Washington, DC: Strategic Planning Associates.

DEREK F. CHANNON

H

halo effects Halo effects were the first threat to performance appraisals identified in the literature (e.g. Thorndike, 1920), and have received a great deal of attention ever since (the most comprehensive review is probably by Cooper, 1981). Although, conceptually, halo effects are believed to result in high intercorrelations among ratings on separate performance dimensions, there has been considerable disagreement over the proper operational definition of halo (e.g. intercorrelations among ratings, standard deviation of ratings across dimensions), as well as the cause for halo effects (e.g. conceptual similarity among performance dimensions, the effects of global evaluations), and even whether halo reflects true relationships among dimensions or some type of RATING ERRORS. Much of the interest in halo effects, though, has been based on the assumption that halo effects do reflect a type of rating error, and so can serve as a proxy for rating (in)accuracy. But, unless we know the "true" underlying covariance among performance dimensions, we cannot be sure that halo reflects the presence of error. Furthermore, the relationship between halo and rating accuracy is debatable, and may be positive rather than negative, although this probably depends upon the definition of accuracy used (*see* RATING ACCURACY). Finally, as the relevance of accuracy as a criterion in performance appraisal research is challenged (Ilgen, 1993), the entire issue may become moot. Instead, halo may be important as an index of within-ratee discriminability, which may be related to ratee reactions to ratings. Further research is needed, however, to determine the utility of such a role (*see* DISTRIBUTIONAL EFFECTS IN PERFORMANCE APPRAISAL).

Bibliography

Cooper, W. (1981). Ubiquitous halo. *Psychological Bulletin*, **90**, 218–44.

Ilgen, D. R. (1993). Performance appraisal accuracy: an illusive or sometimes misguided goal? *Personnel Selection and Assessment*, Eds. Schuler, H., Farr, J. & Smith, M. Hillsdale, NJ: Erlbaum.

Thorndike, E. L. (1920). A constant error in psychological ratings. *Journal of Applied Psychology*, **4**, 25–9.

ANGELO S. DENISI

Hawthorne Effect This effect, observed in field experiments, occurs when:

(1) one or more changes or manipulations are made by researchers in a field setting;
(2) the persons in the target sample experiencing the change(s) are aware of the experimental manipulations; and
(3) the latter alter their behavior *not because of the specific variables manipulated* but because of the attention they receive.

As a result, the researchers may falsely attribute the observed effects on behavior to the variables manipulated rather than the attention. The effect gets its name from the research studies in which it was identified and labeled.

In the late 1920s and early 1930s, several studies were carried out at Western Electric's Hawthorne Works in Chicago, Illinois. The research, conducted by E. Mayo, F. J. Roethlisberger, W. J. Dickson, T. N. Whitehead, and others from the Graduate School of Business Administration at Harvard University, in cooperation with a number of persons at the Hawthorne Works, began as an investigation of the effects of illumination intensity on employees, particularly on employee performance. The goal of the research was to find the optimal level of illumination for work involving the assembly and inspection of relays used in telephone equipment. Therefore, the researchers simply varied the amount of illumination over time and measured changes in performance, among other things. The unanticipated finding was that performance did not covary with illumination but continued to improve over the course of the experiment, even when the level of illumination was reduced to very low levels. The post hoc explanation for the observed pattern of results was that the employees very much appreciated the attention that they received from the researchers, management, and others for being part of the experiment, and their improved performance was one way in which they expressed their appreciation. The explanation stuck, and the phenomenon has been known as the Hawthorne Effect ever since.

Ironically, the Hawthorne Effect was discovered only because, in the eyes of the researchers, their research had "failed." Had performance decreased as the amount of light decreased and vice versa, the Hawthorne Effect would not have been discovered. Since the effects on performance of illumination and those of attention were in opposite directions, the pattern of results fit one explanation, that of the Hawthorne Effect, and not the other.

Often in organizational behavior research in the field, the phenomenon of interest is manipulated in a way that leads to predicted changes in behavior that are in same direction as those that would result from the Hawthorne Effect. For example, interventions designed to empower workers, enrich jobs, increase self-efficacy, focus on quality, or in some other way impact positively on performance may be implemented in such a way that they create a Hawthorne Effect. In such cases, if performance changes as is predicted, based on the construct of interest (empowerment, increased self-efficacy, etc.), the tendency is to attribute the effect to the construct under investigation; the alternative explanation of a Hawthorne Effect is often ignored. At the very least, when the Hawthorne Effect is a possible cause of results that are found, it should be mentioned. Better yet, multiple studies and carefully designed research should be conducted to insure that effects attributed to constructs of interest are, most likely, caused by those constructs and not other common variables confounded with the constructs of interest, particularly those variables considered to cause the Hawthorne Effect.

Bibliography

Roethlisberger, F. J. & Dickson, W. J. (1939). Management and the worker. Cambridge, MA: Harvard University Press.

DANIEL R. ILGEN

Herfindahl-Hirschman index   While a complete analysis of market structure may require information on the market share of each competitor, industrial concentration is frequently measured with a single summary index. Such indices are desirable for both econometric research and in establishing antitrust guidelines. The Herfindahl-Hirschman index (HHI) is among the most widely accepted measures of market concentration. The index is defined as

$$HHI = \sum_{i=1}^{n} S_i^2$$

where S denotes the market share of the ith firm in an industry composed of n firms. The HHI ranges between negligible values for perfectly competitive industries and a maximum value of 1.0 for a pure monopoly.

Considerable theoretical work has related the HHI to industrial behavior. Stigler (1964) related the HHI to the pricing behavior of oligopolies. Adelman (1969) suggested that the HHI has an intuitive "numbers equivalent" interpretation in that 1/HHI is the number of equal-sized firms which will produce a given HHI. Cowling and Waterson (1976) demonstrated that the HHI may be related to profitability in industries with constant marginal cost.

Since the 1980s, the Department of Justice has utilized the HHI as a primary measure of market concentration. For the calculations used in their merger guidelines, the decimal point in the firms' market shares is ignored, thus producing a HHI which is larger by a multiple of 10,000. Accepting this modification, current guidelines specify that markets in which the HHI exceeds 1800 are said to be highly concentrated. Thus, mergers raising an HHI by more than 50 and resulting in an HHI above 1800 are likely to attract in antitrust litigation. Mergers producing an HHI between 1000 and 1800, are likely challenged only if the HHI increases in excess of 100 units. Mergers resulting in an HHI of less than 1000 are unlikely to meet objection.

Bibliography

Adelman, M. (1969). Comment on the "H" concentration measure as a numbers equivalent. *Review of Economics and Statistics*, 51, 99–101.

Cowling, K. & Waterson, M. (1976). Price-cost margins and market structure. *Economica*, 43, 267–74.

Stigler, G. (1964). The theory of oligopoly. *Journal of Political Economy*, 72, 44–61.

ROGER TUTTEROW

hierarchy of effects model   This is a model of MARKETING COMMUNICATIONS developed by Lavidge & Steiner (1961) which has a number of stages through which the buyer/customer passes from unawareness of a product or service to purchase. The cognitive stage is denoted by awareness and knowledge, the affective stage by liking, preference, and conviction, and the conative (or behavioral) stage by a purchase. Measures taken before and after a form of communication is used will enable objective(s) to be set and the success of it to be analyzed. Logical progression through the stages is not always possible – indeed, much depends on the product or service being offered and the target group of receivers.

see also **Communications objectives**

Bibliography

Kotler, P. (1994). *Marketing management: Analysis, planning, implementation and control*, 8th edn, Englewood Cliffs, NJ: Prentice-Hall. Chapter 22.

Lavidge, R. J. & Steiner, G. A. (1961). A model for predictive measurements of advertising effectiveness. *Journal of Marketing* Oct., 61.

DAVID YORKE

hiring persons with disabilities   The hiring of persons with disabilities has become an issue of concern to US organizations primarily due to the Rehabilitation Act of 1973 and the Americans with Disabilities Act of 1990, both of which prohibit employment discrimination against qualified persons with disabilities. Efforts to increase the hiring of persons with disabilities have also been fueled by the public's belief that people with disabilities are an underutilized labor pool (Louis Harris and Associates, 1991), employer surveys reporting that employees with disabilities are a sound investment (e.g. Greenwood and Johnson, 1987), various advocacy groups for people with disabilities, and federal tax credit programs which offer incentives for hiring people with disabilities and reduce the cost of accommodation.

Based on disproportionately low employment rates for persons with disabilities, particularly in higher level positions, it is often assumed that job applicants with disabilities face discrimination in the hiring process (Braddock and Bachelder, 1994). Thus, there has been a great deal of research examining potential sources of bias in hiring decisions. One line of research has focused on personnel selection decisions (based on interviews or resumes) regarding applicants with disabilities. This research, mostly conducted in laboratory settings, has led to mixed results, often reporting negative bias against job applicants with disabilities, but occasionally showing bias in favor of applicants with disabilities (see Stone et al., 1992).

Several factors have been shown to influence bias in hiring decisions towards job applicants with disabilities (see Stone and Colella, 1996, for a review of factors influencing the treatment of employees with disabilities). These factors include interviewer characteristics (e.g. empathy), type of disability, perception of personal blame for the disability, perceived unpredictability of behavior, perceived peril associated with the disability, stereotypes of disability job fit, job characteristics (e.g. amount of public contact), and organization size. Reasons for negative bias include negative stereotypes, low performance expectations, concern over coworker acceptance, and ignorance about the nature of disabilities.

Another issue in the hiring of persons with disabilities is the construction of valid selection procedures and instruments which are not unduly influenced by various disabilities (e.g. Nester, 1984). Testing applicants with disabilities may require that a different testing procedure or medium be used, or that accommodations be made in current procedures. For example, readers may be necessary to give paper and pencil exams to visually impaired applicants and time limits may need to be extended in order to accommodate persons with a variety of disabilities. Such changes in standardized testing procedures will also require further validity work to assure that the test remains fair and valid after modifications.

Another area of concern to employers is the recruitment of persons with disabilities. There are many public and private organizations which assist in the vocational rehabilitation and job placement of persons with disabilities, as well as organizations and programs which assist businesses in recruiting persons with disabilities. One such program is Projects with Industry (PWI), a federally established program which promotes collaborative efforts between rehabilitation specialists and business and industry.

Bibliography

Braddock, D. & Bachelder, L. (1994). *The Glass Ceiling and Persons with Disabilities*, Washington, DC: US Department of Labor, Glass Ceiling Commission.

Greenwood, R. & Johnson, V. A. (1987). Employer perspectives on workers with disabilities. *Journal of Rehabilitation*, 53, 37–45.

Louis Harris & Associates (1991). *Public Attitudes towards People with Disabilities*, Washington, DC: National Organization on Disability.

Nester, M. A. (1984). Employment testing for handicapped people. *Public Personnel Management*, 13, 417–34.

Stone, D. L. & Colella, A. (1996). A framework for studying the effects of disability on work experiences, *Academy of Management Review* (in the press).

Stone, E. F., Stone, D. L. & Dipboye, R. L. (1992). Stigmas in organizations: race, handicaps, and physical unattractiveness. Kelley, K. *Issues, Theory, and Research in Industrial and Organizational Psychology*, New York: Elsevier Science Publishers BV.

ADRIENNE COLELLA

history of business ethics Concern about ethical issues in business goes back as far as history itself; there has always been some form of mandate for people in commerce. The Egyptians were not to take money for passage across the river until after the passenger was safely there. In the Old Testament interest was not to be taken on loans. For Aristotle interest was also not to be levied on loans because money was "consumed" in its first use (like fruit) and therefore had no other use for which interest could be extracted. Cicero asked about price justice for goods in a starving city. Dionesian Roman Law prescribed that justice requires to grant to each person what is his/her due.

Arguments against the position of the Roman Catholic Church towards business can be traced to scholastic theologians, especially to Thomas Aquinas. Some claim that for Aquinas a just price was determined by the inherent nature of the product and not by the market forces of supply and demand, although subsequent studies have shown that the medieval scholars acknowledged market forces in determining business ethics. In the medieval period the guilds furnished protection and standards for their respective groups. The Reformation and the trade in the new world opened new horizons for business and its practices, including slavery, an upcoming middle class of merchants, and a rising sense of nationalism. Much later, Adam Smith's *Wealth of Nations* fits well into the overall surge into developing an industrial society and setting minimum standards for business behavior. Ethical principles such as Kant's categorical imperative, and Bentham's utilitarianism also served the industrial revolution and its new ethical choices. However, no set of ethical principles or practices emerged to guide business practices of employers and employees. In the late nineteenth century the underpinning concepts of business ethics – power and rights – were exercised in such interacting arenas as courts of law, unions, trade associations, and professional societies (*see* POWER), with its new evolutionary social ideology of progress in an industrial society, became prominent. In 1881, Pope Leo XIII reacted by writing his famous social encyclical (letter) on capital and labor. He used natural-law principles and the theories of Thomas Aquinas to fortify his arguments for the rights of labor. The 1886 Haymarket riots in Chicago, however, exemplify conflict between employer and employees during this period of industrial growth.

In the early twentieth century, most of the books on business ethics were general in approach and provided an overview on an issue or a specific aspect or problem. For example, they did not deal with an overall problem of business ethics. The exception was Sharp and Fox (1937), who covered pricing, lying, and other topics which related to the economics of business in their book. Issues dealing with employee rights, the environment, and international ethics would come at a much later date.

The first breakthrough for a general interest in business ethics came in Baumhart's revealing 1961 study, "How Ethical Are Businessmen?" Baumhart's study was published in 1961 when the electrical industry price-fixing scandal shook the United States. It was the first empirical study which showed that ethical issues and problems were found in every industry, in most companies, and on all levels of the managerial pyramid. This revelation came at a time when business enjoyed an outstanding reputation for providing goods and services, where it was assumed that executives and managers acted in an ethical manner.

Following Baumhart's study, the principle-to-solution approach to ethical problems in business was frequently, but not exclusively, pursued through natural law concepts in conferences, textbooks, and general interest books. Furthermore, the manager was himself (*sic*) responsible and accountable: business ethics was personal and individual – it was not corporate. The issues and the problems were generally perceived from an individualistic viewpoint. For example, the highest executives of the General Electric Corporation believed that the company did not have any responsibility for the managers who fixed prices. Padded expense accounts, bribery, "call girls," cheating, lying, pricing, and wages were some of the popular topics which were discussed and written about. Most of the concerns were personal, not corporate: how was this executive or manager responsible for his ethical problem? Courses in institutions of higher learning were generally called Business Ethics and were frequently taught in the philosophy departments, although some were given by business law or management departments (*see* BUSINESS ETHICS).

The 1964 US Civil Rights Act and subsequent social legislation triggered an awareness of concerns which affected employees, the environment, and the community, both local and national. The term business ethics was frequently replaced with the phrase "the social responsibilities of business," thus incorporating prevailing social norms and expectations. The change of name reflected the shift in emphasis from the personal ethics of the manager to the overall position of the company on such issues as racial and sexual discrimination, air and water pollution, plant closing, and employee rights, the companies became legally and ethically responsible for implementing these changes. "Responsibility" as such implies having assumed an obligation and is thus accountable and prescriptive in nature. Responsibility also refers to rights as well as to obligations. Furthermore, the philosophical approach to business ethics shifted from natural law to utilitarianism and Kant's categorical imperative. Rawls' theory of distributive justice became a necessary tool in the teaching of business ethics. By 1975, US colleges and universities offered over 550 undergraduate and graduate courses on business ethics, although most institutions used titles such as "Business and Society." Text books and case books on business ethics proliferated, written primarily by philosophers who specialized in applied ethics. Bowie, Cavanagh, Davis, Donaldson, De George, Frederick, Garrett, Goodpastor, Sethi, Steiner, Velasquez, Walton and Werhane are just a few of the authors who published anthologies and textbooks on business ethics. Centers for research and programs on business ethics as well as endowed chairs multiplied; business ethics became recognized as a distinct discipline in academia. Indeed, in 1976 the prestigious Academy of Management added a "social issues in management" division.

The Watergate Affair and payoffs to foreign government officials in the 1970s shifted emphasis once again in business ethics. Media attention on questions about who told subordinates to act illegally and/or unethically pierced the corporate veil of secrecy; personal accountability within institutional structures became the arena of concern. The question was: "Who told whom to do what as it affected society?" At the same time, payoffs to foreign government officials precipitated the 1977 FOREIGN CORRUPT PRACTICES ACT. It also set the stage of discussing not only the issue of personal accountability but also the question of cross-cultural differences and incompatible legal systems: Whose ethics does a business person follow when she/he is in a foreign country? Finally, business ethicians became concerned with political and social structures that permitted humans to be treated in an inhumane manner, such as apartheid, child labor, and land division. These changes led to a newer view of business decision-making in the form of what authors refer to as "social responsiveness" which both requires a reaction of social pressures but also the "long-run role in a dynamic social system" (Sethi, 1974), which in turn should be anticipatory and preventative. Frederick (1978) calls corporate social responsibility CSR_1, which has a philosophic underpinning. He names corporate social responsiveness CSR_2, which refers to the capacity of the corporation to respond to social pressures; it is a more pragmatic effort in reacting to the corporate environment. While social responsibility relates more clearly to rights and obligations, social responsiveness reacts to pressures which are in effect various forms of power exercised by different groups affecting the corporation. Davis and Blomstrom,

Post, Sethi, Wilson, and others have developed various categories to illustrate social responsiveness. Carroll has combined social responsibility, social responsiveness, and social issues to produce the "corporate social performance model."

Two sets of events in the 1980s encouraged business ethicians to consider 1) insider trading and 2) an unprecedented number of acquisitions and mergers. The former challenged the ethical as well as the legal practices of the financial community. First of all, using insider information unbalanced the competitive environment, but discussion on what constituted insider information left much gray area, while the law challenged violators like Boesky (see INSIDER TRADING LAW (US)).

Freeman (1984) and others developed the notion of stakeholders: "an individual or group who can affect or is affected by the actions, decisions, policies or goals of the organization." The notion of stakeholder broadened the relationship of the firm to different, and perhaps previously disregarded, elements in society, such as special-interest groups, social activists, environmentalists, and institutional social investing (see STAKEHOLDER THEORY). The proliferation of mergers and acquisitions occasioned "downsizing," "rightsizing," and "reorganization" which resulted at times in massive terminations of employees, including executives and managers. Middle management positions were frequently eliminated, employees felt a loss of job security, and they redirected their loyalty in the firm. Furthermore, the term "business ethics" now included the broader view of social issues. Authors included the social responsibilities of business, business and society, and perhaps even public policy under the now more generic "business ethics." Indeed, the founding of the Society for Business Ethics resolved the concern of individual and social issues of business once and forever. Business ethics included both.

In the late 1980s and 1990s business ethics assumed an international flavor. European philosophers and business school professors in particular began to develop their own approaches. Up to this time, the Europeans and others depended primarily on material produced by American scholars. The political and economic changes in the Eastern European countries and the forming of the European Community raised specific issues in business ethics that had not been adequately treated previously by Americans, such as language and cultural changes when working in foreign countries. The European approach has strong philosophical tenets as well as interests in dealing with the ethics of economics. It also questions the moral individualism of American decision-making which is closely linkpersons. Indeed, these new problem-type approaches should have a greater interdisciplinary analysis. The European approach is more collegial and investigates long-term interests of all concerned. Business ethics is thus conceived as a consensual ethic, possibly a result of the different variations of European social democracy. EBEN (the European Business Ethics Network) is the institutionalized network for European ethicians. Enderle, Mahoney, Ryan and van Luijk are familiar names in the European setting.

Political events raise business ethics issues: NAFTA (North American Free Trade Agreement) and GATT (General Agreement on Tariffs and Trade) (see GATT)

These agreements have international implications for business ethics in terms of jobs, relocation, investing, environment, and discrimination, both racial and sexual. It is too early to determine the precise ethical application of these issues, which standards will apply, and how they will be implemented. Furthermore, the legal disintegration of apartheid raises new problems in business ethics, such as ownership of property, foreign investing, and equal job opportunity (*see* EQUAL EMPLOYMENT OPPORTUNITY COMMISSION).

International business ethics is different from national business ethics inasmuch as there is no sovereign power to settle claims; there are different derivative values from different cultures; there are problems of communication; and there are differences in interpretation and application.

The one constant in the history of business ethics has been change: in emphasis, in philosophy, in topics, in cases. Change is also noticeable in accountability: from the individual to the corporation and then returning to the individual within the corporation. Changing economics, financial, and marketing functions shifted production and distribution, which in turn brought new and sometimes different ethical problems. Business ethics has also broadened its scope from national and regional issues to international and global concerns. All this change has produced a complexity in business ethics that requires thorough inquiry and innovative solutions.

Bibliography

Baumhart, S. J., & Raymond C. (1961). How Ethical Are Businessmen? *Harvard Business Review*, **39** (4).

Beauchamp, T. L. & Norman E. Bowie, (eds) (1993). *Ethical Theory and Business* 4th edn. Englewood Cliffs, NJ: Prentice-Hall.

Buchholtz, R. A. (1992). *Business Environment and Public Policy* 4th edn. Englewood Cliffs, NJ: Prentice-Hall.

Cavanagh, G. F. (1976). *American Business Values in Transition*. Englewood Cliffs, NJ: Prentice-Hall.

Carroll, A. B. (1993). *Business and Society: Ethics and Stakeholder Management*, 2nd edn. Cincinnati, Ohio: South-Western.

Davis, K. & Blomstrom, R. L. (1971). *Business, Society and Environment: Social Power and Social Response*, 2nd edn. New York: McGraw-Hill.

De George, R. T. & Pichler, J. A. (eds) (1978). *Ethics, Free Enterprise and Public Policy*. New York: Oxford University Press.

Donaldson, T. & Werhane, P. H. (eds) (1993). *Ethical Issues in Business: A Philosophical Approach*, 4th edn. Englewood Cliffs, NJ: Prentice-Hall.

Frederick, W. C. (1978). From CSR$_1$ to CSR$_2$: The Maturing of Business-and-Society Thought. Graduate School of Business, University of Pittsburgh, 1978. Working paper No. 279.

Frederick, W. C., Post, J., & Davis, K. (1992). *Business and Society: Corporate Strategy, Public Policy, Ethics*, 7th edn. New York: McGraw-Hill.

Freeman, R. E. (1984). *Strategic Management: A Stakeholder Approach*. Boston: Pitman.

McMahon, T. F. (1975). *Report on the Teaching of Socio-Ethical Issues in Collegiate Schools of Business/Public Administration*. Charlottesville, Va: University of Virginia Press.

Sethi, S. P. (ed.) (1974). *The Unstable Ground: Corporate Social Policy in a Dynamic Society*. Los Angeles: Melville Publishing.

Sharp, F. C. & Fox, P. G. (1937). *Business Ethics: Studies in Fair Competition*. New York: Appleton-Century.

van Luijk, H. J. L. (1990). Recent Developments in European Business Ethics. *Journal of Business Ethics*, **9**, 537-44.

Velasquez, M. G. (1982). *Business Ethics: Concepts and Cases*. Englewood Cliffs, NJ: Prentice-Hall.

THOMAS F. MCMAHON

holding company structure   The conventional holding company structure, illustrated in figure 1, is usually found in companies which have attempted to expand or diversify by acquisition. In its classical form, the central office plays no role in the strategy of the constituent member companies within the holding company and, indeed, there may also be no central financial control. In the 1970s such companies were common as an original strategy began to mature or be subjected to excessive pressure. As a consequence, almost invariably after the appointment of a new chairman or chief executive officer, such firms attempted to break out from the mature/decline strategic position by diversifying rapidly through acquisition (*see* ACQUISITION STRATEGY), or by eliminating competition by buying them up. As the holding companies lacked the appropriate post-acquisition capabilities of integrating the new subsidiaries, they were allowed to manage themselves. A classic example would have been the development of GKN, a leading British manufacturer of screws, which expanded and at the same time attempted to eliminate competition by purchasing major competitors. There was no central control and, as a result, within the group the subsidiaries continued to compete with one another, so eliminating the expected benefits. The central office in this structure was virtually nonexistent, consisting only of the chairman and a secretary.

The board structure of such holding companies tends to be made up of CEOs of a number of the subsidiary companies, operating under a chairman who might be a

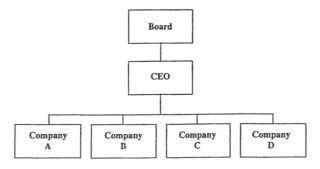

Figure 1 A holding company structure.

nonexecutive, or at least unable to intervene in the operations of the subsidiaries. In the absence of any formalized strategic plans, subsidiaries tend to pursue their own strategies, and are interested in preserving their autonomy rather than being subject to strict financial and strategic control from the central office. When a holding company is established, board membership may well change, and functional specialist directors of the original core company leave the board. This process is necessary in order to change the functional bias of the executive board members, who might otherwise concentrate on the original business to the detriment of new diversifications. However, where the original core business is especially large as, for example, in oil, banking, and tobacco, this change in board emphasis is especially hard to achieve.

A further form of the holding company structure is also current, in that some corporations exist in which, again, no attempt is made to influence the strategy of subsidiaries, although they are subject to tight financial control. Hanson Trust, for example, could be classified as a holding company. The difference between this form and the historic pattern is the sophisticated financial control systems, the central office strategic capabilities in acquisition search, post-acquisition and the imposition of tight financial controls. Thus while no product market strategy is immediately apparent and the break-up and disposal of acquired companies is undertaken, the financial characteristics of the residual activities form part of an ongoing strategy. In the case of Hanson, therefore, disposals help to recover the financing of an acquisition, leaving the residual businesses to generate a high rate of return on a relatively limited capital outlay. The residual businesses also tend to be cash generators, allowing the build up of a cash war chest to finance the next acquisition. This type of holding company, while apparently having no synergistic product market strategy, does have SYNERGY within a financial portfolio concept.

The traditional holding company strategy tends to be basically unstable. Without control there is a natural tendency for subsidiaries to undertake actions which may lead to financial imbalance. Acquisitions may not be adequately integrated or rationalized, and strategic moves may be undertaken which, while increasing corporate size, may also lead to reduced profitability. As a result, most of these holding companies have eventually been acquired by the second type, or have reorganized by adopting a DIVISIONAL STRUCTURE as consultants are brought in to establish greater control.

Functional Holding Company

The functional holding company structure is an intermediate variant that is often used in the early stages of diversification away from the single business stage. Diversification in the early stages normally occurs through acquisition (*see* ACQUISITION STRATEGY) and a new subsidiary is usually grafted on to an existing functional structure, as shown in figure 2.

The constitution of the board of the new enterprise is usually modified to add the CEO – but not the functional directors – of the acquired company. The chairman and nonexecutive directors of acquired companies are often dismissed. The same is true of the CEO if the bid is contested.

This structure is rarely stable. First, in making a diversification, the acquiring company often underestimates the STRATEGIC FIT between itself and the acquiree. Second, the board culture still strongly reflects that of the parent, and board meetings tend to emphasize the affairs of the parent rather than those of the acquiree, even if the new arrival makes a substantial contribution to overall profitability. Third, the constitution of the board is predominantly made up of functional specialists – not general managers. As a result, it is common that the CEO of the acquired company may resign out of frustration. A serious common mistake then is for the parent company to install one of its own senior managers as the new CEO of the acquiree. Performance suffers further, and this tends to be compounded if further acquisitions are undertaken which lead to the establishment of a holding company structure.

Research indicates that, as DIVERSIFICATION develops, one of the two traditional holding company structures is introduced. However, while corporate sales overall tend to expand sharply, profitability declines after a relatively short time. While the initial bout of diversification occurs after a change in the chairman and/or the chief executive, the failure of the diversification moves to produce improved profitability leads to a second change of leadership, which is often introduced from outside the company in order to establish a shift in corporate culture. This is often initiated by board changes and by the introduction of external consultants to rationalize and reorganize the business and to introduce a new structure. In the 1970s and 1980s this tended to mean the introduction of a DIVISIONAL STRUCTURE and/or an SBU structure. In the 1990s even more fundamental changes are taking place in strategy/structure revisions, especially in industries in which changes induced by information technology are transforming cost structures.

Figure 2 A functional holding company structure.

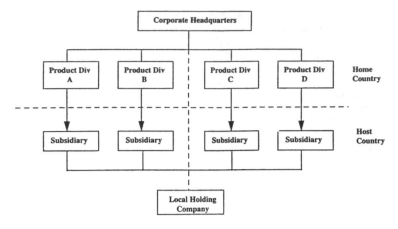

Figure 3 A local umbrella company structure.
Source: Channon & Jalland (1979).

Here the process of re-engineering (*see* VALUE-DRIVEN RE-ENGINEERING) is tending to convert conventional vertical organizational linkages toward customer quality driven horizontal linkages.

Holding company structures may also be widely used for legal and fiscal reasons, which may or may not have organizational management implications. For example, an intermediate holding company might be used to avoid withholding taxes on dividends paid to shareholders resident outside the domicile of particular corporations. Thus Swiss corporations might operate with Panama-based holding companies which receive dividends from some of their overseas subsidiaries that can be distributed to shareholders without withholding.

Similarly, local umbrella holding companies, as shown in figure 3, are often required by multinationals to legally coordinate the individual interests of product divisions. Such a holding company can: (i) present a unified corporate face to local government and markets; (ii) provide a communication channel for details regarding existing and future operations necessary for business unit coordination; (iii) provide an overall corporate perspective on local opportunities; (iv) achieve tax optimization; (v) ensure consistent personnel policies; and (vi) consolidate divisional funds to permit more local borrowing and to provide easier management control for centralized cash and foreign exchange management.

Bibliography

Channon, D. F. (1973). *The strategy and structure of British enterprise.* Cambridge, MA: Harvard Division of Research.
Channon, D. F. & Jalland, M. (1979). *Multinational strategic planning.* New York: Amacon.
Goold, M. & Campbell, A. (1987). *Strategies and styles: the role of the centre in managing diversified companies.* Oxford and Cambridge, MA: Basil Blackwell.
Rumelt, R. P. (1974). *Strategy, structure and economic performance.* Cambridge, MA: Harvard Division of Research.

DEREK F. CHANNON

horizontal integration   This is regarded as an integrative growth strategy and involves acquiring competitors within the same industry, as opposed to a vertically integrative strategy which might involve the acquisition of suppliers (backward integration) or customers (forward integration).

Horizontal integration may not necessarily be undertaken as a means of growth; it might also be employed to rationalize an industry, which is maturing or declining, by removing capacity.

see also **Competitive strategy; Vertical integration**

DALE LITTLER

horizontal structure   In traditional vertical organizations, is divided into functions, then departments, and finally tasks. The primary building block of performance is the individual, with the chain of command rising through the function, and the manager's job is concerned with assigning individuals to tasks and then measuring, controlling, evaluating, rewarding, and sanctioning performance.

This structure has come under increasing pressure in today's rapidly changing environment, in which time and cost pressures are forcing reconsideration of the vertical structure and a move toward horizontal structures, organized around the CORE PROCESS.

In the horizontal form of organization, work is primarily structured around a small number of core processes or work flows, as shown in figure 1 (*see* VALUE-DRIVEN RE-ENGINEERING; CORE PROCESS). These link the activities of employees to the needs of suppliers and customers, so as to improve the performance of all three. Work, and the management of work, are performed by teams rather than individuals. While still hierarchical, the new structure tends to be flatter than traditional functional systems.

The processes of evolution, decision making, and resource allocation shift toward continuous performance improvement. Information and training occur on a "just in time" basis rather than "need to know," while career progression occurs within the process rather than the function, making individuals generalists rather than specialists. While individual rewards may be made, compensation also relates to team performance.

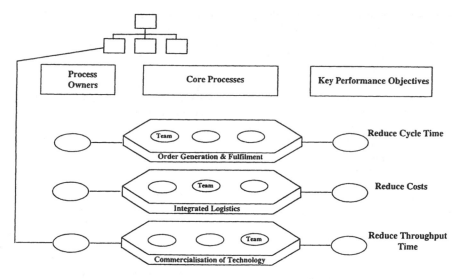

Figure 1 The horizontal organizational structure.
Source: Ostroff & Smith (1992).

A number of key principles have been identified at the center of horizontal organizations. These include the following.

1. Organize Around the Process, not the Task

In a horizontally structured corporation, the focus of performance can be shifted by organizing the flow of work around company-wide processes. This involves selecting a number of key performance indicators, (KPIs), quantitative but not necessarily financial measures, based on customer needs, and tying them to work flows. To achieve this, the corporation's activities need to be subdivided into around three to five "core processes." These might include order generation through to fulfillment, new product development, integrated logistics management, and branch management. The redesign of these processes can produce major one-off gains and then lay the basis for the introduction of continuous improvement strategies.

The structure for such a change involves the creation of a cross-functional team based upon the workflow, not on the individual task (*see* CROSS-FUNCTIONAL MANAGEMENT STRUCTURE). These work flows are then linked to others, both upstream and downstream. Organizing mechanisms for the structure include:

- the appointment of a leader, or team of leaders, to "own" and guide each core process

- assigning, to everyone involved in the process, objectives related to continuous improvement against "end of process" performance measures

- establishing measurement systems for each process, to integrate overall performance objectives with those of all work flows within the process

- reaching explicit agreement on the new staff requirements between upstream and downstream activities

- creating process-wide forums to review, revise, and syndicate performance objectives

2. Flatten the Hierarchy by Minimizing the Subdivision of Work Flows and Non Value Added Activities

In horizontal organizations, hierarchy is still seen as necessary, although ideally core processes can be "owned" by a single team. In reality, effective teams rarely exceed 20–30 people, far fewer than the thousands involved in core processes in large corporations. As a result, some hierarchy is needed, although one or two layers of functional hierarchical structures are normally eliminated.

The mechanism of delayering is used to combine related but formerly fragmented tasks, eliminating activities that do not add value or contribute to the achievement of performance objectives, and to reduce as far as possible the number of activity areas into which each core process is divided. While horizontal organizations are almost invariably flatter than vertical structures, this is not the key objective of restructuring; rather, this is to reshape the organization so that every element contributes directly to the achievement of the KPIs.

3. Assign Ownership of Processes and Process Performance

Leadership is still important in horizontal organizations. Thus teams or individuals are assigned "ownership" of each core process and are responsible for achieving performance objectives. Such individuals and/or teams are often responsible for the activities of thousands of employees engaged in the core process.

4. Link Performance Objectives and Evaluation to Customer Satisfaction

The primary driver in horizontal organizations may well be customer satisfaction rather than justifiability or shareholder value. These latter two terms might well be derived variables of the former.

Vertical organizations tend to drive for financial results and focus attention on the bottom line contribution of each function. In horizontal organizations, by contrast, the primary measure may well be customer satisfaction. This is measured in a variety of ways, many of which are nonfinancial, such as relative market share, growth rate, and market penetration, in the sense in which these are measures of relative competitive position.

As teams develop a clear understanding of how to manage a core process, they often find it useful to evaluate activity areas from the perspective of the external customer. In this way they use customer satisfaction measures to drive all the internal measures of performance.

5. Make Teams, not Individuals, the Principal Building Blocks of Organizational Performance and Design

Managers who organize around work flows treat teams, not individuals, as the key organizational building blocks. Teams regularly outperform individuals due to their greater skill base, broader perspective, and ability to solve complex problems. Moreover, many people find working in teams more rewarding than operating alone.

However, real teams need to be organized and motivated! As individuals they may offer a superior mix of skills, but unless these are orchestrated the result may actually be dysfunctional. For horizontal organizations to be successful, therefore, organization by teams is necessary, but leadership and orchestration of these skills is essential for them to be complementary.

6. Combine Managerial and Nonmanagerial Activities as Often as Possible

When teams are organized horizontally around work flows, it is important to make such teams as self-managing or empowered as possible. The premise behind this concept is that those who participate in the process know it best and, if so motivated, have the most to contribute to improving its productivity. Moreover, as problems develop, decisions can be made quickly and action can be taken in real time without interrupting critical work flows.

By contrast, in vertical organizations the benefits of self-management are constrained to within the function, where actions may ironically cause decreased efficiency in subsequent dependent functions. Moreover, lower hierarchical level personnel may lack the authority to make changes, which need to be approved at senior levels within the organization. When such moves threaten the existing power system, changes may well be resisted.

Horizontal structures combine rather than separate managerial and nonmanagerial activities wherever possible. Teams must therefore be empowered to exercise training and information processing, and be motivated to evaluate and change when, how, where, when, and with whom they interact, and in so doing become the real managers of the process.

7. Treat Multiple Competencies as the Rule, Not the Exception

In horizontal structures, the more skills that individuals bring to the team, the greater is the team's ability to manage the core process for which it is responsible. By contrast, in vertical organizations the trend is toward task specialization to maximize efficiency. This does not mean that horizontal structures can afford to ignore functional specialist skills; therefore they also need to embrace such skills when they are identified as essential.

However, specialist skills are often illusory and may be used to reinforce the existing structure. It is therefore necessary to identify carefully what specialist skills are needed and which can be discarded. Often, this is a political decision rather than an operational one.

8. Inform and Train Personnel on a "Just in Time to Perform" Basis, Not on a "Need to Know" Basis

In vertical organizations, information has often been used as a source of power rather than to improve the performance of a function or relationships between functions. Information has tended to flow on an "up–over–down–back" basis, leading to time delays, and dispersed – and perhaps contradictory – decision making. Despite training and attempts at improved coordination and cooperation in many corporations, interfunctional coordination is far from optimal.

In horizontal organizations, information is ideally made available on a "just in time to perform" basis, and is provided to those responsible for implementation. Moreover, the reward structure is linked to achievement of the core process activity rather than the function; hence it behoves the participants within the process to maximize rather than hinder efficiency.

9. Maximize Supplier and Customer Contact

In horizontal structures, corporations aim to bring their employees into direct, regular contact with suppliers and customers. Such contact increases their insight into the total value added process within an industry. Done well, this provides opportunities for building supplier and customer loyalty and to improve cost efficiency. Managers sometimes resist this vertical integration because it reduces their power and influence over the business process. Evidence suggests, however, that overcoming such resistance provides an important means of strengthening customer-driven performance.

10. Reward the Development of Motivational Skills and Team Performance, Not Just Individual Performance

In horizontal organizations, synchronizing the reward and sanction systems is important for successful implementation. The emphasis on developing the role of the individual within the core process team is very different from the narrow, individualistic competitive approach in the vertical functional system.

For teams to be effective, members must accept mutual accountability on agreed purposes and objectives. Within this structure some individual rewards are permissible; however, the competitive pressure imposed under the functional system, which may lead to sub-optimal behavior, can be dampened. To maximize their rewards, team members must partially sacrifice their own position for the good of the team.

Conclusions

It is not easy to find the correct balance between vertical and horizontal structures. However, it is important to recognize that such a structural transformation may well be necessary, and will need to overcome the existing power structure for successful implementation. Horizontal structures are a natural consequence of re-engineering strategies and, while accepted by top management, may well meet serious resistance in the ranks of middle management who may be "delayered" in the process of change.

Bibliography

Kaplan, R. B. & Murdock, L. (1991). Core process redesign. *McKinsey Quarterly*, no. 2, 27–43.

Ostroff, F. & Smith, D. (1992). The horizontal organisation. *McKinsey Quarterly*, no. 1, 148–68.

DEREK F. CHANNON

human factors engineering Systematic consideration of the human user or operator in the design of systems, tools, consumer products, and environments is a concept known as human factors engineering (HFE). It is also known as human factors, human engineering, ergonomics, and human-centered design. The underlying philosophy is that a machine and its human operator constitute a human–machine system, the effectiveness of which depends on the integration of human and non-human components.

Origin and Rationale

Design professionals, such as engineers and computer scientists, have traditionally sought to develop physical systems that operate reliably and effectively. Nevertheless, there are always some failures, and most (estimates run as high as 60–90 percent) are attributed to "human error" (Wickens, 1992). During the Second World War, psychologists were recruited to help combat human error in the operation of aircraft, radar, and other advanced systems of that era, error that was occurring despite rigorous selection and training of personnel. In many cases it was discovered that *design* features, such as instruments that were easily misread or controls that were easily confused, were implicated (Christensen, 1958). Consequent design changes based on well-established principles of human performance (e.g. attention, perception, memory, motor ability) produced marked improvements.

Thus was born the idea that systematic consideration of human limitations, capabilities, and tendencies in design could pay big dividends. Following the war, the idea persisted and spread. Disciplines other than psychology and engineering became involved, and civilian applications were found in settings as diverse as transportation, manufacturing, and communications (Chapanis, 1959). By 1958, interest had grown sufficiently to prompt the establishment of several organizations committed to the advancement of the HFE concept, notably the Human Factors Society (now the Human Factors and Ergonomics Society), the Society of Engineering Psychologists (a division of the American Psychological Association), and the international Ergonomics Society.

It was recognized early on that HFE would demand more than merely *applying* what is known about human performance to the design and improvement of systems. Often the required knowledge was lacking, making research necessary. Hence the field evolved as a combined science–practice enterprise. Professional journals (e.g. *Human Factors*, *Ergonomics*) were founded that included scientific as well as applied content.

Debate within the HFE community over exactly what mix of science and practice is appropriate, and whether the field is best regarded as an independent discipline or a philosophy that draws a number of disciplines together, has always been lively (Howell, 1994). Some do not consider HFE a psychological specialty despite the disproportionate representation of psychology in its demographics and content (Van Cott and Huey, 1992).

HFE Today

Growth in the size, diversity, and visibility of HFE has continued. There are now over 10,000 professionals who identify with the field. They are being produced by some 59 graduate programs in the United States alone (Van Cott and Huey, 1992), and served by literally dozens of professional institutions (Salvendy, 1987). The knowledge base has exploded, with the most recent general handbook (which is quite dated) running to nearly 2000 pages and barely scratching the surface of the 72 topic areas covered (Salvendy, 1987).

The growing impact of the HFE concept on society is now evident in litigation over the safety of consumer products and working conditions, in government and industry regulations, in product advertising, and in ordinary discourse. "User-friendly" has become a household term. Despite such encouraging signs, however, the discipline still functions in relative obscurity, and human factors considerations are all too often subordinated to those of cost, aesthetics, and machine performance in the design process (Howell, 1992).

A related difficulty is the popular misconception that advanced technology (notably automation), rather than human-oriented design, offers the final solution to the "human error problem." The fallacy in this logic is that automation never completely eliminates the human from the system. It merely redefines roles – in general, limiting human participation to broad supervision and decision responsibilities. Unfortunately, demands on the human increase rather than decline in this role, and the consequence of error can be enormous. Widely publicized mishaps such as the USS *Vincennes* incident, in which a civilian airliner was mistakenly shot down by a US cruiser despite the latter's highly sophisticated information system, serve to underscore this point (Wickens, 1992).

Topics of greatest interest to HFE researchers and practitioners have generally been driven by technological developments (Howell, 1993). This accounts for the current emphasis on issues posed by computer-based systems. The human–computer interaction (HCI) area, for example, is concerned with how to design the "interface" – displays, processing software, controls – to maximize human learning and performance. Similarly, the aforementioned supervisory role of the human in increasingly complex and powerful systems has prompted research on the "mental workload" demands of such systems, human capacities for coping with them, and designs for reducing them.

Another driver of HFE activity is social trends. For instance, changing population demography is currently stimulating considerable interest in design for special user groups (such as the elderly and disabled), an increasingly diverse workforce, and an altered concept of the workplace (*see* FLEXIBLE WORKPLACE/TELECOMMUTING).

Bibliography

Chapanis, A. (1959). *Research Techniques in Human Engineering*, Baltimore, MD: Johns Hopkins Press.

Christensen, J. M. (1958). Trends in human factors. *Human Factors*, 1, 2–7.

Howell, W. C. (1992). Human factors in the workplace. Eds. Dunnette, M. D. & Hough, L. M. *Handbook of Industrial and Organizational Psychology*, Palo Alto, CA: Consulting Psychologists Press.

Howell, W. C. (1993). Engineering psychology in a changing world. *Annual Review of Psychology*, **44**, 231–63.

Howell, W. C. (1994). Human factors and the challenges of the future. *Psychological Science*, 5, 1–7.

Salvendy, G. (Ed.) (1987). *Handbook of Human Factors*, New York: Wiley.

Van Cott, H. P. & Huey, B M (Eds) (1992). *Human Factors Specialists' Education and Utilization*, Washington, DC: National Academy Press.

Wickens, C. D. (1992). *Engineering Psychology and Human Performance*, New York: Harper Collins.

WILLIAM C. HOWELL

human resource-based competitive advantage Human resource-based competitive advantage can be defined broadly as the utilization of employee capabilities to create value for customers in a way that rival firms cannot. This perspective has emerged from resource-based theories in organizational economics where profit and competition focus on internal characteristics of firms rather than external forces in the industry environment (Wernerfelt, 1984). Barney (1991) made the case that a firm's resources lead to sustained competitive advantage when they are: (a) valuable, (b) rare, (c) inimitable, and (d) non-substitutable. More recently, Wright et al. (1994) and Snell et al. (1996) have applied this framework specifically to STRATEGIC HUMAN RESOURCE MANAGEMENT.

The Value of Human Resources

Human resources can add value by either improving efficiency or enhancing a firm's ability to satisfy customer needs (i.e. effectiveness). Research shows that programs designed to create a highly skilled workforce can result in higher productivity, and these improvements provide value to firms over and above the costs incurred (Hunter and Hunter, 1984). For example, employee empowerment programs tend to make performance more sensitive to variations in human skills, knowledge, and attitudes and to ensure that mental effort rather than physical effort is instrumental for creating value and success (Walton and Susman, 1987).

The Rareness of Human Resources

Human resource-based competitive advantage is also based on the assumption that labor supplies are *heterogeneous* across firms (Wright et al., 1994). Many human attributes, such as cognitive ability, are normally distributed in the population, and because of this capability levels even one standard deviation above the mean (i.e. 84th percentile) are, by definition, rare. If companies can attract and retain the best and the brightest employees, and establish programs that maximize their value-added contribution, then they can build a competitive advantage through people.

In addition to the heterogeneity of labor, the question of rareness also depends on the *asset specificity* and *mobility* of the workforce (Becker, 1964). Employee skills that are firm-specific and cannot be transferred to other companies constitute a potential source of sustainable competitive advantage (Lado and Wilson, 1994).

The Inimitability of Human Resources

Human capital can be either acquired on the open market or developed internally. If employee capabilities can be duplicated or imitated by another firm, they cannot be a source of sustainable competitive advantage. Resources are difficult to imitate under two conditions: (a) when the link between a firm's resources and its competitive advantage is *causally ambiguous* (Reed and DeFillippi, 1990), and (b) when internal and external relationships are multifaceted and *socially complex* (Barney, 1991). These two conditions imply that while individual skills and capabilities can be important sources of competitive advantage, it may be the complementarity among them that is most distinctive and sustainable (Snell et al., 1996).

The Substitutability of Human Resources

In the context of human resource-based competitive advantage, if a competitor can substitute another resource (e.g. technology) and achieve the same benefit *vis-à-vis* customers, then human resources would not provide a sustainable source of competitive advantage. The key issue here is *functional equivalence* (i.e. alternative resources that serve the same function are substitutes). In the past, organizations have historically substituted capital for labor where possible, and replaced decision-making with rules and procedures. In these ways, human resources have been readily substituted in traditional organizations, particularly in the context of routine aspects of physical work. However, as employees make the shift from touch labor to knowledge work, their value hinges more on cognitive processes such as problem diagnosis, trouble shooting, and decision-making (Snell and Dean, 1992). These aspects of human capital are not easily substitutable.

In summary, human resource-based competitive advantage refers to leveraging employee skills to outperform rival firms. Particularly in knowledge-based industries, competitive advantage increasingly resides in the people-embodied know-how (Prahalad, 1983), and human resources rather than physical or financial resources are what distinguish market leaders.

Bibliography

Barney, J. (1991). Firm resources and sustained competitive advantage. *Journal of Management*, 17, 99–120.

Becker, G. S. (1964). *Human Capital*, New York: Columbia.

Hunter, J. & Hunter, R. (1984). Validity and utility of alternative predictors of job performance. *Psychological Bulletin*, 96, 72–98.

Lado, A. A. & Wilson, M. C. (1994). Human resource systems and sustained competitive advantage: a competency-based perspective. *Academy of Management Review*, 19, 699–727.

Prahalad, C. K. (1983). Developing strategic capability: An agenda for management. *Human Resources Management*, 22, 237–54.

Reed, R & DeFillippi, R. J. (1990). Causal ambiguity, barriers to imitation, and sustained competitive advantage. *Academy of Management Review*, 15, 88–102.

Snell, S. A. & Dean, J. W. (1992). Integrated manufacturing and human resource management: a human capital perspective. *Academy of Management Journal*, 35, 467–504.

Snell, S. A., Youndt, M. A. & Wright, P. W. (1996). Establishing a framework for research in strategic human resource management: merging resource theory and organizational learning. *Research in Personnel and Human Resources Management*, Ferris, G. R. (ed.), 14, Greenwich, CT: JAI Press.

Walton, R. E. & Susman, G. I. (1987). People policies for the new machines. *Harvard Business Review*, 86, 71–83.

Wernerfelt, B. (1984). A resource based view of the firm. *Strategic Management Journal*, 5, 171–80.

Wright, P. M., McMahan, G. C. & McWilliams, A. (1994). Human resources and sustained competitive advantage: a resource-based perspective. *International Journal of Human Resource Management*, 5, 301–26.

SCOTT A. SNELL

human resource information systems Human resource information systems (HRIS) are systematic procedures for collecting, storing, maintaining, retrieving, and validating data needed by an organization about its human resources, personnel activities, and organization unit characteristics (Milkovich and Boudreau, 1993). A HRIS need not be complex or even computerized. HRIS can be as informal as the payroll records and time cards of a small boutique or restaurant, or as extensive and formal as the computerized human resource data banks of major manufacturers, banks and governments. HRIS can support human resources planning with information for labor supply and demand forecasts, staffing with information on equal employment opportunity, job postings, separations, and applicant qualifications; and TRAINING and development with information on training program costs and trainee work performance. HRISs can also support compensation with information on pay increases, payroll processing, salary forecasts, and pay budgets; and labor–employee relations with information on contract negotiations and employee assistance needs. The purpose is to provide information that is required by human resource stakeholders or supports human resource decisions. HRIS enhances human resource management in several ways, including: (a) reducing the *costs* of gathering, summarizing, and distributing information; (b) business process re engineering, by encouraging decision–makers to carefully consider how to design their HR information processing to be most efficient and effective; and (c) decision support, by providing data that help the recipient to improve decisions about programs or personal choices (Boudreau, 1992).

HRIS must accomplish three significant processes: (a) *input*, which involves adding data to the system; (b) *maintenance*, which involves updating, integrating, and organizing the data; and (c) *output*, which involves manipulating the data to appear in the appropriate format, and then delivering the data to the appropriate destination or person. A growing number of organizations now use computerized systems to implement their HRIS. Such systems may rely on large centralized databases, but more frequently are evolving to exploit large networks of smaller computers, each containing a portion of the human resources data of the organization (Broderick and Boudreau, 1991). Future systems will very likely provide connections to worldwide networks such as the Internet, allowing external information to be imported and combined with the internal information from the organization. Construction of such computerized information requires careful planning, and the cooperation of multiple constituents (Walker, 1993).

As computers become increasingly common in offices, homes and factories, access to HRIS is rapidly increasing. In the past, only a handful of technicians had the skills to obtain HRIS contents. Today, many managers can acquire such information from their desktops or even by phone, and employees are increasingly able to use computers to change their personal data entries, get information about company policies, and even obtain computerized expert system assistance for decisions such as choosing among flexible benefit plans or relocation. As access proliferates, the question of PRIVACY IN ORGANIZATIONS will be increasingly important to human resource managers, especially those who support international human resource management (Boudreau et al., 1994).

Bibliography

Boudreau, J. W. (1992). HRIS: adding value or just cutting costs? *HR Monthly*, May, 8–11.

Boudreau, J. W., Broderick, R. L. & Pucik, V. (1994). Just doing business: human resource information systems in the global organization. *Global Information Systems and Technology: Focus on the Organization and Its Functional Areas*,Eds.Deans, P. C. & Karwan, K. R. Harrisburg, PA: Idea Group Publishing.

Broderick, R. L. & Boudreau, J. W. (1991). The evolution of computer use in human resource management: interviews with ten leaders. *Human Resource Management*, **30**, 485–508.

Milkovich, G. T. & Boudreau, J. W. (1993). *Human Resource Management*, Homewood, IL: Richard D. Irwin.

Walker, A. J. (1993). *Handbook of Human Resource Information Systems*, New York: McGraw-Hill.

JOHN W. BOUDREAU

human resource inventories Inventories, also called stocks, are accumulated stores of employee characteristics within an organization that have value to the organization. Inventories have value to the extent that the characteristics contribute, directly or indirectly, to the achievement of organization objectives.

Characteristics with value to an organization may be either attributes of individual employees or attributes of groups of employees. Individual attributes that may have value are: abilities, age, attitudes, behaviors and traits, beliefs, capitalized value, character or integrity, citizenship, commitment, competencies, condition and health, energy level, knowledge and understanding, longevity or tenure, performance, personality, productivity, protected group classification, satisfaction, skills, service orientation, values, and work ethic. All these attributes may be summed to determine their extent within groups of employees.

In some instances synergistic or critical mass effects tend to occur when many persons in a group have an attribute. The most common synergistic effect is the acting out by employees of a characteristic. Enactment occurs when employees in the group become aware that other persons in the group share the characteristic and when display of the characteristic meets a social need of employees (Weick, 1979).

Individual employee attributes most likely to have synergistic effects within groups are (with their corresponding group attribute in parentheses): behaviors and traits (culture), commitment (loyalty), job satisfaction (morale), and character or integrity (social character).

Are Characteristics Actually Inventoried?
To inventory usually means that the amount of the item in the stock is counted or measured at a given time. In practice, organizations typically inventory human resources only when the characteristic may easily be counted or measured and/or a count or measure is necessary or highly important. For example, many organizations routinely inventory the age and longevity of their employees because turnover can have significant financial implications. Organizations doing federal contract work inventory the protected group status of employees since they may be required by a Presidential executive order to submit this information to the Office of Federal Contract Compliance

Programs. More often, human resource inventories are monitored without actual physical count or measure.

Inventories have long played a central role in the forecasting of work force availability, as part of the employment planning process. Current changes sweeping the workplace appear to be heightening the need for attention to monitoring human resource inventories. For example, workforce flexibility, delivery of product and quick response to changing customer needs, is enhanced by building organizations with flat structures staffed by empowered employees working in teams (see SELF-MANAGING TEAMS). These teams require multiskilled employees, who can perform most of the discrete jobs needed to produce the product or service, and who have problem-solving and interpersonal skills.

Strategic human resource management may identify, often using generic competency models, competencies of special importance to strategic objectives. These competencies, because of their critical importance for organization success, often are measured using ASSESSMENT CENTERS and deficiencies are addressed through corporate universities or academies.

Bibliography

Biles, G. E. & Schuler, R. S. (1986). *Audit Handbook of Human Resource Practices: Auditing the Effectiveness of the Human Resource Functions*, Alexandria, VA: American Society for Personnel Administration.

Grinold, R. C. & Marshall, K. T. (1977). *Manpower Planning Models*, New York: North-Holland.

Jarrell, D. W. (1993). *Human Resource Planning: a Business Planning Approach*, Englewood Cliffs, NJ: Prentice-Hall.

Manzini, A. O. & Gridley, J. D. (1986). *Integrating Human Resources and Strategic Business Planning*, New York: AMACOM, American Management Association.

Weick, K. E. (1979). *The Social Psychology of Organizing*, Reading, MA: Addison-Wesley.

DONALD W. JARRELL

Human Resource Planning Society "The Human Resource Planning Society (HRPS) is committed to improving organizational performance by creating a global network of individuals who function as business partners in the application of strategic human resource management practices" (mission statement of HRPS). One focus of the society is identifying state-of-the-art strategic human resource (HR) issues, utilizing input from HR experts. Additionally, HRPS conducts a yearly conference for all members, a corporate sponsor's conference, and several professional development workshops, and sponsors HR-related research. The approximately 2500 members are typically people who hold more senior and key strategic HR positions. Most members have responsibilities in organization effectiveness, continuity, and/or organizational development.

For further information contact: Human Resource Planning Society, 41 East 42nd Street, Suite 1509, New York, NY 10017. Telephone: 212-490-6387.

OLIVER LONDON

human resource programming Human resource programming is a process for developing action plans to close the gap between the supply of human resources and the demand for human resources over a particular planning period. It is part of human resources planning and occurs after an organizations's human resource needs have been forecasted. Action programs may be needed to increase the supply of employees when demand is greater than supply of employees. Conversely, programs may be required to decrease the number of employees if the forecasts show supply exceeding demand. These gaps may reflect not only quantities of employees but also their quality, skill mix, and DIVERSITY. Additionally, some parts of a firm may be in balance while other areas may experience shortages or surpluses. Effective human resource programming involves generating alternative courses of action, evaluating each, and selecting the best course of action to close the gap. Research and practice suggest that organizations have a number of alternative ways to manage surpluses and shortages of human resources.

Human resource surpluses can be addressed through a number of strategies. Because layoffs have such a negative impact on employees, practitioners and researchers alike suggest the use of first-level strategies like reduction in overtime or work hours and hiring freezes so that attrition may naturally diminish the work force (Greenhalgh et al., 1988). Other defenses against layoffs include RETRAINING, redeployment, job sharing, unpaid vacation, and reduction in pay. More companies have been making use of voluntary early retirement programs to manage surpluses. Such programs offer additional years' credit and bonuses to encourage employees not currently eligible for retirement to retire at an earlier age. A major concern with such programs has been the potential loss of talent. One study of a major employer, however, found no loss in quality of management talent as a result of early retirements (Howard, 1988). Another concern is that employees may feel coerced into retiring through negative changes in their performance evaluations and pressure from supervisors to take the incentive. The Older Workers Benefit Protection Act of 1991, an amendment to the Age Discrimination Act, lays out guidelines for structuring early retirement programs to minimize risk of adverse impact charges from older employees (Stein, 1991).

Once first-level strategies have been exhausted and surpluses still remain, layoffs and DOWNSIZING may be inevitable. In recent years, because of competitive and economic pressures, organizations have turned to downsizing as a strategy to reconcile gaps between demand and supply of human resources. Downsizing is not without its problems. Cascio (1993) reported that few companies are well-prepared for downsizing and that, six months to a year after a downsizing, key firm performance indicators often do not improve. Reasons for this include workload strains on remaining employees, survivors' guilt among those not laid off, and replacement costs for loss of knowledge and skills. Researchers suggest that companies must be careful to plan for downsizing and layoffs. Downsizing should not be undertaken as a short-term, quick fix solution but contemplated in relation to a firm's intended competitive strategies. Attention must be paid not just to head count reduction but also to fundamental changes in the design of work and the structure of the organization (Cascio, 1993). There are a number of practices that can soften the impact of layoffs on employees. These range from early advance notice to outplacement services. Companies having 100 or more employees are required by the Worker Adjustment and Retraining Notification Act (WARN) to provide sixty days' advance notice of plant closings to employees, unions, and state and local officials when fifty or more employees will lose jobs.

Human resource shortages present another kind of challenge. Shortages can be addressed through RECRUITING both internally and externally. Internal recruiting offers the advantage of greater knowledge of job candidates, lower recruitment costs, and less need for orientation. On the downside, reliance on internal recruiting may result in stagnation due to in-breeding. Part of the challenge with external recruiting to fill shortages is identifying those sources that will yield the desired number and quality of employees at the most efficient cost. Instead of recruiting permanent employees, many organizations are increasingly turning to contingent workers to fill employee shortages. Contingent workers include temporaries, part-timers, consultants, subcontractors, and leased employees (Belous, 1989). These approaches offer an organization greater strategic flexibility in matching staffing needs with work demands.

Bibliography

Belous, R. S. (1989). How human resource systems adjust to the shift toward contingent workers. *Monthly Labor Review*, 112, 7–12.

Cascio, W. (1993). Downsizing. What do we know? What have we learned? *Academy of Management Executive*, 7, 95–104.

Greenhalgh, L., Lawrence, A. T. & Sutton, R. I. (1988). Determinants of work force reduction in declining industries. *Academy of Management Review*, 13, 241–54.

Howard, A. (1988). Who reaches for the golden handshake? *Academy of Management Executive*, 2, 133–44.

Stein, L. I. (1991). Through the looking glass: an analysis of window plans. *Labor Law Journal*, October, 665–76.

STELLA M. NKOMO

human resource strategy The term human resource strategy (HRS) currently lacks definitional precision, but it generally refers to a construct denoting the coherent set of decisions or factors that shape and guide the management of human resources (acquisition, allocation, utilization, development, reward) in an organizational context. It is directly related to the business strategy and focuses on the formulation and alignment of human resource activities to achieve organizational competitive objectives.

HRS is a relatively new concept in the field of human resource management (HRM). It has emerged as the HRM function has assumed a more strategic perspective and organizations have come to view employees as essential resources to be managed effectively to achieve strategic business goals. At least three basic concepts of HRS have been articulated: the decisional concept, the human resource issue/action concept, and the human resources priorities concept.

The Decisional Concept

Drawing upon the business strategy literature, Dyer (1984) has formulated a longitudinal or retrospective decisional concept of HRS. He defines the organizational HRS "as the pattern that emerges from a stream of important decisions about the management of human resources" (p. 159). This concept requires a review of important HRM-related organizational decisions over a period of time to determine consistencies and observable patterns. In effect, the emergent pattern of coherent and consistent decisions revealed upon retroactive investigation indicates the strategy that guides HR activity.

In a later work, Dyer and Holder (1988) offer a more proactive decisional concept of HRS. In this case, the HRS is viewed as the collection of major human resource (HR) goals and means to be used in pursuit of organizational strategic plans. When an acceptable business strategy is formulated, key HR goals are defined to support this strategy and the necessary means (i.e. programming and policies) are designed and implemented to meet the goals. For example, if an organization chooses a competitive strategy of low-cost producer, major HR goals to support this strategy could be higher performance and lower headcounts. These, in turn could lead to programs including reduction in force and more increased investment in employee training. This combined set of HR goals and means would be the organizational HRS.

The HR Issue/Action Concept

This approach is based on an issue-oriented focus to develop an organizational HRS. Schuler and Walker (1990) and Walker (1992) argue that in a dynamic, fast changing environment, managers must deal effectively with a series of emerging business issues that can have a significant impact on competitive success. Business issues will involve HR issues that are critical to successful strategy implementation.

These HR issues can be considered gaps that represent opportunities for people to contribute more effectively to the achievement of business strategies. Line managers have to respond to these HR issues in their decision processes. As is necessary, they will define directional actions to address the people-related business issues. These managerial actions and plans will focus, mobilize, and direct the HR activities toward the business issues most important to the firm; and they will form the essence of the organizational HR strategies.

The HR Priorities Concept

This concept of HRS posits that each organization has an identifiable set of dominant HR priorities that are used to align its HR activities, policies, and programs with its strategic business goals (Craft, 1988, 1995). This cluster of key HR priorities, which constitutes the HRS, defines the organization's orientation and attitude toward its employees and it guides the development of HR plans that deal with the personnel aspects of basic business issues. For example, in an organization competing on the basis of innovation, core HR priorities might include employee risk taking, initiative, teamwork and high competence.

The priorities will be basic factors guiding and configuring the HR system (acquiring, developing, rewarding) in response to business needs. Each organization's cluster of priorities (HRS) will differ based on the mix of its competitive strategy, internal organizational factors (e.g. culture, technology), and external environmental factors (e.g. labor market, competitor practice).

While the HRS tends to be stable in the short term, over time it is a dynamic concept since the priorities will evolve and be crafted to meet changing business situations.

Bibliography

Craft, J. A. (1988). Human resource planning and strategy. *Human Resource Management: Evolving Roles and Responsibilities,* Dyer, L. Washington, DC: Bureau of National Affairs. 47–87.

Craft, J. A. (1995). Human resources strategy (unpublished working paper).

Dyer, L. (1984). Studying human resource strategy: an approach and an agenda. *Industrial Relations,* **23,** 156–69.

Dyer, L. & Holder, G. W. (1988). A strategic perspective of human resource management. *Human Resource Management: Evolving Roles and Responsibilities,* Dyer, L. Washington, DC: Bureau of National Affairs.

Schuler, R. S. & Walker, J. W. (1990). Human resources strategy: focusonal Dynamics, **19,** 4–19.

Walker, J. W. (1992). *Human Resource Strategy,* New York: McGraw-Hill.

JAMES A. CRAFT

human resources function   The role of the human resources (HR) function is to attract and select qualified job applicants, to develop performance management and compensation systems that align employee behaviors with organizational goals, and to assist in the development and retention of a diverse workforce to meet current and future organizational requirements (*see* HUMAN RESOURCE STRATEGY). Employees within the HR function also provide support and consulting services to line managers, who are directly responsible for the administration of the firm's human resources (Schuler, 1995). Specific areas of responsibility include job and organizational design, recruitment and selection, performance management, compensation and benefits, employee development and training, HR planning, labor relations, diversity management, and compliance with legal and governmental guidelines.

Bibliography

Schuler, R. S. (1995). *Managing Human Resources,* St Paul, MN: West Publishing Company.

MARK A. HUSELID

impact of mergers and acquisitions

Merger and Acquisition: Definition and Purpose

Mergers and acquisitions rapidly reconfigure assets to better implement strategy by combining independent enterprises. This is effected through the purchase of one organization (classic acquisition), exchange of stock, or simple pooling of assets (classic merger). Typically, 80 percent of such combinations are described as failures (Hawkins, 1988), attributable to poorly blended organizations, culture differences, or turnover of key people (Scott, 1981; Schweiger and Weber, 1989).

Role of Human and Organization Resources

Mergers and acquisitions are complex changes, incorporating rapid growth and modification of organizational culture. For the combination to be successful, employees must accept new objectives and functions within a new structure. Employees may be required to engage in new behaviors or continue previous behavior but in a new organization context. Thus, the merger or acquisition plan should include steps to foster employee behaviors necessary to the combination's success.

Mergers and acquisitions also cause disruptions in individual and organizational performance as a by-product of the changes. Tasks and rules appropriate in the combined organization must be learned or reaffirmed and employees are forced to deal with ambiguity and JOB STRESS, which compel attention to a greater extent than the tasks they are expected to perform. In the face of such transition, there may also be an unfreezing of attitudes allowing for rapid change. If this opportunity is squandered as employees cling to old conventions rather than establish new psychological contracts, an important opportunity to guide the success of the combination is lost.

Human Resource Management Actions

The most common role for the human resource function is fostering communication after the combination is announced. This includes newsletters, telephone hotlines, formal presentations (particularly those explaining benefits and personnel policies), and meetings among counterparts from the different organizations. These programs emphasize one-way communication.

More sophisticated efforts foster employee involvement by soliciting and responding to questions or by establishing project teams. This may involve surveying employees and providing feedback. Teams can decide how things will be done after the combination occurs. Such groups are common at the executive level (e.g. Baxter Healthcare, described in Ulrich et al., 1989) but may also involve supervisory and professional employees (e.g. Ernst & Young, described in Greller et al., 1994). The participative approach increases acceptance, disseminates information, creates opportunities to influence decisions, and builds relationships across organization boundaries.

Human resource issues can be part of the decision to proceed with a particular combination. This may involve developing an acquisition screening procedure that includes questions dealing with operational aspects of personnel, management practices (appraisal, compensation, and so forth), and cultural fit (e.g. Novell, described in Anfuso, 1994). Alternatively, firms may identify a few key indicators, such as sales per employee (Hawkins, 1988), which act as surrogates for more extensive information on culture and business process.

Currently, human resource managers generally become involved after the decision to combine has been made and even after key policies have been set. Under these circumstances, communication is the major tool available for constructive action. Proactive employee relations can identify concerns and morale problems so that management may address them.

Bibliography

Anfuso, D. (1994). Novell idea: a map for mergers. *Personnel Journal*, 48–54.

Greller, M. M., Kesselman, G. A. & Ostling, P. J. (1994) Merging the service organization: the case of Ernst & Young. *Achieving Organizational Success through Innovative Human Resource Strategies*, Eds.Fay, C. H., Price, K. F. & Nihaus, R. J. New York: Human Resource Planning Society.

Hawkins, M. D. (1988). Using human resource data to select merger/acquisition candidates. *Creating the Competitive Edge through Human Resource Applications*, Eds.Nihaus, R. J. & Price, K. F. New York: Plenum.

Schweiger, D. M. & Weber,Y. (1989). Strategies for managing human resources during mergers andempirical investigation. *Human Resource Planning*, 12, 69–86.

Scott, J. H. (1981). *The Effect of Mergers, Acquisitions, and Tender Offers on American Business: a Touche Ross Survey*, New York: Touche Ross.

Ulrich, D., Cody, T., LaFasto, F. & Rucci, A. (1989). Human resources at Baxter Healthcare Corporation merger: a strategic partnership role. *Human Resource Planning*, 12, 87–103.

MARTIN M. GRELLER

imperfect information Perfect information is the strongest information requirement that can be assumed in an economic model. Traditionally, it has been a standard assumption in economic theory. Even though many of the real world markets being modeled (e.g. insurance markets, financial markets, and labor markets) were recognized as having important information imperfections, it was not subject to debate until fairly recently. Stigler's (1961) article, "The economics of information," is recognized as a path-breaking article on the formal modeling of imperfect information.

Incomplete information is a type of imperfect information. For example, one or more parties to a transaction may lack knowledge of some aspect of the transaction that affects their payoffs. When consumers have incomplete information, markets which would be perfectly competitive otherwise have the features of MONOPOLISTIC COMPETITION and firms have some degree of market power. ASYMMETRIC INFORMATION is another type of imperfect information. For example, one party to a transaction may have valuable knowledge of some aspect of the transaction that another party does not. Information asymmetries are an important source of information imperfections which may in turn create problems of moral hazard and adverse selection.

An early article on the effects of imperfect information on the standard conclusions of economic theory is Rothschild and Stiglitz (1976). They examined the effects of imperfect information on competitive insurance markets and found that under plausible conditions an equilibrium did not exist in those markets in the presence of imperfect information. Although their focus was on insurance markets their results also had implications for financial markets and labor markets. In the context of credit markets, Stiglitz and Weiss (1981) show how equilibrium in credit markets can be characterized by rationing in the presence of imperfect information.

One of the implications of Rothschild and Stiglitz (1976) was recognizing imperfect information as a source of market inefficiency. Another was recognizing that specific institutions in markets may be responses to the difficulties of handling problems of imperfect information. This second implication has had a profound influence on recent developments in what has come to be called the "new institutional economics." The approach taken by the imperfect information strand of the new institutional economics is associated primarily with the work of Akerlof and Stiglitz. It is rigorous, specifying assumptions and equilibrium solutions, and making sharp distinctions between different types of information problems. Stiglitz (1986) utilizes the imperfect information theory of institutions to provide an explanation of the existence of certain agrarian institutions as substitutes for incomplete insurance markets, credit markets, and futures markets.

Screening and SIGNALING are two methods individuals use in attempting to overcome problems of imperfect information that arise due to adverse selection. Stiglitz (1975) develops a theory of screening which he uses to analyze the allocation of resources to education. Screening serves to sort individuals on the basis of their qualities. Stiglitz finds that screening in education has productivity returns but it increases inequality, creating a trade-off between distributional and efficiency considerations. Leland and Pyle (1977) develop a signaling model where entrepreneurs seek financing for projects whose true qualities are known only to them. An entrepreneur's willingness to invest in their own project is seen as a signal of the project's quality. They conclude that the value of the firm increases with the share of the firm owned by the entrepreneur, and suggest that financial intermediation is a natural response to asymmetric information.

Bibliography

Leland, H. & Pyle, D. (1977). Informational asymmetries, financial structure and financial intermediation. *Journal of Finance*, 32, 371–87.

Rothschild, M. & Stiglitz, J. (1976). Equilibrium in competitive insurance markets: an essay on the economics of imperfect information. *Quarterly Journal of Economics*, 90, 629–50.

Stigler, G. J. (1961). The economics of information. *Journal of Political Economy*, 69, 213–25.

Stiglitz, J. (1975). The theory of "screening", education and the distribution of income. *American Economic Review*, 65, 283–300.

Stiglitz, J. (1986). The new development economics. *World Development*, 14, 257–65.

Stiglitz, J. & Weiss, A. (1981). Credit rationing in markets with imperfect information. *American Economic Review*, 71, 393–410.

ALEXANDRA BERNASEK

implementation of information systems Implementation processes for information system projects focus on the diagnosis and resolution of concerns that individuals and groups have about changes that an information system project will produce in their work life. The discussion of implementation processes is organized around three topics: (a) the change process; (b) the diagnosis of implementation problems; and (c) management actions for implementation. These three components are illustrated in figure 1.

The Change Process

To be successful, an information systems project must move a work system from its current state to a desired new state. This movement involves passing through three phases: (a) unfreezing; (b) moving; and (c) refreezing (Lewin, 1952). The length of time for a phase depends upon the nature of the system being built, the nature of the organization for which the system is being built, and the management actions used to manage the transition. Failure of the project can occur at each stage.

Implementation involves all the stakeholders to an information systems project: those various groups of people, inside and outside the organization, whose methods of work will be affected by the project. In addition, stakeholders are also groups of people whose actions can affect the success of the project. For an improvement in an order entry system, for example, the stakeholder groups include personnel from credit and collections, distribution, manufacturing, and information systems, plus general managers and owners. Outside of the organization, the stakeholders would include customers, competitors, and suppliers.

Unfreezing involves gaining recognition and acceptance from the stakeholders of the project that changes to the work system are needed. The data used to achieve unfreezing successfully arise at two organizational levels. For the upper management and suppliers of capital to the organization, the required data revolve around projected improvements in organizational performance and increase in value that the project will bring to the organization (e.g. increases in sales, gains in market share, reduction in costs, and improvements in quality). For others, such as mid-level managers, front-line workers, sales people, as well as customers, competitors, and suppliers, interest focuses on what benefits and costs the project will produce for them personally, not for the organization in general.

Moving involves the functionality of the system. Functional requirements are implemented in hardware, software, management policies and procedures, and education and training specifications for the stakeholder groups. Approaches to developing these specifications fall within the domain of systems analysis and design. It is through the successful completion of the systems development process that the projected, as well as unforeseen, benefits and costs used as evidence in the unfreezing stage are achieved.

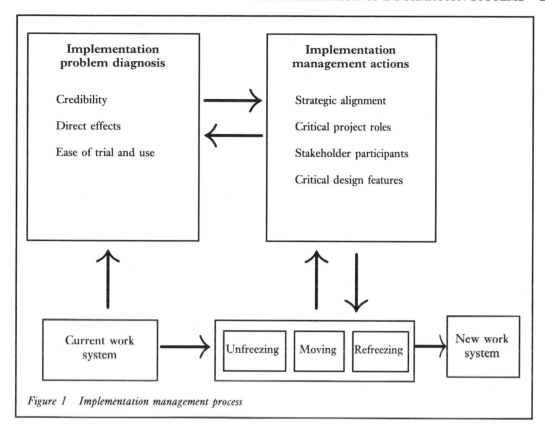

Figure 1   Implementation management process

Refreezing involves ensuring that the new work systems become institutionalized standards of work behavior for the stakeholder groups. The focus is on demonstrating that the benefits and costs, projected in unfreezing and captured by the analysis and design efforts, are delivered to the various stakeholders.

Diagnosis of Implementation Problems

Research on innovation in general, and innovation and information technology, has identified three broad categories of factors to judge the value and acceptability of a proposed project: (a) the credibility of the project proposers and developers and the technology being employed; (b) the direct positive and negative effects of the proposed system; and (c) the ease of trial and use of the proposed system. While each individual stakeholder evaluates a proposed system in terms of these three categories, implementation problem diagnosis focuses upon identifying the typical beliefs about the systems held by different groups of stakeholders. For example, the evaluation of a proposed new order-processing system is done in terms of the beliefs of sales personnel, customers, distribution personnel, and others.

Credibility of proposers, developers, and technology is important because it influences *a priori* perceptions of the implementation project. For example, if the system is being recommended by sales management, the credibility of the sales management in the eyes of the various stakeholder groups is critical. In information systems projects, the reputation of the specific system developers involved in the project, as well as the general credibility of information

systems groups, are important. The reliability of the hardware and software employed in the project is important. If the technology being employed (e.g. voice recognition in an order-processing system) has been used successfully elsewhere, credibility is acceptable. Conversely, if there has been a failed implementation of the technology, credibility will be unacceptable.

Direct effects of the proposed system consist of incremental benefits, incremental costs, and failure consequences. *Incremental benefits* may be monetary or non-monetary. As an example of monetary benefits to a stakeholder, a new sales support system may directly lead to an increase in sales and sales commissions. Most stakeholders do not receive monetary payment; they receive benefits such as the ability to complete a task faster with higher quality. *Incremental costs* for most stakeholders are not monetary. Rather, the costs may be the incremental effort to learn to use the proposed system and pressure to perform at higher levels of productivity with the new system. These incremental costs may be transitory or continuing. *Failure consequences* are encountered if a stakeholder adopts the new system and it temporarily or permanently fails. If, for example, a sales force moves to an electronic customer information database system and the system fails, it will affect sales effort.

Ease of trial and use of the proposed system focuses on five issues. The first two are *physical and intellectual ease of use* and *ease of conversation about the system*. If, for example, stakeholders can talk about and use a new system without learning complex technical procedures and terminology, they will be more likely to view the system favorably. The importance of these two issues explains the significance of graphical user interfaces in END-USER COMPUTING. The third issue is *compatibility* with other parts of the stakeholders' work processes. The more localized the effects of a proposed system, the more favorably it will be viewed. The fourth and fifth issues are ability to test a system *on a limited basis* before committing to full-scale use and ability to reverse the *usage decision*. The ability to try a proposed system on a limited, experimental basis and the ability to discontinue use if the actual system does not live up to expectations increase the likelihood that the system will be viewed favorably.

The three evaluative categories and the issues in them define measures that the proposers and developers of a new system should monitor during the three phases of the change process. Positive responses across key stakeholder groups increase the likelihood that the project will succeed. When a proposed project scores poorly on several issues, a prototyping approach may be used. Extensive training may be required. *Incremental benefits* are critical. Stakeholders will be willing to work to overcome a number of problems if they see a clear benefit in the system. Perception of no benefit or limited benefits by a stakeholder group is almost certain to cause implementation problems and may lead to outright failure of a project.

Management Actions for Implementation

Implementation problem diagnosis for stakeholders defines implementation management problems. There are four broad categories: (a) the alignment of the proposed system with the strategy of the organization; (b) critical roles within each project; (c) participation by representatives of stakeholder groups; and (d) the critical system design features.

Strategic alignment focuses on the relationship between the proposed system and the strategy of the organization. It explains why the system is important to the *success factors* of the organization. While the systems analysis process builds this linkage as it defines the information requirements and capability, the implementation management process assures that all stakeholder groups understand the reasons for the proposed system. Although not all stakeholders will see personal *incremental benefits*, the strategic alignment explanation provides a legitimate reason for the system.

Critical project roles refer to positions and activities of sponsor, champion, and project leader. The sponsor is a senior-level manager in the organization who can legitimize the spending of resources and time on the proposed project. The sponsor is the person who, by his or her support, communicates the alignment of the project with the organization's strategy. The project must also have a *champion*, usually an upper-level manager in the functional organization that will use the system. The champion is usually organizationally above the directly affected organizational stakeholders. From this position, he or she commits the time and energy to manage the negotiations and resolve the political issues that evolve with an information systems project. Champions are usually at some political risk in the organization if the project fails. The *project manager* is the person responsible for managing the day-to-day activities of the project. For information systems, the project manager usually comes from the systems development group in the organization. There should also be a co-project leader from the main user area. This dual project manager approach is necessary to ensure that both the business issues and the technical issues are addressed during the development process.

Stakeholder participation refers to the active and appropriate involvement of the stakeholder groups in the systems analysis and development process. If there is a positive level of trust between the stakeholders and the project proposers and developers, stakeholder involvement can increase the quality of input concerning the functionality required in the system. The involvement of stakeholders also helps to obtain their "buy-in" concerning the changes in work processes that will be required. In terms of the implementation problem diagnostic dimensions discussed in the previous section, involvement is a productive way of achieving favorable perceptions among the various stakeholder groups. In cases where there is little trust between the stakeholders and the proposers and developers, participation can be an alternative to the control process that stakeholders may require before proceeding with the project.

Critical design features refer to system functionality and system user interfaces. These features are necessary to the success of the project, but they are not sufficient. The degree to which they will contribute to the success or failure of the project often depends on how well *strategic alignment*, *critical project roles*, and meaningful *participation* are executed.

Bibliography

Lewin, K. (1952). Group decision and social change, in E. E. Maccoby, T. M. Newcombe and E. L. Hartley (eds), *Readings in Social Psychology*, pp. 459–73. New York: Holt.

NORMAN L. CHERVANY and
SUSAN A. BROWN

impression management   Organizational theorists, researchers, and practitioners have increasingly recognized the importance of *impression management* (also called *self-presentation*) as an explanatory model for a broad range of organizational phenomena. Impression management refers to the many ways that individuals attempt to control the impressions others have of them: their behavior, motivations, morality, and personal attributes like competence, trustworthiness, and future potential. Individuals may also attempt to control the impressions others form of entities besides themselves such as commercial products or a company (Schlenker & Weigold, 1992).

The impression management framework employs a "life as theater" or *dramaturgic* metaphor to describe social and organizational behavior. People are actors, taking many roles (e.g., parent, employee, supervisor), and are keenly aware of audience reactions to their behaviors. Thus, some actors' behavior is an attempt to control or modify the image that relevant audiences have of them and win audiences' moral, social, and financial support. The impression management framework assumes that a basic human motive, both inside and outside of organizations, is to be viewed by others in a favorable manner and to avoid being seen negatively. Individuals act as amateur publicity agents using enhancing impression management tactics (e.g. ingratiation, self-promotion) to look good and protective or defensive impression management (e.g., excuses, apologies) to minimize deficiencies and avoid looking bad.

Impression management has increasingly become a recognized part of organizational behavior theory, research, and practice. Two edited volumes (Giacalone & Rosenfeld 1989; 1991) have systematically applied an organizational impression management perspective to topics such as selection interviews, PERFORMANCE APPRAISAL, LEADERSHIP, CAREER strategies, exit interviews, organizational justice.

Impression management theory – so popular today in organizational settings – had its roots in the pioneering work of sociologist Erving Goffman. In his classic book, *The Presentation of Self in Everyday Life* (1959), Goffman systematically interpreted social behavior utilizing the terminology and methods of the theater. People were seen as social actors attempting to establish (in conjunction with those with whom they were interacting), a "working consensus" through their impression management behaviors. This reciprocal impression management served as a social lubricant: it allowed actors to know how to act and what actions to expect from others.

Beginning in the 1960s, experimental social psychologists (most notably Edward E. Jones' seminal studies of ingratiation) increasingly began utilizing impression management to explain a whole host of research areas including cognitive dissonance, reactance, altruism, and aggression. Rather than having independent theoretical status, however, impression management was often an alternative explanation for established social psychological laboratory phenomena (Baumeister, 1982).

The social psychological legacy of impression management theory also gave it a stigma that it still struggles to overcome. Impression management for many became synonymous with unscrupulous, nefarious, insincere, and deceptive actions. People who practiced impression management did not necessarily believe in the impressions they were claiming, but were saying and doing things to gain favor in the eyes of significant audiences as part of a general motive of manipulative social influence (Tedeschi, 1981; see POLITICS).

This pessimistic view of impression management has gradually moderated during the last decade. The current thinking among most theorists is that impression management behaviors are often sincere components of social and organizational behavior. As Tetlock and Manstead (1985, pp. 61–62) noted, "although some writers have used the term *impression management* to refer to the self-conscious deception of others (e.g., Gaes, Kalle, & Tedeschi, 1978), there is no compelling psychological reason why impression management must be either duplicitous or under conscious control. Impression management may be the product of highly overlearned habits or scripts, the original functions of which people have long forgotten."

In an authoritative review, Schlenker and Weigold (1992) distinguished between *restrictive* and *expansive* views of impression management. The restrictive view sees impression management as a generally negative often deceptive set of behaviors aimed at illicitly gaining social POWER and approval. The now more accepted expansive view sees impression management as a fundamental aspect of social and organizational interactions. It is perhaps best to view impression management behaviors as falling on a continuum ranging from sincere, accurate presentations to conscious deception.

The popularity of impression management in organizational scholarship is a relatively recent phenomenon. While many of the concepts of impression management were utilized in areas such as organizational politics, there were few organizational investigations of impression management before the early 1980s. Not until the mid-1980s did the organizational impression management perspective begin to gain an identity theoretically distinct from the earlier literature on organizational politics and attain a degree of independent status. Thus, although popular in social psychology for over two decades, it is only relatively recently that the organizational impression management literature has expanded into the full range of organizational behavior topic areas. It seems fair to say that impression management now provides explanatory power for a wide range of topics across the organizational sciences.

A number of challenges remain for organizational impression management. Three of note are:

(1) *Can impression management be trained?* Although training in impression management performance and detection has been recommended (Giacalone, 1989), impression management has yet to have true empirically derived practitioner applications. A first step may require viewing impression management as a desirable set of skills rather than a deficit.

(2) *Are impression management motivation and tactics applicable to an increasingly diverse, multinational workforce?* As organizations grow increasingly diverse and multinational impression management may be crucial to members of racial/ethnic minority groups, women, immigrants, and expatriates who often need to please majority group members in positions of greater social power. Understanding how impression management behaviors are interpreted by others can also serve as the basis for smoother interactions and a means for solving potential communication problems among individuals from diverse backgrounds (Rosenfeld, Giacalone & Riordan, 1994).

(3) *Does impression management play a role in functional and dysfunctional interpersonal relationships?* Little impression management research has been done with individuals in ongoing personal and professional relationships. It would be of interest to know what types of impression management behaviors are associated with stable, long-lasting relationships. At the same time, organizations would benefit from understanding conditions that elicit impression management behaviors that are dysfunctional or destructive from the individual or organizational point of view (e.g., substance abuse, sabotage, withholding of effort).

see also **Interpersonal skills**

Bibliography

Baumeister, R. F. (1982). A self-presentational view of social phenomena. Psychological Bulletin, 91, 3–26.

Gaes, G. G., Kalle, R. J. & Tedeschi, J. T. (1978). Impression management in the forced compliance paradigm: Two studies using the bogus pipeline. Journal of Experimental Social Psychology, 14, 493–510.

Giacalone, R. A. (1989, May). Image control: The strategies of impression management. Personnel, 52–55.

Giacalone R. A. & Rosenfeld, P. (Eds) (1989). Impression management in the organization. Hillsdale, NJ: Sage.

Giacalone, R. A. & Rosenfeld, P. (Eds) (1991). Applied impression management: How image making affects managerial decisions. Newbury Park, CA: Sage.

Goffman, E. (1959). The presentation of self in everyday life. Garden City, NY: Doubleday.

Rosenfeld, P., Giacalone, R. A. & Riordan, C. A. (1994). Impression management theory and diversity: Lessons for organizational behavior. American Behavioral Scientist, 37, 601–607.

Schlenker, B. R. & Weigold, M. F. (1992). Interpersonal processes involving impression regulation and management. Annual Review of Psychology, 43, 133–168.

Tedeschi, J. T. (1981). Impression management and social psychological research. New York: Academic Press.

Tetlock, P. E. & Manstead, A. S. R. (1985). Impression management versus intrapsychic explanations in social psychology: A useful dichotomy? Psychological Review, 92, 59–77.

PAUL ROSENFELD
ROBERT A. GIACALONE
and CATHERINE A. RIORDAN

income tax treaties   The United States is a party to a dizzying array of international agreements with other nations, including over 80 income tax treaties now in force or being negotiated. Even the best income tax advice can be thrown to the winds if the subject transaction is between taxpayers from different countries and the taxpayers fail to consider the effects of tax treaties that may exist between their nations. The language of the treaties, although a little stilted with the formulas of international legal expression, is generally understandable in context, and the goal of income tax treaties is clear: to harmonize and simplify tax laws between the two countries, promoting commerce, while avoiding double taxation and fiscal evasion.

Each income tax treaty is a separate agreement between two nations who are a party to the agreement. While in theory each treaty could differ widely from each other treaty, in practice all treaties to which the United States is a party tend to look very much alike, and tend to look like most other income tax treaties in the world, owing largely to the Organization for Economic Cooperation and Development (OECD). In 1963, the OECD member nations developed a model treaty, a basic framework designed to serve as the starting point for tax treaty negotiations between member nations. Modified in 1977, the Model Treaty was accompanied by a Commentary prepared by the OECD that has become a key guide to interpreting the meaning to the terms and expressions used in modern treaties. As a consequence of this general international understanding of the meaning of treaty terms, conflicts between nations over treaty obligations are actually rather rare. If they do occur, the International Court at The Hague adjudicates the dispute. In 1977 and in 1981, the United States adopted its own version of a model treaty, but the Commentary developed by the OECD remains a major guide to interpretation of this US Model Treaty, as well as the OECD versions.

The status of a treaty obligation is a matter for domestic law to determine in each country. Where a treaty obligation is in conflict with a domestic tax law, a country must decide which has priority over the other. In the United States, tax law clearly provides that a treaty provision controls in the event of a conflict of laws if the conflict existed on April 16, 1954, but, thereafter, the later expression of sovereign will controls. As a result, it is possible for Congress to override a treaty obligation by passing a law that contravenes the clear language of a treaty obligation already in existence. In this event, the treaty as a whole remains in force, but the contravened provision is deemed abrogated, and usually the two countries renegotiate the treaty.

In the United States, treaties are negotiated by the executive branch of the federal government, and once approved by the President, sent to the Senate for its advice and consent. Once ratified by the Senate, treaties come into force on the date the two parties to the treaty exchange instruments of ratification – conformed copies of the final treaty. Because all recent US tax treaties start from the same model, it is possible to generalize a great deal about the contents of an income tax treaty, although the specific points that are agreed upon vary from treaty to treaty.

Each income tax treaty must determine what persons have treaty standing, and what taxes are covered by the treaty. Treaty standing is critical because a taxpayer may take advantage of a provision in a treaty only if that taxpayer is covered by the treaty. US tax treaties generally follow the OECD model in providing that all US residents and domestic corporations may benefit from a US tax treaty. Interestingly, this means that a nonresident US citizen may not obtain benefits from a US tax treaty, even though the US asserts its right to tax its citizens – not just its residents – on their world-wide income. Residency is usually carefully described in terms of the geographic area that creates residency for treaty standing purposes, and generally excludes US territories. Residency can be a difficult matter to determine, and treaties often go to great lengths to avoid dual residency by prescribing "tie breaker" rules, designed to insure that any taxpayer is deemed a resident of only one of the two contracting nations in a tax treaty. A treaty may also contain a set of anti-treaty shopping provisions, designed to obtain treaty benefits by creating shell corporations or other subterfuges that appear to create residency.

The taxes covered by the treaty tend to include only US federal income taxes, often exclusive of the personal holding company tax and the accumulated earnings tax. In only a few cases are state income taxes explicitly covered in US treaties, although the fact that nearly 40 states in the United States begin their tax computations with federal income makes these states implicit signatories to each US income tax treaty. Similarly, other countries may or may not cover taxes other than basic federal income taxes.

Once a treaty has established the issues of treaty standing and taxes covered by the treaty, treaties based on the OECD Model Treaty often include permanent establishment provisions. To simplify the issue of the income taxation of business income of a foreign entity or individual, these treaties provide that the business income of a foreign person is taxable in the foreign country only if that person has a permanent establishment in that foreign country. Otherwise, this business income is taxable only in the country of that person's residency. If there were no permanent establishment provision, foreign business income would be taxable in a foreign country if the tax laws in that foreign country sourced the transaction in that foreign country. The rules governing sourcing of transactions vary widely, often leading to double taxation without a permanent establishment provision to harmonize the tax laws of the two countries in a treaty.

A permanent establishment is defined in the US Model Treaty of 1981 to be:

> a fixed place of business through which the business of an enterprise is wholly or partly carried on.

A place of management, a branch, an office, a factory, a workshop, a mine or well, a building site used for 12 months, or an installation, drilling rig, or ship used for more than 12 months to discover or exploit natural resources all qualify as permanent establishments. In addition, if another party other than an agent of independent status has and habitually exercises the power to bind a foreign person to contracts in a foreign country, this person is deemed to create a permanent establishment on behalf of the person that he or she represents in that country.

Following the permanent establishment provisions in treaties are a number of special sourcing rules for nonbusiness income, such as dividends, interest, rents, royalties, and capital gains. These types of income are often taxed to nonresident recipients by using withholdings taxes – taxes withheld by the payor and sent directly to the government – obviating the need to file tax returns in the foreign country. To encourage commerce, treaties often reduce or eliminate these withholdings taxes. In addition, the treaty may include special taxing rules for other types of income, such as the income of teachers or students, or that of artists or sportsmen. Often this kind of income is determined to be tax free, or very beneficially taxed, in the foreign country.

Treaties usually contain a savings clause that clearly limits the applicability of the treaty to international transactions, by providing that nothing in the treaty should be construed as interfering with the right of the country of residency to tax its own residents. As a result, even though a US treaty may declare gains on the sale of personal capital assets tax free, gains on the sale of such assets by a US citizen or resident are clearly taxed in the US.

Treaties also commonly include the identification of a person or official to serve as competent authority to negotiate with the other government to insure that the goal of avoiding double taxation without evasion is met. Competent authorities are often invoked to determine fair transfer prices for goods or services provided by residents of one country to those of the other country, where the parties are related, for example.

Information sharing provisions are also commonly included in treaties, providing for specified levels of cooperation between the contracting states in the pursuit of income taxes in the other country. The United States refuses to enter into such information sharing agreements unless foreign governments agree to treat the information so received with the same level of confidentiality that is required of US tax authorities.

While the language of treaties appears to be somewhat technical in character, reference to model treaties and their commentaries provides a ready basis for reading and understanding the nature of the mutual obligations that nations incur in the network of income tax treaties, and the often extraordinary benefits that the treaties confer on the residents of the contracting states. Clearly, tax planning and practice require that treaty law be carefully screened to insure that international transactions are appropriately taxed.

DALE L. DAVISON

increasing returns There are increasing returns to an input in production when as incremental units of that input are added, the resulting increases in output are rising. Increasing returns typically occur in the early stages of production as the first units of a variable input are added but, as more units are added, diminishing returns set in (*see* LAW OF VARIABLE PROPORTIONS). For example, the increases in output from adding the first workers to a plant should rise as those workers assist each other in production, so the MARGINAL PRODUCT of labor would be rising. Eventually, additional workers will not be as productive and their marginal product will be falling. As with diminishing returns, increasing returns refer to the short run when other factors of production are held constant. When all factors of production are changed, the issue is one of ECONOMIES OF SCALE (or of returns to scale).

ROBERT E. MCAULIFFE

indifference curves These curves are used to describe the preferences of a consumer who is faced with an array of market baskets, or sets of goods, from which to choose. One indifference curve represents all of the different combinations of goods which give the consumer equal total utility. Typically, market baskets containing different quantities of two goods are examined. Ordinarily, as the amount of either of the goods is reduced, utility is lost. As a result, the quantity of the second good must be increased in order to compensate for the loss and to leave the consumer indifferent between the initial and new position. For example, a consumer may indicate that a combination of four pairs of sneakers and one warm-up suit per year gives the same overall satisfaction as does three pairs of sneakers and two warm-up suits or one pair of sneakers and four warm-up outfits. These three combinations would be part of the same indifference curve for that consumer.

As it is generally assumed that more is preferred to less, any combination having more of at least one of the goods and no less of the second good would generate more total utility. Thus, for example, four pairs of sneakers in combination with three outfits would yield more total utility than the first combination identified above (and, by transitivity, more than the other two combinations as well). When other combinations having the same total utility as this new point are identified, a second indifference curve is created. The complete set of such curves is known as an indifference map.

It is important to recognize that the indifference curve represents the consumer's evaluation of these combinations without regard to income or the prices of the two goods. As such, the indifference map identifies a complete ranking of these combinations of goods solely on the basis of the consumer's tastes. The various combinations of goods which the consumer can afford and that set which leads to utility maximization requires the analysis of the consumer's BUDGET CONSTRAINT as well.

A diagram of an indifference curve is drawn with the y-axis measuring the quantities of one good (Y) and the x-axis measuring the quantities of the second good (X). The different combinations which are equivalent in the eyes of the consumer are combined to form a curve which ordinarily is negatively sloped. The slope of the indifference curve indicates the amount of good Y which the consumer is willing to trade in order to receive one extra unit of good X. This is identified as the marginal rate of substitution of X for Y. Each indifference curve is typically bowed inward toward the origin due to the law of diminishing marginal utility which causes the marginal rate of substitution between the two goods to decline. Indifference curves which are farther from the origin represent higher levels of overall utility and are thus more desirable.

Indifference curve analysis can be used to demonstrate how an advertising campaign for a product works to alter consumers' marginal rates of substitution and thus favorably alter their choices toward greater purchases of the good being promoted. Alternatively, the analysis can be used to show how a pricing strategy which lowers the price of one good causes greater consumption of that good through the choice of a new combination on the consumer's indifference map.

Moreover, both the income effect and the substitution effect of the price change can be demonstrated. In addition, indifference curves can be used to examine investment decisions by managers. Combinations of risk and rates of return (in the place of goods X and Y) can be used to create indifference curves which describe varying degrees of RISK AVERSION. The cost of financing capital expenditures can also be examined using this approach.

Finally, important advances have been made by Lancaster (1971) who used indifference curves to describe consumer preferences in terms of product characteristics. By identifying consumers tastes towards combinations of features which a product may hold, *target markets* can be established and marketing strategies concerning PRODUCT DIFFERENTIATION can be developed (*see* PRODUCT ATTRIBUTES MODEL).

Bibliography

Douglas, E. (1992). *Managerial Economics.* 4th edn, Englewood Cliffs, NJ: Prentice-Hall.

Lancaster, K. (1971). *Consumer Demand: A New Approach.* New York: Columbia University Press.

GILBERT BECKER

industrial marketing This is the term originally coined in the 1960s to describe the process of marketing between organizations. The term referred implicitly to organizations engaged in industry (especially "smokestack" industries). During the 1980s it became accepted that the term industrial marketing was inadequate because it failed to reflect the full diversity of marketing activities between organizations, especially between commercial organizations such as banks, publishers, distributors, and retailers. The term BUSINESS-TO-BUSINESS MARKETING was then coined as an alternative, though nowadays the term ORGANIZATIONAL MARKETING is preferred by many authorities because it recognizes that the principles and practice of marketing between organizations is not confined to "businesses" but also extends to a vast range of organizations such as hospitals, orchestras, prisons, armed forces, schools, charities, governments, and unions.

DOMINIC WILSON

industrial relations Industrial relations refers to workplace and societal interactions between workers and employers, and resulting employment-related outcomes. In the USA especially, the term often is used in a narrower sense to refer only to employment relationships where COLLECTIVE BARGAINING is used to establish terms and conditions of employment. In its broadest meaning, industrial relations is "all aspects of people at work" (Kochan, 1980, p. 1).

Industrial Relations as an Area of Study

The term "industrial" connotes heavy industry to many, but most industrial relations scholars use the term broadly, as in distinguishing industrialized societies from agrarian societies. Thus industrial relations refers to relations between employers and workers in all economic sectors.

Industrial relations remains the preferred term for describing the field among scholars. The major professional association is the Industrial Relations Research Association. (Many industrial relations scholars are also active in the Academy of Management's Human Resources Division.) There has been controversy concerning whether the field has become too closely associated with the narrower conception of industrial relations, i.e. union–management relations, and there have been calls for name changes with the intent of better conveying the broad sense of the field (e.g. "employment relations"). In the past ten years especially, many firms and academic programs have tended to downplay or even eliminate reference to "industrial relations" (e.g. in department names).

To fully appreciate multifaceted industrial relations issues, one must draw from varied perspectives, including economics, psychology, sociology, political science, and law. Thus industrial relations is often called an interdisciplinary subject. Industrial relations is studied within business schools and in specialized institutes or schools at many colleges and universities.

Theories and Assumptions

Kochan (1980) has suggested that an important factor distinguishing industrial relations from its contributing disciplines and related areas (e.g. human resources) is a distinctive set of values and assumptions. These include the following propositions:

(1) Labor is more than a commodity.
(2) There is an inherent conflict of interests between employers and employees in terms of economic matters (e.g. wages versus profits), but also in terms of friction in supervisor–subordinate relations.
(3) There are large areas of common interests between employers and employees despite their conflicting interests, and important interdependencies.
(4) There is an inherent inequality of bargaining power in most individual employer–employee relationships.
(5) There is pluralism, the notion that there are multiple competing interests groups in society, each with valid interests.

The dominant paradigm or conceptual framework for the study of industrial relations is the Industrial Relations Systems model advanced by Dunlop (1958). The concept of a system is applied in the sense that industrial relations consists of the "processes by which human beings and organizations interact at the workplace and, more broadly, in society as a whole to establish the terms and conditions of employment" (Mills, 1994, p. 5). Kochan (1980) has observed that like any complex social system, industrial relations systems are best understood by identifying and analyzing their various components and how they interact with one another to produce certain outcomes.

The major components of the industrial relations system are: (a) the actors (workers and their organizations, management, and government); (b) contextual or environmental factors (labor and product markets, technology, and community or "the locus and distribution of power in the larger society:" Dunlop, 1958); (c) processes for determining the terms and conditions of employment (collective bargaining, legislation, judicial processes, and unilateral management decisions, among others); (d) ideology, or a minimal set of shared beliefs, such as the actors' mutual acceptance of the legitimacy of other actors and their roles, which enhances system stability; and (e) outcomes, including wages and benefits, rules about work relations (e.g. standards for disciplinary action against workers), JOB SATISFACTION, employment security, productive efficiency, industrial peace and conflict, and industrial democracy. The basic purposes of the industrial relations systems concept are to provide a conceptual framework for organizing knowledge about industrial relations and for understanding how various components of industrial relations systems combine to produce particular outcomes (and hence why outcomes vary). It is noteworthy that the systems concept does not presume superiority of a particular process for determining employment outcomes.

The precise specification of system components may vary with the level of analysis and from one system to another. Although it has endured, the industrial relations systems concept has been criticized and challenged (e.g. Kochan et al., 1986). Although not denying change, several scholars have argued that even though major transformations in industrial relations may be occurring, they are not inconsistent with traditional understandings of industrial relations or the systems concept (e.g. Lewin, 1987).

Bibliography

Barbash, J. (1984). *Elements of Industrial Relations*, Madison, WI: University of Wisconsin Press.

Chelius, J. & Dworkin, J. (Eds) (1990). *Reflections on the Transformation of Industrial Relations*, New Brunswick, NJ: IMLR Press.

Dunlop, J. T. (1958). *Industrial Relations Systems*, New York: Holt-Dryden.

Fiorito, J. (1996). Industrial relations. *Gale Encyclopedia of Business*, Detroit: Gale Research.

Kaufman, B. E. (1993). *The Origins and Evolution of the Field of Industrial Relations in the United States*, Ithaca, NY: ILR Press.

Kaufman, B. E. & Kleiner, M. M. (Eds) (1993). *Employee Representation: Alternatives and Future Directions*, Madison, WI: Industrial Relations Research Association.

Kochan, T. A. (1980). *Collective Bargaining and Industrial Relations: from Theory to Policy to Practice*, Homewood, IL: Richard D. Irwin.

Kochan, T. A., Katz, H. C. & McKersie, R. B. (1986). *The Transformation of American Industrial Relations*, New York: Basic Books.

Lewin, D. (1987). *Industrial relations as a strategic variable Human Resources and the Performance of the Firm*, Kleiner, et al. (eds), Madison, WI: Industrial Relations Research Association.

Mills, D. Q. (1994). *Labor Management Relations*, **5th edn**, New York: McGraw-Hill.

JACK FIORITO

industrial unions An industrial union represents all workers in a particular industry regardless of their skill levels. Examples of industrial unions include the United Auto Workers, the United Steel Workers, and the Aluminum Workers of America. These unions bargain collectively over wages, hours, and other terms and conditions of employment. Unlike CRAFT UNIONS, which seek to restrict employment, industrial unions seek to expand membership and employment in the industries within which they operate. Thus, job security becomes a very prominent feature of a typical COLLECTIVE BARGAINING agreement. Industrial unions seek both fair wages and job security for their membership.

Bibliography

Kochan, T. A., Katz, H. C. & McKersie, R. B. (1986). *The Transformation of American Industrial Relations*, New York: Basic Books.

Slichter, S. H., Healy, J. J. & Livenash, E. R. (1960). *The Impact of Collective Bargaining on Management*, Washington, DC: Brookings Institution.

JAMES B. DWORKIN

industry life cycle This is the extension of the PRODUCT LIFE CYCLE concept to the industry. When a new product (or product category) has been created, the industry is in the introduction phase of the cycle where the market is small but growing and risk is high because the market is not yet fully established. Firms tend to have high ADVERTISING expenditures in this stage as they inform consumers about the new product. In addition, firms may be more vertically integrated if markets for supporting services and parts have not developed. For example, in the early years of the computer industry, there were few independent producers of peripherals such as disk drives or software, so companies such as IBM and later Digital had to produce these products themselves. During the growth phase of the cycle, the market grows rapidly as new firms enter the industry. New product development, innovations and marketing methods occur during this period as firms compete for higher profits and market share. Eventually as the market becomes saturated, growth slows and the industry reaches the maturity phase of the cycle where profits stabilize and firms tend to compete more on price rather than through PRODUCT DIFFERENTIATION. Following this phase, the industry enters the decline phase with a contracting market and higher EXIT rates among firms. The industry structure tends to consolidate as larger firms acquire weaker rivals, competition focuses on price and costs and industry profits are falling.

As Porter (1980) observed, there are several criticisms of the life cycle approach. Every industry or product will not necessarily pass through each stage of the cycle, nor is it always clear where a specific industry may be in the life cycle. The evolution of the industry and competition between firms may vary between industries rather than follow the course predicted by the life cycle. However, the industry life cycle does offer interesting dynamic predictions regarding entry, exit, competition and profits over time; see Greer (1992) and DECLINING INDUSTRY.

Bibliography

Greer, D. F. (1992). *Industrial Organization and Public Policy.* 3rd edn, New York: Macmillan.

Jacquemin, A. (1987). *The New Industrial Organization: Market Forces and Strategic Behavior.* Cambridge, MA: MIT.

Porter, M. E. (1980). *Competitive Strategy.* New York: Free Press.

ROBERT E. MCAULIFFE

influence This terms means any social process in which an individual's actions or attitudes are affected by the actual or implied presence of one or more others. It is essential to many features of group and organizational functioning, including LEADERSHIP, conformity, and role-taking. Two-way influence is necessary in all of these to achieve mutual ends. Influence usually is distinguished from POWER by an emphasis on persuasion rather than coercion or CONTROL. As Bierstedt put it in a classic phrase, "Influence does not require power, and power may dispense with influence." In many ROLE relationships, power and influence may coexist and be brought to bear variably, as appropriate. Supervisory, managerial, administrative, and executive functions in organizations usually grant power based on authority.

However, these LEADERSHIP roles also require what Katz and Kahn (1978) refer to as "the influential increment over and above mechanical compliance with the routine directives of the organization," in the nature of a following (p. 528). A demand for compliance can limit individual initiative and CREATIVITY, with costs to individual satisfaction and the performance of the organization. Because individuals can interpret and learn from new experiences, they have resources to resist influence and to influence (*see* UPWARD COMMUNICATION) tactics used within hierarchies. These tactics are contingent upon individual circumstances, such as one's level in the organization and years of experience (see, e.g., Kipnis, Schmidt, & Wilkinson, 1980).

Depending upon various situational factors, different tactics are suitable for the achievement of the influence objective within what is acceptable in the agent–target relationship. A questionnaire study of how 128 managers used nine influence tactics was conducted in the field with each manager's subordinates, peers, and boss (Yukl & Tracey, 1992). The results, regarding criteria of target task commitment and manager effectiveness, showed rational persuasion, inspirational appeal, and consultation to be most effective. Ingratiation and exchange were moderately effective with subordinates and peers but not with superiors. Least effective in this study were pressure, coalition, and legitimating.

Influence also may result from imitation, as in modeling, where one or more persons pattern their actions and attitudes on those of another. This process has utility in socializing newer members of an organization into appropriate ways of behaving (*see* SOCIALIZATION). Associated with it is the willingness of those in leadership roles to be influenced by followers through a recognition of mutual interdependence and the development of their leadership skills (see Hollander & Offermann, 1990, p. 185).

see also **Decision making; Interpersonal skills; Resistance to change**

Bibliography

Hollander, E. P. & Offermann, L. R. (1990). Power and leadership in organizations: Relationships in transition. American Psychologist, **45.**, (2), 179–189.

Katz, D. & Kahn, R. L. (1978). The social psychology of organizations. (2nd edn) New York: Wiley.

Kipnis, D., Schmidt, S. & Wilkinson, I. (1980). Intraorganizational influence tactics: Explorations in getting one's way. Journal of Applied Psychology, **65**, 440–452.

Yukl, G. & Tracey, J. B. (1992). Consequences of influence tactics used with subordinates, peers, and the boss. Journal of Applied Psychology, **77**, 525–535.

EDWIN P. HOLLANDER

influence tactics in the performance evaluation process Influence tactics refer to attempts to affect the PERFORMANCE APPRAISAL *process*, and thus, performance appraisal outcomes. Both subordinates and supervisors can influence the performance evaluation process and outcomes, and the usefulness of different tactics appears to be contingent on the context, source, and target of the influence efforts. Additionally, while research began in this area more than 25 years ago, it has gathered increased momentum only within the past five or six years.

Subordinate/Ratee Influence Tactics

Kipnis and his colleagues developed one program of research which focused on subordinate/ratee influence efforts (Kipnis et al., 1980). This program produced a typology, and results using that typology indicate that subordinate ingratiation can lead to higher performance ratings. Furthermore, a tactician influence strategy (emphasizing reason) was more successful for male subordinates and an ingratiator strategy (emphasizing friendliness) was more effective for female subordinates (Kipnis and Schmidt, 1988).

Ferris, Wayne, and colleagues developed a second program of research emphasizing the performance evaluation process and outcomes. Ferris et al. (1989) proposed, and Ferris and Judge (1991) extended, a conceptualization of how influence tactics affect human resources decisions. Findings demonstrate that influence tactics operate through supervisor affect, perceived competence, and perceived similarity to the supervisor. Furthermore, Ferris et al. (1994) found support for a positive link between supervisor-focused (i.e. ingratiation) tactics and performance evaluation through liking, but a negative link between job-focused (i.e. self-promotion) tactics and performance evaluation through liking. Wayne et al. (1995) included a broader set of influence tactics, all three intermediate linkages (i.e. supervisor affect, perceived competence, and perceived similarity to supervisor), and tangible outcomes (i.e. promotions and salary increases), finding that reasoning, favor-doing, and assertiveness positively influenced, and bargaining negatively influenced, human resources decisions through managers' perceptions of subordinate skills, competence, and similarity to the subordinate. Thus, not all influence tactics are similarly perceived or equally effective (Kipnis and Schmidt, 1988).

These research streams are conceptually based on the influence typology described in Kipnis et al. (1980). Other research has suggested that influence tactics beyond this typology may also be used. For example, goal setting can be used to influence the impressions supervisors have of the subordinate, resulting in higher performance ratings. In this regard, Frink (1995) identified self-set goals. In another study, Greenberg (1985) found a positive relationship between self-handicapping (i.e. enhancing the ability to externalize failure by setting unattainable goals) and performance when the performance was relevant to participants' self-image and not contingent on individual inputs. These are examples of early studies in this area, and the relevant linkages have not been fully delineated. It may be that subordinates believe that self-set goals influence supervisor perceptions of subordinate competence and motivation.

Supervisor/Rater Influence Tactics

While the majority of literature concerns the subordinate/ratees' use of impression management, there is also ample reason and opportunity for supervisor/raters to employ impression management strategies in the performance evaluation process. Longenecker et al. (1987) described several alternative political and impression management activities within their sample of business executives. Some of the reasons that supervisor/raters may use influence tactics include maintaining or elevating personal status or rewards by having a highly rated work group, retaining good employees by under-rating their performance, losing poor or unfavored employees by over-rating their performance, rewarding or encouraging improvements, sending signals to subordinates about what the supervisor deems important and unimportant, and so forth (see also Ferris et al., 1991; Ferris and King, 1991; Martocchio and Ferris, 1991; Villanova and Bernardin, 1991).

Conclusion

While the greater portion of performance evaluation theory and research is directed toward measurement issues, the importance of research on influence tactics in performance evaluation is increasingly recognized as a component of the larger focus of social contexts of human resources decisions. This focus is a vital part of human resource management and human resources research (Ferris and Mitchell, 1987).

Bibliography

Ferris, G. R. & Judge, T. A. (1991). Personnel/human resources management: a political influence perspective. *Journal of Management*, 17, 447–88.
Ferris, G. R., Judge, T. A., Chachere, J. G. & Liden, R. C. (1991). The age context of performance-evaluation decisions. *Psychology and Aging*, 6, 622–6.
Ferris, G. R., Judge, T. A., Rowland, K. M. & Fitzgibbons, D. E. (1994). Subordinate influence and the performance evaluation process: test of a model. *Organizational Behavior and Human Decision Processes*, 58, 101–35.
Ferris, G. R. & King, T. R. (1991). The politics of age discrimination in organizations. *Journal of Business Ethics*, 11, 341–50.
Ferris, G. R. & Mitchell, T. R. (1987). The components of social influence and their importance for human resources research. *Research in Personnel and Human Resources Management*, Eds. Rowland, K. M. & Ferris, G. R. (eds), 5.

Ferris, G. R., Russ, G. S. & Fandt, P. M. (1989). Politics in organizations. *Impression Management in the Organization*, Eds. Giacalone, R. A. & Rosenfeld, P. Hillsdale, NJ: Lawrence Erlbaum.
Frink, D. D. (1995). Accountability, impression management, and goal setting in the performance evaluation process (paper presented at the Academy of Management, 55th Annual National Meeting, Vancouver, British Columbia).
Greenberg, J. (1985). Unattainable goal as a self-handicapping strategy. *Journal of Applied Social Psychology*, 15, 87–101.
Kipnis, D. & Schmidt, S. M. (1988). Upward influence styles: Relationship with performance evaluations, salary, and stress. *Administrative Science Quarterly*, 33, 528–42.
Kipnis, D., Schmidt, S. M. & Wilkinson, I. (1980). Intraorganizational influence tactics: explorations in getting one's way. *Journal of Applied Psychology*, 65, 440–52.
Longenecker, C. O., Sims, H. P. Jr & Gioia, D. A. (1987). Behind the mask: the politics of employee appraisal. *Academy of Management Executive*, 1, 313–23.
Martocchio, J. J. & Ferris, G. R. (1991). Performance evaluation in high technology firms: a political perspective. *Journal of High Technology Management Research*, 2, 83–97.
Villanova, P. & Bernardin, H. J. (1991). Performance appraisal: the means, motive, and opportunity to manage impressions. *Applied Impression Management: How Image-making Affects Managerial Decisions* Eds. Giacalone, R. A. & Rosenfeld, P. Newbury Park, CA: Sage Publications.
Wayne, S. J., Graf, I. K. & Ferris, G. R. (1995). The role of employee influence tactics in human resources decisions (paper presented at the Academy of Management, 55th Annual National Meeting, Vancouver, British Columbia).

GERALD R. FERRIS and DWIGHT D. FRINK

information concepts Processing, delivering, and communicating information are essential objectives of the management information system of an organization. The system employs information and communications technology in achieving these objectives. The concept of information is therefore fundamental to the design of an information system.

In the context of information systems, information is data that have been processed into a form that is meaningful to the recipient and is of real or perceived value in current or prospective actions or decisions. Underlying the use of the term are several ideas: information adds to a representation, corrects or confirms previous information, or has "surprise" value in that it tells something the receiver did not know or could not predict. Information reduces uncertainty. It has value in the decision-making process in that it changes the probabilities attached to expected outcomes in a decision situation. It has value in motivation and building expertise about the organization and its processes and values.

The relation of data to information is that of raw material to finished product. An information-processing system processes data into information. Information for one person may be raw data for another. For example, shipping orders are information for the shipping room staff, but they are raw data for the vice president in charge of inventory. Because of this relationship between data and information, the two words are often used interchangeably.

Information resources are reusable. When information is retrieved and used, it does not lose value; in fact, it may gain value through the credibility added by use. This characteristic of stored data makes it different from other resources. Since management information systems deal with information, it would be useful to be able to measure the information provided by the systems and how much comes from informal information channels. There is no adequate method for measuring the information provided by an information system. However, several concepts are useful in understanding the nature and value of information in organizations. These are (a) information theory; (b) message reduction concepts; (c) information quality; (d) the value of information in decision-making; and (e) the non-decision value of information.

Information Theory

The term "information theory" refers to a mathematical theory of communication. The theory has direct application in electronic communication systems. It focuses primarily on the technical level of accuracy in information communication. It is limited in its practical application to management information systems, but it does provide useful insights into the nature of information.

Information theory was formulated by Norbert Weiner, a well-known mathematician, in connection with the development of a concept that any organism is held together by the possession of means for acquisition, use, retention, and transmission of information. Claude Shannon of Bell Laboratories developed and applied these concepts to explain telephone and other communications systems.

The purpose of a communication system is to reproduce at the destination a message selected at the source. A transmitter provides coded symbols to be sent through a channel to a receiver. The message that comes from a source to the transmitter is generally encoded there before it can be sent through the communications channel and must be decoded by a receiver before it can be understood by the destination. The channel is not usually a perfect conduit for the coded message because of noise and distortion. Distortion is caused by a known (even intentional) operation and can be corrected by an inverse operation. Noise is random or unpredictable interference.

As used in the mathematical theory of communication, information has a very precise meaning. It is the average number of binary digits that must be transmitted to identify a given message from the set of all possible messages to which it belongs. If there is a limited number of possible messages that may need to be transmitted, it is possible to devise a different code to identify each message. The message to be transmitted is encoded, the codes are sent over the channel, and the decoder identifies the message intended by the codes. Messages can be defined in a variety of ways. For example, each alphanumeric character may be a message, or complete sentences may be messages if there is a limited, predefined number of possible sentences to be transmitted. The size of the code is dependent on the coding scheme and the number of possible messages. The coding scheme for information theory is assumed to be binary (only 0 or 1 as values).

The information content (or code size in bits) may be generalized as:

$$I = \log_2 n$$

where n = the total number of possible messages, all equally likely. Some examples for a message selected from 8, 2, 1 or 27 possible messages illustrate the formula. If there are eight messages, a code with only three bits can be sent to distinguish among them, i.e. there are three combinations of 0s and 1s in three bits ($n = 8$, $I = \log_2 8 = 3$). If there are only two outcomes, a single bit (0 or 1) value can identify which of the two is intended ($n = 2$, $I = \log_2 2 = 1$). If there is only one message to select from, there is no need to transmit anything because the answer is already known by the receiver ($n = 1$, $I = \log_2 1 = 0$).

If the set of messages is the alphabet plus a space symbol, the number of bits required will average 4.75 per letter, assuming all letters to be equally probable ($n = 27$, $I = \log_2 27 = 4.75$). However, all letters are not equally probable. The probability of an A is 0.0642 but for J is 0.0008. When probabilities are unequal, the average information content is computed by the following formula:

$$I = \sum_{i=1}^{n} p_i \log_2 \frac{1}{p_i}$$

A computationally equivalent form is

$$I = \frac{-\sum_{i=1}^{n} p_i \log_2 p_i}{}$$

A communication is rarely if ever completely composed of information. There are usually redundant elements. Redundancy reduces the efficiency of a particular transmission because more codes are transmitted than are strictly required to encode the message. However, some redundancy is very useful for error control purposes. A message may not be received as sent because of noise in the communication channel. The transmission of redundant data allows the receiver to check whether the received message is correct and may allow the original message to be reconstructed.

Message Reduction Concepts

The mathematical theory of communication deals with the information content of messages that are assumed to be objective. However, the richness of language by which humans communicate, and the constraints on humans and organizations as information processors, means that humans typically receive too much information, and the interpretation of received messages are subject to misunderstanding. Information concepts for information systems therefore also include concepts of message reduction, either by sending or receiving efficiency or by selective distribution.

Two methods for reducing the quantity of information are summarization and message routing. Within organizations, message summarization is commonly utilized to reduce the amount of data provided without changing the essential meaning. Formal summarization is illustrated by accounting classifications. The president of an organization cannot normally review each sale to get information for decisions. Instead, the accounting system summarizes all sales into a "sales for the period" total. The system may provide more meaningful information for decision purposes by summarizing sales by product group, geographical area, or other classification. The level of summarization is dependent on the organizational level of the decision-maker. For example, the president may need only the total sales by area, but the sales manager for the area may need sales by sales representative and sales by product.

In *message routing*, there is a reduction in communication volume by distributing messages only to those individuals or organizational units that require the information for some action or decision. This is illustrated by the transmission of copies of purchase orders to only those departments (production, distribution, billing) that take direct action based on the information on the order. The efficiency of message routing is often thwarted by individuals who have little or no use for information but require their own record of it "just in case."

In addition to message routing, individuals or organizational units exercise some discretion over the content and distribution of messages to control their workloads, to control distribution that may have perceived undesirable effects to the individual or unit handling the message, or as part of a presentation format. Messages may be delayed, modified, or filtered before being sent to a recipient. For example, customer complaints may be delayed, modified, or filtered as the information moves up the organization. Serious indicators of customer dissatisfaction may be blocked.

The way that data are presented will influence or bias the way it is used and the interpretation of its meaning. Three examples of presentation bias are (a) order and grouping in the presentation; (b) exception selection limits; and (c) selection of graphics layout. Order and grouping of data influence the perception of importance and affect the comparisons a user is likely to make. The selection of exceptions to be reported also causes presentation bias. In exception reporting, only those items that vary from an "acceptable level" by a fixed deviation are presented to the decision-maker. The choice of a limit automatically introduces presentation bias. A third example of potential presentation bias is the layout of graphics. Examples of ways in which bias is introduced are choice of scale, graphic, size, and color.

Information Quality

Even if information is presented in such a way as to be transmitted efficiently and interpreted correctly, it may not be used effectively. The quality of information is determined by how it motivates human action and contributes to effective decision-making. Andrus (1971) suggests that information may be evaluated in terms of utilities that, besides accuracy of the information, may facilitate or retard its use.

1 *Form utility*. As the form of information more closely matches the requirements of the decision-maker, its value increases.
2 *Time utility*. Information has greater value to the decision-maker if it is available when needed.
3 *Place utility* (physical accessibility). Information has greater value if it can be accessed or delivered easily.
4 *Possession utility* (organizational location). The possessor of information strongly affects its value by controlling its dissemination to others.

Given a choice, managers have a strong preference for improvement in quality of information over an increase in quantity. Information varies in quality because of bias or errors. If the bias of the presenter is known to the receiver of the information, he or she can make adjustments. The problem is to detect the bias; the adjustment is generally fairly simple.

Error is a more serious problem because there is no simple adjustment for it. Errors may be a result of incorrect data measurement and collection methods, failure to follow correct processing procedures, loss or nonprocessing of data, wrong recording or correcting of data, use of wrong stored data, mistakes in processing procedure (such as computer program errors), and deliberate falsification.

The difficulties due to bias may be handled in information processing by procedures to detect and measure bias and to adjust for it. The difficulties with errors may be overcome by controls to detect errors, internal and external auditing, adding of "confidence limits" to data, and user instruction in measurement and processing procedures, so they can evaluate possible errors in information.

Value of Information in Decision-making

In decision theory, the value of information is the value of the change in decision behavior caused by the information less the cost of obtaining the information. In other words, given a set of possible decisions, a decision-maker will select one on the basis of the information at hand. If new information causes a different decision to be made, the value of the new information is the difference in value between the outcome of the old decision and that of the new decision, less the cost of obtaining the new information. If new information does not cause a different decision to be made, the value of the new information is zero.

The value of perfect information is computed as the difference between the optimal policy without perfect information and the optimal policy with perfect information. Almost no decisions are made with perfect information because obtaining it would require being able to foresee or control future events. The concept of the value of perfect information is useful, however, because it demonstrates how information has value as it influences (i.e. changes) decisions. The value of information for more than one condition is the difference between the maximum value in the absence of additional information and the maximum expected value with additional information, minus the cost of obtaining it. The maximum expected value can change by a change either in the probabilities for the conditions or in the payoffs associated with them.

The quantitative approach suggests the value of searching for better information, but decisions are usually made without the "right" information. Some reasons are that the needed information is unavailable, acquiring the information is too great an effort or too costly, there is no knowledge of the availability of the information, and the information is not available in the form needed.

Non-decision Value of Information

If the value of information were based only on identified decisions, much of the data that organizations and individuals prepare would not have value. Since the market for information suggests that it does have value, there are other values of information such as motivation, model building, and background building.

Some information is motivational; it provides the persons receiving the information with a report on how well they are doing. This feedback information may motivate decisions, but its connection is often indirect.

The information may reinforce an existing understanding or model of the organization. It may provide comforting confirmation that results are within allowable limits. It also aids in learning as individuals receive feedback on the consequences of actions.

The management and operation of an enterprise function with models of the enterprise within the minds of the managers and operations personnel. The models may be simple or complex, correct or incorrect. Information that is received by these individuals may result in change or reinforcement in their mental models. This process is a form of organizational learning and expertise building. Since the models are used in problem-finding, a change in the models will have an influence on identification of problems. The information also communicates organization values and culture, thereby providing a frame of reference for future decisions.

In decision theory, the value of information is the value of the change in decision behavior (less its cost), but the information has value only to those who have the background knowledge to use it in a decision. The most qualified person generally uses information most effectively but may need less information since experience has already reduced uncertainty when compared with the less-experienced decision-maker. Thus, the more-experienced decision-maker may make the same decision for less cost, or a better decision for the same cost, as the less-experienced person. The value of the specific information utilized in a decision cannot be easily separated from the accumulated knowledge of the decision-maker. In other words, much of the knowledge that individuals accumulate and store (or internalize) is not earmarked for any particular decision or problem. A set of accumulated knowledge allows a person to make a better decision, or the same decision at less immediate cost, than one who lacks this expertise.

Application of Information Concepts to Information Systems
Information theory, although limited in scope, provides useful insights about the surprise value and uncertainty reduction features of some information. It emphasizes the value of information in changing decisions. The idea that information has value only in that it alters a decision provides a useful guideline for parsimony of information. A common mistake in information system design is to produce volumes of data in the form of reports because they are easy to produce. In many cases, the actual value of the additional information is zero.

The theory explains that not all communications have information value, but there is value in redundancy for error control. In management information systems, there is substantial noise in the information being communicated due to the unknown but differing backgrounds of humans, their differing frames of reference, varying prejudices, varying levels of attention, physical differences in ability to hear and see, and other random causes. Redundancy can be effectively used to overcome noise and improve the probability of messages being received and interpreted correctly.

Concepts of message reduction suggest ways to improve sending and receiving efficiency and reduce bias. Summarization and message routing reduce information being communicated. Filtering, inference by use of statistics, and presentation choices may improve efficiency but may also introduce bias. The quality of information received is not directly measurable. However, design can focus on achieving utilities associated with information and on processes to reduce bias and errors.

In decision theory, information is associated with uncertainty because there is a choice to be made and the correct choice is uncertain. The reason for obtaining information is to reduce uncertainty so the correct choice can be made. If there were no uncertainty, there would be no need for information to influence choice. Information received will modify the choice by altering the subjective estimate of the probability of success. The decision theory approach focuses the attention of the information system designer not only on the value of information in decision-making but also on the fact that the cost of obtaining more information may not be worthwhile.

Much data are received and stored without reference to decisions being made. However, the data is meaningful to the recipient and is of real or perceived value in current or prospective decisions. It has value in building mental models and expertise that will be useful in future analysis and decision-making.

Bibliography

Andrus, R. R. (1971). Approaches to information evaluation. *MSU Business Topics*, Summer, 4046.

Cherry, C. (1957). *On Human Communication*. Cambridge, MA: MIT Press.

Gilbert, E. N. (1966). Information theory after eighteen years. *Science*, **152**, 320.

Shannon, C. E. & Weaver, W. (1962). *The Mathematical Theory of Communication*. Urbana, IL: University of Illinois Press.

Weiner, N. (1948). *Cybernetics, or Control and Communication in the Animal and the Machine*. New York: Wiley.

GORDON B. DAVIS

information content of accounting numbers A key function of financial markets is to filter information and coordinate the allocation of economic resources. In this setting, information is anything that causes economic agents to revise their beliefs about the future returns from the assets traded in financial markets. In well-functioning markets, economic agents condition their demands for financial markets. In well-functioning markets, economic agents condition their demands for financial assets on their available information (which will include asset prices). Equilibrium prices, through a process of balancing demands with supplies, impound this information. If asset prices change to reflect the latest information, they will direct resources to their most efficient use.

Participants in financial markets gather information about the value of firms from various sources. Some information comes from the activities of individual investors and financial analysts generating private information. Other information comes from public releases by firms themselves. Firms communicate with financial markets through a complex set of formal and informal channels. When management have information about the firm that outside investors do not have, any action by management, e.g., to raise new capital, can signal information about firm value to the market. However, the most visible and regular form of communication by firms to financial markets is the public disclosure of accounting numbers contained in financial statements.

Studies of the information content of accounting numbers investigate the relation between accounting numbers and asset prices or returns. This area of largely empirical research has formed a major part of the agenda of market-based accounting research, otherwise known as capital market research in accounting, over the last thirty years.

We can define a formal test of information content of some accounting number(s), Y_i, from a financial reporting system or generally accepted accounting principles (GAAP) regime, in the general form of null and alternative hypotheses. In the following definition, $f(\tilde{R}_j | y_i)$ is the distribution of asset j's return conditional on available information that includes the accounting number(s) of interest. The corresponding marginal distribution, $f(\tilde{R}_j)$, is conditional on available information excluding the accounting number(s) of interest.

H_N: $f(\tilde{R}_j | y_i) - f(\tilde{R}_j) = 0$ for all $y_i [\, Z,$

H_A: $f(\tilde{R}_j | y_i) - f(\tilde{R}_j) \, i \, 0$ for at least one $y_i [\, Z.$

This definition accommodates the effect on any parameter of the return distribution, including mean, volatility, skewness, etc. It also accommodates any potentially affected financial asset, from the equity stock of the disclosing firm itself, the firm's bonds or other securities, options written on the firm's securities, through to stocks of other firms. However, because the focus is on traded securities and market prices, traditional tests have not examined the information content of accounting numbers for stakeholders with a nontraded claim on the firm.

Most information content studies have examined the effect of an accounting disclosure by a firm on the mean of the firm's return distribution. Here, the alternative hypothesis would state that for the firm's accounting number y_i to possess information content, the firm's unexpected return conditional on y_i must be non-zero. In some studies this requires separate classification of "good news" and "bad news" information signals, y_i. There are also several studies that have investigated the effect on return volatility or variance of announcements of accounting numbers. If accounting numbers have information content, asset price changes, and therefore returns, should be greater in announcement periods than nonannouncement periods. Tests based on return variability may avoid the need for classifying news.

One of the first and most famous pieces of published academic research on the information content of accounting numbers was Ball & Brown (1968). This study offered a rigorous examination of the relation between accounting earnings and stock returns. The study was motivated as a response to accusations that accounting numbers, and earnings in particular, were worthless to investors trying to value firms and were ignored by financial markets. Contrary to popular belief, Ball & Brown found that the information content of earnings numbers, given by the contemporaneous association between earnings changes and a measure of firm-specific stock price change over the period, was considerable. They also found strong evidence of the market anticipating the accounting numbers to be released, suggesting the public disclosure date is not timely,

and weaker evidence of a delayed response to at least part of the public disclosure. For a personal account of the story of Ball & Brown (1968) and subsequent developments (see Ball, 1989).

Many studies following Ball & Brown, using increasingly sophisticated research designs, have confirmed the link between earnings and stock returns. Researchers have consistently found statistically significant *earnings response coefficients* – measuring the effect on stock returns of one unit of unexpected earnings – across alternate samples, periods, research designs, and countries. Subsequent landmarks in this literature are Beaver et al. (1980) and Kormendi & Lipe (1987). Lev (1989) caused a brief pause in this research in suggesting that the explanatory power of earnings for stock returns, and therefore the usefulness of earnings disclosures, was embarrassingly low. Active research areas now include more detailed examination of market anticipation of accounting numbers, their value-relevance, and whether the market responds rationally to accounting numbers. Work of Ohlson (see, for example, Ohlson, 1995), which provides a clearer theoretical link between value and accounting numbers, has stimulated further research.

Research has also investigated the information content of accounting numbers besides historic cost earnings. Much of this has examined the *incremental information content* (IIC) of accounting numbers – their additional information content after controlling for the information in other accounting numbers. The IIC of components of earnings over the bottom line earnings figure would be an example. Evidence on the IIC of cash flows and accruals over earnings is mixed. Similar mixed evidence comes from studies on the IIC of current cost disclosures over historic cost earnings. A major problem in tests of IIC is in hypothesizing the effect of the information. Are higher accruals good news or bad news, or good for some firms bad for others? Later, more sophisticated research designs, specifically addressing this issue, have found IIC that earlier studies failed to detect (see, for example, Ali, 1994).

Future work on information content of accounting numbers is likely to require more detailed theoretical work on *fundamental analysis* – the link between firm value and accounting numbers – and on the time-series properties of accounting numbers. To test and interpret information content of accounting numbers, researchers will need to understand better the context of individual firms' operating and reporting environments. Comparative international studies offer the challenge of examining alternative dimensions of the issue.

Bibliography

Ali, A. (1994). The incremental information content of earnings, working capital from operations, and cash flows. *Journal of Accounting Research*, 32, Spring, 61–74.

Ball, R. (1989). [Ball & Brown, 1968] *Journal of Accounting Research*, 27, (supplement), 202–17.

Ball, R. & Brown, P. (1968). An empirical evaluation of accounting income numbers. *Journal of Accounting Research*, 6, Autumn, 159–78.

Beaver, W. H., Lambert, R. A. & Morse, D. (1980). The information content of security prices. *Journal of Accounting and Economics*, 2, June, 3–28.

Kormendi, R. C. & Lipe, R. (1987). Earnings innovations, earnings persistence, and stock returns. *Journal of Business*, 60, July, 323–46.

Lev, B. (1989). On the usefulness of earnings and earnings research: Lessons and directions from two decades of empirical research. *Journal of Accounting Research*, 27, (supplement), 153–92.

Ohlson, J. (1995). Earnings, book value, and dividends in security valuation. *Contemporary Accounting Research* Spring.

NORMAN C. STRONG

information systems, strategic use of Recent years have seen a change in the role of information systems (IS) from that of support for business operations to a potential weapon to gain strategic advantage. Whereas in the past the value of information systems was seen as resulting from their ability to automate routine processes and transactions, it is now recognized that through their potential to inform and innovate, organizations who adopt and use information systems wisely can gain both a short- and long-term competitive edge.

A well-known example is the introduction by American Airlines of SABRE, a computerized reservation system which has both changed the basis of competition in the airline industry and served as a source of competitive advantage for the airline itself. SABRE was the first on-line reservation system to be developed, and was used by 48 per cent of travel agents in the USA. Its function was primarily to list flight availability, fares, and times, but it also provided a whole range of further information, such as baggage tracking and control, hotel reservations, and crew scheduling. In addition to listing its own flights, the system also listed flights offered by rival airlines. However, American's own flights were displayed first, thus making it more likely that the travel agent would book a passenger on American Airlines than on another airline. So effective was this strategy that other airlines felt the system to be providing American Airlines with an unfair advantage and anti-trust suits followed. The result of these actions was to permit American Airlines to charge other carriers for use of its system. By charging $1.75 for every reservation made through SABRE, of $400 mllion pretax profits on $5.3 billion sales revenue made in 1984, SABRE earned $170 million pretax profits on $338 million reservation revenues.

Examples such as the success of SABRE have encouraged organizations to consider whether there is a potential for them to harness the power of systems to leapfrog the competition, develop new markets, and increase profitability. The approach being adopted by these companies is to try to align the technology investments more closely with the company's business goals. In some instances this requires a complete re-thinking of the business, the processes, and the particular employee skills required, as well as gaining an understanding of the potential of the new technology. A central issue is how organizations identify the factors that will enable them to maximize the technological potential. In recent years a number of characteristics associated with the strategic use of information systems have been highlighted (Ward, 1992), the most pertinent of which are as follows:

The ability of the system to link an organization more closely to its customers or suppliers. Organizations who are successful with IS are those who link their systems together along the value chain most effectively and integrate the information into the organization's value adding process (Porter & Miller, 1985). Consider, for example, the Economost system developed by the McKesson Corporation. McKesson is a wholesale distributor of drugs to independent pharmaceutical outlets. It provided its customers with portable data-collection devices to check and control inventory, automatically process orders, and schedule shipments. Order data were transmitted to McKesson's computer and assembled orders were packed and delivered in a sequence that reflected the arrangement in which the merchandise was packed on the shelves in the customer's store. If a customer ordered their merchandise from another supplier this upset the inventory control system, thus creating additional work and incurring cost. McKesson also provided a claims service for customers of the drug stores. Many of the customers had their prescription purchases covered by medical insurance programs. McKesson provided a plastic identification card for these customers, so that when purchasing prescription drugs they were required to pay only a nominal amount toward the price of the prescription. The remainder of the payment was claimed through McKesson. Because this service was free it encouraged customers to return to the same drugstore. Over a ten-year period following the introduction of Economost, sales increased at McKesson from $900 million to $5 billion. Automation enabled the company to reduce warehouse staff from 130 to 54, eliminate 500 clerical jobs, and reduce merchandise buyers from 140 to 12. The average order size increased from $4,000 per month to $12,000 per month.

The ability of the system to provide information that enables strategic decisions to be made – to know where, when, and how to obtain critical information. Benetton, the largest purchaser of wool in the world, avoids stockpiling by obtaining information on demand for its products from the point of sale systems in its franchised outlets.

The ability of the system to enable an organization to develop new products. Merrill Lynch used information systems to provide a cash management account which combined separate financial products such as cheques, charge cards, and brokerage services into a single product, with the customer's idle funds being immediately transferred into interest-bearing accounts. While Merrill Lynch provided the brokerage facilities, they collaborated with Banc One to provide the necessary banking facilities. Within the first year of its introduction the cash management account attracted $1 billion in assets. Within six years there were 400,000 new accounts in place and the managed assets totaled $85 billion.

As in other areas, the strategic advantages gained by information systems are typically short-lived. What is today's competitive advantage becomes tomorrow's competitive necessity, and continuing enhancements and upgrading of systems is required to stay ahead. However, as companies move toward implementing global strategies the need for information systems development increases. Information itself is a key resource that requires effective support and full-time management. The companies that will succeed in the increasingly global markets will be those whose information systems investments enable access to relevant information in timely and accurate ways.

Bibliography

Porter, M. E. & Miller, V. E. (1985). How information gives you competitive advantage. *Harvard Business Review,* **63** (4) (July–August), 149–60.

Ward, J., Griffiths, P. & Whitmore, P. (1992). *Strategic planning for information systems.* Chichester: John Wiley.

BENITA COX

initial public offerings (IPOs) In contrast to a seasoned offering, an IPO is the offering of shares of a company that are not publicly traded. The most common are IPOs of fixed-income securities, equity securities, warrants, and a combination of equity shares and warrants ("units"). The term IPO is often used to refer only to equity or unit offerings, and the remainder of this entry concentrates only on equity and unit offerings in the United States.

In "best-effort" IPOs, underwriters act only as the issuer's agent; in "firm-commitment" IPOs, underwriters purchase all shares from the issuer and sell them as principal. In the USA, virtually all IPOs by reputable underwriters are sold as firm commitment. Other special IPO categories are (domestic tranches of) international IPOs, reverse leveraged buyouts (where company shares had been traded in the past), real estate investment trusts (REITs), closed-end funds, and venture-capital backed IPOs, etc. Most IPOs begin trading on Nasdaq.

Most IPOs typically allow a company founder to begin to "cash out" (secondary shares), or begin to raise capital for expansion (primary shares), or both. (Issuers sometimes constrain shares granted to insiders from sale for a significant amount of time after the IPO in order to raise outside demand.) Direct underwriter fees and expenses of the IPO typically range from 7–20 percent (mean of about 15 percent). Auditor fees range from US$0–80,000 (mean of about US$50,000), lawyer fees from US$0–130,000 (mean of about US$75,000). In addition, issuers must consider the cost of warrants typically granted to the underwriter, a three- to six-month duration to prepare for the IPO, the costs and time of management involvement, prospectus printing costs, and subsequent public release requirements. Consequently, many firms avoid IPOs despite the advantages and prestige of a public listing, relying instead on private or venture capital, banks, trade credit, leases, and other funding sources. Even IPO issuers tend to issue only a small fraction of the firm, and return to the market for a seasoned offering relatively quickly.

In the USA, numerous federal, state, and NASD issuing regulations have attempted to curtail fraud and/or unfair treatment of investors. Among the more important rules, in section 11 of the 1993 Securities Act, the SEC describes necessary disclosure in the IPO prospectus. Issuers are required to disclose all relevant, possibly adverse information. Failure to do so leaves not only the issuer, but also the underwriter, auditor, and any other experts listed in the prospectus liable. The SEC rules prohibit marketing or sales of the IPO before the official offering date, although it will allow the underwriter to go on roadshows and disseminate a "preliminary prospectus" (called "red herring"). Further, underwriters must offer an almost fixed number of shares at a fixed price, usually determined the morning of the IPO. (Up to a 15 percent over-allotment ("green shoe") option allows some flexibility in the number of shares.) Once public, the price or number of shares sold must not be raised even when after-market demand turns out better than expected. Interestingly, although US underwriters are not permitted to "manipulate" the market, they are allowed to engage in IPO after-market "stabilization" trading for thirty days.

Some countries (such as France) allow different selling mechanisms such as auctions. Other countries (such as Singapore), do not allow the underwriter the discretion to allocate shares to preferred customers, but instead require proportional allocation among all interested bidders.

There are two outstanding empirical regularities in the IPO market that have been documented both in US and a number of foreign markets: on average, IPOs see a dramatic one-day rise from the offer price to the first aftermarket price (a 5–15 percent mean in the USA) and a slow but steady long-term underperformance relative to equivalent firms (a 5–7 percent per annum mean for three to five years after the issue for 1975–84 US IPOs). Prominent explanations for the former regularity, typically referred to as "IPO underpricing," have ranged from the winner's curse (in which investors require average underpricing because they receive a relatively greater allocation of shares when the IPO is overpriced), to cascades (in which issuers underprice to eliminate the possibility of cascading desertions especially of institutional investors), to signaling (in which issuers underprice to "leave a good taste in investors' mouths" in anticipation of a seasoned equity offering), to insurance against future liability (to reduce the probability of subsequent class action suits if the stock price drops), to preselling (where underpricing is necessary to obtain demand information from potential buyers). The consensus among researchers and practitioners is that each theory describes some aspect of the IPO market. Empirical findings related to IPO underpricing also abound. For example, IPOs of riskier offerings and IPOs by smaller underwriters tend to be more underpriced, and both IPOs and IPO underpricing are known to occur in "waves" (while 1972 and 1983 saw about 500 IPOs, 1975 saw fewer than 10 IPOs; 1991–94 saw about 500 IPOs per year). Noteworthy is the hot market of 1981, which saw an average underpricing in excess of 200 percent among natural resource offerings.

Table 1 Total Firm Commitments IPOs

	REITs	*Closed-end funds*	*ADRs*	*Reverse LBO*	*Other IPOs*
1990	0	41	6	13	204
1991	1	37	12	81	405
1992	5	88	35	102	602
1993	44	114	59	68	865
1994	35	39	62	30	638

Explanations for the long-term underperformance have yet to be found. This poor performance is concentrated primarily among very young, smaller IPO firms. (Indeed, IPOs of financial institutions and some other industries have significantly outperformed their non-IPO benchmarks.) Many of the smaller IPO firms are highly illiquid and thus more difficult to short, preventing sophisticated arbitrageurs from eliminating the underperformance.

Because once the IPO has passed, shares of IPOs are tradeable, like other securities, the long-run underperformance of IPOs presents first and foremost a challenge to proponents of specific equilibrium pricing models and efficient stock markets.

Other theoretical and empirical work among IPO firms has concentrated on the role of the expert advisors and venture capitalists in the IPO, subsequent dividend payouts and seasoned equity offerings, institutional ownership, etc. Information on current IPOs is regularly published in the *Wall Street Journal*, the *IPO Reporter, Investment Dealers Digest*, and elsewhere. Securities Data Corp maintains an extensive data base of historical IPOs. Institutional and legal details on the IPO procedure can be found in Schneider et al. (1981).

Bibliography

Beatty, R. & Welch, I. (1995). Legal liability and issuer expenses in initial public offerings. *The Journal of Law and Economics.*

Benveniste, L. M. & Spindt, P. A. (1989). How investment bankers determine the offer price and allocation of new issues. *Journal of Financial Economics*, 24, 343–62.

Drake, P. D. & Vetsuypens, M. R. (1993). IPO underpricing and insurance against legal liability. *Financial Management*, 22, 64–73.

Ibbotson, R., Sindelar, J. & Ritter, J. (1994). The market's problems with the pricing of initial public offerings. *Journal of Applied Corporate Finance*, 7, 66–74.

Loughran T., Ritter J. & Rydqvist, K. (1994). Initial public offerings: international insights. *Pacific-Basin Finance Journal*, 2, 165–99.

Loughran, T. & Ritter, J. R. (1995). The new issues puzzle. *Journal of Finance*, 50, 23–51.

Ritter, J. R. (1984). The "hot issue" market of 1980. *Journal of Business*, 57, 215–40.

Ritter, J. R. (1987). The costs of going public. *Journal of Financial Economics*, 19, 269–82.

Rock, K. (1986). Why new issues are underpriced. *Journal of Financial Economics*, 15, 187–212.

Schneider, C., Manko, J. & Kant, R. (1981). Going public: practice, procedure and consequence. *The Villanova Law Review*, 27.

Welch, Ivo (1989). Seasoned offerings, imitation costs, and the underpricing of initial public offerings. *Journal of Finance*, 44, 421–50.

Welch, Ivo (1992). Sequential sales, learning, and cascades. *Journal of Finance*, 47, 695–732.

IVO WELCH

innovation   Few subjects have received as much attention from social scientists, managers, and public policy makers as innovation. It is the engine for novel changes in social, economic, and political arrangements in organizations and society as a whole (*see* ORGANIZATIONAL CHANGE). An innovation is the creation and implementation of a new idea. The new idea may pertain to a technological innovation (new technical artifacts, devices, or products), a process innovation (new services, programs, or production procedures), or an administrative innovation (new institutional policies, structures, or systems). The idea may be a novel recombination of old ideas, a scheme that challenges the present order, or an unprecedented formula or approach (Zaltman, Duncan, & Holbek, 1973). As long as the idea is perceived as new and entails a novel change for the actors involved, it is an innovation. When the actors who develop and implement the new idea are members or groups of an organization, the venture is considered an organizational innovation or an internal corporate venture, in contrast to efforts undertaken by independent individuals (ENTREPRENEURSHIP), or by organizations working collectively.

Innovations can vary widely in novelty, size, and temporal duration. Some innovations involve small, quick, incremental, lone-worker efforts. Some are unplanned, and emerge by chance, accident, or afterthought. Although the majority of innovations in organizations may be of small scope, larger scale innovations have attracted most attention from practitioners and researches. In particular, the scope of innovations discussed below are those in which most managers and venture capitalists typically invest. They consist of planned, concentrated efforts to develop and implement a novel idea in a climate of substantial technical, organizational, and market UNCERTAINTY; entailing a collective effort of considerable duration; and requiring greater resources than are held by the people undertaking the effort.

Studies of organizational innovation tend to examine two kinds of questions:

(1) What are the antecedent factors? and
(2) How are innovations created, developed and implemented?

The first question usually entails study of the contextual factors (independent variables) which explain statistically variations in the number and kinds of organizational innovations introduced in a given period of time (the dependent variable). The second question involves processual study of the temporal order and sequence of events which unfold in the development of a given innovation. A brief overview of research on these two questions is described below.

Factors Influencing Organizational Innovativeness

Tornatsky and Fleischer (1990) point out that a positive bias pervades the study of innovation. Innovation is often viewed as a good thing because the new idea must be useful – profitable, constructive, or solve a problem. New ideas that are not perceived as useful are not normally called innovations; they are usually called mistakes. Objectively, of course, the usefulness of an idea can only be determined after the innovation process is completed and implemented. Moreover, while many new ideas are proposed in organizations, only a very few receive serious consideration and developmental effort. Since it is not possible to determine at the outset which new ideas are "innovations" or "mistakes," it is important to understand what conditions motivate and enable organizational innovation.

Amabile (1983), Angle (1989), and Kanter (1983) and Tornatsky and Fleischer (1990) summarize a large body of research indicating that innovative behaviors are more likely to occur in organizational contexts that both enable and motivate innovation; it is less likely to occur where either enabling or motivating conditions are absent. The design of an organization's structure, systems, and practices influence the likelihood that innovation ideas will be surfaced, and that once surfaced they will be developed and nurtured toward realization (*see* ORGANIZATIONAL DESIGN).

Several organizational structural features are empirically related to innovative activities. The more complex and differentiated the organization, and the easier it is to cross boundaries, the greater the potential number of sources from which innovative ideas can spring. However, as Kanter (1983) discusses, organizational segmentation and bureaucratic procedures accompany increases in organizational size and complexity (*see* BUREAUCRACY). These often constrain innovation unless special systems are put in place to motivate and enable innovative behavior. Key motivating factors include providing a balance of intrinsic and extrinsic rewards for innovative behaviors. While people work for pay to make a living, incentive pay (i.e., monetary rewards contingent on performance and in addition to base salary) seems to be a relatively weak motivator for innovation; it more often serves as a proxy for recognition. Angle (1989) found that individualized rewards tend to increase idea generation and radical innovations; whereas group rewards tend to increase innovation implementation and incremental innovations.

In addition to these motivating factors, the following kinds of enabling conditions are equally necessary for innovative behavior:

- resources for innovation;
- frequent COMMUNICATIONS across departmental lines, among people with dissimilar viewpoints;
- moderate environmental uncertainty and mechanisms for focusing attention on changing conditions;
- cohesive work groups with open conflict resolution mechanisms that integrate creative personalities into the mainstream;
- structures that provide access to innovation ROLE models and mentors;
- moderately low personnel turnover; and PSYCHOLOGICAL CONTRACTS that legitimate and solicit spontaneous innovative behavior.

Angle (1989) concludes that normal people have the capability and potential to be creative and innovative. The actualization of this potential depends on whether management structures an organizational context to not only motivate but also to enable individuals to innovate.

Many innovations transcend the boundaries of individual firms, industries, and populations or communities of organizations. As a result, economics and organizational researchers have examined innovation from an augmented industry level of analysis (see Sahal, 1981). At this macro level, studies have focused on patterns of cooperation and competition among organizations developing similar, complementary or substitute innovations, as well as the roles of public and private sector actors in the development of an industrial infrastructure for innovation. This infrastructure includes:

(1) institutional arrangements that legitimate, regulate, and standardize a new innovation;
(2) public resource endowments of basic scientific knowledge, financing and insurance arrangements, and pools of competent labor; as well as
(3) proprietary R&D, testing, manufacturing, marketing, and distribution functions that are often required to develop and commercialize a technical or process innovation.

The development of this industry infrastructure significantly influences the odds of innovation success by individual organizations and entrepreneurs. This infrastructure does not emerge and change all at once through the actions of one or even a few organizational actors. Instead, it develops through an accretion of numerous events involving many public and private sector actors over an extended period of time.

The Process of Organizational Innovation

Perhaps the most widely known model of the innovation process is that proposed by Rogers (1983). It represents three decades of Rogers's own research and a synthesis of over 3100 published innovation studies. This model portrays the process of innovation as consisting of three basic stages:

(1) invention of novel idea, which comes from a recognition of market or user needs and advances in basic or applied research;
(2) its development, or the sequence of events in which the new idea is transformed from an abstract concept into an operational reality; and
(3) implementation, or the diffusion and adoption of the innovation by users.

Specialized fields of study have emerged to examine each innovation stage in greater detail. For the idea invention stage, an extensive literature has developed on individual and group CREATIVITY, primarily by psychologists (e.g., Amabile, 1983; Angle, 1989), and on "technology push" versus "demand pull" by economists (e.g., Sahal, 1981). Although less extensively studied than the other stages, the development stage is gaining more research attention from management scholars (e.g., Kanter, 1983; Tushman & Romanelli, 1985; Van de Ven, Angle, & Poole, 1989). Finally, Rogers (1983) notes that no area in the social sciences has perhaps received as much study as the implementation stage.

While a conducive organizational context sets the stage for innovation, the developmental process itself is highly uncertain, ambiguous, and risky. Van de Ven, Angle, and Poole (1989) report recent studies showing that the sequence of events in developing innovations from invention to implementation do not unfold in a simple linear sequence of stages or phases. Instead, the innovation journey tends to unfold in the following ways. In the beginning, a set of seemingly coincidental events occur in an organization which set the stage for initiating an innovation. Some of these gestating events are sufficiently large to "shock" the action thresholds of organizational participants to launch an innovative venture. Soon after work begins to develop the venture, the process proliferates from a simple unitary sequence of activities into a divergent, parallel, and convergent progression. Some of these activities are related through a division of labor among functions, but many are unrelated in any noticeable form of functional interdependence. Many component ideas and paths that were perceived as being related at one time, are often reframed or rationalized as being independent and disjunctive at another time when the innovation idea or circumstances change. Problems, mistakes, and setbacks frequently occur as these developmental paths are pursued, and they provide opportunities either for learning or for terminating the developmental efforts. The innovation journey ends either when the innovation is adopted and implemented by an organization, when resources run out, or when political opposition prevails to terminate the developmental efforts (*see* POLITICS). These messy and complex processes that are being found in recent real-time studies of innovation development are leading researchers to reconceptualize the process of innovation, because the observed processes cannot be reduced to a simple sequence of stages or phases as most process models in the literature suggest.

We may never find one best way to innovate because the innovation process is inherently probabilistic and because there are myriad forms and kinds of innovations. In particular, the characteristics of the innovation processes described above are more pronounced or more complex in innovations of greater novelty, size, and duration. Researchers have found the stages of the innovation process to be more disorderly for technically complex innovations than they are for technically simple innovations. Statistical relationships between the innovation processes and outcomes are much weaker for highly novel radical innovations than they are for less novel incremental innovations. Some organizations appear more successful in developing certain types of innovation. For example, an organization which values and rewards individualism may have the advantage in radical innovation, while a more collectivist system may do better at an incremental one. However, across these organizations differences, studies show that transitions from innovation invention to development to adoption activities often entail shifts from radical to incremental and from divergent to convergent thinking. As innovations approach the culminating institutionalization step, they become more structured and stabilized in their patterns and less differentiated from other organizational arrangements.

The developmental pattern and eventual success of an innovation is also influenced by its temporal duration. Initial investments at the startup of an innovation represents an initial stock of assets that provides an innovation unit a "honeymoon" period to perform its work. These assets reduce the risk of terminating the innovation during its honeymoon period when setbacks arise and when initial outcomes are judged unfavorable. The likelihood of replenishing these assets is highly influenced by the duration of the developmental process. Interest and COMMITMENT wane with time. Thus, after the honeymoon period, innovations terminate at disproportionately higher rates, in proportion to the time needed for their implementation.

In terms of organization size, small organizations appear to have the advantage in starting up innovations, but larger organizations with more slack resources have the advantage of keeping an innovation alive until it is completed. Larger organizations can offer a more fertile ground for sustaining and nurturing spin-off innovations. Yet, as organizations grow in size they seem to rely increasingly on bureaucratic systems and procedures that may be efficient for managing ongoing operations, but may inhibit innovative behavior. So the message to managers of large organizations is to keep finding ways to remain flexible (*see* FLEXIBILITY), to permit sufficient attention and resources to concentrate on innovation, to build access to technical competence, and to listen attentively to the views of those directly responsible for implementation – factors which Nord and Tucker (1987) found were critical success factors for adopting innovations in large organizations.

see also **Open systems; Risk analysis**

Bibliography

Amabile, T. M. (1983). The social psychology of creativity. New York: Springer-Verlag.

Angle, H. A. (1989). Psychology and Organizational Innovation Chapter 5 in A. Van de Ven, H. Angle, M. S. Poole (Eds.) Research on the management of innovation: The Minnesota studies. New York: Ballinger/Harper & Row.

Kanter, R. M. (1983). The change masters. New York: Simon and Schuster.

Nord, W. R. & Tucker S. (1987). Implementing Routine and Radical Innovations. Lexington; MA: D. C. Heath.

Rogers, E. (1983). Diffusion of innovations. (3rd edn) New York: Free Press.

Sahal, D. (1981). Patterns of technological innovation. Reading, MA: Addison-Wesley.

Tornatzky, L. G. & Fleischer M. (1990). The processes of technological innovation. Lexington, MA: D. C. Heath.

Tushman, M. & Romanelli, E. (1985). Organizational Evolution: A Metamorphosis Model of Convergence and Reorientation In B. Staw & L. Cummings (Ed.), Research in organizational behavior. (vol. 7) Greenwich, CT: JAI Press.

Van de Ven, A. H., H. Angle & M. S. Poole (eds.) (1989). Research on the Management of Innovation: The Minnesota Studies. New York: Ballinger/Harper & Row.

Zaltman, G. R., Duncan & J. Holbek (1973). Innovations and organizations. New York: Wiley.

ANDREW H. VAN DE VEN

insider trading law (US) Federal regulation of insider trading occurs through three main sources: Section 16 of the Securities Exchange Act of 1934, Securities and Exchange Commission (SEC) Rule 10b-5, and SEC Rule 14e-3. The SEC rules are enforced by both the SEC and private plaintiffs, while violations of the Securities Exchange Act are crimes that can be prosecuted by the Justice Department. Section 16 of the Securities Exchange Act of 1934 provides the most straightforward regulation of insider trading. This section requires statutorily defined insiders – officers, directors, and shareholders who own 10 percent or more of a firm's equity class – to report their registered equity holdings and transactions to the SEC. Under Section 16, insiders must disgorge to the issuer any profit received from the liquidation of shares that have been held less than six months.

The two SEC rules provide more complex regulation of insider trading. Rule 10b-5 states, in part, that "it is unlawful ... to engage in any act ... which operates as a fraud or deceit upon any person, in connection with the purchase or sale of any security." However, this Rule does not specifically define insider trading. Thus, definitions of insider trading comes from legal and SEC interpretations of Rule 10b-5.

In addressing insider trading cases, the courts have adopted two major theories of liability for illegal insider trading: the classical theory and the misappropriation theory. The "classical theory," which has been adopted by the Supreme Court, states that a person violates Rule 10b-5 if he buys or sells securities based on material non-public information while he is an insider in the corporation whose shares he trades, thus breaking a fiduciary duty to shareholders. The classical theory is also called the "fiduciary breach theory," because it concentrates on those who trade securities of a firm in breach of a duty to the shareholders of that firm. This theory is sometimes referred to as the "abstain or disclose theory," because insiders must abstain from trading on material information about their firm until that information has been disclosed.

The classical theory also states that people who trade on material non-public information provided to them by insiders are also in violation of Rule 10b-5. An example of a violation of Rule 10b-5 under the classical theory is the purchase of stock in a firm by its CEO just before the firm announces it is increasing its dividend. Since advance knowledge of a dividend increase is material information and the CEO is an insider, such trading is illegal. The second major theory of insider trading under Rule 10b-5 is the "misappropriation theory," which has not been adopted by the Supreme Court but has been adopted by most lower federal courts. The misappropriation theory was developed by the SEC to address insider trading by non-insiders. Although many people consider trading on non-public information undesirable, non-insiders who do so are not liable under the classical theory. However, under the misappropriation theory, Rule 10b-5 is violated when a person misappropriates material non-public information and breaches a duty of trust by using that information in a securities transaction, whether or not he owes a duty to the shareholders whose stock he trades. Thus, those receiving "tips" are liable, even if the provider of the tip is not an insider.

SEC Rule 14e-3 allows for prosecution of inside trading by non-insiders. This rule makes it illegal to trade around a tender offer if the trader possesses material non-public information obtained from either the bidder or the target. Thus, in the case of a tender offer, Rule 14e-3 prohibits inside trading even when no breach of duty occurs.

The penalties for violations of insider trading laws can be severe. Money damages can be up to three times the profit made on the trade, while fines can be up to a million dollars. Further criminal violations of these laws can result in jail time.

JEFFRY NETTER and PAUL SEGUIN

institutional theory   Much of the research on organizations since the 1970s focuses on the structure and composition of organizational environments (*see* ORGANIZATION AND ENVIRONMENT). In contrast to research in micro OB or corporate strategy, which stresses the efforts of individual organizations to adapt, most macro-level work maintains that ORGANIZATIONAL CHANGE is shaped largely by changes in the environment. The idea that organizations are deeply embedded in wider institutional environments suggests that organizational practices are often either direct reflections of, or responses to, rules and structures built into their larger environments. This line of institutional analysis traces its origins to research by John Meyer on the effects of education as an institution (Meyer, 1977; Meyer & Rowan, 1977); work by J. Meyer, W. R. Scott, and colleagues (Meyer & Scott, 1983) on the dependence of educational organizations on wider cultural and symbolic understandings about the nature of schooling; research by Zucker (1977; 1983) on the taken-for-granted aspects of organizational life; and work by DiMaggio and Powell (1983) on the

social construction of organizational fields. In recent years, institutional theory and research have developed rapidly and it presently represents a significant strand of work in macro OB. Substantial collections of current research (Powell & DiMaggio, 1991; Scott & Meyer, 1994) present a wide range of applications of institutional analysis to topics as diverse as differences between public and private schools, internal labor markets, art museums, the DIVERSIFICATION strategies of large corporations, and types of accounting systems.

Although ecological and institutional approaches differ markedly in the weight they assign to organization adaptation and managerial cognition, these approaches share a number of key insights. Both focus on the collective organization of the environment, insisting that the environment of organizations made up of other organizations and that processes of legitimation and competition shape organizational behavior (*see* LEGITIMACY). But ecologists attend to demographic processes – organizational foundings, transformations, and deaths (*see* POPULATION ECOLOGY). Institutionalists, in contrast, analyze the diffusion of rules and procedures that organizations are rewarded for incorporating.

Institutional theory combines a rejection of the optimizing assumptions of rational actor models popular in economics with an interest in institutions as independent variables. The constant and repetitive quality of much of organizational life results not from the calculated actions of self-interested individuals but from the fact that practices come to be taken for granted. The model of behavior is one in which "actors associate certain actions with certain situations by rules of appropriateness" (March & Olsen, 1984, p. 741). Individuals in organizations face choices all the time, but in making decisions they seek guidance from the experiences of others in comparable situations and by reference to standards of obligation.

The unit of analysis in institutional research is the organizational field or societal sector. The assumption is that organizations exist in socially constructed communities composed of similar organizations that are responsible for a definable area of institutional life. An organizational field includes key suppliers, consumers, regulatory agencies, professional and labor associations, as well as other organizations that produce a similar service or product.

DiMaggio and Powell (1983) argue that the process by which a field comes to be organized consists of four stages:

(1) an increase in the amount of interaction among organizations within a field;
(2) the emergence of well-defined patterns of hierarchy and coalition;
(3) an upsurge in the information load with which members of a field must contend; and
(4) the development of a mutual awareness among participants that they are involved in a common enterprise.

Processes of Institutionalization

How do organizational practices and structures become institutionalized within a field? Scholars have posited several mechanisms that promote isomorphism, that is, structural similarities among organizations within a field. Some of these processes encourage homogenization within a field directly by leading to structural and behavioral changes in organizations themselves. Others work indirectly by shaping the assumptions and experiences of the individuals who staff organizations. DiMaggio and Powell (1983) posit three general types of institutional pressures:

(1) coercive forces that stem from political influence and problems of legitimacy;
(2) mimetic changes that are responses to uncertainty; and
(3) normative influences resulting from professionalization

These three mechanisms are likely to intermingle in specific empirical settings, but they tend to derive from different conditions and may lead to different outcomes. Indeed, institutional pressures may be cross-cutting and lead to CONFLICT.

Coercive influence results from both formal and informal pressures exerted on organizations by other organizations upon which they are dependent, as well as by strongly held cultural expectations in society at large (*see* CULTURE). In some circumstances, organizational change is a response to government mandate: manufacturers adopt new pollution control technologies to conform to environmental regulations, nonprofits maintain accounts and hire accountants to meet the requirements of the tax laws, restaurants maintain minimum health standards, and organizations hire affirmative action officers to fend off allegations of discrimination.

UNCERTAINTY is a powerful force that encourages mimetic or imitative behavior among the members of an organizational field. When organizational technologies are poorly understood, that is, when managers are unclear about the relationship between means and ends, or when there is ambiguity regarding goals, or when the environment is highly uncertain, organizations often model themselves after other organizations. The modeled organization may be unaware of the modeling; it merely serves as a convenient source of organizational practices that the borrowing organization may use. Models may be diffused unintentionally, indirectly through employee transfer or turnover, or explicitly by organizations such as consulting firms. In this view, the ubiquity of certain kinds of modern management practices is credited more to the universality of mimetic processes than to any concrete evidence that the adopted models enhance efficiency.

A third source of organizational change is normative and stems from the culture of professionalism. Two aspects of professionalism are particularly relevant. One is the growth of professional communities based on knowledge produced by university specialists and legitimated through academic credentials; the second is the spread of formal and informal professional networks that span organizations and across which innovations may diffuse rapidly. Universities and professional training institutions are important centers for the development of organizational norms among professional managers and staff.

Empirical Results

Much of the initial research focused on public sector and nonprofit organizations in such areas as education, health care, mental health, and the arts. The twentieth century has seen a large-scale expansion of the role of government and the professions in these fields. The more highly organized policy making has become, the more individual organizations focus on responding to the official categories and procedures specified by the larger environment. In order to be perceived as legitimate, organizations adapt their formal structures and routines to conform to institutional norms. Hence to the extent that pressures from the environment are exerted on all members of a field, these organizations will become more similar. But pressures for fieldwide conformity may shape only an organization's formal structure (i.e., its organization chart and rules and reporting procedures), while backstage practices may be "decoupled" from official actions.

The concept of isomorphism has been utilized to describe the processes that encourage a unit in a population to resemble other units facing similar circumstances. Such pressures were theorized to be strongest in fields with a weak technical base (e.g., education, the arts, advertising, etc.), with ambiguous or conflicting goals (e.g., professional service firms), and that are buffered from market pressures (i.e., supported by endowment income or public funding, protected by government regulation, etc.). More recently, however, researchers have turned their attention to for-profit firms, examining the adoption of various employment practices, the utilization of different accounting standards, and the diffusion of management policies. This work has proven valuable in extending the reach of institutional analysis to some of the core firms in the US economy, while at the same time showing that organizations do not passively conform to institutional pressures. Rather government or professional mandates can be contested, negotiated, or partially implemented. Work by Edelman (1992) on civil rights law illustrates that the diffusion of new legal practices is not uni-directional; instead a complex interaction emerges in which government compliance standards are shaped by the responses of organizations.

Most institutional studies have focused on organizational practices as responses to the actions of various governing bodies: legislatures, courts, regulatory agencies, certification and accreditation boards, and professional associations. The advantage of this research is that it permits specification of how the environment shapes organizations, allowing researchers to understand the effects of different types of CONTROL systems. These analyses also enhance our understanding of the relationship between environmental complexity and internal organizational structure (*see* ORGANIZATIONAL DESIGN). For example, when environments contain multiple strong centers of authority and legitimacy, we find more levels of administration inside organizations, and greater differentiation across members of a field. When environments are more homogeneous, researchers find less elaborate internal organizational structures and less diversity across organizations.

Summary

Many of the prevailing approaches to ORGANIZATION THEORY assume implicitly that organizations are purposive and are progressing toward more efficient and adaptive forms. The institutional approach takes neither of these assumptions for granted, consequently it raises a different set of questions, asking how and from where do our notions of rationality emerge. This line of work seeks to treat the emergence of modern organizations and the laws and practices that govern them as the objects of study. Institutionalization, or the "process by which a given set of units and a pattern of activities come to be normatively and cognitively held in place, and practically taken for granted as lawful" (Meyer, Boli, & Thomas, 1987, p. 13) becomes the subject of inquiry.

Bibliography

DiMaggio, P. J. & Powell, W. W. (1983). The iron cage revisited: Institutional isomorphism and collective rationality in organizational fields. American Sociological Review, 48, 147–60.

Edelman, L. (1992). Legal ambiguity and symbolic structures: Organizational mediation on civil rights law. American Journal of Sociology, 97, 1531–1576.

March, J. G. & Olsen J. (1984). The new institutionalism: Organizational factors in political life. American Political Science Review, 78, 734–49.

Meyer, J. W. (1977). The effects of education as an institution. American Journal of Sociology, 83, 55–77.

Meyer, J. W., Boli, J. & Thomas, G. (1987). Ontology and rationalization in the Western cultural account. In G. Thomas, J. W. Meyer, F. O. Ramirez & J. Boli (Eds). Institutional Structure, pp. 12–37. Beverly Hills, CA: Sage.

Meyer, J. W. & Rowan, B. (1977). Institutionalized organizations: Formal structure as myth and ceremony. American Journal of Sociology, 83, 340–63.

Meyer, J. W. & Scott, W. R. (Eds) (1983). Organizational environments: Ritual and rationality. Beverly Hills, CA: Sage.

Powell, W. W. & DiMaggio P. J. (Eds) (1991). The new institutionalism in organizational analysis. Chicago: University of Chicago Press.

Scott, W. R. & Meyer, J. W. (1994). Institutional environments and organizations. Thousand Oaks CA: Sage.

Zucker, L. G (1977). The role of institutionalization in cultural persistence. American Sociological Review, 42, 726–43.

Zucker, L. G. (1983). Organizations as institutions In S. Bachrach (Ed), Research in the Sociology of Organizations. (pp. 1–47.) Greenwich, CT: JAI.

WALTER W. POWELL

integrative bargaining   Integrative bargaining refers to situations where the parties' goals are not in direct conflict and each party perceives opportunities for mutual gain. Integrative bargaining is often contrasted with DISTRIBUTIVE BARGAINING, but elements of both may be present in any negotiation.

The Character of Integrative Bargaining

Integrative bargaining focuses on the parties' interests, is cooperative, and stresses the creation of win–win situations. Negotiation is characterized by a joint problem-solving approach whereby problems are identified, solutions proposed, and specific proposals implemented. Negotiators strive to understand the interests and goals each brings to the negotiation and to fashion proposals that meet as many of these objectives as possible. A central notion in integrative bargaining is Pareto optimality. Proposals should be generated and altered until no party can be made better off without the other party being made worse off. Satisfaction of this principle ensures that the parties have realized the full potential for mutual gain inherent in the negotiation.

Integrative Bargaining Strategies

Integrative bargaining strategies support and facilitate a joint problem-solving approach. Negotiators stress their similarities and common interests, downplaying differences. Each party encourages the other to clearly and fully communicate his or her interests and hopes to secure the other's cooperation and trust by fashioning proposals that explicitly recognize and meet the other's needs. Creative suggestions are encouraged and the parties evaluate proposals against both objective standards and notions of equity. Common integrative bargaining strategies include brainstorming, bridging, cost-cutting, and logrolling (see NEGOTIATION TACTICS).

Bibliography

Fisher, R. & Ury, W. (1981). Getting to Yes: Negotiating Agreement without Giving in, New York: Penguin Books.

Lewicki, R. J. & Litterer, J. A. (1985). Negotiation, Homewood, IL: Richard D. Irwin.

Walton, R. E. & McKersie, R. B. (1965). A Behavioral Theory of Labor Negotiations: an Analysis of a Social Interaction System, New York: McGraw-Hill.

PAUL JARLEY

integrity   Integrity, in the sense relevant for business ethics: the quality of moral self-governance. Derived from the Latin word integritas, meaning wholeness, completeness, or purity, integrity has been widely praised both as a virtue and as a quality essential for personal well-being and social effectiveness. Psychologists have found integrity to be essential to an individual's sense of identity and self-worth, enabling the successful navigation of change and challenge. Links between integrity and the ability to gain and maintain the trust of others have often been noted. Many purveyors have counseled that integrity is the cornerstone of worldly success. According to Franklin, "no Qualities [are] so likely to make a poor Man's Fortune as those of Probity & Integrity" (quoted in Beebe, 1992, p. 8).

Although integrity has been defined in a variety of ways, it is generally identified with one or more of the following related characteristics:

Moral conscientiousness. Integrity involves moral conscientiousness and a desire to do what is right. Persons of integrity are trustworthy and resistant to corruption. They can be relied on to be truthful, to be fair, to stand by their promises, to follow the rules – or, at least, to challenge them openly and fairly. Such persons are faithful to the moral requirements of the roles in which they serve. When acting as a fiduciary for others, for example, they can be counted on to exercise independent judgment unbiased by personal advantage (see FIDUCIARY DUTY). They are scrupulous in dealing with conflict of interest or improper influences which might taint their judgment.

Moral accountability. Integrity involves personal accountability. Persons of integrity accept responsibility for themselves and what they do. They rarely appeal to external forces to explain or justify their behavior. They do not pass the buck or seek exculpation in excuses such as "He made me do it," "I was just following orders," "I had no choice." Nor do they see themselves as slaves of their own desires. Integrity is associated with a high degree of self-control and self-awareness.

Moral commitment. Integrity is often identified with having a set of distinctive and strongly held commitments. Persons of integrity have a set of anchoring beliefs or principles that define who they are and what they believe in. They stand for something and remain steadfast when confronted with adversity or temptation. In some instances – for example, Gandhi's commitment to non-violent resistance or Martin Luther King's commitment to civil rights – their anchoring beliefs become the driving force of their lives. Individuals who have no defining commitments, who are too easily swayed by the crowd, who tailor their beliefs to their audience, or who capriciously change their fundamental values are generally thought to be lacking in integrity. While integrity is incompatible with dogmatic adherence to unexamined belief, it does imply constancy of purpose and willingness to take a principled stand.

Moral coherence. Integrity connotes coherence or consistency in a variety of senses: among commitments, among moral judgments, between belief and expression, and between word and deed. Hypocrisy, dishonesty, and self-deception, perhaps the most common failures of integrity, all involve forms of incoherence. Although perfect coherence in all the above senses is unattainable – and perhaps undesirable – persons of integrity generally strive for harmony between principle and practice and for coherence among who they are, who they perceive themselves to be, and how they present themselves to the world. Authenticity and sincerity are often regarded as hallmarks of integrity.

These different aspects of integrity, though related, can sometimes conflict, creating difficult moral dilemmas for decision-makers. For example, managers' role-related obligations may conflict with their personal commitments. Conscientious persons may be torn between blowing the whistle on misconduct they observe and adhering to the conventional bounds of their assigned responsibilities. Despite its associations with harmony and personal well-being, integrity requires that individuals deal with such conflicts and overcome the tensions inherent in them.

While philosophers and psychologists have approached integrity from different perspectives, it is tempting to speculate that the moral expressions of integrity may rest on the psychological foundation of a well-integrated personality. If true, this connection would lend credence to Aristotle's view that virtue and personal well-being are closely linked and rooted in human nature. In this regard, it is interesting to note that Erik Erikson (1950), the well-known psychoanalyst and developmental psychologist, regarded integrity as encompassing ethical and psychological wholeness and as the final and highest stage of personal development.

Though integrity has been widely admired, some philosophers have questioned its usefulness as a moral standard. The philosopher John Rawls, for example, has called integrity a secondary moral concept, one of form rather than content, with no moral purchase until informed by a theory of right and wrong. According to Rawls (1971, p. 519), integrity is compatible with almost any guiding principles or commitments; even a tyrant, he says, could exhibit a high degree of integrity.

Others have argued that while integrity allows for some latitude in content, it is not entirely open-ended. Integrity-conferring commitments must be important, and they must be morally sound (McFall, 1987). There is a note of irony in attributing integrity to the mafioso who only "takes out" those who deserve it. Similarly, a "tyrant with integrity" would appear to be a contradiction in terms insofar as a tyrant is someone who exercises absolute power brutally and in flagrant violation of law and morality. According to this line of thought, integrity is a powerful moral concept precisely because it focuses on form as well as content and because it is compatible with a range of personal commitments.

Whether moral integrity can be properly ascribed to entities other than individual persons has been a matter of debate. In recent years, however, executives and management theorists have become concerned with corporate or organizational integrity. New US standards for sentencing corporations convicted of wrongdoing have reinforced this concern. Under the 1991 Federal Sentencing Guidelines, organizational culpability was made a critical factor in determining corporate fines, thus giving managers added incentives to promote moral self-governance in their companies.

While organizational integrity is sometimes thought to require nothing more than the personal integrity of the organization's members, research suggests that organizational strategies, structures, and systems are important factors in supporting organizational integrity. Research also suggests that individual integrity is best thought of not as a stable personality trait established once and for all in early life, but as a process of interacting with the world which can be supported or inhibited by the context in which the individual acts. These findings imply that executives concerned about organizational integrity should focus both on developing the personal capabilities of individuals in their companies and on establishing the organizational conditions required for moral self-governance.

Bibliography

Badaracco, J. L., Jr., & Ellsworth, R. R. (1989). *Leadership and the Quest for Integrity.* Boston: Harvard Business School Press. (Executive perspectives.)

Beebe, J. (1992). *Integrity in Depth.* College Station: Texas A&M University Press. (A psychological perspective.)

De George, R. T. (1993). *Competing with Integrity in International Business.* New York: Oxford University Press. (A philosophical perspective.)

Erikson, E. H. (1950). *Childhood and Society.* New York: W.W. Norton. (A developmental perspective.)

Halfon, M. S. (1989). *Integrity: A Philosophical Inquiry.* Philadelphia: Temple University Press. (A philosophical perspective.)

McFall, L. (1987). Integrity. *Ethics,* **98**, 5–20 (A philosophical perspective.)

Paine, L. S. (1994). Managing for organizational integrity. *Harvard Business Review* Mar./Apr., 106–17 (An organizational perspective.)

Rawls, J. (1971). *A Theory of Justice.* Cambridge, Mass.: Harvard University Press. (A philosophical perspective.)

Srivastva, S. & Associates. (1988). *Executive Integrity: The Search for High Human Values in Organizational Life.* San Francisco: Jossey-Bass. (Organizational and executive perspectives.)

Taylor, G. (1985). *Integrity: Pride, Shame, and Guilt.* Oxford: The Clarendon Press, 108–41. (A philosophical perspective.)

LYNN SHARP PAINE

integrity testing   Integrity (or honesty) tests are paper and pencil instruments administered primarily to job applicants for the purpose of predicting counterproductive work behavior. Recent estimates suggest that several million such tests are administered in the USA annually, primarily to applicants for entry level jobs with access to money or merchandise. Current research, however, downplays or eliminates the link to the polygraph. It focuses not only on the prediction of employee theft, but on a wide variety of counterproductive behaviors, to include violation of work rules, fraudulent worker's compensation claims, and ABSENTEEISM.

Two basic types of tests can be identified. Overt tests measure attitudes toward theft and other forms of counterproductivity. They commonly ask for a self-report of applicant involvement in various illegal and/or counter-productive behaviors. Personality-oriented tests are con-siderably broader in focus and are not explicitly aimed at theft. They may include items dealing with dependability, conscientiousness, social conformity, thrill-seeking, trouble with authority, and hostility.

A large body of validity evidence shows integrity tests to be positively related to both a range of counterproductive behaviors and supervisor ratings of overall performance. However, most of the research has been done by test publishers, leading skeptics to question whether only successes are being publicized.

There is currently no federal regulation on the use of integrity testing. Women, racial minority groups, and older workers do not systematically perform more poorly on these tests. As a result, there have been no successful challenges to integrity tests under federal anti-discrimina-tion laws. However, two states (Massachusetts and Rhode Island) restrict the use of integrity tests.

Critics express concerns about invasion of privacy and the risks of misclassifying honest applicants. Defenders point to the business justification for inquiry into issues of conscientiousness and counterproductivity. They also note that the standard of comparison for any selection system is not perfect accuracy, but the degree of predictive accuracy achieved by available alternatives.

Bibliography

American Psychological Association (1991). *Questionnaires Used in the Prediction of Trustworthiness in Pre-employment Selection Decisions: an APA Task Force Report*, Washington, DC: US Government Printing Office.

Congress of the United States Office of Technology Assessment (1990). *The Use of Integrity Tests for Pre-employment Screening*, Washington, DC: US Government Printing Office.

Murphy, K. R. (1993). *Honesty in the Workplace*, Pacific Grove, CA: Brooks-Cole.

Sackett, P. R., Burris, L. R. & Callahan, C. (1989). Integrity testing for personnel selection: an update. *Personnel Psychology*, 42, 491–529.

PAUL R. SACKETT

intellectual property Most property can be seen, touched, and is capable of physical measurement and valuation. This is not true of all property. With technolo-gical advancements over the past several decades, a new type of property in the form of ideas or unique processes has been recognized. Especially valuable are ideas and devel-opments associated with advances in computers or communications technology. The person having these ideas or the firm developing a process or way of doing things is said to have developed intellectual property. Intellectual property has become valuable and subject to protection in many countries. Patents and copyrights are two examples of measures to protect intellectual property rights.

The owner of intellectual property can protect it against unauthorized use by filing the forms documenting its existence with the appropriate governmental authorities. A real problem exists in the world today because of the failure of some countries to allow intellectual property rights to be protected or to enforce existing property right protections. Failure to protect intellectual property rights may slow the spread of certain technological advances throughout the world. Unless intellectual property rights protection is provided (with the accompanying right to profit from those rights) organizations may be unwilling to share technolo-gical developments with certain countries.

Several international initiatives and organizations have begun work toward establishing better methods of controlling unauthorized use of intellectual property. The United Nations established the World Intellectual Property Organization (WIPO) and began operations in 1970. The WIPO is charged with promoting international cooperation and coordination related to intellectual property rights protection.

see also **Berne Convention for the Protection of Literary and Artistic Works (1886); World Intellec-tual Property Organization**

JOHN O'CONNELL

intelligence tests An intelligence test is a series of standardized tasks for assessing general cognitive ability. The tasks may be diverse, including, for example, words, numbers, designs, pictures, and blocks. Tests that include more than one item type often arrange them in subtests such as vocabulary, information, block design, comprehension, arithmetic, and picture completion.

Intelligence tests measure a very *general capability*, as reflected in abstract thinking, problem solving, and ability to deal with complexity. This is in contrast to aptitude and achievement tests. Aptitude tests target narrower abilities, such as verbal, mechanical, or spatial aptitude (Anastasi, 1988, p. 15). Achievement tests assess knowledge of specific school curricula, such as reading, science, or history. Intelligence tests tend to require less specific knowledge, sometimes only elementary concepts like in-out or large–small. The distinctions among the three types of test are not always clear. Some aptitude and achievement tests function like intelligence tests when test takers have been equally exposed to the subject matter being tested.

Origins and Use

Alfred Binet and his colleague Theophile Simon con-structed the first modern intelligence test, in 1905, in response to the French government's desire to develop diagnostic and instructional procedures for mentally retarded children. American psychologists developed the first group intelligence tests (called the Army Alpha and Army Beta tests) during the First World War, in response to the Army's need to screen millions of recruits. The Army Alpha required examinees to read; the Army Beta did not.

Interest in mental testing grew rapidly after the First World War. The US military services developed what is today called the Armed Services Vocational Aptitude Battery (ASVAB), and the US Department of Labor developed the General Aptitude Test Battery (GATB). Many schools, colleges, and private employers adopted some of the many new tests on the market for selecting and placing students and employees. The most widely used individually administered tests today are, for school-age children, the Wechsler Intelligence Scale for Children–III (WISC–III) and, for adults, the Wechsler Adult Intelligence Scale–Revised (WAIS–R).

The major uses of intelligence tests include clinical diagnosis of individuals' behavior or achievement problems, vocational and educational guidance, personnel selection and college admissions, and placement into different education and training programs. Good professional practice requires that intelligence test scores be supplemented with other information when high-stakes decisions are being made about individuals (e.g. assigning a child to a special education class).

Individual tests are administered by highly trained professionals who exercise judgment in gaining rapport, administering prompts, and scoring the quality of responses. Group tests can be administered by less-trained individuals because they allow no discretion in administration and scoring.

The construction and use of intelligence tests are governed by professional standards (Anastasi, 1988), principally the Standards for Educational and Psychological Testing (AERA/APA/NCME, 1985).

Trends

Test construction has tended to be atheoretical, but today is more often guided by some explicit theory of intelligence. Those undergirding theories tend to represent broader conceptions of intelligent and adaptive behavior. There is also rising demand for tests that provide more diagnostic information about test takers' particular strengths and weaknesses in mental functioning.

The new technology of computer adaptive testing promises a generation of tests that can be instantly tailored to the ability level of the test taker, thus providing quicker and more accurate assessment. Item response theory is now providing new ways of scaling test scores, leading to more useful developmental norms for score interpretation.

Legal and Social Issues

Test use has risen and fallen during the century, depending on social and legal currents of the time (Wigdor and Garner, 1982). Public concern has focused on test fairness, because mental tests are often used in ways that affect people's lives. Selection and placement are two such uses. While often warranted by the tests' predictive validities, such uses make tests the focus of long-standing sociopolitical debates over equal opportunity.

Common, and sometimes large, racial or ethnic disparities in test scores underlie another major source of concern, fueling claims that intelligence tests are culturally biased. Extensive research (Jensen, 1980; Wigdor and Garner, 1982) has shown, however, that they are not biased against native-born, English-speaking Americans, including blacks. Their use, however, often creates disparate impact, which has provoked much litigation in recent decades. *Griggs* v. *Duke Power Company*, 401 US 424 (1971), *Larry P.* v. *Riles*, 495 F. Supp. 926 (ND Cal. 1979), and similar court decisions have greatly affected the regulation and use of tests in employment and educational settings. Media reports of the foregoing issues have tended in recent years to misreport expert opinion on intelligence testing (Snyderman and Rothman, 1988).

Bibliography

AERA/APA/NCME (1985). *Standards for Educational and Psychological Testing*, Washington, DC: American Psychological Association.

Anastasi, A. (1988). *Psychological Testing*, 6th edn, New Cronbach, L. J. (1990). *Essentials of Psychological Testing*, 5th edn, New York: Harper Collins.

Jensen, A. R. (1980). *Bias in Mental Testing*, New York: Free Press.

Kamphaus, R. W. (1993). *Clinical Assessment of Children's Intelligence*, Boston: Allyn and Bacon.

Snyderman, S. & Rothman, M. (1988). *The IQ Controversy: the Media and Public Policy*, New York: Transaction.

Wigdor, A. K. & Garner, W. R. (1982). *Ability Testing: Uses, Consequences, and Controversies. Part 1: Report of the Committee*, Washington, DC: National Academy Press.

Wolman, B. B. (Ed.) (1985). *Handbook of Intelligence: Theories, Measurements, and Applications*, New York: Wiley.

LINDA S. GOTTFREDSON

interaction approach Extensive research by the IMP (Industrial Marketing and Purchasing) Group of researchers into European buyer–seller purchasing relationships has generated significant insights into how such relationships develop (Håkansson, 1982; Turnbull & Valla, 1986; Ford, 1990). The Group describes these relationships in what has become known as the interaction approach to ORGANIZATIONAL MARKETING. In essence, the interaction approach regards purchasing in organizational markets as a multifaceted and dynamic phenomenon where specific purchases are understood as "exchange episodes" in the evolving relationship between buyer and seller organizations, and between individuals in these organizations. These bilateral exchanges are also seen as part of a much wider and more complex NETWORK of multilateral interactions which bind organizations of suppliers and customers together in seamless "markets."

The interaction approach emphasizes stability and continuity of organizational markets which are evolving through many interrelated buyer–seller relationships, even where a superficial analysis may suggest greater volatility. It is also implied that the textbook dichotomy between "marketing" (by suppliers) and "purchasing" (by customers) may not be the most appropriate way to describe what is essentially a seamless and iterative process (*see* PURCHASING PROCESS). The interaction approach prefers a view of organizational marketing as, in effect, the management of buyer–seller relationships where it is more appropriate to differentiate participants in terms of power, expertise, experience, and cultural affiliation rather than broad organizational membership. This approach also emphasizes the importance of "atmospherics" such as personal objectives and expectations, interpersonal familiarity, and levels of cooperation and dependence in understanding specific "exchange episodes." The elements of the interaction approach are summarized in the interaction model which is discussed elsewhere (*see* ORGANIZATIONAL BUYER BEHAVIOR). Acceptance of the interaction approach has significant implications for the management of organizational marketing. Four of these implications are listed here to illustrate the practical significance of the interaction approach:

- marketing planning should be focused on key customers in target markets (including foreign markets) rather than just on products/services;
- investment in product design and technology should only be made where this is based on an understanding of customer requirements;
- integrated team selling should be developed and managers should be appointed to coordinate all aspects of key customer relationships;
- the supplier's marketing function should be more closely integrated with the customer's purchasing function.

see also **Relationship marketing**

Bibliography

Ford, D. (Ed.) (1990). *Understanding business markets: Interaction, relationships and networks.* London: Academic Press.
Håkansson, H. (Ed.) (1982). *International marketing and purchasing of industrial goods – an interaction approach.* New York: John
Turnbull, P. W. & Valla, J-P. (Eds) (1986). *Strategies for international industrial marketing.* Beckenham: Croom Helm.

DOMINIC WILSON

interaction model   *see* INTERACTION APPROACH

interdependence   Interdependence is a relatively simple concept referring to organizations or groups relying upon the actions of each other in order to function. An import firm is reliant upon an export firm to stay in business, as well as the export firm being reliant on the import firm for the same reason. The two firms are thus interdependent. Regardless of its simplicity, it is an extremely important concept in the context of international trade. Organizations which are too dependent upon the operations of other organizations (suppliers, buyers, distributors, etc.) may have their very existence threatened by the demise of that other organization or a change in contract, etc.).

Interdependencies must be identified and dealt with by management. When situations are identified in which the dependence is too great for management, alternate sources of supply, sale, or distribution must be found. Failure to deal with interdependency situations places the organization's continued existence in the hands of others. To most managements this is an unacceptable condition which must be remedied if at all possible.

Bibliography

Egelhoff, W. G. (1988). Strategy and structure in multinational corporations: A revision of the Stopford and Wells Model. *Strategic Management Journal,* 9, 1–14.
Grosse, R. & Kujawa, D. (1995). *International business: Theory and managerial applications.* 3rd edn, Boston, MA: Richard D. Irwin Inc.
Humes, S. (1993). *Managing the multinational: Confronting the global–local dilemma.* Englewood Cliff, NJ: Prentice-Hall.
Rosenzweig, P. M. & Singh, J. V. (1991). *Organizational environments and the multinational enterprise.* The Academy of Management Review, 16, 340–61.

JOHN O'CONNELL

interest arbitration   Interest arbitration is a procedure used to resolve negotiation disputes over new contract terms (or disputes over interests, rather than disputes over rights under an existing contract as occurs in grievance arbitration). Interest arbitration procedures vary according to (a) the basis for the proceedings (voluntary versus compul-

sory), (b) the number of arbitrators involved (one individual versus a multiple person panel), (c) the rules governing how the arbitration decision will be made (conventional versus FINAL OFFER ARBITRATION), and (d) the formality of the proceedings, and so on.

Most interest arbitration occurs in negotiating disputes involving public employers and unions of their employees, as a result of state or federal collective bargaining legislation that requires that arbitration be used in this manner (it usually is compulsory rather than voluntary). As this implies, arbitration requirements are accompanied by prohibitions on the use of strikes and lockouts. These legislative mandates are sought by public employee unions and resisted by public employers, based on their mutual belief that compulsory arbitration enables unions to negotiate new contract terms from a stronger position than would be the case without such laws, and research evidence supports these beliefs. Research also indicates that the existence of a compulsory arbitration requirement sometimes may reduce union and employer incentives to bargain their own contracts.

Because most private sector employers and unions strenuously object to relinquishing their decision authority to arbitrators (which includes their right to strike or lock out), there is little use of voluntary or compulsory interest arbitration in the private sector.

PETER FEUILLE

intergroup relations   In organizational theory, the term "intergroup relations" refers to the collective behavior of groups in interaction with other groups, either within or between organizations. The classic definition of intergroup relations was provided by Sherif (1966) who suggested that, "Whenever individuals belonging to one group interact, collectively or individually, with another group or its members in terms of their group identification, we have an instance of intergroup behavior" (p. 12).

Several important traditions distinguish how intergroup relations have been conceptualized in organizational theory. Sociological theory and research has generally focused on structural determinants of intergroup behavior. For example, organizational scholars in this tradition have emphasized how differences in goals, task structure, POWER, and STATUS affect intergroup relations. In addition, they have examined the impact of social processes such as COMMUNICATION patterns and social norms on intergroup behavior. In contrast, political perspectives on intergroup relations have focused on how strategic processes such as bargaining, COALITION FORMATION, and collective action influence intergroup relations. Finally, psychological theories have construed intergroup relations primarily in terms of intra-individualistic processes, such as interpersonal attraction, social perception, and TRUST. These theories emphasize the importance of cognitive factors such as stereotyping, as well as motivational underpinnings of intergroup behavior, including the presumed desire on the part of group members to maintain positive social group identities (Brewer & Kramer, 1985). According to these theories, such psychological processes influence intergroup behavior by affecting social judgment and behavior in intergroup contexts.

The major theories of intergroup relations illustrate these differing emphases. *Realistic Conflict Theory* posits that intergroup relations are influenced not so much by cognitive and motivational processes as they are by the inherent competition between groups for crucial but scarce resources. In this framework, interdependence is viewed as the basis of intergroup cooperation and CONFLICT. In contrast, other theories afford greater importance to the social and psychological processes that influence how individuals in social groups construe their interdependence with other groups. For example, *Social Categorization Theory* focuses on how social and organizational processes that categorize people into distinctive groups fosters competitive and conflictual orientations at the intergroup level. Research in this vein has shown that categorization results in a tendency for individuals to view members of their own group (the "ingroup") more positively than "outgroup" members. Along similar lines, it has been shown that, when allocating scarce resources such as REWARDS, individuals tend to confer more favorable treatment on members of their own group over those from other groups. A major presumption of this framework is that an understanding of cognitive processes alone is sufficient to account for intergroup phenomenon such as stereotyping and discrimination. In contrast, *Social Identity Theory* argues that a variety of motivational processes, such as the desire to maintain a positive social identity, also play a formative role in intergroup relations (Tajfel, 1982). According to this perspective, enhancement of the ingroup and derogation of the outgroup serve the important psychological function of bostering individual's self-esteem and the collective esteem of the ingroup. Finally, *Relative Deprivation Theory* examines the role that social comparison processes play in understanding intergroup relations. This theory views intergroup relations as shaped by people's comparisons between what their own group has relative to other groups within an organization. When individuals feel that their group is receiving favorable treatment relative to other groups, satisfaction is likely to be high. In contrast, when they believe their own group is relatively deprived or disadvantaged, discontent is likely to result.

These perspectives are important because of the insight they provide with respect to two central concerns in the study of intergroup relations: intergroup conflict and cooperation. Theory and research on intergroup conflict has attempted to identify the origins and dynamics of conflict between various groups. For example, there exists a considerable literature pertaining to intergroup conflict in industrial settings (usually under the rubric of *labor–management conflict*). Much of this literature draws attention to the role perceptual and social processes – such as ethnocentrism and ingroup bias – play in the development and escalation of intergroup conflicts. As Blake and Mouton (1989) noted, "The striking conclusion from [this] research is that when groups are aware of one another's psychological presence, it is nature for them to feel competition . . . [suggesting] a very basic incipient hostility is operating at the point of contact between primary groups" (p. 192). These insights, in turn, suggest a number of perspectives on reducing intergroup competition and conflict. These perspectives generally take as given the pervasiveness of intergroup rivalry and conflict, and then attempt to address the problem of how to promote cooperation between groups. Several approaches to increasing intergroup cooperation have been proposed,

and reasonable evidence is available to suggest the efficacy of each. First, introduction of superordinate (shared) goals to reduce competition has been shown to help attenuate or override competitive tendencies between groups. Second, certain forms of intergroup contact have been shown to enhance cooperation. Of particular importance is contact in which status differences and interaction patterns that reinforce negative stereotypes are minimized or controlled. In addition, the use of "boundary spanners" (individuals who have roles in both groups) can help correct misperceptions, improve communication and coordination, and reduce distrust between groups. Another important approach has emphasized the positive consequences of "recategorization" as a strategy for achieving intergroup cooperation. The recategorization approach is predicated on the assumption that the deleterious consequences associated with ingroup favoritism and outgroup derogation can be reduced by categorizing individuals in terms of shared or collective identities that draw attention to interpersonal similarities and that increase social attraction between individuals from different groups. Another major focus is on behavioral strategies designed to elicit cooperative interaction and build trust between groups, including the use of RECIPROCITY-based influence strategies, such as tit-for-tat. Finally, recent theory and research on the use of conflict resolution processes such as NEGOTIATION. This includes the use of integrative bargaining involving the groups themselves, as well as various third-party interventions such as mediation and arbitration (*see* INFLUENCE). This is currently one of the most active and promising new directions in the study of intergroup relations.

see also **Industrial relations; Interorganizational relations**

Bibliography

Axelrod, R. (1984). The evolution of cooperation. New York: Basic Books.

Alderfer, C. P. & Smith, K. K. (1982). Studying intergroup relations embedded in organizations. Administrative Science Quarterly, 27, 33–65.

Blake, R. & Mouton, J. (1989). Lateral conflict. In D. Tjosvold & D. Johnson (Eds), Productive conflict management. Edinia, MN: Interaction.

Brett, J. M. & Rognes, J. K. (1986). Intergroup relations in organizations. In P. Goodman (Ed.), Work group effectiveness. San Francisco: Jossey-Bass.

Brewer, M. B. & Kramer, R. M. (1985). The psychology of intergroup attitudes and behavior. Annual Review of Psychology, 36, 219–243.

Kramer, R. M. (1991). Intergroup relations and organizational dilemmas: The role of categorization processes. In B. M. Staw & L. L. Cummings (Eds). Research in organizational behavior, (vol. 13) Greenwich, CT: JAI Press.

Messick, D. M. & Mackie, D. (1989). Intergroup relations. Annual Review of Psychology, 40, 45–81.

Sherif, M. (1966). In common predicament: Social psychology of intergroup conflict and cooperation. New York: Houghton & Mifflin.

Stephan, W. G. (1985). Intergroup relations In G. Lindsey & E. A. Ronson (Eds), The handbook of social psychology. (Vol. 2, 3rd edn). New York: Random House.

Tajfel, H. (1982). Social psychology of intergroup relations. Annual Review of Psychology, 39.

RODERICK M. KRAMER

internal audit An internal audit is one part of the MARKETING AUDIT (the other being external audit) and involves examination of the internal operations, strengths, and weaknesses of an organization. There are many ways to approach this audit but all methods involve, in essence, the allocation of all internal operations and assets into various categories labeled judgementally according to whether they are perceived as "good" or "bad" for the organization. Thus, one method recommends the identification of "strengths" and "weaknesses" while another method would be to identify "core" activities and "peripheral" activities (Prahalad & Hamel, 1990). Porter (1980) suggests that internal activities can be analyzed in terms of "value added" with the implication that operations which add little "value" to the organization's output should be improved, or minimized (if they are unnecessary), or subcontracted (if they lie outside the organization's core competence). All these methods of identifying internal strengths and problems risk, through disaggregation, losing sight of the collective synergies arising from the operations of the organization as a whole. Thus, an activity such as an annual Christmas Party or a weekly newsletter to customers may not seem to add significant value to the organization's offerings but cancellation could have important implications for the perception of an organization's commitment to its stakeholders.

Bibliography

Porter, M. E. (1980). *Competitive strategy: Techniques for analyzing industries and competitors.* New York: Free Press.

Prahalad, C. K. & Hamel, G. (1990). The core competence of the corporation. *Harvard Business Review*, **68**, (3), May–June, 79–91.

DOMINIC WILSON

internal equity/internal consistency Internal equity is one of two organizing concepts (along with EXTERNAL EQUITY/EXTERNAL COMPETITIVENESS) used to define the structure and form of a traditional JOB-BASED PAY system. Internal equity is the degree to which an organization's jobs or positions are ordered hierarchically such that there is congruence with the organization's strategic and business objectives (Milkovich and Newman, 1993, p. 35). Thus, the relative pay differences between jobs (within a single organization) will reflect each job's unique value to the employing organization when the system is internally equitable (Mahoney, 1979). At a more macro level, the structures of pay hierarchies also are likely to reflect societal norms and values.

A high degree of internal equity should promote a sense of equity and fairness among organization members and thus encourage cooperation and organizational citizenship behaviors. Internally equitable systems also are likely to facilitate a willingness to undertake training and seek higher-level positions within the hierarchy.

The principle means of establishing internal equity is through the use of JOB EVALUATION METHODS. Here, the job's essential attributes are rated with respect to their perceived value to the organization. Thus, it is possible for there to be a discrepancy between a job's value as defined by the so-called market wage and how it is positioned within the organization's internal structure. This possible tension between internal and external equity represents a central and difficult area for resolution for wage and salary administrators.

Bibliography

Mahoney, T. A. (1979). Organizational hierarchy and position worth. *Academy of Management Journal*, **22**, 726–37.

Milkovich, G. T. & Newman, J. M. (1993). *Compensation*, Homewood, IL: Richard D. Irwin.

GEORGE F. DREHER

internal labor markets Many of the rules which determine economic outcomes and social welfare originate within the firm and are, in a non-trivial sense, chosen by the firm. Because many workers spend long stretches of their careers within the shelter of enterprises, understanding these rules is very important. These rules have come to be characterized as the internal labor market (ILM).

The central idea of ILMs was set forth by Kerr (1954) in his description of "institutional labor markets." Kerr argued that these labor markets created non-competing groups, and that one of the central boundaries was between the firm and the external labor market. Kerr identified "ports of entry" as the link between the inside and outside and described the implications for labor mobility of the boundaries and rules. Dunlop (1966) coined the term "internal labor market" and provided a description of one of its central rules, that concerning job ladders. In the 1970s, Doeringer and Piore (1971) provided a full description of the rules of blue collar ILMs as well as the tradeoffs among rules (for example, between hiring criteria and training procedures). Doeringer and Piore also began the process of linking analysis of ILMs back to mainstream labor economics through their discussion of how specific human capital helps to cement employee attachment to firms.

Internal labor markets attract scholars of divergent bents. For mainstream economists the challenge is to explain these rules in a framework that preserves the core ideas of maximization and efficiency. Institutional economists do not deny the impact of standard economic considerations, but they emphasize the interplay of economic, political, and social forces. This orientation has been reinforced by recent interest in international comparisons. There is also a vibrant sociology literature. Since stable work groups lead to the formation of norms, customs, and interpersonal comparisons, ILMs provide sociologists with an opportunity to illustrate and explore the importance of these phenomena. In addition, variation across enterprises in extent and content of rules suggests that sociological models which focus on the diffusion and adaption of institutional practices independent of their efficiency properties (for example, the search for legitimacy via mimicry) can be fruitfully applied to ILMs.

The nature of research on ILMs has also expanded. The initial investigations were largely field-based, and the ideas rested upon interviews with firms and unions. Our confidence in these observations has, however, been strengthened by studies based upon representative samples of firms as well as more thorough examinations of particular practices, such as firm-based wage setting, long-term tenure, or part-time work. In the course of this research the original concept, while generally affirmed, has been modified in important ways. For example, there is heightened sensitivity to the fact that a firm is not a unitary employment system, but rather consists of a set of ILM subsystems which may operate on quite different principles (Osterman, 1984).

A central ILM idea is that categories of rules fit together in a logical system, and it does not make sense to isolate one rule and ignore the others. For example, narrow job classifications, wages attached to jobs, few restrictions on the ability of the firm to lay off workers, and strict seniority are a mutually reinforcing set of practices. On the other hand, broad classifications, wages attached to individuals rather than jobs, ease of deployment, and high levels of job security constitute another logical cluster. Anyone familiar with the literature will recognize the first cluster as the "traditional" US model, while the second is a model associated (at least until recently) with leading-edge US firms and with the Japanese.

An important development is the transformation of ILMs in America. From the mid-1940s to the mid-1970s, the traditional model – which is essentially what Doeringer and Piore described – dominated both in the union sector and in largely imitative nonunion firms. Towards the end of this era, a competing model emerged, one which placed much greater emphasis upon direct communication with workers and upon innovations such as team production and quality circles. This structure was motivated in part by its superior performance, and in part by its ability to keep unions at bay. It emerged in a progressive segment of the US nonunion sector (e.g. IBM), but it also gained momentum from the spread of Japanese transplants, such as the Honda factory in Ohio, which organized work along the Japanese model. The more traditional sector, union and nonunion, was torn between adoption of the new (often called "transformed" or "salaried") model and defense of old structures. The playing out and resolving of this tension is the current ILM "story" of greatest interest and importance.

Bibliography

Doeringer, P. & Piore, M. (1971). *Internal Labor Markets*, Lexington, MA: D C Heath.

Dunlop, J. (1966). Job vacancy measures and economic analysis. *The Measurement and Interpretation of Job Vacancies: a Conference Report*, New York: Columbia University Press.

Kerr, C. (1954). The Balkanization of labor markets. *Labor Mobility and Economic Opportunity*, Bakke, E. W., Cambridge, MA: MIT Press.

Osterman, P. (1984). *Internal Labor Markets*, Cambridge, MA: MIT Press.

PAUL OSTERMAN

internal rate of return   The internal rate of return is the discount rate which makes the NET PRESENT VALUE of an asset equal to its current cost. Formally, if an asset which costs P_0 today will generate cash flows of C in each period i for T periods in the future, then the internal rate of return is that value of r^* which solves

$$\sum_{i=1}^{T} \left[\frac{C_i}{(1 + r^*)^i} \right] - P_0 = 0$$

The internal rate of return essentially measures the expected rate of return from an investment and this can be compared with some hurdle rate for CAPITAL BUDGETING decisions. Based on this criterion, an investment should be made if its internal rate of return exceeds the cost of capital. The internal rate of return may not be unique if future cash flows alternate between positive and negative values and the ranking of alternative investments by this criterion may not correspond with rankings from the net present value method; see Edwards, Kay and Mayer (1987) and Brigham and Gapenski (1993). Fisher and McGowan (1983) assert that the internal rate of return is the appropriate measure of the economic rate of return, but Edwards, Kay and Mayer (1987) suggest that adjusted accounting data could be used in economic analysis.

see also **Economic profit**

Bibliography

Brigham, E. F. & Gapenski, L. C. (1993). *Intermediate Financial Management*. New York: Dryden.

Edwards, J., Kay, J. & Mayer, C. (1987). *The Economic Analxford: OUP*.

Fisher, F. M. & McGowan, J. J. (1983). On the misuse of accounting rates of return to infer monopoly profits. *American Economic Review*, 73, 82–97.

ROBERT E. McAULIFFE

international accounting   According to statistics compiled in *The Economist* (Crook, 1992, pp. 6, 9), the volume of cross-border transactions in equity securities has expanded more than tenfold in the course of a decade, increasing from (US) \$120 billion in 1980 to (US) \$1.4 trillion in 1990. The increase in international bank lending has been even more staggering, from \$324 billion in 1980 to \$7.5 trillion in 1991. International business has moved in a very few years from the specialty of a few to the mainstream. Accompanying this trend has been an expanded interest in international accounting. Although there is much diversity in international accounting practice, recent years have been marked by a movement toward international accounting harmonization. This movement has been led by the efforts of the International Accounting Standards Committee and, in Europe, by the accounting directives of the European Union.

Comprehensive reviews of international accounting issues and research are provided by Wallace & Gernon (1991) and Meek & Saudagaran (1990). In recent years, a more rigorous vintage of international accounting research has accompanied the growing volume of international transactions. At a more practical level, several comprehensive international accounting references now exist, such as a handbook edited by Choi (1991), a thorough guide to international practices compiled by Coopers & Lybrand (1993), and a guide to European accounting practices edited by Alexander & Archer (1991).

International Accounting Diversity

The process of comparing financial reports from different countries might seem only to require translating to a common language and a common currency. Although the currency translation process can itself be quite complex, translation alone is a small part of the exercise. There are vast differences in accounting practices that hinder direct comparison among international financial reports – differences that can seem subtle and inconspicuous to the casual user. For example, the requirement to depreciate long-lived assets is common. However, countries' traditions differ widely in assumed useful lives of assets, which leads Bavishi (1993, p. 225) to conclude that "depreciation is probably the most inconsistently applied accounting standard in the world." Moreover, some countries (e.g., the USA downward adjustments in cases of asset impairment). By contrast, other countries (e.g., the UK, the Netherlands, and Australia) permit upward revaluations to reflect changing market conditions. Research indicates that such revaluations can be employed strategically by managers, and are reflected in the prices of firms' equity securities.

A comprehensive analysis of international accounting differences is compiled by Bavishi (1993), while a more concise review of key differences is provided by Peller & Schwitter (1991). Such differences are not arbitrary, but rather have evolved from unique economic and societal forces in different countries. Some of the more important forces are considered below:

Securities markets. Financial reporting serves various constituencies, and the relative importance of these constituencies molds the framework of the reporting process. In countries where investors provide the principal source of capital through securities markets, the accounting standard setting process espouses the objective of providing a "fair view" of financial operations. The USA and the UK are prime examples. It is no coincidence that the securities markets in these two countries together account for 63 percent of the world's total equity capitalization (including both domestic and foreign listings), with the USA having by far the largest domestic capitalization, while the UK dominates in foreign listings (*see* tabulation by the Organisation for Economic Cooperation and Development (1994, p. 27)). A comparison and analysis of US and UK accounting disclosure practices is provided by Frost & Pownall (1994).

Some recent research has compared stock market reactions to accounting reports in different countries (Alford et al., 1993), although Pownall (1993) has cautioned that it is difficult to separate the informativeness of different accounting systems (as reflected in different security price reactions) from more fundamental differences in shareholder clienteles and stock market characteristics. Choi & Levich (1990) (as summarized in Choi & Levich (1991)) conducted a comprehensive survey of securities market participants in various countries, reporting that one-half of the respondents felt that international accounting diversity affected them adversely. Accounting practices in Japan, Germany, and Switzerland were most frequently mentioned as a cause of concern. In these countries, restrictive regulatory accounting standards prevail to varying degrees over the "fair view" model.

Credit markets. The alternative to the "fair view" model of accounting can be labeled a "stewardship" model. This alternative is characteristic of accounting practices in Japan and Germany, where accounting adopts a more rigid and conservative focus, consistent with creditors' demands for a conservative estimate of the assets underlying their loans. It is noteworthy that the historical focus on conservatism in US financial reporting has waned over the years, while conservatism (also known as "prudence") continues to be considered a desirable quality of accounting in several other countries. In fact, one conspicuous difference between the

otherwise similar conceptual frameworks of the International Accounting Standards Committee (IASC) and the US Financial Accounting Standards Board (FASB) is that the IASC includes "prudence" in its list of qualitative characteristics of accounting (IASC, 1994, pp. 44–45), but neither conservatism nor prudence appear in the FASB chart of desirable accounting qualities (FASB, 1980, figure 1). In Japan, which has a traditional heavy reliance on credit financing as well as a large domestic stock market, a dual reporting system has evolved. One report is typical of the conservative, stewardship view of accounting, while the other is intended to be more useful to equity investors. For a discussion of Japanese accounting conservatism in general, see Aron (1991).

Taxation. The importance of the interrelationship between a country's system of taxation and its system of financial reporting cannot be overemphasized. In many countries, the two systems are structurally linked, such that a company pays tax on the same net income that is reported in general purpose financial statements. To varying degrees, alignment between tax and financial accounting is common in continental Europe and Scandinavia (see table 1 of Alford et al. (1993) for a listing by country). This linkage imposes a natural discipline on accounting choice; managers may be hesitant to choose income-increasing accounting methods if those methods also increase taxes. In the USA, taxes and financial reporting are linked by regulation only for inventory costing, which partially explains why there are so many accounting standards in the USA designed to prevent managers from overstating income. Research and development expenditures, to offer one example, must be charged to current expense. This requirement is rare internationally, but the freedom to account for research costs as an asset is not nearly so appealing if this election results in a higher tax liability.

Another consequence of the requirement to report the same net income for tax and financial accounting purposes is the use of *reserves*, a bookkeeping technique that provides an exception to the general rule that equates operating changes in net assets with net income. In effect, reserve accounting involves a reclassification of owners' equity from net income (and hence retained earnings) to various alternative designations. Reserves have typically dominated the owners' equity sections of financial statements in European countries that have a high degree of alignment between tax and financial reporting. Although some owners' equity designations similar to reserves have been introduced for selected items in the USA, the use of reserves in the USA is not nearly as prevalent as it is in Europe.

Taxes also impact intercompany transfer prices for multinational firms. Firms may distribute profits among their various foreign and domestic operations in such a manner as to minimize their global tax liability. Leitch & Barrett (1992) provide a comprehensive review of multinational transfer pricing and related research.

Economic stability. The stability of the monetary unit on which accounting values are based exerts an important influence on accounting systems. The most vivid example is in several countries in South America, where inflation has long been rampant. Accordingly, mandated inflation adjustments are common in the financial reports of South

American and Mexican companies, in contrast to the historical cost standard prevalent elsewhere. Germany provides an interesting counterexample to illustrate this contrast. German experiences with hyperinflation earlier in the 20th century have elevated the perceived importance in Germany of monetary stability. This has resulted in a strict German adherence to the historical cost postulate as an accounting manifestation of that stability.

Emphasis on Social Responsibility. In a capitalist economy, the primary mandate of the business firm is to maximize profit, providing a return to the firm's investors. In addition to the profit motive, however, different countries have different expectations regarding the firm's broader, societal objectives. These differing expectations give rise to different accounting disclosures. In some countries, for example, information regarding the number of employees (addressing the full employment objective) may be considered just as important as disclosure of product lines. Mueller, Gernon & Meek (1994, p. 83) provide the interesting example of the French firm Pernod Ricard's 1991 disclosure of a new air conditioning system, reflecting the company's "concern for constant improvement of working conditions." Another example on a broader scale is the *value-added statement*, a supplement to the traditional income statement that focuses on the applications of "sources of value" to various constituencies, including employees, the government, and investors. International examples of social responsibility accounting are provided by Gray & Roberts (1991) and Gray, Owen & Maunders (1987). As a counterexample, Lynn (1992) documents the virtual absence of social responsibility disclosures in Hong Kong, where a powerful capitalist ethic predominates.

Culture. Differing cultural values in different societies may influence acceptable accounting values, although researchers are only now beginning to systematically investigate such influences (Gray, 1988). Some recent research has applied the cultural typology of Hofstede (1980; 1991) to accounting and auditing issues. Schultz et al. (1993) (considering France, Norway, and the USA) and Kachelmeier & Shehata (1995) (considering China, Hong Kong, and Canada) are two accounting research applications.

International Accounting Harmonization

Given the economic and social forces that have conditial accounting differences, the task of replacing such differences with a harmonized set of comparable accounting standards is quite daunting. Yet, the need for comparability resulting from the surge in international finance has made harmonization a priority that cannot be ignored.

International Accounting Standards Committee. The prominent force in the quest for harmonization is the International Accounting Standards Committee (IASC), an organization that has been in existence for over twenty years. Founded in 1973 as an outgrowth of the efforts of accounting bodies in Canada, the UK, and the USA to foster international comparability, the IASC has grown considerably, and now boasts 109 member bodies in 80 countries. The volume of accounting pronouncements issued by the IASC has grown at a commensurate rate, now published in an annual compilation. The IASC standards comprise an invaluable resource to anyone in business who deals with international accounting.

Notwithstanding this growth, it is important to recognize that the IASC has little if any enforcement power, and that its pronouncements have often been more descriptive than proscriptive. For instance, the original wording of International Accounting Standard No. 9 (1978) on research and development provided that such costs "should be charged as an expense of the period in which they are incurred except to the extent that development costs are deferred..." Standards such as this can essentially be read to permit anything, which has led to the criticism that the IASC is more of a figurehead than a substantive harmonizing agent (Purvis, Gernon & Diamond, 1991). In recent years, however, the IASC has proposed more restrictive standards, most notably its comparability project (Draft E32, as modified and finalized in November 1993). This explains why Purvis, Gernon & Diamond (1991) find a lower degree of national conformity with later IASC standards than with earlier standards.

It is likely that the IASC will continue to grow in stature and influence as international trade continues to escalate. An increasingly frequent international practice is the reconciliation of financial statements prepared under local accounting standards to statements prepared under IASC standards. Research has shown that reconciliations such as these can be of significant importance to securities markets. Amir, Harris & Venuti (1993) provide a US example, where regulations for foreign listings require a reconciliation to US standards. Also, developing countries with little accounting infrastructure may find it both cost-effective and internationally beneficial to adopt the IASC model.

The European Union. In Europe, the European Union (EU) has complemented and to some extent competed with the IASC's harmonization efforts. The most pervasive of EU accounting directives have been its Fourth Directive (issued in 1978), dealing with various accounting issues, and its Seventh Directive (issued in 1983), dealing with consolidated financial reporting for affiliated enterprises. In sum, the spirit of the EU accounting directives has been to shift toward the "fair view" model of the UK and away from the more conservative and rigid models typical of continental Europe. Another objective has been to relax regulatory requirements linking tax generation to general purpose financial reporting (Joos & Lang, 1994).

Despite (or perhaps due to) the ambition of these objectives, countries have been slow to adopt the directives (Mueller, 1991). Even after adoption, evidence suggests that the effect of the EU directives has been more form than substance. For example, Nobes (1993) describes subtle but important differences in how the English words "true" and "fair" were translated in country-specific versions of the Fourth Directive. Emenyonu & Gray (1992) assert that significant accounting differences persist among France, Germany, and the UK in spite of the EU directives. Joos & Lang (1994) provide some market evidence corroborating these assertions. Using a capital markets methodology (i.e., research based upon security prices), they show that the EU directives did not result in any measurable convergence of the valuation relevance of French, German, and UK financial statements.

Other harmonization efforts also exist or may arise. For example, it is possible that the North American Free Trade Agreement may result in accounting pressures among Canada, the USA, and Mexico similar to those present in the European Union. Another region of rapid accounting change is in the former socialist countries of Eastern Europe (Gray & Roberts, 1991) and Russia (Enthoven, 1992), where market-oriented accounting models are just now beginning to emerge. Even in the People's Republic of China, which remains under socialist rule, accounting changes have been rapid and profound (Winkle, Huss & Xi-Zhu, 1994).

Whether harmonization will gain an edge over diversity remains an open question. The growing pressures of international markets strengthen calls for accounting harmonization, while nationalistic pressures from both economic and social sources are likely to resist change.

Bibliography

Alexander, D. & Archer, S.; Eds. (1991). *European accounting guide*. London: Academic Press.

Alford, A., Jones, J., Leftwich, R. & Zmijewski, M. (1993). The relative informativeness of accounting disclosures in different countries. *Journal of Accounting Research*, 31, supplement, 183–223.

Amir, E., Harris T. S. & Venuti, E. K. (1993). A comparison of the value-relevance of US versus non-US GAAP accounting measures using Form 20-F reconciliations. *Journal of Accounting Research*, 31, supplement, 230–64.

Aron, P. (1991). Japanese P/E ratios in an environment of increasing uncertainty. *Handbook of international accounting* F. D. S. Choi, (ed.), Chapter eight, New York: John Willey & Sons.

Bavishi, V. B. (Ed.). (1993). *International accounting and auditing trends*, 1, 3rd edn, Princeton, NJ: Center for International Financial Analysis and Research.

Choi, F. D. S. (Ed.). (1991). *Handbook of international Accounting*. New York: John Wiley & Sons.

Choi, F. D. S. & Levich, R. M. (1990). *The capital market effects of international accounting diversity*. Homewood: Dow Jones-Irwin.

Choi, F. D. S. & Levich, R. M. (1991). Behavioral effects of international accounting diversity. *Accounting Horizons*, 5, June, 1–13.

Coopers & Lybrand (1993). *International accounting summaries: A guide for interpretation and comparison*. 2nd edn, New York: John Wiley & Sons.

Crook, C. (1992). Fear of finance: The world economy. *The Economist*, 324, 19 Sept. (supplement), 1–48.

Emenyonu, E. N. & Gray, S. J. (1992). EC accounting harmonisation: An empirical study of measurement practices in France, Germany and the UK. *Accounting and Business Research*, 23, Winter, 49–58.

Enthoven, A. J. H. (1992). Accounting in Russia: From perestroika to profits. *Management Accounting*, 74, Oct., 27–31.

FASB (1980). *Statement of Financial Accounting Concepts No.2: Qualitative Characteristics of Accounting Information*. Stamford, CT: Financial Accounting Standards Board.

Frost, C. A. & Pownall, G. (1994). Accounting disclosure practices in the United States and the United Kingdom. *Journal of Accounting Research*, 32, Spring, 75–102.

Gray, R., Owen, D. & Maunders, K. (1987). *Corporate social reporting: Accounting and accountability*. London: Prentice-Hall.

Gray, S. J. (1988). Toward a theory of cultural influence on the development of accounting systems internationally. *Abacus*, 24, Apr., 1–15.

Gray, S. J. & Roberts, C. B. (1991). Corporate social and nonfinancial disclosures. *Handbook of international accounting* (Ed.), F. D. S. Choi, (Ed.), Chapter 24. New York: John Wiley & Sons.

Gray, S. J. & Roberts, C. B. (1991). East–West accounting issues: A new agenda. *Accounting Horizons*, 5, Mar., 42–50.

Hofstede, G. (1980). *Culture's consequences: International differences in work-related values*. Beverly Hills: Sage Publications.

Hosfstede, G. (1991). *Cultures and organizations: Software of the mind*. London: McGraw-Hill.

IASC (1994). *International Accounting Standards*. London: International Accounting Standards Committee.

Joos, P. & Lang, M. (1994). The effects of accounting diversity: Evidence from the European Union. *Journal of Accounting Research*, 32, (supplement), 141–68.

Kachelmeier, S. J. & Shehata, M. (1995). Internal auditing and voluntary cooperation in multinational firms: A cross-cultural laboratory experiment. Working paper University of Texas at Austin and McMaster University.

Leitch, R. A. & Barrett, K. S. (1992). Multinational transfer pricing: Objectives and constraints. *Journal of Accounting Literature*, 11, (1992). A note on corporate social disclosure in Hong Kong. *British Accounting Review*, 24, June, 105–10.

Meek, G. K. & Saudagaran, S. M. (1990). A survey of research on financial reporting in a transnational context. *Journal of Accounting Literature*, 9, 145–82.

Mueller, G. G. (1991). 1992 and harmonization efforts in the EC. *Handbook of international accounting*. F. D. S. Choi, ed., Chapter 12, New York: John Wiley & Sons.

Mueller, G. G., Gernon, H. & Meek, G. K. (1994). *Accounting: An international perspective*. Burr Ridge, IL: Business One Irwin.

Nobes, C. W. (1993). The true and fair view requirement: Impact on and of the Fourth Directive. *Accounting and Business Research*, 24, Winter, 35–48.

Organisation for Economic Cooperation and Development (1994). *Financial statistics monthly*. Section 2, October.

Peller, P. R. & Schwitter, F. A summary of accounting principle differences around the world. *Handbook of international accounting*. F. D. S. Choi ed., Chapter 4, New York: John Wiley & Sons.

Pownall, G. (1993). Discussion of the relative informativeness of accounting disclosures in different countries. *Journal of Accounting Research*, 31, supplement, 224–9.

Purvis, S. E. C., Gernon, H. & Diamond, M. A. (1991). The IASC and its comparability project: Prerequisites for success. *Accounting Horizons*, 5, June, 25–44.

Schultz, J. J., Jr,, Johnson, D. A., Morris, D. & Dyrnes, S. (1993). An investigation of the reporting of questionable acts in an international setting. *Journal of Accounting Research*, 31, supplement, 75–103.

Wallace, R. S. O. & Gernon, H. (1991). Frameworks for international comparative financial reporting. *Journal of Accounting Literature*, 10, 209–64.

Winkle, G. M., Huss, H. F. & Xi-Zhu, C. (1994). Accounting standards in the People's Republic of China: Responding to economic reforms. *Accounting Horizons*, 8, Sept., 48–57.

STEVEN J. KACHELMEIER

international business International business takes place when business is carried out across national borders. International business includes import and export activities, trade in services, consulting activities, and any other business related endeavors which cross a nation's borders. International business activities have grown to be a major part of the world's total economic picture. Changes in political positioning of countries and the drive toward privatization of formerly governmental operations will assure the continued growth of international business.

Bibliography

Alkhafaji, A. F. (1990). *International management challenge*. Acton, MA: Copley.

JOHN O'CONNELL

international business ethics   Ethical issues surrounding transnational corporations are numerous and fall into at least eight major categories: bribery and sensitive payments, employment issues, marketing practices, impact on the economy and development of host countries, effects on the natural environment, cultural impacts of transnational operations, relations with host governments, and relations with the home countries.

While discussions of the responsibilities of transnationals has occurred for decades, few analyses cast explicitly in terms of ethics occurred until the late 1970s. It was then that moral philosophers and business academics began exploring specific issues in international business ethics. Since then, two distinct schools of thought have arisen concerning transnational responsibilities: they may be called "minimalist" and the "maximalist" schools. The "minimalist" school argues that a transnational's moral responsibilities are tied directly to its economic purposes: i.e., to make profits for its investors and products or services for the public. Minimalists deny that it is the responsibility of the corporation to help the poor, encourage the arts, or contribute to social causes – except insofar as doing such things is consistent with its more fundamental mission of making profits. Minimalists assert that transnationals have moral responsibilities, but that they can sometimes put them under the heading of "not harming" and not directly violating the rights of others. In contrast, the maximalist believes that corporations are unique in their level of organization and ability to control wealth, and that, in turn, they have the duty to reach out and help others. If housing and water supplies are substandard in the local area, then the company should work toward their improvement. And if malnutrition is a serious problem, the transnational should both develop nutrition programs and facilitate their implementation. Both minimalists and maximalists agree that transnationals should meet certain minimum ethical standards in conducting their business, but they disagree about whether transnationals should exceed this minimum.

The most often-used means of expressing minimum standards is through the moral language of rights. Many international documents which articulate rights, including the United Nations' *Universal Declaration of Human Rights*, have gained broad acceptance among nations. A list of rights to which most nations and individuals would agree is the following:

1 The right to freedom of physical movement.
2 The right to ownership of property.
3 The rights to freedom from torture.
4 The right to a fair trial.
5 The right to non-discriminatory treatment (i.e., freedom from discrimination on the basis of such characteristics as race or sex).
6 The right to physical security.
7 The right to freedom of speech and association.
8 The right to minimal education.
9 The right to political participation.
10 The right to subsistence.

All individuals, nations, and corporations are understood to have correlative duties in connection with these rights. Moreover, most experts agree that these duties include not only refraining from depriving people of the objects of their rights directly, but also, at least in some instances, helping protect people from being deprived of their rights. For example, a transnational operating in a developing country has correlative duties regarding the right to minimal education. In turn, the transnational would violate the right to minimal education if it hired 8-year-old children for full-time, ongoing labor and thus deprived them of the opportunity to learn to read and write. Here the violation would be passive rather than active; it would happen not through the company's actively removing the means for minimal education, but by passively failing to protect the right from deprivation.

Another example of failing to honor a right by failing to protect it from deprivation involves the prospective purchase of land in a Third World nation by a transnational corporation, where the intent is to convert the land to the production of a cash, export crop. Suppose the land in question is owned by absentee landlords but worked by tenant farmers. Suppose further that the tenant farmers each year have been able to take a portion of the crop barely sufficient for their own nutritional needs, but that the conversion of the land to a cash crop (forced by the transnational's purchase) will have the effect of driving the farmers to the slums of a nearby city where they will suffer malnutrition as a result. If this were true, then the transnational may violate the farmers' right to subsistence by its actions, even though it would not have taken food from anyone's mouth. The violation of the right would be passive; it would occur as a result of not honoring the duty to protect the right to subsistence from deprivation.

An approach that is satisfied with merely honoring rights, such as the above, is a "minimalist" approach to international business ethics. In contrast, De George's book, *Competing with Integrity in International Business* (1993), is a good example of the "maximalist" approach. De George advances ten guidelines that he believes apply to American multinationals operating in less-developed countries. According to him, such multinationals should:

1 Do no intentional direct harm.
2 Produce more good than harm for the host country.
3 Contribute by their activity to the host country's development.
4 Respect the human rights of their employees.
5 Respect the local culture and work with and not against it.
6 Pay their fair share of taxes.
7 Cooperate with the local government in developing and enforcing just background institutions.
8 Recognize that majority control of a firm carries with it the ethical responsibility for the actions and failures of the firm.
9 Make sure that hazardous plants are safe and run safely.
10 When transferring hazardous technology to less-developed countries, be responsible for redesigning such technology so that it can be safely administered in the host country.

As De George's rules imply, one of the most difficult contexts for transnational ethics involves clashes between home- and host-country norms or laws. The problem is especially acute when the norm or law appears substandard from the perspective of the transnational's home country. When wage scales, pollution standards, norms prohibiting bribery, and treatment of minorities appear substandard in a foreign country, should the transnational take the high road of adhering to the home-country standards, or should it take the expedient route of embracing the host-country standards?

Embracing either extreme would be morally problematic. Always to adopt the home-country standard would sometimes disadvantage the host country. For example, a transnational that always paid workers in host countries the same wage rates as paid in the home country could damage foreign development in the host country, since attractive wage rates are often the principal incentive for transnational investment overseas. Furthermore, the trade-offs among competing economic and social goods may be different in the host than in the home country. A Third World country barely able to feed its malnourished population may prefer somewhat higher levels of pollution and more productivity (say, of food and fertilizer) than would a developed nation.

On the other hand, always to adopt the host-country standard would be pernicious. Laws and regulations in many developing countries are frequently unsophisticated, and a lack of technological knowledge coupled with inefficient bureaucratic mechanisms may preclude effective government control of industry. Blindly to adopt a developing country's standards for asbestos or for the dumping of hazardous waste could have tragic human consequences. While no simple answers exist, Donaldson, De George, and others have argued that certain principles can be articulated for the purpose of addressing such problems of norms in conflict.

In a directly practical vein, coalitions of governments and transnational corporations are increasingly articulating shared responsibilities in formal documents. Sometimes the responsibilities are formalized as the result of voluntary efforts by companies who are members of the same industry, as in the instance of the World Health Organization's Code on Pharmaceuticals and Tobacco, and the World Intellectual Property Organization's Revision of the Paris Convention for the Protection of Industrial Patents and Trademarks. Sometimes they are formalized as the result of international economic arrangements, as in the instance of the principles of intellectual property circumscribed by the General Agreement on Tariffs and Trade (GATT). And sometimes they are formalized as a result of decisions by truly global institutions, as in the instance of the OECD's *Declaration on International Investment and Multinational Enterprise*.

Bibliography

DeGeorge, R. T. (1993). Competing with Integrity in International Business. (New York: Oxford University Press.)

Donaldson, T. (1989). The Ethics of International Business. (New York: Oxford University Press.)

Donaldson, T. (1991). The ethics of conditionality in international debt. *Millennium: Journal of International Studies*, **20** (2), 155–69.

Enderle, G. (1989). The indebtedness of low-income countries as an ethical challenge for industrialized market economies. *The International Journal of Applied Philosophy*, **4** (3), 31–8.

Guidelines for Multinational Enterprises. (1984). Added to the 1976 *OECD Declaration*. In *International Investment and Multinational Enterprises: Revised Edition 1984*. Paris: Organization for Economic Cooperation and Development, 11–22.

Kline, J. (1985). *International Codes and Multinational Business: Setting Guidelines for International Operations*. Westport, Conn.: Quorum Books.

Moran, T. H. (1977). *Multinational Corporations and the Politics of Dependence: Copper in Chile*. Princeton, NJ: Princeton University Press.

O'Neill, O. (1986). *Faces of Hunger: An Essay on Poverty, Justice, and Development*. London: Allen & Unwin.

Preston, L. E., & Windsor, D. (1991). *The Rules of the Game in the Global Economy: Policy Regimes for International Business*. Dordrecht, The Netherlands: Kluwer.

Shue, H. (1980). *Basic Rights*. Princeton, NJ: Princeton University Press.

Waldman, R. J. (1980). *Regulating International Business Through Codes of Conduct*. Washington, DC: American Enterprise Institute.

THOMAS DONALDSON

international channel management In marketing, the term distribution has two distinct, yet interconnected, meanings. The first refers to the physical movement of goods from the place of manufacture to a location in or close to points of purchase. A location in a point of purchase might be a supermarket; a location near a point of purchase might be a storage facility supplying, say, spare parts to industry in a given region. Distribution in this sense is called logistics or physical distribution management. The second meaning refers to channel management. This contribution is concerned with international channel management.

A marketing channel should not be seen narrowly as a pathway from the point of production to points of purchase by customers. Rather it should be seen as a concatenation of individuals and organizations involved in the process of making goods or services available for use or consumption. Distribution arrangements for making goods and services available for use and consumption in foreign markets are extremely varied. The persons or organizations involved in the distribution process include agents, distributors, other representatives who may be externally appointed (e.g., an export house), locally established sales offices, or franchisees.

The precise choice of these persons and organizations is influenced by factors such as the nature of the product or service, the degree of day-to-day control that the marketing firm wishes to exercise from the outside, its knowledge and experience of given markets, its strategic remit and INTERNATIONAL MARKETING policy. For example, a company supplying mass consumer goods, such as Coca Cola, needs as many outlets as possible supported by an intensive distribution system. By contrast, a selective or exclusive distribution system is required by products such as PCs or Chanel No. 5 respectively.

Consistent with these factors, internationally-operating firms address five specific challenges in the selection and implementation of schemes, which have been highlighted by Terpstra & Sarathy (1994) as follows:

(1) Should the firm extend its domestic distribution approach uniformly to foreign markets or adapt its distribution strategy to each national market?

(2) Should the firm use direct or indirect channels in foreign markets?

(3) Should the firm use selective or widespread distribution?

(4) How can the firm manage the channel?

(5) How can the firm keep its distribution strategy up to date?

This list needs to be qualified in two important ways. First, it needs to be emphasized that, the more sophisticated the operation, the more likely it is that a firm will use a combination of distribution approaches and underpin these approaches through promotional and ADVERTISING support. This latter activity can involve a locally appointed intermediary, such as an advertising agency or a public relations company, which it is not normal to view as a channel member on the grounds that these organizations are only indirectly involved in selling the goods or delivering the service. Second, advances in information technology and modern instant forms of electronic communication now mean that distribution in foreign markets, where IT is well established, is increasingly becoming an information management activity.

It has been argued by Dahringer & Mühlbacher (1991) that small and medium-sized enterprises, on the one hand, and multinational corporations (MNCs), on the other, show a marked tendency to leave matters of distribution to their local representatives or local offices. As a result, too many firms lack a coherent international or global distribution policy, which underpins company guidelines for setting "MARKET SHARE, sales volume, and profit margins for each market, taking account of market-entry alternatives, the desired level of company involvement in the distribution system, and the desirability of ownership of intermediaries." Market control becomes uncertain and the quality of marketing impaired. These arguments tend to reinforce Drucker's famous dictum that distribution, for all its hallowed status in the 4 P's, is still very much marketing's "dark continent."

Whatever the distribution system in given markets, the key factor for firms is to select arrangements that ensure profitability and are suited to the nature of the market in terms of its customer characteristics, structure, and distribution support facilities (e.g., transportation systems, warehousing, and storage). As for channel management, which means in practice the management of relationships with channel intermediaries, specific challenges face international marketers relating to operationally interconnected areas of organization, communication, control, and motivation.

An appropriate organizational form must be developed, which links the supplier with key market intermediaries. This could be an extension of the firm's domestic organizational structure. Its organizational arrangements need to facilitate smooth and prompt exchanges of information with channel intermediaries to maintain a high level of cooperation, secure reliable feedback about the market, and encourage their ideas on all aspects of MARKETING, promotion, and selling in their territories. Apocryphal stories of channel intermediaries being the last people to hear about a price change affecting their market serve as a warning about the difficulties of handling these most important of international business relationships.

Bibliography

Dahringer, L. D. & Mühlbacher, H. (1991). *International marketing: A global perspective.* Reading, MA: Addison Wesley.

Terpstra, V. & Sarathy, R. (1994). *International marketing.* Chicago: The Dryden Press.

NIGEL HOLDEN

international code of business ethics Can international codes of professional ethics be developed to regulate, successfully, professional behavior? Put differently: are the rules of the game the same in Boston, Berlin, and Tokyo? There is evidence that local "customs" may override universal principles, thus making for ethical "diversity." By identifying and understanding the factors which make local cultures unique, and addressing their requirements, the potential effectiveness and acceptability of an "international" code might be enhanced. There is no guarantee of success in this venture: to illustrate the problems, we will examine the code of conduct or guidelines used by the International Federation of Accountants (IFAC) in July 1990.

On the face of it, there are two major reasons why worldwide acceptance of the current version of this Guideline may be problematic. First, societies tend to resist guidelines imposed from without where they are perceived as inconsistent with a society's entrenched cultural norms. Second, as socio-economic conditions vary dramatically from country to country, so, too, do levels of professional proficiency in the countries in which guidelines are to be implemented. While all accountants encounter ethical conflicts, those arising in the context of the high technical proficiency required of accountants in a developed country may be entirely different in kind from those encountered by accountants in developing countries. In this article we will concentrate on highlighting the cultural issues.

Cultural Influences on Ethical Conduct

We will argue that culture plays an important role in relation to ethical standards. If we restrict the meaning of culture to a national or local unit of analysis, as opposed, say, to ethnic or corporate cultures, Hofstede's (1980) definition provides a useful framework. Culture in this sense is "the collective mental programming of the mind which distinguishes the members of one human group from another" (p. 25). As he considered cultures, he concluded that four measures – power distance, uncertainty avoidance, poles of individualism and collectivism, and poles of masculinity and femininity – could be used to differentiate the "collective mental programming" which is culture.

Power distance, a construct originally identified by Mulder (1977), measures how a less powerful subordinate perceives the degree of inequality in power which separates him or her from a more powerful superior.

Uncertainty avoidance, which indexes tolerance for uncertainty in culture, considers three indicators: rule orientation, employment stability, and stress. *Reluctance to break rules*, even when doing so is in the interests of the company, indicates an aversion to uncertainty. *Employment stability* captures a collective tolerance of the risks associated with job change. (Long-term employers who hold scrupulously to rules would measure high on the uncertainty avoidance scale.) While recognizing that *stress* certainly reflects organizational and personality variables, Hofstede attributes some part of it to culture and sees it as reflecting the level of anxiety in a society.

The poles of *Individualism* and *Collectivism* form the third dimension of national culture. Put simply, this dimension captures the extent to which a culture values individual achievement over group cohesion. Individualist societies, such as the United States, regard achievement as personal; collective contributions to one's success tend to be discounted. In contrast, collectivist cultures prize group well-being and group achievement over individual self-interest.

The poles of *Masculinity* and *Femininity* form the final dimension of national culture. This dimension measures the extent to which a culture emphasizes assertive ("masculine") rather than supportive ("feminine") values and also captures the degree to which a culture identifies jobs as gender-based.

Where cultures differ, international codes of ethics, even for a relatively homogenous profession such as accounting, may encounter difficulties. Two broad difficulties suggest themselves: lack of consensus as to what constitutes acceptable behavior and divergent interpretations of the code.

Lack of consensus on acceptable behavior. Since cultures embody generally held beliefs and norms of appropriate behavior in a country, they have consequences for ethical behavior. Consider bribery. Pressure on a subordinate to cover up a supervisor's illegal action, such as accepting bribes, might be evaluated differently by Japanese than Americans because of cultural influences. While an American might interpret this pressure as coercion, a Japanese might willingly participate in a cover-up for collective motives – to save face and protect the reputation of the group.

Intellectual property presents another interesting contrast. In the typically collectivist cultures of Asia, the individual artist or writer is expected to share his or her creation. In contrast, individualist societies emphasize protecting the artist or writer by establishing copyright and patent laws.

Diversity of interpretation. Cultural differences, in the second place, might limit the application of an international code by spawning a diversity of interpretations of the code, with corresponding consequences for implementation. The ideal of a self-regulating profession, in which members identify not with the organization by which they are employed but instead with the code of a profession, may be based on an individualist value system. Several researchers have argued that individualism values prize allegiance not to a group of people, but to a set of standards. As a consequence, practitioners in an individualist society may assume that if a professional chooses in light of the profession's guidelines, this will produce the best long-term results for that profession and for the society. But such an assumption may be antithetical to a collectivist culture.

An Evaluation of the IFAC Guideline

The Guideline identifies six principles fundamental to the accounting profession: Integrity, Objectivity, Professional Competence and Due Care, Confidentiality, Professional Presentation. Some of these could conflict with some cultural norms, and others are geared more toward the needs of developed economies than those of less-developed countries. Figure 1 shows a matrix consisting of Hofstede's cultural dimensions and the IFAC Guideline: cells with text identify areas where cultural diversity might create problems.

Figure 1   A framework for evaluating international codes of conduct applied to IFAC's "Guideline on Ethics"

	Consistency with Cultural Values			
	Power distance	*Individualism/ Collectivism*	*Uncertainty/ Avoidance*	*Masculinity/ Femininity*
Integrity	Loyalty to supervisor	Conflicting loyalties	Compromising professional standards	Exaggeration of ability
Objectivity	Loyalty to supervisor	Value of others' opinions		
Confidentiality	Willingness to follow instructions	Loyalty to family and friends		Acceptability of self-promotion
		Loyalty to professional colleagues	Resolution of ethical conflicts	"Lowballing" and aggressive promotion of the firm
Professional behavior		Independence of audit		Sex discrimination

Power Distance and the dilemmas of the faithful follower. Power distance captures the extent to which subordinates in an organization expect to be instructed by superiors, and willingly obey those instructions. In a "high" power distance culture, the International Guideline's requirements on integrity, objectivity, and confidentiality are likely to create cultural conflicts for subordinates. Consider the first column of figure 1: a subordinate in such a culture would be likely to acquiesce to a superior's unauthorized request for confidential information, and such acquiescence would be regarded as acceptable behavior. A subordinate would also be more likely to remain loyal to his or her supervisor out of respect for the supervisor's position, even when the supervisor acts unethically, or even illegally. More important, such behavior on the part of the subordinate would be culturally acceptable.

Individualism/Collectivism and the dilemmas of personal loyalty. The integrity principle requires the professional accountant to be "straightforward and honest in performing professional services," and the objectivity principle requires that "a professional accountant should be fair and not allow prejudice or bias or influence of others to override objectivity" (IFAC, p. 8). If we take "straightforward and honest" to involve a willingness on the part of individuals to be open to non-members of their group, then cultures will differ markedly. As the second column indicates, a member of a collectivist culture would value the opinion of peers, and indeed would be unwilling to make a decision without their input. A code of conduct which forces individuals to compromise relationships with group members in favor of client confidentiality also conflicts with collectivist cultural norms.

The confidentiality principle states that a professional accountant "should respect the confidentiality acquired during the course of performing the professional services and should not use or disclose any such information without proper and specific authority" (IFAC, p. 9). If a professional discovered that his or her client was close to bankruptcy, the Guideline requires that this information be withheld from close friends and family. However, in a collectivist culture, a failure to warn family and friends who were owed money would be a serious breach of collectivist norms.

Uncertainty Avoidance and the dilemma of being "professional." In the process recommended for the solution of an ethical conflict, the Guideline recommends a hierarchical approach whereby the professional is to review the conflict with his or her superior, or a higher authority if the superior is involved in the conflict problem. While this hierarchical approach might be suitable for a strong uncertainty avoidance culture, with its preference for written rules and intolerance of deviance, a weak uncertainty avoidance culture would be more tolerant of whistleblowing. Furthermore, a professional from a collectivist culture would value the advice of colleagues rather than superiors.

Masculinity/Femininity and the question of professional "presentation." The masculinity dimension has important implications for the accounting profession, in which Western norms of professional conduct include restrictions on advertising and promotion. A masculine culture might be more tolerant of exaggerated self-promotion, and aggressive bidding for new clients.

The norms of a masculine culture which include acceptance of gender-based work-role differences in a country such as Japan (which has the highest masculinity score) would be interpreted as sex discrimination by members of a more feminist culture (such as Sweden).

Toward Internationally Acceptable Ethical Guidelines
As our review of the IFAC's guidelines suggests, "international" professional guidelines may turn out to be ethnocentric, reflecting the ethical and cultural standards of the developed countries whose organizations are most influential in writing them. They therefore risk failing to address ethical dilemmas found primarily in developing countries. Truly international guidelines must be sensitive to the need for guidance of the profession in its normal practice in all countries in which the code will operate.

Bibliography
Hofstede, G. (1980a). *Culture's Consequences.* Beverly Hills, Calif.: Sage.
Hofstede, G. (1980b). Organizational Dynamics. *Motivation, leadership, and organization: Do American theories apply abroad?* Summer, 42–63.
Mulder, M. (1977). *The Daily Power Game.* Leiden, Netherlands: Martinus Nijhoff.

LAURIE PANT
DAVID SHARP

international human resources management (HRM) International human resources management involves managing the factors dealing with persons employed in various fashions by an organization. These factors include: planning for human resource needs; staffing per the plans; training and development, if necessary; developing compensation systems; and evaluating the performance of employees. These factors are the same as those for domestic operations except international HRM must also take into consideration cultural variables between employees' countries of origin, language differences, religious preferences, and a myriad of other factors which differ from country to country. International HRM involves keeping a balance between all employees, thereby allowing employee transfer from country to country. It also allows different management styles to coexist and value differences to be recognized and accommodated.

Bibliography
Acuff, F. (1984). International and domestic human resource functions. *Innovations in International Compensation,* **September**, 3–5.
Brewster, C. & Tyson, S. (1991). International comparisons in *international human resource Management.* London: Pitman.
Dowling, P. J. & Schuler, R. S. (1990). *International dimensions of human resource management.* Boston, MA: PWS-Kent.
Edstron, A. & Lorange, P. (1984). Matching strategy and human resources in multinational corporations. *Journal of International Business Studies,* **15** (2), 125–37.
Ishidi, H. (1986). Transferability of Japanese human resource management abroad. *Human Resource Management,* **259** (1), 103–20.
Martinez, Z. L. & Ricks, D. A. (1989). Multinational parent companies' influence over human resource decisions of affiliates: U.S. forms in Mexico. *Journal of International Business Studies,* **20** (3), 465–87.
Punnett, B. J. (1989). International human resource management in A. Rugman *International Business in Canada.* Toronto, Canada: Prentice-Hall, Canada.

Reynolds, C. (1986). Compensation of overseas personnel in *Handbook of Human Resource Administration*. 2nd edn, New York: McGraw-Hill.

Schuler, R. S. (1993). World class HR departments: Six crucial issues. *The Singapore Accounting and Business Review*, Inaugural Issue, September,

Tung, R. L. (1984). Strategic management of human resources in the multinational enterprise in *Human Resource Management*. New York: John Wiley & Sons.

JOHN O'CONNELL

international integration   This is the process of molding a company's various international activities into a single, unified organization. The integration process centralizes management decisions, thereby reducing the autonomy of foreign subsidiaries or affiliates. The process of international integration allows management to view the organization as truly a single entity with focused goals and objectives instead of a group of independent operations which may or may not have the best interests of the parent company in mind. International integration is generally a precursor to the development of a true global organization.

Bibliography

Peak, M. H. (1991). Developing an international style of management. *Management Review*, 80, 32–5.

JOHN O'CONNELL

international location   The international location decision is one which is concerned with the location of facilities at the highest level. It is a decision that needs to be made by any organization involved in international operations. Such organizations can include subsidiaries of multinational enterprises, international joint ventures, licensees or franchising operations. They may be involved in a range of different activities such as local assembly, offshore manufacturing or the complete production of goods for global markets. International organizations are also increasingly becoming involved in the delivery of services, particularly since the barriers preventing them being transferred across national boundaries are progressively being removed.

In many respects the international location decision is similar to any decision regarding the location of facilities for a domestic organization. Tangible factors can be taken into account, such as the cost of land, cost of buildings, labor costs, transport costs, etc. Similarly there are intangible factors to be considered, such as environmental constraints and ease of communications.

Perhaps the main thing that distinguishes an international location decision from a domestic one is its strategic dimension. Many organizations choose a particular international location with a view to exploiting the long-term possibilities offered and not simply to meet short-term objectives. Therefore, many of the established techniques for evaluating alternative locations or determining an "optimum" location are only of partial relevance.

The actual method used to determine the location of an international operation will tend to vary according to its type.

Local assembly normally takes place where tariff barriers exist on imported goods, or the assembly costs in the parent company are high, thereby making the products too expensive in the local market. The solution is therefore to use local labor to assemble CKD (complete knock down) or SKD (semi-knock down) kits, thereby avoiding import tariffs or taking advantage of lower local labor costs. Location decisions in this case need to consider the logistics of supplying parts and the availability of suitable low-cost labor.

Offshore manufacturing is where products are made in a foreign country to the design of, and often using parts supplied by, an original equipment manufacturer (or OEM), then reexported to the country of the OEM or to third countries. Therefore it is often restricted to assembly operations with the purpose of exploiting one or more of the local advantages such as reduced labor costs, specialized skills or lower overheads. Where there is a tariff on imported materials this is often overcome by locating in an "export processing zone," which is a tariff free area for export-oriented companies. Location decisions in such situations are influenced by the local costs of production, the incentive and taxation regime, and the ease with which materials, parts, and finished goods can be transported into and out of the country in question.

Complete production of goods for the global market is the approach to international operations commonly encountered in multinational corporations. It is often chosen because it offers the opportunity of achieving good economies of scale since production for every market takes place at just one single location and is fully integrated. Here, the location decision involves finding the best place to manufacture the product, taking into account a wide range of factors such as design capability, engineering competence, and availability of low-cost productive resources, as well as the need to minimize transport costs. This last factor is not too easy to determine because the materials, parts and finished goods can come from, and go to, an enormous number of other countries. The distribution of finished goods can also present difficulties because of the ever changing nature of the market in terms of customer location and product mix.

An alternative and overlapping approach to international location is to consider the configuration of a company's network at an international level. Four configuration strategies have been identified.

Home Country Configuration

The simplest strategy for an organization trading around the world is not to locate plants outside its home country and to export its products to foreign markets. The reason for this might be, for example, that the technology employed in the product is so novel that it needs to be manufactured close to its research and development headquarters. Alternatively, the home location of the company might be part of the attraction of a product (e.g. high fashion garments from Paris).

Regional Configuration

An alternative strategy is to divide the company's international markets into a small number of regions and make each region as self-contained as possible. So, for example, the Pacific region's market would be served by an operation or operations, in that region. Companies might adopt this strategy because their customers demand speedy delivery and prompt after-sales service. If products or services were created outside the region it might be difficult to provide such a level of service without regional warehouses and service centers.

Global Co-ordinated Configuration

The opposite of the regional strategy is the global co-ordinated configuration. Here each plant concentrates on a narrow set of activities and products and then distributes its products to markets around the world. So, for instance, a company might take advantage of low labor costs in one region and the technical support infrastructure in another in order to seek to exploit the particular advantages of each site or region. However, by doing so it does place a co-ordination requirement on the headquarters of the company. All product allocations, operations capacities and movement of products are planned centrally.

Combined Regional and Global Co-ordinated Configuration

The regional strategy has the advantage of organizational simplicity and clarity, the global co-ordinated strategy of well exploited regional advantages. Firms often attempt to seek the advantages of both by adopting a compromise between them. Under such a strategy regions might be reasonably autonomous, but certain products could still be moved between regions to take advantage of particular regional circumstances.

Bibliography
Dicken, P. (1992). *Global shift*. London: Paul Chapman.
DuBois, F. C. & Oliff, M. D. (1992). International manufacturing configuration and competitive priorities. In C. A. Voss, *Manufacturing strategy: Process and content*. London: Chapman and Hall.

DAVID BENNETT

international management   The process of planning, staffing, organizing, and controlling international business activities. International management thinking is normally not a part of domestic business operations. When an organization first ventures into international trade activities, management is not prepared to face its challenges. Consultants are often used to fill in the gaps in knowledge and approach to multinational business activities. As the organization grows in terms of its reliance on international business for market growth and profits, managers begin to more fully appreciate other cultures and economic systems. Language skills and cultural awareness increase. More growth results in managers striving to standardize their products for worldwide distribution. The world begins to appear as a single market and management must be prepared to deal with all aspects of that market.

Bibliography
Austin, J. E. (1990). *Managing in developing countries: Strategic analysis and operating techniques*. New York: Free Press.
Beamish, P., Killing, J. P. & Lecraw, D. J. (1991). *International management text and cases*. Homewood, IL: Irwin.
Daniels, J. D. & Radebaugh, L. H. (1993). *International dimensions of contemporary business*. Boston, MA: PWS-Kent Publishing.
Davidson, W. H. & de la Torre, J. (1989). *Managing the global corporation*. New York: McGraw-Hill.
Deresky, Helen (1994). *International management*. 1st edn, New York: HarperCollins.
Hodgetts, R. H. & Luthans, F. (1994). *International management*. 2nd edn, New York: McGraw-Hill Inc.
Lane, H. W. & Distefano, J. J. (1988). *International management behavior*. Scarborough, Ontario: Nelson Canada.
Lessem, R. (1989). *Global management principles*. London: Prentice-Hall International.
Mahini, A. (1988). *Making decisions in multinational corporations – managing relations with sovereign governments*. New York: John Wiley & Sons.
Mendenhall, M., Punnett, B. & Ricks, D. (1995). *Global management*. Cambridge, MA: Blackwell Publishers.
Punnett, B. J. & Ricks, D. (1992). *International business*. Boston, MA: PWS-Kent.

JOHN O'CONNELL

international market entry and development strategies   The term "market entry and development strategies" has advantages over the term "market entry" in that the shorter expression focuses attention only on methods of entry, whereas the reality of INTERNATIONAL MARKETING is that the method of entry is a prelude to market penetration, the process of business development and consolidation within a foreign market over time. In other words, the selection of method of market entry or combination of methods is directly connected to both the overall business strategy for the market in question and the scale of investment allocated to achieve the strategic objectives.

For convenience, market entry and development strategies can be classified into direct and indirect methods. It is also possible to make a distinction between strategies which involve marketing only and those which involve marketing and production. Each strategy involves trade-offs between market control and degree of risk. Table 1 neatly captures these distinctions.

Table 1   Market entry and development strategies

Indirect entry	Direct entry
• exporting	• import houses
• direct mail (from outside)	• wholesale or retail purchasing groups
• export management companies	• public trading agencies
• export trading companies	• export departments
	• foreign sales representatives or branch offices
• licensing	
• franchising	
• production or management contracts	• joint ventures
	• direct foreign investment
	• acquisitions

The principal methods of market entry and development include EXPORTING, licensing, FRANCHISING, management contracts, turnkey contracts, international joint ventures, and cooperation agreements of which so-called strategic alliances are a prime example.

Market entry decisions are among the most important that internationally operating firms must make. A first consideration is that they depend on the quality and accuracy of information inputs obtained through international marketing research. A second is that the decisions made have a direct bearing on the evolution of the main MARKETING STRATEGY for the selected foreign market. The point to emphasize is not only that one particular method or combination of methods entails a specific investment, but that every method comes with operational implications. Broadly speaking, market entry and development decisions cover four key areas: control issues (are key decisions affecting operations in the market taken by a firm's local representatives or by an independent center such as a firm's international headquarters?); initial resource commitment; subsequent resource commitments; and definition of objectives.

In the case of consumer products, decisions on market entry and development involve decisions on, say, channel management (see INTERNATIONAL CHANNEL MANAGEMENT) or ADVERTISING campaigns. Miscalculations arising from wrong advertising or channel management decisions can result in unforeseen and therefore unwelcome costs in the form of product modifications, redeployment or reselection of market intermediaries. Nor can price rises be excluded. For firms supplying technical goods and operating primarily (though not necessarily exclusively) in industrial markets, strategy will be determined by the defirm's intention to enter the market and take up a position there by means of either some kind of collaboration (as through a technology transfer activity) or a more direct ("aggressive") penetration strategy.

NIGEL HOLDEN

international marketing Over recent years the theoretical underpinnings and definitional scope of international marketing have been both challenged and augmented by scholars. The impulses for this reappraisal of international marketing reflect changes in the international business environment, which have given rise to new market structures and forms of inter-firm cooperation. For example: the "classic" distinction between domestic and international marketing has become increasingly problematical; the emphasis on global products for global markets, so attractive in the 1980s, is now generally seen to be naive, if not out of place; similarly, a long-standing tendency to associate international marketing with nations' overall international competitiveness no longer reflects the nature and trends of modern business; the glib formulation that international marketing is the application of the domestic MARKETING CONCEPT to international scenarios does not always stand up to scrutiny; and pan-European marketing, itself a slippery concept, is becoming notionally distinct from international marketing.

These points then suggest a shift in the definitional scope of international marketing, particularly over the last ten years or so, even if the basic operational tasks associated with the management of international marketing activities have remained constant: the task of marketing of goods and services across national or other boundaries (such as linguistic and cultural ones within the European Union); the task of marketing within foreign markets; and the task of coordinating the marketing effort in multiple markets (see Terpstra & Sarathy, 1991).

The key challenge facing practitioners is all about understanding how the interplay of global, regional, and local processes affects their decisions about what to offer to their international customers and how to implement a well-planned business approach that is responsive to local conditions. The point to emphasize is that these decisions span an exceptionally broad range of issues of a strategic and tactical nature, ranging from major decisions about the scale of investment in particular markets to minor decisions, which nevertheless require detailed market knowledge, such as the wording and format of labels.

It is then not surprising that authors of international marketing texts show a wide divergence in their definitions of international marketing. Paliwoda (1993) emphasizes the relationship between international marketing and national competitiveness. Dahringer & Mühlbacher (1991) find limitations with the long-standing approach which emphasizes the need for a distinct MARKETING MIX for each MARKET. For them, the task lies in concentrating on "product markets (groups of customers with shared needs), emphasizing their similarities regardless of the geographic areas in which they are located." They call this approach "global marketing," but emphasize that it does not ignore differences among markets. Many leading corporations, e.g., Texas Instruments, General Electric, Sony, and Toyota, practice this kind of global marketing as opposed to producing and selling so-called global products for global markets, now an increasingly discredited concept.

Perhaps the most enduring concept of international marketing is the one which links international marketing to internationalization – the international extension of a firm's activities into and within foreign markets. A seminal paper in this regard was by Johanson & Wiedersheim-Paul in 1975. Advocates of what might be termed "the internationalization approach" have generated various models suggesting the processes whereby firms take up positions in markets by stages.

This approach has led to a preoccupation of European marketing scholars with firms' internationalizing activities as networking behavior. Supported by extensive empirical studies of predominantly industrial suppliers and buyers, this approach in effect views international marketing as a form of management of relationships within NETWORKS (see Ford, 1990). American marketing scholars are less inclined to accept this behavioral interpretation and prefer to see and study international marketing as a global strategic function. American marketers tend to see internationalization in terms of the globalization of business – by which they frequently mean *American* business.

On the other hand, there is close agreement between European and American scholars that international marketing is a potentially incremental activity in the sense that firms select the degree of involvement with foreign markets. The degree of commitment begins, as it were, with direct selling overseas (i.e., EXPORTING), and ends with a complex business investment in foreign markets such as a production facility or international joint venture. Firms which engage heavily in international business operations tend not to make a distinction between home and overseas business. For example, Zeneca, the major UK pharmaceuticals producer, makes this a plank of its MISSION STATEMENT.

The creation of the Single European Market in 1993 has stimulated interest, on both sides of the Atlantic, in so-called "Euro-marketing" and there is a perennial debate about the mythic or actual status of the "Euro-consumer." But, perhaps the most significant feature of the Single European Market in terms of international marketing thinking is that this *planned* market of 340 million consumers can be seen to be a new and empirically significant battleground for arguably the most important operational issue in international marketing: namely, whether products can be marketed in more or less standardized formats or whether they should be adapted to suit local tastes and needs.

All in all, the subject-matter of international marketing is diffuse and certainly difficult to crystalize into an adequate definition which captures the essence of all marketing activity, namely that it is a management function in its own right *and* a business philosophy about the centrality of customer satisfaction to a firm's success. Also, a serviceable definition must somehow reflect the variety of locales of business and emphasize that international marketing is a learning activity. The definition we propose is that international marketing is the systematic internationally-based quest for customers in MARKET environments (*see also* MARKETING ENVIRONMENT) involving a business approach that interprets customer requirements in terms of local behavior, tastes, and modes of thought.

These market environments themselves form what is traditionally known as the INTERNATIONAL MARKETING ENVIRONMENT, the wide arena in which marketers plan and execute their marketing programs. This international marketing environment is traditionally divided into sets of macro- and micro-level factors and influences, which in their totality act as a constraint, or even an impetus, on firms for developing and maintaining their international business commitments (*see also* MACRO ENVIRONMENT and MICRO ENVIRONMENT). These factors are variously classified under headings such as economic, cultural, social, legal, political, and technological. The macro-environmental factors can be global in their reach and impact, whereas the micro-level factors are associated with a distinct foreign market and are therefore "culture-specific." The more the environmental factors become culture-specific, the more they are likely to be bound up with local attitudes, values, and nuances of buyer behavior (*see also* CONSUMER BUYER BEHAVIOR). Experience suggests that marketers have most difficulty handling and apprehending attitudes and values, especially where there exists a major cultural gap.

Information from and about foreign markets stemming from international marketing research activity is the key input for strategic and tactical decisions regarding policies and practices concerning product development, pricing, promotion, the establishment of market positions after the initial entry, and responses to competitive pressures. The information gathered by means of marketing research supplies input for decisions about three key questions of strategic significance: which markets to target for special attention; which markets to earmark for specific development; which method of market entry (*see also* INTERNATIONAL MARKET ENTRY AND DEVELOPMENT STRATEGIES) and market maintenance to adopt. In everyday business practice the processing of information is a slow and exacting task, for the decision-making process must take into account the risks associated with each possible line of action.

Sometimes firms' activities, especially where promotion and ADVERTISING are concerned, go against the grain of local culture or sensitivities or simply bemuse the target market. For example, there is increasing evidence that consumers in former socialist countries of Eastern Europe find Western advertisements uninformative and unappealing intellectually. But, perhaps the most important transformation in the practice of international marketing is that as a business activity its operations are shifting from a competitive stance to a cooperative one. Super-regional environments such as the EU and ASEAN and even the Triad, which is a purely notional structure linking the USA, the EU, and Japan, are creating business conditions in which even very big (often technologically leading) firms must combine resources with partner businesses, who may otherwise be direct competitors in many product areas. Such international strategic alliances and other inter-firm and cross-border business formats suggest that in future a major task of international MARKETING MANAGEMENT will be to handle relationships involving sets of (occasionally competitive) partners in cooperative ventures. These relationships are going to become increasingly international with inter-firm cooperation spanning a multiplicity of cultures, languages, and outlooks. Thus, the international marketing manager of the future will almost need more competencies in communication and relationship management than even in the immediate past. Slowly, international marketing textbooks and curricula at business schools and management courses both for students and practitioners are reflecting this important change.

Bibliography

Dahringer, L. D. & Mühlbacher, H. (1991). *International marketing: a global perspective.* Reading, MA: Addison-Wesley.

Ford, D. (Ed.) (1990). *Understanding business markets.* London: Academic Press.

Johanson, J. & Wiedersheim-Paul, F. (1975). The internationalization process of the firm: Four Swedish case studies. *Journal of Management Studies,* **12**, October, 305–322.

Paliwoda, S. J. (1993). *International marketing.* Oxford: Butterworth-Heinemann.

Terpstra, V. & Sarathy, R. (1991). *International marketing.* Chicago: The Dryden Press.

NIGEL HOLDEN

international marketing environment   The marketing environment is commonly defined as the set of actors and forces that influence the success of a company's marketing program. The important observation to be made regarding the marketing environment is that it is simultaneously complex, competitive, and dynamic. This observation is particularly pertinent so far as INTERNATIONAL MARKETING is concerned; it is unlikely that anyone can fully comprehend or understand the environment and beyond identifying broad and usually ill-defined forces or currents there can be little in the way of a common environmental diagnosis. In fact it is misleading to talk of "the" environment as the environment of a firm is partially defined or even created by itself. The success of Body Shop, for example, is presumably in part a reflection of the founder's early appreciation of the growing influence of "green" issues. The "same" environment was clearly perceived differently by established firms in the cosmetics industry.

What meaning can we attach to the notion of an international marketing environment? It is clearly not a seamless whole spanning many or all countries. On the other hand, it is not just a collection of different national environments as this would make international marketing almost redundant as a separate field of study. International marketing belongs somewhere between these two poles and international marketing environments can be viewed in some sense as the linkages between different national environments. This linkage can, in principle, be viewed in two quite different ways: interdependence or integration. Traditional trade theories, for example, implicitly adopt the interdependence view, whereas the notion of "GLOBALIZA- TION" that is popular within international business and management studies (including marketing) implies an integration view. Globalization is held to be a force that is either dissolving national differences or is transcending these differences. Levitt's (1983) view of the globalization of markets is one good example. Another is Badarocco's view regarding the globalization of knowledge and technology (1991). One can also meaningfully talk of the globalization of competition (Prahalad & Hamel, 1988) or the globalization of business, where this refers to growing integration of business activities in different countries within the multinational corporation.

Globalization is driven, essentially, by economic and particularly technological forces reducing the costs of and barriers to resource mobility including the mobility of people, money, and (of course) knowledge of all sorts. The same forces have also reduced radically the costs of organizing and managing economic activity across space.

By contrast, political forces, generally speaking, are acting as a break on globalization. Protectionism, which is largely a manifestation of economic nationalism, is still a powerful force and the success of GATT (now called the World Trade Organization) in removing non-tariff barriers to trade has at best been limited. In fact, protectionism is more entrenched as it is increasingly exercised by regional blocks rather than by individual countries. For example, the dispute between France and the USA relating to the former's restrictions on service imports was enmeshed in the dispute between the EU and the USA. The tensions within the EU itself also reveal the relevance of political forces. There is increasing resistance to further integration and some European countries show great reluctance to trading off national for regional sovereignty.

The slogan that marketers "should think globally and act locally" is meant to emphasize the fact that international marketers face a hierarchy of environments. Irrespective of how the linkages between different national marketing environments are construed, the environment of a particular country remains highly relevant to success or failure in that market. Environmental analysis should, therefore, concern itself with the international level as well as the national or local levels. International analysis should

be used to indicate which countries may be avoided (on account, for example, of their instability or hostility to foreign business) and which countries could potentially be targeted. But the "real" marketing tasks relate to designing a MARKETING MIX for countries that are selected for entry or expansion programs, and clearly require a thorough understanding of the specific conditions of these countries. Furthermore, decisions regarding the feasibility and desirability of standardizing the marketing approach for several countries should be informed by a careful analysis of the relevant markets.

Even ardent advocates of globalization as the basis of marketing strategies cannot overlook the significant diversities that still divide national markets. Thus, it is obvious that differences in climate, topography, and other physical conditions will always be with us and will remain a significant influence on buyer behavior (see CONSUMER BUYER BEHAVIOR). For example, it is unlikely that a product (e.g., a washing machine) designed to perform well in the arid climates of Greece or Spain will give an equally satisfactory service in Denmark or Sweden. More generally, the apparent homogeneity in customer preferences across countries, evidenced by their purchase of standardized products and global brands, may in fact mask significant behavioral or attitudinal differences of relevance to international marketers. Notably, recent research has shown that consumers in different countries and cultures show different degrees of involvement with a number of standardized global products (Zaichowsky & Sood, 1989; Sood, 1993). Cultural influences are clearly deeply rooted and are very durable and marketers should be highly sceptical of "evidence" of growing convergence. The key challenge facing practitioners concerns understanding how the interplay of global, regional, and local environments affects their decisions about what to offer to their international customers and how to implement a well-planned business approach that is responsive to local conditions. The point to emphasize is that these decisions span an exceptionally broad range of issues of a strategic and tactical nature, ranging from major decisions about the scale of investment in particular markets to minor decisions, which nevertheless require detailed market knowledge, such as the wording and format of labels.

Bibliography

Badaracco, J. (1991). *The knowledge link: How firms compete through strategic alliances*. Boston, MA: Harvard Business Press School.

Levitt, T. (1983). The globalization of markets. *Harvard Business Review*, 22, May–June, 41–53.

Prahalad, C. & Hamel, G. (1988). Creating global strategic capability. In N. Hood & J. Vahne (Eds), *Strategies in global competition*. London: Routledge.

Sood, J. (1993). A multi-country approach for multinational communication. *Journal of International Consumer Marketing*, 5, 29–50.

Zaichowsky, J. & Sood, J. (1989). A global look at consumer involvement and use of products. *International Marketing Review*, 6, 20–34.

MO YAMIN

international marketing organization In the planning of their INTERNATIONAL MARKETING strategies firms must play close attention to the matter of organization. The creation of suitable organizational structures is in fact a central element of strategy formulation: it cannot be separated from the operational aspects of strategy. The creation of suitable organizational structures is, however, exceptionally complicated and is influenced by a host of factors, which cannot have quite the same significance for any two firms no matter how similar they may appear to be in their size (i.e., turnover and number of employees), product profile, and market specialization.

On the other hand, it is possible to identify eight main clusters of variables which firms need to take into account to ensure that their chosen organizational form serves as an effective mechanism of control for coordinating across the markets in which they operate. These eight variable clusters are: the size of the business – overall volume and the contribution of foreign sales; the number of markets in which the firm operates; the nature and level of involvement in foreign markets; the firm's international business goals; its international experience; the nature of its products, including its technical complexity and back-up needs; the width and diversity of the product line; and the precise nature of the marketing task.

In deciding on a suitable organization structure, companies traditionally choose between forms, which are based on four broadly alternative principles of divisionalization. The first principle is the international division, which is a specialist structure responsible for handling all aspects of a company's activities with foreign markets. These activities can be very diverse. In addition to overseeing relationships with all its international markets and intermediary partners, the international division will be called upon to: be responsible for foreign currency operations; deal with foreign governments and its own; handle all documentation pertaining to the supply of products to foreign customers; and work with key business partners such as exhibition contractors and advertising agencies. The establishment of a separate international marketing division is not favored by all companies on the grounds that such a structure creates an artificial distinction with domestic marketing operations. The argument for this organizational form is that international marketing is so specialized that it warrants this separation.

The second principle of organization is the product division. The rationale here, which is favored by several major international companies, is that a division based on a product (or suite of related products) enables the company to plan its business around products and product managers who will be exceptionally knowledgeable about them and fully aware of customer needs in all markets. The product division is popular with firms offering technical products requiring strong after-sales support and service. Therefore, a key role of the product manager is not only to advise on product marketing strategy, but also to act as a troubleshooter.

Against that form of organization, companies also make use of the geographical principle. In this case, companies divide their worldwide markets into distinct territories such as North America (i.e., USA and Canada), the Middle East, South America, the European Union etc. In this structure, the division is peopled by area specialists, one of whose skills may be knowledge of a foreign language. The rationale here is that doing business in specific geographically connected groups of markets requires considerable area knowledge, a kind of knowledge that the peripatetic

product manager can never acquire, literally because he is never anywhere long enough and geography and the geopolitical associations that go with it do not lend themselves to tidy, self-contained, classification. For example, until the end of the 1980s it was convenient to treat the Soviet Union and the socialist countries of Eastern Europe as a more or less homogeneous region from a marketing point of view. Today, this region has become a set of increasingly distinctive business regions, each requiring a high degree of specialized knowledge.

The fourth divisional form is known as functional. This structure is prominent in the case of companies – such as those operating in the oil and gas industries – where production and marketing methods are homogenous. In reality, it is rare that one encounters a company that adopts one of these organizational structures in the pure form as described here. The need for specialization is ever to be balanced with the need to integrate functions and competencies across organizational boundaries. This state of affairs gives rise to a fifth structure known as the matrix organization. This structure takes account of the fact that foreign subsidiaries or intermediary partners may report to one group at company headquarters. Thus, it is organizationally straightforward for local managers to deal directly with HQ staff responsible for marketing, production, research and development and so forth. This arrangement has a certain elegance, while representing a pragmatic attempt to add flexibility to relationships between HQ and local representation. Nevertheless, there are drawbacks. For example, a principle of the matrix system is that the majority of interactions involve lower-level management and that adequate resources – human, financial, and technical – support these interactions. However, when senior managers are drawn into exchanges, this can lead to factionalism and time-consuming haggling over resource allocations. Despite these limitations, the matrix structure tends to be the favored form of organization in large, internationally operating, companies.

In operational terms, the key facet of any organizational structure is that it facilitates those activities for which it has been designed. It should not be overlooked that, in addition to serving as a means of achieving customer closeness, an effective organizational structure must prove amenable for the fulfilling of key tasks of international MARKETING MANAGEMENT. Companies frequently have difficulty combining operational effectiveness with managerial efficiency; and, as a result, breakdowns in communication occur between market places and the strategic center of the company. Organizational designers, therefore, need to be very clear about the organizational structure they opt for. The reality of international marketing operations is that the established structure will perforce undergo modification, planned or unplanned. A major influence in this respect concerns the management of information. Thus, the international marketing organization should be designed with a very clear view of information needs.

According to Dahringer & Mühlbacher (1991), there are a number of activities in respect of which an information system is needed for undergirding the formal organizational arrangements. These activities are: monitoring the INTERNATIONAL MARKETING environment; elaboration of strategic decisions (e.g., pertaining to market expansion or divestment); performance monitoring of product markets and geographical regions; assessment of resource-allocation decisions and their impact on the company's overall success; exchanging and integration of experiences gained in different parts of the company; and communicating information about the firm and its products, activities, and achievements to relevant business partners. The information system must be able to gather, store, update, and disseminate information efficiently.

Whatever organizational structure a firm adopts for its international marketing operations, a suitable information system (*see* MARKETING INFORMATION SYSTEMS) must be in place. Without this, competence for other major management tasks of international marketing, namely planning and control, will be severely impaired. It is still not fully appreciated by firms that international marketing success is closely correlated with a superior capacity to handle environmental information. This has been demonstrated by Japanese firms in the last two decades.

Bibliography

Dahringer, L. D. & Mühlbacher, H. (1991). *International marketing: A global perspective*. Reading, MA: Addison Wesley.

NIGEL HOLDEN

international pricing policy Pricing decisions have long been held to be among the most difficult that managers must make. Chisnall (1995) points out five key factors which influence pricing decisions: nature and extent of demand; competitors' activities (influenced by trading structure); costs of production and marketing; pricing objectives (business policy); and product life cycle.

When it comes to pricing for international markets, these factors and the levels of complexity associated with them take on extra dimensions. The fact that all these factors play themselves out differently from market to market makes standard price policy a virtual impossibility and suggests that an international pricing policy must be one that is not narrowly focused on the setting of the product price. Ideally, as Dahringer & Mühlbacher (1991) note, an international pricing policy must take account of "the intended strategic position of the company as well as the positioning of its product lines and individual products."

International pricing decisions cannot be as easily standardized as decisions concerning product policy or promotional strategy. This is because so many uncontrollable influences can have a bearing on price. Furthermore, many of these influences are subject to rapid fluctuation: an obvious example of this kind concerns currency exchange rates. Other factors, such as changes to tax regimes in foreign markets or the rate of inflation there, can bring about significant changes in purchasing power, the degree of demand, and the nature of competition.

A number of factors which impact on pricing decisions for international markets have been classified by Daniels & Radebaugh (1994): different degrees of governmental intervention; greater diversity of markets; price escalation for exports; changing relative values of currencies; differences in fixed versus variable pricing practices; and strategies to counter international competitors.

Each of these factors is now considered. With respect to government intervention, this can take three main forms: exchange rate policies, balance of payments policies, and regulations. The first two influence the financial environment, having a direct bearing on business confidence. The third can manifest itself in the form of price controls. In order to protect a home industry or to avoid dumping, a government can use its regulations in various ways, for example to: impose price ceilings, restrict price changes, or tax profits (for example, by limiting the amount that can be expatriated).

Concerning diversity of markets, Dahringer & Mühlbacher (1991) isolate four general classifications from country to country and which influence markedly the price that a market will tolerate for a given product: customers, competition, business groups, and economic conditions. Customers not only, in principle, establish through demand the real value of products, but also determine the theoretical price ceiling of a given product. Competition has a tendency to keep prices low. Business groups possibly, with their country's government, establish the framework of competition and may cooperate, formally or informally, to set the price parameters for a given industry sector. With respect to economic conditions, four factors exert the greatest influence over prices: growth rates, exchange rates, inflation, and income distribution. All of these factors are interrelated, and influence an economy's dynamism and its openness to foreign products.

Price escalation refers to the additional charges imposed on the basic production cost of a product. There may be as many as 20 of these cost elements on a product which is destined for export. These cover various ex-works transportation costs, administrative fees, international carriage and associated insurance, special packaging, and so forth.

Exchange rates not only establish monetary differentials among nations; they are also subject to fluctuation, and any currency in which goods may be finally quoted is subject to pressures which affect the ultimate perceived value of goods and therefore their relative value and affordability. One such pressure is inflation which can either be exported or imported. As Daniels & Radebaugh (1991) point out, inflationary pressures affect pricing in two significant ways: the receipt of funds in a foreign currency, when converted, buys less of the company's own currency than had been expected; and the frequent readjustment of prices is necessary to compensate for continual cost increases.

Changes in exchange rates have, of course, the effect of making goods appear either cheaper or more expensive. This means that an element of international pricing strategy must be to make best guesses about any such changes in order to set a price that does detract from consumers' perceived value. This form of prediction is far from easy. Nor should it be forgotten that exchange rates not only influence a company's prices, they also determine the cost of its own purchases from foreign sources.

A crucial aspect of pricing policy for international operations is that prices are often subject to extensive negotiation between suppliers and foreign customers, who may in the first instance be a market intermediary and not an end-user. In the case of a "one-off" capital project, such as a chemical plant or renovation of an airport, the purchaser would aim to secure a lower price, e.g., by modifying his requirements. There is also flexibility over payment and credit terms as well as over service arrangements or programs for training the purchaser's personnel. In other words, companies can shift their pricing strategy from one based on fixed price to one based on variable price.

A major consideration behind a variable price strategy is frequently a recognition of the need to counter international competitors. If the main competition in a foreign market comes from within, then the external supplier is able to set his price according to levels influenced by the domestic competition. Where, however, it encounters the same international competition in various markets, the company must develop a pricing policy which recognizes this fact. In other words, its pricing for international markets cannot be mainly influenced by internal market factors; the global competitive environment must be taken into account.

So far the discussion has concerned pricing as an element of business development linking suppliers to foreign markets. However, there is another form of international pricing that takes account of the fact that major internationally operating businesses supply goods internationally from one company location to another, e.g., from the point of production in one country to a subsidiary in another country. The pricing arrangement in this case is termed TRANSFER PRICING. A major motivation for this pricing option is that it provides major companies with a mechanism for side-stepping higher tax penalties in some countries.

As Daniels & Radebaugh (1994) explain: "If the corporate tax rate is higher in the parent company's country than in the subsidiary's country, the parent will set a low transfer price on products it sells to the subsidiary in order to keep profits low in its country and high in the subsidiary's country. The parent will also set a high transfer price on products sold to it by the subsidiary." In practice, transfer pricing may become very complicated, partly due to interdivisional rivalries within the same (vast) organization. Furthermore, because the transfer price is said to be arbitrary, i.e., is not set in accordance with market conditions, it can often prove difficult to evaluate subsidiary performance. It is for these reasons that transfer pricing is not always preferred to pricing methods that are market-oriented.

Bibliography

Chisnall, P. (1995). *Strategic business marketing*. Hemel Hempstead, UK: Prentice-Hall.

Dahringer, L. D. & Mühlbacher, H. (1991). *International marketing: A global perspective*. Reading, MA: Addison Wesley.

Daniels, J. D. & Radebaugh, L. H. (1994). *International business: Environments and operations*. Reading, MA: Addison Wesley.

NIGEL HOLDEN

international product adaptation   Marketing adaptation is the opposite of standardization and conveys the idea that marketers may tailor their marketing program to the specific conditions of the different countries in which they operate. A distinction is usually made between "mandatory" and "discretionary" adaptation (Hill & Still, 1984; Walters & Toyne, 1989). Mandatory adaptations are those that are dictated by the physical, legal, political, or economic factors in a country. For example, voltage levels and power sockets of electrical equipment need to conform to local requirements; in some countries safety or anti-pulsion/emission regulation may be particularly restrictive and may make it impossible for the firm to offer a standardized product. In

fact, however, research indicates that the majority of adaptations are not mandatory and according to one estimate, more than 70 percent of adaptations made are discretionary (Hill & Still, 1984).

Jain (1989) provides a rigorous examination of factors that affect the balance between program standardization and adaptation and offers a number of specific hypotheses relating to their impact on the degree of standardization. These factors fall into five categories: the nature of the target market; the market position of the firm in different countries; the nature of the product itself; environmental factors; and organizational factors. The observed pattern of standardization seems to confirm Jain's analyses. For example: the nature of the product is a strong predictor of standardization; standardization is more common for industrial as compared to consumer products; and products for which buyer behavior is culturally determined tend to be more adapted than products for which consumer choice is dependent on functional performance (e.g., food products compared to electrical goods).

see also **International product standardization**

Bibliography

Hill, J. & Still, R. (1984). Adapting products to LDC tastes. *Harvard Business Review*, March–April, 92–101.

Jain, S. (1989). Standardisation versus adaptation: Some research hypotheses. *Journal of Marketing*, 53, January, 70–79.

Walters, P. & Toyne, B. (1989). Product modification and standardization in international markets: Strategic options and facilitating policies. *Columbia Journal of World Business*, 29, Winter, 37–44.

MO YAMIN

international product life cycle   This is a relatively new theory (originating in the mid-1960s) attempting to describe the evolution of products through various stages: (1) local sales in the country in which the product was first produced; (2) exporting the goods; (3) production in a country which formerly imported the goods; and (4) becoming an import to the country in which the production process for the goods was originally developed. Through the cycle the original producing country eventually becomes an importer of the goods.

When an organization develops the technology to successfully produce a quality product (which is in demand) at low cost, that product will secure a local market relatively quickly. Take for example, color televisions. When color televisions first came on the market, local companies which had the technology produced and sold most of the TV sets. As more and more sets were sold more companies entered the market to produce and sell goods. TVs were exported as the local demand was met. As exports grew, the demands of high quantity production brought about standardization of product to take advantage of economies of scale.

As overseas sales prospered, it became evident that if the costs of transportation, tariffs, etc. could be saved, lower costs and competitive advantage would accrue to the company. Overseas production units are then established to service the foreign markets. More and more of domestic product is transferred to foreign factories as it becomes evident that labor and materials costs are also less. As more production takes place overseas, competition develops in foreign countries to meet their own demand. Eventually, production in developing countries supplants the production of the originator of the color television. Less costly production may eventually lead the original innovative country (the developer of the color TV) to become an importer of the item to meet its own demand. In the advanced industrialized nations this has occurred with automobile production, textiles, computers, and other products as well.

Bibliography

Albaum, Gerald, Strandskov, Jesper, Duerr, Edwin & Dowd, Lawrence (1994). *International marketing and export management.* 2nd edn, Wokingham: Addison-Wesley.

Davidson, W. H. & de la Torre, J. (1989). *Managing the global corporation.* New York: McGraw-Hill.

Root, E. R. (1994). *Entry strategies for international markets.* New York: Lexington Books.

Toyne, B & Walters, Peter, G. P. (1993). *Global marketing management.* Boston: Allyn and Bacon.

JOHN O'CONNELL

international product standardization   There is an inevitable tension between standardization and adaptation within marketing, whether domestically or internationally. The fact that customers have different preferences, and given marketing's commitment to customer "satisfaction," implies a pressure toward adaptation or even the customization of the offering to individuals or small groups. However, customization has been (until very recently, at any rate) considered to the existence of economies of scale and other technological and economic constraints suggesting that most people (with the exception of the very rich) must tolerate some degree of standardization or uniformity in what they purchase and consume. The evolution of marketing from "mass" to "target" marketing reflects this tension; "mass" marketing simply ignores diversity or the desire for variety ("you can have any color as long as it is black"). Target marketing, by contrast, starts by assuming pervasive diversity and searches for groups or SEGMENTS that may have similar preferences for a particular offering. However, the tension between standardization and adaption is particularly important for the international marketer, as the potential for economic benefits from standardizing across countries could be very substantial while the diversities may be very great due to significant differences in culture and other environmental conditions between countries (*see* INTERNATIONAL MARKETING ENVIRONMENT).

In INTERNATIONAL MARKETING, complete program standardization means offering the same product or product line at identical prices through identical distribution systems and promotional policies to customers in different countries. Program standardization is, thus, concerned with the degree to which different elements in the MARKETING MIX are treated in the same or a similar manner by a firm that operates internationally. Process standardization, on the other hand, refers to the uniformity in the approach chosen by a multinational firm in analyzing market potential and the formulation of MARKETING PLANNING for different countries. The vast majority of the literature is concerned, however, with program standardization.

The main attraction of standardization is clearly the scale economies that may result from it, not only in production but also in R&D and product development and possibly in advertising and promotional expenditure. Levitt (1983) puts particular emphasis on technology and scale factors in advocating standardization. An uninterrupted production run from one center will allow the firm to move rapidly up the learning curve, thus reducing per-unit cost very rapidly. Operating on a large scale will also provide sourcing efficiencies, e.g., purchasing large amounts of raw materials and other inputs gives a multinational the power to bargain with suppliers. Doglus & Wind (1987) are more skeptical and point out that economies of scope and flexible manufacturing increasingly make it feasible to make adaptation without incurring increasing costs or diseconomies of scale. Economies of scope arise if it is cheaper to produce a number of different products or product varieties together in one plant than it is to produce each in a separate plant. The basis for economies of scope is a number of interconnected technical developments known as "flexible" manufacturing systems.

In spite of much debate between the advocates of standardization and adaptation, little is known regarding the impact of standardization on corporate performance and until recently the performance issue had not received any research attention. Samiee & Roth's (1992) work is probably the first systematic investigation of the link between standardization and performance. They found no significant difference in performance between firms that stressed standardization and those that did not.

see also **International product adaptation**

Bibliography

Doglus, S. & Wind, Y. (1987). The myth of globalization. *Colombia Journal of World Business*, 22, 19–30.

Levitt, T. (1983). The globalization of markets. *Harvard Business Review*, 22, May/June, 92–102.

Samiee, S. & Roth, K. (1992). The influence of global market standardisation on performance. *Journal of Marketing*, 56, April, 1–17.

MO YAMIN

international selection   This is the process used to determine which employees will be considered for overseas assignments. The factors associated with international selection have both similarities to and differences from the selection process for home country (domestic) employment. Both types of selection include basic qualifications for work competency (work skills, technical knowledge, etc.); work ethic (absenteeism rate, etc.) and general managerial skills. The expatriate, however, must have a number of additional qualities in order to be successful. These qualities normally include among other factors: flexibility in thought and action; ability to listen; empathy; acceptance of change; tolerance of cultural differences; and good language skills.

One of the major problems with expatriate selection is that having a different selection process for local and international positions may run foul of laws against discrimination in some countries. For example, it is difficult for a person in a country which provides equal rights to men and women to accept that in other countries women may not be able to obtain driver's licenses, cannot go out unescorted, or a number of other things which would be blatant discrimination in their own countries. Is it justifiable under these conditions to avoid hiring women for jobs in such a country? A difficult question and one which must be dealt with considering both the laws against discrimination in various countries and practical considerations of getting a job done.

Bibliography

Brown, R. (1987). How to choose the best expatriates. *Personnel Management,* **June,** 67.

Harvey, M. (1985). The executive family: An overlooked variable in international assignments. *Journal of International Business Studies.* Columbia Journal of World Business, 785–800.

Heller, J. E. (1980). Criteria for selecting an international manager. *Personnel,* May–June, 47–55.

Martinez, Z. L. & Ricks, D. A. (1989). Multinational parent companies' influence over human resource decisions of affiliates: U.S. forms in Mexico. *Journal of International Business Studies,* **20** (3), 465–87.

Punnett, B. J., Crocker, O. & Stevens, M. A. (1992). The challenge for women expatriates and their spouses: Some empirical evidence. *International Journal of Human Resource Management,* **3** (3), 585–92.

Tung, R. L. (1984). Strategic management of human resources in the multinational enterprise in *Human Resource Management.* New York: John Wiley & Sons.

Zeira, Y. & Banai, M. (1985). Selection of expatriate managers in MNC's: The host environment point of view. *International Studies of Management and Organization,* **15** (1), 33–51.

JOHN O'CONNELL

International Standards Organization (ISO) The ISO was established in 1946 to develop standards for measurements used in the scientific field, international trade, commerce, and industry. The development of the organization was in response to common problems associated with differing systems of measurement existing in different countries. It is the goal of the ISO to develop uniformity of measures applicable to international commerce.

JOHN O'CONNELL

interorganizational relations (IOR) This is a general term which directs attention to the sources, kinds, and consequences of linkages between and among organizations as social actors. Three general foci have animated studies of interorganizational relations: understanding the establishment and maintenance of dyadic cooperative interorganizational linkages; understanding the emergent processual dynamics (e.g., POWER, STATUS) in sets of these linkages; and understanding the properties of IOR networks and their effects across industries, organizational fields, and public policy domains.

The rise of OPEN SYSTEMS approaches in organizational theory provided the initial impetus for developing models of interorganizational relations. Scholars began focusing on the acquisition of needed inputs and the disposal of completed outputs as major determinants of ORGANIZATIONAL EFFECTIVENESS. This early work reflected prevailing research paradigms: the legacy of structural–functionalism and its focus on efficient goal attainment processes, as well as the prevalence of survey methods and case studies, and the emphasis on unit, or focal organization, analysis (Whetten, 1987). Findings corroborated the recognition that linkages with other organizations served as the conduits for resource exchanges; this work stimulated inquiries that focused on ways to improve IOR coordination, particularly in task-focused multiorganizational units, referred to as action sets (e.g., service delivery systems or distribution channels). These studies of IORs provided systematic evidence of the ways organizations used purposeful linkages with other organizations to accomplish goals and to manage uncertain environments (*see* UNCERTAINTY). The role of boundary spanning actors and practices figured prominently in these studies – interorganizational linkages were viewed as extensions of relationships between organizational representatives (Aldrich & Whetten, 1981). The results tended to support the importance of awareness of common interests and organizational initiatives grounded in these perceptions for linkage formation.

A second area of research has focused on aggregates of dyadic linkages, comprising an "organization set" for a focal organization (analogous to a role set for individual actors). These studies focused on the structural properties of IORs, including the consequences of asymmetries of power and status, and on COMMUNICATION patterns and frequency. This widened conception of the forms and kinds of IORs redirected research to fundamental questions about the relations between structure and process in organizational dynamics, the focus on purposive organizational action, and the nature of organizational forms (*see* ORGANIZATIONAL DESIGN). These studies often maintained an organization set perspective, although the size and complexity of the networks examined in these studies tended to increase over time. For example, in studies of the dispersion of INNOVATIONS or the flow of INFLUENCE between organization the "networks" examined consisted of aggregates of overlapping organization sets. This analysis yielded improved understanding of the relationship between such aggregate set attributes as size and diversity and focal organization members' perceptions of effective performance.

Subsequent analyses broadened the focus beyond cooperative activity, to examine more general patterns of relations within sets of organizations. For example, studies of the social network structure of economic activity describes the prevalence and persistence of various forms of linkage among business elites; these include a wider array of IOR types, including interlocks among boards of directors, alliances such as joint ventures, and flows of personnel between firms and between industries (Mizruchi & Galaskiewicz, 1993). Work in this area has examined the relationship between diverse measures of network centrality, reputation, and the effects of vertical versus horizontal and local versus nonlocal linkages, to argue for the importance of these ties in coordinated action. The evidence provides support for familiar resource dependence accounts of linkage dynamics, as well as for the effects of social and economic class interests on linkage patterns.

New lines of work on IORs examine the life cycle-processes of linkage development and their substantive content (Ring & Van de Ven, 1994) (*see* ORGANIZATIONAL CHANGE). The empirical results of these inquiries challenge static structural analyses, emphasizing coordination as a process over time, rather than as either a simple cause or effect of organizational and network properties. These inquiries also suggest the value of more attention to the substance of linkages. In general, the results here highlight the dynamic, situated character of many IOR arrangements and open up questions about the changing conditions that support diverse types of linkages. The attention to process represents one challenge to structural analysis. Other research directions provide further challenge, highlighting the emergence of new organizational forms that blur the distinctions between a focal organization and its network (Alter & Hage, 1993); evidence from emerging industries like biotechnology, from reinvigorated industrial regions, and from comparative studies of markets and states all provide evidence of the prevalence of new "hybrid" organizational forms (Powell, 1990).

The third stream of IOR research extends the work on organization–environment relations (see ORGANIZATION AND ENVIRONMENT), conceptualizing environments as structured networks that serve as both opportunities for and constraints upon organizational behavior. Work in this area investigates the structuring processes within inter-organizational fields, their determinants and their effects over time (Scott, 1983). The focus on the historical, cultural, and network elements of interorganizational fields provides an alternative to more abstract, dimension-based treatments of environments. DiMaggio (1986), for example, applies blockmodeling techniques to partition these networks-as-environments into analyzable units; this kind of work redescribes complex fields of organizations in ways that combine earlier insights about asymmetries of POWER and STATUS with the attention to nonlocal and indirect ties in the structuring of organizational fields and networks. Other recent empirical studies trace the consequential mechanisms and the direct and indirect effects of state and other collective actors for embedded organizations (Fligstein, 1990; Hamilton & Biggart, 1988). The recognition that wider institutional arrangements matter for IOR dynamics is salutary (see INSTITUTIONAL THEORY).

Theory and empirical research on intergroup relations have taken diverse avenues in recent years. On the one hand, core questions about the dynamics of cooperative linkages have persisted and have been recently reinvigorated by the interest in the business strategy literature on new organizational forms and on various types of corporate alliances (see STRATEGIC MANAGEMENT). On the other hand, broader currents in the study of social organization have reinforced and extended the early attention to cooperative linkages, such that interorganizational relations have come to include an increasingly expansive set of concerns, linked by common attention to extraorganizational levels of analysis. Much of the contemporary study draws from network imageries and methodologies, examining the consequences of social linkages for a broad range of organizational outcomes and drawing attention to the embeddedness of organized social and economic action.

see also Intergroup relations; Coalition formation; Industrial relations

Bibliography

Aldrich, H. & Whetten, D. A. (1981). Organization-sets, action-sets, and networks: making the most of simplicity. In W. H. Starbuck (Ed.), Handbook of organizational design. (Vol. 1, pp. 385–408.) Oxford: Oxford University Press.

Alter, C. & Hage, J. (1993). Organizations working together. Newbury Park CA: Sage.

DiMaggio, P. (1986). Structural analyses of organizational fields: A blockmodel approach. In B. Staw & L. L. Cummings (Eds), Research in organizational behavior, 8, 335–370.

Fligstein, N. (1990). The transformation of corporate control. Cambridge, MA: Harvard University Press.

Hamilton, G. & Biggart, N. (1988). Market, culture, and authority: A comparative analysis of organization and management in the Far East. In C. Winship & S. Rosen (Eds), Organizations and institutions, a supplement to American Journal of Sociology, 94, S52-S94.

Mizruchi, M. S. & Galaskiewicz, J. (1993). Networks of interorganizational relations, in Sociological Methods & Research, 22, (1), 46–70.

Powell, W. W. (1990). Neither market nor hierarchy: Network forms of organization. Research in Organizational Behavior., 12, 295–336. Ring, P. S. & Van de Ven, A. H. (1994). Developmental processes of cooperative interorganizational relationships. Academy of Management Review, 19, (1), 90–118.

Scott, W. R. (1983). The organization of environments: Network, cultural, and historical elements. In J. W. Meyer & W. R. Scott (Eds), Organizational environments: Ritual and rationality, pp. 155–175. Beverly Hills, CA: Sage.

Whetten, D. A. (1987). Interorganizational relations In J. Lorsch (Ed.), Handbook of organizational behavior, (pp. 238–253). Englewood Cliffs, NJ: Prentice-Hall.

DAVID A. WHETTEN and
MARC J. VENTRESCA

interpersonal communications Interpersonal communications are the basis of informal channels of marketing communications, sometimes referred to as word-of-mouth communications (see WORD-OF-MOUTH COMMUNICATIONS), when consumers/buyers talk to each other about product-related issues. To understand interpersonal communications requires consideration of personal influence, group influence including reference groups, and opinion leaders.

Personal influence is the change in attitudes and/or behavior as a result of interpersonal communications. Personal influence can be initiated by a potential consumer seeking advice and information, or after purchase – as a provider of information and opinions. It is a two-way influence unlike that of the MASS MEDIA, and it may be visual as well as verbal.

The occurrence of personal influence depends on product variables (e.g., visibility, complexity, degree of perceived risk, stage in the diffusion process), and consumer variables (e.g., life stage, product experience, personality). Companies try to affect the extent of personal influence in their advertising and promotion, personal selling, and sales promotion activities. For example, in their advertising they may simulate personal influence with user stereotypes, testimonials, and group activities; or stimulate it, e.g., by encouraging people to talk about a product.

In the realm of interpersonal communications, not all individuals wield equal influence. Some, opinion leaders, are more influential and others may turn to them for information and advice. Katz & Lazerfeld (1955) believe that people are most influenced by those they are in contact with in everyday life, i.e., by people most like themselves, e.g., doctors for health issues and close friends for the purchase of consumer durables. Research has not been able to clearly identify opinion leader traits, e.g., with respect to demographics, personality, lifestyles, or media habits (e.g., Myers & Robertson, 1972). Further, it has not been possible to identify opinion leaders across product categories; opinion leadership is primarily product specific (e.g., King & Summers, 1979).

Group influence is an important aspect of social influence. All groups have values, beliefs, and norms, and expect individual members to share these and conform to them and behave in appropriate ways. Consumers are, therefore, influenced by a number of groups which may be categorized as primary (e.g., family, friends, neighbors, work associates) or secondary where there has been some deliberate choice in belonging and there is a more formal structure and rules (e.g., political parties, church affiliation, leisure and sporting clubs).

There are pressures on consumers to conform to group beliefs, values, and norms, and there is evidence in the consumer behavior literature that this does occur. The family is the most important source of group influence on an individual, in particular in his or her formative years. However, one of the distinguishing characteristics of Western culture (*see* CULTURE) is the declining influence of the family.

A specific type of group influence of interest to marketers is reference group(s) influence. These are groups which consumers identify with and are used as reference points in determining judgements, beliefs, and behavior. They set standards which are the source of personal behavior norms. They may be membership or aspirant groups. Examples of aspirant groups are personalities whose lifestyles are characterized by luxury products/consumption; and soccer stars who are emulated by small boys (and others) – as typified in the purchase of "football strips and apparel."

Bearden & Etzel (1982) studied reference group influence and the conspicuousness of a product and its brands, and suggested that reference group influence can be strong or weak for product and/or brand. For example, the purchase of a car and the model chosen are both subject to such influence, whereas for satellite television reference group influence prevails with respect to product ownership but not for "brand" choice.

Interpersonal communications are complementary to MASS MEDIA communications, and consumers use both types depending on the product, stage in the decision-making process, and perceptions of risk. Interpersonal communications provide a two-way communication process, are usually seen as more trustworthy than the mass media, and are harder to selectively ignore or tune out. However, they may also be providing unrealistic or inaccurate information and are, indeed, usually communicating evaluations and opinions rather than factual information.

Bibliography

Bearden, W. O. & Etzel, M. J. (1982). Reference group influence on product and brand purchase decisions. *Journal of Consumer Research*, 9, (2), Sept., 183–94. Also in H. H. Kassarjian & T. S. Robertson (Eds) (1991). *Perspectives in consumer behaviour*, 4th edn, pp. 435–51. Prentice Hall.

Engel, J. F., Blackwell, R. D. & Miniard, P. W. (1990). *Consumer behavior*, 6th edn, Orlando, FL: The Dryden Press. Chapter 5.

Hawkins, D. I., Best, R. J. & Coney, K. A. (1992). *Consumer behavior: Implications for marketing strategy*, 5th edn, Home-wood, IL: Irwin. Chapter 5.

Katz, E. & Lazerfeld, P. F. (1955). *Personal influence*. Glencoe, IL: Free Press.

King, C. W. & Summers, J. O. (1979). Overlap of opinion leaders across consumer product categories. *Journal of Marketing Research*, 7, Feb., 43–50.

Myers, J. H. & Robertson, T. S. (1972). Dimensions of opinion leadership. *Journal of Marketing Research*, 9, Feb., 41–6.

Schiffman, L. G. & Kanuk, L. Z. (1991). *Consumer behavior*, 4th edn, Prentice-Hall. Chapters 11, 17.

Solomon, M. R. (1992). *Consumer behavior*. Needham Heights, MA: Allyn & Bacon, Chapter 11.

BARBARA LEWIS

interpersonal skills   Whereas the term "SKILLS" refers generally to an individual's capability for effective action, interpersonal skills refers to *the capability to accomplish individual and/or organizational goals through*. In organizations, many types of goals are primarily accomplished through interaction, and each of these goal types corresponds to a certain type of interpersonal skill. For example, individuals in organizations must accomplish the goal of communicating effectively with others. The capability to accomplish this goal is referred to as "COMMUNICATION skill." As another example, individuals are sometimes in a position where they want to ensure the success of a group meeting. The capability to accomplish this goal may be referred to as skill in facilitating meetings. Goals may be stated broadly or specifically, and so may skills; e.g., "interpersonal" versus "reflective listening" skills.

Interpersonal skills are distinguished in principle from other types of skills which are also pertinent to organizational life. These include:

(1) *intrapersonal* skills, where goals involve self-change, such as self-awareness, time management, or STRESS management;
(2) *learning* skills, where goals involve obtaining and using new information;
(3) *cognitive* skills, where goals are accomplished primarily through cognitive processes; and
(4) *job* skills, where goals involve effective job performance.

Interpersonal skills are a type of "action" skill, wherein goal accomplishment requires significant exercise of behavior. While these skill types are conceptually distinct, they are typically used in concert in organizations.

Importance of Interpersonal Skills
Interpersonal skills are a uniquely important subset of the skills considered as valuable in organizations. Much of human intelligence is believed to have evolved to cope with the complexities of human interaction. Thus we would expect the exercise of interpersonal skills to involve a large part of intrinsic human capability. The importance of interpersonal skills is also underscored by its inclusion as one aspect of wisdom.

In understanding the relevance of interpersonal skills to organizations it is important first to understand the types of goals which may be accomplished through the exercise of interpersonal skills. These goals can generally be classified as "direct" and "indirect." Direct goals have to do with changes in others as a direct result of interaction; e.g., in others' orientation, COMMITMENT, TRUST, support, knowledge, motivation, etc. Indirect goals have to do with the larger impact of direct goal accomplishment. For example, interaction with another may result in the other's support for a policy (direct change), which in turn leads to a majority organizational vote to adopt the policy (indirect change).

Managers accomplish their work largely through the indirect effects of their interactions. Consequently, most of managerial time is spent in interpersonal interactions via phone, in meetings, and in face-to-face interactions with individuals (see MANAGERIAL BEHAVIOR; Mintzberg, 1975). Interpersonal skills, therefore, are critical for managerial effectiveness. Moreover, modern organizations have shifted toward more decentralized, interactive, and participatory designs (see DECENTRALIZATION; MATRIX ORGANIZATION). In them, those doing the primary work of the organization are meeting more, doing more work in groups, and taking on greater managerial responsibilities (see AUTONOMOUS WORK GROUPS; SELF-MANAGING TEAMS). For this reason interpersonal skills have become increasingly important for organizational members at all levels.

Skills and Competencies

Some authors have used the terms "COMPETENCY" and "skill" interchangeably. The two are similar, but by no means identical. To paraphrase Boyatzis (1982, p. 21), an interpersonal competency consists of an underlying characteristic of an individual which contributes to effective and/or superior performance in a given type of interpersonal setting. For example, "developing others," "use of unilateral power," and "spontaneity" are competencies which have been found to contribute to effectiveness in situations requiring "directing subordinates" (ibid, p. 230).

Skills and competencies are alike in that both are regarded as individual attributes which contribute to situational effectiveness. They differ, however, in two important ways. First, the relation between skills and situational effectiveness is closer: a skill has to do with effective action in relation to a particular goal. The relation between competencies and situational effectiveness, on the other hand, is less direct: many competencies may contribute to effectiveness toward particular goal, and a particular competency may contribute to effectiveness toward a variety of goals.

The second difference is that competencies include a wider variety of individual attributes than do skills. Whereas the concept of skill has only to do with the capability for effective action, competencies may also include motives (e.g., concern for impact), traits (e.g., self-control), and social roles (e.g., oral presentations).

Types of Interpersonal Skills and Their Relationships

Much of the study of interpersonal skills has centered around identifying skills which are important in organizations. At this point four major types of interpersonal skills can be distinguished, each centering around a basic type of goal, and each including one or more skills:

1. COMMUNICATIONS. Goal: Establishing effective communication between self and others, and among others. Skills include establishing a supportive climate, listening, NETWORKING, giving feedback, oral and written communication, use of communications technology, and language.

2. INFLUENCE. Goal: Effecting changes in others. Skills include persuading, asserting, MOTIVATION, PERFORMANCE APPRAISAL, mentoring, counseling, DELEGATION, and disciplining.

3. NEGOTIATION and CONFLICT MANAGEMENT. Goal: Developing beneficial agreement among parties. Skills include bargaining, diagnosing the other party, assessing negotiation sessions, mediation, and implementing negotiation tactics.

4. FACILITATION. Goal: Helping groups and organizations to operate effectively. Skills include conducting a meeting, TEAM BUILDING, participative problem solving, GROUP DECISION-MAKING, facilitation, ORGANIZATIONAL CHANGE, and LEADERSHIP.

The importance and expression of these skills can be expected to vary among organizations and over time. Remember that interpersonal skills are means of accomplishing certain types of goals. As organizations and their structures change, different kinds of goals may become more or less important. For example, as organizations become increasingly international, the ability to enter and establish effective work relationships in a culturally different organization may become increasingly important (see INTERNATIONAL MANAGEMENT). Thus, "entry" skills may eventually be added to our list of interpersonal skills. Moreover, as information technology develops, new methods of interpersonal interaction may become available. For example, the use of "groupware" may lessen the need for group facilitation skills, and increase the need for computer group session management, or "chauffeuring" skills.

Nature of Interpersonal skills

While the concept of skill has been in widespread use for many years, its primary users have been practitioners, such as educators, job trainers, and therapists working with the handicapped. Their interests have generally been in enabling their target groups to enact fairly straightforward behavioral routines. These practitioners have tended, often implicitly, to place skills in a behavioristic context. A basic premise of this context is that behaviors are learned and maintained by a system of stimuli, which elicit a desired set of behaviors, or "skill" response, which are followed in turn by REINFORCEMENT.

Initial efforts to put interpersonal phenomena into a skills framework have tended to place them in a behavioristic context as well. Thus, interpersonal skills have been regarded as a set of fairly specific behavioral routines, and interpersonal skillfulness equated with the accurate demonstrations of these behaviors upon the appropriate cue. These early efforts have met with limited success, and this has led to a closer examination of the nature of interpersonal skills (Bigelow, 1993). The conclusion: the phenomenon of interpersonal skillfulness departs from behavioral premises in a number of ways:

1. *Response inspecificity*. Whereas a behavioristic approach requires clear descriptions of desired behaviors, skillful interaction is interactive and complex, often involving multiple, possibly conflicting goals and resulting dilemmas. It is usually not possible either to identify one best response or to describe desired responses behaviorally. Thus the set of possibly appropriate interpersonal

behaviors is not closed, but open, requiring CREATIVITY and ongoing learning.

2. *Lack of cues*. Whereas a behavioristic approach requires cueing of behaviors, it is usually not possible to discern unambiguous cues for behavior in interpersonal situations. Thus, a part of interpersonal skillfulness consists of the ability to "cue" one's own behavior.

3. *Cognition*. Whereas a behavioristic approach does not include cognition, skilled interaction often requires significant cognition. For example, during an interaction a person may be weighing the implications of what the other said, vicariously projecting the impact of various tactics, assessing the success of a line of action, or considering modifying his/her goals for the interaction. Thus, a part of interpersonal skill learning must include development of associated cognitive processes.

4. *Learning resistance*. Whereas a behavioristic approach assumes the skill learner is indifferent to the content of what is learned, interpersonal skill learners have already developed orientations and practice theories (i.e., implicit behavioral programs driving their behavior, Argyris & Schon, 1978) which already dominate their interactions. These prior learnings can strongly interfere with attempts to develop new behaviors. Thus, the learning of interpersonal skills must include the surfacing, examination, and reassessment of what the individual has already learned.

In sum, our picture of the interpersonally skilled practitioner is becoming much richer than that implied by behaviorism. Interpersonally skilled people are able to orient themselves to situations. They take into account not only the situation, but their prospective broader impact beyond the encounter itself. They have developed a repertoire of interaction tactics and are able to draw on them as needed, or may develop new tactics as the situation warrants. During interaction, they monitor their progress, and may change tactics or goals if necessary. They are able to learn on their own, both from their own encounters and from the encounters of others (*see* LEARNING ORGANIZATION).

Skill Learning

An increased reliance on interpersonal skills in organizations has led to concern as to where organizations will obtain interpersonally skilled participants. Many candidates for organizational positions are not very interpersonally skilled, by reason of youth and/or inexperience. This is particularly the case in individualistic cultures such as the United States (Adler, 1991, pp. 26–28), which do little to prepare individuals to operate effectively in group or organizational settings.

In response, many organizations have developed skill TRAINING programs for employees, and have attempted to enhance on-the-job learning. Moreover, some have suggested that colleges of business, which have traditionally emphasized cognitive skills, should also address interpersonal skills in their curriculum.

Currently a number of approaches to classroom learning are in use. These include:

(1) a *social learning* approach, based on Bandura's (1977) model, involving the steps of self-assessment, con-

ceptual learning, skill modeling, application to cases and practice situations, and application to life situations;

(2) a *self-managed* learning approach, which empowers individuals to take responsibility for their own learning; and

(3) a *situational learning* approach, which focuses on practice in holistic managerial situations and the development of "skillfulness," as opposed to development of separated skills.

These approaches are not entirely distinct in that each has elements which could be used in other approaches, and each has its own pros and cons (e.g., Bigelow, 1993).

Perhaps the thorniest problem faced in skill learning is the assessment of results. Traditional assessment methods involving objective or essay exams are more geared toward assessing cognitive rather than skill accomplishment. Even when unbiased self-assessment can be obtained through self-administered instruments or portfolios, learners often do not have the insight to assess their own skills. The most promising approach appears to be the "action" or "performance" examination, in which learners are required to demonstrate their skill. Yet these require considerable investment in training of examiners, and are time-consuming to administer. Moreover, they measure skill capability only, and not disposition to actually use skills. Until viable and reasonably accurate measures of skill accomplishment are developed it will be difficult for educators to improve their pedagogy, and for institutions to make claims about the skillfulness of their graduates.

see also **Impression management; Trust**

Bibliography

Adler N. J. (1991). International dimensions of organizational behavior. Boston: PWS–Kent.

Argyris, C. & Schon, D. (1978). Organizational learning: A theory of action perspective. Reading, MA: Addison-Wesley.

Bandura, A. (1977). Social learning theory. Englewood Cliffs, NJ: Prentice-Hall.

Bigelow, J. D. (1993). Teaching managerial skills: A critique and future directions. Paper presented at the Organizational Behavior Teaching Conference, Bucknell University (June).

Boyatzis, R. R. (1982). The competent manager: A model for effective performance. New York: Wiley.

Mintzberg, H. (1975). The manager's job: Folklore and fact. Harvard Business Review, 53, 49–71.

Porter, L. W. & McKibbin, L. E. (1988). Management education and development: Drift or thrust into the 21st century? New York: McGraw-Hill.

Bradford, D. L. (Issue Editor) (1983). Special issue on "Teaching managerial competencies." The organizational behavior teaching Journal (vol. 2). [A seminal issue, much of which continues to be relevant.]

Bigelow, J. D. (1991). Managerial skills. Explorations in practical knowledge. Newbury Park, CA: Sage. [Provides a variety of viewpoints on skills.]

JOHN D. BIGELOW

investment banking   The earliest known banks, temples, operated as repositories of concentrated wealth. They were among the first places where a need for money and money-changers emerged. The word bank traces to the French word *banque* (chest) and the Italian word *banca* (bench). These early meanings capture the two basic functions that banks perform: (1) the safe-keeping or risk-control function (chest); and (2) the transactions function including intermediation and trading (bench). Taking investment to mean the outlay of money for income or profit, an investment bank functions as a safekeeper, risk manager, trader, and intermediary with respect to the outlay of money for income or profit.

Although modern investment banks (also called securities firms) engage in numerous financial activities, especially in a world characterized by globalization, securitization, and financial engineering, two activities represent the heart of investment banking: bringing new securities issues (debt and equity) to market; and making secondary markets for these securities. The first activity captures the underwriting function while the second reflects the broker/dealer function. As brokers, investment banks bring parties together to trade securities while, as dealers, they trade from their own inventory.

To understand the full range of financial services provided by investment banks, consider the six basic functions performed by a financial system: clearing and settling payments, pooling or subdividing resources, transferring wealth, managing risk, providing price information, and dealing with incentive problems. Since investment banks are a major component of financial systems in developed countries, they play a prominent role in performing most of these functions. In the United States because of the separation of commercial and investment banking (Glass–Steagall Act of 1933), investment banks perform all of these functions except clearing and settling payments, a task performed mainly by commercial banks in the USA. In contrast, in Germany and Japan where such artificial barriers between investment and commercial banking do not exist, the activities of commercial and investment banks are commingled, and interwoven with the activities of non-financial firms.

In Japan, banks own shares in businesses, which also own shares in the banks. Although cross-holdings tend to be nominal, the practical effect links dissimilar companies together for mutual support and protection. These cross-shareholding groups, called *keiretsu*, provide a unique approach to corporate control based on continuous surveillance and monitoring by the managers of affiliated firms and banks.

The German model links universal banks and industrial companies through the *Hausbank* approach to providing financial services (i.e. reliance on only one principal bank). In addition, incentive compatibilities and monitoring are accomplished by bank ownership of equity shares, bank voting rights over fiduciary (trust) shareholdings, and bank participation on supervisory boards. The *Hausbank* relationship results in companies accessing both capital-market services (e.g. new issues of stocks and bonds) and bank-credit facilities through their "universal bank." By providing all of the financing needed to start a business (e.g. seed capital, initial public offerings of stock, bond underwritings, and working capital), German banks gain *Hausbank* standing. On balance, in the German model, bank–industry linkages involve strong surveillance and monitoring by banks and the potential for a high degree of control in maximizing shareholder value as banks have an equity stake and fiduciary obligations with respect to depository shares.

The investment banking industry in the USA has three tiers: large, full-line firms that cater to both retail and corporate clients; national and international firms that concentrate mainly on corporate finance and trading activities; and the rest of the industry (e.g. specialized and regional securities firms and discount brokers). Examples of key players in the top two tiers are Merrill Lynch in the top tier and Goldman Sachs, Salomon Brothers, and Morgan Stanley in the second tier. In addition, due to the piecemeal dismantling of Glass–Steagall, major US commercial banks such as BankAmerica, Bankers Trust, Chase Manhattan, Chemical, Citicorp, and J. P. Morgan (listed alphabetically) are important global players as investment banks, especially in derivatives activities.

Although the primary regulator of the securities industry in the USA is the Securities and Exchange Commission (SEC, established in 1934), the New York Stock Exchange (NYSE) and National Association of Securities Dealers (NASD) provide self-regulation and monitoring of day-to-day trading practices and activities. Two important SEC rules governing underwriting activities are Rule 415 and Rule 144A. Rule 415 ("shelf registration") permits large issuers to register new issues with the SEC up to two years in advance, and then "pull them off the shelf" (i.e. issue them) when market conditions are most favorable. Rule 144A establishes boundaries between public offerings and private placements of securities. In a public offering, securities are offered to the public at large; in a private placement, securities are "placed" with one or more institutional investors.

Since investment banking can be defined by what investment banks or securities firms do, let us look at the major functions they perform. Investment banks underwrite and distribute new issues of debt and equity. When firms issue securities for the first time, this is called an initial public offering or IPO. How IPOs are priced is an important research question in empirical finance. Securities may be underwritten either on a best-efforts basis, where the investment banker acts as an agent and receives a fee related to the successful placement of the issue, or on a firm-commitment basis, where the investment bank buys the entire issue and resells it making a profit on the difference between the two prices or the bid–ask spread. A common practice in underwriting public offerings is to form a syndicate to ensure raising enough capital and to share the risk. Trading, market making, funds management (for mutual and pension funds), and providing financial and custodial services, are other functions performed by investment banks.

Financial innovation has been a substantial force in capital markets, and investment banks have played a leading role in this area (e.g. in the development of securitization and in the engineering of risk-management products called "derivatives"). First-mover or innovative investment banks tend to be characterized by lower costs of trading, underwriting, and marketing. Evidence (Tufano, 1989) suggests that compensation for developing new products centers on gaining market share and maintaining reputational capital as opposed to "monopoly pricing" before imitative products appear.

Bibliography

Bloch, E. (1986). *Inside investment banking, IL: Dow Jones–Irwin.*

Hayes, S. L., III & Hubbard, Philip M. (1990). *Investment banking: A tale of three cities.* Boston, MA: Harvard Business School Press.

Marshall, J. F. & Ellis, M. E. (1994). *Investment banking and brokerage: The new rules of the game.* Chicago, IL: Probus Publishing Company.

Tufano, P. (1989). Financial innovation and first-mover advantages. *Journal of Financial Economics*, **25**, 213–40.

JOSEPH F. SINKEY, JR.

ISO 9000   ISO 9000 is an internationally developed and recognized series of quality standards that focus on a company's *management practices*. Businesses certified by third-party agencies join a registry of ISO–certified companies. This stamp of approval provides comparative advantages to certified companies. Additionally, European Union companies can minimize certain legal liabilities by applying ISO 9000 standards and choosing ISO–certified suppliers (Chase and Aquilano, 1995).

The ISO 9000 series consists of five separate standards. The ISO 9000 standard provides basic definitions and concepts and summarizes how to select and use the other standards in the series. Essentially, ISO 9000 directs a firm to document what it does and do what it has documented. ISO 9004 lists the essential elements that make up a quality system and contains guidelines for operation. The remaining standards constitute a hierarchical set of quality requirements covering various aspects of the business. ISO 9003, the least stringent, deals only with final testing and inspection. ISO 9002 covers production and installation requirements. ISO 9001, the most comprehensive standard, covers all elements of ISO 9002 and 9003, while also addressing design, development, and service capabilities.

Organizations often ponder the relative merits and timing of ISO 9000 certification and MALCOLM BALDRIGE NATIONAL QUALITY AWARD (MBNQA) application. The MBNQA award emphasizes customer satisfaction and business results (Rabbitt and Bergh, 1993). Generally, ISO 9000 is a good starting point to help organizations prepare for MBNQA application. MBNQA assumes that internal processes, the focus of ISO 9000, are in control.

Bibliography

Arter, D. R. (1992). Demystifying the ISO 9000/290 series standards. *Quality Progress*, **November**, 66.

Chase, R. B. & Aquilano, N. J. (1995). *Production and Operations Management: Manufacturing and Services*, Burr Ridge, IL: Richard D. Irwin.

Huyink, D. S. (1994). *ISO 9000: Motivating the People, Mastering the Process, Achieving Registration!*, Burr Ridge, IL: Richard D. Irwin.

Rabbitt, J. T. & Bergh, P. A. (1993). *The ISO 9000 Book*, White Plains, NY: Quality Resources.

WILLIAM E. YOUNGDAHL

J

JIT/MRP JIT/MRP is a combination of two popular approaches to operations planning and control, namely just-in-time (JIT), and materials requirements planning (MRP). Although seen as alternative approaches for some years after the popularization of JIT in the 1980s, the two approaches are now seen as being, to some extent, complementary. Certainly just-in-time is seen as having much to contribute to the strengthening of conventional MRP systems. Two major aspects of JIT philosophy especially, simplification and the elimination of waste, can be applied to the improvement and focusing of MRP design.

JIT concepts help to address a number of potential weaknesses in the way that MRP is designed and executed. These include the following:

- Although MRP can be seen as a pull system (*see* push and pull planning and control) driven by the master production schedule, the way it is used is actually as a push system. Inventory is driven through the factory in response to detailed, time-phased plans by part number.
- MRP is usually operated as a computer-based system which may require substantial investment in hardware, software, and systems support. It has a complex, centralized structure which may result in the operation losing sight of customer needs.
- MRP depends on a large amount of data, from bills of material to routing and stock records. This makes it particularly vulnerable to problems of data accuracy.
- Understanding MRP is a lengthy process for users, therefore training may be expensive and time consuming.
- MRP assumes fixed lead times. Batches of parts are moved from one operation to the next according to these set lead times. This, to some extent, disguises the real performance of the operation. It is easy to become preoccupied with improving the planning and control system performance (data accuracy, etc.) at the expense of more fundamental improvements.
- Because of the lengthy processing time to update MRP records, it is often run in batch mode on a weekly basis. Many versions today have "net change" options which enable records for selected parts to be updated daily. MRP is therefore only responsive on a daily or weekly basis, thus records are often out of step with reality.

Perhaps most significantly, while MRP excels at planning and co-ordinating materials, it is relatively weak in its control of the timing of material movements and the complexity of MRP may become a liability at shop floor level, where control systems are comparatively cumbersome and unresponsive. Yet the comparative simplicity resulting from such JIT techniques as leveled scheduling and kanban can greatly help to simplify shop floor control of parts, especially those which are made at regular intervals, sometimes termed "runners" and "repeaters". Further, JIT concepts can be used to attack many of the wasteful assumptions which are often built into MRP, such as fixed reorder rules and scrap allowances.

There are a number of ways in which the overall control of complex operations through MRP and the improvement-oriented simplicity of JIT can be combined at a technical level. Two general approaches to this are particularly influential.

The first is to use different planning and control systems for different products. Using the runners, repeaters, and strangers terminology, pull scheduling using *kanbans* can be used for "runners" and "repeaters," while MRP is used for "strangers." For "strangers," works orders are issued to explain what must be done at each stage and the work itself is monitored to push materials through manufacturing stages. One advantage of this approach is that by increasing responsiveness and reducing inventories of runners and repeaters, it encourages operations to increase their number by design simplification.

The other approach is to use MRP for overall control and JIT for internal control. So, for example, MRP is used for the planning of supplier materials to ensure that sufficient parts are available to enable them to be called off "just-in-time." The master production schedule is broken down by means of MRP for supplier schedules (forecast future demand). Actual material requirements for supplies are signaled by means of *kanbans* to facilitate JIT delivery. Within the factory, all material movements are governed by *kanban* loops between operations.

The relative complexity of product structures (gauged by the number of levels in the BILL OF MATERIALS), and of process routing (gauged by the number of processes through which parts must travel), both have an important influence on which planning and control system is used. Where there are simple structures and routings, internal material control merits simple systems such as JIT-based systems. As complexity increases, so the power of the computer is needed to break down forecast demand into supplier schedules through MRP, but much internal control can still be carried out by means of pull scheduling. As structures and routings become more complex, so the opportunities for pull scheduling reduce, and MRP is needed to co-ordinate material movements. Network planning and control systems are needed for the most complex structures and routings.

Bibliography

Karmarkar, U. S. (1989). Getting control of just-in-time. *Harvard Business Review*, **67**, 5.

Vollman, T. E., Berry, W. L. & Whybark, D. C. (1992). *Manufacturing planning and control systems*. Homewood, IL: Irwin.

ALAN HARRISON

job analysis Job analysis is the systematic process of uncovering and describing the components of a job. The process may be all-encompassing or more narrow, depending upon the needs of the job analyst. The analyst may explore the goals of the work, the work procedures and processes (duties, tasks, and so forth; Harvey, 1992), the kinds of personal attributes required of people to complete the work (KSAOs), and the work context, broadly defined to include the physical environment as well as the business environment. For example, for the job of police officer, the goals of the work might include enforcing laws, promoting the safety of the public, and maintaining community relations. The work procedures and processes might include such activities as giving traffic citations, resolving domestic disputes, and testifying in court. The personal characteristics might include the ability to remember laws, physical strength, and skill in operating a patrol car. The work context might include such items as working outdoors. The police officer reports to a police sergeant within a particular civic and geographic context (consider, for example, how the job might differ from Miami, Florida to Ann Arbor, Michigan).

Job analysis can be considered to be a managerial activity because it helps solve so many human resource problems (McCormick, 1979; Gael et al., 1988). However, it may also serve society at large. Among the vast uses of job analysis are producing a written description of the nature of the job (a JOB DESCRIPTION), providing information used to set salaries (JOB EVALUATION METHODS), and planning for the future of people at work in the company (human resources planning). Job analysis also forms the basis for training programs (TRAINING and development), hiring and promoting workers (staffing), defending the job-relatedness of employment practices, and defining the job in such a way that job performance can be evaluated (performance measurement). Societal purposes include vocational guidance for students.

Job analysis employs a variety of approaches to uncover and describe components of a job. Such approaches can be captured in four categories: (a) the kinds of job data collected; (b) the methods of gathering data; (c) the sources of job information; and (d) the methods of data analysis (Levine, 1983). The kinds of data collected include such items as responsibilities, products and services, machines, tools, work aids, and equipment, and work and worker activities. The sources of information include the job analyst (the person doing the job analysis), the job holder, the job holder's supervisor, training specialists, and technical experts such as chemists or college professors. The data analytic approach can include units of work (task, duty, or job dimensions), worker trait requirements, such as mental and physical capabilities, and quantitative scales applied to the work. For an example of a quantitative approach, job holders could be given a survey that asks them to rate each task in their job in terms of its difficulty to learn. The way we carry out a job analysis will depend on what we are trying to accomplish (Levine et al., 1988). We might proceed differently, for example, if we are interested in staffing than if we are interested in job evaluation. In staffing, we would concentrate on what personal characteristics (e.g. skill in word processing) job applicants need in order to be successful on the job. In evaluating jobs to set salaries, we would concentrate on the aspects of jobs that differentiate them in terms of pay, such as degree of fiscal responsibility.

Bibliography

Gael, S., Cornelius, E. T. III, Levine, E. L. & Salvendy, G. (1988). *The Job Analysis Handbook for Business, Industry and Government*, New York: Wiley.

Harvey, R. J. (1992). Job analysis. *Handbook of Industrial and Organizational Psychology*, Eds. Dunnette, M. D. & Hough, L. M. 2, Palo Alto, CA: Consulting Psychologists Press.

Levine, E. L. (1983). *Everything You Always Wanted to Know about Job Analysis*, Tampa, FL: Mariner.

Levine, E. L., Thomas, J. N. & Sistrunk, F. (1988). Selecting a job analysis approach. *The job analysis handbook for business, industry and government*. Eds. Gael, S., Cornelius, E. T. III, Levine, E. L. & Salvendy, G.1, New York: Wiley.

McCormick, E. J. (1979). *Job Analysis: Methods and Applications*, New York: AMACOM.

MICHAEL T. BRANNICK
and EDWARD L. LEVINE

job-based pay   Job-based pay refers to pay structures based on any form of JOB EVALUATION METHODS, focusing on job contents and/or job specifications. Job-based pay systems may be contrasted with knowledge-based or skill-based pay systems that use knowledge, skills, abilities, and other characteristics (*see* KSAOs) of each incumbent to determine pay. Thus, job evaluation methods of classification, factor-comparison, Hay method, and point and ranking would all yield a job-based pay system whereby an incumbent's base pay is determined by the job he or she occupies rather than KSAOs. Most employers use job-based pay, but knowledge- and skill-based systems are growing.

THOMAS H. STONE

job characteristics   These refer to objective properties of the work itself that are likely to contribute to the work effectiveness and satisfaction of employees. The characteristics that have received the most research attention have been suggested by Job Characteristics Theory (Hackman & Oldham, 1980). At its most basic level, the theory argues that the presence of five core job characteristics prompt a number of beneficial personal and work outcomes (e.g., high satisfaction, attendance and performance, and low turnover). The five characteristics are defined as follows:

Skill variety.   The degree to which a job requires a variety of different activities in carrying out the work, involving the use of a number of different skills and talents of the person.

Task identity.   The degree to which the job requires completion of a whole, identifiable piece of work – that is, doing a job from beginning to end with a visible outcome.

Task significance.   The degree to which the job has a substantial impact on the lives of other people, whether those people are in the immediate organization or the world at large.

Autonomy.   The degree to which the job provides substantial freedom, independence and discretion to the individual in scheduling the work and in determining the procedures to be used in carrying it out.

Task feedback.   The degree to which carrying out the work activities required by the job provides the individual with direct and clear information about the effectiveness of his or her performance.

The most frequently used measures of these characteristics are included in the Job Diagnostic Survey (JDS; Hackman & Oldham, 1975, 1980). The JDS asks individual jobholders to indicate the extent to which each of the five core characteristics is present in his or her job. In addition to the JDS, a companion instrument, the Job Rating Form (JRF; Hackman & Oldham, 1980) has been used to obtain measures of the job characteristics from individuals who do not themselves work on the focal job (e.g., supervisors or outside observers). Research has demonstrated that there is substantial agreement between the assessment of job characteristics made by jobholders and those made by outside observers (Kulik, Oldham, & Hackman, 1987).

In general, research has shown that measures of the core job characteristics are associated with the positive outcomes specified by Job Characteristics Theory (Fried & Ferris, 1987; Loher, Noe, Moeller, & Fitzgerald, 1985). For example, research has demonstrated that the higher the job scores on the five characteristics, the higher the employee's performance, JOB SATISFACTION, and attendance (see ABSENTEEISM). Moreover, employees who are strongly desirous of growth and development opportunities at work respond even more positively to jobs high on the five characteristics than individuals who have little interest in growth opportunities at work.

These results have important implications for the redesign of jobs in organizations (see JOB DESIGN, JOB ENRICHMENT). Specifically, they suggest that boosting jobs on the five characteristics can result in substantial improvements in the effectiveness and well-being of employees. What remains unclear in this literature are the effects of job characteristics on other work and nonwork outcomes (see NONWORK/WORK). For example, we know little about the effects of job characteristics on employees' CREATIVITY at work or upon their relationships with family members.

see also Job analysis; Motivation

Bibliography

Fried, Y. & Ferris, G. R. (1987). The validity of the job characteristics model: A review and meta-analysis. Personnel Psychology, 40, 287–322.

Hackman, J. R. & Oldham, G. R. (1975). Development of the job diagnostic survey. Journal of Applied Psychology, 60, 159–170.

Hackman, J. R. & Oldham, G. R. (1980). Work redesign. Reading, MA: Addison-Wesley.

Kulik, C. T., Oldham, G. R. & Hackman, J. R. (1987). Work design as an approach to person-environment fit. Journal of Vocational Behavior, 31, 278–296.

Loher, B. T., Noe, R. A., Moeller, N. L. & Fitzgerald, M. P. (1985). A meta-analysis of the relation of job characteristics to job satisfaction. Journal of Applied Psychology, 70, 280–289.

GREG R. OLDHAM

job description   The job description is a written summary of the nature of a job (see Ghorpade, 1988). The most common elements in a job description include: (a) a job identification that includes the job title; (b) a job overview that states the mission of the job and the products and services produced by the worker; (c) the primary tasks involved in the job; (d) a list of equipment, machines, and tools used; (e) raw materials, goods, data, or other materials used in the job; (f) the processes used to transform materials into products and services; (g) guidelines and controls that limit the discretion of the worker, such as supervision; (h) required knowledge, skills, abilities, and other characteristics (see KSAOs); (i) a description of the work context, such as working conditions; and (j) a statement of the qualifications required, such as a license or level of education.

Supervisors use job descriptions as a basis for assigning work and clarifying performance expectations. Job holders can use job descriptions to help understand their own jobs and jobs further up the job ladder that they may hold one day. Job descriptions are also a primary tool in PERFORMANCE APPRAISAL, in which supervisors evaluate the JOB PERFORMANCE of incumbents, and in JOB EVALUATION METHODS, with which the salaries of jobs within an organization are determined. Job descriptions may also play a role in RECRUITING and staffing functions, where they inform all parties of the nature of the work to be performed, thus helping to ensure a good match between people and jobs.

The centrality of the job description to human resource practices is currently being questioned by some organizations because of rapid changes in jobs. Such changes are in response to the dynamic nature of today's business environment. In addition, many organizations have placed increased reliance on teams that require flexible assignment of duties (see SELF-MANAGING TEAMS).

Bibliography

Ghorpade, J. (1988). Job Analysis: a Handbook for the Human Resource Director, Englewood Cliffs, NJ: Prentice-Hall.

MICHAEL T. BRANNICK
and EDWARD L. LEVINE

job design   Organizations have particular functions to accomplish if they are to meet their objectives. Those functions comprise a number of tasks, which are then grouped to form jobs undertaken by individuals. Job incumbents typically are trained to carry out their prescribed tasks, and given a certain degree of discretion over how they do so. The term "job design" refers to the outcome of this process and may be defined as the specification of the content and methods of jobs. Other terms often used as synonyms for job design include "work design" and "job" or "work structuring." "Work organization" is also frequently used to encompass job design, but usually signifies a broader perspective linking jobs more explicitly to their organizational context.

In principle, the concept of job design applies to all types of jobs and to the full range of possible job properties. Within OB, however, a more particular emphasis has developed, which has two aspects. First, with regard to types of work, attention has been directed mainly at lower level jobs within larger organizations, such as those involving clerical and especially shopfloor work. Second, with respect to job properties, the primary focus has been on generic JOB CHARACTERISTICS such as the variety of tasks in jobs, and the amount of discretion job incumbents have in completing those tasks. Interest in job design has centered on two main issues. One concerns the impact of job design on job attitudes and behavior; the other concerns the technological and organizational factors which influence the design of jobs. These emphases are best understood in the context of the historical development of shopfloor jobs and associated research.

Historical Context

From around the turn of the twentieth century, the trend in job design in manufacturing has been one of job deskilling or job simplification. The replacement of small craft-based enterprises with larger factories, the emergence of mass production, and the application of the principles of SCIENTIFIC MANAGEMENT, are among the factors which encouraged organizations to design jobs so that they involved a narrow set of closely prescribed tasks. The rationale for this strategy was that simplifying jobs in this way would reduce costs, by making errors less likely, enabling less skilled labor to be recruited and by shortening TRAINING times. The archetype of this process is the assembly line, where jobs can be so simplified that they entail the continuous repetition of a single operation with a short cycle time, minimal discretion over how to carry out the task, and no control over the pace of work.

The practice of job simplification gave rise to concerns about its psychological effects, and inspired some of the earliest research in OB. In the United Kingdom this was a focus of work conducted during the 1920s by the publicly funded Industrial Fatigue Research Board. That research, involving such jobs as tobacco weighing, cigarette making, cartridge case assembly, and bicycle chain assembly, was mainly formulated in terms of the psychological effects of the lack of task variety, that is, of repetitive work. Not surprisingly, the evidence suggested that employees did indeed find repetitive jobs monotonous and boring. As this area of inquiry developed in the United Kingdom, the United States and elsewhere during the next few decades, evidence also began to emerge of a link between repetitive work and employee STRESS and mental health. Research during the 1950s and 1960s began also to consider how the restriction of job discretion or autonomy brought about by job simplification affected job incumbents, and showed similar and often stronger psychological effects. This is a key component of current approaches to job design as will be described later.

Job Redesign

Evidence of the undesirable effects of simplified job designs gave rise to various proposals for and initiatives in *job redesign*. This normative term, widely used in the literature instead of the more neutral "job design," reflects the historical background outlined above. Job simplification is cast as the traditional approach to job design, and job *redesign* refers to deliberate attempts to reverse its effects by building into jobs greater task variety, autonomy, and associated characteristics. Suggestions for job redesign naturally reflect findings regarding simplified jobs. Thus one of the earliest proposals, focused on the reduction of repetitiveness by increasing task variety, was for job rotation, which involves individuals moving between different jobs at regular intervals. "Horizontal job enlargement" has the same objective, but increases task variety by incorporating into jobs a wider range of component tasks of a similar kind. Other proposals are more concerned with augmenting responsibility or autonomy. This is the thrust of both "vertical job enlargement" and JOB ENRICHMENT, which entail increasing the degree to which individuals can control the planning and execution of their work, usually including responsibilities and tasks which otherwise would be undertaken by specialist support or supervisory staff. Job enrichment is a term coined by Herzberg to denote the approach to job redesign based on his two-factor theory (1966), but which is now used more generally. A final type of proposal directed at enhancing the discretionary content of work, but which differs in taking the WORK GROUP rather than the job as the main unit of analysis, derives from sociotechnical theory (*see also* below), and is for the implementation of AUTONOMOUS WORK GROUPS or self-managed teams (*see* SELF-MANAGEMENT).

Major Theoretical Approaches

Current approaches to job design are more broadly based than the early work. Two theoretical frameworks have been particularly influential, and have yet to be superseded. The first of these is the JOB CHARACTERISTICS, Oldham, 1976), which specifies five "core job dimensions" (namely autonomy, feedback, skill variety, task identity, and task significance) as predictors of work motivation, work performance, JOB SATISFACTION, labor turnover and absence (*see* ABSENTEEISM). The strength of the effects of the job characteristics on the outcomes is predicted to be affected by individual differences, in particular, being stronger for employees with greater growth need strength and (in later formulations of the model) for those with higher contextual satisfaction and more knowledge, SKILLS, and ABILITY.

The second main approach derives from sociotechnical theory. The emphasis in this case is on job design for groups of employees, the major proposal being for the implementation of autonomous work groups. Theorists identify six design criteria for promoting work effectiveness, individual well-being and the quality of working life more generally. These are that the work should: be reasonably demanding and provide variety; afford the opportunity to learn and to continue learning; include an area of decision making that employees can call their own; offer social support and recognition; be of wider social relevance; and lead to a desirable future (Cherns, 1976). There is no particular recognition of individual differences in this approach, but otherwise the specified variables are very similar to those of the Job Characteristics Model.

Examples

A series of studies by Wall, Clegg and colleagues illustrates empirical work in this area (Wall & Martin, 1994). For example, the redesign of work in a department in a confectionery factory led to the institution of two autonomous work groups, each taking responsibility for organizing their own work, within the constraints of meeting production targets and of normal health and safety requirements. The groups set their own speed of work, allocated tasks amongst themselves, and took responsibility for daily operational decisions. The results were impressive and significant: levels of productivity and job satisfaction increased, whilst reports of individual strain fell. A further study in a different organization compared the use of autonomous group work in a greenfield factory designed for such purposes, with a more traditional factory making similar products. This demonstrated that workers much preferred autonomous working, although interestingly the managers found it very challenging. Levels of operational efficiency were comparable across the two factories, although the indirect support costs were considerably lower in the new factory.

A series of studies in an electronics company substantiates the claim that people much prefer more enriched jobs. Furthermore, enriching individual's jobs led to substantial improvements in operational performance when there was uncertainty in the work system. Part of the improvement was "logistical," the operators were on hand to resolve difficulties as they arose. Part was also motivational, in the sense that the operators prefer to have and take responsibility. However, it is clear there was also a learning explanation to these improvements in performance. For example, operators learned to anticipate problems and acted to prevent them occurring (Wall & Jackson, 1994).

A further point should be stressed. Each of these studies revealed the importance of the surrounding organization within which jobs are designed or redesigned. Choices about the tasks for which individual operators or groups of operators take responsibility have a substantial impact on the work of others, most notably their supervisors (if there are any) and managers, and other staff in indirect support roles (e.g., in quality and engineering). The organizational context within which jobs are designed or redesigned is probably the major issue for people attempting practical changes in this area, and the failure to take this into account the main reason for lack of success.

Current Issues and Future Directions

Interest in job design which waxed during the 1970s, making it then one of the most prominent areas of inquiry within OB, waned during the 1980s. However, it is now resurfacing in response to the new strategies, practices, and technologies emerging in manufacturing and elsewhere. Organizations are placing increased emphasis on enhancing their competitiveness through improved quality, flexibility, and responsiveness to customer (or client) demand; and supporting this through the use of ADVANCED MANUFACTURING TECHNOLOGY, just-in-time inventory control, total quality management, business process reengineering and other initiatives. It is widely recognized that these developments have implications for the nature of jobs, and that success depends on their being supported by appropriate job designs (e.g., Buchanan & McCalman, 1989; Lawler, 1992). This renewed emphasis on job design has highlighted the limitations of existing knowledge and thus clarified directions for further development.

One issue on which existing evidence is relatively conclusive is that of the effect of job design on attitudes. Evidence consistently supports the theoretically specified link between job design variables, especially autonomy, and job satisfaction. With regard to performance, in contrast, findings have been more variable. It is likely that this relationship varies according to unspecified contingencies, and those need to be determined. As in the examples described earlier, one such contingency, suggested by organizational theory, is UNCERTAINTY. It is possible that designing more autonomous jobs benefits performance under conditions of greater uncertainty, but that the effect declines as job requirements become more predictable. That is a particular issue that deserves serious attention. More importantly, however, it exemplifies the now apparent more general need in job design research for the development of a wider perspective and greater integration with cognate areas of inquiry (Wall & Jackson, 1994).

Four other areas of job design requiring such development are high on the agenda. The first concerns mental health. It is interesting that although this featured as a dependent variable in early studies it has subsequently been neglected by mainstream approaches. As if to rectify this neglect, there has emerged a separate area of inquiry on job stress, in which mental health is the focus and autonomy a key predictor variable (e.g., the Demands–Control Model, Karasek & Theorell, 1990). Those areas are ripe for integration. A second need is to broaden the range of job content variables taken into account within job design. Research on new technologies and work practices in particular has pointed to the potential relevance of such factors as cognitive demand and cost responsibility. This relates to a third need which is for the development of a stronger cognitive emphasis. At present job design is founded on motivational assumptions. Recent evidence suggests that at least some of the effects of job design operate through enhancing job incumbents' understanding of their tasks. The role of underlying cognitive mechanisms is worthy of investigation in its own right, and would benefit through being linked to developments in cognitive psychology. Finally, it is apparent the effect of technology on job design has been neglected. Especially important in the context of new technology is the issue of prospective design, where social scientists and users work alongside development engineers in the design and implementation of systems to ensure that they are not specified in such a way as to preclude job design alternatives that would be of benefit (Clegg, Cooch, Hornby, Maclaren, Robson, Carey, & Symon, 1994). These and other developments are now underway.

see also **Operations management; Organizational design**

Bibliography

Buchanan, D. A. & McCalman, J. (1989). High performance work systems: The Digital experience. London: Routledge.

Cherns, A. (1976). The principles of sociotechnical design. Human Relations, **29**, 783–792.

Clegg, C. W. Cooch, P. Hornby, P. Maclaren, R. Robson, J. Carey, N. & Symon, G. (1995). Methods and tools to incorporate some psychological and organisational issues during the development of computer-based systems. SAPU memo 1435

Hackman, J. R. & Oldham, G. R. (1976). Motivation through the design of work: Test of a theory. Organizational Behavior and Human Performance, **15**, 250–279.

Herzberg, F. (1966). Work and the nature of man. Cleveland, OH: World Publishing.

Karasek, R. & Theorell, T. (1990). Healthy work: Stress, productivity and the reconstruction of working life. New York: Basic Books.

Lawler, E. E. (1992). The ultimate advantage: Creating the high involvement organization. San Francisco: Jossey-Bass.

Wall, T. D. & Jackson, P. R. (1994). Changes in manufacturing and shopfloor job design. In A. Howard (Ed.), The changing nature of work. San Francisco: Jossey-Bass.

Wall, T. D. & Martin, R. (1994). Job and work design. In C. L. Cooper & I. T. Robertson (Eds.). Key reviews in organizational behavior: Concepts, theory and practice. Chichester: Wiley.

TOBY D. WALL and CHRIS W. CLEGG

job enrichment In its most general form, this involves expanding a job's content to provide increased opportunities for the individual employee to experience personal responsibility and meaning at work, and to obtain more information about the results of his or her work efforts. In practice, job enrichment programs often focus on improving a job's standing on JOB CHARACTERISTICS, specifically: autonomy, task feedback, task significance, SKILL variety, and task identity. Several specific "implementing principles" have been identified (Hackman & Oldham, 1980; Hackman, Oldham, Janson, & Purdy, 1975) which can be used to boost a job on these characteristics and, therefore, to enrich the job itself. These are defined as follows:

Combining tasks. This refers to putting together existing, fractionalized tasks to form new and larger modules of work. When tasks are combined, all tasks required to complete a piece of work are performed by one person, rather than by a series of individuals who do separate small, parts of the job.

Forming natural work units. This involves giving employees continuing responsibility for work that has been arranged into logical or inherently meaningful groups. For example, an individual employee might be given responsibility for all work within a particular geographical area or for all work that originates in a particular department of a larger organization.

Establishing client relationships. This refers to putting the employee in direct contact with the "clients" of his or her work (e.g., customers or employees in other departments) and giving the employee personal responsibility for managing relationships with those clients.

Vertical loading. This involves giving the employee increased control over the work by "pushing down" responsibility and authority that were once reserved for higher levels of management (*see* SPAN OF CONTROL). Thus, vertical loading can involve giving the employee discretion in setting schedules, determining work methods, and deciding when and how to check the quality of work produced.

Opening feedback channels. This involves removing blocks that isolate the employee from naturally occurring data about his or her performance at work. Specifically, this may involve giving the employee the opportunity to inspect his or her own work and providing standard summaries of performance records directly to the employee.

The major objectives of job enrichment are to improve the JOB SATISFACTION, MOTIVATION, and work effectiveness of employees. Numerous studies have examined the effects of job enrichment on such outcomes, and the results have generally been positive (see Ford, 1969; Herzberg, 1976). For example, in a review of 32 empirical studies, Kopelman (1985) concludes that job enrichment programs typically result in a 17.2 percent increase in work quality, a 6.4 percent increase in work quantity, and a 14.5 percent decrease in ABSENTEEISM. Moreover, 80 percent of the studies that included measures of job satisfaction showed some improvement after job enrichment.

In addition, other research suggests that the outcomes of job enrichment will be even more positive when employees involved are strongly desirous of opportunities for growth and self-direction at work. Unfortunately, there remain a number of questions about the practice of job enrichment. One of the most serious of these concerns the durability of the effects of job enrichment interventions. Most empirical investigations have examined the effects of enrichment for periods of less than 12 months. Therefore, it is not yet clear that employees will find the enriched jobs stimulating and challenging after extended periods of time – or will find that the jobs provide insufficient opportunities for personal responsibility and continued growth.

see also **Job design; Organizational design**

Bibliography

Ford, R. N. (1969). Motivation through the work itself. New York: American Management Association.

Hackman, J. R. & Oldham, G. R. (1980). Work redesign. Reading, MA: Addison-Wesley.

Hackman, J. R., Oldham, G. R., Janson, R. & Purdy, K. (1975). A new strategy for job enrichment. California Management Review, 17, 57–71.

Herzberg, F. (1976). The managerial choice. Homewood, IL: Dow Jones-Irwin.

Kopelman, R. E. (1985). Job redesign and productivity: A review of the evidence. National Productivity Review, 4, 237–255.

GREG R. OLDHAM

job evaluation methods Job evaluation is a systematic process designed to aid in establishing pay differentials across jobs within a single employer (Milkovich and Newman, 1996, p. 127). It is an alternative to person-based (e.g. competency-based pay) and market pricing approaches. Job evaluation is a judgmental process based on a systematic appraisal of JOB DESCRIPTIONs. The culmination of this appraisal process is a hierarchy of jobs denoting their relative complexity and value to the organization. When matched with data about market pay rates, job evaluation provides the critical link between the organization's internal job structure and the external market and establishes the organization's pay structure (Schwab, 1980; Milkovich and Newman, 1996). Job evaluation is a crucial process for establishing a pay structure that is internally equitable, externally competitive, and consistent with the goals of the organization (*see also* EXTERNAL EQUITY/ EXTERNAL COMPETITIVENESS).

Two essential components are usually assessed in job evaluation: job content and job value. Job content refers to the type of work performed, the knowledge, skills, and abilities (*see* KSAOs) required to perform that work, working conditions, degree of responsibility assumed, and so on. Job value refers to the relative contribution a job makes to organizational goals, its value in external markets, or its worth relative to some other agreed upon standard. Job evaluation methods differ in terms of how they appraise job value and content, and how they position jobs based upon these values and content assessments. The most popular job evaluation method is the POINT JOB EVALUATION METHOD.

Bibliography

Milkovich, G. T. & Newman, J. M. (1996). *Compensation*, 5th edn, Homewood, IL: Richard D. Irwin.

Schwab, D. P. (1980). Job evaluation and pay setting: concepts and practices. *Comparable Worth: Issues and Alternatives*, Livernash, E. R. Washington, DC: Equal Employment Opportunity Council.

MATTHEW C. BLOOM

job involvement   Job involvement is an attitude toward the work role and its context. Conceptual definitions of job involvement have been of two basic types (see, for example, Lodahl and Kejner, 1965; Rabinowitz and Hall, 1977). One regards it as reflecting the degree to which a person's sense of esteem is affected by JOB PERFORMANCE. The other views it as the centrality of work and the job context to the individual's self-image. Unfortunately, however, there are many other views on the nature of the job involvement construct and there is currently no consensus on the most appropriate measure of this construct (Rabinowitz and Hall, 1977). Moreover, as is true of the conceptual definitions of many constructs, popular definitions of job involvement tend to confuse it with its antecedents (e.g. WORK VALUES) and consequences (e.g. performance-based esteem changes; Stone-Romero, 1994).

Researchers and theorists have equated job involvement, directly or indirectly, with such constructs as work centrality, morale, intrinsic motivation, JOB SATISFACTION, and the Protestant work ethic (Rabinowitz and Hall, 1977). Recently, however, Paullay et al. (1994) argued that job involvement differs from both the Protestant work ethic and work centrality. The Protestant work ethic is a value orientation that has several components, including the normative belief that individuals should be involved in their work (Weber, 1930; Wollack et al., 1971). Work centrality reflects the degree to which individuals view work (independent of a specific job) as being an important activity in life (Dubin, 1956). Job involvement reflects the degree to which individuals feel attracted or attached to the tasks that make up their jobs (i.e. job involvement role) and the setting in which such tasks are carried out (i.e. job involvement setting). Research by Paullay et al. showed that job involvement role, job involvement setting, work centrality, and Protestant work ethic are distinct, although related, constructs.

Fishbein and Ajzen's (1975) attitude model can aid in the conceptualization of the job involvement construct. The model specifies that: (a) attitudes toward an attitude object are a function of individuals' values and beliefs; (b) attitudes, in conjunction with subjective norms, are precursors of behavioral intentions; and (c) these intentions determine actual behavior. Applying this framework to the attitude of job involvement suggests that: (a) socialization consistent with such value orientations as the Protestant work ethic leads individuals to value the performance of job-related tasks and to view work as central to their lives; (b) this value orientation predisposes them to become involved with their jobs and their work settings; (c) when such work-related values are combined with beliefs about the nature-specific jobs and their settings, individuals manifest job involvement (i.e. an attitude of attraction to the job and its context); and (d) this attitude leads individuals to develop behavioral intentions that are reflective of it and, thereafter, to behave in attitude consistent ways (e.g. perform at above average levels). This view of job involvement clarifies relationships between job involvement and its antecedents and consequences, helps to explain the results of prior research on relationships between job involvement and other variables (see Rabinowitz and Hall, 1977, for a review), and provides a basis for predicting how such interventions as EMPLOYEE INVOLVEMENT and job redesign programs will affect job involvement and its consequences.

Bibliography

Dubin, R. (1965). Industrial workers' worlds: a study of the "central life interests" of industrial workers. *Social Problems*, 3, 131–42.

Fishbein, M. & Ajzen, I. (1975). *Belief, Attitude, Intention, and Behavior: an Introduction to Theory and Research*, Reading, MA: Addison-Wesley.

Lodahl, T. M. & Kejner, M. (1965). The definition and measurement of job involvement. *Journal of Applied Psychology*, 49, 24–33.

Paullay, I. M., Alliger, G. M. & Stone-Romero, E. F. (1994). Construct validation of two instruments designed to measure job involvement and work centrality. *Journal of Applied Psychology*, 79, 224–8.

Rabinowitz, S. & Hall, D. T. (1977). Organizational research on job involvement. *Psychological Bulletin*, 84, 265–88.

Stone-Romero, E. F. (1994). Construct validity issues in organizational behavior research. *Organizational Behavior: the State of the Science*, Eds. Greenberg, J. Hillsdale, NJ: Lawrence Erlbaum Associates.

Weber, M. (1930). *The Protestant Ethic and the Spirit of Capitalism*, Winchester, MA: Allen & Unwin.

Wollack, S., Goodale, J. G., Wijting, J. P. & Smith, P. C. (1971). Development of the survey of work values. *Journal of Applied Psychology*, 55, 331–8.

EUGENE F. STONE-ROMERO

job loss   Job loss is used interchangeably with layoffs and generally refers to loss of employment due to plant closings, work slowdowns, corporate downsizings, or organizational restructuring (Leana and Feldman, 1992).

Evidence exists that job loss has a negative impact on the unemployed, on his or her family, and on friends and coworkers. People who have lost their jobs have been found to be more anxious, depressed, unhappy, and dissatisfied with life in general. Job loss also has strong effects on psychosomatic illnesses such as sleeping disorders, eating disorders, overuse of sedatives, dermatitis, headaches and listlessness. Spouses of the unemployed often suffer psychological problems similar to those of the job loser. There is also evidence that job loss may contribute to the rate of marital separation and divorce. The results of several laboratory and field studies on coworkers of laid-off employees suggest that these so-called survivors often lower their productivity, develop poorer job attitudes, and voluntarily leave their employers in the wake of coworkers' layoffs (Brockner, 1988; Leana and Feldman, 1994).

Individuals cope with job loss in a variety of ways. These coping strategies have been categorized as problem-focused coping (i.e. JOB SEARCH, RETRAINING) or symptom-focused coping (i.e. seeking social support). Some level of both is necessary for successful adjustment and re-employment (Leana and Feldman, 1994).

Four corporate interventions have been most frequently used to soften the effects of layoffs. These include: advance notification, severance pay and extended benefits, retraining programs, and outplacement programs (Leana and Feldman, 1992).

Bibliography

Brockner, J. (1988). The effects of work layoffs on survivors: Regional Behavior, Staw, B. (ed.), 10, Greenwich, CT: JAI Press.

Leana, C. R. & Feldman, D. C. (1992). *Coping with Job Loss: How Individuals, Organizations, and Communities Respond to Layoffs*, New York: Lexington Books.

Leana, C. R. & Feldman, D. C. (1994). The psychology of job loss. Eds. Ferris, G. & Rowland, K. *Research in Personnel and Human Resources Management*, 12, Greenwich, CT: JAI Press.

CARRIE R. LEANA

job performance   Job performance is defined as that aspect of the work behavior domain that is of relevance to job and organizational success (Austin et al., 1991). As such, it represents a sample of the universe of behaviors an individual performs in the course of work that is relevant to judging success. Job performance is a key construct in human resource management, because criteria for promotion, as well as for selection validation purposes, are frequently drawn from the job performance domain.

Representing and Understanding Job Performance

Job performance is a complex construct that is multidimensional, multiply determined, and potentially dynamic. Understanding job performance requires one to recognize that patterns of behavior in organizations can be prescribed through formal, bureaucratic means, such as job descriptions, and through informal and more subjective means, such as role-sending, role-making, and role negotiation. Traditional definitions of job performance have concentrated on the former, more technical, objective and quasi-static job-based domain. More recent conceptualizations of job performance have been expanded to include less formally established activities, such as citizenship behavior and a willingness to assume responsibility and leadership beyond those detailed in a formal job description. No doubt, this more inclusive conceptualization of job performance reflects the complexity of today's work organizations.

Job performance is multidimensional. There is abundant evidence that job performance, even for low-complexity jobs, is multidimensional (Campbell et al., 1990; Borman, 1991), and reflects both task and contextual aspects of the job (Borman and Motowidlo, 1993). Task proficiency is what has been traditionally studied as job performance and consists of the technical core (i.e. creating goods and services). Contextual performance reflects behaviors that enhance or detract from the environment surrounding the technical core.

Moreover, just as task performance is almost perfectly identified with established task elements of a job, contextual performance consists exclusively of emergent task elements that may be actively constructed or passively accepted by a worker. Because contextual performance more closely resembles "role performance," these activities and contributions may vary from worker to worker, even among those nominally assigned the same job classification. The implications are that performance dimensions may not only vary from one setting to another, as Bailey (1983) has argued, but also within a setting, where multiple roles are enacted by individuals performing the same "job."

Job performance is multiply determined. Just as no single dimension can successfully represent the complexity of performance, no single predictor sufficiently accounts for performance variability, or, more appropriately, for the patterns of behavior that define job success. Moreover, if one accepts that both tasks and contextual aspects of performance are important, the implications for selection include expansion of the predictor domain and acknowledgement that single predictor–single criterion combinations are inevitably deficient, both conceptually and practically. In particular, motivational and personality constructs would appear as logical candidates for providing incremental understanding of contextual performance, just as knowledge, skill, and ability constructs would seem to support task performance. Borman et al. (1995) have shown that contextual aspects of performance, such as "dependability," can account for as much, or more, of the variance in supervisor ratings of performance as do knowledge, ability, and proficiency.

Job performance is dynamic. The dynamic nature of performance on most jobs makes its representation by any measure at any one point in time somewhat deficient, contaminated, and less relevant than if measured at another time. Dynamic criteria reflect these shifts in the underlying structure of job success, and are reflected in changes in rank ordering of employees over time (Ghiselli, 1956). For example, the demands of the job, work aids, and worker proficiency may change over time as new technology or work methods are introduced, while performance standards are not calibrated to reflect these changes. The practical implications include timing of appraisals, appraisal accuracy, and the potential for inaccurate estimates of selection validity and utility. Models that reflect the interaction between persons and work systems seem well equipped to explain this dynamic variance.

Bibliography

Austin et al. (1991). Construct validation of performance measures: definitional issues, development, and evaluation of indicators. *Research in Personnel and Human Resources Management*, Eds. Rowland, K. M. & Ferris, G. R. Greenwich, CT: JAI Press.

Bailey, C. T. (1983). *The Measurement of Job Performance*, Aldershot: Gower Press.

Blumberg, M. & Pringle, C. D. (1982). The missing opportunity in organizational research: some implications for a theory of work performance. *Academy of Management Review*, 7, 560–9.

Borman, W. C. (1991). Job behavior, performance, and effectiveness. *Handbook of Industrial and Organizational Psychology*, Eds. Dunnette, M. D. & Hough, L. M.2, Palo Alto, CA: Consulting Psychologists Press.

Borman, W. C. & Motowidlo, S. J. (1993). Expanding the criterion domain to include elements of contextual performance. *Personnel Selection*, Eds. Schmitt, N. & Borman, W. C. San Francisco: Jossey-Bass.

Borman, W. C., White, L. A. & Dorsey, D. W. (1995). Effects of ratee task performance and interpersonal factors on supervisor and peer performance ratings. *Journal of Applied Psychlgy*, 80, 168–77.

Campbell, J. P., McHenry, J. J. & Wise, L. L. (1990). Modeling job performance in a population of jobs. *Personnel Psychology*, 43, 313–33.

Ghiselli, E. E. (1956). Dimensional problems of criteria. *Journal of Applied Psychology*, 40, 1–4.

PETER VILLANOVA, JAMES T. AUSTIN,
and WALTER C. BORMAN

job satisfaction   This is probably one of the most researched constructs in organizational behavior. Literally thousands of articles have been written about its definition and meaning, its antecedents, and its consequences. Job satisfaction may be defined as the emotional state resulting from the appraisal of one's job and as such can be negative, positive, or neutral. A basic element in this definition is that job satisfaction has to do with an affective state or how one "feels" about one's job in contrast to simply describing a job (*see* EMOTIONS IN ORGANIZATIONS).

There are a variety of theories which help explain how job satisfaction comes about. One theoretical structure suggests that job satisfaction is a function of what one expects from a job compared to what is actually present in the job. Another theoretical structure suggests that job satisfaction is a function of the degree to which individual's needs are fulfilled; still another argues that satisfaction is a function of the degree to which a job fulfills important work values. All this connote reactions to some degree of fit or misfit between people and jobs.

Job satisfaction may be thought of as an "overall appraisal" of one's job, and be broken down in several different job facets such as achievement, working conditions, advancement opportunities, etc. Some controversy exists regarding whether an overall measure of job satisfaction has the same meaning as measuring satisfaction on different job facets and summing over these facets to obtain a composite measure. In addition, some research suggests that job satisfaction may be described along two relatively independent dimensions – intrinsic satisfaction which involves achievement, recognition, and other features associated with the work itself, and extrinsic satisfaction which involves working conditions, supervision, and other components of the environmental context in which the work is performed. An important early framework was developed by Frederick Herzberg who argued that these two general independent types of events affected satisfaction and dissatisfaction differently. He argued that intrinsic factors (called "Motivators") could only enhance job satisfaction, and that extrinsic factors (called hygiene factors) would only operate to reduce or eliminate job dissatisfaction. This theory, known as the "two-factor" motivator–hygiene theory was used as a starting point for JOB ENRICHMENT and enlargement efforts on the part of organizations. Subsequent research has shown that this model was perhaps too simplistic and that both intrinsic and extrinsic factors operate to influence both satisfaction and dissatisfaction.

There have been a variety of efforts to measure job satisfaction. Perhaps two of the best-known efforts are:

(1) the Minnesota Job Satisfaction Questionnaire (MSQ) which assesses job satisfaction along 20 separate job facets where separate composites are computed for Intrinsic, Extrinsic, and General Job Satisfaction; and
(2) the Job Description Index (JDI) where satisfaction is assessed along the following dimensions: work, pay, promotions, co-workers, and supervision.

Many factors have been hypothesized to contribute to job satisfaction. These may be broken roughly into two major categories: Individual or person factors and environmental factors. Individual or person factors include demographic variables such as age, race, gender, etc., as well as trait factors associated with individuals (e.g., IQ, self-esteem, dominance, etc.). Research evidence has established that job satisfaction is significantly associated with general mental health indices, with several PERSON-

ALITY variables, age, and even genetic factors. Such personal variables are sometimes labeled to trait-like, stable, and reliable individual differences which correlate with satisfaction. Environmental variables are facets associated with the job and organization such as working conditions, variety in the work, pay, autonomy, interpersonal relations among coworkers. A voluminous body of research has established significant relationships between a variety of these environmental factors and job satisfaction. For example, skill variety in jobs, the degree of task or work significance, and the degree of feedback are significantly associated with job satisfaction. One of the ongoing debates today is how much independent and joint influence do these two broad factors have in determining job satisfaction.

There is also a sizable research base examining the consequences of job satisfaction. One of the more closely studied relationships has been between job satisfaction and job performance. While some have argued that high job satisfaction leads to higher levels of job performance, others have suggested that the relationship is reversed and that high performance leads to high satisfaction, but only if performance is rewarded. A sizeable number of research studies have been conducted to investigate the empirical relationship, and the findings indicate that the relationship is modest but generally significant (Iaffaldano & Muchinsky, 1992). The correlations generally range in the high teens to low 20s. Other research studies show a similarly modest relationship between satisfaction and ABSENTEEISM, but a more substantial relationship between satisfaction and turnover. In addition, satisfaction has been shown to be significantly associated with the COMMITMENT individuals have with the organization, and overall citizenship within the organization.

see also **Job design**

Bibliography

Arvey, R. D., Carter, G. W. & Buerkley, D. K. (1991) Job satisfaction: Dispositional and situational influences. In C. L. Cooper & I. T. Robertson (Eds), International review of industrial and organizational psychology. (vol. 6, pp. 359–383).
Cranny, C. J., Smith, P. C. & Stone, E. F. (1992). Job satisfaction: How people feel about their jobs and how it affects their performance. New York: Lexington Press.
Iaffaldano, M. T. & Muchinsky, P. M. (1992). Job satisfaction and job performance: A meta-analysis. Psychological Bulletin, 97, 251–273.
Locke, E. A. (1985). The nature and causes of job satisfaction. In M. D. Dunnette (Ed.), Handbook of industrial and organizational psychology, (pp. 1297–1349). Chicago, IL: Rand McNally.

RICHARD D. ARVEY

job search Job search is the process of gathering information about potential job opportunities. It is the individual corollary of RECRUITING and together they form the basis for successful person-job matching. Job search frequently has been imbedded within the construct of employee withdrawal under the assumption that it results from the same factors that lead to turnover. However, the temporal relationship between intention to search and the intention to quit is ambiguous, suggesting that job search serves many purposes in addition to facilitating turnover. Some employed people search without any intention to leave a current position. For example, job search can be used to establish networks of influential contacts, to leverage improved employment conditions with the current employer, or to convince oneself that the current employment arrangements are attractive relative to alternatives (Bretz et al., 1994).

Job search among the employed is thought to be motivated by a combination of "push" and "pull" factors. The push process reflects the degree to which current life or work situations cause enough dissatisfaction to justify the costs of finding and evaluating alternatives. The pull process reflects the market's reaction to one's human capital, or the degree to which an individual's accomplishments make one a target for external recruitment activity.

Critical aspects of the job search process include: (a) the amount of information sought; (b) the nature of the information sought; and (c) the source of the information (Schwab et al., 1987). The amount of information sought encompasses both extensive and intensive search behaviors. Extensive search involves identifying potential job opportunities. Intensive search involves collecting detailed information about each alternative, and has been shown to relate to many positive outcomes, including shorter unemployment durations and higher probabilities of finding an acceptable job (Rynes, 1991).

The type of information sought changes over the course of the search. At first, people engage in extensive search to generate alternatives, followed at later stages by intensive search to learn more about the alternatives. However, the job choice literature is inconclusive regarding the evaluation process. One model suggests that job offers are evaluated simultaneously against one another, while competing models suggest that job seekers consider alternatives sequentially as they become known (Schwab et al., 1987). Under most circumstances it is reasonable to believe that job search is sequential, and that jobs are evaluated against pre-established standards on a few important criteria, such as (a) the nature of the work required, (b) the rewards the job offers, and (c) the degree of person–organization "fit" based on job requirements (Bretz and Judge, 1994).

Job applicants typically assign greater credibility to informal than to formal sources of job information. Specifically, friends, relatives, and organizational representatives other than the recruiter are presumed more likely to give REALISTIC JOB PREVIEWS and are thus perceived as more credible. These sources generally yield better post-hire results as well. The effects of recruitment on applicant decisions have been debated, but recent research indicates that RECRUITING does significantly affect job search and choice behaviors (Rynes et al., 1991).

Bibliography

Bretz, R. D., Boudreau, J. W. & Judge, T. A. (1994). Job search behavior of employed managers. *Personnel Psychology*, 47, 275–301.

Bretz, R. D. & Judge, T. A. (1994). The role of human resource systems in job applicant decision processes. *Journal of Management*, 20, 531–51.

Rynes, S. L. (1991). Recruitment, job choice and post-hire consequences: a call for new research directions. *Handbook of Industrial and Organizational Psychology*, Eds. Dunnette, M. D. & Hough, L. 2nd edn, Palo Alto, CA: Consulting Psychologists' Press. 399–444.

Rynes, S. L., Bretz, R. D. & Gerhart, B. (1991). The importance of recruitment in job choice: a different way of looking. *Personnel Psychology*, 44, 487–521.

Schwab, D. P., Rynes, S. L. & Aldag, R. J. (1987). Theories and research on job search and choice. *Research in Personnel and Human Resources Management*, Eds. Rowland, K. M. & Ferris, G. R. 5, Greenwich, CT: JAI Press. 129–66.

ROBERT D. BRETZ JR

job-skills training   Job-skills training initiatives are designed to identify and target improvement in the basic skills individuals need to be successful in the workplace. Job-skills training is of increasing interest to employers because new business realities (e.g. global competition, rapid technological change) have created demand for a higher level of skills for all workers. The domain of basic skills includes the traditional "three Rs" (reading, writing, and arithmetic) as well as problem-solving, teamwork, and capacity to learn (Carnevale et al., 1990a). The most effective job-skills training has employed a job-specific methodology which links learning to job performance and encourages retention by requiring repeated use of trained skills (Carnevale et al., 1990b).

Bibliography

Carnevale, A. P., Gainer, L. J. & Meltzer, A. S. (1990a). *Workplace Basics – the Essential Skills Employers Want*, San Francisco: Jossey-Bass.

Carnevale, A. P., Gainer, L. J. & Meltzer, A. S. (1990b). *Workplace Basics – Training Manual*, San Francisco: Jossey-Bass.

TIMOTHY T. BALDWIN

job stress   Job stress is defined as the mind–body arousal resulting from physical and/or psychological demands associated with a job. It may lead to enhanced job performance up to an optimum level of stress; conversely, it may place an employee at risk of distress if the job stress is too intense, frequent, or chronic (Selye, 1976). Understanding job stress is important so as to reduce job strain (or job distress) and job burnout and to implement effective stress management programs.

Sources of Job Stress

Job stress is triggered by a wide variety of job demands. These include task-specific demands, role demands, interpersonal demands, and physical demands (Quick and Quick, 1984). These demands are not inherently, or necessarily, harmful, and the degree of stress they elicit in a person depends in part on the individual's cognitive appraisal of that demand. Lack of control over and uncertainty about aspects of the psycho-social and physical work environments in industrialized nations are major sources of job stress (Sutton and Kahn, 1987). Extreme working environments, such as those of military fighter pilots or oil field service personnel in arctic climates, create unique physical and/or peak demands. Whether the job stress level is healthy or unhealthy is determined in part by the prevalence of job strain within a given work population.

Costs of Job Strain

Job strain, an adverse consequence of job stress, may be costly to organizations and may take one of three individual forms: psychological, medical, or behavioral. Common forms of psychological distress are depression, job burnout, anger, and sleep disturbances. Common forms of medical distress are backaches and headaches, ulcer disease and cardiovascular problems. Common forms of behavioral distress are substance abuse, violence, and accident proneness. High strain jobs, characterized by high job demands and low employee control, have significantly higher incidence rates of distress, such as myocardial infarction (Karasek et al., 1988).

Organizational costs may accrue from employees' psychological, medical, and behavioral distress. The direct organizational costs of job strain take the form of turnover, ABSENTEEISM, performance problems on the job, and workers' compensation, court-ordered, or negotiated cash awards. In addition, there are indirect organizational costs of job strain which may be reflected in low morale, low job satisfaction, faulty decision-making, and distrust in working relationships.

Individual Differences in the Stress–Strain Relationship

Individual predispositions and vulnerabilities influence the degree to which job stress may become job strain. Gender and personality are two key individual differences in this regard. Women are more predisposed to a variety of non-fatal forms of distress, such as depression, while men are more predisposed to a variety of fatal forms of distress, such as cardiovascular disease. Excessive anger enhances the conversion of job stress into job strain, while personality hardiness enables individuals to maintain low levels of strain in the presence of high stress levels (Spielberger et al., 1988).

Stress management programs may help prevent job stress from becoming one or another form of job strain (job distress). Employee assistance programs can help employees who experience identifiable job strain, distress and/or job burnout. Health promotion programs may also help employees to manage job stress.

Bibliography

Karasek, R. A., Theorell, T., Schwartz, J. E., Schnall, P. L., Pieper, C. F. & Michela, J. L. (1988). Job characteristics in relation to the prevalence of myocardial infarction in the US health examination survey (HES) and the health and nutrition examination survey (HANES). *American Journal of Public Health*, 78, 910–18.

Quick, J. C. & Quick, J. D. (1984). *Organizational Stress and Preventive Management*, New York: McGraw-Hill.

Sutton, R. I. & Kahn, R. L. (1987). Prediction, understanding, and control as antidotes to organizational stress. *Handbook of Organizational Behavior*, Lorsch, J. W. Englewood Cliffs, NJ: Prentice-Hall.

Selye, H. (1976). *Stress in Health and Disease,* Boston: Butterworths.

Spielberger, C. D., Krasner, S. S. & Solomon, E. P. (1988). The experience, expression, and control of anger. *Health Psychology: Individual Differences and Stress*, Janisse, M. P. New York: Springer Verlag.

JAMES CAMPBELL QUICK
AND DEBRA L. NELSON

joint venture strategy   Joint ventures may well prove to be a useful, and indeed necessary, way to enter some new markets, especially for multinational firms. In some markets which restrict inward investment, joint ventures may be the only way to achieve market access. Within joint ventures, clear equity positions are usually taken by the participants; such holdings can vary substantially in size, although it is usually important to establish clear lines of management decision making control in order to achieve success.

A lesser form of participation, which may or may not involve equity participation, involves STRATEGIC ALLIANCES. Joint ventures do tend to have a relatively high failure rate. Nevertheless, they also enjoy a number of specific advantages.

Advantages of Joint Ventures

First, for the smaller organization with insufficient finance and/or specialist management skills, the joint venture can prove an effective method of obtaining the necessary resources to enter a new market. This can be especially true in attractive developing country markets, where local contacts, access to distribution, and political requirements may make a joint venture the preferred, or even legally required, solution.

Second, joint ventures can be used to reduce political friction and local nationalist prejudice against foreign-owned corporations. Moreover, political rules may discriminate against subsidiaries that are fully foreign-owned, and in favor of local firms, through the placing of government contracts or through discriminating taxes and restrictions against foreign firms importing key materials, machineryt of trading blocs such as the European Union and NAFTA, intergovernmental negotiations have seen the introduction of tariff walls to protect the participants. As a result, despite the development of GATT, the use of joint ventures to gain access to trading bloc markets has increased, especially by firms from the Pacific Rim.

Third, joint ventures may provide specialist knowledge of local markets, entry to required channels of distribution, and access to supplies of raw materials, government contracts, and local production facilities. Japanese companies have actively exploited joint ventures for these purposes. Triad alliances have thus often led to Japanese manufacturers linking with European and/or North American manufacturers to provide badge engineered products, which have enhanced the global volume production of the Japanese suppliers and gained them access to Western developed country markets without political friction. Similarly, after the first oil-price shock, the Japanese moved swiftly to use joint ventures in order to gain access to secure supplies of oil. As a result, while Western oil companies supplied some 80 per cent of Japan's oil imports in 1973, by 1995 this had been reduced to around 25 per cent, the balance being supplied via Japanese corporations operating via joint ventures.

Fourth, in a growing number of countries, joint ventures with host governments have become increasingly important. These may be formed directly with state-owned enterprises or directed toward national champions. Such ventures are common in the extractive and defense industries, where the foreign partner is expected to provide the necessary technology to aid the developing country partner.

Fifth, there has been growth in the creation of temporary consortium companies and alliances, to undertake particular projects which are considered to be too large for individual companies to handle alone. Such cooperations include new major defense initiatives, major civil engineering projects, new global technological ventures, and the like.

Finally, exchange controls may prevent a company from exporting capital and thus make the funding of new overseas subsidiaries difficult. The supply of know-how may therefore be used to enable a company to obtain an equity stake in a joint venture, where the local partner may have access to the required funds.

Disadvantages of Joint Ventures

Despite the advantages of joint ventures, there remain substantial dangers that need to be carefully considered before embarking on a joint venture strategy.

The first major problem is that joint ventures are very difficult to integrate into a global strategy that involves substantial cross-border trading. In such circumstances, there are almost inevitably problems concerning inward and outward transfer pricing and the sourcing of exports, in particular, in favor of wholly owned subsidiaries in other countries.

Second, the trend toward an integrated system of global cash management, via a central treasury, may lead to conflict with local partners when the corporate head-quarters endeavors to impose limits or even guidelines on cash and working capital usage, foreign exchange management, and the amount, and means, of paying remittable profits. As a result, many multinationals that generate joint ventures may do so outside a policy of global strategy integration, making use of such operations to service restricted geographic territories or countries in which wholly owned subsidiaries are not permitted.

A third serious problem occurs when the objectives of the partners are, or become, incompatible. For example, the MNC may have a very different attitude to risk than its local partner, and may be prepared to accept short-term losses in order to build market share, to take on higher levels of debt, or to spend more on advertising. Similarly, the objectives of the participants may well change over time, especially when wholly owned subsidiary alternatives may occur for the MNC with access to the joint venture market.

Fourth, problems occur with regard to management structures and staffing of joint ventures. This is especially true in countries in which nepotism is common and in which jobs have to be found for members of the partner's families, or when employment is given to family members of local politicians or other locals in positions of influence. From the perspective of MNCs, seconded personnel may also be subject to conflicts of interest, in which the best actions for the joint venture might conflict with the strategy and objectives of the MNC shareholder.

Finally, many joint ventures fail because of a conflict in tax interests between the partners. Many of these could actually be overcome if they were thought through in advance; however, such problems are rarely foreseen. One common problem occurs as a result of start-up losses. Due to past write-offs, accelerated depreciation, and the like, it is common for capital-intensive businesses to report operating losses in their first few years. It is therefore possibly more attractive for the local partner if these losses can be used to offset against other locally derived profits.

To obtain such tax advantages, however, certain minimum levels of shareholdings may be necessary, and this may be in conflict with the aspirations of an MNC partner. The precise nature of the shareholding structure of joint ventures therefore needs to be considered at the formation stage in order to maximize fiscal efficiency and avoid this form of conflict.

The Joint Venture Agreement

Because of the potential difficulties that can occur with joint ventures, they should be formulated carefully and the Articles of Association only drawn up after consideration of the objectives and strategies of the participants, both at the time of formation and as they might reasonably be expected to evolve in the future. Furthermore, such an agreement should set out, in clear language, the rights and obligations of the participants, taking care that differences in interpretation due to translation are not introduced when more than one language is used. The country of jurisdiction under which any disputes would be settled also needs to be clearly stated. The joint venture agreement should then cover the following points:

- the legal nature of the joint venture and the terms under which it can be dissolved
- the constitution of the board of directors and the voting power of the partners
- the managerial rights and responsibilities of the partners
- the constitution of the management and appointment of the managerial staff
- the conditions under which the capital can be increased
- constraints on the transfer of shares or subscription rights to nonpartners
- the responsibilities of each of the partners in respect of assets, finance, personnel, R&D, and the like
- the financial rights of the partners with respect to dividends and royalties
- the rights of the partners with respect to the use of licenses, know-how, and trademarks in third countries
- limitations, if any, on sales of the joint venture's products to certain countries or regions
- an arbitration clause indicating how disputes between partners are to be resolved
- the conditions under which the Articles of the joint venture agreement may be changed
- consideration of how the joint venture can be terminated

Bibliography

Channon, D. F. & Jalland, M. (1979). *Multinational strategic planning*. London: Amacom/Macmillan. See pp. 200–6.

Farok, Contractor & Lorange, P. (1988). Why should firms cooperate? In Farok, C. & Lorange, P. (eds). *Cooperative strategies in international business*. Lexington, MA: Lexington Books.

Harrigan, K. R. (1985). *Strategies for joint ventures*. Lexington, MA: D. C. Heath.

DEREK F. CHANNON

K

kaizen The Japanese term "kaizen" means "continuous improvement" and is an all embracing concept covering just-in-time, total quality control, and kanban. It applies at all levels in Japanese corporations. A kaizen program can be subdivided into three areas based on complexity and hierarchical level, namely:

- management-oriented kaizen
- group-oriented kaizen
- individual-oriented kaizen

Management-oriented Kaizen

Under the Japanese system, continuous improvement is considered to be an activity that involves everyone. Managers are expected to devote half their time to seeking ways to improve their job, and those of the personnel for whom they are responsible. Sometimes these tasks become blurred, as blue collar workers also come up with ways of changing production processes as part of their own kaizen programs, whereas this task is technically the responsibility of management.

The kaizen projects undertaken by management involve problem solving expertise and professional and engineering knowledge. Particular use is made of the "Seven Statistical Tools." These are used by managers, but are also displayed within the factory and at the level of the work group. These tools (some of which are described in greater detail elsewhere) are as follows:

1. *Pareto diagrams.* These classify problems according to cause and phenomenon, normally with 80 per cent of cost being accounted for by 20 per cent of factors.
2. *Cause and effect diagrams.* Also called "fishbone diagrams," these are used to analyze the characteristics of a process and the factors that determine them.
3. *Histograms.* These display the data from measurements concerning the frequency of an activity, a process, and the like.
4. *Control charts.* Two types in use; they detect abnormal trends with the help of line graphs. Sample data are plotted to evaluate process situations and trends.
5. *Scatter diagrams.* Data concerning two variables are plotted to demonstrate the relationship between them.
6. *Graphs.* These depict quantitative data. Graphic displays are widely used in Japanese culture, compared with Western reliance on numerical tabulations.
7. *Checksheets.* These are designed to tabulate the outcome through routine checking of a situation.

These statistical tools are used by all levels within the organization, are prominently displayed throughout working areas, and all personnel are trained to use them.

Opportunities for improvement are to be found everywhere. However, kaizen is also the application of detail – each contribution may be small but the cumulative effect is dramatic. In particular, kaizen is concerned with waste elimination, just-in-time, and TQC. Management-oriented kaizen may also involve group activities: *ad hoc* and temporary organizational units, such as kaizen teams, project groups, and task forces, may be created to undertake a specific task, and then dispersed upon its completion.

Group-oriented Kaizen

In group work, kaizen is achieved via quality circles and other small group activities that use statistical techniques to solve problems. It also involves workers operating the full PDCA cycle and requires the groups to identify problems, analyze them, implement and test new practices, and establish new working standards. Groups are rewarded not so much with money, but with prestige. Group achievements are communicated throughout the organization, partially via cross-functional structures: groups engaged in one business activity, and evaluating tasks similar to those of other groups, are expected to learn from one another in order to maximize productivity.

At all levels in the Japanese corporation, these small groups are no longer informal but, rather, have become an integral component of continuous improvement. The advantages of this practice are seen as follows:

- the setting of group objectives and working toward their achievement reinforces the sense of team working
- members share and coordinate their respective roles better
- labor–management communication is improved
- morale is improved
- workers acquire more skills and develop cooperative attitudes
- the group becomes self-sustaining and solves problems that are normally considered the province of management
- labor–management relations are significantly improved

Individual-oriented Kaizen

At this level, kaizen involves the individual identifying ways of improving the productivity of the job. In particular, individuals contribute via the use of suggestion schemes. While in the West such schemes tend to be poorly supported, in Japan targets are now set for the number of suggestions to be contributed by work groups and individuals. As a result, in large corporations the number of suggestions can amount to many millions, and each year the number increases. When sharp appreciation of the yen has taken place, as in 1987 and 1994–5, the number of suggestions has increased dramatically – in part because workers were hired under the assumption of permanent employment – in an attempt to maintain relative competitive advantage. The main areas for suggestions in the Japanese system have been identified as follows:

- improvements in one's own work
- savings in energy, materials, and other resources
- improvements in the working environment

- improvements in jigs and tools
- improvements in office working practices
- improvements in product quality
- ideas for new products
- customer services and customer relations
- other

Kaizen policies are the norm in Japanese corporations. While sharp increases in the exchange rate make Japanese practices less competitive from time to time, the positive response of the workforce as a result of kaizen programs attempts to rapidly restore the Japanese productivity advantage. The low level of fear of forced redundancy has a significant impact on workers who, basically, may well suggest ideas which – if implemented – might actually eliminate their own jobs.

Bibliography

Cooper, R. (1994). *Sumitomo Electric Industries Ltd: the kaizen program*, Case 9-195-078. Cambridge, MA: Harvard Business School.

Masaaki Imai (1986). *Kaizen*. New York: McGraw-Hill.

DEREK F. CHANNON

keiretsu structure This is a specific structural form found in Japan. It occurs essentially in both horizontal and vertical forms, although groupings are also found in production and distribution. There are six main horizontal keiretsu; Mitsubishi, Mitsui, Sumitomo, Sanwa, Fuji, and Dai Ichi Kangyo. The first three of these are industrial groups which are based on leading prewar Japanese ZAIBATSU STRUCTURE; family-based industrial groups, the origins of which date back to Japan's initial industrialization. Originally each zaibatsu had a central holding company which set strategy. After World War II, the holding companies were eliminated, but the post-occupation Japanese government later allowed the industrial groups to reform, led by Mitsubishi. By the end of the 1950s, the historic zaibatsu-based groups had created Presidents' Councils as coordinating vehicles, and the groups had integrated, in part by taking cross-shareholdings in one another, as a protective device against possible hostile takeover bids. The other three major keiretsu groups developed during the 1960s, each based on the nucleus of one of the major city banks (strictly, the Dai Ichi Kangyo group is based on the merger of two groups, following the creation of the Dai Ichi Kangyo bank from the merger of the Dai Ichi and Nippon Kangyo banks). A further industrial group also exists, centered on the Industrial Bank of Japan (IBJ). However, the participants in this group, which includes most major Japanese corporations, do not have the same relationship with the bank and are also members of one of the other horizontal groups. A horizontal keiretsu group is illustrated in figure 1. There are several characteristics of these industrial groups that make them different than Western structures.

First, they all contain financial service companies which can provide finance to other members when necessary: each contains a commercial bank, a trust bank, and a life insurance company. Historically, the commercial bank took in short-term deposits and lent short- to medium-term. In recent times, and especially outside Japan, these organizations have mirrored their Western competitors and added investment banking services. The trust bank took in long-term funds and would lend long. Similarly, the life insurance company would also provide long-term loan funds. While the internal financial concerns do not provide all of the funds needed within an industrial group, and there is a restriction of a maximum of 5 per cent of total shares in any company that can be held by a bank, they do provide a special, formal relationship between the industrial members and the financial sector, quite unlike the position in Western structures.

Second, each group contains at least one trading company, known as the soga shosha. These act as trading companies, intelligence gatherers, financiers, and project coordinators in a way that can support other group members. In turn, the other group members form a

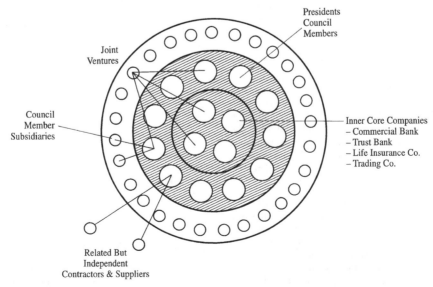

Figure 1 A Japanese horizontal keiretsu group.

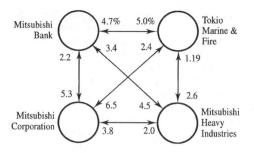

Figure 2 Japanese industrial group cross-shareholdings.
Source: Dodwell Marketing Consultants (1992).

cross-section of the economy: thus there will be a chemical company, a metal manufacturer, a heavy engineering concern, and the like

Third, the cross-shareholdings between group members make it virtually impossible for external institutions to subject group members to predatory acquisition threats (*see* ACQUISITION STRATEGY). The linkages between a number of Mitsubishi Group companies are shown in figure 2. Shares in the trading company Mitsubishi Corporation are held by member companies such as Mitsubishi Bank,

Tokio Marine and Fire Insurance, and Mitsubishi Heavy Industries. In all, about one-third of the company's shares are held by other Mitsubishi Group concerns. In turn, the trading company owns shares in other Mitsubishi companies.

By contrast to Western core business strategies, keiretsu groups have tended to continue to increase their level of diversification. Where new business areas develop, such as ocean mining, it would be quite natural for a keiretsu to enter the industry by forming a separate jointly owned subsidiary to exploit such a market opportunity; again, as in the case of fusion technologies, bringing together the elements of such a technology from across the group to create a new subsidiary.

Fourth, in the case of economic adversity in a particular member company, other group members will rally to its support, the financial members providing monetary assistance, while other group members might provide employment on a "loan" basis. In addition, personnel may be assigned to subsidiaries or affiliates. Usually, the major group companies send their managers to lower order companies as senior officers or directors. The bank in particular will often send a senior executive, as CEO, to any group member in financial difficulty. The average rates of directors sent by group members among the six major groups in 1990 were around 60 per cent, with the highest

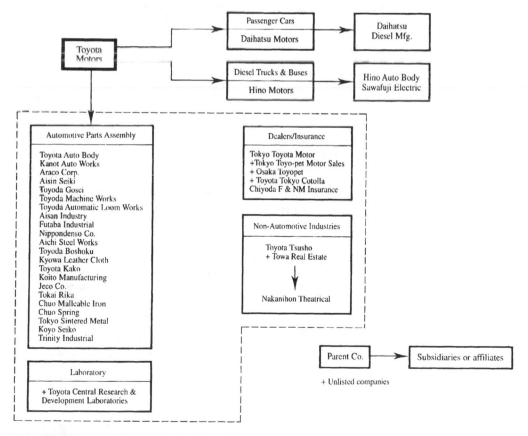

Figure 3 A vertical keiretsu group – the Toyota Motor Group.
Source: Dodwell Marketing Consultants (1992).

rate being 97 per cent for Mitsubishi and the lowest 41 per cent for Mitsui. In addition to appointments from within, the leading group companies also employ senior retiring government civil servants (this process is known as *amakudari* or "the descent from heaven").

Fifth, while each group will have many hundreds of members, there is a leading group of companies within the structure which form the Presidents' Council, or Shacho-Kai. The number of companies represented in such a structural element varies substantially, depending upon the roots of the keiretsu. Ideally, such a council should contain one representative from each industry. In the Mitsubishi Group this is approximately the case; but in the Dai Ichi Kangyo Group this is not so, as this group results from the merger of two major groups, each of which had its own set of companies. The councils meet regularly, on a specific day in each month. While the Presidents' Councils do not set specific group strategy, they do review external factors which affect member companies. The leader of the Presidents' Council in each individual group tends to come from one of a limited number of core companies, which varies between groups. In addition, other regular meetings occur between group member companies at vice-presidential level, and between specialists in planning and public relations.

Vertical keiretsu are groups in which there is a vertical relationship between a core company and its supplying subsidiaries or associates. Typical examples structure of the Toyota Group, which consists of the automobile manufacturer, its sales unit, and its suppliers, is shown in figure 3. While some of the subsidiaries are wholly owned, others are not; but Toyota may have a shareholding and an extremely close relationship. Such groups emphasize industries in which the parent companies are involved. Subsidiaries and affiliates are usually controled by shareholdings and/or the appointment of the CEO and/or other directors.

Keiretsu groups also occur in Japan within the service industry sector; such as the Seibu–Saison Group, which incorporates financial services, department stores, food retailers, entertainment, restaurants, hotels, and transportation.

The keiretsu form of organization found so extensively in Japan is unique to that country, and is a key element of the ability of Japanese companies to take a longer-term view. It contrasts with the stock market pressures experienced by Western companies, which have forced them to modify strategy in many cases and adopt structures which emphasize short-term profitability. The nearest equivalent to the keiretsu is probably the CHAEBOL STRUCTURE of Korea.

Bibliography

Chen, M. (1995). *Asian management systems.* London: Routledge.
Dodwell Marketing Consultants (1992, 1994). *Japanese industrial groups.* Tokyo: Dodwell Marketing Consultants.
Tokyo Business Today (1989). Intimate links with Japan's corporate groups. *Tokyo Business Today*, January, 14–19.

DEREK F. CHANNON

key job/benchmark job The terms "key job" and "benchmark job" are generally used interchangeably. A benchmark job is a job that matches, in terms of content, a similar job in the external labor market. If the content of a company's job is identical to that of the external market match, the average wage paid for the external job can be taken as the going market rate. Benchmark jobs have several characteristics: (a) they are stable in content across time; (b) they are stable in content across companies; (c) this content is well known across individuals in organizations; (d) their current pay rates are generally acceptable; and (e) the pay differentials among them are reasonably stable. This stability allows such jobs to be included in salary surveys. Compensation experts, seeking to find what others pay for these jobs, ask for wage data from a number of labor market competitors (or contract with consulting firms). This information across numerous benchmark jobs gives a picture of the external market rate.

JERRY M. NEWMAN

knowledge teams Knowledge teams are groups of employees who perform interdependent KNOWLEDGE WORK and who are collectively responsible for a product or service. Knowledge teams are often composed of members with a number of different highly advanced discipline bases. Each carries values, algorithms, information, and skills that may be only partially overlapping (Dougherty, 1992), making communication and collaboration difficult. The team integrates the work of these specialists.

Variants of knowledge teams include: (a) work teams, such as new product development or systems integration teams, that deliver service or produce a product; (b) integrating teams that coordinate across parts of the organization; (c) management teams that integrate parts of the organization by providing strategic and operational direction, allocating resources, and ensuring that the organization is appropriately designed, and by insuring that there is an effective performance management system in place; and (d) process improvement teams that examine and make changes to the work processes of the organization (Mohrman et al., 1995). Knowledge teams may be SELFMANAGING TEAMS, but there are some design challenges that limit team independence. If deep–discipline knowledge bases are required, cross-training is limited and the organization must find ways to keep discipline knowledge current. Knowledge teams are often highly interdependent with other organizational teams and units, requiring integrating mechanisms across teams.

Knowledge teams are examples of horizontal management. Team members do the coordination, assignment, and management of tasks among disciplines that have traditionally been done hierarchically. Increased use of knowledge teams reflects pressures for faster time-to-market and better customer responsiveness, as well as for effectively dealing with the complexity of organizational trade-offs and decisions in the global economy (Galbraith, 1994).

Bibliography

Dougherty, D. (1992). Interpretive barriers to successful product innovation in large firms. *Organizational Science*, 3, 179–202.
Galbraith, J. R. (1994). *Competing with Flexible, Lateral Organizations*, San Francisco: Jossey-Bass.

Mohrman, S. A., Cohen, S. G. & Mohrman, A. M. Jr (1995). *Designing Team-based Organizations: New Forms for Knowledge Work*, San Francisco: Jossey-Bass.

SUSAN ALBERS MOHRMAN

knowledge work The terms *knowledge work* and *knowledge workers* are commonly used to describe the kind of work and workers critical to organizational success in post-industrial society. Today knowledge is considered a primary resource for organizations (Drucker, 1988) and a source of wealth and competitive advantage for nations (Porter, 1990). Work increasingly involves the processing and production of symbols rather than physical materials. Knowledge work requires employees who can (a) use their own knowledge base; (b) acquire new information; (c) combine and process information to produce and communicate new information outputs; and (d) learn continuously from their experiences. Information technology provides support for these basic knowledge work functions and has had some unanticipated impacts on knowledge workers and their productivity.

Use of Personal Knowledge Base
In order to perform knowledge work successfully, individuals must employ their own *intellectual capital*: a personal base of knowledge that includes both factual and procedural information. Knowledge workers build their intellectual capital through education and experience. Information technology can supplement the knowledge base stored in a knowledge worker's memory. For example, DATABASE MANAGEMENT SYSTEMS enable knowledge workers to store more information and retrieve and combine it in more ways than information stored in memory or in paper-based systems. Knowledge workers can build their own personal knowledge base by entering data directly or by importing data extracted from corporate databases and external sources. The personal database becomes a unique, external archive of the intellectual capital of the knowledge worker.

Acquisition of New Information
Acquisition of new information from print resources is facilitated by bibliographical data storage and retrieval systems that provide references to (or, in some cases, full text of) books, articles, and other printed materials. New information about one's own company can be retrieved from corporate databases, and information external to an organization pulled from a variety of commercial online services (e.g. Dow Jones). This new information can be stored in the personal database of the knowledge worker (as previously described) and/or manipulated (as described below).

Combine, Process, Produce, and Communicate Information
Knowledge workers use a variety of information technologies to manipulate information. Systems like word processing and desktop publishing support combinations of information from a variety of sources and of different types (text, numeric, graphic) to produce new documents. Processing of information may be accomplished by specialized applications (e.g. tax preparation software) in which decision and processing rules are already included and data can be entered or imported from other systems. Processing may also be accomplished via software that allows users to develop their own applications (e.g. spreadsheet programs). Technologies such as electronic mail, groupware, and information networks enable knowledge workers to share information with both individuals and groups. Portable computers equipped with Fax/modems, supported by worldwide networks, allow knowledge workers to compute anytime, anywhere and to keep in constant contact with their office and colleagues.

Continuous Learning from Experiences
A key advantage of using information technology for knowledge work is the ability of information systems to capture task data and processes. Once a knowledge worker bears the cost of learning how to use a technology and/or builds a system to perform a task, a record of task inputs, processes, and outputs can be made. These computerized records can be recalled for subsequent task performance. When tasks are complex and repeated, but are not performed again for some time interval, the computer files can help knowledge workers remember what they learned from the last time they performed the task.

For example, suppose a manager uses a spreadsheet program to support budgeting. The manager will need to enter the data for that year in the appropriate categories, enter formulae that represent the relationships between the categories, and enter text that labels the categories and calculated data. The spreadsheet may be formatted so that a final document can be printed. Some benefits from using the spreadsheet program are realized immediately, since it enables the manager to consider many more budget alternatives than are feasible via hand calculations. Additional benefits are realized when the budget spreadsheet is retrieved at the next budget cycle, since the spreadsheet contains the content, rules, and format for the budgeting task. Only new or changed data or rules must be entered. The spreadsheet is a stored recipe for budgeting that the manager or others can recall and reuse. This helps prevent individual knowledge workers and the organization from "losing the recipe" for important tasks.

The organization can also benefit from using expert system technology to capture the intellectual capital of knowledge workers. EXPERT SYSTEMS can make an individual's expertise available even after that person has left the firm, and also can make it possible to extend that expertise to other, less knowledgeable, employees in the firm.

Impacts on Knowledge Workers and their Productivity
It seems logical that information technology support for the main functions of knowledge work would lead to increased productivity. Computer systems equipped with a variety of software and communications capabilities are standard tools for knowledge workers, and as common as telephones in offices. The seemingly insatiable demand for more hardware with additional capabilities in increasingly smaller packages, and for software to support new and existing tasks, would appear to reflect the value of information technology for knowledge work.

However, economic data from the 1980s indicate that productivity in knowledge work-intense sectors has not improved with increased investment in information technology and has not realized performance benefits commensurate with the large and continuing costs of information technology acquisition and support. There are several possible reasons for this "missing technology payback" in knowledge work. One central reason may be that knowledge-worker productivity is not accurately measured. While the benefits from information technology that replaced workers was easy to measure in reduced labor costs, information technology support for knowledge workers is intended to assist and enhance task performance. Higher-quality information products may not be captured by productivity measures. When technology speeds task performance, the knowledge worker may "use up" that efficiency gain in striving for non-measured improvements in task processes or outputs. Or, as described above, many of the benefits from technology use may accrue in the future, when a task is repeated. Poor or no productivity gains may also be caused by changes in the division of labor, since knowledge workers may be assigned a larger task set because they have computer support. For example, some companies eliminate or drastically reduce the number of secretaries because the professional workers have tools such as word processing and electronic mail. Another reason for the missing technology payback is the high, continuing costs of using information technology: the organization experiences increased back office costs to build and keep technology systems working and the individual bears costs to learn and use information technology.

Bibliography

Drucker, P. F. (1988). Management and the world's work. *Harvard Business Review*, **66**, 65–76.

Porter, M. E. (1990). *The Competitive Advantage of Nations.* New York: Free Press.

ROSANN COLLINS

KSAOs KSAOs refer to the knowledge, skill, ability, and other personal characteristics required for good job performance on a specific job. Knowledge is what a person knows that is relevant to the job (e.g. knowledge of legal procedures for a police officer). Skill is what a person is able to do on the job. This includes both mental tasks (e.g. skill in doing algebra) and physical tasks (e.g. skill in driving an automobile). Ability is the capacity to learn a skill (e.g. cognitive ability is the capacity to learn mental skills). Abilities include mental abilities, physical abilities, and PSYCHOMOTOR ABILITIES. Other personal characteristics, not covered by the first three, include attitudes, beliefs, personality characteristics, temperaments, and values. All four classes of human characteristics can be assessed with psychological tests, as well as with other assessment devices. KSAOs are commonly assessed for purposes of personnel selection.

Some JOB ANALYSIS methods provide specifications of the KSAOs necessary for a particular job. KSAO requirements can also be tied to individual job tasks, which is helpful in designing jobs. The ability to associate KSAOs with individual tasks is important for compliance with the Americans With Disabilities Act. KSAO requirements that are associated with noncritical tasks can be relaxed to make reasonable accommodation for a disabled employee.

PAUL E. SPECTOR

Lanchester strategy Although it is less well known than their adoption and adaptation of the quality management theories of Duran and Deming, a number of Japanese companies have evolved a concept of strategic marketing based on the ideas of F. W. Lanchester, who developed a theory of military fire power.

On the basis of World War I battles, Lanchester proposed that the outcome of military combat depended not only on unquantifiable factors such as surprise or luck but also upon factors which could be formulated in a precise mathematical form. He therefore developed two differential equations known as the linear law and the square law. The first of these applied in battles that consisted of the sum of a series of man-to-man duels, in which the total size of each army was essentially irrelevant, and the rate of change of an army over time was negatively related to the weapon efficiency of the opposing force. Thus if army m, with a force of m and a weapon efficiency of b, fought army n of size n and weapon efficiency a, then army m would win when:

$$\frac{m_0}{n_0} > \frac{a}{b}$$

where the subscript zero refers to "zero time."

On a modern battlefield, however, Lanchester argued that a concentration of fire power was possible and that direct man-to-man conflict was therefore replaced. Thus, casualties suffered by one army were related to both the armed efficiency and size of the opposing force. In these circumstances, army m would win if:

$$\frac{m_0{}^2}{n_0{}^2} > \frac{a}{b}$$

This was Lanchester's square law.

These concepts were subsequently expanded to include more complex situations, and it was shown that the principles appeared to be useful predictors of casualties during the American capture of Japanese-held islands in the Pacific during World War II.

Japanese consultants have made use of Lanchester's principles to provide insights into business competition. It was proposed by Onada (1979) that a battle between two armies was comparable to the competitive struggle between a market leader and its competitors. In this struggle military strength was equated with MARKET SHARE; tactical military forces (front line troops) became the strength and capability of the sales force; strategic forces (equivalent to the airforce) were pricing, advertising, and product development; and the rate of reinforcement was equivalent to the rate at which each side "captured" potential customers. The potential or uncommitted customers represented the pool of "reserves" on which a company could draw to increase its fighting strength or market share.

The theory required acceptance of the assumption that the rate at which a company could "capture" customers from the uncommitted pool was proportional to its existing market share. Thus, if two companies with shares of 20 per cent and 10 per cent respectively made the same marketing efforts as before, then the ratio at which they captured customers would be 2 : 1.

Target conditions were then established for a number of situations. In the first of these, Onada in a strong position to defend his position against all competitors with a market share greater than 42 per cent. This was identified as the "premium" position, in which the market share leader could afford to devote more attention to strategic marketing (advertising, pricing, etc.) than to tactical marketing.

Two other target positions were also established at the 74 per cent and 26 per cent levels of market share. A market leader with only a 26 per cent share was vulnerable, while one with a 74 per cent share was considered to be very safe. These two conditions were defined as "polyopoly" and "monopoly" respectively.

The derivation of these market share targets led to a number of propositions about market leadership and the stability of market structures:

- in monopoly and premium markets, the leader is safer than in other markets, and these market share patterns will tend to be stable
- to maintain position, market leaders in monopoly and premium markets need to outperform competitors in strategic marketing
- in polyopoly markets, market leadership will change more frequently, because no competitor will easily gain significant advantage

In addition to these three market conditions, two further conditions, duopoly and oligopoly markets, were defined. These were explained by introducing the concept of the "shooting range." The limits of competition were identified at equilibrium as 74 per cent and 26 per cent respectively. If the competition was between two companies the shooting range was therefore 3 : 1. Outside this range no "saddle" point exists and the competitive power of a smaller company cannot affect the position of a larger one. In a market in which many competitors attack each other, Lanchester's square law was said to operate, and the shooting range was defined as the square root of 3, or approximately 1.7.

Some analysis of these Japanese concepts has been undertaken using the PIMS database; this did not support the stability of the monopoly and premium structures. Nevertheless, the concepts have been widely accepted and used within Japan, and by Japanese companies, in attacking global markets. In this respect, the use of Lanchester's concepts has not been to optimize stable positions but as a *modus operandi* of attack, utilizing concentration of force with a view to eliminating entrenched leaders. An illustration of a Lanchester strategy for market domination in Kanagawa Prefecture, Japan, is shown in figure 1.

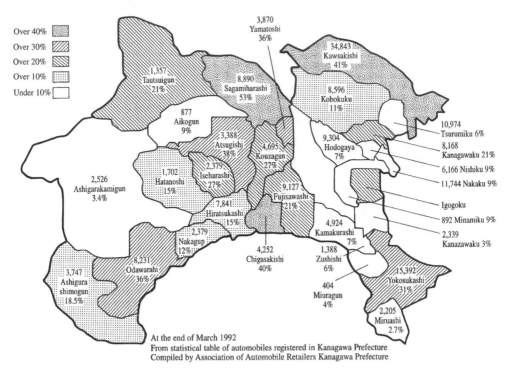

Figure 1 Using Lanchester theory for market domination: the ratio of market share by cities and countries.
Source: Nagashima, S. (1992). *100 management charts*. Tokyo: Asian Productivity Organisation.

While the concept is not well appreciated in the West, it bears some resemblance to the Boston Consulting Group's concept of the Rule of Three and Four and McKinsey and Company's concept of the micromarket, in which unless one firm can gain an adequate share of market it should contemplate strategic withdrawal.

Bibliography

Campbell, N. C. G. & Roberts, K. J. (1986). Lanchester market strategies. *Strategic Management Journal* (May–June).
Onada, T. (1979). *Science to win the competition: the development of Lanchester's strategic models*. Tokyo: Kaihatsu-sha (in Japanese).
Taoka, N. (1977). *The Lanchester laws*. Tokyo: Biginesusha (in Japanese).
Taoka, N. (1982). *Practical applications of Lanchester strategy*. Tokyo: Biginesusha (in Japanese).

DEREK F. CHANNON

law of demand   A fundamental principle of economics states that an inverse relationship exists between a change in the price of any product and the resulting change in its quantity demanded in the market. More formally the law of demand states that, CETERIS PARIBUS, as the price of a good rises its quantity demanded falls and as the price of a good falls its quantity demanded rises in the market. It is important to note that the motivating force behind the change in consumer behavior here is a change of price rather than, and without any other, change occurring in variables such as consumer tastes and income, which also make up the DEMAND FUNCTION.

The price change influences the adjustment in quantity demanded through two separate effects. The income effect is that portion of the change in quantity demanded which is due to the change in consumer purchasing power resulting from the price change. For example, when the price of a product decreases, the existing (and unchanged) level of consumer income now has greater real purchasing power. This makes consumers of the good in question richer and induces an increase in the number of units purchased. The substitution effect recognizes that in the calculus of consumer decision making, individuals are also concerned with the price of a product relative to the prices of any substitutes which are available. Since the ceteris paribus condition in the law holds these other prices constant, a fall in the absolute price of a good causes a decrease in its price relative to all others. This makes the good in question more attractive to consumers who then substitute away from other goods toward this good. Both effects normally reinforce the inverse relationship between price and quantity demanded.

The near universal applicability of this consumer behavior to a wide array of goods has elevated the principle to the status of an economic law. Even the demand for goods which are absolute necessities, such as water, tends to follow this law. Studies have shown that when faced with higher water prices, while people do not necessarily drink less water they will economize on its other uses. Also, what often appears to be a counter example to the law is actually a situation in which one or more of the other variables in the demand function have changed and the ceteris paribus condition has been broken.

Economic laws are not always obeyed and thus the law of demand is not without exceptions. Individuals sometimes violate the law, for example when a "snob effect" occurs and a higher price induces increased purchases. Here the individual's demand shows a positive relation between the product's price and the quantity demanded. The market demand for this product sometimes, but not always, continues to maintain the inverse relation indicated by the law. A second example where the law of demand may be violated concerns markets where new goods are involved. Bagwell and Riordon (1991) indicate that a higher price for a new product may induce increased sales as it sometimes acts as a signal of higher quality in markets where information is imperfect.

Managers should be aware that the law indicates that a price change will ordinarily have an important impact on a firm's sales volume and total revenue, and thus its profitability. Although the law identifies the direction of the change in quantity demanded resulting from a price change, it does not indicate the size of the change. This size change is central to the overall impact of the price change on revenues (*see* ELASTICITY).

Bibliography

Bagwell, K. & Riordon, M. (1991). High and declining prices signal product quality. *American Economic Review*, 81, 224–39.

Douglas, E. (1992). *Managerial Economics: Analysis and Strategy*. 4th edn, Englewood Cliffs, NJ: Prentice-Hall.

Miller, R. (1994). *Economics Today*. 8th edn, New York: HarperCollins.

GILBERT BECKER

law of variable proportions Sometimes referred to as the law of diminishing returns, the law of variable proportions is concerned with the effect of changes in the proportion of the factors of production used to produce output. As the proportion of one input increases relative to all other inputs, at some point there will be decreasing marginal returns from that input. Adding more units of an input, holding all other inputs constant, will at some point cause the resulting increases in production to decrease, or equivalently, the MARGINAL PRODUCT of that input will decline. Among the inputs held constant is the level of technology used to produce that output. This is an empirical law and is therefore a generalization about the nature of the production process and cannot be proven theoretically; see Friedman (1976), Stigler (1966) and DIMINISHING RETURNS. Applied to management, Friedman argues that the law of variable proportions requires firms to produce by using inputs in such proportions that there are diminishing average returns to each input in production.

Bibliography

Douglas, E. J. (1992). *Managerial Economics*. 4th edn, Englewood Cliffs, NJ: Prentice-Hall.

Friedman, M. (1976). *Price Theory*. 2nd edn, Chicago: Aldine.

Stigler, G. J. (1966). *The Theory of Price*. 3rd edn, New York: Macmillan.

ROBERT E. MCAULIFFE

leadership Although systematic research into the topic of leadership is a product of the twentieth century, interest in identifying the properties that make leaders effective is almost as old as recorded history. Bass and Stogdill (Bass, 1990) noted that discussions relating to leadership and leadership effectiveness can be found in the Greek and Latin classics, the Old and New Testaments of the Bible, the writings of the ancient Chinese philosophers, and in the early Icelandic sagas. Bass (1990), in an exhaustive review of the present era's leadership literature, cites over 3000 empirical studies.

Despite the attention given to the topic there appear to be almost as many definitions of leadership as there are researchers in the field. Consider the following definitions found in the literature:

> Leadership is "the initiation and maintenance of structure in expectation and interaction" (Stogdill, 1974, cited in Yukl, 1994, p. 2.)
>
> Leadership is ". . . the behavior of an individual when he is directing the activities of a group toward a shared goal." (Hemphill & Coons, 1957, cited in Yukl, 1994, p. 2.)
>
> Leadership is ". . . interpersonal influence exercised in a situation, and directed through the communication process, toward the attainment of a specified goal or goals." (Tannenbaum, Weschler, & Massarik, 1964, cited in Yukl, 1994, p. 2.)
>
> Leadership is ". . . the process of instilling in others shared vision, creating valued opportunities, and building confidence in the realization of the shared values and opportunities." (Berlew, 1974.)
>
> "Leadership is leaders inducing followers to act for certain goals that represent the values and the motivations – of both leaders and followers." (Burns, 1978.)
>
> "Leaders are those who consistently make effective contributions to social order, and who are expected and perceived to do so." (Hosking, 1988, cited in Yukl, 1994, p. 3.)
>
> Leadership is ". . . a process of giving purpose (meaningful direction) to collective effort, and causing willing effort to be expended to achieve purpose." (Jacobs and Jaques, 1990, cited in Yukl, 1994, p. 3.)
>
> Leadership is "a process by which members of a group are empowered to work together synergistically toward a common goal or vision, that will create change and transform institutions, and thus improve the quality of life. The leader is a catalytic force or facilitator who by virtue of position or opportunity empowers others to collective action accomplishing the goal or vision." (Astin, 1993.)

Note that a rather significant shift occurred in the mid-1970s with the definitions offered by Berlew and Burns. Berlew was the first to introduce the concept of shared VALUES and follower confidence building. Berlew's discussion also emphasized the creation of organizational excitement, and emotional appeal of the leader into the managerially oriented leadership literature. In the definitions of leadership offered by Berlew (1974), Burns (1978), Hoskings (1988), Jacobs and Jacques (1990), and Astin (1993), we see the definition of leadership progressively broadened to include contributing to social order, introducing major change, giving meaning and purpose to work and to organizations, empowering followers, and infusing organizations with values and ideology.

For analytic and expository purposes it is useful to distinguish between leadership, management, and supervision.

Leadership Contrasted with Management

Zaleznik (1977) has argued that there is a substantial difference between leadership and management. Zaleznik's position reflects the differences in the definitions listed above. Zaleznick reserves the term leadership for individuals who determine the major objectives and the strategic courses of organizations and introduce major change rather than individuals who transmit and enforce rules and policies, or implement goals and changes initiated by individuals at higher organizational levels.

Leadership is defined as behavior on the part of an individual which appeals to ideological values, motives, and self-perceptions of followers and results, in turn, in:

(1) unusual levels of effort on the part of followers above and beyond their normal role or position requirements; and
(2) follower willingness to forego self-interest, and make significant personal sacrifices in the interest of a collective vision, *willingly*.

Management is defined as rational–analytic behavior of a person in a position of formal authority directed toward the organization, coordination, and implementation of organizational strategies, tactics, and policies. The essential distinction between leader behaviors and MANAGERIAL BEHAVIORS is that managerial behaviors are rational–analytic and impersonal and leader behaviors appeal to follower motives and are interpersonally oriented. Leaders set the direction for organizations or collectivities. Managers provide the intellectual content necessary for organizations to perform effectively.

Examples of leader behaviors are articulation of a collective vision; infusing organizations and work with values by communicating and setting a personal example regarding the values inherent in the vision; making sacrifices and taking personal risks in the interest of the vision and the collective; motivating exceptional performance by appealing to the values, emotions, and self concepts of followers; inspiring followers by showing confidence, determination, persistence, and pride in the collective; and by engaging in symbolic behavior such as serving as a spokesperson for the collective.

Examples of managerial behavior are planning, organizing, and the establishment of administrative systems. These particular managerial behaviors are included because there is empirical evidence demonstrating that these behaviors distinguish effective managers from others, despite the fact that they are not interpersonal in nature.

Note that according to these definitions managers are individuals in positions of formal authority. In contrast, leaders may or may not hold positions of formal authority. Leaders assert INFLUENCE by virtue of unique personal attributes and behaviors. Managers obtain compliance from subordinates on the basis of legitimate position influence and formal authority, and reward and coercive POWER (*see*

LEGITIMACY). In contrast, leaders influence followers to internalize the values of the collective vision and identify with the collective on the basis of referent power rather than, or in addition to, positional authority. Leaders are followed willingly, and therefore those whom they motivate to action are referred to as followers rather than subordinates.

Subordinates of managers comply with the manager's directions only as long as the manager exercises formal authority and applies reward or coercive power. In contrast, followers of leaders continue to identify with the collective and internalize the values inherent in the collective vision in the absence of the leader.

Of course, some individuals in positions of authority may function as both managers and leaders. Such individuals will thus have some subordinates who minimally comply with normal levels of position requirements as well as some followers who go above and beyond the call of duty in the interest of a collective vision.

Leadership Contrasted with Supervision

Supervision is defined as behavior on the part of a person in a position of authority concerned with monitoring, guiding, and providing corrective feedback and support for subordinates or followers in their day-to-day activities. Examples of supervisory behaviors are showing individualized consideration, providing equitable recognition and REWARDS, scheduling and programming, problem solving, GOAL-SETTING, ROLE and goal clarification, coaching, direction, monitoring operations, PERFORMANCE APPRAISAL and feedback, providing guidance and on-the-job training, and the effective use of incentives to motivate followers.

The formal appointment of individuals to positions of authority in formal nonvoluntary organizations make followers dependent on leaders for their livelihood. Further, in formal organizations the leader–follower relationship is usually characterized by frequent face to face interaction between leaders and followers (Mintzberg, 1983).

The consequences of these two attributes of the leader–follower relationship – dependency and face-to-face interaction – are that leaders need to engage in instrumental management behaviors to organize, coordinate, and facilitate follower performance. These two attributes of the leader–follower relationship also require supportive behaviors to provide for followers a psychologically satisfying work environment. Consequently, effective leadership in formal organizations requires leaders to engage in not only strategic initiatives and the introduction of major changes, but also in the exercise of the management and supervisory behaviors described above.

Theories of Leadership

The vast number of empirical social scientific studies concerning leadership has yielded a small number of theories, which attempt to explain the PERSONALITY characteristics and behaviors distinguishing effective from ineffective leaders. While none of the theories are definitive, there is rather solid empirical evidence in support of each. Reviews of this evidence can be found in Bass (1990) and Yukl (1994).

These theories can be classified into three categories: instrumental theories, inspirational theories, and theories of informal leadership. Instrumental theories (House & Mitchell, 1974; Fiedler & Garcia, 1987; Wofford, 1982) are theories of supervision as defined above. These theories stress task and person oriented leader behaviors which facilitate, or are instrumental to, effective follower performance. They emphasize such task oriented leader behaviors as goal setting, coaching, direction, performance appraisal, and feedback, and the effective use of incentives to motivate followers. They also emphasize the use of such person oriented behaviors as showing consideration, joint participation, counseling, providing support, and empowering followers through delegation of authority and encouragement (*see* DELEGATION; EMPOWERMENT).

There are several inspirational (House, 1977; Conger & Kanungo, 1987), transformational theory (Burns, 1978; Bass, 1990), and visionary theory (Bennis & Nanus, 1985) (*see* LEADERSHIP). These are theories of leadership, as the term leadership is defined above, emphasizing ideological and emotional appeal by the infusion of values into work and organizations. This is accomplished by articulating an inspirational vision, values, and norms; communicating challenging performance expectations and confidence in followers; displaying exemplary behavior, and engaging in symbolic behaviors which encourage intrinsic motivation, COMMITMENT, and pride in work.

Theories of informal leadership (Hollander, 1964; Bowers & Seashore, 1966) emphasize the kinds of behavior associated with "emergent" or informal leadership by individuals who are not formally appointed to positions of authority. These theories stress individual contribution to group goals, facilitation of the work of others, and providing direction, collaboration, and support for co-workers.

There is a substantial amount of support for all three classes of theories (Bass, 1990; Yukl, 1994). This evidence demonstrates that task and person oriented behaviors described in the instrumental theories generally, but not always, differentiate effective supervisors and managers from others. The leader behaviors described by the inspirational theories generally, and quite consistently, differentiate outstanding or exceptionally effective leaders from others.

The leader behaviors described by the theories of informal leadership have also been shown to differ others, however the number of supporting studies remains small.

When tested individually, the behaviors specified in all of the above theories have been shown to have positive effects on follower psychological states such as follower satisfaction with, and commitment to leaders. However, the various combinations of leader behaviors remain to be tested empirically. In this context, scholars have raised the possibility that some instrumental behaviors, especially the exercise of contingent reward and punishment behaviors, are incompatible with and undermine the effect of inspirational behaviors. This issue remains to be resolved in future research.

Conclusion

The considerable amount of empirical evidence and theory relevant to the practice of leadership is impressive. Despite this knowledge a substantial number of issues remain to be addressed. Available knowledge has not been brought to bear on such issues as management selection, the introduction of change, resolution of CONFLICT, the exercise of upward INFLUENCE in orgranizations. There is little theory or empirical evidence concerning how leaders exercise political influence in organizations. Further, a number of specific situational variables that enhance, constrain, or substitute for leadership have not been adequately researched.

The generality of prevailing theories remains to be specified and verified. Finally, it is noteworthy that the cultural constraints on what leader behaviors can be exercised and what leader behaviors are effective have not been explicated. Most prevailing theories of leadership have a definite North American cultural orientation: individualistic rather than collectivistic; oriented toward self-interest rather than duty; oriented toward rules and procedures rather than norms; emphasizing assumptions of rationality rather than asthetics, religion, or superstition; and assuming centrality of work and democratic value orientation (*see* NATIONAL CULTURE).

A substantial body of cross cultural social psychological, sociological, and anthropological research informs us that there are many cultures that do not share the assumptions of North American leadership theories. As a result there is a need for empirically grounded theory to explain differential leader behavior and effectiveness across cultures (*see* CULTURE). In the past five years there has been an increase in the volume of cross cultural leadership research. This should, in a matter of only a few years, yield important insights concerning culture specific leadership and the generality of US based leadership theory.

Despite the limitations stated above it is safe to conclude that a there is a substantial amount of available knowledge concerning the exercise and effectiveness of leadership, and there are a sufficient number of remaining issues and questions to occupy the time of social scientists for a considerable, and indefinite duration.

Bibliography

Astin, H. & Leland, C. (1991). Women of influence, Women of vision. A cross generations study of leaders and social change. San Francisco: Jossey-Bass.

Bass, B. M. (1990). Bass & Stogdill's Handbook of leadership. (3rd edn) New York: The Free Press.

Bennis, W. & Nanus, B. (1985). Leaders: The strategies for taking charge New York: Harper & Row.

Berlew, D. E. (1974). Leadership and organizational excitement. *California Management Review*, **17** (2)

Bowers D. G. & S. E. Seashore (1966). Predicting organizational effectiveness with a four-factor theory of leadership. Administrative Science Quarterly, **11**, 238–263.

Burns, J. M. (1978). Leadership. New York: Harper & Row.

Conger, J. A. & R. A. Kanungo (1987). Toward a behavioral theory of charismatic leadership in organizational settings. Academy of Management Review, **12**, 637–647.

Fiedler, F. E. & Garcia, J. E. (1987). New approaches to leadership, cognitive resources and organizational performance. New York: Wiley.

Hollander, E. P. (1964). Leaders, groups, and influence. New York: Oxford University Press.

House, R. J. (1977). A 1976 theory of charismatic leadership. In J. G. Hunt & L. L. Larson (Eds), Leadership: The cutting edge. Carbondale, IL: Southern Illinois University Press.

House, R. J. & Mitchell J. R. (1974). Path goal theory of leadership. Journal of Contemporary Business, **5**.

Mintzberg, H. (1983). *Power in and around organizations.* Englewood Cliffs, NJ: Prentice Hall.

Wofford, J. C. (1982). An integrative theory of leadership. *Journal of Management,* 8, 27–47.

Yukl, G. (1994). *Leadership in organizations.* (3rd edn) Englewood Cliffs, NJ: Prentice-Hall.

Zaleznik, A. (1977). Managers and leaders: Are they different? *Harvard Business Review.* May–June, 47–60.

ROBERT J. HOUSE

learning curve (economics)   The learning curve refers to the reduction in AVERAGE TOTAL COST which occurs as workers gain experience from producing a product over time and for this reason it is also called the experience curve. Unlike ECONOMIES OF SCALE where long run average costs decrease when more output is produced per period of time, the learning curve shows the reduction in average costs arising from the total accumulated volume of production to date. Therefore if a firm produced 2 million units per month at MINIMUM EFFICIENT SCALE (MES) and the average cost per unit was $10, if there were learning effects in production, they would cause the average cost curve to shift down over time. In this example, the firm might find that its average costs of production fell to $8 per unit once the firm had produced 24 million units over a year, even though production remained at 2 million units each month.

One of the first theoretical treatments of learning effects was provided by Arrow (1962) and learning curves have been estimated for a variety of industries; see Ghemawat (1985) for a survey. When significant learning effects exist, they can confer strategic advantages (*see* FIRST-MOVER ADVANTAGES) to those established firms which increase their production volumes quickly to reduce their costs; see Porter (1980). To take advantage of the learning curve managers should set prices for new products below the level which would only maximize current period profits recognizing that future costs will be lower and profits higher.

This aspect of pricing with a learning curve makes it difficult to establish whether a firm has engaged in PREDATORY PRICING, because a firm may price below AVERAGE TOTAL COST anticipating lower costs in the future from learning effects. Since this form of pricing is a legitimate business practice and leads to more efficient production, it is difficult to determine whether pricing below average cost is actually predatory in nature; see Carlton and Perloff (1994).

Some care is required when estimating learning curves because the effects occur over time but as time passes other factors (such as factor prices) which affect average costs will also change. A simple but common representation of the learning curve would be:

$$AC_t = AC_0 \times CV_t^{\lambda} \times e^{u_t} \qquad (1)$$

where AC_t is the *real* average cost per unit of production in period t, AC is the real average cost in the initial period of production, CV_t represents the cumulative volume of output produced up to period t, λ is the ELASTICITY of average costs with respect to volume, and u_t is an error term (with e the natural exponent). Since equation (1) relates current real average costs of production to the initial cost and the total volume produced, it omits the costs of factors of production which, if they have changed during

the sample period, will cause estimates of the learning curve to be biased; see Berndt (1991). In fact, Berndt shows that unless the effects of changes in input prices can be captured by an appropriate deflator and there are constant returns to scale, estimates of the learning curve based on equation (1) will be biased.

If we ignore the biases mention above, how would a manager estimate the learning curve? Taking logarithms of both sides of equation (1) yields:

$$\ln(AC_t) = \ln(AC_0) + \lambda(CV_t) + u_t \qquad (2)$$

which can be estimated by linear regression. As Berndt observed, it is important to use general price deflators to obtain real unit average costs, since a price deflator for the industry will already include learning effects and will therefore mask the cost reductions we wish to estimate. Once λ has been estimated, average real costs will decrease according to

$$AC_{\text{new}} = (2^{\lambda}) \times AC_{\text{old}} \qquad (3)$$

when total volume doubles. For example, if the estimated value of λ were - 0.25, then costs would decrease by 25 percent of their previous level when production volume doubled and the learning curve would have a 75 percent slope.

Bibliography

Arrow, K. J. (1962). The economic implications of learning by doing. *Review of Economic Studies,* 29, 153–73.

Berndt, E. R. (1991). *The Practice of Econometrics.* Reading, MA: Addison-Wesley.

Carlton, D. W. & Perloff, J. M. (1994). *Modern Industrial Organization.* 2nd edn, New York: HarperCollins.

Douglas, E. J. (1992). *Managerial Economics.* 4th edn, Englewood Cliffs, NJ: Prentice-Hall.

Ghemawat, P. (1985). Building strategy on the experience curve. *Harvard Business Review,* 63, 143–49.

Porter, M. E. (1980). *Competitive Strategy.* New York: Free Press.

ROBERT E. MCAULIFFE

learning curves (operations management)   Learning curves are the functions which predict the reduction of labor input per unit of manufactured output. The concept can be applied at both micro and macro levels.

At the micro level when a worker is first trained to carry out a specific task, the performance on that task will naturally be poor. As the worker gains experience and develops the work-specific skills, performance will improve. The rate at which such improvement is made will depend on a number of factors such as the complexity of the work, the cycle time of the work, the ability of the workers, and their experience of similar work. However, in all cases, the rate of improvement will decrease over time as the worker becomes more proficient. A learning curve is a graphical representation of the improvement in performance and for most work follows a general asymptotic pattern. The graph normally relates performance (measured as job completion time) either to time on the job, or to the number of job cycles completed.

Where work measurement is used to establish the standard time for a job, it is possible to plot on the curve the desired end-point of an induction or training period and to measure operator performance over time against this end-point. Where a learning curve has been established by prior observation of a range of workers adjusting to the same work, it is possible to measure the progress of a new worker to the present time, and then to predict further rates of progress from the shape of the curve. Where a payment system based on individual performance is in use, it is common to add a "learner allowance" to the standard time to form an "allowed time" for a trainee. Similarly, where a payment system is based on team or group performance, it is common to compensate the team for the poor performance of new members of the team. If learning curves are available for the work, any allowance or compensatory payments can be adjusted over time as the trainee moves along the curve.

At the macro level learning curves can be used to relate the total cost per unit (or value added per unit) to the cumulative output. At this level they are often called "experience curves." The relationship between cost and output usually assumes that costs decrease by the reciprocal of some function of cumulative output. This is often expressed as the amount cost decreases for each doubling of cumulative output. So, for example, an 80 percent experience curve means that costs reduce to 80 percent of their value when cumulative output doubles. For simplicity this relationship can be drawn on logarithmic scales which will show a straight line relationship.

Bibliography

Abernathy, W. J. & Wayne, K. (1974). Limits to the learning curve. *Harvard Business Review*, **52**, (8), 109–19.

JOHN HEAP

learning organization The concept of organizations as dynamic systems having capacities of self-changing, and the ability to develop and more optimally satisfy the changing desires of stakeholders. Learning organizations embody, probably as a result of deliberate management strategy, a high proportion of the processes of organizational learning.

The concept achieved popularity in the 1990s as a follow on from the "excellence" movement of the 1980s. "Excellent" organizations have not maintained this status. Failure of adaptation or learning has been the obvious explanation.

Theories and descriptions of the learning organization treat organizations as bounded systemic entities interacting with environments, having survival and growth as their main concerns (*see* SYSTEMS THEORY). Learning organization theories offer accounts of this process. Senge (1990) interprets organizational learning as overcoming systems patterns (archetypes) interfering with survival and development. Argyris and Schon (1978) suggest that a difficulty in changing fundamental purposes and visions (double loop learning) as well as operating procedures (single loop learning) is a major cause of organizational failure. Garratt (1987) advocates a "hands off, brains on" approach to the conduct of the roles of Directors, Presidents, and Vice-Presidents so that broad vision and strategic action is not sacrificed to reactive trouble shooting.

Pedler, Burgoyne, and Boydell (1991) describe organizational learning as depending on the balance and connection of the four processes of collective policy, group operations, individual action, and individual thought. This process is achieved through eleven organizational behaviors and

features: experimental strategy moves, member participation in policy making, transparency of internal information through information technology, decision and feedback oriented accounting systems, internal coordination through lateral NEGOTIATION, REWARD for INNOVATION and problem solving, clear but flexible structures, information gathering by boundary workers, imitation of and experimentation with other organizations, cultures encouraging learning from mistakes, cultures and structures to encourage individual self-development (*see* ORGANIZATIONAL CULTURE).

A number of other theoretical issues link to the Learning Organization concept which offers a novel point of conceptual integration between them: questioning how firms achieve adaptation if hierarchical control is substituted for free market behavior in transaction cost theory. The consequent interest in the flexible firm appears in labor process theory as the source of new demands on labor (*see* FLEXIBILITY). New forms of human resource management involving greater employee COMMITMENT, involvement, and incorporation into the performance and adaptation of corporate activity (*see* EMPLOYEE INVOLVEMENT). The POPULATION ECOLOGY theory of organizations raises the possibility that organizations change through variation at their foundation followed by natural selection, rather than an intrinsic ability to learn. Conventional approaches to corporate strategy see organizations as observing (*see* STRATEGIC MANAGEMENT), predicting, and reacting to their environments, but alternative formulations suggest a more proactive approach in which organizations create or enacting their contexts (Bougon, 1992) with minds that may be able to remember and learn.

The Learning Organization concept raises, when considered in conjunction with these other theoretical perspectives, questions of: the difference between learning and change; the entity that learns (individual, organization, industry sector, nation-state, society, or processes of ordering); the nature and problems of discontinuation in learning (*see* ORGANIZATIONAL CHANGE); the fundamental source of purpose and order in human activity.

see also **Organization and environment**

Bibliography

Argyris, C. & Schon, D. A. (1978). Organizational learning: A theory in action perspective. Reading, MA: Addison-Wesley.
Bougon, M. G. (1992). Congregate cognitive maps: A unified dynamic theory of organization and strategy. Journal of Management Studies, **29**, (3), 369–389.
Garratt, R. (1987). The learning organisation. London: Fontana/Collins.
Pedler, M., Burgoyne, J. G. & Boydell, T. (1991). The learning company: A strategy for sustainable development. London: McGraw-Hill.
Senge, P. (1990). The fifth discipline: The art and practice of the learning organisation. New York: Doubleday.

JOHN BURGOYNE

leasing An agreement between two parties to rent an asset is a leasing arrangement. The owner of the leased asset, the lessor, receives a set of fixed payments for the term of the contract from the lessee. If the lease contains a provision that allows the lessee to cancel at any time or if the lessor is responsible for insurance and maintenance, then it is called an operating lease. Financial leases are long term, carry no cancelation options, and the lessee is responsible for all insurance and maintenance.

It has been pointed out in a number of studies (see Smith and Wakeman, 1985) that leasing would not exist in the absence of capital market imperfections like taxes, transaction costs, and agency costs. The demand for short-term leasing arrangements stems from the need to eliminate the transactions costs of buying and selling an asset (Flath, 1980). In the absence of transaction costs, Myers et al. (1976) show that lessee and lessor tax rates must differ for a leasing arrangement to be advantageous. A number of other firm and asset characteristics that increase the likelihood of leasing have also been identified (Smith and Wakeman, 1985). Empirical evidence suggests that the market value of both lessee and lessor stock rises upon announcements of new leasing arrangements (Slovin et al., 1990; Vora and Ezzell, 1991).

Sale and Leaseback

In a sale and leaseback, an asset is sold and simultaneously leased back by the seller. The rights to ownership are transferred to the buyer/lessor while the seller/lessee enjoys the rights to services provided by the asset. The financial effects of a sale and leaseback are: (1) the lessee gets an immediate inflow of cash equal to the selling price of the asset, while the lessor receives (2) a promise of a stream of fixed lease payments in the future; (3) the salvage value of the asset; and (4) the depreciation tax shields.

Although the sale and leaseback offers the same advantages to the lessee that an ordinary lease arrangement would, it has been suggested that the sale-and-leaseback can also be used as a device to expropriate wealth from the senior claimholders to the common stockholders of the lessee since it rearranges the priority of the claims against the lessee in favour of the lessor (Kim et al., 1978). The empirical evidence suggests that the market value of lessee common stockholders rises when a sale and leaseback is announced (Slovin et al., 1990 and 1991; Vora and Ezzell, 1991), the source of the gain does not seem to be wealth expropriation since the value of lessee preferred stock remains unchanged (Vora and Ezzell, 1991). In fact, as suggested in a number of studies (e.g. see Myers et al., 1976) savings in taxes seems to be the motivating factor behind such sale and leasebacks (Vora and Ezzell, 1991).

Net Advantage to Leasing (NAL)

This is the present value of the benefits that are provided by leasing an asset instead of purchasing it via other financing alternatives. If the NAL of a lease is positive, leasing is preferred over the purchase. In the absence of transaction costs, savings in taxes is considered to be the paramount benefit of leasing. It has been shown that a necessary condition for the NAL to be positive for both lessee and lessor, is that their tax brackets must differ (Myers et al., 1976; Miller and Upton, 1976; Lewellen et al., 1976). The intuition is that an organization that is non-tax-paying or even in a low tax bracket would be better off by transferring its depreciation and interest tax shields to a company that pays taxes at a higher tax rate. This can be easily accomplished by entering into a leasing arrangement (either for assets that are newly put into use or for existing assets – by entering into a sale and leaseback). In return for the tax shields, the lessee receives consideration in the form of lower lease payments relative to its outflows under other financing alternatives.

Bibliography

Flath, D. (1980). The economics of short-term leasing. *Economic Inquiry*, 18, 247–59.

Kim, E. H., Lewellen, W. G. & McConnell, J. J. (1978). Sale-and-leaseback agreements and enterprise valuation. *Journal of Financial and Quantitative Analysis*, 13, 871–83.

Lewellen, W. G., Long, M. S. & McConnell, J. J. (1976). Asset leasing in competitive capital markets. *Journal of Finance*, 31, 787–98.

Miller, M. H. & Upton, C. W. (1976). Leasing, buying and the cost of capital services. *Journal of Finance*, 31, 761–86.

Myers, S. C., Dill, D. A. & Bautista, A. J. (1976). Valuation of financial lease contracts. *Journal of Finance*, 31, 799–819.

Slovin, M. B., Sushka, M. E. & Polonchek, J. A. (1990). Corporate sale-and-leasebacks and shareholder wealth. *Journal of Finance*, 45, 289–99.

Slovin, M. B., Sushka, M. E. & Polonchek, J. A. (1991). Restructuring transactions by bank holding companies: the valuation effects of sale-and-leasebacks and divestitures. *Journal of Banking and Finance*, 15, 237–55.

Smith, C. W. Jr. & Wakeman, L. M. (1985). Determinants of corporate leasing policy. *Journal of Finance*, 40, 895–908.

Vora, P. P. & Ezzell, J. R. (1991). Leasing vs. purchasing: direct evidence on a corporation's motivations for leasing and consequences of leasing. Working paper, Penn State University.

PREMAL VORA

legitimacy This concept operates at multiple levels of analysis; it pertains to individuals, behaviors, organizations, industries, or institutions (in general, focal actor). Legitimacy is a relational concept created and maintained by other actors in the relevant social system. The essence of legitimacy is that a focal actor is *accepted* or *judged appropriate* by the social system in which the actor is embedded; a legitimate actor is one who is congruent with the beliefs and norms of a social system. This acceptance can be taken-for-granted, preconscious, and understood intuitively and unquestioningly. The institution of marriage and the structure of authority based on rank in the military are examples of this type of acceptance. Alternatively, social actors confer legitimacy on a focal actor by deliberately evaluating them; for instance, the sale of shares of stock by a company to the general public requires regulatory approval in many countries. The process by which legitimacy is gained (or lost) is called (de)legitimation.

The standards which social actors use to judge legitimacy can exist at a societal level, within a group or organization, or at an intermediate social system such as an industry. In general, the standards for legitimacy are derived from formal laws and rules, legal norms, and social norms and VALUES (Katz & Kahn, 1978) (*see* ORGANIZATIONAL CULTURE). The evaluation of legitimacy may result from attributes of the focal actor, from the characteristics of the focal actor's ROLE in a social system, or from a combination of the two (*see* STATUS).

Legitimacy most often has been examined as a base of POWER and INFLUENCE within groups and organizations (French & Raven, 1968; Katz & Kahn, 1978; Michener & Burt, 1971; Zelditch & Walker, 1984). French and Raven (1968) proposed three structural foundations of legitimate power. The first is the cultural values of a social system, such as a respect for age or experience. The second is the acceptance of the structure of authority in a social system; for example, in bureaucratic organizations individuals accept the hierarchy of offices as legitimate (*see* BUREAUCRACY). Third, legitimate power may be exerted by a person designated by a legitimizing agent as having the right to exercise power; for instance, a company president may designate a vice president to form and lead a task force which will solve a particular company problem. Personal attributes also contribute to legitimacy; two such attributes are perceived competence and fairness (Michener & Burt, 1971) (*see* PROCEDURAL JUSTICE).

Organizational legitimacy refers to the appropriateness of an organization's goals and procedures. Much research examined organizational legitimation, and Galaskiewicz (1985) identified two ways organizations legitimated themselves. First, they identified with cultural symbols or legitimate figures in the environment through interlocking directorships or by obtaining endorsements. Second, business organizations enhance their legitimacy by donating to charitable organizations.

see also **Politics**

Bibliography

French, J. R. P. Jr. & Raven, B. (1968). The bases of social power. In D. Cartwright & A. Zander (Eds), Group dynamics. (3rd edn, pp. 259–269). New York: Harper & Row.

Galaskiewicz, J. (1985). Interorganizational relations. In R. H. Turner & J. F. Short, Jr. (Eds), Annual review of sociology, (vol. 11, pp. 281–304).

Katz, D. & Kahn, R. L. (1978). The social psychology of organizations, (2nd edn) New York: Wiley.

Michener, H. A. & Burt, M. A. (1971). Legitimacy as a base of social influence. In J. Tedeschi (Ed.), Perspectives on social power, (pp. 311–348). Chicago: Aldine.

Legitimacy and the stability of authority. In E. J. Lawler, Jr. (Ed.), Advances in group processes, (vol. 1, pp. 1–25).

DAVID L. DEEPHOUSE

lemons market In information theory, a "lemons market" is a market in which the degree of ASYMMETRIC INFORMATION between buyers and sellers is very high, and, in the extreme, may result in market failure. Akerlof (1970) provided an intuitive and logical exponent of this theoretical result by reference to a used car market. In a used car market, there may be cars that are of good quality and those that are "lemons." Since sellers are generally better informed than buyers regarding the quality of the car and buyers are not easily able to discern car quality, buyers will be unwilling to pay the "good car" price for a car of uncertain quality, so they value a car at the average price. In the extreme, owners of good cars will be unwilling to sell their cars at the prevailing price and ultimately, the only cars in the market will be those that no one wants and the market will fail.

The solution to this problem requires that market participants act to reduce the level of information asymmetry. For example, buyers might invest in additional information by hiring experts or gaining expertise themselves. Sellers may attempt to better convey information, although they will have to bear some costs to make their claims of value believable to potential buyers.

The logic and intuition used in the used car example has been extended to several other markets that exhibit imperfections due to information asymmetry. Spence (1974) suggests that the willingness of a potential employee to incur the costs of education and training is a reliable signal of quality that can be used to overcome the information asymmetries in the labor market. In insurance markets, the inability of insurers to accurately identify the risk class of potential policyholders creates the potential for market failure. If premiums are set at a rate based on the risk of the pool of potential policyholders, the good risks will choose to forgo insurance and the pool of policies will make losses for the insurer. However, Rothschild and Stiglitz (1976) suggest that the willingness of good risks to forgo full insurance (e.g. through deductibles and co-insurance) may provide a reliable signal that will allow the insurer to charge them appropriate premium rates. The result is that there will be two kinds of policies in the market: partial insurance policies at lower rates for the good risks, and full insurance at higher rates for the higher risks.

In the context of financial markets, information asymmetry exists between managers and shareholders. In addition, incentive conflicts make managers' favorable public announcements regarding the firm's future prospects less credible. Therefore, it is necessary that managers signal information to investors in a credible way, e.g. their willingness to accept compensation in the form of stock options. The high degree of regulation of information in the financial markets is, in part, designed to reduce information asymmetry that could lead to reduced investor confidence and market failure.

Bibliography

Akerlof, G. A. (1970). The market for 'lemons': quality uncertainty and the market mechanism. *Quarterly Journal of Economics*, **August**, 488–500.

Brigham, E. F. & Gapenski, L. C. (1996). *Intermediate Financial Management*. 5th edn, Fort Worth, TX: Dryden.

Rothschild, M. & Stiglitz, J. (1976). Equilibrium in competitive insurance markets: an essay on the economics of imperfect information. *Quarterly Journal of Economics*, **November**, 629–49.

Spence, M. (1974). *Market Signalling*. Cambridge, MA: Harvard University Press.

VICKIE L. BAJTELSMIT

leveled scheduling In planning and control in operations it is possible to consider the leveling of scheduled material movements so that each movement is co-ordinated with the others when work cycles repeat. "Co-ordination" here refers to the timing and volumes of material movements. This consideration can be extended from the factory to suppliers and customers so that material movements are co-ordinated throughout the supply chain. Leveled scheduling is an important aspect of just-in-time philosophy, and plays a key role in the Toyota production system, where it is referred to as *heijunka*.

According to the runners, repeaters, and strangers classification, runners and repeaters are prime candidates for leveled scheduling. Strangers must be scheduled by alternative means, such as material requirements planning (*see* JIT/MRP).

Leveled scheduling involves distributing volume and mix evenly over a given production timespan. Output thereby matches customer demand as closely as possible at any instant during that timespan. The development of leveled scheduling is illustrated in figure 1. Suppose that

Low	Degree of leveling	High →
High	Set-up times	Low →
Low	System flexibility	High →

Large batches	Small batches	Mixed-model assembly
200 A 120 B 80 C	5 A 3 B 2 C	AABABCABCA

Figure 1 Leveled scheduling

we begin with a weekly production schedule for a range of three products A, B, and C which runs at 200 of product A, 120 of B, and 80 of product C. Assume that the customer for these products is using them evenly across the product range. Then producing them in large batches according to weekly usage will create inventories of finished product, and lead to production peaks which impose excessive work on one team at a time in preceding processes. Instead, it is better to level the finished product schedule as much as possible, and to downdate that leveling to production of sub-assemblies and components as well. To begin, the batch sizes could be reduced to five of product A followed by three of product B followed by two of product C. But even greater leveling of "runners" can be produced by scheduling in the sequence AABABCABCA. This is called a mixed-model assembly sequence, and achieves maximum repetition in the shortest cycle. Mixed model assembly allows close tracking of changes to mix in demand for the products, and finished product inventory should be at a minimum. However, mixed model assembly is the most extreme approach to leveled scheduling in terms of set-ups. Therefore, it only becomes possible as set-up reduction leads to short set-up times. Also, mixed model assembly places increased pressure on operators, who must cope with constantly changing product mixes. Use of error-proof devices (*see* FAIL-SAFING) to make it impossible to produce non-conforming products therefore becomes a necessary feature of this approach.

Leveled scheduling places a number of demands on a production system. Operators must be capable of switching quickly between different product mixes, transferring between areas of high demand and areas of low demand, and taking on different tasks. The processing capacity of each machine also needs to be harmonized. A frequent temptation is to use the capacity of a machine to the fullest, but leveled scheduling principles indicate that the output of each process should be leveled to whatever is needed to produce the required output. This often means that machines are "derated," inasmuch as the output from them is deliberately reduced so that it is co-ordinated with other processes.

A related concept is that of the "band width" (Vollman et al., 1992) of a production system, which is a measure of its surge capacity to handle changes in volume and mix across a given range. If the objective of leveled scheduling is to be able to make any product in any sequence with no disruption, many processes only need to meet full surge capacity occasionally. Such processes are therefore usually run below capacity, and may often be shut down.

Bibliography

Schonberger, R. J. (1982). *Japanese manufacturing techniques: Nine hidden lessons in simplicity.* New York: Free Press.

Shingo, S. (1988). *Non-stock production: The Shingo system for continuous improvement.* Cambridge, MA: Productivity Press.

Shingo, S. (1989). *A study of the Toyota production system from an industrial engineering viewpoint.* Cambridge, MA: Productivity Press.

Vollman, T. E., Berry, W. L. & Whybark, D. C. (1992). *Manufacturing planning and control systems.* Homewood, IL: Irwin.

ALAN HARRISON

leveraged buy-out strategy Leveraged buy-outs (LBOs) occur when the management of a company purchase it from existing shareholders and effectively become the owners. The target is typically a public company or a subsidiary of one which is taken private, with a significant portion of the cash purchase price being financed by debt. This debt is secured not by the credit status of the purchaser but by the assets of the target company. The debt used has usually been high-yield securities of substandard investment grade quality, commonly referred to as "junk bonds." During the late 1980s and early 1990s in the USA, and to some extent in Western Europe, LBOs were very popular, and some financial institutions specialized in the issuance of junk bonds. With the arrival of the credit crunch of the mid-1990s and a number of highly visible failures amongst LBOs and investment banks, the movement lost ground. However, with returning liquidity in the banking system, there are signs of a new surge of interest in the mid-1990s.

An important criterion for an LBO is a gap between the existing market value of the firm and the value determined by a reappraisal of the assets or by the capitalization of expected cashflows. Moreover, after an LBO the incoming management are often able to achieve dramatic savings in the business's operating costs.

LBOs tend to be mature businesses with a demonstrable record of stable consistent earnings, a significant market share, and experienced in place management. Manufacturing and retailing businesses are attractive because they also contain a basis for asset secured loans or stable income streams for unsecured or subordinated debt. Low capital intensive service businesses are less popular because of their narrow asset bases.

LBOs are said to be attractive to all those involved. Typically, the target concern's top management approaches an investment banker with an LBO proposal. In some cases, specialist banks may take the initiative. The bankers then package an LBO deal, usually involving commercial bankers, insurance and finance companies, pension funds, and the like. The final deal will provide the incumbent management with the opportunity to purchase a stake in the common stock that is much greater than they would be able to obtain on the basis of their individual resources, provided that they can successfully secure the debt. Usually, however, the management group's resources still only provide a small percentage of the initial investment.

This equity gap has led to the creation of a new form of financing known as mezzanine-level finance. Such lenders are often limited partnerships with wealthy investors, venture capitalists and pension funds as limited partners, supported by an investment banking firm acting as a general partner. In addition to investing in common equity, mezzanine lenders also hold securities senior to management equity but subordinate to secured debt. Most mezzanine financiers are short- to medium-term investors who expect to resell their share of the equity a few years after purchase to realize a substantial capital gain.

LBOs are far from risk-free. First, an LBO offer may serve to attract more bidders, although this is not a problem if the primary objective is to achieve the best value for existing shareholders. Second, and more important, is the risk of insolvency. Since revolving bank lending is a primary means of financing LBOs, they are very sensitive to increases in interest rates as a result of their highly leveraged position.

The risk of diversification is also a potential problem. LBO firms tend to be relatively undiversified and from mature industries. The process of diversification, especially from a single business strategy or a dominant business strategy, suffers a high failure rate. Furthermore, as LBOs revert to private status, results reporting becomes much less transparent than with publicly owned concerns, increasing the risk to lenders.

Bibliography

Diamond, S. C. (Ed.). (1985). *Leveraged buyouts*. Homewood, IL: Dow Jones Irwin.

Law, W. A. (1988). Leveraged buyouts. In J. P. Williamson (Ed.), *Investment banking handbook*. New York: John Wiley.

Shaked, M. A. (1986). *Takeover madness*. New York: John Wiley. See chapter 3.

DEREK F. CHANNON

licensed production   The holder of a patent, trademark, or copyright may allow another organization to use its property rights in the production of goods. An organization is "licensed" to use the rights or processes of another. A commission or royalty is commonly paid in such licensing arrangements. This arrangement is common when an organization in one country desires to legally use the rights or processes of an organization in another country.

JOHN O'CONNELL

life cycle strategy   An alternative to the "growth share" and "market attractiveness competitive position" portfolio models was developed by Arthur D. Little Inc. (hereafter, ADL) based on the concept of the life cycle as illustrated in figure 1. As with the other portfolio models, the ADL approach first identifies the life cycle position of a business as a descriptor of industry characteristics. Second, the competitive strength of a business is represented by six categories (dominant, strong, favorable, tenable, weak, and nonviable). The combination of these two variables is illustrated in figure 2 as a six by four matrix, on which the position of each business unit suggests a number of logical strategic alternatives, as shown. In using this system the corporation is first segmented into a series of relatively independent business units. Second, the life cycle position of each business is carefully assessed (note that the product life cycle need not necessarily be the same as the business life cycle). Third, the competitive position of each business is carefully assessed.

The label "strategy center" was assigned by ADL to each business that others had defined as a strategic business unit (*see* SBU STRUCTURE). To reach their conclusions on strategy centers, ADL defined them in terms of competitors, prices, customers, quality/style, substitutability, and divestment or liquidation. The first four of these indicate

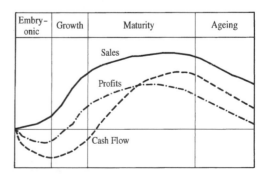

Figure 1   Yearly sales, cashflow, and profits through the industry life cycle stages.
Source: Arthur D. Little Inc.

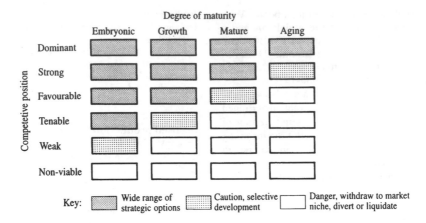

Figure 2   *The life cycle portfolio matrix*
Source: Arthur D. Little Inc.

that a strategy center contains a specific set of products for which it faces a specific set of customers and competitors which are also affected by price, quality and style change. Moreover, all products within a strategy center should be close substitutes for one another. A strategy center could also probably survive as an independent business if divested.

The position of a business within its industry life cycle is determined by eight factors. These descriptions are market growth rate, market growth potential, breadth of product lines, number of competitors, distribution of market share among competitors, customer loyalty, barriers to entry, and

technology, as illustrated in table 1. Strategy centers do not usually fall into a single life cycle phase for every descriptor, and some judgement therefore needs to be made as to the overall life cycle position of a business. Embryonic businesses are usually characterized by high growth, rapid technological change, pursuit of a rapidly widening range of customers, fragmented and changing shares of market, and new competitor entries. By contrast, a mature industry is characterized by stability in known customers, technology, and market shares, with well established and identifiable competitors. Interestingly, it is sometimes possible, usually as a result of technological

Table 1   Factors affecting the stage of the industry life cycle for a strategy center.

Descriptors	*Stages of industry (maturity)*			
	Embryonic	Growth	Mature	Ageing
Growth rate				
Industry potential				
Product line				
Number of competitors				
Market share stability				
Purchasing patterns				
Ease of entry				
Technology				
OVERALL				

Source: Arthur D. Little, Inc.

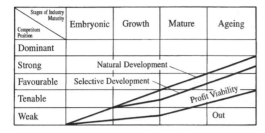

Figure 3 Natural strategic thrusts.
Source: Arthur D. Little, Inc.

change, to convert mature or emerging industries back into embryonic industries. For example, in motor insurance, Direct Line Insurance has transformed the industry over only eight years by selling policies direct and achieving a growth rate of *c*.70 per cent per annum against the background of a relatively static growth rate for the industry as a whole. Most industries, however, work through the life cycle on a steady basis.

The competitive position of a business is assessed by ADL via a series of qualitative factors rather than the use of quantitative factors such as relative market share. Five categories of competitive position are identified: dominant, strong, favourable, tenable, and weak. The sixth position – nonviable – demands immediate or rapid exit. A dominant position is rare, and comes about because a competitor has managed to establish a quasi-monopoly or has achieved technological dominance. Such positions could be claimed by IBM in computers and Kodak in color film. However, both positions have come under attack in recent years. IBM has failed to dominate the personal computer market which, because of technological advances, has become an increasing threat to IBM's core mainframe computer business. Similarly, Kodak has begun to face a major threat from electronic digital imaging in its core business of amateur color film, a silver halide based "wet" process activity. A "strong" business, by contrast, enjoys a definite advantage over competitors, usually with a relative market share of greater than 1.5 times. "Favorable" means that a business usually enjoys a unique characteristic; for example, dominance of a specific niche, access to dedicated raw materials, or a special relationship with an important distribution channel. A tenable position means that the firm has the facilities to remain within a market but has no distinctive competence. Nevertheless, the position is such that survival is not a serious issue. Finally, a weak position is not tenable in the long term. Such businesses should either be developed to a more acceptable position or exited.

For portfolio balance using the life cycle model, the firm needs a balanced mix of activities, with mature businesses generating a positive cashflow that can be used to support embryonic or growth operations. Success is also determined by having as many businesses as possible in dominant or favorable positions.

Once the portfolio of businesses has been determined, ADL has developed three further aids to assist managers of strategy centers in formulating strategy. The first of these concepts was labeled by ADL as *families of thrusts*. The consultants agreed that there were four families of activities

Table 2 Grouping of generic strategies by main areas of concern.

Marketing strategies

F	Export/same product
I	Initial market penetration
L	Market penetration
O	New products/new markets
P	New products/same markets
T	Same product/new markets

II	*Integration strategies*
A	Backward integration
G	Forward integration

III	*Go overseas strategies*
B	Development of overseas business
C	Development of overseas production facilities
J	Licensing abroad

IV	*Logistic strategies*
D	Distribution rationalization
E	Excess capacity
M	Market rationalization
Q	Production rationalization
R	Product line rationalization

V	*Efficiency strategies*
N	Methods and functions efficiency
V	Technological efficiency
W	Traditional cost cutting efficiency

VI	*Market strategies*
H	Hesitation
K	Little jewel
S	Pure survival
U	Maintenance
X	Unit abandonment

Source: Arthur D. Little, Inc. (1974)

which covered the spectrum of business development. These were "natural development," "selective development," "prove viability," and "withdrawal." The fit of each of these families is indicated in figure 3. A "natural development" position is likely to represent a position at industry maturity with a strong, competitive position which, as a result, justifies strong support to maintain or enhance the strategic position. A "selective development" strategy implies concentration of resources into attractive industry segments or where the firm has destructive competitive advantage. "Prove viability" status requires management to come up with a strategy that enhances strategic position or exit. "Withdrawal" clearly suggests exit, the speed of which needs to be clarified to avoid undue haste.

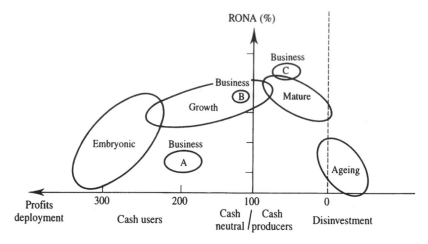

Figure 4   A typical ronagraph
Source: Arthur D. Little Inc.

Having identified the family of strategic thrust that is most appropriate for a specific business, management is now challenged to select a specific strategic thrust for the business. For example, the following thrusts have been applied to the natural development family:

- *Start-up* could be applied in an embryonic stage business to achieve a high share position while the market growth is high.
- *Growth with industry* applies when the firm is content with its industry position and seeks to maintain market share. This position prevails under dominant or strong conditions and at industry maturity.
- *Gain position gradually* is a stance that is applicable when a modest share increase is required to consolidate industry position.
- *Gain position aggressively* is similar to the double or quit position or question mark business. The firm seeks to aggressively build share in an attractive industry while the growth rate remains high.
- *Defend position* applies when the firm already enjoys a dominant or strong position. As part of a defensive strategy, spending should be at whatever level is necessary to maintain the existing position. The relative cost of defense tends to be much lower for industry leaders than for attackers, due to ECONOMIES OF SCALE and ECONOMIES OF SCOPE.
- *Harvest* is relevant at all stages of the life cycle. The key factor for consideration is the speed of harvest. From a strong position, harvesting may be slow, with the cashflows generated being deployed more effectively in newer businesses. Rapid harvesting occurs from positions of strategic weakness and may imply strategies of sale or closure.

The third concept developed by ADL is that of generic strategy (not to be confused with Porter's concept, which is discussed elsewhere). ADL conceived 24 generic strategies, which were then grouped into a series of subcategories as shown in table 2. The three concepts of families, strategic thrusts, and generic strategies were then linked into an overall matrix to demonstrate strategic position.

In the ADL methodology, the position of a business in the life cycle impacts upon its financial performance. A tool used by ADL to assess this is the ronagraph which is illustrated in figure 4. This shows, on the vertical axis, the return on net assets (RONA) generated by each business in the corporate portfolio and, on the horizontal axis, the internal deployment of cashflows. At 100 per cent all cash generated is redeployed within the business, which thus becomes cash neutral. Above 100 per cent the business becomes a cash user, while below 100 per cent a business is a cash generator. In addition, a negative value implies a divestment strategy. On the ronagraph each business unit is represented by a circle, the area of which is proportional to the net investment attached to the business.

In addition to RONA, a number of other indicators are also expected to reflect industry maturity. These include profit after tax, net assets, net working capital/sales, fixed costs/sales, variable costs/sales, profit after tax/sales, and net cashflow/sales.

The final step in the ADL methodology consists of assessing the level of risk associated with a business unit strategy. This involved a substantial level of subjectivity, but ADL have identified a number of factors which contribute to such risk, including the following:

- *Maturity and competitive position* – derived from the position of the business within the life cycle matrix. The greatest risk occurs for embryonic businesses with a weak market position, and the lowest for a business with a dominant position in a mature industry.
- *Industry* – some are much less predictable than others at the same stage of maturity.
- *Strategy* – aggressive strategies tend to be inherently more risky.
- *Assumptions* – future predictions enjoy varying degrees of probability and hence greater or lesser degrees of risk.
- *Past performance* – while the past is no necessary predictor of the future, stable historic records tend to be less risky than no records or inconsistent ones.

- *Management* – historic management performance counts, although this can be subject to change by events such as mid-life crisis, illness, and the like.
- *Performance improvement* – the gap between actual and predicted performance is also important. Dramatic improvements tend to be much more risky than gradual extensions of existing performance.

While the ADL model is a useful addition to the range of portfolio models, like the others it needs to be used with care. Criticisms of the approach include, first, the usefulness of the life cycle approach, which has been challenged by many as to its validity. Second, where a life cycle can be accepted, the stages of each position vary widely in terms of time. Third, industry activity does not necessary evolve into a well behaved S-curve. Markets can be rejuvenated and maturity can become growth through changes in fundamental industry characteristics. Firms can also fundamentally transform life cycle positions by innovation and repositioning. Finally, the nature of competition varies greatly from industry to industry. Thus fragmented industries may concentrate, while others go in the other direction. Automobiles, for example, have concentrated; while personal computers have moved from fragmentation to concentration and back to fragmentation in the short time interval of around 20 years. Nevertheless, used wisely, the life cycle portfolio model provides a useful addition to the development of the strategic management tool kit.

Bibliography

Arthur D. Little Inc. (1974). *A system for managing diversity.* Cambridge, MA: Arthur D. Little Inc. December.

Arthur D. Little Inc. (1980). *A management system for the 1980s.* San Francisco: Arthur D. Little Inc.

Hax, A. C. & Majluf, N. (1984). *Strategic management.* Englewood Cliffs, NJ: Prentice-Hall. See pp. 182–206.

DEREK F. CHANNON

life cycles *see* LIFESTYLES

lifestyles Consideration of consumer lifestyles incorporates an awareness of demographic variables and life cycles. Consumer behavior researchers and marketers are interested in trends in consumer DEMOGRAPHICS with respect to: birth rates and age profiles; marriage and divorce rates; number and spacing of children; size and composition of households/families, and extent of single-person households; incomes and occupation; levels of employment including participation of women in the labor force; and type and location of residence. These all impact on consumer needs, attitudes, and behavior, and are often discussed in relation to life cycles and lifestyles.

The term life cycle refers to the progression of stages through which individuals and families proceed during their lives, with the consequent financial situation and needs for goods and services. The traditional life cycle stages were from: bachelor stage to newly married; full nest 1,2,3; empty nest 1,2; solitary survivor in labor force; and solitary survivor retired (see Wells & Gubar, 1966). However, several modernized family life cycles have been put forward (e.g., Murphy & Staples, 1979; Gilly & Enis, 1982) in response to demographic trends such as smaller family sizes, postponement of marriage, and rising divorce rates.

Consumer lifestyle refers to a consumer's pattern of living which influences and is reflected by consumption behavior. It is the result of interactive processes between social and personal variables surrounding individuals in childhood and throughout life, e.g., family, reference groups, culture. It embodies patterns that develop and emerge from the dynamics of living in a society. Further, economic influences provide constraints and opportunities in the development of lifestyle.

Lifestyle encompasses a person's pattern of living in the world as expressed in terms of activities, interests, and opinions (e.g., see Wells & Tigert, 1971). Activities refer to how people spend their time: at work, home, community, special activities, hobbies, clubs, vacation, sport, and entertainment. Interests refer to what they place importance on in their immediate surroundings: family, home, job, community, recreation, fashion, and media. Opinions are in terms of their view of themselves and the world around them: e.g., social issues, politics, business, economics, education, and culture. These variables are considered together with demographics, and the basic premise of lifestyle research is that the more marketers know and understand about customers, the more effectively they can communicate and market to them. It provides a three-dimensional view of customers. The term PSYCHOGRAPHICS is used interchangeably with lifestyle, but may also include PERSONALITY variables.

One example of lifestyle is the VALS framework (see Solomon, 1992), which is based on some 30 to 40 demographic and attitudinal characteristics. From this, three broad groups of consumer are identified (in the US population): need-driven, outer-directed, and inner-directed. These are further divided into nine value lifestyle groups: survivors, sustainers, belongers, emulators, "I am me," experientals, societally conscious, and integrated – with associated impact on consumer needs, attitudes, and behavior.

Another example of lifestyle is ACORN-typing (see CACI, 1993), used as an indicator of SOCIAL CLASS. This incorporates geodemographic data (*see* GEODEMOGRAPHICS), from the most recent census, to include: age, sex, marital status, occupation, economic position, education, home ownership, and car ownership: to provide a full and comprehensive picture of socioeconomic status. From these data, and postcode information, ACORN types are developed to profile consumers in terms of their attitudes and behavior – with respect to products and services bought, leisure activities, media habits, and financial position.

Bibliography

CACI (1993). London: CAtx1CI Information Services.

Engel, J. F., Blackwell, R. D. & Miniard, P. W. (1990). *Consumer behavior*, 6th edn, Orlando, FL: The Dryden Press. Chapter 21.

Gilly, M. C. & Enis, B. M. (1982). Recycling the family life cycle: A proposal for redefinition. In A. Mitchell (Ed.), *Advances in consumer research* (vol. 9, pp. 271–276). Ann Arbor, MI: Association for Consumer Research.

Hawkins, D. I., Best, R. J. & Coney, K. A. (1992). *Consumer behavior: Implications for marketing strategy*, 5th edn, Homewood, IL: Irwin. Chapters 3, 7, 11.

Loudon, D. L. & Della Bitta, A. J. (1993). *Consumer behavior*, 4th edn, McGraw-Hill Int. Chapter 7.

Murphy, P. E. & Staples, W. A. (1979). A modernised family life cycle. *Journal of Consumer Research* June, 12–22.

Plummer, J. (1974). The concept and application of life style segmentation. *Journal of Marketing*, 38, Jan., 33–37.

Schiele, G. W. (1974). How to reach the young customer. *Harvard Business Review*, 52, Mar.–Apr., 77–86.

Schiffman, L. G. & Kanuk, L. Z. (1991). *Consumer behavior*, 4th edn, Prentice-Hall. Chapter 5.

Solomon, M. R. (1992). *Consumer behavior*. Needham Heights, MA: Allyn & Bacon.

Wells, W. D. (Ed.) (1974). *Lifestyle and psychographics*. Chicago: American Marketing Association.

Wells, W. D. (1975). Psychographics: A critical review. *Journal of Marketing Research*, 12, May, 196–213.

Wells, W. D. & Gubar, G. (1966). Life cycle in marketing research. *Journal of Marketing Research* Nov., 355–363.

Wells, W. D. & Tigert, D. J. (1971). Activities, interests and opinions. *Journal of Advertising Research*, 11, 27–35.

BARBARA LEWIS

line balancing   Line balancing is a technique used in connection with the design of product layout or "lines." The term "balancing" is used because one of its main objectives is to minimize the idle time and spread it as evenly as possible across the work stations.

When balancing a line the following factors need to be taken into account:

- the required output rate or cycle time (which depends on the demand for the product);
- precedence constraints (these are restrictions on the order in which tasks can be done; in other words certain tasks will have "predecessor tasks" which must be done first);
- zoning constraints (these are restrictions on where certain tasks or combinations of tasks should, or should not, take place);
- whether there is a need for work station duplication or replication (this would be the case when any task takes longer than the available cycle time).

The line balancing problem comprises two aspects: determination of the required number of stations, and the assignment of tasks to each station with the objective of maximizing efficiency (by minimizing idle time and spreading it evenly across work stations).

The effectiveness of the balance decision is measured by the "balance loss" of the line. The balance loss is the time invested in making one product which is lost through imbalance, expressed as a percentage of the total time investment. For a paced n stage line the time lost through imbalance is the cumulative difference between the stations' allocated work times and the cycle time allowed by the pacing of the line. For unpaced lines it is the cumulative difference between each stage's work time and that of the stage with the largest work time (this effectively governs the cycle time of the whole line).

A very simple line balancing problem may be solvable by "trial and error." Most practical problems, however, are extremely complex, requiring thousands of tasks to be assigned across hundreds of work stations and with numerous precedence and zoning constraints to be taken into account.

To solve such problems a large number of heuristic algorithms have been developed, such as the Kilbridge and Wester method and the ranked positional weights technique. Being based on heuristics, or "rules" which have been tested empirically, such techniques can provide good, though not necessarily optimal, results. More recently, simulation has grown in popularity as an approach to balancing lines and a visual interactive simulation can allow the line designed to immediately see the effect of any modifications made.

Product layouts have traditionally been used to produce highly standardized products, but today the demand is for a greater variety of products or models. Therefore two types of line are now in widespread use and require a modification to the traditional line balancing approach. These are multimodel lines, where the line is reorganized periodically to produce different models or variants, and mixed model lines, where the line is designed to allow simultaneous production of any model or variant without reorganization.

The aim in multimodel line balancing should be to minimize total production cost, taking account of the additional factor of change-over costs. For very large batches the problem degenerates into the successive application of single model line balancing.

The main costs of an operator changing from one product to another are connected with reallocation of inventory and equipment to work stations and LEARNING CURVES of operatives in new jobs. To reduce these the number of stations and location of equipment should be constant whenever possible, and work elements common to more than one model should always be performed by the same operator. Since work content and production requirements vary between models the cycle times are the best factors to manipulate in reducing idle time, but balancing efficiency may be sacrificed for compatibility. The total balance loss will be the average per model, weighted in proportion to production ratios. A sensible ploy is to balance the line for the most popular model and to adjust this basic arrangement by empirical methods for the other models. If this is unsatisfactory, the steps may be repeated but centered on the model of second highest production volumes, etc.

For very small batches the problem is akin to the mixed model line. Here, achieving a good long-term balance is more difficult and depends on the sequencing of model types proceeding down the line. One approach is to balance the line using a range of task times for each activity.

Bibliography
Wild, R. (1972). *Mass production management*. London: Wiley.

DAVID BENNETT

localization (of employees)   This concerns replacing expatriates with host country nationals (HCNs) as the opportunity arises. The cost of sending expatriates overseas is extremely high. High level management personnel may cost an additional several hundred thousand dollars to send overseas. Although that figure may be extreme the cost for any expatriate is much higher than local labor. Localization of employees is the process of replacing expatriates with local hires as expatriate assignments come to an end. The need for expatriates is usually the greatest in the early periods of a company's overseas activities. Once time has allowed local labor to be trained (in technical as well as managerial pursuits) lower cost employees can successfully take the place of expatriates.

Bibliography

Black, J. S. (1988). Work role transitions: A study of American expatriate managers in Japan. *Journal of International Business Studies*, **19** (2), 277–94.

Pulatie, D. (1985). How do you ensure success of managers going abroad. *Training and Development Journal* December, 22–4.

Ronen, S. & Tung, R. L. (1981). Selection and training of personnel for overseas assignments. *Columbia Journal of World Business*, Spring, 68–78.

JOHN O'CONNELL

localization of industry   Industries tend to locate in areas in which there is a ready supply of raw materials, labor, or other services necessary for the production of goods. In the past some organizations developed "company towns" where workers not only lived but shopped for goods and services and went to work in the company facility. With the advent of global enterprises the tendency to localize industry has declined. With the entire world as a potential location for various segments of a company's operations, localization of industry is not as common as in the past.

JOHN O'CONNELL

location theory   An economic theory that a manufacturer will consider transportation costs as a major location determinant. If true, this theory states that a manufacturer will locate its manufacturing and distribution activities at locations having the lowest transportation costs for incoming raw materials and outgoing finished products.

JOHN O'CONNELL

locus of control   This is a personality construct denoting people's generalized expectancies for CONTROL of REINFORCEMENTS or REWARDS. People who believe that they can control reinforcements in their lives are termed internals. People who believe that fate, luck, or other people control reinforcements are termed externals. The locus of control concept is most frequently attributed to Rotter (1966). He also developed the most commonly used scale to assess the construct (Rotter, 1966).

Locus of control has been one of the most popularly studied PERSONALITY variables in the organizational behavior domain. In his review of organizational studies Spector (1982) noted that internality is associated with high levels of effort, MOTIVATION, job performance and JOB SATISFACTION. Internals tend to exhibit initiative on the job and prefer participative supervisory styles. Externals, on the other hand, are more conforming to authority and prefer directive supervisory styles. Research has found that externality (feeling that one has little control) is associated with counterproductive behavior in response to frustration. Externals are more likely than internals to respond to frustrating events at work by engaging in aggression against others, sabotage, starting arguments, and stealing (see Perlow & Latham, 1993).

The higher performance of externals has been explained by the concept of expectancy from Vie theory. Internals tend to have greater expectancies than externals that they

can be effective in task accomplishment. If they see the job as leading to desired rewards, internals should be more motivated to perform. Recent research has shown, however, that internals may not always be better performers. Blau (1993) found that internals did better at job tasks requiring initiative, but externals did better in highly structured routine tasks. Thus internals and externals may be suited for different kinds of jobs, depending upon their need for compliance or initiative.

Since Rotter's initial work scales have been developed to assess locus of control in specific domains relevant to organizations, including economic locus of control, health locus of control, safety locus of control, and work locus of control (Spector, 1988). These specific scales tend to correlate more highly with variables within their domains than does the general Rotter scale. Spector (1988), for example, found that work locus of control had stronger correlations than general locus of control with work related variables, such as JOB SATISFACTION.

see also **Personality**

Bibliography

Blau, G. (1993). Testing the relationship of locus of control to different performance dimensions. Journal of Occupational and Organizational Psychology, 66, 125–138.

Perlow, R. & Latham, L. L. (1993). The relationship between client abuse, and locus of control and gender: A longitudinal study in mental retardation facilities. Journal of Applied Psychology, 78, 831–834.

Rotter, J. B. (1966). Generalized expectancies for internal versus external control of reinforcement. Psychological Monographs, 80, (1, Whole No. 609).

Spector, P. E. (1982). Behavior in organizations as a function of employees' locus of control. Psychological Bulletin, 91, 482–497.

Spector, P. E. (1988). Development of the work locus of control scale. Journal of Occupational Psychology, 61, 335–340.

PAUL E. SPECTOR

logistics   This is a management function concerning the process of physical distribution and stockholding. It deals with the planning, allocating, and controlling of a firm's resources and their movement around the organization or between organizations in a smooth, uninterrupted, and timely flow. Within a retail system this would include the flow of goods from the site of manufacture to the final consumer. The allocation of financial and human resources would also be the responsibility of logistics management.

Efficiency of allocation is of great importance to ensure that there is no over- or under-supply and that resources are distributed at lowest possible cost. This requires consideration of stockholding costs, packaging and transport costs, etc.

Bibliography

Christopher, M. (1977). *Distribution, planning and control, a corporate approach*. Farnborough, Hants: Gower.

STEVE WORRALL

long run cost curves   For the firm, the long run refers to the length of time required so that all inputs in production are variable. There are no fixed costs in the long run. Since the firm is free to choose its capacity level in the long run, this is also considered the planning horizon. The long run is not fixed in calendar time but may vary across industries and even between firms within the same industry if their contractual commitments differ. From the perspective of the industry, Stigler (1966) suggested that the long run was the time required for a market or industry to fully adjust to "new conditions" and the period of adjustment required would depend upon the questions under consideration.

The long run average cost (LRAC) curve is the planning curve for the firm because it shows the minimum average cost of production using plants of varying sizes. As such it envelopes the short run average cost (SRAC) curves for different capacity levels and is typically assumed to be U-shaped. Associated with the long run average cost curve is a long run marginal cost (LRMC) curve which lies below the LRAC curve when the LRAC is falling (due to ECONOMIES OF SCALE), intersects the LRAC curve at its minimum, and lies above the LRAC curve when the LRAC curve is rising (when DISECONOMIES OF SCALE occur) as in figure 1 below.

The LRMC curve reflects the change in total costs when an additional unit of output is produced, given that all inputs are adjusted optimally (including capital). When capital expenditures are discrete and cannot be adjusted to produce one additional unit, such as when the scale of the plant is changed, the LRMC curve shows the changes in total costs moving to the next scale of operation; see Sexton (1995). In these cases, the LRAC curve will not be as smooth as in figure 1 and will follow the individual short run average cost curves more closely. If a manager anticipated sales of 1 million units per period, then she would choose capacity level $SRAC_1$ above. However, if sales were expected to be 1.5 million units per period, $SRAC_2$ would be the best capacity choice and in this example, it is also the MINIMUM EFFICIENT SCALE. For this plant, both the LRAC and SRAC curves are at their minimum points at 1.5 million units of output per period and so the LRMC curve intersects the short run marginal cost ($SRMC_2$) curve at this point as well. It should also be noted that for each point on the long run marginal cost curve, a short run marginal cost curve passes through it. Since some factors of production are fixed in the short run, the short run marginal cost curve should be steeper than

the long run marginal cost curve where all factors of production can be adjusted optimally; (see Friedman (1976), Shughart, Chappell and Cottle (1994) and SHORT RUN COST CURVES).

The output level of 1.5 million units at a price P_L represents the long run equilibrium for a firm in a competitive industry, where the representative firm earns zero ECONOMIC PROFIT and operates a plant at the minimum efficient scale. At this price, there will be no net entry into or net exit from the industry unless the conditions of supply or demand change.

Bibliography

Friedman, M. (1976). *Price Theory*. 2nd edn, Chicago: Aldine.
Sexton, R. L. (1995). *Microeconomics*. Englewood Cliffs, NJ: Prentice-Hall.
Shughart, W. F., Chappell, W. F. & Cottle, R. L. (1994). *Modern Managerial Economics*. Cincinatti, OH: South-Western Publishing.
Stigler, G. J. (1966). *The Theory of Price*. 3rd edn, New York: Macmillan.

ROBERT E. MCAULIFFE

lot sizing in MRP   Lot sizing (or batching) in MRP refers to the modification of the net requirement quantities before they are translated into planned orders in a material requirements planning (MRP) system (*see* NETTING PROCESS IN MRP).

If net requirements were translated directly into planned orders, it would result in manufacturing component schedules and purchasing schedules which did not take any account of the cost of machine set-ups or the cost of ordering. In other words, making the requirements as they occur on a period by period basis, otherwise known as the lot-for-lot policy, may certainly reduce overall stockholding costs, depending on the size of planning period chosen, but may increase costs incurred through excessive set-up and ordering activities for small batches.

To take account of the total costs of managing the materials, that is holding costs and ordering or set-up costs, batch sizing rules or ordering policies may need to be

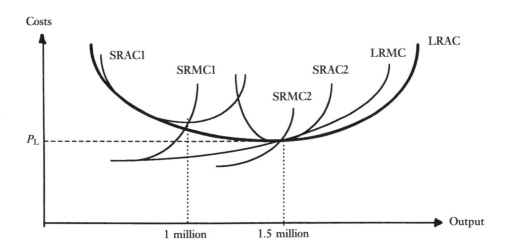

Figure 1   Long run and short run cost curves

applied to the net requirements to produce planned orders for the manufacturing or purchasing of items.

There are basically three different groups of methods of batching requirements together. These are fixed quantity batching rules, fixed period coverage batching rules, and dynamic batching rules.

Fixed quantity batching rules essentially state that every time an item is manufactured or bought it is done so in batches of minimum size X, or multiples of X. The fixed multiple batch size may be determined by a physical constraint of a manufacturing process, for example furnace or oven size, by considering the quantity that would normally be produced in one shift or in one week, or, most frequently, by the size of container that is used to transport the item.

The minimum fixed quantity batch size is usually determined by some form of economic calculation. This could take account of price breaks or discounts for quantity or it might use the so-called economic order quantity (EOQ) formula as used in traditional inventory management approaches. However, it should be noted that in a MRP system environment, the assumptions upon which the EOQ calculation is based are not valid, that is; a continuous review inventory system is not in operation and there may not be continuous demand and a gradual depletion of the stock of the item (*see* inventory control systems). Consequently, although the EOQ may be a guide to the best batch size, it cannot be guaranteed that its implementation will result in minimizing total inventory operating costs.

Fixed period coverage batching rules calculate a batch size by batching together the net requirements for the next y periods ahead. The coverage period may be chosen to fit in with a cycle scheduling approach to shop load on a three weekly repeated cycle with one third of components starting in week one, one third in week two and so on. If the choice is not determined by this constraint, an economic coverage period may be calculated by relating the economic order quantity calculation to an equivalent number of time periods' coverage.

With dynamic batching rules, the computer uses an algorithm which attempts to arrive at a batching schedule which minimizes inventory operating costs. Dynamic rules include the following: least unit cost, least total cost (part period algorithm), McLaren's order moment and Wagner-Whitin.

As an example, the least total cost (part period) algorithm consists of computing the cumulative holding costs and stopping at the batch size just short of the point where cumulative holding costs exceed the set-up cost. It makes the cost comparison by first calculating the ratio of the set-up cost to the holding cost per period known as the part period value (PPV), i.e. how many parts may be held for how many periods whose holding cost will equate to the set-up cost. For example, if the set-up cost for an item was $500 and the holding cost was $0.3 per period, the PPV would be 500/0.3, which equals 1667 part periods.

Each type of batching rule has its own advantages and disadvantages. The fixed quantity rule is easily understood and may fit in well with manufacturing process constraints or suppliers' standard order sizes. However, it suffers from the drawbacks of generating orders at irregular intervals and, compared to the other methods of batching, it generates higher stock levels. In a non-repetitive manufacturing environment it can also generate extra stocks which may become obsolete. Since the fixed period coverage rule is directly related to the future period's requirements it is more economical in terms of the overall stock level generated and, as mentioned previously, it may fit in well with the balancing of the workload on the shop floor. However, it may result in sizes of batches which fluctuate considerably, especially if there are periods with zero net requirements. Theoretically the dynamic batching rules are superior to the other two methods of batch sizing in the reduction of costs. However, they suffer the disadvantages of not being understood as easily and of generating differing batch sizes at uncertain time intervals which, in turn, may lead to difficulties in shop loading.

Bibliography

Vollman, T. E., Berry, W. L. & Whybark, D. C. (1992). *Manufacturing planning and control systems*. New York: Irwin.

PETER BURCHER

M

macro environment The environment of an organization (*see* MARKETING ENVIRONMENT) is generally regarded as consisting of a MICRO ENVIRONMENT and a macro environment which is composed of several major elements over which the organization has little, if any, influence. The major forces in the macro environment tend to be viewed as: social, economic, legal, political, economic, and technological. It is generally assumed that organizations will identify the major trends and possible future developments in these various components of the macro environment and the possible threats to their existing business and the opportunities for future developments (*see* SWOT ANALYSIS). In this sense, organizations are often depicted as being reactive, although it is clear that they can be active in certain areas, through major technological innovation and attempts at influencing the policy-making and legislative processes. An organization's environmental analysts can be very selective with respect to those aspects of the macro environment on which they focus and in their interpretation of them.

see also **Environmental analysis**

Bibliography

Brownlie, D. B. (1994). In M. J. Baker (Ed.), *The marketing book*, 3rd edn, Oxford: Butterworth-Heinemann. Chapter 7.
Sanderson, S. M. & Luffman, G. A. (1988). Strategic planning and environmental analysis. *European Journal of Marketing*, **22**, (2), 14–27.

DALE LITTLER

macro marketing Macro marketing embraces marketing's role in society and can be defined as "the delivery of a standard of living to society." The aggregation of all organizations' marketing activities includes transportation and distribution, and so the efficiency of the system for moving goods from producers to consumers may substantially affect a society's well-being. Thus, macro marketing is the aggregate of marketing activities within an economy, or the marketing system within a society, rather than the marketing activities of a single firm.

Bibliography

Zikmund, W. G. & d'Amico, M. (1995). *Effective marketing: creating and keeping customers*. St Paul, MN: West Publishing Co. Chapter 1, p. 21.

BARBARA LEWIS

maintenance of software Software maintenance is the modification of an existing software system by information systems professionals. It applies to both system software and applications. It involves three types of activities: repairs, improving technical performance, and enhancement. Repairs are required when incorrect or incomplete software code renders the system defective. Changes to software features, such as rewriting the code to take advantage of processing efficiencies, may be made to improve technical performance. Enhancements are additions, changes, or deletion of software functionality. Repairs tend to dominate the maintenance activity for the first few months of operation of a new software system. Later, most of the maintenance is enhancement. Sometimes maintenance is performed by the system developers, but often it may be the responsibility of a separate maintenance group.

Productivity in Software Maintenance

Software maintenance is an expensive activity. At least half of information system resources in organizations are devoted to software maintenance activities. On a life-cycle basis, more than three-quarters of the investment in software occurs after it has been implemented. It is thought that many problems in software maintenance are caused by inadequacies in the initial software design (Schneidewind, 1987). Poor choices in software development may result in low-quality software that is difficult to modify. A particularly problematic aspect of the software that ensues from bad design is software complexity. Software complexity refers to the characteristics of the data structures and procedures in the code that make the software hard to understand. There have been several studies that suggest the importance of software complexity for performance in software maintenance. Experimental studies by Curtis et al. (1979) and Gibson and Senn (1989), as well as others, indicate that software complexity is a major factor in software maintenance performance.

Software complexity is believed to interfere with the critical maintenance activity of software comprehension. Software that is large in size or that has complicated data interactions or logic paths is difficult to understand. There are several measures of software complexity. The most noted are Halstead's (1977) software science metrics, which measure software volume, and McCabe's (1976) cyclomatic complexity metric, which counts the number of decision paths in the software. These measures, as well as others, can be used to assess the quality of software design. Such assessment is important to ensure that maintainability is built in to the software when it is initially constructed.

Maintenance Management Concerns

There are several managerial issues related to software maintenance. A critical task is to effectively manage the system portfolio, or set of systems. As software systems age, they tend to become more complicated, with frequent modifications and enhancements. In addition, there may be few information systems personnel and users familiar with these systems. Thus, a key maintenance management decision concerns whether to continue to repair a system or replace it entirely. Another maintenance management concern is how to organize the software maintenance function. Software maintenance can be organized together with software development, so that IS personnel work on both development and maintenance tasks. Another alternative is a life-cycle arrangement where there are separate development and maintenance staffs. While this arrangement has potential advantages for quality assurance and user service, it may have disadvantages of coordination and political costs. Motivation of maintenance personnel is a final important managerial concern. Studies by Couger and Zawacki (1980) and Swanson and Beath (1989) indicate that information systems personnel may not consider maintenance work to be sufficiently interesting or challenging. Especially when technological obsolescence is prevalent, information system workers may fear that unless they are continuously involved in development work, their skills will deteriorate, and this will not only affect their future earning power, but also their ability to do work they enjoy.

Future of Software Maintenance

Several software development innovations, such as structured programming techniques, computer-aided software engineering, software reuse and object-oriented programming, promise to reduce the software maintenance burden. In addition, there have been tools and techniques developed to improve software maintenance performance. Some of the most prominent maintenance aids include software code analyzers, code restructurers, and reverse engineering tools. These software development and maintenance practices may lower the need for maintenance and increase the maintainability of systems.

Bibliography

Couger, J. D. & Zawacki, R. A. (1980). *Motivating and Managing Computer Personnel.* New York: John Wiley.

Curtis, B., Sheppard, S. B., Milliman, P., Borst, M. A. & Love, T. (1979). Measuring the psychological complexity of software maintenance tasks with the Halstead and McCabe metrics. *IEEE Transactions on Software Engineering*, SE-5 (2), 96–104.

Gibson, V. R. & Senn, J. A. (1989). System structure and software maintenance performance. *Communications of the ACM*, 32 (3), 347–58.

Halstead, M. (1977). *Elements of software science.* New York: Elsevier North-Holland.

McCabe, T. J. (1976). A complexity measure. *IEEE Transactions on Software Engineering*, SE-2 (4), 308–20.

Schneidewind, N. (1987). The state of software maintenance. *IEEE Transactions on Software Engineering*, SE-13 (3), 303–10.

Swanson, E. B. & Beath, C. M. (1989). *Maintaining information systems in organizations.* New York: John Wiley.

SANDRA SLAUGHTER

make/buy decision   An important alternative to PURCHASING goods or services is to supply them from internal sources. Equally, before undertaking internal production of goods or services it is important to consider whether external purchasing might provide a more efficient or preferable alternative. Make or buy decisions can also apply to internal services such as marketing, research, planning, accounting, and design, which may be better undertaken by external specialists with economies of scale and specialized investments (Anderson & Weitz, 1986). This issue has many strategic and operational implications beyond the relatively simple aspect of cost control. In-house supplier arrangements appear to offer potential advantages of management control, of cost manipulation (e.g., in TRANSFER PRICING), of acquitting minimum national content requirements where the alternative is international sourcing, of flexible production management, and of using what might otherwise be under-utilized assets. But there can also be significant problems of cost control, quality, delivery, and service where the commercial pressures of market

forces are (or are perceived to have been) "suspended." Decisions in this area are frequently concerned with political, cultural, personal, historic, and strategic issues rather than with the more routine purchasing concerns.

Bibliography

Anderson, E. & Weitz, B. (1986). Make-or-buy decisions. *Sloan Management Review*, 27, Spring, 3–19.

Ford, D., Cotton, B., Farmer, D. & Gross, A. (1993). Make-or-buy decisions and their implications. *Industrial Marketing Management*, 22, Aug., 207–214.

Venkatesan, R. (1992). Strategic sourcing: To make or not to make. *Harvard Business Review*, 70, (6), Nov.–Dec., 98–107.

DOMINIC WILSON

Malcolm Baldrige National Quality Award of American goods and services and to counter foreign competition, the US Congress established the Malcolm Baldrige National Quality Award (MBNQA) in 1987. Named for a former Secretary of Commerce, the award recognizes US companies "for business excellence and quality achievement."

The 1996 award criteria framework contains seven categories (each contributing points to a total of 1000): (a) leadership (90 points); (b) information and analysis (75 points); (c) strategic planning (55 points); (d) human resource development and management (140 points); (e) process management (140 points); (f) business results (250 points); and (g) customer focus and satisfaction (250 points). Categories contain from two to five subcategories. The human resource development and management category, for example, has four subcategories: (a) HUMAN RESOURCES PLANNING and evaluation; (b) human performance work systems; (c) employee education, training and development; and (d) employee well-being and satisfaction.

The MBNQA competition involves a four-stage process: application review by Baldrige examiners; review and evaluation of applicants surviving stage 1; site visits by Baldrige judges to applicants surviving stage 2; and judges' review and final recommendations. This competition is not free. Applicants pay a non-refundable $100 fee to determine their eligibility. If eligible, manufacturing and service firms then pay a $4500 application fee, while small businesses pay $1500. Site visits entail additional fees. Annual MBNQA winners are expected to share information on their quality strategies with other US organizations at "quest for excellence conferences."

Reactions to the MBNQA have been mixed, and applicant levels have declined since the award's early years. Critics argued that the MBNQA evaluated business activities or processes without evaluating business outcomes to determine if total quality management activities actually made a difference in firm performance (Greising, 1994). Evaluation criteria have since been changed to require information about business performance.

Some firms pursue the MBNQA to get an assessment of their standing relative to this benchmark of quality performance. Other firms do not enter the Baldrige competition, but use the criteria for an internal analysis of their quality status. Most of the entrants view the competition not as an attempt to "win" something, but as an effort to change their corporate culture. They view the Baldrige not as an end in itself, but as a first step on a journey to ever improving quality (Blackburn and Rosen, 1993).

While many of the Baldrige winners have gone on to (continued) business success, others have run into difficulties. IBM, the Cadillac Division of General Motors, and the Wallace Company (a 1991 small-business winner that declared bankruptcy shortly after winning its award) are examples in this latter group.

The MBNQA is one of a number of quality awards offered around the world, including the Deming Prize award by the Japanese Union of Scientists and Engineers and the European Quality Award presented by the Foundation for Quality Management. While not an award, the ISO 9000 certification process certifies that a plant's processes are in compliance with the certification guidelines, on the assumption that such compliance leads to quality outcomes.

Copies of the award criteria and the application form are available from: MBNQA, National Institute of Standards and Technology, Gaithersburg, MD 20899-[09, USA. Telephone: 301-975-2036. Fax: 301-948-3716

Bibliography

Blackburn, R. & Rosen, B. (1993). Total quality and human resources management: lessons learned from Baldrige Award-winning companies. *Academy of Management Executive*, 7, 49–66.

Garvin, D (1991). How the Baldrige Award really works. *Harvard Business Review*, 69, 80–95.

Greising, D. (1994). Quality: how to make it pay. *Business Week*, **August 8**, 54–9.

RICHARD S. BLACKBURN

management by objectives   At the individual level, management by objectives (MBO) is an interactive process whereby a manager and an employee (a) jointly identify and agree upon the subordinate's work goals, (b) define each of their responsibilities for achieving the agreed upon goals, and (c) then use goal accomplishment as a guide for examining and evaluating the subordinate's performance (Odiorne, 1965). At the organizational level, MBO is a process for managing and guiding the firm in a consistent and logical way. At this level, MBO requires senior management to develop clear, long-range organizational objectives. Mid-level management then uses these objectives to form appropriate shorter-range objectives. In turn, these become the basis for the traditional manager–employee MBO discussion and individual goal-setting. Conducted properly, this cascading process insures that objectives at different levels of the organization and within different groups mesh together, and result in the attainment of the firm's overall goals. Regardless of individual or organizational level, the defining characteristics of MBO are the creation of specific, measurable goals in important areas, and the use of these goals to monitor and guide progress.

Theoretical Underpinnings of MBO

Although Drucker (1954) and a number of other practitioners championed MBO in the 1950s, the research of Locke (1968) and his colleagues on goal-setting provides the theoretical foundation for understanding the workings of MBO. Goal-setting research explains why objectives should be specific and challenging, why participation in

setting objectives may be important, and why periodic feedback on goal attainment is essential.

Effectiveness of MBO

In spite of being a widely implemented motivation and PERFORMANCE APPRAISAL technique, the evidence supporting MBO effectiveness is mixed. While MBO has great potential for improving performance, practical difficulties abound, and firms have often found successful implementation difficult. Top management must first create an organizational culture supportive of an objectives-oriented approach. Without this, MBO effects are likely to be short term, with benefits dissipating within a year or two.

Common criticisms of MBO are that such systems generate too much paperwork, and that they over-emphasize quantitative goals at the expense of more qualitative objectives. However, these criticisms do not point up any theoretical weakness in the technique, and may simply underscore the need for thoughtful, careful implementation.

MBO may also create a conflict of interest for the employee. Since financial and other rewards are typically tied to successful goal achievement, it is in the subordinate's interest to set easily achievable goals. Yet goal-setting research consistently demonstrates that performance is highest with challenging goals. Thus, the goal-setting aspect of MBO may take the form of a struggle, with the employee attempting to set easy targets (to insure achievement), while the supervisor strives to set more challenging goals (to increase performance and insure unit success). This possibility highlights the critical role mutual trust and supportiveness play in any effective MBO implementation. Without these qualities, the firm will not reap the full benefits of MBO's substantial potential.

Bibliography

Carroll, S. & Tosi, H. (1973). *Management by Objectives: Applications and Research*, New York: Macmillan and Company.

Drucker, P. (1954). *The Practice of Management*, New York: Harper.

Locke, E. (1968). Toward a theory of task motivation and incentives. *Organizational Behavior and Human Performance*, 3, 157–89.

Odiorne, G. (1965). *Management by Objectives: a System of Managerial Leadership*, New York: Pitman.

Raia, A. (1974). *Managing by Objectives*, Glenview, IL: Scott, Foresman.

DONALD J. CAMPBELL

management contracting   A firm can enter foreign markets under a contract to manage a new or existing commercial operation in those markets. For example, a manufacturer has a proven record of aggressive and efficient management in its home country. The manufacturer may be approached not to provide product but instead management expertise for a start-up operation or an existing operation having problems in a foreign country. This places the management of the original manufacturer into a foreign operation in which international experience may be gained. Success in one management contract may lead to additional contracts and eventually equity ownership in foreign firms. The only real problems associated with management contracts is that they remove top management from the home country operation, are normally temporary, and may incur the blame for a problem which previously existed in a foreign company.

see also **Market entry strategies**

JOHN O'CONNELL

management information system   The terms management information system (MIS), information system (IS), and information management (IM) are synonyms. They refer both to an organization system that employs information technology in providing information and communication services and the organization function that plans, develops, and manages the system.

Definition of MIS as a System

The *management information system* is a system within an organization that supplies information and communication services and resources to meet organization needs. The system consists of information technology infrastructures to provide information processing and communication capabilities and application systems for delivery of specific information resources and services.

The infrastructures are core technology systems, databases, and information management personnel. The infrastructures provide capabilities and services for applications. Application systems deliver information resources and services for specific organizational functions or purposes. Types of applications include systems embedded in products or services, transaction processing, communications, cooperative work support, reporting and analysis, decision support, and management support. The applications employ both automated and manual procedures. They are human–technology systems because the results are obtained through an interaction of human users with the technology. The applications are model-based, i.e. the designs reflect models of decision-making, human–machine interfaces, social interaction, organization behavior, customer service, and so forth.

The objectives of the MIS infrastructures and applications are to meet an organization's information and communication needs, improve productivity in organizational activities, add value to organizational processes, and assist the organizational strategy. The systems apply information technology and information resources to functionality and performance in products and services, quality and scope in analysis and decision-making, communication and sharing in cooperative work, and improved, faster operational and management processes at all levels. In a well-designed MIS, the different applications are not independent; they are interconnected subsystems that form a coherent, overall, integrated structure for information and communication services.

Definition of MIS as an Organization Function

The management information system *organization function* plans, develops, implements, operates, and maintains the organization's information technology infrastructures and the organization's portfolio of applications. It also provides support and advisory services for systems developed and operated by individuals and departments.

The function employs, trains, and manages personnel with specialized knowledge and expertise for these purposes. The system development processes of the information management function include methods, techniques, and technologies for analyzing business processes, identifying system requirements, developing and implementing systems and related organization changes, and maintenance of systems. The management processes of the function include interaction with organizational strategic planning to identify ways information technology systems may be used to achieve competitive advantage and other strategic goals, planning of infrastructures and applications, management of information system projects, operation of systems, consultation services to users, and evaluation of MIS performance.

The MIS function is needed by an organization because of organizational reliance on information technology, the size of the investment, the need for organizational coordination and standards for the information system, and the need for expertise in processes for planning, development, and management of the information and communication infrastructures and applications for an organization. The reliance on information technology is pervasive in transactions and other business processes; few organizations could operate competitively without it. The investment in information technology has, in recent years, been a significant part of the investment budget of organizations. The need for a function to coordinate information technology in the organization is increased as information technology innovation is diffused across all functions. Information technology use in business functions depends on an information technology infrastructure, organization-wide applications, and standards for systems that cross functional and organizational boundaries. The MIS function performs this important role. A fourth reason for the MIS function is the expertise required for planning, developing, operating, and managing the information technology infrastructure and organization applications.

Body of Knowledge Associated with MIS

The use of information technology is so pervasive that a certain level of expertise must be distributed broadly across the organization. Individuals and workgroups within other organization functions may have significant responsibility for their own information management activities or local systems involving information technology. However, the management information system function has responsibility for maintaining expertise sufficient to assist individuals, groups, departments, and functions in their information management, to provide integration across the organization, and build and maintain the corporate information infrastructures and standards necessary for integrated information processes. The expertise associated with the MIS function consists of:

1 *Information strategies and structures*. Information system strategies and structures provide an organization with the capacity and capability for obtaining and using information, for applying information technology in its processes and systems, and for using information and systems in its competitive strategy. The MIS function applies expertise in strategy and structures in the process of PLANNING FOR INFORMATION SYSTEMS.

2 *Business process and information system development*. The information management function has special expertise in the design and implementation of business processes and systems. Information technology is a key element in

most designs. Although all organization functions have some responsibility for their systems, the information management function has an ongoing expert role with primary technical responsibility for systems analysis and design, development, and integration.

3 *Organization and administration of the information management function*. This area includes organization of responsibilities for the functioning, hiring, and training of information systems personnel, budgeting and planning of activities, and ASSESSMENT OF MANAGEMENT INFORMATION SYSTEM performance. Information system specialists are expected to have expertise to perform advisory and consulting services to users, build and maintain technical infrastructures, analyze requirements, and acquire or build solutions that employ information technology.

4 *Information management operations*. The operations within the domain of MIS include the operation of organization-wide systems for information processing and communications. The activities include scheduling, operating, and controlling information and communications facilities, organization applications, and organization databases.

The body of knowledge for planning, implementing, and operating the MIS for an organization rests upon a number of underlying disciplines or bodies of knowledge. As examples, it relies on the software engineering principles and computational algorithms of computer science, the organization behavior and management principles of the field of management, the concepts and principles of human behavior in human–technology systems from cognitive psychology, principles of cooperation and communication from the field of communications, system concepts and INFORMATION CONCEPTS from a variety of fields, and analysis of costs, benefits, and productivity from economics. From these reference disciplines, MIS has built a body of knowledge about the design, implementation, operation, and evaluation of information system infrastructures and applications in organizations.

Evolution of the MIS Concept

When computers were applied to business data processing in 1954, the first applications were document and report preparation based on batch input of transactions. Payroll checks, customer order documents, inventory analyses, and related reports are examples. In large part, computer technology was employed in early applications as a substitute for clerical labor and electromechanical devices. The systems were often referred to as electronic data processing (EDP) systems. Innovative organizations soon applied the computer to management reporting and analysis. The files that had been prepared for transaction document processing and transaction reporting provided the basis for more timely, analytical management reports. The computer made possible the use of quantitative modeling in support of business decisions. To reflect this change in emphasis from data processing to management support, the systems and function began to employ the term *management information systems*. The term included support for various levels of management and for decision-making.

The concept also included data as an organization resource. The data resource concept was implemented with

DATABASE MANAGEMENT SYSTEMS. Prior to computers, transaction data files were viewed as being "owned by" or the responsibility of a single business function. The marketing files were the responsibility of the marketing department, the accounts receivable records were the responsibility of the accounting department, and so forth. Database management systems and databases freed the organization from functional constraints on the use of data. Data were defined as organization resources to be managed for broad organization use. Retrieval software was made available to selectively search and retrieve from the databases. Any authorized person could employ the software to access the databases.

Data could be organized, analyzed, and alternatives modeled in order to support decision-making. Since many models are applicable across the organization, a model base of analytical tools was developed to support decision-making and decision-making access to data. Software was provided as part of the MIS to support individual modeling of decisions and access to data for the model. Software was added to the system to support group decision-making and cooperative work (*see* computer-supported cooperative work; DECISION SUPPORT SYSTEMS; EXECUTIVE INFORMATION SYSTEMS; GROUP DECISION SUPPORT SYSTEMS).

An extension of the MIS concept was the STRATEGIC USE OF INFORMATION TECHNOLOGY to improve the competitive position of the organization and achieve competitive advantage. The MIS planning process became more closely tied to the strategy of the organization. The MIS function is expected not only to respond to requirements as defined by other business functions but interact in the planning process to suggest innovative uses of information technology to improve products, services, and business processes. This new set of applications includes interorganizational applications that apply information technology to reduce cycle time and improve communications and transaction handling between the organization and its suppliers and customers.

The Structure of an MIS

The structure of an information system may be visualized as infrastructures plus applications. The applications have a conceptual structure based on the purposes or needs being met and the functions of the organization that employ them. The three infrastructures that provide the general capacity and capabilities for information access and processing are technology, data, and personnel. The infrastructures enable specific applications and activities.

1 The *technology infrastructure* consists of computer and communication hardware, system software, and general purpose software systems. The computer hardware consists of computers and related storage, input, and output devices. The communications hardware contains devices to control the flow of communications within internal networks and with external network providers. Computer hardware is made operational through system software that provides generalized functions necessary for applications. Computer operating systems, communications software, and network software are examples. Generalized software is not specific to a single application but provides facilities for many different applications. An example is a database management system to manage databases and perform

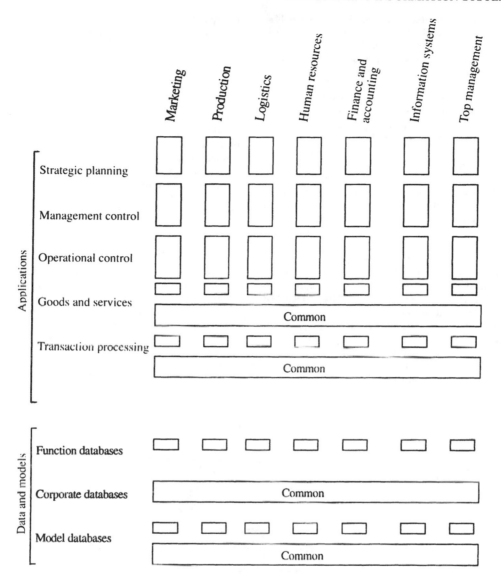

Figure 1 Organizational MIS applications, data, and models

access and retrieval functions for a variety of applications and users.

2 The databases form a *data infrastructure*. They provide for storage of data needed by one or more organizational functions and one or more activities. There will be a number of databases based on organization activities. Planning of the database infrastructure involves determining what should be stored, what relationships should be maintained among stored data, and what restrictions should be placed on access. The result of database planning and implementation with database management systems is a capacity to provide data both for applications and *ad hoc* needs. Comprehensive databases designed for *ad hoc* use may be termed DATA WAREHOUSING.

3 The information systems *personnel* can be viewed as a third infrastructure, which includes all personnel required to establish and maintain the technology and database infrastructures and the capacity to perform user support, development, implementation, operation, and maintenance activities. The personnel may be divided between an MIS function and functional areas. There may be, for example, general purpose user support personnel in the MIS function and functional information management support personnel in the functional areas of the organization.

The application portfolio provides the specific processing and problem-solving support for an organization. It consists of the application software and related model bases and knowledge bases. The application software consists of applications that cross functional boundaries and applications identified with a single function. Although there is significant integration of applications because of the use of common databases and use of the same application by more than one function, the application portfolio reflects a federation of systems rather than a totally integrated system. A single, integrated system is too complex; the selective integration by interconnections among the federation of systems is more manageable and robust. A visualization of the MIS based on the application portfolio consists of applications in direct support of each business function (marketing, production, logistics, human resources, finance and accounting, information systems, and top management) plus general-purpose applications and facilities. Although the database management system provides general-purpose support, it also supports databases common to many functions and databases unique to a function. The applications can also be classed as being associated with transaction processing, products and services, and management. The management applications can be classified as related to operational control, management control, and strategic planning. This conceptual structure is illustrated in figure 1.

In terms of the use of technology and the frequency of use of the software, the applications in figure 1 differ in several respects. The transaction processing and goods and services applications tend to support lower-level management and operating personnel. The applications tend to

incorporate programmed decision processes based on decision rules and algorithms. Applications supporting higher-level management processes are less structured and require human interaction to specify the decision process and data to be used. Because of these differences, the application structure of a management information system is often described as a pyramid (figure 2).

Information System Support for Management Activities

In addition to its use in transaction processing, business processes, and within products and services, information systems support management processes such as planning, control, and decision-making. This use of information technology can provide significant value to the organization. The Anthony framework is used by both academic researchers and business practitioners to model and classify the information system support for management. The three levels of the Anthony hierarchy define the nature of the management support applications.

1 *Operational control* ensures that operational activities are conducted efficiently and effectively according to plans and schedules. Examples of applications in support of operational management are scheduling, purchasing, and inquiry processing for operations. The decisions and actions cover short time periods such as a day or a week. An example of processing in support of operational control is the sequence of operations to authorize an inventory withdrawal. The balance on

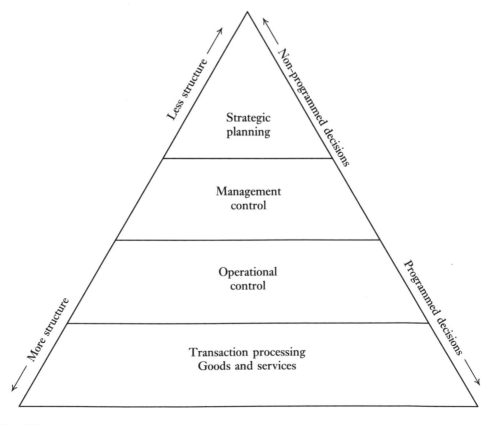

Figure 2   The MIS as a pyramid

hand and on order is examined to determine the need for a replenishment order. The size of the replenishment order is based on reorder quantity algorithms to control inventory levels. An order document is prepared automatically for review and acceptance or modification by a purchasing analyst before it is released.

2 *Management control* focuses on a medium–term time period such as a month, quarter, or year. It includes acquisition and organization of resources, structuring of work, and acquisition and training of personnel. Budget reports, variance analysis, and staffing plans are typical of management control applications.

3 *Strategic management* applications were designed to assist management in doing long-range strategic planning. The requirements include both internal and external data. The emphasis is on customer trends and patterns and competitor behavior. Market–share trends, customer perceptions of the organization and its products and services, along with similar perceptions for competitors, and forecasts of technology changes, are examples of information useful in strategic management.

A set of applications and retrieval/report facilities within an MIS designed especially for senior executives has been termed an EXECUTIVE INFORMATION SYSTEM (EIS). It focuses on the unique needs of senior management. These include an ability to formulate executive–level inquiries, construct special information requests, explore various alternative analyses, and so forth. The databases used for an EIS include portions of the corporate transactions databases, selected summary and comparative data, and relevant external data.

Information System Support for Decision-making
The decision-making support provided to an organization by its information system can be described in terms of Simon's three phases of the decision-making process: intelligence, design and choice. The support for the intelligence phase of discovering problems and opportunities consists of database search and retrieval facilities. For example, an analyst investigating collections policy can use retrieval software to obtain data on customers, sales, and collections for a representative period. The decision design phase in which decision alternatives are generated is supported by statistical, analytical, and modeling software. In the collections example, the decision design might involve correlation of collection times with customer characteristics and order characteristics. The support for the choice phase includes decision models, sensitivity analysis, and choice procedures. A choice procedure for a collections policy might involve the use of models to compare collection policies on various dimensions and rank order the policies.

EXPERT SYSTEMS support decision-making by rule-based or knowledge-based systems. The most commonly used rule-based systems incorporate decision procedures and rules derived from the decision-making processes of domain experts. Data items presented to the rule-based system are analyzed by the expert system and a solution is suggested based on the rules derived from experts. The decision may be supported by an explanation facility that details the rules and logic employed in arriving at the decision. Unlike expert systems based on rules, neural networks are a decision-support procedure based on the data available for a decision. The neural network is established (or recalibrated) by deriving the factors and weights that will achieve a specified outcome using an existing set of data. The factors and weights are applied to new data to suggest decisions. An example of neural network use is decision-making relative to credit worthiness for a loan or credit approval for a transaction.

The term DECISION SUPPORT SYSTEM is defined as a set of applications within an MIS devoted to decision support. Although some writers distinguish between MIS and DSS, the MIS concept is typically defined to include a DSS. The concept of a DSS incorporates the Anthony framework and the decision-making categories of Herbert Simon (1977). The classic description of the concept is by Gorry and Scott Morton (1971). Their framework for a DSS classifies decisions as structured, semi–structured, and unstructured within the three levels of management. Structured decisions can be incorporated in the programmed procedures of computer software, but unstructured (and many semi-structured) decisions are best supported by analytical and decision models and analytical and modeling tools. These facilities aid human decision-makers to deal with difficult problems that cannot be solved with algorithms. The concept of a DSS incorporates human–system interaction as the human decision-maker formulates scenarios, models alternatives, and applies analytical procedures in order to explore alternative solutions and evaluate consequences.

The Future of the MIS System and Function
Systems based on information technology have become an integral part of organization processes, products, and services. The data available for analysis and decision-making have increased with the capabilities for computer based storage and retrieval. The infrastructures have become more complex as more information technology is distributed to individuals and departments. The planning, design, implementation, and management of information resources have become more complex and more vital to organizations. The need for a specialized MIS function has increased. Although some routine functions may be outsourced, the critical functions that affect competitive advantage are likely to remain part of an MIS function in the organization.

Information technology is still changing rapidly, and new opportunities for business use continue to emerge. The rate of innovation and change and the investment implications also underlines the need for an MIS function to support organizational use of information technology for information access, processing, and communication.

Bibliography

Anthony, R. N. (1965). *Planning and Control Systems: A Framework for Analysis*. Cambridge, MA: Harvard University Press.

Davis, G. B. & Olson, M. H. (1985). *Management Information Systems: Conceptual Foundations, Structure, and Development*, 2nd edn. New York: McGraw-Hill.

Gorry, G. A. & Scott Morton, M. S. (1971). A framework for management information systems. *Sloan Management Review*, 13 (1).

Simon, H. A. (1977). *The New Science of Management Decision*, rev. edn. Englewood Cliffs, NJ: Prentice-Hall.

GORDON B. DAVIS

management localization   Management localization is a term which takes on different meanings depending on the specific international human resource management context under consideration. In extreme circumstances, the term may indicate complete nationalization of the enterprise or that ownership is transferred to foreign-country nationals. In less extreme contexts, the term means that the enterprise's managerial practices and approaches have been adapted to those appropriate for the foreign country or local conditions (Negandhi and Welge, 1984).

The term is also used to describe greater flows over time of host-country nationals into subsidiaries' key managerial positions and the delegation to them of greater decision-making authority (Serapio, 1995). Scholars have argued that, in the absence of host-country managers having authority to make decisions, real management localization does not occur just because host-country nationals have been placed in key managerial positions.

Research on international human resource management literature has typically defined management localization more narrowly to describe the flow of host-country nationals into management positions, the promotion of host-country nationals, and the corresponding replacement of home-country nationals over time (Negandhi and Welge, 1984; Serapio, 1995). Other variations in the use of the term occur in its operationalization for research purposes. One such study, involving the subsidiaries of Japanese companies in the USA, has operationalized the term as the percentage of total managers accounted for by host-country (US) nationals, and has traced these percentages over a five-year time series, beginning with the start of operations in the host country (Serapio, 1995). Another example of the term's operationalization is provided by a study of subsidiaries of companies having their corporate head-quarters. Comparisons are made of the percentages of managers accounted for by host-country nationals at top, middle, and lower level positions (Negandhi and Welge, 1984).

Bibliography

Negandhi, A. & Welge, M. (1984). *Beyond Theory Z: Globalization Strategies of American, German, and Japanese Multinational Companies*, Greenwich, CT: JAI Press.
Serapio, M. (1995). Management localization in Japanese subsidiaries in the United States. Shenkar, O., *Global Perspectives on Human Resource Management*, Englewood Cliffs, NJ: Prentice-Hall.

MANUEL G. SERAPIO JR

management prerogatives   Management prerogatives are those rights of a management to direct its workforce which have not been restricted by COLLECTIVE BARGAIN-ING. Many labor agreements specify a "management rights" or "residual rights" clause that all those rights which have not been specifically restricted or modified by a specific provision of the labor agreement remain exclusively with management.

JOHN C. SHEARER

managerial behavior   The behavior of managers has been the subject of research since the 1950s. This research, prompted partly by an academic concern to examine how far management theory applied in practice and partly by a practical concern to furnish evidence on which management education, training/development, recruitment, and PER-FORMANCE APPRAISAL might be based, has occurred in a variety of contexts and has employed a variety of methods.

Clearly, what constitutes "managerial behavior" depends on how "managers" and "behavior" are defined. Conventionally, managers have been regarded as those taking responsibility for the work of at least one other individual and designated as "managers" by their employing organization. However, with the diminution of hierarchy and the erosion of departmentalization and line-staff distinctions, together with the concomitant growth of self-managed teams, JOB ENRICHMENT and cross-functional projects, the boundaries between managers, professionals, and non-managers have become less clear-cut. Distinguishing exclusively *managerial* behavior is increasingly difficult. Moreover, since "management," as a broad process, is not synonymous with what "managers," as an occupational category, do, the claim of some research on managerial behavior to have "disproved" classical management theory is questionable.

As for "behavior," research faces the problem of distinguishing among managerial *work*, *jobs* as clusters of work and *behavior* within jobs; between what managers are *expected* to do and what they *actually* do; and between the *ends* (tasks/responsibilities) and *means* (actions/behavior) of managerial work. In practice, studies of actual behavior in the context of jobs defined organizationally as "managerial" have predominated. From these have resulted conceptual models which seek to depict and explain managerial behavior and a set of empirical findings which shed light on its content and form.

Among the models which have been developed are: the conception of managers as subject to "demands," "constraints," and "choices" (Stewart, 1982; 1991); managerial work as a configuration of "interpersonal," "informational," and "decisional" roles (Mintzberg, 1973); the view of managers developing and pursuing "agendas" through "networks" of contacts (Kotter, 1982); analysis of the "expectations" surrounding managerial positions (Machin, 1982); and the notion of how different "managerial divisions of labor" impinge on managerial behavior (Hales, 1993). These models demonstrate a discernible shift over time away from viewing managerial behavior as an aggregate of static elements toward a greater appreciation of its dynamic and processual character.

Research findings demonstrate both commonalities and variations in managerial behavior. The *content* of managerial behavior (i.e., *what* managers do) commonly involves both specialist/professional and general managerial elements, with the latter including some combination of:

1. Acting as a figurehead, representative, and point of contact of a work unit or team.
2. Monitoring and disseminating information.
3. Negotiating with subordinates, superiors, colleagues, and those outside the organization.
4. Monitoring workflow, handling disturbances, and problem solving.
5. Allocating human, material, and financial resources.
6. Recruiting, training, directing, and controlling staff.
7. Networking, forming contacts, and liaising with others.

8. Innovating, by seeking new objectives or methods of working.
9. Planning and scheduling work.
10. Engaging in "informal" activities such as instrumental socializing and organizational POLITICS.

The *form* of managerial behavior (*how* managers work) commonly exhibits the following characteristics:

(a) Fragmentation, with commuting between short, interrupted activities.
(b) Frequent reaction to, rather than initiation of, events and the requests of others.
(c) A concern with ad hoc, day-to-day exigencies.
(d) NEGOTIATION over the boundaries, content, and style of performance of the manager's job.
(e) Embeddedness, with decisions and plans developed in the course of other activities.
(f) A high level of interaction with others, often face-to-face.
(g) Pressure, CONFLICT, and contradictory demands.
(h) A degree of choice over what gets done and how.

Whilst these basic characteristics have remained fairly stable over time, a number of important developments and shifts in emphasis have taken place, stemming from increasingly fluid and ambiguous managerial job responsibilities. In particular, managers' behavior has become less focused on allocating and administering resources within a clearly defined work unit and more concerned with innovating, securing resources, and activities which span unit and organizational boundaries. Consequently, it has become more fragmented, exigent, embedded, and interactive, concerned less with vertical relationships, involving the direction and CONTROL of subordinates, more with horizontal and external relationships, involving networking, and negotiation with a broad set of constituencies.

As well as these variations over time, there are also well-documented variations in managerial behavior by individual, position, function, organization, industry, and culture. Variations in ROLE configurations, balance of work content, allocation of time, work patterns, contact patterns, interaction with others, and degree of choice have all been demonstrated (Stewart, 1991). One problem, however, is that some of this variation is as much an artefact of different research approaches as a reflection of substantive differences in managerial behavior. Consequently, studies reliant on single methods, such as diaries, observation or structured questionnaires, have given way to multimethod studies. The body of knowledge on managerial behavior remains somewhat disconnected, however.

Constructing a more integrated framework for analyzing managerial behavior is, therefore, one of a number of likely future developments in the field. Tackling the question of what constitutes *effective* managerial behavior is another, given the importance attached to managerial activity as a determinant of organizational performance. Only recently has research addressed this question directly (Luthans, Hodgetts, & Rosencrantz 1988), not least because of difficulties in establishing agreed criteria of effectiveness (*see* ORGANIZATIONAL EFFECTIVENESS). Thus, whether the reactive, fragmentary, and exigent nature of much managerial behavior indicates managerial ineffectiveness in applying rational planning and control or an effective way of handling the ambiguities of managing within complex organizations remains a matter of debate.

The connection between managerial behavior and its context requires further exploration and explanation in the light of current changes to that context. The link between BUREAUCRACY and managerial behavior is well documented (Hannaway, 1989; Jackall, 1989) but rapid organizational RESTRUCTURING means that the general relationship between forms of organization structure/culture and managerial behavior needs to be better understood. So too does the influence of national culture on managerial behavior, given the increasing internationalization of managerial relationships and careers (*see* INTERNATIONAL HUMAN RESOURCE MANAGEMENT; EXPATRIATES).

see also **Job design; Leadership; International management; Women managers**

Bibliography

Hales, C. P. (1986). What do managers do? A critical review of the evidence. Journal of Management Studies, 23, (1), 88–115.
Hales, C. P. (1993). Managing through organisation. London: Routledge.
Hannaway, J. (1989). Managers managing: The workings of an administrative system. Oxford, UK: Oxford University Press.
Jackall, R. (1989). Moral mazes: The world of corporate managers. Oxford, UK: Oxford University Press.
Kotter, P. (1982). The general managers. New York: Free Press.
Luthans, F., Hodgetts, R. M. & Rosencrantz, S.A. (1988). Real managers. Cambridge, MA: Ballinger.
Machin, J. L. J. (1982). The expectations approach. Maidenhead, UK: McGraw-Hill.
Mintzberg, H. (1973). The nature of managerial work. New York: Harper & Row.
Stewart, R. (1982). Choices for the manager. Englewood Cliffs, NJ: Prentice-Hall.
Stewart, R. (1991). Managing today and tomorrow. Basingstoke, UK: Macmillan.

COLIN L. HALES

managerial ethics and the ethical role of the manager The ethical dimension of management is determined by the social role that managers are understood as playing. Three possibilities are especially worthy of consideration. They are: principal or client, that managers are trustees for various corporate constituencies, and that managers are partners with governmental officials in an integrated system of political authority.

If managers are agents acting on behalf of a principal/client, the moral dimension of management is the same as in any agency relationship (*see* AGENCY THEORY) In such a relationship, the agent consents to act on behalf of and under the direction of the principal, who in turn consents to have the agent's actions count as the principal's for moral or legal purposes. The duties of an agent are performance (to do what he or she has undertaken to do), obedience (to accept the reasonable directions of the principal, which may involve performing the undertaken task in what seems to be a mistaken way), and loyalty (not to act contrary to the interests of the principal).

The moral strength of these duties is influenced by the intrinsic moral importance of the task the agent has undertaken to perform, but is not exhausted by it. The duties of an agent can have considerable moral force even when the task undertaken has no intrinsic moral importance if the interests of the principal would be seriously damaged by failure to perform the task, or to perform it well. Of special significance here is the case where the principal is not knowledgeable enough to determine whether the agent is performing well or to instruct the agent on how to proceed. The problem of the control of an expert agent by a relatively inexpert principal is sometimes called an "agency problem."

The model of agency is applicable to the provision of many professional services, and it is characteristic of paradigmatic professions such as the law that the agent is much more knowledgeable than the principal/client. Thus the moral problems that arise when an agent has expertise that the principal lacks are central to professional ethics. In addition to prohibitions against exploiting the vulnerability of the principal/client, professional ethics may call for the abridgment of the duty of obedience. If employing the means suggested by an inexpert client would, in the judgment of the agent, be extremely foolish, the agent may have no duty to comply.

Managers of corporations are often thought to be agents of the shareholders, but this claim is not supported by the law. The law of corporations does not regard the directors (or the other managers) as having the same duties to the shareholders that agents have to principals. For example, one of the duties of agents is obedience to the reasonable directions of the principal or principals, but although shareholders sometimes make corporate decisions directly by voting their shares, corporate constitutions usually provide no way that the shareholders as a group can routinely give instructions to managers. And while legal relations do not necessarily determine moral relations, the lack of an institutional mechanism that would enable shareholders to give instructions to managers also argues against the view that managers function morally as the agents of the shareholders. The difficulties encountered in regarding the managers of corporations as agents of the shareholders leads to the second way of characterizing the moral dimension of management. This approach can be introduced by noticing that the idea that the primary moral task of managers is to serve the shareholders can be accommodated without regarding managers as agents of the shareholders. They can be regarded instead as trustees. A trustee has a FIDUCIARY DUTY to advance the interests of the beneficiary of the trust, but has no duty to obey the beneficiary. Even if legally managers are not trustees for the shareholders, the model of trusteeship may provide a more accurate representation of the moral relation between managers and shareholders than the model of agency.

The primary importance of the model of trusteeship, however, is that it provides an alternative way of accommodating the fact that the interests of the share-holders are not the only interests that managers must take into account. The model of agency accommodates this fact by saying that an agent may not do on behalf of a principal anything that would violate the rights of other people. A similar point can be made in connection with the model of trusteeship. A trustee may not advance the interests of a beneficiary in any way that would violate the rights of other people. But the model of trusteeship also seems to allow another possibility. We can say that, morally, managers have the status of trustees not only for the shareholders but also for some other groups.

This is the core of the "stakeholder" model of managerial ethics (see STAKEHOLDER THEORY). The fact that the interests of certain groups other than the shareholders – most importantly, employees, customers, suppliers, and neighbors of corporate facilities – are routinely affected by managerial decisions is registered by regarding them as having, like the shareholders, a "stake" in managerial decisions. And the idea of trusteeship is used to explain how these interests are to be reflected in managerial decision-making. Morally, managers are trustees for all routinely affected groups, with the same duty to protect or advance their interests (without violating the rights of people who fall outside them) that they have to protect or advance the interests of the shareholders.

This way of representing the moral significance of the interests of non-shareholders for managerial decision-making is not free of difficulty, however. There is no transaction that establishes a relation of trusteeship between non-shareholder groups and managers. Apparently, then, the possession by managers of this role must be derived from some general moral principle according to which each moral agent is a trustee for all others – or all others whose interests he or she routinely affects. But this drains from the role of trustee any distinctive content capable of distinguishing it from other relations in which individuals might stand to each other, and reveals the stakeholder view as a variant of the moral theory of utilitarianism, according to which each is required to maximize the total aggregate satisfaction of all affected interests.

Whether or not the stakeholder view is best regarded as a variant of utilitarianism, it shares an important defect with utilitarianism. It provides no way of regarding some, but not all, interests routinely affected by managerial decisions as creating legitimate moral claims. If we wish to characterize routinely affected interests in a way that reflects such distinctions, the conceptual apparatus of rights or fairness with which we started is preferable. Some interests are such that frustrating them violates stringent rights or constitutes serious unfairness, while others, equally strongly felt by those whose interests they are, lack this feature. So a right-based way of representing the moral claims of non-shareholders, whether routinely affected or not, actually yields a subtler view than the stakeholder theory. The members of routinely affected groups sometimes have rights that constrain what managers may do to promote narrower organizational goals.

There is a third way of understanding the social role of managers. Managers can be regarded as serving not the shareholders, or all the stakeholders, but rather as serving the employees. On this view, the shareholders join consumers, suppliers, and neighbors as an affected group that has a right to fair treatment in the course of managerial efforts to promote narrower organizational goals. To be more precise, they become investors, understood as suppliers of a certain kind – suppliers of capital – who have a right to a fair price for what they provide, which in this case means an adequate return on investment. But they have no right that managers derive organizational goals from their interests. These goals are rather determined by the concerns, especially the moral concerns, of the employees.

The justification for this way of looking at the social role of managers arises from an important difference between employees and other groups affected by managerial decisions. Managers have authority over employees. But where there is authority, consideration must be given to what makes it legitimate. In the governmental sphere, legitimate authority is authority that serves the interests of those over whom it is exercised. Legitimate rulers rule in the interests of the governed. That is, they have the job of facilitating mutually beneficial cooperation among the governed. If managerial authority is relevantly similar to governmental authority, then managers should be regarded not as servants of the shareholders or all the stakeholders, but as servants of the employees with the task of facilitating mutually beneficial cooperation among them.

If managers have this social role, their primary moral duty is to exercise authority in a way that enables the employees more successfully to achieve their moral aims in their work (while appropriately respecting the rights of other groups). To the extent that managers are understood as exercising the legal property rights of non-employee owners, these must be defined so that the directive power they confer on managers does not exceed legitimate authority.

This approach can be challenged by questioning whether managerial authority is relevantly similar to the authority of governments. Earlier we saw that the law of corporations does not regard managers as agents of the shareholders. But legally, employees often have the status of agents of their employers. In corporate contexts, this means that employees are agents of the corporation that employs them. Managers are supervising agents to whom the corporation's authority as principal has been delegated. Viewed in this way, managerial authority is different from the authority of governments. On standard contractarian political theories, for example, the people are not the agents of the state; rather the government is an agent or trustee of the people. Defenders of this third view of the social role of managers must, then, do more than simply point out that managerial authority has to be legitimate. They must vindicate the claim that what makes managerial authority legitimate is the same thing that makes the authority of governments legitimate. One way of doing this is explored in McMahon (1994).

In the political sphere, it is generally accepted that cooperation-facilitating authority should be democratically exercised, at least in the sense that those exercising it should be elected by those over whom it is exercised. So this third approach points to the conclusion that managers should be elected by the employees. But legitimate social purposes may be served by corporate constitutions that also give investors some role in choosing managers – as in the system of codetermination – and strong unions may provide a way of satisfying the demand for democracy without instituting the election of managers by employees.

On all the moral structure of managerial decision-making is the same. There is some goal that managers are understood as responsible for promoting, and there are constraints, deriving from rights, on what managers may do to promote these goals. The three views differ only on what the goal of managers is: either to advance the interests of the shareholders, to advance the aggregate interests of all the stakeholders, or to facilitate mutually beneficial cooperation among the employees. Ordinarily, constraints deriving from rights limit absolutely what can be done to

promote non-moral goals, but it may be possible to regard some managerial goals as underwritten by deeper moral considerations. In cases of this sort, the constraints on managerial action provided by rights may have to be balanced against the moral benefits associated with the goals. Many moral problems have this structure.

A further question can be raised about the moral dimension of management. Are the moral considerations that managers face the same as those faced by ordinary citizens, or are the requirements of morality strengthened or weakened in the domain of management? Two possibilities must be distinguished here.

The first is that although the moral considerations that managers face in their capacity as managers are the same as those faced in ordinary life, the factual situation of managers combines with these considerations in such a way that actions that would be impermissible for ordinary citizens become permissible for managers. For example, the closing of a plant may devastate a whole town, and an ordinary citizen would not normally be justified in doing something that had this effect. But managers may be faced with a situation in which the failure to take this step would result in greater losses to the employees and others down the road, and thus the balance of ordinary moral considerations may justify it.

The second way that managerial morality could depart from ordinary morality is that managers could face a different set of moral considerations than ordinary citizens. Of particular interest here is the idea that in the world of business, some ways of treating people that would ordinarily be prohibited are permissible. This point must be distinguished from the previous one. The claim is not that moral considerations applicable to all sometimes justify managers in performing actions that ordinary citizens would not be justified in performing, but rather that certain moral considerations applicable to ordinary life are inapplicable to the business world.

This claim is dubious, however. Managerial ethics depends on the social role of management, and it is hard to think of any legitimate social purposes that would be served by regarding the world of business as one in which some ordinary moral considerations do not apply. The closest we can come is to make the converse point. There is a class of moral considerations that identify social states of affairs the promotion or maintenance of which is important from the moral point of view. These morally important social values include the preservation of the environment, the advancement of knowledge, the development of culture, the fostering of community, the promotion of social prosperity, and the protection of public health. Considerations of this kind have little significance outside organizational contexts since nothing much can be done to affect them. Thus they are not a part of the morality of ordinary life. But like governmental officials, the managers of large non-governmental organizations must take these values into account, and the moral desirability of promoting them may sometimes outweigh – and thus justify departing from – more familiar moral considerations. To say this, however, is to say that managers must be sensitive to more, rather than fewer, moral considerations than ordinary people.

Bibliography

Dahl, R. (1985). *A Preface to Economic Democracy*. Berkeley: University of California Press.

Frascona, J. (1964). *Agency*. Englewood Cliffs, NJ: Prentice-Hall.

Goldman, A. (1980). *The Moral Foundations of Professional Ethics*. Totowa, NJ: Rowman and Littlefield.

Mason, E. (1959). *The Corporation in Modern Society*. Cambridge, Mass.: Harvard University Press.

McMahon, C. (1994). *Authority and Democracy: A General Theory of Government and Management*. Princeton: Princeton University Press.

Nagel, T. (1978). Ruthlessness in public life. In S. Hampshire *Public and Private Morality*. Cambridge: Cambridge University Press, 75-91.

CHRISTOPHER MCMAHON

managerial value differences   Managerial value differences in the cross-cultural context require that we take into consideration the interaction of the personal values of managers – as influenced by their cultural heritage – and the work environment demands – as influenced by the political and economic ideology of the country. Specifically, cultural influences are those that differentiate one society or one societal cluster from another (e.g. Eastern, Western). History, religion, and proximity tend to be important factors in differentiating the cultural values of societies (Ronen and Shenkar, 1985). Conversely, ideological influences (e.g. capitalism, socialism) tend to emanate from the economic and political systems within which an individual must function (Ricks et al., 1990). Therefore, cultural influences tend to reflect regional differences, while ideological influences tend to be more cosmopolitan in that these influences tend to be shared across societies with common business ideologies.

Thus, both culture and ideology shape managerial values. The more unique one culture is from another and/or the more unique one ideology is from another, the more likely it is that the managers from these various culture–ideology mixes will differ in their values and the resultant work behaviors that they exhibit to perform their managerial duties (Ralston et al., 1993). The importance of recognizing the causes of these differences and understanding how to deal with them lies in the need to function efficiently and effectively in the global environment, even when this environment is markedly different from the typical domestic situation with which the manager is familiar.

Managerial value differences manifest themselves in organizations in a wide variety of ways and behaviors. These differences frequently can be observed in managers' degree of delegation, respect for authority, individual versus group orientation, means of communications, ethical standards, and style of motivation and leadership.

Bibliography

Ralston, D. A., Gustafson, D. J., Cheung, F. & Terpstra, R. H. (1993). Differences in managerial values: a study of US, Hong Kong, and PRC managers. *Journal of International Business Studies*, **24**, 249–75.

Ricks, D. A., Toyne, B. & Martinez, Z (1990). Recent developments in international management research. *Journal of Management*, **16**, 219–53.

Ronen, S. & Shenkar, O. (1985). Clustering countries on attitudinal dimensions: a review and synthesis. *Academy of Management Review*, **10**, 435–54.

DAVID A. RALSTON

managing the human resource planning process   Human resource planning may be done in response to the organization business planning process or as an integral part of the business planning process. Whichever the approach, certain initial steps need to be followed (Jarrell, 1993, pp. 146–53):

(1) Set objectives for the planning process. Although specific objectives will vary depending on the needs of particular organizations, the main objective must be to bring about focused management of the human resources of the organization.

(2) Identify key participants. Planning should begin with participants who played key roles in the management of human resources in the past. Participants may change as the planning process evolves, but at a minimum should include the chief executive officer, the chief human resource officer, and selected line managers. Human resource specialists, as well as other members of the organization, may be added as the need for specific planning knowledge and skills becomes apparent.

(3) Establish that part of the organization philosophy or mission statement that concerns human resources.

(4) Collect information about that part of the organizational environment of importance to human resource management (*see* ENVIRONMENTAL SCANNING). Sectors of the environment of special importance to human resource planning are cultural, demographic, economic, political, social, and technological.

(5) Compare the human resource competencies of the organization with those of competitors. This comparison will help to determine strategies appropriate for the organization.

(6) Formulate a HUMAN RESOURCE STRATEGY. A strategy may be as simple as the decision to excel in one of the classical human resource management functions, such as staffing or development. Or a strategy may be a bundle of interrelated human resource activities that cut across traditional functional lines (MacDuffie, 1995).

(7) Implement the chosen strategies. Implementation requires a long-term collaborative effort by human resource professionals and line managers. Steps must be taken to insure that control systems applied to this strategy implementation are appropriate for the longer term (Hain, 1983).

(8) Evaluate the planning process in terms of its expected outcomes, both direct and indirect (Hax, 1985).

(9) Manage issues that arise under the strategic plan. Issues should be used as feedback for improving the planning process and keeping it current. Issues management normally is more efficient if done for the human resource function as part of an organization-wide effort.

The planning process outlined above can be used where a formal approach is needed as a guide and where little or no pre-existing information and planning methodology have been accumulated. As the planning process evolves, planners should tailor the planning process to their unique needs.

Bibliography

Hain, T. (1983). Commentary on Dyer. *Human Resource Management*, **22**, 272–3.

Hax, C. (1985). A new competitive weapon: the human resource strategy. *Training and Development Journal*, **89**, 76–82.

Jarrell, D. W. (1993). *Human Resource Planning: a Business Planning Approach*, Englewood Cliffs, NJ: Prentice-Hall.

MacDuffie, J. P. (1995). Human resource bundles and manufacturing performance: organizational logic and flexible production systems in the world auto industry. *Industrial and Labor Relations Review*, **48**, 197–221.

DONALD W. JARRELL

marginal cost   The marginal cost is the change in total costs due to a unit (or incremental) change in output. For discrete changes in output, marginal cost is given by:

$$MC = \frac{\Delta TC}{\Delta q} \qquad (1)$$

where MC is the marginal cost, ΔTC is the change in total costs, and Δq is the change in output. In the short run, fixed costs do not vary with output so marginal costs can also be written as:

$$MC - \frac{\Delta TVC}{\Delta q} \qquad (2)$$

where ΔTVC is the change in TOTAL VARIABLE COST. If the total cost function is known or has been estimated, marginal cost would be the derivative of total costs with respect to output. Therefore, if total costs are:

$$TC = 1000 + 5 \times q + 8 \times q^2 \qquad (3)$$

marginal costs would be:

$$MC = \frac{d TC}{dq} = 5 + 16 \times q \qquad (4)$$

Understanding marginal costs is crucial for optimal decision making because, unless there are resource constraints, any activity should be continued as long as the additional (or marginal) benefits exceed the marginal costs. If two or more activities have marginal benefits which exceed their marginal costs but a manager cannot fully fund all of them, then each activity should be funded until each provides the same marginal benefits per dollar. For any *change* in an activity (production, pricing, advertising, etc.) a manager must compare the marginal benefits of the change against the marginal costs to make the best decision.

For example, consider a manager whose only variable input is labor. The change in total costs will then be the change in labor input (ΔL) multiplied by the wage rate (w), and since marginal costs are the change in total variable costs divided by the change in quantity (Δq), from equation (2) we have:

$$MC = \frac{\Delta TVC}{\Delta q} = \frac{w \times \Delta L}{\Delta q} = w \times \left\{ \frac{\Delta L}{\Delta q} \right\} \qquad (5)$$

The term in braces is the inverse of the MARGINAL PRODUCT of labor, so (5) shows the relationship between marginal costs, variable input costs (the wage rate, w) and productivity (the marginal product of labor). An increase in the cost of variable inputs, w, will increase the marginal cost

of production while an increase in productivity (a rise in the marginal product of labor) will reduce marginal costs, as would be expected; see Shughart, Chappell and Cottle (1994) and Friedman (1976).

As Baumol (1977) notes, managers frequently use average values rather than marginal values when making decisions, and this can lead to incorrect conclusions. This occurs because much of the accounting information provided to managers is in the form of average or total figures. In addition, marginal calculations may require information a company does not yet have, such as the marginal benefits and costs of an increase in advertising. The important issue is not whether past advertising expenditures have generated net revenues which exceeded the costs, but whether any increase (or decrease) in advertising is justified. Finally, because marginal costs reflect the change in total costs for the last unit(s) produced, they reflect changes more quickly than average total costs which are based on the costs for all units produced to that point. Thus even if the average increase in net revenues from advertising fell by a small amount, the *marginal* change could be substantial and profits could be increased by reducing advertising expenditures.

Bibliography

Baumol, W. J. (1977). *Economic Theory and Operations Analysis*. Englewood Cliffs, NJ: Prentice Hall.

Douglas, E. J. (1992). *Managerial Economics*. 4th edn, Englewood Cliffs, NJ: Prentice-Hall.

Friedman, M. (1976). *Price Theory*. 2nd edn, Chicago: Aldine.

Shughart, W. F., Chappell, W. F. & Cottle, R. L. (1994). *Modern Managerial Economics*. Cincinatti, OH: South-Western Publishing.

ROBERT E. MCAULIFFE

marginal pricing   Marginal pricing is a term used to refer to those occasions when price is calculated to cover only the variable costs of production and/or distribution and little or no contribution is required towards fixed costs and profit margins. Clearly, this is an unusual and uneconomic level for prices and one which could not be sustained for long. Marginal pricing might be used during a temporary fall in demand (e.g., during an economic recession or a price war) to keep assets "ticking over" pending the return of more normal trading conditions. The alternative is to reduce radically (or even suspend) operations which can lead to even less attractive consequences such as deterioration of skills, reduced customer loyalty, loss of reputation, and erosion of brands. Marginal pricing might also be used to secure what is expected to be a favored position with respect to future sales (as with introductory offers).

DOMINIC WILSON

marginal product   The marginal product of any input, such as labor or capital, measures the change in total product as a result of a small change in the usage of that input, holding all other inputs constant. For example, the marginal product of labor or capital is the additional output from using one more labor or machine hour.

The marginal product of an input that is infinitely divisible can be obtained by taking the partial derivative of the production function with respect to that input. In the relevant range of production, marginal product is positive. An increase in the marginal product (or an increase in productivity) of an input means that through better technology, more efficient management, or an increase in work effort, the company is able to obtain more output from the same amount of inputs. Alternatively, marginal product can be improved through the restructuring of the company by decreasing the number of work hours while holding the addition to total output constant.

The total product and marginal product curves demonstrate the LAW OF VARIABLE PROPORTIONS which states that as the quantity of a variable input increases, holding the amount of other productive factors constant, beyond some point the marginal product of the variable input begins to decrease; total product continues to increase though at a decreasing rate. DIMINISHING RETURNS arise because the fixed amount of plant and equipment is gradually spread among an even greater number of workers, leaving a smaller amount of capital for each one.

By enabling us to measure the change in total product as a result of a change in a variable input, marginal product permits comparisons with the short run cost of production. If the costs of labor and machine hours are known, we can calculate the MARGINAL COST by dividing an input's cost by the marginal product of the input. Therefore, marginal costs are inversely related to the marginal product of the variable inputs. For example, when the marginal product of labor is falling, the marginal cost of output is increasing, and vice versa. When the marginal product of labor is constant, additional units can be produced with constant marginal cost.

Knowledge of the marginal products of inputs enables managers to determine the short-run optimal level of employment of capital and labor in the production process. To maximize total profit inputs should be hired up to the point where the marginal input cost equals the marginal revenue product of labor. Marginal input cost is defined as the amount that an additional unit of the variable input adds to total cost. Marginal revenue product is defined as the amount that an additional unit of the variable unit adds to total revenue and equals the marginal product of the variable input times the marginal revenue resulting from the increase in output produced.

Bibliography

Douglas, E. J. (1992). *Managerial Economics*. 4th edn, Englewood Cliffs, NJ: Prentice-Hall.
Shughart, W. F., Chappell, W. F. & Cottle, R. L. (1994). *Modern Managerial Economics*. Cincinatti, OH: South-Western Publishing.

LIDIJA POLUTNIK

marginal revenue   Marginal revenue is the change in the total revenue resulting from a one unit increase in the sales of a product. It is important to a firm because PROFIT MAXIMIZATION requires the firm's managers to find the output level where this extra revenue equals the MARGINAL COST of production. While greater sales resulting from price reductions generally cause marginal revenue to fall, marginal cost eventually rises with greater output. Thus, any output below the level where the two are equal leaves the possibility for additional profits to be made, but output

beyond that level costs more to produce than the gain in revenues from the additional sale.

The nature of the relation between marginal revenue and the level of output sold varies with the basic market structure under consideration (*see* BASIC MARKET STRUCTURES). Under PERFECT COMPETITION the firm, being too small to influence market outcomes, can sell as much output as it desires without changing the market price. As such, for any additional sales, the marginal revenue is constant at the level of the market generated price. In other words, the firm faces a demand which is perfectly elastic for its own product.

Under OLIGOPOLY and other forms of imperfect competition, additional sales may occur as a result of a change in the quality of the product or a change in advertising, or they may be brought about by a change in the product's price. The LAW OF DEMAND indicates that, all else being equal, an increase in the number of units sold requires a reduction in price. In the absence of PRICE DISCRIMINATION, the marginal revenue from an additional unit sold tends to decline as the lower price needed to generate a larger number of unit sales tends to more or less offset the gains from the increased quantity sold (*see* ELASTICITY). Moreover, the estimation of marginal revenue becomes more difficult in oligopoly since the amount of additional sales resulting from a price reduction depends in part on the reaction of rivals, who may or may not respond with price cuts of their own.

Bibliography

Carlton, D. W. & Perloff, J. M. (1994). *Modern Industrial Organization*. 2nd edn, New York: HarperCollins.
Douglas, E. (1992). *Managerial Economics: Analysis and Strategy*. 4th edn, Englewood Cliffs, NJ: Prentice-Hall.

GILBERT BECKER

marginal utility   Marginal utility is defined as the change in the total utility resulting from the consumption of one additional unit of a good by a consumer. For any individual good, consumer behavior typically follows the law of diminishing marginal utility which states that in any given time period, as the rate of consumption of a good rises, the additional utility, or satisfaction, acquired by the consumer eventually declines.

It can be shown that for an individual who is purchasing several goods simultaneously, the maximization of total utility requires equating the marginal utility per dollar spent on each good. More formally, this ideal combination of goods occurs when

$$\text{MU}_1/P_1 = \text{MU}_2/P_2 = \ldots = \text{MU}_i/P_i \qquad (1)$$

where MU and P indicate the marginal utility and price of the ith good. An imbalance between any two of these ratios, for example

$$\text{MU}_2/P_2 > \text{MU}_1/P_1 \qquad (2)$$

would result in a situation where a reallocation of the consumer's income toward purchasing more of good 2 would cause a net increase in total utility. This is because the additional satisfaction gained from consumption of an extra unit of good 2 would more than offset the loss of utility from the decreased consumption of good 1. An inequality such as in equation (2) would occur if, for example, the price of the second good, P_2, was decreased. The equation demonstrates why a decrease in the price of this good would lead to a shifting away from good 1 and an increase in the purchase of good 2. This helps to generate the negative relationship between the price of good 2 and its quantity demanded, which is the foundation of the LAW OF DEMAND. Similarly, equation (2) can be used to demonstrate how a manager may create a more favorable position for a product by using increased advertising. This strategy, when successful, creates imbalances between the ratios by altering the marginal utility of one good relative to the others.

The marginal utility of income, to a gambler, or profit, to an investor, can be used to identify the three categories of risk behavior which individuals may portray. An individual is identified as a risk lover if his marginal utility of income grows as his level of income rises. An individual is said to show RISK AVERSION if the marginal utility of an extra dollar of income falls as income rises, and risk neutrality if the marginal utility of an extra dollar of income is constant. A risk averter typically sees risk as being undesirable and is only willing to tolerate greater uncertainty in an outcome if rewarded with a greater expected return. A risk lover is a gambler who prefers the increased uncertainty.

Bibliography

Douglas, E. (1992). *Managerial Economics: Analysis and Strategy*. 4th edn, Englewood Cliffs, NJ: Prentice-Hall.

Mansfield, E. (1993). *Managerial Economics: Theory, Applications, and Cases*. 2nd edn, New York: Norton.

GILBERT BECKER

market The term "market" is clearly an important concept in the field of marketing, yet while much debate has taken place on what constitutes an appropriate definition of "MARKETING," less attention has been directed in marketing literature toward the nature of markets. This is increasingly being recognized as an omission, given that many analytical techniques rely on concepts such as MARKET SHARE and MARKET SEGMENTATION (Curran & Goodfellow, 1990).

The original use of the term "market" referred to a physical location where buyers and sellers come together in order to exchange products and services. Since then, the term has been developed in the field of economics to refer variously to any network of dealings between buyers and sellers of a particular product, or to refer to products which are regarded as close substitutes. The latter is often referred to as the substitutability criteria, two products being contained in the same market where the cross-elasticity of demand between the two is greater than a pre-assigned number (x). However, there is little agreement in the field as to the criteria by which x might be specified.

Elsewhere, the term "market" has been used extensively to describe aggregate demand for a specific product (the "automobile" market) or in a specific physical area (the "European market"). Markets have also been viewed in broader "need" terms (the "transportation" market) and demographic terms (the "female" market) or any combination of these variables.

In contemporary marketing, however, the "market" is most commonly used to refer to the existing or target group of customers for a particular product or service. For example: "All the potential customers sharing a particular need or want who might be willing or able to engage in exchange to satisfy that need or want" (Kotler, 1991, p. 8). "Individuals who, in the past, have purchased a given class of product" (Sissors, 1966). "An aggregate of people who, as individuals or organisations, have needs for products in a product class and who have the ability, willingness and authority to purchase such products . . . people seeking products in a specific category" (Dibb et al., 1991). This view is endorsed in the literature on MARKET SEGMENTATION, the process by which overall market definition is subdivided into identifiable sets of buyers similar in terms of demographic, psychographic, or other profiles.

The prevalent view is, then, one of markets as units of analysis with clearly defined boundaries. Yet perspectives offered elsewhere suggest a somewhat more complex understanding of markets. Strategic management literature offers a number of further perspectives, Abell (1980), for example, proposing a three-dimensional concept of markets, with the dimensions as customer group (who is being served with respect to factors such as demographics, user industry, or buyer behavior); customer function (what "need" is being satisfied); and technology (how the customer function is being satisfied). A "market" is consequently defined by the performance of given functions in given customer groups and includes all the substitutable technologies to perform these functions. Such definitions recognize that competing suppliers may define a market in different ways, as may individuals at different levels within the same organization, a recognition shared by Day (1981), who identifies two different perspectives for defining markets, top down and bottom up. Top down, or strategic, definitions reflect the needs of strategists to understand the capacity and competitive potential of the business and specify markets in terms of organizational competitive capabilities and resource transferability. Bottom up, or operational, definitions reflect the narrower tactical concern of marketing managers and define markets in terms of patterns of customer requirements, usage situations, and "needs," which can be served in many ways.

Another dimension of market definition is apparent in the literature on BUSINESS-TO-BUSINESS MARKETING, where it is recognized that the importance of individual customers is often considerable and the relevance of aggregate markets therefore lessened. Here, the concept of a "market" might refer to only a single customer (see Grönroos, 1989, for further discussion of this).

A number of authors have also identified a disparity between the way markets are defined in marketing literature and in practice. Jenkins et al. (1994) elicited definitions of the term "market" from a sample of marketing managers and found that the majority tended to define markets in terms of products or channels (e.g., "the food retail market"), with only a minority of the sample offering definitions in terms of groups of consumers.

It is accepted by some authors at least, then, that the understanding of markets is likely to vary to a greater or lesser extent from marketer to marketer even within a particular organization, significantly from organization to organization with similar offerings, and radically from sector to sector. Others further assert that "the market," whether defined in terms of existing or potential customers, products, or organizational capabilities, is a volatile concept, where boundaries are arbitrary and seldom clear-cut, where definitions are multi-dimensional, and where perspectives shift with changing individual, corporate, and user views of product offerings and changes in the nature and availability of these offerings (see Curran & Goodfellow, 1990; Jenkins et al., 1994).

Bibliography

Abell, D. F. (1980). *Defining the business: The starting point of strategic planning.* Englewood Cliffs, NJ: Prentice-Hall.

Curran, J. G. M. & Goodfellow, J. H. (1990). Theoretical and practical issues in the definition of market boundaries. *European Journal of Marketing,* **24**, (1), 16–28.

Day, G. S. (1981). Strategic market analysis and definition: An internal approach. *Strategic Management Journal,* **2**, 281–299.

Dibb, S., Simkin, L., Pride, W. M. & Ferrell, O. C. (1991). *Marketing: Concepts and strategies.* European edn, London: Houghton Mifflin Co.

Grönroos, C. (1989). Defining marketing: A market-oriented approach. *European Journal of Marketing,* **23**, (1), 52–60.

Jenkins, M., le Cerf, E. & Cole, T. (1994). How managers define consumer markets. In M. Jenkins & S. Knox (Eds), *Advances in consumer marketing.* The Cranfield Management Research Series. London: Kogan Page.

Kotler, P. (1991). *Marketing management: Analysis, planning.* Englewood Cliffs, NJ: Prentice-Hall.

Sissors, J. (1966). What is a market? *Journal of Marketing,* **30**, (3), July, 17–21.

FIONA LEVERICK

market definition An economic definition of the term "market" is the group of all firms willing and able to sell a similar product or service to the same potential buyers. As such, the market definition for a given product is the identification of the relevant group of sellers which may be seen as being in competition with one another for the sale of a particular product. Two boundaries are used to define a market:

(1) the product boundary and
(2) the geographic boundary.

Properly identifying these boundaries for a particular market will result in a more accurate count of the number and size distribution of firms in that market. This information is useful for a firm in developing its competitive strategy. The information is essential for the government and the courts in developing ANTITRUST POLICY and in deliberating antitrust cases. For example, the Clayton Act proscribes mergers which substantially lessen competition "in any line of commerce" (i.e. product market) and "in any section of the country" (i.e. geographic market).

The central issues in market definition are where and how these boundaries are to be drawn. Various theoretical and practical tests have been developed. The relevant product market boundary determines a set of competitors in terms of the substitutability of the product. For markets under PERFECT COMPETITION the product boundary is relatively easy to establish since the product is homogeneous across firms. Where PRODUCT DIFFERENTIATION exists, this boundary becomes blurred. Here, cross elasticities are tools which have been used for decades.

The cross elasticity of demand between two goods measures the percentage change in unit sales of one firm's product given a 1 percent change in the price of a rival's product. As such it measures the degree to which the two goods are substitutes in the eyes of consumers. A high cross elasticity measure indicates close substitutability and thus the firms in question should be counted as being in the same market. Similarly, cross elasticities of supply must be considered. High values for this measure indicate a firm's willingness and ability to produce more of their own good in reaction to a rival's price increase. It may also indicate a similarity in technological process between firms and the potential to switch product lines and readily and easily enter a product market where price has been increased above the competitive level. For antitrust purposes, the condition of entry is important to evaluate as potential entry often can diminish the effectiveness of existing firms' attempts to abuse market power. As a result, both measures of cross elasticities are needed to properly define the relevant product market.

Scherer and Ross (1990), and others have identified several difficulties arising in the application of these measures. First, what constitutes a "high" value for cross elasticity is necessarily an arbitrary decision. Second, two different estimates for the cross elasticity of demand between two goods A and B will be generated for the relatively similar cases of a 1 percent price increase in product A and a 1 percent price decrease in product B. Third, the correct estimation of elasticities requires using price changes originating from the competitive price level. As a result, the courts have also attempted to generate "common sense" product market definitions by identifying product groups in terms of their different product attributes.

One theoretically appealing new method for market boundary delineation, developed by Boyer (1979), has recently been put to use by the federal government. Boyer argues that a market can be identified, from the point of view of a single firm, as the smallest group of rivals necessary to organize in order to successfully act as a cartel. If this group of firms could raise prices without bringing about reaction by other firms which was sufficient to force a retreat in the cartel price hike, then these other firms can correctly be seen as being outside of the market. This may be due to their producing a sufficiently different (non-substitutable) product, or because of the fact that their business takes place in a geographically distinct location. If, on the other hand, the initial group of firms in question could not successfully collude for a significant period of time without feeling the disciplinary effects of the other rivals increasing their supply, then the relevant market should be expanded to include these firms. One nice feature of this method is that it can be used to define the relevant geographic market as well as the product market boundary.

In revising its guidelines for mergers in 1982, the Department of Justice introduced a variation of Boyer's method to define markets. The method uses what is known as the 5 percent rule, or SSNIP (a small but significant non-transitory increase in prices). This involves examining a hypothetical monopolist existing at the site of the proposed merger and evaluating its ability to raise price (by 5 percent) above the current level for a sustained period. If the potential SSNIP would not be successful in the eyes of antitrust officials because of the reactions of rivals outside of the area being considered, the definition of the market will be expanded. This method, with modest revisions, was retained in the most recent 1992 merger guidelines.

The proper definition of the relevant market can be crucial in these and other antitrust cases. An expanded market definition which includes a greater number of rivals will naturally tend, for example, to diminish the market share of the merging firms and thus make the merger less potentially onerous in the eyes of the antitrust enforcers. Boyer's work recognized that problems similar to those involved in the use of cross elasticities still exist with the new approach. Moreover Scherer and Ross argue that the use of the 5 percent rule in a market in which market power already exists will tend to yield biased market definitions which could increase the likelihood of allowing mergers which are being examined.

see also **Merger guidelines, 1992**

Bibliography

Boyer, K. (1979). Industry boundaries. Calvani, T. & Siegfried, J. *Economic Analysis and Antitrust Law*. Boston: Little, Brown.

Greer, D. (1992). *Industrial Organization and Public Policy*. 3rd edn, New York: Macmillan.

Howard, M. (1983). *Antitrust and Trade Regulation*. Englewood Cliffs, NJ: Prentice-Hall.

Scherer, F. & Ross, D. (1990). *Industrial Market Structure and Economic Performance*. 3rd edn, Boston: Houghton Mifflin.

US Department of Justice, & Federal Trade Commission (1992). *Horizontal Merger Guidelines*. Washington DC: US Government Printing Office.

GILBERT BECKER

market demand   The term market demand most usually refers to the total demand for a product or service over a specific period of time. It is used in relation to either individual products or services or product or service categories.

FIONA LEVERICK

market efficiency   The term market efficiency is used to explain the relationship between information and share prices in the capital market literature. Although the tests of market efficiency were reported as early as 1900, it was not until 1953 that the idea of market efficiency was put forward by Maurice Kendall. The concept was a byproduct of a chance discovery through his paper on behavior of prices of stocks and commodities. He discovered that security prices follow a random walk that implied that price changes were independent of one another. The formal definition of "market efficiency" was given by Fama (1970). Fama classified market efficiency into three categories namely, weak form, semi-strong form, and strong form. According to Fama a market is efficient in weak form if stock price changes cannot be predicted based on past returns, and semi-strong efficient if stock prices instantaneously reflect any new publicly available information. The strong form of the market efficiency hypothesis states that prices reflect all types of information whether available publicly or privately.

The weak form of the market efficiency hypothesis is that stock returns are serially uncorrelated and have a constant mean. The market is considered weak-form efficient if current prices fully reflect all information contained in historical prices, which implies that no investor can devise a trading rule based on past price patterns to earn abnormal return. A weaker and economically more sensible version of the hypothesis says that prices reflect information to the point where the marginal benefits of acting on the information (profits to be made) do not exceed the marginal costs (Jensen, 1978). This view led to many early tests of weak-form efficiency and has influenced the interpretations of the various anomalies in stock returns that have been documented so far.

Based on mixed results for and against the efficient market hypothesis Fama (1991) made changes in all the three categories. In order to cover a more general area of testing weak form of market efficiency, tests for return predictability and forecasting of returns with variables like dividend yields, interest rates, etc. have been included. Also issues such as cross-sectional predictability for testing asset-pricing models and anomalies like size effect (Banz, 1981), seasonality of returns like the January effect (Keim, 1983; Roll, 1983) and day of the week effect (Cross, 1973; French, 1980) have been included under the theme of return predictability. In the semi-strong form of market efficiency it is assumed that the prices of securities will change immediately and rationally in response to new information and the market neither delays nor overreacts or underreacts in response to the new information. This means that investors cannot earn excess returns by developing trading rules based on publicly available information. When announcement of an event can be dated to the day, daily data allow precise measurement of the speed of the stock price response which is the central issue for market efficiency. Event studies have become an important part of research in capital markets since they come closest to allowing a break between market efficiency and equilibrium pricing issues and give direct and mostly supportive evidence on efficiency. Event studies such as those of Ahrony and Swary (1980), Mandelker (1974), and Kaplan (1989) document interesting regularities in response of stock prices to dividend decisions, changes in corporate control, etc.

Strong-form efficiency assumes that prices fully reflect all new information, public or private. The tests of private information help to ascertain whether such information is fully reflected in market prices. Fama (1991) reviews tests for private information and concludes that the profitability of insider trading is now established. Insider trading refers to the use of private information to earn abnormal profits. The evidence that some investment analysts have insider information (Jaffe, 1974; Ippolito, 1989) is balanced by evidence that they do not (Brinson et al., 1986; Elton et al., 1991). The concept of an efficient stock market has stimulated both insight and controversy since its introduction to the economics and financial literature. The efficient market hypothesis addresses the consequences of competition in financial markets in determining the equilibrium values of financial assets. Perhaps the most important implication of the hypothesis is that the market price of any security reflects the true, or rational, value of security; thus in an efficient market, investors are assured that the securities they purchase are fairly priced. A precondition for this strong version of the hypothesis is that information and trading costs, the costs of getting prices to reflect information, are zero.

The fact that in practice the investors have to incur trading costs and that not all behave homogeneously in response to the information has led to a huge amount of research producing evidence for and against the proposition that financial markets are efficient. However, in spite of these controversies the efficient market hypothesis has contributed to our understanding of how and when economic and industry information is encoded in the prices of securities. The hypothesis has also provided very useful insights on the role of information in determining stock prices.

The early evidence seemed unexpectedly consistent with the theory. The large amount of research in the area of market efficiency tests with the help of common models of market equilibrium like the one factor Sharpe–Lintner–Black (SLB) model, multifactor asset pricing models of Merton (1973) and Ross (1976), and consumption-based intertemporal asset pricing model of Rubinstein (1976), Lucas (1978), and Breeden (1979), provide evidence that the market efficiency is a maintained hypothesis.

However, several recent papers have uncovered empirical evidence which suggests that stock returns contain predictable components. Keim and Stambaugh (1986) find statistically significant predictability in stock prices using forecasts based on certain predetermined variables. Fama and French (1988) show that long-holding-period returns are significantly negatively serially correlated, implying that 25 to 40 percent of the variation of longer-horizon returns is predictable from the past returns. Lo and MacKinlay (1988) reject the random walk hypothesis and show that it is inconsistent with the stochastic behavior of weekly returns, especially for smaller capitalization stocks. Empirical evidence of anomalous return behavior in the form of variables like P/E ratio, market/book value ratio (Fama and French, 1992) has defied rational economic explanation and appears to have caused many researchers to strongly qualify their views on market efficiency.

The efficient market hypothesis is frequently misinterpreted to imply perfect forecasting abilities. In fact, it implies only that prices reflect all available information. When we talk of efficient markets, we mean that the market is functioning well and prices are fair. Thus in assessing the efficiency of the market on the basis of observed behavior of stock returns, and observed predictability of returns in particular, one must judge whether the observed behavior is rational. Given the subjectivity of judgment of rational behavior, it is not surprising that the question of whether markets are efficient is hotly debated.

Bibliography

Ahrony, J. & Swary, I. (1980). Quarterly dividend and earning announcements and stock holders returns: an empirical analysis. *Journal of Finance*, 35, 1–12.

Bachelier, L. (1900). *Théorie de la spéculation*. Paris: Gauthiers-Villars.

Banz, R. W. (1981). The relationship between return and market value of common stocks. *Journal of Financial Economics*, 9, 3–18.

Black, F. (1972). Capital market equilibrium with restricted borrowings. *Journal of Business*, 45, 444–65.

Breeden, D. T. (1979). An intertemporal asset pricing model with stochastic consumption and investment opportunities. *Journal of Financial Economics*, 7, 265–96.

Brinson, G. P., Hood, L. R. & Beebower, G. L. (1986). Determinants of portfolio performance. *Financial Analysts Journal*, 42, 39–44.

Cross, F. (1973). Price movements on Fridays and Mondays. *Financial Analysts Journal*, 29, 67–79.

Elton, E. J., Gruber, M. J., Das, S. & Hlavka, M. (1993). Efficiency with costly information: a reinterpretation of evidence from managed portfolios. *Review of Financial Studies*, 6, 1–22.

Fama, E. (1970). Efficient capital markets: a review of theory and empirical work. *Journal of Finance*, 25, 383–417.

Fama, E. F. (1991). Efficient capital markets II. *Journal of Finance*, 46, 1575–618.

Fama, E. F. & French, K. R. (1988). Permanent and temporary components of stock returns. *Journal of Political Economy*, 96, 246–73.

Fama, E. F. & French, K. R. (1992). The cross-section of expected stock returns. *Journal of Finance*, 47, 427–66.

French, K. R. (1980). Stock returns and the weekend effect. *Journal of Financial Economics*, 8, 55–69.

Ippolito, R. A. (1989). Efficiency with costly information: a study of mutual fund performance 1965–84. *Quarterly Journal of Economics*, 104, 1–23.

Jaffe, J. (1974). Special information and insider trading. *Journal of Business*, 47, 410–28.

Jensen, M. C. (1978). Some anomalous evidence regarding market efficiency. *Journal of Financial Economics*, 6, 95–101.

Kaplan, S. (1989). The effect of management buyouts on operating performance and value. *Journal of Financial Economics*, 24, 217–54.

Keim, D. B. (1983). Size-related anomalies and stock return seasonality. *Journal of Financial Economics*, 12, 13–32.

Keim, D. B. & Stambaugh, R. F. (1986). Predicting returns in stock and bond markets. *Journal of Financial Economics*, 17, 357–90.

Kendall, M. G. (1953). The analysis of economic time series. Part I: prices. *Journal of the Royal Statistical Society*, 96, 11–25.

Lintner, J. (1965). The valuation of risk assets and the selection of risky investments in stock portfolios and capital budgets. *Review of Economics and Statistics*, 47, 13–37.

Lo, A. W. & MacKinlay, A. C. (1988). Stock market pricetion test. *Review of Financial Studies*, 1, 41–66.

Lucas, R. E. (1978). Asset prices in an exchange economy. *Econometrica*, 46, 1429–45.

Mandelker, G. (1974). Risk and return: the case of merging firms. *Journal of Financial Economics*, 1, 303–36.

Merton, R. C. (1973). An intertemporal capital asset pricing model. *Econometrica*, 41, 867–87.

Roll, R. (1983). Vas ist das? "The turn of the year effect and the return premia of small firms." *Journal of Portfolio Management*, 9, 18–28.

Ross, S. A. (1976). The arbitrage theory of capital pricing. *Journal of Economic Theory*, 13, 341–60.

Rubinstein, M. (1976). The valuation of uncertain income streams and the pricing options. *Bell Journal of Economics*, 7, 407–25.

Sharpe, W. F. (1964). Capital asset prices: a theory of market equilibrium under conditions of risk. *Journal of Finance*, 19, 425–42.

SUNIL POSHAKWALE

market entry strategies A market entry strategy is the method chosen by a company to begin selling, or conduct other activities, in a foreign country. Entry into a foreign market can be as easy as picking up a telephone and contacting an overseas buyer for your goods. Entry could also involve a start-up operation which duplicates a company's operations in its home country. The type of market entry strategy chosen depends upon a number of factors, including the following: amount of available investment capital; degree of risk one is willing to assume; knowledge of foreign markets; knowledge of working with diverse cultures; knowledge of export/import transactions; available distribution systems; time commitment; ability to handle stress and uncertainty; potential profit; and a number of other factors as well. The following lists some of the more common market entry strategies.

1 Assembly operations – An organization sends parts for a product to a foreign plant for final assembly. The products are then sold in the foreign market or exported to other countries. Assembly plants may allow a company to take advantage of low cost labor in the most labor-intensive portion of production. There may also be lower duties and other taxes because unfinished products are imported instead of finished products. Assembly plants also allow a foreign manufacturer to meet host country requests for more domestic production while at the same time allowing the manufacturer to maintain control over production by using its own subproducts as supplies and materials for the foreign assembly plant. A potential problem, especially with plants located to pacify foreign governments needs for domestic production, is that the foreign government may institute quotas on the amount of foreign parts which may be used in the host country.

2 Contract manufacturing – Some companies use manufacturers in foreign countries to make (or assemble) their product and distribute them through the foreign manufacturer's existing marketing channels. Thus, entry to the country is achieved with the assistance of local companies using proven marketing channels. Although the cost of this type of method is usually a substantial portion of the product revenues, it allows a company to test the market for its goods and become more familiar with doing business overseas.

3 Exporting – This is one of the simplest methods of foreign market entry. The product is exported to a buyer who then distributes it to the foreign market. Market entry of the product is achieved without considerable investment of either time or capital. The key to exporting is knowing the components of the export transaction very well. If knowledge is not present there are a number of export agents available to assist the exporter of products (see EXPORT AGENT).

4 Joint venturing – A joint venture is an agreement between two companies to coproduce and distribute a product. A separate entity is commonly established to handle a joint-venture arrangement. Joint ventures normally involve a foreign company and a host country company. Some countries require some local equity participation in all companies operating within their borders. A joint venture is a way of meeting equity participation requirements. One of the major problems associated with joint ventures (in addition to usually high capital investment needs) is obtaining the right joint-venture partner. If partners are not compatible, do not understand each other's cultures, do not have a common language, or do not share basic intentions regarding the outcome of the joint venture, the chances of the arrangement succeeding are reduced.

5 Franchise agreement – This is an agreement in which a company holding the rights to a product, trademark, process, etc. allows another company to make and distribute the product or use the trademark under a contractual agreement. The franchise agreement spells out the details, which usually include the geographic area in which the franchise is good, the fees to be paid to the franchisor, as well as any other requirements the franchisor is able to place in the contract. A franchise agreement is a method of entering a foreign market by having a local business (hopefully an established and highly reputable business) distribute and/or produce a foreign firm's product. This builds name recognition and provides a good foundation from which to add more foreign franchises or to begin owned operations overseas.

6 Licensing – Licensing provides the right to a foreign company to use trademarks, patents, and other protected property rights in return for a licensing fee. The company holding the property rights is able to obtain distribution through an established business in a foreign country and avoid the problems with high capital outlays and competing in a country in which it is relatively unknown. Licensing may also be a way of gaining some protection from pirating or invasion of intellectual property rights because it sells these rights to an existing foreign company, which is more likely to be able to protect them in the host country. Licensing also allows a company to enter a market in which foreign entry restrictions are high or currency convertibility problems exist. A license fee flows out of the country as an expense of the local business, instead of a repatriation of profits to a foreign parent company.

7 Management contracting – A firm can enter foreign markets under a contract to manage a new or existing commercial operation in those markets. For example, a manufacturer has a proven record of aggressive and efficient management in its home country. The manufacturer may be approached not to provide product but instead management expertise for a operation having problems in a foreign country. This places the management of the original manufacturer into a foreign operation in which international experience may be gained. Success in one management contract may lead to additional contracts and eventually equity ownership in foreign firms. The only real problems associated with management contracts is that they remove top management from the home country operation, are normally temporary, and may incur the blame for a problem which previously existed in a foreign company.

8 Manufacturing – The establishing of capability to produce goods in a foreign country. This method allows the greatest control of the overseas operation but also the greatest investment in capital, management time, and effort. Often direct investment in facilities is achieved through the purchase of an existing company's assets in a foreign country but many large companies build new facilities when they expand. The decision to purchase or build a manufacturing plant in another

country may be forced upon a company by competition or foreign government demands for local representation.

9 Piggyback exporting – Piggyback exporting describes a situation in which one company markets its products through the distribution channels of a second company. Two major reasons for piggyback marketing are: (1) a local company desires to enter multinational markets but lacks the money, experience or possibly the inclination to learn what is necessary to be successful in the international marketplace; (2) an existing multi-national company is seeking to fill out its product lines to stay competitive overseas. Piggybacking involves products which compliment one another instead of competing. This method of exporting is one of the least problematic of all of the methods of entering foreign markets. Of course, success is dependent upon who the partners are and the commitment to making the partnership function effectively.

10 Wholly owned subsidiaries – This form of market entry provides a company full control over its foreign operations. This method of market entry requires large capital investment, commitment of time and effort, and normally a willingness of some employees/management to travel to and live in a foreign country. Fully owned subsidiaries are commonly existing businesses acquired by the company. If this is so the investment in management and expatriate time and effort may not be as significant as with a start-up operation.

Bibliography

Albaum, Gerald, Strandskov, Jesper, Duerr, Edwin & Dowd, Lawrence (1994). *International marketing and export management.* 2nd edn, Wokingham: Addison-Wesley.

Buzzell, R. D., Quelch, J. A. & Bartlett, C. A. (1995). *Global marketing management: Cases and readings.* Reading, MA: Addison-Wesley.

Cateora, P. R. (1993). *International marketing.* 5th edn, Homewood, IL: Irwin.

Grosse, R. & Kujawa, D. (1995). *International business: Theory and managerial applications.* 3rd edn, Boston, MA: Richard D. Irwin Inc.

Kaynak, E., & Ghauri, P. N. (eds) (1994). *Euromarketing: Effective strategies for international trade and export.* Binghamton, NY: Haworth Press Inc.

Majaro, S. (1977). *Marketing: A strategic approach to world markets.* London: George Allen and Unwin.

Mendenhall, M., Punnett, B. & Ricks, D. (1995). *Global management.* Cambridge, MA: Blackwell Publishers.

Toyne, B. & Walters, Peter, G. P. (1993). *Global marketing management.* Boston: Allyn and Bacon.

JOHN O'CONNELL

market penetration   This is one of the strategies identified in Ansoff's (1965) directional policy matrix (*see* DIRECTIONAL MATRIX). It is generally regarded as aiming at increasing the firm's MARKET SHARE within its existing markets. This can be achieved in at least one of three ways: increasing purchases by existing customers, winning over the consumers of competitors' offerings, and converting non-users to purchasers of the firm's offerings.

Bibliography

Ansoff, H. I. (1965). *Corporate strategy.* New York: McGraw-Hill. Chapter 6.

DALE LITTLER

market segment   *see* MARKET SEGMENTATION

market segmentation   Smith (1956) first defined market segmentation as "a rational and more precise adjustment of product and marketing effort to consumer or user requirements, it consists of viewing a heterogenous market (one characterised by divergent demand) as a number of smaller homogenous markets." If it is assumed, or known, that all consumers in a market have similar needs and wants, then an undifferentiated or total market approach can be adopted by a company using a single MARKETING MIX to satisfy consumers. The Coca Cola company's early marketing of only one drink, of only one size, is an example of this approach. If the market has heterogeneous needs, then a TARGET MARKET approach can be adopted. Here, an organization attempts to subdivide the market into clusters of customers with similar requirements and tailor its marketing mix to each cluster. This approach involves additional costs for product modifications and associated administrative, promotional, and inventory costs. In completely heterogeneous markets, where each customer's requirements are different, the only way to satisfy everyone is by offering tailor-made or bespoke products. Nowadays, this is more prevalent in organizational markets (*see* ORGANIZATIONAL MARKETING). However, in some consumer markets, producers still design their products for individual consumers, e.g., tailor-made clothes and shoes. This type of customized marketing is becoming increasingly possible, even in traditional mass markets, with the use of modern and flexible manufacturing technology, which allows shorter runs of products to be profitable. It should be noted that the idea of market segmentation can be used by profit-making and not-for-profit organizations alike (*see also* SEGMENTATION VARIABLES).

The Process of Market Segmentation

The first step is usually some form of needs assessment, e.g., benefit segmentation, in order to decide whether or not groups of buyers seek different product benefits and hence will value different product features (*see* SEGMENTATION VARIABLES). (The starting point is not restricted to benefit segmentation, but must be something which is closely related to the customer needs.) Since markets are defined in terms of demand or customer needs/requirements, marketers must know how these needs vary by segment in order to design products to meet them. For example, the shoe market is best characterized by identifying customer needs of protection, durability, style, size, price, etc., rather than by the age, sex, or social class of the market. Green (1977) distinguished two methods commonly used when deciding on how a market should be segmented. First, is a priori segmentation in which management decides the basis for segmentation, such as product purchase, customer type, or respondent's favorite brand. Respondents are classified into favorite brand segments, for example, and then further examined in terms of their differences on other characteristics. The second, post hoc segmentation, is a cluster-based segmentation design in which segments are determined on the bases of a clustering of respondents on a set of relevant attributes, e.g., benefits, needs, attitudes.

The second step is to describe how the benefit segments differ in their buying loyalties, shopping behaviors, media usage, and sensitivity to various marketing tactics. In this descriptive phase are included all the "normal" SEGMENTATION VARIABLES which are discussed by numerous authors. If the benefit segments do not vary significantly on any of these descriptor variables, they will be very difficult to reach and target with tailored marketing mixes. The choice of descriptor variable is not easy, partly because of the enormous number of possible variables which could be used and partly because of the often questionable link between the selected base(s) for the segmentation and the descriptor.

A number of authors do not take needs as the starting point for segmentation and argue that, in practice, segmentation may not follow the logical two-step approach. Often descriptor or profile variables, which can be easily measured, are identified first, then the segments so described are examined to see if they show different behavioral responses. This approach of looking for measurable and identifiable variables, then examining their influence on behavior, can be criticized for moving the marketer's attention away from customer requirements and toward implementation issues. Sometimes a product is designed for a particular segment of consumers whose collective need also happens to be accurately characterized by a description of their group association; various clubs and organizations, e.g., the Brownies, or football supporters clubs, etc. might be examples. In these relatively few cases, the two approaches do overlap.

A recent survey found that the similarity of needs within segments and the feasibility of marketing action were the two most important criteria used to form segments. Stability of the segment over time was third most important, while the difference of needs between segments, and the potential for increased profit and return on investment were fourth and fifth. The simplicity of assigning customers to segments was least important (Abratt, 1993).

Good market segmentation can result in numerous advantages including: (1) a closer matching of a company's products with customers' needs, which leads to increased customer satisfaction and implementation of the MARKETING CONCEPT; (2) checking the basic assumptions and understanding about customers in the market, which can lead to improved communication with customers; (3) identifying new marketing opportunities from segments that have not been hitherto exploited; (4) increased COMPETITIVE ADVANTAGE by viewing a market in different ways from one's competitors; it also keeps organizations alert to changes in market conditions, competitors' actions, and environmental opportunities and threats; (5) better COMPETITIVE STRATEGY, because companies that do not understand how the market is divided up risk competing head on against larger organizations with superior resources; it can allow a company to dominate a segment – which is not often possible in the total market; and (6) enabling two different pieces of research containing separate data to be combined by means of a common classification (see GEODEMOGRAPHICS).

However, not all authors agree that market segmentation is necessarily a profitable strategy, especially when the market is so small that marketing to a portion of it is not profitable; when heavy users make up such a large proportion of the sales volume that they are the only relevant target; or when one brand dominates the market and draws its appeal from all segments of the market (Young, Ott & Feigin, 1978). In markets where consumers are willing to accept lower prices in exchange for less-tailored products and where there is a high potential for product and marketing economies by eliminating or fusing market segments, counter-segmentation should be considered (Resnik, Turney & Mason, 1979).

The question of profitability can be one of the principal limitations of market segmentation. Bonoma & Shapiro (1984) highlight two major cost factors associated with segmentation. One is the number of segments approached: the more a market is segmented the more costly it is. Second, is that some elements of the MARKETING MIX are more expensive to change than others. The least expensive tactic is tailoring communications. Specialized prices are harder to administer and can have a substantial impact on profits. By far the most expensive change to implement is product change. Bonoma & Shapiro advocate the practical strategy of using the least expensive tools first so long as the segments are responsive to these changes. In practice, however, Abratt (1993) found that product changes and sales promotion campaigns were the marketing actions most often used by companies to target different segments, while different advertising appeals and prices were used less often. Changing the sales force and distribution systems were used least often. A further limitation is the inability to predict the nature and number of market segments that confront a new product in advance of the product being introduced (Frank et al., 1972). If the product has to be altered after introduction to meet the needs of different segments, this can be more expensive for the company and may reduce how well the company capitalizes on its first mover advantages. Conventional practice is to conduct an attitude and usage study in the test market area once the product has been introduced. However, from this it is impossible to tell if the segments which develop existed prior to being exposed to the product and advertisements, etc. One way to overcome this problem consumers and ask them to indicate the concept's applicability to their situation and the benefits that could be derived therefrom (Moriarty & Venkatesan, 1978). A final limitation is that segments may not be stable in the longer term, because of changing consumer values, DEMOGRAPHICS, and LIFESTYLES.

Target Segment Selection

Many authors have written about the criteria used to assess the usefulness of segmentations, but one of the most commonly used sets includes the criteria of measurability, substantiality, accessibility, and actionability (Kotler, 1991). Measurability is the degree to which size and purchasing power of segments can be measured. Substantiality is the degree to which segments are large and/or profitable enough for the organization to pursue. Accessibility is the extent to which segments can be effectively reached and served, and actionability is the degree to which an effective marketing program can be formulated for attracting and serving the segments. Mitchman (1991) adds meaningful to the list, which relates to the similarity of needs within the segments, i.e., when there is low intrasegment variability. Wind (1978) considers other factors, namely: the reliability of the data from which the segments were derived and the temporal stability of resultant segments.

Piercy & Morgan (1993) suggest that little explicit concern has been shown about the difference between strategic and operational aspects of segmentation, and they study the "fit" between segment requirements and company strengths. If the proposed segments do not fit in with the company's long-run objectives or the company does not possess the relevant skills and resources then the segmentation is less likely to be successful. Strategic marketing segmentation models may be better judged by such criteria as the ability to create and sustain competitive differentiation and advantage; INNOVATION in how the market is attacked; compatibility with the MISSION STATE-MENT; providing a coherent focus for thinking in the organization; and consistency with corporate values and culture. It is important, however, that organizational compatibility does not become the governing criterion for segment selection, since organizations should be able and prepared to adapt to segments identified, rather than to target only those which are compatible with existing organizational strengths and weaknesses (see SWOT ANALYSIS).

Finally, some authors have advocated the use of Porter's five forces framework as criteria for determining a segment's structural attractiveness (see COMPETITIVE STRATEGY). A survey of marketing practice found that the ability to reach buyers in the market and the competitive position of their firm in the market were the two most highly rated criteria used by practitioners to select target segments. These were followed by the size of the market, compatibility of market with companies, objectives/resources, profitability, and expected market growth.

see also **Organizational segmentation; Segmentation variables**

Bibliography

Abratt, R. (1993). Market segmentation practices of industrial Marketers. *Industrial Marketing Management*, 22, 79–84.

Bonoma, T. V. & Shapiro, B. P. (1984). Evaluating market segmentation approaches. *Industrial Marketing Management*, 13, 257–268.

Frank, R., Massy, W. & Wind, Y. (1972). *Market segmentation*. Englewood Cliffs, NJ: Prentice-Hall.

Green, P. E. (1977). A new approach to market segmentation. *Business Horizons*, 20, 61–73.

Kotler, P. (1991). *Marketing management: Analysis, planning, implementation and control* 7th edn, Englewood Cliffs, NJ: Prentice-Hall.

Mitchman, R. (1991). *Lifestyle market segmentation*. New York: Praeger.

Moriarty, M. & Venkatesan, M. (1978). Concept evaluation and market segmentation. *Journal of Marketing*, 42, July, 82–86.

Piercy, N. F. & Morgan, N. A. (1993). Strategic and operational market segmentation: A managerial analysis. *Industrial Marketing Management*, 22, 79–84.

Resnik, A. J., Turney, P. B. B. & Mason, J. B. (1979). Marketers turn to "Countersegmentation." *Harvard Business Review*, 57, Sept–Oct., 100–106.

Smith, W. (1956). Product differentiation and market segmentation as marketing strategies. *Journal of Marketing*, 21, July, 3–8.

Wind, Y. (1978). Issues and advances in segmentation research. *Journal of Marketing Research*, 15, Aug., 317–337.

Young, S., Ott, L. & Feigin, B. (1978). Some practical considerations in market segmentation. *Journal of Marketing Research*, 15, Aug., 405–412.

VINCE MITCHELL

market share   Widely believed to be a critical factor in the determination of competitive position, many firms focus on the achievement of market share gain as a critical strategic factor. However, great care must be exercised in the pursuit of market share. In the Boston Consulting Group model, the GROWTH SHARE MATRIX relative market share is used as a surrogate for cumulative production volume, a critical term in experience effect analysis (*see* EXPERIENCE AND LEARNING EFFECTS). It is assumed that the higher the level of market share is, the more a firm will have produced of a particular product. The firm with the highest relative share should therefore enjoy a lower cost than its smaller rivals (assuming that all firms are on the same experience curve). As defined in the BCG model, relative market share is the share of the firm subdivided by that of the largest single competitor. By definition, therefore, only one firm within a market can enjoy a relative share greater than one. The widespread awareness and adoption of this model has contributed to the belief in the importance of market share. Note, however, that the model refers to *relative share*, not absolute share.

The PIMS model makes use of two market share terms; namely, absolute share and relative share. The PIMS definition of relative share is also different: it is the share of the business under analysis divided by the sum of the shares of the three largest competitors. The PIMS model's use of absolute share also avoids the problem with use of the BCG model in that it has little meaning in fragmented industries. The PIMS model also argues that market share, although a significant variable in the determination of profitability, is actually a derived variable and that relative product quality is its driver. PIMS clearly supports the BCG contention that market share is an important determinant of business profitability. In the PIMS model, however, it is but one of a large number of variables. Moreover, for the variable to be of value, clear market identification is essential. While PIMS uses two market share terms in its analysis, it also emphasizes product quality, productivity, and capital intensity. As a result, making use of these latter variables it is possible to eliminate the advantage of high market share. Japanese competitors have been especially successful at utilizing these variables as a way of countering the volume advantage of US-based competitors in industries, such as machine tools, automobiles, and electronics.

A major problem with the use of market share is its difficulty in measurement. First, it is essential to define exactly what the market is before a firm's share can be measured. This is actually extremely difficult in practice. The PIMS model expends great effort in defining the served market of a business. This is usually some combination of product, customer, and geography that a business chooses to serve. Serious problems of definition can, however, still occur. Moreover, market boundaries can and do shift. For example, in the early 1980s the US General Electric company believed itself to be in a strong market share position in the USA in product areas such as consumer electronics and appliances. While this was true, these markets were in the process of globalizing, and if a global market definition had been adopted GE's position would have been recognized as much weaker. In some industries such as retailing, the correct market share is also extremely difficult to select. This could, for example, refer to national position, regional position, or that immediately surrounding an individual store.

While market share is therefore seen to be important, great care must be exercised in its definition and usage as a strategic variable. Nevertheless, different levels of market share have been shown to suggest alternate operating strategies. Businesses can thus be defined as high, medium, and low market share concerns. Dependent upon the position of a business, different strategies are suggested.

Strategies for High-share Competitors

While high market share does often generate lower costs in high experience effect markets, this may not always be the case. For example, although Kodak enjoys a worldwide volume advantage over Fuji Film, the latter is the lower-cost producer. Nevertheless, industry leaders are often able to maintain their position, especially when they control activities such as distribution and promotion. Three contrasting strategic positions have been identified for industry leaders:

1. *Stay on the offensive.* Under this strategy, the best offense is the best defense. Leadership and competitive advantage is sustained by achieving FIRST MOVER ADVANTAGE through continuous innovation and improvement. This forces competitors to adopt follow-on strategies. It also provides the possibility of locking up distribution channels and increasing customer switching.
2. *Fortify and defend.* This strategy attempts to build barriers to entry for competitors (*see* BARRIERS TO ENTRY AND EXIT). The range of possible specific actions includes:

- raising the cost structure of competitors, as a result of increased promotion, customer service, and R&D
- introducing alternative brands to match competitor product attributes
- increasing customer switching costs
- broadening the product line to maximize store shelf space, to reduce competitor distribution capacity, and to fill niche positions
- introducing fighting brands to maximize price range offering
- adding capacity ahead of the market to try to deter capacity investment, especially by smaller competitors
- driving for experience gains as a result of greater cumulative production volume
- patenting alternate technologies
- signing up exclusivity deals with key suppliers and distributors

This strategy is best for companies with a strong dominance position that are not subject to monopolies legislation. Such a business may well be a cash cow but can be maintained with a long-term future by continuous adequate investment to maintain position. The critical danger from this strategy is the risk of flanking attacks which endeavor to shift the grounds on which the business is founded.

3. *Follow the leader.* This strategy forces small-share competitors to conform to policies established by the industry leader. Clear signals are established for weaker competitors by: rapid responses to price attacks; heavy promotion spend when challengers threaten; special deals for customers and/or distributors; pressure applied to distributors to reduce competition shelf space availability; and the poaching of key competitor personnel from competitors attacking the leader. On occasion, such behavior can breach ethical standards, and care must be taken to insure that grounds for legal attack by smaller competitors are not provided. The "dirty tricks" campaign by British Airways against Virgin is a classic recent example, in which the industry leader, exasperated by the success of its smaller rival, adopted illegal tactics to try to limit Virgin's progress.

Strategies for Medium-share Competitors

Most product markets tend to be at least oligopolistic. Many have multiple competitors. As a result, most competitors are not industry leaders but, rather, medium-share concerns. Despite their medium-share positions, such businesses may operate a number of wholly viable strategies that are profitable and attractive. Some such companies operate as fierce challengers to industry leaders, while others appear content to accept their subordinate position. Those firms keen to strengthen their strategic position are recommended to adopt the indirect approach rather than engage in head-on confrontation.

In industries in which a substantial experience effect prevails, low-share competitors need to achieve similar cost positions by tactics such as lower capital intensity, higher productivity, use of debt leverage, and superior product quality. Alternately, such firms should aim to achieve differentiation by technological leadership, alternate distribution systems, re-segmentation of the market, and reconfiguration of the value chain. Where ECONOMIES OF SCALE or experience effects are more limited, the strategic options open to medium-share firms are greater and include the following:

1. *Vacant niche.* Such a strategy involves focusing on customer segments that have been neglected by industry leaders. Ideally, such niches should be sufficiently large to justify specialization in product development, distribution, and the like, and to provide profitable opportunities. Such niches might include health foods in the food industry, feeder and commuter airlines, specialist magazines, and investment and insurance products targeted at the middle aged.
2. *Specialist.* This strategy focuses on supplying the needs of specific market segments. Competitive advantage is gained through the differentiation achieved by specialization. Examples include Apple Computers in desktop publishing, Hewlett Packard in specialist calculators, and Baxters in speciality soups.
3. *Superior quality.* This strategy combines segment and/or product differentiation coupled with "superior" quality, where quality is based on customer perception. Customers are then prepared to pay higher prices for

such product offerings. Examples include specialist foods from Marks and Spencer, Chivas Regal Whisky, Smirnoff Vodka, Wedgwood china, and branded perfumes.

4. *Passive follower*. Many medium-ranking competitors are content to maintain follower positions behind established industry leaders. Their strategies do not seek confrontation but react to the leader's moves rather than initiating attack policies. Under such stable market conditions – especially as growth slows, but does not drift into decline – medium-ranking competitors are able to maintain satisfactory levels of profitability.

5. *Growth via acquisition*. One strategy to rapidly strengthen market position is by the acquisition of or merger with competitors (*see* ACQUISITION STRATEGY). Such moves may rapidly create high-share positions and reap economies of scale. Industries which have undergone such restructuring include pharmaceuticals, brewing, airlines, heavy chemicals, accountancy, global media, and the like. The dangers in such a strategy stem largely from problems of integration, especially in supposed mergers, where potential clashes between the cultures of new partners may result in dysfunctional behavior.

Despite their nonleadership position, medium-ranked businesses often enjoy attractive profits and established market positions. In the food and drink product sectors for example, food distributors offer at least two branded products, not least to maintain pressure on industry leaders. In many industrial and other consumer product areas, this is also the case. The handicap of lower market size can thus be circumvented by: segment-focused strategies in which price confrontation is avoided; superior technical and quality positions; lower costs and superior productivity; strategies which reinforce differences from the industry leader; and a focus on alternative distribution strategies and differentiation in advertising and promotion.

Strategies for Low-share Businesses

A number of strategic options are open to businesses with low-share positions. When a low-share position is coupled with low growth or a high cost of product development, unless the parent company can afford to attack and gain share by market means or acquisition, harvesting or rapid exit strategies seem to be recommended.

When it is possible, harvesting maximizes the cash that can be extracted from such a business. Under such a strategy, all unnecessary expenditure is cut, R&D is minimized, and new investment is limited to the maintenance of operations, provided that shareholder value is not destroyed. Prices are raised or maintained rather than cut in a tradeoff of market share for cashflow. A number of indicators have been identified of when a harvesting strategy seems most appropriate:

- in industries with unattractive long-term prospects
- when growing share would be too expensive and insufficiently profitable
- when market share defense is too expensive
- when share is not dependent on the maintenance of competitive effort

- when resources can be deployed elsewhere to improve shareholder value
- when the business is not critical to core activities
- when the business does not add special features to the corporation's overall portfolio

Bibliography

Buzzell, R. D., Gale, B. T. & Sutton, R. G. (1975). Market share – a key to profitability. *Harvard Business Review*, **53**, 97–108.

Buzzell, R. D. & Gale, B. T. (1987). *The PIMS principles*. New York: The Free Press. See chapter 3.

Hammermesh, R. B., Anderson, M. J. & Harris, J. E. (1978). Strategies for low market share businesses. *Harvard Business Review*, **56**, 95–103.

Kotler, P. (1978). Harvesting strategies for weak products. *Business Horizons*, **21** (5).

Kotler, P. (1978). *Marketing management*. Englewood Cliffs, NJ: Prentice-Hall. See pp. 397–412.

Porter, M. E. (1985). *Competitive advantage: creating and sustaining superior performance*. New York: The Free Press. See chapter 15.

Thompson, A. & Strickland A. J. (1993). *Strategic management*, 7th edn. New York: Irwin. See pp. 226–68.

Woo, C. Y. & Cooper, A. C. (1982). The surprising case for low market share. *Harvard Business Review*, **60**, 106–13.

DEREK F. CHANNON

market structure Market structure consists of those relatively fixed features of a firm's environment which identify the competitive nature of the industry. As such it is related to market power, market performance and ANTITRUST POLICY. Its first element is the number and size distribution of the sellers in the market. As the number of sellers increases, the market moves toward PERFECT COMPETITION and market power tends to diminish. Several measures of the size distribution of firms, including various concentration indices and the HERFINDAHL-HIRSCHMAN INDEX emphasize the collective market shares of an industry's leading firms. High values in these indices indicate a potential for market power. The market share of a single firm may also help to explain the market's structure and competitive conditions (*see* PRICE LEADERSHIP). The second element of market structure is the number and size distribution of buyers, which is important as it offers an indication of the extent of their countervailing power which exists.

A third vital element of market structure is the condition of entry. High BARRIERS TO ENTRY are a central feature of MONOPOLY and are common to oligopoly. The condition of entry is important in understanding the competitive process in two ways. First, it helps to explain the number and size distribution of firms currently in the market. Second, it helps to evaluate the potential for new competitors. Some researchers cite this element of structure as being uniquely important. Baumol, Panzar and Willig (1982) maintain that in the absence of any barriers to entry or exit markets become contestable and the number of rivals, their size and other structural variables become irrelevant in determining the outcome of market performance (*see* CONTESTABLE MARKETS). Their research cites examples such as the airline industry where high resource mobility and low barriers to entry into new geographic markets assures market efficiency. Despite this, Shepherd (1984) and others have argued that the number of truly contestable markets is extremely limited and that the level of competition already in existence in a market is of far greater importance than the degree of potential competition.

Two other elements of market structure are the degree of PRODUCT DIFFERENTIATION and the extent of X-efficiency existing in the market. Both influence the nature of industry costs and the strategic behavior among the rivals within the market. Both may also play a role in determining the condition of entry by increasing the costs and risk of entry.

The structure of a market is dependent on several factors, the two most basic of which are the underlying consumer demand and the industry's production cost conditions. Industry technology which offers substantial ECONOMIES OF SCALE relative to market demand may require large firm size and greater market concentration and thus limit the room for and number of existing rivals. In addition, these circumstances may limit the number of potential new entrants, which may face cost disadvantages stemming from an inability to produce at MINIMUM EFFICIENT SCALE (*see* BARRIERS TO ENTRY; ENTRY DOCUMENTS).

Market structure may also be influenced by government policy ranging from patent laws and licensing requirements, which influence entry, to antitrust policy such as restrictions on mergers, which may influence the number and size distribution of existing rivals. Finally, limit pricing and other forms of STRATEGIC BEHAVIOR by rival firms to alter the structure of a market.

The work by Porter (1980) on competitive strategy emphasizes the importance of market structure to successful business management. Five basic forces (including potential entrants, substitute goods industries and the rivalry of materials suppliers) which exist in every market are identified. Porter demonstrates that from these forces evolve the competitive strategies which firms must adopt to be profitable. He argues that a sound evaluation of market structure and MARKET DEFINITION is essential for managers in order to properly develop offensive and defensive strategies, assess the company's strengths and weaknesses, and examine its ability to cause changes in market structure.

Analysis of market structure is also important in the development of industrial policy. Shepherd (1982) uses an analysis of market structure to investigate the extent to which goods in the US economy are produced in competitive markets. He uses structural elements to create categories such as "effective competition" (wherein industries have low concentration ratios, unstable market shares and low entry barriers) and "tight oligopoly" (where concentration ratios exceed 60 percent, and barriers are medium or high). He finds that more than 75 percent of the economy's national income in 1980 is generated in markets which were competitive. Moreover, this percentage has increased sharply (from somewhat more than 50 percent) since the 1950s. Shepherd cites active government antitrust policy as the primary explanatory variable and imports as a secondary variable causing this shift. The policy implications here, and surrounding market structure in general, are controversial.

Bibliography

Bain, J. (1956). *Barriers to New Competition*. Cambridge: Harvard University Press.

Baumol, W., Panzar, J. & Willig, R. (1982). *Contestable Markets and the Theory of Industry Structure*. New York: Harcourt Brace Jovanovich.

Carlton, D. & Perloff, J. (1994). *Modern Industrial Organization*. 2nd edn, New York: HarperCollins.

Porter, M. (1980). *Competitive Strategy: Techniques for Analyzing Industries and Competitors*. New York: Free Press.

Shepherd, W. (1982). Causes of increased competition in the U.S. Economy, 1939–1980. *The Review of Economics and Statistics*, **64**, 613–26.

Shepherd, W. (1984). 'Contestability' vs. competition. *American Economic Review*, **74**, 572–87.

GILBERT BECKER

marketing Marketing was apparently first taught as a business subject in 1902, at the University of Wisconsin, although the first textbooks on the subject were not written until several years later (Bartels, 1962, 1970; Converse, 1951). The concept has no single universally agreed definition and perspectives on the nature of marketing have shifted considerably over time. Halbert (1965) has suggested that this is due to marketing having no recognized central theoretical basis such as exists for many other disciplines and the natural sciences in particular.

The development of "marketing" is often seen in terms of at least three "eras" (see, for instance, Gilbert & Bailey, 1990; Webster, 1988). The first of these is most commonly termed the "production" era (Keith, 1960) and is considered to have taken place between 1870 and 1930, when the primary focus of marketing was limited to overcoming constraints on supply, rather than paying attention to sales methods or customer requirements. The production era was apparently followed by the "sales" era, between 1930 and 1950, where marketing's responsibility was to sell what the organization produced, with a consequent focus on sales techniques. The shift from the production era to the sales era has been attributed to increased competition in many industrial sectors (Keith, 1960). Finally, the "marketing" era signified a widespread adoption of the "customer orientation" generally held to be part of the modern MARKETING CONCEPT. A number of authors, however, dispute the existence of either the production or sales eras (see, for instance, Fullerton, 1988), pointing to a number of varied and vigorous marketing efforts by manufacturers during these periods, especially the growth of chain stores (pre-1900), department stores (1850), advertising agencies (by 1900), and supermarkets focusing on self-service and low prices (by 1930 in the USA and by 1945 in Europe).

More recent examples of the various definitions of "marketing" include those of the UK's Chartered Institute of Marketing ("the management process which identifies, anticipates and satisfies customer requirements efficiently and profitably") and the American Marketing Association, which reviewed 25 definitions in 1985 and arrived at its own contribution ("marketing is the process of planning and executing the conception, pricing, promotion and distribution of ideas, goods and services to create exchanges that satisfy individual and organizational objectives"). EXCHANGE is seen by many authors as the central concept underlying marketing.

A number of attempts have been made to categorize definitions of "marketing." Crosier (1988), for example, reviewed over 50 definitions, placing them into three broad groups. The first group consisted of definitions which conceived of marketing as a process connecting a producer with its market via a marketing channel, such as "the primary management function which organises and directs the aggregate of business activities involved in converting customer purchase power for a specific product or service into effective demand for a specific product or service and in moving the product or service to the final consumer or user so as to achieve company set profit or other objectives" (Rodger, 1971). The definitions of McCarthy & Perreault (1993) and Runyon (1982), among others, might be seen as falling into this category. The second group consisted of definitions which viewed marketing as a concept or philosophy of business (*see* MARKETING CONCEPT), e.g., "selling is preoccupied with the seller's need to convert his product into cash; marketing with the idea of satisfying the needs of the consumer by means of the product and the whole cluster of things associated with creating, delivering and finally consuming it" (Levitt, 1960). Crosier's third category of definitions emphasized marketing as an orientation present to some degree in both consumer and producer: the phenomenon which makes the process and the concept possible. However, only one example of such a definition was provided by Crosier, and this was felt by many researchers to be an unconvincing argument in favor of a third category of definitions (*see* MARKETING ORIENTATION).

A number of challenges to the definitions of the scope of marketing outlined by Crosier have emerged. The first of these might be seen as emanating from the field of NOT-FOR-PROFIT MARKETING, where Kotler & Levy's (1969) article extended the scope of marketing to cover activities undertaken for primary aims other than that of profit, including those of organizations such as educational establishments, churches, politicians, national interest groups, or charities, or, indeed, the activities related to internal marketing. Kotler & Levy referred to such not-for-profit marketing as SOCIETAL MARKETING, a term which has more recently come to develop a somewhat different meaning (see below and SOCIETAL MARKETING).

A second challenge developed from the area of SOCIETAL MARKETING, which has been described by some authors as the "fourth era" of the development of marketing (Bell & Emory, 1971; Abratt & Sachs, 1989). Societal marketing criticizes traditional marketing definitions for their emphasis on material consumption and short-term consumer gratification, without considering the long-term societal or environmental impact of marketing activities. It is often seen as a response to both the CONSUMERISM movement and wider criticisms of the ills of marketing. Societal marketing does not generally deny that the basic goal of a business enterprise is to ensure its long-term profitability and survival; however, it does counsel businesses to be fair to consumers, enabling them to make fully informed and intelligent purchase decisions, and to avoid marketing practices that have negative consequences for society. (See also Bartels, 1974; Dawson, 1969; Dickinson et al., 1986; Elliot, 1990; McGee & Spiro, 1990; SOCIAL RESPONSIBILITY; SOCIETAL MARKETING.)

A third challenge has stemmed from those who consider that definitions involving a focus on customer "needs" discourage major product innovations in favor of low-risk product changes, given that when consumers are asked to verbalize their needs, they tend to build on the familiar (Kaldor, 1971; Hayes & Abernathy, 1980).

A fourth challenge comes from authors like Grönroos (1989), who suggest that existing definitions do not capture the essence of BUSINESS-TO-BUSINESS MARKETING or SERVICES MARKETING, both of which revolve primarily around customer relationships (*see* RELATIONSHIP MARKETING). Grönroos offers an alternative definition of marketing as "to establish, develop and commercialise long term customer relationships, so that the objectives of both parties are met" (57).

Finally, marketing could be defined as an academic discipline, with a recognizable body of theory in relation to the study of the issues and processes described above, although, as Halbert (1965) suggests, there might be some disagreement among marketing acaof such a body of theory. Marketing is taught on the majority of university business and management degree courses throughout the world.

Bibliography

Abratt, R. & Sacks, D. (1989). Perceptions of the societal marketing concept. *European Journal of Marketing*, **23**, (6), 25–33.

Bartels, R. (1962). *The development of marketing thought*. Homewood, IL: Irwin.

Bartels, R. (1970). Influences on development of marketing thought 1900–1923. In R. Bartels (Ed.), *Marketing theory and metatheory* (pp. 108–125). Homewood, IL: Irwin.

Bartels, R. (1974). The identity crisis in marketing. *Journal of Marketing*, **38**, 73–76.

Bell, M. L. & Emory, C. W. (1971). The faltering marketing concept. *Journal of Marketing*, **35**, (4), Oct., 37–42.

Converse, P. D. (1951). Development of marketing theory: Fifty years of progress. In H. Wales (Ed.), *Changing perspectives in marketing* (pp. 1–31). Urbana, IL: University of Illinois Press.

Crosier, K. (1988). What exactly is marketing? In M. J. Thomas & N. E. Waite (Eds), *The marketing digest* (pp. 16–27). London: Heinemann.

Dawson, M. (1969). The human concept: The new philosophy for business. *Business Horizons*, **12**, 29–38.

Dickinson, R., Herbst, A. & O'Shaughnessy, J. (1986). Marketing concept and customer orientation. *European Journal of Marketing*, **20**, (10), 18–23.

Elliot, G. R. (1990). The marketing concept: Necessary but sufficient? An environmental view. *European Journal of Marketing*, **24**, (8), 20–30.

Fullerton, R. A. (1988). How modern is modern marketing? Marketing's evolution and the myth of the "Production" Era. *Journal of Marketing*, **52**, (1), Jan., 108–125.

Gilbert, D. & Bailey, N. (1990). The development of marketing: A compendium of historical applications. *Quarterly Review of Marketing*, **15**, (2), Winter, 6–13.

Grönroos, C. (1989). Defining marketing: A market-oriented approach. *European Journal of Marketing*, **23**, (1), 52–60.

Halbert, M. (1965). *The meaning and sources of marketing theory*. Marketing Science Institute Series. New York: McGraw-Hill.

Hayes, R. H. & Abernathy, W. J. (1980). Managing our way to economic decline. *Harvard Business Review*, **57**, July–Aug., 67–77.

Kaldor, A. G. (1971). Imbricative marketing. *Journal of Marketing*, **35**, (2), Apr., 19–25.

Keith, Robert J. (1960). The marketing revolution. *Journal of Marketing*, **24**, 35–38.

Kotler, P. & Levy, S. (1969). Broadening the concept of marketing. *Journal of Marketing*, 33, (1), Jan., 10–15.

Levitt, T. (1960). Marketing myopia. *Harvard Business Review*, 37, July–Aug., 45–56.

McCarthy, E. J. & Perreault, R. (1993). *Basic marketing*, 11th edn, Homewood, IL: Irwin.

McGee, L. W. & Spiro, R. K. (1990). The marketing concept in perspective. *Business Horizons*, 31, (3), 40–5.

Rodger, L. W. (1971). *Marketing in a competitive economy*. London: Associated Business Programmes.

Runyon, K. E. (1982). *The practice of marketing*. Columbus, OH: C. E. Merrill.

Webster, F. E. Jr (1988). The rediscovery of the marketing concept. *Business Horizons*, 31, (3), 29–39.

FIONA LEVERICK

marketing audit A marketing audit is an analysis, conducted from the perspective of the marketing function, of the environment surrounding an organization and its offerings (*see also* ENVIRONMENTAL ANALYSIS). The aim of the audit is to examine systematically an organization's operations, offerings, markets, and environment so as to find ways to improve marketing performance. This could result, for example, in recommendations that products be adapted to meet new customer requirements, or that old markets be exited, or that fresh investments be considered

The marketing audit is generally conducted in two interrelated parts: the INTERNAL AUDIT (examining the internal operations and assets of the organization) and the external audit (examining the environment surrounding the organization). This process is similar to the SWOT ANALYSIS recommended for strategic marketing planning where strengths and weaknesses (the "SW" of SWOT) equate to the internal audit, while opportunities and threats (the "OT" of SWOT) correspond to the external audit.

Bibliography

Kotler, P., Gregor, W. & Rodgers, W. (1977). The marketing audit comes of age. *Sloan Management Review*, 18, Winter, 25–43.

Wilson, A. (1982). *Marketing audit checklists*. Maidenhead: McGraw-Hill.

DOMINIC WILSON

marketing communications Organizations are involved in a range of marketing communications exchanges; e.g., a manufacturer may communicate with its middlemen, customers (existing and potential), and various publics. Its middlemen communicate with their customers and various publics. Customers engage in WORD-OF-MOUTH COMMUNICATIONS with other customers and consumers, and each group can provide communication feedback to every other group, especially through the marketing research activities of organizations.

Marketing communications comprise a mix of techniques or tools known as the COMMUNICATIONS MIX (and sometimes referred to as the promotional mix), by which a message is delivered from one party in the communications exchange to another.

Schramm (1971) was one of the first to discuss the marketing communications process. This is summarized in Kotler (1994). This model answers the questions (1) who (2) says what (3) in what channel (4) to whom (5) with what effect? All communications involve "senders" and "receivers;" the "senders" being concerned with messages and channels, i.e., the ways in which messages are carried/delivered to an audience. Marketing communicators require that the message sent is the one that is received, but they are aware of consumers' selective processes (of exposure, attention, distortion, and recall), and intervening variables, referred to as noise (i.e., factors over which the communicator has no control, not least of which are messages being sent to target groups simultaneously), which may interfere with the process.

Kotler (1994) refers to the five major tools of the marketing communications mix available to an organization, namely: ADVERTISING, DIRECT MARKETING, SALES PROMOTION, PUBLIC RELATIONS and PUBLICITY, and PERSONAL SELLING. An alternative consideration of the mix is a classification into two broad dimensions: first, whether or not the communications are paid for, and second, whether they are personal, i.e., where there is some direct contact between the sender and the receiver, or impersonal where there is not. Examples include:

Paid and personal: PERSONAL SELLING, telemarketing
Paid and impersonal: ADVERTISING, SALES PROMOTION, PUBLIC RELATIONS, DIRECT MAIL, PACKAGING
Non-paid and personal: social channels, i.e., word-of-mouth communications, INTERPERSONAL COMMUNICATIONS
Non-paid and impersonal: PUBLICITY

Personal communications tend to be more important when products are expensive, risky, have social significance, or are purchased infrequently; and buyers seek information, product experiences, and the knowledge of others. Impersonal communications are less insistent than personal channels, and so can easily be avoided or tuned out. Further, they are subject to the consumer psychological processes of selective attention, perception, and retention.

This classification allows for the communication to be initiated by consumers as well as supplier organizations (*see* TWO STEP FLOW MODEL).

Effective communication/promotion involves a number of activities. These include: identifying the target audience and its characteristics, e.g., individuals, groups, families, and businesses, and their socioeconomic profiles, personality, perceptions of risk, and stages in the buying process, etc.; determining the COMMUNICATIONS OBJECTIVES, e.g., to create awareness, knowledge, liking, preference, conviction, or purchase; designing the message; selecting the communication channels, both personal and impersonal, which will vary between consumer and organizational markets; allocating the communications budget and deciding on the promotional mix, which will be influenced by funds available, the nature of the market and the stage in the product life cycle, etc.; measuring the communications results; and managing the marketing communications program.

Bibliography

Dibb, S., Simkin, L., Pride, W. M. & Ferrell, O. C. (1994). *Marketing concepts and strategies*. European edn, Boston, MA: Houghton Mifflin Co. Chapter 14.

Kotler, P. (1994). *Marketing management: Analysis, planning, implementation and control*, 8th edn, Englewood Cliffs, NJ: Prentice-Hall. Chapter 22.

Schramm, W. (1971). How communications works. In W. Schramm & D. F. Roberts (Eds), *The process and effects of mass communications*. Urbana, IL: University of Illinois Press.

BARBARA LEWIS

marketing concept   The marketing concept has been seen variously as a statement of the philosophy of marketing, an approach to doing business, or a broad umbrella governing business activity. It is seen by many as synonymous with "marketing" itself, definitions of marketing as a concept or philosophy of business comprising one of the three types of definitions of "marketing" identified by Crosier (1988) (*see* MARKETING).

The marketing concept is generally held to have three major components (see McGee & Spiro, 1990). The first of these is a so-called "customer orientation," whereby an understanding of customer "needs," wants, and behavior is the focal point of all marketing action. The second is a focus on what is usually termed either coordinated activities or integrated effort, with the entire organization sharing the customer orientation by emphasizing the integration of the marketing function with areas such as research, product management, sales, and advertising. The third is a profit orientation, with attention directed primarily toward profit, as opposed to sales volumes, although clearly a profit focus is not appropriate for all organizations (e.g., NOT-FOR-PROFIT MARKETING). Reflecting these three areas, Kotler (1994) defined the marketing concept as "a customer orientation backed by integrated marketing as the key to attaining long term profitable volume." Other authors have gone on to emphasize a fourth component: a long term-orientation, in order to deflect criticisms of the marketing concept as focused only on the current, articulable "needs" of consumers (*see* MARKETING).

There has been some concern that the marketing concept as defined above is not broad enough to cover the more recent developments in the scope of marketing. In particular, developments in the area of SOCIETAL MARKETING have led to a number of restatements of the marketing concept to include a focus on consumers' and society's long-term interests (*see* SOCIAL RESPONSIBILITY). This had led some authors to produce a more "modern" statement of the marketing concept based on the three elements of consumer satisfaction, company profits, and community welfare (Abratt & Sacks, 1989).

Bibliography
Abratt, R. & Sacks, D. (1989). Perceptions of the societal marketing concept. *European Journal of Marketing*, 23, (6), 25–33.
Crosier, K. (1988). What exactly is marketing? In M. J. Thomas & N. E. Waite (Eds), *The marketing digest* (pp. 16–27). London: Heinemann.
Kotler, P. (1994). *Marketing management: Analysis, planning, implementation and control*, 8th edn, Englewood Cliffs, NJ: Prentice-Hall.
McGee, L. W. & Spiro, R. K. (1990). The marketing concept in perspective. *Business Horizons*, 31, (3), 40–45.

FIONA LEVERICK

marketing control   It is clear that effective strategic marketing management (*see* STRATEGIC MARKETING; MARKETING MANAGEMENT) suggests establishing predetermined targets against which actual performance can be assessed. This is the essence of marketing control.

There are at least two major areas where marketing control will be applied: to the marketing strategy; and to the marketing budget. In the case of marketing strategy, control is viewed as the final phase of the four-stage strategy process (*see* STRATEGIC PLANNING), and is primarily concerned with ensuring that the strategy is developing according to plan so that the established objectives will be realized. If deviations are identified, the implications can be analyzed and appropriate action taken. It may be necessary to adjust expectations or even the strategy where the outcomes differ significantly from expectations and cannot be reconciled with the original strategy. In some instances, the strategy may have to be abandoned where the deviations are such as to make it commercially unviable.

Budgetary control involves monitoring the extent to which the various cost and revenue streams match with those defined in the budget. Assessments are likely to be undertaken regularly (in some cases daily, made possible by the use of computerized data capture and processing systems). Among the variables managers may monitor are: sales/profits and sales/profit variances; market share; and expenses to sales ratios. In addition, it is important to watch more qualitative indicators such as customer attitudes (say, through tracking studies) and complaints.

Firms also need to evaluate periodically the profitability of products, channels of distribution, customers and order sizes, as well as the efficiency of key marketing activities, such as advertising and sales. Firms may employ benchmarking, i.e., compare their costs and efficiencies against the "best practice" elsewhere.

Bibliography
Bureau, J. R. (1995). Controlling marketing. In M. J. Baker (Ed.), *The marketing book* (pp. 565–585). Oxford: Butterworth-Heinemann.

DALE LITTLER

marketing decision support systems   A marketing decision support system is an information system that allows marketing decision-makers to interact directly with both databases and models. As such, it is an improvement on MARKETING INFORMATION SYSTEMS. A decision support system consists of the computer hardware and communication interface, databases, relevant marketing models and software, and the marketing decision-maker. The aim is to help the decision-maker, not only by allowing access to past and current data, but also by providing answers to "what if . . . " questions through the incorporation of marketing models deemed appropriate by the decision-maker.

To be effective a marketing decision support system should have the following characteristics: it should be understood by the managers using it; it should be perceived as useful by these users; it should be complete on important issues (e.g., on important factors where hard objective data are not available, the system should allow the use of the subjective assessments of the user rather than ignore those factors); it should be easy for the manager to use and interact with without the need for an intermediate computer expert; it should be flexible and give sensible answers; and it should be evolutionary in the sense that it is capable of being extended at a later date.

One of the problems is getting marketing decision-makers to use decision support systems. This will be helped if: the potential users are involved in the design of the system; the decision-makers specify the decisions where they would like support (probably frequently occurring decisions); the marketing models/theories and databases being used have the decision-makers' approval; and successful use of the system can be demonstrated, probably, in the first instance, by helping with simple problems.

Examples of marketing decisions that have been aided by decision support systems include media scheduling, sales force management, store location, warehouse location, and competitive bidding.

Bibliography

Churchill, G. A. (1991). *Marketing research: Methodological foundations*, 5th edn, Chicago: The Dryden Press. Chapter 2.

MICHAEL GREATOREX

marketing environment   The marketing environment is made up of the actors and forces that directly or indirectly influence the company's marketing operations and performance and which are generally thought to be outside the company's power of control. The distinction is often made between the MICRO ENVIRONMENT, which is made up of actors in the company's immediate environment, such as suppliers, market intermediaries, customers, or competitors, and the MACRO ENVIRONMENT, which is made up of wider societal forces that affect all of the actors in the micro environment, such as legal, cultural, economic, technological, demographic, or political trends.

see also **Marketing management**

FIONA LEVERICK

marketing ethics   Marketing ethics can be seen as the moral principles that define "right" or "wrong" behavior in marketing. "Unethical" marketing activity might include, for example, deceptive advertising, misleading selling tactics, price fixing, and the deliberate marketing of harmful products. While marketing ethics are frequently referred to in conjunction with the concept of SOCIAL RESPONSIBILITY, the two areas have been differentiated by the criteria that social responsibility is an organizational concern while ethics are the concern of the individual manager or business decision-maker (Carroll, 1981). Other authors have identified the process of ensuring that marketing decisions are taken according to ethical principles as just one aspect of a wider concept of corporate social responsibility (*see* SOCIAL RESPONSIBILITY).

The study of marketing ethics has become an important area for research, paralleling a growing body of literature in the field of business ethics more generally (see Smith & Quelch, 1993 for a more thorough discussion of ethical issues in marketing). While there exists no totally accepted statement about what is ethical in marketing, two major philosophies, deontology and utilitarianism, have dominated the study of ethics and these have been used as the basis for a general theory of marketing ethics (see Hunt & Vitell, 1986).

Deontology refers to the existence of prima facie ideals that can direct our thinking, behavior being judged on the basis of whether or not it infringes these universal rules. Kant (1964 translation) suggests that ethical actions should be based on reasons the decision-maker would be willing to have others use. That is, one should not act unless one is willing to have the maxim on which one acts become a universal law. This approach would, for example, require a marketer to ask if he or she would be willing to live in a world where all producers were making a product known to be harmful to some people in its normal use. Rawls (1971) provides a more modern statement of deontology, suggesting that an action is ethical if it involves true freedom of choice and action, is available to all, injures no one, and is of benefit to some.

Utilitarianism, on the other hand, is concerned with maximizing the greatest good for the greatest number of people. Alternative marketing actions would thus be judged on the basis of the consequences for all the people affected by the actions, according to a cost-benefit analysis. If the net result of all benefits minus all costs is positive, the action would then be ethically acceptable. Compared to deontology, which views the individual as the major concern and unit of analysis, utilitarianism is societal in nature, being more concerned with the welfare of society as a unit.

Utilitarianism, in particular, has been criticized on a number of points. First, difficulties are likely to be encountered in attempting to quantify "benefits" and "costs." It also involves the problem of concealing major negative occurrences to a small segment of people by allowing them to be offset by a relatively minor increase in "benefits" to large segments.

Bibliography

Carroll, A. B. (1981). *Business and society.* Boston, MA: Little, Brown & Co.

Hunt, S. D. & Vitell, S. (1986). A general theory of marketing ethics. *Journal of Macromarketing*, 6, Spring, 5–16.

Kant, I. (1964). *Groundwork of the metaphysics of morals.* Translation by H. J. Paton. New York: Harper & Row.

Rawls, J. (1971). *A theory of justice.* Cambridge, MA: Harvard University Press.

Smith, N. C. & Quelch, J. A. (1993). *Ethics in marketing.* Boston, MA: Irwin.

FIONA LEVERICK

marketing exchange   *see* EXCHANGE

marketing information systems   A marketing information system is designed to generate, analyze, store, and distribute information to appropriate marketing decision-makers on a regular basis. The definition of marketing information systems is similar to that of marketing research except for the emphasis on the regular supply of information to marketing managers in marketing information systems as opposed to the emphasis on the gathering of information in marketing research. The growth in the use of marketing information systems has been facilitated by improvements in computer hardware and software, and contemporary marketing information systems are very much computer driven.

Marketing information systems are designed around individual decision-makers, the decisions they are required to make, and the information needed to make those decisions. The information includes both that required on a regular and that required on an ad hoc basis. The underlying data may be collected internally or externally. The information is presented in a form requested by the decision-maker. The key task is to specify what information each individual decision-maker requires, when it is required, and in what format. The end result is a series of customized reports that go to the appropriate decision-makers.

As the volume of information in a marketing information system increases over time, a large memory and easy access becomes important; technical improvements in the form of laser compact discs are meeting this need.

Marketing information systems are being superseded by MARKETING DECISION SUPPORT SYSTEMS which are more versatile in the way the decision-maker is able to interact with the database and which, because of the ability to include marketing modeling in marketing decision support systems, permit the decision-maker to ask "what if . . . " questions rather than merely retrieve data.

Bibliography

Churchill, G. A. (1991). *Marketing research: Methodological foundations*, 5th edn, Chicago: The Dryden Press. Chapter 2.

MICHAEL GREATOREX

marketing management   The term "marketing management" is generally used to refer to the management activities undertaken in the practice of marketing in organizations. The conventional view of marketing management found in most standard marketing textbooks is of a process whereby the marketing manager uses marketing resources to perform a highly defined and "logical" series of activities and responsibilities (see Baker, 1991; Dibb et al., 1991; Kotler, 1994; McCarthy & Perreault, 1993). Dibb et al. (1991), for instance, see marketing management as the process of "planning, organising, implementing and controlling marketing activities to facilitate and expedite exchanges effectively and efficiently." The execution of this process defines the marketing manager's areas of responsibility and the nature of his or her work.

The specific activities involved in marketing management will depend to a great extent on the type of markets the business is operating in. The activities involved, for instance, in marketing to consumers and marketing to other businesses may differ significantly (*see* BUSINESS-TO-BUSI-NESS MARKETING; CONSUMER MARKETING). At a general level, however, standard marketing textbooks frequently divide marketing management activities into the four areas of analysis, planning, implementation, and control.

Analysis refers to the gathering and preparation of information about the markets the organization is currently operating in or which it plans to enter, in terms of identifying and evaluating present and emergent customer "needs" and potential opportunities for business expansion. Such analysis is often seen as being undertaken by studying both the organization's current MARKETING ENVIRON-MENT and identifying future trends.

Planning is most commonly seen as a systematic process of assessing opportunities and resources, setting marketing objectives, developing a MARKETING STRATEGY, and formulating measures for implementation and control (*see*

MARKETING PLANNING). In this way, marketing managers are required to make decisions on target markets, market positioning, product and service development, pricing, distribution channels, physical distribution, communication, and promotion. The result of these activities is often contained in a marketing plan.

Implementation refers to the activities necessary to translate the marketing plan into action. It might include organizing marketing resources and developing the internal structure of the marketing unit, coordinating marketing activities, motivating marketing personnel, and effectively communicating within the unit. Bonoma (1985), however, reviewed 17 marketing textbooks and found implementation to be a generally neglected area of marketing management, with most emphasis directed toward analysis, planning, and control.

Finally, the marketing control process involves the measurement of results and evaluating progress according to standards of performance such as MARKET SHARE, cost sales ratios, advertising/sales ratios, or, more commonly in the case of BUSINESS-TO-BUSINESS MARKETING, techniques such as customer PORTFOLIO ANALYSIS or customer profitability analysis. Expected performance standards against which results are judged would commonly be specified as part of the marketing plan. Indeed, analysis, planning, implementation, and control might be seen as a continuous marketing management process in which during planning, guidelines for implementation are set and expected results specified for the control process, and feedback from the control process is used in the development of new plans.

This "textbook" view of marketing management embedded in the work of, for example, Kotler (1994) and McCarthy & Perreault (1993) has, however, been criticized on a number of counts (see Brownlie, 1991, for a summary of criticisms). In particular, the view of the marketing management process driven by "rational" marketing planning has been questioned by authors such as Brownlie (1991) and King (1985), who suggest that such a normative model of marketing management bears little relation to what practicing marketing managers actually do, being based instead on what textbook writers think marketing managers *ought to* do. According to Brownlie, much marketing management literature overlooks the part played by individual managerial judgement, vision, and experience, qualities seen as especially relevant in the area of marketing as opposed to, say, finance or production, given that the data on which marketing decisions are made are often unreliable and consumers often behave "irrationally" or unexpectedly, making a focus purely on analytical techniques inappropriate. Whereas marketing management may be reduced to a sole focus on analconsumer goods sectors, it is questioned whether this is representative across other sectors and levels of responsibility.

References are frequently made on this point to the work of authors such as Kotter (1982) and Mintzberg (1973), who have both looked at the nature of managerial work. Kotter, for instance, followed 15 general managers for a month and found that activities such as building networks, developing agendas, executing marketing activities, establishing values and norms, maintaining relationships, working through meetings and dialogues, establishing multiple objectives, spending time with others, and using rewards to secure support and desired behavior were more common in successful organizations than were planning and analysis activities. Mintzberg (1973) found that managers spend a great proportion of their time in oral communication and face-to-face contact rather than in formulating written plans.

A more accurate portrayal of marketing management might also reflect the increasingly wider focus of marketing itself (see MARKETING), to include the activities undertaken in SERVICES MARKETING, BUSINESS-TO-BUSINESS MARKETING, and NOT-FOR-PROFIT MARKETING, and also marketing activities directed toward parties in the organization's MARKETING ENVIRONMENT other than those individuals and organizations who purchase goods and services, such as stakeholders, publics, or employees.

Bibliography

Baker, M. J. (1991). *Marketing: An introductory text*, 5th edn, Basingstoke: Macmillan.

Bonoma, T. V. (1985). *The marketing edge: Making strategies work*. New York: Free Press.

Brownlie, D. T. (1991). Putting the management into marketing management. In M. J. Baker (Ed.), *Perspectives on marketing management*, Vol 1. Chichester: John Wiley.

Dibb, S., Simkin, L., Pride, W. M. & Ferrell, O. C. (1991). *Marketing: Concepts and strategies*, European edn, London: Houghton Mifflin Co.

King, S. (1985). Has marketing failed or was it never really tried? *Journal of Marketing Management*, 1, (1), 1–20.

Kotler, P. (1994). *Marketing management: Analysis, planning, implementation and control*, 8th edn, Englewood Cliffs, NJ: Prentice-Hall.

Kotter, J. (1982). *The general managers*. New York: Free Press.

McCarthy, E. J. & Perreault, R. (1993). *Basic marketing*, 11th edn, Homewood, IL: Irwin.

Mintzberg, H. (1973). *The nature of managerial work*. New York: Harper & Row.

FIONA LEVERICK

marketing mix   The term "marketing mix" was first used by Professor Neil Borden of Harvard Business School to describe a list of the important elements or ingredients that make up marketing programs, the idea having been suggested to him by Culliton's (1948) description of a business executive as a "mixer of ingredients" (Borden, 1964). More recently, McCarthy & Perreault (1987) have defined the marketing mix as the controllable variables that an organization can coordinate to satisfy its target market. The essence of the concept is the idea of a set of controllable marketing variables or a "tool kit" (Shapiro, 1985).

Some diversity of opinion exists as to the components of the marketing mix. Borden's own list is probably the longest, containing merchandising/product planning, pricing, branding, channels of distribution, personal selling, advertising, promotion, packaging, display, servicing, physical handling, fact finding and analysis, and market research. The best-known marketing mix is McCarthy's 4Ps, product, price, promotion, and place. However, this has been widely criticized as simplistic and misleading, especially in the areas of BUSINESS-TO-BUSINESS MARKETING, SERVICES MARKETING, and NOT-FOR-PROFIT MARKETING, and more recently Kotler (1986) has added politics and public relations and Booms & Bitner (1981), participants, physical evidence, and process to McCarthy's 4Ps.

see also **Marketing management**

Bibliography

Booms, B. H. & Bitner, M. J. (1981). Marketing strategies and organization structures for service firms. In J. Donnelly & J. R. George (Eds), *Marketing of services* (pp. 47–51). Chicago: American Marketing Association.

Borden, Neil H. (1964). The concept of the marketing mix. *Journal of Advertising Research* 2–7.

Culliton, J. W. (1948). *The management of marketing costs*. Division of Research, Graduate School of Business Administration, Harvard University.

Kotler, P. (1986). Megamarketing. *Harvard Business Review*, 64, (2), Mar.–Apr., 117–124.

McCarthy, E. J. & Perreault, W. D. Jr (1987). *Basic marketing*, 9th edn, Homewood, IL: Irwin.

Shapiro, B. P. (1985). Rejuvenating the marketing mix. *Harvard Business Review*, 63, Sept.–Oct., 28–34.

FIONA LEVERICK

marketing organization   The modern marketing department has had an evolution consisting of at least five phases, ranging from the simple sales department to the modern marketing company. In the early stages, many of the activities now associated with marketing would have been undertaken by a number of different functions, often in an uncoordinated manner. Thus, the sales department may have been responsible not only for managing the sales activity, but also for advertising and rudimentary market research; pricing may have been shared by accounting, sales, and production; while design and product development may have been the responsibility of research and development. As the importance of marketing became increasingly recognized, it emerged as a distinct corporate activity responsible for at least managing in a more coordinated fashion different activities that were seen to have some bearing on the development of the product and more generally on the relationship with the customer. Contemporarily, marketing is widely acknowledged as a core organizational activity, often with representation at board level.

The marketing activity can be structured according to functions; geographical areas; products; and customer types.

In the functional form, marketing is organized in terms of distinct specialisms, such as marketing research, sales, and product development, that report to a marketing manager or director. However, in organizations in several markets, there is clearly a need for marketing responsibility to be shared among several managers, each of whom may have responsibility for particular products and/or market areas. Marketing may also be organized in terms of geographical regions. A naive division may be between overseas and domestic operations. However, companies operating in several countries may have managers for different groups of countries, e.g., Asia Pacific; South America; Europe; or even specific countries. Within countries, there may also be managers for particular areas, such as the South West or the North East.

The product manager system developed as individual products became increasingly important. Under the general marketing management structure, "assistant" marketing managers were appointed to manage various aspects of the increasingly complex product portfolio. Individual managers, often referred to as brand or product managers, are given responsibility for coordinating all the marketing activities, such as advertising, marketing research, product development as well as, in some cases, responsibility for profit, of specific major products or brands.

Alternatively, marketing may be organized according to the customers or markets it serves, this being particularly appropriate where the firm markets to diverse customer groups with significantly differing requirements. Individual managers may be responsible for all the marketing effort for customer groups or markets and even for individual customers where the level of demand merits this. Hanan (1974) has termed this approach "market centring" and argues that it provides the company with a distinct competitive advantage because of the detailed knowledge of the customer or market that in theory the market manager should acquire. Such a structure would appear to support RELATIONSHIP MARKETING.

These approaches to marketing organization are not mutually exclusive, and the marketing activity may be a combination of two or more of these forms. For example, marketing may have functional managers supporting product and market managers. There may, in addition, be managers responsible for geographical regions.

Marketing may have representation at board level and may be expected to be an active participant in the development of overall organizational strategy. It may be a service activity providing marketing advice both to the board and to individual business or operating units. Individual business units or divisions may have individual marketing activities or departments; while marketing may be part of the matrix structure of an organization ensuring that marketing contributes to every major activity. Increasingly, it is argued that marketing should be embedded in the culture of an organization and that it should be recognized that all those whose activities in any way have some impact on the customers should be seen as, in effect, part-time marketers.

All decision makers can have access to cuswhich can be disseminated throughout the organization using computerized information systems (see MARKETING INFORMATION SYSTEMS). It could be argued that this might herald the end of the era of marketing as an important functional activity. Marketing may at best in the future be a minimal service activity, advising managers, responsible for particular relationships, on various facets of marketing, much of which may be outsourced to specialist agencies.

Bibliography

Hanan, M. (1974). Recognize your company around its markets. *Harvard Business Review* November–December.

Spillard, P. (1994). Organisation for marketing. In M. J. Baker (Ed.), *The marketing book* 3rd edn, (pp. 54–88). Oxford: Butterworth-Heinemann.

DALE LITTLER

marketing orientation A marketing orientation is usually seen as the company orientation necessary in order that the MARKETING CONCEPT is put into practice. It is often contrasted with the "production orientation" and "sales orientation" associated with the "production era" and "sales era" of the development of marketing thought respectively (see MARKETING; MARKETING CONCEPT).

A number of writers have gone into more detail on the precise nature of a "marketing orientation" in relation to the various activities associated with MARKETING MANAGEMENT. For example, according to McCarthy & Perreault (1993), marketing activities and the product offering are seen as guided primarily by customer "needs;" the role of market research is seen as to determine customer "needs" and how well the company is satisfying them; innovation activity is focused primarily on locating new opportunities, in, for example, products or technologies; profit (as opposed to sales volume) is the critical objective of marketing activity; packaging is designed for customer convenience and as a selling tool (over and above simply the protection of the product); inventory levels are set with customer requirements and costs in mind (rather than at the convenience of the supplier); the focus of advertising is to promote the needs-satisfying benefits of the product or service; the role of sales force, coordinated with the efforts of the rest of the firm, is to help customers to buy only if the product fits their needs; and so on. Somewhat more succinctly, Shapiro (1988) notes three key features of a marketing orientation: information on all important buying influences permeates every corporate function; strategic and tactical decisions are made interfunctionally and interdivisionally; and divisions and functions make well coordinated decisions and execute them with a sense of commitment.

Many authors (Doyle, 1985; Hooley & Lynch, 1985; Saunders & Wong, 1985; Witcher, 1990) have argued that UK companies in particular have found it difficult to develop a marketing orientation and that this has been a significant contributor to the decline in the UK's worldwide competitive position (see also Kheir-El-Din, 1991, for a review of this literature). Doyle et al. (1987), for example, found that almost 50 percent of a sample of UK companies acknowledged that they were unclear about the main types of customer in their markets and what the requirements or preferences of these customers were. The corresponding figure for a sample of Japanese companies was 13 percent. More recently, similar deficiencies were found in a sample of UK manufacturers involved in business-to-business marketing (Chartered Institute of Marketing/University of Bradford Management Centre, 1995).

Bibliography

Chartered Institute of Marketing/University of Bradford Management Centre (1995). *Manufacturing: The marketing solution.* Oxford: Chartered Institute of Marketing Report.

Doyle, P. (1985). Marketing and the competitive performance of British industry. *Journal of Marketing Management*, 1, (1), 87–98.

Doyle, P., Saunders, J. & Wright, L. (1987). *A comparative study of US and Japanese marketing strategies in the British market.* Warwick University Report.

Hooley, G. J. & Lynch, J. E. (1985). Marketing lessons from the UK's high flying companies. *Journal of Marketing Management*, 1, (1), 67–74.

Kheir-El-Din, A. (1991). The contribution of marketing to competitive success. In M. J. Baker (Ed.), *Perspectives on marketing management*, Vol. 1. Chichester: John Wiley.

McCarthy, E. J. & Perreault, R. (1993). *Basic marketing* 11th edn, Homewood, IL: Irwin.

Saunders, J. & Wong, V. (1985). In search of excellence in the UK. *Journal of Marketing Management*, 1, (2), 119–137.

Shapiro, B. P. (1988). What the hell is market-oriented? *Harvard Business Review*, **66**, Nov.–Dec., 119–125.

Witcher, B. J. (1990). Total marketing: Total quality and the marketing concept. *Quarterly Review of Marketing*, **15**, (2), Winter, 1–6.

FIONA LEVERICK

marketing performance   MARKETING PLANNING may involve the definition of targets or performance indicators. Measures commonly employed include product sales, costs, and market share. The company may also monitor the ability to meet customer specifications, delivery times, stock levels, tender success rates, the efficiencies of various operations, and such like.

DALE LITTLER

marketing plan   *see* MARKETING PLANNING

marketing planning   Marketing, like other functions and the organization as a whole, may have a plan which sets out the objectives and the means of achieving these. The plan can be viewed as a blueprint for future action. It will also set out targets against which performance can be monitored (*see* MARKETING CONTROL; MARKETING PERFORMANCE). The process of marketing planning, frequently prefaced with "strategic," is often depicted as consisting of a number of stages (Leppard & McDonald, 1991) involving: the gathering of information on the company's internal operations and its external environment; the identification of the strengths, weaknesses, opportunities, and threats (*see* SWOT ANALYSIS); the definition of the assumptions regarding the company and its environment; the setting of the marketing objectives in the light of the first three stages; the formulation of strategies aimed at achieving these objectives; the devising of programs setting out the timing of activities, costs, and revenues; the definition of responsibilities and the means of monitoring performance. The plan should ensure that the organization has in place the rudiments for implementing, monitoring, and controlling the strategy (Bonoma & Crittenden, 1988). The plan might contain specific objectives in terms of: sales, profits, and market share; the pricing strategy and policies; the communications strategy; and various other elements of the traditional MARKETING MIX necessary for the organization to meet its strategic objectives.

Such marketing plans may be undertaken, inter alia, at the level of the product or at the level of the strategic business unit.

In the marketing literature the distinction between corporate, strategic, and marketing planning has become blurred: all are often depicted as involving a similar methodology, for example. However, it is reasonable to assume that corporate planning embraces all of the different activities of the organization, whereas marketing planning should be regarded as focusing on the means by which marketing can play its part in facilitating the attainment of corporate objectives. In this sense then, (strategic) marketing planning is operational, a stance which appears compatible with that adopted by Greenley (1986).

It could be argued that marketing planning would apply particularly to large firms, which have the resources to direct the extensive analysis that such planning demands,

and which operate in stable, and therefore relatively predictable, environments (see Mintzberg, 1973).

Bibliography

Bonoma, T. V. & Crittenden, V. L. (1988). Managing marketing implementation. *Sloan Management Review*, **29**, Winter, 7–14.

Leppard, J. W. & McDonald, M. H. B. (1991). Marketing planning and corporate culture: A conceptual framework which examines management attitudes in the context of marketing planning. *Journal of Marketing Management*, **7**, (3), July, 213–36.

Greenley, G. E. (1986). *The strategic and operational planning of marketing*. Maidenhead: McGraw-Hill, 89–139.

Mintzberg, H. (1973). Strategy making in three modes. *California Management Review*, **16**, (2), Winter, 44–53.

DALE LITTLER

marketing strategy   In essence, marketing strategy embraces the customer targets or segments and the means, in terms of the MARKETING MIX elements, to be employed for these. Foxall (1981), for example, regards marketing strategy as being an indication of how each element of the marketing mix will be used to achieve the marketing objectives. Some such as Kotler (1994) argue that corporate or business strategy should be heavily influenced by marketing, on the grounds that strategy is concerned with the match between the organization and its environment, and that marketing, because of its unique position at the interface between the organization and the environment, must therefore be a prime mover in strategy formulation. It seems reasonable that marketing should be regarded as having a perspective critical to strategic management because it is primarily concerned with operationalizing the MARKETING CONCEPT. However, the other functional activities, such as those concerned with technological development, must also take into account wider environmental considerations; while many activities (finance, manufacturing, logistics, research and development) all contribute to the development and achievement of wider corporate goals.

Others, such as Greenley (1986) take a more limited view of marketing strategy, arguing that it is operational, i.e., it is oriented towards implementing the overarching strategy of the organization. It is likely that marketing strategy is shaped by and also shapes overall CORPORATE STRATEGY.

Greenley (1993) suggests that marketing strategy has five elements: market positioning and segmentation, involving the selection of segments for each product market; product positioning, involving decisions on the number and type of products for each segment; the selection of the marketing mix; market entry – how to enter, re-enter, position, or reposition products in each segment; and the timing of strategy and implementation given that, as Abell (1978) argues, there are only limited periods during which the fit between key requirements of a market and the particular competencies of a firm competing in that market is at an optimum. The marketing strategy is likely to be modified according to different stages of the PRODUCT LIFE CYCLE.

Bibliography

Abell, D. F. (1978). Strategic windows. *Journal of Marketing*, **42**, (3), 22–25.

Foxall, G. R. (1981). *Strategic marketing management*. London: Croom Helm.

Greenley, G. E. (1986). *The strategic and operational planning of marketing*. Maidenhead: McGraw-Hill.

Greenley, G. (1993). An understanding of marketing strategy. *European Journal of Marketing*, **23**, (8), 45–58.

Kotler, P. (1994). *Marketing management: Analysis, planning, implementation and control*, 8th edn, Englewood Cliffs, NJ: Prentice-Hall. Chapter 3.

DALE LITTLER

Markov analysis Markov analysis is named for the Russian mathematician Andrei Andreevich Markov, who died in 1922. A Markov chain or a Markov process is defined as a sequence of events in which the probability of each event depends upon the outcome of previous events.

Use in Organizations

At the organizational level, Markov analysis may be applied to describe and forecast the process of human resource flows or movements within, into, and out of the organization. Since there are a finite number of human resource movements which may occur in an organization (promotion, demotion, transfer, exit, new hire) Markov analysis may be used for investigating the rates of such movements over time or between two time periods (t and $t + k$).

The Markov analysis process begins by translating the existing organizational structure into a series of mutually exclusive and exhaustive states which individuals may occupy. These states correspond to job titles and are created on the basis of organizational function (marketing, accounting, operations, and so forth) and hierarchical level within function (Walker, 1980). In addition, an exit state is created to reflect movement out of the organization. States are arranged in a matrix, with the rows representing the states at time t and the columns representing the states at time $t + k$.

For the individuals in each state at t, the number and proportion occupying each state at $t + k$ is computed. For each row, the numbers of individuals in the cells represent the distribution of people by job title who stayed in the same position during the year, who moved to another position or who exited the organization. For each row the number of individuals in each cell at $t + k$ is divided by the row total at time t. The resultant proportions are defined as *transitional probabilities*, the probability of remaining in the initial state, of moving to another state or cell within the matrix, or exiting the organization (Heneman and Sandver, 1977).

The diagonal elements of the matrix represent the proportion of individuals who did not change states from t to $t + k$. The off-diagonal elements of the matrix represent the proportion of persons who moved from one state to another or who exited the organization from t to $t + k$. For each row of the matrix, the sum of the probabilities must equal 1 because the number of moves in the system is finite and the states are mutually exclusive and exhaustive. The matrix may be multiplied by itself to represent the movement of people in the organization over successive time periods.

Markov Analysis as a Forecasting Tool

Markov analysis may prove useful to human resource planners to help forecast shortages of employees in certain critical job titles over time (Mahoney and Milkovich, 1971).

Some recent applications of Markov analysis employ the technique as a tool in strategic human resource management (Bechet and Maki, 1987).

Limitations of Markov Analysis

Some authors have pointed out the limitations of Markov analysis and warn human resource managers to view personnel flows as stochastic or probabilistic rather than as deterministic and forecastable events (Vroom and MacCrimmon, 1968). Methodological problems such as sample size, choice of the time interval between t and $t + k$, multiple employee moves during a time period, and accuracy of personnel data may limit the usefulness of Markov analysis for human resources planning purposes (Heneman and Sandver, 1977).

Bibliography

Bechet, T. P. & Maki, W. R. (1987). Modeling and forecasting focusing on people as a strategic resource. *Human Resource Planning*, **10**, 209–17.

Heneman, H. G. & Sandver, M. G. (1977). Markov analysis in human resource administration: applications and limitations. *Academy of Management Review*, **2**, 535–42.

Mahoney, T. A. & Milkovich, G. T. (1971). The internal labor market as stochastic process. *Manpower and management science*, Eds. Bartholomew, D. J. & Smits, A. R. Lexington, MA: Lexington Books.

Vroom, V. H. & MacCrimmon, K. R. (1968). Toward a stochastic model of managerial careers. *Administrative Science Quarterly*, **13**, 26–46.

Walker, J. W. (1980). *Human Resource Planning*, New York: McGraw-Hill.

MARCUS HART SANDVER

mass media Mass media are impersonal channels by which the communicator can communicate directly with the target audience. The major mass media are cinema, television, radio, posters, newspapers and magazines. Although the communicator has a high degree of control over the content of the message, mass media channels are relatively inflexible in that in general the message cannot be adapted to suit the particular requirements of the audience. They can often be seen to involve the imposition of a message on an audience, and they cannot be adapted to suit specific moods or relevant wants. The use of domestic video recorders enables consumers to be more discerning in their consumption of television advertising messages, while selective exposure, selective perception, and selective retention can be powerful filtering processes affecting the effectiveness of mass media communications. Technological developments, such as advertising via the Internet, are already facilitating greater interactivity between the consumer and the communicator.

It may not be possible to aim communications at narrowly defined targets through mass media channels, because by definition these channels tend to have a wide appeal, although the readership of, for example, many magazines and the viewers of certain television programs and cinema films can be specialized. In the future, it is likely that the proliferation of cable, satellite, and terrestrial digital television will enable the targeting of specific clusters of consumers.

see also **Communications mix; Marketing communications**

DALE LITTLER

materials management

There are many definitions of materials management. Lee and Dobler (1977) identified that there was little agreement, at that time, on what functions were involved in materials management, LOGISTICS and physical distribution management. They define materials management as "an integrated management approach to planning, acquisition, conversion, flow and distribution of production materials from the raw materials state to the finished product state." Implicitly their definition refers to finished products within one firm, rather than the flow of materials through the entire supply chain down to the ultimate consumer. More recently some authorities have defined materials management as the cost and control of materials, incorporating all functions involved in obtaining and bringing materials into the plant; this appears to exclude movement through the plant and from the plant. However, others define materials management as including purchasing, inbound transport, storage, materials handling, inventory control, and production scheduling.

The definition of materials management appears now to be covered by the phrase supply chain management.

Underlying all the definitions is that materials management is a cross-functional, integrative approach to managing materials and information associated with materials Cross-functional management of the materials flow from the supply end of the business to the demand end of the business is intended to yield the following benefits:

- *Increased speed of material flow*: which results in reduced lead time; this enables shorter lead times to be quoted to customers which, in speed oriented businesses, can provide the business with a competitive advantage.
- *Greater flexibility and ability to respond to change*: integrating the materials flow allows the organization to respond customer volume changes or range changes as examples.
- *Reduced cost*: managing materials through the organization rather than in functional departments allows business wide visibility of inventories, allowing inventory reduction.
- *Greater dependability*: the integrated processes under materials management compared to separated functional processes can make material and order tracking easier in the organization, ensuring greater dependability (*see* DELIVERY DEPENDABILITY).
- *Improved quality*: in an organization that integrates the materials flow processes, quality problems are visible and made more visible to all parts of the materials flow. This also means that there is less waste in the organization arising from poor quality.

Bibliography

Cavinato, J. (1984). *Purchasing and materials management*. St Paul, MN: West Publishing.

Lee, L. & Dobler, D. (1977). *Purchasing and materials management*. New York: Tata McGraw-Hill.

Zenz, G. (1994). *Purchasing and the management of materials*. 7th edn, New York: Wiley.

CHRISTINE HARLAND

matrix organization

The distinctive feature of a matrix organization is that some individuals report to two (or even more) bosses. This form of organization, the only major type of organizational design with its origins in the twentieth century, violates the classic principle of unitary command ("one-person–one-boss"). It is employed when firms must:

(i) tightly coordinate or balance two or more dimensions such as resources (e.g., functional expertise) and businesses (e.g., products or projects);
(ii) while facing uncertainties that require high information processing; and
(iii) strong constraints on financial and human resources.

The matrix can be viewed as a diamond with three roles: the top manager who heads up and balances the dual chains of command; two or more matrix bosses who share common subordinates, and the individuals who report to the two different matrix bosses. However, a point to be emphasized is that matrix organization is more than this matrix structure. The dual structure must be supported by matrixed processes such as joint GOAL-SETTING, dual evaluation systems, by matrix LEADERSHIP behavior and individual skills, and by a matrix culture that constructively resolves conflicts and balances power (Davis & Lawrence, 1977).

The origins of matrix organization are to be found in the US space program of the 1960s, where the challenge was to meet President Kennedy's target of putting man on the moon by 1970, requiring highly complex project coordination, while meeting Congressional cost constraints. The term was supposedly coined by mathematically training engineers to describe this evolution in project management. Today, one recognizes that matrix organization takes different shapes on a continuum. Taking the continuum between function and project-oriented organization as an example, at each extreme are nonmatrix traditional organizations, where functional and project hierarchies are coordinated by general management at the top (*see* TOP MANAGEMENT TEAMS). Then there is the unbalanced matrix where one party is dominant (the secondary reporting lines are often denoted by dotted lines on organizational charts). In the full or balanced matrix, described above, the authority and responsibility of both project and functional managers is equal.

Matrix never applies to an entire organization. In balanced or unbalanced forms, it is applied to temporary projects, or it is an overlay on part of the organization. Almost all complex organizations, notably multinational corporations, display some matrix overlays. A local personnel manager in Germany reports directly to his or her country manager but has a "dotted line" responsibility to coordinate certain issues with the regional or corporate vice president for human resources.

Matrix organization attracted much attention in the 1970s when the pioneering works on this form of organization were written. The purported advantages are an increase in lateral COMMUNICATION and the amount of information that the organization can handle, better deployment of and flexibility in the use of human and other resources, increased MOTIVATION and personal development, and better achievement of technical excellence. But there are many disadvantages such as high levels of CONFLICT which may lead to power struggles between resource and business managers; ambiguity over resources, pay and assignments; difficulties in control ("passing the buck" and abdication of responsibility); the cost of support, information processes and meetings; slow DECISION MAKING; higher levels of STRESS (*see* ROLE CONFLICT). A number of organizations that introduced matrix in the 1970s reverted to traditional structures in the 1980s, leading some influential observers to comment that matrix organizations are so complex as to be virtually unmanageable. Davis and Lawrence (1977) argue that they are so difficult (because processes and culture must also be matrixed) that one should not consider this way of organizing unless there are no other alternatives.

In what settings and under what conditions is matrix management appropriate? The environment is one parameter. It may be considered when a high degree of both differentiation and integration is required, coupled with strong resource and cost constraints. This is often true for complex projects in construction, aerospace, investment banking and consulting services. This applies also to organizations that draw upon a pool of common expertise to develop different products or services for segmented markets, especially when technology and customer needs change frequently. The culture of the firm is another parameter (*see* ORGANIZATIONAL CULTURE). Matrix organization will not function well in bureaucratic or mechanistic cultures with strong vertical reporting lines, low competence in managing change, and minimal interdepartmental bureaucracy. There is also evidence that certain national cultures, those with a strong attachment to traditional authority, are less receptive to matrix organization. And as a generalization, it appears that project or business oriented matrices are more effective than balanced matrices, while functional or resource matrices are least effective.

What are the internal requirements of a matrix organization for it to be effective? There is insufficient research to provide a clear answer. The list is endless, typically organized into a number of headings (e.g., matrix = matrix structure + matrix systems + matrix culture + matrix behavior (Davis & Lawrence, 1977)). The roles and responsibilities of the managers and individual contributors within the matrix must be spelt out, and the necessary COMPETENCES provided through staffing and training. For example, the general manager at the apex of the matrix diamond must push responsibility down, maintain a certain distance, ensure clear goals, but be skilled at intervening in conflicts. Planning and control systems need to be tailored to the matrix organization. Unless a multidimensional measurement, reporting, and evaluation system is built, lack of clear accountability may lead to confusion and conflict escalation. Human resource systems must be adjusted, with implications for CAREER pathing, skill development (notably in teamwork, negotiation, and conflict management), appraisal, and compensation.

There has been surprisingly little research since the 1970s on matrix, partly because of the disillusionment and partly because of reduced interest in issues of organizational form and design. Both practitioners and researchers have turned their attention to how lateral relations (coordination and teamwork) can provide the flexibility of matrix without its disadvantages. Indeed, Ford and Randolph (1992) note that there are two dimensions of matrix management:

(i) the dual or multiple authority relationships (formal reporting lines); and
(ii) the horizontal communication linkages and teamwork that matrix organization intends to foster.

Reviewing the studies on matrix and project management, they suggest that most of the disadvantages appear to stem from the former, while most of the advantages originate from the latter.

Some organizations today appear to be moving "beyond matrix" in the sense of creating multidimensional management processes that provide flexibility to simple and unitary decision-making structures. Many multinational corporations exist in three- or four-dimensional matrix environments. Pressured by global competition, they must organize by product, geography, and function, often also having to satisfy customer segments that cut across product or geographic lines (e.g., global accounts) and to manage CORE COMPETENCES embedded in different parts of the firm. However, formal three- or four-dimensional matrix structures might paralyze decision making.

Many of these firms believe in keeping the lines of the formal authority structure as simple as possible, typically focusing on business/product lines or geographic lines. Matrix organization and project groups are utilized on an *ad hoc* basis and "dotted reporting lines" are used to manage important independencies. But these dotted lines are complemented by other horizontal linkage mechanisms – coordination committees, councils, task forces, temporary project teams, workshops, and personal relationships. And while there is a unitary authority structure, the key managers in this formal line of authority have broad and balanced perspectives that allow them to take the appropriate decisions, fostered by formative experiences in both functional and business roles. From the point of view of decision-making authority, matrix management can be seen not as a structure but as a frame-of-mind (Bartlett & Ghoshal, 1990).

This emerging organization looks more like a network of relationships and perspectives, and "network" appears to be a more appropriate metaphor today than the matrix of the space agency engineers in the 1960s.

see also **Span of control**

Bibliography

Bartlett, C. A. & Ghoshal, S. (1990). Matrix management: Not a structure, a frame of mind. Harvard Business Review, **68**, (4), 138–145.

Davis, S. M. & Lawrence, P. R. (1977). Matrix. Reading, MA: Addison-Wesley.

Ford, R. C. & Randolph, W. A. (1992). Cross-functional structures: A review and integration of matrix organization and project management. Journal of Management, **18**, (2), 267–294.

Janger, A. R. (1979). Matrix organization of complex business New York: Conference Board Report No. 763.
Kingdon, D. R. (1973). Matrix organization. London: Tavistock.

PAUL EVANS

matrix structure Often found in complex multinationals, matrix structures involve a combination of geography and product, as illustrated in figure 1.

In multinational corporations that have multiple product lines, country organizations will normally have a manager, and may operate production units and certain sales and marketing teams for the corporation's product groups sold in that country. However, product divisions, to which geographic management will be subordinate, will tend to set strategy for each worldwide product division as a whole. Reporting relationships are therefore complex, with many executives reporting to more than one central unit.

Country managers report primarily to the area management and are responsible overall for the activities country. They will also usually act as the corporation's representative for external affairs within a country. Each country may be treated as a profit center, but under some matrix systems and for a variety of reasons (for example, tax treatment, location of high-cost facilities or services, and the like), the maximization of profitability by country may well be subordinate to regional or global product and profit considerations. In multinational corporations the management of international tax is especially important, as is management of the exchange rate risk.

Below the country manager level, operations tend to be divided by product group. The management of such groups have dual reporting relationships to the country manager and to their own product divisions. In many matrix structures the latter relationship overrides the former, again increasing the difficulty of assessing country units on a pure profit basis. In the banking industry, for example, the use of worldwide account teams to service key global customers may well result in the sacrifice of profitability in one country in order to provide a superior customer service worldwide. Similarly, banks relinquish profits on scarce risk lending capacity in difficult countries in order to provide such capacity to selected worldwide key account customers at lower rates.

In general, the importance of the geographic component of matrix structures has diminished over time, and in some companies the position of an overall country manager has disappeared, with each main product division operating as a global business in its own right. Matrix structures are complex and difficult to manage. There is frequent rivalry between the perceived interests of geographic units and product groups. The general trend, however, has been that the greater the degree of overseas product diversity, the more likely it has been that product considerations take precedence.

A specific problem that has affected corporations operating multinational matrix structures has been the dominance of headquarters operations staffed predominantly by home country nationals in attempting to set the strategies of overseas subsidiaries. Where domestic product groups have attempted to set global strategy, there has often tended to be a lack of knowledge of overseas conditions, and policies have often been established on the basis of domestic conditions. This is especially true of US multinationals, but also applies to MNCs from other countries – most recently to the emerging Japanese MNCs. While, clearly, the US domestic market is usually paramount, the failure to appreciate international conditions and to allow non-US nationals sufficiently strong

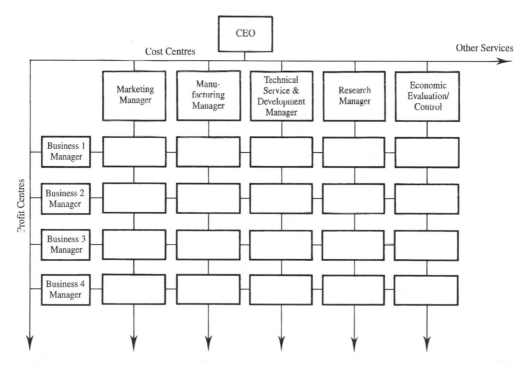

Figure 1 The form of a matrix organization.

geographic inputs into policy making has often led to the growth of overseas competition that has proved damaging. The contrast with Japanese corporations in this respect is marked. Japanese corporations very carefully examine local markets and design strategies to meet local product needs and minimize political friction, although foreigners have not been significantly accepted by these corporations.

The Japanese have also structurally attempted to coordinate not merely by product and geography but also by function. In this, production especially is coordinated on a worldwide basis and cross-functional product divisional teams endeavor to insure that any interdivisional rivalries are minimized, while gains made in one division are transferred rapidly to others. This elimination of rivalries leads to cooperation in the production of hybrid products, using fusion technology to cut across divisional boundaries. Marketing is less coordinated on a worldwide basis and localized marketing strategies may well be used. By contrast, in many Western companies operating a DIVISIONAL STRUCTURE and/or an SBU STRUCTURE, the boundaries between divisions or SBUs may well make such cooperation difficult, especially when reward structures are based on unit rather than corporate performance. In such circumstances sharing profits or accepting costs from another unit may apparently diminish unit performance despite actually or potentially improving overall corporate results.

Bibliography

Bartlett, C. A., Bartlett, A. & Sumantra, G. (1990). Matrix management not a structure, a frame of mind. *Harvard Business Review*, **68** (4), 138–45.

Davis, S. M. & Lawrence, P. R. (1978). Problems of matrix organisations. *Harvard Business Review*, **56** (3), 131–42.

Galbraith, J. R. (1971). Matrix organisational designs. *Business Horizons*, **15** (1), 29–40.

DEREK F. CHANNON

McKinsey 7S model   While, historically, a relationship was established between strategy and structure, the concept has been broadened by McKinsey and Company to encompass a framework linking strategy and a number of other critical variables. It has been argued that the strategy–structure model is an inadequate description of critical elements in the successful implementation of strategy, and that a successful "fit" between those elements and corporate strategy is essential to insure successful implementation. The McKinsey model is illustrated in figure 1.

McKinsey and Company believe that there are seven broad areas which need to be integrated to achieve overall successful strategy implementation. Apart from strategy itself and formal organizational structure, the other variables that they have identified are as follows: shared values, attitudes, and philosophy; staffing and the people orientation of the corporation; administrative systems; practices and procedures used to administer the organization, including the reward and sanction systems; organizational skills, capabilities, and core competencies; and the management style of the corporation as set by its leadership. This model is called by McKinsey the 7S framework.

Structure

In the McKinsey model, it is argued that while formal structure is important, dividing up the organizational task

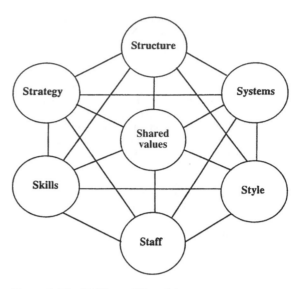

Figure 1 The McKinsey 7S model.
Source: Waterman et al. (1980, p.7).

is not the critical structural problem: rather, it is developing the ability to focus on those dimensions that are currently important to the evolution of the corporation, and being ready to refocus as critical dimensions shift.

Systems

By systems, McKinsey and Company mean the procedures, formal and informal, which make the organization work. It is important to understand how the organization actually works: it is often reliant on informal rather than formal systems.

Style

Although it is often underestimated, management style, and especially that of the CEO, is an important determinant in what is strategically possible for the corporation.

Staff

In the McKinsey model, the nature of the people factor is broadened and redefined. Consideration of people as a pool of resources, who need to be nurtured, developed, guarded, and allocated, is seen to turn this dimension into a variable that needs to be given close attention by top management.

Skills

Given a chosen strategy, this variable enables the corporation to evaluate its capabilities realistically in the light of the critical factors required for success. One particular problem may actually be in weeding out old skills, which can be a significant block to necessary change and can prevent the development of new skills.

Conclusion

At the core of the model are superordinate goals and shared values around which the organization pivots. These values define the organization's key beliefs and aspirations and form the core of its corporate culture. Corporations needing to change their values endeavor to undergo dramatic transformations which involve fundamental reappraisals of all aspects of activities. Sometimes such changes are introduced as re-engineering projects (*see*

VALUE-DRIVEN RE-ENGINEEERING). A major reason for the high failure rate of these projects is their lack of success in implanting new shared values that can embrace the radical changes required to achieve the dramatic stretch targets set by such programs.

Bibliography

Waterman, R. (1982). The seven elements of strategic fit. *Journal of Business Strategy* no. 3, 68–72.

Waterman, R., Peters, T. & Phillips, J. (1980). Structure is not organisation. *The McKinsey Quarterly*, summer, 2–20.

DEREK F. CHANNON

mediation   While mediation has traditionally been an adjunct to labor negotiations and international conflict, its use is increasingly being extended to resolve differences in families and communities, at work, and across levels of government. As a mode of dispute processing, mediation involves an outsider, a so-called third party, who assists the principal parties in the resolution of their differences. Mediation is generally a voluntary process where the mediator lacks formal decision-making authority. Because of its voluntary nature, the ability of parties to actively participate in the resolution of their own differences, and the relative speed of the process, mediation is often seen as a better, more satisfying and harmonious, more efficient, less costly way for society to deal with its conflicts.

Although mediation has long been part of labor negotiations, only recently has it spread to other disputing arenas in organizations. Mediation is being used to settle legal claims between firms, and is now a step in many grievance and complaint procedures, including the role of ombudsman. In addition, informal mediation is coming to be recognized as a necessary part of team work and organizational change, and as a function of management generally.

Mediators assist parties by giving them a forum to air their differences, vent their feelings and frustrations, explore options for settlement, and appreciate the consequences of no agreement (Moore, 1986). What mediators actually do in a dispute, whether they push for settlement or try to alter how parties relate and communicate with each other, is a function of their diagnosis of the conflict, their relationships with the parties, and their background and training, among other factors (Kressel and Pruitt, 1989; Bush and Folger, 1994; Kolb et al., 1994).

Bibliography

Bush, R. B. & Folger, J. (1994). *Mediation at the Crossroads*, San Francisco: Jossey-Bass.

Kolb, D. M. & Associates (1994). *When Talk Works: Profiles of Mediators*, San Francisco: Jossey-Bass.

Kressel, K. & Pruitt, D. (1989). *Mediation of Social Conflict*, San Francisco: Jossey-Bass.

Moore, C. (1986). *The Mediation Process*, San Francisco: Jossey-Bass.

DEBORAH M. KOLB

mentoring programs   Mentoring programs are initiatives designed to encourage relationships that support learning and development of targeted employee populations (e.g. new hires, high potentials, individuals from diverse backgrounds). They are generally established to create *accountability for development* and *accessibility to developmental relationships* (see STRATEGIC ISSUES IN DIVERSITY).

Mentoring programs vary in specific objectives, degree of structure, number of participants, associated training and education, and monitoring and evaluation methods.

Sometimes formally assigned relationships remain superficial or become destructive, participants have unrealistic expectations for the program and fail to seek other opportunities for development, and/or those who do not participate feel unfairly excluded. These unintended negative consequences are minimized when program objectives and design are aligned with an organization's culture and HUMAN RESOURCE STRATEGY, participation is voluntary, and adequate education and training are provided.

There are a number of alternatives to mentoring programs that can foster developmental relationships for a wide range of employees. These include: (a) job assignments that require individuals who have complementary development needs to collaborate; (b) PERFORMANCE APPRAISAL and COMPENSATION STRATEGY practices that recognize and reward mentoring and coaching behaviors; (c) SUCCESSION PLANNING processes that explicitly monitor the mentoring and coaching needs of candidates for leadership positions; (d) work teams that have mentoring as one of their primary purposes; and (e) various homogeneous and heterogeneous groups whose purposes are to promote personal learning through dialogue. Given trends of globalization, flatter and team-oriented organizations, increasing work force diversity and rapid technological change, multiple strategies to promote mentoring are essential. The maximum value of mentoring programs is achieved when they are implemented (and aligned) with related human resource practices.

Bibliography

Kram, K. E. & Hall, D. T. (1996). Mentoring in a context of diversity and turbulence. *Human Resource Strategies for Managing Diversity* Eds. Lobel, S & Kossek, E. Oxford: Blackwell Publishers.

Murray, M. (1991). *Beyond the Myths and Magic of Mentoring: How to Facilitate an Effective Mentoring Program*, San Francisco: Jossey-Bass.

Noe, R. A. (1988). An investigation of the determinants of successful assigned mentoring relationships. *Personnel Psychology*, 41, 457–79.

KATHY E. KRAM

merger guidelines, 1992   These guidelines are the third set of guidelines offered to the business community in the past quarter century. They are an effort to clarify the circumstances under which the current administration will challenge a merger which it believes to be in violation of the Clayton Act. The guidelines offer a five-step approach to the analysis of a merger:

(1) the definition of the market and measure of industry concentration,

(2) the evaluation of the potential adverse effects of the proposed merger,

(3) the analysis of the condition of entry into the market (see BARRIERS TO ENTRY),

(4) the existence of potential efficiency from the merger and

(5) the examination of the circumstances in the case where one of the merging firms is failing.

Once the market boundaries are defined using the method known as the five percent rule, or SSNIP (*see* MARKET DEFINITION), the market is classified as being highly concentrated (if the post merger HERFINDAHL-HIRSCHMAN INDEX, HHI, has a value greater than 1800), moderately concentrated (if, after the merger, 1000 HHI 1800), or unconcentrated (if the post merger HHI 1000). While a challenge in the latter case is unlikely, in general the likelihood of a challenge increases, all else constant, for higher levels of concentration and for larger changes in the level of concentration.

The second and third steps involve numerous tests and screens which evaluate factors inherent in the industry which facilitate or limit collusion which could arise as a result of the merger.

Evidence indicating a diminished capacity for the abuse of market power will tend to lessen the likelihood of a challenge. When the reverse is true, the likelihood of a challenge is enhanced. In addition, the extent to which the proposed merger may offer a unique method for achieving ECONOMIES OF SCALE or other cost savings is considered as a possible defense in cases which might otherwise be challenged. Finally, the guidelines recognize that the threat of increased market power is minimized in cases where one of the merging firms is in imminent danger of failure. As such, a challenge is not likely as long as the failing firm has made a good faith effort to find an alternative partner with which there exists a decreased potential danger to competition arising from a merger.

These guidelines are largely an extension of those presented in 1982–84. Both sets of guidelines are generally accepted as being more lenient toward firms which wish to merge than those introduced in 1968. In an examination of recent antitrust activity Lande (1994) finds that of 61 mergers challenged by the Federal Trade Commission between 1987 and 1992 only one involved a merger with a post merger HHI value less than 2000. In addition, only four challenges involved mergers where the change in the HHI was less than 400 points. He cites this and other evidence as indicative of the attenuation of aggressiveness in antitrust enforcement.

Heightened concerns by business over increasing foreign competition during the past decade may have fueled the discussion of a need for greater leniency in the guidelines, but foreign competition's effect on the leniency of the new guidelines appears to be limited. While the two most recent sets of guidelines specifically recognize the need to include foreign imports in the definition of the market, they also clearly recognize that trade restrictions may limit the ability of foreign firms to respond to domestic price increases.

see also **Antitrust policy**

Bibliography

Lande, R. (1994). Beyond Chicago: will activist antitrust arise again? *Antitrust Bulletin*, **39**, 1–25.

Mueller, W. & O'Connor, K. (1993). The 1992 horizontal merger guidelines: a brief critique. *Review of Industrial Organization*, **8**, 163–72.

Ordover, J. & Willig, R. (1993). Economics and the 1992 merger guidelines: a brief survey. *Review of Industrial Organization*, **8**, 139–50.

US Department of Justice (1992). *Horizontal Merger Guidelines*. Washington, DC: US Government Printing Office.

US Federal Trade Commission Bureau of Competition (1992). *How 1992 Guidelines Differ from Prior Agency Standards*. Washington, DC: US Federal Trade Commission.

GILBERT BECKER

merit pay   Merit pay refers to pay increases based on PERFORMANCE APPRAISAL (Heneman, 1992). The higher the rating of an employee's performance, the larger the pay increase granted to the employee. The size of the pay increase allocated is dependent upon the employee's position in the rate ranges as assessed by the compa-ratio. The larger the compa-ratio for an employee, the smaller the size of the increase granted in order to keep the employee's salary within the rate range. Under a traditional merit pay plan, pay increases are made a permanent addition to the employee's salaries. Under a lump sum merit pay plan, pay increases are bonuses not made as permanent additions to employees' salaries. Merit pay plans are used in over 80 percent of US organizations, primarily for exempt employees (Peck, 1984). Merit pay is one form of PAY FOR PERFORMANCE.

Merit pay has been shown to be related to positive attitudes toward work, including PAY SATISFACTION (see JOB SATISFACTION). The evidence regarding the relationship of merit pay to subsequent productivity is mixed, with some studies showing an improvement in productivity and others a decrease (Heneman, 1992). Merit pay is often criticized as being associated with an entitlement culture.

In order for merit pay plans to be effective, two conditions must be met (National Research Council, 1991). First, performance appraisal ratings must have criterion relevance, be free from RATING ERRORS, and be accurate. Second, pay increases must be large enough to differentiate poor from excellent performers.

Bibliography

Heneman, R. L. (1992). *Merit Pay: Linking Pay Increases to Performance Ratings*, Reading, MA: Addison-Wesley.

National Research Council (1991). *Pay-for-performance: Evaluating Performance Appraisal and Merit Pay*, Washington, DC: National Academy Press.

Peck, C. (1984). Pay and Performance: the Interaction of Compensation and Performance Appraisal. New York: The Conference Board.

ROBERT L. HENEMAN

methodologies of business ethics research   comprise the variety and justification of methods by which business ethics research is undertaken. Business ethics research conventionally is divided into two approaches: normative and descriptive. Normative research is concerned with evaluating or prescribing the behavior of business persons and organizations. Descriptive research, by contrast, focuses on describing individual and organizational behavior so that it can be explained and possibly predicted. This conventional division of business ethics into two fairly distinct fields can be criticized as theoretically untenable and ethically undesirable (see below). But the distinction between normative and descriptive business ethics research *at least* captures a variety of important *surface* differences of current practice in the field, even if those differences fade at a deeper level of scrutiny.

Normative research focuses on what ought to be, and typically is the province of persons trained in philosophy, religious studies, or related liberal arts subjects. Such persons may see themselves filling the role of external critic of established business practices. By contrast, descriptive business ethics research usually is performed by applied social scientists, and often takes place within business organizations and business schools. It displays a more pragmatic approach to issues, and arguably is less prone to take a critical stance toward the established norms and goals of business. More importantly, mainstream social science theory (at least in the US) generally forgoes questions of what ought to be in favor of queries into what is. The goal is to explain the behavior of business organizations and their members. Business policies and practices are studied to discover what influences them and what they in turn influence. Although questions of their ethical propriety may be important, those are questions which range beyond the scope of conventional social science inquiry.

Language and Style

These different institutional homes and academic outlooks incorporate significant differences of style and language. Mainstream empiricists utilize the consensually agreed upon methods of their social scientific training, whether it be laboratory experimentation, business database studies, or surveys. Research is guided by relatively formal design criteria which, if judiciously followed, are thought capable of supporting explanatory models of business behavior. Data typically are analyzed utilizing a variety of quantitative statistical methods (e.g. regression analysis).

By contrast, philosophically driven research includes nothing like the highly specified research methods of social science. Although there is methodological self-reflection in normative ethics generally, it tends to be individualized to the task and author at hand. Any generally applicable normative method is best described informally in terms of intellectual virtues such as consistency, clarity, avoidance of emotional manipulation, etc. Thus, whereas descriptive work has relatively standardized forms of method and presentation, normative work is much more eclectic and idiosyncratic.

Differences of language and presentation, plus different attitudes toward methodological uniformity, can contribute to misunderstanding. For example, normative theorists usually use the phrase "ethical behavior" to refer to behavior which in fact is ethically proper. Descriptive researchers, however, use the term "ethical" in a non-normative sense. For them, "ethical behavior" denotes the behavior of a person or organization confronted with ethical issues or choices, regardless of whether or not the behavior in question is normatively proper.

Assumptions about Human Agency

The normative and descriptive domains invoke explanatory models that rest upon distinct and sometimes unstated assumptions about human agency. The normative approach typically assumes that actions are performed with some degree of autonomy and responsibility. For some (metaphysical – as distinct from political – libertarians), this assumption entails a denial that ethical action easily can be placed in the kind of causal or nomological nexus empiricists usually seek. For other normative theorists (sometimes called "soft" determinists), the assumption of autonomy and responsibility attendant to ethical deeds suggests that not all causal factors are on equal footing.

Autonomous and responsible actions involve the agent's choices, *even if* those choices are causally determined. Thus only causal factors that work through a person's choices preserve autonomy and moral responsibility.

Searches for the causal antecedents of behavior, then, can be problematic to normative theorists, as the goal of such a search conflicts with a normative assumption about human agency. To some normative theorists, success on the part of the empiricist in finding the sources of behavior risks compromising one's ability to impute normative significance to the behavior. Moreover, to some normative theorists, ethically proper action is self-explanatory, needing no additional explanation in social scientific terms.

In contrast, management researchers – even if they admit that in some sense individuals should be considered ethically responsible for their actions – nevertheless are more interested in finding causal determinants of ethical behavior (e.g. reward systems, codes of conduct, individual characteristics). External determinants of behavior are more interesting and useful for study because they are factors a manager can control. For example, a manager can manipulate reward systems in order to influence subordinates' behavior. In the descriptive approach, both ethically proper and improper actions are viewed as complex phenomena that should be explained by a combination of causal factors. Even whistleblowing, often presumed to be an example of autonomous, ethically proper action, is understood by social scientists to be the product of multiple internal and external causal factors.

Role of Abstraction vs. Empirical Detail

Modern normative ethical theory typically (though not universally) pursues a standard of moral reasoning or action which holds for persons in general. Consequently, normative theory often is framed at an abstract level, and is distanced from the specifics of any particular social setting. Even though normative inquiries often rely on the detailed study of real-life cases in business ethics, that kind of empirical detail often merely provides a venue for applying normative theories or unearthing implicit counter-intuitive implications of such theories. It is only at the level of dealing with particular issues that normative theory is context sensitive; its general principles typically are framed in context-neutral fashion.

While normative business ethics thus displays a bias toward abstraction, descriptive business ethics leans in the opposite direction. Even though the abstract concepts of empirical psychology and sociology may play key roles in empirical business ethics research, those concepts are expected at some point to be empirically or observationally defined so that they can be concretely measured. Thus, the social scientist may devalue the philosopher's moral judgments because they cannot be evaluated by standardized empirical tests, nor be used to predict or explain behavior. But the social scientist's statements about "ethical" behavior may seem of secondary value to a normative theorist, because they do not address the evaluative questions of right and wrong.

Basis for Evaluating Theoretical Claims

The "method" of normative ethical theory – insofar as there is a common one – involves achieving what Rawls (1971) calls a reflective equilibrium between theoretical constructions (i.e., general normative principles) and persons' considered moral judgments. Everything from the formal sciences to common norms and intuitions is relevant in this process. Importantly, actual moral practice functions among the criteria for evaluating moral theories; were a normative theory to prescribe gratuitous punishment, we would have at least *prima facie* grounds for rejecting the theory. But these grounds are only *prima facie*; inconsistency with current moral practice in no way *necessitates* the rejection of a normative principle. After all, the point of such principles is to guide and possibly correct current practice. Normative claims and principles, in short, are to be evaluated according to an open-ended array of evidence, concerns, and insights, all tied together by generalized standards of good argument (e.g. no unseemly emotional appeals, no efforts to intimidate, etc.) rather than by some precisely defined methodology.

In descriptive business ethics, the initial stages of theory development may proceed in somewhat intuitive fashion. However, on the conventional account an acceptable theory ultimately must contribute to one's ability to explain and predict. Thus, theory justification is accomplished via a putatively natural scientific model of empirical confirmation or disconfirmation, or through the theory's pragmatic ability to predict behavior and solve problems. Although critics of this conventional view of science argue that (a) the ideas of empirical confirmation and disconfirmation are beset with conceptual problems, and (b) that a variety of non-rational factors enter into the acceptance or rejection of a theory, the bulk of descriptive research on business ethics maintains this traditional empiricist (or neo-positivist) view of the goals and methods of inquiry.

Conventional Empirical Approaches

The prominent research methods within conventional descriptive business ethics fall within two broad categories: experimental and correlational research. Within both categories, researchers are expected to begin with hypotheses rooted in social science theory. They then are to design a study that will test the hypothesized relationships.

Experimental approaches are used when the researcher wants to investigate a causal relationship between two variables, essentially investigating whether some phenomenon, X, "causes" another, Y. Experiments can be conducted in laboratory or field settings. The experimenter manipulates one or more independent variables (X, above), and then measures variations in the dependent variable (Y, above). The two major criteria for evaluating experimental research are *internal* and *external* validity. If an experiment is internally valid, the researcher can be confident that the independent variable "caused" the dependent variable. Laboratory experiments are generally thought to be higher in internal validity because the investigator has maximum control over the independent variables. For example, a laboratory experimenter might hypothesize that individuals would be more likely to steal under certain circumstances, and then randomly assign subjects to conditions that represent either the presence or absence of those circumstances. External validity has to do with the generalizability of the research results. Laboratory experiments are lower in external validity because they are conducted in artificial settings that strip away much of the complexity of real-life settings. Field experiments are higher in external validity because they are conducted in actual organizational settings, but they are lower in internal validity because the antecedent conditions (the Xs) are more difficult to control.

Correlational approaches are used when the research has hypothesized relationships among variables which cannot be manipulated by the researcher. Data to test the hypotheses may come from archival sources, or from surveys the researcher administers. For example, the researcher might hypothesize that individuals' cynicism toward business ethics will be higher for business school students and lower for older, more experienced members of the business community. A survey could be conducted of members of both groups, and their responses could be compared. Or, the research might hypothesize that corporate crime is higher in firms that are in financial difficulty. In this case, archival data about convictions and financial performance could be collected and subjected to correlational analysis.

Alternative Empirical Approaches

There is, however, descriptive business ethics research which departs from the standard, quantitatively oriented methods. These approaches involve a variety of qualitative techniques which eschew numerical analysis for some form of in-depth verbal description or textual and verbal analysis. This research does not claim to provide generalizable claims in the fashion of quantitatively oriented research, but often is presented as a basis for building theories which can then be tested by more conventional quantitative techniques. Constructing a robust theoretical model of some category of phenomena may require intimate familiarity with it, familiarity best obtained by extensively talking to, observing, or living among the people involved. Qualitative research, in the fashion of interviews and ethnographic research such as participant observation, provides the basis for that kind of in-depth understanding.

The theoretical account resulting from qualitative research *may* be shaped into a formal model and then subjected to quantitative empirical test. But more radical non-quantitative research questions this possibility, and argues for the unavoidably malleable, interpretive character of all social or behavioral phenomena. In this view, any efforts to quantitatively assess phenomena by "objective" means (such as survey research) disguise the fact that the resulting portrait is *artificially* static. Quantitative methods, according to this alternative view, treat essentially interpretive phenomena as considerably more fixed and objective than we are entitled to claim.

More importantly, radically interpretive empirical research rejects the assumption of a normative/empirical distinction which underlies the conventional approaches to business ethics research. Rather, it argues that even the mainstream empiricist methodology imposes a normative standard on its subjects. Conventional empiricists may go so far as to admit that normative concerns lead them to study some phenomena rather than others (e.g. ethical concerns may prompt one to study the effects of certain forms of organizational discipline). But conventional empiricists would argue that standardized empirical methods guarantee that any conclusions will be value-neutral, favoring no particular ethical position. To the critic of conventional methodology, however, such "objective" methods inherently favor a particular set of ethical claims (usually held to be those of the status quo or dominant power structure). For example, conventional empirical research on the effects of punishment on employees focuses on whether or not punishment is effective in changing behavior. But in doing so, this ostensibly neutral research assumes a consequentialist view of punishment (i.e., behavioral consequences are all that matters), and defines the relevant consequences from a managerial standpoint (rather than from the standpoint of, e.g., a labor union organizer). To the critic, then, empirical business ethics research – despite its methodological and stylistic differences from normative research – does not avoid normative issues so much as hide them.

Integrative Approaches

The more radically interpretive approach to empirical methodology, then, suggests the possibility of more integrative approaches to business ethics inquiry, in which normative and empirical considerations are not so readily isolated. Various types of integrative methods are well known in other fields. Kohlberg's work on moral development, to take just one example, uses normative principles or categories not only to label levels of moral development, but also to carry out some of the explanatory work in accounting for an individual's transition from one type of moral reasoning to another. (In Kohlberg's view, people move toward higher levels of moral reasoning in part *just because* they are higher, i.e., morally preferable.)

Within business ethics research, however, integrative methodologies are rare. Most typically, they occur when the empirical methods used are of the more interpretive, qualitative sort. (Jackall's *Moral Mazes* (1988) exemplifies this approach, simultaneously describing the ethical assumptions and standards of managerial work *and* the normative ethical problems attendant to those standards.) Integrative empirical work in the conventional quantitative tradition is rarer, however, as the underlying assumptions of that approach usually work against integrative tendencies. Extant work which attempts such integration generally uses normatively articulated categories to initially frame issues and phenomena, which then are analyzed according to conventional empirical methods (e.g. Victor & Cullen, 1988).

see also **Business ethics**

Bibliography

Donaldson, T. (1994). When integration fails. *Business Ethics Quarterly*, 4, (2), 157–71.

Jackall, R. (1988). *Moral Mazes: The World of Corporate Managers.* New York: Oxford University Press.

Rawls, J. (1971). *A Theory of Justice.* Cambridge, Mass.: Harvard University Press.

Trevino, L. K. (1992). Experimental approaches to studying ethical/unethical behavior in organizations. *Business Ethics Quarterly*, 2, (2), 121–36.

Trevino, L. K. & Weaver, G. R. (1994). Business Ethics/Business Ethics: One field or two? *Business Ethics Quarterly*, 4, (2), 113–28.

Victor, B. & Cullen, J. (1988). The organizational bases of ethical work climates. *Administrative Science Quarterly*, 33, 101–25.

Victor, B. & Stephens, C. U. (1994). Business ethics: A synthesis of normative philosophy and empirical social science. *Business Ethics Quarterly*, 4, (2), 145–57.

Weaver, G. R. & Trevino, L. K. (1994). Normative and empirical business ethics: Separation, marriage of convenience, or marriage of necessity? *Business Ethics Quarterly*, 4, (2), 129–33.

GARY R. WEAVER
and LINDA KLEBE TREVINO

micro environment The environment of an organization is generally viewed as comprising two components: the MACRO ENVIRONMENT and the micro environment which, unlike the former, consists of elements or activities with which the organization interacts directly and over which it can therefore exert influence, if not control. The major aspects of the micro environment are: competitors; suppliers; CHANNELS OF DISTRIBUTION; customers; and the media (*see* MASS MEDIA).

DALE LITTLER

minimum efficient scale (MES) The MES represents the smallest output level for a firm at which long run average costs are at a minimum (*see* LONG RUN COST CURVES). If the long run average cost curve were U-shaped and continuous, then the MES firm size would be unique. However, statistical estimates of cost curves for various industries suggest that long run average cost curves are L-shaped where there are significant ECONOMIES OF SCALE at low levels of output which are exhausted relatively quickly, then average costs remain constant; see Johnston (1960) and Scherer, Beckenstein and Kaufer (1975). This means that the MES represents a lower bound on firm size but not an upper bound.

Estimates of the MES have also been obtained using engineering surveys and survivor studies. With engineering surveys, industrial engineers and other experts provide information concerning the expected changes in costs as the scale of operations increases and from this the MES is determined. Recognizing the difficulties in estimating the MES, Stigler (1958) suggested that those firms which survived in the competitive environment should be the most efficient. Survivor studies examine the changes in the number of firms in different size classes over time to determine the optimum size plant (or, as Stigler suggested, optimum range of sizes). In the short run, firms may not be operating at the optimal scale, so reliable survivor estimates must be based on industries in long run equilibrium. Unlike engineering studies, these studies use data from operating firms, but those firm sizes which survive could have done so through anti-competitive behavior or because of BARRIERS TO ENTRY which would not reflect efficiency. Nevertheless, survivor studies tend to confirm the results obtained from the engineering and statistical cost studies: there appears to be a wide range of optimum plant sizes suggesting a range of output levels where long run average costs are constant.

Knowledge of the plant-level MES in an industry is important to understand the feasible number of firms which could operate in the industry. Scherer, Beckenstein and Kaufer (1975) concluded from their estimates of MES that actual concentration ratios in US industries are much higher than required by the estimated minimum efficient scale. If correct, these estimates indicate that antitrust policies which would break up large firms might not cause inefficiency. However ECONOMIES OF SCOPE are also important in industry and estimates of economies of scale and the MES may fail to detect these additional causes of larger firm size, so any policy actions must be carefully considered. (See Gold (1981) for a critical survey of the theoretical issues regarding firm size.)

The behavior of costs for plants operating at less than MES is also important. If costs increase significantly when plants are smaller than the MES, then the disadvantages of small size are much greater and this could deter entry into the industry.

Bibliography

Gold, B. (1981). Changing perspectives on size, scale, and returns: an interpretive survey. *Journal of Economic Literature*, 19, 5–33.
Johnston, J. (1960). *Statistical Cost Analysis*. New York: McGraw-Hill.
Scherer, F. M., Beckenstein, A. & Kaufer, E. (1975). *The Economics of Multi-plant Operation: An International Comparisons Study*. Cambridge, MA: Harvard University Press.
Stigler, G. J. (1958). The economies of scale. *Journal of Law and Economics*, 1, 54–71.

ROBERT E. MCAULIFFE

mission The "mission" of a company is an important element in establishing the strategy of the organization. Establishing the mission itself is usually a difficult and demanding task. Top management tends to agonize for long periods of time over the development of a mission statement: the process involves negotiation and compromise, but is usually leadership led – and depends upon a critical input from the CEO. Surprisingly, perhaps, despite all the effort expended, many mission statements tend to seem full of platitudes and motherhood statements.

Mission statements need to be communicated throughout the organization. Top management must also demonstrate their importance by "living" them as an example. In this way a clear mission statement can become an important inspiration to employees and can lead to commitment and loyalty to the corporation. Once established, missions are difficult to change, as they become critical ingredients in the corporate culture. For example, IBM has attempted to change its mission several times, but the critical elements established by the company's founder, Thomas Watson, still encourage the IBM sales function to attempt to achieve "quota" by the year end, rather than seeking to provide customers with "solutions," or to promote nonmainframe sales.

Good mission statements tend to be simple and easy to understand at all levels of the organization. They stimulate enthusiasm and commitment amongst employees; they are challenging; they are short and easily absorbed and accepted; and they are frequently repeated. For example, in the US General Electric Company, the mission for each business is to "be number one or two in the world or sell it, close it or fix it." Such a statement is readily understood and memorable.

Many Japanese companies have long emphasized a corporate mission or philosophy. Each strategic plan, lasting on average three years, has a clearly identifiable name which is well known throughout the organization. The key ingredients of such plans are fully communicated throughout the organization, and employees take on the corporate mission and values until such time as the strategy is changed.

A well developed mission statement helps top management in a number of ways. First, it crystallizes top management's own view of the long-term strategic position of the firm. Second, it helps to insure that the behavior of lower-order personnel is directed toward achievement of the corporate mission. Third, it conveys a message to external stakeholders, such as financial institutions that may influence their investment strategies. Fourth, it insures organizational confidence, in that top management knows where it wishes to drive the corporation. Fifth, it provides a pathway for establishing longer-term strategy.

Bibliography

Thompson, A. A. & Strickland, A. J. (1993). *Strategic management*, 7th edn. Homewood, IL: Irwin. See pp. 24–7.

DEREK F. CHANNON

mission statement The mission statement is generally presented as the first stage in the strategic planning (*see* MARKETING PLANNING; STRATEGIC PLANNING) process, depicted as consisting of a number of stages, although it may in fact be formulated at any time. Greenley (1986) suggests that the mission statement has several aims, including: to provide the purpose for the organization; to express the philosophy that will guide the business; to articulate the vision of where the firm will be in the future; to define the business domain, i.e., the customer groups and needs, and the technology to be employed; and to motivate employees by providing them with a clear sense of purpose and direction. Campbell & Tawadey (1992) have devised the Ashridge Mission Model which has four elements: purpose ("why the company exists"); strategy ("the commercial rationale" which embraces the business domain in which the firm is aiming to compete and the competitive advantages that it aims to exploit); standards and behaviors ("the policies and behavior patterns that guide how the company operates"); and values ("the beliefs that underpin the organization's management style, its relations to employees and other stakeholders, and its ethics"). Overall, the mission statement might be expected to provide answers to the questions posed by Drucker (1973): What is our business? Who is the customer? What is value to the customer? What will be our business? What should our business be? It is believed that the mission statement should be aspirational and provide a shared sense of purpose, thereby giving a focus for the efforts of all in the organization. It has various audiences, often with different requirements, including customers, shareholders, employees, and suppliers.

However, mission statements may often be general and bland, perhaps for fear of providing competitors with information about future strategies and because they need to appeal to different constituencies. They may also reflect what the company has been or is doing, rather than what it intends to do.

Bibliography

Abell, D. (1980). *Defining the business: The starting point of strategic planning*. Englewood Cliffs, NJ: Prentice-Hall. Chapter 3.
Campbell, A. & Tawadey, K. (Eds), (1992). *Mission and business philosophy*. Oxford: Butterworth-Heinemann. Chapter 1.
Drucker, P. (1973). *Management: Tasks, responsibilities, practices*. New York: Harper & Row. Chapter 7.

Greenley, G. E. (1986). *The strategic and operational planning of marketing*. Maidenhead: McGraw-Hill.

DALE LITTLER

modified re-buy Robinson, Faris & Wind (1967) suggest a division of organizational buying into three categories: NEW TASK, modified re-buy, and straight re-buy. The category of modified re-buy refers to those occasions when there are significant differences in the terms of the purchasing contract under review (e.g., changes in price, technical specifications, delivery arrangements, packaging, design, quality). The significance of these differences might reflect changes in the customer's requirements (e.g., changed specifications or delivery arrangements), or in the customer's competitive position (e.g., entering new markets, developing improved products), or in a supplier's offerings (e.g., increased price, new product features), and will generally require a significant renegotiation of the contract though not usually a change of supplier.

Bibliography

Robinson, P. T., Faris, C. W. & Wind, Y. (1967). *Industrial buying and creative marketing*. Boston, MA: Allyn & Bacon.

DOMINIC WILSON

monopolistic competition a MARKET STRUCTURE characterized by a large number of firms where every firm has some control over its products. The concept was introduced by Edward Chamberlin (1933) to study deviations in terms of prices and the number of firms in the market from perfect competition.

The basic market characteristics of a monopolistically competitive industry are the following:

- There is a large number of firms, and every firm has a small market share.
- Every firm sells a differentiated product from its competitors (*see* PRODUCT DIFFERENTIATION), and therefore it faces a downward-sloping demand for its product).
- There is free entry and exit of companies into and from the industry in the long-run, which usually leads to lower market share and zero ECONOMIC PROFITS.
- Because of the large number of firms in the industry, each firm does not consider the reactions of its rivals in its own decisions.

The market structure of monopolistic competition is suitable to study several different questions which cannot be easily addressed in the context of other market structures. First, since every firm in the industry sells a different variety, the level of product variety in the market can be assessed along with its social welfare implications. Second, this market structure allows economists to explore the reasoning behind companies' decisions on the type, the design, and the selection of the varieties (brands) they offer in the market. Finally, the implications of brand selection on companies' pricing policies can be also assessed.

In analyzing the monopolistically competitive market structure, two major families of models have been developed. *Chamberlinian-type models*, sometimes also called the *representative consumer models*, and *Hotelling-type models*, also known as location or address models.

Chamberlinian Models

Introduced by Chamberlin (1933) and extended by Dixit and Stiglitz (1977), the *Chamberlinian model* is a representative consumer model with a large number of firms, each one of which offers a distinct product variety in the market. In the model, consumers desire product variety itself and perceive every brand as an equally good substitute for every other brand available. Thus the representative consumer does not have an "ideal" variety which he prefers the most. Firms produce one variety each and compete only in terms of price so they do not compete in the design and the particular characteristics of their products.

The number of different varieties in the market is equal to the number of firms in the industry. Firms will enter in the market until all profitable opportunities are exhausted (zero economic profits). Overall, the model predicts that monopolistically competitive industries will have a large number of varieties when there are low fixed costs in production, and/or a low elasticity of substitution between different varieties, and/or a large market demand.

Overall, these models predict that the product variety provided in the market can either be greater or less than optimal because of two contradicting forces. On the one hand, a firm will enter the market with a new brand if it believes entry will be profitable, but the new brand may take business from other firms already in the market. Since the entrant does not worry about the negative effect it will have on established firms, there tends to be too much entry and too many varieties. Offsetting this force is the fact that society may benefit more from a new brand than it costs to produce, but if the firm cannot practice price discrimination, it cannot capture all the benefits to society from introducing a new brand and this force tends to reduce the number of brands.

Hotelling-type Models

In this family of models, consumers have an "ideal" variety for every product they consume. Introduced by Hotelling (1929), the model assumes that consumers are uniformly distributed along the product characteristics space and each one has an ideal product variety. The product characteristics space is a straight line, bounded, and can be considered equivalent to the market for the product. There are also many firms in the market, and each one produces one brand of the product. Firms decide about the particular attributes (*see* PRODUCT ATTRIBUTES MODEL) of these brands by choosing the location of their brands along the product characteristics space. Brands compete with only their neighboring products on either side of their location in the product characteristics space. Hence, the degree of substitution between different brands is not the same for all brands.

Hotelling showed that in a case of a *duopoly* (a market with just two firms), when companies do not compete in terms of price, it is optimal for them to locate next to each other in the middle of the product characteristics space. The reason for this is that consumers will purchase from the store which is closest to them in the market. Since the firms do not compete on price, only their location matters to customers. This result, known as *minimum product differentiation*, depends on specific assumptions of the model. High market demand, low fixed costs (weak

ECONOMIES OF SCALE), and weak substitution between different varieties, lead to high product variety in the market.

Generalizing Hotelling's results, Eaton and Lipsey (1975) show that in a case of a large number of firms, there is an equilibrium where firms locate in pairs along the product characteristics space with some space between the pairs. In other words, there is some *clustering* of varieties in the market. Other researchers derive Hotelling's result of *minimum product differentiation* by assuming instead that consumers are not uniformly distributed along the product characteristics space, but instead, that they are clustered around certain points (in some cases in the middle of the product characteristics space). In other words, consumers tend to prefer some varieties relative to others. Then, companies have incentives to locate in those areas of high demand (*thick markets*). This is one of the causes of geographic concentration of economic activity in large metropolitan areas (*spatial agglomeration*).

Finally, Lancaster (1979), introduced a model where consumers perceive products as bundles of characteristics, and have preferences over different collections of characteristics and not necessarily over individual products. Therefore, by combining different products in their consumption, they can end up with the set of characteristics and qualities they find most desirable. Called the *characteristics approach*, this model allows formalization of different situations like whether products can or cannot be combined in consumption, or whether such combinations preserve the characteristics of the separate products.

Monopolistic Competition and Price Markups
Recent research has studied how the entry and exit of firms in a monopolistically competitive market influences the pricing policy of companies and especially their price markups. In the context of the Chamberlinian models, price markups are constant and not related to entry and exit because the degree of substitution between different varieties is constant and not influenced by the number of brands in the market. In terms of Hotelling-type models though, price markups are inversely related to the entry of firms since market entry implies a larger number of brands, stronger competition, a higher price elasticity of demand and lower price markups. The conclusion is that periods of high market demand and therefore high market entry (for example an economic boom or a seasonal increase in market demand during Christmas), are associated with lower price markups. Weitzman (1982) and others, present theoretical justification for this result, while Barsky and Warner (1995) offer some empirical support.

Bibliography

Barsky, R. B. & Warner, E. J. (1995). The timing and magnitude of retail store markdowns: evidence from weekends and holidays. *The Quarterly Journal of Economics*, CX, 321–52.
Chamberlin, E. (1933). *The Theory of Monopolistic Competition*. Cambridge, MA: Harvard University Press.
Dixit, A. K. & Stiglitz, J. E. (1977). Monopolistic competition and optimum product diversity. *American Economic Review*, 67, 297–308.
Eaton, B. C. & Lipsey, R. G. (1975). The principle of minimum differentiation reconsidered: some new developments in the theory of spatial competition. *Review of Economic Studies*, 42, 27–49.
Hotelling, H. (1929). Stability in competition. *Economic Journal*, 39, 41–57.
Lancaster, K. J. (1979). *Variety, Equity, and Efficiency*. New York: Columbia University Press.
Perloff, J. M. & Salop, S. C. (1985). Equilibrium with product differentiation. *The Review of Economic Studies*, 52, 107–20.
Salop, S. C. (1979). Monopolistic competition with outside goods. *The Bell Journal of Economics*, 10, 141–56.
Weitzman, M. (1982). Increasing returns and the foundation of unemployment theory. *The Economic Journal*, 92, 787–804.

KOSTAS AXARLOGLOU

monopoly A monopoly exists when there is a single seller of a product in the industry. As a consequence, the monopolist's DEMAND CURVE is the same as industry demand and is thus downward sloping. A monopolist must be protected by BARRIERS TO ENTRY to remain a single seller while earning ECONOMIC PROFIT. The monopolist may be protected by licensing requirements, patents, its own strategic behavior, or ECONOMIES OF SCALE which prevent entry into the industry.

Since the industry demand curve facing the monopolist is the *average revenue* curve, when it is decreasing the MARGINAL REVENUE curve must lie below it. To maximize profits the monopolist will produce until marginal revenue equals MARGINAL COST, a condition all profit-maximizing firms must fulfill regardless of MARKET STRUCTURE (*see* PROFIT MAXIMIZATION). The marginal revenue curve lies below the demand curve because, in the absence of price discrimination, the monopolist must lower the price to all consumers of the product in order to sell an additional (marginal) unit.

The monopolist earns profits by reducing output relative to the level of production under PERFECT COMPETITION. The optimal markup of price over marginal cost for a monopolist is inversely related to the absolute value of the elasticity of demand. The monopolist will charge a higher price markup over marginal cost when consumers have fewer substitutes (market demand is less elastic).

The Social Costs of Monopoly
In the preceding discussion it was stated that a monopolist will set its price above marginal cost, while in perfectly competitive markets, price equals marginal cost. This means that some consumers who are willing to pay the cost to society of producing this product do not receive it and this is called DEADWEIGHT LOSS. Consider an example where, for simplicity, there are no fixed costs in production, so that the long run marginal cost ($LRMC$) is equal to long run average cost ($LRAC$) in figure 1 below.

To maximize profits the monopolist will produce Q_m units of output (where MR = MC) and the market price for Q_m units will be P_m. If this industry were perfectly competitive it would produce until $P = MC$ which would be Q_c units sold at price P_c above. Compared with a perfectly competitive industry, the monopolist produces less output and charges a higher price. In the figure above, the rectangle P_m, M, B, P_c is the monopolist's profit which is a transfer from consumers (who lose this amount in CONSUMER SURPLUS) to the monopolist. Since this transfer makes consumers worse off and the monopolist better off, the welfare consequences cannot be judged on the grounds of Pareto optimality. However the triangle M, B, C is lost consumer surplus which is not gained by the

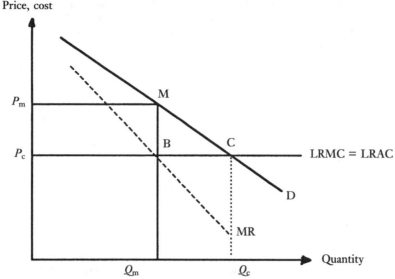

Figure 1   Profit maximizing price and output under monopoly

monopolist. This is the DEADWEIGHT LOSS to society from a monopoly. Once the monopolist has earned its profits, hypothetically it should be willing to produce additional units for those consumers who are willing to pay the marginal cost of production (that is, those consumers along the demand curve between points M and C). This production would make consumers (and therefore society) better off and leave the monopolist no worse off, so it is a more efficient (Pareto optimal) allocation. Since the monopolist does not produce and sell these additional units, this loss in allocative efficiency is one of the costs to society from monopoly.

Another potential cost of monopoly is what Leibenstein (1966) termed X-inefficiency, the failure to minimize production costs. Without the pressure of competition, a monopolist has less incentive to be efficient and may waste resources in production. Therefore the monopolist's costs would not be equal to those achievable under perfect competition and so the social costs of monopoly would include the monopolist's higher costs of production in addition to the deadweight loss.

Potential monopoly profits may encourage firms or individuals to expend resources attempting to acquire or maintain a monopoly. Such behavior is called rent-seeking and if these expenditures do not create benefits to society, then the effort to monopolize is costly to society. Posner (1975) argued that if firms compete for these monopoly profits, they would expend resources until the net expected profit was zero, and this meant that the social cost of monopoly was all of the monopolist's profits. Although this represents an extreme upper bound, some resources are wasted in rent-seeking behavior and this increases the costs to society from a monopoly (see Tirole (1988)).

Monopolies can be beneficial to society under certain conditions. When there are ECONOMIES OF SCALE, a single firm may be able to serve the market more efficiently than several firms. Governments grant monopoly licenses to firms and individuals through patents in an effort to encourage innovation. In this case, rent-seeking behavior can have socially desirable benefits which society promotes.

Bibliography

Arrow, K. J. (1962). Economic welfare and the allocation of resources for inventions. Nelson, R. *The Rate and Direction of Inventive Activity*. Princeton, NJ: Princeton University Press.
Leibenstein, H. (1966). Allocative efficiency vs. 'X-efficiency'. *American Economic Review*, 56, 392–415.
Martin, S. (1994). *Industrial Economics*. 2nd edn, New York: Macmillan.
Posner, R. (1975). The social costs of monopoly and regulation. *Journal of Political Economy*, 83, 807–27.
Shughart, W. F., Chappell, W. F. & Cottle, R. L. (1994). *Modern Managerial Economics*. Cincinatti, OH: South-Western Publishing.
Tirole, J. (1988). *The Theory of Industrial Organization*. Cambridge, MA: MIT.

ROBERT E. MCAULIFFE

moral status of corporations   The moral status of the corporation is dependent on the moral features of the corporation and dependent on the moral status of the members of the corporation. At the heart of the philosophical sub-field called business ethics are central questions of metaphysics, ethical theory, and social philosophy related to the status of the business corporation. Of chief concern are these questions: Is the corporation ontologically distinct from the individual persons who compose it? Does the corporation have responsibilities, and to whom? Does the corporation have moral rights and are they equivalent to those of individual humans? Does the regulation of corporations pose special moral problems? Questions of ontology, responsibility, and rights have always been the proper purview of philosophy and so it is easy to understand why philosophers have gravitated recently to these questions in business ethics.

The moral status of the corporation is intimately linked with its metaphysical status, for only if the corporation is a distinct moral entity, specifically a moral agent, does the corporation have a distinct moral standing, separate from the entities (individual human persons) who make it up. Of course, the corporation could have an auxiliary or dependent moral status even if the corporation was not a moral agent. While this is in itself an important point, most of what follows will ignore this alternative. Instead, the focus will be on questions of agency, responsibility, and rights of a corporation *per se*.

The corporation exists, but what kind of existence is this? There are at least three ways to answer this question. First, the corporation may exist in the way that a "heap" exists, as merely the category which stands for the collection of entities which happen to compose it. Second, the corporation may exist as a "unity," where the form of the corporation (its organizational structure) is what renders it unique, but where the substance of the corporation is entirely made up of other things. Third, the corporation may exist somehow in its own right, as a formally and substantially "unique thing."

The question of whether the corporation is an agent can be addressed in a similar way to the question of whether the corporation exists. First, a corporation may be an agent in the sense that "corporate action" is merely a shorthand way to refer to how discrete individual human persons act. Second, a corporation may be an agent vicariously through the various actors who make up the corporation and who are facilitated in their actions by the corporation's organizational structure. Third, a corporation may be an agent in its own right, perhaps as much an actor as is the collection of body parts that make up a human actor. The law treats corporations as full-fledged legal persons that can act in their own right. This is commonly known as "the legal fiction of the corporate person," and hence it is not necessarily useful in determining whether the corporation is a moral person.

One way to approach the question of corporate agency is to ask whether the common-sense understanding of corporate actions can be reduced to individual human actions. In this context the corporation cannot really act on its own; only individual human persons can act. But it is very difficult to make sense completely of corporate actions, such as "Gulf Oil Company acquired XYZ Company," without referring to corporations, or to features of individual human persons. Of course, merely because it is hard to make these complete reductions does not yet tell us that corporate agents should be admitted into our moral universe. But until complete reductions are made, it is intelligible to think of corporations as moral agents.

If corporations are moral agents, what kind of agents are they? Corporations may be full-fledged moral agents or they may be partial or vicarious agents. In order to be full-fledged moral agents there must be some sense in which they can act in a morally significant way on their own. Following the model of individual human action, a locus of choice or intention must be found from which moral actions could issue. The corporate boardroom is the most obvious place to look for such choice or intention. Here the individual choices or intentions of the board members are transformed so that what emerges is a collective choice or intention. For the choices to be the choices of a full-fledged moral agent they must at least resemble the choices that a

single human individual would make. But there is a wide diversity of viewpoints about what constitutes choice for a single human individual, and it is not clear what criteria must be satisfied for a collective choice to be ascribable to a corporation. Nonetheless, the more these choices and intentions resemble those cases of individual human choice or intention, the stronger the case for thinking that a corporation is a full-fledged moral agent.

Vicarious or secondary agency is a weaker form of corporate agency than full-fledged agency. One way to understand vicarious agency is in terms of individual humans who have been authorized to represent the corporation, thereby providing the corporation with a way in which it can act *through* the actions of these individuals. It is common to speak of an employee "acting within the scope of his or her authority." Such expressions belie a moral fact: that for certain previously established purposes, a given act can be given two descriptions. The act always remains primarily an act of a discrete individual human; and the act is secondarily (or vicariously) also an act of a corporation. Whenever authority has been so conveyed, then it is relatively easy to establish this weaker sense of moral agency on the part of a corporation.

Corporations may be morally responsible for harms in several different ways. Most obviously, if a person is harmed directly as a result of a corporate intentional decision, then the corporation is morally responsible for this harm. Responsibility may also apply to corporations for harms that result from negligence, recklessness or simple omission. Such cases are more or less problematic, depending on the difficulty of telling whether the corporation's contribution to a harm was in some sense morally faulty. In Anglo–American law there are three main types of fault: intentional wrongdoing, negligence, and recklessness.

Corporations can engage in intentional wrongdoing and hence be morally responsible and blameworthy on this basis. It is rare that a corporation sets out to do wrong to a person in the same way that an individual agent might intend to do harm to another out of revenge or anger. The most obvious explanation for the rarity here is that corporations do not have any recognized way of displaying or feeling anger or revenge. The corporation can make decisions, and those decisions may be based on the emotional reactions of the members of the board of directors. Nonetheless, corporations could decide to harm a person especially if it would advance the interests of the corporations to do so. But normally the threat of adverse publicity will make this very unlikely. Far more common is that corporations decide to do things which will risk harm to persons so as to more expeditiously advance their interests.

Corporate negligence is the most common basis upon which corporate moral responsibility can be based. Negligence is the failure to display due care, that is, care which a reasonable person would take. Decision-making in the corporate domain is so focused on serving the goals of the charter, or the interests of investors, etc., that it is relatively common for corporations to fail to take into account the possible harms of their decisions. But for these failures to constitute moral negligence, it must also be the case that reasonable people would have taken those possible harms into account. An interesting example concerned a decision by the Boeing Company to build their 727 line of aircraft so that all of the backup electrical systems were in the same part of the plane. In the event of an accident it was possible that all of the backup systems could be disabled at once, leaving the plane unmaneuverable and the passengers on the plane in great peril. Of course, no one at Boeing intended to harm anyone by making this decision. But it did seem unreasonable for them to have done this, given the risks of harm to their passengers. This is a fairly straightforward case of corporate moral negligence.

An example of corporate moral recklessness concerned a decision by the Ford Motor Company to place the gas tank on the Ford Pinto in a position so close to the back of the car that it could explode upon fairly low-speed collisions. What made this case one of recklessness was that key members of Ford's management knew of the problem and knew that it would cost very little to fix it, but decided to take the risk. Here a rare internal memorandum surfaced which indicated that Ford had actually calculated how many people were likely to die and how much Ford would be likely to lose in wrongful-death lawsuits, compared to how much it would cost to fix the Pintos so that it was far less likely the gas tanks would explode. This was judged in a court of law in Indiana to be reckless because of the decision to go ahead with a known risk that no reasonable person would inflict on the populace. The moral assessment would be similar.

In addition to the responsibilities to individual persons, corporations also have more broadly based social responsibilities. While it is controversial how extensive these responsibilities are, nearly everyone recognizes the responsibility that corporations have not to harm or risk harm to the larger society, by such acts as discriminatory hiring or polluting the water sources in a particular locale. Milton Friedman, a well-known critic of most social responsibilities for corporations, has said that the chief social responsibility of business corporations is to make a profit. But even this view supports the general idea that there are various customs in each locale, concerning what are appropriate and inappropriate actions which affect the overall well-being of a society.

On the other side of the balance sheet from corporate moral responsibilities, are corporate moral rights. Corporate moral rights can be divided into commercial and non-commercial rights. Commercial rights generally concern rights to property, rights to profit, and generally rights to determine how the corporation is run. Non-commercial corporate rights concern such things as rights to free speech, and generally rights to exert influence in the public domain. The basis of rights can come from the moral agency of the corporation, or from the moral interests of the corporation. In either case, the ascription of moral rights to corporations is based on an analogy to the ascription of moral rights to persons.

Commercial rights of corporations are moral if they affect moral duties, liberties, privileges, or immunities. The property rights of corporations are moral rights if, for instance, they restrict the range of moral options that individuals or groups have in behaving toward that corporation. Property rights generally are rights to the exclusive (or nearly exclusive) ownership and use of a given thing. In most modern corporations, ownership and control are divided to the extent that, while the shareholders own

the corporation, it is normally management (in a sense employed by the shareholders) which controls the activities of the corporation. The property rights of a modern corporation create moral options related to control for managers and moral options related to ownership for shareholders, but the divided nature of corporate property makes it often hard to tell who should be afforded what moral privilege or immunity.

Corporate rights to profit are even harder to ascertain morally. While it seems reasonable that corporations are morally entitled to keep whatever surplus value is generated from their production processes, things get cloudier when these profits are generated by windfalls or exploitative conditions. Indeed, the moral right to profit seems to virtually everyone to be limited based on how that profit was generated. The same could be said of all commercial corporate rights. Since commercial rights themselves are justified by their social productiveness, when the overall social effect is negative, rights may be restricted as well. The corporation generally has the right to decide how it is run as long as its being run this way is not likely to be harmful to the overall social welfare.

Non-commercial rights of corporations derive their moral force from analogy with similar rights for individual humans. The Anglo-American legal tradition recognizes corporations as legal persons with very similar rights to other persons. Morally, to the extent that corporate agents resemble human agents, corporations will have a basis for rights to free speech similar to that which human persons have. But the problem with this strategy is that corporations are not the kind of agents whose voices necessarily add to the political process when they participate. Indeed, corporations have a history of drowning out the rest of the voices in a political debate. And these corporations are rarely the kind of agents who are vulnerable and hence in need of the kind of protection which free-speech rights afford. For these reasons, most corporations will not have the same, or as weighty, non-commercial rights as will individual humans.

Finally, corporations may be considered morally virtuous or morally evil, but from a more roundabout route. While a plausible case can be made for seeing corporations as limited agents, it is far harder to see them as having characters that can be morally assessed except in a very derivative form. But the leading members of a corporation may convey a character to a corporation by the way these members conduct themselves while acting on the behalf of the corporation. It is also possible for a succession of virtuous leading members of a corporation to convey good character to a corporation over many years. But should the moral characters of the leading members change, then so will the "character" of the corporation. The regulation of corporations does not pose the same sort of moral problems as it does for individual humans, except in limited cases of rights violation, since the lack of distinct moral character of the corporation means that there is no *prima facie* basis for respecting corporate autonomy.

Bibliography

Berle, A. A. & Means, G. C. (1933). *The Modern Corporation and Private Property.* New York: Macmillan.
Copp, D. (1979). Collective actions and secondary actions. *American Philosophical Quarterly*, 16, 177–86.

De George, R. (1990). *Business Ethics*, 3rd edn, New York: Macmillan.

Donaldson, T. (1982). *Corporations and Morality*. Englewood Cliffs, NJ: Prentice-Hall.

French, P. A. (1984). *Collective and Corporate Responsibility*. New York: Columbia.

Fuller, L. L. (1967). *Legal Fictions*. Stanford, Calif.: Stanford University Press.

May, L. (1987). *The Morality of Groups*. Notre Dame, Ind.: Notre Dame University Press.

Soloman, R. C. (1992). *Ethics and Excellence: Cooperation and Integrity in Business*. New York: Oxford University Press.

Velasquez, M. (1983). Why corporations are not morally responsible for anything they do. *Business and Professional Ethics Journal*, **2**, 1–18.

Werhane, P. (1985). *Persons, Rights, and Corporations*. Englewood Cliffs, NJ: Prentice-Hall.

LARRY MAY

motivation This term refers to the psychological mechanisms governing the direction, intensity, and persistence of actions *not* due solely to individual differences in ABILITY or to overwhelming environmental demands that coerce or force action (see Vroom, 1964). The field of motivation seeks to understand, explain, and predict:

(a) which of many possible goals an individual chooses to pursue (direction of action);
(b) how much effort an individual puts forth to accomplish salient goals (intensity of action); and
(c) how long an individual perseveres toward goal accomplishment, particularly in the face of difficulties (persistence of action).

The topic of motivation has a long history in the field of basic and applied psychology (see, e.g., Weiner, 1980). Work motivation represents a specialty area in the broader field of human motivation that focuses directly on theories, research, and practices that have implications for individual behavior in the context of work, and may be applied to a variety of human resource management activities, including selection, TRAINING, and managerial practices.

In the organizational behavior domain, the term motivation often refers to a critical management activity; that is, to the techniques used by managers for the purpose of facilitating employee behaviors that accomplish organizational goals. Managerial practices designed to enhance employee performance are rarely straightforward applications of particular work motivation theories, but rather are uniquely tailored activities that incorporate motivational notions within the broader context of the organization's culture, dynamics, and practices (*see* ORGANIZATIONAL CULTURE). The tailoring of motivational techniques to the specific organizational context makes evaluation of the true validity of motivational approaches to organizational productivity difficult. Nonetheless, in a review of 207 published experiments using psychologically based programs (including motivational programs such as GOAL-SETTING, MANAGEMENT BY OBJECTIVES, and other supervisory methods), Katzell and Guzzo (1983) found that over 80 percent of published studies showed evidence of productivity improvement on at least one measure. These results suggest that motivational techniques used by managers can have direct effects on organizational outcomes.

Motivation Tenets

Three assumptions guide contemporary thinking and research on human motivation. First, motivation is not directly observable. What is observed is a stream of behavior and the products of those behaviors. Motivation is *inferred* from a systematic analysis of how characteristics of the individual, task, and environment influence behavior and aspects of job performance. Second, motivation is not a fixed attribute of the individual. Unlike motives (which are often defined in terms of stable individual differences in dispositional tendencies), motivation refers to a dynamic, internal state resulting from the independent and joint influences of personal and situational factors. As such, an individual's motivation for specific activities or tasks may change as a consequence of change in any part of the system. In other words, modern approaches do not view motivation as an individual trait (*see* PERSONALITY), but rather as an individual state affected by the continuous interplay of personal, social, and organizational factors.

Third, motivation has its primary effect on behavior (covert and overt); that is, what an individual chooses to do and how intensely an individual works to accomplish his/her goal. The distinction between motivational effects on behavior versus job performance is of critical importance for understanding motivation effects in the work domain. In the workplace, changes in motivation may or may not affect job performance depending on how job performance is defined and evaluated. Programs designed to enhance job performance by increasing employee motivation may be unsuccessful if job performance is not immediately or substantially affected by an individual's on-task effort.

The processes by which motivation influences behavior and performance are best represented as comprised of two interrelated psychological systems; goal choice and goal striving (or self-regulation; see, e.g., Heckhausen, 1991; Kanfer & Hagerman, 1987; Kanfer, 1990). Cognitive theories of motivation describe goal choice as a DECISION-MAKING/COMMITMENT process in which choice is determined jointly by personal factors and the individual's perceptions of the situation. The product of this process, an individual's intentions or goals, provide a mental representation of a future situation that signifies a desired end-state. Relative to intentions, goals define more specific end-states. Commitment to a goal serves to direct the individual's attention, mobilize the individual's effort toward goal attainment, and encourage goal persistence. Intentions and goals may relate to the individual's behavior (e.g., my goal is to work overtime for three hours today) or to an outcome the individual seeks to attain (e.g., my goal is to obtain a promotion). Person and situation characteristics influence goal choice as well as the specificity at which goals are articulated.

Theories that describe the decision-making process with respect to goal choice (e.g., Vroom, 1964) have frequently been used to successfully predict a variety of behaviors in which goals are readily attainable (e.g., choice among job offers). However, when goals involve difficult or prolonged tasks that require sustained effort in the face of difficulties, prediction of performance requires additional consideration of the individual's commitment to the goal as well as other motivational processes.

Goal striving refers to the motivational mechanisms set into motion by adoption of difficult goals for which accomplishment requires active self-regulation of one's cognitions, emotions, or actions. Goals, such as learning a complex new skill or earning a college degree require self-regulatory, or volitional processes by which the individual can develop subgoals, monitor his/her performance, and evaluate activities with respect to goal progress. Deficits in the goal striving system may thwart successful transition of a goal into action and obscure or weaken the effect of motivation on performance.

Work Motivation Overview

Numerous theories of work motivation have been proposed over the past 60 years. Comprehensive reviews by Campbell and Pritchard (1976) and Kanfer (1990) document major advances in work motivation through the mid-1970s and from the mid-1970s to 1990, respectively. Descriptions of major motivational approaches in the context of organizational behavior are provided in Steers and Porter (1987). In concert with theoretical advances, a tremendous variety of programs and techniques have been developed for use in organizational settings. Although the popularity of particular motivation theories or techniques wax and wane, there is little evidence to indicate any decline in basic or applied interest in the topic over the past two decades. Motivation theories, research, and practices remain a topic of central importance in industrial/organizational psychology, organizational behavior, executive development, and managerial and job training programs.

Historical Trends

The history of the application of scientific principles for enhancing work performance via changes in an individual's motivation corresponds closely to theoretical and empirical developments in the study of human behavior and the workplace. Early management theories, such as Taylor's SCIENTIFIC MANAGEMENT, made reference to the long-standing practice of using financial compensation to spur motivation and job performance. The emergence of personality and learning theories in psychology during the early 1900s led to the development of motivational programs aimed at enhancing performance by creating organizational conditions that facilitated the match between employee need satisfaction and increased on-task effort. During the 1940s through the 1960s, explosive growth in theorizing and research on the determinants of choice led to the development of models aimed at enhancing prediction of individuals' workplace behaviors, such as turnover. During this same period, results of the Hawthorne studies provided striking evidence for the influence of social norms and other nonfinancial incentives on work motivation and performance.

The rise of behaviorism during the mid-1900s stressed the importance of operant learning and REINFORCEMENT as a means of altering workplace behavior. Organizational interventions using behavior modification techniques were developed to enhance performance on a variety of dimensions, such as safety. At the same time, progress in the field of task characteristics led to greater consideration of the motivating potential of jobs. Integration of this work with intrinsic motivation theorizing led to the development of interventions aimed at enhancing motivation and performance through job redesign. Similar in some respects to earlier work by Herzberg that focused on psychological determinants of JOB SATISFACTION, job redesign efforts aimed to strengthen employee motivation by creating work environments that promoted a sense of achievement, perceptions of competence, and autonomy (*see* JOB ENRICHMENT).

The past two decades have witnessed tremendous growth in the use of goal setting and management by objectives programs. These programs, based upon a view of human behavior that espouses goals as the immediate precursors of action, focus largely on the process of setting, establishing commitment to, and following-through on specific and challenging goals.

Goal-based approaches currently dominate the basic and applied literature. However, most organizational researchers and practitioners recognize that there is no one "best" theory or program. As a result, there has been a growing trend to develop broad formulations that subsume or complement major tenets of goal choice, behavioral, and goal striving theories of action (see, e.g., Naylor, Pritchard, & Ilgen, 1980; Kanfer & Ackerman, 1989; Locke & Latham, 1990). From a practical perspective, the broadening of theories has placed a greater burden on practitioners to conduct a careful analysis of the motivational problem in order to select an appropriate intervention perspective.

Key Perspectives

Modern approaches to motivation may be organized into three related clusters:

(1) personality-based views;
(2) cognitive choice/decision approaches; and
(3) goal/self-regulation formulations.

The following section highlights major assumptions, theories, and findings from each perspective.

Personality-based views of motivation emphasize the influence of relatively enduring characteristics of persons as they affect goal choice and striving. Three types of personality-based work motivation perspectives may be distinguished. The first type pertains to models based upon broad theories of personality, such as Maslow's Need Hierarchy Theory (Maslow, 1954). In these approaches, workplace behavior and satisfaction are posited to be powerfully determined by an individual's current need state within a universal hierarchy of need categories. By understanding which needs were most salient to an individual (e.g., affiliation, self-actualization needs), organizations could enhance work performance and satisfaction by creating environments that facilitated need satisfaction. Although this perspective is well known, scientific research has consistently failed to provide support for basic tenets of the model or to demonstrate that this model is useful in predicting workplace behaviors.

The second type of personality perspective derives from considering the influence of a single or small set of universal or psychologically based motives that may affect behavior and performance. A great deal of work in this perspective has focused on the role of individual differences in the strength of achievement motives (i.e., need for achievement). Substantial research in this area indicates that individuals who score high on tests of achievement motivation are more likely to select appropriately challenging task goals and to persist longer than persons who score low on this trait (Heckhausen, 1991).

During the mid-1900s, attention also focused on the role of universal motives, such as the need for competence, self-determination, and fairness. In contrast to achievement motivation theories, motive theories such as Deci's Cognitive Evaluation Theory and Adam's EQUITY THEORY do not stress individual differences in the degree of the motive, but rather stress the conditions that arouse the motive and its influence on behavior. In equity theory, for example, arousal of the justice motive occurs when the individual perceives imbalance in the ratio of his/her inputs and outcomes relative to others (see DISTRIBUTIVE JUSTICE).

Unlike broad personality theory formulations, motive-based theories more fully specify the organizational conditions that instigate motive-based behaviors, as well as the cognitive processes by which the motive affects behavior. Newer formulations of these motive-based approaches in the areas of intrinsic motivation and equity/fairness enjoy substantial popularity in the work motivation literature.

The third personality perspective on work motivation emerged in the early 1980s as a direct result of advances in basic research in personality. During the past two decades, personality researchers made significant progress in the identification and measurement of basic personality dimensions. The results of this work led to general agreement regarding the existence of five basic personality dimensions, or traits: (1) neuroticism; (2) extraversion; (3) openness to experience; (4) agreeableness; and (5) conscientiousness. Of the five factors, conscientiousness, also called will to achieve and dependability, represents the trait dimension most closely associated with motivation. Recent investigations of the association between personality dimensions and job performance indicate that conscientiousness shows consistent relations with several dimensions of job performance (see, e.g., Barrick & Mount, 1991). These results have led to renewed interest in delineating how individual differences on motivationally related traits might affect work behavior and performance, particularly in service sector jobs.

Cognitive choice/decision approaches emphasize two determinants of choice and action: (1) the individual's expectations (i.e., the individual's perception of the relationship between effort and performance level, as well as between performance level and salient outcomes); and (2) the individual's subjective valuation of the expected consequences associated with various alternative actions (i.e., the anticipated positive or negative effect associated with attainment of various outcomes). These formulations, known as Expectancy Value (ExV) theories, are intended to predict an individual's choices or decisions, not necessarily subsequent performance. In most models, individuals are viewed as rational decision makers who make choices in line with the principle of maximizing the likelihood of positive outcomes. (Note, however, that ExV models predict choice behavior on the basis of the individual's perceptions; misperceptions of the environment or relationship between effort, performance, and outcomes may yield "poor" decisions.) In the motivational realm, choices may be made with regard to direction (goal choice), intensity (goal striving), or persistence of a specific course of action.

The popularity of these approaches reached a peak in the early 1980s. During the 1970s and 1980s, organizational research focused on testing key tenets of these models and investigating the predictive validity of various models. Results from this period indicated several limitations and difficulties associated with basic assumptions of the ExV models, and lower than expected levels of predictive validity for task and job performance criteria (though predictive validity for job choice has been substantially better; see Mitchell (1982) for a review). Limitations of ExV models in predicting ongoing workplace behaviors led to a general decline in the use of classic formulations in field research during the 1980s, and to the development of modern, integrative choice frameworks, such as Naylor, Pritchard, and Ilgen's (1980) theory of organizational behavior, and Beach and Mitchell's (1990) Image Theory. Both these theories incorporate several of the classic assumptions of ExV theorizing, but use a broader framework of decision making that includes individual differences in personality as well as other motivational processes, such as self-regulation.

Goal/Self-Regulation formulations of work motivation emphasize the factors that influence goal striving, or the translation of an individual's goals into action (see COGNITIVE PROCESSES). In organizational psychology, the most well-known goal setting model was developed by Locke and his colleagues (see Locke, Shaw, Saari, & Latham, 1981; Locke & Latham, 1990), and focuses on the relationship between goals and work behavior. Other broader formulations that specify the psychological processes involved (Lord & Kernan, 1989), resource allocation theory (Kanfer & Ackerman, 1989), and social–cognitive theory (Bandura, 1986).

Early organizational goal setting research examined the effects of explicit goal assignments that varied in difficulty. The majority of these studies indicated higher levels of performance among persons assigned difficult and specific goals (e.g., make six sales this week), compared to persons assigned "do your best" goals. Subsequent research has sought to more fully examine the boundary conditions of this robust effect. Results of this research indicate two critical preconditions for demonstration of the positive goal-performance relationship; namely, that the individual accept the goal assignment and that the individual be provided with performance feedback. Several studies further suggest that specific, difficult goal assignments may be more effective when used with relatively simple tasks (e.g., simple arithmetic tasks) than with complex tasks (e.g., supervision, programming).

More recently, cybernetic control, resource allocation, and social–cognitive theories have been used to more closely examine how particular attributes of the goal, the person, and the situation influence goal striving and performance. Studies from these theoretical perspectives indicate further conditions that mediate the effect of goals on task performance. Findings suggest that task demands, percepts of self–efficacy, goal commitment, and orientation toward task accomplishment are also important determinants of the effectiveness of goal setting methods.

Summary

The plethora of work motivation theories and motivational techniques underscores both the complexity of understanding and predicting individual behavior as well as the substantial progress that has been made in this domain. Oldof Maslow's Need Hierarchy Theory, Adams' Equity Theory, and Vroom's Expectancy Theory have given way to new approaches that build upon advances in cognitive psychology, information processing, personality, and self-regulation. These newer perspectives, including for example, Locke and Latham's (1990) goal-setting model, Kanfer and Ackerman's (1989) integrative resource model of learning and performance, and Lord and Kernan's (1989) control theory, often incorporate elements of older theories, but do so in ways that reduce the sharp distinctions between various approaches. New approaches differ from older conceptualizations in other ways as well. For example, contemporary models of motivation place a central emphasis on the role of goals as the primary concept for linking individuals and organizations. In addition, these approaches typically focus on predicting specific job behaviors, rather than an overall job performance or satisfaction criterion.

Although there has been substantial progress in the theoretical field of work motivation, the dynamics of the modern workplace continue to raise important questions and challenges to the field. Two topics of particular relevance for the coming decade are indicated below.

(1) The social/cultural context of work. There is widespread agreement regarding the influence of the social context as an important determinant of work motivation and performance. This has led to the inclusion of broad "social factors" in several motivation models. But, until recently, little attention was paid to understanding the unique and dynamic motivational processes operative in workgroup or team contexts. The growing use of team approaches to performance in organizations has renewed interest in this facet of motivation theory and research. In response, several ongoing programs of research, aimed at understanding workteam processes (see, e.g., Gersick, 1988; Swezey & Salas, 1992), have begun to delineate how attributes of the team and the task affect the goals, motivation, and behaviors of individual team members.

In a related vein, results of cross-cultural research indicate that the use and effectiveness of motivational techniques depends in part on the congruence of the motivational approach with the cultural values of the society in which it is used. Erez (1993) points out that motivational approaches consistent with collectivistic, group-oriented values (e.g., quality circles, AUTONOMOUS WORK GROUPS, participation in goal setting) tend to be more effective when used in collectivistic cultures such as Japan, China, and Israel. In contrast, motivational programs consistent with individualistic values (e.g., individual job enrichment, individual goal setting, individual incentive plans) are used and reported more effective in individualistic cultures, such as the United States. Erez (1993) further argues that, with the growing internationalization of the workforce, the ultimate success of managerial techniques depends critically on their congruence with the cultural values of the particular organization and its social environment.

(2) Managing motivation. Traditional views of work motivation imply that employees are relatively passive recipients of managerial and organizational efforts to maximize work motivation by providing appropriate work conditions and incentives. However, this view is problematic for two reasons. First, theory and research over the past three decades clearly indicates that individuals are active agents in the motivation process. Employees interpret and respond to managerial practices in light of personal goals, schemas, and beliefs. Research in the areas of employee SOCIALIZATION, procedural justice (*see* PROCEDURAL JUSTICE), and leadership indicates that motivation is affected not only by what the manager and/or organization offers the individual, but by the way in which practices are implemented. Procedural justice research, for example, indicates that the process by which incentives are allocated or layoffs are realized exerts an important effect on employee attitudes and behavior, independent of the outcome.

Second, and perhaps more importantly, demographic, technological, and economic changes in the workplace, forecasted to continue through the end of this century, will likely continue to erode managerial control over employee motivation. Increasing workforce diversity, for example, is associated with growing diversity in employee goals and attitudes toward traditional motivational incentives, such as pay. Similarly, the development of new technologies that permit employees to work in locations far removed from the manager makes traditional supervisory methods for increasing employee motivation more difficult to implement and raises new motivational issues, such as how to encourage work goal commitment and increased task effort in nontraditional work environments, such as the home.

For these reasons, further advances in work motivation theory and practice are most likely to come from integrative approaches that explicitly consider how the *employee* controls his/her motivation in response to managerial/organizational practices. In this goal-striving perspective, motivation may be represented as a job-related competency and employee resource, that is, a resource that organizations can help to develop and that managers and employees co-manage. Recent training programs, based on self-regulation principles aimed at cultivating employee skills in managing work-related goals and actions, for example, represent a promising avenue for potentially reducing substantial organizational costs associated with supervision, ABSENTEEISM, and poor performance.

Bibliography

Bandura, A. (1986). Social foundations of thought and action: A social cognitive theory. Englewood Cliffs, NJ: Prentice-Hall.

Barrick, M. R. & Mount, M. K. (1991). The big five personality dimensions and job performance: A meta-analysis. Personnel Psychology, **44**, 1–26.

Beach, L. R. & Mitchell, T. R. (1990). Image theory: A behavioral theory of decision making in organizations. In B. Staw & L. L. Cummings (Eds), Research in organizational behavior, (Vol. 12, pp. 1–41). Greenwich, CT: JAI Press.

Campbell, J. P. & Pritchard, R. D. (1976). Motivation theory in industrial and organizational psychology. In M. D. Dunnette (Ed.), Handbook of industrial and organizational psychology, (pp. 63–130). Chicago: Rand McNally.

Cropanzano, R. (Ed.), (1993). Justice in the workplace. Hillsdale, NJ: Erlbaum.

Deci, E. L. & Ryan, R. M. (1980). The empirical exploration of intrinsic motivational processes. In L. Berkowitz (Ed.), Advances in experimental social psychology, (Vol. 13, pp. 39–80). New York: Academic Press.

Erez, M. (1993). Toward a model of cross-cultural industrial and organizational psychology. In M. D. Dunnette & H. Triandis (Eds), Handbook of industrial and organizational psychology, (Vol. 4) Consulting Psychologists Press.

Gersick, C. J. G. (1988). Time and transition in work teams: Toward a new model of group development. Academy of Management Journal, 31, 9–41.

Heckhausen, H. (1991). Motivation and action. New York: Springer-Verlag.

Kanfer, R. (1990). Motivation theory and industrial/organizational psychology. In M. D. Dunnette & L. Hough (Eds), Handbook of industrial and organizational psychology Volume 1. *Theory in industrial and organizational psychology*, (pp. 75–170). Palo Alto, CA: Consulting Psychologists Press.

Kanfer, R. (1992). Work motivation: New directions in theory and research. In C. L. Cooper & I. T. Robertson (Eds), International review of industrial and organizational psychology, (vol. 7, pp. 1–53). London: Wiley.

Kanfer, R. & Ackerman, P. L. (1989). Motivation and cognitive abilities: An integrative/aptitude-treatment interaction approach to skill acquisition. Journal of Applied Psychology – Monograph, 74, 657–690.

Kanfer, F. H. & Hagerman, S. M. (1987). A model of self-regulation. In F. Halisch & J. Kuhl (Eds), Motivation, intention, and volition, (pp. 293–307). New York: Springer-Verlag.

Katzell, R. A. & Guzzo, R. A. (1983). Psychological approaches to productivity improvement. American Psychologist, 38, 468–472.

Katzell, (1990). Work motivation: Theory and practice. American Psychologist, 45, 144–153.

Locke, E. A. & Latham, G. P. (1990). A theory of goal setting and task performance. New York: Prentice-Hall.

Locke, E. A., Shaw, K. N., Saari, L. M. & Latham, G. P. (1981). Goal setting and task performance: 1969–1980. Psychological Bulletin, 90, 125–152.

Lord, R. G. & Kernan, M. C. (1989). Application of control theory to work settings. In W. A. Herschberger (Ed.), Volitional action, (pp. 493–514). Amsterdam: Elsevier Science, North-Holland.

Maslow, A. (1954). Motivation and personality. New York: Harper & Row.

Mitchell, T. R. (1982). Expectancy-value models in organizational psychology. In N. T. Feather (Ed.), Expectations and actions: Expectancy-value models in psychology, (pp. 293–312). Hillsdale, NJ: Erlbaum.

Naylor, J. C., Pritchard, R. D. & Ilgen, D. R. (1980). A theory of behavior in organizations. New York: Academic Press.

Steers, R. M. & Porter, L. W. (1987). Motivation and work behavior, (4th edn.) New York: McGraw-Hill.

Swezey, R. W. & Salas, E. (Eds), (1992). Teams: Their training and performance. Norwood, NJ: Ablex.

Vroom, V. H. (1964). Work and motivation. New York: Wiley.

Weiner, B. (1980). Human motivation. New York: Holt, Rinehart, & Winston.

RUTH KANFER

multicultural   Multiculture may be defined as having more than one culture represented. The term is used to describe culturally diverse workplaces, living units, and any other situation or activity where more than one culture exists. The existence of multicultural conditions is so prominent in today's world that managers must become aware of differences and learn how to deal with common problems that arise.

see also **Cross-cultural training**

JOHN O'CONNELL

multilateral netting   Multilateral netting is an important cash management tool for organizations having operations and currency flows between a number of nations. Each time currency payments must be made there are transaction costs and delays. If an organization could make fewer, but larger currency transfers, transaction costs could be reduced and delays minimized. This is where multinational netting comes in. As an example, assume an organization has operations in three countries. Each operation transfers currency to each other country once per day. Each operation is paying for some goods or services from a country while at the same time receiving payment from that country for goods or services it provided. Thus, a total of six transactions take place (payment of the three operations). Instead of transferring money directly to the country, a multilateral netting approach would have each operation transfer its payments to a single "coordination center." The coordination center would "net out" (deduct the outflows from the inflows) the individual transactions between the three country operations. The difference would then be sent to each operation (a total of three transactions) at a lower transaction cost and with greater speed.

see also **Cash management**

Bibliography

Celi, L. J. & Rutizer, B. (1991). *Global cash management.* 1st edn, New York: Harper Business (HarperCollins).

Kuhlmann, A. R., Mathis, F. J. & Mills, J. (1991). *First steps in treasury management: Prime cash.* 2nd edn, Toronto, Canada: Treasury Management Association of Canada.

JOHN O'CONNELL

multinational bargaining   Multinational bargaining is a concept developed in the 1970s, when the growth and spread of firms operating in more than one nation appeared vulnerable to activity orchestrated by unions known as international trade secretariats. Some of these union bodies with worldwide memberships, such as the International Chemical and Energy Workers, the International Union of Food and Allied Workers, and the International Metalworkers' Federation, all based in Geneva, claimed that a new concept encompassing union and management delegates bargaining across national borders would be the wave of the future. The European Trade Union Confederation, based in Brussels, and its industry groups were also seen as active participants in this process. A number of serious obstacles has prevented the development of multinational collective bargaining:

(1) *Different legislation* – no two countries have the same labor laws or practices. Bargaining rights, union structures, and bargaining structures are different and difficult to reconcile from one country to another.

(2) *Employer opposition* – employers almost universally oppose multinational bargaining since they see nothing to be gained from the process. Most business leaders see multinational bargaining as a potential complicating factor that would add a third level of risk to work stoppages.

(3) *Union opposition* – some unions fear that multinational bargaining will result in a transfer of power from national union officials to those who lead multinational organizations.

(4) *Lack of employee interest* – employee interest in multinational union action is close to being nonexistent. Workers in one country are not likely to support their fellow employees in another country.

Bibliography

Northrup, H. R. & Rowan, R. L. (1974). Multinational collective bargaining activity: the factual record in chemicals, glass, and rubber tires. *Columbia Journal of World Business*, **Spring and summer**, 112–24 and 49–63.

Northrup, H. R. & Rowan, R. L. (1979). *Multinational Collective Bargaining Attempts: the Record, the Cases, and the Prospects*, Philadelphia: Industrial Research Unit, The Wharton School, University of Pennsylvania.

Rowan, R. L. & Northrup, H. R. (1975). Multinational bargaining in the telecommunications industry. *British Journal of Industrial Relations*, 13, 257–62.

RICHARD L. ROWAN

mutual funds Mutual funds are equity claims against prespecified assets held by investment companies (firms that professionally manage pools of assets). Thus, a share of a mutual fund is an equity claim, typically held by an individual, against a professionally managed pool of assets.

Mutual funds provide four benefits to individual investors. First, since most mutual funds are well diversified, these funds allow individuals with limited capital to hold diversified portfolios. Second, since mutual funds are professionally managed, an individual investor can obtain the benefits of professional asset management at a fraction of the cost of privately retaining a professional manager. Third, mutual funds can provide superior liquidity both during the holding period of the fund and at liquidation. Since transaction costs are not typically proportional to order dollar values, mutual funds can rebalance portfolios at a lower proportional cost than an individual investment can. Furthermore, to liquidate a portfolio, mutual funds require the sale of only a single security (the fund). Finally, mutual funds reduce book-keeping and clerical costs by automatically reinvesting dividends or coupons and by providing quarterly performance reports and annual consolidated statements for investors' tax purposes.

Mutual funds carry several costs for investors. Management fees, charged daily against the net asset value of the fund, are summarized, aggregated and reported quarterly. Load funds charge a one-time fee to the investor whenever shares are purchased (a "front-end" load) and/or sold (a "back-end load"). Some back-end load fees are contingent on the holding period. For example, a back-end load fee of (5 percent – 1 percent × years held) means that an investor can escape the back-end load fee if the shares are held for five years or more. Such contingent back-end fees are often called "contingent deferred sales loads." Finally, investment companies may charge mutual fund holders "12b-1 fees" to reimburse the investment company for marketing, advertising, reporting, and maintaining investor relations.

The most important dichotomy in the analysis of mutual funds is the distinction between open-end and closed-end funds. In an "open end fund," purchases and sales of shares in the fund can be made through the investment company at any time. Thus, the number of shares outstanding and the amount of capital under management vary constantly. Further, such transactions occur at the stated net asset value (NAV). The NAV, which is calculated at least daily, is the current market value of the fund's assets divided by shares outstanding.

In contrast, shares of a "closed-end fund" are issued by the investment company only once and are fixed thereafter. As a result, individuals wishing to buy or sell shares of an established closed-end fund must identify a counterparty willing to take the other side of the transaction. This is why closed-end funds, but not open end funds, are listed on stock exchanges. Often, secondary market transactions of a closed-end fund occur at prices that differ from the fund's NAV. Funds with market prices above their NAV trade at a premium; funds with market prices below their NAV trade at a discount. Closed-end funds do not charge an explicit front-end load fee. Instead, this fee is charged implicitly, through the difference between the higher purchase price and the NAV of the fund.

A second important distinction between mutual funds is their investment "style." Some funds are "passively" managed; that is, holdings of the mutual fund are rarely altered and the fund mimics a benchmark index such as the Standard and Poor's 500 Index. However, the vast majority of mutual funds are "actively" managed, with portfolio holdings frequently altered according to management discretion. One example of an actively managed style is "market timing," where a manager dynamically alters a fund's weights in stocks, bonds, and short-term debt in anticipation of future moves.

Actively managed funds are classified by the type of assets they hold. For example, some funds invest only in tax-exempt municipal bonds, while others invest only in mortgage-backed debt obligations. Equity funds are normally classified as growth funds (containing speculative stocks with low dividend yields), income funds (containing less volatile, higher yield stocks, and sometimes bonds), or balanced funds (containing elements of both growth and income funds).

Furthermore, some equity funds consider only foreign issues, while others, called "country funds," invest only in equities in one particular foreign country. Since many countries restrict foreign investment, a closed-end fund may be the only viable avenue for investing in a particular country. Thus, a foreign country closed-end fund is likely to trade at a premium.

In the USA, mutual funds, and the investment companies that manage them, are regulated under the Investment Company Act of 1940. Under this Act, the Securities and Exchange Commission is granted authority to regulate mutual funds. Investment companies, like the equity market, are regulated by disclosure, rather than merit, regulation. Consequently, mutual fund regulation focuses on mandatory disclosure of information, including the filing of a prospectus at the time of issue as well as quarterly and annual reports. To prevent potential conflicts of interest, regulation limits the holdings of brokers and underwriters in a mutual fund.

PAUL SEGUIN

national culture   When research and other publications dealing with cultural questions are reviewed it may appear that each country has its own unique culture. This is because most research is carried out in a specific country and the assumption is often made that "country" corresponds with "culture." Nothing could be further from the truth. A "national" culture is that of the majority of a country's citizens. The values, beliefs, and attitudes of the majority can and do coexist with a large number of other cultures. One has only to look at the diversity of cultures within the United States for an example of a multicultural country. Still, the US national culture would probably include descriptors such as: individualism, creative, oriented towards accumulation of material goods, and others. As for cultures remaining only within a certain country's boundaries, one may look to Great Britain as a bold example of national culture spreading to many other parts of the world. If a person goes to most of the former British colonies he/she will find a multitude of British cultural attributes alive and well. A national culture may be capable of definition and useful as a first look at what will face a future expatriate. Closer inspection of most countries will reveal the existence of a great number of other cultures.

JOHN O'CONNELL

National Labor Relations Board   The National Labor Relations Board (NLRB) is a federal agency created under the National Labor Relations Act of 1935. The NLRB is headquartered in Washington, DC, with approximately forty regional and field offices scattered across the United States. Its five-member board is appointed by the President and confirmed by the US Senate. The board has two functions: (a) preventing, investigating, and remedying unfair labor practices committed by employers and unions; and (b) conducting secret ballot elections of designated bargaining units to determine whether employees desire union representation. Unfair labor practice charges are initially handled by the regional offices, with appeals to the five-member board. Representation elections are usually held on the premises of the employer.

DAVID A. GRAY

national origin   National origin is one of the protected categories under Title VII of the CIVIL RIGHTS ACT OF 1964. This category of protection is interpreted synonymously with ancestry; it protects individuals based on the country of origin of the individuals themselves or of their forebears. It also protects individuals from discrimination based on their *perceived* ancestries. The term "national origin" is not synonymous with citizenship; although it is illegal to discriminate on the basis of national origin, it is not illegal to discriminate (under Title VII) on the basis of alienage *per se*. Aliens are protected under Title VII only to the extent that they are discriminated against on the basis of race, color, religion, sex, or national origin.

RAMONA L. PAETZOLD

national treatment   An agreement between countries to treat imported products and services (between signatories of the agreement) in the same manner as domestically-produced goods and services. This is an example of free trade at its highest level. Essentially, national treatment removes barriers which may have hampered free trade. National treatment is the basic goal of the General Agreement on Tariffs and Trade (GATT).

see also **Reciprocity**

JOHN O'CONNELL

nationalization   Nationalization is the action of a government to transfer possession of private property to the government. Many countries have nationalized whole industries on the premise that ownership transfer is in the public's best interests. Compensation is generally offered but there are no guarantees it will be sufficient to pay for loss of value and future profits of the nationalized firm. Nationalization has been most common in extractive industries (mining, energy), communications and financial services (insurance companies and banks). Nationalization is considered a political risk for which insurance coverage may be available.

see also **Political risk; Political risk insurance**

Bibliography

Coplin, W. D. & O'Leary, M. K. (1994). *The handbook of country and political risk analysis.* New York: Political Risk Services.

Gregory, A. (1989). Political risk management in A. Rugman (ed.). *International Business in Canada*, pp. 310–29. Scarborough, Ontario: Prentice-Hall, Canada.

Kennedy, C. R., Jr. (1991). *Managing the international business environment: Cases in political and country risk.* Englewood Cliffs, NJ: Prentice-Hall.

JOHN O'CONNELL

negligent hiring   Negligent hiring claims are made when an employee injures another individual (whether or not the victim is a coworker) and the victim can prove not only that the employee was unfit for the position, but also that the employer knew that the employee was unfit, or, had the employer investigated the employee's background prior to hiring that individual, the employer would have known that the employee was unfit. The victim must show that the injury was a direct result of the employment relationship, such as an assault committed by an employee who comes into a customer's home to repair an appliance.

BARBARA A. LEE

negligent retention   Negligent retention claims may be filed against an employer when one of its employees injures or otherwise harms another individual, and the victim asserts that the employer knew that the employee was either dangerous or unfit for the job. Employers who know that an employee has been violent, has engaged in sexual, racial, or other unlawful forms of harassment, or has been dishonest may be liable under this legal theory if the employee repeats the behavior and someone, whether another employee, a client or customer, or a member of the general public, is harmed.

BARBARA A. LEE

negotiation   It has been argued that customer/supplier negotiations have traditionally tended to be part of a "zero-sum game" and that an advantage for one side (e.g., a discount) was "won" through a disadvantage for the other (Dion & Banting, 1988). This is, of course, an over-simplified view of the complex field of customer/supplier negotiations and there would have been many exceptions to this exaggeratedly aggressive picture of negotiation. Nevertheless, this image seems to have had a powerful influence on the sales negotiation literature, much of which has focused on techniques for manipulating customers into sales agreements which, by definition, they would otherwise have negotiated further or even declined. A more sophisticated view of marketing negotiation now prevails whereby "win-win" situations are sought in which both supplier and customer gain from negotiation. An example of this mutually beneficial approach is the idea of long-term customer/supplier partnerships where commitment and trust on both sides replace the traditional image of suspicion and hostility. In reality, different circumstances and personnel will require different negotiating styles and this has always been the case. The fundamental principle remains that effective negotiation depends not just on skill and techniques but on understanding the position of all parties involved – a principle which lies at the heart of marketing more generally.

Bibliography

Carlisle, J. & Parker, R. (1990). *Beyond negotiation.* Chichester: John Wiley.
Dion, P. A. & Banting, P. M. (1988). Industrial supplier–buyer negotiations. *Industrial Marketing Management,* 17, (1), Feb., 43–48.
Fisher, R. & Brown, S. (1988). *Getting together: building a relationship that gets to Yes.* Boston, MA: Houghton Mifflin Co.
Lancaster, G. & Jobber, D. (1985). *Sales technique and management.* London: Pitman.
Lidstone, J. B. J. (1991). *Manual of sales negotiation.* Aldershot: Gower.
McCall, I. & Cousins, J. (1990). *Communication problem solving.* Chichester: John Wiley. Chapter 6, 89–115.

DOMINIC WILSON

negotiation tactics   Negotiation tactics are the methods used by bargainers to reach their negotiation goals. Most negotiation scholars distinguish between tactics intended to attain a high distributive outcome (i.e. claim value) and those intended to attain a high integrative outcome (i.e. create value) (Walton and McKersie, 1965; Raiffa, 1982; Lewicki et al., 1994) (*see* DISTRIBUTIVE BARGAINING; INTEGRATIVE BARGAINING). This distinction is useful for understanding negotiation tactics, provided it does not obscure the idea that, in practice, attempting to claim and create value simultaneously is a fundamental tension faced by negotiators (Lax and Sebenius, 1986). As such, tactics of both types may be used in combination, or one tactic may even be used to accomplish both goals.

Because each negotiation party typically has incomplete information about the opponent's true preferences, tactics are used to convey and gather information. Tactics intended to claim value may convey information to the opponent about one's own bargaining situation (e.g. unwillingness to concede) or one's commitment to undertake a course of action (e.g. threats to reach an impasse). Tactics intended to create value may, for example, convey information to the opponent about one's true preferences on the issues being negotiated. Other tactics, such as those intended to gather information about the opponent's preferences, may be used to either claim or create value. This latter example demonstrates that while certain tactics are often used to send or gather particular types of information, it is often the use of the information and the accuracy with which it is transmitted that link the tactic to a particular outcome.

Many specific tactics are described in the negotiation literature. Some examples include making an extreme first offer, threatening to walk away if concessions are not granted, or using silence to elicit information from the opponent. Most tactics involve risk. Distributive tactics may increase the chance that the opponent will become more competitive. Some integrative tactics, such as revealing one's true preferences, create the opportunity for an opponent to take advantage of this information. Because of these risks, choosing an appropriate tactic or set of tactics can be difficult. Adding further complexity, the timing with which tactics are employed can moderate their effectiveness. Ethical considerations also frequently arise when a negotiator considers using tactics that convey incomplete, misleading, or even false information.

Contextual factors typically have a strong influence on the probability that various tactics will succeed. One of the most important factors in choosing tactics is the opponent. For example, while some opponents are likely to reciprocate contentious tactics, others may give in to them. Of course, being able to predict the reactions of the other party to a particular tactic can greatly simplify the decision regarding which tactics to use. Frequently, however, tactics are most effective when applied forcefully, and this very force decreases the predictability of the opponent's reaction. Choosing appropriate tactics remains, in Raiffa's (1982) words, an art as well as a science.

Bibliography

Lax, D. A. & Sebenius, J. K. (1986). *The Manager as Negotiator: Bargaining for Cooperation and Competitive Gain,* New York: The Free Press.
Lewicki, R. J., Litterer, J. A., Minton, J. W. & Saunders, D. M. (1994). *Negotiation,* Boston: Richard D. Irwin.
Neale, M. A. & Bazerman, M. H. (1991). *Cognition and Rationality in Negotiation,* New York: The Free Press.
Raiffa, H. (1982). *The Art and Science of Negotiation,* Cambridge, MA: Harvard University Press.
Walton, R. E. & McKersie, R. B. (1965). *A Behavioral Theory of Labor Negotiations,* Ithaca, NY: ILR Press.

JEFFREY T. POLZER

net present value Used in CAPITAL BUDGETING decisions, a project's net present value (NPV) is the discounted cash flow of benefits from that project. To calculate the NPV for a given investment, the net cash flow for each period must be calculated and discounted at the appropriate discount rate (the firm's COST OF CAPITAL is frequently used). Therefore, if an asset which costs P_0 today will generate cash flows of C in each period i for T periods in the future, then the net present value is

$$NPV = \sum_{i=0}^{T} \left[\frac{C_i}{(1+r)^i} \right]$$

where C_0 will equal the cost of the asset, $-P_0$, representing a negative cash flow (an outlay) in the initial period. The cash flows from the investment must be calculated as after-tax values and all of the effects of the investment on the firm's cash flows must be considered. One feature of the NPV method of evaluating projects is that it assumes cash flows can be reinvested and earn the firm's cost of capital; Brigham and Gapenski (1993) argue this is more appropriate than the reinvestment assumption using the INTERNAL RATE OF RETURN method. The NPV approach also provides a more consistent ranking of alternative investment decisions for capital budgeting than other methods; see Brigham and Gapenski (1993) and Edwards, Kay and Mayer (1987).

Profit-maximizing firms will maximize the present value of the firm by choosing those projects which have the highest NPV per dollar invested. In the example above, the cost of capital used to discount the cash flows from the investment is assumed to be constant over the life of the investment but this need not be the case and the NPV calculation can easily be modified to accommodate this change; see Brigham and Gapenski (1993), Edwards, Kay and Mayer (1987) and Shughart, Chappell and Cottle (1994).

If inflation is expected to occur during the life of the investment, then the estimated cash flows must be adjusted accordingly. The net present value above can be calculated using real (constant purchasing power) dollar values for both cash flows in the numerator and the discount rate in the denominator. Or managers can adjust estimated cash flows and the discount rate for expected inflation in their calculations. In either case, managers should be careful to note whether their firm's revenues adjust in the same manner as costs when inflation occurs.

see also **nominal income and prices; real prices**

Bibliography

Brigham, E. F., Gapenski, L. C. (1993). *Intermediate Financial Management.* New York: Dryden.

Edwards, J., Kay, J., Mayer, C. (1987). *The Economic Analysis of Accounting Profitability.* Oxford: OUP.

Shughart, W. F., Chappell, W. F., Cottle, R. L. (1994). *Modern Managerial Economics.* Cincinatti, OH: South-Western Publishing.

ROBERT E. MCAULIFFE

netting process in MRP The MRP netting process is the way material requirements planning carries out calculations on a level by level basis down through a BILL OF

Part no. *A*

Week no.	10	11	12	13	14	15	16
Master schedule	400	300	200	200	300	200	400

Part no. *X* (BOM = 6 per item *A*)   Lead time = 4 weeks

Week no.		10	11	12	13	14	15	16
Gross requirements		2400	1800	1200	1200	1800	1200	2400
Scheduled receipts			6000					
Projected stock	3200	800	5000	3800	2600	800	0	0
Net requirements							400	2400
Planned orders			400	2400				

Figure 1 An example of offsetting

MATERIALS which converts the master production schedule of finished products into suggested or planned orders for all the sub-assemblies, components, and raw materials. These calculations or requirements generation runs are likely to be carried out on the computer every week, or more frequently on a net change basis.

At each level of assembly breakdown, MRP undertakes three steps in its calculations before continuing to the next lower level. These steps are as follows:

(1) It generates gross requirements for the item by "exploding" the "planned order" quantities of the next higher level assembly, by reference to the bill of material structure file. For example, for a finished product A which requires six components X; a "planned order" of 200 As in week 15 would be exploded to give gross requirements of 1,200 Xs in week 15.

(2) The gross requirements are amended by the amount of inventory of that item that is expected to be available in each week, i.e. on hand from previous week plus scheduled receipts. This information is obtained from the inventory status file and the amended requirements are called the net requirements. For example, if in week 15 a total of 800 Xs are expected to be available, the gross requirement of 1,200 is amended to give a net requirement of 400 Xs in week 15.

(3) The net requirements are then offset by the relevant lead time for the item to give planned orders for initiating the manufacture or purchase of the item. For example, if the lead time for the Xs is 4 weeks, the net requirements of 400 Xs in week 15 are offset as in figure 1.

To summarize, in its simplest form, material requirements planning would calculate the requirements and planned orders for Xs for each period of the planning horizon as in figure 2. This calculation assumes that the only use of X is in the assembly of A. If this were not the case, and if its usage was common to other products assembled by the organization, then the gross requirements for X would have been the aggregated requirements generated from the planned orders of all the assemblies using X. This simplified approach to the calculation of requirements has, so far, assumed that the net requirements would be translated directly into planned orders, resulting in manufacturing component schedules and purchasing schedules which do not take any account of the cost of machine set-ups or the cost of ordering. It may therefore be necessary to modify the net requirements by the application of batching rules or ordering policies (see LOT SIZING IN

MRP). Similarly, no account has been taken of the need for any unplanned occurrences or short-term changes in supply or demand. In such cases it may be necessary to incorporate safety factors into the MRP calculations.

Bibliography

Luscombe, M. (1993). *MRPII: Integrating the business.* Oxford: Butterworth Heinemann.
New, C. (1973). *Requirements planning.* Epping: Gower Press.
Vollmann, T. W., Berry, W. L. & Whybark, D. C. (1992). *Manufacturing planning and control systems.* New York: Irwin.

PETER BURCHER

network   The research into European buyer–seller purchasing relationships has developed the concept of interaction (see INTERACTION APPROACH) whereby supplier–customer relationships are understood in terms of a set of evolving and mutually-dependent exchanges bound not only by commercial logic but also by factors of social and operational "comfortableness." The IMP research evolved from studies of procurement practices between suppliers and customers in European industrial markets where the importance of an informal network of personal contacts was quickly recognized as crucial to the day-to-day work of procurement personnel. At a more aggregated level, organizations in a market will share many such relationships in what can be analyzed as a network of bilateral and multilateral relationships (Håkansson & Snehota, 1989). It may even be useful to define organizational markets in terms of the common factors shared by a network of organizational relationships rather than the more usual simplistic reference to products or services. More recently, the network concept could be seen as an important stimulus to research interest in issues of interorganizational collaboration and strategic alliances, e.g., in terms of NEW PRODUCT DEVELOPMENT (Håkansson, 1987) and technology management (Håkansson, 1990).

see also **Relationship marketing**

Bibliography

Håkansson, H. (1987). Product development in networks. In H. Håkansson (Ed.), *Industrial technological development – A network approach* (pp. 84–128). London: Croom Helm. (Also (abridged) in D. Ford (Ed.), *Understanding business markets: Interaction, relationships and networks*, (pp. 487–507). London: Academic Press.
Håkansson, H. (1990). Technological collaboration in industrial networks. *European Management Journal*, 8, (3), 371–9.
Håkansson, H. & Snehota, I. (1989). No business is an island: The network concept of business strategy. *Scandinavian Journal of Management*, 4, (3), 187–200.

DOMINIC WILSON

Week no.	11	12	13	14	15	16
Net Requirements					400	
Planned Orders	400					

Figure 2 An example of calculating requirements

networking Research about networking and networks can be complicated. Understanding what networking is and the nature of networks is not complicated. Networking at its most basic is the process of contacting and being contacted by people in our social network and maintaining these linkages and relationships. A network, then, is a set of relations, linkages, or ties among people. A connection between people consists both of content (type of connection) and form (strength of the connection).

Content may include information exchange or simply friendship ties. The strength of the connection may be determined by the number of contacts made between people over time. Of course, strength can also be measured by the degree of intensity of the relationship, e.g. how long a singular contact is maintained, compared with the number of contacts made.

Like individuals, organizations are embedded in multiple networks, e.g., resource and information exchange. A domain of organization networks studied extensively is board of director interlock networks. Early research into these networks attempted to show collusion among competitors via their interlocking board members, but more recently Zajac (1988) has found little evidence to support this interpretation. Most researchers today view the interlock network as a way to exchange information rather than exert explicit control (Useem, 1984).

Much research has been conducted on networks. According to Davis and Powell (1992), the information content, maintenance, and mapping of network ties has received most attention whereas, for example, the consequences of an organization's position in various networks has hardly been studied. According to Burt (1980), methodological advances have been made, but theory is underdeveloped.

Fischer, Jackson, Stueve, Gerson, Jones, & Baldassare (1977) have contributed to the field by suggesting that networks can best be understood according to a choice-constraint approach, that is, a network is the result of individual choices made within certain social constraints. Social structures, such as class, determine whether and to what degree these choices can be made.

Tichy, Tushman, and Fombrun (1979) state that the study of networks can be traced to three broad schools of thought: sociology, anthropology, and role theory. From these studies, the key properties of networks have been identified as:

(1) transactional content – what is exchanged between members, e.g., information;
(2) nature of the links – the strength and qualitative nature of the relationships, e.g., the degree to which members honor obligations or agree about appropriate behavior in their relationships; and
(3) structural characteristics – how members are linked, the number of clusters within the network, and certain individuals representing special nodes within the network; in other words, not all members are equally important; some, for example, are GATEKEEPERS.

Tichy et al. (1979) also describe ways of analyzing organizations according to a network framework. They conclude that the social network framework can be used to study and understand more effectively:

(a) INTERORGANIZATIONAL RELATIONS relationships;
(b) organizations and their boundaries;
(c) career patterns and career succession;
(d) organizational change (see ORGANIZATION DEVELOPMENT AND CHANGE);
(e) ORGANIZATIONAL DESIGN configuration; and
(f) POWER and political processes (see POLITICS).

Networking in organizations is usually an informal process, that is, the contacts and interactions among people do not as a rule conform to the formal organization chart – which is usually in the form of a hierarchy. Today formal hierarchy is being viewed more as a hindrance than a help to ORGANIZATIONAL EFFECTIVENESS. The need to coordinate activities of organizational members is significantly greater today than in the past. Getting products to market more rapidly, providing quality service (which now is more dependent on numbers of people rather than a single individual), and partnering more with contractors, vendors and other organizational constituents are but a few of the many forces impinging on organizations to be more rapidly responsive. Some believe the "network organization" is a more effective alternative to hierarchy (Rockart & Short, 1991).

It would appear, then, that with the:

(a) need for more and faster responsiveness; and
(b) increasing reliance on information technology,

networking will be of growing importance in organizations.

Understanding and using networks can have practical outcomes, as illustrated by Granovetter (1973). Assume you are looking for a job. You are more likely to be successful via the weak ties in your social network than by the strong ones. Close friends are likely to have many of the same contacts and sources as yourself. More distant acquaintances travel in different circles and therefore provide a link to contacts you would not otherwise have. Thus, while certain kinds of networking may be frivolous, for example, a set of friends who share with you the same interest in, say, Stephen King novels, other networks in your life may provide highly useful information and assistance.

see also **Coalition formation; Intergroup relations**

Bibliography

Burt, R. S. (1980). Models of network structure. *Annual Review of Sociology*, 6, 79–141.
Davis, G. F. & Powell, W. W. (1992). Organization–environment relations. In M. D. Dunnette & L. M. Hough (Eds), Handbook of industrial and organizational psychology, (2nd edn, vol. 3, pp. 316–375). Palo Alto, CA: Consulting Psychologists Press.
Fischer, C. S., Jackson, R. M., Stueve, C. A., Gerson, K., Jones, L. M. & Baldassare, M. (1977). Networks and places: Social relations in the urban setting. New York: Free Press.
Granovetter, M. (1973). The strength of weak ties. *American Journal of Sociology*, 78, 1360–1380.
Rockart, J. F. & Short, J. E. (1991). The networked organization and the management of interdependence. In M. S. S. Morton (Ed.), The corporation of the 1990s: Information technology and organizational transformation, (pp. 189–219). New York: Oxford University Press.
Tichy, N. M. Tushman, M. L. & Fombrun, C. (1979). Social network analysis for organizations. *Academy of Management Review*, 4, 507–519.

Useem, M. (1984). The inner circle: Large corporations and the rise of business political activity in the U.S. and U.K. New York: Oxford University Press.

Zajac, E. S. (1988). Interlocking directorates as an interorganizational strategy: A test of critical assumptions. *Academy of Management Journal*, 31, 428–438.

W. WARNER BURKE

new employee orientation   "Orientation is the planned introduction of new employees to their jobs, their co-workers, and the policies, processes, and culture of the organization" (Cook, 1992, p. 133). Most organizations offer an employee orientation program coordinated by the human resource department. A carefully planned orientation program creates a favorable impression of the organization, gives employees the information they need to get started in a new job, and helps to reduce the stresses of coping with an unfamiliar environment.

An ideal new employee orientation program should have two components, administered by different individuals. First, there should be one or more formal presentations by human resource professionals aimed largely at administrative and organization-wide issues. Some of these issues must be dealt with on the first day at work; others can wait for several weeks until there is a small group of newcomers who can be oriented as a class. The formal sessions might include the following: (a) rules and procedures (pay and benefits, work hours, employee handbook); (b) safety procedures, fire evacuation procedures; (c) administrative formalities (payroll forms, insurance enrollment forms); (d) tour of the facility; and (e) information about the organization's history, mission, goals, and values (perhaps including a talk by a senior manager or a videotaped message from the CEO).

The second component of new employee orientation is conducted on-the-job by the immediate supervisor. A checklist provided to the immediate supervisor assures that all relevant information is covered over the course of the first few weeks on the job. Topics to be included in the orientation by the superior include: (a) information about the job, duties, procedures, manuals, performance expectations, workstation, equipment, location of needed resources, authority to make decisions, and so forth; (b) introduction to coworkers, including possible assignment of a "buddy" to answer questions; (c) information about the department, goals, rules, schedules, work flow, and relationships to other departments and clients; and (d) discussion of career goals, training needs, performance appraisal and promotion practices, and so forth.

Bibliography

Cook, M. F. (1992). Orientation. *The AMA Handbook for Employee Recruitment and Retention*, Cook, M. F., New York: AMACOM. 133–48.

Wanous, J. P. (1992). *Organizational Entry: Recruitment, Selection, Orientation and Socialization of Newcomers*, Reading, MA: Addison-Wesley.

CYNTHIA D. FISHER

new product development   New product development, or NPD, "is the process that transforms technical ideas or market needs and opportunities into a new product that is launched onto the market" (Walsh et al., 1992, 16). New products can make a profound contribution to competi-tiveness and this is particularly acute in an era of accelerating technological change, general shortening of the PRODUCT LIFE CYCLE, and increasingly intense competition. The most common representation of the NPD process is as a series of decision stages or activities (Kotler, 1984, 5th edn). Cooper & Kleinschmidt (1986) identify 13 stages of the NPD:

(1) screening of new product ideas;
(2) preliminary market assessment;
(3) preliminary technical assessment;
(4) detailed market study/market research;
(5) business/financial analysis;
(6) physical product development;
(7) in-house product testing;
(8) customer tests of product;
(9) test market/trial sell;
(10) trial production;
(11) pre-commercialization business activities;
(12) production start-up; and
(13) market launch.

However, the traditional sequential model of NPD has been criticized for ignoring the interactions that occur between the stages and the interactions between different departments, as well as with external agencies, such as customers and suppliers (Hart, 1995). The uncertainties of NPD are recognized and relate to both market uncertainties and technological uncertainties. The more radical the NPD, then the greater the difficulty in making ex ante assessments of the technical and market opportunities. A considerable amount of research has been devoted as to how to improve the likelihood of new product success. However, there is little agreement as to what constitutes "success," and various indicators have been used, such as different financial measures and different units of analysis, which means that direct comparison of the results of separate studies is not feasible. Nonetheless, some themes have emerged from the different studies that appear to have some bearing on the positive outcome of NPD. These include: people factors, such as commitment of senior managers (Maidique & Zirger, 1984); organizational factors, e.g., effective interfunctional cooperation (Pinto & Pinto, 1990); and operational factors, such as the use of market research (Johne & Snelson, 1988). Marketing has been identified as having a significant role. Rothwell (1977) points to the role of marketing and publicity and of understanding "user needs," and Cooper (1994) notes the value of having a "strong market orientation and customer focus." The constant interaction of R&D, design, production, and marketing from the very early stages of NPD to market launch have been associated with success (e.g., Cooper & Kleinschmidt, 1986). The presence of a "PRODUCT CHAMPION" has also been acknowledged as a "success" factor. Product development is not always about new products – product modifications, extensions, and style change are also aspects of product development.

To devise, produce, and implement new products and modifications to existing products entails input from different functions, notably marketing, R&D, and production. Their input has to be integrated to ensure that products are made that correspond with customer needs and are made economically and without time delays.

Different approaches to the management of product development activities have been identified. "Over the wall" refers to a functionally divided organization wherein product ideas are continually passed back and forth between functions, so that marketing undertakes some development work, then passes this onto R&D which carries out more development and then passes the ideas back to marketing, and so on. This process can mean that the idea stays in development for a long time. A different approach is that of the "rugby scrum" whereby product development teams are formed with representatives from each function, all of which make an ongoing contribution to the product's development. This organizational approach can facilitate a quicker time to market than the "over the wall" approach (Walsh et al., 1992).

Different functions may not communicate easily with one another and the interface between R&D and marketing, in particular, has received attention (Gupta, Raj, & Wileman, 1995). A recent study found that effective interface between marketing and design was likely to occur in organizations with a culture of openness, close location of marketing and design functions and a multi-disciplinary team approach to product development (Davies-Cooper & Jones, 1995).

Bibliography

Cooper, R. G. (1994). New products: The factors that drive success. *International Marketing Review*, 11, (1), 60–77.

Cooper, R. G. & Kleinschmidt, E. J. (1986). An investigation into the new product process: Steps, deficiencies and impact. *Journal of Product Innovation Management*, 3, (1), 71–85.

Davies-Cooper, R. & Jones, T. (1995). The interfaces between design and other key functions in product development. In M. Bruce & W. Biemans (Eds), *Product development: Meeting the challenge of the design–marketing interface*. Chichester: John Wiley.

Gupta, A. K., Raj, S. P. & Wileman, D. (1985). R&D and marketing dialogue in high-tech firms. *Industrial Marketing Management*, 14, 289.

Hart, S. (1995). Where we've been and where we're going in new product development research. In M. Bruce & W. Biemans (Eds), *Product development: Meeting the challenge of the design–marketing interface*. (Chapter 1) Chichester: John Wiley.

Johne, F. A. & Snelson, P. (1988). Marketing's role in successful product development. *Journal of Marketing Management*, 3, (3), 256–268.

Kotler, P. (1984). *Marketing management: Analysis, planning and control*. 5th edn, Englewood Cliffs, NJ: Prentice-Hall. Chapter 10, p. 309.

Maidique, M. A. & Zirger, B. J. (1984). A study of success and failure in product innovation: The case of the US electronics industry. *IEEE Transactions on Engineering Management*, EM-31, (4), Nov., 192–203.

Pinto, M. B. & Pinto, J. K. (1990). Project team communication and cross functional co-operation in new program development. *Journal of Product Innovation Management*, 7, 200–212.

Rothwell, R. (1977). The characteristics of successful innovations and technically progressive firms (with some comments on innovation research). *R&D Management*, 7, (3), 191–206.

Walsh, V., Roy, R., Bruce, M. & Potter, S. (1992). *Winning by design: Technology, product design and international competitiveness*. Oxford: Basil Blackwell. Chapters 1 & 5.

MARGARET BRUCE

new task Robinson, Faris & Wind (1967) suggest a division of organizational buying into three categories: new task, MODIFIED RE-BUY, and straight re-buy. Of these categories, new task is the most complex and refers to those occasions when it is necessary to identify new sources for goods or services. This may be because a previous source is no longer satisfactory, or because the requirement itself is new. In principle, will be involved in new task buying but in practice this will depend on the scale and significance of the purchase in question. Thus, new task purchasing in the defence sector (e.g., for an aircraft carrier) might take years, whereas new task purchasing for ballpoint pens (e.g., in a bank) might be done very quickly.

Bibliography

Robinson, P. T., Faris, C. W. & Wind, Y. (1967). *Industrial buying and creative marketing*. Boston, MA: Allyn & Bacon.

DOMINIC WILSON

non-compete agreements If an employer employs an individual or individuals with specialized training or knowledge, or whose skills are highly valuable to that employer and its competitors, the employer may require the employee to sign a non-compete agreement. These agreements restrict the employee from working for competing organizations, typically for a limited period of time and within a limited geographic area. Non-compete agreements that completely bar an employee from any employment in his or her occupation are usually not enforced by the courts because they are viewed as unreasonable.

BARBARA A. LEE

nonresident convertibility A nonresident of a country normally has the right to exchange local deposits of that country's currency for any other currency. Thus, a Canadian citizen with pound sterling in a London bank could exchange the pound sterling for any other currency. This is referred to as "nonresident convertibility."

JOHN O'CONNELL

nonwork/work This refers to the relationship between one's work and nonwork life. Work generally refers to activities or attitudes undertaken in an employing organization. Nonwork has generally referred to activities and attitudes related to one's family, yet also includes what Zedeck (1992) considers, a personal sphere, where leisure activities, hobbies, and health-related activities occur. Zedeck (1992) further notes that the nonwork concept includes other spheres such as religion, community, and social. Yet, the most studied area of the nonwork/work literature has been the relationship between one's employing organization and one's family.

The need for research in the nonwork/work area became prevalent with the onset of the Industrial Revolution and the increasing separation of work from family life. In the past decade, interest in the nonwork/work field has continued to grow, as researchers recognize the interrelatedness of the nonwork/work spheres, and as the relationship between these two spheres becomes more diverse. For example, the definitions of nonwork/work have changed over time. Family no longer solely means a male headed household, but has become broadened to mean two or more people having influence over each other's lives, sharing a sense of identity and shared goals (Zedeck, 1992). This new definition encompasses both same and different sex partners. The definition of work has also evolved over time. Zedeck (1992) reminds us that work is something that is done, not only in the traditional work environment, but for many (e.g., homemakers, telecommunicators), work is something that is done within the home environment. With these changes in definitions, it becomes obvious that the way researchers view the nonwork/work relationship has evolved historically.

History of Findings

Research related to nonwork/work issues began in the 1930s (Voydanoff, 1989). Findings from this period consistently suggested that male *un*employment and female *em*ployment had negative effects on both children and the family (Voydanoff, 1989). While this era of research recognized a "relationship" between one's nonwork and work lives, the primary focus was on the negative effects of work on family. The notion that the family might also influence work life had not yet been considered.

Subsequently, the focus of the nonwork/work research slowly began to shift to a position of viewing nonwork and work lives as interdependent, and in the 1960s to increase attention to the dual-career couple. Much of this research focused on the additional STRESS and tradeoffs of dual career couples in both their nonwork and work lives. Voydanoff (1989) notes that research during this era began to recognize the "unpaid contribution" of wives of professionals and managers to their husbands' careers. According to Voydanoff (1989) it was often the work the wife's career, due to geographic mobility, and demands on the wife's time.

Voydanoff (1989) notes that while earlier research examined primarily men's *un*employment, women's *em*ployment, and dual career couples, recent research has focused on the structural and psychological characteristics of work, and the relationship between JOB CHARACTER-ISTICS and JOB SATISFACTION. Nonwork/work research has also begun to investigate the relationship between job characteristics and stress and health. Structural aspects of the job, such as working hours, compressed work week schedules, and geographic mobility have been shown to affect family life. Weekend work is generally shown to be negatively related to quality of family life (Voydanoff, 1989), the compressed work week schedule is positively related to family satisfaction (Tippins & Stroh, 1991), and job-related geographic mobility has mixed results (Brett, Stroh, & Reilly, 1992a).

Models to Study Nonwork/work Issues

Combined with earlier research on nonwork/work issues, Kanter's (1977) influential review encouraged researchers to begin to think of the nonwork/work environment as an interface and theorists began to develop models to help explain the relationship.

The spillover theory suggests that work-related activities/satisfaction can affect nonwork life and nonwork responsibilities/satisfaction may also affect one's work life. For example, a person's marital satisfaction may affect their relationship to the work place (Brett, Stroh, & Reilly, 1992b).

Not all researchers accept the spillover theory. Other research argues in favor of a compensation theory. This theory suggests there is an inverse relationship between nonwork/work such that individuals compensate for shortcomings in one domain by satisfying needs in the other. For example, a person who is dissatisfied with their family or nonwork life may seek greater levels of satisfaction from their work life environment (Zedeck, 1992).

A third model explaining the relationship between nonwork/work is the segmentation theory, based on the premise that nonwork/work lives are distinct and one domain has no influence on the other. For example, family life satisfies needs for affection, intimacy, and relationships, while work life satisfies needs for competition and instrumental relationships (Zedeck, 1992).

In reality, all three models can be accepted insofar as they describe different relationships which may be obtained under particular circumstances.

Conclusion

The emphasis on the way one's family life can affect one's work life as well as one's work life affecting one's family life has given way to new, more applied research efforts on how to balance adequately the work/family interface. The practical implications of this research in terms of human resource policy and working arrangements are varied. Economic and social pressures have forced many organizations to implement more progressive maternity, paternity, and child care related policies in efforts to attract and retain talented managers of both sexes who want to create more balance in their lives. Flexitime and job sharing are two examples of work restructuring that have been found to be useful in helping employees balance the work/family interface (*see* JOB DESIGN).

see also Women at work

Bibliography

Brett, J. M., Stroh, L. K. & Reilly, A. H. (1992a). What is it like being a dual-career manager in the 1990s? In S. Zedick (Ed.), Work and families, and organizations, (pp. 138–167). San Francisco: Jossey-Bass.

Brett, J. M., Stroh, L. K. & Reilly, A. H. (1992b). Job transfer. In C. L. Cooper & I. T. Robinson (Eds), *International review of industrial and organizational psychology*, (pp. 323–362). Chichester, UK: Wiley.

Kanter, R. M. (1977). Work and family in the United States. New York: Russell Sage Foundation.

Tippins, M. & Stroh, L. K. (1991). Shiftwork: Factors impacting workers biological and family well-being. *Journal of Applied Business Research*, 7, (4), 131–135.

Voydanoff, P. (1989). Work and family: A review and expanded conceptualization. In E. B. Goldsmith (Ed.), Work and family, (pp. 1–22). London: Sage.

Zedeck, S. (1992). Exploring the domain of work and family concerns. In S. Zedick (Ed.), Work and families, and organizations, (pp. 1–32). San Francisco: Jossey-Bass.

LINDA K. STROH

not-for-profit marketing   Not-for-profit marketing is part of "non-business" marketing (together with SOCIAL MARKETING) which relates to marketing activities conducted by individuals and organizations to achieve some goal other than ordinary business goals of profit, market share, or return on investment. Marketing concepts and techniques can be applied to not-for-profit organizations in both the public and private sectors and includes, for example: government agencies, health care organizations, educational institutions, religious groups, charities, political parties, performing arts.

For example, universities facing increasing costs may use marketing to compete for both students and funds, e.g., defining markets better, improving their communication and promotion, and responding to needs of students and other publics. One of the main characteristics of many not-for-profit organizations is that their support does not come directly from those who receive the benefits which the organization produces, e.g., funding for students' education comes from student fees, government sources, endowments, industry sponsorship, research grant awarding bodies.

Bibliography

Blois, K. J. (1994). Marketing for non-profit organisations. In M. J. Baker (Ed.), *The marketing book*. London: Heinemann.

Christy, R. (1995). The broader application of marketing. In G. Oliver (Ed.), *Marketing Today*. (Chapter 24, pp. 500–527). Hemel Hempstead, UK: Prentice-Hall.

BARBARA LEWIS

O

observation   Observation is a method of collecting data on a topic of interest by watching and recording behavior, actions, and facts. Informal, unstructured, observation is an everyday means of collecting marketing information. However, planned observation is likely to produce better information than casual observation. Observation can in fact be structured or unstructured, with disguised or undisguised observers, in a natural or a contrived setting, using human and/or electronic/mechanical observers.

Observation is used instead of, or in conjunction with, surveys involving interviews utilizing questionnaires or depth interviews. Observation is less suitable than interview techniques for measuring attitudes, needs, motivations, opinions, etc., except where the subjects being studied are unable to communicate verbally, e.g., children and animals. Observation is unsuitable for studying events that occur over a long period of time or that are infrequent or unpredictable when an excessive amount of time and money may be required to carry out the research. Observation is suitable for traffic counts, for packaging experiments, for retail audits, etc., where data are more economically gathered through observation than through interviews. Sometimes data are collected by observation and through questionnaires and the results compared.

Structured observation is used when a problem has been defined precisely enough for there to be a specification of the behavior and actions to be studied and the ways in which the actions will be coded and recorded. Unstructured observation is used in exploratory research where the problem has not been identified and where the observer has less guidance about what to note and record. Structured observation implies prior knowledge of the subject under study, of hypotheses to be tested, or inferences to be made. For this latter reason, trained human observers may be preferred to mechanical observers as a human observer can make such inferences in a way that a machine cannot. Perversely, this is a potential weakness of the method, relying as it does on the subjective and possibly biased judgement of the observer.

In disguised observations the subjects do not know that they are being observed. Disguised observations are used in order to overcome the tendency for subjects to change their behavior if they know that they are being watched. Mystery shopping, where observers take on the role of store or bank customers in order to assess the level of service offered by sales staff, is one example of disguised observation. Other examples of disguised observation include the use of two-way mirrors or hidden cameras. Undisguised observations include the measurement of TV audiences based on a sample of households in which on-set meters record when a TV set is in use and to which channel it is tuned.

Sometimes it is possible to study behavior in natural settings. Counting how many people turn right and how many turn left at the top of an escalator in a department store can be done in a natural setting. Likewise, the effect of new point of sale display material for a product may be

studied by observing the sales of the product in a supermarket by counting the numbers in stock at the beginning and at the end of a period and adjusting for additions to stock; this is observation research done in a natural setting. However, the researcher often wants to control for intervening variables by researching in a laboratory, which is obviously an unnatural setting. As well as controlling intervening variables, laboratory research allows stimuli to be invoked and response measured in situations where occurrences of the stimulating event in real life might be uncommon. This is one way in which laboratory research can be a quick way of obtaining data. Laboratory research also permits easier use of electronic and mechanical devices to record behavior.

Among the electronic and mechanical devices that are used to record behavior are those that record physiological changes in subjects when they are subject to stimuli. For example, the galvanometer is used to measure the emotional arousal of subjects exposed to advertising copy by measuring the changes in electrical resistance caused by the sweating that is brought on by emotional arousal. The eye camera records eye movements of subjects looking at newspaper advertisements. Other electronic/mechanical devices include the on-set meters used to measure TV audiences and the scanners that are used by panels of shoppers to read the bar-codes on their purchases.

Bibliography

Malhotra, N. K. (1993). *Marketing research: An applied orientation.* Englewood Cliffs, NJ: Prentice-Hall. Chapter 7.

MICHAEL GREATOREX

occupational choice   Occupational choice refers to the process by which individuals select an occupation or career field to pursue CAREER CHOICE. Recent comprehensive reviews of the theoretical approaches to occupational choice may be found in Brown and Brooks (1990) and Osipow (1990). An examination of the research on occupational choice and related phenomena is published annually in the October issue of the *Journal of Vocational Behavior.*

Theoretical Approaches to the Study of Occupational Choice
Several different, although not mutually exclusive, theoretical perspectives on the occupational choice process have emerged over the years. One of the most popular has been the *matching approach*, which asserts that individuals tend to choose occupations that match their unique set of needs, motives, values, and talents. Holland's (1985) typology of personality and occupational environment and the work adjustment theory of Dawis and Lofquist (1984) are prominent examples of this approach.

The *developmental* approach views occupational choice as a process that unfolds and evolves over time. The most influential developmental perspective has been provided by Super (1990), who proposed that people progress through different stages of career development that permit them to form a self-concept and express that self-concept in an occupational decision.

Other researchers focus on the psychological *decision-making process* that guides a person in the selection of a specific occupation. This perspective has examined how people combine and weigh information about different occupations to arrive at an occupational choice, and has studied the reasons why people may become undecided about what occupational path to pursue. One decision-making approach, social learning theory, emphasizes the role of self-efficacy expectations – personal beliefs about competence in a particular area – in occupational choice (Hackett and Betz, 1981). It is believed that people tend to enter occupations for which they hold strong self-efficacy expectations.

Additional Issues in the Study of Occupational Choice

In addition to the ongoing development and refinement of theories on how people select occupations, it is expected that research will continue to address a number of significant and timely issues. One burgeoning area of study is the role of gender in occupational choice. It is increasingly questioned whether the theories on men's occupational choice are applicable to women or whether unique theories of women's occupational choices need to be developed (Fouad, 1994). A similar question has been raised about the occupational choices of American minorities (Smith, 1983). It is possible that the unique barriers and obstacles experienced by minority group members render traditional theories of occupational choice less relevant for this group. Finally, research on the occupational choices of adult employees is likely to expand in the years ahead. Corporate DOWNSIZING and restructuring will require adults of all ages to re-evaluate their career goals and redirect their careers into different occupational areas. Considerable research will be required to help this growing segment of the population.

Bibliography

Brown, D. L. & Brooks, L. (eds) (1990). *Career Choice and Development: Applying Contemporary Theories to Practice*, San Francisco: Jossey-Bass.

Dawis, R. V. & Lofquist, L. H. (1984). *A Psychological Theory of Work Adjustment*, Minneapolis: University of Minnesota.

Fouad, N. A. (1994). Annual review 1991–1993: vocational choice, decision-making assessment, and intervention. *Journal of Vocational Behavior*, **45**, 125–76.

Hackett, G. & Betz, N. E. (1981). A self-efficacy approach to the career development of women. *Journal of Vocational Behavior*, **18**, 326–39.

Holland, J. L. (1985). *Making Vocational Choices: a Theory of Vocational Personalities and Work Environments*, **2nd edn**, Englewood Cliffs, NJ: Prentice-Hall.

Osipow, S. H. (1990). Convergence in theories of career choice and development: review and prospect. *Journal of Vocational Behavior*, **36**, 122–31.

Smith, E. J. (1983). Issues in racial minorities' career behavior. *Handbook of Vocational Psychology*, **1**, Eds. Walsh, W. B. & Osipow, S. H. Hillsdale, NJ: Lawrence Erlbaum Associates.

Super, D. E. (1990). A life-span, life space approach to career development. *Career choice and development: Applying contemporary theories to practice*, Eds. Brown, D. & Brooks, L. San Francisco: Jossey-Bass.

JEFFREY H. GREENHAUS

offshore   In international trade and finance the term offshore refers to any situation in which deposits, investments, production, or other activities take place in a country other than the home country of the investor, producer, or owner of the deposits. Thus, a US resident placing dollars in a bank in Switzerland would have an offshore deposit. The Swiss bank would be considered an offshore banking facility.

JOHN O'CONNELL

offshore banking   Locations that offer services, tax benefits, and confidentiality to foreign depositors. The term offshore banking is often synonymous with "tax haven."

JOHN O'CONNELL

offshore funds   Funds kept in banks outside of the owner's country are referred to as offshore funds.

JOHN O'CONNELL

oligopoly   This market structure is usually composed of a few firms with market power and is characterized by strong and recognized interdependence among them. It is an important market structure and is frequently observed in industry.

Market characteristics

The major characteristics of an oligopolistic market structure are the following:

- The industry is composed of a few firms which are the major suppliers in the market.
- The number of firms in the industry does not change significantly through time because there are barriers to potential entrants in the market.
- Companies produce either a relatively homogeneous product (as in the steel or the aluminum industry) or a differentiated product (as in the ready-to-eat cereal industry).
- Each firm takes into consideration its competitors' reaction to its own decisions.
- Due to the small number of companies in the industry, there are strong incentives for competition as well as cooperation among them.
- Both producers and consumers in the industry have IMPERFECT INFORMATION.

Since there are few companies in an oligopolistic industry, each firm has some market power. Economists have developed several measures to estimate the degree of economic concentration in the hands of few firms in an industry (*see* HERFINDAHL-HIRSCHMAN INDEX). The US Department of Commerce produces the Census of Manufacturers which reports concentration ratios for about 450 manufacturing industries in the US. In 1987, for six-tenths of these industries, the four-firm concentration ratio was below 40 percent, for three-tenths of them it was in the range of 41–70 percent, and for the remaining one-tenth it was over 70 percent. Apparently, sectors of the US manufacturing sector are significantly concentrated. Industries such as the motor vehicles and car bodies industry (SIC-3711) with a 90 percent concentration ratio, the aircraft industry (SIC-3721) with a 72 percent concentration ratio, and the cereal breakfast foods industry (SIC-2043) with an 87 percent concentration ratio, are just a few examples of industries with high levels of concentration in US manufacturing.

Models of oligopolistic behavior: homogeneous products

In this and the following sections, several theories of oligopoly are presented for markets with homogeneous (identical) products.

The extensive interaction and interdependence among companies in an oligopolistic industry makes the study of this market structure a rather complicated and challenging task. However, the variety of models could be seen as a virtue of the literature and not as a flaw, since the behavior of companies in this market structure depends on the particular characteristics of each industry and will vary across industries.

The crucial element of an oligopolistic industry is the fact that the outcome of a company's actions depends on the reaction of its competitors to its decisions. Consequently, the company must consider its competitors' reaction to its own decisions. In economic theory, this element is formalized by the company's *reaction function*. Economists frequently analyze oligopolistic competition by using game theory, since it allows them to study the interactions and strategies involved among companies in an oligopolistic market structure. Also, in studying oligopolistic industries, and due to the specific characteristics of this market structure, economists employ a special type of market equilibrium, called *Nash equilibrium*, due to the American mathematician J. Nash who defined it in 1951. In this equilibrium, each firm is doing the best it can, given what its competitors are doing, therefore, the company does not have an incentive to change its actions unilaterally.

Presented below, there is a brief discussion of the most important models of oligopolistic behavior in markets where firms produce identical products. Oligopoly models are often classified under two major families: *static models* and *dynamic models*. This review will focus on static models of oligopoly.

Static models

These models analyze the strategic interactions among companies in an oligopolistic structure from a static, and therefore, *timeless* point of view. There are two major classifications of the models: *non-cooperative models*, and *cooperative models*.

Cournot competition is a non-cooperative model, where each firm believes its competitors will not react to its output decision. If there are *n* identical firms in the market and market demand for the product depends on price, the company's profit maximizing price markup is:

$$\frac{P - c}{P} = \frac{1}{ne_p},$$

where P is the price each company receives based on the total output, Q, produced in the market by all of the firms, c is the firm's marginal cost of production and e_p the price elasticity of industry demand.

The Bertrand Model. Another non-cooperative model, suggested by the French economist J. Bertrand in 1883 (see *Carlton and Perloff*, 1994), assumes that companies compete in prices instead of the level of their production. Assuming that companies produce homogeneous products, consumers will buy from the company with the lowest price. This means that each company has an incentive to lower its price to achieve higher sales. Consequently, firms continue to reduce their prices until they are equal to the per unit (marginal) cost of production. The Nash equilibrium occurs when $P = MC$, the same result as with perfect competition. This result does not depend on the number of companies in the market, and even in the case of a *duopoly* (two firms in the market) the result is preserved. Since Bertrand competition is very intense, companies frequently prefer to compete with other means, other than prices.

Collusion. A cooperative model, it is based on the fact that some or all the companies in an industry decide jointly to maintain a certain level of prices (*price fixing*) or production, and thus reduce competition. Although illegal in the US, it exists in industries in other countries. Companies realize that price wars result in significant losses and through collusion, they agree to alleviate competition and keep their prices at a profitable level. However, the collusive agreements can be very fragile, not only because they are illegal in some countries, but mainly because there are strong incentives for individual companies to cheat on the agreement, to undercut their competitors, and increase their profits.

Empirical studies

Researchers are primarily interested in two questions: the degree of flexibility of prices in oligopoly and the relation between market concentration, barriers to entry and profitability. The studies are based upon data which come from different industries at the same point in time (*cross-section data*), or from one or more industries over time (*time-series data*).

Carlton (1986) calculated price rigidity as the average length of time during which prices were unchanged in different US industries. He found that price rigidity differed significantly across industries, from about 5.9 months in household appliances to 19.2 months in chemicals. Encaoua and Geroski (1984), using data from different countries, found that high industry concentration implied slow adjustment of prices to cost changes, and therefore high price rigidity.

Hall (1987) found that price markups were relatively high in a wide range of US manufacturing industries. Domowitz, Hubbard, and Petersen (1986), using data from US manufacturing during 1958–81, found that price markups were higher in more concentrated industries. Overall, these studies point in the direction that there is some positive relation between market concentration and price rigidity.

Market concentration and profitability. In his path-breaking study, J. Bain (1951), collected data from 42 different US industries which he split in two samples: the high concentration sample, with concentration ratios above 70 percent, and the low concentration sample, with concentration ratios below 70 percent. He found that the rate of return (income per book value of the stockholders' equity) was 11.8 percent for the high concentration industries, versus 7.5 percent for the low concentration industries. He also found that high industry concentration was associated with high barriers to entry and high profits.

Although considered a contestable market by some, several studies of the airline industry concluded that concentration in a certain route connecting two cities does influence air fares. Bailey, Graham, and Kaplan (1985) used time service data and found that if concentration doubled from 50 percent to 100 percent, fares would increase by 6 percent. Borenstein (1989) also found that concentration affected fares in city-pair markets. Overall, these studies show some modest positive relation between industry concentration and air fares. However, all these results must be interpreted with caution, since they are based on accounting profits data which might not be a good proxy for economic profits.

Bibliography

Bailey, E. E., Graham, D. R. Kaplan, D. P. (1985). *Deregulating the Airlines*. Cambridge, MA: MIT.

Bain, J. S. (1951). Relation of profit rate to industry concentration: American manufacturing, 1936–1940. *Quarterly Journal of Economics*, 65, 293–324.

Borenstein, S. (1989). Hubs and fares: dominance and market power in the US airline industry. *Rand Journal of Economics*, 20, 344–65.

Carlton, D. (1986). The rigidity of prices. *American Economic Review*, 76, 637–58.

Carlton, D. W. Perloff, J. M. (1994). *Modern Industrial Organization*. 2nd edn, New York: HarperCollins.

Domowitz, I., Hubbard, R. G. Petersen, B. C. (1986). The intertemporal stability of the concentration-margins relationship. *Journal of Industrial Economics*, 17, 1–17.

Encaoua, D. Geroski, P. (1984). Price dynamics and competition in five countries. *University of Southampton Working Paper no. 8414*

Hall, R. (1986). Market structure and macroeconomic fluctuations. *Brookings Papers on Economic Activity*, 2, 285–322.

Mann, M. (1966). Seller concentration, barriers to entry, and rates of return in thirty industries, 1950–1960. *The Review of Economics and Statistics*, 48, 290–307.

Means, G. C. (1935). Industrial prices and their relative inflexibility. *Senate Document 13, 74th Congress, 1st session*. Washington, DC: US Government Printing Office.

Nash, J. F. (1950). Equilibrium points in N-person games. *Proceedings of the National Academy of Science*, 36, 48–9.

Rotemberg, J. Saloner, G. (1986). A supergame-theoretic model of price wars during booms. *American Economic Review*, 76, 390–407.

Stigler, G. J. Kindahl, J. K. (1970). *Behavior of Industrial Prices*. New York: National Bureau of Economic Research.

Sweezy, P. (1939). Demand under conditions of oligopoly. *Journal of Political Economy*, 47, 568–73.

Weiss, L. W. (1974). The concentration-profits relationship and antitrust. Goldschmid, J. *et al.* edn, *Industrial Concentration: The New Learning*. Boston: Little, Brown.

KOSTAS AXARLOGLOU

on-the-job training   On-the-job training (OJT) involves assigning trainees to jobs and encouraging them to observe and learn from experienced job incumbents or supervisors. OJT is the most widely used training strategy and is favored for its low cost and the opportunity it provides for immediate feedback. It also facilitates positive transfer of training by allowing trainees to learn with the actual materials, personnel, and machinery that comprise the job. Unfortunately, OJT is often used haphazardly and its success is contingent on the capacity and willingness of job incumbents to take time from regular work duties to provide effective instruction and guidance.

TIMOTHY T. BALDWIN

one step flow model   The one step flow model of communications presents mass communications (*see* MASS MEDIA), mainly ADVERTISING, as acting directly on each member of the target audience. This often-called "hypodermic needle" model of communications (the communication passing directly to individual members of the audience) contrasts markedly with the TWO STEP FLOW MODEL, which depicts communications as being filtered through intermediaries called opinion leaders (*see* INTERPERSONAL COMMUNICATIONS). Many individuals are likely to receive information from mass communications, although selective exposure, selective perception, and selective retention will act as filters. Mass communications may create awareness and even interest, but then further information may be sought or received through interpersonal channels, such as from opinion leaders (*see* INTERPERSONAL COMMUNICATIONS).

DALE LITTLER

open systems   When applying SYSTEMS THEORY to organizations, OB scholars conceptualize them as being open systems exchanging information and resources with their environment (*see* ORGANIZATION AND ENVIRONMENT; STAKEHOLDER ANALYSIS). This perspective draws attention to how organizations and their environments mutually influence each other. It seeks to explain how organizations maintain functional autonomy while adapting to external forces.

As open systems, organizations seek to sustain an input–output cycle of activities aimed at taking in inputs of information and resources from the environment, transforming them into outputs of goods and services, and exporting them back to the environment. This cycle enables organizations to replenish themselves continually so long as the environment provides sufficient inputs and the organization delivers valued outputs.

Considerable research has gone into understanding how organizations manage these information and resource flows. One perspective focuses on how organizations process information in order to discover how to relate to their environments. Another view concentrates on how organizations compete for resources through managing key resource dependencies. Still another perspective focuses on how organizations gain LEGITIMACY from environmental institutions so they can continue to function with external support (*see* INSTITUTIONAL THEORY).

In managing information and resource flows, organizations, like all open systems, seek to establish Boundaries around their activities. These organizational boundaries must be permeable enough to permit necessary environmental exchange, yet afford sufficient protection from external demands to allow for rational operation.

Organizational scholars devote considerable attention to understanding the dual nature of organizational boundaries. They study various boundary spanning roles that relate the organization to its environment, such as sales, public relations, and purchasing. They examine how organizational members perceive and make sense out of environmental input, and how organizational boundaries vary in sensitivity to external influences. Research is also aimed at identifying different strategies for protecting transformation processes from external disruptions while being responsive to suppliers and customers.

Viewed as open systems, organizations use information about how they are performing to modify future behaviors. This information feedback enables organizations to be self-regulating. It enables them to adjust their functioning to respond to deviations in expected performance. According to the system's law of requisite variety, however, organizations must have a sufficient diversity of responses to match the variety of disturbances encountered if self-regulation is to be successful.

Extensive research has been devoted to understanding how organizations control and regulate themselves. Using modern information technology, organizations develop a variety of methods for setting goals, obtaining information on goal achievement, and making necessary changes. They also devise different structures and processes for learning from this information about how to improve performance (see continuous improvement; LEARNING ORGANIZATION).

As open systems, organizations display the property of equifinality. They can achieve objectives with varying inputs and in different ways. Consequently, there is no one best way to design and manage organizations, but there are a variety of ways to achieve satisfactory performance.

Organizational scholars have devoted considerable attention to identifying different choices for designing and managing organizations. They have shown a range of ORGANIZATIONAL DESIGN options that can achieve success in particular situations.

see also **Organizational effectiveness; Population ecology**

Bibliography

Aldrich, H. (1979). Organizations and environments. New York: Prentice-Hall.
Galbraith, J. (1977). Organization design. Reading, MA: Addison-Wesley.
Pfeffer, J. & Salancik, G. (1978). The external control of organizations. New York: Harper & Row.

THOMAS G. CUMMINGS

operational centers   A financial center in which actual banking transactions take place. A center where money is deposited or passed through is referred to as a "booking" center. New York financial centers are considered operational centers, whereas a financial center in the Bahamas is usually considered a booking center.

JOHN O'CONNELL

operations role   The "role" of the operations function refers to the set of long-term strategic responsibilities which are seen as being its prime concern, and from that the part it has to play in achieving competitive success. Usually the term is used to mean the underlying rationale of the function.

The best known approach to defining operations role considers the organizational aims or aspirations of the operations function. Hayes and Wheelwright (1984) developed a four-stage model which can be used to evaluate the competitive role and contribution of the operations function of any type of company. The model traces the progression of the operations function from what is the largely negative role (called stage 1 operations) to it becoming a central element of competitive strategy (called stage 4 operations).

Stage 1, or "internal neutrality," is the very poorest level of contribution by the operations function. In a stage 1 organization the operation is considered a "necessary evil." The other functions regard the operations function as holding them back from competing effectively. Operations has little which is positive to contribute towards competitive strategy; it is unlikely even to have developed its resources so as to be appropriate for the company's competitive position. The best that the function can hope for is to be ignored inasmuch as when operations is being ignored it is not holding the company back. The rest of the organization would not look to operations as the source of any originality, or competitive drive. In effect the operations function is aspiring only to reach the minimum acceptable standards implied by the rest of the organization. It is trying to be "internally neutral," a position it attempts to achieve not by anything positive but by avoiding the more obvious mistakes.

Stage 2, or "external neutrality," envisages the operation breaking out of stage 1 by meeting the minimum internal performance required and comparing itself with similar companies or organizations in the outside market. This may not immediately result in the company taking a leading position in the market, but at least it is aspiring to reach that position and is measuring itself against the performance of competitors. Although not particularly creative in the way they manage, such operations are trying to "be appropriate," by adopting "best practice" from their competitors. In taking the best ideas and norms of performance from the rest of their industry they are trying to be "externally neutral."

Stage 3, or "internally supportive," operations have probably reached a leading position in their market. They may not be better than their competitors in every aspect of operations performance but they are broadly up with the best. Nevertheless, good as they may be, stage 3 operations aspire to be clearly and unambiguously the very best in the market. They try to achieve this by gaining a clear view of their competitive or strategic goals after which they organize and develop operations resources to excel in the things which the company needs to compete effectively. Not only are they developing "appropriate" resources, they are taking on the role of the "implementers" of strategy. The operation is trying to be "internally supportive" by providing a credible operations strategy.

Stage 4, or "externally supportive," operations go further in attempting to capture the emerging sense of the growing importance of operations management. In essence, a stage 4 company is one which sees the operations function as providing an important foundation for its future competitive success. Operations looks to the long term. It forecasts likely changes in markets and supply, and it develops operations-based strategies which provide the company with the performance which will be required to compete in future market conditions. In effect the operations function is becoming central to strategy making. Stage 4 operations are creative and proactive. They are likely to organize their resources in ways which are innovative and capable of adaptation as markets change. Essentially they are trying to be "one step ahead" of competitors in the way that they create products and services and organize their operations, which Hayes and Wheelwright describe as being "externally supportive." Operations are not only developing "appropriate" resources and "implementing" competitive strategy, they are also an important long-term "driver" of strategy.

The Hayes and Wheelwright four-stage model may be a simplification but two points are worth considering. First, it assesses the performance of operations by the function's aspirations. Second, as companies move from stage 1 to stage 4 there is a progressive shift in the contribution of operations from being negative and merely operational to being positive and strategic. For both reasons the model has become widely used by both academics and practitioners.

see also **Manufacturing strategy; Service strategy**

Bibliography

Hayes, R. H. & Wheelwright, C. (1984). *Restoring our competitive edge: Competing through manufacturing*. New York: Wiley.
Slack, N., Chambers, S., Harland, C., Harrison, A. & Johnson, R. (1995). *Operations management*. London: Pitman Publishing.

NIGEL SLACK

opinion leaders *see* INTERPERSONAL COMMUNICATIONS

opportunity costs Opportunity costs are fundamental to economics, yet they are frequently overlooked in business practice. The opportunity cost of any decision or choice made by consumers or firms is the value of the next best choice which was sacrificed. For example, consider a division within a firm which produces computer chips which are used by another division to assemble computers. The computer-assembly division would prefer to obtain the chips at the production cost of the manufacturing division (say, \$100 per chip) to increase its profits. However, if those chips can be sold in the market at \$250 per chip, then every internal sale of chips to the assembly division has an opportunity cost of \$250 to the company. Furthermore, if the company earns a 10 percent return on the capital it has invested in computer assembly but could earn 15 percent elsewhere, then this company should leave this industry in the long run; see Shughart, Chappell and Cottle (1994) for their discussion of internal transfer pricing between divisions.

The distinction between ECONOMIC PROFIT and ACCOUNTING PROFIT is based on the concept of opportunity costs. Suppose a company owns a building and does not pay rental expenses. Then accounting practices would not count those fees as costs to the firm. But if the building could be leased or rented, that represents the opportunity cost of using the building and should be considered in managerial decisions to maximize profits. If managers never consider alternative uses for the resources of the firm, how can they know that they have found the best use? The calculation of economic costs includes these opportunity costs and ensures that the scarce resources of the firm and of society are used where they are most needed.

Bibliography

Douglas, E. J. (1992). *Managerial Economics*. 4th edn, Englewood Cliffs, NJ: Prentice-Hall.
Shughart, W. F., Chappell, W. F. Cottle, R. L. (1994). *Modern Managerial Economics*. Cincinatti, OH: South-Western Publishing.

ROBERT E. MCAULIFFE

organization and environment The environment is a key concept in the study of organizations. Essentially, an organization's environment is everything that lies outside the organizational boundary. That is, other organizations, the society in which it operates, governmental agencies and institutions, the economic system, labor markets, financial systems, and so on. These factors make up what is known as the "general environment." Organizations generally do not have to deal with the whole environment in its totality, particular parts of the environment will have special importance. These make up the "task environment" and include the organization's own customers, suppliers, shareholders, bankers, and so on (*see* STAKEHOLDER ANALYSIS). Within the organization, individual subunits will develop relationships with particular parts of this task environment. So, for example, the finance department will deal with external financial institutions and specific governmental agencies such as the Inland Revenue, while the purchasing department will deal with suppliers and their agents. Each department will therefore manage the interface between themselves and a segment of the total task environment, acting on behalf of the organization as a whole.

Although the environment is often discussed as though it is completely separate from the "focal" organization, in reality, organizational boundaries are not always easy to distinguish with absolute precision. For example, are contracted-in cleaners or catering staff, those working on temporary contracts, or consultancy and advisory staff really part of the organization or not? Furthermore, the organization only selectively accepts environmental inputs – it is not necessarily open to everything. For these reasons the organization may be said to be a "relatively" OPEN SYSTEM, with semipermeable boundaries.

An open systems view sets the organization in the context of the environment. It recognizes that in order to survive, the organization must interact with its environment, obtain resources from it, transform them into products or services and export them back into it.

The environment represents UNCERTAINTY for the organization. This is because organizations cannot exist without these resource exchanges and they therefore do not have complete control over everything they need. Other organizations are in a position to exert influence over the flow of critical inputs. Uncertainty can bring instability since what is uncertain is less predictable. Organizations therefore need to "buffer" themselves from the possibly damaging effects of the environment. Boundary-spanning departments can help by "environmental scanning," monitoring what is going on outside the organization to try and forecast change. Part of the work of research and development departments, marketing, and the human resource function, for example, is to monitor the environment to predict changes in products and TECHNOLOGY, customer requirements, and labor markets. By doing this they hope to establish a secure supply of resources and take proactive decisions to ward off threats and take advantage of opportunities. Individuals such as the chief executive and senior managers also perform this function, developing networks and relationships outside the organization. Interlocking directorates are a specific way in which senior personnel form linkages across organizations, sitting as directors, often in a nonexecutive capacity, on the boards of a number of different organizations and influential agencies (see NETWORKING; INTERORGANIZATIONAL RELATIONS). In this way they can gather information, build alliances and promote their own organizational interests, or, as it is sometimes argued, the interests of their social sector or class (see COALITION FORMATION).

It is clear that organizations do not all face the same environment. Furthermore, the nature and characteristics of the environment may be different for different organizations. Environments differ in their degrees of *complexity* and *turbulence*. Complexity refers to the number of environmental factors with which the organ-ization has to deal. For example, particularly since deregulation, the banking industry now has to deal with a number of different competitors (insurance companies, building societies, credit companies) all seeking to offer financial services to customers. Banks are therefore facing an increasingly complex environment. In contrast, for many years universities faced a relatively simple environment. The turbulence of the environment refers to the degree of change that is present. A fashion company would be a good example of a firm operating within a fairly turbulent environment. Changes in fashion are rapid, continuous, and relatively unpredictable. In contrast, until the advent of lagers in the 1980s, the British beer industry faced a fairly stable environment. The market was growing, but growth was relatively constant and predictable.

The levels of complexity and turbulence are obviously linked to the degree of uncertainty faced by managers. The greater the rate of environmental change and the number of factors to be considered, the less predictable the environment becomes and the greater the uncertainty for managers having to make sense of it.

Theories of organization differ about what managers have to do to cope with this situation, and the degree to which they have the freedom to manage environmental demands.

Contingency theory takes as its central focus the way in which the organization needs to adapt to environmental constraints. In this view the successfulness of an organization is predicated on the "fit" between an organization and the environment in which it operates. A number of factors need to be taken into account in order to ensure congruency. For example, Burns and Stalker (1961) suggested that environmental features will influence the effectiveness of the structural arrangements that the organization adopts. When the environment is fairly simple and relatively stable a mechanistic structure will work reasonably well. Hierarchical lines of COMMUNICATION that allow information to flow up and down the organization are sufficient, decisions are taken centrally, and precise job specifications and routinized procedures allow tasks to be performed in standardized ways that facilitate stability (see BUREAUCRACY). But where the environment is highly volatile, firms need to respond quickly to changing demands. This requires communication to be more free-

flowing across the organization as well as through the usual hierarchical channels. Whoever has information about changes needs to be able to pass this on, and DECISION MAKING is more decentralized (see DECENTRALIZATION). Job specifications and procedures are more flexible in order to speed up decision making. Organic structures help firms to perform more effectively in this kind of environment.

Lawrence and Lorsch (1967) noted that with more dynamic environments there is a need for organizations to separate out activities to a greater extent to cope more directly with specific segments of the environment. This differentiation has to be complemented by a reciprocal degree of integration – coordinating mechanisms that bring the differentiated parts together again for the effective working of the whole organization.

However, one comment in relation to this school of thought is that the environment is not defined with precision. This makes it difficult for managers to know which indicators are critical in signaling whether there is an appropriate or inappropriate environmental fit. And if there is not, there are few prescriptions about the actions they need to take to regain congruency.

Child (1972) responded to this early work in the contingency framework by arguing that much of this did not make enough provision for the concept of strategic choice by managers. His argument was that managers often have a far greater range of options open to them than is generally allowed by more deterministic views. They are not always constrained by environmental demands but can sometimes shape their own environments by choosing to operate in certain markets and offer particular products. This is especially true in the case of larger organizations, or those operating in monopolistic situations. The power of multinational and global companies to influence their competitive environment and the policies of host governments is well documented. Certainly, the ability of managers to make strategic decisions should not be underestimated (see STRATEGIC MANAGEMENT). This suggests that the allocation of power in the organization and the use of influence by subunits has a greater part to play than the contingency approach allows.

A further point here is that the environment itself is mediated by the managers' own interpretations. The environment is not "given" but has to be experienced and made sense of. This enactment leaves room for differing interpretations and understandings. Selective perception and biases may influence this process and so affect the actions which managers take.

The resource dependence approach (Pfeffer & Salancik, 1978) also subscribes to much of the above. In viewing organizations as resource exchanging entities, this perspective sees the environment as playing a central part in any study of organizations. Organizations need to obtain external resources in order to survive, and since these are located in the environment it has a central role to play in organizational functioning. The resource dependence approach holds that a key function for managers is to manage this interface, as well as managing the internal organizational processes. For Pfeffer and Salancik, organizations can either try to change their environments or form interorganizational relationships to control or absorb uncertainty. Methods of changing the environment would include political lobbying to secure favorable trading or competitive conditions and choosing to operate in different market sectors. The development of interorganizational relationships can be accomplished in a number of ways. For example, by contracting arrangements, joint ventures, interlocking directorates, mergers, and acquisitions. All these measures seek to reduce the dependence the organization has on its environment by securing access to external resources, including information.

The POPULATION ECOLOGY approach goes further than this. It too places the environment at the center of organizational analysis, but it is rather more pessimistic about the ability of managers to influence their situation. The view is that organizations do not so much adapt to their environment, but need to be selected by it if they are to survive. This is very similar to the Darwinian model of evolution. Organizations are subject to a process of natural selection, whereby the "fittest" survive, the rest do not. To survive, organizations need to find a niche where the environmental resources they require are available.

In the population ecology view, the environment is seen to have a number of dimensions in addition to the ideas of complexity and turbulence discussed above. The "capacity" of the environment refers to how rich or lean its stock of resources is. Rich environments provide more resources for growth but also attract more organizations so competition is fiercer. Environmental "concentration" describes a situation where environmental elements (such as customers, or clients) are relatively concentrated, whereas "dispersion" indicates they are scattered. Organizations will generally find it easier to operate within a more concentrated environment. Finally, the dimension of "domain consensus–dissensus" refers to the degree to which there is agreement about the area of operation of an organization. If claims to a domain or market are contested then domain dissensus will result.

This perspective goes beyond the analysis of individual organizations to study organizations as populations and tries to provide a general explanation for growth and death (*see* ORGANIZATIONAL CHANGE). Growth, if it happens at all, happens in stages. The first stage is when organizational forms begin to vary. Some of these forms are then selected and survive – others do not. This is the second stage. The final stage is retention, when those that are selected are duplicated or reproduced.

From the above discussion it will be seen that the environment occupies a central place in the analysis of organizations. But, as has been shown, the concept is much debated. A great deal of discussion focuses on the degree to which organizational actors are constrained by externalities or how far they have a measure of strategic choice. A central theme here is the discourse surrounding the free-will – determinism dialectic. Certainly, the environment is not always all-powerful and the ability of larger organizations to control external forces should not be overlooked.

The environment is a complex concept and definitions of its constituent parts are offered with varying degrees of precision and specificity. However, one significant point is that environments are perceived and interpreted by organizational actors. In this way, managers can and do shape their own environments.

see also **Five forces model; Organizational effectiveness; Systems theory**

Bibliography

Aldrich, H. (1979). Organizations and environments. Englewood Cliffs, NJ: Prentice Hall.

Burns, T. & Stalker, G. M. (1961). The management of innovation. London: Tavistock.

Child, J. (1972). Organizational structure, environment and performance: The role of strategic choice. Sociology, (6), 1–22.

Lawrence, P. R. & Lorsch, J. W. (1967). Organization and environment. Cambridge, MA: Harvard University Press.

Pfeffer, J. & Salancik, G. R. (1978). The external control of organizations: A resource dependence perspective. New York: Harper & Row.

SUSAN MILLER

organization development and change Organization development and change, also known as organization development (OD), is a field of applied behavioral science focused on understanding and managing organizational change. OD is both a field of social and managerial action and a field of scientific inquiry (Woodman, 1989; Cummings and Worley, 1993). The action side of the field is of greatest interest for human resource managers and professionals, although successful change programs rely on valid, scientifically acquired knowledge of individual, group, and organizational behavior. From a training perspective, OD is not a single change management technique, but rather a collection of techniques that have a certain philosophy and body of knowledge in common.

Definitions and Characteristics

Some formal definitions of organizational change and development help to frame the boundaries and identify the focus of the field. *Organization development* is "a system-wide application of behavioral science knowledge to the planned development and reinforcement of organizational strategies, structures, and processes for improving an organization's effectiveness" (Cummings and Worley, 1993, p. 2). *Organizational development* is "a set of behavioral science-based theories, values, strategies, and techniques aimed at the planned change of the organizational work setting for the purpose of enhancing individual development and improving organizational performance, through the alteration of organizational members' on-the-job behaviors" (Porras and Robertson, 1992, p. 722). *Organization development* "means creating adaptive organizations capable of repeatedly transforming and reinventing themselves as needed to remain effective" (Woodman, 1993, p. 73).

Organizational development is typically characterized by: (a) developing individual commitment to needed change; (b) changing whole systems and processes, in contrast to piecemeal change approaches; (c) relying on action research and other collaborative change philosophies and techniques; and (d) emphasizing both organizational effectiveness and human fulfillment through the work experience. In addition, another key characteristic of OD is particularly instructive for the training function in organizations. OD typically places equal emphasis on solving immediate organizational or work group problems and on the long-term development of an effective, adaptive organization. Thus, the most effective training, from the OD perspective, is that which not only helps employees solve current problems but prepares them to solve future problems facing the organization.

Organization Development and Human Resource Management

Surveys of the Fortune 500 industrials and the Fortune 500 service firms indicate that the practice of organization development, as well as the location of OD staff in these large corporations, is most commonly found within the human resource management function (McMahan and Woodman, 1992). For example, the lead OD professional in these firms typically reports directly to a vice president of human resources. Further, among the change management issues identified by these surveys as crucial to organizational success is the problem of linking human resource activities to business strategy. The organizational training function can make major contributions to organizational effectiveness by linking with and supporting the firm's internal OD activities. In general, the field of organizational development and change provides a promising arena for human resource managers to contribute to organizational effectiveness.

Bibliography

Cummings, T. G. & Worley, C. G. (1993). *Organization Development and Change*, **5th edn**, Minneapolis/St Paul: West.

McMahan, G. C. & Woodman, R. W. (1992). The current practice of organization development with the firm. *Group and Organization Management*, 17, 117–34.

Porras, J. I. & Robertson, P. J. (1992). Organizational development. theory, practice, and research. *Handbook of Industrial and Organizational Psychology*, 3, **2nd edn**, Eds. Dunnette, M. D. & Hough, L. M. Palo Alto, CA: Consulting Psychologists Press.

Woodman, R. W. (1989). Organizational change and development: new arenas for inquiry and action. *Journal of Management*, 15, 205–28.

Woodman, R. W. (1993). Observations on the field of organizational change and development from the lunatic fringe. *Organization Development Journal*, 11, 71–4.

RICHARD W. WOODMAN

organizational buying behavior The exchange relationship between buyers and sellers has long been studied in the context of consumer markets and is now also recognized as being central to an understanding of organizational markets, though with significant differences. Research into organizational buying behavior has developed from an analysis of individual purchases in organizational markets, to an examination of the broader strategic implications of buyer/seller relationships and of the environmental, corporate, and personal influences permeating the purchasing context.

Much of the early research was concerned with attempts to develop models of organizational buying behavior and three models of organizational buying behavior are discussed here. For a concise review of this research see Parkinson & Baker, 1986 (especially Chapters 4, 5 & 7), while Turnbull provides a convenient discussion of the Sheth, Webster & Wind model, and interaction models (Turnbull, 1994). It should be noted that none of these "models" claims to be predictive; all three are attempts to describe a complex process as a necessary preliminary to further analysis. Consequently, it is difficult to "test" the theoretical status of these models.

Webster & Wind modeled the process as a set of four contextual influences (macro environment, organization, group, individual) with particular emphasis on the role of organizational culture and individuals as the ultimate decision-makers in the buying process (Webster & Wind, 1972). Although Webster & Wind present their model as a sequence with each area of influence leading progressively to the next, it is important to understand that the relationship between these influences is generally iterative rather than sequential. Sheth's (1973) model included the concept of multiple sources and participants in a buying process which was acknowledged as having significant psychological aspects as well as rational aspects. Both the Sheth and the Webster & Wind models take the buying decision as the unit of analysis, yet much of the work undertaken by the IMP (Industrial Marketing and Purchasing) Group of researchers suggests that greater insights into the buying process may be available from taking the relationship between organizations as the unit of analysis (*see* INTERACTION APPROACH). The IMP research has developed a model of buying behavior in organizational markets as an interaction between individuals within organizations, conducted in an atmosphere formed by the context and experience of previous exchange episodes and surrounded by the macro-environmental features common to previous models (Håkansson, 1982; Campbell, 1985). In this presentation, decisions could be thought of as the "punctuation" in a continuing stream of interaction, and best understood in the long-term context of the relationship.

Arguably, there are also many contemporary macro-environmental and competitive dynamics which could be regarded as stimuli to interorganizational relationships, such as acceleration of the widely recognized phenomena of globalization, increasing competition, environmental complexity (*see* MARKETING ENVIRONMENT), and escalating R&D costs. Under these pressures a routine purchasing relationship can evolve into a STRATEGIC ALLIANCE, especially as the foundation for such relationships may have as much to do with mutual familiarity and trust as it does with strategic logic. This encourages a much wider understanding of the scope and significance of "buying behavior" in organizational markets than has generally been recognized and emphasizes the importance of understanding such relationships in their long-term dynamic and strategic context rather than, perhaps, as a series of recurring exercises in cost control. Research into the process of how such relationships develop over time, and the implications arising for MARKETING MANAGEMENT, are therefore increasingly relevant to organizations seeking to develop their competitiveness through strategic alliances.

Buyer–seller relationships in organizational markets are now accepted as a highly complex area and one of considerable strategic importance. Research continues into both these aspects: e.g., the work of Johnston & Bonoma (1981) examining the intricate dynamics and systems at work in the BUYING CENTER itself; and Ford's (1984) further work arguing that skill in the management of such relationships can itself become a strategic asset and an important factor in the selection of interorganizational partners. Nevertheless, it is difficult to avoid the conclusion that research into organizational buying behavior seems to have been less productive than that into CONSUMER BUYING BEHAVIOR, perhaps because organizational buying is highly complex, difficult to categorize (other than simplistically), and explanations depend on many personal and contingent variables.

see also **Relationship marketing**

Bibliography

Campbell, N. C. G. (1985). An interaction approach to organizational buying behaviour. *Journal of Business Research*, 13, (1), 35–48.

Ford, D. (1984). Buyer–seller relationships in international industrial markets. *Industrial Marketing Management*, 13, (2), May, 101–112.

Håkansson, H. (Ed.) (1982). *International marketing and purchasing of industrial goods – An interaction approach*. New York: John Wiley.

Johnson, W. J. & Bonoma, T. V. (1981). The buying centre: Structure and interaction patterns. *Journal of Marketing*, 45, Summer, 143–156.

Parkinson, S. T. & Baker, M. J. (1986). *Organisational buying behaviour: Purchasing and marketing management implications*. Basingstoke: Macmillan.

Sheth, J. N. (1973). A model of industrial buyer behaviour. *Journal of Marketing*, 37, (4), Oct., 50–56.

Turnbull, P. W. (1994). Organizational buying behaviour. In M. J. Baker (Ed.) (1994). *The marketing book* 3rd edn, London: Heinemann, pp. 216–237.

Webster, F. E. Jr & Wind, Y. (1972). *Organizational buying behavior*. Englewood Cliffs, NJ: Prentice-Hall.

DOMINIC WILSON

organizational change The study of organizational change is at the very core of management and organizational behavior. Organizational change is a difference in form, quality, or state over time in an organizational entity. The entity may be an individual's job, a work group, an organizational subunit, strategy, or product, or the overall design of an organization (*see* ORGANIZATIONAL DESIGN). Change in any of these entities can be calculated by measuring the same entity at two or more points in time on a set of dimensions, and then calculating the differences over time in these dimensions. If the difference is greater than zero (assuming no measurement error), we can say that the organizational entity has changed. Much of the voluminous literature on organizational change focuses on the nature of this difference, what produced it, and what are its consequences. Change can take many forms; it can be: planned or unplanned, incremental or radical, and recurrent or unprecedented. Trends in the process or sequence of changes can be observed over time. These trends can be accelerating or decelerating in time, and move toward equilibrium, oscillation, chaos, or randomness in the behavior of the organizational entity being examined. Thus, the basic concept of organization change involves three ideas:

(1) difference;
(2) at different temporal moments; and
(3) between states of the same organizational unit or system.

As this definition suggests, changes in an organizational system can occur at various levels of analysis, including the individual, group, organization, population or networks of organizations, and even larger communities or societies of organizations (*see* SYSTEMS THEORY). Understanding organizational change therefore requires careful focus on what level of analysis is being examined if one is to understand how changes occurring at these various levels interrelate. Organizational change is often mediated through individual actors. Therefore, Van de Ven and Poole (1988) argue that theories of organizational change should show how macro variables affect individual motives and choices and how these choices in turn change the macro–organization.

The topic of change depends on what events or variables are used to measure differences in an organizational entity over time. If an organization is viewed as a social system, the changes observed may include the following issues:

- changes in composition (e.g., personnel mobility, recruitment, promotion, or lay-offs, and shifts in resource allocations among organizational units);
- changes in structure (e.g., alterations of the organization's governance structure, centralization of decision making, formalization of rules, monitoring and control systems, and inequalities of STATUS or POWER among units or positions);
- changes in functions (e.g., organizational or subunit strategies, goals, mandates, products, or services);
- changes in boundaries (as brought about by mergers and acquisitions, or divestitures of organizational units, establishing joint ventures or STRATEGIC ALLIANCES, modifying membership admission criteria, organizational expansions or contractions in regions, markets, products/services, and political domains);
- changes in relationships among organizational levels and units (e.g., increases or decreases in resource dependencies, work flows, COMMUNICATIONS, CONFLICT, cooperation, competition, CONTROL, or culture among organizational entities);
- changes in performance, including effectiveness (degree of goal attainment), efficiency (cost per unit of output), and morale of participants (e.g., JOB SATISFACTION or quality of WORKING LIFE (*see* ORGANIZATIONAL EFFECTIVENESS)); and
- changes in the environment (ecological munificence or scarcity, turbulence, UNCERTAINTY, complexity, or heterogeneity) (*see* ORGANIZATION AND ENVIRONMENT).

Changes in any of these substantive areas can be planned or unplanned. In the late 1960s and 1970s, much attention to planned organizational change came from scholars and practitioners identified with organizational development (OD). Beckhard (1969, p. 9) defined OD as "an effort (1) *planned*, (2) *organization-wide*, and (3) *managed* from the top to (4) increase *organization effectiveness* and *health* through (5) *planned interventions* in the organization's processes using *behavioral science* knowledge" (italics in original). While Beckhard's definition implies a relatively conservative change strategy, Bartunek (1993) discusses other OD views that are more revolutionary in purpose and focus on bottom-up rather than top-down strategies for change. OD encompasses a variety of behavioral science interventions and action research methods that may help organizational participants make decisions, solve problems, overcome resistance, resolve conflicts, and play roles as needed to implement a planned change (*see* RESISTANCE TO CHANGE). OD takes a normative and interventionist orientation that is useful to management consultants and change agents who are frequently called upon to help undertake a variety of changes that are planned and desired by organizational executives.

Other management and organizational scholars have taken a more descriptive and positive approach to organizational change. Recognizing that varying degrees of change and stability are facts of any organization over time, much of the literature has distinguished between two modes of change:

(1) incremental (first-order) change which channels an organizational entity in the direction of adapting its basic structure and maintaining its identity in a stable and predictable way as it changes; and

(2) radical (second-order) change, which creates novel forms that are discontinuous and unpredictable departures from the past (see review by Meyer, Brooks, & Goes, 1990).

Typically, observed changes represent small, incremental, convergent, or continuous differences in localized parts of the organization, without major repercussions to other parts of the system. The organization as a whole remains intact, and no overall change of its former state occurs in spite of the incremental changes going on inside. While first-order changes may represent radical transformations *of* organizational subunits, they typically represent only incremental or continuous changes *in* the overall organizational system. Indeed, system stability often requires these kinds of incremental changes. Occasionally, large differences may occur in all (or at least the core) components of the system, producing a radical transformation or mutation *of* the overall organization. These second-order changes lead us to treat the new organizational system as fundamentally different from the old one.

The borderline between these extremes is somewhat fluid. Incremental changes in organizational units may accumulate and affect the core of the system, producing a radical change *of* the overall organization. Path dependencies or positive feedback may exist among incremental change events so that the timing of the changes may lead to major transformations. These incremental and radical changes in organizations may also alternate over time. For example, in Tushman and Romanelli's (1985) punctuated equilibrium model, organizational metamorphosis is explained by long periods of incremental, first-order changes that refine an organization's operations, products, and services. These convergent periods are occasionally punctuated by short periods of technological ferment, which may produce radical and discontinuous second-order changes in the organization.

Theories Explaining Organizational Change Processes
Explaining how and why organizations change is a central and enduring quest of scholars in management and many other social science disciplines (see reviews in Sztompka, 1993; and Van de Ven & Poole, 1994). The processes or sequences of events that unfold in these changes are very difficult to explain, let alone to manage. Van de Ven and Poole (1994) identify four different theories that are often used to explain how and why organizational changes unfold: life cycle, teleology, dialectics, and evolution. These four theories will be reviewed here, for they represent fundamentally different explanations of organizational change in any of the substantive areas or topics listed before. Each theory focuses attention on a different set of generating mechanisms and causal cycles to explain what triggers change and what follows what in a sequence of organizational changes.

Life cycle theory.   Many OB scholars have adopted the metaphor of organic growth as a heuristic device to explain changes in an organizational entity from its initiation to its termination (see applications in Huber and Glick, 1993). Witness, for example, often-used references to the life cycles of organizations, products, and ventures, as well as stages in the development of individual CAREERS, groups, and organizations: startup births, adolescent growth, maturity, and decline or death. Life cycle theory assumes that change is immanent; that is, the developing entity has within it an underlying form, logic, program, or code that regulates the process of change and moves the entity from a given point of departure toward a subsequent end that is already prefigured in the present state. What lies latent, rudimentary, or homogeneous in the embryo or primitive state becomes progressively more realized, mature, and differentiated. External environmental events and processes can influence how the immanent form expresses itself, but they are always mediated by the immanent logic, rules, or programs that govern development.

The typical progression of events in a life cycle model is a unitary sequence (it follows a single sequence of stages or phases), which is cumulative (characteristics acquired in earlier stages are retained in later stages) and conjunctive (the stages are related such that they derive from a common underlying process). This is because the trajectory to the final end state is prefigured and requires a specific historical sequence of events. Each of these events contributes a certain piece to the final product, and they must occur in a certain order, because each piece sets the stage for the next. Each stage of development can be seen as a necessary precursor of succeeding stages.

Life cycle theory is rooted in the approach of the gross anatomist in biology who observes a sequence of developing fetuses, concluding that each successive stage evolved from the previous one. From this perspective, change is driven by some genetic code or prefigured program within the developing entity. This view can be extended to include a number of historically driven processes of cognitive development in which each stage logically presupposes the next, such as when the development of manipulative skills precedes writing. There is no reason to suppose organizational systems could not have such processes as well.

Life cycle theories of organizations often explain development in terms of institutional rules or programs that require developmental activities to progress in a prescribed sequence. For example, a legislative bill enacting state educational reform cannot be passed until it has been drafted and gone through the necessary House and Senate committees. Other life cycle theories rely on logical or natural properties of organizations. For example, Rogers' (1983) theory posits five stages of INNOVATION: need recognition; research on the problem; development of an idea into useful form; commercialization; and diffusion and adoption. The order among these stages is necessitated both by logic and by the natural order of Western business practices.

Teleological theory. Another family of process theories uses teleology to explain development. This approach underlies many organizational theories of change, including functionalism, DECISION MAKING, adaptive learning, and most models of strategic choice and GOAL SETTING. A teleological theory is based on the assumption that change proceeds toward a goal or end state. It assumes that the organization is populated by purposeful and adaptive individuals. By themselves or in interaction with others they construct an envisioned end state, take action to reach it, and monitor their progress. Thus, this theory views development as a cycle of goal formulation, implementation, evaluation, and modification of goals based on what was learned or intended. The theory can operate in a single individual or among a group of cooperating individuals or organizations who are sufficiently like-minded to act as a single collective entity. Since the individual or cooperating entities have the freedom to set whatever goals they like, teleological theory inherently accommodates CREATIVITY; there are no necessary constraints or forms that mandate reproduction of the current entity or state.

Unlike life cycle theory, teleology does not presume a necessary sequence of events or specify which trajectory development will follow. However, it does imply a standard by which development can be judged: development is that which moves the entity toward its final state. There is no prefigured rule, logically necessary direction, or set sequence of stages in a teleological process. Instead, these theories focus on the prerequisites for attaining the goal or end-state: the functions that must be fulfilled, the accomplishments that must be achieved, or the components that must be built or obtained for the end-state to be realized. These prerequisites can be used to assess when an entity is developing; it is growing more complex, it is growing more integrated, or it is filling out a necessary set of functions. This assessment can be made because teleological theories posit an envisioned end state or design for an entity and it is possible to observe movement toward the end state vis-à-vis this standard.

Teleological models of development incorporate the systems theory assumption of equifinality; i.e., there are several equally effective ways to achieve a given goal. There is no assumption about historical necessity. Rather, these models rely on voluntarism as the explanatory principle. They posit a set of functions or goals desired by an organizational unit, which it must acquire in order to "realize" its aspirations. Changes in organizations are viewed as movements toward attaining a desired purpose, goal, function, or desired end state. There is no hard and fast order in which the organization must acquire the means and resources to achieve this goal.

While teleology stresses the purposiveness of the individual as the generating force for change, it also recognizes limits on action. The organization's environment and its resources of knowledge, time, money, etc., constrain what it can accomplish. Some of these constraints are embodied in the prerequisites, which are to some extent defined by institutions and other actors in the entity's environment. Individuals do not override natural laws or environmental constraints, but make use of them in accomplishing their purposes.

Once an entity attains this end state does not mean it stays in permanent equilibrium. Influences in the external environment or within the entity itself may create instabilities that push it to a new developmental path or trajectory. Theories that rely on a teleological process cannot specify what trajectory development will follow. They can at best list a set of possible paths, and rely on norms of rationality to prescribe certain paths (*see* ORGANIZATION AND ENVIRONMENT).

Dialectical theory. A third family, dialectical theories, is rooted in the assumption that the organization exists in a pluralistic world of colliding events, forces, or contradictory values that compete with each other for domination and control. These oppositions may be internal to an organization because it may have several conflicting goals or interest groups competing for priority. Oppositions may also arise external to the organization as it pursues directions that collide with those of others (see Burawoy & Skocpol (1982)).

Dialectical process theories explain stability and change by reference to the relative balance of POWER between opposing entities (*see* CONFLICT). Stability is produced through struggles and accommodations that maintain the status quo between oppositions. Change occurs when these opposing VALUES, forces, or events gain sufficient power to confront and engage the status quo. The relative power of an opposing paradigm or antithesis may mobilize to a sufficient degree to challenge the current thesis or state of affairs and set the stage for producing a synthesis. More precisely, the status quo subscribing to a thesis (A) may be challenged by an opposing entity with an antithesis (Not-A), and the resolution of the conflict produces a synthesis (which is Not Not-A). Over time, this synthesis can become the new thesis as the dialectical process recyles and continues. By its very nature, the synthesis is something created new, discontinuous with thesis and antithesis.

Creative syntheses to dialectical conflicts are often not assured. Sometimes an opposition group mobilizes sufficient power to simply overthrow and replace the status quo, just as many organizational regimes persist by maintaining sufficient power to suppress and prevent the mobilization of opposition groups. In the bargaining and conflict resolution literature the desired creative synthesis is one that represents a win–win solution, while either the maintenance of the status quo or its replacement with an antithesis are often treated as win–lose outcomes of a CONFLICT engagement. In terms of organizational change, maintenance of the status quo represents stability, while its replacement with either the antithesis or the synthesis represents a change, for the better or worse.

In general, a process theory that focuses on the intercourse of opposites can explain organizational changes that move toward:

(1) equilibrium;
(2) oscillation; and
(3) chaos.

First, organizational stability and inertia result when the routines, goals, or values of the status quo are sufficiently dominant to suppress opposing minority positions, and thereby produce incremental adaptations flowing toward equilibrium. For example, an existing ORGANIZATIONAL CULTURE, structure, or system can remain intact by undertaking incremental adaptations that appease or diffuse opposing minority positions. Such equilibrium-maintaining adaptations underlie many structural–functional theories of exchange, power, and order. Second, organizational business cycles, fads, or pendulum swings occur when opposing interest groups, business regimes, or political parties alternate in power and push the organization somewhat farther from a stable equilibrium. Such cycles explain recurrent periods of organizational feast and famine, partisan mutual adjustment among political parties, and alternating organizational priorities on efficiency and innovation. Third, seemingly-random organizational behaviors are produced when strong oscillations or shifts occur between opposing forces that push the organization out of a single periodic equilibrium orbit and produce multiple equilibria and bifurcations, each bounded by different strange attractors. Currently there is growing interest in recent advances in catastrophe theory and chaos theory to explain such seemingly random behavior in organizations. Thus, different patterns for resolving dialectical oppositions can push an organization to flow toward equilibrium, to oscillate in cycles between opposites, or to bifurcate far from equilibrium and spontaneously create revolutionary changes.

Evolutionary theory. Although evolution is sometimes equated with change, evolution is used here in a restrictive sense to focus on cumulative and probabilistic changes in structural forms of populations of organizations (*see* POPULATION ECOLOGY). As in biological evolution, change proceeds through a continuous cycle of variation, selection, and retention. Variations, the creation of novel forms, are often viewed to emerge by blind or random chance; they just happen. Selection occurs principally through the competition among forms, and the environment selects those forms that optimize or are best suited to the resource base of an environmental niche. Retention involves the forces (including inertia and persistence) that perpetuate and maintain certain organizational forms. Retention serves to counteract the self-reinforcing loop between variations and selection (Aldrich, 1979). Thus, evolutionary theory explains changes as a recurrent, cumulative, and probabilistic progression of variation, selection, and retention of organizational entities.

Alternative theories of social evolution can be distinguished in terms of how traits can be inherited, whether change proceeds gradually and incrementally or rapidly and radically, and whether the unit of analysis focuses on populations of organisms or species. A Darwinian perspective argues that traits can be inherited only through intergenerational processes, whereas a Lamarkian argues that traits can be acquired within a generation through learning and imitation. A Lamarkian view on the acquisition of traits appears more appropriate than strict Darwinism for organization and management applications of social evolution theory. As McKelvey (1982) discusses, to date no adequate solutions have been developed to identify operationally an organizational generation and an intergenerational transmission vehicle.

Social Darwinian theorists emphasize a continuous and gradual process of evolution. In *The Origin of Species*, Darwin wrote, "as natural selection acts solely by accumulating slight, successive, favourable variations, it can produce no great or sudden modifications; it can act only by short and slow steps." Other evolutionists posit a saltational theory of evolution, such as punctuated equilibrium, which Tushman and Romanelli (1985) introduced to the management literature. Whether an evolutionary change proceeds at gradual versus saltational rates is an empirical matter, for the rate of change does not fundamentally alter the theory of evolution – at least as it has been adopted thus far by organization and management scholars.

The paleontologist, Gould (1989), argues that another basic distinction between Darwinian evolution and his punctuated equilibrium theory is hierarchical level. This distinction has not yet been incorporated in the management literature, but ought to be. Gould points out that classical Darwinism locates the sorting of evolutionary change at a single level of objects. This sorting is natural selection operating through the differential births and deaths of organisms, as exemplified in many population ecology studies of organizational birth and death rates (see reviews in Hannan & Freeman (1989)). Gould's punctuated equilibrium model adds a hierarchical dimension to evolutionary theory by distinguishing this sorting (a description of differential birth and death) from speciation (a causal claim about the basis of sorting). "Speciation is a property of populations (organisms do not speciate), while extinction [a sorting process] is often a simple concatenation of deaths among organisms" (Gould, 1989, p. 122). This multilevel view of evolution is important for understanding how organizational adaptation and selection can occur at multiple levels (both the species and organism levels). Adaptation is the class of heritable characters that have a positive influence on the fitness of an organism within a constraining situation. Selection focuses on the evolutionary process of choosing new situations (i.e., variations). So selection assumes variation, while adaptation assumes fitting within a selected environment.

Conclusion

Life cycle, teleology, dialectics, and evolutionary theories provide four useful ways to think about and study processes of change in organizations. The relevance of the four theories will differ depending upon the conditions surrounding the organizational change in question. Specifically, Van de Ven and Poole (1994) propose that the four theories explain processes of organizational change and development under the following conditions:

- Life cycle theory explains change processes within an entity when natural, logical, or institutional rules exist to regulate the process.
- Teleological theory explains change processes within an entity or among a cooperating set of entities when a new desired end-state is socially constructed and consensus emerges on the means and resources to reach the desired end-state.
- Dialectical theory explains change processes between conflicting entities when the aggressor entities are sufficiently powerful and choose to engage the opposition through direct confrontation, bargaining, or partisan mutual adjustment.
- Evolutionary theory explains change processes between a population of entities when they compete for similar scarce resources in an environmental niche.

Thus, to explain organizational change in any content area, one applies the theory that best fits the specific conditions. Of course, changes in organizations are often more complex than these propositions suggest. Conditions may exist to trigger interplays between several change theories and produce interdependent cycles of change. While each of these types has its own internal logic or generating mechanism, confusion and complexity arise when these logics interact. To deal with some of these complexities, it is helpful to distinguish the myriad ongoing changes in organizational life into those that are routine versus novel and the level of analysis at which they occur.

To stay in business, most organizations follow routines to reproduce a wide variety of recurring changes, such as adapting to economic cycles, periodic revisions in products and services, and ongoing instances of personnel turnover and executive succession (*see* SUCCESSION PLANNING).

These commonplace changes within organizations are typically programmed by preestablished rules or institutional routines, and can be analyzed and explained using a life cycle theory of change. At the industry or population level, competitive or environmental selection for shifts in resources typically govern the rates of reproduction (and resulting size and number) of various forms of organizations. Evolutionary theory is useful for explaining these population-level changes as the probabilistic workings of variation, selection, and retention processes.

Occasionally, organizations also experience unprecedented changes for which no established routines or procedures exist. They include many planned (as well as unplanned) changes in organizational creation, innovation, turnaround, reengineering, cultural transformation, merger, divestiture, and many other issues the organization may not have experienced (*see* TURNAROUND STRATEGY; mergers and acquisitions). These kinds of novel changes can be usefully analyzed and explained with a teleological theory if they are triggered by a reframing or frame-breaking goal of powerful people in control of the organization. Alternatively, a dialectical theory might better explain the novel change process when conflicts and confrontations between opposing groups occur to produce a synthesis out of the ashes of the conflict engagements.

The processes through which these novel changes unfold are far more complex and unpredictable than routine changes because the former require developing and implementing new change routines, while the latter entail implementing tried-and-tested routines. Novel changes entail the creation of originals, whereas routine changes involve the reproduction of copies. Novel changes are organizational innovations, whereas routine changes are business as usual.

An important concluding caveat is to recognize that existing theories of organizational change are explanatory, but not predictive. Statistically, we should expect most incremental, convergent, and continuous changes to be explained by either life cycle or evolutionary theories, and most radical, divergent, and discontinuous changes to be explained by teleological or dialectical theories. But these actuarial relationships may not be causal. For example, the infrequent statistical occurrence of a discontinuous and radical mutation may be caused by a glitch in the operation of a life cycle model of change. So also, the scale-up of a teleological process to create a planned strategic reorientation for a company may fizzle, resulting only in incremental change.

see also **Strategic management**

Bibliography

Aldrich, H. (1979). Organizations and environments. Englewood Cliffs, NJ: Prentice-Hall.
Bartunek, J. M. (1993). The multiple cognitions and conflicts associated with second order organizational change. In J. K. Murningham (Ed.), Social psychology in organizations: Advances in theory and research. (Chapter 15) Englewood Cliffs, NJ: Prentice Hall.
Beckhard, R. (1969). Organization development: Strategies and models. Reading, MA: Addison-Wesley.
Burawoy, M. & Skocpol, T. (1982). Marxist inquiries: Studies of labor, class, and states. Chicago: University of Chicago Press.
French, W. L. & Bell, C. H. Jr. (1978). Organization development: Behavior science interventions for organization improvement. Englewood Cliffs, NJ: Prentice Hall.
Gould, S. J. (1989). Punctuated equilibrium in fact and theory. Journal of Social and Biological Structures, **12**, 117–136.
Hannan, M. T. & Freeman, J. (1989). Organizational ecology. Cambridge, MA: Harvard University Press.
Huber, G. P. & Glick, W. H. (1993). Organizational change and redesign: Ideas and insights for improving performance. Oxford, UK: Oxford University Press.
McKelvey, B. (1982). Organizational systematics: Taxonomy, evolution, classification. Berkeley, CA: University of California Press.
Meyer, A. D., Brooks, G. R. & Goes, J. B. (1990). Environmental jolts and industry revolutions: Organizational responses to discontinuous change. Strategic Management Journal, **11**, 93–110.
Rogers, E. (1983). Diffusion of innovations, (3rd edn) New York: Free Press.
Sztompka, P. (1993). The sociology of social change. London: Blackwell.
Tushman, M. L. & Romanelli, E. (1985). Organizational evolution: A metamorphosis model of convergence and reorientation. In B. Staw & L. Cummings (Eds), Research in organizational behavior, (vol. 7) Greenwich, CT: JAI Press.
Van de Ven, A. H. & Poole, M. S. (1988). Paradoxical requirements for a theory of organizational change. In R. Quinn & K. Cameron (Eds), Paradox and transformation: Toward a theory of change in organization and management. New York: Harper Collins, Ballinger Division.
————— (1994). Explaining development and change in organizations Minneapolis, MN: University of Minnesota. Strategic Management Research Center, Discussion Paper #189.

ANDREW H. VAN DE VEN

organizational culture The interest in organizational culture during the 1980s – to practitioners and researchers alike – was stimulated by two factors. The first of these was the impact of Japanese enterprises in international markets, and the search to identify a possible link between national culture and organizational performance. The second factor was the perceived failure of the "hard S's" – systems, structure, and strategy – to deliver a competitive advantage, and the belief that this elusive success was more a matter of delivering the "soft S's," such as staff, style, and shared values. However, the early attempts to prescribe a specific culture and manipulate cultural change met with little success, and have led to a reappraisal of what the concept of "culture" involves.

Smircich (1983) provides a useful framework for reappraising the concept. She classifies the perspectives of culture as falling into two broad camps. In the first perspective culture is seen as a "product," something an organization "has." In such an approach, organizational culture is deemed to be capable of classification and manipulation (usually by management). By contrast, in the second perspective organizational culture is regarded as more of a "process," something an organization "is." According to this perspective, "culture" is much more difficult to pin down and pigeon-hole, and does not lend itself to manipulation.

Culture as a "Product"

This perspective generates a spectrum of definitions, ranging from those that emphasize the surface indicators to those that try to tap some deeper meaning. The surface manifestations include definitions such as "how things get done around here," or culture as a "stock of values, beliefs, and norms widely subscribed to by those who work in an organization." In this vein, an influential approach has been Handy's division of cultures into four types: power, role, task, and person (Handy, 1978). Deeper definitions refer more to culture as "mental processes or mindsets characteristic of organizational members."

Hofstede (1990) defines culture as the "software of the mind." His work, conducted in over 50 countries, has concentrated on unearthing national cultural differences and determining how these influence organizational life. He claims that organizations have to confront two central problems: how to distribute power and how to manage uncertainty. He then identifies five value dimensions which, he claims, discriminate between national groups, and which influence the way in which people perceive that an organization should be managed to meet these two key problems. The dimensions are as follows:

- power distance, i.e., the extent to which people accept that power is distributed unequally
- uncertainty avoidance, i.e., the extent to which people feel uncomfortable with uncertainty and ambiguity
- individualism/collectivism, i.e., the extent to which there is a preference for belonging to tightly knit collectives rather than a more loosely knit society
- masculinity/feminity, i.e., the extent to which gender roles are clearly distinct (masculine end of the spectrum) as opposed to those where they overlap (feminine end of the spectrum)
- Confucian dynamism, i.e., the extent to which long-termism or short-termism tends to predominate

Hofstede's work is only based on employees of one organization. Furthermore, the extent to which one country can be said to have an homogeneous culture is problematic. Nevertheless, Hofstede's work has been highly influential. It attempts to explain why differing national cultural mind-sets will cause difficulties when a manager from one country goes to work abroad. Difficulties can also be predicted when two organizations from countries with different cultural mind-sets attempt to merge. Adler's work (1991) on differing national negotiating styles is also useful for gaining an understanding of cultural differences between nations. It is interesting to speculate whether globalization will increase the need to understand national cultural differences (as multinationals seek to manage diverse workforces) or whether the need will decrease as globalization brings about an homogenization of national cultures.

In terms of the desire to "learn from Japan," it is possible to identify specific cultural values in Japanese society which might influence economic performance, such as the importance attached to reciprocity between those of different status. However, there are successful organizations in other parts of the world in which these conventions are flouted. Indeed, even within Japan, there is a range of organizational practices as to how employees are treated. It is also difficult to disentangle the effects of culture on performance from other factors, such as industrial structure, manufacturing practices, and the role of the state (Dawson, 1992). The evidence on the attempts to introduce Japanese practices in other countries is also mixed (for the UK experience, see Oliver & Hunter, 1994).

The "culture as a product" perspective has also focused on the role of comparative organizational cultures within a country. Here an attempt has been made to provide a rigorous test as to what sort of a culture will lead to high performance. Denison (1991) argues that the four specific variables that influence performance are involvement, consistency, adaptability, and mission. Denison notes how these variables are, to some extent, contradictory: for example, consistency in terms of having agreement can sometimes inhibit adaptability. It is also important that a culture is appropriate to its environment, so it is unlikely that there is one universal culture that suits all environments. On the other hand, environments change much more rapidly than organizational cultures, which can take many years to develop. Kotter & Heskett (1992) claim that cultures in which there is a strong consensus that key stakeholders should be valued, leadership at all levels is seen as important, and the culture underpins an appropriate strategy, can serve as valid generalizations, but these claims have yet to be put to the test. Brown (1994) carries a useful summary of both this issue and of the literature on models of organizational cultural change, of which Schein's model (1985) is the best-known.

Culture as a Process

Smircich's other perspective sees culture as a root metaphor for understanding organizations. This perspective makes it difficult to define culture. Organizations do not so much *have* cultures; it is more that they *are* cultures. This has implications for those who wish to try to change a culture.

The "culture as root metaphor" concept sees culture as something that is collectively enacted, where all who experience a culture at first hand become part of its generation and reproduction. To assume that one group (usually management) can unilaterally modify a culture is thus to mistake its essential properties. This is not to deny that culture changes – indeed, its enactment is a continuous process – but it usually changes in unintended ways. It is important also to recognize that collective enactment does not mean harmony and agreement; the power to enact is not equally shared amongst all groups.

The concept also has implications for those who wish to research cultures: the researcher inevitably becomes part of the enactment process (Weick, 1983). Trying to fix a culture and establish typologies is just an interpretation, one more part of the enactment process. As Martin (1993, p. 13) puts it: "Culture is not reified – out there – to be accurately observed."

However, this does not mean that the concept of "culture" is valueless except as a stick to beat those who see it as a product. Morgan (1986) argues that culture can be a powerful metaphor for enabling thought about organizations, drawing attention to the importance of patterns of subjective meaning, of images, and of values in organizational life.

Conclusion

The life cycle of organizational culture mirrors that of many other alleged managerial panaceas, running through the stages of initial enthusiasm, followed by a critical backlash, and ending up with a more widely based consensus on the limited applicability of the concept, which often highlights the complexity of management as a discipline.

Culture as a "product" has already gone through this cycle. It soon became clear that "culture" is not something that can easily be manipulated. Indeed, culture as a "process" seems a more powerful perspective in that it recognizes that culture depends upon human interaction – it is continuously being produced and re(created). To believe that one group can unilaterally change an existing culture according to some blueprint is mistaken. Culture does change – but often slowly and in unpredictable ways. Managers who wish to establish a blueprint might be better advised to go for a greenfield site and then carefully control recruitment and selection (Wickens, 1987). There is also the danger of thinking of culture as a monolithic entity to which all organizational members subscribe. Martin (1993) terms such a view "integrationist" and contrasts it with a "differentiation" focus, which stresses the importance of subcultures and the potential for conflict between these subcultures.

Even if a particular culture could be established by managerial fiat, the links between culture and organizational performance are not well-established. Assuming that cultures can be measured and pigeon-holed, there is no clear evidence that one particular type of culture is always associated with success – indeed, some of the features which are claimed to be linked with success are themselves contradictory. Furthermore, the sheer complexity of the factors involved in organizational performance makes it difficult to pin-point the exact contribution made by culture alone.

Bibliography

Adler, N. (1991). *International dimensions of organisational behaviour*. Boston, MA: PWS-Kant.
Brown, A. (1994). *Organisational culture*. London: Pitman.
Dawson, S. (1992). *Analysing organisations* (2nd edn), London: Macmillan.
Denison, D. (1991). *Corporate culture and organisational effectiveness*. New York: John Wiley.
Handy, C. (1978). *The gods of management*. Harmondsworth, UK: Penguin.
Hofstede, G. (1990). *Cultures and organisations: software of the mind*. Maidenhead, UK: McGraw-Hill.
Kotter, J. P. & Heskett, J. L. (1992). *Corporate culture and performance*. New York: The Free Press.
Martin, J. (1993). *Cultures in organisations*. Oxford: Oxford University Press.
Morgan, G. (1986). *Images of organisations* Sage.
Oliver, N. & Hunter, G. (1994). The financial impact of Japanese production methods in UK companies. Paper no. 24. Cambridge, UK:
Schein, E. H. (1985). *Organisational culture and leadership*. London: Jossey–Bass.
Smircich, L. (1983). Concepts of culture and organisational analysis. *Administrative Science Quarterly*, **28**, 339–58.
Weick, K. (1983). Enactment processes in organisations. In B. Staw & G. Salancik (eds), *New directions in organisational behaviour*. Malabar, FL: Robert E. Krieger.
Wickens, P. (1987). *The road to Nissan: flexibility, quality, teamwork*. London: Macmillan.

MICHAEL BROCKLEHURST

organizational design This term is used rather loosely to refer to the choosing of structures and associated managerial processes to enable an organization to operate effectively. The term, therefore, includes at least five interconnected concepts:

1 *Organization* can be taken to cover a wide range of types such as business, NOT-FOR-PROFIT, private, public, service, or manufacturing organizations. The extent to which societies have a capacity to organize, Stinchcombe (1965) argues, will be dependent upon a number of factors such as the literacy rate, degree of communication, existence of a money economy, political revolution, and the density of social life. As most of these factors are on the increase around the world, the rate of increase of organizational formation can be expected to be maintained and hence the need to design them more effectively to be ever more urgent.

2 *Design* implies a deliberate attempt to find an effective organizational form and, therefore, a managerial authority to put into effect such structures, usually seen as a fundamental responsibility of top management (*see* TOP MANAGEMENT TEAMS). In democratic organizations design would be more likely to also involve the total membership.

3 *Structure* can be seen as rules for making decisions. Organization theory has developed many variables and dimensions of structure concerning variables such as the degree of specialization, formalization, or centralization (*see* DECENTRALIZATION).

4 *Effectiveness* (*see* ORGANIZATIONAL EFFECTIVENESS) refers to the performance of an organization as measured against a range of norms. Organizations generally have to satisfy heterogeneous and variable norms coming from a wide constituency of supporters (or stakeholders). Following the principle of bounded rationality organizations, when faced with contradictory norms of performance, tend to concentrate upon a relatively small number of norms demanded by their most powerful constituency.

5 *Choice* in the particular pattern of structures and processes adopted exists. If there was no choice and all organizations were designed the same, the notion of organizational design would be meaningless. The notion of choice also indicates that specific decisions about structures can be made in organizations.

Although it could be said that traditional organizations such as the church were "designed," the earliest organizational design principles that may be recognized as belonging to modern management theory came from a group of practicing managers and engineers who wrote eruditely about their work. Interest in organizational theory developed in the post-World War II period as a result of the increasing complexity of organizational and managerial problems, and in appreciation of the need to adapt designs to the contingencies of the environment and technology (*see* ORGANIZATION AND ENVIRONMENT).

Under the heading of sociotechnical systems a number of far-reaching studies conducted by researchers at the Tavistock Institute immediately post-World War II on organizational change in British coal mines and in an Indian textile factory can be seen as concerned with organizational design. Mention of organizational design in the American organizational literature appears around 1960 (Rubenstein & Haberstroh, 1965) and in March's edited *Handbook of Organizations* (1965). It was the era of large-scale American military and quasi-military organizations, the style that of systems analysis, simulations, and various optimizing methods. The American space agency NASA and the RAND Corporation were major sponsors of such work.

The four editions of Daft's (1992) book *Organization Theory and Design*, and Nystrom and Starbuck's (1981) *Handbook of Organizational Design* point to the sustained interest in this topic. In particular, these books draw together a number of themes which were previously left to relatively separate management subjects such as strategic management, marketing, production, and the like.

Some Principles

Attempts have been made to develop systematic theoretical underpinnings to organizational design issues by drawing upon a growing body of literature on organizational information systems and DECISION MAKING. Ashby's (1956) Law of Requisite Variety provides one such basis. This law states that informational variety is needed to cope with variety. Hence, if a production process is highly variable in the quality of its output, informational variety is needed to solve the coordination problem.

Building upon Ashby's Law is a tradition of treating organizational design as a problem of an optimal control theory of decision making. A decision-based theory of organizational design (Huber, 1990) draws attention to developments management information systems design (*see* COMMUNICATIONS).

Thompson's book (1967) *Organizations in Action* provides a framework for thinking about organizational design which still has an immense influence. Building upon the work of Simon, March, and Cyert with their view of organizations as indeterminate behavioral systems, Thompson's propositions show how an organization can cope with the often conflicting demands of technical and organizational rationality.

Many of Thompson's ideas were taken up by later writers on organizational design, particularly the three types of coordination methods (rules, plans, and mutual adjustment) and the three types of interdependencies for which each is most suited, respectively, pooled, sequential, and reciprocal interdependency. Galbraith (1977) developed detailed propositions regarding organizational design,

in particular, concerning the need for horizontal and vertical communication in organizations.

The theory of BUREAUCRACY has also been a major source of influence upon principles of organizational design, particularly by those principles which emphasize the need to specify job descriptions and formal hierarchical reporting relationships. It has been shown (Pugh and Hickson 1989) that an organization tends to increase centralization of decision making as its dependency in the environment increases; a highly dependent organization is one that relies for a high percentage of its inputs upon a small number of sources, or which sends a high percentage of its output to a small number of outlets. An alternative more horizontal coordination mechanism is structuring of activities, meaning that control resides in the standardized procedures that are set up. Once set up, structuring allows a high degree of DELEGATION although writing the rules in the first place and dealing with exceptions will require centralization.

Galbraith (1977) devised a typology of vertical and horizontal linkage mechanisms according to the degree of coordination and the information capacity needed. Vertical linking providing the least information capacity is hierarchical referral, with rules and plans, adding levels in the hierarchy and finally vertical information systems providing increasing degrees of information capacity. Horizontal linking mechanisms, in order of increasing information capacity, are paperwork, direct contact, liaison roles, task forces, and teams. These proposed linkage mechanisms are basically similar to the coordinating mechanisms suggested by Thompson and illustrate the underlying accepted organizational design paradigm.

The transactions costs approach to organizations (Williamson 1975) also reflects attempts to see the coordination problem of organization in terms of the type of information, and the cost of acquiring that information for effective decisions to be made (*see* TRANSACTION COST). What has become known as institutional economics proposes that markets are replaced by hierarchies when informational variety is insufficiently high to match the complexity of the transactions being conducted.

OPEN SYSTEMS theory of organization design emphasizes the relationship between task environment and structure. Organizations create boundary structures to cope with environmental uncertainties and interdependencies. As environments get more complex, organizations tend to differentiate their structures more indicating the need for more integration, that is, coordination effort.

Related to an open-systems perspective are theories that more specifically link organizational structure and business strategy. Chandler (1962) noted how the American corporation tended to develop divisionalized or m-form organization structures in response to increasing size and diversified markets. Miles and Snow (1978) developed four types of strategy (*see* STRATEGIC GROUPS) (the defender, prospector, analyzer, and reactor) and argued that, for effectiveness, firms need to find the right match between environment, structure, and technology.

Due to the development of greater interorganizational linkages there has been increasing emphasis upon cooperative strategies and the need to manage boundary transactions more effectively (*see* INTERORGANIZATIONAL RELATIONS). Designs for this purpose include just-in-time management, joint ventures, use of contracts, and coopting. Increasing attention has also turned to the issue of corporate governance and the need to ensure an appropriate membership of governing bodies.

Determinants and Outcomes

Organizational design principles attempt to determine relationships between independent and dependent variables in order to achieve effectiveness. Departmentalization (who is grouped with whom) is a major dependent variable of organizational design. Four principal ways of departmentalizing have been outlined, namely, by function (or process), by product (or service), by area, or by client. Functional departmentalization puts people of a similar skill together in groups representing different stages in the production of a product or service. The advantages of a functional organization are that they allow development of professional skills; the disadvantages are that workers lose contact with the overall product and its associated customers.

Product departmentalization puts people of a similar product (or service) together in groups. This arrangement provides the advantage of greater commitment to matching the product to customer need but with the disadvantage of losing professional skill development.

Functional and product departmentalizations are therefore the inverse of each other but these are not mutually exclusive types, however, and most organizations are hybrids. The MATRIX ORGANIZATION is an attempt to provide the benefits of both functional and product types without the disadvantages of each, although this can be difficult in practice. The project form of organization is similar to the matrix except that projects have a definite life (Knight, 1976) (*see* project management).

Another approach to determining relationships between variables is to define "bundles" of variables which occur together in particular configurations. Some configurations are empirically defined, such as that of Pugh and Hickson (1989) who identify four types of bureaucracy according to the two dimensions of degree of structuring of activities and concentration of authority:

(1) Full bureaucracy occurs when structuring of activities and concentration of authority is high.
(2) Workflow bureaucracy occurs when structuring is high but concentration of authority is low: in this type, control of the work is so precisely programmed into instructions that little direct decision making by management is needed.
(3) Personnel bureaucracy occurs when structuring is low but authority is concentrated: formal procedures are now replaced by direct intervention by top management, or by outside fiat.
(4) Nonbureaucracy occurs when neither direct authority nor structuring is used: under these conditions a number of things can happen, one of which is for a more collective form of organization based upon TRUST to take over whereby participants come to control their own work more closely.

Markets and hierarchies represent two broad contrasting organizational types which are able to cope with different types of transactions, the hierarchy being more costly but better able to cope with more complex information. A third generic collective type of institutional arrangement for managing transactions (Butler, 1991) has also been suggested. In the collective, the coordination of transactions is governed by means of trust and mutual adjustment. The collective is therefore the most suitable form of organization when complexity is very high since it allows the development of trust and the use of special languages and a generally highly rich informational environment.

Mintzberg (1983) combined Thompson's propositions of coordination with a general SYSTEMS THEORY defining the subsystems needed by an organization to produce five organizational configurations. These are: the simple structure, machine bureaucracy, professional bureaucracy, divisionalized form, and the adhocracy. Each configuration displays a prime coordinating mechanism, a key part of the organization, a number of design parameters concerning especially the type of decentralization used, and the situational factors to which each is most suited. For example, the simple structure uses direct supervision for coordination, the key part of the organization is the strategic apex, the main design parameters are centralization combined with an organic structure, and the situational factors pertain to small size, youth, and a homogeneous dynamic environment.

The configurational approach to organizational design has produced a large number of typologies and the problem is finding some underlying logic to these configurations. The relationship between technology and organizational design has received a lot of attention. Woodward (1965) classified manufacturing technology on a continuum from craft through batch to process production. It was found that craft and process technologies shared small SPANS OF CONTROL and a high ratio of skilled to unskilled workers while mass production was high on these features. Other structural features, such as the proportion of support staff, showed a linear increase from craft to process production.

Perrow's (1970) four types of technology is posited in terms of task analyzability and variability. The routine type requires the most structuring of activities whilst the nonroutine requires a very flexible structure; craft and engineering types can be seen as possessing intermediate structures. More recent theories about the connection between technology and structure emphasize the need for flexibility. The use of automation, computer-aided design (CAD), computer-aided manufacturing (CAM), and ADVANCED MANUFACTURING TECHNOLOGY have tended to emphasize the ability to introduce product design more rapidly with a vision, as yet not widely realized, of designs being transferred directly to manufacturing instructions without many intermediate steps (Dudley & Hassard, 1990).

A fundamental variable is organizational size which can be both an independent and a dependent variable of organizational design. As an independent variable increase in size leads to an exponential rise in management costs, in return the organization can gain economies of scale. In order to cope with the complexities of increased size, organizations tend to routinize their activities or break them down into autonomous units.

From a strategic viewpoint size can be used as a means of gaining advantage in the task environment. Organizations can grow organically by going through a certain life cycle (*see* ORGANIZATIONAL CHANGE). To grow can also be a deliberate strategy since by extending the domain of customers and suppliers a firm can gain more secure support for itself. Growth can also occur by means of acquisition (see MERGER GUIDELINES) and can include a deliberate attempt to move out of a local market to national, international, and global markets. Although the principles of organizational design should remain the same, the main difference would be the requirement to take into account a wider range of cultures and to cope with extensive communication problems over long distances. Reductions in size, or DOWNSIZING, is not necessarily a completely reversible process. Recent research is showing that downsizing can also be accompanied by increases in routinization.

Ideological Aspects

Ideological and cultural aspects of organizational design have received increasing attention. The distinction between the two terms is somewhat blurred but there appears general agreement that variables capturing the underlying beliefs and VALUES of organizational members and of the wider society need to be in a model of organizational design. These beliefs and values provide a kind of organizational lens through which the context, ways of making decisions, and appropriate structures are viewed.

There is, however, also a feedback link from structure to ideology. Particular types of structure will tend to foster particular types of ideology. For example, if structure sets rules emphasizing highly individualistic profit based pay, it would be surprising if such an organization managed to develop a robust ideology, that is, an ideology which encourages team work and concern for overall organizational objectives.

We might expect connections between cultural symbols and structures since structures themselves can become symbolic of the intentions of management. For example, reward systems indicate what kinds of behaviors are approved; executive pay can therefore become very indicative of the key contingencies at any one time. As with ideology, culture provides a repertoire of managerial recipes which are used in organizational design.

Critiques and Syntheses

A critique of a coordination and decision cost paradigm of organizational design comes from the postmodernism position which denies the notion of organizational rationality by arguing that theories of organization are in themselves self-fulfilling and deny the essential chaos of social life. However, chaotic as the post-modern world may be, the goods and services consumed in that society can only be produced by means of high levels of intended rationality even though that rationality may be, at some later point, found to rest upon an illusion. It seems unlikely, therefore, that interest in organizational design will diminish. Developments within organizational theory which may impact upon organizational theory design practice, such as fuzzy sets analysis and chaos theory, may give mathematical tools that can be used to make sense out of the inherent indeterminacy of complex situations.

A more specific current concern in this direction is seen in the interest in organizational learning as a major dimension of organizational effectiveness (see also LEARNING ORGANIZATION). The notion of an organization as an error-coping and learning device shifts attention from rationality to the need for developing new knowledge. Organizational design, therefore, needs to create the conditions for learning to take place. Argyris and Schon (1978) have elaborated two types of learning which link with the two types of error outlined above. Errors of under-capacity only allow single loop learning, that is, learning to do better what is already being done. Double loop learning involves learning to do new things to enable the organization to adapt to complexity.

INSTITUTIONAL THEORY provides a critique of the dominant paradigm of organizational design which focuses upon the need to minimize coordination costs. The institutional view sees organizational structures as strongly determined by their institutional settings and that the dominant organizational design paradigm as too rationalistic, a view which is particularly appropriate to professional, educational and public service types of organizations. Organizations, therefore, attempt to increase their legitimacy by adopting structures which are institutionalized in society rather than structures which are the most efficient for the task of producing products and services. This search for LEGITIMACY means that structures can take on a ritualistic role in order to satisfy institutionalized norms.

A critical omission in much of the organizational design literature concerns the issue of how to achieve change. Organizational design has tended to concentrate upon providing propositions connecting variables on how to improve effectiveness, but change is a technical, political, and cultural problem, although more recent books on organizational design now include sections on achieving change (Butler, 1991; Daft, 1992). A number of structural ideas have been suggested to allow organizations to make changes which can, in general terms, be seen as ways of managing the tension between organizational rigidity and flexibility. The ambidextrous organization would incorporate both crisp and fuzzy structures simultaneously. When, for example, introducing a new technology a fuzzy structure would be used but as learning develops a more crisp structure would be needed. The use of venture teams, idea champions, and entrepreneurship are ways of introducing change.

An attempt has been made to bring together these related approaches to the problem of organizational coordination through an institutional model of organizational design (Butler, 1991). This model divides the environment of an organization into the task and institutional environments. The task environment is where the competitive exchange resources (with suppliers, customers, and the like) occur and here the main problem is managing resource dependence. The institutional environment sets norms of performance for an organization and here the main problem is that of gaining legitimacy. Legitimacy can be acquired in a number of ways, for instance, by performing well in the task environment or by adopting appropriate structures. Achieving legitimacy by satisfying minimum performance norms becomes the first objective of organizational design and, in order to achieve this, attention needs to be paid to the interrelationship between four sets of variables:

(1) the technical and task context within which an organization operates, of which the notion of complexity is the key descriptor;

(2) the structures adopted;
(3) the ideologies held by organizational participants; and
(4) the DECISION MAKING processes.

Underlying the model is the notion that organizational design should be aimed at error coping and learning rather than output optimizing (*see* LEARNING ORGANIZATION). In coping with complexity errors will be made. If structures are too rigid and ideologies too narrowly focused for the degree of complexity, errors of decision under-capacity are made; the problem becomes lack of organizational adaptability. If structures are too fuzzy and ideologies too robust, errors of decision over-capacity are made; the organization here achieves high adaptability but at the expense of efficiency. The institutional model sees organizational design as a dialectic between conflicting features and alerts designers to how a wide range of aspects of the institutional environment can impact upon design parameters. In particular, changes in the political, social and cultural, and economic segments of the environment can radically alter the performance norms to which an organization has to attend.

The Future
Until the 1980s the general trend was for organizations to grow and organizational theory was generally built upon this premise. Since then reductions in size have become common. Reducing the number of people does not necessarily mean a reduction in output, turnover, or capital employed. Number of people employed has been the usual measure of size in organizational theory since the subject is most concerned with organization as a social rather than as a financial or a technical phenomenon. Whether size increases or decreases makes no difference to the principles of an intendedly rational organizational design but will make a difference to the process of change.

The availability of networks of low-cost personal computers combined with the enormous information processing capacity of larger computers means that networks of organizations can be created; airline booking and bank telling systems are archetypes (*see* NETWORK-ING). This is allowing organizations to develop flatter, less centralized, but probably more routinized, structures. Research continues to show, however, that formal executive information systems are not used much by senior managers since, in making the more complex higher-level decisions, they prefer to rely less upon formal and more upon informal information.

In most Western economies there has been an increase in the number of small firms and it is increasingly being observed that organizations do not need to employ people but can buy in goods and services from a network of small suppliers. Taken to the limit the proposition of downsizing poses an interesting paradox for organizational design since it would mean the replacement of large organizations in the formal sense by transactions contract governance. Manufacturing a motor car, for instance, would be a matter of buying in sufficient goods and services and managing a vast network of contracts. Such an image suggests that some of the conventional variables of structure will have to change. However, the underlying principles of transaction costs, requisite informational variety, and requisite decision capacity should still hold.

Bibliography
Argyris, C. & Schon, D. A. (1978). Organizational learning: A theory of action perspective. Reading, MA: Addison-Wesley.
Ashby, W. R. (1956). Self-regulation and requisite variety. In F. E. Emery (Ed.), Systems thinking. Harmondsworth, UK: Penguin. (1969), Ch. 6. Originally in W. R. Ashby Introduction to Cybernetics. New York: Wiley. (1956), Ch. 11.
Butler, R. J. (1991). Designing organizations: A decision-making perspective. London: Routledge.
Chandler, A. D. (1962). Strategy and structure: Chapters in the history of the industrial enterprise. Cambridge, MA: MIT Press.
Daft, R. L. (1992). Organization theory and design., (4th edn) St Paul: MN. West.
Dudley, G. & Hassard J. (1990). Design issues in the development of computer integrated manufacturing (CIM). Journal of General Management, 16, 43–53.
Galbraith, J. R. (1977). Organization design. Reading, MA: Addison-Wesley.
Huber G. P. (1990). A theory of the effects of advanced information technologies on organizational design, intelligence and decision making. Academy of Management Review, 15, 1.
Knight, K. (1976). Matrix organization: A review. Journal of Management Studies, 13, 11–130.
March, J. G. (Ed.), (1965). Handbook of organizations. Chicago: Rand McNally.
Miles, R. E. & C. C. Snow (1978). Organizational Strategy, Structure and Process. New York: McGraw-Hill.
Mintzberg, H. (1983). Structures in fives: Designing effective organizations. Englewood Cliffs, NJ: Prentice-Hall.
Nystrom, P. C. & Starbuck, W. H. (Eds), (1981). Handbook of organizational design, (vols. I & II) Oxford, UK: Oxford University Press.
Perrow, C. (1970). Organizational analysis: A sociological view. London: Tavistock.
Pugh, D. S. & Hickson, D. J. (1989). Writers on organizations. Newburg Park, CA: Sage.
Rubenstein, A. H. & Haberstroh, C. J. (Eds), (1966). Some theories of organization. Homewood, IL: Irwin & Dorsey.
Stinchcombe, A. (1965). Social structure and organizations. In J. G. March (Ed.), Handbook of organizations, (Ch. 4) Chicago: Rand McNally.
Thompson, J. D. (1967). Organizations in action. New York: McGraw-Hill.
Trist E. L., Higgin G. W., Murray H. & Pollack A. B. (1963). Organizational choice. London: Tavistock.
Williamson O. E. (1975). Markets and hierarchies: Analysis and Anti-Trust Implications: A Study in the Economics of Internal Organization. New York: Free Press.
Woodward, J. (1965). Industrial organization: Theory and practice. Oxford, UK: Oxford University Press.

RICHARD BUTLER

organizational effectiveness This has been defined in a variety of ways but no single definition has been accepted universally (Cameron & Whetten, 1983). This is because organizational effectiveness is inherently tied to the definition of what an organization is. As the conceptualization of an organization changes, so does the definition of effectiveness, the criteria used to measure effectiveness, and frameworks and theories used to explain and predict it. For example, if an organization is defined as a goal seeking entity, effectiveness is likely to be defined in terms of the extent to which goals are accomplished. If an organization is defined as the central focus of a social contract among constituencies, effectiveness is likely to be defined in terms of constituency satisfaction. To understand what is generally agreed upon about organizational effectiveness, it is helpful to discuss several of its important attributes. In particular, effectiveness:

(1) is a *construct*,
(2) it is grounded in the *VALUES* and *preferences* of constituencies; and
(3) it must be *bounded* to be measured.

As a *construct*, effectiveness cannot be observed directly. This is because constructs are abstractions "constructed" to give meaning to an idea. In other words, organizational effectiveness cannot be pinpointed, counted, or objectively manipulated. It is an idea rather than an objective reality. In addition, effectiveness is reflective of the *values and preferences* of various constituencies. What one group may prefer or label as effective may not be the same as that of another group. Moreover, preferences may knowingly or unknowingly change, sometimes dramatically, over time among individuals. The attachment of effectiveness to goodness or to excellence makes judgments of effectiveness inherently subjective and valued-based. This helps explain why no single definition of effectiveness is universal. Different constituencies have different preferences, different values, and different evaluation criteria.

This does not mean, of course, that effectiveness cannot be measured. But in order for acceptable criteria of effectiveness to be identified, the *boundaries* of the construct must be clearly delineated. This means that the answers to seven questions must be answered which specify the construct boundaries:

(1) From whose perspective is effectiveness being judged (e.g., customers, stockholders, employees)?
(2) On what domain of activity is the judgment focused (e.g., service delivery)?
(3) What level of analysis is being used (e.g., individual satisfaction, organizational profitability, industry competitiveness)?
(4) What is the purpose for judging effectiveness (e.g., to recognize achievements, to identify weaknesses, to eliminate waste)?
(5) What time frame is employed (e.g., immediate snapshot indicators versus long-term trend lines)?
(6) What type of data are being used for judgments (e.g., employee perceptions, financial results, customer satisfaction)?
(7) What is the referent against which effectiveness is judged (e.g., effectiveness compared to an ideal standard, compared to past improvement, compared to stated goals)?

Every judgment of effectiveness must answer these seven questions, either explicitly or implicitly, in order to reach a conclusion. When the answer to each question is clearly specified, then acceptable criteria of effectiveness can be clearly identified. Unfortunately, in the organizational behavior literature few writers have been careful enough to specify their answers to each of these questions, so comparable measurements of effectiveness have been difficult to find (see Whetten & Cameron 1994).

Certain common approaches to the definition and measurement of organizational effectiveness have emerged over time; each "era" with its own underlying definition of effectiveness. For example, the earliest models of organizational effectiveness emphasized "ideal types," that is, forms of organization that maximized certain attributes. Max Weber's characterization of BUREAUCRACY as the ideal form of organization is an obvious and well-known example. The most common criterion of effectiveness under this model was efficiency (maximum output with minimum input). The more nearly an organization approached the ideal bureaucratic characteristics – which were designed to produce maximum efficiency – the more effective it was. In other words, the more specialized, formalized, and centralized, the better.

Subsequent models of organizing challenged this bureaucratic model, however, suggesting that many effective organizations were actually nonbureaucratic. The most effective organizations, they argued, were cooperative and participative. Effective organizations satisfied the needs of their members by providing adequate inducements to sustain required contributions. They controlled employee activities via goals, participation, or decision processes, not rules. They became legitimated by linking their role in society to social values (e.g., Likert, 1967).

Over the years, several ideal type approaches have been widely used. The most common model used organizational goal accomplishment as the ideal indicator of effectiveness. If stated goals are achieved, the organization is effective. Advocates of a "natural systems" view of organizations, however, argued that effectiveness ultimately depends on obtaining critical resources (*see* SYSTEMS THEORY; OPEN SYSTEMS). The more resources acquired (e.g., revenues, personnel, recognition), the more effective. Others emphasized the organization's COMMUNICATION and "interpretation" systems, the satisfaction of organizational members, the achievement of profitability, and the consistency of activities with principles of social equity (see Pfeffer & Salancik, 1978; Scott, 1992). The common ingredient among all these models was an advocacy of one definitive, universalistic definition and set of criteria for assessing organizational effectiveness. Organizations are effective if they are characterized by the ideal criteria.

Challenges to this universalistic approach to effectiveness, coupled with mounting frustration over the truth of the claims of the competing models, gave rise to the "contingency theory" approach to effectiveness (e.g., Lawrence & Lorsch, 1967). This approach argued that effectiveness is not a function of the extent to which an organization reflects the qualities of an ideal profile, instead, it depends on the match between an organization's profile and environmental conditions. Definitions of effectiveness were built on the idea of "fit" between certain environmental characteristics and certain organizational characteristics, such as between mechanistic organizational forms and stable, simple environments, and organic forms with rapidly changing, complex environments.

The critical difference between the ideal type and the contingency theory approaches to effectiveness is that the former assumes that "one size fits all." Effective organizations are distinguished by a universal set of attributes. In contrast, contingency approaches argue that organizations are effective only to the extent to which they match the conditions of their environments (*see* ORGANIZATION AND ENVIRONMENT).

A third approach to effectiveness arose when the focus shifted away from the abstract *constructs* (i.e., dimensions) associated with the organization itself and began to focus on the expectations of the organization's constituencies. Effective organizations were defined as those that had accurate information about the expectations of strategically critical constituents and that had adapted internal processes, goals, and values to meet those expectations. Proponents of the "strategic constituencies" perspective viewed organizations as highly elastic entities in a dynamic force field of constituencies that manipulated organizational form and performance (*see* Connolly, Conlon, & Deutsch, 1980) (*see* STAKEHOLDER ANALYSIS). The organization was molded to the demands of powerful interest groups such as stockholders, unions, regulators, customers, and top management. Effectiveness became linked, therefore, to concepts such as customer satisfaction, learning, adaptability, and LEGITIMACY. The assumption was that organizations are effective if they satisfy their customers, or if they are learning systems, or if they are adaptable to constituency demands, or if they acquire legitimacy with their publics (*see* LEARNING ORGANIZATION).

When the expectations of these various constituencies diverged from or contradicted one another, however, organizations were faced with a dilemma. Which constituencies should the organization satisfy and which criteria should be emphasized? Four alternatives emerged in the organizational behavior literature (see Zammuto, 1984):

(1) strive to provide as much as possible to each constituency without harming any other constituency;
(2) strive to satisfy the most powerful or dominant constituency first;
(3) favor the least advantaged constituencies who are most likely to be harmed; and
(4) adapt to the changing set of constituency expectations and respond as rapidly as possible to all of them.

In other words, conscious choices were required under this approach regarding which constituency or set of demands received priority.

This strategic constituencies approach to effectiveness, then, differs from the previous two approaches – ideal type and contingency theory – by emphasizing dynamic criteria of effectiveness. Rather than relying on ideal attributes or on appropriate fit to define effectiveness, this approach relies on key constituencies to determine the most appropriate criteria.

An especially visible manifestation of this strategic-constituencies approach is the current quality movement (*see* TOTAL QUALITY MANAGEMENT). The term quality has overtaken effectiveness, in fact, as the construct of choice in describing and assessing desirable performance in the organizational behavior literature. This represents a significant change in the organizational behavior literature because prior to the late 1980s, quality was treated as a predictor of effectiveness, not a substitution for it. Quality referred to the rate of errors or defects in goods-producing organizations, to institutional reputation in educational organizations, to ambiance and talent in arts organizations, to recovery rates in health care organizations, and to customer satisfaction levels in service organizations. In every case quality was *one* of the desired attributes organizations wanted to pursue, and a qualifier in describing a product or service, i.e., high-quality products, high-quality education, high-quality art, high-quality health care.

However, with the increased visibility achieved by several quality gurus (e.g., Edwards Derning, Joseph Juran, Philip Crosby, Kaoru Ishikawa), quality became an ultimate objective, something of a *summum bonum*, for organizations. "Quality is defined by the customer" was a commonly accepted definition, through which organizational processes, attributes, behavior, and achievements were relevant only if they helped achieve customer satisfaction. At the present time, this perspective, and the strategic constituencies approach it represents, is currently the most frequently utilized approach to effectiveness.

However, the recognition that tensions exist among the demands placed on organizations, that different customers may possess different expectations, and that focusing exclusively on customer satisfaction implies a reactive orientation gave rise to a fourth approach to effectiveness – a paradox approach (Cameron, 1986a). This approach emphasized the paradoxical nature of effective organizational performance. It incorporated elements of each of the three previous models in defining effectiveness as, for example, both fitting with and enacting the external environment, being both responsive to external constituencies (e.g., customers) and being independent of them, being both short- and long-term focused, being both flexible and rigid, being both centralized and decentralized, and being both efficient and malleable. Organizational behavior that is most highly effective, it was argued, is that which is characterized by seemingly paradoxical attributes.

One study concluded, for example, that the presence of simultaneous opposites in organizations created the highest levels of effectiveness, as well as improvements in effectiveness over time, particularly under conditions of environmental turbulence (Cameron, 1986b). Another pointed out that "it is not just the presence of mutually exclusive opposites that makes for effectiveness, but it is the creative leaps, the flexibility, and the unity made possible by them that leads to excellence . . . the presence of creative tension arising from paradoxical attributes helps foster organizational effectiveness" (Cameron, 1986a).

In other words, proponents of this definition of effectiveness argued that effectiveness refers not just to matching an ideal profile, nor matching environmental conditions, nor responding to constituency expectations. Instead, they emphasized that effectiveness is inherently tied to organizations that are simultaneously defensive and aggressive, entrepreneurial and conservative, consistent and inconsistent, reinforcing and destroying traditions, growing and declining, tightly coupled and loosely coupled.

This paradoxical approach to effectiveness also had impact on the definition of quality. Among some (especially the Japanese), quality began to focus on more than the mere pursuit of customer satisfaction, by encompassing attributes of process, structure, and employee behavior as well as the production of products and services. It has taken on the broader meaning and more encompassing label of total quality management.

Despite the fact that organizational effectiveness lies at the center of all theories of organizations (i.e., all theories of organization ultimately rely on the fact that some way to organize or behave is *more effective* than others) despite the fact that organizational effectiveness is an ultimate dependent variable in organizational behavior (i.e., all relationships among organizational elements assume that achieving effectiveness is an ultimate objective), and despite that fact that individuals and organizations are constantly required to maintain accountability for effectiveness (i.e., individuals and organizations are regularly appraised on their performance, which assumes that one kind of performance is more effective than another), one common definition of effectiveness has remained elusive. However, at least four approaches to effectiveness are currently available, each of which has legitimacy and value.

Bibliography

Cameron, K. (1986a). Effectiveness as paradox: Consensus and conflict in conceptualizations of organizational effectiveness. Management Science, 32, 539–553.

Cameron, K. (1986b). A study of organizational effectiveness and its predictors. Management Science, 32, 87–112.

Cameron, K. & Whetten, D. A. (1983). Organizational effectiveness: A comparison of multiple models. New York: Academic Press.

Connolly, T., Conlon, E. & Deutsch, S. (1980). Organizational effectiveness: A multiple-constituency view. Academy of Management Review, 5, 211–217.

Lawrence, P. & Lorsch, J. (1967). Organization and environment. Cambridge, MA: Harvard University Press.

Likert, R. (1967). The human organization. New York: McGraw-Hill.

Pfeffer, J. & Salancik, J. (1978). The external control of organizations. New York: Harper & Row.

Scott, R. (1992). Organizations: Rational, natural, and open systems. Englewood Cliffs, NJ: Prentice-Hall.

Whetten, D. & Cameron, K. (1994). Organizational effectiveness: Old models and new constructs. In J. Greenberg (Ed.), Organizational behavior: The state of the science. NJ: Lawrence Earlbaum.

Zammuto, R. (1984). A comparison of multiple const models of organizational effectiveness. Academy of Manag Review, 9, 606–616.

KIM S. CAMERON

organizational life cycle While it is possible to identify the formal structure of a corporation, at any moment in time this picture is static. In reality, organizations actually evolve, and the pattern of their progress has been observed by many researchers, leading to a number of similar models of evolution which may be termed organizational life cycles. Two such models are illustrated in figures 1 and 2.

Initially, firms tend to be created by individual entrepreneurs or groups. Such firms tend to operate a relatively undiversified product market strategy. Most decisions are taken by the owner–entrepreneur and such firms cannot usually afford professional management skills in most functions. As a result, the organizational structure is informal and there is a lack of professional standards. Most small firms do not progress beyond this stage: this is often by design, in addition to the fact that they do not enjoy strategies that are capable of substantial growth. In such firms it is also difficult for founding entrepreneurs to give up decision making authority to others, and this also tends to block growth prospects. Board structures in such concerns tend to be dominated by the founder and his or her family, and since such concerns are usually privately owned, few have nonexecutive board members.

For those firms which do grow, however, size usually adds some complexity although, as long as the historic product market strategy remains viable, diversification is

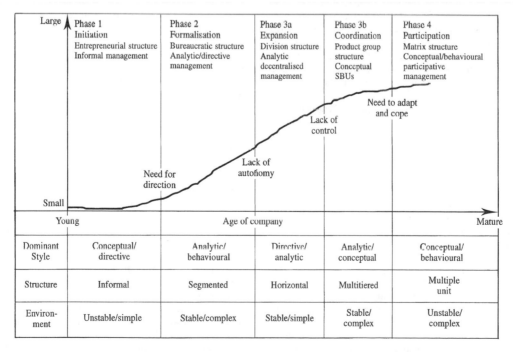

Figure 1 Match of management with organizational life cycle.
Source: Rowe et al. (1994).

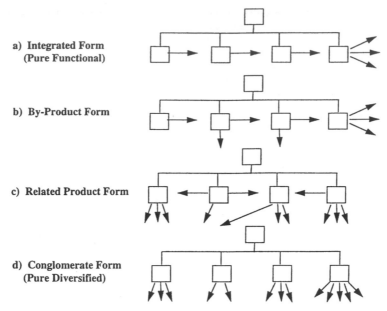

a) Integrated Form
(Pure Functional)

b) By-Product Form

c) Related Product Form

d) Conglomerate Form
(Pure Diversified)

Figure 2 Stages in the transition to the pure diversified form.
Source: Mintzberg (1989).

limited. Nevertheless decision making is necessary and professional management is usually added to create a FUNCTIONAL STRUCTURE. Decisions, while usually still dominated by the founding entrepreneur until his or her death, involve functional specialists operating under direction.

The first major corporate crisis usually occurs with the death or retirement of the founder; unless, of course, he or she is unable to prevent the firm from entering an operational crisis, which also usually results in the removal of the founder. The organizational structure then tends to become a centralized bureaucracy and continues to pursue the original strategy established by the founder, but it lacks the original streak of imagination shown in the creation of the firm.

Eventually, the original strategy tends to mature and – often after the appointment of a new leader – the firm searches for new areas of activity into which to diversify. Such strategic moves usually occur through acquisition, and by this stage many such firms may well have become public companies. Most firms attempt to diversify into product market areas perceived by management to be related to the historic core activities. Unfortunately, this often turns out not to be the case, and many such DIVERSIFICATION moves fail to achieve the expectations of the acquirer.

The organizational changes that accompany such strategic moves tend to result in the adoption of a HOLDING COMPANY STRUCTURE. Initially, a functional holding company system is usually introduced, with the board consisting of the original functional executives together with the CEO of any newly acquired concern. While such diversification moves may well lead to significant increases in corporate sales, profits usually do not grow commensurately. As a result, a further crisis may well develop and the share price may decline, often leading

to a change in either the chairman or the chief executive, or both.

At this point it is common for management consultants to be brought in to help the company introduce a divisional or business unit structure (*see* SBU STRUCTURE), together with suitable management information planning and control systems: the firm is ill equipped to introduce these on its own. The new structure also assists in the development of a cadre of general managers capable of continuing the strategy of diversification. A particular problem occurs with diversification away from a dominant business strategy position, especially where the main business is significantly larger than the diversification moves. In these circumstances the main focus of the board remains centered on the functions of the traditional core business or on geographic areas of operation.

While most diversification strategies move from a single or dominant business to related diversified areas, some firms adopt a conglomerate strategy. While both strategies involve divisional or business unit structures, historically, conglomerate businesses operated with a very small central office, while related diversified concerns tended to have larger central offices, which were required to coordinate activities between operating units. Improved information technology, re-engineering, and the like have tended to result in reductions in the size and scope of the central office of all diversified concerns.

Concurrently with higher levels of product market diversification, many larger firms have also adopted multinational strategies, or environmental and technological factors have required the integration of cross-functional activities. In such firms, a form of MATRIX STRUCTURE has therefore tended to be adopted.

Different leadership styles also tend to be needed at the different stages of the organizational life cycle. In the initial phase, the successful executive is entrepreneurial and creative, usually with a strong dominant personality. Many such individuals tend to come from socially depressed backgrounds and have ethnic origins that involve Jewish, Muslim, or Asian ethics.

In phase 2 (see figure 1) the successful executive focuses on pursuing growth with the original strategy, while introducing a formal functional structure coupled with appropriate financial controls and rudimentary planning systems. The management style tends to be analytic, but to lack the imagination necessary to evolve new strategies.

At the start of phase 3, a new chairman and/or chief executive is charged with breaking out of the historic strategy, usually through acquisition. This is generally accomplished by forceful leadership, with tight centralized control. As a result, the new strategy often fails to achieve its objectives; newly acquired executives find it difficult to work under such a leadership style, and the acquiring firm lacks the appropriate information and control systems to manage a diversified enterprise. As a result, a further leadership change often occurs, to introduce a style embracing a combination of analytic and behavioral skills. Such a leader has a broad strategic vision, a capacity to deal with complex situations, and the ability to achieve results by operating through other managers.

In phase 4, the best leadership style tends to be a combination of analytic, conceptual, and behavioral skills, together with a clear vision for the future direction of the corporation. Such leaders are capable of dealing with high uncertainty, coping with rapid change in the environment and technology, and delegating responsibility across a complex matrix structure.

Bibliography

Channon, D. F. (1973). *The strategy and structure of British enterprise.* Cambridge, MA: Harvard Division of Research.

Galbraith, J. R. & Kaganjian, R. K. (1986). *Strategy implementation.* Los Angeles: West.

Greiner, L. E. (1972). Evolution and revolution as organisations grow. *Harvard Business Review*, 56 (August–September).

Hansen, A. H. (1985). CEO management style and the stages of development in new ventures. Unpublished paper Sasem, OR: Atkinson Graduate School of Management.

Mintzberg, H. (1979). *The structuring of organisations.* Englewood Cliffs, NJ: Prentice-Hall.

Mintzberg, H. (1989). *Mintzberg on management.* New York: The Free Press.

Rowe, A. J., Mason, R. O., Dickel, K. E., Mann, R. B. & Mockler, R. J. (1994). *Strategic management*, 4th edn. Reading, MA: Addison-Wesley. See chapter 11.

Scott, B. R. (1971). The stages of corporate development, part 1. Unpublished paper. Boston, MA: Harvard Business School.

DEREK F. CHANNON

organizational marketing Organizational marketing can be thought of as the activity of marketing between organizations, as opposed to marketing between organizations and individual customers, usually referred to as CONSUMER MARKETING. However, such a simple clarification masks many problems of interpretation and definition. For example, the term "organization" includes many groups which are not primarily concerned with generating profit, such as charities, political parties, military groups, local societies, hospitals, and so on.

It is worth highlighting two central issues in organizational marketing which have profound implications for

marketing and for understanding organizations more generally. The first issue concerns organizational objectives, the guiding light of marketing activities. With the increasing realization of how widely marketing can be applied to organizational activities, organizational devices can no longer be thought of in quite such straightforward terms as "profit maximization" or "shareholder asset growth." For example, it is clear that, at least in principle, charities are concerned with altruism, that orchestras have cultural objectives, that armies aim at enforcement, and that government agencies are directed at efficient administration rather than generating profits. No doubt, many of these objectives are also applicable to conventional business organizations and their constituent sub-units. It is important to appreciate this multi-faceted and overlapping nature of organizational objectives because this kaleidoscope of objectives provides the direction and momentum for marketing activities.

The second issue is the importance of understanding relationships as interactions, rather than as an episodic series of encounters where "manipulative suppliers" engage with "suspicious customers" (Han et al., 1993). Understanding interorganizational relationships as continuing interactions (*see* INTERACTION APPROACH) is important not only to understanding organizations but also to understanding the competitive and strategic dynamics of markets (Håkansson & Snehota, 1989). While the idea of a collaborative interactive relationship is implicit in the idea of marketing as a mutually advantageous exchange, as Chisnall (1995) points out, marketing (more accurately "selling") in business markets has long been presented as an antagonistic zero-sum game where the customer's gain is the supplier's loss. This raises many conceptual and practical questions, not least of which is the difficulty of reconciling traditional views of organizational relationships as necessarily competitive with the increasing representation of these relationships as fundamentally mutually dependent and collaborative.

Both these issues are inextricably linked also with the role of the manager in STRATEGIC MANAGEMENT as an individual with personal objectives and discretionary power rather than, as seems to have been assumed in much of the marketing literature, as a strictly rational organizational servant routinely enacting corporate executive policies (Pettigrew, 1975).

It could be argued, therefore, that organizational marketing is not only an important aspect of marketing but also that it has raised issues with profound implications for a better understanding of marketing and of organizations more generally. In line with these developments in the understanding of the role of marketing, organizational marketing can be seen not simply as the marketing of products and services between organizations but more broadly as the management and development of EXCHANGE relationships between organizations.

As a rule, organizational markets are more complex and larger than consumer markets, if only because for every consumer market there are usually several upstream organizational markets manufacturing and supplying the products marketed to consumers. There are also many large and complex organizational markets providing services where conventional payment may not be involved (e.g., churches, charities, schools, hospitals) or where there may be no direct connection with consumers at all (e.g., military forces).

Another important distinguishing feature of organizational markets is the nature of DEMAND. Demand in organizational markets is derived from a combination of many factors, depending on the market in question. For example, in industrial markets demand is derived from the requirements of downstream suppliers of various consumer goods and services. In government markets demand may also be a function of poland legislative commitments, economic circumstances, political priorities, and lobbying. Forecasting this derived demand is, therefore, highly complex and depends on understanding the needs and circumstances not only of immediate organizational customers, but also of subsequent supplier/customer exchanges right down the value chain to the eventual consumer. Inevitably, many organizations are unable to do much more than respond to the anticipated requirements of their immediate customers. One potentially useful approach to this problem of forecasting demand in organizational markets is to build particularly close relationships with selected customers in various key segments. There can, of course, be many other reasons for building such relationships but the advantage with respect to forecasting problems is that such relationships can provide intimate insights not otherwise available into the competitive position of strategic customers and so of their markets and customers more broadly. (See also RELATIONSHIP MARKETING.)

Much of the theory discussed above seems most obviously appropriate to the more important occasions of organizational marketing – to NEW TASK purchasing and major accounts, to complex customer requirements and intensely competitive markets. However, it should not be forgotten that much of organizational marketing is concerned with routine purchasing in relatively familiar circumstances and with few immediate implications for competitive positions or strategic dynamics. On such occasions the application of the processes and principles discussed above remains relevant but the practice of organizational marketing is more likely to reflect compromises based on experience, work priorities, and common sense.

Bibliography

Chisnall, P. M. (1995). *Strategic business marketing*, 3rd edn, Englewood Cliffs, NJ: Prentice-Hall.

Håkansson, H. & Snehota, I. (1989). No business is an island: The network concept of business strategy. *Scandinavian Journal of Management*, 4, (3), 187–200.

Han, S-L., Wilson, D. T. & Dant, S. P. (1993). Buyer–supplier relationships today. *Industrial Marketing Management*, 22, (4), Nov., 331–338.

Pettigrew, A. M. (1975). The industrial purchasing decision as a political process. *European Journal of Marketing*, 5, Feb., 4–19.

DOMINIC WILSON

organizational purchasing see ORGANIZATIONAL BUYING BEHAVIOR

organizational segmentation The goal of organizational segmentation is to divide a large organizational MARKET into smaller components that are more homogeneous with respect to product needs. Griffith & Pol (1994) argue that segmenting organizational markets is generally a more complex process than segmenting consumer markets since: organizational products often have multiple applications, organizational customers can vary greatly from one another, and it is sometimes difficult to decide which product differences are important.

Bonoma & Shapiro (1984) identify a general approach to segmentation, characterized by ease of implementation, which reflects a major trend in and criticism of organizational segmentation studies. Recently, Dibb & Simkin (1994) have reiterated the complaint that selection of segmentation variables is related to the ease of implementation rather than to how valid the segments are in terms of grouping customers with similar requirements. While academics stress validity, the priority of the practitioner is often to identify segments which can be effectively targeted with a marketing program. In a recent survey of the variables which industrial marketers use in segmentation, the results suggest that variables are chosen more for convenience and actionability than for grouping purchasers with similar needs. The survey found that geographic segmentation bases were the most often used – by 88 percent of the sample. PSYCHOGRAPHICS, e.g., purchaser risk perceptions, were used by only 50 percent of companies, while the most theoretically sound and meaningful base, that of benefit segmentation, was used by only 38 percent of companies (Abratt, 1993). Bonoma & Shapiro (1984, 259) argue that: "Clearly a benefits-orientated approach is the more attractive in the theoretical sense, but more difficult for managers to implement . . . often management and researchers face an interesting 'segmentation tension' between the theoretically desirable and the managerially possible."

While it is acknowledged that any starting point for segmentation should be user requirements in the form of needs and benefits (see MARKET SEGMENTATION; SEGMENTATION VARIABLES), the discussion here focuses on the additional descriptor variables which are only used in organizational markets. These have been grouped into macro variables, based on organizational characteristics, and micro variables based on decision-making characteristics.

Macro Variables

These include standard industrial classification (SIC), organizational size, and geographic location. SIC describes an organization's main type of business, e.g., forestry, and is one of the most common variables used to describe business segments. Although this type of information is quite superficial, it is widely available in a standardized and comprehensive form and allows a firm to assess the potential size of a market segment. When using SIC codes, two cautions must be noted. First, all establishments with the same SIC code do not necessarily engage in the same activities. For example, in the grocery store category, large grocery stores sell more than just grocery items. Second, establishments in a given category do not necessarily account for all, or even a large proportion, of the activity in that category.

Organizational size data in terms of total sales volume or number of employees can easily be obtained and related to an organization's need for some products, e.g., insurance and health care plans which can be modified depending on the number of employees in an organization. However, size can be measured in many ways: total size, size by division, size and number of individual branches, sales value, asset value, other types of activity measure, and number of employees, which can sometimes be related tangentially to purchaser requirements. Dickson (1994) describes two "natural" organizational segmentation variables as being the size of the account and growth potential of the account. If an organization has much of its business with a relatively small number of clients, it cannot help but adopt a RELATIONSHIP MARKETING approach. Such individual relationship segmentation makes consideration of other broader segmentation variables somewhat redundant, but not all companies are in a position to adopt this relationship approach.

Geographic location can indicate purchaser needs when the itself is dependent upon the geography of the area, for example, coal mining and other natural resource industries. Purchasing practices and expectations of companies may also vary by location, e.g., in Central and Eastern Europe. Convenient though it may be to use simple spatial geography to separate complicated purchasing practices or expectations, the variable used to segment the market in this case should be purchasing practice, not geographic location. Using simple geography as anything other than a descriptor variable can be problematic if further criteria are not specified. For example, which geographical location of the business should be used: the site of the buying office, where the products are received, or where they are used? As Griffith & Pol (1994) point out, the first is of concern to sales management, the second to logistics managers, and the third to field service people, installation crews, etc.

Micro Variables

These include choice criteria such as productivity and price. This is akin to benefit segmentation (*see* SEGMENTATION VARIABLES). Decision-making unit (DMU) characteristics identify the nature of the individuals within the DMU and the benefits they perceive. Different members within an organization may value different attributes and benefits. The type of purchasing structure in organizations can also be important, e.g., centralized purchasing is usually associated with purchasing specialists who become experts in buying a range of products.

see also **Market segmentation; Positioning**

Bibliography

Abratt, R. (1993). Market segmentation practices of industrial marketers. *Industrial Marketing Management*, 22, 79–84.

Bonoma, T. V. & Shapiro, B. P. (1984). *Segmenting the industrial market*. Lexington, MA: D. C. Heath & Co.

Dibb, S. & Simkin, L. (1994). Implementation problems in industrial market segmentation. *Industrial Marketing Management*, 23, 55–63.

Dickson, P. R. (1994). *Marketing management* international edn, Orlando, FL: The Dryden Press.

Dickson, P. R. & Ginter, J. L. (1987). Market segmentation, product differentiation and marketing strategy. *Journal of Marketing*, 51, 1–10.

Griffith, R. L. & Pol, L. G. (1994). Segmenting industrial markets. *Industrial Marketing Management*, 23, 39–46.

VINCE MITCHELL

organizational socialization   Organizational socialization is the process of learning the ropes in an organization, or moving from naive newcomer to fully informed insider.

As newcomers become socialized, they learn about the organization and its history, values, jargon, culture, and procedures. They also learn about their work group, the specific people they work with on a daily basis, their own role in the organization, the skills needed to do their job, and both formal procedures and informal norms. Socialization functions as a control system in that newcomers learn to internalize and obey organizational values and practices.

Socialization takes place over weeks or months. It occurs through both formal methods, such as NEW EMPLOYEE ORIENTATION, training, coaching, and MENTORING PROGRAMS, and by informal methods, such as advice from coworkers, observation, experience, and trial and error.

Some authors have distinguished three stages in the socialization process. The first stage is anticipatory socialization, and includes the learning and adaptations newcomers make prior to actually joining the organization. The selection process can be one source of information about the organization, and correct anticipatory socialization should be facilitated by REALISTIC JOB PREVIEWS. The second stage is sometimes called "encounter." In this stage, the newcomer may suffer from reality shock and unconfirmed expectations if anticipatory socialization was found to be inaccurate. This is often a traumatic period of rapid learning, during which the newcomer is regarded as a rookie by others in the organization. The third stage has been called mutual acceptance, adaptation, or metamorphosis. In this stage, the newcomer makes a place for him or herself and becomes accepted as a full insider. The newcomer may change his or her values or work styles to fit the organization, but also may negotiate some accommodation by the organization for his or her own preferences.

Effective socialization results in greater JOB SATISFACTION, organizational commitment, and self-confidence at work, and reduces stress and the likelihood of turnover.

Bibliography

Chao, G. T., O'Leary-Kelly, A. M., Wolf, S., Klein, H. J. & Gardner, P. D. (1994). Organizational socialization: Its contents and consequences. *Journal of Applied Psychology*, 79, 730–43.

Fisher, C. D. (1986). Organizational socialization: an integrative review. *Research in Personnel and Human Resource Management*, 4, 101–45.

Ostroff, C. & Kozlowski, S. W. J. (1992). Organizational socialization as a learning process: the role of information acquisition. *Personnel Psychology*, 45, 849–74.

Wanous, J. P. (1992). *Organizational Entry: Recruitment, Selection, Orientation and Socialization of Newcomers*, Reading, MA: Addison-Wesley.

CYNTHIA D. FISHER

outsourcing   This refers to the activity of purchasing goods or services from external sources, as opposed to internal sourcing (either by internal production or by purchasing from a subsidiary of the organization). In practice, the term tends to be used in connection with a purchasing decision to change from an internal source to an external source. For example, an organization may decide that in future it will "outsource" part of its distribution operation by purchasing distribution services from an organization specializing in this field. The advantages of "outsourcing" can include cost reduction (external sources may enjoy scale economies), access to specialist expertise, and greater concentration on an organization's "core competence" (by avoiding "peripheral" operations). The potential disadvantages of outsourcing can include reduced control over the operations involved and so less flexibility in responding to unexpected developments. It is, therefore, important to take into account both the strategic and the operational implications of outsourcing.

There has been a notable increase in the use of outsourcing during the 1980s and 1990s, for example in UK local government and health markets. It could be argued that this has arisen as a direct consequence of increasing competitive pressures which have forced organizations (often against their cultural predispositions) to outsource "uncompetitive" activities to external specialists and to focus on areas of more sustainable and profitable differentiated competence.

see also **Make/buy decision**

DOMINIC WILSON

overall reciprocity   This takes place when two countries agree to offer one another virtually unrestricted trade concessions. It is the broadest form of reciprocity. Overall reciprocity is one of the ultimate goals of nations belonging to trading groups or blocs. Achievement of overall reciprocity has been found to be an extremely difficult objective.

see also **Reciprocity**

JOHN O'CONNELL

own branding   This is the process whereby a product or service name is developed for or by a retailer for their exclusive use. In some cases the producer of a branded good will produce a similar product for a retailer giving it a different name as chosen by that retailer. In other cases the retailer may contract to have the product manufactured independently. Examples would include Marks and Spencer's "St Michael" range and Sainsbury's "Classic Cola."

Own brand goods are usually positioned in the market place to compete directly with the manufacturers' brands (often appearing next to them in the store) and may even have a very similar appearance and usage characteristics. In other cases stores may stock only their exclusive brands (e.g., Body Shop).

In pursuing such a marketing strategy the retailer may be attempting to create consumer loyalty for his brand and take market share from the competitors. This strategy may also raise the retailer's profile in the consumer's mind. In addition, own branding may allow a retailer to gain an advantage over competitors without own brand products as the perceived quality of own brands increases while still being offered to the customer at a price lower than manufacturers' brands. Dore (1976) recommends a 15 percent discount on similar branded goods.

Problems with an own brand strategy can include increased pressure on limited store display space, and the possible confusion of customers due to an abundance of very similar products.

Bibliography

Dore, B. (1976). Own labels – are they still worth the trouble to grocers? *Advertising and Marketing*, 13, (2), 58–63.

James, G. & Morgan, N. J. (Eds) (1994). *Adding value: Brands and marketing in food and drink*. London: Routledge.

STEVE WORRALL

P

P:D ratios   The P:D ratio of an operation is the ratio of its customer lead time to the total throughput time of its materials. An external customer of an operation judges the speed of any operation by the total waiting time between asking for a product and receiving it. This is the "demand" time, D. But to the operation it is the whole throughput cycle, P, which is important because that is how long the operation will have to manage the flow of materials and information. In a typical make-to-stock manufacturer such as those making consumer durables, customer's demand time, D, is the sum of the times for transmitting the order to the company's order processing system, processing the order to the warehouse or stock point, picking and packing the order, and its physical transport to the customer (the "deliver" cycle). Behind this visible order cycle lie other cycles. The "make" cycle involves scheduling work to the various stages in the manufacturing process. Physically this involves withdrawing materials and parts from input inventories and processing them through the various stages of the manufacturing route and the "purchase" cycle (the time for replenishment of the input stocks) involving transmitting the order to the supplier and awaiting their delivery. For this type of manufacturing the "demand" time which the customer sees is very short compared with the total throughput cycle, the sum of the deliver, make, and purchase cycles, P.

Contrasting with the make-to-stock company is the company which both makes and develops its products to order. Here D is the same as P. Both include an "inquiry" cycle, a "develop" cycle for the design of the product, followed by "purchase," "make," and "delivery" cycles.

Most companies operate with more than one P and more than one D.

Reducing total throughput time P will have varying effects on the time the customer has to wait for demand to be filled. For many customized products, P and D are virtually the same thing. The customer waits from the material being ordered through all stages in the production process. Speeding up any part of P will reduce the customer's waiting time, D. On the other hand, customers who purchase standard "assemble to order" products will only see reduced D time if the "assemble" and "deliver" parts of P are reduced and savings in time are passed on.

Generalizing, D is smaller than P for most companies. How much smaller D is than P is important because it indicates the proportion of the operation's activities which are speculative, that is carried out on the expectation of eventually receiving a firm order for the work. The larger P is compared with D, the higher the proportion of speculative activity in the operation and the greater the risk the operation carries.

But the speculative element in the operation is not there only because P is greater than D; it is there because P is greater than D and demand cannot be forecast perfectly. With exact or close to exact forecasts, risk would be non-existent or very low no matter how much bigger P was than D. When P and D are equal, no matter how inaccurate the forecasts, speculation is eliminated because everything is made to a firm order. Reducing the P:D ratio becomes, in effect, a way of taking some of the risks out of manufacturing planning.

see also **Supply chain management**

NIGEL SLACK

packaging   In the past, commodities were typically sold as loose items, the most widely used form of packaging was a paper bag, and packaging had a purely functional role, i.e., to protect the product. Today, however, the plethora of competing products from which the prospective buyer has to choose points to packaging's role in product promotion by communicating the product's features, benefits, and image. Yavas & Kaynak (1981) argue that an effective package design is a promotional tool and should: attract the prospective buyer, communicate rapidly and clearly, create a desire for the product, and trigger a sale. Southgate (1994) suggests that creative packaging adds value and helps to achieve brand preference. A badly designed package may communicate to the consumer that the product it contains is of low value. Conversely, a well-designed package is evidence of the care and attention that has gone into the product. A package has to sell the product at the point of sale and act as the sales tool in self-service environments.

Bibliography

Southgate, P. (1994). *Total branding by design*. London: Kogan Page, p. 21.

Yavas, V. & Kaynak, E. (1981). Packaging: The past, present and the future of a vital marketing function. *Scandinavian Journal of Materials Administration*, 7, (3), 35–53.

MARGARET BRUCE

parallel loans   A loan between two organizations in a foreign country which turns out to actually involve four organizations in two countries. A parallel loan is a method of offsetting a loan made to a subsidiary in another country. Here is how it works: a subsidiary company in country A needs money to operate. Instead of getting money directly from its parent company (which would involve selling parent company currency and buying subsidiary country currency) a parallel loan agreement is worked out. Subsidiary company number 1 borrows local funds from subsidiary company number 2. The parent companies of both subsidiaries (which are both located in a second country) arrange another loan between each other in their home currency. The second loan offsets the first loan.

Bibliography

Eiteman, D. K., Stonehill, A. J. & Moffett, M. H. (1992). *Multinational business finance*. 6th edn, Reading, MA: Addison-Wesley Publishing.

JOHN O'CONNELL

part-time employment   Part-time employment implies an average working week shorter than the standard – or full-time – week in the same job. Part-time work is associated with the service sector and with female employment but its incidence varies (Rubery and Fagan, 1993) according to country-specific patterns of industrial organization, labor market regulation, and gender relations (Rubery, 1989). Part-time work adds to the flexibility of employment arrangements, allowing for variations in working and operating time at lower costs than full-time work. Its advantages to employers include the opportunity to adjust labor hours to meet variable demand during the day or week, to extend operating hours, to cover unsocial hours, and to increase work intensity through minimizing paid rest periods. Other advantages include opportunities to minimize employment during periods of slack demand, to reduce variable and overhead costs through paying lower basic pay rates, and to exclude part-timers from bonuses, unsocial hours premia, fringe benefits, or social protection contributions. Under European law, application of inferior terms and conditions for part-timers may be regarded as indirect discrimination against women. Part-time work can be used to meet employee needs, to facilitate women staying in or re-entering employment, to provide employment opportunities for students, or a transition into retirement. Even so, the question remains as to whether part-time work is a bridge, facilitating access to employment, or a trap (Buchtemann and Quack, 1989), confining workers, particularly women, to low-paid jobs with limited career prospects.

Bibliography

Buchtemann, C. & Quack, S. (1989). Bridges or traps? Non-standard employment in the Federal Republic of Germany. *Precarious jobs in labour market regulation: the growth of atypical employment in Western Europe*. Eds. Rodgers, G. & Rodgers, J. (eds), Geneva: International Labour Organisation.

Rubery, J. (1989). *Precarious forms of work in the United Kingdom Precarious jobs in labour market regulation: the growth of atypical employment in Western Europe*, Eds Rodgers, G. & Rodgers, J. Geneva: International Labour Organisation.

Rubery, J. & Fagan, C. (1993). Occupational segregation of men and women in the European community. *Social Europe Supplement*, March, 93, 3.

JILL RUBERY

pattern bargaining   Pattern bargaining is an approach to COLLECTIVE BARGAINING where the objective is to spread the terms of employment achieved in one union–management relationship to other bargaining relationships within an industry (automotive, rubber, airlines, and so forth). In pattern bargaining a union negotiates a favorable or "model" agreement with a single employer (or one firm). The union subsequently seeks to reach similar wage and contract terms with other firms in the industry with which the union has a bargaining relationship. Pattern bargaining may also reflect NEGOTIATION TACTICS within one company. The union (or the employer) in a decentralized bargaining arrangement seeks to apply an early contractual settlement to other sites within the same company.

Bibliography

Ready, K. J. (1990). Is pattern bargaining dead? *Industrial and Labor Relations Review*, 43, 272–9.

DANIEL G. GALLAGHER

pay for knowledge, skills, and competencies   Plans that pay employees for their knowledge, skills, and competencies are called pay for knowledge, pay for learning, skill-based pay, and many other names. Here we use the shorthand "skill-based pay" and "SBP" to refer to these plans.

SBP plans pay employees for their repertoire of knowledge, skills, and competencies, not the job they are performing at one point in time. Pay increases are associated with increases in knowledge, skills, or competencies that the organization values, not job changes or increased seniority. Typically, employees must pass some type of formal certification of increased skill before obtaining pay increases. This contrasts with job-based pay systems, where pay typically changes immediately when the job changes. Advancement opportunities for employees tend to be greater under SBP than under job-based pay.

Different types of learning may be rewarded through SBP. Skill depth reflects increasing knowledge about one topic. The skilled trades apprenticeship systems and the technical ladder for professionals are examples of depth-oriented SBP systems. Skill breadth refers to increasing knowledge that is relevant to but different from the employee's job or position. For example, employees may be rewarded for learning all the jobs in a work team or manufacturing plant. This is the form most commonly associated with the term "skill-based pay." SBP plans may also reward the development of self-management skills.

Skill-based pay is the most widely used form of person-based pay. In 1993, 60 percent of Fortune 1000 firms used SBP with at least some employees, up from 40 percent in 1987 (Lawler et al., 1995). Firms using SBP typically cover less than 20 percent of the workforce. SBP plans are now found in every type of manufacturing and service delivery technology and in almost every kind of organizational setting (Jenkins et al., 1992).

Research on skill-based pay is limited. Available research includes survey studies, including one survey of 97 SBP plans (Jenkins et al., 1992), and some case studies (e.g. Ledford, 1991). The results suggest that employees tend to respond favorably to skill-based pay. Most organizations using SBP report few problems and a wide variety of organizational benefits, such as increased productivity and quality. These benefits appear to result from employee flexibility and the facilitation of employee self-management. A consistent finding is that SBP appears more often and is more successful in settings with a high level of employee involvement.

An area of great practitioner interest is the application of the concept to knowledge workers, such as managers and professionals. The SBP concept often is relabeled "competency-based pay" in these settings. There is virtually no research on this type of pay system. Boyatzis's (1982) study of managerial competencies is the foundation for much consulting practice in this area. The differences in the nature of professional work have led to the evolution of new forms of SBP (Ledford, 1995). For example, employees in some firms negotiate learning contracts as part of the PERFORMANCE APPRAISAL system. Others reward employees with BONUSES rather than base pay increases where the underlying knowledge base quickly becomes obsolete.

Bibliography

Boyatzis, R. E. (1982). *The Competent Manager: a Model of Effective Performance*, New York: John Wiley & Sons.

Jenkins, G. D. Jr, Ledford, G. E. Jr, Gupta, N. & Doty, D. H. (1992). *Skill-based Pay: Practices, Payoffs, Pitfalls, and Prospects*, Scottsdale, AZ: American Compensation Association.

Lawler, E. E. III, Mohrman, S. A. & Ledford, G. E. Jr (1995). *Creating High Performance Organizations: Practices and Results of Employee Involvement and Total Quality Management in Fortune 1000 Companies*, San Francisco: Jossey-Bass.

Ledford, G. E. Jr (1991). Three case studies on skill-based pay: an overview. *Compensation and Benefits Review*, 23, 11–23.

Ledford, G. E. Jr (1995). Paying for the skills, knowledge, and competencies of knowledge workers. *Compensation and Benefits Review*, 27, 55–620.

GERALD E. LEDFORD JR

pay for performance Pay for performance, defined as the explicit link of financial reward to individual performance, covers a variety of different pay systems. These systems do, however, share a common structure. Any performance-based pay scheme is founded upon three features: setting performance criteria for the individual employee; assessing whether those criteria have been met; and linking the assessment to financial reward. The various types of systems can be distinguished using these three features.

Performance criteria may be related to what the individual brings to the job in terms of behavioral traits or more tangible outputs, targets or goals (*see* BONUSES). The assessment of those criteria may take different forms in terms of who carries it out (line manager, personnel specialist, peers), when it is carried out (once a year or more frequently), and how it is conducted (formally or informally). The linking of the assessment to reward may be through a consolidated or non-consolidated payment and a general cost of living increase may or may not be incorporated.

There has been much rhetoric surrounding the value and viability of pay for performance. Policy-makers in Britain, for example, have been strongly supportive of the principle. Other commentators, including some of the major management gurus, such as Deming, Peters and Moss Kanter, have been more critical, highlighting its negative impact upon teamwork and cooperation.

Beyond the rhetoric, the evidence suggests that in the United States pay for performance is extensive, while in Britain it is spreading. A survey by the American Association in the late 1980s found that practically all firms relied on annual performance appraisal by supervisors as an input into pay decisions. In Britain the Workplace Industrial Relations Survey 1990 (Millward et al., 1992) found that 40 percent of establishments had individual performance pay for senior and middle managers. It is nevertheless apparent that paying for individual performance is to some degree culturally bound. The Anglo–American emphasis on rewarding individual performance is not matched in certain Eastern countries. Trompenaurs (1993) has stressed the limited attraction of such a pay system in Japan, where seniority and group-based pay have predominated.

The managerial reasons for introducing performance-related pay have varied. It has been used as an *ad hoc* and opportunistic response to immediate pressures (Smith, 1992). Thus, in Britain many organizations have implemented such schemes as a way of recruiting and retaining scarce staff groups. Alternatively some have sought to control their paybill more effectively through targeted pay increases. Other organizations have used pay for performance more strategically to develop a performance culture, to encourage communication between managers and their staff, to facilitate the development of certain management skills, and to foster greater employee commitment (Kessler, 1994).

A number of operational difficulties with such schemes have been highlighted. Major problems have been noted in setting performance criteria for employees involved, for example, in routine or caring work. Subjectivity has been a major concern in relation to assessment. Moreover, the limited amounts of money devoted to paying for performance have often been too small to motivate.

The effectiveness of pay for performance has been challenged by studies which suggest that pay for performance has very little positive impact on motivation (Thompson, 1993). At the same time it is clear that many of the objectives underlying the use of performance pay are less easily measured. The use of performance pay to pursue the longer-term goal of changing organization culture suggests that such schemes may well have considerable life left in them yet.

Bibliography

Kessler, I. (1994). Performance pay. *Personnel Management in Britain*, Sisson, K. Oxford: Blackwell Publishers.

Millward, N., Stevens, M., Smart, D. & Hawes, W. (1992). *Workplace Industrial Relations in Transition*, Aldershot: Dartmouth.

Smith, I. (1992). Reward management and HRM. *Reassessing Human Resource Management*, Eds. Turnbull, P. & Blyton, P. London: Sage Publications.

Thompson, M. (1993). *Performance Related Pay: the Employee Experience*, Brighton: Institute of Manpower Studies.

Trompenaars, F. (1993). *Riding the Waves of Culture*, London: Economist Books.

IAN KESSLER

pay grade/job family Pay grades or job families are classes into which jobs of similar value to the firm are grouped. Because job evaluation is a somewhat subjective process, small differences in the value of jobs may be attributable to subjective error. To lessen the impact of this error on job holders, jobs of similar value are grouped together, classified as one pay grade, and treated identically for compensation purposes. That is, jobs in the same grade have the same minimum worth (pay minimum) and the same maximum worth (pay maximum). Individuals move through pay grades as a function of their individual worth to the firm. Jobs that have work of the same nature, but require different skill and responsibility levels, and that represent steps in a typical promotion path, are identified as part of the same job family.

JERRY M. NEWMAN

pay satisfaction Pay satisfaction is defined as the amount of positive or negative feelings that individuals have towards their pay (Miceli and Lane, 1991). It can be measured using the pay satisfaction questionnaire (PSQ) which is broken down into several pay dimensions towards which individuals have feelings (Heneman and Schwab, 1985). These dimensions are pay level, pay raise, benefits, and structure or administration. Satisfaction with pay level is the perceived satisfaction with direct wages or salaries, whereas satisfaction with pay raises refers to perceived satisfaction with changes in pay level. Satisfaction with structure or administration is defined as perceived satisfaction with the internal pay grades and with the methods used to distribute pay. Satisfaction with benefits concerns perceived satisfaction with indirect payments to the employees.

Pay satisfaction is important as research has shown it to be related to ABSENTEEISM, turnover, and union vote (Heneman, 1985). Possible causes of pay satisfaction include perceived and actual job characteristics (e.g. autonomy), person characteristics (e.g. seniority), and pay plan characteristics (e.g. JOB EVALUATION METHODS, pay secrecy, MERIT PAY, pay innovations, REWARD SYSTEMS). Each dimension of pay satisfaction may have different causes. Hence, for example, the amount of dental insurance offered by an employer is likely to impact benefits satisfaction, but not impact satisfaction with structure or administration.

Bibliography

Heneman, H. G. III (1985). Pay satisfaction. *Research in Personnel and Human Resources Management*, 3, Eds. Rowland, K. M. & Ferris, G. R. Greenwich, CT: JAI Press.
Heneman, H. G. III & Schwab, D. P. (1985). Pay satisfaction: its multidimensional nature and measurement. *International Journal of Psychology*, 20, 129–41.
Miceli, M. P. & Lane, M. C. (1991). Antecedents of pay satisfaction: a review and extension. *Research in Personnel and Human Resources Management*, 9, Eds. Rowland, K. M. & Ferris, G. R. Greenwich, CT: JAI Press.

ROBERT L. HENEMAN

peer ratings To obtain peer evaluations of job performance in organizations, typically coworkers of the organization member to be evaluated are asked to rate him or her on overall performance or on multiple dimensions of performance (job knowledge, planning and organizing, etc.). Reasons for generating peer ratings include providing feedback on performance, obtaining criterion scores for selection or other kinds of research, making predictions of future performance, providing information to aid in promotion decisions and salary allocation, or some other administrative action.

An advantage of peer assessment (relative to SUPERVISORY RATINGS) is that often peers work more closely with the organization member being evaluated than does his or her supervisor. Thus, peers should have better knowledge of his or her performance. A disadvantage is that peers will often have less experience than supervisors of making performance evaluations; therefore, they may tend to provide ratings with more error or bias.

The quality of peer ratings has usually been evaluated according to inter-rater reliability (i.e. how closely two or more peers agree in their independent evaluations of the same organization members), agreement with other rating sources (e.g. supervisor or self-ratings), leniency (i.e. whether the ratings are overly high), or, when appropriate, accuracy regarding the prediction of subsequent perfor-

mance. We now summarize the results in each of these areas.

Kane and Lawler (1978) reviewed 14 studies using peer ratings and found a mean inter-rater reliability of 0.45. This is not very high, but it suggests at least a moderate level of agreement between peer raters evaluating the same persons. Regarding agreement across different rating sources, Harris and Schaubroeck (1988) conducted a meta-analysis of inter-rater agreement across supervisor, peer, and self-ratings. Results for peer ratings were: mean peer–supervisor reliability = 0.62; mean peer–self reliability = 0.35. The peer–supervisor agreement results are encouraging for the reliability of both rating sources.

Regarding leniency, research has shown that self-ratings are most lenient and supervisor ratings are least lenient (Borman, 1991). Peer ratings fall between these two sources. Finally, research, primarily in the military, has demonstrated that peer assessments of leadership can successfully predict subsequent performance as a leader (e.g. Hollander, 1965).

A prevailing opinion about peer ratings is that they are a valuable source of performance information. Peers are likely to provide performance data somewhat different to what the more commonly gathered supervisor ratings provide. Accordingly, experts recommend obtaining performance ratings from multiple sources (e.g. supervisors and peers) (*see* 360 DEGREE APPRAISALS).

Bibliography

Borman, W. C. (1991). Job behavior, performance, and effectiveness. *The Handbook of Industrial and Organizational Psychology*, 2, Eds. Dunnette, M. D. & Hough, L. M. Palo Alto, CA: Consulting Psychologists Press.
Harris, M. M. & Schaubroeck, J. (1988). A meta-analysis of self–supervisor, self–peer, and peer–supervisor ratings. *Personnel Psychology*, 41, 43–62.
Hollander, E. P. (1965). Validity of peer nominations in predicting a distant performance criterion. *Journal of Applied Psychology*, 49, 434–8.
Kane, J. S. & Lawler, E. E. (1978). Methods of peer assessment. *Psychological Bulletin*, 85, 555–86.

WALTER C. BORMAN

penetration pricing Penetration pricing is the term used to describe a PRICING strategy whereby an organization uses a low price in marketing a new product so as to develop a large MARKET SHARE very quickly. For example, penetration pricing might be used by a new entrant aiming to develop a substantial competitive position in a market dominated by an established rival. Alternatively, the strategy might be used to launch a new product where the initial barriers to competitive entry were thought to be low and there was a risk of rivals developing imitative products quickly.

Following successful entry to a market using a penetration pricing strategy, price levels can subsequently be raised (e.g., where the price had been promoted as a temporary introductory discount), although raising prices is often problematic and can generate undesirable market signals. More usually, prices set through a penetration policy are held largely unchanged and become profitable as unit costs decrease in line with the economies of scale made available through growing market share. Scale economies and capital investment requirements in production and distribution can then provide significant barriers to deter new entrants. Thus, the effect of successful penetration pricing is often to accelerate not only the rate of adoption (*see* ADOPTION PROCESS), but also the early stages of the PRODUCT LIFE CYCLE and the emergence of competitive market structures. Alongside these potential advantages, penetration pricing also carries the risks associated with commitment to relatively long-term policies (including reduced competitive flexibility). In short, penetration pricing is likely to be appropriate where there is widespread potential demand for the offering, where this demand can be accessed quickly by the supplier, where significant scale economies are available, and where rivals could otherwise develop imitative offerings promptly.

DOMINIC WILSON

perceived risk The concept of perceived risk can be looked on as an extension of the general conceptual framework of the CONSUMER DECISION-MAKING PROCESS, which may be described as problem-solving activity in which a consumer attempts to identify product performance and psychological goals and to match them with products/brands. However, this involves risk in the sense that any action will produce consequences which cannot be anticipated with anything approaching certainty, and some of which are likely to be unpleasant. Consumers cannot conceive of all possible consequences and those which they are aware of they cannot anticipate with a high degree of certainty.

Consumers may be uncertain with respect to buying goals; their nature, acceptance levels, relative importance, and current levels of goal attainment. They may be uncertain as to which products/brands will best satisfy acceptance levels of buying goals, i.e., the problem of matching goals with purchases. Further, consumers may see adverse consequences if a purchase is made, or not made, and the result is a failure to satisfy buying goals. These consequences relate to: performance goals, i.e., functional ones; psychosocial goals; and the time, money, and effort invested to attain the goals. So one can refer to types of risk as: financial, which is a function of price, length of commitment to a product; social, related to visibility of a product; and physiological, e.g., to do with consumption and harmful physiological effects as with smoking. Roselius (1971) refers to time, hazard, ego, and money losses or risks.

Consumers develop strategies to reduce perceived risk so that they can act with relative ease and confidence in buying situations where information is inadequate and where the consequences of their actions are in some way unknown or incalculable. They either increase certainty (decrease uncertainty) by information handling, or decrease the amount at stake – i.e., the consequences which would occur. Typically, risk handling is largely concerned with dealing with uncertainty and so can be equated with information handling. In respect of buying goals and needs, consumers generate information needs and to satisfy them they acquire, process, and transmit information.

Information acquisition may be accidental or sought from marketer dominated channels, INTERPERSONAL COMMUNICATIONS, or from neutral sources – e.g., consumer reports. Information processing involves evaluation and decisions with respect to use, storage, and forgetting, followed by possible transmission of information to others. Alternatively, to reduce the consequences, consumers can reduce or modify their goals and expectations, avoid or postpone purchases, or purchase and absorb any unresolved risk. Numerous strategies for reducing risk have been researched (see, e.g., Bauer, 1967; Cox, 1967; and Cunningham, 1967) and include: BRAND LOYALTY, to economize on effort, substitute habit for deliberate action/decision; reliance on advertising, to give confidence; consumer reports, to provide objective information – e.g., evidence of government or private testing; personal influence, e.g., word-of-mouth communication with those with experience of the product/brand; group influence, usually stronger when the wisdom of one's choice is difficult to assess; impulse buying, to suppress possible consequences from consciousness and rush through the buying process; store used, its image, reputation, and product range; most or least expensive brand; demonstration, e.g., test driving of cars; special offers; service, to include money back guarantees and exchanges; reliance on well-known brands; and endorsements, e.g., testimonials from experts and personalities.

People use different styles in their choice between increasing certainty and decreasing the consequences of purchases, which depend on their buying goals, products under consideration, personality, and degree of buying maturity or experience. These may relate to: clarifying the purchase situation – typically reacting to ambiguity by seeking new information and increasing understanding; or simplifying – typically avoiding new information and relying on experience of other people.

Bibliography

Bauer, R. A. (1967). Consumer behavior as risk taking. In D. F. Cox (Ed.), *Risk taking and information handling in consumer behavior*. Division of Research, Harvard Business School.

Cox, D. F. (Ed.) (1967). *Risk taking and information handling in consumer behavior*. Division of Research, Harvard Business School.

Cunningham, S. M. (1967). The major dimensions of perceived risk. In D. F. Cox (Ed.), *Risk taking and information handling in consumer behavior*. Division of Research, Harvard Business School.

Roselius, T. (1971). Consumer rankings of risk reduction methods. *Journal of Marketing*, 35, Jan., 56–61.

Taylor, J. W. (1974). The role of risk in consumer behavior. *Journal of Marketing* Apr., 54–60.

BARBARA LEWIS

perfect competition Perfect competition is one of the four BASIC MARKET STRUCTURES which exist in the economic classification system for markets. Although relatively few examples exist where markets completely fit the criteria for this market type, it is one of great focus in economics as it establishes a theoretical benchmark for the criteria needed to achieve socially optimal market performance.

The criteria necessary for perfect competition are as follows:

(1) The market contains a large number of buyers and sellers, each of which is small relative to the size of the whole market.

(2) The product being produced by the rivals in this market is homogeneous and thereby lacking in features – ranging from product attributes (*see* PRODUCT ATTRIBUTES MODEL) to quality differences to sales and service differences – by which each firm's product can be differentiated from its rival's in the eyes of consumers.

(3) Firms in the market have knowledge of and access to the same technology for producing the product, and both buyers and sellers have perfect information as to other conditions in the market.

(4) The entry of new firms into the market may be described as being relatively easy to achieve in that no substantive barriers to entry or exit deter new firms wishing to join the market.

Largely as a result of these criteria, managers of individual firms in this type of market find that they have no control over the price of their product as the combined forces of the market's supply and demand determine the market price for all firms. As such, perfectly competitive firms are said to be *price takers*. In addition, the ease of new entry, in theory, fosters a long run outcome in which price is high enough to cover all costs but does not offer any positive ECONOMIC PROFIT. Moreover, the threat of new entry promotes efficiency by forcing existing firms to minimize costs or be driven out of the market.

Markets most closely fitting the criteria for perfect competition often involve financial markets; commodities, such as agricultural goods; services, such as independent truckers; or the market for unskilled labor.

see also **Oligopoly; Monopolistic competition; Monopoly**

Bibliography

Hirschey, M.   Pappas, J. (1995). *Fundamentals of Managerial Economics.* 5th edn, Fort Worth: Dryden.

GILBERT BECKER

performance appraisal   Performance appraisal is the process of identifying, observing, measuring, and developing human performance in organizations (Carroll and Schneir, 1982). This description is a widely accepted definition of appraisal (Cardy and Dobbins, 1994). Each of the components of this definition refers to an important portion of the appraisal process. The *identification* component refers to the process of determining what areas are to be focused on. Identification typically involves job analysis as a means of identifying performance dimensions and developing rating scales. In terms of the rater, identification means that the evaluator must somehow determine what to examine concerning the ratees. What is identified, of course, should be performance-related criteria and not performance-irrelevant characteristics.

The *observation* component indicates that all appraisal criteria must be sufficiently observed so that fair and accurate judgments can be made. Infrequent observation or observation of nonperformance characteristics will lead to poor ratings.

The *measurement* component refers to the central feature of appraisal. The rater must somehow translate the observations into a value judgment representing the level of the ratee's performance. As pointed out by Banks and Roberson (1985), raters are, in essence, human testing devices. As such, they need to be similarly calibrated (i.e. use similar standards to evaluate ratees' performance). The comparability of measurement standards across raters is an important but under-researched area.

The *development* component suggests that performance appraisal should be more than simply the assessment of past performance. To be complete, appraisal should also focus on improving future performance. This requires that raters be effective performance coaches and that ratees accept appraisal feedback. Problems with any of the other components may make the development phase an impossibility.

This definition is a description of what appraisal should be. Unfortunately, characteristics of the typical appraisal system often fall far short of this ideal (*see* DYSFUNCTIONAL PERFORMANCE APPRAISALS).

Performance appraisal is a central human resource management function, since it is an input or component of so many other human resource management activities (e.g. Landy et al., 1982). Subjective performance ratings are the common criteria against which performance is evaluated. The ratings may also be used to assess the effectiveness of a training program or the validity of a selection mechanism.

Performance ratings also drive a variety of personnel actions. For example, promotions are often largely determined by performance ratings. Training, salary increases, layoffs, and terminations may also be directly tied to performance appraisal.

While appraisal is important in its own right, its involvement in so many other human resource management activities makes it a critical human resource management function.

Bibliography

Banks, C. G. & Roberson, L. (1985). Performance appraisers as test developers. *Academy of Management Review*, **10**, 128–42.

Cardy, R. L. & Dobbins, G. H. (1994). *Performance Appraisal: Alternative Perspectives*, Cincinnati, OH: South-Western.

Carroll, S. J. & Schneir, C. E. (1982). *Performance Appraisal and Review Systems: the Identification, Measurement, and Development of Performance in Organizations*, Glenview, IL: Scott, Foresman.

Landy, F., Farr, J. L. & Jacobs, R. R. (1982). Utility concepts in performance measurement. *Organizational Behavior and Human Performance*, **30**, 15–40.

ROBERT L. CARDY
and GREGORY H. DOBBINS

performance diaries   Performance diaries are typically used for PERFORMANCE APPRAISAL purposes. Raters use diaries to record critical work behaviors of ratees whom they observe during the appraisal period (Bernardin and Walter, 1977). Diaries also may be used in other ways, such as when role incumbents are asked to record their own behaviors as part of a JOB ANALYSIS, criterion validation, or self-management study. In performance appraisal, the purpose of a performance diary is to document the occurrence of target behaviors and the conditions under which they occur, thereby facilitating evaluations of performance and related personnel decisions.

Event-contingent Sampling

Performance diaries can be thought of as a behavior sampling technique. Raters are encouraged to keep diaries in order to increase the sample of observations upon which evaluations are made. Several behavior sampling techniques exist (see Wheeler and Reis, 1991), but the most common technique for performance diaries is event-contingent sampling. In event-contingent sampling, individuals record specific events (e.g. task behaviors) each time they are observed and note important characteristics of the event. This type of sampling represents a CRITICAL INCIDENTS TECHNIQUE approach to performance measurement.

The Promise of Performance Diaries

RATING ACCURACY has been a longstanding concern among human resource management practitioners and researchers. Research on raters' cognitive processes suggests that memory decay and biased observation result in a low correspondence between actual behaviors and ratings. For example, raters use different cues, such as knowledge about the ratee or job, as well as the purpose of the appraisal, to form impressions of ratees, which then influence the amount and types of information to which raters attend (Ilgen et al, 1993). Performance diaries have been offered as a way to reduce memory and observation biases (Lee, 1985).

There are several ways in which performance diaries may increase rating accuracy. First, diaries reduce memory demands placed on raters. They provide raters with a "hard copy" of their observations at the time ratings are made, thereby reducing subjectivity and bias in recall (DeNisi et al., 1989).

Second, diary-keeping reinforces the importance and relevance of certain behaviors at the time of observation. By making behaviors more salient, diaries may reduce the influence of global impressions on observation. Combining diaries with BEHAVIORALLY ANCHORED RATING SCALES may be an especially effective technique for focusing rater attention on critical behaviors (Bernardin and Walter, 1977; Bernardin and Beatty, 1984).

A third benefit, proposed by cognitive researchers, is that diaries structure the way information is organized in memory. The organization of performance information in memory has been related to recall and rating accuracy (Williams et al., 1990), and organizing performance diaries by person categories, as opposed to task categories or no specific categories, may hold the most promise for improving accuracy (DeNisi et al., 1989; DeNisi and Peters, 1992).

A fourth benefit of diaries is that they improve estimates of the frequency, distribution, and intensity of ratee behavior. Such information is often under-utilized in traditional performance appraisals.

Concerns Surrounding the Use of Diaries

A common problem with performance diaries is response decay: rates of responding by raters tend to decrease over time, due to fatigue or motivation loss. A second concern is participant cooperation. The benefits of performance diaries will only be realized to the extent that raters are willing to use them properly. Also, diary-keeping is not immune to the observational biases mentioned earlier. Impressions of ratees and contextual cues will influence how behavior is interpreted and recorded, in addition to how it is observed.

Summary

If managed properly, performance diaries may be a useful tool in the performance appraisal process. Current research suggests that diary-keeping should emphasize specific behaviors related to task success, and should be organized by persons. Rater training and incentives should be used to ensure that a sufficient number of incidents is sampled, that a distribution of performance is attained, and that environmental conditions affecting performance are identified (Bernardin and Beatty, 1984).

Bibliography

Bernardin, H. J. & Beatty, R. W. (1984). *Performance Appraisal: Assessing Human Behavior at Work*, Boston, MA: Kent Publishing.

Bernardin, H. J. & Walter, C. S. (1977). Effects of rater training and diary-keeping on psychometric error in ratings. *Journal of Applied Psychology*, 62, 64–9.

DeNisi, A. S. & Peters, L. H. (1992). Diary keeping and the organization of information in memory: a field extension (paper presented at the Annual Meeting of the Society for Industrial and Organizational Psychology, Montreal, Canada, May).

DeNisi, A. S., Robbins, T. & Cafferty, T. P. (1989). Organization of information used for performance appraisals: role of diary-keeping. *Journal of Applied Psychology*, 74, 124–9.

Ilgen, D. R., Barnes-Farrell, J. L. & McKellin, D. B. (1993). Performance appraisal research in the 1980s: what has it contributed to appraisals in use? *Organizational Behavior and Human Decision Processes*, 54, 321–68.

Lee, C. (1985). Increasing performance appraisal effectiveness: matching task types, appraisal process, and rater training. *Academy of Management Review*, 10, 322–31.

Wheeler, L. & Reis, H. T. (1991). Self-recording of everyday life events: origins, types, and uses. *Journal of Personality*, 59, 339–54.

Williams, K. J., Cafferty, T. P. & DeNisi, A. S. (1990). The effect of appraisal salience on recall and ratings. *Organizational Behavior and Human Decision Processes*, 46, 217–39.

KEVIN J. WILLIAMS

performance evaluation (international managers) Managers (or any other employee) are expected to successfully perform a number of tasks and/or assignments for an organization. In order to determine the extent of a manager's success in carrying out required activities, periodic appraisals of performance are strongly advised. To be effective, a performance evaluation must concentrate on those factors which are within a manager's control and are included in a clear statement of the manager's scope of authority and responsibility. To judge the performance of a manager on the basis of factors which are uncontrollable or not within the scope of authority or responsibility granted is unfair and not responsive to the purpose of an evaluation. Although an evaluation system that includes factors over which a manager has no control may not result in a poor rating of the manager, it will result in a rating that does not realistically portray the achievements of the manager within his/her stated job objectives.

Areas of performance measurement usually used for managers include: meeting budgets; production goals; sales goals; quality of product or service measures; profitability of department; and market share. All of these items are normally subject to measurement and control on the part of the manager when a domestic operation is being reviewed. However, international managers may not have the same degree of control over these or other factors when business is carried out in another country. Evaluation factors must be reviewed in terms of the conditions in the host country. Profits may be restricted because of local laws or tax structures; market penetration may be closely monitored and governed by the host government; production figures, etc. may be partially determined by the continued availability of trained labor, raw materials and other resources, some of which may be in short supply or in intermittent supply in a foreign country; and quality and service measures may not be comparable with home country operations because of the inability to obtain data or different standards which may apply in the host country.

Evaluating the managers of foreign operations requires a good deal of work to establish the standards by which comparisons will be made. Using the experience of former expatriate managers and sharing of ideas in professional meetings are two ways of gaining additional insight into the problem. The three most important things to remember are: (1) the areas of evaluation must be under the control of the manager to be evaluated; (2) the evaluators must be well versed and aware of the host country environment in which the manager is expected to perform; and (3) the input of the expatriate manager must become a part of the evaluation process in order to explain the peculiar differences the manager has encountered in running an overseas operation.

Bibliography

Carroll, S. J. & Schneier, C. E. (1982). *Performance appraisal and review systems.* Glenview, IL: Scott, Foresman.

Caudron, D. (1991). Training ensures success overseas. *Personnel Journal*, **70**, 27–30.

Dowling, P. J. & Schuler, R. S. (1990). *International dimensions of human resource management.* Boston, MA: PWS-Kent.

JOHN O'CONNELL

performance management   Performance management should be the primary goal of any appraisal system. While measurement is important, what is critical is what is done with the evaluations. A complete appraisal process includes informal day-to-day interactions between managers and workers as well as formal face-to-face interviews, all aimed at improving ratees' levels of effectiveness.

Appraisal interviews, part of the formal performance management system, are typically done annually to provide feedback to ratees. The appraisal interview often involves discussion of both performance and salary. However, some companies have shifted to a system, referred to as split reviews, in which performance and salary discussions occur in separate interviews. However, research has found that discussion of salary in an appraisal review session has a positive impact on how employees perceive the usefulness of the review (Prince and Lawler, 1986). Discussion of salary may have a positive impact by increasing the meaningfulness of the interview session for both the rater and the ratee.

Formal appraisal interviews are typically conducted once a year and, thus, may not have a lasting impact on performance (Bernardin and Beatty, 1984). Informal day-to-day performance feedback is probably more useful for that purpose.

Effective performance management requires: (a) identifying and controlling system influences on performance; (b) developing an action plan and empowering workers to reach solutions; and (c) directing communication at performance, rather than at the performer (Gomez-Mejia et al., 1995).

Identification of system factors involves careful study of the work situation by the rater and ratee. System factors are any influences on performance that are external to the worker. A joint and systematic consideration of possible external influences on performance can help to create a partnership between the rater and ratee and be an important basis for the improvement of performance. Once the system factors are identified, the rater and ratee can work together to try to eliminate or reduce their influences on performance.

Developing an action plan and taking an empowered approach means that the rater should help the ratee to identify ways to effectively deal with the work situation. Empowering the worker to deal with the work situation requires that the rater be a coach rather than a director or controller. Making suggestions, providing immediate feedback, helping to eliminate unnecessary constraints, and other coaching activities can create a supportive work environment and lead to meaningful and long lasting performance improvement.

Communication between a rater and ratee is critical to effective performance management. How a rater communicates with a ratee about performance can determine whether performance improves or declines. Communication should address the characteristics of the performance and not characteristics of the performer. In addition, communication that might cause the ratee to be defensive should be avoided.

Bibliography

Bernardin, H. J. & Beatty, R. W. (1984). *Performance Appraisal: Assessing Human Behavior at Work*, Boston: Kent.

Gomez-Mejia, L. R., Balkin, D. B. & Cardy, R. L. (1995). *Managing human resources*, Englewood Cliffs, NJ: Prentice-Hall.

Prince, J. B. & Lawler, E. E. (1986). Does salary discussion hurt the developmental appraisal? *Organizational Behavior and Human Decision Processes*, **37**, 357–75.

ROBERT L. CARDY
and GREGORY H. DOBBINS

performance standards   Performance standards are criteria against which individuals' behaviors and outcomes are judged in order to evaluate their performance. There are three features which define performance standards (Bobko and Colella, 1994). First, standards have an *evaluative* component. That is, they serve as criteria for judging effectiveness. Second, standards are *externally established.* Finally, performance standards are usually considered to be *established entities*, which usually remain stable over time and across individuals. Locke and Latham (1990, p. 7) define performance standards as "a rule to measure or evaluate things." They distinguish between standards and goals, by defining the latter as the "aim or end of an action." Bobko and Colella (1994) further distinguish between goals and standards by pointing out that standards are usually consistent across individuals, whereas goals are usually assigned on an individual basis.

Performance standards are essentially ubiquitous in organizations. Common examples include sales quotas, standards for making partners in a law firm, and manufacturing piece rate systems. Standards are used in a variety of personnel decisions, including, but not limited to, PERFORMANCE APPRAISAL, training, promotion, and PAY FOR PERFORMANCE. Despite the frequent presence of performance standards in organizational life, little research has directly focused on issues such as how organizations currently set standards, how they should set standards, and the consequences of various standard setting procedures (Murphy and Cleveland, 1991). Much more research has been conducted on selection standards rather than performance standards. The education literature, in particular, has focused a great deal on standard setting in education (see Pulakos et al., 1989) for a review.

Despite this lack of research, several practical guides to setting performance standards exist. For example, Carlyle and Ellison (1984) suggest that standards should be concrete and specific, practical to measure, meaningful, realistic and based on a sound rationale, and consistent across similar jobs.

Bobko and Colella (1994) suggested that standards that exist for evaluative purposes can also influence the motivation and job satisfaction of those to whom the standards are applied. These authors reviewed a variety of literatures related to standard setting (e.g. goal setting and feedback literatures) and proposed characteristics of standards that are likely to influence employee job motivation and satisfaction. These characteristics include who sets the standards, whether outcomes and rewards are tied to meeting these standards, the difficulty of the standards, whether some standards conflict with other standards, the specificity of the standards, whether the standards are focused on behaviors versus outcomes, the valence of the standards, how standards are framed, whether employees participated in standard setting, single versus multiple standards, and whether the standard is static or can be expected to change.

Bibliography

Bobko, P. & Colella, A. (1994). Employee reactions to performance standards: a review and research propositions. *Personnel Psychology*, 47, 1–29.
Carlyle, J. & Ellison, T. (1984). Developing performance standards. *Performance Appraisal: Assessing Human Behavior at Work*. Eds. Bernardin, J. & Beatty, R. Boston: Kent.
Locke, E. & Latham, G. (1990). *A Theory of Goal Setting and Task Feedback*, Englewood Cliffs, NJ: Prentice-Hall.
Murphy, K. & Cleveland, J. (1991). *Performance Appraisal: an Organizational Perspective*, Boston: Allyn and Bacon.
Pulakos, E., Wise, L., Arabian, J., Heon, S. & Delaplane, S. E. (1989). *A Review of Procedures for Setting Job Performance Standards*, Alexandria, VA: US Army Research Institute.

ADRIENNE COLELLA

personal influence *see* INTERPERSONAL COMMUNICATIONS

personal selling Personal selling is the process of informing customers and potential customers and persuading them to purchase products and services through oral personal communication in an exchange situation, either face to face or on the telephone. It is a two-way channel of communication (*see* MARKETING COMMUNICATIONS) which has a number of advantages: customers can inquire, discuss, or even bargain; there is immediate, interactive response; a company can get feedback; and the company can relate to specific consumer needs. Personal selling aids in the cultivation of buyer–seller relationships (*see* RELATIONSHIP MARKETING), especially in organizational buying (*see* ORGANIZATIONAL BUYING BEHAVIOR).

The characteristics and personality of sales people is important, in particular because persuasion techniques, including the use of inducements, may be relevant. Customers may see personal selling activities as biased and react negatively to their obligation to listen and to persuasion techniques, etc. It is an expensive form of communication, and potential customers may not always be accessible.

Personal selling takes place in the home, in stores and other organizations (i.e., in business-to-business interactions) and involves the sales force and sales persons who as well as providing information may be active in tasks such as order taking, delivery, and market research.

see also **Communications mix; Marketing communications; Sales management**

Bibliography

Dalrymple, D. J. & Cron, W. L. (1995). *Sales management: Concepts and cases*. New York: John Wiley.
Lidstone, J. (1994). In M. J. Baker (Ed.), *The marketing book*, 3rd edn, Oxford: Butterworth-Heinemann. Chapter 19.

DAVID YORKE

personality As far back as 1937, Gordon Allport identified fifty different definitions for the term personality. The most widely used scientific definition identifies personality as that set of nonphysical and nonintellectual psychological qualities which make a person distinct from other people.

Status within OB

Within the field of organizational behavior, personality has been defined, measured, and studied in vastly different ways. Moreover, the very value of personality constructs in understanding organizational behavior has itself been a matter of much controversy over the decades and has been questioned on both conceptual and empirical grounds. Conceptual criticism has come from both ends of the theoretical spectrum. On the one hand, radical humanists see the use of personality dimensions as reductionist, as breaking apart the essential uniqueness of each individual. On the other end of the theoretical spectrum, radical behaviorists see the study of personality as attempting to measure variables not directly observable, an incursion into the "black box" which falls beyond the scope of scientific inquiry.

On empirical grounds, the proved contributions of personality variables to our understanding or work behavior have been limited. Positive findings, when they appear, are often of marginal significance and personality effects within a given research area are often inconsistent. These disappointing results within OB are consistent with empirical findings in other areas of personality research. Best known is Mischel's (1968) famous critique of personality research in which he claimed, after reviewing the literature, that behavior is inconsistent across situations, and that rarely do personality variables account for more than 10 percent of the variance in criterion behaviors of interest. Mischel argued that behavior is largely determined by situational factors.

Many scholars within OB, following Mischel (1968), have made the same argument, that behavior in work organizations is largely situationally determined. Accordingly, the thrust of research on JOB ENRICHMENT, expectancy Vie theory of work MOTIVATION, job attitudes and many other areas has emphasized situational determinants. The approach recommended to organizations for creating a motivated work force, for example, is not necessarily to hire people who are dispositionally high in motivation, but rather to expand job scope, alter reward contingencies, and empower the work force.

Weiss and Adler (1984) questioned this bias against personality, arguing that the potential for personality in theory, research, and practice within OB has, in fact, scarcely been explored. In area after area, research typically does not adequately test for personality effects. Often personality is of secondary interest to the researcher and is accordingly treated marginally, given little thought, and studied in inappropriate settings using inappropriate designs. A conservative evaluation of the role of personality within OB, conclude Weiss and Adler, is that this role has simply not yet been adequately examined.

The negative view of personality was so widely accepted within OB for so long that there are whole areas of personality research which once were productive and then almost completely abandoned. Selection testing, the study of work attitudes, and LEADERSHIP all were areas in which decades of interest in personality were followed by decades of uninterest. Only very recently have researchers in these areas begun reexamining the value of personality. The past few years indeed have generally seen some increased interest in personality within OB, marked by the publication of several important summaries of theory and research on this topic (e.g., Barrick & Mount, 1991; Brockner, 1988; Furnham, 1992; Hogan, 1991).

Personality Traits

OB researchers and practitioners have studied a wide range of personality constructs. Among the more widely studied are self-esteem, self-efficacy, achievement motivation, LOCUS OF CONTROL, and extroversion. These constructs all reflect a particular conception, which describes personality in terms of traits. There have been other approaches to conceptualizing personality, the most prominent being psychoanalytic approaches. These non-trait approaches have contributed insightful analyses of important aspects of behavior in organizations e.g., organizational neurosis. Psychodynamic approaches have also been used in clinical applications to human resources management, such as in treating psychopathology that impacts on work behavior or in screening out high-risk candidates for positions that involve potential danger to the public (e.g., police officers and airline pilots). However, the overwhelming preponderance of empirical personality research in OB has adopted traits as the unit of analysis.

Personality traits are seen as internal psychological structures or properties that relate to regularities in behavior. For example, people scoring high on a measure of conscientiousness are more likely than those scoring low in that trait to attend to details when performing a task, to double-check calculations before submitting financial projections to their manager, and to exert a high level of energy to achieve an assigned objective.

A somewhat different conception of traits has been advanced by Hogan (1991) who has suggested that personality traits can better be understood as dimensions of a person's social reputation. That is, if your behavior leads others to see and describe you as conscientious, then you are high in the trait of conscientiousness, whether or not this trait really exists internally.

Personality traits are generally thought of as dimensions or continuous variables. People are seen as being arrayed on a continuum with respect to the attribute in question, being low, medium, or high in self-esteem, for instance. Thinking of personality traits as continuous variables corresponds to how ability attributes (e.g., intelligence, individual differences) are generally conceptualized. Continuous trait measures are also amenable to the correlation-based statistical techniques that have been the primary tools of organizational researchers. There is some evidence, though, that a few personality traits may be more fruitfully conceptualized as typologies or class variables. The extent to which people are or are not disposed to adapt their behaviors and attitudes to environmental cues, entitled Self-Monitoring, is one such typology. Programmatic research (Gangestad & Snyder, 1985) supports the notion that high- and low- self-monitors are really two different types of people, and not merely opposite ends of a single continuum. There is similar evidence that the trait of STRESS-proneness is a class variable yielding two distinct types of people, Type A and Type B.

Rather than developing their own models of personality, OB researchers almost always draw on personality constructs and measures from existing personality models, although unfortunately without always examining in-depth the theoretical and empirical base from which these constructs and measures are drawn. Some OB researchers, though, have both drawn on and contributed to basic personality theory. For example, Brockner (1988) has developed a model of self-esteem and behavioral plasticity, defined as the susceptibility of people low in self-esteem to social influence. Brockner has systematically examined that influence on the expectations, motivations, and attributions of those high and low in self-esteem before, during and after task performance (*see* ATTRIBUTION). This work has contributed to both OB and basic self–esteem theory.

OB researchers have similarly developed an appreciation of work in personality theory identifying dispositional differences in emotionality and have applied these developments to better understand the causes and consequences of JOB SATISFACTION. Staw and his colleagues (see Judge, 1992, for a summary of this area) first demonstrated the surprisingly strong consistency of job attitudes over relatively long periods of time (3–5 years), even as respondents change jobs and organizations. Later research showed that general tendencies toward a positive or negative evaluation of life evidenced as early as the teen years can predict specific job attitudes decades later. People with optimistic, emotionally positive, dispositions are consistently more satisfied on the job than those with more negative, anxious, pessimistic, and cynical dispositions. Subsequent research demonstrated the role of these differences in affective disposition in the complex linkages between job satisfaction, other work attitudes and stress. Recent evidence from studies of identical twins reared apart suggests that these dispositional differences in positive and negative emotionality may actually be reflected in genetic effects on job attitudes, though the linkage remains controversial.

These two examples represent a trend toward the more serious consideration of basic personality theory when its constructs are incorporating OB models.

Role in OB Models

There are essentially four ways that personality has been treated in models of work behavior:

1. *As simple predictors.* In these models a single personality trait is hypothesized to have a direct effect on some relevant criterion variable. For example, a measure of Extraversion is expected to predict sales performance. These simplistic bivariate models are conceptually limited; most complex behaviors of interest to organizations cannot be adequately explained by isolated personality traits. Indeed, these models have also proved to be empirically limited; rarely does a single trait explain more than a small proportion of variance in work-relevant criteria. Moreover, although much of the OB research fitting this model is actually cross-sectional in design — that is, both the personality trait and the criterion are measured at the same point in time – significant correlations between traits and criteria are too often interpreted in terms of the personality variable having had a causal effect on the criterion in question. It is a well-known principle that correlation is not necessarily proof of causality.

2. *Interacting with other factors.* In this more sophisticated conceptualization, the effects of a personality variable on a criterion are considered at least partially dependent on another factor, most commonly a situational factor. For example, people high in Achievement Motivation will show more effort than those low in Achievement Motivation only in competitive situations. In noncompetitive situations, no significant difference in task effort is expected between those high and low in Achievement Motivation. This kind of interaction model underlies work on PERSON–JOB FIT, the notion being that people will be most content and productive in work situations that are suited to the individual's ability and personality dispositions. Correspondingly, some interaction models posit that the effects of a situational factor on behavior depend on a personality factor. For instance, high-pressure work environments are more likely to produce symptoms of stress in those with Type A rather than Type B personalities. The interactive effect of two or more personality constructs on behavior can and has been studied in the same way. As an example of this configural approach, McClelland's Leadership Motive Pattern (*see* LEADERSHIP) predicts that the most effective leaders will be those who are high in need for power, low in need for affiliation, and high in Activity Inhibition (*see* POWER). In contrast with models focused on single personality predictors, interactive models can be used to investigate more complex multivariate relationships.

3. *As impacted by situations.* In both the simple and complex models described above, personality is seen as a causal factor. It is possible to treat personality as a dependent variable, impacted by situational factors. Long-

itudinal research has shown, for instance, that long-term assignment to simple, repetitive work results in a decrease in an individual's cognitive complexity and flexibility. Personality has been conceptualized as the dependent variable in studies on the effects of rural versus urban upbringing on adult work needs and of job mobility on LOCUS OF CONTROL. The Management Progress Study (Howard & Bray, 1988) conducted over a 20-year period at AT&T similarly showed how certain personality traits can change as a function of CAREER advancement (*see* CAREER STAGES). Obviously, research on how work experiences affect personality are of immense theoretical and practical interest, especially since most people spend such a large portion of their waking hours in the work place. However, it is important to remember that adult personality traits are likely to change slowly and only with prolonged exposure to psychologically salient environmental factors. Testing models of this type requires carefully planned longitudinal research.

4. *In dynamic interplay with situational factors.* Even more rare are those dynamic models which describe some process in which personality, behavior and situations are seen as continuously influencing each other. The following model serves as an illustration. More Dogmatic individuals, if given a choice, will prefer to interact with people whose opinions are likely to be similar to their own. Prolonged exposure to like-minded others will subsequently strengthen the confidence that Dogmatic people have in the veracity of their own opinions, making their thinking become more rigid over time. This type of polarization of traits over time, in fact, was noted for several of the personality factors studied in the AT&T longitudinal study (Howard & Bray, 1988). Managers who were initially high in achievement orientation were more likely to advance up the managerial hierarchy than those low in achievement orientation. As a consequence of having advanced, achievement orientation grew stronger over time. The opposite was true for those who failed to advance. These dynamic models suggest that the most important role for personality may be through the influence of personality traits on the choices people make about which situations to enter. Once in a particular situation, indeed situational forces may have the dominant role in shaping how people behave, as Mischel (1968) and others have argued. It should also be noted that in any given study based on dynamic models of the reciprocal influences of personality and on personality, the personality construct of interest may be treated as both the dependent and independent variable. Sophisticated multivariate techniques are now available for untangling the effects of personality and situational factors on each other.

Whatever the role assigned to personality in OB models, these models also vary in the extent to which the links between the personality construct and the criterion of interest are specified. Brockner's (1988) Behavioral Plasticity Model very clearly specifies how self-esteem is ultimately linked to plasticity. Those low in self-esteem are more concerned with securing social approval. Consequently, they are more attentive than those high in self-esteem to social cues relevant to approval, such as negative feedback or INFLUENCE attempts.

When these cues occur, people low in self-esteem are more likely to notice and respond with conformity, a strategy more likely to bring the desired approval from others. In contrast, Fiedler's contingency theory of leadership, for example, hypothesizes that leaders with a relations-oriented personality are most effective in certain leadership situations and least effective in other situations. However, the theory does not specify the mediating processes which link the leader's personality to work group performance. Several reviews of the literature have shown that carefully thinking through the potential linkages of personality and job performance (e.g., by first conducting a JOB ANALYSIS to identify tasks that might be impacted by a particular trait) enhances the chances of finding significant validities for measures of personality in predicting performance criteria (see VALIDITY).

Although there are various ways, then, that personality could potentially be incorporated within OB models, it is clear that most existing models have either ignored personality altogether or have assigned to it a conceptually limited role. Many of the models that do incorporate personality variables fail to adequately specify how those variables are linked to criteria of interest. Few studies have employed longitudinal designs; the emphasis has been on correlational designs or relatively short-term experimentation. Consequently, it has not been possible within OB to adequately study the effects of work on personality or the dynamic interplay of personality and situations. Hopefully, the future will see the emergence of more elaborate, conceptually rich, treatments of personality in OB theory to guide productive research and application.

Predictive Power

The availability of multiscaled inventories widely used in organizations to measure personality has been partially responsible for atheoretical approaches to studying personality in OB. These inventories yield scores on 10–30 different traits, allowing researchers to take a "shot-gun" approach; since it is probable that a few of these traits will significantly correlate with a criterion. Not surprisingly, this body of research produced little by way of consistent and meaningful findings.

One of the major developments in personality psychology has been the consolidation of this assortment of individual, particularistic traits into a more coherent taxonomy, the Big Five Model (Barrick & Mount, 1991; McCrae & Costa, 1987). The Model proposes five broad dimensions of personality: Extraversion (or Surgency), Stability (or Neuroticism), Agreeableness (or Likability), Conscientiousness (comprising achievement-orientation and Dependability), and Openness. Several personality inventories have been developed around the structure of the Big Five Model and specifically validated for use in employment settings (e.g., the NEO Personality Inventory, McCrae & Costa, 1987). These inventories have demonstrated a high degree of stability over time, perhaps because they measure fewer, more abstracted, personality dimensions than did the earlier inventories.

Using the Big Five model to statistically summarize previous research, Barrick and Mount (1991) found that Conscientiousness is moderately predictive of a range of performance criteria across a range of occupational categories. Some of the other Big Five dimensions were specifically related to particular criterion categories for particular occupational groups. The analysis by Barrick and Mount (1991) as well as other statistical reviews make it very clear that, at best, within simple predictive models, individual Big Five dimensions will have only moderate power in predicting job performance criteria. However, it is important to note that these broad personality dimensions have little or no relationship to the mental ability dimensions so often used to predict performance criteria. Consequently, measures of the Big Five may well significantly enhance the predictive power of existing ability-focused models of individual performance.

Although the Big Five Model has brought some coherence to the study and measurement of traits, there is still controversy about whether five broad dimensions is adequate to describe individual differences in personality. Different scholars, and various inventories, break the Big Five down into a list of anywhere from 6 to 11 somewhat more narrowly defined dimensions. For example, Hogan (1991) distinguishes between two aspects of Extraversion, Sociability, and Ambition. Those proposing a longer list of dimensions argue that the Big Five do not allow for fine-tuned analyses of personality profiles, especially needed when diagnosing the suitability of job candidates. On the other hand, it should be noted that one of the earliest, most sophisticated and enduring of trait taxonomies, that developed by Hans Eysenck (see Furnham, 1992), consists of just three broad dimensions: Neuroticism, Extraversion, and Psychoticism.

Attempts to enhance the predictive power of personality variables go beyond consideration of how those constructs are categorized and address the organizational context in which personality-criteria relationships are examined. One critical contextual factor is situational strength. Strong situations are those which provide people with: salient and clear cues, a high degree of structure, uniform expectancies about what will or will not happen, and incentives for the performance of a particular response pattern. Strong situations, then, constrain the range of behaviors that people are likely to exhibit and consequently minimize the impact of individual differences. Weak situations are ambiguous, low in structure, and allow for a wide range of behaviors. It is in weak situations that personality factors are most likely to make a difference.

One relatively unstructured context in which personality has been shown to have an impact is NEGOTIATION. For example, people high in the trait of Machiavellianism are more effective in novel bargaining situations and, based on past success in such situations, also set higher negotiating goals relative to those low on this trait (see GOAL-SETTING). In stronger, more structured situations within organizations, personality is unlikely to predict criterion behaviors.

Also, it should be clear that a trait is unlikely to predict any criterion if the population under study shows little range on the trait. For example, since it unlikely that shy, retiring types would apply for a high-pressure commission sales position, there is little reason to expect Surgency to predict sales performance within this particular population of sales applicants. Relative homogeneity on organizationally relevant traits may be the rule, rather than the exception, within work environments. Organizations tend to create homogeneity with respect to particular personality traits by differentially attracting people of a certain type, selecting those who most closely fit the desired type, and causing relatively high rates of attrition among those not fitting in. Thus, the personality traits most likely to predict behavioral criteria are those criterion-relevant traits on which people in the sample vary widely, a relatively uncommon set of circumstances within a single organization.

Serious consideration of the relevance of personality to behavior in a particular context can also enhance the predictive power of personality variables. As an illustration, Field Independent individuals have consistently been found to be more instrumentally oriented and effective on group tasks than Field Dependent people. However, research on these relationships has almost always employed structured tasks in a mechanistic group environment. In performing unstructured tasks in an organic T-group type setting, Field Dependents are actually more task-oriented and effective than Field Independents. In such contexts, the self-focused, autonomous, individualistic style of Field Independent types tends to place psychological distance between themselves and other group members and to minimize their contributions to the more emotion-centered group process (Gruenfeld & Lin, 1984). By analyzing critical contextual factors and developing a clear, theory guided understanding of how linkages between personality and behavior are affected by these contextual factors, researchers can arrive at creative interactive hypotheses and more accurate predictions of behavior.

Criteria

There are three critical facets of criteria that are likely to impact on predictor–criterion relationships. These facets are: (a) criterion type; (b) criterion level; and (c) time of criterion measurement.

(a) *Type*. As noted above, individual personality traits typically have at best a moderate relationship with mean, total, or typical job performance criteria. However, personality traits may relate to the reliability or consistency of an individual's performance across tasks, situations, or time. Similarly, personality traits are only weakly related to the effectiveness of an appointed group leader, but are related to an individual's informal emergence as a group's leader. The key here, as noted above, is to carefully analyze the criterion to identify personality-sensitive elements.

(b) *Level*. Virtually all personality research in OB has focused on the prediction of individual-level criteria. In contrast, Staw and Sutton (1993) have proposed an approach they entitle "macro organizational psychology," using individual-level personality traits to explain organizational-level criteria. For example, there is some evidence that the personality of the organization's leader may influence organizational structure. In one study, CEOS who were high in need for achievement were found to create more centralized structures, establish more individual organizational units so that concrete results could be more clearly monitored, and engage in more planning activity requiring integration across units. As expected, these effects of CEO personality on organizational structure were stronger in newer and smaller firms. Similarly, the personality of those organizational members with high visibility to the organization's exchange partners may impact on organizational-level exchange behaviors.

(c) *Time*. Another criterion-relevant issue concerns the period of time over which criterion measures are aggregated. Low correlations typically found in personality research may be due to poor reliability in behavioral criterion measures. When criterion measures are collected over several occasions and aggregated into composite scores, their stability increases and their correlations with personality predictors increase as well. Thus, personality is more likely to predict employee lateness aggregated over a year's time than lateness during any given week of that year.

In addition, the effects of personality on criterion measures may vary over the course of time. Specifically, basic ability factors, and most importantly general mental ability, seem to account for much of the variance in performance early on, when the employee is learning the job. Personality comes to play a more significant role once this skill acquisition phase is over. In a sample of airline reservation agents, for instance, correlations of personality measures with performance over the first 3 months after the completion of training were not significant. Personality measures were significantly correlated with reservationist performance when criterion measures were collected after 6 months and 8 months on the job.

In sum, developments within basic personality theory and research and within OB have created an intellectual climate that is more conducive than in the recent past to a serious consideration of the role of personality and organizational behavior.

see also **Role; Leadership**

Bibliography

Barrick, M. R. & Mount, M. K. (1991). The big five dimensions and job performance: A meta-analysis. Personnel Psychology, **44**, 1–26.

Brockner, J. (1988). Self-esteem at work. Lexington, MA: Lexington Books.

Furnham, A. (1992). Personality at work. London: Routledge.

Gangestad, S. & Snyder, M. (1985). To carve nature at its joints: On the existence of discrete classes in personality. Psychological Review, **92**, 317–349.

Gruenfeld, L. W. & Lin, T. R. (1984). Social behavior of field independents and dependents in an organic group. Human Relations, **37**, 721–741.

Hogan, R. (1991). Personality and personality measurement. In M. D. Dunnette & L. M. Hough (Eds), Handbook of industrial and organizational psychology. Palo Alto, CA: Consulting Psychologist Press.

Howard, A. & Bray, D. W. (1988). Managerial lives in transition. New York: Guilford.

Judge, T. A. (1992). The dispoin human resources research. In G. R. Ferris & K. M. Rowland (Eds), Research in personnel and human resource management. Greenwich, CT: JAI Press.

McCrae, R. R. & Costa, P. T. Jr. (1987). Validation of the five-factor model of personality across instruments and observers. Journal of Personality and Social Psychology, **52**, 81–90.

Mischel, W. (1968). Personality and assessment. New York: Wiley.

Staw, B. M. & Sutton, R. (1993). Macro-organizational psychology. In J. K. Murnighan (Ed.), Social psychology in organizations. Englewood Cliffs, NJ: Prentice-Hall.

Weiss, H. M. & Adler, S. (1984). Personality and organizational behavior. In B. M. Staw & L. L. Cummings (Eds), Research in organizational behavior. Greenwich, CT: JAI Press.

SEYMOUR ADLER

person–job fit   This refers to the extent to which the dispositions, abilities, expectations, and performance contributions of an individual worker match the job demands, situational demands, expectations, and available REWARDS of a particular job. Individuals bring to their respective jobs a set of dispositions and expectations about what they can and want to accomplish at work and what they expect in return. They also contribute their effort, talents, skill, ability, education, and experience. In return, they expect certain outcomes, including (but not limited to) financial compensation, security, stimulation, and opportunities for growth, development, and advancement.

At the same time, individual jobs require certain things of the people who perform them. In particular, job incumbents must have the physical, cognitive, and emotional skills and abilities necessary to meet minimum performance requirements, as well as the MOTIVATION to perform at an adequate level. At a more general level, organizations also expect certain levels attendance, various forms of "citizenship behaviors," and other contributions. In exchange, the organization provides direct and indirect compensation and other forms of inducement (*see* EQUITY THEORY).

The higher the level of congruence between what an individual provides to and expects from the organization and what the organization expects from and provides to the individual, the greater the degree of person–job fit. When the person–job fit is poor, several outcomes are possible. Individual STRESS, frustration, anxiety, job dissatisfaction, and low performance are all likely outcomes (*see* JOB SATISFACTION). As a consequence, the organization may find it necessary to replace the worker and/or to invest heavily in additional training or to seek a new job assignment for the individual.

It is also important to recognize that person–job fit is likely to change over time. For example, a job that seems exciting, motivating, and stimulating to an organizational newcomer may seem boring and tedious after a longer time. Similarly, as such contributors to person–job fit as job demands, salary, ability, and motivation change, the overall level of congruence may also change.

see also **Personality; Job design; Psychological contract**

Bibliography

Brousseau, K. R. (1983). Toward a dynamic model of job–person relationships: Findings, research questions, and implications for work system design. Academy of Management Review, 8, 33–45.

RICKY W. GRIFFIN

PEST analysis   A number of major variables lie well outside the control of the organization: PEST analysis is a broad-brush instrument that can be used in attempts to define and measure their effects. PEST is an acronym of the four categories of change factor: Political, Economic, Social, and Technological. It is therefore essentially an environmental checklist of those external elements which both influence and constrain the attraction of industry profitability. Often used in conjunction with Porter's FIVE FORCES MODEL, it has become a powerful tool for reducing the parameters of risk.

Political Change and Intervention

In most Western countries, political legislators are expressly forbidden to benefit commercially from their legal enactment, despite overt infringements of this principle seen currently in Italy and France. How, then, should the business world influence and forecast likely political intervention? Consider the following situations:

- *Regional.* Will a change of government in the UK, from Conservative to Labour, increase financial support for business start-ups in Northern Ireland?
- *National.* Will the Clinton administration in the US intervene in the investment terms of the Ford Motor Company's decision as to where to site the new Jaguar plant?
- *International.* Given the explosion of Sino–Western joint ventures within Southern China, who will succeed Diang Xiaping as Premier, and will the social market policy be reversed?

Each of these potential situations requires careful evaluation to determine strategic risk and opportunity. Who will be the decision makers? Who will be the key influencers? How can the top manager reduce the lead time from early warning to strategic modification?

Dependency on the Economic Cycle

Demand for every product or service is to some degree dependent upon the economic cycle. Is demand within any product/market segment a leader or a laggard relative to GNP momentum? Some show increased demand during the first phases of the economic cycle downturn; for example, gourmet convenience food. Some, such as two-star restaurant bookings, show the reverse. Relative to the economic cycle, what fiscal and monetary mechanisms are likely to be chosen by central government? Specifically, how will this affect disposable income expenditure patterns, or the cost of funding working capital? Would it be prudent to take on fixed-interest long-term debt rather than a floating rate shorter-term facility?

In response to this economic uncertainty, much progress has been made in both macro- and sectorial econometric model-building; leading, *inter alia*, to better inventory control and to a reduction in the cost of corporate capital.

Social Demographic, Attitudinal, and Religious Change

From a corporate perspective, what social changes will affect contemporary strategic positioning and – given robust forecasting – what competitive advantage could be established? Take, for example, the falling reproduction rates in Wein Germany and the UK, the figure is approximately 1.6. When combined with an increase in life expectation, who will fund the retirement pension? Can the state fulfil historic provision from the public purse? This social trend has led to the private sector developing new products, particularly private portable pensions, private medical schemes, sheltered housing developments, "third age" holidays, and vocational courses within the university sector.

Consider the rise of pressure groups: the anti-smoking lobby has recorded successes in restaurants, on hotel floors, and on aircraft. The strong positive correlation between smoking and heart disease has been linked to a marked reduction in Western adult male consumption of tobacco products, while – perversely – it has had no impact on female teenagers. Should the tobacco companies re-focus their advertising and promotional activity on a smaller niche and/or diversify more rapidly into related products – see, for example, Philip Morris and Miller?

The third, and increasingly important, category is that of religious fundamentalism, often associated with extreme nationalism. Should Western oil and gas companies invest for the long term in Kakastan? Given the terrorist targeting of tourists in Algeria and Egypt, should holiday companies begin to wind down from hotel contracts in Tunisia? Will the Parsees of India, a minority religion who dominate much of private-sector enterprise, be better long-term joint venture partners than the majority Hindus?

Technological Vulnerability

It is axiomatic that we live in a world of rapid technological change – all the more reason to be proactive in corporate response. Organizations should regularly review the commercial impact of emerging new technologies upon activity costs along the value chain. Take the example of constant-velocity joints: GKN, who claim a 35 per cent world market share, invest heavily in friction research (tribology) in the major technological universities. The reasoning behind this strategy is that, since the 1960s, engine brake horse power, from the same cubic capacity, has quadrupled – and vehicle top speed has doubled. Correspondingy, automobile manufacturers demand component technology of equivalence. Consider advances in data compression and transmission. Will this reduce the need for as many medical general practitioners, or for legal experts? Will neural networks replace branch bank managers? How soon will interactive video disk technology replace ageing professors!

Any company which fails to monitor technological advance within the area of its existing core competencies exacerbates the risk of product/market obsolescence.

Constructing a PEST Framework

PEST analysis is an attempt to reduce strategic risk by SCENARIO PLANNING. It is not intended to be a precise technique in quantification but is specific to individual products and/or markets. It therefore follows that each PEST, although following the same general outline, will specify different item variables, to which different weightings will be allocated. Given the enormous number of potential variables, it is sensible to limit the PEST analysis to no more than five items within each of the main PEST headings in the first instance. The first step is to determine the probability rankings of each item variable; and the second is to evaluate the quantitative and qualitative effect of these occurring upon the achievement of corporate objectives. By multiplying probability by effect, a crude ranking index of corporate vulnerability – or opportunity – is established. This index is next refined by eliminating those items with insufficient impact, so that more detailed analysis can be conducted of the significant variables.

Bibliography

Fahey, L. & King, W. (1977). Environmental scanning for corporate planning. *Business Horizons*, **20** 4.

Hofer, C. W. & Schendel, D. (1978). *Strategy formulation: analytical concepts*. St Paul, MN: West Publishing.

Rowe, A. J., Mason, R. O., Dickel, K. E., Mann,

R. B. & Mockler, R. J. (1994). *Strategic management*, 4th edn. Reading, MA: Addison-Wesley.

Utterback, J. (1979). Environmental analysis and forecasting in strategic management. In C. Hofer, D. Schendel (eds), *A new view of business policy and planning*. Boston, MA: Little Brown.

William, R. E. (1976). *Putting it all together, a guide to strategic thinking*. New York: Amacom.

DAVID NORBURN

physical abilities   Physical ability refers to the capability or capacity to develop or learn a physical skill, such as climbing a ladder or hammering nails. Many individual physical abilities exist that involve both motor (e.g. running speed) and perceptual (e.g. visual acuity) functions. Abilities that combine both physical and psychological factors (e.g. information processing or perception) are termed PSYCHO-MOTOR ABILITIES. An example would be eye–hand coordination. Many job tasks require a combination of specific physical abilities involving both motor and psychological components. In personnel selection, however, a physical equivalent to INTELLIGENCE TESTS does not exist. Where physical ability testing is used, it tends to focus on specific abilities rather than overall physical capability.

PAUL E. SPECTOR

picketing   Picketing, in its usual (primary) form, is the stationing of persons outside the premises of an employer with which a union has a labor dispute (Cihon and Castagnera, 1993). This is done for the purpose of giving notice of the existence of the dispute, and is usually intended to persuade persons not to deal with the employer. It has at times been described as inherently coercive (*Cory Corporation*, 84 NLRB 972, 1949) and at times as free speech (*Thornhill* v. *Alabama*, 310 US 88, 1940). Currently US law permits peaceful picketing unless it is mass picketing, is pursued for purposes of gaining union recognition, or is part of SECONDARY BOYCOTTS.

Bibliography

Cihon, P. J. & Castagnera, J. O. (1993). *Labor and Employment Law*, **2nd edn**, Belmont, CA: Wadsworth.

Taylor, B. J. & Witney, F. (1992). *Labor Relations Law*, **6th**, Englewood Cliffs, NJ: Prentice-Hall.

HOYT N. WHEELER

PIMS structural determinants of performance   Profit performance varies enormously from business to business and within a business over time. In developing strategy, both corporate and business unit management need to be able to realistically appraise the level of performance that should be expected for a given business, and to be clear as to what factors explain variations in performance between businesses, and within a business over time. Important guidelines which help address these questions have been developed from the Profit Impact of Market Strategy (PIMS) program. For a fuller description of the background of the PIMS program, see Schoeffler et al. (1974).

Background to the PIMS Methodology

At the heart of the PIMS program is a business unit research database that captures the real-life experiences of over 3,000 businesses. Each business is a division, product line, or profit center within its parent company, selling a

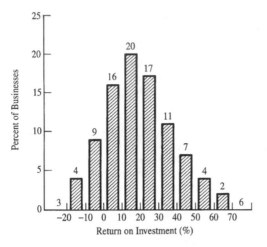

Figure 1   The distribution of return on investment in the PIMS database. ROI is defined as follows: pre-tax after deduction of corporate expenses but prior to interest charges divided by average investment where this is equivalent to the historic net book value of plant and equipment plus working capital (i.e., total assets less current liabilities). Note that four year averages are used for all figures.
Source: PIMS Associates

Table 1   Key determinants of R.O.I. in the PIMS data base

Category of factor	Impact on ROI as factor increases
Marketplace standing	
Market share	+
Relative market share	+
Served market concentration	+
Market environment	
Real market growth	+
Selling price inflation	+
Market differentiation	+
Purchase amount immediate customers	–
Importance of purchase to end user	–
Differentiation from competitors	
Relative product quality	+
Relative price	+
Relative direct cost	–
% Sales new products	–
Marketing/sales revenue	–
R&D/sales revenue	–
Capital and production structure	–
Investment/sales revenue	–
Investment/value added	–
Receivables/investment	+
Fixed capital/investment	–
Capacity utilization	+
Unionization	–
Labor effectiveness*	+

* Based on a productivity submodel.
Source: PIMS Associates

distinct set of products and/or services to an identifiable group of customers, in competition with a well defined set of competitors, for which meaningful separation can be made of revenue, operating costs, investment, and strategic plans. The business's served market is defined as the segment of the total potential market which it is seriously targeting by offering suitable products and/or services and toward which it is making specific marketing efforts. On this basis each business reports, in standardized format, over 300 items of data, much of it for at least four years of operations.

The information collected covers, *inter alia*, the market environment, competitive situation, internal cost and asset structure, and profit performance of the business. A full listing of the information captured by the PIMS database is given by The Strategic Planning Institute's *PIMS data manual*. A useful summary of the manual is given in Buzzell & Gale (1987).

The businesses in the database have been drawn from some 500 corporations, spanning a wide variety of industry settings. These corporations are based for the most part in North America and Europe.

The distribution of return on investment in the database is shown in figure 1. As can be seen, profit varies widely among the businesses, with 16 percent of the sample showing negative returns and 12 percent consistently achieving in excess of 50 percent ROI. An understanding of why one business should be loss-making while another achieves premium returns lies at the heart of strategy formulation. To explain this variance, cross-sectional analysis is carried out on the database to uncover the general patterns or relationships that account for these profit differentials. The fundamental proposition that underpins this approach is that the name of a business has no bearing on its level of performance. What matters are the structural characteristics that describe the business, factors such as market share, growth rate, customer concentration, product quality, and investment intensity.

Research on the database has identified some 30 factors that are statistically significant at the 95 percent probability level or better in explaining the variance in profitability across businesses. These factors, which operate in a highly interactive way, collectively explain nearly 80 percent of the variance in ROI across the database. The more powerful factors are listed in table 1 under four categories: marketplace standing, market environment, differentiation production structure.

It should be noted at the outset that part of the explanation of variance is definitional. This comes about because some of the profit-explaining variables, such as investment/sales revenue, contain elements which are also present in the construction of the dependent variable, ROI. However, the emphasis is on behavioral relationships. Definitional elements are included in the independent

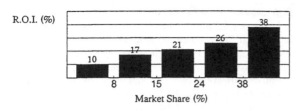

Figure 2   Marketplace standing and profitability are closely related.
Source: PIMS Associates

variables only when it is impossible to separate out the behavioral and definitional effects of a particular factor.

Key Research Findings from the PIMS Database

The more powerful relationships listed in table 1 are now considered one and two variables at a time in relation to the dependent variable ROI. While this approach sacrifices the insights contained in multifactor interactions, it has the benefit of reducing complexity and helps to develop an understanding of the basic building blocks. To this extent it provides insight and guidelines to aid business judgement rather than hard dogma.

Marketplace Standing

There are several measures of a business's marketplace standing: market share (the business's sales expressed as a percentage of total sales made within the served market), market share rank, and relative market share (the business's market share divided by the sum of the shares of its three leading competitors). Whichever measure is adopted, a strong positive correlation between marketplace strength and profitability is observed. Figure 2 shows the relationship between market share and profitability. Businesses with strong market share (above 38 percent in the upper quintile of the distribution) achieve on average a 38 percent ROI, compared to only 10 percent for their low-share counterparts (below 8 percent in the lower quintile of the distribution).

While the data in figure 2 show that strength of marketplace standing and profitability are strongly related, the question remains as to why we observe the effect. The numbers are a fact, but hypothesis and further examination are required to explain the relationships. It should be remembered that market share in and of itself is not important: it is an output measure which reflects a business's historic and potential ability to gain substantive competitive advantages within its activities and in the marketplace. Factors which explain the underlying reasons why share may help profitability are shown in table 2. For a fuller discussion of the benefits of market share, see Buzzell et al. (1975).

Powerful as these factors are, the fact remains there is nothing inevitable about the relationship between share and profitability. Over 30 percent of the businesses in the

Table 2   Potential benefits of strong market standing.

---

* *"Experience curve" and "learning curve" benefits*
Widely publicized by the Boston Consulting Group, the experience curve effect sees cost per unit come down in a fairly predictable manner as cumulative volume doubles.

* *Economics of scale and scope*
Can drive down cost per unit throughout the cost structure of a business as well as benefitting balance sheet productivity. Key areas for potential benefit are seen to be:
  – purchases: stronger negotiating stance with suppliers leads to preferential terms
  – manufacturing: plant scale and run length
  – distribution: drop size and drop density
  – marketing/R&D: spreading fixed cost component over a larger number of units
  – investment productivity
    ● improved asset utilization
    ● improved ability to control all current asset components and extend current liabilities

* *Relative perceived quality*
Higher market visibility offering the "low-risk" option for buyers in many instances. Scale benefits should give ability to establish stronger brand and better control distribution.

* *Competitive ability*
    – potential to act as "industry statesman"
    – opportunities to set and administer prices
    – size may deter competitive attack
    – size will heighten ability to control the chain from supplier to customers
    – better ability to spread risk and explore more competitive avenues

---

Source: PIMS Associates

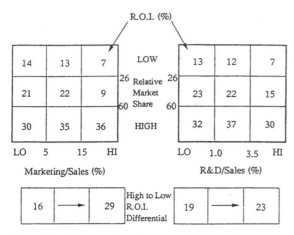

Figure 3 Share tends to have more leverage in marketing and R&D intensive settings.
Source: PIMS Associates

database with market shares above 40 percent have ROI's below the average of 22 percent. These businesses have often become victims of their own success, wedded to historic investment decisions and burdened with complexity costs. For a fuller discussion of below average performance for high-share businesses, see Woo (1984).

The benefits of market share are particularly marked in marketing- and R&D-intensive environments, as can be seen in figure 3. The two variable cross-tables divide the database into equal thirds on the basis of relative market share and then into low and high marketing and R&D environments. Each cell contains approximately 300 businesses, and the numbers in the cells refer to the average ROI achieved by the businesses that fall into that cell over a four year time period.

When marketing expenditure is below 5 percent of sales revenue, the ROI's achieved by low-share businesses are 14 percent, as compared to 30 percent for their high-share counterparts – a differential of 16 points. On the other hand, in marketing-intensive environments the importance of market share on profit is much more pronounced, with ROI going from 7 percent to 36 percent, a 29 point differential. A similar relationship manifests itself in the case of market share and R&D expenditure.

What the PIMS data highlight is the danger of low market share in an environment which is either marketing- or R&D-intensive. This is because both marketing and R&D have many of the characteristics of a fixed cost. Businesses with small market shares often find that they have to spend as much as their larger competitors on these activities, but do not have the same volume over which to spread the costs. The result is that they are trapped in the low-profit cells. When faced with such a trap, the strategic alternatives appear to be to reduce the role of marketing and R&D, to strengthen share either organically or by merger/alliance, or to re-segment to dominate a niche within the market. If none of these possibilities appears to be feasible, the small-share competitor will be faced with the large-share competitor's "virtuous circle," shown in figure 4.

Differentiation from Competitors

A business's value-for-money position versus competitors is a critical determinant of competitive advantage. PIMS assesses this position by judging a business's relative competitive standing in terms of quality and price. It then examines how that offer is supported by new product activity, marketing, and R&D expenditure and the extent to which price is underpinned by the relative direct cost position of the business. "Relative perceived quality" is seen as the key driver of business performance under this category of factor.

Quality in the PIMS database is defined from the perspective of the external marketplace. Customers evaluate the total benefit bundle of products and services offered by the business and rank it relative to leading competitors as being superior, equivalent, or inferior. The "relative perceived quality" measure used by PIMS is then computed by subtracting the percentage of product and service attributes that are judged as being superior to competitors from the percentage which is judged as inferior.

Relative perceived quality has a major positive impact on profitability, as can be seen in figure 5. Businesses whose offer is judged as clearly superior to that of competitors on average achieve more than twice the ROI of businesses whose offer is judged as inferior.

Not only is the relationship between quality and return one of the key determinants of performance in the database, but it is extremely robust in all types of business and marketplace situations. Businesses that achieve a significant quality advantage relative to their competitors can choose to benefit in one of two ways: either they can charge premium prices or grow market share at competitive pricing levels, or some combination of both.

The relationship between market share, quality, and profitability is shown in figure 6. The combination of share and quality is extremely powerful, with ROI in the high-quality/high-share cell averaging 39 percent.

Figure 6 also shows that quality and share are correlated.

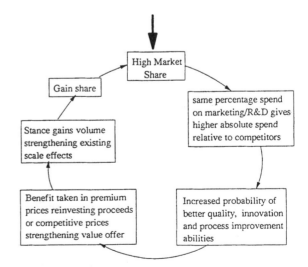

Figure 4 High share competitors vicious circle
Source: PIMS Associates

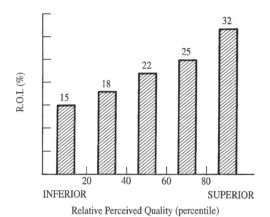

Figure 5 Relative perceived quality is closely related to profitability.
Source: PIMS Associates

Thus, although the database was split into equal thirds on both quality and share, 45 percent of businesses lie on the top left to bottom right diagonal. The implications appear to be that high-share businesses that offer poor quality weaken in position, while weak-share businesses that offer high quality strengthen in position – both extremes may be transitory in nature and represent only 13 percent of the sample.

Capital and Production Structure
Within this category of factor, the most powerful of the PIMS findings relates to investment intensity. The definition of investment in this context is fixed capital, measured on an historic basis as the net book value of plant and equipment, plus working capital, defined as current assets less current liabilities. Investment intensity itself is measured in two ways: first, investment is ratioed to sales revenue in the conventional manner; and, second, investment is ratioed to the value added actually generated by the business (where value added is defined as net sales revenue less all outside suppliers' inputs).

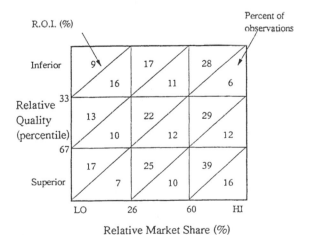

Figure 6 Market position and quality are partial substitutes for each other
Source: PIMS Associates.

Both measures are simultaneously employed to assess investment intensity, as many businesses have low levels of investment to sales (turn their asset base frequently) but because of a high bought-in component have high levels of investment to value added. Having cautioned that a balanced view on the overall investment intensity of a business is only achieved by using both measures in combination, on an individual basis each measure is similarly related to profit performance in the PIMS data base, and here the more familiar investment/sales revenue ratio is employed to illustrate the investment intensity effect.

As the investment intensity in a business rises, so the ROI that it achieves falls dramatically. This finding is the most powerful negative relationship in the database, with ROI's averaging only 8 percent for investment intensive businesses, compared to 38 percent for low investment intensity businesses. The finding is consistent with the experiences of many businesses in sectors such as airlines, shipbuilding, base chemicals, low alloy steel, refining, smelting, and commodity pulp and paper, which in large degree achieve at best modest rates of return.

Part of the reason for the relationship is definitional. As the investment level in a business increases, it simultaneously increases the denominator of the ROI ratio, hence dragging down the value of the ratio. That there is a behavioral element to the investment intensity effect is vividly illustrated if the return on sales (ROS) achieved at different levels of investment is considered. If a business is to hold ROI as investment intensity increases, ROS should increase smoothly. In practice, ROS is at best flat, and in fact starts to tail off at higher levels of investment intensity. Moreover, it should be remembered that return has been taken pre-tax and pre-interest, with no financial charge made on the amount of investment used in the business. If even a modest capital charge rate is applied to a business's returns to reflect its investment, the relationship would start to turn sharply down. If businesses were sufficient to offset the level of investment that they need to sustain their sales, there is indeed a powerful behavioral element to the ROI/investment intensity finding.

What explains this behavioral element? Part of the reason may lie in the fact that management often focus their attention on profit margin on sales, rather than on the more

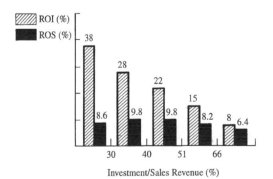

Figure 7 Investment intensity is a major drag on profitability
Source: PIMS Associates

important criterion of return on investment. The more substantive explanation, however, relates to the destructive nature of competition that typically accompanies high levels of investment intensity.

When a business is capital intensive, management not unnaturally becomes concerned about capacity utilization. When this drops, either because of a weakening in demand or because of new capacity addition by competitors, the knee-jerk reaction is to cut price. When one competitor cuts price, the rest of the industry typically follows, and the result is a price war. The tendency to cut price is particularly marked in fixed capital intensive businesses, because the value of the marginal sale always appears to be so attractive.

The problem is compounded because fixed capital intensity frequently represents a major barrier to exit. When a company has sunk a lot of money into a business, it is often reluctant to exit: it becomes desperate to make the investment come good. It convinces itself that the problems of the business are transitory and that all it needs to do is "hang in" and better times will follow. This is a comforting illusion that does little for a business.

Overview

At the start, it was observed that profit performance varies enormously from business to business and within a business over time. Several of the key research findings arising from the PIMS database that help to explain this variance in performance have been discussed.

Care must be cautioned in interpretation. Comprehensive insight is not obtained by examining one or two factors at a time: it requires a multifactor approach in order to start to capture the complexities and tradeoffs in business. To this end, PIMS researchers have developed several models that help assess the level of ROI, cashflow, productivity, and so forth that should be expected for a business, given its structural make-up. Once these benchmarks have been established, attention can be focused on the next stage of strategy formulation; that of managing change. It can be extremely misleading to use the *general* findings presented for this purpose. That market share is generally closely related to profitability is observable; but that is not to argue, of course, that a business should try to grow share in all instances – the feasibility and cost–benefit tradeoff of such a move needs close examination. To this end, other modeling techniques and the database itself, via matched sample analysis, provide important empirical vehicles for the identification and evaluation of particular strategy moves by researchers and practitioners alike.

The authors would like to acknowledge the assistance of John Hillier of the Strategic Planning Institute in researching the PIMS database.

Bibliography

Buzzell, R. D. & Gale, B. T. (1987). *The PIMS principles.* New York: The Free Press. See Appendix A.

Buzzell, R. D., Gale, B. T. & Sultan, R. G. M. (1975). Market share – a key to profitability. *Harvard Business Review*, **53** (1), 97–106.

Schoeffler, S., Buzzell, R. D. & Heany, D. F. (1974). Impact of strategic planning on profit performance. *Harvard Business Review*, **52** (2), 137–45.

Strategic Planning Institute (n.d.). *PIMS data manual.* Cambridge, MA: Strategic Planning Institute.

Woo, C. (1984). Market share leadership – not always so good. *Harvard Business Review*, **62** (1), 50–6.

KEVIN JAGIELLO and GORDON MANDRY

planning for information systems   Information systems (IS) planning is an organizational administrative process that involves the consideration of alternative methods for employing information, computing, and communications resources in furtherance of the organization's objectives and its overall "business" strategy. IS planning takes place at a number of different levels in the organization. At the highest level of strategic IS planning, the relationship between the organization's objectives and strategy and its IS resources is articulated. At a much lower level, IS project planning involves the specification of the activities, resources, and relationships that will be required to develop a new computer system, install and implement new hardware and software, or perform any other complex task involving computer resources.

Strategic IS Planning

Strategic IS planning is the core of IS planning since it directly involves the translation of organizational objectives and strategy into data, applications, technology, and communications architectures that can best support the implementation of that strategy and the achievement of the organization's overall objectives. It also involves the assessment of the "product-market" opportunities that may be supported by existing and planned information resources (i.e. identifying whether the organization's information resources and competencies may suggest opportunities for it to carry on its activities in ways that may make it more competitive in the market).

Figure 1 shows these two major elements of strategic IS planning in terms of two arrows that connect an "organizational strategy set" and an "information resources strategy set." The former represents the organizational mission, objectives and strategies that have been developed through a strategic "business" planning process. The right-facing arrow shows that the information resources strategy set (composed of the information resources strategy and information infrastructure) is derived from the organizational strategy set. The left-facing arrow describes the assessment of information resources that may be conducted to identify important changes in the organizational strategy set.

Evolution of IS Planning

Tracing the development of IS planning can serve to describe its various levels, since the forms of IS planning that represented its highest and most sophisticated level in past eras are still conducted today. Higher (more strategic) levels of planning have been added to the previously existing planning activities in each era as the IS planning field has evolved. This approach also offers the opportunity of identifying the underlying concepts and techniques associated with each planning paradigm.

The pre-strategic planning era.   In the early computer era, the most sophisticated level of IS planning involved assessing the future computing needs of the enterprise and ensuring that adequate and appropriate computing capacity was available to fulfill those needs. An associated planning task was that of evaluating and selecting the

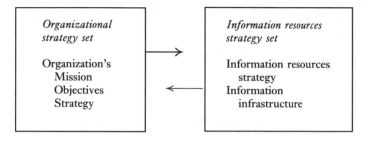

Figure 1   Strategic IS Planning

applications and systems development projects that would be funded and implemented by the enterprise. At the project level, project plans were developed to ensure that appropriate milestones were identified and that specific activities and tasks were assigned to appropriate IS professionals.

The systems development life-cycle (SDLC) was the primary conceptual basis for planning in this era. The SDLC for information systems evolved from the basic SDLC for complex systems. The SDLC postulated that the development of all complex systems naturally evolved through a sequential series of phases that were most appropriately managed in different ways, and which demanded different mixes of resources to complete effectively and efficiently. An extremely simplified version of the SDLC is shown at the center of figure 2 where it is labeled "Traditional SDLC."

In this era, the multi-project levels of planning (capacity planning and project selection and evaluation) were based on the concepts of forecasting and project selection, respectively. Capacity planning involved the forecasting of computing requirements and planning for the acquisition, installation, and testing of new generations of hardware and software. Project evaluation and selection were conceptually based on the project selection methodologies that had largely been previously developed and used in the research and development (R&D) context.

Because "cost avoidance" was the major criterion for project evaluation in this pre-strategic era, this project selection procedure was relatively straightforward, primarily involving the estimation of the costs that could be avoided if manual systems were to be automated. This criterion usually resulted in the approval of projects that were at the operational or operational control levels. Those projects that substituted computer systems for human operatives or those that measured and controlled the performance levels of operations were accepted as being cost-effective. Projects whose rationale depended on the sometimes intangible benefits that they might produce were difficult to justify because of the emphasis on the cost-avoidance criterion and the relatively greater ease of forecasting costs versus benefits.

The highest level plan that came into being in some organizations during the latter part of this pre-strategic era was the "IS master plan." This plan demonstrated the intended relationships among the various systems and subsystems that the organization operated or planned to develop. The need for a master plan was recognized by organizations that had developed independent and incom-

patible systems. While such systems may well have been individually effective to operate, they could not be readily integrated to provide information that might be of use to higher-level management. Illustrative of this situation were the many banks that had developed expensive and operationally effective product-oriented computer systems. Their checking account systems, loan systems, and trust systems, for example, had databases that were not readily cross-referenced to enable a marketing manager to readily determine which of the bank's many products and services were utilized by a given customer. The master plan was intended to ensure systems integration. The adoption of this notion was the precursor to the IS strategic planning era.

The early strategic IS planning era. The simple idea of deriving the IS strategy directly from the overall organizational strategy, and thereby of developing the IS resources that best supported the organization's strategy, had profound effect on IS planning and on IS development activities (King & Cleland, 1975; King, 1978). When IBM incorporated the notion into this widely known business systems planning (BSP) methodology, strategic IS planning came into widespread use (IBM, 1981).

This expanded domain for IS necessitated a change from the simple, cost-avoidance IS project selection criterion that had been in common use to more sophisticated criteria that gave greater consideration of the potential benefits that might result from an IS project. Because cost remained a necessary consideration and benefits were often intangible and difficult to quantify, the net result was a multi-dimensional criterion that was conceptually similar to those that had been in use in R&D project selection for some time.

For the first time in the history of many firms, IS applications whose benefits were intangible, and/or more difficult to forecast than was cost avoidance, came to be given higher priority. The result was that top managers developed a greater appreciation of the IS function as a potential contributor to business value rather than viewing IS merely as a service function.

The expanded planning horizons of IS and the emphasis on assessing and evaluating systems in more sophisticated ways have been conceptualized in terms of the expanded life-cycle shown in figure 2 (King & Srinivasan, 1983). Figure 2 shows a simplified version of the "traditional SDLC" embedded in a broader life-cycle that also includes strategic planning, systems integration planning, evaluation, and divestment phases. These phases serve to extend

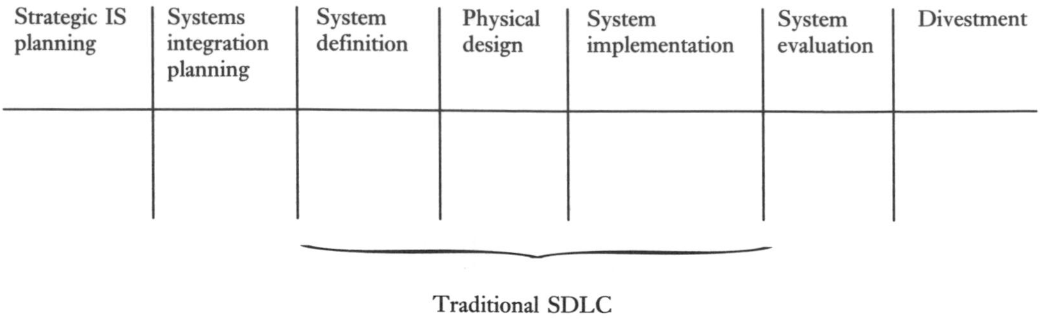

Strategic IS planning	Systems integration planning	System definition	Physical design	System implementation	System evaluation	Divestment

Traditional SDLC

Figure 2   Expanded systems development life-cycle

the traditional SDLC, which applies to a single system, to a broader organizational context. The systems integration planning phase primarily involves the sort of systems integration functions that are implicit in the earlier notion of a "master plan." The strategic planning phase involves the development of an IS strategy that is derived from, and which directly supports, the business strategy.

In figure 2, the two phases that are shown to begin after the traditional SDLC – evaluation and divestment – reflect the growing attention that has come to be paid to the formal evaluation of systems and the need to phase out systems. In the evaluation phase, other measures, such as user satisfaction and business value assessments, are commonly used to complement traditional cost, time, and technical performance measures. These two phases further recognize that an IS, like any complex system, has a finite useful life. These phases not only reflect the need to evaluate systems, but *the need to plan for the shutdown, replacement, and phasing out of systems.* In the earlier eras of IS planning, little attention was given to divestment, leading many firms to make the implicit assumption that systems would function forever. This assumption inevitably leads to decisions concerning systems maintenance, updating, and modification that might be significantly different from what they would be under the assumption of a finite useful lifespan for a system.

Strategic planning for information resources: the modern era. In the 1980s, the initial notion of strategic IS planning was expanded to include the idea described by the left-facing arrows in figure 1. This involved the recognition that information resources could become a basis for new organizational strategy as well as being supportive of existing organizational strategy. This idea, enunciated by King and Zmud (1981), has come to be a basic concept of the IS field.

The systems that have been developed as a result of the planning process described by the left-facing arrow in figure 1 are variously described as "strategic systems," and "competitive weapons" (i.e. systems that impact the "product-market" strategies of organizations). Among such systems are Merrill Lynch's Cash Management Account (CMA), a "product" whose core technology is information processing, and American and United Airlines' reservation systems, which have been employed to achieve competitive advantages in the market rather than serving merely for transaction processing.

This new view of "information resources," as contrasted with "information systems," reflects both the greater organizational importance of computer-related entities and the rapid development of a wide variety of useful communications and information technologies that greatly transcend the traditional computer hardware and software dimensions of IS. Local area networks, wide area networks, DATABASE MANAGEMENT SYSTEMS, word and document processing, EXPERT SYSTEMS and many other technology-based entities are now physically and/or conceptually integrated into an overall set of information resources that must be jointly planned for and managed. Moreover, in the modern information era, the important role of data *per se*, without regard to the technology that is used to collect, process, and disseminate it, has also increasingly been recognized. An organization can utilize these entities much as it has traditionally employed its human, financial, and physical resources to create business value.

The evolution of the criteria used to evaluate and select systems has moved toward a focus on "sustainable competitive advantage" in the era of strategic systems. Systems that have the potential to produce an identifiable advantage over competition, sustainable over time, are those that will be given highest priority (e.g. Sethi & King, 1994). Systems that promise cost avoidance or temporary competitive advantage will generally be less highly valued (unless, of course, in the former case, cost leadership is a strategy that is intended to produce an advantage in the market).

Current Trends in IS Planning
At least three major trends in IS planning are readily identifiable: (a) the integration of IS planning into overall organizational planning; (b) the integration of planning for various communications and information technologies; and (c) the development of planning for business process re-engineering as an element of IS planning.

Integration of IS planning and organizational planning. The recognition of strategic planning for information resources as a "free-standing" administrative activity may be beginning to reach the limits of its value. With the emerging view of information resources as one of the important kinds of resources that a general manager can employ to achieve organizational objectives, many organizations have embarked on the integration of IS planning with overall strategic "business" planning processes.

Although this trend is not universal, it is clearly identifiable and, if successful, will undoubtedly become a major theme of future developments in the area.

When strategic planning for information resources becomes a process conducted under the aegis of the organization's general manager with the heavy involvement of non-IS personnel, it will have emulated the evolution of IS from a backroom technical service function to one that is not only important to the organization but also includes the significant involvement of non-IS personnel in its management.

Integration of communications and information technology planning. At the same time as IS planning is being integrated into overall organizational planning, its scope is being expanded because of the physical and conceptual integration of technologies. As electronic data interchange (EDI), telecommunication systems and a wide variety of other technologies become less distinguishable from computer systems, and as the requirements for organizations to employ these various technologies in an integrated manner becomes clear, information resources planning has expanded to address a broad range of communications and information systems and technologies.

Planning for business process re-engineering. Planning for business process re-engineering (BPR) is also one of the important trends in IS planning. The redesign of business processes has become a major organizational activity that usually has a high information systems and technology content. As such, BPR projects must be designed, selected, and implemented just as any other IS project. Since BPR is potentially of great strategic importance to the enterprise, in some organizations BPR planning is treated as an element of strategic IS planning.

Conclusion

Planning for information resources has become a complex and sophisticated administrative process. Its increasing integration into overall organizational strategic planning processes parallels the increasing regard of information resources as one of the most important varieties of resources that are at the disposal of managers in the pursuit of their organizational objectives. This development vividly contrasts with earlier eras when computer systems were backroom service functions of relatively limited importance to business and when information systems planning was a straightforward capacity and requirements-driven process.

The increasingly important and visible role of the IS function and of communications and information resources represents both opportunity and challenge for the field. In earlier eras, failures of computer systems to perform in the manner that was expected were often not of enormous significance to overall organizational performance. Therefore, IS planning was not usually instrumental in determining long-run overall organizational success. Now, we can, with increasing frequency, identify situations in which organizational success is primarily based on the ability to develop and exploit information resources. In the future, such situations are likely to proliferate as are situations in which the decline and fall of organizations can be explained by their failure to do so. In such an environment, IS planning is of fundamental importance.

Bibliography

IBM (1981). *Business Systems Planning: Information Systems Planning Guide.*

King, W. R. (1978). Strategic planning for management information systems. *MIS Quarterly,* **2 (1),** 27–37.

King, W. R. & Cleland, D. I. (1975). A new method for strategic systems planning. *Business Horizons,* **18 (4),** 55–64.

King W. R. & Srinivasan, A. (1983). Decision support systems: planning, development and evaluation, in R. Schultz (ed.), *Applications of Management Science,* vol. 3. JAI Press.

King, W. R. & Zmud, R. (1981). Managing information systems: policy planning, strategic planning and operational planning, *Proceedings of the Second International Conference on Information Systems.* Boston, MA, December.

Sethi, V. & King, W. R. (1994). Development of measures to assess the extent to which an Information Technology application provides competitive advantage. *Management Science,* **40 (12),** 1601–27.

WILLIAM R. KING

point job evaluation method The point job evaluation method has the following characteristics: (a) it uses COMPENSABLE FACTORS; (b) each factor is subdivided into degrees which are numerically scaled; and (c) each factor is given a weight that reflects its relative importance (Milkovich and Newman, 1993, p. 131). A job receives a point total in this method that represents the sum of points for each degree of compensable factor associated with the job. This provides a quantitative measure of the relative worth of each job, which facilitates the development of a pay structure and pay grades.

The advantage of the point job evaluation method is that the quantitative rating scales provide for relatively stable and consistent results (Belcher and Atchison, 1989, p. 196). The disadvantages of the point job evaluation method are that it is costly and takes time to develop and implement unless a ready-made plan is purchased.

Bibliography

Belcher, D. W. & Atchison, T. J. (1989). *Compensation Administration,* **2nd edn,** Englewood Cliffs, NJ: Prentice-Hall.

Milkovich, G. T. & Newman, J. M. (1993). *Compensation,* **4th edn,** Homewood, IL: Richard D. Irwin.

DAVID B. BALKIN

political action committees and labor unions Labor unions have used political action committees (PACs) to influence elections and lawmakers. PACs raise money that may be contributed to political candidates. Research has indicated that PAC contributions may have considerable impact on the electoral and legislative processes (Kau and Rubin, 1981; Masters and Zardkoohi, 1987).

The Role of Labor PACs

Labor unions formed PACs in the New Deal era to raise money to channel to candidates for elective office (Delaney and Masters, 1991). Since the Taft–Hartley Act of 1947 and, more recently, the Federal Election Campaign Act of 1971, unions have been prohibited from using regular sources of income (e.g. dues) for contributions to congressional and presidential candidates (Epstein, 1976). Federal election law, however, allows unions to raise money from their members on a strictly voluntary basis for PACs, which, in turn, may contribute up to $5,000 to each federal candidate per election.

PACs are one of the most important means unions have to influence politics, although in-kind assistance (e.g. get-out-the-vote drives) is also quite significant (Masters and Delaney, 1987). Since the 1970s, union PAC receipts and contributions have grown considerably, offsetting the decline in union membership (Masters et al., 1989–90). Union PAC receipts (adjusted for inflation) rose from nearly $35 million in 1980 to nearly $50 million in 1992, despite unions losing several million members during this period. Research has shown that union PAC activity is correlated with a union's membership composition and industry location (Delaney et al., 1988).

PAC Influence

The impact of PACs has been widely debated and researched (Masters and Delaney, 1987). While no singular conclusion has been reached, several studies indicate that union PAC contributions may have offset the decline in union membership in maintaining union political influence (Moore et al., 1995).

Bibliography

Delaney, J. T., Fiorito, J. & Masters, M. F. (1988). The effects of union organizational and environmental characteristics on union political action. *American Journal of Political Science*, 32, 616–41.

Delaney, J. T. & Masters, M. F. (1991). Unions and political action. *The State of Unions*, Eds. Straus, G., Gallagher, D. & Fiorito, J. Madison, WI: Industrial Relation Research Association.

Epstein, E. M. (1976). Labor and federal elections: the new legal framework. *Industrial Relations*, 15, 257–74.

Kau, J. B. & Rubin, P. H. (1981). The impact of labor unions on the passage of economic legislation. *Journal of Labor Research*, 2, 133–46.

Masters, M. F., Atkin, R. & Delaney, J. (1989–1990). Unions, political action, and public policy. *Policies Studies Journal*, 18, 471–80.

Masters, M. F. & Delaney, J. T. (1987). Empirical research on union political activities: a review of the literature. *Industrial and Labor Relations Review*, 40, 336–53.

Masters, M. F. & Zardkoohi, A. (1987). Labor and Congress: PAC allocations and legislative voting. *Advances in Industrial and Labor Relations*, Eds. Lewin, D., Lipsky, D. B. & Sockell, D. (eds), 4, Greenwich, CT: JAI Press. 79–118.

Moore, W. J., Chachere, D. R., Curtis, T. D. & Gordon, D. (1995). The political influence of unions and corporations on COPE votes in the US Senate, 1979–1988. *Journal of Labor Research*, 16, 203–22.

MARICK F. MASTERS

political influences in career planning   Traditional career planning is based on rational self-assessments of fit between individual characteristics and organizational need, framed within human capital theories of career attainment. A political perspective on careers recognizes that organizations involve an interplay of competing interests and finite resources. In such environments, career planning is defined in terms more of self-interest and power or resource acquisition than of the efficiency with which individual characteristics (e.g. goals, values, interests) mesh with organizational needs (Pfeffer, 1989).

Both organizational- and individual-focused variables can act as political influences on careers. The primary organizational influence is POWER. Cohort and interest groups with power shape career-relevant processes such as hiring, promotion, internal mobility, and succession so as to maintain their power (Pfeffer, 1989). Factors such as congruence with power groups' demographic composition and cultural values are important to career success, as are status and position in formal and informal organization networks.

Individual-focused variables involve political behaviors or tactics that are used to enhance career opportunities. Of several classifications of political behavior, Kipnis's taxonomy has generated the most organizational research (Ferris and Judge, 1991). Self-promotion and impression management may be accomplished by several tactics, including assertiveness, ingratiation, rationality, sanctions, exchange, upward appeal, blocking, and coalitions. Judge and Bretz (1994) found that tactics that encourage the appearance of job competence (e.g. taking credit for others' accomplishments) have been found to be ineffective in promoting career success, whereas tactics that elicit positive affect from superiors and important decision-makers (e.g. ingratiation) appear effective.

Bibliography

Ferris, G. R. & Judge, T. A. (1991). Personnel/human resources management: a political influence perspective. *Journal of Management*, 17, 447–88.

Judge, T. A. & Bretz, R. D. (1994). Political influence behavior and career success. *Journal of Management*, 20, 43–65.

Pfeffer, J. (1989). A political perspective on careers: interests, networks, and environments. *Handbook of Career Theory*, Eds. Arthur, M. G., Hall, D. T. & Lawrence, B. S. New York: Cambridge University Press.

KEVIN W. MOSSHOLDER

political risk   Political risks are associated with government actions which deny or restrict the right of an investor/owner: (1) to use or benefit from his/her assets; or (2) which reduce the value of a firm. The most well known of the political risks include: war, revolutions, government seizure of property (expropriation, nationalization, or confiscation), and actions to restrict the movement of profits or other revenues from within a country. The impact of political risk sources of loss varies from the total destruction of assets (war); to the ability to operate but without the right to return profits to a home country (currency inconvertibility); to the taking of private property for the social good (expropriation, nationalism, confiscation). The following is a listing of governmental actions which could affect the value of a business or restrict an owner's rights to use or benefit from the business.

1 Confiscation – This is one of the major political risks faced by multinational enterprises. Confiscation is the taking of private property by a government without any offer of compensation. Governments which confiscate privately-owned property of foreign organizations usually use the excuse that the foreign firm was exploiting the country or that relations between the government and the foreign country are too strained to allow any representative of the foreign country to continue in business. Businesses considering large capital investment in a country should check the status of political risk "before" such investment takes place.

2 Contract repudiation – From time to time a contractor will enter into a contract with a foreign government

only to find that the contract cannot be fulfilled. This may be because the government terminates the contract without showing cause, refuses to pay for delivered goods, cancels the contractor's license to operate, or otherwise causes cancellation of the contract. Contracts with private buyers are subject to the same set of circumstances, although legal remedies may be available which are lacking when dealing directly with government contracts. Although most contracts are fulfilled without problem, a sufficient number are not honored to support the growth of a specific type of insurance to protect against contract repudiation.

3 Currency inconvertibility – A government may restrict the right of foreign firms to repatriate (send home) profits to their home country. Thus, all profits remain in the foreign country. If an organization does not have other operations in that country, or the owners do not have residence there, this may cause great hardship. Inconvertibility may arise because of the passage of new laws or because of administrative slowdown. Administrative slowdown refers to situations in which the government bureaucracy of a foreign country slows (either intentionally or unintentionally) the process to convert currency to such a point that it becomes a financial burden to foreign-owned companies. Insurance is available for both causes of currency inconvertibility.

4 Discriminatory taxation – Charging higher tax rates to foreign companies than for domestic companies. This type of protectionist action is not as common as it has been in the past but it still exists in many countries. The system of taxation in a foreign country must be considered when determining the method by which a company will enter that country. For example, if a local company is charged lower tax rates than a foreign-owned company, a local joint venture may be in order.

5 Embargo – To embargo is to prohibit or forbid the movement of certain or all goods to a certain country or countries. One of the most recent embargoes was that placed against Iraq after its invasion of Kuwait in the early 1990s. As of the writing of this book (mid-1996) much of that embargo is still in place. As with the United Nations sanctioned embargo of Iraq, most embargoes are implemented in times of war or to attempt to force political change by other than military force. Embargoes are difficult to implement and even more difficult to enforce over long periods of time. Embargoes not only harm the country to which they are imposed, but also all of the international export of goods to that country.

6 Expropriation of property – The government seizure of private property owned by a foreign company, with compensation being offered. Expropriation is normally aimed at a specific company whereas "nationalization" generally affects an entire industry. Expropriation may occur because of host country feelings that the foreign company is taking advantage of the host country and its people; or because of disagreements between the company and the government; or for any other reason deemed acceptable to the host government.

7 Nationalization – Nationalization is the action of a government to transfer possession of private property to the government. Many countries have nationalized whole industries on the premise that ownership transfer is in the public's best interests. Compensation is generally offered but there are no guarantees it will be sufficient to pay for loss of value and future profits of the nationalized firm. Nationalization has been most common in extractive industries (mining, energy) and communications and financial services (insurance companies and banks). Nationalization is considered a political risk for which insurance coverage may be available.

8 War risk – Actual damage caused by war, rebellion, insurrection, invasion, or use of military force to invade sovereign territory with the intent of exerting governing control. Although the definition of war varies considerably depending upon the legal jurisdiction, the fact that war or warlike actions cause severe damage to property is of the greatest interest in the present context. Generally, war risk insurance is not available in any standard market. When war risk is covered by insurance it is most likely to be under a marine insurance policy with war risk added. Land-based property damage by war is rarely covered by any insurance contract, although it is sometimes available through insurance companies that write political risk insurance.

9 Wrongful calling of guarantees – The unfair collection of a letter of credit, on-demand bond, or other guarantee of performance established by a company on behalf of a government. Companies are often required to put up a good faith guarantee of their performance before being allowed to begin work on a contract for a foreign government. For example, a road contractor may be required to provide 10% of the bid amount to a government before the government will allow construction to begin. The guarantee is supposed to provide the government with leverage to force the contract to be accomplished on time and in a workmanlike manner. Wrongful calling occurs when the government causes non-performance to occur. Cancellation of the contractor's permit to work in a country or restrictions on working hours could result in non-performance, thereby making the guarantee collectible by the government. Such collection is an example of a wrongful calling of a guarantee.

Bibliography

Cosset, J. & Roy, J. (1991). The determinants of country risk ratings. *Journal of International Business Studies*, **22** (1), 135–42.

Gregory, A. (1989). Political risk management in A. Rugman, *International Business in Canada*, pp. 310–29. Scarborough, Ontario: Prentice-Hall, Canada.

Howell, L. D. (1994). The political sociology of foreign investment and trade: Testing risk models for adequacy of protection. *AGSIM Faculty Publication*, No. 94–105.

Mathis, F. J. (1990). International risk analysis in R. T. Moran, *Global Business Management in the 1990s*. Washington, D.C.: Beacham.

Micallef, J. V. (1981). Political risk assessment. *Columbia Journal of World Business*, **16** (2), 47–52.

Yaprak, A. & Sheldon, K. T. (1984). Political risk management in multinational firms: An interrogative approach. *Management Decisions* 53–67.

JOHN O'CONNELL

political risk insurance Political risks are associated with government actions that deny or restrict the right of an investor/owner: (1) to use or benefit from his/her assets; or (2) which reduce the value of a firm. The most well known of the political risks include: war, revolution, the government seizure of property (expropriation, nationalization, or confiscation), and actions to restrict the movement of profits or other revenues from within a country. Although not all political risks are subject to insurance coverage, insurance is available for a number of government actions which act to take away or reduce the value of a foreign firm.

Political risk insurance is usually not available for the actions of a company's home government. Thus, if a United States company was subjected to high taxes or fines, political risk insurance would not provide coverage. However, if a US company was confiscated by the Libyan government the confiscation losses could be covered by political risk insurance. The discussion which follows is meant to provide general information on common coverages and restrictions in political risk insurance. Each insurer writing such coverage must be contacted to determine the exact details of their various political risk programs. Common political risk coverage includes:

1 Comprehensive export credit insurance coverage – This insurance provides coverage for losses (above those normally expected in the course of business) caused by a buyer failing to make payment due to political and commercial risks. Political risks are those associated with acts of government, whereas commercial risk includes insolvency of a buyer or other economic reasons for nonpayment. Another type of loss commonly covered by the broader forms of this coverage is if a foreign buyer cannot convert currency in order to make payment to the insured. Coverage is generally very broad, but one cannot rely on the name of an insurance contract (e.g., "comprehensive") to imply coverage. Each contract must be carefully reviewed in making a purchase decision.

2 Confiscation, expropriation, and nationalization coverage – Insurance companies usually do not differentiate between confiscation, expropriation, and nationalization because each involves the actions of a government to deprive a company of its assets or the profits derived from those assets. If compensation is paid by a government the amount received acts to reduce the payment by the insurance company. Depending on the insurance company, coverage is often found for buildings, inventory, or mobile equipment, all of which is located in a foreign country. Policies covering worldwide exposure are preferred by insurers because it provides a good spread of risk. Although single country coverage is available, the company that picks and chooses countries to insure and those to go without, often pays as much as if its entire worldwide exposure was covered. The reason for this is that the countries chosen offer the greatest risk, and thus carry the highest premiums. The insurer would probably be willing to offer an average rate for all exposures which would have been much lower than that offered for the highest risk countries.

3 Contract repudiation coverage – This type of political risk insurance provides coverage for noncompliance with contracts by a foreign government. An insured doing business with a foreign government faces the risk that the government will not comply with the contract, thereby causing loss to the insured. For example, a building construction contractor expects to be paid when the building is completed, but may not be paid if the government terminates the contract or makes it impossible for the contractor to complete the project on schedule thereby forcing a default. Insurance against contract repudiation commonly provides coverage for: unilateral government termination of a contract without cause; nonpayment of a government for service or other contracts; license termination which forces the company to default; embargoes which make completion impossible; and other government actions as outlined in each policy. Some insurers will also offer coverage for war risk which causes contract cancellation.

4 Inconvertibility of currency coverage – The inability to convert local currency into a company's home currency. This is an important consideration for an organization seeking to repatriate profits or dividends from a foreign operation. Insurance against losses arising from inconvertibility is available from speciality international insurance markets. Insurance commonly protects against one or both of the following situations:

(a) A change in a law or regulation which restricts the right to convert currency. As long as there is an official method of currency conversion before the insurance contract goes into force, coverage usually applies for changes in the law from that point forward. Most policies require that normal convertibility be delayed at least 60 to 90 days beyond the normal conversion period.

(b) An administrative delay on the part of the country's exchange authority which delays the ability to exchange currency. Most policies require the delay to be a minimum number of days beyond the period normally required for conversion. If either of these situations occur, the insurer converts the currency for the insured into the currency designated in the contract.

5 Wrongful calling of guarantees coverage – The unfair collection of a letter of credit on-demand bond, or other guarantee of performance established by a company on behalf of a government. Companies are often required to put up a good faith guarantee of their performance before being allowed to begin work on a contract for a foreign government. For example, a road contractor may be required to provide 10% of the bid amount to a government before the government will allow construction to begin. The guarantee is supposed to provide the government with leverage to force the contract to be accomplished on time and in a workman-like manner. Wrongful calling occurs when the government causes non-performance to occur. Cancellation of the contractor's permit to work in a country or restrictions on working hours could result in non-performance, thereby making the guarantee collectible by the government. Such collection is an example of a wrongful calling of a guarantee. Exporters are also subject to wrongful calls of guarantees when required to bid on supplying goods to foreign governments.

Insurance policies for wrongful calling usually provide coverage if the call on the guarantee was caused by the action of a government, such as the cancellation of an import or export license or other action that causes the non-performance. This is one type of political risk insurance in which the actions of a home government may also be covered. Persons interested in this type of coverage must contact their insurer or broker because coverage details periodically change and differ between insurers.

see also **Political risk**

JOHN O'CONNELL

political union A political union exists when two or more countries agree to allow some or all of their individual political decisions to be made by a body outside of their own, existing, governments. A third-party government to which countries transfer governing power is referred to as a "supranational" organization or one which spans national boundaries. A good example of a supranational organization is the European Community Parliament which exercises control over the E.C., thereby taking some of the powers previously held by each member country of the community.

JOHN O'CONNELL

politics Politics in organizations may be defined as POWER in action. Specifically, this refers to behaviors designed to INFLUENCE others to reach an outcome one favors. Such behaviors usually reflect competing individual (CAREER) and collective (subunit) interests that must somehow be managed for an organization to be effective. Politics exist in varying degrees in all organizations, as the article will indicate.

Old Paradigms: Politics is Bad
Virtually every major management scholar writing on politics, including Kanter, Kotter, and Pfeffer, has emphasized that it was a neglected subject until the mid-1970s, and it still lags relative to other specialties. They argue that politics was seen traditionally as representing the nonrational, underside of organizational life, deflecting people away from task performance, emphasizing instead devious, Machiavellian maneuverings for personal career or group (e.g., department, division) advantage. Politics, as Bennis was quoted to have said, "is the organization's last dirty secret."

A dichotomy was often posed between "rational," "businesslike" organizations and "political" ones. In the former, decisions regarding strategy, organization design, and personnel, for example, were presumably made "on their merits." Managers were seen as using "objective" (financial, economic, organizational, and behavioral) approaches, e.g., optimization models, SWOT analysis, motivational theory. Political organizations, by contrast, were seen as making decisions by manipulation, logrolling, and compromise, reflecting mainly turf and personal career interests.

New Paradigms: Power and Politics are Universal and Can Be Good
Since the early 1960s, several streams of writing have converged, arguing for the universality of politics in organizations. They also argue that politics may well be functional for individual and ORGANIZATIONAL EFFECTIVENESS, holding organizations together, aligning them with their environments, and distinguishing successful from unsuccessful managers (*see* ORGANIZATION AND ENVIRONMENT).

One stream from Simon, Cyert, and March emphasizes the cognitive limits to rationality in DECISION MAKING, given managers' limited information, noting that many decisions ultimately involve matters of judgment and are made and implemented by shifting coalitions, depending on their importance to different groups.

Sociologist James Thompson argued that many important organizational decisions – e.g., on strategy – involve matters on which there is no consensus regarding goals and no clearly established or agreed on programs or means. The result, again, is an intrusion of politics, with decisions emerging as resultants from negotiations among various coalitions, rather than as rationally planned through the use of sophisticated analytic techniques or models (*see* COALITION FORMATION; NEGOTIATION).

Lawrence and Lorsch (1967) observed that all organizations differentiate into various subunits, as they adapt to their environments, with these subunits establishing separate functions, interests, and tendencies toward territoriality– e.g., across departments, divisions, and levels. A critical problem is then one of integration, usually through bargaining and, again, that involves politics.

Political scientists added their perspective in the 1960s and 1970s, arguing that organizations may be seen as collections of interest groups or stakeholders. One of the main tasks of the manager, so they argue, is to negotiate agreements with these stakeholders in establishing organizational goals. This theme is picked up in Pfeffer and Salancik's work (1978) on resource dependency.

A particularly relevant contribution in this regard is David Hickson and Derek Pugh's strategic contingencies theory of power. It posits that power gravitates to those individuals and subunits whose expertise enables them to control for the organization's critical uncertainties. Effective organizations, from this perspective, are those whose dominant coalition have the skills most relevant to the dominant issues those organizations are facing.

John Kotter argues that the manager must negotiate with more and more individuals and groups who fall outside the chain of command, as organizations become less hierarchical and more horizontal, and as more decisions are made in cross-functional teams. He writes of the "power gap" that managers increasingly face, as they attempt to manage these stakeholders. Managing dependency, then, is a central task of all managers, particularly those at higher levels.

An underlying theme from all these writings is that organizations are not just tools for rational action whose decisions may be systematically programmed and implemented. They have both increased in complexity – with many more stakeholders than before – and in environmental uncertainty – faced with much more change that is harder to read and predict. For both reasons, managing effectively under such circumstances is incredibly challenging. The recent emphasis on politics as a central feature of organizational life takes up an important component of that challenge.

Key Substantive Issues in Politics

There are many ways of conceptualizing key issues in organizational politics. Pfeffer's is particularly useful, dividing the field into four broad questions:

(1) assessing politics by developing a map indicating the key players, their goals and resources, and how they play the game;
(2) developing a power base;
(3) using it through various tactics; and
(4) the role of politics in shaping organizational change.

This framework is particularly useful for practicing managers. Thus, for a manager to be effective in getting decisions implemented, it is critical to gain the support of key players with stakes in the decision. Gaining that support requires building a political base and then applying it in various influence tactics e.g., framing or defining the issue, timing, using data and analysis to legitimate one's positions, exercising interpersonal influence, and using the appropriate symbolism (the manager as "evangelist") necessary to get others to collaborate (see LEGITIMACY). This is not, of course, a linear process, and effective managers are engaged constantly in various political resource building activities and power tactics.

Ultimately, politics is only important as it shapes how things get done in organizations, particularly how organizations adapt (see ORGANIZATIONAL CHANGE). This last issue on the consequences of politics for organizational performance is critical.

Still another way of conceptualizing the field is in terms of the politics of key relationships and career stages for managers. This is Kotter's approach, as he characterizes the relational and life cycle contexts of managers.

Some Illustrative Propositions

This field is a long way from being easily codified. It is possible, however, to indicate some propositions. One set relates to the following conditions under which organizational decisions are more likely to be political: In highly differentiated organizations, where subunits are very interdependent, where there is considerable resource scarcity, on high stakes decisions whose outcomes are important for several participants, and where authority and power are widely dispersed. In addition, the larger the organization, the more uncertain its environment, the more it is dependent on outside groups, the more ambitious its goals, the more complex and sophisticated its technology, the more consolidated it is geographically, the less its measurement systems clearly measure individual performance, and the less the reward system rewards individual performance, the more political the organization is likely to be.

Taking a more micro perspective, those managerial positions that have more responsibilities, more direct and indirect reports, and more formal authority will be more political by virtue of having in each instance more job related dependence. In general, those decisions where discretion is high, where there is much ambiguity, and where it is difficult to apply techno–economic criteria, are more likely to be political. This would include strategic decisions at high levels, decisions around interdepartmental or interdivisional coordination, those relating to budgets, resource allocation across subunits, and purchasing,

ORGANIZATION DESIGN, and many personnel decisions, e.g., promotions and transfers.

Finally, from Pfeffer, power is likely to be most effectively exercised when it is done so in unobtrusive ways, when it makes decisions and processes stemming from its exercise look rational, and when it involves much coalition building. Given industrialized societies' cultural emphasis on rationality and objectivity, any appearance of manipulation or Machiavellianism may lead to a manager being seen as unethical and losing coalition support.

Examples of political behavior that reflect this rationalistic bias include the selective use of objective criteria, the use of outside consultants, controlling the agenda (which issues get discussed and in what order), selective hiring and promotions, and coopting potential opponents, often through committees. Each of these tactics often involves managing appearances and may be represented as appealing to objective criteria in making decisions. In actual fact, it is a way of breaking a deadlook on highly complex decisions where there are no clear, objective solutions, where power is widely dispersed among multiple players with different interests, where the stakes for the organization and these players are high, and where the costs of a continuing stalemate are too great to allow it to continue. Such political tactics thus become the means of generating a consensus enabling the organization to make and implement decisions that are vital to its future and on which it had been unable to act in the past.

Future Directions

Even though the new emphasis on politics is a significant advance over traditional writings, one main objective from past paradigms still prevails: Make organizations more effective. The only difference is that politics is a new tool in such an effort.

Little attention is given in this new politics literature, however, to what is meant by effectiveness or to the question of effectiveness for whom. In particular, there is little emphasis on how politics may contribute to inequality in organizations, to "unfair treatment" of particular categories of employees (women, black people or other minorities), or to social harm that organizations may incur on the communities and society in which they are located. Following from that, little attention has been given to how politics might be used within organizations to effect social change in humanistic ways in relation to these issues.

Organizations may be seen as tools through which elites maintain their dominance by controlling their employees and by preventing noncompliance with organization goals and policies. A distinction may be made between power to and power over. In the former, the emphasis is on how politics may be harnessed for career mobility for managers and for organizational adaptation, narrowly defined by the senior managers of organizations (see TOP MANAGEMENT TEAMS). In the latter, it is on domination and control.

An alternative research agenda that might well flow from these points would be to look more critically at the ways senior managers use politics to control stakeholder demands. The larger context of such research might be to devise ways of enabling dispossessed stakeholders to use political skills and analysis to effect more organizational responsiveness to their concerns. This might be a way of promoting social change by developing the countervailing power of an underclass who may well be victimized by the top down decisions of senior managers. While such decisions may be defined in existing paradigms as contributing to organizational effectiveness, that may be a narrow definition, reflecting the interests of those senior managers who make the decisions. A more humanistic and social change oriented politics, driven by such perspectives as critical theory in the organizations field might well move it in such intriguing new directions.

Another agenda for politics research would take as its starting point new trends and organizational forms in the 1980s and 1990s. One is mergers and acquisitions. Though the conglomerate craze of the 1970s and 1980s has passed, growth through mergers is still common throughout industrialized nations. The political problems of postmerger integration – e.g., who will gain control, over what functions and levels – are major issues for managers. A second is the politics of DOWNSIZING, an experience many corporations are going through, though with few guidelines on how to manage it.

Still a third trend is for corporations to form STRATEGIC ALLIANCES and joint ventures to stabilize their market position in globally competitive industries. The large US auto companies – GM with Toyota or Ford with Nissan – are examples. Managing the power struggles involved in these ventures is a critical issue.

Finally, such new forms as the "horizontal corporation" and the "virtual corporation" generate their own politics. With regard to the former, earlier was mentioned the interest in the politics of managing cross-functional teams. We need to know much more about that process. The virtual corporation involves the out-sourcing that many corporations have engaged in, to shed nonessential businesses in an era of down-sizing. Working out the political dynamics of such relationships with subcontractors requires major political skills.

In conclusion, between the humanistic politics of the dispossessed in organizations and the politics of emerging organizational forms, a rich agenda of future research should generate new knowledge – both for managers and for academics. This is a field with a promising future.

see also **Collective bargaining; Organizational culture**

Bibliography

Cyert, R. M. & March, J. G. (1963). A behavioral theory of the firm. Englewood Cliffs, NJ: Prentice-Hall.
Gandz, J. & Murray, V. V. (1980). The experience of workplace politics. Academy of Management Journal, **23**, 237–251.
Hickson, D. et al. (1971). A strategic contingencies' theory of intraorganizational power. Administrative Science Quarterly, **16**, 216–229.
Kanter, R. (1977). Men and women of the corporation. New York: Basic Books.
Kotter, J. (1985). Power and influence. New York: Free Press.
Kotter, J. (1979). Power in management. New York: Amacom.
Lawrence, P. R. & Lorsch, J. W. (1967). Organization and environment. Cambridge, MA: Harvard University Press.
Pfeffer, J. (1981). Power in organizations. Marshfield, MA: Pitman.
Pfeffer, J. (1992). Managing with power. Boston: Harvard Business School Press.
Pfeffer, J. & Salancik, G. R. (1978). The external control of organizations: A resource dependence perspective. New York: Harper & Row.
Thompson, J. (1967). Organizations in action. New York: McGraw-Hill.

DAVID ROGERS

polygraph testing Polygraph testing is a specialized procedure used for the purpose of identifying persons who fail to answer questions honestly. The polygraph, commonly referred to as a "lie detector," is used for this purpose. It monitors physiological responses, including cardiovascular, respiratory and electrodermal patterns, as an examinee answers a set of questions.

Research makes it clear that there is, in fact, no direct physiological response that indicates deception on the part of the examinee. A sharp jump in one or more physiological indicators in response to a direct question about the theft of money, for example, still leaves unanswered the "reason" for that physiological response. Many plausible reasons might exist (e.g. the individual has stolen and fears being detected, the individual has not stolen but fears being wrongly accused, the individual suddenly remembers that he or she forgot to feed the parking meter), making a conclusive inference of dishonesty unwarranted. As a result, examination techniques have been developed in an attempt to differentiate between various possible causes for a physiological response to a particular question.

The accuracy of polygraph examinations remains a matter of considerable dispute. Levels of accuracy above 90 percent have been reported in some technically sound studies investigating a single specific event (e.g. "who took the money from the safe?"). However, the vast majority of polygraph investigations in the employment context have not been investigations into a specific criminal act, but, rather, are broad, multifaceted pre-employment inquiries. Even if accuracy were as high as 90 percent in the inquiry into a single event, error rates would compound in a pre-employment inquiry where the range of issues might include theft, drug use, and work habits, among others. The American Polygraph Association concludes that there is a high accuracy rate with trained examiners and proper examination procedures. In contrast, the American Psychological Association concluded that the scientific evidence in support of polygraph use is unsatisfactory.

Use of the polygraph by private employers was heavily restricted by the Employee Polygraph Protection Act of 1988, which prohibited requiring or requesting that applicants or employees submit to a polygraph examination. Exemptions are provided for highly regulated examinations of employees who are suspects in an ongoing investigation, and for examination of applicants by a very limited set of employers (e.g. manufacturers of controlled substances). Most states also regulate or restrict polygraph exams, with some state regulations also covering government employees.

Federal regulation covers mechanical devices used to diagnose an individual's honesty. Thus, devices such as voice stress analyzers are covered. However, federal regulation does not cover oral or written inquiries into honesty, such as written honesty tests or INTEGRITY TESTING.

Bibliography

Ben-Shakar, G. & Furedy, J. J. (1990). *Theories and Applications in the Detection of Deception*, New York: Springer-Verlag.

Congress of the United States Office of Technology Assessment (1983). *Scientific Validity of Polygraph Testing*, Washington, DC: US Government Printing Office.

Raskin, D. C. (1986). The polygraph in 1986: Scientific, professional, and legal issues surrounding application and acceptance of polygraph evidence. *Utah Law Review*, 29, 29–74.

Saxe, L., Dougherty, D. & Cross, T. (1985). The validity of polygraph testing: scientific analysis and public controversy. *American Psychologist*, 40, 355–66.

PAUL R. SACKETT

population ecology This theoretical perspective attempts to explain organizational diversity as resulting from natural selection processes. The perspective was introduced in 1977 by Michael Hannan and John Freeman, who proposed that the organizations we see around us can be understood as the survivors of past processes of organizational founding and dissolution (Hannan & Freeman, 1989). The theory and methods of organizational ecology attempt to explain the empirical record of these processes, and have expanded in scope to include the study of organizational aging, growth, change, and performance (*see* ORGANIZATIONAL CHANGE).

Environmental Selection

The primary unit of analysis is the "organizational form," the various "blueprints" that guide organization building. A basic ecological principle is that selection processes favor one organizational form over all others in a given niche, or segment of the organizational environment (*see* ORGANIZATION AND ENVIRONMENT). Based on this idea, studies typically model how conditions of the organizational environment select among organizational forms. The estimates of these models can then be used to determine an environment's "carrying capacity" for a particular organizational form – the number of a particular form that can be supported in a given environment.

The initial Hannan and Freeman paper (1977) discussed the survival prospects of specialist and generalist organizational forms. They predicted, and later found, that specialist organizations are favored over generalists under most conditions. Only when resource availability is highly variable and the time between variations is long did they predict an advantage for generalists.

Other work has extended the study of environmental selection processes to include political and social forces (*see* POLITICS). Work in this vein finds that political upheaval tends to increase both failure and founding rates – jeopardizing existing forms while freeing up resources for the founding of new organizations. Carroll and Huo (1986) looked at the effects of both the task and institutional environments on newspaper organizations, finding that institutional factors were most important for predicting vital rates while aspects of the task environment most strongly predicted organizational performance (*see* ORGANIZATIONAL EFFECTIVENESS).

Formal government policies and regulations have become standard variables explaining the vital rates of organizations. In most cases these variables are found to have their expected effects, but under some conditions public policies have had unintended consequences due to ecological dynamics. Other work has looked at how organizational viability is affected by institutional affiliations.

Resource partitioning. While most research has treated the structure of environmental niches as given, Carroll (1985) proposed a model that accounts for the evolution of niche structure over time. In his resource partitioning model, Carroll argued that the availability of niches for specialists changes when an organizational population becomes more concentrated. As concentration increases, generalists become more suited to the "mass market" but less tailored to particular specializations. Consequently, his model predicts that increasing concentration actually increases the niches available to specialists, making them more viable. Carroll found evidence in support of this prediction in his study of newspaper publishing organizations, and recent work on other populations also supports the model.

Ecological Interdependence

A growing body of research looks at selection forces endogenous to organizational populations – where organizations affect one another's life chances.

Density dependence. Interest in ecological interdependence has sky-rocketed since Hannan developed the so-called "density dependent" model (Hannan & Carroll, 1992). The model is based on the idea that both LEGITIMACY and competition increase with the density (number) of organizations in a population. When an organizational population is new it lacks legitimacy. At this point increases in numbers enhance legitimacy considerably but intensify competition only a little. At high levels of density, however, additional increases in density add little to the legitimacy of the form but increase competition significantly due to overcrowding. Together, these arguments predict that increases in density at low levels increase founding rates and decreases failure rates, while in-density at high levels should drive founding rates down and failure rates up. A sizable empirical record mostly supports these predictions (Singh & Lumsden, 1990).

Other work has sought to specify the geographic levels of analysis where competition and legitimation occur, under the idea that legitimation may develop more broadly across societies while competition is more localized. Results do not break into this neat pattern, however, but suggest:

(1) that higher-level patterns may conceal important differences between rural and urban areas, and
(2) that entrepreneurship may be driven more by local factors while the ultimate fates of these organizations may depend on broader regional competition.

Carroll and Hannan extended the density-dependence model to include "density delay" – a reduction in an organization's viability experienced over its lifetime due to competition at the time it was founded. Two ideas combine for density delay. First, organizations are thought to be made more frail when they are founded under crowded, high-density conditions. Second, this initial frailty is argued to be permanent since it effects the characteristics "imprinted" into an organization at its time of founding. Other generalizations of the density model look at how competition depends on organizational size and experience.

Multiform models. Why do different forms of organizations sometimes coexist in the same domain? Ecologists typically answer this question by proposing that the environment is segregated into distinct niches were the conditions are right for different organizational forms (*see*

STRATEGIC GROUPS). The more that these niches are segregated by institutional boundaries, technological barriers, and the like, the less "overlap" will exist between them and so the less their organizational forms will compete. With competition attenuated, different organizational forms can coexist in equilibrium.

Empirical tests have searched for such differentiation in several ways. The most widely used approach is to apply the density-dependence model, specifying density effects between forms. McPherson (1983) developed a different approach by conceiving of competition among particular organizations, and then directly measuring the extent to which they depend on common resources.

Extending the idea of segregated niches, Hannan, Ranger-Moore, and Banaszak-Holl (1990) proposed that competition is "size-localized," so that similar-sized organizations compete more strongly than organizations of different sizes. The idea is that size typically co-varies with many other aspects of an organization's form. If organizations of similar forms tend to occupy the same niche, and so compete more strongly, then we should see greater competition among organizations when they are more similar in size. Baum and Mezias (1992) find support for this prediction and extend the model.

A new application of multiform competition models was developed by Carroll and Swaminathan (1992), who argue that the concept of organizational form is essentially the same as the idea of strategic group developed in the strategy literature (see STRATEGIC MANAGEMENT). With this in mind, multiform competition models have been used to test hypotheses about strategic behavior and its effects on competition.

Population dynamics. The evolution of organizational populations is also shaped by the effects of foundings and failures at one point in time on ensuing foundings and failures, so-called population dynamics. Failures are followed by foundings, since they free-up resources – although periods of extremely high failure rates act to lower founding rates by dissuading potential entrepreneurs. By contrast, observed foundings in one period encourage potential entrepreneurs and so increase the ensuing founding rate. However, this effect is reversed at high levels since very large numbers of foundings deplete resources for further organizing.

Organization-level Processes

Ecological theory can be applied to the evolution of individual organizations (Aldrich, 1979), and ecological processes are often modeled using data where individual organizations are the units of analysis. Consequently, researchers have investigated regularities that vary from organization to organization – especially age- and size-dependent failure, organizational change, and organizational growth.

Age- and size-dependent failure. Researchers have argued that organizations are more likely to fail when they are young, since the internal roles and routines as well as the external position, legitimacy, and relations of a new organization are not yet well developed. Researchers in organizational ecology have usually found support for this so-called "liability of newness".

More recently, some have questioned the ubiquity of this effect. Halliday, Powell, and Granfors (1987) studied US state bar associations. They described these organizations as "minimalist" in that they incur low costs and are supported by other organizations, and did not find that they suffer a liability of newness from a liability of smallness. Others have found that the liability of newness does not start immediately when an organization is born, but only after an initial period when a new organization can survive on its initial resource endowment.

Barron, West, and Hannan (1994) argue that the finding of negative age-dependent failure rates reflects only an uncontrolled "liability of smallness". In a study of credit unions, they find that controlling for organizational size, organizations are more likely to fail as they get older – evidence of internal problems that become worse over time (senescence) and obsolescence.

Organizational change. A controversial tenant of the ecological perspective is that organizations are unlikely to change in dramatic ways, and are likely to fail when they do try to change. In what is known as Structural Inertia Theory, Hannan and Freeman laid out the logic behind this tenet. Their central argument is that selection processes favor inert organizations. Organizations are rewarded for performing reliably, and for being able to account rationally for their behavior. Such reliability and accountability are greater for organizations with stable routines that resist change. Thus selection forces tend to favor the creation of inert organizations.

This theory has testable implications for the "core" organizational characteristics. With respect to the likelihood of change, it implies that organizations become more stable as they age and grow. ROLES, political coalitions, routines, and ties to other social actors in the environment (among other factors) tend to resist change. Furthermore, these forces become well established – and so more resistant to change – as time passes and as organizations grow in size. This implies that organizations become less likely to change as they age and grow. Should change occur, however, this stabilizing process is restarted. The newly changed organization has not yet had time for new internal processes, structures, and external ties to stabilize. Consequently, change rachets up the likelihood of additional change – an effect that again falls away as time passes.

When change does occur it is predicted to be hazardous, since organizational action often generates unanticipated consequences. Furthermore, even when organizations do change as planned, this is not sufficient for success. The question is whether an organization can change fast enough to match its environment – which typically also is changing. For these reasons, dramatic organizational change is predicted to make organizations again as likely to fail as a new organization – essentially "resetting" the liability of newness clock. As time passes, however, organizations are predicted to recover from the shock of having changed, as internal processes and routines develop and external legitimacy and ties are again secured. Thus the hazard associated with change should wear off over time – if the organization does not die first.

Amburgey, Kelly, and Barnett (1993) found support for the predictions of structural inertia theory in a thorough test on the Finnish newspaper industry, and Barnett (1994) found that technological change increased failure rates among telephone companies. By contrast, Haveman (1992) found that change enhanced viability among savings and loans during a period when not changing implied nearly certain failure. Other studies have shown mixed effects, probably because they analyzed changes in peripheral as well as core characteristics.

Organizational Growth

Organizations differ dramatically in size, and several studies attempt to explain these differences from an ecological perspective. Researchers typically start with the null hypothesis that proportionate organizational growth is random and independent of current size – so-called "Gibrat's law." Studies then test whether ecological dynamics can account for deviations from this baseline model. In most cases, researchers have applied theoretical propositions developed in studies of vital rates to explain organizational growth. For instance, Barron, West, and Hannan (1994) find support for the density-dependence model in their analysis of credit union growth.

see also **Interorganizational relations; Institutional theory; Organizational design**

Bibliography

Aldrich, H. E. (1979). Organizations and environments. Englewood Cliffs, NJ: Prentice-Hall.

Amburgey, T. L. Kelly, D. & Barnett, W. P. (1993). Resetting the clock: The dynamics of organizational change and failure. Administrative Science Quarterly, 38, 51–73.

Barnett, W. P. (1994). The liability of collective action: Growth and change among early American telephone companies. In J. Baum & J. Singh (eds), Evolutionary Dynamics of Organizations. New York: Oxford University Press.

Barron, D. N. West, E. & Hannan, M. T. (1994). A time to grow and a time to die: Growth and mortality of credits 1914–1990. American Journal of Sociology.

Baum, J. A. C. & Mezias, S. J. (1992). Localized competition and organizational failure in the Manhattan hotel industry, 1898–1990. Administrative Science Quarterly, 37, 580–604.

Carroll, G. R. (1985). Concentration and specialization: Dynamics of niche width in populations of organizations. American Journal of Sociology, 90, 1262–1283.

Carroll, G. R. & Huo, Y. P. (1986). Organizational task and institutional environments in ecological perspective: findings from the local newspaper industry. American Journal of Sociology, 91, 838–873.

Carroll, G. R. & Swaminathan, A. (1992). The organizational ecology of strategic groups in the American brewing industry from 1975–1990. Industrial and Corporate Change, 1, 65–97.

Halliday, T. Powell, M. J. & Granfors, M. W. (1987). Minimalist organizations: Vital events in state bar associations: 1870–1930. American Sociological Review, 52, 456–471.

Hannan, M. T. & Carroll, G. R. (1992). Dynamics of organizational populations: density, competition, and legitimation. New York: Oxford University Press.

Hannan, M. T. & Freeman, J. (1977). The population ecology of organizations. American Journal of Sociology, 83, 929–984.

Hannan, M. T. & Freeman, J. (1989). Organizational ecology. Cambridge, MA: Harvard University Press.

Hannan, M. T. Ranger-Moore, J. & Banaszak-Holl, J. (1990). Competition and the evolution of organizational size distributions. In J. V. Singh (Ed.), Organizational evolution: New Directions, pp. 246–268. Newbury Park, CA: Sage.

Haveman, H. A. (1992). Between a rock and a hard place: Organizational change and performance under conditions of fundamental environmental transformation. Administrative Science Quarterly, 37, 48–75.

McPherson, J. M. (1983). An ecology of affiliation. American Sociological Review, 83, 340–363.

Singh, J. V. & Lumsden, C. J. (1990). Theory and research in organizational ecology. Annual Review of Sociology, 16, 161–195. Palo Alto, CA: Annual Reviews.

WILLIAM P. BARNETT

portfolio analysis In marketing, portfolio analysis is used at both a business and a product level, but the discussion here will be in terms of businesses. The aim is to assess the current mix of businesses in terms of balance of, for example, growing as against maturing businesses. Portfolio analysis techniques generally prescribe the actions to be taken with regard to these businesses, such as, invest, abandon, etc.

The most popular framework for portfolio analysis is that proposed by the Boston Consulting Group (*see* BCG MATRIX) which classifies businesses in terms of two major parameters (relative MARKET SHARE and market growth). Other analytical frameworks which employ a composite of variables have subsequently been developed, although essentially they all have the same end in view: of providing an easily employable means of evaluating a mix of businesses and prescribing the courses of action to be adopted.

Two of these, the Shell directional policy matrix and the A. D. Little competitive position–industry maturity matrix, are reviewed in Abell & Hammond (1979) and Hofer & Schendel (1978). The limitations of these approaches are discussed in Day, 1977 and Wensley, 1981. Some criticisms made are that: strategy aimed at securing a high market share regardless of context is questionable; there are difficulties in defining the market, and the cut-off points to decide between "high and low" of market share and growth; and the approaches focus on generalized strategic recommendations which might stifle creative solutions.

Bibliography

Abell, D. F. & Hammond, S. (1979). *Strategic market planning.* Prentice-Hall, 213–219.

Day, G. (1977). Diagnosing the product portfolio. *Journal of Marketing,* 41, Apr., 29–38.

Hofer, C. W. & Schendel, D. (1978). *Strategy formulation: Analytical concepts.* St Paul, MN: West Publishing.

Wensley, R. (1981). Strategic marketing: Betas, boxes or Basics. *Journal of Marketing,* 45, 173–182.

DALE LITTLER

portfolio management Portfolio management (Strong, 1993) is concerned with distributing investible liquidity across a range of available assets and liabilities with the objective of providing risks and returns that achieve performance objectives. Portfolio management therefore comprises objective setting (establishing the relative importance of delivering capital and income growth and providing stability of principal and income to actual or prospective investors), asset allocation (where the available funds are distributed across geographic markets and security categories to exploit broad market and currency movements) and security selection (the choice of particular securities in each category that offer the best value in terms of portfolio objectives).

So far as objective setting is concerned this is conducted in either a direct or indirect mode. Direct objectives emerge from detailed customer financial reviews conducted in approved form by financial intermediaries licensed by a regulatory authority. Alternatively pension or insurance fund trustees might set portfolio managers income and growth objectives relative to a specific benchmark such as the *Financial Times*/Actuaries All Share Index. Indirect objective setting arises where portfolios in the form of mutual funds (unit trusts and investment trusts in the UK) are offered to the public in which case the basic strategy in terms of exposure to equities or bonds or to UK, European, or Far Eastern markets will be outlined in a prospectus. Arising from this strategy a benchmark in terms of the growth, income, and capital stability characteristics of a particular index (e.g. European equity, North American bond) will be defined and the security reported in that category by the financial press.

Historically the distinction between portfolio management and investment management arises from new ideas about risk diversification introduced in the 1950s by Harry Markowitz (1952) with the observation that the variability of returns for a collection of assets depended on the correlation of asset returns with each other and not just on the weighted average of the individual assets. Diversifying investments across a range of substantially uncorrelated securities, whether within one country or increasingly internationally (Levy and Sarnat, 1970) provides portfolio managers with lower variability for the same return or a higher return for the same variability than any single one of the underlying national or international securities.

The theory of diversification was developed by Sharpe (1963) and Lintner (1965) to show that where large numbers of securities are used to create a fully diversified portfolio the effect is to eliminate the specific risks relating to each particular asset, leaving only the systematic risk, the common risks to which all securities are exposed. This systematic risk or market risk is effectively equivalent to the riskiness of the market portfolio and provides the reference benchmark for risk pricing used in the capital asset pricing model or CAPM.

Depending on diversification strategy, portfolio management may be active or passive. Passive portfolio management aims to replicate the performance, say, of a particular stock index by neutral weighting whereby asset distribution in the portfolio matches the proportions of each asset or asset class in the index to be proxied. In contrast under active portfolio management elements in the portfolio are either overweight (overrepresented) or underweight (underrepresented) relative to the target index. The intention is to produce outperformance relative to the target index by overrepresentation of assets or asset classes expected to outperform the relevant index. Active management therefore involves frequent rebalancing of both the asset allocation and the individual underlying security holdings to reflect changes in the expected risks and returns.

This rebalancing will aim to exploit timing effects. The relative returns for different countries and for the different types of security such as equities bonds and money market balances within a country vary with economic conditions of growth, inflation, etc. By overweighting the portfolio with the asset most likely to outperform under the anticipated economic climate the portfolio manager aims to outperform a portfolio that maintains unchanged weightings throughout the economic cycle.

If the choice of assets is simplified to comprise simply high risk (equity) investments that generally outperform under economic recovery and low risk (bonds and cash) that outperform in conditions of economic slowdown and recession, timing effectiveness can be measured relative to a benchmark portfolio with fixed equity and bond/cash proportions. In principle the benchmark portfolio could be fully invested in equities with the bond/cash proportion zero, but a fund manager wishing to increase equity exposure relative to the benchmark could borrow cash to invest more than 100 percent of portfolio value in equities. Significant leverage (using debt to purchase equities in excess of the total value of the fund) is encountered both in closed end funds and in the speculative hedge funds, but open-ended mutual funds are prohibited from borrowing and in practice most portfolios contain liquidity either to meet imminent liabilities (pension payouts, insurance claims, fund withdrawals) or from uninvested new contributions. To reflect this, the benchmark portfolio might have 20 percent cash/bonds and 80 percent equity. If the equity index yields 7 percent and money market rates are 5 percent an active fund with a 30 percent/70 percent allocation will earn 0.3×5 percent + 0.7×7 percent or 6.4 percent, an underperformance relative to the benchmark return (0.2×5 percent + 0.8×7 percent or 6.6 percent) of 0.2 percent.

The timing stances of a variety of funds in respect of cash, bonds and equities are illustrated in a sample of portfolio recommendations published regularly by *The Economist* (table 1).

Strictly performance comparison between portfolios should specifically adjust for the *ex ante* risks taken by the portfolios, otherwise portfolio managers would simply increase risk levels to improve returns. The CAPM model provides a framework for risk adjustment by using beta or the correlation of returns of a security or portfolio with the returns of the market portfolio as a proxy for riskiness with the market portfolio definitionally having a beta of one.

Table 1 Sample Portfolio Recommendations (%)

	Merrill Lynch	Lehman Brothers	Nikko Securities	Daiwa Europe	Credit Agricole	Credit Suisse
Equities	45	50	65	55	65	30
Bonds	40	40	30	40	35	48
Cash	15	10	5	5	0	22

Source: *Economist* 7 January 1995, p. 72.

The beta is then multiplied by the risk premium or historical outperformance of equities relative to government bonds to provide a risk adjusted benchmark return. Thus if the risk premium is 7 percent then a portfolio with a beta of 1.5 has to achieve returns 7 percent higher than a portfolio with a beta of 0.5 before outperformance is demonstrated. Unfortunately in recent years the risk premium has been rather volatile; see table 2.

Table 2   Real Returns on Investment in US dollar terms, 1984–93 annual average.

	Equities	Bonds	Cash
France	18	14.5	9.5
Holland	17.5	11.5	8
Britain	15	8.5	7.5
Germany	14	9	7.5
Switzerland	13.5	8	6.5
Italy	13	14	9.5
Japan	13	13.5	10
USA	12	11	3
Australia	10.5	11	6
Canada	3.5	11	5.5

Source: *Economist* 14 May 1994.

As an alternative Merton (1981) argued that as returns of an all-equity portfolio are more variable (risky) than an all-bond portfolio, risk differences due to composition should be proxied by using option performance. Perfect timing is equivalent to holding cash plus call options on the entire equity portfolio with benchmark adjustments using reduced options to reflect any equity proportion.

The two best known portfolio performance yardsticks are the Sharpe measure and the Treynor measure. Sharpe (1966) measures return differences from average relative to the standard deviation of returns, while Treynor measures return differences from average relative to beta, or systematic risk.

Within the overall asset allocation, active portfolio management involves security analysis aimed at picking the best value way of investing allocated funds in asset categories such as bonds, deposits, real estate, equities, and commodities. Portfolios, though, mainly emphasize bonds and equities for the simple reason that they have high liquidity (reasonable quantities can be bought or sold at market price) and low transaction costs. In analyzing securities, portfolio managers utilize either fundamental analysis or technical analysis. Fundamental analysis utilizes financial and non-financial data to locate undervalued securities which relative to the market offer growth at a discount, assets at a discount or yield at a discount. Although brokerage houses, among others, invest heavily in such analysis if successful it would contradict the efficient market hypothesis (EMH) which argues that the market prices of securities already incorporate all information in the market and that therefore it is impossible in the long term to outperform the market. Nevertheless, relatively simple transformations such as Gordon's growth model

(Gordon, 1963) relating share prices shares to dividends and dividend growth are widely used in security selection. There is an extensive literature, including Fama (1969), on signaling where factors such as dividend changes or investment announcements are used to explain security price changes.

The arbitrage pricing theory APT developed by Ross (1976) provides a more general formal framework for analyzing return differences based on the basis of multiple factors such as industry, size, market to book ratio, and other economic and financial variables.

Not surprisingly, the possibility of beating the passive or buy and hold strategies indicated by the EMH has attracted considerable attention, with Banz (1981) among the first to detect an anomaly in the risk-adjusted outperformance of small firms followed by Keim's (1983) analysis of a January effect. End of month, holiday, and weekend effects together with price/book anomalies have also been reported, but with an overall effect small relative to transaction costs. Despite this limited success market practitioners continue to offer simple guidelines that they have used to produce exceptional returns. Jim Slater (Slater, 1994) reports favorable results for a stock picking exercise that uses principles developed by the legendary Warren Buffett and more recently by O'Higgins and Downes (1992) who report in *Beating the Dow* that picking the ten highest yielding shares from the 30 Dow Jones Industrial Index and then investing in the five cheapest (in dollar price) of these shares produced a gain of 2,800 percent against a 560 percent gain on the Dow over eighteen years. It is unclear, though, what these authors have to gain by disclosing such valuable procedures.

Technical analysis or chartism is an alternative and widely used technique in portfolio management. In direct contradiction to the weak-form version of the EMH, which states that all information contained in past securities prices is incorporated in the present market price, technical analysts use past patterns to project trends. These patterns may be simply shapes described for example as "head and shoulders," "double tops," "flags," and so on or more elaborate short- or long-term trend lines, all of which are used to generate buy or sell signals. Evaluations of technical analysis have generally run into problems because of subjectivity in classifying signals, but recent work in neural networks (Baestans et al., 1994) has provided objective evidence of information in the trend lines used by technical analysts, much of it in non-linear components neglected in some econometric analysis.

The relatively recent development of large, liquid derivative markets – security and index options and futures – has revolutionized the asset allocation process because it allows portfolio managers to proxy the exposure of one asset allocation despite holding a portfolio consisting of a completely different set of assets. A bond or money market portfolio together with equity index futures contracts effectively proxies an equity portfolio. An equity portfolio together with the purchase of put options and sale of call options is similarly equivalent to a fixed interest portfolio. Portfolio managers are able to use derivatives to segment risks asymmetrically. An equity portfolio or index future hedged by put options gives the downside stability of a bond portfolio and the upward opportunities of an equity portfolio. This allows the portfolio manager to create funds with partial or full performance guarantees where investors are offered half any upward movement in the equity market plus the return of their original investment.

Index-based derivatives are particularly popular with portfolio managers because they provide market diversification with very low transaction costs and none of the trading and monitoring activity involved in maintaining a portfolio of securities that mimicked the index. A portfolio manager wishing to hold a long-term position in equities but at the same time wanting a flexible asset allocation will typically use an index transaction to adjust exposure. A sale of an index future on 20 percent of the portfolio is equivalent to a 20/80 bond equity portfolio.

The possibility of altering positions in this way without transactions on the spot market has generated a number of new techniques. Program trading, for example, involves buying or selling bundles of shares. A portfolio manager with a bundle of shares that provide an adequate proxy for the market index may use programme trading to arbitrage between the spot market and index futures, with the transaction itself being computer initiated. In other words if index futures rise in value it may be profitable to buy a bundle of shares that proxy the index in the spot market. Alternatively the index future price may fall and a portfolio manager who has bought in the forward market may then program sell in the spot market, depressing the spot market which then transmits a further downward signal to the futures market, arguably increasing the risk of a major price melt down (Roll, 1988).

The second major development is dynamic hedging. Because of the low cost and flexibility of futures markets a portfolio manager can optimize the portfolio on a continuous rather than one off basis. Dynamic hedging incorporates the possibility of new information and the dynamic hedge ratio for a portfolio reflects the quantity of an option that must be traded to eliminate a unit of risk exposure in a portfolio position. This depends on the delta, which measures the sensitivity of the value of an option to a unit change in the price of the underlying asset, and/or the ratio of the dollar value of the portfolio to the dollar value of the futures index contract multiplied by the beta or systematic risk of the portfolio.

Bibliography

Baestans, D., Van den Berg, W. M. & Wood, D. (1994). *Neural solutions for trading in financial markets.* London: F. T. Pitman.

Banz, R. (1981). The relationship between return and market value of common stocks. *Journal of Financial Economics*, 9, 3–18.

Fama, E. (1969). The adjustment of stock prices to new information. *International Economic Review*, 9, 7–21.

Gordon, M. J. (1963). Optimal investment and financing policy. *Journal of Finance*, 18, 264–72.

Keim, D. (1983). Size related anomalies and stock return seasonality: further empirical evidence. *Journal of Financial Economics*, 12, 12–32.

Levy, H. & Sarnat, M. (1970). International diversification of investment portfolios. *American Economic Review*, 60, 668–75.

Lintner, J. (1965). The valuation of risk assets and the selection of risky investments in stock portfolios and capital budgets. *Review of Economics and Statistics*, 47, 13–37.

Markowitz, H. (1952). Portfolio selection. *Journal of Finance*, 7, 77–91.

Merton, R. C. (1981). On market timing and investment performance. I. An equilibrium theory of value for market forecasts. *Journal of Business*, 54, 363–406.

O'Higgins, M. & Downes, J. (1992). *Beating the Dow; high return, low risk method for investing in the Dow-Jones Industrial Stocks with as little as $5000.* New York: Harper Collins.

Roll, R. (1988). The international crash of October 1987. *Financial Analysts Journal*, 45, 20–9.

Ross, S. (1976). The arbitrage theory of capital asset pricing. *Journal of Economic Theory*, 13, 341–60.

Sharpe, W. F. (1963). A simplified model for portfolio analysis. *Management Science*, 9, 227–93.

Sharpe, W. F. (1966). Mutual fund performance. *Journal of Business*, 39, 119–38.

Slater, J. (1994). *The Zulu principle revisited.* London: Orion.

Strong, R. A. (1993). *Portfolio construction, management and protection.* St Paul, MN: West Publishing.

Treynor, J. (1965). How to rate management of investment funds. *Harvard Business Review*, 43, 63–75.

DOUGLAS WOOD

positioning   In an attempt to emphasize the non-product aspects of positioning, Ries & Trout (1982) define it as: "not what you do to the product. Positioning is what you do to the mind of the prospect." Ries & Trout's focus on the end product of positioning strategies, namely, the "position" the product holds in the minds of consumers, brings to the fore Kelly's work (1955) on the idiosyncratic way in which people see the world. Recently, Marsden & Littler (1995) have argued that only in terms of the consumers' own construing of products will marketers find meaningful "units" of segmentation, and it remains important that marketers define, categorize, and describe products from the consumers' point of view. However, psychological positioning must be supported by the reality of the product otherwise the positioning created by other elements of the MARKETING MIX will be undermined by the use experience and will not be sustainable in the long term.

When developing a positioning strategy, marketers need a good understanding of how their product differs from others. Kotler (1991) suggests that differences should be: (1) important to a sufficient number of buyers; (2) distinctive, i.e., the difference is not offered in the same way, or at all, by competitors; (3) superior to others in achieving the same/more benefit; (4) communicable and visible to buyers; (5) difficult to copy; (6) affordable to the target market; (7) profitable and possible for the company to engineer.

Few products are superior to their competitors on all their attributes. What is required is that they differ on key dimensions that are important to the target customers. Some marketers advocate promoting only one benefit – a unique selling proposition or USP, since buyers tend to remember "number one" messages better than others – particularly in today's over-communicated society (Reeves, 1960; Ries & Trout, 1982). Others believe that it is possible to employ a double-benefit positioning strategy, e.g., Volvo is positioned on two benefits, safety and durability. One of the main advantages of using benefit or need-based segmentation is that it is the most useful in determining the positioning strategy. If other variables, e.g., age, are used initially, at some stage the marketer needs to return to benefits in order to effect a positioning strategy. When deciding which position to adopt, a company should promote its major strengths, provided that the target market values these strengths.

To overcome the problem that many companies face of how to unlock the psychological grip which large brands have on the market, a company can: strengthen its own position with the message of "because we're number two we try harder;" unlock new unoccupied positions which are valued by consumers; and deposition or reposition the competition, e.g., identify a competitor's weakness through comparative advertising (Ries & Trout, 1982). A further strategy is the "exclusive club strategy." Since people tend to remember number one, it is important to become number one on something. What counts is to be number one on some valued attribute, not necessarily size. However, if the number one position along a meaningful attribute cannot be achieved, a company can promote the idea that it is one of, for example, the Big Three in the industry. The idea was first used by the third largest US car manufacturer Chrysler, although the concept can be extended to any reasonable number (below ten) in any industry where there is some justification for it in the industry's structure (Kotler, 1991).

Occasionally, products will require repositioning because of changing customer tastes and/or poor sales performance. Jobber (1995) identifies four repositioning strategies: (1) *image repositioning*, where the product is kept the same in the same market, but its image is altered via changes to the COMMUNICATIONS MIX. This is akin to what Ries & Trout (1982) view as positioning and is the purest form of repositioning proposed by Jobber as it focuses solely on changing perceptions, not the reality of a product, in consumers' minds; (2) *product repositioning* in which the product is adapted to meet the needs of the target market more closely; (3) *intangible repositioning* which involves a different market segment being targeted with the same product, e.g., Lucozade's attempts to target sporty young adults; (4) *tangible repositioning* when both target market and product are changed.

see also **Market segmentation; Segmentation variables**

Bibliography

Jobber, D. (1995). *Principles and practice of marketing*. Maidenhead: McGraw-Hill. Chapter 7, 200–233.

Kelly, G. A. (1955). *The psychology of personal constructs*, vols 1 and 2, New York: Norton.

Kotler, P. (1991). *Marketing management: Analysis, planning, implementation and control*, 7th edn, Englewood Cliffs, NJ: Prentice-Hall. Chapter 10, 262–277.

Marsden, D. & Littler, D. (1995). *Product construct systems: A personal construct psychology of market segmentation*. Association for Consumer Research Conference, Copenhagen, June.

Reeves, R. (1960). *Reality in advertising*. New York: Knopf.

Ries, A. & Trout, J. (1982). *Positioning: The battle for your mind*. New York: Warner Books.

VINCE MITCHELL

positive discipline The definitional core of positive discipline is the rejection of traditional PROGRESSIVE DISCIPLINE as dysfunctionally punitive. Non-punitive or positive discipline, by contrast, is an approach to disciplining employees that focuses on instilling self-discipline in them by reasoning with them, rather than externally imposing discipline on them by punishing them. Positive discipline's rejection of punitive, progressive discipline leads many of its proponents to claim that it represents discipline without punishment (Redeker, 1989).

Outwardly, positive discipline resembles the operational characteristic of progressive discipline in that successive managerial responses to misconduct are increasingly severe. However, more emphasis is placed on counseling employees instead of simply warning them. Furthermore, no suspensions are involved in positive discipline systems. The step prior to termination is a *paid* day off of work, variously referred to by names such as "decision-making leave" or "decision day." The purpose of paid time off is to provide the disciplined employee with a last opportunity to reflect on his or her ability to conform with the organization's behavioral expectations. Therefore, at least until the point of termination, management imposes no penalties on employees in an effort to encourage them to conform to organizational standards.

Positive discipline systems have come under fire from some managers who question the provision of paid time off for marginal employees. Moreover, some arbitrators have expressed skepticism over whether employees are genuinely "put on notice" when they are not penalized for prior instances of misconduct (Sherman and Lucia, 1992). Nevertheless, the high profile success that numerous employers have experienced with non-punitive discipline systems (Bryant, 1984) has led to continuing interest in such programs throughout the 1990s.

Bibliography

Bryant, A. (1984). Replacing punitive discipline with a positive approach. *Personnel Administrator*, **10**, 79–87.

Redeker, J. R. (1989). *Employee Discipline*, Washington, DC: BNA.

Sherman, M. R. & Lucia, A. J. (1992). Positive discipline and labor arbitration. *The Arbitration Journal*, **47**, 35–41.

MARK R. SHERMAN

postretirement benefits In addition to pensions, many companies provide retirees and their dependents with benefits such as medical care, life insurance, housing, etc. In the USA, the costs of these other postretirement benefits (OPEB) tend to represent the largest portion of a company's total costs of benefits. For example, OPEB for General Motors Corp. exceeded $37 billion in 1993. Traditionally, the majority of OPEB plans in the USA have not been funded. Companies now have to accrue the projected cost of postretirement benefits during an employee's working life, as required by Statement of Financial Accounting Standard (SFAS) No. 106, "Employers' Accounting for Postretirement Benefits Other Than Pensions." In a single employer defined benefits plan, the benefits are specified in monetary terms or by type. The provisions of SFAS No. 106 are effective for fiscal years starting after December 15, 1992 for all public companies and for nonpublic companies with more than 500 plan participants (the relevant year is 1994 for companies with non-US plans and others).

Assumptions

The employer's best estimate of relevant future events are based on some explicit assumptions about:

Discount rate: The discount rate used to determine the present value of future expected benefit payments required to meet the plan's obligations should be based on currently available rates of return on high-quality fixed-income investments with similar timing of cash flows and benefits.

Expected long-term rate of return: This rate (for funded plans) reflects the average rate of return expected on current and future (contributed) plan assets, which considers the current returns being earned on the plan assets currently invested and returns expected to be available from reinvestment.

Demographic assumptions: These are assumptions regarding employee turnover, retirement age, mortality, dependency status, gender, and work force reductions.

Per capita claims cost: This represents the current cost of providing postretirement health care benefits for one year at each age of benefit eligibility.

Health care cost trend rate: This rate reflects the expected rate of change in average per capita claims cost, due to factors other than changes in the demographic characteristics of plan participants, which considers inflation, technological advances, health care delivery patterns, and changes in health status of plan participants.

OPEB Obligations

The expected postretirement benefit obligation (EPBO) is the actuarial present value of the postretirement benefits expected to be paid under the terms of the substantive plan (i.e., the plan as it is understood by the employer and the plan participants). The portion of the EPBO representing the present value of benefits attributed to the employee's service rendered to date, assuming the plan continues in effect and that all assumptions about future events are met, is referred to as the accumulated postretirement benefit obligation (APBO).

The APBO obligation and the plan assets are measured as of the company's reporting year-end date (or a date not more than three months prior to that date) based on the assumptions used for the previous reporting period or adopted during the current year.

Attribution

OPEB costs are spread over or attributed to the employee's service period using the projected unit credit actuarial method (also called the benefit/years-of-service method). Under this method, the same amount of expected postretirement benefit costs is allocated to each year of the employee's attribution period.

Recognition of Net Periodic Postretirement Benefit Cost

The employer must recognize and report the net periodic costs of postretirement benefits (NPPBC) associated with the plan, which includes: (1) service cost for the change in expected postretirement benefit obligation (EPBO) attributable to employee service for the period; (2) interest cost for the increase in the accumulated postretirement benefit obligation (APBO) resulting from the passage of time; (3) actual return on plan assets calculated as the difference between the fair market value of plan assets at the beginning and at the end of the reporting period, adjusted for contributions and benefit payments made during the period; (4) prior service cost representing an amortized share of the increase in APBO due to retroactive plan amendments; and (5) gains and losses representing, in general, changes in the APBO and the plan assets resulting from changes in either assumptions or experience different from that assumed. In the case of funded plans, the gain or loss component includes the difference between the actual and the expected return on plan assets.

Balance Sheet Recognition and Disclosure

An asset, labeled prepaid cost of other postretirement benefits, is reported in the balance sheet if the amounts contributed to the plan or paid to or for the plan participants during the reporting period exceed the net periodic costs of postretirement benefits (NPPBC). This asset represents the fair market value of plan assets in excess of the accumulated postretirement benefits. A liability, labeled accrued cost of other postretirement benefits, is reported in the balance sheet if the NPPBC exceeds the amounts contributed to the plan or paid to or for the plan participants during the reporting period. This liability represents the amount of the APBO in excess of the fair market value of any plan asset.

Additional disclosures are required to inform the readers about plan assumptions, funding, and policy actions.

Defined Contribution Plans

These plans specify how contributions to the individual's account are to be determined. In such a plan, other postretirement benefits (OPEB) are limited to the amounts contributed.

Miscellaneous Issues

A multi-employer plan is one to which contributions are made by two or more unrelated employers (usually according to collective bargaining agreements) and is administered by a joint board of trustees comprised of management and labor representatives of the contributing employers. Each employer reports in its own financial statements: (1) NPPBC for the amount of the required contribution to the plan for the particular reporting period, and (2) a liability for any unpaid contributions required for the period.

Specific adjustments are also required for firms involved in business combinations, for settlements relieving the employer from APBO obligations, and for plan curtailments.

MARY STONE and JAN E. BARTON

power   This can be defined as the probability of carrying out one's own will despite resistance (Weber, 1947). It is neither all-or-none, nor generalizable across situations. To have power is relative, not absolute, since it relies on the specifics of the context and the relationships there.

Power and INFLUENCE are not the same. Although the terms are sometimes used as if synonymous, behaviors associated with them have been found to be distinctive from one another (e.g., Hinkin & Schriesheim, 1990). Influence is usually more dependent upon persuasion than upon explicit or implicit coercion. However, in given circumstances, power and influence may be intertwined. This is seen when those in authority employ persuasion rather than power, since restraint in its use saves unnecessary costs in resistance and negative feelings.

Power need not be exercised to get results. It holds a potential for gaining intended effects. An evident instance occurs when a person cannot be forced to do something, but is aware of the negative later consequences of failing to comply. This is seen, for example, if a person is concerned about a needed letter of recommendation. Furthermore, power implies various psychological states, i.e., motivational, perceptual, as well as behavioral. McClelland (1975) has investigated the motive to exert power over others which he finds has many implications, interpersonally and organizationally. For example, people with a strong power motive may present themselves well when seeking a post but prove to be disastrous choices once selected. They may also perceive situations in power terms, and act accordingly, as exemplified in Machiavellianism.

Organizational power is basically structural insofar as it comes from imposed authority. Pfeffer (1981) observes that most studies of power in organizations focus on hierarchical power, i.e., the power of supervisors, or bosses over employees. There are, however, at least two other forms that power may take, in addition to power over. These are power to and power from, represented respectively by power sharing or empowerment (see EMPLOYEE INVOLVEMENT), and the ability to fend off the unwanted power demands of others (Hollander & Offermann, 1990).

The "power and POLITICS" view of organizations considers such realities by looking at the ways individuals and groups in organizations contend for resources and other desired ends. This affords a more reality-based picture of the organizational world than is presented by seeing only formal structures, or accepting images of common purposes being sought with little CONFLICT.

Special attention is given to resources and REWARDS, including promotions, pay, and other career goals, sought by individuals and units within the organization. Control of these is illustrative of position-based legitimate power that comes with authority, but can be accorded by the acceptance of others (see LEGITIMACY). Higher status as a leader usually equates with having more benefits to allocate at one's discretion, which represents reward power in the short and long range.

Though power is imputed to an organizational role, actualizing it depends upon who occupies it and how that person is perceived by others, and relates to them. In short, power becomes a reality when others perceive it and respond accordingly. Some power still depends more on personal qualities, such as relevant knowledge and expertise than on position, and is designated expert power.

Power and Leadership

Power is not the same as leadership, but is a feature of it. Analyses of leadership and power usually begin with the basis on which one person, a leader, is able to exert power over others. In organizations the most fundamental sources of power are structural and personal. These refer to position or place and to individual qualities, respectively, including "Resource dependency" (Pfeffer, 1981). Excessive reliance on power can have negative effects, but the reverse is also true. A failure to employ power can be limiting. As Gardner (1990) says, "Leaders who hold high rank in organized systems have power stemming from their institutional position, and they do not hesitate to use that power to further their purposes. They may be very persuasive, but they do not live by persuasion alone – rather by persuasion interwoven with the exercise of power" (p. 56).

Holding and wielding power have unintended effects, as Kipnis (1976) details in The Powerholders. It is not the fate of the powerholder that concerns Kipnis so much as it is the destructive effects of excessive power on relationships. He presents a set of concepts about the "metamorphic effect of power," going beyond Lord Action's famous adage that "Power tends to corrupt; absolute power corrupts absolutely," and analyzing its redounding effects. Four corrupting influences of power are seen to operate:

(1) the desire to have power becomes an end in itself, with implication for the means–end relationship;
(2) access to power tempts the individual to use institutional resources for illegitimate self-benefit;
(3) false feedback is elicited from others, with an exalted sense of self-worth; and
(4) others' worth is devalued with a desire to avoid having close social contacts with them.

Uses and Abuses of Power

The uses of power come from its perception as well as its reality. In the process of NEGOTIATION, for example, the perception of power is important both for one's self and others. Bargainers who perceive themselves as more powerful will delay concessions, while those who perceive themselves as less powerful may be encouraged to try to build their power, or make unilateral concessions. The self-definition of relative power therefore can be consequential to the outcome.

Similarly, in exercising "legitimate power" it is still necessary to have the "endorsement" of followers, who must perceive its appropriateness (Hollander, 1992). Granting the effect of position, a leader's acquiescence to group pressure may depend upon a sense of that affirmation. A leader experiencing low endorsement from followers accordingly may feel it necessary to use coercive power on them so that it becomes a response to weakness and a sense of threat.

Even in a clear social exchange, power does play a part, though Blau (1964) accentuated the distinction between a noncoercive social exchange relationship versus one characterized by power. Coercive power may operate in various subtle ways so that the idea of having noncoercive choice is illusory. In such cases, dependence is made more prominent. This occurs for instance when discontent produces a desire to resign from an organization, but one is reminded of what would be lost by such a course of action.

Harassment, sexual or otherwise, exemplifies the power-dependence connection which underlies organizational relationships. Throughout one's CAREER, there is the continuing need to have the approval of superiors, not least for later recommendations. It is therefore understandable that the less powerful are seen to be more vulnerable and open to exploitation by the more powerful. Sexual harassment is one variant of the coercive use of power as it applies to gender distinction.

Another instance of it is seen in negative power, which is saying no to a request, a proposal, program, or whatever, to substantiate the greater power of the rejector, independently of the merits of the case at hand. It may be designed to keep down younger, threatening members of the organization. This tactic sometimes takes the form of asking questions to trivialize and dismiss the points being raised.

Lukes (1974) has considered overt and covert conflicts in power relations. In the overt case, both parties are aware of a manifest conflict of interest. However, one party may see benefits in obscuring the conflict, and keeping it covert, lest others look behind the scenes to see who in fact is "pulling the strings."

Sharing Power

Whatever the leader's source of power, the quantitative variable of how much power is of fundamental importance, as the social psychologist Mark Mulder noted in the 1950s. He said, for example, that power differences can act as an impediment to authentic worker participation in organizations. A good part of this effect may be due to variations in available information and expertise related to STATUS in organizations. Accordingly, low status participants may feel even more frustration when exposed to a supposed participation situation where they are not equipped with these resources. Hence his conclusion that no participation is preferable to sham participation.

There also may be informal as well as formal power in organizations. These can be highly dispersed, with people of both lower and higher status having access to power. Informal power may be exercised by people who are relatively low on the status ladder – such as secretaries, bookkeepers, and hospital attendants – but who are structurally well placed. Such positions provide for opportunities to control others, not because of a grant of authority or personal qualities, but by their location in the organization.

An emphasis on power over others has tended to obscure the important place of power to, as well as power from (Hollander & Offermann, 1990). Among other things considered are the benefits of, and sources of resistance to, delegation and empowerment of followers. On balance, by sharing power and allowing followers to influence them, leaders foster leadership skills in others, as well as achieving other gains through their greater participation and involvement.

Delegation comes out of a cognitive growth approach to job enrichment, and represents distributing power beyond traditional participation. Self-managed work teams exemplify groups to whom such authority has been successfully delegated (Goodman Devadas, & Hughson, 1988). Despite such evidence, there are clear barriers to extending a process of power sharing in organizations.

The largest barrier to employee empowerment is the commonplace belief that the amount of power is fixed in an organization. This zero-sum conception supports the fear that power granted to others is lost to one's self or unit. Banas (1988) reported the difficulties in introducing an employee involvement program at the Ford Motor Company, until supervisor concerns were allayed about losing their authority and jobs (*see* RESISTANCE TO CHANGE).

Finally, there is the reality of accountability. In many organizational settings, even with assurances to the contrary, supervisors are ultimately held responsible for decisions made in their units. This source of resistance to power sharing needs to be understood and addressed, given the sensitivities and concerns that power generates about one's strengths and vulnerabilities in the organization.

see also **Decision making; Leadership;**

Bibliography
Banas, P. A. (1988). Employee involvement: A sustained labor/management initiative at the Ford Motor Company. In J. P. Campbell & R. J. Campbell (Eds), Productivity in organizations, pp. 388–416. San Francisco: Jossey-Bass.
Blau, P. M. (1964). Exchange and power in social life. New York: Wiley.
Gardner, J. York: Free Press.
Goodman, P. S. Devadas, R. & Hughson, T. L. (1988). Groups and productivity: Analyzing the effectiveness of self-managing teams. In J. P. Campbell & R. J. Campbell (Eds), Productivity in organizations, pp. 295–327. San Francisco: Jossey-Bass.
Hinkin, T. R. & Schriesheim, C. A. (1990). Relationships between subordinate perceptions of supervisory influence tactics and attributed bases of supervisory power. Human Relations, **43**, 221–237.
Hollander, E. P. (1992). Legitimacy, power, and influence: A perspective on relational features of leadership. In M. M. Chemers & R. Ayman (Eds), Leadership theory and research: Perspectives and directions. San Diego: Academic Press.
Hollander, E. P. & Offermann, L. (1990). Power and leadership in organizations: Relationships in transition. American Psychologist, **45**, 179–189.
Kipnis, D. (1976). The powerholders. Chicago: University Chicago Press.
Lukes, S. (1974). Power: A radical view. London: Macmillan.
McClelland, D. (1975). Power: The inner experience. New York: Irvington.
Pfeffer, J. (1981). Power in organizations. Marshfield, MA: Pitman.
Weber, M. (1947). The theory of social and economic organization. (Translated and edited by T. Parsons & A. M. Henderson.) New York: Oxford University Press.

EDWIN P. HOLLANDER

predatory dumping When a country sells goods in another country at much lower than market prices in either country the practice is called "dumping." Dumping is an unfair trade practice which is subject to additional tax and other penalties. If goods are sold in the manner described above with the intent of putting local competition out of business, the practice is referred to as "predatory dumping." Predatory dumping is used to achieve market penetration much more quickly than otherwise possible. It is also an unfair trade practice.

Bibliography
Viner, J. (1991). *Dumping: A problem in international trade.* Caldwell, NJ: Augustus M. Kelley Publishers.

JOHN O'CONNELL

predatory pricing Predatory pricing is where heavy discounting is used as a deliberate attempt to drive out competition with a view to achieving a subsequent monopoly situation where prices can be raised to exploitative levels. Predatory pricing is illegal in many countries, although it can sometimes be difficult to distinguish unambiguously between vigorous discounting (e.g., in "price wars") and more unethical or illegal practices such as dumping and predatory pricing.

DOMINIC WILSON

pre-departure briefing A pre-departure briefing is normally given to expatriates to make certain that important items have been taken care of both as an individual and as an employee of the company. It is the final discussion and farewell before the employee leaves for an assignment. This briefing should emphasize the support systems for the employee and family members which are available as well as bolster their confidence prior to the actual move. The real reason for a pre-departure briefing is to make certain that "surprises" during travel or upon arrival are kept to a minimum.

JOHN O'CONNELL

present value Cash flows which arrive at different times should not be compared until they are adjusted for the amount of time that elapses between each inflow. For example, an immediate inflow of $1000 is not the same as ten annual inflows of $100 each, although each is nominally equal to $1000. The reasons they are not the same are:

(1) profitable investment opportunities exist, which means that the $1000 immediate inflow is better than the stream of ten $100 inflows;
(2) inflation exists, so the purchasing power of the two alternatives is not the same;
(3) time preference exists, i.e. individuals will choose to have current consumption in preference to consumption later, unless they are compensated for deferring consumption.

These three reasons are related but conceptually distinct. All three of them, and one more besides, which is the risk of the cash flows, are embedded in the opportunity discount rate (ODR), which is the rate used to discount the cash flows.

The amounts that are coming in later time periods need to be discounted in order to be commensurate with an amount that is now in hand. The process of discounting the cash flows that are to arrive in the future is called calculating the present value. A payment which is to arrive in one year's time, in order to be compared to a payment which is arriving today, must be divided by the amount $(1+r)$, where r is the annual opportunity discount rate. This discounting is required because funds which are in hand today could earn a return over the course of the year of r. A payment which is arriving in two years' time, in similar fashion, needs to be divided by the amount $(1+r)^2$, before it can be compared to a payment which is arriving today. The number which is calculated by adding the value of the payment arriving today, plus the discounted value of future payments, is called the present value.

In algebraic terms, if payments are CF_0, CF_1, CF_2, ..., CF_n arriving today, one year from today, two years from today, and yearly until year n, then the present value (PV) of this flow of funds is calculated as:

$$PV = CF_0 + \frac{CF_1}{(1+r)^1} + \frac{CF_2}{(1+r)^2} + \ldots + \frac{CF_n}{(1+r)^n} \quad (1)$$

Or, more generally, if payments are received once a year until year n:

$$PV = \sum_{i=0}^{n} \frac{CF_i}{(1+r)^i} \quad (2)$$

It should also be noted that in the present value calculations above, the interest rate used to discount the cash flows, r, is assumed to be the same over the n years. For investment decisions, managers may want to consider the effects that

variations in the discount rate would have on their net present value calculations.

Bibliography

Brigham, E. F. Gapenski, L. C. (1993). *Intermediate Financial Management*. New York: Dryden.
Edwards, J., Kay, J. Mayer, C. (1987). *The Economic Analysis of Accounting Profitability*. Oxford: OUP.

JOHN EDMUNDS AND ROBERTO BONIFAZ

price discrimination Price discrimination is where different prices are charged to different customers. There are many reasons why it may be necessary to vary the price of a particular product or service, though this practice can sometimes seem inequitable and so may be resisted by customers and avoided by suppliers. Important variables which can affect costs and so provide a basis for reasonable price discrimination include: the costs of distribution to differing markets, the shelf life of the product in different climatic conditions, discounting for volume, the need for incentives to ease supply management, the imposition of local taxes, and the adoption of SKIMMING PRICING or PENETRATION PRICING strategies in new markets. There can also be considerable variation in price sensitivity and demand within the market for a particular offering which may lead to variation in pricing (Shapiro et al., 1991) although the ruthless exploitation of vulnerable demand through inflated prices (profiteering) is both unethical and illegal in many countries.

see also **Price elasticity**

Bibliography

Shapiro, B. P., Rangan, V. K., Moriarty, R. T. & Ross, E. B. (1991). Managing customers for profits (not just sales). In R. J. Dolan (Ed.), *Strategic marketing management* (pp. 307–319). Boston, MA: Harvard Business School.

DOMINIC WILSON

price elasticity Price elasticity refers to the effect on demand of changes in price and is similar to the concept of price-sensitivity. In elastic (or price-sensitive) markets a small change in price can result in a large change in demand (e.g., interest rates in money markets), whereas in inelastic (or price-insensitive) markets even substantial changes in price tend to have relatively little effect on demand (e.g., luxury goods). Traditionally, inelastic demand has been seen as typical of "basic" needs such as food, health, housing, and education but it is notable that in all these cases the element of inelasticity refers only to aggregated demand and there can be very considerable price elasticity within subsections of these markets (e.g., respectively, for delicacies, health insurance, mansions, private education). The elasticity (or price-sensitivity) of demand may also be affected by variables such as the availability of product alternatives, variants, and substitutes, or the availability of product prerequisites (e.g., driving lessons, petrol supplies, and spare parts for would-be motorists) (Reibstein & Gatiguan, 1984). The concept of price elasticity continues to be important in many markets and even small price changes can have significant consequences for consumer loyalty (e.g., supermarket groceries, newspapers). The following formula can be used to estimate price elasticity:

Price elasticity of demand = % change in demand / % change in price

Bibliography

Hanssens, D. M., Parsons, L. J. & Schultz, R. L. (1990). *Market response models: Econometric and time series analysis.* Boston, MA: Kluwer Academic Publishers.

Hoch, S. J., Kim, B.-D., Montgomery, A. L. & Rossi, P. E. (1995). Determinants of store-level price elasticity. *Journal of Marketing Research,* 32, (1), Feb., 17–29.

Reibstein, D. Optimal product line pricing: The influence of elasticities and cross elasticities. *Journal of Marketing Research,* 21, (3), 259–267.

DOMINIC WILSON

price leadership   Where an organization is able to exert considerable influence (whether active or tacit) over rivals' PRICING decisions then it is said to be the price leader. This influence is often a reflection of a dominant MARKET SHARE (as with IBM in mainframe computer markets during the 1960s and 1970s) but it can result from other factors such as reputation for quality (Marks & Spencer clothing) or reputation for value (MFI furniture). Where a group of suppliers together dominate a market in an effective oligopoly (as with petrol retailing, sports shoes, broadcasting) then they may exercise price leadership collectively (though one or two of them may well be more influential than the others) and this might have to be regulated by government or independent administrators to avoid price collusion and unfair practices.

DOMINIC WILSON

price promotions   Some pricing decisions involve a short-term adjustment to the price of an existing product/ service, possibly prompted by disappointing sales caused by an economic downturn, competitors' activities, seasonality, etc. Such adjustments should be made using an estimate of price elasticity, i.e., how much will sales volumes change with a change in price and what will be the likely contribution margin, i.e., the difference between price and average variable cost? Price promotions need not result in a net profit increase in the short term – they may be used to attack competitive offerings. However, price promotions must be used with care. While they might have a beneficial short-term effect, their continuing use may demean the product/service in the mind of the customer/buyer.

see also **Pricing methods; Pricing objectives**

Bibliography

Day, G. S. & Ryans, A. B. (1988). Using price discounts for a competitive advantage. *Industrial Marketing Management,* 17, (1), Feb., 1–14.

Wilcox, J. B., Howell, R. D., Kuzdrall, P. & Britney, R. (1987). Price quality discounts. Some implications for buyers and sellers. *Journal of Marketing,* 51, (3), July, 60–70.

DAVID YORKE

price/earnings ratio   The price/earnings (P/E) ratio is a valuation tool calculated as current stock price divided by annual earnings per share. The earnings statements from the previous twelve months are typically used, although P/ E forecasts are calculated with twelve-month earnings estimates. P/E can be used to value individual stocks or the market as a whole.

Corporate P/E

The P/E ratio is used as a fundamental benchmark to relate a stock's price to corporate performance. The company's management may influence the ratio through accounting practices, the management of growth and market expansion and the capital structure. The price, however, is driven by the investment community's confidence in the predictability of stable or optimistic earnings. This sentiment reflects projections about earnings, profitability, and cost of capital, as well as intangible factors such as confidence in the quality of management and the prospects of the industry.

Graham and Dodd (1934) cite the multiplier of ten as the historically accepted valuation standard before the 1927–29 bull market. Given the volatility of the elements affecting P/E, it is impossible to adhere to firm parameters of "acceptable" rates of valuation. High P/E ratios, which may be 25/1 or more are to be expected for growth stocks with a promising outlook. P/E ratios in the range of 20/1 may be expected for moderate-growth companies with stable earnings.

It is difficult to compare P/E values for companies from one country to another. Differing accounting conventions and methods to state earnings and value assets contribute to distortions which may be hard to control for. Cultural biases towards understating or inflating earnings also affect the validity of comparison.

In the research of stock performance, the P/E ratio has been examined theoretically as it is correlated to other factors such as risk, firm size, and industry effects. The efficient market hypothesis states that security prices reflect all current and unbiased information and that securities with higher risk should bring higher rates of return. Basu (1977) examined the investment performance of stocks and determined that low P/E portfolios earned higher risk-adjusted rates of return than high P/E securities, thus indicating market inefficiency. Banz (1981) examined the "size effect" and determined that small firms have higher risk-adjusted returns than large firms, and that P/E may be a proxy for the size effect. Peavy and Goodman (1983) showed that stocks with low P/E multiples outperform high P/E stocks after controlling for the "industry effect" which occurs when characteristically low or high P/E industries skew the results in an analysis of an undifferentiated group.

Market P/E

The P/E ratio of the S&P 500, FT-A 500 or other market indices may be examined as a predictor of future market profitability as a whole. Bleiberg (1989), however, could conclude only generally that based on historic P/E ratios of the S&P 500 and the distribution of subsequent returns, stock returns will be higher (lower) in the periods following low (high) P/E multiples, and that the market will do better as the P/E ratio falls. He illustrated that from 1959 to 1965 the S&P produced an annualized rate of return of 11.1 percent, despite the fact that the P/E ratio never fell below 16 and quite often hovered at highs between 18 and 22.

The P/E ratio serves best as an indicator of the present sentiments of the investment community, either with respect to one stock or the market as a whole. It can swing with volatility up or down based on the intangible values and estimates used to judge the premium of an issue or the health of the general investing climate. Although general inferences can be made about the patterns which emerge from the trends of the P/E ratio movement, there is no clear evidence that it can be reliably used to profitably time the market.

Bibliography

Banz, R. W. (1981). The relationship between return and market value of common stocks. *Journal of Financial Economics*, 9, 3–18.

Basu, S. (1977). Investment performance of common stocks in relation to their price–earnings ratios: a test of the efficient market hypothesis. *Journal of Finance*, 32, 663–81.

Bleiberg, S. (1989). How little we know … about P/Es, but perhaps more than we think. *Journal of Portfolio Management*, 15, 26–31.

Graham, B. & Dodd, D. L. (1934). *Security analysis*. New York: Whittlesey House, McGraw-Hill.

Peavy, J. W., III & Goodman, D. A. (1983). The significance of P/Es for portfolio returns. *Journal of Portfolio Management*, 9, (2), 43–7.

MICHELLE A. ROMERO

pricing At its simplest, price is the value placed on that which is exchanged between a supplier and a customer. However, price is a highly complex and multi-faceted issue, reflecting the complexity of EXCHANGE processes. For example, price can be expressed in many different forms – rent, royalties, interest rates, taxes and gratuities are all forms of "price" – and need not be expressed in monetary terms at all (as in barter, or countertrade). It could be argued that pricing is the most important of the MARKETING MIX elements since the price an organization sets for its offerings will play a large part in determining an organization's revenues, profitability, and competitiveness. Whereas this is a useful reminder of the significance of pricing, it should also be understood that no single element of the marketing mix can be isolated from the mix as a whole in terms of its effects and significance. Thus the factors, objectives, and strategies relevant to pricing will also be relevant to other aspects of the mix and, indeed, to other functional aspects of the organization's operations.

Management decisions concerning price should reflect PRICING OBJECTIVES which in turn should be consistent with the overall objectives of marketing strategies (*see* MARKETING STRATEGY) and of business and corporate strategies (*see* CORPORATE STRATEGY). Pricing decisions are arrived at, in principle, through PRICING METHODS and can result in prices which are high, low, or neutral with respect to rival offerings, costs, or customer perceptions. To illustrate the complexity of objectives and strategies in pricing, consider the example of a product which may be priced well above the cost of its production and distribution though well below that charged by less efficient rivals and yet still be perceived by potential customers as being poor value (perhaps because of weak promotional strategies). Many organizations will find it necessary to adopt a range of pricing strategies, reflecting differences among the products in their portfolio of offerings, while also attempting to ensure a degree of consistency, perceived fairness, and competitiveness in pricing necessary to generate profit and satisfy customers. It is this mix of complex, and sometimes conflicting, dynamics which makes pricing so difficult and so important.

Much of the specialist literature on pricing refers to consumer products and relatively little attention has been paid to pricing issues in the contexts of organizational markets (Laric, 1980), services markets (Schlissel & Chasin, 1991), or international marketing (Lancioni, 1989). Nevertheless, there are several well-established and excellent general guides to the theory and practice of pricing (e.g., Nagle, 1987; Gabor, 1988; Winkler, 1989), while a convenient brief review of the literature is provided by Diamantopoulos (1991).

Bibliography

Cohen, S. S. & Zysman, J. (1986). Countertrade, offsets, barter, and buybacks. *California Management Review*, 28, Winter, 41–56.

Diamantopoulos, A. (1991). Pricing: Theory & practice – A literature review. In M. J. Baker (Ed.), *Perspectives on marketing management*, Vol. 1. Chichester: John Wiley.

Gabor, A. (1988). *Pricing: Concepts and methods for effective marketing*, 2nd edn, Aldershot: Gower.

Korth, C. M. (Ed.) (1987). *International countertrade*. New York: Quorum Books.

Lancioni, R. A. (1989). The importance of price in international business development. *European Journal of Marketing*, 23, (11), 45–50.

Laric, M. V. (1980). Pricing strategies in industrial markets. *European Journal of Marketing*, 14, (5/6), 303–321.

Monroe, K. B. (1973). Buyers' subjective perceptions of price. *Journal of Marketing Research*, 10, Feb., 70–80.

Nagle, T. T. (1987). *The strategy & tactics of pricing: A guide to profitable decision-making*. Englewood Cliffs, NJ: Prentice-Hall.

Schlissel, M. R. & Chasin, J. (1991). Pricing of services: An interdisciplinary review. *Service Industries Journal*, 11, (3), July, 271–286.

Winkler, J. (1989). *Pricing for results*. London: Heinemann Business Paperbacks.

DOMINIC WILSON

pricing methods "Pricing methods" refer to the methods by which prices are decided for any particular product or service. There is an important distinction to be made between price decisions for existing offerings and those for new offerings. Setting the price for an existing (or "established") product is relatively straightforward as substantial market data are often available (reflecting customer response to previous price levels). However, it should be recognized that not all organizations collect such data rigorously, nor is it always easy to isolate the effect of price variation from shifts in other elements of the MARKETING MIX. It is also the case that even established offerings can experience sudden changes in the market environment (*see* MARKETING ENVIRONMENT) which can undermine the relevance of previous data and so question long-standing pricing policies – e.g., in times of economic recession; or at the launch of rival offerings; or when there are dramatic changes in legislation, technology, or consumer expectations.

Nevertheless, the pricing of new products is generally more complex than that of established products as crucial issues such as cost, demand, and competitive response are likely to be relatively unfamiliar. The problems of setting prices for innovative offerings can be so complex that sometimes these decisions are, in effect, intuitive and heuristic (Oxenfeldt, 1973). However, three more rigorous methods have also been identified for determining prices for relatively new products and services: cost-plus pricing, demand-based pricing, and going-rate pricing, each of which is discussed below.

The cost-plus pricing method is an approach which, with deceptive simplicity, sums the costs incurred in producing and distributing a good, adds an appropriate profit margin (or mark-up) according to company policy, and so generates an appropriate price (also known as mark-up pricing). A significant variant of this approach is rate-of-return or target return pricing which adds in to these calculations the cost of the capital investment involved in production and distribution, aiming to fix a price which will yield a target rate of return on this investment. This variant is more typical of those occasions when substantial investment is required for the development, production, and launch of a new product or service, resulting in particular priority to achieving a prompt return on such investment. The problem with such an approach to pricing is that it makes assumptions about DEMAND and competitive response which can be frail, especially for a new product or service (one might consider the UK Channel Tunnel as an example here). An interesting reversal of this target return approach, which responds to these problems, is that of target costing, favored by some Japanese multinational suppliers of consumer goods. This approach reverses the stream of calculations mentioned above, starting not with price. The desired profit margin is then deducted leaving a figure to cover all costs. The issue then is whether or not the offering can be produced and marketed within these costs.

The calculation of these prices is based on the following crude formulae:

Cost-plus or Mark-up price = unit cost / (1 – % markup)

[where Unit cost = variable cost + (fixed cost/ forecast unit sales)]

Target return price = unit cost + ((% target return x capital invested) / forecast unit sales)

While ensuring an important priority to cost issues, cost-plus pricing methods have a number of difficulties. First, it can be surprisingly difficult to allocate all relevant costs to individual product variants, even where a standard cost accounting system is already in use. Some costs can only be allocated very approximately (e.g., production, inventory, customer service, central administration, R&D, strategic planning, multiple product, or non-specific promotions). Second, this approach takes no account of the discounting and competitive flexibility which provide the area of discretion necessary for negotiating contracts in organizational markets. Third, the approach takes no direct account either of competitive offerings or of the price sensitivity of demand (see PRICE ELASTICITY). And fourthly, costs can vary considerably over time yet it is impractical (and undesirable) constantly to vary price. Nevertheless, the approach is useful for its apparent reasonableness (assuming appropriate margins), its focus on cost control, and its compatibility with existing management accounting systems.

The second fundamental approach is that of the demand-based pricing method which uses a mix of market research, managerial experience, and intuition to arrive at a price which, it is assumed, reflects demand. Here too, there are problems. First, the assessment (at best) reflects demand prior to the introduction of the new product which is, presumably, differentiated from previous offerings in some significant way. This problem can be anticipated to some extent through market research techniques (such as focus groups, price recall tests, and buyer response surveys) and by TEST MARKETING. Second, difficult assumptions have to be made about the future response not only of demand but also of competitors. Third, demand is often influenced by qualitative factors such as self-image or risk tolerance, factors which may not easily be registered in the quantitative terms necessary for pricing decisions. Fourth, demand-based prices in consumer markets can only reflect an aggregate assessment of demand since it would be impractical in most cases to vary prices for each purchase in response to the specific motivations and circumstances of individual customers (an important exception here is pricing by auction). In organizational markets, the individual nature of many supplier–customer relationships makes it possible (even common) to adjust prices in response to specific demand. So consumer prices cannot usually reflect demand directly, even if this could be measured accurately. And fifth, the widespread market and competitive research required by this approach can be costly and time-consuming (and may risk leaking news of the product to rivals). Despite these difficulties, the demand-based pricing method is likely to ensure that priority is given to the customer's perspective.

A third method of determining prices for new products is one which seeks to minimize competitive disruption by setting prices which are thought to reflect what might be the going rate for a parallel product. This is sometimes also referred to as imitative pricing. Relatively few "new" products or services are completely different to anything already on the market and most will compete, in effect, with existing alternatives or substitutes. By setting prices in line with such established offerings it may be possible to sidestep some of the problems of assessing price-sensitivity to new products (see PRICE ELASTICITY) while also perhaps avoiding immediate competitive response. Prices can subsequently be adjusted to reflect observed demand for whatever differentiating features may be offered by the new product. It may well be sensible to avoid provoking strong competitive responses during the initial, vulnerable, stages of a new product's life cycle, especially perhaps where the extent of differentiation is not immediately apparent or involves significant changes in customer learning.

The three main methods of pricing discussed above reflect the three principal problems of determining prices for new products – uncertainty about costs, demand, and competitive response. Cost-based pricing focuses on costs and assumes that demand and competitive response are predictable; demand-based pricing focuses on customer response while paying relatively little attention to cost or rivals; going-rate pricing prioritizes maintaining the competitive status quo over issues of cost or demand. All approaches have difficulties and advantages and all should ideally be considered when making pricing decisions (Gabor, 1988).

A fourth method of setting prices is also worth mentioning: hedonic pricing or perceived value pricing (Kortge & Okonkwo, 1993). This is an interesting approach originating from the field of economics which regards products and services as "clusters of desirable attributes" and attempts to allocate a "price" component to each attribute such that the eventual price calculation is the sum of the hedonic price components. For example, a washing machine may merit different price components according to such variables as its spin speed, the time taken by its wash cycles, the availability of economy settings, the strength of its brand, the ease of servicing, its appearance, its power consumption, and so on. Statistical regression and correlation analysis of existing washing machines can identify the apparent price which the consumer seems prepared to pay for these attributes in existing washing machines and so new models can be designed and priced accordingly (Hartman, 1989). This approach presents problems in researching consumer response to genuinely innovative attributes and in its apparent disregard for cost issues, but the concept seems useful, especially perhaps in high-price mature consumer markets such as white goods, cars, furniture, holidays, and housing.

Sensible pricing decisions will, of course, draw on all four pricing methods (Tellis, 1986) though perhaps with a mixture of formal and more intuitive methodologies which will reflect not only the logic of the products/services and their anticipated markets, but also the culture of the organizations involved and the personal preferences of individual decision-makers. As with all organizational decision-making processes, it would be foolish to ignore the sociopolitical dynamics and personal interests which are likely to be powerful factors affecting the individual decision-makers involved.

Bibliography

Cooper, R. & Kaplan, R. S. (1988). Measure cost right: Make the right decisions. *Harvard Business Review*, 66, Sept.–Oct., 96–103.

Gabor, A. (1988). *Pricing: Concepts & methods for effective marketing*, 2nd edn, Aldershot: Gower.

Hartman, R. S. (1989). Hedonic methods for evaluating product design and pricing strategies. *Journal of Economics & Business*, 41, (3), Aug., 197–212.

Kortge, G. D. & Okonkwo, P. A. (1993). Perceived value approach to pricing. *Industrial Marketing Management*, 22, (2), May, 133–140.

Nagle, T. T. (1987). *The strategy and tactics of pricing*. Englewood Cliffs, NJ: Prentice-Hall.

Nagle, T. T. (1993). Managing price competition. *Marketing Management*, 2, Spring, 36–45.

Oxenfeld, A. R. (1973). A decision-making structure for price decisions. *Journal of Marketing*, 37, Jan., 48–53.

Smith, G. E. & Nagle, T. T. (1994). Financial analysis for profit-driven pricing. *Sloan Management Review*, 35, (3), Spring, 71–84.

Tellis, G. J. (1986). Beyond the many faces of price: An integration of pricing strategies. *Journal of Marketing*, 50, Oct., 146–160.

DOMINIC WILSON

pricing objectives   An organization might have many objectives in determining its pricing policies. Some of the more typical pricing objectives include: ensuring continuity of cash flow (encouraging attention to payback period); increasing market share (favoring low price strategies such as PENETRATION PRICING; maintaining the competitive status quo (favoring neutral pricing strategies and a focus on non-price competition); and, of course, achieving sufficient profit to offset the costs and risks involved in making the offering available. Finally, in times of economic or competitive difficulty the prime objective of organizations may simply be to survive, resulting in pricing policies such as MARGINAL PRICING which would not normally be considered. It is particularly important that pricing objectives be consistent with the objectives of other elements of the MARKETING MIX, e.g., a product priced to imply quality and prestige (such as a perfume or a liqueur) would seem absurd if promoted and packaged as a commodity product. Equally, the pricing objectives should be consistent with the strategic objectives of the business and the organization as a whole, for example, a supermarket aiming to appeal to a wide range of customers would offer some products such as coffee forms (economy, premium, luxury) with different levels of quality and price.

Bibliography

Marn, M. V. & Rosiello, R. L. (1992). Managing price: Gaining profit. *Harvard Business Review*, 70, Sept.–Oct., 84–94.

Oxenfeldt, A. R. (1973). A decision-making structure for price decisions. *Journal of Marketing*, 37, Jan., 48–53.

DOMINIC WILSON

pricing process   In theory, the pricing process can be represented as having several interconnected but distinguishable "stages," though in practice it will rarely be appropriate to go through all of these stages completely except on the most elaborate and important occasions of new task purchasing (see Corey, 1991 for a concise overview). According to this theoretical and idealized model, the pricing process starts with the identification of PRICING OBJECTIVES (derived from strategic marketing objectives), then analyzes the level of DEMAND and price sensitivity in the target market, while also analyzing the relevant cost structure and profit expectations, and evaluating rival offerings, before selecting an appropriate pricing policy (such as PENETRATION PRICING or SKIMMING PRICING), and an actual set of prices for the product range. In effect there are four broad and overlapping phases in this "process": first, the setting of objectives; second, the analysis of costs, demand, rival offerings, potential profits, and the development of varying scenarios to test the assumptions involved; third, the determination of specific prices and the degree of discretion to be associated with each nominal price; fourth, the monitoring and (if necessary) adjustment of the pricing decisions compared to assumptions concerning demand and competitive response. It would, of course, be sensible to assume that this pricing process was a seamless part of the product development and marketing process rather than a discrete sequence.

Bibliography

Corey, E. R. (1991). Pricing: The strategy and process. In R. J. Dolan (Ed.), *Strategic marketing management*. Harvard Business School, 253–269.

DOMINIC WILSON

pricing strategy   Historically the main determinant of buyer choice, pricing strategy produces revenue in corporate strategy. The choice of pricing strategy is therefore a key determinant in achieving corporate success. There are many options open to the firm in assessing pricing strategy, which are significantly influenced by a number of key factors. Buyers are less price sensitive under the following conditions:

- unique value effect – when products are unique
- substitute awareness effect – when they are unaware of realistic alternatives
- difficult comparison effect – when they are unable to differentiate between product offerings
- total expenditure effect – when the purchase use is a low part of discretionary expenditure
- end-benefit effect – when the cost is a small proportion of the total cost
- shared cost effect – when costs are shared with another party
- sunk investment effect – when costs are related to a cost which has already been incurred
- price quality effect – when the product is seen by consumers as having higher quality, prestige, and the like
- inventory effect – when they cannot store the product

Given the customers' demand schedule, the cost function of the business, and the pricing strategy of competitors, a number of pricing strategy options are available, including the following:

- *Mark-up pricing*. The most common strategy used in the West involves adding a mark-up to the cost of a product. Many companies compute the cost of producing a product and add a specific margin.
- *Perceived value pricing*. Many companies presently base their pricing on perceived value as identified by the buyer. The price is set to maximize perceived buyer value by using both price and nonprofit features. Companies such as Dupont and Caterpillar have made heavy use of this method.
- *Target pricing*. The price is based on a target position within the market. This method is widely used by Japanese companies and in industries such as auto-mobiles. From the target price, given a desired rate of return, the required production cost can be calculated and steps taken to remove cost at all stages in order to achieve the target.
- *Value pricing*. A number of companies have charged a low price for high-value products, representing a particular bargain for consumers. In automobiles in recent times, the Lexus was specifically priced lower than comparable Mercedes Benz models, despite its high value. Other examples might include Virgin Airways, Wal-Mart, and Direct Line Insurance.
- *Going rate pricing*. In this form of pricing, prices are decided in relationship to those of the competitors. Such a method may well apply to medium-share companies competing against high-share competitors. Typical examples also apply in relatively undifferentiated products such as gasoline.
- *Sealed bid pricing*. This is widely used in industries such as construction, and increasingly in industries in which OUTSOURCING is becoming important.

- *Penetration pricing*. This is often used to maximize rapid market entry by discounting and special deals. It has been used by recent entrants in automobiles from new countries such as Malaysia and Korea.
- *Skimming pricing*. This is used by some competitors to maximize profit returns by maintaining the highest possible price for as long as possible. Examples might include compact disks.
- *Experience curve pricing*. Some companies have made extensive use of experience effects (*see* EXPERIENCE AND LEARNING EFFECTS) to set future pricing tactics. Texas Instruments has been a major exponent of this technique, and the effect is important in industries such as electronics in which substantial experience effects operate.

Factors Impacting External Price Strategies
The choice of pricing strategy adopted by the firm will also depend on a number of criteria. It should:

- be consistent with overall corporate strategy
- be consistent with buyer expectations and behavior
- be consistent with competitor strategies
- be monitored and modified to reflect industry changes
- be monitored for changes in industry boundaries

There are also constraints on the range of pricing options that are available. These include the following:

- *Corporate image*. The external image of the corporation affects its ability to adopt a specific pricing strategy. For example, a producer of low-cost automobiles would find it extremely difficult to successfully be perceived to be a producer of luxury cars: a downmarket low-priced supermarket chain would find it difficult to move up market in price. The corporation also needs to consider the impact of its pricing strategies on others, such as shareholders, consumer pressure groups, regulatory authorities, and government agencies.
- *Geography*. Many companies charge different prices for goods and services in different parts of the world, depending upon local market conditions and regulations.
- *Discounts*. Many corporations offer discounts based on demand for both volume and value. Large users can usually command significant discounts. Discounts may also be offered for early payments and penalties imposed for late payments.
- *Price discrimination*. Many companies differentiate between customers, product or service form, place and time.

Bibliography
Channon, D. F. (1986). *Bank strategic management and marketing*. Chichester: John Wiley.
Forbis, J. L. & Mehta, N. T. (1981). Value based strategies for industrial products. *Business Horizons* (May–June), 32–42.
Kotler, P. (1994). *Marketing management*, 8th edn. Englewood Cliffs, NJ: Prentice-Hall.
Kotler, P. & Armstrong, G. (1989). *Principles of marketing*. Englewood Cliffs, NJ: Prentice-Hall.
Nagle, T. T. (1987). *The strategy and tactics of pricing*. Englewood Cliffs, NJ: Prentice-Hall.

DEREK F. CHANNON

primary data   Primary data are collected specifically to address a particular research issue. Primary data are required when SECONDARY DATA are unavailable or insufficient. They are more likely to be used in the later decision-making stages of a research project. Primary data are collected about such things as the demographic, socioeconomic, psychographic, and lifestyle characteristics of the subjects of research as well as their attitudes, opinions, awareness, knowledge, intentions, motives, and behavior. Methods of collecting primary data are set out in the section on PRIMARY RESEARCH.

Bibliography

Churchill, G. A. (1991). *Marketing research: Methodological foundations*, 5th edn, Chicago: The Dryden Press, 305–314.

MICHAEL GREATOREX

primary research   Primary research collects data (*see* PRIMARY DATA) specifically to address a particular research issue. The broad categories of methods of collecting primary data are qualitative (*see* QUALITATIVE RESEARCH) and quantitative, which can be broken down into OBSERVATION, surveys (*see* SURVEY RESEARCH) involving the questioning of respondents, and experiments (*see* EXPERIMENTATION).

Qualitative methods include depth interviews, FOCUS GROUPS, and PROJECTIVE TECHNIQUES and are often used in exploratory research. Surveys use structured questionnaires to obtain the desired information, usually from a sample of the population of interest. The questionnaires may be administered personally by an interviewer, in the street or in the home or using the telephone; alternatively a computer or the postal system may be used. Responses are numerically analyzed using computer statistical packages.

Both qualitative methods and surveys aim to obtain information on respondents' attitudes, opinions, motives, etc., with unstructured (qualitative methods) or structured (surveys) interviews. Qualitative methods are aimed at discovering the hidden or underlying factors that more direct methods may not reveal.

OBSERVATION is a method of collecting data on a topic of interest by watching and recording behavior, actions, and facts.

EXPERIMENTATION is a type of primary marketing research in which the experimenter systematically manipulates the values of one or more variables (the independent variables), while controlling the values of other variables, to measure the effect of the changes in the independent variables on one or more other variables (the dependent variables).

Primary research may be done on an ad hoc basis, where the data are collected from the respondents once only, or continuously, where data are collected from the same respondents on a regular basis. Examples of continuous research include consumer panels, members of which keep diaries about their purchases, TV audience measurement by the Broadcasters' Audience Research Board (BARB), and retail audits. One advantage of continuous research is the opportunity to observe trends.

Bibliography

Churchill, G. A. (1991). *Marketing research: Methodological foundations*, 5th edn, Chicago: The Dryden Press. Chapter 7.

MICHAEL GREATOREX

principal–agent problem   The general problem of motivating one person or organization to act on behalf of another is known as the principal–agent problem. The principal–agent problem arises when the principal hires an agent to perform tasks on his behalf and the agent thereby influences the welfare of the principal. The principal–agent relationship provides a useful framework for analyzing situations in which there is asymmetric information and when there is a need to design a contract or monitor the behavior of parties. Moral hazard and adverse selection are also examples of the principal–agent problem.

For example, a typical firm is owned by shareholders (principals) who hire professional managers (agents) to run the company. The manager may be more interested in maximizing the firm's market share, size and growth in order to provide him and his subordinates greater opportunities for promotion. Furthermore, managers may prefer to make investments whose payoffs come earlier rather than later, avoid risks, shirk, and otherwise fail to maximize the profits of the firm. Although economists commonly assume profit maximization when describing the decision making of a firm, the incentives of managers often differ from those of the shareholders and the efforts of the managers are impossible or too expensive to monitor. This would not be a problem if an enforceable contract could be drawn up that specified every duty of the manager and matched performance incentives to outcomes perfectly. Given that incomplete contracts occur frequently, due to bounded rationality, the firm's profit is less than the profit maximizing level and the difference is referred to as the residual loss.

Agency costs arise as principals try to ensure that the agents will act in the best interest of the principal. There are three types of agency costs: monitoring costs, bonding costs and the residual loss of a principal (Jensen and Meckling, 1976). The principal–agent framework is employed to analyze the role of monitoring and bonding activities in reducing the residual loss of the principal. Monitoring costs occur when the principal employs resources to observe the efforts of the agent or creates incentives for the agent to undertake actions that are more likely to assure efficient use of resources within the firm. For example, an employee receiving a fixed salary may be able to shirk on the job, thus the firm needs to develop a way of monitoring the performance, as well as, the honesty of the agent. Markets can also perform the monitoring function. In particular, the market for corporate control and the labor market for managers penalize managers who manage companies poorly. Thus, poor managers face a greater probability of unemployment and company takeovers, lower salaries, or a reputation for having brought a firm into bankruptcy (Fama, 1980).

In order to guarantee performance, the agent may be required to post a bond. If the agent does not fulfill the terms of their agreement, then he must forfeit the bond. Edward Lazear (1979) showed that for workers who expect to make a career within an organization, it may be to the advantage of both parties to align the incentives of the employee and the employer by paying the employee below his marginal product early in the career and above his marginal product later in the career. This rising wage pattern is similar to a worker posting a bond to be collected later in his career. In this compensation scheme it becomes efficient for the employee to work diligently in order to avoid being fired before the deferred rewards can be collected (i.e. or the bond is forfeited). For this scheme to be effective, employees must find the firm's promise to be credible and the employer must provide for mandatory retirement. Similarly, stock options and bonuses that can be exercised by the manager only when he retires or leaves in a mutually agreeable way create incentives for managers to maximize long-run profits of a firm. If the behavior of the manager is not acceptable to the owners of the firm, the manager faces reductions in the value of the deferred compensation.

Structuring the employee and managerial compensation packages is one of the ways in which the owners of a firm minimize the residual loss. In addition, owners of a firm who monitor the market price of their shares can thereby infer whether the agents are acting in their best interest; on the basis of that information alone they can buy and sell shares and limit the amount of residual losses imposed on them by the actions of the management. Hence, the power of stockholders to sell their stake in the firm promotes efficiency in the use of resources. In addition, a principal–agent problem is avoided when the owner of a firm also serves as the manager; in this case, the firm eliminates the agency costs and any residual loss.

Bibliography

Fama, E. F. (1980). Agency problems and the theory of the firm. *Journal of Political Economy*, 88, 272–84.

Jensen, M. C. & Meckling, W. H. (1976). Theory of the firm: managerial behavior, agency costs, and ownership structure. *Journal of Financial Economics*, 3, 305–60.

Lazear, E. (1979). Why is there mandatory retirement? *Journal of Political Economy*, 87, 1261–84.

Shughart, W. F., Chappell, W. F., Cottle, R. L. (1994). *Modern Managerial Economics*. Cincinatti, OH: South-Western Publishing.

LIDIJA POLUTNIK

prisoner's dilemma   The prisoner's dilemma is a classic illustration in GAME THEORY. Two suspects are arrested by the police and are charged with a minor crime. They are also suspected of a major crime but there is not enough evidence to convict them without a confession. The two prisoners are separated and are offered the following deal:

(1) If one prisoner confesses to the major crime and implicates the other, he will serve 6 months in jail while the other will serve 6 years in jail.
(2) If neither prisoner confesses to the major crime, each will be convicted of the minor offense and will serve 1 year in prison.
(3) If both prisoners confess to the major crime, they will both serve 3 years in prison.

The "payoffs" to the two prisoners, Al and Bill depend on the choice made by the other. These are shown in the matrix below where Al's payoff is shown in parentheses.

The interesting feature of these payoffs is that the best strategy for each suspect individually is to confess. Consider Al's payoffs from choosing to confess compared with the payoffs from choosing to be silent. Whether Bill chooses to confess or be silent, Al's best strategy is to confess, and the same result holds for Bill. Thus both

		Bill	
		Confess	Be silent
Al	Confess	(–3) –3	(–.5) –6
	Be silent	(–6) –.5	(–1) –1

prisoners are worse off pursuing their individual self interest than if they agreed to be silent.

The strategy pair (confess, confess) is a *Nash equilibrium* because it is the best response for each player given the strategy of the other, i.e. neither player can do better knowing the strategy chosen by the other. The prisoners would choose the same strategies if they used the minimax or maximin criterion to evaluate their decisions; see Rasmusen (1989).

If the players developed reputations to make the threat of punishment a credible threat, then the prisoner's dilemma can be avoided. Rasmusen notes that reputation can be important in a variety of repeated games such as duopoly (where the strategies are to maintain the current price or cut the price), employer–worker relations (where the worker chooses to work hard or slack off), product quality under imperfect information (where the firm chooses to produce a high quality product or a low quality product) and entry deterrence (where the incumbent firm may retaliate aggressively or accommodate an entrant).

see also **signaling**

Bibliography

Gibbons, R. (1992). *Game Theory for Applied Economists*. Princeton, NJ: Princeton University Press.

Rasmusen, E. (1989). *Games and Information*. Oxford, UK: Blackwell.

ROBERT E. MCAULIFFE

privacy in information systems   Privacy is comprised of two separable parts: *physical* privacy and *information* privacy. When one's physical space is intruded upon, this is a violation of one's physical privacy. When information about someone is collected, used, or shared inappropriately, this is a violation of someone's information privacy. Our concern here is with information privacy, a significant and growing issue for information systems managers. As corporations find their data management activities receiving more scrutiny from a privacy perspective, information systems managers should be aware of exposure and be accountable to their organizations (Straub & Collins, 1990).

Dimensions of Information Privacy Concern
Individuals often indicate that they are "concerned" about their privacy. Public opinion polls in the United States and Canada show that such concerns are at record levels (Equifax Inc., 1992, 1993). It is surprisingly difficult to dissect these concerns and to ascertain exactly what is troubling respondents, since the factors contributing to such concerns are fairly complex. In fact, the research of Smith et al. (1995) indicates that there may be four primary dimensions of information privacy concern and two

secondary dimensions. The primary dimensions are as follows:

1 *Collection.* Individuals often perceive that large quantities of data regarding their personalities, background, and actions are being accumulated, and they often resent this. Laudon (1986) coined the term "dossier society" to describe our increasing reliance on personal data and the increasing collection of such data. While few individuals dispute an organization's right to collect data which is pertinent to a particular decision (e.g. household income on a credit-card application), many resent being asked for personal data not clearly tied to a specific transaction.

2 *Unauthorized secondary use.* Sometimes, information is collected from individuals for one purpose but is used for another, secondary, purpose without authorization from the individuals. Even if contained *internally* within a single organization, unauthorized use of personal information will very often elicit a negative response. For example, some credit-card issuers have come under attack for utilizing data about their cardholders' transactions in their own marketing campaigns. Specific examples of such secondary, internal uses include "sugging," a practice in which data is collected ostensibly for research only to be used later for marketing purposes (Cespedes & Smith, 1993). Concerns about secondary use are often exacerbated when personal information is disclosed to an *external* party (i.e. another organization). The sale or rental of direct mail or telemarketing lists often falls into this category. This concern is an important one as the number of interorganizational systems increases, a trend enabled by computing and telecommunications advances.

3 *Errors.* Many individuals believe that companies are not taking enough steps to minimize problems from errors in personal data. Although some errors might be deliberate (e.g. a disgruntled employee maliciously falsifying data), most privacy-related concerns involve instead *accidental* errors in personal data. Provisions for inspection and correction are often considered as antidotes for problems of erroneous data, but many errors are stubborn ones, and they seem to increase in spite of such provisions. Also at issue are questions of responsibility for spotting errors: does a system rely on individuals to monitor their own files, or is there a structure for such monitoring in place? Although errors are sometimes assumed to be unavoidable problems in data handling, whether controls are or are not included in a system represents a value choice on the part of the system designers.

4 *Unauthorized access.* Who is allowed to access personal information in the files? This is a question not only of technological constraints (e.g. access control software) but also of organizational policy. It is often held that individuals should have a "need to know" before access to personal information is granted. However, the interpretation of which individuals have, and which do not have, a "need to know" is often a cause of much controversy. Technological options now exist for controlling such access at file, record, or field level. But how those options are utilized and how policies

associated with those uses are formed represent managerial judgments.

The secondary dimensions are:

1 *Reduced judgment.* As organizations grow in size and data-processing capabilities, they tend to rely more often on "standard operating procedures" than on individual decisions. Their use of automated decision-making processes may lead people to feel that they are being treated more as "a bunch of numbers" than as individuals. Laudon (1986, pp. 3–4) has noted that "decisions made about us . . . rely less and less on personal face-to-face contact, on what we say, or even on what we do. Instead, decisions are based on information that is held in national systems and interpreted by bureaucrats and clerical workers in distant locations." As systems are increasingly designed so that these decisions are automated, and when there are few provisions for referring decisions to human beings at appropriate times, concerns about this dimension of decision-making increase. While privacy advocates often claim that "reduced judgment" is a privacy concern, it is actually somewhat tangential and can be viewed as an issue of organizational design.

2 *Combining data.* Concerns are sometimes raised with respect to combined databases which pull personal data from numerous other sources, creating what has been termed a "mosaic effect." Even if data items in disparate databases are seen as innocuous by themselves, their combination into larger databases appears to some to be suggestive of a "Big Brother" environment. This is a somewhat tangential dimension of information privacy, since the concerns associated with combined data are actually subsumed by the "Collection" and "Unauthorized secondary use" dimensions.

Corporate Approaches to Managing Privacy

In a study of banks, insurance organizations, and a credit-card issuer, Smith (1994) reported that a consistent policy-making cycle can be observed as corporations grapple with information privacy issues. The cycle contains three parts: drift, external threat, and reaction. By delegating decisions about management of personal data to mid-level managers, and by allowing different organizational units to establish different sets of practices, which sometimes conflict with one another, corporations allow their privacy policies to *drift.* Corporations may experience an *external threat* in the form of negative media attention, legislative scrutiny (e.g. congressional committee hearings), or a competitive threat (e.g. consumer complaints or a competitor's use of privacy protection as a marketplace weapon). In response to an external threat, corporation executives become involved in a defensive *reaction* period of assessment and official policy-making. Often, task forces are convened to deal with such crises. Differences in practices across the organization are then confronted. In many cases, more conservative approaches to managing personal data are embraced, and these new approaches are codified in new policies.

At one health insurer, the *drift* period was characterized by the creation of a variety of practices across organizational units in which individuals' medical claim data were either protected with rigid controls or were provided to outsiders with varying degrees of discretion. Internal access controls also varied widely during this period, with some individuals being allowed to see medical data inappropriately. The *external threat* was in the form of a new state law which regulated the collection and use of AIDS test data. This prodded a *reaction*, an extensive reassessment of the existing practices at an executive level and a codification of a new, omnibus policy.

Fair Information Practices

The most widely quoted guidelines for "fair" management of personal data are found in the 1973 Code of Fair Information Practices developed by the US Department of Health, Education, and Welfare (as presented in CPSR, 1989):

- There shall be no personal data record-keeping systems whose very existence is secret.
- There must be a way for a person to find out what information about the person is in a record and how it is used.
- There must be a way for a person to prevent information about the person that was obtained for one purpose from being used or made available for other purposes without the person's consent.
- There must be a way for a person to correct or amend a record of identifiable information about the person.
- Any organization creating, maintaining, using, or disseminating records of identifiable person data must assure the reliability of the data for its intended use and must take precautions to prevent misuse of the data.

Smith (1994) suggested that the Fair Information Practices should be updated to also include:

- There must be no deception in data-collection practices.
- A person should be given the opportunity to "opt out" of any information practices he or she finds inappropriate.
- Only individuals with a legitimate "need to know" should have access to personal data.
- Disparate data files should not be combined unless the conditions regarding data collection and "opt out" have been met.

Privacy Regulation

Many different models of privacy regulation exist around the world. While overall legislative activity regarding information privacy is flourishing internationally, no single, standard policy regarding privacy issues has emerged. As described in Milberg et al. (1995), the predominant models appear to be those represented in figure 1. The models vary significantly in terms of governmental involvement in day-

to-day corporate operations. At the low government involvement side (left end) of the continuum, the government assumes a "hands-off" role and allows corporations to monitor themselves, with reliance on injured individuals to pursue their own remedies in the court system. At the high government involvement side (right end) of the continuum, the government assumes authority to license and regulate all corporate uses of personal data, including the right to conduct inspections inside corporations and to examine all proposed applications of personal data before they are implemented.

The models can be described as follows:

1 *The self-help model* depends on data subjects' challenging inappropriate record-keeping practices. Rights of access and correction are provided for the subjects, but they are responsible for identifying problems and bringing them to the courts for resolution.

2 *The voluntary control model* relies on self-regulation on the part of corporate players. The law defines specific rules and requires that a "responsible person" in each organization ensures compliance.

3 *The data commissioner model* utilizes neither licensing nor registration, but relies on the ombudsman concept through a commissioner's office. The commissioner has no powers of regulation but relies on complaints from citizens, which are investigated. The commissioner also is viewed as an expert who should offer advice on data handling; monitor technology and make proposals; and perform some inspections of data-processing operations. This model relies to a great degree on the commissioner's credibility with legislature, press, and the public.

4 *The registration model* acts much like the licensing model with one exception: the governmental institution has no right to block the creation of a particular information system. Only in a case where complaints are received and an investigation reveals a failure to adhere to data-protection principles would a system be "deregistered." Thus, this model provides more remedial than anticipatory enforcement of principles.

5 *The licensing model* creates a requirement that each databank containing personal data be licensed (usually upon payment of a fee) by a separate government institution. This institution would stipulate specific conditions for the collection, storage, and use of personal data. This model anticipates potential problems and heads them off, by requiring a *prior* approval for any use of data.

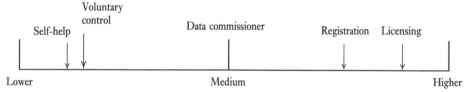

Figure 1   Regulation models: lower, medium, and higher refer to the level of government regulation in corporate privacy management
Source: Milberg et al. (1955)

The United States is usually described as intermingling the self-help and voluntary control models. Germany is often viewed as a good example of the data commissioner model, the United Kingdom as the registration model, and Sweden as the licensing model. Some countries have no data protection laws at all (see Bennett, 1992; Madsen, 1992, for additional details).

Bibliography

Bennett, C. J. (1992). *Regulating Privacy: Data Protection and Public Policy in Europe and the United States*. Ithaca, NY: Cornell University Press.

Cespedes, F. V. & Smith, H. J. (1993). Database marketing: new rules for policy and practice. *Sloan Management Review*, **34** (4), 7–22.

Computer Professionals for Social Responsibility (1989). *The CPSR Newsletter*, **7** (4), 16.

Equifax Inc. (1992). *Equifax Canada Report on Consumers and Privacy in the Information Age*. Quebec: Equifax Canada.

Equifax Inc. (1993). *Harris–Equifax Health Information Privacy Survey 1993*. Atlanta, GA: Equifax Inc.

Flaherty, D. H. (1989). *Protecting Privacy in Surveillance Societies*. Chapel Hill, North Carolina: University of North Carolina Press.

Laudon, K. C. (1986). *Dossier Society: Value Choices in the Design of National Information Systems*. New York: Columbia University Press.

Linowes, D. F. (1989). *Privacy in America: Is your Private Life in the Public Eye?* Urbana, IL: University of Illinois Press.

Madsen, W. (1992). *Handbook of Personal Data Protection*. New York: Macmillan.

Milberg, S. J., Burke, S. J., Smith, H. J. & Kallman, E. A. (1995). A cross-cultural study of relationships between values, personal information privacy concerns, and regulatory approaches. *Communications of the ACM*, **38** (12), 65–74.

Smith, H. J. (1994). *Managing Privacy: Information Technology and Corporate America*. Chapel Hill, North Carolina: University of North Carolina Press.

Smith, H. J., Milberg, S. J. & Burke, S. J. (1995). Information privacy: measuring individuals' concerns about corporate practices. Unpublished working paper, Georgetown University.

Reindenberg, J. R. (1992). The privacy obstacle course: hurdling barriers to transnational financial services. *Fordham Law Review*, **60** (6), S137–S177.

Rule, J. B. (1974). *Private Lives and Public Surveillance: Social Control in the Computer Age*. New York: Schocken Books.

Rule, J. B., McAdam, D., Stearns, L. & Uglow, D. (1980). *The Politics of Privacy: Planning for Personal Data Systems as Powerful Technologies*. New York: Elsevier.

Straub, D. W. & Collins, R. W. (1990). Key information liability issues facing managers: software piracy, proprietary databases, and individual rights to privacy. *MIS Quarterly*, **14** (2), 43–6.

Westin, A. F. (1967). *Privacy and Freedom*. New York: Atheneum Publishers.

H. JEFF SMITH and DETMAR W. STRAUB

privacy in organizations Organizational privacy is a state or condition in which an individual (i.e. job applicant, current employee, or former employee) can (a) control the release and possible subsequent dissemination of personal information, (b) regulate both the amount and nature of social interaction in the workplace, (c) exclude or isolate himself or herself from unwanted (auditory, visual, etc.) stimuli in the workplace, and, thus, (d) behave free from the control of others (Stone and Stone, 1990). Organizational privacy is of considerable importance because organizations collect, store, and use large amounts of information about

individuals for such purposes as personnel selection, PERFORMANCE APPRAISAL, training, needs assessment, human resources planning, and attitude assessment (Privacy Protection Study Commission, 1977; Stone and Stone, 1990). Organizations also structure the physical and social environments of work (e.g. through office and plant layout, structuring of work roles) in ways that facilitate the attainment of organizational goals. Unfortunately, the same actions may be viewed as intrusive by individuals because they have the potential to violate expectations of organizational privacy or legal rights to privacy (e.g. Privacy Act of 1974). In response to such violations, individuals may form negative attitudes toward the organization, engage in counterproductive behaviors at work, file GRIEVANCES against the organization, institute litigation against the organization, and engage in other acts aimed at insuring organizational privacy (Privacy Protection Study Commission, 1977; Harris and Westin, 1979; Stone and Stone, 1990). In view of this, organizations must be sensitive to organizational privacy issues.

Bibliography

Harris, L. & Westin, A. F. (1979). *The Dimensions of Privacy: a National Opinion Research Survey of Attitudes toward Privacy*, Stevens Point, WI: Sentry Insurance Company.

Privacy Protection Study Commission (1977). *Personal Privacy in an Information Society*, Washington, DC: US Government Printing Office.

Stone, E. F. & Stone, D. L. (1990). Privacy in organizations: theoretical issues, research findings, and protection mechanisms. *Research in Personnel and Human Resources Management*, **8**, 349–411.

EUGENE F. STONE-ROMERO
and DIANNA L. STONE

privatization Privatization is the transfer of a controlling interest in a state-owned organization to private ownership.

A wider definition also embraces any substantial transfer of state asset ownership or control to the private sector, including any government activity intended to reduce the role of the state, or of central or local government, in any particular industry or organization. This can include the issue of new equity in the capital market, the setting up of independent holding companies to distance government from the management of state enterprises, competitive purchasing practices, or even noninterference pledges made in relation to state holdings. As most privatized organizations used to provide goods or services on behalf of the state while they were part of its administrative structure, it is important to make the distinction between the state's obligation to make available and its obligation to be involved with all aspects of such provision. The logistics of postal services may be delegated, for example, while the financing (subsidy) of uniform national tariffs can remain the responsibility of the government, if this is considered to be desirable.

In summary, although privatization is a concept that, strictly, only has to do with ownership of assets, it is very difficult to understand and explain it without consideration to the related organizational matters of control and the setting of organizational goals, priorities and constraints, and the type and methods of management.

Rationale

There exist a number of different reasons to privatize, and these can typically be understood in ideological, financial, or political terms. Although not necessarily mutually exclusive, tradeoffs are often involved; and the ranking of reasons depends, among other aspects, on the country and industry involved, and the place of any particular privatization in the privatizing country's program.

The ideological rationale is based on the neoliberal view that the market is superior to government planning as a means of allocating resources. Therefore, exposure to the market for corporate capital and control in substitution to the allocation mechanisms employed by most governments encourages the development of a closer link between consumer and producer, and enhances the flow of information as well as accountability, leading to higher allocative efficiency. In addition, such exposure can enlarge a small national capital market both in terms of size and the number of participants and, in the extreme, be used to convert a planned economy into a market-based economy. Also, privatization can offer the opportunity to introduce or enhance competition in the product market (as the existence of a privileged state-owned competitor may mean that competitive production is unfeasible), with all the beneficial implications which this can have according to the same ideology. Finally, privatization segregates many activities from the all-encompassing state, and this permits more precise measurement of the rationality and cost of government involvement.

The financial rationale for privatization, increasingly used by administrations holding a wide range of political beliefs, is based on short-term monetary considerations and justifies the exchange of state assets for liquid funds by the need to raise revenue for the vendor government, often to finance current expenditure and reduce the public-sector borrowing requirement (PSBR). In financial terms, privatization can be seen as the exchange of a perpetual series of cashflows for an up-front payment. A short-termist government would always be willing to sell below value, while the private sector would only pay more if it believed that it could undertake the management better. Another, associated, reason to privatize is to allow financial decision making in the organization to be carried out without regard to public spending, thereby often allowing the undertaking of investments which, although sound in their own right, may be deferred in view of more urgent government priorities.

The final privatization rationale involves political and electoral considerations. The ability of the government to reallocate wealth and resources, and through pricing and method of sale to strongly influence the composition of many organizations' ownership, enables it to attack opposition strongholds and form interest groups who benefit from the process (or would be expected to suffer as a result of its discontinuation or reversal), thereby creating a captive electorate.

Related Actions

A number of government actions are often associated with privatization. Although they can often take place without privatization, and privatization can conceivably be implemented without them, these actions are frequently interlinked with privatization in critical ways, particularly as they take an active role in dissipating its effects.

The first such action is liberalization (DEREGULATION). In a deregulated market, state-owned firms have no justification for receiving subsidies or any other preferential treatment, so they can only survive if they are as efficient as any other competitor. Public ownership in a deregulated market, therefore, becomes irrelevant. Therefore privatization, although not strictly necessary, may well follow. Similarly, a privatized company cannot be allowed to maintain strong monopoly powers, so it must be controlled by means of competition and/or regulation. As a result, privatization is likely to lead to a combination of regulation and deregulation.

A second action is the decoupling of the organization's finances from those of the state, enabling the organization to raise funds directly from the markets. A state-owned organization may be able to raise some project funding directly from the market to circumvent some of the problems of combined funding which have already been discussed but, ultimately, this is likely to lead to loss of state control and, if carried out to any great extent, loss of ownership and privatization. Similarly, and almost by definition, a privatized enterprise ought to have its finances separated from those of the state.

The third action is a change in the employment status of the organization's personnel, who cease to be part of the traditionally well protected civil servant family and become private employees. This typically implies reduced job security. Civil servant status for employees of public-sector organizations is often a matter of legal necessity, although it may be possible to alter the employment status of the employees concerned by moving them to private companies which are contracted to perform the same tasks. In essence, however, this is tantamount to partial privatization. Privatization, in turn, is associated with the drawing up of new employment contacts on a private basis.

Bibliography

Dunsire, A., Hartley, D. & Dimitriou, B. (1988). Organisational status and performance: a conceptual framework for testing public choice theories. *Public Administration Review*, 66 (4), 363–88.

Goodman, J. B. & Loveman, G. W. (1991). Does privatization serve the public interest? *Harvard Business Review*, 69, 26–38.

Jensen, M. C. (1989). Eclipse of the public corporation. *Harvard Business Review*, 67, 61–74.

Kay, J. A. (1988). The state and the market: the UK experience. Occasional paper no. 23, Group of Thirty, London.

Kay, J. A. & Thompson, D. (1986). Privatisation: a policy in search of a rationale. *Economic Journal*, 96, 18–32.

Vickers, J. & Yarrow, G. K. (1988). *Privatization: an economic analysis*. Cambridge, MA: MIT Press.

STEPHANOS AVGEROPOULOS

privatization options   Over the last decade, the sales of state-owned enterprises (SOEs) have reached dramatic levels on a worldwide scale. For instance, in Europe, they are expected to grow at the rate of US$30 to US$40 billion annually till the turn of the century and in Russia alone, 25,000 firms need to be privatized (see Boycko et al., 1994).

In spite of these impressive figures, there is no consensus over the optimal means and financial strategies that are necessary for a successful privatization. Moreover, the empirical evidence regarding the "success" of privatizations in achieving their stated objectives has been mixed. Studies such as those conducted by Kay and Thompson (1986) argue that privatizations did not promote economic efficiency. However, more recent empirical analyses such as Megginson et al. (1994) suggest otherwise.

Alternative Methods of Privatization

At the theoretical level, there is no model that explains the diversity of the methods of sale. It is generally accepted that there is no single "best" method and that each case should be examined on its own merit (see Baldwin and Bhattacharyya, 1991).

Public Offerings of Shares. This option involves the partial or complete sale to the public of an SOE's shares. It frequently dominates alternate modes of privatization and has often been of record-breaking proportions. The offer can be on a fixed price basis, in which case the issuer determines the offer price before the sale. Perotti and Serhat (1993) find evidence from twelve countries that such sales tend to be made at highly discounted fixed price offerings. Alternatively, the offer can be made on a tender basis where the investors indicate the price they are willing to pay.

Private Sales of Shares. In a private sale of shares, the government sells the shares to a single entity or a group. The sale can be a direct acquisition by another corporate entity or a private placement targeting institutional investors. Megginson et al. (1994) point out that France and Mexico systematically used this method to transfer ownership to a few large "core" shareholders.

Pricing strategies involve a negotiation or a competitive bidding process. The disclosure policy can be an auction.

Cornelli and Li (1995) warn that the investor with the highest bid may not necessarily be the one who will run the privatized firm in the most efficient way. They give examples of Fiat, Mercedes-Benz, and Volkswagen which recently acquired majority stakes of makers. These companies may not necessarily believe that the acquired factories *per se* have great potential value. They may have been motivated to acquire them mainly to gain a foothold in the local markets.

Private Sale of SOEs' Assets. The transaction basically consists of the sale of specific assets rather than the sale of the company's shares.

Fragmentation. This method consists of the reorganization of the SOE into several entities that will be subsequently privatized separately, e.g. the break up of a monopoly.

New Private Investment in an SOE. This operation takes place when the government adds more capital by selling shares to private investors, usually for rehabilitation and expansion purposes. This method dilutes the government's equity position.

Management and Employee Buyout. This transaction refers to the new acquisition of a controlling interest in a company by a small group of managers. Employees can also acquire a controlling equity stake with or without management. The assets of the acquired company are usually used as collateral to obtain the financing necessary for the buyout.

Leases and Management Contracts. These options involve a transfer of control, rather than ownership, to the private sector. In a lease, the lessee operates the SOE's assets and facilities and bears some burden of maintenance and repair in exchange for a predetermined compensation. The lessee has to make the payment regardless of the profitability of the firm.

The management contractor, on the contrary, assumes no financial responsibility for the running of the enterprise. A World Bank report (1995) found that although management contracts have not been widely used, they were generally successful when attempted. Using a worldwide search, they found only 150 management contracts, mainly in areas where output is easily measurable and improvements tangible.

For a review of the techniques discussed above, see also Vuylsteke (1988).

Mass Privatization. Mass privatization is very popular in Eastern Europe and other former centrally planned economies in Central Asia. It involves a rapid give away of a large fraction of previously state-owned assets to the general public. Boycko et al. (1994) cite numerous examples of mass privatization such as free grants of shares to workers and managers in the enterprises employing them; distribution of vouchers to the whole population, with the subsequent exchange of these vouchers for shares in SOEs; and free grants of shares of mutual funds, specially created to manage a portfolio of shares of SOEs, to the whole population.

Pre- and Post-Privatization Options

If the chosen method is through a public equity offering, the government and the new management have several pre- and post-privatization options concerning the strategy to maximize the revenues from such a privatization. Errunza and Mazumdar (1995) assume that a SOE's debt may be perceived as a junior secured debt contract. Thus the risk premium on a SOE's debt is less than that of a comparable private firm. This difference in risk premium is the value of the government's loan guarantee. When a SOE is privatized, this guarantee may be potentially removed leading to a wealth transfer from debt holders to equity holders. Other factors such as production efficiencies, monopoly power, government debt guarantees, tax shields, and bankruptcy costs affect the value of this loan guarantee and hence the potential gains from privatization. Errunza and Mazumdar (1995) believe there are various optimal government financial strategies that would maximize the gains from privatization:

1. The value gains from privatization are likely to be relatively smaller when implemented by governments with overall riskier public sector operations. Further, the government should prioritize its privatization program by selling off its most heavily subsidized firms.
2. The government should prioritize its privatization program by selling off firms from minor sectors first, and under certain conditions, the government could improve the valuation gains to equity holders by undertaking riskier investment strategies prior to privatization. Similarly, value gains from a privatization are higher for firms with the highest levels of debt.

3. A more active role by the government in the management of the company even after privatization may not necessarily be detrimental to the firm's shareholders since it may enhance tax shields and wealth transfers from debtholders. Moreover, to maintain SOE ownership in domestic private hands, appropriate tax subsidies and restrictions should be considered.

4. SOEs that were well managed prior to privatization, or have fully exploited any monopoly power in the product market, or may be handicapped with bureaucratic malaise or trade union pressures after privatization, would be less attractive to investors, *ceteris paribus*. Indeed, the prospects for the new management, of capitalizing on unrealized gains would be smaller under these scenarios.

5. Finally, if post-privatization bankruptcy costs are significant, then the firm may be forced to reduce its debt level as well as opt for safer investments. The first hypothesis is empirically validated by Megginson et al. (1994).

Bibliography

Baldwin, C. & Bhattacharyya, S. (1991). Choosing the method of sale: a clinical study of Conrail. *Journal of Financial Economics*, 30, 69–98.

Boycko, M., Shleifer, A. & Vishny, R. W. (1994). Voucher privatization. *Journal of Financial Economics*, 35, 249–66.

Cornelli, F. & Li, D. D. (1995). Large shareholders, private benefits of control, and optimal schemes of privatization. London Business School. Working paper.

Errunza, V. R. & Mazumdar, S. C. (1995). Privatization: a theoretical framework. McGill University. Working paper.

Kay, J. & Thompson, D. (1986). Privatization: a policy in search of a rationale. *Economic Journal*, 96, 18–38.

Megginson, W., Nash, R. & Van Randenborgh, M. (1994). The financial and operating performance of newly privatized firms: an international empirical analysis. *Journal of Finance*, 49, 1231–52.

Perotti, E. & Serhat, G. (1993). Successful privatization plans. *Financial Management*, 22, 84–98.

Vuylsteke, C. (1988). *Techniques of privatization of state-owned-enterprises. Vol. I. Methods and implementation.* Washington, DC: World Bank. Technical paper 88.

World Bank (1995). *Bureaucrats in business: The economics and politics of government ownership.* New York: Oxford University Press. Policy research report.

VIHANG R. ERRUNZA, SUMON C. MAZUMDAR
and AMADOU N. R. SY

privatization, valuation of state-owned enterprises   When enterprises change from being state-owned to being privately owned, some values need to be assigned to the enterprise's assets and obligations in order to determine the enterprise's equity. Because of the absence of market prices in the past, it is difficult to assign values to the enterprise's composition of assets and liabilities. Book values at the time of privatization may not be indicative of the underlying economic values of the assets because of the use of administered prices and arbitrary booking in the past. The problem is compounded by the existence of inflationary and unstable economic conditions, which render a higher degree of volatility in the prices observed in a newly created market system.

The process of coping with these problems differs among countries and became crucial with the breakup of the Soviet Union and the movement of numerous countries into privatization. In Poland, for example, the legal system requires the use of two different methods of valuation to assist in gauging the value of an asset or a liability. For example, the discounted future cash flow and the replacement cost can be used to check the validity of the calculation of one another. Furthermore, in Poland, the object of valuation might be the entire enterprise, a segment of an enterprise, or individual assets of a state-owned enterprise. This range of alternatives complicates the choice of valuation methods, especially since the anticipated cash flows are judgmental and subject to unknown inflationary effects.

In Poland the concept of "property" is defined by the Civil Code as being related to a specific entity and is synonymous with "possession." For accounting purposes, "property" means assets and, for a business entity, consists of both the material (tangible) substance and the intangible elements which are related to the organization and use of the material substance (e.g., goodwill). As with Western systems, tangibles include land, buildings and constructions with fixtures and fittings, technical equipment, and current assets. Fixed assets consist of intangibles, defined as fixed property elements, other than tangibles, including acquired computer software, patents, licenses, and goodwill. The object of valuation in the process of privatization is generally the enterprise "property," which is defined as the totality of various tangible and intangible elements. Indeed, an enterprise is defined in the legal codes as a set of tangible and intangible elements intended to perform economic tasks, which embraces everything that forms the enterprise's constituent parts that are to be directed at such functioning that allows a maximum utilization of their use value, i.e., their profit-yielding ability.

Methods of Valuation in Privatization

In the case of Polish privatization, appraisal of an enterprise follows one of three methods: property-based methods, income-based methods, and mixed methods (based on both property and income).

Property-based methods.   Property-based methods consist chiefly in determining the value of the property components of a privatized enterprise on the basis of either book values (entries) or market values, where the latter includes (1) liquidation value, or (2) replacement value. The book value of net assets is the easiest method to apply because it is assumed that the value of an enterprise equals its book value minus liabilities in accordance with the basic balance-sheet formula.

The liquidation method allows one to establish the value of assets of an enterprise at a level closest to their terminal market value. Liquidation value is regarded as total cash realizable upon the liquidation of an enterprise or sale of its individual assets (usually by means of tender or liquidation). This method is particularly useful for an enterprise that is not considered a going concern. In contrast, the income-based method is preferred for profitable businesses.

The replacement value equals the amount of capital outlay needed to reproduce the same productive capacities at a given point in time. The replacement value relates mainly to fixed assets, but is also used in valuing patents, licenses and concessions, organization of distribution channels, and recruitment and training of employees.

Income-based methods. These methods assume that an enterprise is worth the asset based yielding the profits it can earn. Two such methods are in use: (1) the market multiplier method, which is a simple capitalization of the profit realized by the enterprise being privatized, and (2) discounting of future cash flows generated by such an enterprise.

For income-based valuation purposes, it is assumed that a given enterprise will continue to function as a state-owned enterprise in order to determine its value to the State Treasury, so the following generally accepted principles are adopted: (1) the enterprise is a going concern; (2) prudence, which is an expectation of average results that takes into account various external and internal prospects and threats in order to determine the enterprise's earning power; (3) most efficient use of assets; and (4) accurate, fair, reliable, and efficient valuation.

In order to measure the economic value of Polish enterprises, the privatization practice includes the assessment of: (1) volume of future income (revenue); (2) volume of expected costs; (3) volume of future profits; (4) discount rate of future income realized without the element of risk; (5) uncertainty in the realization of anticipated income; (6) terminal value; and (7) duration of an enterprise's life, constituting the basis for calculating future revenue and expenditure.

A crucial element in appraising the value of an enterprise is the choice of the discount rate. Due to the prevalent inflationary conditions in Poland, the chosen rate is often fixed at a higher level than is usually accepted for comparable undertakings in developed market economies. In general, however, the application of the discounted profit or cash flow method is difficult because there is an insufficiently developed capital market or transactions market to provide a relevant pricing frame of reference.

Mixed methods. Mixed methods of valuation (based on both property and income) assume that the worth of a business is a combined result of the value of assets and the discounting of income. Some of the mixed methods used include: (1) the average value method, also known in the literature as the German or Berlin method; and (2) the Anglo–Saxon methods in their original version, which have been employed by European Economic Community experts.

In general, each of the methods used in the valuation of privatized enterprises has its own limitations and reliance on appraisals by experts who use a combination of these methods is mandated by the long absence of established market prices and the reliance on administered prices. As these conditions change, market prices will form a more useful frame of reference and valuation will tend to be more structured.

ALICJA A. JARUGA and
ALDONA KAMELA-SOWINSKA

procedural justice Procedural justice involves the fairness of means (methods for determining results), much as DISTRIBUTIVE JUSTICE involves the fairness of ends (outcomes, the results themselves). Thibaut and Walker (1975) suggested that people want "process control" over

dispute resolution or allocation methods, akin to participation or a "voice" in decision-making. People want a say in decisions affecting them. Expressing opinions and arguments about one's interests can substitute (somewhat) for not choosing outcomes directly. People value this fairness substitute both as a means of trying to influence a decision-maker (instrumental value) and for the inherent satisfaction of speaking out (expressive value).

Other procedural fairness criteria exist (Leventhal et al., 1980). One, representativeness, overlaps with voice, process control, and participation: a fair procedure reflects the concerns of each affected group (e.g. grievance process with union steward representing labor's interests). Additional criteria include consistency (same procedure each time, for everyone), accuracy (e.g. objective data collection), correctability (e.g. appeal systems), bias suppression (no favoritism), and ethicality (norms of socially appropriate conduct). With respect to ethicality as fair interpersonal treatment, some writers distinguish between the procedural justice of making decisions and the "interactional justice" of implementing them (e.g. prior notice, timeliness). The latter refers especially to fairness perceived because of adequate, sincere explanations and interpersonally sensitive conduct (e.g. politeness, consideration). The perceived fairness of both a procedure itself and its implementation increases decision acceptance along with the degree to which outcomes are also considered fair.

Bibliography

Cropanzano, R. & Folger, R. (1991). Procedural justice and worker motivation. *Motivation and Work Behavior,* Eds. Steers, R. & Porter, L. New York: McGraw-Hill.

Folger, R. & Greenberg, J. (1985). Procedural justice: an interpretive analysis of personnel systems. *Research in Personnel and Human Resources Management,* 3, Eds. Rowland, K. & Ferris, G. Greenwich, CT: JAI Press.

Greenberg, J. (1990). Organizational justice: yesterday, today, and tomorrow. *Journal of Management,* 16, 399–432.

Leventhal, G. S., Karuza, J. & Fry, W. R. (1980). Beyond fairness: a theory of allocation preferences. *Justice in Social Interaction,* Mikula, G. New York: Springer Verlag.

Lind, E. A. & Tyler, T. R. (1988). *The Social Psychology of Procedural Justice,* New York: Plenum.

Justice: a Psychological Analysis, Hillsdale, NJ: Lawrence Erlbaum Associates.

Tyler, T. R. & Smith, H. J. (1996). Social justice and social movements. *Handbook of Social Psychology,* **4th edn,** Eds. Gilbert, D., Fiske, S. T. & Lindzey, G. New York: McGraw-Hill.

ROBERT FOLGER

process mapping For many years, theories on business management have been functionally based, but now organizations are viewing themselves as a collection of interrelated and interdependent processes. A process is a coordinated set of activities which meets a customer requirement – it represents the customer's view of the organization rather than the internal view displayed by the organigram. Many organizations are now undergoing Business Process Reengineering (BPR) to change from a FUNCTIONAL STRUCTURE to an HORIZONTAL STRUCTURE.

To achieve this change, time, commitment, and control are required, particularly from the CEO/chairman. Employees need regular communication to convince them of the necessity for change, to gain their commitment and confidence, and to maintain their enthusiasm during difficult stages of projects. Communication is essential not only between team members undertaking the study but also between the team and the business. Effective communication helps staff members understand the purpose of a process, where they fit into it, and how the process contributes to company goals. Successful projects require the participation of cross-functional, trained teams, often supported by an external consultant to act as a facilitator to draw out key goals and objectives.

Most organizations have an "organigram" but very few have analysed the flow of work across the functions or even within them. This kind of analysis is increasing within companies, and is a powerful way of spotting how the organization could work more effectively and either save time/costs or increase quality, or both. However, if improvements are to be made to processes, a clear understanding of them is required before any can be implemented.

One of the most effective ways to gain an understanding of existing processes is to draw them on a "map". Such maps enable them to be easily read and understood and are key in the description, analysis, and communication processes. Typically, between five and 20 major processes are used to encompass the key activities of the organization. These should support the key objectives and goals of the organization.

Use of Process Maps

Within BPR, there are various phases in which process maps may act as a focus.

Process capture and business modeling. This phase is where the "as is" processes of the organization are mapped. This is important for process redesign, as time spent in this phase provides a number of benefits. Specifically, it:

- identifies "quick win" solutions
- provides a common understanding for the team involved
- identifies other potential areas for improvement
- highlights particular failures affecting areas of the organization; for example, customers

Process maps can highlight duplicated activities and interactions in the organization and those which do not add value.

Process redesign. Following the initial process analysis, the processes are analyzed and redesign opportunities are discussed by the team. Ideas are discussed within the team and simulations may be carried out to investigate the various "what if" possibilities and assess the impact of potential changes.

Process support. Teams that have been involved in the initial stages of process mapping will be involved in support as changes/new processes are implemented.

Process analysis flows are very effective when overlapped onto organizational structures. Companies are typically organized into functional, vertical hierarchies such as Marketing, Operations, Distribution, Finance, and Human Resources. Organizational charts typically reflect this functionality, with a high degree of hierarchy. Often, status, power, control, ambition, and rank are more important to people than efficiency, lateral cooperation, and customer service. However, organizations delivering to customers depend on key processes that often cut across functional vertical hierarchies. Many companies are thus moving to a CROSS-FUNCTIONAL MANAGEMENT STRUCTURE, to manage and deliver superior CORE PROCESS performance. Process maps help the understanding of the interaction between departments and identify "hand offs" that can then be addressed (see figure 1).

JULIA CHANNON

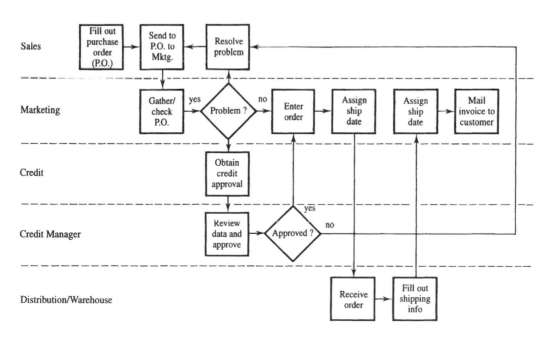

Figure 1   Cross functional map: flow diagram

processing methods for information systems Processing methods are generally associated with transaction processing. Transaction processing is a basic organization activity. Without transaction processing, business transactions would not be completed. Without it, bills would not be paid, sales orders would not be filled, manufacturing parts would not be ordered, and so on. Without it, data for management activities would not be available.

Transaction Processing Cycle

The transaction processing cycle begins with a transaction that is recorded in some way. Although hand-written forms are still very common, transactions are often recorded directly to a computer by the use of an online terminal. Recording of the transaction is generally the trigger to produce a transaction document. Data from the transaction is frequently required for the updating of master files; this updating may be performed concurrently with the processing of transaction documents or by a subsequent computer run.

The capturing of data on documents or by direct entry is a necessary first step preceding other activities in processing the transaction. For example, a sales order is manually prepared on a sales order form by a salesperson, a telephoned order is entered in a computer by a telephone salesperson, a cash withdrawal is entered in an automatic teller machine by the customer, and a reservation is entered by a travel agent using an online reservation terminal.

When a transaction is recorded manually, a copy of the document is usually used for data preparation. The transaction is keyed into a file using a terminal or data entry computer. The records of the transactions are used for processing. Many times, the documents involved are partially or completely coded. A bank check is precoded with the customer number and bank number; the amount of the check must be added. A turnaround document may be coded with much of the transaction data. An example is the part of the invoice returned with the payment; the turnaround portion may often be read with optical scanning.

Data validation is the testing of input data records to determine if they are correct and complete. This cannot be accomplished with complete assurance, but reasonable validation is usually possible. Validation tests applied against each data item or set of items may include tests for missing data, valid field size for each data item, numerical data class test, range or reasonableness test, valid or invalid values test, and comparison with stored data. Identification numbers and processing codes are very sensitive to errors. They can be validated for size, range, and composition of characters. An additional, very effective, validation technique for codes is a check digit. It is a redundant digit derived by computations on the identification number and then made a permanent part of the number. During data preparation and input validation, the check-digit derivation procedure is repeated. If the procedure results in a different check digit, there has been an error in recording or entering the identification number.

When input data items have been validated, the transactions are processed. Subsequently, two major activities occur during transaction processing: updating of machine-readable stored data (master file) related to or affected by the transaction, and preparation of outputs such as transaction documents and reports. In both of these activities, control information is also produced.

Transaction data output can be classified as to its purpose. There are three major reasons for producing transaction documents or other transaction output: (a) informational to report, confirm, or explain proposed or completed action; (b) action to direct a transaction to take place or be completed; and (c) investigational for background information or reference by the recipient. Action documents include shipping orders, purchase orders, manufacturing orders, checks, and customer statements. These documents instruct someone to do something. For example, a purchase order instructs a vendor to ship, a check instructs a bank to pay, etc. When action is taken, the completed action (or lack of completion) is reported back to the organizational unit initiating the action. A sales order confirmation verifies receipt of an order. Lists of checks not paid by banks represent a confirmation of completed action (if not on list, checks have been paid) and lack of completed action (by being listed as unpaid). A single document or different copies of it may serve both action and informational purposes. For example, one copy of the sales order confirmation may be sent to the customer to confirm the order; a second copy may be used as an action document to initiate filling of the order.

Some transaction records are distributed to other departments in the organization to provide background information for recipients in the event that they need to respond to inquiries or need them for other reference. With online systems, a reference copy of the transaction can be stored in a computer file and may be retrieved via a terminal by anyone who is authorized and has need of the information. Transaction documents may also be used for managerial information or control scanning, as when a purchasing manager scans all purchase orders to spot unusual occurrences. In general, however, managerial information purposes are better met by reports or analyses which summarize transactions.

When transactions are processed, a listing of data about each transaction is usually prepared. The listing includes control totals for the number of transactions processed, total dollar amount of transactions, etc. The listing represents a batch of transactions or, for online processing, processing during a period of time. It provides a means of processing reference and error control.

Methods for Processing Transactions

There are three different methods commonly used for processing transactions and updating master files: (a) periodic data preparation and periodic batch processing (usually termed batch processing); (b) online entry with subsequent batch processing; and (c) online entry with immediate processing (termed online processing). The choice of methods should reflect the underlying process being supported. If the underlying process is transaction-oriented with immediate completion of the transaction desirable (as with order entry), online processing is indicated. If the process is periodic (as with payroll), batch processing is adequate.

Batch processing involves the accumulation of transactions until a sufficient number has been assembled to make processing efficient or until other considerations, such as a report cycle, initiate processing. The processing of batches can be daily, weekly, or monthly, depending on the volume of transactions and other considerations.

Batch processing of transactions can be very efficient in terms of data preparation and processing of transactions. One major disadvantage of periodic batch processing is the delay in detecting and correcting errors. This is an especially serious problem for errors that can be found only when the transaction is compared against the master file. For example, if a transaction is coded with an apparently valid customer number for a nonexistent customer, the error will not be detected until processing is attempted against the customer file. The delay makes it difficult to trace the transaction back to the origination point and identify the correct customer.

With a batch system, the user prepares data input as a batch of transactions recorded over a period of time such as a day or week. A user responsible for processing data in a batch system must prepare input data in the exact format and with the exact codes required by the processing program, prepare control information used to ensure that no records are lost or remain unprocessed, and check output received for errors (including checking against the control information prepared with input data). The user is also responsible for reviewing error reports, preparing corrections, and submitting corrections for processing.

When *transactions are entered at an online terminal*, the transaction is entered directly into the computer and validated immediately. The processing itself may be performed immediately or at a subsequent time as with periodic batch processing. One important advantage of online entry over periodic data preparation and input is that most of the validation may be performed while the transaction is being recorded. Many errors can therefore be corrected immediately while the person entering the transaction is available for correction. Often the user or customer originating the transaction is still available to make appropriate changes. In addition, the master files can be accessed for the detection of errors such as nonexistent master file records. In online entry with subsequent batch processing, the computer is used for direct data entry and validation, but valid transactions are stored for later periodic batch processing.

In *online entry with immediate processing*, the transaction is validated online and then processed immediately if valid. A response with the result of processing or a confirmation of completion of processing is generally provided to the user at the input terminal. The advantages of this approach are the same as direct entry with subsequent processing (i.e. immediate validation with opportunity for immediate corrections by the person doing the input) plus the additional advantage of immediate processing with immediate results. The master files are always up to date. For instance, after an item is sold, the inventory master file reflects the actual state of the inventory for that item. The disadvantages of immediate versus periodic batch processing (requires greater computer power and often data communications) and the extra procedures required to produce adequate control information and to safeguard the files against accidental or deliberate destruction during online updating.

In online processing, the user has a terminal or microcomputer for the input of transactions and output of results. The terminal is connected by communication lines to a remote computer where processing actually takes place. Transactions are entered and processed one at a time as they occur (in real time). The user generally has to be identified to the system as an authorized user before transactions are accepted. System sign on and authorization usually uses a password protection scheme. Users may have different authorization levels which determine what types of transactions they may perform. For instance, a user may be authorized (via his or her password) to process certain update transactions (e.g. a sale) but not others (e.g. alteration of payroll data). The mode of operation is a dialog. The dialog may be extensive and provide tutorial and help information for entry of data, or it may be very limited and require the user to understand what data to enter and how it should be entered. A user responsible for processing data in an online system must enter transactions in the proper format based on a dialog, a visual form, or instructions in a manual; respond to error messages (since the system should reject any invalid data) with corrected input; and review control information. At the end of a period of processing transactions, the user signs off, so that an unauthorized user may not subsequently enter data.

Retrieval in Transaction Processing

Many online systems use data retrieval software to support transaction processing. Even in applications where batch updating is appropriate, the capability to access related records during transaction preparation is often desired. For instance, a bank may install online terminals so that customers may inquire about the status of their accounts. A customer complaint department in a retail catalog company may check the status of an order when a customer calls. In these examples, online inquiry into master files is required.

Inquiries associated with a transaction-processing system tend to be fairly structured, so that they may be programmed to use a standard set of commands that can be mastered fairly easily. In some systems, commands can be assigned to special function keys on the keyboard so that the operator needs only to press a single key rather than type in a command. Terminals that are only to be used for inquiries, such as terminals for customer use on a bank floor, may be specially designed with only function keys.

Information Processing Controls

Control of transaction processing begins with the design of the document for initially recording the transaction. If the document is manually prepared, it should be designed to minimize errors in completing it. This requires adequate space, unambiguous directions and labels, and a sequence of recording that is natural to the preparer. Boxes, lines, colors, labels and menus of alternatives are some of the methods used to aid the preparer. One serious problem is how to make sure every transaction is recorded and entered into processing. Interruptions or carelessness may cause a transaction to not be recorded or the source document to be misplaced. To prevent or detect such errors and omissions, the transaction processing system may have one or more controls such as the following: (a) prenumbered source document; (b) record anticipating a transaction (such as payment due); (c) document produced as a byproduct; or (d) comparison with related transaction controls.

The use of a terminal to enter the original transaction has the advantage that a machine-readable record is produced at the same time as source documents needed for the transaction. If a source document is misplaced or lost, the computer record permits the tracking or reconstructing of the missing record. Accuracy and completeness considerations for source document design also apply to input screen design for the visual display terminal. Since online entry may also be performed without a source document (as with order entry by telephone), the machine record may be the only "document."

In the flow of control in batch processing, it is best to establish a control total of documents before data preparation. The control total can be a record count, a financial total, or a "hash total" of numbers such as account numbers, which are not normally summed (hence the total is meaningless except for control purposes).

During the data-preparation process, the control totals are checked to verify that no transactions are missing and that items used in control totals have been entered correctly. The control total is input with the data and checked by computer as part of data validation, processing, and output. The control totals appear on batch reports and on other control reports. The output (after adjusting for rejected transactions) should match the control total for the input batch. Computer programs and control personnel make control total comparisons during processing; users check controls on output against control totals for data they submitted for processing. This checking provides a simple but powerful control procedure to ensure that all transactions in the document batch are processed.

In the case of online input from documents, there is no control total of transactions prior to entry. However, if there are reasonable control procedures to enforce entry of all transactions, control totals can be developed for logical batches of input (transactions that are logically grouped by some common feature). The logical batches provide a basis for listings for reference, follow-up, comparison with physical evidence, and so on. For example, the log of all transactions entered is sorted, and logical batches of transactions are prepared by terminal, by operator, by type of transactions, etc.

There are special control considerations with online processing. The files change continuously, and therefore any error can disrupt a file and create additional errors as subsequent transactions are processed. The straightforward preprocessing batch control totals cannot be used to check batches before updating. Some examples of controls illustrate how control in online processing is handled. Restart procedures tell input personnel which transactions were lost if a system goes down. A separate backup file copy and transaction log are used for making file correction.

Processing Reference Control

The audit trail (or a processing reference trail) is the trail of references (document numbers, batch numbers, transaction references, etc.) which allows tracing of a transaction from the time it is recorded through to the reports in which it is aggregated with other transactions, or the reverse, tracing a total back to amounts on individual source documents. The processing trail is required for internal clerical, analytical, and management use because of the frequent need to examine the details behind a total or to trace what happened to a transaction. It is also needed

by external auditors and is required by certain tax regulations for tax-related records.

An audit trail should always be present. Its form may change in response to computer technology, but three requirements should be met:

1 Any transaction can be traced from the source document through processing to outputs and to totals in which it is aggregated. For example, each purchase of goods for inventory can be traced to inclusion in the inventory totals.
2 Any output or summary data can be traced back to the transactions or computations used to arrive at the output or summary figures. For example, the total amount owed by a customer can be traced to the sales and payments that were used to arrive at the balance due.
3 Any triggered transaction (a transaction automatically triggered by an event or condition) can be traced to the event or condition. An example is a purchase order triggered by a sale that reduced inventory below an order point.

GORDON B. DAVIS

product A product can be an idea, a service, a good, or a combination of these. For Kotler (1984) a product "is anything that can be offered to market for attention, acquisition, use or consumption that might satisfy a want or need." Obviously, the products of manufacturing firms are tangible, while those of service industries are intangible. A household insurance package is an example of a product that is a service. Such examples indicate the difficulty of clearly distinguishing between a product and a service (see SERVICE PRODUCT). The product is regarded as encompassing a set of benefits and is often referred to as the product (or service) offering.

Bibliography

Kotler, P. (1984). *Marketing management: Analysis, planning and control*, 5th edn, Englewood Cliffs, NJ: Prentice-Hall. Chapter 15, pp. 462–463.

MARGARET BRUCE

product attributes model Developed by Kelvin Lancaster (1971), the product attributes model sets out to explain consumer behavior as a process of choosing bundles of product characteristics or attributes inherent in goods and services, rather than simply choosing bundles of goods or services themselves. The basic assumption of the model is that the consumer's choice is based on maximizing utility from the product attributes subject to a budget constraint. The model is particularly useful in analyzing differentiated product markets, in which specific products that are substitutes for each other are distinguished by their embodiment of a specific set of characteristics.

For purposes of exposition, a two-dimensional graph reveals the model's main features (see Douglas 1992 for textbook treatment and examples), and links it to the traditional BUDGET CONSTRAINT and indifference curve analysis of consumer behavior (see INDIFFERENCE CURVES). Figure 1 shows three specific products, each offering a specific amount of attribute X and attribute Y in

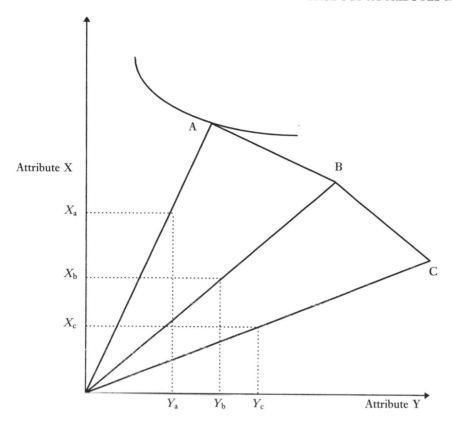

Figure 1   Product attributes and consumer choice

constant proportions. Each unit of product A contains X_a of attribute X and Y_a of attribute Y, for example. Similarly, each unit of products B and C offers the attribute bundles (X_b, Y_b) and (X_c, Y_c), respectively. The attributes could represent calories (X) and vitamin content (Y) for competing brands of soups, for example. While some attributes can be measured objectively in this way, it may also be useful to consider more subjective attributes, such as "atmosphere" and "quality of food" in distinguishing among restaurants, for example. Subjective attributes do, however, imply that the attribute content of a particular product may be determined largely by the perceptions of the individual consumer (see discussion of advertising below). For a given budget constraint and set of prices for the products, the end points A, B, and C represent the limits of consumption along each attribute ray, and the line segment ABC defines the budget (or efficiency) frontier for the consumer. The consumer's choice is made by maximizing utility, as defined by the consumer's set of indifference curves, subject to the budget constraint. In this model, we interpret the slope of an indifference curve at a particular point (marginal rate of substitution) as the rate at which the consumer is willing to trade off units of attribute Y for an additional unit of attribute X to remain at constant utility. Thus, the consumer's choice is influenced by his or her preference pattern in attribute space. As shown in figure 1, this consumer shows a strong preference for attribute Y and therefore chooses product A; a strong

preference for attribute X would lead him or her to choose C. In this regard, the proliferation of differentiated products in a particular market can be explained as the result of the dispersion of tastes for various attributes among the population of consumers.

Note that the consumer will spend the entire budget on a single product A, B, or C if the highest indifference curve just touches the respective end point. If the highest indifference curve touches a point on the line segment between two attribute ray end points, then the consumer would choose to split consumption between the two adjacent products. If the product's consumption is indivisible (as in the case of an automobile or house), then such consumption splitting would be impossible, and the consumer's choice would be determined by the highest indifference curve that touches an end point; see Douglas (1992).

The product attributes model also allows an analysis of strategic behavior by firms and its effect on consumer choice. A decrease in the price of a product moves the end point further out along the ray, for example. Advertising can change the perception of the product in terms of attribute content and proportion (length and slope of the product ray) or the consumer's tastes for attributes (shape of individual consumers' indifference curves). Product positioning strategy may focus on opportunities based on "gaps" in the attribute space between rays, or may target existing products for direct competition.

Bibliography

Douglas, E. J. (1992). *Managerial Economics.* 4th edn, Englewood Cliffs, NJ: Prentice-Hall.

Lancaster, K. (1971). *Consumer Demand: A New Approach.* New York and London: Columbia University Press.

KENT A. JONES

product champion   Product champion is a term used to refer to those individuals with a commitment to, or belief in, a new product, which is strong enough to overcome organizational resistance to the new product idea (Maidique, 1980). Schon (1963) studied 15 major inventions of the 20th century and observed that certain highly committed individuals, or champions, were likely to play a role in successfully commercializing these inventions: "no ordinary involvement with a new idea provides the energy to cope with the indifference and resistance that major technical change provokes;" champions of new innovations "display persistence and courage of heroic quality." Various studies have associated the existence of a product champion as a differentiating factor between innovations regarded as successful and those regarded as less successful (SPRU, 1972; Roberts & Fusfield, 1981). Roberts & Fusfield (1981) suggest that product champions are critical in NEW PRODUCT DEVELOPMENT, "recognizing, proposing and pushing a new (product) idea." However, the product champion may serve to play a detrimental role precisely because of his/her unshaking commitment to, or belief in, the new product in question in order to overcome resistance to the new idea. This may occur when commitment leads to continued expenditure on a relatively unpromising venture, rather than withdrawing resources before considerable losses are incurred (Leverick & Littler, 1994).

Bibliography

Leverick, F. & Littler, D. A. (1994). Marketing in the process of managing ambiguity: The development of telepoint in the UK. Manchester School of Management Working Paper, UMIST: UK.

Maidique, M. A. (1980). Entrepreneurs, champions and technological innovation. *Sloan Management Review*, 3, 299–307.

Najak, P. R. & Ketteringham, J. M. (1985). *Breakthroughs.* London: Mercury Books.

Roberts, E. B. & Fusfield, A. R. (1981). Staffing the innovation technology based organization. *Sloan Management Review*, 22, (3), 19–34.

Schon, D. A. (1963). Champions of radical new inventions. *Harvard Business Review*, 41, (2), 77–86.

SPRU (1972). *Project SAPPHO: A study of success and failure in innovation.* SPRU, University of Sussex, UK.

MARGARET BRUCE

product concept   The product concept is a basic outline of the features and values of the product. This should be based on the core benefit(s) proposition which is a summary of the advantages the product will offer to the customer. In addition, the proposition should highlight the main features which differentiate it from the competition. The first definition of the product concept will tend to be general, but over time, as a result of market research and management deliberation, it will gradually become more refined. Examples of product concepts are: a kettle that can be easily filled through the spout and enables the user to boil only small quantities of water at a time; and an ergonomically designed secretarial chair that adapts with ease to different tasks of the secretary and prevents backache. In these cases, more work is required to define some of the basic features outlined, for example, what is a "small volume of water?"

Bibliography

Kotler, P. (1984). *Marketing management: Analysis, planning and control*, 5th edn, Englewood Cliffs, NJ: Prentice-Hall. Chapter 10.

Littler, D. A. (1984). *Marketing and product development.* Oxford: Philip Allan. Chapter 7.

MARGARET BRUCE

product cost determination   Accuracy in product costing is an important issue in managerial accounting and control. For purposes of product profitability analysis and continuous cost improvement, it is no longer considered sufficient to obtain aggregate cost figures only that are used for external financial reporting. With increasing global competition in the market place, the trend is towards setting a *target selling price* with a *target product quality* as a first step in new product planning. This is very different from the traditional approach where the selling price is set by estimating the product cost and adding to it a desired profit margin and where an acceptable level of quality is the aim. The new trend is to attain the highest product quality or at least to meet the target quality level at the target price. Thus, if the estimated product cost is below the target cost obtained by deducting a profit margin from the target price, the task is to increase quality further rather than to accept a higher profit margin. If the estimated product cost is higher than the target cost, then alternative product designs are sought or the profit margin reduced, rather than increasing the target selling price or reducing target quality. This is the currently proven way to obtain a desirable market share for the product. As a consequence, it is more important than ever to accurately determine product costs.

One of the major components of product cost, which affects estimation, involves the application of overheads. This issue has led to the development of activity-based costing approaches. However, a theoretically sound application of overhead should be based on the opportunity cost of producing the product including its consumption of common resources.

Opportunity Cost as Transfer Price

A transfer price is set for the service rendered by one organizational unit to another within the firm. The purposes of charging a transfer price are to accurately measure the full cost of the product and to induce the various organizational units to act in the best interest of the firm. There are two reasons for a transfer price to have an incentive role in a firm: these are (1) goal incongruence among the organizational unit managers and the firm manager, and (2) information asymmetries among the units. The measurement of product cost and the incentive issues are generally not tackled together in the literature on agency modeling. Multi-period considerations can mitigate the incentive issue but not the measurement problem. The approach proposed here addresses both the measurement and incentive issues: i.e., the extent of utilization of the common service center by decentralized units.

A theoretically sound definition for the transfer price when one unit provides a service to another unit within a firm is to set it equal to the incremental costs plus opportunity costs. The incremental costs are usually taken to be the incremental variable costs of providing the service but may include incremental fixed costs as well. In theory, opportunity costs are zero if there is excess capacity in the service center unit. If the servicing unit is operating at full capacity, the opportunity cost is calculated so that the total transfer price is equal to the market price of the product being transferred. In the case of a service, such as machinery repair, the market price is the price the outsiders will charge for this service. Thus, the opportunity cost apparently takes on only two extreme values. With the introduction of demand and scheduling uncertainty, however, this analysis is no longer appropriate.

Job Opportunity Cost in a Common Service Center

Consider a common service center that provides service to several jobs. The jobs may originate from many organizational units. Service rendered may be the repair of machinery, computer consultancy, or even a production process whose facility is shared by several jobs. The capacity of the service center is limited. If a specific job requires service when the center is occupied serving other jobs, it will have to wait in a queue for its turn. Viewing it in reverse fashion, if a job seeks to utilize a common service center, it creates a delay. The uncertainty involved in the actual arrival times precludes one from stating the exact delay caused by any specific job on the other jobs. Nevertheless, one can work with expected delays instead, provided one can determine the rate of demand by jobs for the service and the capacity of the service center. Formulas from queuing theory may be used to determine the expected delay experienced by jobs at the service center. The cost due to delay experienced by the jobs is the opportunity cost of serving any other job. If this job is not processed, the delay and hence potential cost will not be experienced by the other jobs. Equivalently, this is the cost of consuming part of the common service center resource by the job.

The cost incurred to set up a service center is a sunk cost and should not directly enter into the determination of product cost needed for managerial decision-making. What should be part of the product cost is the opportunity cost of using the service. This idea is problematic if one assumes no uncertainty with respect to demand and service times. The problem arises because (1) either there is excess capacity in the service center, in which case the opportunity cost is zero, or (2) the service center is operating at full capacity, in which case the opportunity cost is at its maximum equal to the market price less incremental variable costs.

Taking into account the uncertainties with respect to demand and service times implies that capacity cannot be fully utilized (i.e., there must be times during which the center is idle) otherwise the queue length will become infinitely long. (For a proof of this statement, see a standard book on queuing theory.) It does not follow, however, that the opportunity cost is zero. Even though there is excess capacity, many jobs may be delayed prior to obtaining service due to the uncertain nature of demands and service times. Any job that seeks to use the center will, on average, cause a delay for other jobs that may arrive.

In order to provide concrete expressions for this idea, let us suppose that the cost of delaying a job by one unit of time is H and the expected delay experienced at the center by any job demanding service is D, so that the expected cost due to delay for one job is HD. If the demand rate is A per period, then the expected total cost due to delay per period for all the jobs using the service center is AHD.

If we consider a single job, the delay experienced by all the jobs in the service center by the entrance of this specific job is the marginal value of the total expected delay cost per period, which is equal to $[HD+\{AH\}.dD/dA]$ (where the symbol dD/dA denotes the derivative of D with respect to A). The first component is the delay cost for the entering job itself and the second component is the opportunity cost of serving the job, namely, the delay imposed on the other jobs.

For given probability characterizations of the demand and service processes, formulas for D are available from queuing theory. For example, if the demand process has a Poisson distribution and the service process has an exponential distribution with expected service time, S, the expected delay is given by the formula, $D = S/(1-SA)$. The opportunity cost is equal to $SAH/(1-SA)$. This is the amount to be applied to the job for utilizing the service in addition to all the variable costs of providing the service. This applied cost ranges from zero to a maximum equal to the market price for the service less variable service costs.

Service Center Capacity Determination

Suppose one treats the service center as a cost center. The capacity of the service center is chosen so that the benefit obtained from using the service center is equal to the fixed and variable costs of operating the service center. If the benefit is greater than the costs, jobs will find it advantageous to use the service center and consequently congest the center. This will reduce the benefit for all. This reduction is applied as the opportunity cost of delay. At equilibrium, equality will prevail.

The benefit obtained is the avoidance of paying the market price for the service, less the cost of delay in the service center. Symbolically, the expected benefit from the service center = the expected market price – the expected delay cost for the job. At equilibrium capacity, the market price = the transfer price for service + variable cost of service. The transfer price then is equal to the applied opportunity cost of delay caused to the other users.

Putting it all together, the expected benefit from the service center = applied opportunity cost + variable cost of service – expected delay cost to the job. At equilibrium capacity, equate this to the fixed and variable costs of providing service at the service center. Then, the fixed cost of operating the center = applied opportunity cost – expected delay cost to the job. If the equality does not hold and the fixed operating cost is greater than the right side, the firm should use an outside facility. If it is less, then there is underutilization of the center.

Service Center Volume Variance

Any positive difference between the fixed cost per period and the applied opportunity cost less the delay cost per period for all the jobs using a service center denotes the extent of underutilization. This is theoretically defined to be the service center volume variance.

By introducing an opportunity cost concept for application of service center costs an equilibrium usage of the center by its users will be induced such that the benefits obtained are equal to the costs of operating the center. This is a desirable property of a cost center.

Bibliography

Balachandran, K. R. & Srinidhi, B. N. (1987). A rationale for fixed charge application. *Journal of Accounting, Auditing and Finance*, 2, Spring, 151–83.

Balachandran, K. R. & Srinidhi, B. N. (1988). A stable cost application scheme for service center usage. *Journal of Business Finance & Accounting*, 15, Spring, 87–100.

Balachandran, K. R. & Srinidhi, B. N. (1990). A note on cost allocation, opportunity costs and optimal utilization. *Journal of Business Finance & Accounting*, 17, Autumn, 579–584.

Balachandran, K. R. & Radhakrishnan, S. (1995). Delay costs and incentive schemes for multiple users. *Management Science*.

Cooper, R. D, & Kaplan, R. S. (1992). Activity-based systems: Measuring the cost of resource usage. *Accounting Horizons*, 6, Sept., 1–13.

Cooper, R. B. (1981). *Introduction to queuing theory* Elsevier North Holland, Inc.

Radhakrishnan, S. & Balachandran, K. R. (1995). Stochastic choice hazard and incentives in a common service facility. *European Journal of Operational Research*.

KASHI R. BALACHANDRAN and
JEFFREY L. CALLEN

product deletion   This is the process of eliminating a product that does not perform at a level considered adequate according to certain criteria. Most companies base their decisions to delete weak products on poor sales and profit potential, low compatibility with the firm's business strategies, and unfavorable market outlook (Lambert & Sterling, 1988). The decision to eliminate a product is based on its impact on the overall PRODUCT MIX of the firm and if a weak product is no longer making a contribution and the resources employed can be more effectively deployed, then it may be deleted. Once the decision to delete has been made, the need to minimize costs and to retain customer goodwill (e.g., providing assurances that spare parts will be available for a certain period) may affect whether the "weak" product is immediately dropped, or phased out gradually. The phase out approach can either attempt to exploit any strengths left in the product, e.g., by a price reduction to boost sales, or let the product decline with no change in marketing strategy.

Bibliography

Dibb, S., Simkin, L., Pride, W. & Ferrell, O. C. (1994). *Marketing: Concepts and strategies*, 2nd European edn, Boston, MA: Houghton Mifflin Co. Chapter 9, pp. 242–244.

Lambert, D. M. & Sterling, J. U. (1988). Identifying and eliminating weak products. *Business*, July–Sept., 3–10.

MARGARET BRUCE

product development   *see* NEW PRODUCT DEVELOPMENT

product differentiation   When firms in an industry sell products which are each distinct in the eyes of consumers, those products are said to be differentiated. Eaton and Lipsey (1989) suggested that differentiated products could be any set of closely related products in consumption and/or production. The degree of substitution between differentiated products varies and depends upon consumers' tastes in consumption, their information about other brands and upon ECONOMIES OF SCOPE in production.

When firms produce differentiated products, each firm acquires some market power and faces a downward–sloping demand curve for its brand. If consumers prefer particular brands relative to others, they have fewer substitutes in consumption and so product differentiation reduces the ELASTICITY of the demand for the firm's product(s). Caves and Williamson (1985) noted that product differentiation requires two conditions: consumers must believe that differentiated goods within a product class are close substitutes for each other (relative to other products outside that class) and yet, consumers must find the differentiated brands to be imperfect substitutes so that each firm faces a downward-sloping demand curve. They found that IMPERFECT INFORMATION and complex product attributes combined with fixed costs were sufficient to explain product differentiation in US and Australian manufacturing industries.

Products may be differentiated *horizontally*, or they may be *vertically differentiated*. Horizontal differentiation occurs when consumers have diverse preferences and do not agree on which product is best. Vertical differentiation exists when all consumers may agree which product is best in terms of quality but purchase different brands because of differences in prices or in their incomes.

In his classic study, Hotelling (1929) concluded that, in the absence of price competition, market competition will lead to *minimal product differentiation* where firms offer virtually identical products to appeal to as many consumers as possible. Although this result is not always an equilibrium configuration (see Ireland (1987) and Tirole (1988) and the sources cited there), it does explain the lack of diversity in broadcast television programming, political platforms and other cases where price competition does not occur.

If price competition does occur, the firms will want to increase product differentiation to reduce the intensity of price competition. As product differentiation increases, each firm has more local monopoly power and competes less for sales, so equilibrium prices will rise. In fact, firms have incentives to pursue *maximal* differentiation to reduce price competition and will choose to locate at the extremes of the market (see Tirole (1988)).

When firms compete in markets with differentiated products, there are forces which tend to increase the level of differentiation (and may possibly create a fragmented industry structure) and forces that work in the opposite direction toward *minimal* differentiation. As previously discussed, firms would prefer to increase differentiation to avoid price competition, all else equal. But as Tirole observed, firms will also want to locate near consumers and this reduces product differentiation. For example, if consumers were clustered at the center of a one-mile road, we would expect firms to locate near the center of the market where the density of consumers was highest. This means that if consumers' tastes are not very different, the brands offered in the market should not be very different. Another force reducing differentiation is positive externalities between firms which cause them to cluster together. These externalities arise when the costs of supplying firms in the industry fall when they share a common geographic location or when resources are more easily acquired (such as hiring computer professionals from nearby universities or competitors). Or, if firms share a geographic location, such as a shopping mall, they can reduce consumer search costs and raise their total demand even if price competition is intensified. Finally, Tirole notes that firms will tend to cluster when there is no price competition. It should also be noted that the amount of product differentiation supplied by a free market is unlikely to be the optimal level: unregulated markets may create too much or too little product variety (see Tirole (1988)).

Firms may also choose their locations strategically to create BARRIERS TO ENTRY in address models. Eaton and Lipsey (1989) show that firms could earn positive ECONOMIC PROFITS even when entry is "free" and Schmalensee (1978) argued that firms in the ready-to-eat breakfast cereals industry prevented entry through product proliferation. Both conclusions arise from strategic product positioning by incumbent firms. If the firms in the industry chose their locations strategically, they could locate in such a way that each firm earned economic profits and yet any firm which tried to enter the industry would be unable to cover its fixed costs. For example, if there are product development costs which are SUNK COSTS once a firm enters the industry, then established firms could locate brands throughout the product space so that an entrant's best location would be between two existing brands. As long as the entrant's share of this area is less than its sunk costs, entry will be deterred, even though established firms earn economic profits. Schmalensee argued that there were brand-specific sunk costs of advertising in the ready-to-eat breakfast cereals industry and that the established firms offered so many brands that they literally crowded the product space and prevented entry. Eaton and Lipsey (1989) note that in these models there may be economic profits even with free entry, the free-entry industry equilibrium will not be unique, product variety will not be optimal and monopoly power may persist as established firms make strategic decisions to deter entry.

Bibliography

Archibald, G. C., Eaton, B. C. & Lipsey, R. G. (1986). Address models of value theory. Stiglitz, J. E. and Mathewson, G. F. *New Developments in the Analysis of Market Structure.* Cambridge, MA: MIT.

Caves, R. E. & Williamson, P. J. (1985). What is product differentiation, really? *Journal of Industrial Economics,* 34, 113–32.

Dixit, A. & Stiglitz, J. E. (1977). Monopolistic competition and optimum product diversity. *American Economic Review,* 67, 297–308.

Eaton, B. C. & Lipsey, R. G. (1989). Product differentiation. Schmalensee, R. & Willig, R. D. *Handbook of Industrial Organization.* New York: North-Holland.

Hotelling, H. (1929). Stability in competition. *Economic Journal,* 39, 41–57.

Ireland, N. J. (1987). *Product Differentiation and Non Price Competition.* New York: Blackwell.

Lancaster, K. J. (1966). A new approach to consumer theory. *Journal of Political Economy,* 74, 132–57.

Salop, S. C. (1979). Monopolistic competition with outside goods. *Bell Journal of Economics,* 10, 141–56.

Schmalensee, R. (1978). Entry deterrence in the ready-to-eat breakfast cereal industry. *Bell Journal of Economics,* 9, 305–27.

Tirole, J. (1988). *The Theory of Industrial Organization.* Cambridge, MA: MIT.

ROBERT E. MCAULIFFE

product innovation   This is the "first introduction of a new product into commercial or social use" (adapted from Freeman, 1992). The process of product innovation is concerned with all of the various activities – R&D, marketing, production, etc. – involved in converting a new idea or discovery into a novel product in commercial or social use. The term can cover a spectrum of different possibilities, ranging from minor adaptations or extensions, such as a new formulation and a new flavor or color of an existing product, to the more technologically advanced, such as a compact disc player. Innovations can be categorized in terms of their effects on demand and their perceived degrees of "innovativeness." Robertson (1971) defines three categories of innovation:

Continuous: this is the least disruptive and is likely to involve a modification to an existing product, rather than the creation of something new;

Dynamically continuous: this can involve the development of something new or alterations to existing products, but not the creation of new consumption patterns;

Discontinuous: the creation of new consumption patterns and the development of previously unknown products.

The new product may entail changes in form, components, materials, packaging, or technology, so that products may have different dimensions of "newness." They may: be functionally new or perform an existing function in a new way; be technically new, involving new materials, new ingredients, and sometimes new forms; or have new styles. What really matters is that consumers perceive a product as new, e.g., stylistic innovations, such as changes to packaging, often are intended to generate a perception of newness.

Bibliography

Freeman, C. (1982). *The economics of industrial innovation.* London: Frances Pinter.

Robertson, T. J. & Thomas, S. (1971). *Innovative behaviour and communication.* New York & London: Holt, Rinehart & Winston.

MARGARET BRUCE

product life cycle (economics)   From a variety of perspectives, researchers have hypothesized that products are characterized by patterns of evolution which have been called product life cycles. In most of these theories, new products evolve over time from "young" to "old," and the various stages of the cycle can be documented, because they are associated with certain observable characteristics; see INDUSTRY LIFE CYCLE and Clark (1985) for descriptions of the nature of the cycles. Thus, life cycle theory highlights the importance of product, in addition to process, innovation. Product innovation implies that technology is dispersed through the introduction of new products, whereas process innovation implies that technology is introduced through new production processes. The continuum of product life cycles, arising from product innovation, potentially has implications for patterns of trade, strategic behavior among firms, and even marketing strategies.

For example, Vernon (1966) suggests that international trade patterns are driven by the fact that new products are "born" in technologically superior developed countries, but when technology becomes standardized, production moves to less developed countries, where labor is cheaper. Based on the Schumpeterian notion of the innovative entrepreneur, other research investigates product life cycles in the context of strategic competition and innovation among firms. Recent marketing research simply tries to document the existence of product cycles using the implied observable characteristics of product cycle models. In practical terms, the existence of these product cycles can have implications for the speed at which manufacturers get new products on the market, the available recovery period for research and development, and the decision to innovate versus imitate. See Klepper (1992) for a full description and bibliography concerning product life cycles.

Bibliography

Clark, K. B. (1985). The interaction of design hierarchies and market concepts in technological evolution. *Research Policy*, 14, 235.

Klepper, S. (1992). Entry, exit, and innovation over the product life cycle. Presented at the 1992 Conference of the International Joseph A. Schumpeter Society, Kyoto, Japan.

Segerstrom, P. S., Anant, T. C. A., & Dinopoulos, E. (1990). A Schumpeterian model of the product life cycle. *American Economic Review*, 80, 1077.

Vernon, R. (1966). International investment and international trade in the product cycle. *Quarterly Journal of Economics*, 80, 190.

LAURA POWER

product line analysis   A product line includes a group of items that are related because of marketing, technical, or end use considerations. An optimum product line consists of items that reflect different consumer needs and target methods. A balanced PRODUCT MIX is needed to ensure that new products are being developed and marketed to replace or augment those products that are in decline.

Bibliography

Dibb, S., Simkin, L., Pride, W. & Ferrell, O. C. (1994). *Marketing: Concepts and strategies*, 2nd European edn, Boston, MA: Houghton Mifflin Co. Chapter 7, 201-202.

MARGARET BRUCE

product manager   The product manager is responsible for a product, a product line, or several distinct products in a group. A product manager plans the marketing activities for the product by coordinating a mix of functions including distribution, promotion, and price. The areas the product manager has to deal with include packaging, branding, R&D, engineering, and production and s/he has to continually appraise the product's performance in terms of growth targets, market share, working capital targets, and return on assets managed. Littler (1984) highlights two main criticisms of the product manager approach for product development. First, a lack of authority commensurate with the responsibilities of the position and, second, the relatively low status of the product manager function so that young and often inexperienced recruits are placed at this position.

Bibliography

Littler, D. A. (1984). *Marketing and product development*. Oxford: Philip Allan.

MARGARET BRUCE

product market diversification matrix   Originally developed by Ansoff, the product market diversification matrix, shown in figure 1, originally divided a company's product market activities into four key areas, each of which suggested a particular strategy.

Current products produced for current markets suggest strategies of attempting to maintain or increase existing levels of market penetration.

The introduction of current products into new markets suggests strategies aimed at extending product reach. Many new products when first introduced have actually ended up being most successful in markets for which they were not originally conceived. One particular strategy which has proved effective in opening new markets has been the exploitation of new or unused distribution channels.

New products for existing markets suggest a strategy of new product development. These should be introduced taking full cognizance of actual market needs, rather than attempting to force products developed internally, without paying due attention to customer needs.

The diversification cell, that of new products for new markets, is the most dangerous, as the company knows little about either the products or the markets. As discussed elsewhere, many DIVERSIFICATION moves have therefore resulted in strategic failure, and thus great care needs to be taken when embarking on such a strategy. While a

	Current Products	New Products
Current Markets	Market Penetration Strategy	Product Development Strategy
New Markets	Market Development Strategy	Diversification Strategy

Figure 1 The product market diversification matrix.
Source: Ansoff (1987, p. 109).

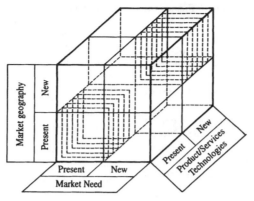

Figure 2   Dimensions of the geographic growth vector
Source: Ansoff (1987)

RELATED DIVERSIFIED STRATEGY might gain greater stock market acceptance, the concept of relatedness needs careful attention, as experience indicates that what is initially thought of as a related activity may indeed turn out differently. For example, until recently banking and insurance were seen as separate industries, but by redefining industry boundaries both can be categorized as "financial services" and hence related. The ability of each specialist function to absorb the culture and methods of the other is often difficult and fraught with danger.

Ansoff subsequently refined his original concept to include the added complexity of geography (see figure 2). In this three-dimensional format, the matrix can be used to define the strategic thrust and the ultimate scope of the business. As shown, the firm can opt for one of a number of variations of market need, product/service technologies, and geographic scope to define a served market. The second component of portfolio strategy, as defined by Ansoff, is the competitive advantage that the firm seeks to achieve in each served market. The third component consists of the synergies that might be achieved between business (*see* SYNERGY), while the last is the degree of strategic flexibility that can be achieved.

Strategic flexibility can be achieved in two ways. The first method is external to the firm, through diversifying the firm's geographic scope, needs served, and technologies, so that any sudden change in any of the strategic businesses areas does not produce serious repercussions.

Second, strategic flexibility can be achieved by making resources and capabilities easily transferable among the businesses. Ironically, optimizing one of the four components of the portfolio strategy growth vector is likely to depress the firm's performance with regard to the other components. In particular, maximizing synergy is very likely to reduce strategic flexibility.

Bibliography

Ansoff, I. (1987). *Corporate strategy*. Harmondsworth, UK: Penguin. See pp. 108–11.

DEREK F. CHANNON

product market   Two broad categories of products and services exist: consumer and organizational. Consumers buy products to satisfy their personal wants, whereas organizational buyers seek to satisfy the goals of their organizations.

Consumer goods can be divided into different categories: convenience, shopping, specialty, and unsought products. Convenience goods are relatively inexpensive, frequently purchased, and rapidly consumed items on which buyers exert only minimal purchasing effort, e.g., bread, soft drinks, and newspapers. Shopping products are items that are chosen more carefully than convenience products, e.g., shoes, furniture, and cameras. Specialty products possess one or more unique features and buyers will expend considerable effort to obtain them, e.g., a Gucci watch. Unsought products are bought irregularly to solve a given problem, e.g., emergency car repairs. Organizational products include raw materials; major equipment; accessory equipment, e.g., tools, calculators; component parts; process materials which are used indirectly in the production of other products, e.g., fiber for products such as computer print ribbon; consumable supplies; and industrial services. The same item can be a consumer and an industrial product, e.g., when consumers buy envelopes for their homes, they are treated as consumer goods; when a company buys envelopes, then they are classified as organizational goods. The ultimate use of the product – for consumers to satisfy their personal wants and for companies to use in the firm's operations – governs the classification.

Bibliography

Kotler, P. (1994). *Marketing management: Analysis, planning and control* 5th edn, Englewood Cliffs, NJ: Prentice-Hall.

MARGARET BRUCE

product mix   This refers to the total array of products that a company markets, and it consists of new, growing, mature, and declining products. A product mix may, in turn, consist of one or more product lines. A product line is composed of variations of a basic product, e.g., Cadbury's chocolate bars. The depth of the product mix is measured by the number of different products offered in each product line and the width of the product mix measures the number of product lines offered by a company. Some companies have a narrow product mix, e.g., Perrier's Mineral Water, whereas a company selling ice-cream with many flavors, such as Haagan-Daz, has a narrow product mix but great product depth. A "balanced" product mix or portfolio is required to ensure that new products are being developed to replace or augment those in decline or in maturity and that there are products with a positive cash flow to finance the development of new products.

Bibliography

Dibb, S., Simkin, L., Pride, W. & Ferrell, O. C. (1994). *Marketing: Concepts and strategies*, 2nd European edn, Boston, MA: Houghton Mifflin Co.

MARGARET BRUCE

product modification This means changing one or more of the product's characteristics and may involve reformulation and repackaging to enhance its customer appeal. Modifications can give a competitive advantage, e.g., a company may be able to charge a higher price and enhance customer loyalty. Dibb et al. (1994) classify modifications into three distinct types: quality, function, and style. Quality modifications relate to the product's dependability and durability; functional modifications relate to the effectiveness, convenience, and safety of products (e.g., washing machines that use less heat and water), and style modifications alter the sensory appeal of the product (such as its taste, texture, sound, and appearance). Such modifications can act to differentiate products in the market place, e.g., BMW cars have an immediately recognizable style.

A number of issues have to be considered before deciding whether or not to keep the product, change it, or eliminate it. What is the customer appeal? The product may have lost its distinctiveness because of the introduction of new products or improvements of its main rivals. By reformulating the product, it may be possible to regain its competitive edge. What is the vulnerability of the product to technological innovation and competition? The company needs to assess the opportunities and threats posed by technological change. What are the interdependencies of the product and others in the mix and how would modification impact upon the overall cost structure?

Bibliography

Dibb, S., Simkin, L., Pride, W. & Ferrell, O. C. (1994). Identifying and eliminating weak products. *Business*, July–Sept., 3–10.
Littler, D. A. (1984). Marketing and product development. Oxford: Philip Allan.

MARGARET BRUCE

product planning The product life cycle suggests that there is a need to monitor the performance of existing products, to devise appropriate policies for those products, and to develop new products where necessary. All this is the essence of product planning. Littler (1984) points out that product planning entails the creation of procedures to evaluate product performance, and to plan the modification, where necessary, of existing products aimed at extending their lives; the deletion of weak products that have reached the terminal stage of their lives; and the development and marketing of new products. The thrust of product planning is to ensure that companies have a "balanced" product mix in the sense that there are new products being developed or marketed to replace or augment those in decline, or maturity, and that there are products with a positive cash flow that can be used to finance the development of new products. In addition, it is important to ensure that there is a balanced portfolio of new products so that those which are highly risky (but offer the prospect of a high return) are balanced by those which have a low element of risk but also a

correspondingly low return. Companies should periodically review their products and identify those products that are satisfying customer needs and yielding returns and those that are not. Managers have to consider the potential of the market and company objectives and set performance criteria to review product performance. Action should be taken to modify or delete those products which do not meet the company's performance criteria. Such criteria may include: sales and profit history of the product, relative profitability, future potential, customer appeal, and vulnerability to technological developments and competitors' actions. As well as considering weak products, new product opportunities need to be identified and investment put into new product development. Innovative products have to be developed as the differential advantages of existing products are undermined by technological change and competitors' actions. In some sectors, the pace of technological change is so rapid that product life cycles are less than one year old (Cane, 1991). New products generate additional sales and profits. They can add value by offering more perceived customer values and so help to sustain a COMPETITIVE ADVANTAGE. Thus, the development of new products should be a facet of the overall product planning process to ensure that new products are available to replace the loss in sales and profits resulting from the maturity and demise of existing products.

Bibliography

Cane, A. (1991). A race that does not lose face. *Financial Times*, May 19, 1991.
Littler, D. A. (1984). *Marketing and product development*. Oxford: Philip Allan.

MARGARET BRUCE

product portfolio The product portfolio covers all the products that a company markets. The portfolio may consist of several product lines; or alternatively different individual products; or a blend of both. In theory, an organization will strive to ensure that it has products at different stages of the PRODUCT LIFE CYCLE so that, for example, there are new products being introduced to replace those products entering their decline stage. The firm may also strive for a balanced product portfolio in terms of risk and/or cash flow. Frameworks such as the BCG MATRIX, developed for business portfolio analysis, can also be employed in the analysis of product portfolios.

DALE LITTLER

product positioning This concerns the decisions and activities intended to create and maintain a firm's PRODUCT CONCEPT in the customer's mind. Attempts are made by companies to position new products so that they are seen to possess the features most desired by the target market. Product positioning is linked to segmentation so that effective product positioning helps to serve a specific market segment by creating an appropriate concept in the minds of customers in that market segment. A product can be positioned to compete directly with another product, e.g., Pepsi with Coca Cola, or it can be positioned to avoid competition, e.g., 7UP in relation to other soft-drink products.

Every product offered to a market needs a positioning strategy so that its place in the total market can be communicated to the target market. Alternative bases for constructing a product-positioning strategy have been identified. Wind (1982) includes positioning on specific product features, positioning for a specific user category, and positioning against another product. Perceptual maps visually summarize the dimensions or primary needs that customers use to perceive and judge products and they present the relative position of brands in terms of these dimensions. For pain relievers, for example, "effectiveness" and "gentleness" may be used as the dimensions to construct the perceptual maps and different offerings can be plotted according to these two dimensions. More than two dimensions of primary needs can be used to create perceptual maps; e.g., alternative modes of transport can be compared on the basis of "quickness and convenience," "ease of travel," and "psychological comfort." Plotting the perception of the new and existing brands on perceptual maps can help evaluate the brands and assess their competitive position and can point to new opportunities. Measures of preference are needed which suggest what potential buyers might want in a new product to determine whether or not the product is desirable (Thomas, 1993).

Bibliography

Thomas, R. J. (1993). *New product development: Managing and forecasting for strategic success.* New York: John Wiley.
Urban, G. L. & Hauser, J. R (1993). *Design and marketing of new products,* 2nd edn, Englewood Cliffs, NJ: Prentice-Hall.
Wind, Y. J. (1982). *Product policy: Concepts, methods and strategy.* Reading, MA: Addison Wesley.

MARGARET BRUCE

production sharing A creative arrangement under which companies in different countries agree to cooperate in the production and distribution of a product. Differences in customs laws and the prices of resources make such cooperative agreements feasible. Maquiladora production in Mexico is an example of production sharing. Foreign countries ship unfinished or unassembled goods to plants located in special trade zones in Mexico. The goods are finished and/or assembled (at low wage rates) and returned for distribution. Another name for production sharing is "outward processing."

Bibliography

Dunning, J. (1981). *International production and multinational enterprise.* London: Allen and Unwin.

JOHN O'CONNELL

profit maximization Although this goal is not always consistent with that of sales (revenue) maximization and other objectives of the firm, profit maximization is generally identified as one of the primary goals of most businesses. Since the level of profit is measured as the total revenue of the firm minus its total costs, profit maximization requires finding the level of output at which the difference between these two measures is a maximum. This level of output can be found by using marginal analysis where the MARGINAL REVENUE from one additional unit sold is compared with the marginal cost of its production. The general rule for profit maximization requires that managers find that level of output where marginal revenue and marginal cost are equal, since at this level of output no extra profits could be earned by increasing or decreasing production. At output levels

where the marginal revenue from an additional unit to be sold exceeds the cost of its production, additional profits can be made by increasing the level of output. Similarly, if the marginal cost of the last unit already produced was in excess of the additional revenue received from its sale, the marginal profit from that unit would be negative and its production and sale would have reduced total profits. In this case, the firm's output level should be decreased as this would increase total profits.

This method is universally applicable to firms regardless of the MARKET STRUCTURE in which they compete. Competitive firms, having no control over price, and monopolists, wherein management supply decisions may significantly influence price, may both use this technique to assure the highest level of profits possible. In addition, many alternative applications of this method may be used. For example, managers of retail shops who are considering extending their daily store hours or opening for business on weekends need to examine the marginal revenues and marginal costs of these additional hours to assure that the profit maximizing number of hours are chosen. Similarly, with respect to hiring decisions, choosing the optimal (profit maximizing) number of workers to hire requires the examination of the marginal gains and costs of additional workers.

see also **economic profit**

Bibliography

Hirschey, M. Pappas, J. (1995). *Fundamentals of Managerial Economics.* 5th edn, Fort Worth: Dryden.
Mansfield, E. (1993). *Managerial Economics.* 2nd edn, New York: Norton.

GILBERT BECKER

profit sharing Profit sharing is a type of VARIABLE COMPENSATION policy that provides employees with income that is based on the profitability of the entire organization or selected subunits (Florkowski, 1987, p. 622). Profit sharing can instill in employees a sense of partnership with other employees and managers across organizational units, because each employee is entitled to recive a share in the success of the organization, as measured by profits. Profit sharing gives the firm's managers some flexibility to reduce its labor costs when resources are scarce and profits are low by reducing employee earnings, as an alternative to using layoffs (Gomez-Mejia and Balkin, 1992). Employees may gain additional job security from this practice.

The three basic types of profit sharing plans are (a) cash, (b) deferred, and (c) combination cash–deferred plans (Kruse, 1993). Cash profit sharing plans provide a cash bonus payment to employees on a quarterly or annual basis. Deferred profit sharing plans put the employee's share of the profits into a tax-deferred profit sharing trust, which is a retirement benefit. The income is not taxed until the employee retires. The combination cash–deferred plan combines cash and deferred contributions in one plan.

Bibliography

Florkowski, G. W. (1987). The organizational impact of profit sharing. *Academy of Management Review,* 12, 622–36.
Gomez-Mejia, L. R. & Balkin, D. B. (1992). *Compensation, Organizational Strategy, and Firm Performance,* Cincinnati, OH: South-Western.

Kruse, D. L. (1993). *Profit Sharing*, Kalamazoo, MI: W. E. Upjohn Institute for Employment Research.

DAVID B. BALKIN

program trading The New York Stock Exchange defines a program trade as the simultaneous trading of at least fifteen stocks with a total value of over US$1 million and, since May 1988, has required the reporting of program trades, classified under seventeen categories. These categories include index arbitrage, which accounted for half of NYSE program trading in 1989 (Quinn et al., 1990), index substitution, portfolio insurance, tactical asset allocation, and portfolio realignment. During June 1989, the average program trade on the NYSE was valued at US$9 million and involved shares in 177 different companies (Harris et al., 1990). Program trading is neither defined nor recorded by the London Stock Exchange.

The 1987 stock market crash was initially blamed on program trading in general, and portfolio insurance in particular (Brady, 1988). This blame was based on the possible market impact of these very large trades, and on the feature of some portfolio strategies which require selling (buying) a basket of shares in an already falling (rising) market, so amplifying the initial price movement. However, the general conclusion from a large number of subsequent studies (see Miller, 1988; Furbush, 1989) is that there is little theoretical or empirical evidence to support this view. Subsequent NYSE regulations limit the scope and nature of program trading (e.g. by limiting the use of the Super DOT system) during unusual market conditions.

Program trading involves the simultaneous trading of a basket of shares, and this may or may not involve computers. Although index arbitrageurs use computers both to monitor the relationship between actual and no-arbitrage prices in real time, and to deliver the program trading instructions to the floor of the NYSE (via Super DOT), many non-program traders also rely on computers to provide information on trading opportunities and to submit orders to trade.

One effect of program trading may be to increase the measured volatility of a market index based on trade prices. Usually, roughly equal numbers of shares in the index will have been bought and sold so that the bid–ask spread tends to cancel out. However, just after a program trade to buy (sell) many shares, most of the prices used in the index calculation will be ask (bid) prices and movements in the index will be exaggerated by about half the bid–ask spread. A different effect is that a program trade temporarily ensures that most of the last trade prices are recent, so removing the "stale" price effect (which biases measured volatility downwards). While both of these effects will increase measured volatility, neither of them implies any economically adverse consequences of program trading.

Modest increases in measured US stock market volatility associated with program trading have been found by Duffee et al. (1992) and Thosar and Trigeorgis (1990), while Grossman (1988) found no such increase. A modest increase is consistent with the bid–ask and stale price effects (Harris et al., 1990).

Bibliography

Brady, N. F. (Chairman) (1988). *Report on the Presidential Task Force on Market Mechanisms.* Washington, DC: US Government Printing Office.

Duffee, G., Dupiec, P. & White, A. P. (1992). A primer on program trading and stock price volatility: a survey of the issues and the evidence. *Research in financial services. Private and public policy.* Vol. 4, Kaufman, G. G. Greenwich, CT: Jai Press Inc., 21–49.

Furbush, D. (1989). Program trading and price movement: evidence from the October market crash. *Financial Management*, 18, 68–83.

Grossman, S. J. (1988). Program trading and market volatility: a report on interday relationships. *Financial Analysts Journal*, 44, 18–28.

Harris, L., Sofianos, G. & Shapiro, J. E. (1990). Program trading and intraday volatility. NYSE Working Paper No. 90-03.

Miller, M. H. (Chairman) (1988). *Final Report of the Committee of Enquiry Appointed by the CME to Examine the Events Surrounding 19 October 1987.* Chicago Mercantile Exchange.

Quinn, J., Sofianos, G. & Tschirhart, W. E. (1990). Program trading and index arbitrage. *Market volatility and investor confidence.* Report to the Board of Directors of the NYSE New York: Appendix F.

Thosar, S. & Trigeorgis, L. (1990). Stock volatility and program trading: theory and evidence. *Journal of Applied Corporate Finance*, 2, 91–6.

JOHN BOARD and CHARLES SUTCLIFFE

progressive discipline Until the recent growth in popularity of POSITIVE DISCIPLINE, the relationship between progressive discipline and CORRECTIVE DISCIPLINE has been viewed as inextricable. In the early 1950s, Arbitrator Shister illustrated this close definitional relationship in the *Bell Aircraft* case. He reinstated a worker because management failed to use "proper corrective disciplinary procedures." He went on to identify those procedures as progressive discipline and defined the term as follows: "What progressive discipline does mean is that progressively more severe penalties may be imposed on each given employee each time any offense is repeated. Progressive discipline also means that after a specified number of offenses, regardless of whether the offenses are identical or not, the company may have the right to discharge the given employee" (Redeker, 1989).

The normal stages of progressive discipline include oral warning, written warning, suspension, and ultimately termination. The presumption is that each successive phase will "place the employee on notice" that the type of misconduct exhibited will be met with increasingly severe consequences. Labor contracts and employee handbooks that incorporate progressive discipline provisions generally specify a series of disciplinary steps, a limitation period preventing the consideration of old discipline, and a disclaimer for types of gross misconduct that may be met with summary discharge. Where management inappropriately ignores the principles of progressive discipline in a collective bargaining context, arbitrators have shown no reluctance to overturn discipline. Even outside the context of grievance arbitration, courts in some states have been willing to give legal force to progressive discipline policies embodied in employee handbooks.

Bibliography

Elkouri, F. & Elkouri, E. (1985). *How Arbitration Works*, 4th edn, Washington, DC: BNA.

Fairweather, O. (1984). *Practice and Procedure in Labor Arbitration*, **2nd edn**, Washington, DC: BNA.

Redeker, J. R. (1989). *Employee Discipline*, Washington, DC: BNA.

MARK R. SHERMAN

project financing During the next decade it is estimated that much more than US$1 trillion will be needed to finance power projects, transport facilities, and other infrastructure around the world. Privatization continues to create a large demand for capital. International consortiums are being formed to finance these large projects. The project finance industry, while it has matured considerably, still faces tremendous risk. Commercial banks were the traditional source of funding for project finance until 1990, when investment bankers started taking large deals to capital markets. Besides traditional project financiers, companies and developers are also turning to pension funds and limited partnerships for capital.

In a general loan, the issuance of securities or simply borrowing the money and the payment of the loan are not specifically associated with the cash flows generated by a given project or economic unit. Generally loan collateral does not have to be generating income to pay for the loan. In contrast, cash flow from the operation of the project is the sole source of return to lenders and equity investors in project financing. The project may be supported through guarantees, output contracts, raw material supply contracts, and other contractual arrangements.

In project financing, securities are issued or loans are contracted that are directly linked to the assets and the income generating ability of these assets in the future. In other words, project financing means that securities are issued or loans are contracted that are based on the expected income generation of a given project or economic unit. By the same token, the collateral, if any, are the assets related to the project or belonging to the economic unit. A project is financed on its own merits and not on the general borrowing ability of the economic unit that is sponsoring it.

Project financing may be called off-balance sheet financing because it may not affect the sponsor's income or balance sheet. It has no effect on the sponsor's credit rating as well because the financing is not provided based on the income generation ability of the sponsor and does not use the sponsor's assets as collateral.

The sponsor of the project to be financed has to show its commitment and possibly give guarantees to the lenders on the repayment of the loans. It is obvious that the lenders will agree to project financing only if they have some sort of commitment from the sponsor, which is the economic unit with assets in place and borrowing power, to back up the project financing and to carry out the project's execution properly. So project financing does not mean that the project is totally independent from the sponsors, who have to show commitment to the project to satisfy the lender's assessment of the project's credit risk.

Sometimes a project cannot be financed off the balance sheet, if it has not commenced yet. Lenders use standard credit analysis tools to verify the project's attractiveness. They do not see the project as equity or as venture capital. Therefore, the sponsor may have to commit resources at the initial stages of the project to get it off the ground and later seek off-balance sheet financing.

There are many reasons for the sponsor to look for project financing. In general, a sponsor would prefer not to have the project reported on its balance sheet, so that it does not affect its financial ratios or credit standing. The sponsor desires that its credit risk and that of the project be judged independently. There could be many reasons why the sponsor would seek project financing, including advantages available only to the project. Some sources of subsidized or favorable financing may only be available for the project itself. The project may be able to meet legal and other restrictions while the sponsor may not. This type of situation often arises when the project is being carried out in a foreign country or in areas of business with special needs.

Project financing is made up of the securities or loans that are contracted by the project, the sponsors and other institutions that may be involved. The securities can be any type of debt securities, from the usual short- and long-term securities such as commercial paper or bonds to other securities particularly designed to tap a specific source or to capture a specific advantage provided by the project. The entities involved may also make a difference. Sometimes it may be better that one of the sponsor's subsidiaries or associated joint ventures will carry out or provide guarantees to the project.

Designing project financing involves executing the appropriate credit analysis of the project with conservative estimates, assessing all the legal, tax, and any other relevant restrictions and advantages stemming from the nature of the project, selecting institutions or entities that should participate in the project in its different stages and determining the securities and types of loans that will be issued. Project financing is a type of financial engineering and participants must carefully analyze several issues including the economics of the transaction, sponsorship, construction, technology, and environmental needs.

Several changes have occurred related to the sources and access to economic development project financing. Capital constraints are increasing the cost of doing business, lenders are requiring additional recourse and guarantees. Equity capital is tight and bank credit criteria have been tightened. Many commercial lending institutions are constrained by regulatory or reserve requirements or internal policies in lending to projects in developing nations as a result of country, political, currency and other risks associated with such lending. Successful financing of projects in developing nations will often require support from the host nation.

Bibliography

Bemis, J. R. (1992). Access to and availability of project financing. *Economic Development Review*, **10**, 17–19.

Forsyth, G. J. & Rod, J. R. (1994). Project finance and public debt markets. *International Financial Law Review, Capital Markets Yearbook* 5–10.

Nevitt, P. K. (1988). *Project financing*. 2nd edn, London: Euromoney Publications.

Siddique, S. (1995). Financing private power in Latin America and the Caribbean. *Finance and Development*, **32**, 18–21.

REENA AGGARWAL and RICARDO LEAL

projective techniques Projective techniques are a group of QUALITATIVE RESEARCH methods which are useful when it is felt that a typical direct questionnaire may not be appropriate in providing the information sought. Projective techniques include word association tests where the respondent is required to give the first word that comes to mind after the interviewer presents a word, e.g., a brand name, in a sequence that includes the words of interest along with several neutral words. Two further techniques are sentence completion and story completion where it is felt that respondents will give revealing answers as they relax their conscious defense. Construction techniques require the respondent to construct dialogue, e.g., to fill in a balloon on a cartoon, or to compose a story behind a picture. Third person techniques allow the respondents to project their own attitudes and opinions on to someone else, such as an average person, rather than acknowledge that they are their own attitudes, opinions, etc.

Projective techniques, based on methodologies devised by clinical psychologists, require specialists to conduct and to interpret the responses.

Bibliography

Malhotra, N. K. (1993). *Marketing research: An applied orientation.* Englewood Cliffs, NJ: Prentice-Hall. Chapter 6.

MICHAEL GREATOREX

promotion *see* MARKETING COMMUNICATIONS; SALES PROMOTIONS

psychographics Psychographics is the general term used to describe the measurement of psychological characteristics of consumers. While personality traits and values are of major concern, many authors also include, in this category, lifestyle data such as activities, interests, hobbies, and opinions (*see also* LIFESTYLES; PERSONAL-ITY). Mitchman (1991) argues that the great diversity of consumer lifestyles in the 1980s and '90s has made market segmentation more difficult in many markets. The general increasing wealth of Western countries, the rise in demand for more psychological value in products, increasing competition, and the better-tailored MARKETING MIX, are factors pushing marketers to develop more precise and effective SEGMENTATION VARIABLES.

Numerous comparisons show that the predictive validity of psychographic variables is likely to be substantially higher than for demographic variables, e.g., Burger & Schott (1972), King & Sproles (1973), Nelson (1969), Wilson (1966) (*see* SEGMENTATION VARIABLES). In the light of this, psychographics have become more popular over the past two decades. However, there is still no single widely-accepted definition. When Wells (1975) published his critical review of the subject, he found no less than 32 definitions in 24 articles. Some researchers have used standard personality tests, while others have developed their own scales unique to their purpose. The dominant method of developing psychographic measures has been to use long scales of items/questions which are rated/answered by respondents. The highly-structured nature of these questionnaires allows easy administration to relatively large samples of consumers. Once the data are collected, a common set of statistical procedures is used to derive the psychographic segments which usually involves the use of factor analysis, cluster analysis, and discriminant analysis.

An example of a generic psychographic segmentation tool is VALS–2 (Values and Lifestyles). SRI International

(of Menlo Park, California) attempted to develop a standard psychographic framework to be used in analyzing US consumers. They identified eight major groups: Strugglers, Makers, Strivers, Believers, Experiencers, Achievers, Fulfilled, Actualizers. It is obvious from the SRI analyses that the categories broadly reflect Maslow's hierarchy of needs ranging from Strugglers at the bottom, who are powerless, narrow focused, risk averse, and conservative, to the Actualizers at the top, who are optimistic, self-confident, involved, outgoing, and growth orientated.

An acclaimed alternative to VALS is LOV (List of Values) which includes segments based on self-respect, security, warm relationships with others, being well-respected, self-fulfilment, self-accomplishment, sense of belonging, fun and enjoyment of life (Kahle & Kennedy, 1988). The researchers have claimed that LOV: (1) has greater predictive validity than VALS in consumer behavior trends; (2) is easier to administer; and (3) is better able to diminish communication errors, because it is easier to preserve the exact phrase from a value study and incorporate it into an advertisement.

A European value-based segmentation includes: Material Hedonists, Rational Materialists, Empathetic Risk-takers, Self-actualizers, and Safety-orientated (Puohiniemi, 1991). Other research on European lifestyles by the RISC organization has identified six "Eurotypes" from 24 Eurotrends, namely: Traditionalists, Homebodies, Ration-alists, Pleasurists, Strivers, and Trendsetters. Whereas most lifestyle research provides only a "snapshot" analysis, the RISC approach offers a continuous measurement of sociocultural trends.

Lifestyle and value-based segmentation have been criticized for being too general to be of great use and their international application is limited because lifestyles vary from country to country (Sampson, 1992). Sampson argues that it is possible to understand human social behavior to a limited degree only, by studying values in isolation. This is because values are too general and cannot deal with issues that relate to specific product consumption and brand-choice behavior in different markets. Therefore, while it may be important to understand value change in longer-term strategic marketing planning, in the short term, value analysis is of limited worth. Sampson advocates a model which has four psychological axes: outward expressiveness to inward repression, and stereotype masculinity (e.g., strength) to stereotype femininity (e.g., softness). The model has been tested in the USA, South Africa, South East Asia, Japan, and 17 European countries, and claims to be superior to lifestyle and value-based segmentation because peoples' loves, hates, fears, hopes, aspirations, and hang-ups are more similar than their lifestyles.

A number of psychographic segmentations have been developed for specific markets. For example, Moschis (1992) has developed a segmentation tool for the 55 years+ market. The "gerontographic" clusters include: Healthy Hermits, Ailing Out-goers, Frail Recluses, and Healthy Indulgers. Pernica (1974) reported that purchasers of stomach remedies can be divided into Severe Sufferers, Active Medicators, Hypochondriacs, and Practicalists.

Despite the usefulness of some psychographic segmen-tation studies in understanding consumers, the technique is not without its problems. Cost is one major problem, since the time and money involved questionnaires and obtaining, analyzing, and interpreting psychographic and lifestyle data can be significant. It is also difficult to draw firm conclusions based upon the results of any single study and reported replications of studies, which would allow discernible patterns to be seen, are few (see e.g. Novak & MacEvoy, 1990). The consumer research literature also contains several critical articles questioning the reliability (and validity) of psychographic concepts and measures (see Lastovicka, 1982; Wells, 1975).

see also **Market segmentation; Segmentation variables**

Bibliography

Burger, P. C. & Schott, B. (1972). Can private brand buyers be identified? *Journal of Marketing Research*, 9, May, 219–222.

Kahle, L. & Kennedy, P. (1988). Using the list of values (LOV) to understand consumers. *The Journal of Services Marketing*, 2, Fall, 49–56.

King, C. W. & Sproles, C. B. (1973). The explanatory efficacy of selected types of consumer profile variables in fashion change agent identification. Institute Paper No. 425, Krannert Graduate School of Industrial Administration, Purdue University.

Lastovicka, L. (1982). On the validity of life style traits: A review and illustration. *Journal of Marketing Research*, 19, Feb., 126–138.

Mitchman, R. (1991). *Lifestyle market segmentation*. New York: Praeger.

Moschis, G. (1992). Gerontographics: A scientific approach to analysing and targeting the mature market. *Journal of Services Marketing*, 6, (3), Summer, 17–27.

Nelson, A. R. (1969). A national study of psychographics. Paper delivered at the International Marketing Congress, American Marketing Association, June.

Novak, T. P. & MacEvoy, B. (1990). On comparing alternative segmentation schemes: The list of values (LOV) and lifestyles (VALS). *Journal of Consumer Research*, 17, June, 105–109.

Pernica, J. (1974). The second generation of market segmentation studies: An audit of buying motivation. In W. D. Wells (ed.), *Life style and psychographics* (pp. 277–313). Chicago: American Marketing Association.

Puohiniemi, M. (1991). Value-based segmentation, social change and consuming orientations. In ESOMAR Seminar on The Growing Individualisation of Consumer Life-styles and Demand: How is Marketing Coping With It? *Helsinki Proceedings*.

Sampson, P. (1992). People are people the world over: The case for psychological market segmentation. *Marketing and Research Today* Nov., 236–245.

Wells, W. (1975). Psychographics – A critical review. *Journal of Marketing Research*, 12, May, 196–213.

Wilson, C. L. (1966). Homemaker living patterns and marketplace behavior – A psychometric approach. In J. S. Wright & J. L. Goldstucker (Eds), *New ideas for successful marketing* (pp. 305–347). Chicago: American Marketing Association.

VINCE MITCHELL

psychological contract As with any other form of contract, the concept of the psychological contract implies an agreement between parties whereby each commits to future actions. These actions are seen as a form of exchange between the parties: if you do this, I will do that. The word "psychological" is used in contrast with formal legal contracts, especially in employment. The psychological contract has thus come to mean those aspects of the employment relationship between organization and employee over and above the legal requirements. However, "psychological" in this context also carries the connotation of perception. Psychological contracts are in the eye of the beholder.

The concept was first used by Argyris (1960), who emphasized that many psychological contracts were implicit in nature, and that considerable benefits were to be gained for both parties if they were made explicit. For Argyris, the employment relationship as a whole was interpretable as a psychological contract.

The parties to the psychological contract may differ in their perceptions of its terms. There may be ambiguity about what each has agreed to do or when and how they will do it. There may even be ambiguity about whether a psychological contract exists in the first place; for example, a temporary worker employed on strictly formal terms of employment might believe a CAREER was on offer. Moreover, this ambiguity may not itself be perceived; each party may believe that the other shares exactly the same view of the contract as they hold themselves. This may even be true if the psychological contract has been made verbally explicit: "We will develop you further if you stay with us for a reasonable period after initial training." What does "develop" imply? What is a "reasonable period?"

The scope for disagreement about the nature and the fulfilment of the psychological contract is therefore considerable. There are, perhaps, three mitigating factors. First, custom and practice in the organization or sector; for example, in the banking and finance sector until 10 years ago, the universal assumption was of a security-for-loyalty contract. Second, general social norms, such as keeping agreements and RECIPROCITY, can support the contract. Third, there is evidence that there is considerable agreement among reasonable third parties as to what the contract is and whether it is fair.

Why is the concept of current importance? As the social, economic, political, and business environments change ever more rapidly, so do organizations in their efforts to keep pace. Changes in ORGANIZATIONAL DESIGN, processes, and personnel imply changes in the nature of the psychological contracts operating. Partly as a consequence of environmental change, organizations are determined to optimize the use of their so-called human resources to achieve business objectives. In an effort to achieve such optimization, they expect more and more from their employees. They even try to alter the fundamental VALUES and assumptions of their workforce by means of culture change programmes (*see* ORGANIZATIONAL CHANGE; ORGANIZATIONAL CULTURE). Furthermore, especially during the recent global recession, demanning, delayering, and casualization of labor have increased. By way of response, individuals have increasingly seen their employment and their careers as entirely their own affair, and their employability as their main asset.

As employment becomes more an organizational career than a job, a contract becomes more relational than transactional. In other words, specific agreements of exchange (e.g., wage rates for overtime) give way to more general exchanges based on TRUST and reliance. Where there is a long delay between formation and fulfillment of the psychological contract (as, e.g., with the promise of career development by the organization) then trust that the bargain will be fulfilled is of the essence. In relational contracts, the elements of the bargain are not agreed independently of each other. Rather, there is a general exchange of support, the social and emotional nature of which has often been likened to family or ORGANIZATIONAL CITIZENSHIP. The good family member and the good citizen will go the extra mile, beyond the call of duty.

The corollary is clear. Just as both parties invest much in a relational contract, so the costs are greater when that relationship breaks up. When promised promotion is withheld or job security shattered by compulsory redundancy, strong emotional reactions to the perceived violation of trust may result. If the relational contract is broken but the individual remains in employment, they may contribute less than before. It is not merely that the perceived terms of the contract have been broken, it also is how they are broken that concerns. People made redundant often express more anger about how they were told than about the redundancy itself. In theoretical terms, they feel that procedural as well as distributive injustice has been done them (*see* DISTRIBUTIVE JUSTICE; PROCEDURAL JUSTICE).

While the concept of the psychological contract and its implications appears to be relevant and powerful, there is relatively little empirical research directly aimed at testing its predictions. What research there is has been well summarized by Rousseau. It is mostly concerned with demonstrating that expectations of reciprocal exchange of both a transactional and a relational nature do exist in employees' minds; and that external observers are capable of agreeing what the contract is, and how equitable it appears (*see* EQUITY THEORY).

While the concept of the psychological contract is fruitful, there remain at least two issues which need to be addressed. First, if the contract is between the individual and the organization, who exactly is "the organization?" A recruiter might promise training for which the recruit's line manager will not release them. A professional mentor offers technical development, while the HR Director expects cross-functional job change. Different people representing "the organization" have different expectations regarding the terms of the contract. A response is to argue that this is all part of the ambiguity inherent in the contract. However, this still leaves the identity of the parties incompletely determined.

The second issue relates to POWER. For the idea of contract to have any validity, the parties have to be reasonably commensurate in the power that each wields. Otherwise, there is a degree of dependency which prevents bargaining between free and equal partners. In particular, where there is mainly a buyer's labor market, as during recession, power is clearly with the organization. Unequal contracts may result, with the organization expecting more and more COMMITMENT for less and less security or prospects.

see also **Organizational culture; Exchange relations; Socialization**

Bibliography

Arggris, C. (1960). Understanding organizational behavior. IL: Dorsey.

Greenberg, J. (1990). Organizational justice: Yesterday, today, and tomorrow. Journal of Management, 16, 399–432.

Handy, C. (1985). The future of work. Oxford, UK: Basil Blackwell.

Herriot, P. (1992). The career management challenge. London: Sage.

Kanter, R. M. (1989). When giants learn to dance. New York: Simon & Schuster.

Rousseau, D. M. & Anton, R. (1991). Fairness and implied contract obligations in job terminations: The role of contributions, promises and performance. Journal of Organisational Behavior, 12, 287–299.

Rousseau, D. M. & Parks, J. M. (1993). The contracts of individuals and organizations. In L. L. Cummings & B. M. Stow (Eds), Research in organizational behaviour, Vol. 15, pp. 1–43. Greenwich, CT: JAI Press.

Weick, K. E. & Berlinger, L. A. (1988). Career improvisations in selfdesigning organisations. In M. B. Arthur, D. T. Hall & B. S. Lawrence (Eds), Handbook of Career Theory. New York: Cambridge University Press.

PETER HERRIOT

psychomotor abilities   Psychomotor ability is the capability or capacity to develop or learn a skill that involves both physical and psychological functions. PHYSICAL ABILITIES involve motor activities of the body or limbs, such as running or throwing. Psychological functions include information processing and perception. Examples of psychomotor abilities include eye–hand coordination and balancing. Combinations of physical and psychological functions are important in the performance of many job skills, including the operation of machinery and the use of hand tools.

PAUL E. SPECTOR

public relations   Public relations is an element in the marketing COMMUNICATIONS MIX and may be defined as "the deliberate, planned and sustained effort to establish and maintain mutual understanding between an organisation and its publics" (Jenkins, 1988). Thus, it is a conscious and positive attempt to maintain an organization's image. Groups, or publics, at whom public relations activities are aimed, include customers and potential customers, shareholders, employees, competitors, suppliers, and government. A variety of techniques may be used in implementing a positive public relations program, including press releases/conferences, newsletters, the production of brochures, posters, and support of community activities.

see also **Publicity; Sponsorship**

Bibliography

Jenkins, F. (1988). *Public relations techniques*. London: Heinemann.

Kotler, P. (1994). *Marketing management: Analysis, planning, implementation and control*, 8th edn, Englewood Cliffs, NJ: Prentice-Hall. Chapter 23.

DAVID YORKE

public sector bargaining   This term refers to the structure and practice of COLLECTIVE BARGAINING between government employers and unions of their employees. As in the private sector, collective bargaining in government consists of (a) the contract negotiation process between union and management representatives over wages, hours, and other employment terms, and (b) the contract administration process whereby union and management representatives handle disagreements over how the contract's terms should be applied to workplace situations on a day-to-day basis (*see* GRIEVANCES, GRIEVANCE PROCEDURE).

Collective bargaining emerged on a large scale in the public sector during the 1965–75 period, accompanied by great controversy. Supporters argued that public employees need unions and bargaining to advance their workplace interests as much as private employees do. In contrast, opponents argued that it is inappropriate for public employees to deal with their employers through a power-based interaction process, and that public employee strikes are especially inappropriate. While these arguments raged, most states and the US government enacted legislation which protects unionization and bargaining rights for their employees, and government employees by the millions joined unions and engaged in bargaining. Most public sector laws limit the scope of negotiations and prohibit work stoppages, and some mandate INTEREST ARBITRATION. Government is now the most highly unionized sector in the American economy, with 45 percent (in 1994) of public employees represented by unions. Research evidence indicates that unionized public employees usually are paid more than their nonunion counterparts.

PETER FEUILLE

publicity Publicity is "non-personal communications in news story form, regarding an organisation and/or its products and services, that is transmitted through a mass medium at no charge (to the organisation)" (Dibb et al., 1994).

Media editors wish to publish information and news stories about organizations and their products, services, etc. to encourage favorable consumer response to the media sources (e.g., sell more newspapers). At the same time, organizations want the information presented in the media to be favorable, so as to stimulate consumer demand for their product/service or create favorable attitudes toward the company (e.g., as a result of community involvement). Many organizations will, therefore, prepare publicity material, i.e., company- and product-oriented information and news, which is made available to the media editors (and sometimes directly to consumers and other interested parties), in the hope that this may reach the company's target audience. However, publicity is generally controlled by the MASS MEDIA and, therefore, may be favorable or unfavorable with respect to a company and its products (e.g., in consumer reports).

The main advantage of publicity for the receiver/consumer is its credibility, typically attributed to an independent source.

Bibliography
Dibb, S., Simkin, L., Pride, W. & Ferrell, O. C. (1994). *Marketing: Concepts and strategies* European edn, Boston, MA: Houghton Mifflin Co. Chapter 15.

DAVID YORKE

purchasing process The purchasing process or buying process in ORGANIZATIONAL MARKETING has been analyzed and modeled as a cycle with various "phases" or "stages." Robinson, Faris & Wind (1967) not only distinguished three "buy classes" (which they refer to as "NEW TASK," "MODIFIED RE-BUY," and "straight re-buy") but also correlated these "buy classes" with eight "buy

phases" in a buygrid model derived from their empirical research. These eight "buy-phases" are:

(1) Anticipation and/or recognition of need
(2) Determination of features and quantity of required item
(3) Specification of purchase requirement
(4) Search for potential sources
(5) Acquisition and analysis of proposals from potential sources
(6) Selection of one (or more) supplier(s)
(7) Negotiation of purchase arrangements and terms
(8) Feedback and evaluation of the flow of purchase
(Robinson, Faris & Wind, 1967 – as cited in Webster & Wind, 1972, 24)

This representation of the purchasing process as a cycle of buy phases is useful for descriptive purposes but it should not be taken literally as a managerial model since it lacks any predictive power or causative explanation of buying decisions (Webster & Wind, 1972). Nor would it be appropriate to regard the buygrid model as necessarily sequential, or serial, or involving all the identified steps and no others. Nevertheless, the buygrid model is not without value. It supports various practical observations and intuitive conclusions, such as what Robinson et al. refer to as "creeping commitment" (the increasing reluctance of customers to consider new suppliers as the purchasing process unfolds); and the different significance of the buy phases in different buy class situations.

It may be more realistic to envisage an extended purchasing process as continuing beyond the stages of "receipt" and "inspection" through a subsequent stage of "payment" (a stage prone to its own complexities and problems) and then through periodic "review" phases towards eventual re-buy situations (if the supply has proved to be acceptable) or reverting to the new task process (if the supply is no longer acceptable). Purchasing practice can, of course, be very different from the theoretical and full-blown process described here for illustrative purposes. Twelve approximately discernible stages (which may overlap or be omitted depending on circumstances) might be envisaged in such an extended purchasing process and these twelve stages are presented below as an illustration in general terms of how the process might be observed for more complex new task purchases:

(1) Perception of requirement
(2) Analysis and assessment (including establishment of provisional specifications, probable size and frequency of order, possible costs, MAKE/BUY DECISION, profiles of potential suppliers)
(3) Criteria setting (identification and ranking of the most important purchasing criteria)
(4) Negotiation (including request for quotations, prototype submission, pilot studies, trials, visits to suppliers' premises and reference sites, pursuit of references, capacity and liquidity assessment)
(5) Value engineering (systematic evaluation of the functions of the short-listed offerings to assess which of the offerings is best able to provide the customer's needs at the lowest net cost taking into consideration all relevant aspects)

(6) Decision (the outcome of the previous stages is considered in the context of broader aspects, where appropriate, and final negotiations may be conducted at senior levels to adjust any residual uncertainties until agreement is struck with one favored supplier)

(7) Delivery and receipt (delivery procedures will have been agreed but receiving procedures are often overlooked, can vary considerably and can often lead to administrative confusion, frustrating delays, deterioration of goods, and problems of disputed payment)

(8) Inspection (usually on arrival and before receipt but this may not be practicable because of weather, nature of packaging, type of good/service, or congestion in receiving area)

(9) Storage (preferably only briefly but this will vary according to contract terms, storage life, cost of storage, safety stocks, and so on)

(10) Payment

(11) Review (all procurement arrangements should be subject to review which should take close account of the views of production management and workers as well as consulting finance (for scrap and obsolescence rates), goods receiving (for delivery performance), quality control, and product engineering (for compatibility with any proposed changes to product design or production systems))

(12) Reassessment of requirement in anticipation of major changes (e.g., in product design, in suppliers, in technology).

Bibliography

Robinson, P. T., Faris, C. W. & Wind, Y. (1967). *Industrial buying and creative marketing.* Boston, MA: Allyn & Bacon.

Webster, F. E. Jr & Wind, Y. (1972). *Organizational buying behavior.* Englewood Cliffs, NJ: Prentice-Hall.

DOMINIC WILSON

— Q —

qualitative research Qualitative marketing research aims to find out what is in a consumer's mind. It is a major methodology used in exploratory research by helping the researcher become familiar with a problem from the respondent's point of view. Qualitative research studies feelings, opinions, needs, motives, attitudes, beliefs, past behavior, etc., which are difficult to observe directly or to obtain data on using structured approaches such as questionnaire surveys (*see* SURVEY RESEARCH).

Qualitative methods include (one-to-one) depth interviews and FOCUS GROUP interviews; these methods are less structured than the major alternative quantitative approaches such as those using questionnaires. They also include PROJECTIVE TECHNIQUES which concentrate on association, completion, and construction techniques.

There are several reasons for the use of the less structured qualitative approach. People may be unwilling to answer, truthfully and directly, embarrassing questions or questions that reflect on their status or which are subject to social pressure. The interviewer may, then, have to investigate such topics indirectly. The researcher may be unable, especially at an exploratory stage, to devise a questionnaire that will allow respondents to describe fully their emotions, behavior, etc. in a complicated situation. An unstructured approach allows the respondents to choose how to report on their feelings, needs, motives, attitudes, values, etc. In a depth interview, a well-trained interviewer is able to follow up a respondent's answer to a question and probe deeper into the respondent's thinking and this may lead in unanticipated ways to the uncovering of underlying or hidden information.

A major difficulty of qualitative research is the subjective nature of the analysis, interpretation, and reporting of the results. A problem is the requirement for highly trained interviewers, usually psychologists. Interviewer bias can also be a problem. Samples are often small and unrepresentative and, thus, it is difficult to generalize results from qualitative studies to the population of interest as a whole.

Qualitative research is most useful in the problem definition stage of the marketing research process where the researcher, while aware that there is a marketing problem, is trying to define or articulate the problem prior to attempting to solve it. Quantitative research, on the other hand, is more useful at the later, decision-making, stage of the marketing research process.

Bibliography

Malhotra, N. K. (1993). *Marketing research: An applied orientation.* Englewood Cliffs, NJ: Prentice-Hall. Chapter 6.

MICHAEL GREATOREX

quality of working life The term "quality of working life" (QWL) refers to people's reactions to work, particularly personal outcomes related to job satisfaction, mental health, and safety. Attention to QWL issues started initially in Scandinavia and Europe in the 1960s and spread to North America in the 1970s. The major impetus was the growing concern among industrialized nations for the health, safety, and satisfaction of workers. In Norway and Sweden, QWL has become a national movement fostered by cultural and political forces advocating employee rights to meaningful work and participation in work decisions. In the United States and Canada, QWL has been more pragmatic and localized, often limited to work situations where unions and management have a strong commitment to improving working conditions.

QWL research has focused on three major issues:

(1) identification of work conditions that contribute to QWL;
(2) development of methods and techniques for enhancing those conditions; and
(3) understanding how QWL affects productivity.

Researchers have discovered a number of conditions that affect whether employees experience work as satisfying, psychologically healthy, and safe. These include: challenging jobs, development of human capacities, safe and healthy work environment, adequate and fair compensation, and opportunity for balancing work and home life. Considerable attention has been directed at developing methods for improving these conditions. Among the QWL innovations that have been implemented successfully in modern organizations are job enrichment, autonomous work groups, flexitime, and employee involvement. A key finding of this applied research is that the success of these QWL interventions depends on a variety of contingencies in the work setting having to do with individual differences, technology, and task environment.

An assumption underlying QWL research is that there is a positive linkage between QWL and productivity. This derives from the idea that increased satisfaction with work will motivate employees to perform at higher levels. Research has shown, however, that the satisfaction-causes-productivity premise is too simplistic and sometimes wrong. A more realistic explanation for how QWL can affect productivity is that QWL innovations, such as job enrichment and participative management, can improve employee communication, coordination, and capability. These improvements, in turn, can enhance work performance. QWL innovations can also improve the well-being and satisfaction of employees by providing a better work environment and more fulfilling jobs. These positive work conditions can indirectly increase productivity by enabling the organization to attract and retain better workers.

Over the past two decades, both the term QWL and the meaning attributed to it have undergone considerable change and development. Concerns about employee well-being and satisfaction have expanded to include greater attention to organization effectiveness, particularly in today's highly competitive, global environment. QWL research and practice have given rise to current attention to employee involvement and empowerment, reflecting the need to make organizations more decentralized and responsive to customer demands. Today, QWL finds expression primarily in union–management cooperative projects in both the public and private sectors. These involve committees, comprised of employees and managers, that seek to address common workplace issues falling outside collective bargaining, such as safety, quality, technology management, and job satisfaction.

Bibliography

Cummings, T. & Molloy, E. (1977). Improving productivity and the quality of work life. New York: Praeger.

Davis, L. & Cherns, A. (eds) (1975). The quality of working life. New York: Free Press.

Thomas G. Cummings

questionnaire design Questionnaires are associated mainly with Survey research but are used sometimes as part of experimental research (*see* Experimentation). A questionnaire is a formalized set of questions for obtaining information from respondents. A questionnaire can be administered in a face-to-face personal interview, by telephone, by computer, or by post.

Questionnaires are used to measure: (1) behavior; past, present, or intended; (2) knowledge; (3) attitudes and opinions; and (4) demographic and other characteristics useful for classifying respondents.

The critical concern in questionnaire design is the minimization of measurement error, i.e., minimizing the difference between the information sought by the researcher and that produced by the questionnaire. The factors that need to be considered in questionnaire design include (1) specification of required information; (2) question content; (3) question wording; (4) response format; (5) question order; (6) physical characteristics; and (7) pilot testing.

Software is available to aid the design of questionnaires and in telephone and computer interviewing to provide the questions and collect the responses as they are made.

The specification of the required information is an essential part of the research process and a necessary prerequisite of good questionnaire design. It is also necessary to consider who the respondents will be and what the interview technique will be – postal, computer, telephone, or personal.

The next consideration is to determine individual question content. Are the data to be produced by a particular question needed? Will a particular question produce the specified data? Are several questions needed rather than one? A common error is to ask two questions in one, resulting in a question that the respondent has difficulty in answering unambiguously. Will the respondent not answer the question because (1) it is outside the competence of the respondent, (2) the respondent has forgotten the answer, (3) the respondent cannot articulate the answer, or (4) the subject is embarrassing or private and the respondent is unwilling to provide an answer?

The wording of the question is important. Simple, frequently used, and well-understood words are preferred. Leading questions such as "Most people agree that corporal punishment is wrong, do you?" or "Do you think patriotic Britons should buy Japanese cars?" should be avoided. Questions should give alternatives equal prominence, for

instance a resident of Glasgow might be asked "Do you prefer to travel by air, train, or road when going to London?"; just asking whether they prefer to travel by air would bias the answers (see Tull & Hawkins, 1987). When using a battery of rating scales, say, Likert scales, the statements should be a positive and negative mixture; indeed, different questionnaires, with the direction of the statements varying, could be prepared and distributed randomly to the respondents.

The response format is a choice between open-ended and closed questions. In open-ended questions the respondent is free to offer any reply using his/her own words. This precludes the influencing of the respondent by the list of response categories. Responses that are different to the researcher's expectations can be forthcoming, making open-ended questions suitable for exploratory research. On the other hand, respondents dislike writing answers on questionnaires and so this reduces the usefulness of self-completion questionnaires; for interviewer-administered questionnaires, the summarization and recording of answers is left to the interviewers, whose abilities and biases may vary. Eventually, responses to open-ended questions have to be coded, which may lead to misinterpretation of responses and certainly adds to cost.

In closed questions a list of possible response categories is provided for respondents to choose and record their choice. Closed, or multiple choice questions, are easier for the interviewer and the respondent. They increase response rates, reduce interviewer bias, and data analysis is easier. However, multiple choice questions are more difficult to compose as the list of possible answers needs to be complete, a problem whose solution requires preliminary research. The list can bias answers, not only because some response categories may be omitted but also due to the order in which the categories are listed. For this reason, several questionnaires with different response category orders may be produced and distributed at random in postal surveys; in computer surveys the order may be easily varied; and in personal interviews several prompt cards with different orders of alternatives may be produced and used at random.

The question sequence can affect replies: the rule is to start with general topics and gradually become more specific. Routes through the questionnaire may need to be devised depending on the responses to early questions: thus, owners of a product may be asked one set of questions, non-owners a different set. Initial questions should be simple and interesting, otherwise respondents may refuse to complete the interview. For the same reason, demographic and classification questions should be left until the end unless they are needed immediately, e.g., to establish whether or not the respondent is qualified to fill a quota in quota sampling.

The physical characteristics should make the questionnaire easy to use, especially when branching questions are used to decide on routes through the questionnaire. Physical appearance is especially important in postal surveys in order to secure the cooperation of the respondent.

Questionnaires should be piloted in order to see if the questions are understood by the respondents and mean the same thing to the respondent as the researcher intended, that the lists of response categories are complete, that the questionnaire is not too long, and that the routes through the questionnaire are appropriate and can be followed by the interviewers or respondents.

Bibliography

Malhotra, N. K. (1993). *Marketing research: An applied orientation.* Englewood Cliffs, NJ: Prentice-Hall. Chapter 12.

Tull, D. S. & Hawkins, D. I. (1987). *Marketing research: Measurement and method* 4th edn, New York: Macmillan. Chapter 7.

MICHAEL GREATOREX

quota One of the most common ways of establishing a barrier to free trade is to establish a quota for specific goods. A quota establishes a quantitative limit on the amounts of goods that can be imported. Quotas may be expressed in terms of weight (so many tons of grain), value (no more than $1,000,000 in value of a good), units (no more than 1000 trucks of a certain type), or more recently in terms of a percentage of final value (no more than 50% of the final value of a good may come from outside the country). Quotas are often used as retaliatory measures for what a country perceives as unfair trade practices of another nation.

see also **Barriers**

JOHN O'CONNELL

R

rate ranges A rate or pay range is the minimum to maximum level of pay assigned to a PAY GRADE/JOB FAMILY or class in a pay structure. The midpoint of a range usually corresponds to the employer's wage or pay policy line. Employees paid at this level are judged to be performing at a satisfactory level. Range minimum reflects the lowest value placed on jobs in the range while the maximum indicates the most the job(s) are worth to that employer. Setting rate ranges involves issues of both INTERNAL EQUITY/INTERNAL CONSISTENCY and EXTERNAL EQUITY/EXTERNAL COMPETITIVENESS. Conceptually, rate ranges are related to SD_y in staffing (*see* SELECTION MODELS).

THOMAS H. STONE

rater training Rater training is used in a variety of different situations in which raters are required to provide subjective judgments of another person's performance effectiveness. For example, rater training is used to teach supervisors how to provide appropriate PERFORMANCE APPRAISALs of their subordinates. It is also used to train interviewers and assessors in how to properly evaluate candidates in EMPLOYMENT INTERVIEWS and ASSESSMENT CENTERS, respectively. Rater training is important because subjective judgments of performance tend to introduce distortion into the measurement process. Well-developed rater training programs have been shown to increase the quality and effectiveness of subjective ratings.

Characteristics of Effective Rater Training Programs

In general, effective rater training applies the basic principles of learning. Successful rater training programs have been characterized by four key learning components:

(1) Lecture. Trainees receive oral instruction on the training objectives.
(2) Practice. Trainees are given an opportunity to practice making ratings. This is often accomplished by having trainees practice observing and rating videotaped performances.
(3) Group discussion. Trainees are provided with an opportunity to discuss and provide rationales for their practice ratings.
(4) Feedback. Trainees are given immediate feedback on their practice ratings. The content of the feedback is specific and reflects the training objectives.

Rater Training Approaches

Although different rater training techniques have been advocated, these programs can generally be classified into two major categories: rater error training and rater accuracy training (*see also* RATING ERRORS and RATING ACCURACY).

Rater Error Training

Performance evaluations are often affected by various RATING ERRORS, or faults in human judgment that occur when one individual evaluates another. These rating errors (e.g. HALO EFFECTS, leniency effects, and central tendency effects) can lessen the reliability, validity, accuracy, and usefulness of ratings. Accordingly, early rater training programs focused on teaching raters how to avoid making common rating errors by providing definitions and examples of the errors and how they can be avoided in a rating situation (see Latham et al., 1975, for an example of an error training program). Although rater error training approaches have been shown to successfully reduce common rating errors, they have not been particularly effective in increasing rating accuracy, which is the crucial criterion in judging the quality of ratings.

Rating accuracy is the extent to which a set of ratings reflect a ratee's true or actual performance level. Although error training is still an aspect of some rater training programs, recent approaches to rater training have focused more directly on improving rater accuracy.

Rater Accuracy Training

Several approaches for increasing the accuracy of ratings have been offered. For example, Banks and Robertson (1985) describe an approach to accuracy training called assessment skills training. This training focuses on training raters in how behavior relevant to different performance dimensions of interest might be manifested in different job situations. Hedge and Kavanaugh (1988) describe observational training in which raters are taught how to make appropriate and accurate behavioral observations. These authors also describe a decision training program, which focuses on the processes by which accurate judgments about performance effectiveness are made.

One approach to accuracy training, in particular, has received considerable research attention. The strategy, labeled frame-of-reference (FOR) training (Bernardin and Buckley, 1981), typically involves training raters about the multidimensional nature of performance, defining the different performance dimensions relevant to the situation or job, providing sample behaviors that represent different levels of effectiveness on the different dimensions, and providing practice and feedback to trainees in how to make accurate ratings. The primary objective of FOR training is to train raters to use common conceptualizations about performance and what constitutes different levels of effectiveness when they are making evaluations of others. This FOR approach to training has been shown to be more effective in increasing rating accuracy than other types of (or no) training (Pulakos, 1984, 1986; McIntyre et al., 1984; Athey and McIntyre, 1987).

In summary, rater training programs that focus directly on increasing rater accuracy yield higher quality ratings than other approaches to rating training. The design of any rater training program should, however, incorporate the key learning components (i.e. lecture, practice, discussion, and feedback) to achieve optimal results.

Bibliography

Athey, T. R. & McIntyre, R. M. (1987). Effect of rater training on rater accuracy: levels of processing theory and social facilitation theory perspectives. *Journal of Applied Psychology*, **72**, 567–72.

Banks, C. G. & Robertson, L. (1985). Performance appraisers as test developers. *Academy of Management Review*, **10**, 128–42.

Bernardin, H. J. & Buckley, M. R. (1981). Strategies in rater training. *Academy of Management Review*, **6**, 205–12.

Hedge, J. W. & Kavanaugh, M. J. (1988). Improving the accuracy of performance evaluations: comparison of three methods of performance appraiser training. *Journal of Applied Psychology*, **73**, 68–73.

Latham, G. P., Wexley, K. N. & Pursell, E. D. (1975). Training managers to minimize rating errors in the observation of behavior. *Journal of Applied Psychology*, **60**, 550–5.

McIntyre, R. M., Smith, D. & Hassett, C. E. (1984). Accuracy of performance ratings as affected by perceived purpose of rating. *Journal of Applied Psychology*, **69**, 147–56.

Pulakos, E. D. (1984). A comparison of error training programs: error training and accuracy training. *Journal of Applied Psychology*, **69**, 581–8.

Pulakos, E. D. (1986). The development of training programs to increase accuracy with different rating tasks. *Organizational Behavior and Human Decision Processes*, **38**, 76–91.

ELAINE D. PULAKOS

rating accuracy Rating accuracy refers to the correspondence between PERFORMANCE APPRAISAL ratings and actual performance levels. Because acceptable measures of actual performance (often referred to as "true scores") are often difficult to obtain in field settings, rating accuracy is often inferred on the basis of the psychometric characteristics of the ratings. For example, a number of RATING ERRORS measures (e.g. measures of HALO EFFECTS, leniency effects, central tendency effects) might be used to evaluate ratings. In the absence of such errors, accuracy is sometimes assumed. However, research on rater error measures and other indirect measures of accuracy suggests that these measures cannot be used to determine the accuracy of performance ratings (Sulsky and Balzer, 1988; Murphy and Balzer, 1989). The measurement of rating accuracy requires the development of some normative standard or true score.

Standards for Evaluating Accuracy

Rating accuracy measures are most often encountered in laboratory research studies (e.g. Borman 1977; Murphy et al., 1982), where it is possible to videotape the performance being evaluated and develop normative true scores. These scores are obtained from multiple expert raters, who have opportunities to observe and evaluate ratings under optimal conditions (e.g. multiple observations of each tape, freedom from distractions). If adequate evidence of convergent and discriminant validity can be demonstrated in these expert ratings, the mean over several experts is accepted as a good approximation of the true performance level, and rating accuracy can be evaluated by comparing an individual rater's evaluations with these expert true scores.

Alternatively, accuracy can be assessed using behavior-recognition measures. In this method, raters are asked whether or not they have observed certain behaviors, and their ratings are checked against videotapes of the performance observed. A number of indices based on signal detection theory can be used to assess raters' sensitivity and biases in remembering or recognizing specific behaviors (Sulsky and Balzer, 1988; Murphy, 1991). Behavior-based methods are thought to assess the accuracy of observation and memory, whereas true score-based measures are thought to assess the accuracy of evaluative judgments about performance.

Accuracy Measures

Measures of accuracy based on comparisons between performance ratings and some normative true score must often be broken down into multiple components; simple differences between ratings and true scores are generally uninterpretable. Cronbach (1955) showed that differences between any rating and some set of standards reflected at least four distinct facets of accuracy: (a) accuracy of the overall mean rating (elevation); (b) accuracy in distinguishing among ratees (differential elevation); (c) accuracy in distinguishing overall strengths from overall weaknesses (stereotype accuracy); and (differential accuracy). There is considerable evidence that these aspects of accuracy are largely independent of one another, unrelated to a number of alternative accuracy measures, and unrelated to a number of indirect measures of accuracy (Sulsky and Balzer, 1988; Murphy and Balzer, 1989).

Is Accuracy Always Desirable?

As Murphy and Cleveland (1995) note, performance ratings have a number of purposes in organizations, and the accurate measurement of job performance might be only one of the many goals pursued by raters, ratees, and organizations. Rating accuracy is most desirable when ratings lead directly to administrative decisions (and when there is clear consensus that these decisions should be made on the basis of current job performance), or when they are used for strictly development purposes. Accuracy may be less desirable (and may even interfere with more important uses of performance appraisal) when ratings are used to motivate employees, or to communicate implicit standards and norms (Murphy and Cleveland, 1995).

Bibliography

Borman, W. C. (1977). Consistency of rating accuracy and rater errors in the judgment of human performance. *Organizational Behavior and Human Performance*, **20**, 238–52.

Cronbach, L. J. (1955). Processes affecting scores on "understanding of others" and "assumed similarity". *Psychological Bulletin*, **52**, 177–93.

Murphy, K. R. (1991). Criterion issues in performance appraisal research: behavioral accuracy vs. classification accuracy. *Organizational Behavior and Human Decision Processes*, **50**, 45–50.

Murphy, K. R. & Balzer, W. K. (1989). Rater errors and rating accuracy. *Journal of Applied Psychology*, **74**, 619–24.

Murphy, K. R. & Cleveland, J. N. (1995). *Understanding Performance Appraisal: Social, Organizational and Goal-oriented Perspectives*, Thousand Oaks, CA: Sage Publications.

Murphy, K. R., Garcia, M., Kerkar, S., Martin, C. & Balzer, W. K. (1982). The relationship between observational accuracy and accuracy in evaluating performance. *Journal of Applied Psychology*, **67**, 320–5.

Sulsky, L. M. & Balzer, W. K. (1988). The meaning and measurement of performance rating accuracy: some methodological concerns. *Journal of Applied Psychology*, **73**, 497–506.

KEVIN R. MURPHY

rating errors Rating errors refer to distortions in PERFORMANCE APPRAISAL ratings that are assumed to reduce RATING ACCURACY. A wide variety of rating errors have been described in the research literature (Saal et al., 1980), but most discussions of these errors focus on HALO EFFECTS, leniency effects, and central tendency effects.

Rating errors represent differences between characteristics of the ratings and assumed characteristics of the performance to be evaluated. Halo errors are thought be the result of raters generalizing from their overall impressions of each subordinate when evaluating specific aspects of performance (Murphy et al., 1993). Errors of this sort will inflate the intercorrelations among ratings of separate aspects of performance, and can make it difficult to validly distinguish individual strengths and weaknesses. Leniency errors occur when ratings are unrealistically high; rating inflation is often assumed to result from raters' unwillingness to face the consequences of giving low ratings, even when they are clearly deserved (Murphy and Cleveland, 1995). Central tendency errors occur when raters do not distinguish between individuals and/or between specific aspects of performance.

Causes and Consequences of Rating Errors

Although some rating errors may be the result of conscious distortions on the part of the rater (e.g. raters might knowingly inflate ratings to avoid confrontations with ratees; Murphy and Cleveland, 1995), they are usually thought to reflect faulty cognitive processes used by raters in evaluating their subordinates. The cognitive processes that contribute to halo errors have been widely studied and there is extensive evidence that attention, encoding and memory biases can all contribute to halo (Murphy et al., 1993). While leniency and central tendency errors may have both cognitive and motivational causes, they are likely to be strongly affected by rating norms in an organization.

Rating error indices have long been used as indirect measures of rating accuracy, based on the assumption that the sorts of cognitive and motivational distortions that lead to these errors will also decrease the accuracy of ratings. However, there is little evidence that rating errors in fact lead to inaccuracy (Murphy and Balzer, 1989), and the use of rating error measures as criteria for evaluating ratings has been widely criticized (Murphy et al., 1993). Indeed, there is evidence that some "rating errors" (e.g. halo) can *increase* the accuracy of performance ratings (Nathan and Tippins, 1990).

Two strategies have been pursued in attempting to reduce halo, leniency and/or central tendency. First, a number of rater training programs have been developed. Although it is possible to train raters to avoid halo, leniency, and the like, this type of training does not appear to increase the accuracy or usefulness of rating. Second, a number of behaviorally oriented rating scale formats have been developed, with the goal of increasing the accuracy of ratings (e.g. BEHAVIORALLY ANCHORED RATING SCALES, BEHAVIORAL OBSERVATION SCALES). However, there is little evidence that the use of these rating scales reduces rating errors or inaccuracy. To date, no method of reducing rating errors *and* increasing the accuracy and usefulness of ratings has been developed.

Are Rating Errors a Serious Problem?

Measures of halo, leniency, and central tendency have long been used as criteria for evaluating performance ratings, training programs, rating scales, and so forth. Use of rating error measures as criteria, however, is no longer justified.

They do not provide information about the accuracy of ratings, the success of training, or the usefulness of scale formats. Obtaining information about the means, variances and intercorrelations among ratings has some value, but none of these measures permits direct inferences about the *quality* of rating data (*see* RATING ACCURACY).

Bibliography

Murphy, K. & Balzer, W. (1989). Rater errors and rating accuracy. *Journal of Applied Psychology*, 74, 619–24.

Murphy, K. R. & Cleveland, J. N. (1995). *Understanding Performance Appraisal: Social, Organizational, and Goal-oriented Perspectives*, Thousand Oaks, CA: Sage Publications.

Murphy, K., Jako, R. A. & Anhalt, R. L. (1993). The nature and consequences of halo error: a critical analysis. *Journal of Applied Psychology*, 78, 218–25.

Nathan, B. R. & Tippins, N. (1990). The consequences of halo "error" in performance ratings: a field study of the moderating effects of halo on validity study results. *Journal of Applied Psychology*, 75, 290–6.

Saal, F. E., Downey, R. G. & Lahey, M. A. (1980). Rating the ratings: assessing the quality of rating data. *Psychological Bulletin*, 88, 413–28.

KEVIN R. MURPHY

rationalization   Rationalization involves seeking efficiency by restructuring an organization. Also known as re-engineering a firm or downsizing, restructuring seeks to reduce the costs of operation through: streamlining processes, reducing unnecessary staff, closing unprofitable operations, concentrating on profitable operations, and generally seeking out the most efficient ways to increase the long-run viability and profitability of a firm. Rationalization has become a very important part of international business activities in the 1990s.

JOHN O'CONNELL

realistic job previews   A realistic job preview (RJP) is a type of external RECRUITING strategy. An RJP contains accurate information about job duties (which can be obtained from a JOB ANALYSIS) and especially about the major sources of satisfaction and dissatisfaction on the job (which can be obtained from exit interviews or attitude surveys). This information is communicated to job applicants *prior* to organizational entry. The RJP can be done during the EMPLOYMENT INTERVIEW, be handed out as a brochure, be shown as a video, or be discussed during a job visit (with, for example, potential coworkers), or in any combination of these methods.

The RJP is designed to increase the degree of "fit" between newcomers and the organizations they join. Although the RJP may initially increase stress for job candidates, its ultimate effect will be to increase newcomer JOB SATISFACTION, and commitment to the organization, and to decrease turnover. The most recent review of RJP research (Wanous, 1992, pp. 78–82) concluded that RJPs increase the "job survival" for newcomers in business organizations by approximately 10 percent (3 percent in the military). This means that a business organization in which 70 percent of new recruits survive one year would be expected to have a 77 percent survival rate if the RJP were used in its RECRUITING efforts.

There are several explanations for the effects of RJPs on turnover. First, the information provided in an RJP helps job candidates to choose more effectively among job offers. Second, the RJP can "vaccinate" expectations against disappointment after organizational entry, because the most dissatisfying job factors have already been anticipated. Third, the information in an RJP can help newcomers to cope more effectively with their job duties as well as newcomer stress, thus enhancing JOB PERFORMANCE and lowering involuntary turnover. Finally, an RJP can enhance the perceived trustworthiness of the organization to job candidates, thus increasing their initial commitment to the organization.

Several guidelines for designing an RJP have been specified (Wanous, 1992, p. 61–4). First, self-selection should be explicitly encouraged; that is, job candidates should carefully consider whether to accept or reject a job offer. Second, the RJP "message" must be credible. This can be facilitated by using actual employees as communicators. Third, the medium used and the message presented must "match" each other. For short RJPs, a video is acceptable, but for those containing a lot of information, brochures are preferable. Interviews are excellent when job candidate questions are expected, because a two-way conversation can take place. Fourth, feelings, not just sterile facts, must be part of an RJP. Fifth, the balance between positive and negative information should closely match the realities of the job itself. Finally, the preview should normally be done early in the RECRUITING process, before job candidates expend too much energy trying to obtain a job offer. (An exception would be to position the RJP at the end of executive selection.)

Research continues to specify the boundaries for using RJPs. First, the severity of an organization's turnover problem among the newly hired is one limiting factor. If the turnover rate is very high (e.g. most newcomers quit before one year) the job may be so undesirable that RJPs would have little effect. Similarly, in organizations with very low turnover, RJPs may not be able to produce additional reductions. Based on current research, the RJP is most effective when the job survival of newcomers is in the 50–80 percent range (Wanous, 1992). Second, if the relevant labor market has relatively few job openings, the RJP will have little effect on a job candidate's job choice. Third, RJPs appear to be more effective when job candidates have some previous job knowledge or work experience, because they can make better sense of the information provided than can naive candidates (Meglino et al., 1993).

RJPs may also be relevant for other aspects of human resource management. They could easily be used for preparing managers for international assignments. Some staffing techniques (see SITUATIONAL INTERVIEW; ASSESSMENT CENTERS) also communicate realistic information and, as a result, could augment an RJP.

Bibliography

Dawis, R. V. & Lofquist, L. H. (1984). *A Psychological Theory of Work Adjustment*, Minneapolis: University of Minnesota Press.

Meglino, B. M., DeNisi, A. S. & Ravlin, E. C. (1993). Effects of previous job exposure and subsequent job status on the functioning of a realistic job preview. *Personnel Psychology*, **46**, 803–22.

Premack, S. L. & Wanous, J. P. (1985). A meta-analysis of realistic job preview experiments. *Journal of Applied Psychology*, **70**, 706–19.

Vandenberg, R. J. & Seo, J. H. (1993). Placing recruiting effectiveness in perspective: a cognitive explication of the job-choice and organizational entry period. *Human Resource Management Review*, **2**, 239–73.

Wanous, J. P. (1992). *Organizational Entry: Recruitment, Selection, Orientation, and Socialization of Newcomers,*, Reading, MA: Addison-Wesley.

Weitz, J. (1956). Job expectancy and survival. *Journal of Applied Psychology*, **40**, 245–7.

JOHN P. WANOUS

reciprocity This is a strong, pervasive, ancient norm that can be represented by three sayings: one negative ("An eye for an eye; a tooth for a tooth."), one positive ("You scratch my back, I'll scratch yours."), and one general ("Do unto others as you would have others do unto you."). The positive and general sides of reciprocity have considerable social value: if people fulfill each others' expectations, everyone is well served. Ignoring negative reciprocity, however, provides the basis for unfulfilled expectations and interpersonal CONFLICT.

Cialdini (1985) notes that all societies subscribe to the norm of reciprocity. Organizationally, reciprocity is most obvious during COLLECTIVE BARGAINING, where reciprocating concessions is an almost immutable norm that contributes toward the resolution of labor–management conflict.

But reciprocity's positive side can be turned around and used manipulatively (see INFLUENCE): having received a favor, an individual may feel obligated to reciprocate. Thus, a subordinate who flatters the boss can establish subtle pressures for the boss to reciprocate. Differentiating between a favor (positive reciprocity) and a sales strategy (manipulative reciprocity), then, becomes an important interpersonal and organizational skill (see INTERPERSONAL SKILLS). Unfortunately, most people's needs for social affirmation also encourage flattery. Thus, while reciprocity provides the potential for enormous interpersonal good, it also can tempt people toward ingratiation rather than actual work performance (see IMPRESSION MANAGEMENT).

see also **Exchange relations; Game theory**

Bibliography

Cialdini, Robert B. (1985). Influence: Science and practice. (2nd edn) Glenview, IL: Scott Foresman.

J. KEITH MURNIGHAN

recruiting Recruiting consists of organizational activities that provide a pool of applicants for the purpose of filling job openings. Successful recruitment requires careful planning and strategy development, well-designed recruitment actions, and the evaluation of past efforts (Rynes, 1991).

Recruitment Planning

Recruitment planning should be carefully integrated with an employer's HUMAN RESOURCE STRATEGY. Among the issues that an employer should address in recruitment planning are: (a) does it wish to fill positions internally or externally (see RECRUITING SOURCES), (b) what are the job specifications for the open positions, (c) is AFFIRMATIVE

ACTION a consideration, and (c) what are its budgetary constraints?

Recruitment Strategy Development

In developing a recruitment strategy, an employer should address numerous issues. Among the most important of these are (a) what is the relevant labor market from which it will recruit, (b) what is the recruitment message it wants to convey, and (c) what recruitment method(s) will it use to communicate this message?

In deciding upon the relevant labor market from which to recruit (e.g. PhD chemists), an employer should consider a variety of factors (e.g. are members of the targeted group likely to be qualified for and interested in the jobs the employer has to fill?). For legal compliance reasons, employers have made special efforts to recruit members of protected groups. To effectively recruit members of protected groups, an employer needs to carefully plan its actions. For example, some recruitment methods (e.g. employee referrals) may be less effective in reaching members of protected groups than other methods (e.g. publicizing positions at a minority job fair). In a similar vein, recruiters who are comparable in relevant background characteristics (e.g. race) to the type of persons being recruited may be seen as having more credibility (Breaugh, 1992).

A key issue in recruitment strategy development is deciding what information about the job and the organization to convey to applicants (Rynes, 1991). If an employer's goal is to attract a large number of applicants, then its recruitment message is likely to present only the positive features of a job. However, such a recruitment message is one-sided, can be perceived as deceptive, and can result in undesirable outcomes (e.g. employee turnover) for the organization (Wanous, 1992). In contrast to a deceptive recruitment message, REALISTIC JOB PREVIEWS provide applicants with an accurate view of the job. The provision of accurate information has been shown to have benefits for both individuals (job satisfaction) and employers (less turnover). In making decisions about the design of recruitment communications, an employer should consider whether it is conveying the type of information that will help applicants make good job choice decisions.

Once it has determined the information that it wants to convey, an employer needs to decide upon the recruitment method(s) that will most effectively fill positions. Early recruitment communications should attract attention and generate interest (Breaugh, 1992). During the course of the recruitment process, other recruitment methods (e.g. conversations with job incumbents) can provide detailed information about the job opening. Given the number of recruitment methods that can be utilized (e.g. job posting, executive search), it is impossible to discuss all of them. Nevertheless, each recruitment method has its pros and cons. For example, the use of employee referrals allows current employees to screen prospective employees and provide realistic job previews. However, the use of employee referrals tends to have adverse impact on protected groups.

Recruitment Activities and Recruitment Evaluation

Given that an employer has carefully considered its recruitment strategy, carrying out recruitment activities (e.g. writing job advertisements, training recruiters) should

be a fairly straightforward process. Once an organization has completed its recruitment actions for filling a job opening, it should evaluate those efforts (Heneman and Heneman, 1994). Among the criteria an employer could assess are: (a) the number of applications generated by each recruitment method; (b) the yield ratio for each step of the recruitment process; (c) the cost per recruit; (d) the number of minority job applicants recruited; and (e) first year performance of new hires. The results of an employer's evaluation of recruitment activities can be used in future recruitment planning and strategy development.

Bibliography

Breaugh, J. A. (1992). *Recruitment: Science and Practice*, Boston: PWS-Kent Publishing.
Heneman, H. H. & Heneman, R. L. (1994). *Staffing Organizations*, Middleton, WI: Mendota House.
Rynes, S. L. (1991). Recruitment, job choice, and post-hire consequences. *Handbook of Industrial and Organizational Psychology*, Eds. Dunnette, M. D. & Hough, L. M. Palo Alto, CA: Consulting Psychologists Press.
Wanous, J. P. (1992). *Organizational Entry*, Reading, MA: Addison-Wesley.

JAMES A. BREAUGH

recruiting sources Recruiting sources are methods used by organizations to transmit information about open positions to potential applicants. These sources can differ in the type of applicants reached, amount of information transmitted, and cost. Recruiting sources can be categorized into two types: *internal* and *external* recruiting sources. Internal recruiting sources refer to methods that transmit information to *current* employees. The most common internal source is job posting, in which position information is directly provided to employees. Interested employees may choose to apply. Breaugh (1992) describes "closed" internal sources whereby applicants may *not* know that they are being considered for a position. Examples include nominations by supervisor(s), replacement charts developed by top management, and computerized job–person matching systems.

External recruiting sources refer to methods directed to individuals who are not current employees. The most common external sources are: brochures, videotapes, advertisements in newspapers, magazines and professional periodicals, announcements on radio, television and electronic networks, job fairs, employee referrals, internships, and educational site visits.

Research has attempted to compare the results of various recruiting sources in terms of such variables as job satisfaction, tenure, and job performance. Rynes (1991) concludes that no consistent differences among sources have been determined. These inconsistencies may partially reflect the fact that satisfaction, tenure, and performance are influenced by several factors, besides recruitment. In addition, Williams et al. (1993) found that applicants frequently use multiple recruiting sources. Therefore, the effects of an individual recruitment source may be difficult to assess.

Bibliography

Breaugh, J. A. (1992). *Recruitment: Science, and Practice*, Boston: PWS-Kent.
Rynes, S. L. (1991). Recruitment, job choice, and post-hire consequences. *Handbook of Industrial and Organizational*

Psychology, Eds. Dunnette, M. D. & Hough, L. M. Palo Alto, CA: Consulting Psychologists Press.

Williams, C. R., Labig, C. E. Jr & Stone, T. H. (1993). Recruitment sources and posthire outcomes for job applicants and new hires: a test of two hypotheses. *Journal of Applied Psychology*, **78**, 163–72.

ROBERT D. GATEWOOD

red circle jobs   A red circle job indicates that the incumbent is paid more than the maximum for the job or range rate. Many red circle rate jobs suggest pay structure control problems, such as managers who have raised employees' pay above rate range maximums. However, red circle rates may also occur if a new job evaluation results in a lower evaluation of some jobs. The common practice for handling red circle jobs is to freeze the pay at that level for the current incumbent until either the job moves within the rate range as a result of wage structure adjustments over time or the incumbent leaves the job.

THOMAS H. STONE

reference price   In order to protect itself from predatory pricing practices or dumping, the European Community (EC) has established minimum prices which must be charged for certain imported commodities. Agricultural commodities are the target of most reference prices. When the price of an import falls below its reference price, a surcharge is imposed on that item. Reference prices are part of the EC's attempt to protect local producers from foreign competition.

Bibliography

Viner, J. (1991). *Dumping: A problem in international trade*. Caldwell, NJ: Augustus M. Kelley Publishers.

JOHN O'CONNELL

regulatory cost advantage   Regulatory cost advantage occurs when the cost of complying with regulations governing an organization's actions are extremely high in the home country whereas those regulations do not exist (or if in existence, the cost of compliance is far less) in a host country.

Three current examples of regulatory cost advantage exist in the environmental pollution area; legal liability arena; and health and safety work regulations. Do companies locate in countries because laws are less stringent than in the company's home country? There is some evidence to indicate that companies have moved because of what they consider an oppressive legal system in the United States (high cost of litigation; uncertainty; high liability insurance costs); because of strict pollution liability regulations and responsibility; because of requirements to provide social types of insurance and pension plans; because of reduced safety and loss control requirements; as well as for other reasons. Regulatory cost advantages as a reason to locate a facility are transitory at best. Environmental legislation is sweeping the globe; legal reform is beginning in the United States (the country facing the most serious legal liability exposure); and common markets are slowly equalizing social benefits and programs between member countries.

The real question to be posed to companies taking advantage of regulatory cost advantages is an ethical one. Does an organization have the right to treat the environment or the people of a foreign nation with less respect than in the home country because there are fewer laws in that nation to offer protection? Sometimes taking advantage of reduced regulatory costs adds to the economic development of a nation, but the question must be asked: "At what cost?" Those firms which locate for cost advantages, but also are considerate of the host country, will have a better long-run chance of succeeding than those who are inconsiderate.

JOHN O'CONNELL

reinforcement   Operant reinforcement refers to a procedure, a behavior change process, and a single event. As a procedure, reinforcement is the creation of a contingency between an operant behavior and a known reinforcer. As a process, reinforcement is the increased rate of an operant behavior above its naturally occurring base-line rate when occurrences of the behavior are followed by occurrences of a known reinforcer. As a single event, reinforcement refers to an instance in which a reinforcer follows an operant behavior, i.e., "the response produced a reinforcement" or each time the student correctly imitated the model's behavior a reinforcement was delivered. Operant behavior rates and patterns of rates during both reinforcement and extinction, at least under laboratory conditions, depend on the schedule of reinforcement experienced during a person's exposure to operant reinforcement procedures. Schedules of reinforcement are rules specifying conditions under which a reinforcer will follow a behavior. A fixed ratio (FR-N) schedule specifies that every Nth response will be followed by a reinforcement. When $N = 1$ the FR-N schedule is called a continuous reinforcement schedule, or CRF. A variable ratio (VR-N) schedule specifies that the N between reinforced behaviors vary randomly within some range so that on average every Nth behavior is followed by reinforcement. Slot machines or one armed bandits exemplify VR-N schedules that exert powerful (sometimes addictive) control over operant behaviors. The following equation is a feedback function for ratio schedules: $R = B/N$, where R is rate of reinforcement received, B is rate of behavior performances, and N is the ratio schedule value. It clearly indicates that, if performance occurs on ratio schedules, a virtually perfect correlation between performance rate, B, and reinforcement rate, R, will occur regardless of values taken by N. In part, this functional relationship accounts for the fact that ratio schedules support very high performance rates. Fixed interval (FI-t) schedules specify that the first response to occur after passage of t time units since the last reinforcement occurred will be followed by reinforcement. Variable interval (VI-t) schedules specify that the interval of time that must elapse between one reinforcement and the next reinforcement vary over some range so that the average time between reinforcements will be t. Empirical evidence indicates that in general (i.e., except for exceedingly small values of t, and large values of N, respectively, for interval and ratio schedules), ratio schedules virtually always support higher behavior rates than do interval schedules. The fixed time (FT-t) schedule specifies that a reinforcement be delivered every t time units contingent only upon the person being in a specific location when the reinforcement is delivered. Concurrent reinforcement schedules (e.g., conFR/VI = concurrent FR and VI) specify that two or more alternative schedules be continually available so the person can continually choose between them.

Applications of operant conditioning procedures in organizations resemble applications of the law of gravity in everyday affairs in that both applications represent analogue of the processes originally described and quantified under controlled laboratory conditions. In organizations reinforcements can be contingent on performance but follow with too long a delay to be isomorphic with reinforcement as it occurs under laboratory conditions (Malott, 1992). Nevertheless, effective use has been made of laboratory based operant learning concepts in the design of field interventions, and the process can be described in terms of recently refined operant concepts (see Agnew & Redmon, in Mawhinney, 1992b). Field interventions typically involve procedures of behavior specification, observation (measurement), and scheduling consequences contingent on performances, e.g., constructing ratio-like schedules of incentives and bonus pay (*see* BONUSES; PAY FOR PERFORMANCE). For example, Latham and Dossett (see Latham & Huber, in Hopkins & Mawhinney, 1992) constructed continuous (CRF) and variable ratio four (VR-4) schedules of monetary pay contingencies among 14 beaver trappers who were randomly assigned to either the CRF or VR-4 schedule of bonus pay added to their normal wages. The amount of bonus pay per occasion of "reinforcement" was, respectively, $1.00 and $4.00 contingent on each beaver trapped and the reinforcement schedule. Note that the feedback functions for the two schedules are as follows: CRF: $R = \$1 \bullet B/1$ and VR-4: $R = \$4 \bullet B/4$; thus, net value of reinforcements received (rate times amount) was equal across the two schedules for equal performance rates. The number of beavers trapped per trapper hours worked was 0.44 prior to the intervention and 0.63 during the intervention. During the intervention, trapper hours per beaver trapped were 0.67 under the CRF and 0.58 under the VR-4 schedule. A reinforcement schedule-by-experience level of the trappers was observed; inexperienced trappers performed at a higher rate on the CRF and experienced trappers performed at a higher rate on the VR-4 schedule. This interaction conforms with operant-based laboratory results that suggest skill learning occurs more rapidly on CRF schedules while maintenance can be achieved with VR schedules of partial reinforcement. The cost per beaver caught fell from $16.75 prior to the intervention to $12.86 during the intervention. Verbal reports indicated high satisfaction with the intervention among the unionized trappers and their supervisors. Performance increases in the classic Hawthorn Experiments (*see* HAWTHORN EFFECT) have been related to operant conditioning (see Parsons, in Hopkins & Mawhinney, 1992) and the pay and cultural practices of the highest paid and most productive work force in the United States, and perhaps the world, within the Lincoln Electric Company can be considered applied principles of operant conditioning whether the formal principles guided development of that work environment or not (see Handlin, in Hopkins & Mawhinney, 1992). Verbal praise and other forms scheduled, can be powerful reinforcements often

rivaling monetary reinforcement in their effects on behavior.

PREE refers to Partial Reinforcement Extinction Effect, in which partial reinforcement (number and random order of reinforced and unreinforced occurrences of B during reinforcement) results in greater resistance to extinction (number of responses occurring before responding ceases) during an extinction procedure (Capaldi, 1966). Researchers have provided experimental subjects with histories of continuous and partial (and irregular) reinforcement of their decisions to allocate limited resources among alternative investments or industrial projects and then exposed them to extinction procedures. As predicted by PREE, subjects with histories of partial irregular reinforcement were more resistant to extinction and allocated more resources to failing investments and projects, than subjects who provided a history or regular (more predictable) partial or simply continuous reinforcement (Hantula & Crowell, 1994). These results may well have implications for executive level DECISION MAKING.

Recent develops in the literature include analyses of linkages between operant learning processes and the role they may play in understanding and dealing with practical issues such as ORGANIZATIONAL CULTURE analysis and change (Mawhinney, 1992b), pay-for-performance (*see* PAY FOR PERFORMANCE) (Hopkins & Mawhinney, 1992), and quality improvement (Mawhinney, 1992a) (*see* TOTAL QUALITY MANAGEMENT). For current accounts of social learning theory, safety, ethics, and other topics viewed from an operant stand point, see *Organizational performance: Behavior analysis and management* (Johnson, Redmon, & Mawhinney, 1995).

Bibliography

Capaldi, E. J. (1966). Partial reinforcement: A hypothesis of sequential effects. Psychological Review, 11, 459–477.

Hantula, D. A. & Crowell, C. R. (1994). Intermittent reinforcement and escalation processes in sequential decision making: A replication and theoretical analysis. Journal of Organizational Behavior Management, 14 (2), 7–36.

Hopkins, B. L. & Mawhinney, T. C. (Eds), (1992). Pay for performance: History, controversies, and evidence. New York: Haworth Press.

Johnson, M., Redmon, W. K. & Mawhinney, T. C. (Eds), (1995). Organizational performance: Behavior analysis and management. New York: Springer-Verlag.

Malott, R. W. (1992). A theory of rule-governed behavior and organizational behavior management. Journal of Organizational Behavior Management, 12 (2), 45–65.

Mawhinney, T. C. (1992a). Total quality management and organizational behavior management: An integration for continual improvement. Journal of Applied Behavior Analysis, 25, 225–243.

Mawhinney, T. C. (Ed.), (1992b). Organizational culture, rule-governed behavior and organizational behavior management: Theoretical foundations and implications for research and practice. New York: Haworth Press.

THOMAS C. MAWHINNEY

reinvoicing Tax considerations play a large role in international trade. One of the methods used by multinational firms to reduce the impact of taxes is to establish an offshore organization which acts as the receiver of imports for the parent corporation. The agent company is established in a country with favorable corporate tax rates and regulations. Goods purchased on behalf of the parent company are sold to the offshore company which then reinvoices the goods to increase their price to the parent company. The parent company has a high cost of raw materials which lowers its domestic taxable income. The offshore company shows high profits which are taxed at favorable rates. The offshore company may then be able to finance the parent company's activities through low- or no-cost loans or through other investments in the parent company.

Bibliography

Celi, L. J. & Rutizer, B. (1991). *Global cash management.* 1st edn, New York: Harper Business (HarperCollins).

Eiteman, D. K., Stonehill, A. J. & Moffett, M. H. (1992). *Multinational business finance.* 6th edn, Reading, MA: Addison-Wesley Publishing.

JOHN O'CONNELL

related diversified strategy   Businesses adopting this strategy are defined as corporations which had diversified into activities with some apparent similarities to their original activities. Such diversification centered on a "core skill" such as a technology. Technologies of this kind included chemical, electrical, and mechanical engineering, and firms in these industries were natural and early diversifiers. They were also early adopters of the multi-divisional structure form of organization in response to the growing complexity of the business as product market diversity increased. In the Harvard studies of the early 1970s, such businesses were defined as those in which less than 70 per cent of sales were generated from any one concern.

Firms in technology- or skill-based industries, where the skill or technology led naturally to the production of a wide range of end products meeting the needs of a variety of markets, were amongst the earliest diversifiers. While acquisition was an important element in their diversification strategies, significant growth also occurred as a result of internal development. In chemicals and electrical engineering the level of research expenditure was relatively high, although it was low in mechanical engineering. Nevertheless, the skills of metal manipulation proved to be readily transferable to a wide variety of different end uses.

While overall concentration and capital intensity was high in specific segments, the wide market scope of these industries had not precluded new competitive entries. Furthermore, the constant rapid change of technology frequently transformed the pattern of strategic advantage. In general, despite technical SYNERGY or STRATEGIC FIT, the degree of integration between the different corporate activities was low. There were cases in which one unit supplied raw materials or components to another, but usually all activities had a direct interface with outside markets. Therefore, while some central coordination of interdependent activities might be desirable, this was usually low, relative to the product flow of the corporation as a whole. As a result, while some concerns were early adopters of a multidivisional form of structure and were latterly converted to an SBU STRUCTURE, the large central office predicted for such businesses was sharply reduced during the 1980s and 1990s.

In industries which were historically relatively specialized, such as food, textiles, paper and packaging, and printing and publishing, and without a readily transferable technology, diversification occurred largely by acquisition. While a number diversified to conglomerate strategies, most firms in these sectors of industry endeavored to achieve a strategic fit in which relatedness occurred more through efforts to service common customers, use of common distribution channels, and the like. In addition, as in the textile and paper industries, a number of firms adopted vertical integration strategies by entering additional stages in the processing of materials.

Growth rates and profitability within the nontechnological diversifiers tended to be low. In specific segments, however, there were high-growth segments, such as convenience foods, plastic packaging, and synthetic fibers. Furthermore, competition tended to increase in these sectors as a result of new market entrants, many of which were international operators.

In the 1970s and 1980s, diversification occurred within both the manufacturing industry and service sectors. Moreover, there was a significant volume of activity between these sectors, such that by the mid-1990s it tended to be increasingly misleading to classify businesses as either manufacturing- or service-dominated.

By the mid-1990s, related diversification has become the most important single diversification strategy amongst large corporations throughout the developed world. This applied to both manufacturing-based and service-based businesses, and hybrid strategies are also becoming common. Concurrently with product market diversification, many of these concerns have also adopted international – and an increasing number, global – strategies, dependent upon the industries in which they are engaged. The management of such businesses now almost invariably corresponds to some form of DIVISIONAL STRUCTURE, SBU STRUCTURE, or MATRIX STRUCTURE amongst Western concerns while, in the East, Japanese concerns are usually participants in vertical and/or horizontal keiretsu – or chaebol in Korea (*see* CHAEBOL STRUCTURE; KEIRETSU STRUCTURE).

As identified by Chandler (1966), it was believed that such businesses needed a large central office to coordinate interrelationships between the related divisions, and this was indeed normal until the late 1970s. The impact of improved information technology and the use of the SBU STRUCTURE led to delayering and reduction in the size of such central offices. By the late 1980s, pressures on cost had therefore led to sharp reductions in the central overheads of related diversified corporations, with a strong focus on strategic control and finance. Such thin head office structures should not, however, be confused with the traditional HOLDING COMPANY STRUCTURE, in which no central strategic control was exercised.

Bibliography

Chandler, A. D. (1966). *Strategy and structure.* New York: Anchor Books.

Channon, D. F. (1973). *Strategy and structure of British enterprise.* Cambridge, MA: Harvard Division of Research.

Channon, D. F. (1976). *The service industries: strategy, structure and financial performance.* London: Macmillan.

Wrigley, L. (1970). Divisional autonomy and diversification. Unpublished doctoral dissertation, Harvard Business School.

DEREK F. CHANNON

relationship marketing Relationship marketing can be seen as stemming from a growing body of literature expressing dissatisfaction with conventional marketing theory when applied to the areas of BUSINESS-TO-BUSINESS MARKETING and SERVICES MARKETING, with Berry (1983) being one of the first researchers to introduce the concept. The major concern is that the traditional marketing paradigm, based on the marketing mix and the concept of exchange, was developed using assumptions derived from studies of the US market for consumer goods and the resulting short-term transactional focus is inappropriate for business-to-business and services marketing where establishing longer term relationships with customers is critical to organizational success.

In contemporary marketing, the term relationship marketing is most commonly used to describe a long-term approach to marketing strategy, in which developing and maintaining relationships with individual customers is seen as of fundamental importance, rather than taking a "one sale at a time" approach. It has many similarities with the International Marketing and Purchasing (IMP) Group's approach to business-to-business marketing (see BUSINESS-TO-BUSINESS MARKETING), where the notion of building long-term relationships with business customers is well documented. Relationship marketing has been used to refer to the development and enhancement of relationships with bodies other than external customers, such as the organization's own staff, as well as its suppliers, referral sources, influence markets, and recruitment markets.

Writing on relationship marketing, Grönroos (1990) proposed a marketing strategy continuum, ranging from "transaction marketing," which was seen as more suitable for consumer packaged goods, through to relationship marketing, which was seen as more suitable for business-to-business marketing and, especially, services marketing. However, the relationship marketing concept has been extended to the area of CONSUMER MARKETING. Copulsky & Wolf (1990), for example, use the term in a highly specific sense to refer to the building of a database of current and potential consumers which records a wide range of demographic, purchase, and lifestyle information. The database is then used to select suitable customer targets for the promotion of products or services (direct mail is particularly commonly used), the message contained in the promotion being differentiated according to customer characteristics and preferences. The response of each customer to this and any further promotional activity is tracked to monitor the cost of acquiring the customer and the lifetime value of his or her purchases.

The rationale forwarded for the use of the relationship marketing concept in consumer markets is the high degree of correlation between customer retention and profitability. Established customers, it is suggested, tend to buy more, are predictable, and usually cost less to service than new customers. They also tend to be less price-sensitive and may provide free word-of-mouth advertising and referrals. Retaining customers makes it more difficult for competitors to enter a market or increase share in that market and also avoids the often considerable cost of recruiting new customers.

Relationship marketing has been linked in its later development to issues of organizational structure, with advice to base organizational design around company-wide processes, as opposed to business functions (see, for example, McKenna, 1991).

Bibliography

Berry, L. L. (1983). Relationship marketing. In L. L. Berry et al. (Eds), *Emerging perspectives on services marketing* (pp. 25–28). Chicago: American Marketing Association.

Copulsky, J. R. & Wolf, M. J. (1990). Relationship marketing: Positioning for the future. *Journal of Business Strategy* July–Aug., 16–20.

Grönroos, C. (1990). Relationship approach to marketing in service contexts: The marketing and organisational behaviour interface. *Journal of Business Research*, **20**, Jan., 3–11.

McKenna, R. (1991). *Relationship marketing*. London: Century Business.

FIONA LEVERICK

relativism, cultural and moral *Cultural relativism* is a descriptive claim that ethical practices differ among cultures; that, as a matter of fact, what is considered right in one culture may be considered wrong in another. Thus truth or falsity of cultural relativism can be determined by examining the world. The work of anthropologists and sociologists is most relevant in determining the truth or falsity of cultural relativism, and there is widespread consensus among social scientists that cultural relativism is true.

Moral relativism is the claim that what is really right or wrong is what the culture says is right or wrong. Moral relativists accept cultural relativism as true, but they claim much more. If a culture sincerely and reflectively adopts a basic moral principle, then it is morally obligatory for members of that culture to act in accordance with that principle.

The implication of moral relativism for conduct is that one ought to abide by the ethical norms of the culture where one is located. This position is captured by the popular phrase "When in Rome, do as the Romans do." Relativists in ethics would say "One ought to follow the moral norms of the culture." In terms of business practice, consider the question, "Is it morally right to pay a bribe to gain business?" The moral relativist would answer the question by consulting the moral norms of the country where one is doing business. If those norms permit bribery in that country, then the practice of bribery is not wrong in that country. However, if the moral norms of the country do not permit bribery, then offering a bribe to gain business in that country is morally wrong. The justification for that position is the moral relativist's contention that what is really right or wrong is determined by the culture.

Is cultural relativism true? Is moral relativism correct? As noted, many social scientists believe that cultural relativism is true as a matter of fact. But is it?

First, many philosophers claim that the "facts" aren't really what they seem. Early twentieth-century anthropologists cited the fact that in some cultures, after a certain age, parents are put to death. In most cultures such behavior would be murder. Does this difference in behavior prove that the two cultures disagree about fundamental matters of ethics? No, it does not. Suppose the other culture believes that people exist in the afterlife in the same condition that they leave their present life. It would be very cruel to have one's parents exist eternally in an unhealthy state. By killing them when they are relatively active and vigorous, you insure their happiness for all eternity. The *underlying* ethical principle of this culture is that children have duties to their parents, including the duty to be concerned with their parents' happiness as they approach old age. This ethical principle is identical with our own. What looked like a difference in ethics between our culture and another turned out, upon close examination, to be a difference based on what each culture takes to be the facts of the matter. This example does, of course, support the claim that as a matter of fact ethical principles vary according to culture. However, it does not support the stronger conclusion that *underlying* ethical principles vary according to culture.

Cultures differ in physical setting, in economic development, in the state of their science and technology, in their literacy rate, and in many other ways. Even if there were universal moral principles, they would have to be applied in these different cultural contexts. Given the different situations in which cultures exist, it would come as no surprise to find universal principles applied in different ways. Hence we expect to find surface differences in ethical behavior among cultures even though the cultures agree on fundamental universal moral principles. For example, one commonly held universal principle appeals to the public good; it says that social institutions and individual behavior should be ordered so that they lead to the greatest good for the greatest number. Many different forms of social organization and individual behavior are consistent with this principle. The point of these two arguments is to show that differences among cultures on ethical behavior may not reflect genuine disagreement about underlying principles of ethics. Thus it is not so obvious that any strong form of cultural relativism is true.

But are there universal principles that are accepted by all cultures? It seems so; there does seem to be a whole range of behavior, such as torture and murder of the innocent, that every culture agrees is wrong. A nation-state accused of torture does not respond by saying that a condemnation of torture is just a matter of cultural choice. The state's leaders do not respond by saying, "We think torture is right, but you do not." Rather, the standard response is to deny that any torture took place. If the evidence of torture is too strong, a finger will be pointed either at the victim or at the morally outraged country: "They do it too." In this case the guilt is spread to all. Even the Nazis denied that genocide took place. What is important is that *no* state replies that there is nothing wrong with genocide or torture.

In addition, there are attempts to codify some universal moral principles. The United Nations Universal Declaration of Human Rights has been endorsed by the member states of the UN, and the vast majority of countries in the world are members of the UN. Even in business, there is a growing effort to adopt universal principles of business practice. In a recent study of international codes of ethics, Professors Catherine Langlois and Bodo B. Schlegelmilch (1990) found that although there certainly were differences among codes, there was a considerable area of agreement. William Frederick has documented the details of six international compacts on matters of international business ethics. These include the aforementioned UN Universal Declaration of Human Rights, the European Convention on Human Rights, the Helsinki Final Act, the OECD Guidelines for Multinational Enterprises and Social Policy, and the United Nations Conduct on Transnational Corporations (in progress) (Frederick, 1991). The Caux Roundtable, a group of corporate executives from the United States, Europe, and Japan, are seeking worldwide endorsement of a set of principles of business ethics. Thus there are a number of reasons to think that cultural relativism, at least with respect to basic moral principles, is not true, that is, that it does not accurately describe the state of moral agreement that exists. This is consistent with maintaining that cultural relativism is true in the weak form, that is, when applied only to surface ethical principles.

But what if differences in fundamental moral practices among cultures are discovered and seem unreconcilable? That would lead to a discussion about the adequacy of moral relativism. The fact that moral practices do vary widely among countries is cited as evidence for the correctness of moral relativism. Discoveries early in the century by anthropologists, sociologists, and psychologists documented the diversity of moral beliefs. Philosophers, by and large, welcomed corrections of moral imperialist thinking, but recognized that the moral relativist's appeal to the alleged truth of cultural relativism was not enough to establish moral relativism. The mere fact that a culture considers a practice moral does not mean that it is moral. Cultures have sincerely practiced slavery, discrimination, and the torture of animals. Yet each of these practices can be independently criticized on ethical grounds. Thinking something is morally permissible does not make it so.

Another common strategy for criticizing moral relativism is to show that the consequences of taking the perspective of moral relativism are inconsistent with our use of moral language. It is often contended by moral relativists that if two cultures disagree regarding universal moral principles, there is no way for that disagreement to be resolved. Since moral relativism is the view that what is right or wrong is determined by culture, there is no higher appeal beyond the fact that culture endorses the moral principle. But we certainly do not talk that way. When China and the United States argue about the moral rights of human beings, the disputants use language that seems to appeal to universal moral principles. Moreover, the atrocities of the Nazis and the slaughter in Rwanda have met with universal condemnation that seemed based on universal moral principles. So moral relativism is not consistent with our use of moral language.

Relativism is also inconsistent with how we use the term "moral reformer." Suppose, for instance, that a person from one culture moves to another and tries to persuade the other culture to change its view. Suppose someone moves from a culture where slavery is immoral to one where slavery is morally permitted. Normally, if a person were to try to convince the culture where slavery was permitted that slavery was morally wrong, we would call such a person a moral reformer. Moreover, a moral reformer would almost certainly appeal to universal moral principles to make her argument; she almost certainly would not appeal to a competing cultural standard. But if moral relativism were true, there would be no place for the concept of a moral reformer. Slavery is really right in those cultures that say it is right and really wrong in those cultures that say it is wrong. If the reformer fails to persuade a slaveholding country to change its mind, the reformer's antislavery position was never right. If the reformer is successful in persuading a country to change its mind, the reformer's antislavery views would be wrong – until the country did in fact change its view. Then the reformer's antislavery view would be right. But that is not how we talk about moral reform.

The moral relativist might argue that our language should be reformed. We should talk differently. At one time people used to talk and act as if the world were flat. Now they don't. The relativist could suggest that we can change our ethical language in the same way. But consider how radical the relativists' response is. Since most, if not all, cultures speak and act as if there were universal moral principles, the relativist can be right only if almost everyone else is wrong. How plausible is that?

Although these arguments are powerful ones, they do not deliver a knockout blow to moral relativism. If there are no universal moral principles, moral relativists could argue that moral relativism is the only theory available to help make sense of moral phenomena.

An appropriate response to this relativist argument is to present the case for a set of universal moral principles, principles that are correct for all cultures independent of what a culture thinks about them. This is what adherents of the various ethical traditions try to do. The reader will have to examine these various traditions and determine how persuasive she finds them. In addition, there are several final independent considerations against moral relativism that can be mentioned here.

First, what constitutes a culture? There is a tendency to equate cultures with national boundaries, but that is naive, especially today. With respect to moral issues, what do US cultural norms say regarding right and wrong? That question may be impossible to answer, because in a highly pluralistic country like the United States, there are many cultures. Furthermore, even if one can identify a culture's moral norms, it will have dissidents who do not subscribe to those moral norms. How many dissidents can a culture put up with and still maintain that some basic moral principle is the cultural norm? Moral relativists have had little to say regarding criteria for constituting a culture or how to account for dissidents. Unless moral relativists offer answers to questions like these, their theory is in danger of becoming inapplicable to the real world.

Second, any form of moral relativism must admit that there are some universal moral principles. Suppose a culture does not accept moral relativism, that is, it denies that if an entire culture sincerely and reflectively adopts a basic moral principle, it is obligatory for members of that culture to act in accord with that principle. Fundamentalist Muslim countries would reject moral relativism because it would require them to accept as morally permissible blasphemy in those countries where blasphemy was permitted. If the moral relativist insists that the truth of every moral principle depends on the culture, then she must admit that the truth of moral relativism depends on the culture. Therefore the moral relativist must admit that at least the principle of moral relativism is not relative.

Third, it seems that there is a set of basic moral principles that every culture must adopt. You would not have a culture unless the members of the group adopted these moral principles. Consider an anthropologist who arrives on a populated island: How many tribes are on the island? To answer that question, the anthropologist tries to determine if some people on some parts of the island are permitted to kill, commit acts of violence against, or steal from persons on other parts of the island. If such behavior is not permitted, that counts as a reason for saying that there is only one tribe. The underlying assumption here is that there is a set of moral principles that must be followed if there is to be a culture at all. With respect to those moral principles, adhering to them determines whether there is a culture or not.

But what justifies these principles? A moral relativist would say that a culture justifies them. But you cannot have a culture unless the members of the culture follow the principles. Thus it is reasonable to think that justification lies elsewhere. Many believe that the purpose of morality is to help make social cooperation possible. Moral principles are universally necessary for that endeavor.

Bibliography

Benedict, R. (1934). *Patterns of Culture*. New York: Penguin Books.

Bowie, N. (1988). The moral obligations of multinational corporations. In S. Luper-Foy, *Problems of International Justice*. Boulder, Colo.: Westview Press.

Frederick, W. C. (1991). The moral authority of transnational corporate codes. *Journal of Business Ethics*, **10**, (3).

Harman, G. (1975). Moral relativism defended. *The Philosophical Review*, **84**, 3–22.

Hatch, E. (1983). *Culture and Morality*. New York: Columbia University Press.

Krausz, M. & Meiland, J. (1982). *Relativism: Cognitive and Moral*. Notre Dame: University of Notre Dame Press.

Ladd, J. (1973). *Ethical Relativism*. Belmont, Calif.: Wadsworth.

Langlois, C. & Schlegelmilch, B. B. (1990). Do corporate codes of ethics reflect national character? Evidence from Europe and the United States. *Journal of International Studies*, **21**, (9), 519–39.

Mackie, J. (1977). *Ethics: Inventing Right and Wrong*. Harmondsworth: Penguin Books.

Rachels, J. (1993). *The Elements of Moral Philosophy* 2nd edn, New York: McGraw-Hill.

Sayre-McCord, G. (1991). Being a realist about relativism (in ethics). *Philosophical Studies*, **61**, 155–76.

Wong, D. (1984). *Moral Relativity*. Berkeley: University of Californina Press.

NORMAN E. BOWIE

religion   Religion is one of the protected categories under Title VII of the CIVIL RIGHTS ACT OF 1964. It is defined in the Act to include "all aspects of religious observance and practice, as well as belief" (section 701 (j)). Courts have interpreted religion to include moral or ethical beliefs that play the role of religion in a person's life (as long as they are sincerely held), but courts have also held that religion does not include beliefs that are viewed to be political in nature, or that form the basis of a social ideology. Atheists receive protection under this protected category, because atheism fits within the statutory definition of religion.

RAMONA PAETZOLD

relocation and orientation   International human resources management involves preparing expatriates for transfer to overseas locations. The relocation and orientation process is carried out to assure that the expatriate suffers as little inconvenience as possible. One of the reasons for expatriate failure is improper preparation for the new assignment. Expatriates must be trained in the language, culture, values, forms of communication, and other nuances of the country of assignment. Preparations must also be completed for the move itself: passports and other travel papers; movement of personal property; temporary quarters; schools for children; and other needs. The expatriate must also be compensated in a manner to take care of inconvenience and extra costs not found in the home country. The entire relocation and orientation process is involved, time consuming and expensive, but must be successfully accomplished to give the expatriate the best chance for success.

see also **Compensation package; Expatriate; Expatriate training**

JOHN O'CONNELL

repatriation   The return of an employee from a foreign country to the home country upon completion of an assignment or upon illness, injury, or death. Also the return of profits from a foreign company to the home country of the parent.

JOHN O'CONNELL

replacement charts   Replacement charts are a human resource forecasting technique that describe a firm's organization structure in terms of individuals who occupy various managerial and professional positions. For each position the incumbent and potential replacements are identified along with information such as potential for advancement, experience or skills needed to qualify for next position, gender (for aid in diversity planning), and age (only for retirement planning).

Replacement charts should be computerized and provide a description of how vacancies can be filled by a firm's INTERNAL LABOR MARKETS. They should be updated annually or when changes in strategic directions occur. Updates should be guided by ongoing assessments of potential replacements – matching their current knowledge, skills, abilities, and other characteristics (*see* KSAOs) against not only present position requirements but also those needed to meet anticipated future needs of the position. Assessments should include KSAOs needed for horizontal as well as vertical moves. The former require more broad-based experience and responsibilities, often of a cross-functional nature, to meet the needs of today's flatter structures.

Before the number of qualified replacements for a current or future position can be determined, a method of comparing potential replacement candidates with the position's requirements is needed. This requires sound JOB ANALYSIS techniques and an up-to-date human resource inventories bank (Gatewood and Rockmore, 1986). When it is done properly, job families (*see* PAY GRADE/JOB FAMILY) can be developed that serve to identify potential CAREER PATHING and aid in individual career planning.

Bibliography

Gatewood, R. D. & Rockmore, B. W. (1986). Combining organizational manpower and career development needs: an operational human resource planning model. *Human Resource Planning*, **9**, 81–96.

NICHOLAS J. MATHYS

reporting assumptions   The domain of accounting has areas that differ primarily in function and purpose. Financial accounting is concerned with the measurement and reporting of all the firm's transactions. An aggregate report of those transactions is made available to investors and other external users on a periodic basis. This report must follow accounting policies and standards considered generally acceptable. These are the policies adopted by the rule-making bodies of the profession, which are in constant flux to adapt to changes in the economic environment and business activities. Accountants who are not employees of the reporting firms, and thus are independent, must examine the financial report prepared by the firm's management and offer an opinion as to whether the report has followed the accounting policies in effect on the date the report is signed.

Managerial and cost accounting deals with measurement and reporting of information on the internal activities of the firm in such a way that would benefit management in decision-making, planning, and control. The nature of these tasks requires more disaggregated information and frequent measurement and reporting.

Another facet of accounting includes accounting for taxation, which in many countries is governed by the prevailing tax laws and regulations and is much less impacted by professional accounting rules. Over the years, the development of the accounting body of knowledge has resulted in adhering to certain broad assumptions, conventions, and concepts.

Going Concern and Valuation

As with any venture, the success or failure of a business enterprise could not be known with certainty until it is concluded. Consequently, entrepreneurs start business enterprises with life spans not known in advance. In fact, many firms outlast their founders. This uncertainty about the duration of a business enterprise has led accountants to assume indefinite survival unless compelling evidence to the contrary comes to light. Accountants refer to this assumption as the "going concern."

Adhering to the going concern assumption implies that (1) managers will continue making operating, investment, and financing decisions that add value to the firm, and (2) resources (assets) owned by the firm are then viewed as stores of benefits to be realized at future dates. To realize those benefits, the firm's assets are to be used in the normal course of business, not under distress conditions, which has implications for the measurement of values to be assigned to various assets. In particular, the value of an asset must emanate from the future benefits the asset is capable of generating. Those benefits are generally identified in terms of cash flows.

If the cash flow streams associated with those expected future benefits are known, they can be represented in a common denominator using present-time monetary units (say, the dollar). This is accomplished by discounting future cash flows to present values using appropriate discount rates and taking account of the timing of each flow. The present value of future flows to be generated by using an asset is the economic value of that asset.

It is a rare occasion, however, to know the amounts and timing of future cash flows. Thus, the economic values of various goods and services cannot be determined merely by a simple calculation. Yet, people exchange goods and services all the time even with this lack of knowledge. In a world of rational expectations, people use known information to predict future outcomes, including the cash flow stream expected to be generated from using an asset. Different people make different predictions, resulting in their making different bids or asking for different prices. An exchange takes place when bid and ask prices match. Thus, it is reasonable to assume that exchange prices represent the traders' best expectations of economic values at the time of the exchange. Accountants acknowledge this relationship and use the amount of cash given up to value the asset acquired in exchange.

As time passes and more information is generated about the performance of various assets, traders in the market place use the new information to revise their earlier predictions of the amounts, timing, and uncertainty of various cash flow streams. In the absence of perfect foresight, this revision is assumed to mirror changes in the economic value of the asset. Thus, assets similar to those held by the firm might be acquired at different times for amounts higher or lower than the firm is reporting them on the books; i.e., the current (replacement) cost differs from book values.

Similarly, assets held by the firm might be sold for prices higher or lower than their book values. In this case, exit values, or realizable values are different from book values.

Once an asset is acquired, accounting policy-makers have generally decided to use the value at the time of exchange for booking the asset, but typically ignore changes in values represented by deviations of either current replacement cost or exit values from book values. To make sure that users know that changes in asset values following acquisition are ignored, the market value at the time of acquiring the asset is denoted "historical cost." Because of the ability to verify the calculation of historical cost, it was considered more objective than other competing measures. Its relevance for decision-making, however, is questioned.

Another source of variation in asset values is the change in the purchasing power of the monetary unit used in valuation. Changes in the prices of assets, goods, and services do occur because of inflationary conditions and technological advances. To reflect the effect of inflation on the financial conditions of the firm, financial statements that are based on historical costs are adjusted using a general price level index. The outcome of this process is known as financial statements in constant dollars.

The different reasons for changes in value has generated corresponding conceptual differences between historical cost, current (replacement) cost, exit values and historical cost adjusted for general price level changes. Although contemporary accounting practice is essentially based on a historic cost model, the ad hoc nature of making accounting policies resulted in producing financial statements that are in effect a depository of mixed measurements and judgments using different valuation rules. The end result of these measurement errors flows to the owners' equity section on the balance sheet.

Conservatism and Revaluation

While the heritage of accountants is to favor the use of historical cost due to its alleged objectivity, they deviate from this tradition when it becomes convenient to selectively update historical cost by adjusting for changes in market values. In some countries like the United Kingdom, Australia, and New Zealand, firms are allowed to substitute market values (or estimates thereof) for historical cost when the market values of assets held by the firm are judged to be materially different from historical cost (i.e., book values). Since many used assets have no ready second-hand markets, estimates and appraisals are often relied upon, which requires an extra effort in assuring users of information about the reliability of the newly reported information.

This practice of allowing upward revaluation of assets is not shared by the accounting profession in many countries. Universally, however, accounting policy-makers fully agree on the necessity of asset revaluation only when evidence shows material *decline* of market (or equivalent) values below book values. Only if there is a significant impairment of assets do accounting policies require substituting market values for historical cost.

This general asymmetric adherence to market value changes (i.e., ignore them if market value is higher than book values, but take them into account if the reverse is true) has been the hallmark of accounting policies for reporting information about the firm to its stockholders, creditors, and other external users of information. Adopting conservative policies is a deep-rooted tradition that has failed to adapt to changes in the socioeconomic environment. Up until the start of the 20th century, the typical business firm was small in comparison with modern corporations and was managed by their owners. Both features, the size and coupling of ownership and management, allowed owners to exercise control over the business firm's activities by means of direct observation and personal involvement. The need to inform others outside the firm was very limited. However, when owners sought financing from lending institutions, lenders, who were at an informational disadvantage as compared to the owner-manager, requested that: (1) the firm must follow conservative policies for investing and operating as well as in its accounting for financial reporting, and (2) the firm must disclose privately to bankers and lenders sufficiently disaggregated information about the performance of the firm so that they can undo the conservative reporting and understand the true economic picture of the firm. To date, these conditions have a lasting and, to a large extent, a progress-hindering effect on the development of accounting policies.

Conservative accounting policies essentially call for ignoring expected gains or anticipated increases in values, but must recognize the effects of expected losses or decline in values. Information users other than management must not be informed about good news until an exchange takes place, but bad news is to be told and taken into account as soon as it is anticipated with a reasonable degree of confidence. For example, if a firm holds goods in inventory, the decline in the market value of this inventory implies that a loss is likely to occur at a future date. To the extent that the market value falls below book value, a loss must be recognized when this expectation is formed. In contrast, an increase in the market value of inventories above book value must not be reported for external users until the earning cycle is complete. This conservative approach has led to concocting the lower-of-cost-or-market (LOCOM) measurement rule.

Since market values could refer to either current (replacement) cost or exit value, various combinations of LOCOM have evolved. In addition, the physical flow of inventory is irrelevant because accountants could assume an entirely different flow for costing purposes.

Because of its appeal to lenders and to those who fear the consequences of optimism, LOCOM was extended to other assets such as short-term investments. Even in recent times when policy-makers have shown more inclination to use market (or equivalent, fair) values for some accounting measurements, LOCOM was retained for some types of investments, while "management intent" has replaced LOCOM for other types. In fact, the book measurement of accounts and notes receivable also follow LOCOM, where market is defined as net realizable value; estimating uncollectible amounts effectively produces net realizable value.

Conservatism has also led to ignoring assets when measurements require judgment. While business firms undertake research and development activities with the anticipation of generating future benefits, most accounting policy-making around the world has followed the US lead bincurred and thereby ignoring the valuation of those benefits.

Accounting Period and Temporal Allocation
Adhering to the going concern assumption was one way of recognizing that the business firm will live indefinitely, but it also raised the problem of evaluating the success of a business venture. The issue is complicated by the fact that the duration of expected future benefits that are associated with any asset varies by its interaction with other assets. Different assets are likely to have different expected productive lives, but often enough the practice of accounting allows using different productive lives for the same assets, especially under varying conditions. An accounting convention has evolved to partition the unknown life of the firm into known periods, which has the advantage of standardizing the period to which various activities can be attributed. The typical reporting period is one year, with corporations in the more developed countries reporting on a quarterly basis. External users, however, are demanding more timely and more frequent reporting. For assets having expected benefits longer than one year (i.e., long-lived assets) attribution of benefits to a given period can be conceptually undertaken by assessing the change in its economic value during that period. However, the accountants' preoccupation with objective and verifiable calculations, that has initially led to a preference for using a historic-cost basis, has also led to developing what are called "systematic and rational" methods of attributing costs to reporting periods. Typically, such methods involve estimating the useful life of an asset and choosing one of several alternative methods of allocating its historic cost to the different periods encompassed by that life. These intertemporal allocation methods are known as depreciation (for tangible assets) and as amortization (for intangible assets). Some allocation methods do not differentiate between the extent of asset use in different periods (e.g., straight line), while others attempt to allocate larger proportions to earlier periods (accelerated) based on various assumptions, including maintenance cost, technological obsolescence, and conservatism.

It is important, however, to note that none of these methods attempts to relate periodic allocation of cost to the actual degree of consuming the benefits stored in a long-lived asset. In effect, the so-called "systematic and rational" aspects of these methods lie in their calculation feature. It is, therefore, often argued that book values of long-lived assets are the products of two independent decisions: (1) the valuation, or more appropriately the cost measurement, decision that basically maintains the historic cost basis, and (2) the intertemporal allocation decision, which is rarely related to the degree of asset utilization or its economic depreciation.

A. RASHAD ABDEL-KHALIK

requirements determination for information systems   There are three levels at which information requirements need to be established in order to design and implement computer-based information systems:

1 *Organization-level information requirements*. These requirements are used to define an overall information system architecture and to specify a portfolio of applications and databases. Often termed "enterprise analysis," the process of organization-level information requirements determination obtains, organizes, and documents a complete set of high-level requirements. The requirements are factored into databases and a portfolio of applications that can be scheduled for development.
2 *Organization database requirements*. These arise both from applications and *ad hoc* queries. User *ad hoc* query requirements and application requirements are referred to as conceptual or logical requirements because the user views of data are separated from the organization of data in physical storage. Requirements for physical database design are derived from user requirements and hardware and software environments.
3 *Application-level information requirements*. An application provides information processing for an organizational unit or organizational activity. There are essentially two types of information system application requirements: social and technical. The social or behavioral requirements, based on job design, specify objectives and assumptions such as work organization and work design objectives, individual role and responsibility assumptions, and organizational policies. The technical requirements are based on the information needed for the job or task to be performed. They specify outputs, inputs, stored data, and information processes.

There are different strategies for determining information requirements. One of these strategies, asking indirectly, is used when requirements cannot be obtained by asking directly or by a study of an existing system. Because of its importance and value in information requirements determination, the asking indirectly strategy will be our focus in this discussion.

Strategies for Determining Information Requirements
There are three broad strategies for determining information requirements:

1 *Asking directly*. In this strategy, the analyst obtains information requirements from persons in the business

processes by asking them to describe their requirements. From a conceptual standpoint, this strategy assumes that users have a mental model (or can build one) to explain their information requirements. These conditions may hold in very stable systems for which a well-defined structure exists or in systems established by law, regulation, or other outside authority.

2 *Deriving from an existing information system.* Existing information systems that have an operational history can be used to derive requirements for a proposed information system for the same type of organization or application. The types of existing information system that are useful in deriving requirements for future systems are the system to be replaced, a system in a similar organization, and a proprietary system or package. In this strategy, users and analysts start with (anchor on) an existing system and adjust from it. If the information system is performing fairly standard operations and providing fairly standard information for business processes that are stable, the use of an existing system as an anchor may be appropriate.

3 *Asking indirectly by eliciting characteristics of business processes.* Requirements for information stem from the activities of the business processes. In eliciting requirements, questions focus on the activities and responsibilities that lead to the need for information. This approach is therefore especially appropriate when the business processes are changing or the proposed information system is different from existing patterns (in its content, form, complexity, etc.), so that anchoring on an existing information system or observations of information needs will not yield a complete and correct set of requirements.

When an initial set of requirements has been elicited by one of the methods, the requirements may be extended, modified, and refined by using a prototype of the application to allow users to adjust initial requirements through experimentation with an evolving information system.

Improving the Process of Eliciting Requirements Indirectly
Four recommendations for improving the process of eliciting information requirements indirectly are to (a) consider cross-functional requirements and sharing of information; (b) use group interviews for stakeholders; (c) use sets of questions that elicit different patterns of thinking about requirements; and (d) use a prototype of the system to elicit user refinements and extensions to requirements.

Elicit cross-functional requirements. Many users and analysts view systems as functional as opposed to cross-functional (Wetherbe & Vitalari, 1994). This perspective is too narrow. For example, when developing a new budgeting system, a focus on the information needed by the budget managers or budgeting staff members is not sufficient. People other than budgeting staff make use of budgeting information.

Order processing illustrates the need to develop systems cross-functionally. To process orders, sales people have to decide which customers to call on, what to sell them, and what is available to sell. Credit must decide which customers can have credit and how much, which customers need past-due notices, and which customers' credit should be discontinued. The warehouse must decide what and how much inventory to stock, when to reorder, when to unload slow-moving inventory, and which customers to allocate limited inventory to. Shipping must decide such things as what merchandise to send to which customers, what orders can be shipped together to save delivery costs, and when trucks should depart. These decisions are summarized in table 1.

Table 1 Decision centers involved in order processing

Decision center	Activity	Examples of major decisions
Sales staff	Selling merchandise	Which major customers to call What to sell customers What is available to sell
Credit department	Accounts receivable management	Which customers to allow credit How much credit to allow Which customers need past-due notices Which customers' credit should be discounted
Warehouse	Inventory management	What inventory to stock How much inventory to stock When to reorder stock When to unload slow-moving stock Which customers to allocate available inventory
Shipping department	Packing and shipping orders	What merchandise to sell to what customers What orders can be shipped together to save delivery cost When trucks should depart

A system should provide information so that all decisions can be improved. In eliciting requirements ts to improve the quality of the decision, cross-functional factors that should be considered include customer importance to the business, customer need for prompt delivery of the order, the profitability of each order, credit status of customer, shipping schedule for delivery to each customer, and customer reaction if a previous order was late.

For example, consider the last decision listed for the warehouse department in table 1 of allocating available inventory to customers. If the warehouse has five orders but only enough inventory to fill three, it must make a resource allocation decision. Typically, this decision is made on a first-in-first-out (FIFO) basis. That seems equitable and fair, given the information they have available to them. This rule can result in a bad decision. What if a customer who does a lot of business with the company needs this shipment promptly, recently received an order late and was furious about it, is paying a high profit margin on the order, pays bills promptly, and a truck is routed to deliver a shipment to another customer nearby the same afternoon. A FIFO decision may cause the inventory to be allocated to someone who hardly ever does business with the company, to whom the order is not urgent, who yields a low profit margin, does not pay bills on time, and a truck is not going into the vicinity for the next three weeks, during which time inventory could have been re-stocked. Note that the information needed to improve the decision-making in the warehouse comes from outside the warehouse. For example, customer need, importance, and profitability come from sales, credit worthiness comes from credit, and shipping schedule comes from shipping.

Use group interviews. In the determination of information requirements, the system design team usually interviews managers individually instead of using a group process (also known as joint application design). Doing each interview separately places cognitive stress on a manager and hinders his or her ability to respond adequately to questions.

A second reason for a joint application design is that different functional areas of an organization have different agendas in developing a new information system. For example, in the order-processing system portrayed in table 1, each decision center is likely to emphasize different design criteria. Sales may view the primary importance of order processing as ensuring prompt and correct delivery of orders to customers. Credit, on the other hand, may view

the agenda as primarily ensuring that the company receives full payment for all orders. Those responsible for inventory management are, of course, interested in facilitating good inventory management, reducing inventory costs, etc., while those responsible for shipping are interested in ensuring good routing of trucks to minimize delivery costs. It is difficult to achieve this overall perspective if each manager is interviewed individually.

Use questions that elicit different patterns of thinking. System developers often ask the direct question: "What information do you need from the new system?" Such a direct question is not helpful to managers desiring better information for problem-solving, decision-making, and business processes. The reason the direct question may not work well is that managers think in terms of the need for information and not the list of information needed.

Good problem-solvers creatively elicit answers to requirements through indirect questions. For example, in determining what lawn mower someone needs, questions such as "How big is your yard? How steep is it? Do you have fences or trees?" are indirect questions that determine appropriate blade width, horsepower, or the need for a rear or side bagger. Those designing information systems need to follow the same approach, and executives should request that they do so.

A straightforward, useful indirect question approach to interviewing executives (instead of simply saying "What information do you need?") to determine information requirements has been developed at the MIS Research Center at the University of Minnesota (Wetherbe, 1988). The technique is based upon three different but overlapping sets of requirement determination questions as shown in table 2. By combining questions from these three different approaches, a comprehensive, reliable determination of conceptual information requirements can be achieved. This method is explained in more detail in the next section.

Use a prototype to elicit user refinements. After providing an initial set of requirements, users should be allowed to extend and refine their conceptual requirements and provide detailed information requirements through trial and error. Trial and error, or experiential learning, is an important part of problem-solving. It is also a part of determining detailed information requirements. It can be incorporated into the system design process through the use of a prototype or mock-up of the system. Using state-of-the-art technology, a prototype of a new system can

Table 2   Comprehensive interview approaches, implementations and developers

Comprehensive approach	Information system implementation	Developers
Specify problems and decisions	The executive interview portion of business systems planning (BSP)	IBM
Specify critical factors	Critical success factors (CSF)	Rockart
Specify effectiveness criteria for outputs and efficiency criteria for processes used to generate outputs	Ends/means analysis (E/M analylsis)	Wetherbe and Davis

usually be constructed quickly. As in manufacturing, much can be learned about final requirements through a prototype before "building the new factory."

Users should be able to observe and experience a prototype within a few days of being interviewed. This prototype can then be shaped into a final design within a few weeks. Once the prototype is accepted, a realistic schedule and budget can be established for building the system. Although systems must evolve over time and should be built with evolution in mind, a system that is initially "right" will not need substantial immediate modifications. Evolutionary change of such a system is therefore much more manageable.

The Eliciting Process in Asking Indirectly

Before conducting the interview, an agreement on the overall purpose of the business activity should be established in a joint application design session. For example, for the order-processing system discussed above, the objective of the system could be to ensure prompt, correct delivery of orders to customers, maintain credit integrity, facilitate inventory management, and ensure good shipment routing and scheduling. Once this has been established, questions can be asked that determine information needed to ensure that those objectives are accomplished. As explained earlier, a robust approach employs questions that overlap in their coverage (table 2). The three sets of questions trigger different patterns of thinking.

Elicit problems and decisions. These questions define information requirements by asking indirect questions about problems and decisions. Example questions are:

1 What are the major problems encountered in accomplishing the purposes of the organizational unit you manage? For example, in an order-processing system, problems include being out of stock too often, allocating limited inventory to the wrong customers, and sending

off trucks unaware that another order going to the same destination will be arriving at the dock within an hour.
2 What are good solutions to those problems? For example, to solve the problem of being out of stock too often requires better inventory management. To solve the problem of incorrectly allocating orders requires letting the warehouse know the importance of customers and the importance of orders to specific customers. It would also be helpful to know customer credit status. To solve the scheduling of truck departure problems requires letting shipping know the destination of orders that are being processed but have not yet arrived at the shipping dock.
3 How can information play a role in any of those solutions? For example, to improve inventory management, out-of-stock and below-minimum reporting could be provided electronically. Also, an automatic reordering system could be implemented. Electronic access to customer importance, importance of order, and credit status could allow the warehouse to make appropriate allocation decisions when inventory is limited. If the shipping department has access to orders received and in process, it can make better decisions over routing and scheduling trucks.
4 What are the major decisions associated with your management responsibilities? Major decisions for order processing include which customers to call on and what to sell them, credit, inventory, reordering, allocation of limited inventory, and scheduling and routing deliveries.
5 What improvements in information could result in better decisions? Table 3 illustrates the way decisions relate to information requirements.

Elicit critical success factors (CSF). A second line of questions is based on critical success factors. Table 4 provides an illustration of critical success factor/information results.

Table 3   Decisions elicited for order-processing system

Decision	Information
Which customers to call on and what to sell them?	Customer-order history; inventory available
Credit for whom? How much? When to discontinue?	Credit rating; current status of account, payment history
What and how much inventory to stock? When to reorder?	Inventory on hand; sales trends on inventory items; market forecasts
How to allocate limited inventory?	Priority of order; importance of customer; credit status of customer; shipping schedule
When to unload slow-moving inventory?	Sales trends
Destination of ordered inventory?	Customers' addresses
What orders can be shipped together to save delivery costs?	Shipping schedule and customers' destination for orders awaiting shipment

Table 4   Critical success factors and information requirements

Critical success factor	Information
Adequate inventory to fill customer orders	Percentage of orders filled on time – overall and also categorized by customer and product
Prompt shipment of orders	Deliver time – overall and also categorized by customer
High percentage of customer payments	Delinquency report on nonpaying customers
Vendors (suppliers) promptly fill reorders	Exception report on vendor reorders not filled on time

1   What are the critical success factors of the organizational unit you manage? (Most managers have four to eight of these.) For example, critical success factors for order processing include adequate inventory to fill customer orders, prompt shipment of orders, high percentage of customer payments made, and vendors (suppliers) promptly filling reorders.

2   What information is needed to monitor critical success factors? For example, to determine if adequate inventory is available, management needs summary and exception reports on percentage of orders filled on time. In addition to overall reports, orders should also be categorized by customer and product. To determine if orders are being shipped promptly, management needs to have summary and exception reports on delivery time, including reports categorized by customers.

Elicit effectiveness and efficiency (ends/means).   Effectiveness measures relate to the outputs or ends from a process whereas efficiency measures relate to the resources (means) employed. Ends/means questions elicit requirements by getting managers to think about both effectiveness and efficiency and information needed to monitor it (Wetherbe, 1988). Questions to elicit this thinking are:

1   What is the end or good or service provided by the business process?

2   What makes these goods or services effective to recipients or customers?

3   What information is needed to evaluate that effectiveness?

4   What are the key means or processes used to generate or provide goods or services? For example, means for order processing include processing orders, processing credit requests, and making shipments.

5   What constitutes efficiency in the providing of these goods or services? For example, efficiency for order processing is achieving low transaction costs for orders and credit checks. It is also minimizing shipment costs.

6   What information is needed to evaluate that efficiency? Examples of information needed to assess efficiency include cost per transaction with historical trends, and shipment cost categorized by order, customer, region, and revenue generated.

Tables 5 and 6 illustrate the use of effectiveness and efficiency questions in an ends/means analysis for order processing.

The method of using these three sets of indirect questions as a basis for obtaining a reasonably correct and complete set of information requirements is both simple and powerful. It is simple because it consists of components that can be learned by an analyst and a manager in a relatively short time. It is powerful because it overcomes

Table 5   Eliciting effectiveness information for order-processing system

Ends	Effectiveness	Information
Fill customer orders	Customer orders delivered as ordered, when expected, and as soon or sooner than competition	Summary and exception reports on customer deliveries; number of order corrections made; comparative statistics on delivery service *v.* competition
Provide customer service	Promptly provide credit to qualified customers	Customer credit status and payment history
	Quick response to and reduction of customer complaints	Report of number and type of complaints by customers and average time to resolve complaint
	Customers are satisfied	Customer attitudes toward service perhaps determined by customer surveys

Table 6 Eliciting efficiency information for order-processing system

Means	Efficiency	Information
Process orders	Low transaction cost	Cost per transaction with historical trends
Process credit request	Low transaction cost	Cost per transaction with historical trends
Make shipments	Minimize shipment costs	Ship cost categorized by order, customer, region, and revenue generated

human limitations in thinking about information requirements.

The redundancy in the questions increases the reliability of the structured interview results. For example, note that the set of problem questions may identify poor allocation of limited inventory to customers. The need to allocate limited inventory may also be identified as a *decision* that must be made. In other words, if the concept of allocating limited inventory is not recalled as a problem, it can still be identified as a decision, and so forth.

Bibliography

Wetherbe, J. C. (1988). *Systems Analysis and Design.* St Paul, MN: West Publishing Company.
Wetherbe, J. C. & Vitalari, N. P. (1994). *Systems Analysis and Design.* St Paul, MN: West Publishing Company.

JAMES C. WETHERBE

resistance to change Change is basic to life. Whether compelled by circumstances or intentionally planned, it is often essential to survival. But organizations and individuals vary widely in the way they deal with the necessity to adapt to new conditions. Such adaptation may take various forms: redesigning jobs; altering organizational structure; adding and/or removing members; and modifying prevailing norms and relationships that are part of the ORGANIZATIONAL CULTURE.

Among the major sources of resistance to change are the protection of material interests, fear of the unknown, and mistrust based upon bad past experience. There also may be an underlying concern about upsetting comfortable social arrangements represented in group norms, STATUS, hierarchy, and REWARD systems. Exemplifying this, Miller and Rice (1967) reported that organizational groups may defend an outmoded task procedure because of such concerns. Yet, organizations require adaptative change to overcome their rigidities, including conformism, the rejection of new ideas, territoriality, favoritism, and other dysfunctional practices.

Introducing change requires a multistep process. A pioneer in developing a group dynamics approach to creating social change, psychologist Kurt Lewin in the 1940s emphasized a threestep group process:

(1) introducing an innovation with information aimed to satisfy a need;
(2) overcoming resistance by group discussion and DECISION MAKING; and
(3) establishing a new practice.

Prevailing practices are seen to be in a "quasi-stationary equilibrium," i.e., a steady though impermanent balance, that must be "unfrozen" before new practices can be introduced through a group process. Nadler and Tushman (1989) have advanced these points with regard to MOTIVATION for change, the transition state to be managed during and after, and the political dynamics of the situation needed for its support. As a general matter, those likely to be affected by a change should be informed and have a stake in the process shaping it.

The process of overcoming resistance is especially furthered by problem recognition when a need becomes manifest, as with scarcity in time of war, depression, or other calamity. The sheer availability of new information also contributes to the possibility of change, particularly with the widespread presence of instantaneous media. Among other things, information gives awareness of more alternatives for action. However, these are perceived within the frames provided by the conceptual models held by organization members, especially leaders. Resistance to change may therefore be based on a limited conception of organizational functioning, as with strict reliance on a hierarchical mechanical structure rather than a more adaptable organic one (Burns & Stalker, 1968).

On pragmatic grounds, however, a rational basis may exist for resistance to change. This is evident in the case of managers who see themselves being displaced by such organizational practices as SELF-MANAGING TEAMS, delayering, and DOWNSIZING. The understandable concerns of those affected need to be recognized and addressed by such means as an information-based group process. It is also essential to see resistance as part of a system of relationships, as Miller and Rice (1967) have observed.

At the macro level, this system is embedded in the organization's culture, represented in the prevailing norms, VALUES, and beliefs underpinning the structures, COMMITMENTS, and actions there (Kilmann Saxton, & Serpa, 1985). While it may make for comfortable stability, culture also presents rigidity in the face of needed change, unless an effective LEADERSHIP process can be instituted. This is one of the major contributions which can be made through techniques of ORGANIZATIONAL DEVELOPMENT (OD), to encourage organization renewal and change. This process may need to cope with a reluctance to air disagreements, because of an avoidance of emotional conflict.

Other conceptual models have emphasized such factors as "momentum" (Miller & Friesen, 1980) in describing an organization's evolution toward a structure that provides coherence in a single interpretive scheme, an archetype. To change it, rather than simply make incremental changes within it, has been called "frame-breaking" versus "frame-bending" by Nadler and Tushman (1989). In bringing about strategic change, such structural elements as these need to be recognized, understood, and dealt with, as part of overcoming resistance to it (see, e.g., Greenwood & Hinings, 1993).

see also **Conflict; Employee involvement; Organizational change; Politics**

Bibliography

Burns, T. & Stalker, G. M. (1968). The management of innovation, **2nd edn**, London: Tavistock.

Greenwood, R. & Hinings, C. R. (1993). Understanding strategic change: The contribution of archetypes. Academy of Management Journal, 36, 1052–1081.

Kilmann, R. Saxton, M. & Serpa, R. (Eds), (1985). Gaining control of the corporate culture. San Francisco: Jossey-Bass.

Miller, D. & Friesen, P. (1980). Momentum and revolution in organization adaptation. Academy of Management Journal, 23, 591–614.

Miller, E. J. & Rice, R. K. (1967). Systems of organization. London: Tavistock.

Nadler, D. A. & Tushman, M. (1989). Organizational framebending: Principles for managing reorientation. Academy of Management Executive, 1, 194–204.

Robertson, P. J. Roberts, D. R. & Porras, J. I. (1993). Dynamics of planned organizational change: Assessing empirical support for a theoretical model. Academy of Management Journal, 36, 619–634.

EDWIN P. HOLLANDER

restructuring This is the deliberate modification of formal relationships among organizational components. Three concepts are fused together in the word restructuring: *re* meaning to do again, *structure* referring to the formal arrangements among organizational components, and *ing* implying a process. Hence, restructuring refers to a process of changing already existing relationships among organizational elements (*see* ORGANIZATIONAL DESIGN). There are two ways to restructure: by changing actual organizational components or by changing the relationships among components. An organization can restructure, in other words, by adding, eliminating, splitting, or merging components within a structure; or it can restructure by strengthening, weakening, reversing, or redefining the relationships among components.

In its most common form, organizational restructuring usually involves actions such as delayering (removing hierarchical layers from the organization); redesigning work processes (mapping processes and removing the non-value-added steps or redundancies); and eliminating structural elements (outsourcing, selling off, or dismissing units, activities, or jobs within the organization). However, restructuring can involve much more than just the manipulation of organizational components. Organizations have a wide variety of structural elements that can be reconfigured, such as financial structures, market structures, technological structures, information structures, and organizational structures. These various types of structures are reconfigured in different ways. Financial restructuring can be accomplished, for example, by renegotiating loan agreements, changing the investment portfolio, selling off unproductive divisions, or outsourcing products or services to an external provider (as illustrated by several major airlines that restructured their financial debt in the last decade in order to remain viable and to begin anew in the industry). Market restructuring can be accomplished by

reconfiguring the product portfolio or by moving the competitive market position of an organization so that it competes in a different market niche (as illustrated, for example, by a major retailer which changed from competing on the basis of price with lower-end merchandise to competing on the basis of quality and image with upper-end merchandise). Technological and informational restructurings are generally accomplished through the application of new technologies, including automation, computerization, and NETWORKING (*see* ADVANCED MANUFACTURING TECHNOLOGY). Despite the obvious importance of these various types of restructuring, organizational restructuring – the alteration of arrangements among internal organizational components, including sub-units, hierarchical relationships, and work processes – is the phenomenon of most interest to students of organizational behavior.

Recently, two terms have been used so often in the popular literature as substitutes for restructuring that they deserve special mention. One is the concept of DOWNSIZING, and the other is the concept of re-engineering. In other words, restructuring, downsizing, and re-engineering have been used as synonyms by many writers even though they have clearly distinctive meanings. Restructuring is used as a substitute for downsizing, for example, in order to avoid the negative connotations associated with job loss or contracting organizational size. However, when organizations have experienced pressure to reduce redundancy or waste, to eliminate headcount, or to increase efficiency through downsizing, few actually engage in restructuring. Past research has shown that downsizing has mainly involved personnel reductions, not the restructuring of organizational elements. Similarly, re-engineering refers to a zero-based redesign of an organization's processes, structures, or relationships. Restructuring does not assume that the entire old way of doing things or of structuring relationships is abandoned and recreated. It assumes remodeling rather than new construction. Consequently, restructuring is not an appropriate synonym for downsizing or for re-engineering.

At least two different orientations are prominent in the theory and practice of organizational restructuring. The two approaches can be arranged on a continuum, anchored on one end by an assumption that managers have complete control over the process of restructuring, and anchored on the other end by the assumption that managers have no control over the process of restructuring. The scholarly and popular literature, thus far, have been dominated by the assumptions represented by the managerial Control end of the continuum.

On the one hand, for example, rethe prerogative and responsibility of an organization's management. It is an activity designed to improve the efficiency, productivity, or effectiveness of the organization, and so is an important part of the managers' role (*see* ORGANIZATIONAL EFFECTIVENESS). Restructuring is motivated by maladaptation or nonalignment with the environment or by competitive opportunities or pressures. For example, Miller and Friesen (1980) found that organizations are restructured in a limited number of archetypical forms when faced with competitive pressures, among which they labeled consolidation, DECENTRALIZATION, professionalization, and entrepreneurial revitalization. Miles and Cameron (1982) found that the firms in the US tobacco industry restructured in three dominant ways in reaction to a hostile and turbulent external environment – defending current practices and incremental restructuring (domain defense), aggressive changes and redesigned forms of organization (domain offense), and completely new structures and original competitive activities (domain creation). Meyer (1992) identified four types of restructuring in hyperturbulent environments:

(1) incremental change within the organization;
(2) framebreaking change within the organization;
(3) incremental change in the organization's relationship to its environment; and
(4) transformation and creation of new relationships and structures in the external environment (see ORGANIZATION AND ENVIRONMENT).

Freeman and Cameron (1993) found that organizations facing financial pressures adopted either a reorientation approach to restructuring or a convergence approach to restructuring. A reorientation approach involves major, strategic changes in hierarchical arrangements and the nature of the work. Restructuring entire units and clusters of subunits in an organization characterizes reorientation. A convergence approach involves minor, tactical changes in work and working relationships. Restructuring the tasks and job relationships in a firm is typical of a convergence approach. A reorientation approach to restructuring has been associated with higher levels of effectiveness over time when organizations face threatening conditions.

The other end of this continuum reflects an assumption that restructuring is outside the purview of management action and is a product of uncontrolled circumstances. Restructuring occurs not because of planned managerial action but because of evolutionary processes and environmental inertia. Theoretical perspectives represented by the POPULATION ECOLOGY or natural selection models, or by the evolutionary life cycles models, exemplify the most common form of unmanaged restructuring. For example, several theorists who represent the population ecology perspective (e.g., Hannan & Freeman, 1977) argue that a variety of organizational and environmental constraints inhibit managers' impact on an organization's structure. The structures, processes, and COMPETENCIES of surviving organizations are almost entirely determined by the demands of the external environment, according to this view. Organizational restructuring that does not match the requirements of the environment results in organizational demise. Hence, if one looks at organizations over time, successful restructuring is a product of environmental selection or environmental determinism rather than managerial choice. The environmental dictates what restructuring will occur and that restructuring will usually occur in slow, evolutionary patterns, although it may also be experienced on rare occasions in revolutionary spurts. Another variation on this deterministic theme is represented by writers on organizational life cycles. One representative study, for example, was conducted by Quinn and Cameron (1983), who found that new organizations restructure in predictable ways over their early life cycles. These stages of restructuring are similar to the progression of group stage development (see GROUP

DEVELOPMENT). The initial structures of organizations, they found, are generally characterized by loosely coupled elements and an entrepreneurial orientation. Subsequent sequential restructurings include a change to teamwork and integration, then a change to hierarchical structures and a focus on control, and finally a restructuring which emphasizes and is aimed at optimizing external relationships and competitive market success.

The challenge for future research on restructuring is to reconcile the two ends of the continuum. For example, Orton (1994) studied the 1976 reorganization of the U.S. intelligence community. By studying original memos, notices, notes of conversations, and minutes, Orton created a six-stage model of reorganizing processes. First, organization members confronted limitless frontiers of actions, statements, influences, and ideas. Second, organization members pulled out of that frontier – through action, perception, discussion, and discovery – small brackets or boundaries on which they focused attention. Third, organization members generated mental maps that made sense of the frontiers, brackets, or boundaries. Fourth, organization members combined their individual-level mental maps to build an overall, agreed-upon organization-level foundation for a restructuring. Fifth, organization members decided upon a set of restructuring initiatives which were presented together as a deliberate organization design. Sixth, the restructuring alternatives were absorbed into and, consequently, changed the existing structure. Over time, Orton argued, emergent restructuring becomes deliberate restructuring.

In sum, organizational restructuring may involve many aspects of an organization, and it may take many forms. What is common about restructuring in all its forms, however, is that it is a process in which already existing elements and their interrelationships are permanently altered. Restructuring is currently a popular way in which organizations are trying to make themselves more effective.

see also **Organizational change; Merger guidelines; Job design**

Bibliography

Freeman, S. J. & Cameron, K. S. (1993). Organizational downsizing: A convergence and reorientation perspective. Organization Science, **4**, 10–29.

Hannan, M. & Freeman, J. (1977). The population ecology of organizations. American Journal of Sociology, **82**, 929.

Meyer, A. D. (1992). Adapting to environmental jolts. Administrative Science Quarterly, **27**, 515–537.

Miles, R. & Cameron, K. S. (1982). Coffin nails and corporate strategies. Englewood Cliffs, NJ: Prentice-Hall.

Miller, D. & Friesen, P. (1980). Archetypes of organizational transition. Administrative Science Quarterly, **25**, 268–299.

Orton, J. D. (1994). Reorganizing: An analysis of the 1976 reorganization of the US Intelligence Community. Unpublished doctoral dissertation. University of Michigan.

Quinn, R. E. & Cameron, K. S. (1983). Organizational life cycles and shifting criteria of effectiveness: Some preliminary evidence. Management Science, **29**, 33–51.

KIM S. CAMERON and J. DOUGLAS ORTON

retail banking Historically retail banking was a relatively simple business. Commercial banks, operating essentially via a branch network, took in consumer deposits which were then usually used to provide loans, in most countries on overdraft, to the corporate sector. In return for deposits held in current accounts the banks provided free transaction services largely by the use of cheques in most developed economies. Personal loans to consumers were also available but did not constitute a significant proportion of a bank's loan portfolio. There was little or no segmentation of the consumer market.

As late as the end of the 1960s electronic personal products were in their infancy, automated teller machine (ATM) networks undeveloped, and credit finance, while accepted as a necessity by commercial banks, was treated as a peripheral and somewhat unsavoury product.

The role of the branch was to provide a complete service range to all forms of clients. The branch manager was expected to both operate as administrator, credit assessor (within narrow limits) and to have knowledge of the domestic services provided by the bank. International services were usually provided by specialist international branches. The system tended to be paper based, negative in customer attitude and focus, slow, expensive, and seriously lacking in marketing and selling efforts (see Channon, 1988).

The structure of the industry in the UK had been stable for over fifty years until 1968 when the first major merger occurred between banks with the creation of the National Westminster. In West Germany the major banks were not really interested in retail banking leaving this to the Landesbank, while in France retail custom was approached in a similar manner to the UK. In the USA retail banking was largely provided by small local institutions due to legal constraints at state level on geographic coverage. An exception to this was the state of California where state-wide branching was permitted. This led to the development of large multi-branch institutions such as the Bank of America, while elsewhere retail banking tended to be the province of local community banks. In Japan, the leading city banks were also much more concerned with corporate clients than with personal customers.

By the mid-1970s around the world retail banking could be considered to be a Cinderella business with personal customers tolerated rather than sought after and many poorer customers predominantly serviced by savings banks, mortgage institutions, and the like which tended to be denied access to the bank-dominated clearing systems, usually with the tacit support of central banks. Interest rates were usually fixed in conjunction with the central banks and competition was minimal.

The Impact of Deregulation

In the mid-1970s Citibank, operators of a branch network in New York, questioned the viability of its retail banking operation. At this time it operated some 260 branches and employed 7,000 people. The bank concluded that retail banking could be viable but only if costs were strictly controlled. Customers were carefully segmented to only service profitable accounts and technology was used to substitute for premises and people.

In addition, led by savings and loans banks, it became normal to offer interest on current accounts and to unbundle interest and transaction costs. Moreover, US regulations provided opportunities to non-banks to offer some retail financial services to selected customer groups which were superior to those offered by the banks themselves and at the same time cost less. The most notable of these was the development of the cash management account (CMA), a product developed by Merrill Lynch for retail customers with over US$20,000 in cash or securities. This new account was to revolutionize retail banking (Kolari and Zardkoohi, 1987).

In 1978, US regulations restricted interest rates paid to 5.25 percent while domestic inflation was high and money market rates were running at some 18 percent. In return for a small annual fee the CMA allowed investors to withdraw bank deposits and place them into the account which aggregated the funds into a mutual fund. Money was invested in the capital markets at the going market rate. At the same time investors were provided with a cheque book and a Visa card. To avoid being classified as a bank and thus being subject to the banking regulations, the two services were operated by Bank One of Columbus, Ohio, one of a new breed of emerging, high technology banks.

Investors also received a comprehensive monthly statement of all transactions conducted using the CMA. The statement showed to investors assets held in money market funds, stocks and bonds, dividends and interest received, securities trading, check and credit card transactions, margin loans taken and paid off and interest charged.

Funds placed in the CMA could be in the form of cash, stocks, and bonds. All cash was placed in one of a series of money market funds which paid interest at market rates. All dividends and interest received were automatically swept into the money market funds unless required to cover transactions incurred. If transactions exceeded available cash then this would automatically trigger sales of assets held in money market funds.

By the mid-1990s the repercussion of the CMA and its derivatives had had a major impact on retail banking around the world. Despite its dramatic success, however, even today few banks have sufficiently developed their information technology capabilities to be able to provide a similar product on a fully integrated basis (Snirreff, 1994).

The success of the money market funds forced regulators to relax control on interest rate ceilings. In addition the use of technology allowed banks, and in particular Citibank, to transform the cost structure of the industry and turn retail banking into an increasingly attractive proposition. By the mid-1980s Citibank had reduced its branch network in New York to 220 branches and its staff to 5,000, yet service quality was improved by the introduction of over 500 ATMs. Market share of assets doubled and profitability increased dramatically. This success was soon mirrored elsewhere, as commercial banks began to rediscover the potential of retail banking and turned away from the blind pursuit of the large corporate market.

Retail Market Diversification

By the mid-1990s commercial banks had rapidly increased the range of retail banking products on offer. This had been stimulated by new moves into the market by other non-banks such as retailers, insurance companies, consumer appliance manufacturers, and the like. Uninhibited by regulatory constraint which applied to banks, these institutions often enjoyed a significant cost advantage over the banks as well as in many cases being more innovative and marketing oriented.

Up until the early 1970s most institutions could be classified as operating in distinct sectors with readily definable boundaries. By the mid-1990s there had been a dramatic convergence of all these specialist institutions such that each tended to operate in the others' traditional marketplace.

Thus banks have become heavily involved in mortgage finance while housing specialists have transformed themselves into full retail banks. Retailers offered credit cards, loans, investment products, insurance, and the like. Capital goods manufacturers and automobile producers provided house finance, leasing, trade finance, credit cards, with a company such as General Electric Capital Services being a market leader in some twenty-six financial service industry segments, including being the largest operator of store credit cards in the world. Increasingly it had become more difficult to precisely define a bank except that such institutions were classified by being subject to bank regulatory authorities, while most non-bank retail financial service providers took great pains to avoid being formally classified as banks.

By 1994, British banks were all involved in investment management products, both debit and credit cards, were introducing telephone banking, personal financial advice, consumer loans, a wide variety of deposit products, interest-bearing transaction accounts, an increasingly diverse range of mortgage products and retail share shops. Overall in Europe, where deregulation had proceeded further, banks had strongly entered the market for insurance products notably for life products. Mortgage protection and household insurance were significant areas in non-life. Keen to increase the throughput of their expensive branch networks, the banks had been relatively successful in developing their insurance business. *Bancassurance* or *Allfinanz* was a key element in the developing strategies of many major European banking and insurance groups.

Delivery System Transformation

The traditional vehicle for the delivery of retail banking, the branch network has come under increasing pressure in recent times. This can be attributed to a number of causes. First, the increased diversification of banks has led to specialization, and in particular the separation of corporate and retail banking. As a result, corporate accounts tended to be serviced via specialist corporate branches, and serviced by relationship officers, who are trained to perform a very different task to that of the traditional branch manager. Second, it had become recognized that retail customers did not require a full service range from every branch but rather within a location area simple transaction branches or ATMs could fulfil customer requirements at sharply reduced levels of costs (Prendergast and Marr, 1994). The micromarket concept substitutes low cost, limited service delivery systems within a defined geographic area for full service branches, except where considered essential (Aractingi, 1994).

Third, the role of the branch manager needed to be modified or eliminated by the use of centralized technology. Fourth, further labor savings could be achieved by the use of smart ATMs or in branch machinery and electronic data capture so sharply reducing the number of in branch personnel needed. Fifth, branches had come under serious pressure from alternative delivery systems with dramatically lower costs while also offering customers the opportunity to determine the time and place when they conducted their banking transactions.

These pressures in the mid-1990s were leading an increasing number of banks to rationalize their networks and their employees with little or no loss in customer service or satisfaction. New branch configurations and delivery system combinations are therefore developing rapidly such as the hub and spoke concept (see Channon, 1988). At the same time there had been a rapid move to open plan branch configurations, specialist branches such as mortgage shops, fully automated branches and limited service operations. Despite these efforts, however, the cost of operating branch networks remained high. In the UK the average cost–income ratio for operating a retail branch network was around 55 percent. This compared very unfavorably with a telephone banking operation where nearly all banking services, except cash dispensing, twenty-four hours per day and year round could be provided with a cost–income ratio of as low as 20 percent.

Other Delivery System Alternatives

In addition to telephone banking which by 1995 in the USA already accounted for some 25 percent of transactions, other new delivery systems included smartcards (which can be used as a substitute for cash), smart ATMs, home banking, and virtual reality systems either in branches or via home computer systems. Substantial experimentation was underway around the world in each of these alternative service delivery mechanisms and by the millennium it is expected that the further cost pressure would result in additional sharp rationalization and re-engineering of traditional branch-based banking.

Future Prospects

Retail banking has evolved rapidly since its Cinderella position at the beginning of the 1970s. Technology has resulted in many new non-traditional entrants able to gain competitive advantage, a massive increase in consumer product choice and mode of service delivery, strategic convergence between historically separated financial service providers, separation of corporate from retail banking, a move to electronic versus paper based systems and the adoption of a marketing orientation.

For the future, traditional branch-based retail banking can expect to continue to decline, integrated data bases will permit even more refined customer segmentation and product design, staff numbers will continue to fall as paper-based systems are converted to electronic systems and the customer determines the time, the place, the institution, and the product to be used in retail banking operations.

Bibliography

Aractingi, E. (1994). The next great downsizing initiative. *Journal of Retail Banking*, **16**, 19–22.
Channon, D. F. (1988). *Global banking strategy*. New York: John Wiley.
Kolari, A. & Zardkoohi, A. (1987). *Bank costs, structure and performance*. Lexington, MA: D. C. Heath.
Prendergast, G. & Marr, N. (1994). Towards a branchless banking society. *International Journal of Retail and Distribution Management*, **22**, 18–26.
Snirreff, D. (1994). The metamorphosis of finance. *Euromoney*, **25**, 36–42.

DEREK CHANNON

retail buying   This is concerned with the acquisition by retailers of a suitable range of stock from suppliers for sale within their stores (or in the case of mail order – catalogs). The organization of the function varies widely among retail firms. The retail buying team takes on the role of implementing corporate strategy by offering to the consumer an assortment of goods that is consistent with that strategy. Decisions have to be taken by the buying team concerning the desired quality, price to the consumer, profit levels, and contract terms with suppliers.

The buyer's role is vital in securing a "good" deal that allows the retailer to compete successfully in the market place. This may entail purchasing the goods at the lowest possible price thus allowing greater profits. The buyer needs negotiating skills and an in-depth understanding of the supplier's business. In addition, the buyer should have an understanding, often based on a combination of intuition, experience, and market research, of what the final consumer might buy, often (depending on manufacture and distribution lead times) several months before the goods are available in the high street. In increasingly competitive markets the buyer must also have an eye for something new to offer the consumer.

Buying mistakes can be costly, especially if a chosen product does not sell well or the right price has not been achieved with the manufacturer. This may allow competitors to undercut the retailer's price.

The main responsibilities of the buyer are likely to include product and supplier selection, negotiation, pricing, evaluation of past purchase decisions, market monitoring, and forecasting – depending on the size of the organization and the structure of its buying department.

Buying decisions may be taken individually or in committee, again depending on the individual company. It may be that the decision to move into a new line of merchandise would be taken at board level, leaving the individual product decisions to the buying team.

The role of the buyer is becoming increasingly important within the commercial environment and more sophisticated as levels of competition increase and the consumer becomes more knowledgeable about the products available (McGoldrick, 1990).

Bibliography

Fulop, C. (1964). *Buying by voluntary chains*. London: George Allen & Unwin.

McGoldrick, P. J. (1990). *Retail marketing*. Maidenhead: McGraw-Hill, p. 207.

STEVE WORRALL

retail distribution channels   Retail distribution channels include both store and non-store selling media such as mail order and catalog shopping, home shopping, and teleshopping. These represent the end of the manufacturer–wholesaler–retailer distribution channel and serve consumers directly. In some channels each activity is performed by independent firms but there is a growing trend toward vertical integration, whereby companies are performing more than one level of activity in the channel, e.g., most large grocery retailers, such as Safeway and Aldi, do their own wholesaling and also control physical distribution tasks. Others, such as Marks & Spencer and The Gap, are involved at all levels including product design, manufacture,

and quality testing. "Indeed, Marks and Spencer has been described as a manufacturer without factories" (McGoldrick, 1990).

Vertical integration enables the retailer to make significant cost savings, enhancing the efficiency of the distribution channel through greater control over the planning and operation of the flow of merchandise to the stores. Many retailers are investing in quick response (QR) delivery systems, which are highly efficient inventory management systems. EPOS and EFTPOS collect information concerning the day's sales at store checkouts and relay the data to enormous, highly efficient, and automated warehouse or distribution centers. Here, stock orders are rapidly made up and dispatched to the stores the same or the following day. The enhanced efficiency minimizes the handling of goods, reducing stock damage and shrinkage, and has eliminated the need for large in-store stock rooms, allowing additional store floor area to be devoted to selling activities, e.g., Next, the high street clothing retailer, has a highly efficient EPOS system and a centralized automated distribution network, that have eliminated the need for in-store stock rooms altogether.

Manufacturers' exclusive hold over merchandise production and design matters has gradually been eroded since the 1950s and "[b]ecause of the growing number of regional, national and international retail chains, retailers have more power in the distribution channel than ever before" (Berman & Evans, 1995). The retail multiples' control of the distribution channel stems from their enormous buying power, through which they are able to dictate production terms and prices, driving down manufacturer margins and further strengthening their own position. Even retailers which are smaller in terms of asset base have been able to gain economies of scale, rapid growth, and channel buying power through establishing networks of retail franchises.

O'Reilly (1984) recognized four key economic factors which might reduce the retailers' channel power:

(1) Surplus floor space, arising from rapid expansion.
(2) Intensification of retail competition.
(3) Serious decline in high street property values.
(4) The massive scale of retailers' long-term investment in their distribution systems.

Since 1984, with world recession and continued retail property investment in shopping malls and out-of-town shopping centers, all of these factors have begun to take effect to varying degrees. It remains to be seen whether or not this will impact upon the retailers' control and power in the distribution channel.

The store distribution channel produces by far the main retail sales volume. However, new retail formats and technology associated with the distribution of goods, such as home shopping and interactive teleshopping, dictate that the precise level of distribution assigned to each channel will continue to be dynamic until equilibrium between the different retail distribution channels is reached.

see also **EFTPOS; EPOS; Retail franchises; Wholesalers**

Bibliography

Berman, B. & Evans, J. R. (1995). *Retail management*. Englewood Cliffs, NJ: Prentice-Hall.

McGoldrick, P. J. (1990). *Retail marketing*. Maidenhead: McGraw-Hill.

O'Reilly, A. (1984). Manufacturing versus retailers; the long term winners? *Retail and Distribution Management*, **12**, (3), 40–41.

Rosenbloom, B. (1990). *Marketing channels*. Orlando, FL: The Dryden Press.

STEVE GREENLAND

retail environment   *see* RETAILING

retail franchises   These are franchising grants selling rights within a given geographical area for franchising goods and services. The franchising company provides a recognized brand name, goods, equipment, and services, such as training in merchandising and management, receiving in return a fee or a percentage of turnover, or both. Franchising has a long history but emerged as a major element in retailing during the 1980s when it accounted for around 10 percent of the retail market. This distribution method is continuing to grow in the retail sector due to the numerous advantages franchising has to offer both franchiser and franchisee (Baron & Schmidt, 1991). Facilitating rapid and reduced risk expansion opportunity, franchising has assisted national and international network development for retailers such as Kentucky Fried Chicken, Blockbuster Video, Benetton, and The Body Shop.

Bibliography

Baron, S. & Schmidt, R. A. (1991). Operational aspects of retail franchises. *International Journal of Retail and Distribution Management*, **19**, (2), 13–19.

Morgenstein, M. & Strongin, H. (1992). *Modern retailing*. Englewood Cliffs, NJ: Prentice-Hall.

STEVE GREENLAND

retail image   Retail image refers to the way in which the retailer is perceived by the public. One of the earliest definitions, specifically in relation to retail stores, was provided by Martineau (1958), who describes retailer image as: "the way in which the store is defined in the shopper's mind, partly by its functional qualities and partly by an aura of psychological attributes."

Bibliography

Martineau, P. (1958). The personality of the retail store. *Harvard Business Review*, **36** (1), 47–55.

McGoldrick, P. J. (1990). *Retail marketing*. Maidenhead: McGraw-Hill.

STEVE GREENLAND

retail pricing   This is the process for deciding the price to be charged to the customer for a product or service. This may be a complex activity involving a number of considerations such as the desired profit level; the price charged by competitors; an understanding of what the market will bear; and promotions being run on a particular product. Within a competitive retail market customers tend to be relatively price aware, holding a perception of the price competitiveness of the major retailers.

A number of pricing options are open to the retailer, depending on whether, for example, market penetration, profit maximization, undercutting the competition, or creating a quality image are the desired goals. For most retailers maximizing sales and/or profitability are the key

intentions. In order to achieve this, an understanding of how price will affect demand is required.

The pricing decision cannot be taken in isolation from other MARKETING MIX decisions. A consistent strategy of merchandise choice, promotion/advertising, store location, and pricing should be adopted in order to attract and retain customers.

Once decided, the price charged for a good or service tends to be varied from time to time such as at the "end of season sale," upon the arrival of updated and improved goods, or as a competitive response to the activities of other retailers.

Across many sectors of retailing, the phenomenon of price discounting has come to the fore. This tends to dilute the power of the seasonal "sale" as customers come to expect low prices and adequate levels of service and product quality all year round.

A number of marketing promotions can be offered to the customer based upon the price charged for an item. The "two for the price of one" device is widely used as is the "price promise" where a retailer will promise to beat any price available for the same product elsewhere.

see also **Pricing**

Bibliography

Gabor, A. (1988). *Pricing concepts and methods for effective marketing*, 2nd edn, Aldershot: Gower.

STEVE WORRALL

retailing   This embraces those activities concerned with selling goods or services to the final consumer or another person acting on his/her behalf.

Retailing need not take place exclusively in a shop setting. Home shopping via a printed catalog and mail order is a firmly established phenomenon. Less widely available is television-based shopping through a fiber optic cable, although this continues to grow. The future is likely to see wider use of computer-based shopping "online" with the use of a modem and standard telephone line.

Retailing takes place in many forms. The typical examples include everyday shopping for clothing and food, etc. However, retailing is also the method by which we acquire mortgages or investment policies from banks and building societies. It is also the medium through which dental treatment is received and paid for; airline or concert tickets are booked over the telephone or through an agent; soft drinks are bought from vending machines.

Although highly visible to the consumer on the high street or through catalogs and home shopping systems, the retail industry is heavily involved in a wide range of activities. These include storage, distribution, and selling a product or service at a price that is competitive, of a quality that is appropriate, at a time that is convenient, and at the greatest possible convenience to the customer.

In order to fulfil this role, the most successful retailers have become highly effective in a number of management disciplines, including personnel management, financial control and accounting, LOGISTICS, STRATEGY development, distribution, and MARKETING. In some cases retailers have also become involved in manufacturing.

For a store-based retailer, siting the outlet at the best possible location is a primary concern. In order to achieve high visibility, and thus achieve passing trade, the best store site is likely to be in the high street of a town or in a shopping mall. The better locations tend to command higher rents, leaving the retailer faced with a trade-off between higher operating costs but potentially higher sales. For some stores, notably larger supermarkets and DIY outlets, an "out-of-town" site may be more appropriate given the importance of car-borne trade and the need for large car parking lots. Other retailers may choose to locate in a "retail park;" these tend to include electrical goods superstores, furniture stores, and car accessory retailers.

Retail companies should also develop a strong understanding of their customer profile. By targeting different segments of the population, retailers are able to tailor their offerings closely to the needs of customers. Some retailers may aim themselves at the affluent, fashion-conscious section of society, whereas others appeal to the less well off or the price conscious.

By understanding their customers' socioeconomic background, lifestyles, and beliefs, retailers are able to develop marketing strategies in order to serve their target customers more profitably. Such strategies entail manipulating the various elements of the "MARKETING MIX" to provide an image and service appropriate to the customer. Therefore, merchandise would be selected, pricing levels decided, store interiors designed, and marketing communications developed (advertising, promotions, etc.) to appeal to the target customer.

Retailers' performance in the market place is heavily influenced by the forces within the business environment (see MARKETING ENVIRONMENT). These consist of economic, political, sociocultural, demographic, technological, and physical influences (Kotler, 1988). In recent years, increasing competition and recessionary forces affecting many retail sectors have, in part, led to cost cutting, price reductions, and lowered profits. Other forces include the growing internationalization of retailing, with a number of operators expanding overseas as international trade becomes less restricted. Other issues such as Sunday trading, EPOS and scanning services, legislation affecting part-time workers, and possible planning restrictions on out-of-town sites are likely to continue to impinge on retail activity.

Retail companies are typically organized into chains of stores and may own several hundred outlets across the country all trading under the same "fascia." Other forms of organization include franchise agreements where a trader pays a proportion of his profits to the parent retailer in exchange for trading under his name (e.g., Benetton); concessions involving a retailer trading from a small store sited within a larger store; market traders who pay a local authority for the use of a market stall site; and independent retailers who may own one or two stores (e.g., the traditional corner shop, butcher, or baker).

Non-store retailing through the medium of a printed catalog is also a highly competitive business. In recent years, the quality of such publications has increased dramatically and the manner of trading has vastly improved with better customer service through telephone ordering, credit and debit card payment facilities, easier exchange policies, and quick postal or vehicle delivery. This has been largely due to the innovative practices of companies such as Next, Cotton Traders, and Racing Green, along with a number of overseas operators which have succeeded in selling or giving away catalogs as supplements to Sunday newspapers. Sales agents are still used by some catalog retailers although recruiting, motivating, and retaining such staff has proved difficult.

Bibliography

Ghosh, A. (1990). *Retail management*. Chicago: The Dryden Press.
Kotler, P. (1988). *Marketing management: Analysis, planning, implementation and control*, 6th edn, New York: Prentice-Hall, 135.
Morgenstein, M. & Strongin, H. (1992). *Modern retailing, management principles and practices*, 3rd edn, Prentice-Hall.

STEVE WORRALL

retraining   Retraining refers to teaching individuals the knowledge, skills, and abilities (*see* KSAOs) that will be necessary for them to obtain jobs in new occupations or organizations. In contrast to training, retraining refers to teaching individuals knowledge, skills, and abilities related to jobs outside their current occupations or outside their current organizations. Retraining is frequently used to retool individuals whose career paths (*see* CAREER PATHING) have become obsolete due to changes in technology, to prepare individuals to assume jobs in different industries or organizations after they have been laid off, or to prepare individuals to take new positions after a structural reorganization of the firm has led to the elimination of their present jobs (Leana and Feldman, 1992).

Bibliography

Leana, C. R. & Feldman, D. C. (1992). *Coping with Job Loss: How Individuals, Organizations, and Communities Respond to Layoffs*, New York: McGraw-Hill.

DANIEL C. FELDMAN

revenue recognition, expenses, gains and losses

Revenue Recognition

Early accounting practices focused on the listing of assets and liabilities at periodic intervals. Changes in the values of assets and liabilities were noted directly in these accounts. As the transactions of entities became more numerous and more complex, another method of measuring and explaining the changes in assets and liabilities emerged, resulting in the income statement or statement of operations. Income statements became common only during the current century.

Assets and liabilities are considered real or permanent accounts because they reflect the actual resources of an entity and the claims against those resources. Income statements include the nominal or temporary accounts of revenues, expenses, gains, and losses. These are termed nominal or temporary accounts because they represent explanations of the changes in the real or permanent accounts. Nominal or temporary accounts are closed out at the end of each period after their explanatory purposes have been captured in the income statement. With the development of the income statement, direct measurement of changes in assets and liabilities gave way to indirect measurements guided primarily by concepts of revenue recognition and expense matching. Although not always articulated clearly, the concepts of revenue recognition and expense matching have dominated the measurement of income in practice for several decades.

Revenues are often described as the accomplishments and expenses as the efforts for an operating period. Revenues are defined in US Financial Accounting Standards Board (FASB) Statement of Financial Accounting Concepts No. 6, "Elements of Financial Statements" (1985) (SFAC 6) as, "inflows or other enhancements of assets of an entity or settlements of its liabilities (or a combination of both) from delivering or producing goods, rendering services, or other activities that constitute the entity's ongoing major or central operations" (para. 78). Revenue would result from the sale of merchandise in the typical merchandising or manufacturing entity and the performance of services for organizations such as accounting, engineering, or legal firms.

Judgment is often required to determine the appropriate time period to record revenue. "Revenue recognition" occurs when the revenue is formally recorded in the accounting records. A current explanation of the revenue recognition concept is found in FASB Statement of Financial Accounting Concepts No. 5, "Recognition and Measurement in Financial Statements of Business Enterprises" (1984) (SFAS 5). Paragraph 83 of this document states " . . . recognition involves consideration of two factors: (a) *being realized or realizable* and (b) *being earned*, with sometimes one and sometimes the other being the most important consideration." Realization is the process of an asset being converted to cash or claims to cash. The FASB made an important distinction between revenue realization and revenue recognition. Prior accounting literature often referred to the realization concept using explanations similar to what is now more clearly defined and labeled as the revenue recognition concept.

Revenue Realization

Revenue recognition requires sufficient evidence of revenue realization. This often involves the exercise of judgment although standards have been issued in several areas to guide the judgment process. The point of sale or delivery of product is the most common time where evidence of realization is judged to be sufficient. This has been described by at least one author as the critical event (Myers, 1959). There are numerous exceptions made to the point of sale for revenue recognition especially in specialized industries outside the traditional manufacturing and merchandising entities. Exceptions having a relatively long accounting history include production under construction contracts and the production and acquisition of inventories of precious metals or agricultural products. There are several other exceptions made to the common point of sale with a shorter accounting history in newer industries such as franchising and computer software development. Installment sales, where collection of all of the cash installments is highly uncertain, is another exception where revenue may not be recognized at the point of sale.

The nature of an asset received in a potential revenue transaction can make a difference in determining the state of realization. The receipt of cash or cash equivalents generally is regarded as proof of realization. The receipt of noncash assets inherently represents an earlier state in the realization process, may or may not offer sufficient evidence of realization, and may also create measurement problems concerning the value of the assets received. Notes and accounts receivables are generally viewed as acceptable evidence of the amount of cash to be realized after estimates of uncollectible amounts have been made and, therefore, constitute sufficient realization. In case of extreme uncertainty of collection and insufficient information to estimate the uncollectible amount, realization is not sufficiently assured and the installment method exception of revenue recognition that defers profit to the time of collection may be followed. The receipt of an asset similar to the one given up is generally regarded as proof that realization has not occurred and revenue is typically not recognized. An example would be the exchange of one tract of land for another. US Accounting Principles Board Opinion No. 29, "Accounting for Nonmonetary Transactions" (1973), describes the accounting treatment for this type of exchange transaction.

The second major factor in the recognition of revenue is the earning process. It is commonly understood that all major functions of an entity support the earning process and that the "earning" of income or profit is a continuous process from the acquisition of revenue-producing inputs to the completion of collection and product warranty service activities. Allocation of a portion of the earnings or income to each of these activities would be difficult and arbitrary. For example, there is no natural basis for determining how much of the profit from the sale of an item was "earned" by the efforts of the salesperson versus the efforts of the production foreman. The test for revenue recognition is whether the earning process has been sufficiently completed. As with realization, this requires judgment, although accounting guidelines exist in several areas to guide the judgment process. The point of sale again serves as the most common point where the earning process is judged as sufficiently complete, with follow-up activities such as collection and product warranty service viewed as incidental.

Further consideration of the two major revenue recognition factors of realization and the earning process assist in an understanding of the normal emphasis placed on point of sale as well as the common exceptions noted above. For most manufacturing and merchandising entities the point of sale is the first time that a known exit market value (sales price) exists. The market price is established at that point in a bargained transaction between two parties with an assumed conflict of interest. Typically either cash is transferred or a receivable is established in a fixed amount at that time. As for the earning process, most of the significant activities have been completed by that point. Exceptions are made for production under construction contracts, precious metals, and agricultural products largely because the sales price is either established or highly determinable in advance of sale or delivery and the acquisition and production activities significantly outweigh sale and any other potential subsequent activities.

Revenue and Expense Matching

The recognition of revenue is only the first step in the measurement of net income. The matching of expenses with revenues is the second step. There are three levels of matching. The best matching is achieved where expenses can be directly associated with the resulting revenue. Sales commissions paid to salespersons is an example of such an expense. A second category of expenses is where an association between revenues and expenses is assumed but cannot be determined directly. Depreciation of assets used in the production of revenues and the determination of cost of goods sold using an assumed flow of goods (e.g. FIFO) are examples of this category. This matching is generally referred to as systematic and rational allocation. While depreciation and inventory cost flow methods are systematic, the degree of rationality is often difficult to access in the absence of stated criteria for the selection of a particular method. The third level of matching is typically referred to as period expensing. These expenses are costs that have been determined to have expired during the period of measurement but cannot be associated with the revenue for that period or any other specific period. Administrative salaries and depreciation on office equipment are two examples of expenses in this category.

Many expenses allocated to specific time periods are estimated. Expenses resulting from future costs such as bad debts, product warranty service, and employee retirement are estimated. Expenses determined through systematic and rational allocation of prior costs such as depreciation are also estimated. Determining product costs in a manufacturing process requires many estimates and assumptions.

Gains and losses are also components of net income but are differentiated from revenues and expenses. The primary basis for differentiation lies in the nature of the transaction, event, or circumstance that caused or created the item. Gains and losses are associated with nonoperating peripheral and/or incidental transactions and events. A loss created by damage from a fire or flood, inventory that became unsalable, and assets seized in a foreign country after a revolution are potential examples. A gain or loss from the sale of an operating asset is another example. The use of an operating asset is a central or major continuing activity that creates an expense such as depreciation or maintenance. The sale of an asset normally used in operations is considered to be a peripheral or incidental transaction since an entity does not operate for the purpose of selling its productive assets. Another characteristic of a loss, unlike an expense, is that it represents a cost that expired without producing a benefit.

Gains and losses are determined on a net rather than a gross basis. Due to the influence of conservatism, gains require a higher degree of certainty than losses for recognition to occur. Gains generally need to have been validated by a specific transaction involving the item while the incurrence of losses need only be probable to be recognized. US Financial Accounting Standards Board (FASB) *Statement of Financial Accounting Standard No. 5*, "Accounting for Contingencies" (1975) (SFAS 5), offers guidance on the recognition of contingent gains and losses. Although this standard is not widely criticized, one could argue that the recognition of both gains and losses should be based on the same level of probability without differentiation in treatment.

The FASB has issued several standards providing specific accounting and reporting guidance, including revenue recognition, for certain industries. For example, SFAS 45, "Accounting for Franchise Fee Revenue" (1981), established accounting and reporting standards for the unique circumstances created in franchise agreements. Revenue recognition guidelines are given for both initial and continuing franchise fees. SFAS 48, "Revenue Recognition When Right of Return Exists" (1981), lists six criteria that must be fulfilled before revenue can be recognized when return rights exist. SFAS 50, "Financial Reporting in the Record and Music Industry" (1981), discusses how to account for revenue from license agreements. SFAS 51 "Financial Reporting by Cable Television Companies" (1981), establishes accounting and reporting standards for costs, expenses, and revenues relating to the construction and operation of cable television systems. SFAS 53, "Financial Reporting by Producers and Distributors of Motion Picture Films" (1981), discusses how to account for revenue generated by films licensed to movie theaters and to television. SFAS 60, "Accounting and Reporting by Insurance Enterprises" (1982), offers guidance on accounting for insurance premium revenue. SFAS 63, "Financial Reporting by Broadcasters" (1982), primarily focuses on cost issues but also discusses how to account for barter revenue. SFAS 65 "Accounting for Certain Mortgage Banking Activities," addresses how to account for fees related to mortgage banking. SFAS 66, "Accounting for Sales of Real Estate" (1982), establishes how to recognize revenue and profit from real estate sales.

Although the nine standards identified above address different situations, all are similar in offering specific guidance to assist in determining when the realizability and earnings criteria set forth in SFAC 5 have been met in these specialized situations. For example, SFAS 53 indicates that a film distributor should recognize revenue from films licensed to television when the license period begins and all of the following five conditions have been met: the license fee for each film is known, the cost of each film is known or reasonably determinable, collectibility of the full fee is reasonably assured, each film has been accepted by the licensee in accordance with the agreement, and the film is available for its first showing. Fulfillment of these conditions provides strong evidence of the amount of cash inflows to be received from the license agreement (realization) and the earnings process efforts of the film producer/distributor are deemed to be substantially completed when the film is made available for the first showing.

The exercise of judgment is supported but not eliminated in situations where specific revenue recognition guidelines exist. Revenue recognition is a very broad and pervasive issue in accounting. Specific guidelines do not exist for the majority of circumstances. The measurement and determination of the appropriate point to record revenues often require the exercise of good professional judgment. The revenue recognition criteria set forth in SFAC 5 and specific financial reporting standards are important and valuable guidelines to assist in making these critical judgments. In conjunction with revenue recognition, the proper matching of expenses against revenues is necessary in order to determine net income. Matching criteria assist in arriving at a proper matching of revenues and expenses, but considerable judgment is often required and sometimes arbitrary allocations are necessary. Gains and losses are reasonably clear concepts and are appropriately distinguished from revenues and expenses. The exercise of good professional judgment in accounting for gains and losses is also required, especially in determining the amount and status of a loss.

Bibliography

Myers, J. (1959). The critical event and recognition of net profit. *Accounting Review* Oct. (1959).

JOHN K. SIMMONS

reverse culture shock   When an employee returns to the home country after an extended assignment, he/she (or family members) may be subjected to what many refer to as reverse culture shock. Reverse culture shock occurs because things have changed in the home country. Friends and neighbors have moved, new schools are attended, fellow employees have gone into management or departed the company, the clothing fads are different, music has changed, and numerous other things have changed that the expatriate might have felt would be the same. Culture shock may also be the result of a different standard of living than was achieved in the host country. Often expatriates have servants or chauffeurs for the first time, or a larger home, or any number of other items they will not have access to in the home country.

Reverse culture shock can be anticipated and dealt with by an organization in the same manner as culture shock was anticipated when the employee first moved overseas. Orientation programs for coming home, and mentors or other contacts, can keep the family abreast of changes at home. Good communications allow the employee to be aware of what is happening in the home office.

Bibliography

Black, J. S. & Gregerson, H. B. (1991). When Yankee comes home: Factors relating to expatriate and spouse repatriation adjustment. *Journal of International Business Studies*, 22 (4), 471–94.
Feldman, D. C. & Thompson, H. B. (1993). Expropriation, repatriation, and domestic geographical relocation: An empirical investigation of adjustment to new job assignments. *Journal of International Business Studies*, 24 (3), 507–30.
Moran, R. T. (1989). Coping with re-entry shock. *AGSIM Faculty Publication*, No. 89–05.
Napier, N. K. & Peterson, R. B. (1990). Expatriate reentry: What do repatriates have to say? *Human Resource Planning*, 14, 19–28.

JOHN O'CONNELL

reward systems   Also known as compensation systems and pay systems, reward systems refer to outcomes that an individual receives in an organization. Such outcomes occur in a variety of types. For example, *extrinsic* rewards include wages, salaries, BONUSES and fringe benefits (insurance, health care, retirement plan, and so forth). *Intrinsic* rewards include praise, recognition, esteem, self-competence, and so forth. To enhance organizational effectiveness, reward systems should be designed to reinforce organizational objectives. Thus, they are tied to and should be integrated with the processes of setting goals and evaluating performance.

Reward systems can contribute to the organization's effectiveness in three ways: (a) the reward system can help attract the best human assets to the firm; (b) the reward system can help retain good performers; (c) the reward system can motivate to affect performance.

Reward systems reflect one of two underlying organizational cultures or orientations about rewards. The first is a *performance culture*, also referred to as PAY FOR PERFOR-

MANCE and merit-based systems. These can occur at the individual level (piece rate or bonus/commission plans), group level (profit centers, cost reduction sharing), and plant or company level (PROFIT SHARING, SCANLON PLAN). Performance culture reward systems link intrinsic and extrinsic rewards to measured outcomes of individuals, groups, or the organization. These outcomes should reflect individual, group, or organizational level goals. In this culture, a larger percentage of an employee's pay is at risk.

A second culture or orientation about rewards is the *entitlement culture*. In this system, rewards are distributed based on factors such as seniority, job level or grade, education, or training. Persons meeting certain levels of each factor receive predetermined levels of reward for that factor. In this culture, a smaller proportion of the employee's pay is at risk.

Bibliography

Henderson, R. I. & Risher, H. W. (1987). Influencing organizational strategy through compensation leadership. *New Perspectives on Compensation*, Eds. Balkin, D. B. & Gomez-Mejia, L. R. Englewood Cliffs, NJ: Prentice-Hall.
Kerr, J. L. (1988). Strategic control through performance appraisal and rewards. *Human Resource Planning*, 11, 215–24.
Lawler, E. E. III (1984). The strategic design of reward systems. *Readings in Personnel and Human Resource Management*, Eds. Schuler, R. S. & Youngblood, S. A. St Paul, MN: West Publishing.
Markham, S. E. (1988). Pay-for-performance dilemma revisited: empirical example of the importance of group effects. *Journal of Applied Psychology*, 172–80.
Newman, J. M. (1987). Selecting incentive plans to complement organizational strategy. *New Perspectives on Compensation*, Eds. Balkin, D. B. & Gomez-Mejia, L. R. Englewood Cliffs, NJ: Prentice-Hall.

STEVE H. BARR

rewards   Theories of MOTIVATION seek to explain and predict the direction, intensity, and persistence of behavior (Kanfer, 1990). In other words, what does a person choose to do, how hard does s/he work at it, and for how long? These motivational outcomes are typically thought (e.g., Vie theory) to be a function of both the person (e.g., values) and the environment (e.g., perceived rewards and their perceived likelihood), and whether an aspect of the environment is perceived as a reward depends on the person's VALUES. Therefore, it is somewhat difficult (perhaps even misleading) to speak in terms of general taxonomies of rewards because they tell us only what people, on average, find rewarding, and may not be terribly accurate for understanding what different individuals find rewarding.

Many different literatures have something to say about what people generally find rewarding. Content theories of motivation such as Maslow's need hierarchy theory and Alderfer's existence, relatedness, and growth theory identify hierarchies of needs ranging from physiological and safety up through esteem and self-actualization. Herzberg's motivation–hygiene theory focuses on identifying factors that either contribute to satisfaction or help avoid dissatisfaction.

The literature on JOB SATISFACTION and its measurement has built on such theories to identify a number of specific reward areas. The Job Descriptive Index (JDI; Smith, Kendall, & Hulin, 1969) asks about the work itself (e.g., routine, satisfying), pay, promotion opportunities, supervision, and coworkers. The Minnesota Satisfaction Questionnaire (MSQ; Weiss, Dawis, England, & Lofquist, 1967) asks about these and other facets of satisfaction. The pay dimension has been further broken down by Heneman and Schwab (1985) in the Pay Satisfaction Questionnaire, which measures pay structure–administration, and benefits.

A good deal of work has also gone into developing instruments to measure work-related values for use in predicting occupational choice (*see* CAREER CHOICE), job satisfaction, and worker satisfactoriness (i.e., performance). Dawis (1991) summarizes five such scales, including the Minnesota Importance Questionnaire (MIQ). The MIQ measures the value attached to ability utilization, achievement, activity, advancement, authority, company policies and practices, compensation, coworkers, CREATIVITY, independence, moral VALUES, recognition, responsibility, security, social service, social STATUS, supervision – human relations, supervision – technical, variety, and working conditions.

Finally, studies of job choice and job preferences suggest at least two factors that influence the rank ordering of importance people attach to rewards. First, self-reports of reward preference often yield different results than less direct assessments methods such as policy capturing (e.g., Zedeck, 1977). For example, money is typically found to be very important when a policy-capturing methodology is used, but less important when self-reports are used. One explanation is that self-reports are more subject to social desirability bias (Schwab, Rynes, & Aldag, 1987) and money tends to be seen as a more pedestrian, less noble sounding value than are some others (e.g., challenge). Another finding from the job choice and preference literature is that the measured importance of a reward depends on its variability (Rynes, Schwab, & Heneman, 1983). Therefore, if companies all have the same pay, but have different advancement opportunities, pay will not be an important factor in job choice, but advancement opportunities will matter in such choices. Pay is not unimportant, but its importance in the decision only comes to light if there is sufficient variance in pay.

Although it is difficult to take these diverse and rich literatures and boil their findings down into a short list of key rewards, one such list is as follows (Noe, Hollenbeck, Gerhart, & Wright, 1994):

Pay level – A person's job is typically the primary source of his or her income.
Challenge and responsibility – For many people, work plays an important role in establishing their self-concepts.
Job security (see JOB LOSS*)* – Work force reductions in the United States have become commonplace, making this an increasingly important concern among employees.
Advancement opportunities – The opportunity to advance one's career and move on to new challenges is attractive to most people.
Geographic location – Dual career and other family issues often mean that choice and flexibility with respect to work location is important (*see* NONWORK/WORK).
Benefits – Health care, retirement income, and so forth, are major factors in ensuring employee health and income security.

Additional rewards – This preceding list obviously excludes a great many factors that are likely to be important to significant segments of the population. Some of these were discussed previously.

see also **Pay for performance**

Bibliography

Dawis, R. V. (1991). Vocational interests, values, and preferences. In M. D. Dunnette & L. M. Hough (Eds), Handbook of industrial and organizational psychology, (2nd edn, vol. 2) Palo Alto, CA: Consulting Psychologists Press.
Heneman, H. G. III & Schwab, D. P. (1985). Pay satisfaction: Its multidimensional nature and measurement. International Journal of Psychology, 20, 129–141.
Kanfer, R. (1990). Motivation theory and industrial and organizational psychology. In M. D. Dunnette & L. M. Hough (Eds), Handbook of industrial and organizational psychology, (2nd edn, vol. 1) Palo Alto, CA: Consulting Psychologists Press.
Noe, R. A., Hollenbeck, J. R., Gerhart, B. & Wright, P. M. (1994). Human resource management: Gaining a competitive advantage. Burr Ridge, IL: Austen Press/Irwin.
Rynes, S. L., Schwab, D. P. & Heneman, H. G. III (1983). The role of pay and market pay variability in job application decisions. Organizational Behavior and Human Performance, 31, 353–364.
Schwab, D. P., Rynes, S. L. & Aldag, R. J. (1987). Theories and research on job search and job choice. In K. Rowland & G. Ferris (Eds), Research in personnel and human resources management, (vol. 5, pp. 129–166). Greenwich, CT: JAI Press.
Smith, P. C., Kendall, L. & Hulin, C. L. (1969). The measurement of satisfaction in work and retirement. Chicago: Rand McNally.
Weiss, D. J., Dawis, R. V., England, G. W. & Lofquist, L. H. (1967). Manual for the Minnesota satisfaction questionnaire. (Bulletin No. 22) Minneapolis: University of Minnesota, Minnesota Studies in Vocational Rehabilitation.
Zedeck, S. (1977). An information processing model and approach to the study of motivation. Organizational Behavior and Human Performance, 18, 47–77.

BARRY GERHART

right of establishment   Right of establishment provides those parties having direct foreign investments with the same protections offered to domestic investors. This means a foreign investor has the right to establish control over a firm in a host country under the same protections (legal and otherwise) as are afforded to a citizen of that country.

see also **National treatment**

JOHN O'CONNELL

right to work   Section 14(b) of the US National Labor Relations Act allows states to prohibit unions from negotiating collective bargaining agreements that require workers to become union members to obtain or retain employment. Proponents of state right to work laws argue that workers should be allowed to choose freely whether to join a union or not. Because unions are legally obligated to represent members and nonmembers equally, unionists argue that right to work laws unfairly allow nonmembers to receive the benefits of unionization (e.g. negotiated wage increases) without incurring any costs (e.g. union dues). As of 1995, 21 states had such laws.

Bibliography

Haggard, T. R. (1977). Compulsory Unionism, the NLRB, and the Courts: a Legal Analysis of Union Security Agreements,, Philadelphia: The Wharton School, Industrial Research Unit.

Kuhn, J. W. (1961). Right to work: symbol or substance? *Industrial and Labor Relations Review*, 14, 587–94.

JOHN T. DELANEY

rights arbitration   Rights (grievance) arbitration is the type of ARBITRATION that stems from employee rights negotiated and written in COLLECTIVE BARGAINING agreements. These rights accrue to employees by the fact that they are employees in positions covered under the collective bargaining agreement; in other words, they are BARGAINING UNIT employees.

Typically the final step in the GRIEVANCE PROCEDURE involves rights arbitration, which takes place in a hearing before a neutral arbitrator selected by the parties. At the hearing the union advocate and management advocate present their respective positions through evidence provided by witnesses and documents related to the relevant contract language and the issue being decided by the arbitrator. At the conclusion of the hearing, the parties decide whether to present oral closing arguments or submit a post-hearing brief (a written version of the facts, relevant contract language, arguments supported by arbitral authority, rebuttals to the opposite party's position, and the requested decision of the arbitrator). The arbitrator then studies the evidence presented by the parties and makes a decision based on the relevant contract language in the collective bargaining agreement and the evidence presented by the parties.

The rights arbitration procedure is considered a peaceful and effective mechanism for resolving disputes that arise during the life of a collective bargaining agreement and is a substitute for the STRIKE by the union and the lockout by the employer. Rights arbitration is an example of workplace self-governance in that the parties themselves design the system which best fits their needs. The parties determine whether there will be a single arbitrator or a board of arbitrators and whether to have a permanent or *ad hoc* (for only one case) arbitrator(s). They also define the authority of the arbitrator by negotiating an arbitration clause in the collective bargaining agreement and by defining the issue to be presented to the arbitrator prior to presenting the evidence at the hearing. The arbitrator interprets the contract language that the parties have negotiated to apply to their workplace. The parties themselves select the arbitrator who will rule on the evidence which the parties present through witnesses and documents. The Code of Professional Responsibility for Arbitrators in Labor–Management Disputes has been established by the National Academy of Arbitrators and the major appointing agencies to govern behavior of arbitrators and their relationships with the union and management. The appointing agencies are the American Arbitration Association, the Federal Mediation and Conciliation Service, and the National Mediation Service.

The arbitrator's decision is usually written and includes the facts in the case, the issue(s) presented, the relevant contract provisions, positions of the parties, analysis of the parties' evidence and positions, and the final decision. Arbitrator decisions are rarely overturned by appeal to the courts as long as the arbitrator bases his or her decision on the contract language and evidence presented.

After decades of experience with rights arbitration in the USA, arbitral standards and guidelines have been developed for arbitral decision making (see bibliography). These include burden of proof, levels of proof, past practice, intent of the parties, and so forth, which guide the arbitrator's decision-making. About 10 percent of the decisions submitted by the arbitrators to the major reporting services (*Labor Arbitration Reports* by Bureau of National Affairs and *Labor Arbitration Awards* by Commerce Clearing House) are published.

Because of its success in the union–management arena, rights arbitration has been introduced in the nonunion sector through employee-promulgated arbitration. This type of arbitration typically occurs in situations where the employee handbook specifies that termination will be only for just cause and/or where arbitration is used for resolving conflicts over statutory claims, such as employment discrimination on the basis of age, disability, race, or gender. In these types of cases, rights arbitration is considered more of a substitute for a court trial than a substitute for a strike or lockout. In some cases, the introduction of employer-promulgated arbitration is viewed as a union avoidance instrument or union substitution device.

Bibliography

Bornstein, T. & Gosline, A. (Eds) (1990). *Labor and Employment Arbitration*, New York: Matthew Bender.
Cooper, L. & Nolan, D. R. (1994). *Labor Arbitration: a Coursebook*, St Paul, MN: West Publishing.
Elkouri, F & Elkouri, E. A. (1985). *How Arbitration Works*, **4th edn**, Washington, DC: Bureau of National Affairs.
Schoonhoven, R. J. (Ed.) (1991). *Fairweather's Practice and Procedure in Labor Arbitration*, **3rd edn**, Washington, DC: Bureau of National Affairs.
Zack, A. M. (Ed.) (1984). *Arbitration in Practice*, Ithaca, NY: Cornell University.

WILLIAM H. HOLLEY

risk analysis   Risk can be simply defined as exposure to change. It is the probability that some future event, or set of events, will occur. Hence, risk analysis involves the identification of potential adverse changes and the expected impact on the organization or portfolio as a result. There are many types of risk to which organizations can be exposed, some that are more easily identified and quantified and others that seem beyond control. A few of the more common risks that require analyses and management include price (or market) risks, credit (or default) risks, legal and regulatory risks, and operational risks.

When evaluating risks, a deviation in an outcome from that which is expected is not necessarily for the worse. In fact, with unbiased expectations, propitious deviations are just as likely as unfavorable ones. Nevertheless, downside risks, or the possibilities of unwanted outcomes, are typically of greatest interest to analysts. For example, in the first half of 1986, world oil prices plummeted, falling by more than 50 percent. While this was a boon to the economy as a whole, it was disastrous to oil producers and companies that supply machinery and equipment to energy industry producers. How could companies that are sensitive to changes in oil prices manage the risks associated with a downward plunge in the price of oil?

Generally speaking, there are three different ways to manage financial risks: purchase insurance, proactively manage the firm's assets and liabilities, and hedging. These approaches are not mutually exclusive; they can be used alone or in conjunction with one or both of the other two approaches.

The first approach, buying insurance, is only viable for certain types of financial risk: predictable risks whose probabilities can be assessed with a fairly high degree of certainty. Insurable risks typically include the risk of loss from fire, theft, or other disaster. Insured organizations pay an insurance premium for the removal of the risk. In effect, the insured risks of many individual firms are transferred to the insurer, but, because the individual risks are not highly correlated (that is, they are unsystematic) the insurer's per firm risk is quite small. In other words, since the risks are independent of one another, the premiums received from all the firms tend to offset the payments to the firms that suffer a loss. This is a simple application of portfolio theory.

The second approach to managing financial risks involves the careful balancing of a firm's assets and liabilities so as to meet the firm's objectives and minimize its risk exposure. The key to using this approach is holding the right combination of on-balance sheet assets and liabilities. Ideally, asset/liability management should strive to match the timing and the amount of cash inflows from assets with the timing and the amount of cash outflows from liabilities. However, precisely matching cash flows can be extremely difficult and expensive. Therefore, firms should concentrate instead on making the value difference between assets and liabilities as insensitive to exogenous shocks as possible. This is commonly referred to as portfolio immunization.

The final approach, hedging, involves the taking of offsetting risk positions. This is similar to asset/liability management except that hedging usually involves off-balance sheet positions. A hedge is a position that is taken as a temporary substitute for a later position in another asset (liability) or to protect the value of an existing position in an asset (liability) until the position can be liquidated. The financial tools most often used for hedging are forwards, futures, options, and swaps. Collectively, these tools are commonly referred to as derivative instruments, or derivative contracts.

The appropriate approach to managing financial risks depends on the complexity of the risks and the sophistication of the risk manager. Risks that are insurable and more easily priced can be managed by purchasing insurance. However, most financial risks are not insurable. Thus, risk managers often employ either asset/liability management techniques or hedging strategies. While these two approaches to risk management are similar, the former usually involves on-balance sheet positions and the latter off-balance sheet activities. However, hedging strategies are often superior to asset/liability management activities because they can be implemented quicker and often do not require the sacrifice of better, more profitable, opportunities.

Bibliography

Fabozzi, F. J. & Zarb, F. G. (1986). *Handbook of financial markets: Securities, options and futures.* Homewood, IL: Dow Jones-Irwin.
Knight, F. H. (1921). *Risk, uncertainty and profit.* New York: Houghton Mifflin.
Smith, C. W., Jr. (1995). Corporate risk management: theory and practice. *Journal of Derivatives*, 3, 21–30.

THOMAS F. SIEMS

risk aversion Decisions involving risk are modeled as lotteries consisting of a set of possible outcomes and a probability distribution across these outcomes. In this environment, optimal decisions depend not only upon the outcomes and their associated probabilities, but also upon a decision-maker's attitude toward risk. An agent is said to be risk averse if he prefers the expected value of a lottery to the lottery itself.

For example, consider a simple lottery of flipping a coin for which one receives $20 if the coin turns up "heads" and $0 if the coin is a "tails." The mathematical expectation or expected value of this lottery is $10. Facing a choice between the coin flip or accepting $10 with perfect certainty, a risk-averse agent will strictly prefer the certain $10. In fact, a risk-averse agent will accept some amount less that $10 rather than accepting the coin flip. The amount with which the agent is indifferent to the lottery is the certainty equivalent of the lottery.

In contrast, an agent who strictly prefers the coin flip to the certain $10 is said to be risk-preferring. A decision maker who is indifferent between the two prospects is said to demonstrate risk neutrality.

The primary framework for the analysis of choices involving risk is the expected utility hypothesis associated with von Neumann and Morgenstern (1944). In their theory, if an agent meets certain rationality axioms, then his preferences over outcomes may be characterized by a continuous utility function. Then, an agent will evaluate lotteries in terms of expected utility rather than expected value. If an agent is risk averse, his utility function will be concave in income. In contrast, risk-preferring and risk-neutral agents have utility functions which are convex and linear respectively.

Since attitude toward risk is subjective, it is not surprising that agents may differ in the degree of risk aversion. Since risk-averse agents have concave utility functions, one might expect the curvature of the utility function to relate to the degree of risk aversion. Following Arrow (1971) and Pratt (1964), risk aversion may be measured by the following coefficient of absolute risk aversion, ARA:

$$ARA = -u''/u'$$

where u'' is the second derivative of the utility function with respect to income and u' is the first derivative. This coefficient is a measure of the concavity of the utility function that is scaled to be invariant to linear transformation of the utility function. Friedman and Savage (1948) argue that individuals may be risk-averse over some ranges of wealth while risk-preferring over other ranges. Empirical evidence suggests that most individuals become less risk averse as their income increases.

Risk aversion has a crucial role in the theory of both insurance and financial securities markets. Insurance markets exist so that risk-averse agents may spread their risk among market participants. That insurance purchasers are willing to pay premiums in excess of the expected value of their losses demonstrates their risk aversion. In financial markets, investors require a higher return from risky securities. The latter example shows that risk aversion does not imply that an individual will not accept risky propositions, but rather that they will require additional compensation to do so.

Bibliography

Arrow, K. J. (1971). *Essays in the Theory of Risk-Bearing*. Amsterdam: North-Holland.

Friedman, M. Savage L. J. (1948). The utility analysis of choices involving risk. *Journal of Political Economy*, **56**, 279–304.

Pratt, J. (1964). Risk aversion in the small and in the large. *Econometrica*, **32** , 122–36.

von Neumann, J. Morgenstern, O. (1944). *Theory of Games and Economic Behavior*. Princeton: Princeton University Press.

ROGER TUTTEROW

role   A role is a delineation of the set of recurrent behaviors appropriate to a particular position in a social system (*see* SYSTEMS THEORY). The social system may range from an informal group to a formal organization. Every social system consists of multiple interdependent positions, each defined by a role. Roles specify many aspects of these relationships, including the authority and STATUS relationships within the system. As with social systems, roles can be informal or formal. Informal roles may evolve or be negotiated as a social system such as a group develops. In work organizations, formal roles are often specified by JOB DESCRIPTIONS.

Roles help us to determine what we should do in order to meet others' expectations, as well as what to expect from others. They are specific to particular positions within particular social systems. Although a person may belong to many different groups and organizations, the role an individual occupies in one social system may be completely different from the role that same individual occupies in other social systems. Furthermore, an individual may occupy more than one role within the same social system.

There are many examples of relatively generic roles that exist in most organizations. The role of boss (i.e., superior, supervisor, manager, etc.) delineates many recurrent behaviors such as evaluating, rewarding, correcting, disciplining, and generally overseeing the work of sub-ordinates in an assertive manner. Likewise, subordinates are expected to behave respectfully and responsively toward their bosses. A person in the role of mentor is expected to be nurturing, patient, and helpful (*see* MENTORING PROGRAMS). A secretary's role includes behaving courteously and in a businesslike manner. While these general roles are fairly universal, many organizational roles delineate much more specific behaviors. However, the exact content of specific role behaviors depends on the particular organization in which the roles are located. For example, a manager in the marketing department of a particular organization may be expected to communicate weekly with a particular production manager, send a summary report to the vice-president of marketing every other week, oversee and evaluate the work of six marketing assistant managers, and entertain certain customers of the company once a month. These specific expectations are unique to the role occupied by the marketing manager in this particular organization.

Because people occupy multiple roles within their social systems, they frequently experience ROLE CONFLICT, when the expectations specified by a person's multiple roles are incompatible. Professionals in organizations often experience role conflict. For example, a corporate lawyer may feel pressures to behave in differing ways from her dual roles as member of the legal profession and employee of the corporation. This latter case is an example of interrole conflict in which there exist incongruent expectations from members of two different role sets. This is distinct from intrarole conflict, which occurs when incongruent expectations are present within a single role set.

Role conflict is one of several role-related concepts that facilitate an understanding of the phenomenon of performing a role. Closely related to role conflict is ROLE AMBIGUITY, which is uncertainty about what is expected regarding role performance. Role ambiguity is minimized when role differentiation occurs. Role differentiation refers to the establishment of clear definitions for group members of their specific duties and responsibilities to the group, and how these duties and responsibilities contribute to the realization of the group's goals. Ideally, organizations will go beyond simply making sure that each member have a role and know what it entails. The roles assigned to group members should also maximize each individual's opportunities to contribute to the objectives of the individual and the social system.

Kahn, Wolfe, Quinn, Snoek, and Rosenthal (1964; see also Katz & Kahn, 1966) constructed a comprehensive theoretical development of roles. In this conceptualization, each role is surrounded by a role set which is the collection of people who are concerned with the performance of the occupant of the role. Role episodes consist of role sending, role receiving, and role expectations. When the expectations associated with a particular role are overwhelming to the occupant of the role, ROLE OVERLOAD occurs. Alternatively, role underload results when there are too few role demands (*see also* ROLE OVER/UNDERLOAD).

Together these role-related concepts form ROLE THEORY. Role theory is closely related to situated identity theory, which posits that people learn about their role by taking the perspective of others in their role set (Mead, 1934). Because everyone undertakes this process, a mutual understanding develops about what each person's role is. This perspective emphasizes the interpersonal nature of roles; because roles are defined by the expectations of others, conceptually they are in interpersonal phenomenon (Gerth & Mills, 1967). This is true even though roles are often studied with the individual as the unit of analysis.

The concept of role has been very useful to researchers theoretically, but formulating hypotheses about roles requires a specification of which conditions surrounding the role are to be tested. A role is difficult to operationalize without narrowing the inquiry to specific types of role conditions. Thus, research on roles has generally taken the form of looking for correlates of role conditions. Role conditions refer to the role conflict or role ambiguity associated with the role, role overload and role underload, and the other specific concepts discussed above. Research in several domains of organizational behavior are relevant to roles, for example, research on perception, COMMUNICATIONS, and expectancies. Even though research on these latter topics is not necessarily couched in terms of roles, there are clear connections between these phenomena and role theory.

There are several directions in which research on role conditions could usefully progress. Surprisingly, even after hundreds of studies on various role conditions, there is still debate about the definition of constructs and how best to measure them (King & King, 1990). It is promising that several researchers have been working on conceptually and operationally disentangling these role conditions. As convergence is reached on how to define accurately and measure these constructs, the findings from previous research on correlates of role conditions can be pooled together to determine the robustness of these findings (Jackson & Schuler, 1985). As relationships between role conditions and personal and organizational characteristics are determined to be robust, it will be useful to investigate factors that moderate and mediate these relationships to further specify the boundary conditions under which these effects are strongest (see Pierce, Gardner, Dunham, & Cummings (1993) for an example of this type of research).

Because of the interpersonal nature of roles and role conditions, integrating the study of networks with the study of roles may increase our understanding of roles within the broader social system. For example, early theorizing on roles suggested that there are objective role conditions and subjective (or perceived) role conditions, but little empirical research investigates the match between objective and subjective role conditions. Network analysis could shed light on how expectations from other people in the role set match the perceived expectations of the person occupying the role. Similarly, network methods could be used to determine how formal organizational roles (defined by JOB DESCRIPTIONS, for example) match the informal roles that develop in organizations.

Several current organizational trends may dramatically affect the expectations, and thus the role conditions, of organizational members. For example, how does organizational demography affect role conditions in an increasingly diverse workforce? How does technology, especially regarding communication, affect how role expectations are sent and received? New roles are beginning to emerge in many organizations for people who are technologically proficient. An example of a behavior that is expected from someone in this type of role is to disseminate information about new technologies to less proficient members of the organization. These emerging roles are especially important because surprising degrees of status and power may accompany them. Another important question is how organizational restructuring and the increased use of temporary employees affect the expectations of employees and the patterns of role relationships within organizations. Decreased loyalty to the organization may result in people attaching more importance to their roles outside the organization, especially when role conflict occurs. These issues highlight the importance of furthering our understanding of how roles affect behavior in organizations.

see also **Attribution; Managerial behavior; Stress**

Bibliography

Gerth, H. & Mills, C. (1967). Institutions and persons. In J. G. Manis & B. N. Meltzer (Eds), Symbolic interaction: A reader in social psychology. Boston: Allyn & Bacon.

Jackson, S. & Schuler, R. (1985). A meta-analysis and conceptual critique of research on role ambiguity and role conflict in work settings. Organizational Behavior and Human Decision Processes, **49**, 8–104.

Kahn, R., Wolfe, D., Quinn, R., Snoek, J. & Rosenthal, R. (1964). Organizational stress: Studies in role conflict and ambiguity. New York: Wiley.

Katz, D. & Kahn, R. (1966). The social psychology of organizations. New York: Wiley.

King, L. & King, D. (1990). Role conflict and role ambiguity: A critical assessment of construct validity. Psychological Bulletin, **107**, 48–64.

Mead, G. (1934). Mind, self and society. Chicago: University of Chicago Press.

Pierce, J., Gardner, D., Dunham, R. & Cummings, L. (1993). Moderation by organization based self-esteem of role condition-employee response relationships. Academy of Management Journal, **36**, 271–288.

JEFFREY T. POLZER

role ambiguity This denotes uncertainty about the expectations, behaviors, and consequences associated with a particular ROLE. Specifically, a person has a need to know others' expectations of the rights, duties, and responsibilities of the role, the behaviors that will lead to fulfillment of these expectations, and the likely consequences of these role behaviors. Role ambiguity results when these three types of information are nonexistent or inadequately communicated. Organizational factors (e.g., rapidly changing organizational structures, job FEEDBACK systems) and individual factors (e.g., INFORMATION PROCESSING biases) may cause role ambiguity. Consequences of role ambiguity may include tension, job dissatisfaction, and TURNOVER. It is useful to distinguish objective role ambiguity from the subjective role ambiguity experienced by the person in the role. A JOB DESCRIPTION is an example of a formal organizational mechanism that may alleviate role ambiguity. Kahn, Wolfe, Quinn, Snoek, and Rosenthal (1964), were the first to extensively develop these elements of role ambiguity within an organizational context. Research indicates that role ambiguity is positively correlated with both ANXIETY and propensity to leave (the role) and negatively correlated with several factors such as organizational COMMITMENT, work involvement, and JOB SATISFACTION.

see also **Job characteristics; Stress: Uncertainty**

Bibliography

Kahn, R., Wolfe, D., Quinn, R., Snoek, J. & Rosenthal, R. (1964). Organizational stress: Studies in role conflict and ambiguity. New York: Wiley.

JEFFREY T. POLZER

role conflict This is the experience of contradictory, incompatible, or competing role expectations. It occurs when an individual has two or more salient roles in a situation which include expectations to act in incompatible ways (inter-role conflict), or when expectations within one role are incompatible with each other (intra-role conflict). CONFLICT between a role and an individual's values or beliefs is also referred to as role conflict. Role conflict is often assumed to be an uncomfortable state. Current research focuses on characteristic role conflicts like those between family and work, union member and family breadwinner, and foreign and native cultures; situations that evoke role conflict; the resolution of role conflict; and the evolution of roles within an individual's life. Meta-analyses (*see* VALIDITY GENERALIZATION) have shown role conflict to be "moderately" (r = 0.30) related to dissatisfaction with job content and coworkers (*see* JOB SATISFACTION) and with turnover.

Many studies rely on an eight-item scale, *The Role Conflict Scale*, developed by Rizzo, House, and Lirtzman (1970). Studies of its construct validity have concluded it has adequate validity.

see also **Job design; Role; Stress**

Bibliography

Rizzo, J. R., House, R. J. & Lirtzman, S. I. (1970). Role conflict and ambiguity in complex organizations. Administrative Science Quarterly, 15, 150–163.

CATHERINE A. RIORDAN

role distancing   This is behavior (e.g., explanations, apologies, or joking) undertaken by the occupant of a ROLE with the intent of communicating to others that the individual's actions should be attributed to the role rather than to the individual. The person's intention is to create or maintain separateness between herself and the role. The individual is not denying her occupancy of the role; instead, the individual is denying that she would act the same way if it were not for the role. The most likely cause of role distancing is the pressure exerted from another role to act inconsistently from the expectations of the first role (i.e., ROLE CONFLICT). Role distancing behaviors suggest that the individual has some resistance to the role. An example of role distancing is when a teacher explains to students that his disciplinary actions for the student's inappropriate behaviors are not due to him being a mean person, but instead are due to his role as a teacher. The concept of role distancing is embedded in the field of sociology and is most comprehensively developed in Erving Goffman's book *Encounters* (1961).

see also **Attribution**

Bibliography

Goffman, E. (1961). *Encounters: Two studies in the sociology of interaction.* Indianapolis: Bobbs-Merrill.

JEFFREY T. POLZER

role over/underload   Role overload occurs when an individual experiences excessive role demands. *Quantitative* overload is when there is too much to do. *Qualitative* overload is when the individual does not have the experience or ability to carry out role demands. Having more than one demanding role at the same time, like parent and professional, or a job position which includes many weighty responsibilities, are two frequently researched examples. Role underload is the opposite condition in which the individual has very few role demands, or the demands are very easily accomplished. Underload can also be quantitative or qualitative.

Both overload and underload are job stressors. They, in conjunction with other job stressors and the amount of control individuals feel they have over job demands, have been found to be predictive of STRESS-related illness. Anecdotal accounts of death from overwork ("karoshi") have come from Japan. The relationship of overload and underload to organizational variables like ABSENTEEISM, JOB SATISFACTION and accidents is inconsistent, probably affected by other moderating variables. Burnout and "rustout" are believed to be potential consequences of overload and underload, respectively. Time management techniques are used to deal with problems of quantitative overload.

see also **Role**

Bibliography

Lazarus, R. S. & Folkman, S. (1984). Stress, appraisal and coping. New York: Springer-Verlag.

CATHERINE A. RIORDAN

roles and role morality   Roles are positions in business or the professions to which different social functions attach; role morality is the assumption of different normative ethical systems for different roles. The central issue here is whether different social roles require distinct norms or moral frameworks to guide their behavior. For there to be truly distinct role moralities, it is not sufficient that those in different social roles or professions enter into unique relations with others. All social roles involve relations that uniquely define them to be the roles they are. Instead, moral considerations that arise elsewhere must be weighed differently, must be systematically augmented or diminished in their weight, against opposing considerations in proper moral deliberations in these social contexts. An occupant of the role, for example a lawyer or business manager, must be called upon to ignore certain moral rights, or certain utilities or disutilities, that would otherwise be morally decisive.

Often such special norms reflect some value central to the definition of the social role in question, and the norm gives that value extra weight for the occupant of the role. Lawyers are called upon to ignore the interests of third parties in zealously pursuing the legal objectives of their clients within the bounds of law. Journalists routinely ignore what others might properly perceive as rights to privacy in developing news stories for their reading publics. In business, the central values lie in efficient use of resources in providing desired goods to the consuming public and in providing stockholders a good return on their investments. Thus, some have argued (e.g. Friedman, 1979) that business managers ought not to forgo profit (which measures efficiency and provides returns) on perceived moral grounds.

From the point of view of moral theory, however, the basic question is how such special norms can be morally acceptable, how the concept of distinct role moralities is even coherent. From the point of view of a rights based or individualist moral theory, it seems that we can override moral rights only for the sake of protecting more central or important rights in the context in question. Otherwise, rights must be voluntarily waived or previously forfeited by wrongdoing in order to be safely ignored. This fundamental demand of the moral framework seems to hold in all social contexts. From the point of view of a utilitarian or collectivist moral theory, it seems that we can impose costs or forgo benefits only to prevent greater harm or realize greater collective good, and once more this constraint appears to govern all contexts to which the theory applies. Thus, if business managers perceive that pursuit of maximal profit imposes serious harm on the public (say in decisions regarding product safety, waste disposal, or relocation), how can it be morally coherent to suggest that such pursuit is their proper role?

The answer is that such norms are at least possible, or coherent, given sufficient complexity in a moral framework. In a multi-leveled framework there can be a distinction between an agent's perception of a morally required course of action and her authority to act on that perception. This distinction exists in several moral theories, including Mill's (1955), and it rests on the fact of fallibility in moral perception and moral reasoning. A major argument by defenders of adversarial legal systems to the conclusion that lawyers ought not to restrain their clients on extra-legal moral grounds is that their moral perceptions may be eccentric or incapable of objective justification. Similarly, if a business manager seeks to sacrifice style or raise prices in order to impose safer products on the public, despite market research that indicates contrary preferences, the result may be not what she predicts, but loss of market share to the competition.

In other cases the justification of special norms does not appeal to fallibility in gauging the consequences of actions considered one at a time, but instead to the results of every occupant of the social role reasoning directly from those consequences. Waste disposal provides a good example here. Each small business may reason correctly that the effect of its disposing of wastes in the cheapest way possible is negligible. But if all reason in the same way, the result can be disastrous to the health of the entire community. Here it seems that a special norm restricting the pursuit of maximum profit is in order. Norms governing other roles may be justified in the same way. A teacher should grade based only on quality of work submitted, even though the effect of taking other considerations into account in individual cases might be known to be utility maximizing. A journalist's passing up a single story because of qualms about privacy might not harm the public, but the cumulative effect of all journalists foregoing stories because of such qualms might be significant deprivation of information to the public. Such norms result in a consistency or uniformity in the behavior of role occupants beyond that achievable without them.

It can be argued that norms of the type just considered are either not special or not necessary. A Kantian will hold that moral reasoners must always think of everyone's acting in the way proposed. But this test is not always relevant. Telling a lie in order to avoid a greater evil can be justified, even though if everyone lied in similar circumstances, the strategy might be useless and hence unjustified. It is permissible not to vote in a local election even though the result of no one's voting would be disastrous. The universalizing test is relevant only when many individuals would act in a cumulatively harmful way on the basis of (individually) correct consequentialist reasoning in the absence of special constraint. This criterion does apply to various social roles, as indicated above, generating special norms and hence role moralities.

It can be argued, as in the pollution example, that a business manager ought not to impose higher costs on his corporation unless these are required by law. The appeal here would be to a moral division of labor (between managers and legislators), and it would reinstate the profit principle as the sole fundamental norm for business. Those who defend special-role moralities often make such appeals, but they must be closely scrutinized. Any justification of special-role moralities, even if coherent, must be carefully criticized, given the sacrifice of normally important moral factors involved.

Bibliography

Bayles, M. (1989). *Professional Ethics*. Belmont, Calif.: Wadsworth, ch. 2.

Fried, C. (1978). *Right and Wrong*. Cambridge, Mass.: Harvard University Press, ch. 7.

Friedman, M. (1979). The social responsibility of business is to increase its profits. In T. Donaldson & P. H. Werhane (eds), *Ethical Issues in Business*. Englewood Cliffs, NJ: Prentice-Hall, 191–7.

Goldman, A. H. (1980). *The Moral Foundations of Professional Ethics*. Totowa, NJ: Rowman & Littlefield.

Kadish, M. R. & Kadish, S. H. (1973). *Discretion to Disobey*. Stanford, Calif.: Stanford University Press, chs. 1, 2.

Mill, J. S. (1955). *On Liberty*. Chicago: Gateway.

Wasserstrom, R. (1975). Lawyers as professionals: Some moral issues. *Human Rights*, 5, 1–24.

ALAN H. GOLDMAN

S

safe arrival notification Showing concern for expatriate employees is very important for a business. One of the areas of concern for most employees is that family and friends be notified when they safely reach their destination. An employer can go a long way in showing real concern for employees by notifying selected persons of the expatriate's safe arrival at the assignment destination. This is a simple task, but one that can create goodwill and loyalty between employer and employee.

JOHN O'CONNELL

sales management Sales management is responsible for the organization and performance of the sales force. More specifically, this will include: defining the task of the sales force, organization into sales territories, planning sales call cycles, recruiting and training of personnel, setting objectives, establishing budgets, motivation of personnel, and performance evaluation against objectives. From the evaluation, sales management can determine strengths and weaknesses and initiate any changes in line with corporate objectives and support.

Bibliography

Adams, T. (1988). *Successful sales management.* London: Heinemann.
Churchill, G. A. Jr, Ford, N. M. & Walker, O. C. Jr (1985). *Sales force management: Planning, implementation and control.* Homewood, IL: Irwin.
Kotler, P. (1994). *Marketing management: Analysis, planning, implementation and control,* 8th edn, Englewood Cliffs, NJ: Prentice-Hall. Chapter 25.

DAVID YORKE

sales promotion Sales promotion(s) is a part of the marketing COMMUNICATIONS MIX and is an activity and/or material that acts as a direct inducement, offering added value and incentive for a product to resellers, sales persons, or end customers.

Sales promotions are designed to stimulate dealer or trade purchases and, in turn, in consumer markets to: get customers to try a new brand; encourage favorable opinions; match competitors' actions; increase sales frequency and amounts, etc. Most sales promotions are short term, and they tend to be used more intensively in the marketing of fast-moving-consumer goods where BRAND switching and perceived homogeneity of the offerings prevails. They are relatively more easy to isolate and evaluate than other elements in the communication mix.

Trade promotions include buying allowances, free goods, cooperative advertising, dealer sales contests, and display materials. Consumer promotions include samples, coupons, PRICE PROMOTIONS, redeemable vouchers for gifts, contests, combination offers, trading stamps, and clubs (e.g. Tesco Club Card). Promotions may also be targeted at the sales force, e.g. contests and prizes.

Bibliography

Blattberg, R. C. & Nelsin, S. A. (1990). *Sales promotion: Concepts, methods and strategies.* Englewood Cliffs, NJ: Prentice-Hall.
Kotler, P. (1994). *Marketing management: Analysis, planning, implementation and control,* 8th edn, Englewood Cliffs, NJ: Prentice-Hall. Chapter 23.
Peattie, S. & Peattie, K. (1994). Sales promotion. In M. J. Baker (Ed.), *The marketing book,* 3rd edn, (Chapter 22, pp. 534–554). Oxford: Butterworth-Heinemann.
Wilmhurst, J. (1993). *Below-the-line promotion.* Oxford: Butterworth-Heinemann.

DAVID YORKE

salesforce compensation Salesforce compensation is defined as the financial and non-financial rewards given to salespeople whose primary responsibilities include contacting customers and prospects with the objective of obtaining commitments to buy the goods or services offered by the salesperson (Ingram and LaForge, 1992). The salespeople may also be responsible for providing supporting services to customers. Compensation is provided by the organization (or individual) employing the salesperson in return for the salesperson's satisfactory job performance.

Financial compensation for salespeople may consist of a salary and/or some form of incentive compensation. Incentives may be a commission paid on the amount of products sold or a bonus that is determined by the amount sold, activities performed, or the sales manager's assessment of the salesperson's performance. Financial compensation systems range from 100 percent salary to 100 percent commission. Non-financial compensation may include various forms of recognition of the salesperson's contribution to the organization (e.g. President's Club).

The method of financial compensation is usually determined by the job requirements and the extent of control and direction that sales management wishes to have over the salesperson's efforts (Anderson and Oliver, 1987). Salary-only compensation provides the most control over the salesperson, whereas commission-only compensation essentially allows the salesperson to determine the amount and allocation of his or her selling effort. Salary-based compensation plans typically include some opportunity for incentive compensation. For example, salary might represent 70 or 80 percent of compensation, with the remainder comprised of bonus or commission pay (Cravens et al., 1992).

Bibliography

Anderson, I. & Oliver, R. L. (1987). Perspectives on behavior-based and outcome-based salesforce control systems. *Journal of Marketing,* **October,** 85–6.
Cravens, D. W., Ingram, T. N., LaForge, R. W. & Young, C. E. (1992). Hallmarks of effective sales organizations. *Marketing Management,* **Winter,** 56–67.
Ingram, T. N. & LaForge, R. W. (1992). *Sales Management,* **2nd edn,** Fort Worth, TX: Dryden Press. 414–15.

DAVID W. CRAVENS

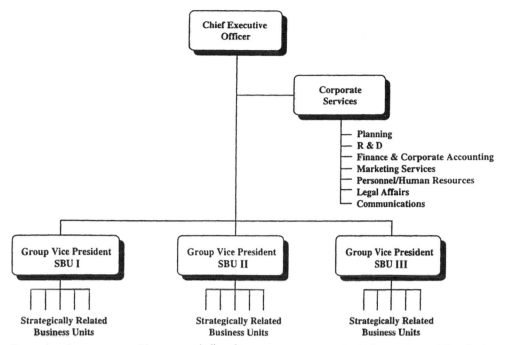

Figure 1 The SBU form of organizational structure.
Source: Hale (1978)

Strategic advantages: provides a strategically relevant way to organize the business-unit portfolio of a broadly diversified company; facilitates the coordination of related activities within an SBU, helping capture the benefits of strategic fits in the SBU; promotes cohesiveness among the new initiatives of separate but related businesses; allows strategic planning to be done at the most relevant level in the enterprise; makes the task of strategic review by top executives more objective and effective; helps allocate corporate resources to areas with greatest growth opportunites.

Strategic disadvantages: it is easy for the definition and grouping of businesses into SBUs to be so arbitrary that the SBU serves no other purpose than administrative convenience. If the criteria for defining SBUs are rationalizations and have little to do with the nitty-gritty of strategy coordination, then the groupings lose real strategic significance; the SBUs can still be myopic in charting their future direction; the establishment of SBUs adds another layer to top management; the roles and authority of the CEO, the group vice president, and the business-unit manager have to be carefully worked out or the group vice presidents get trapped in the middle with ill-defined authority; unless the SBU head is strong willed, very little strategy coordination is likely to occur across business units in the SBU and performance recognition gets blurred with credit for successful business units tending to go first to the corporate CEO, then to business-unit head, and last to the group vice president.

SBU structure   In the 1970s, faced with high levels of complexity, the US General Electric Company, in conjunction with McKinsey and Company, developed the organizational concept of the Strategic Business Unit (SBU). The company's departments, which formed the previous operating structure of GE, were subdivided into 43 SBUs.

These units varied considerably in size. Some SBUs were grouped together to form "divisions," while others were large enough to stand alone. However, each unit was essentially a complete business, and contained all the necessary functions to operate independently. To be classified as an SBU, a business had to be able to clearly identify its actual and potential customers and competitors, and to be able to design comprehensive strategies to reach them, with clearly defined resources, an appropriate management structure and the ability to achieve objectives profitably and at an acceptable measure of risk.

With the introduction of the SBU structure, the then GE President, Reg Jones, was able to personally evaluate the strategic plans of all the units and, at the corporate center, to allocate resources to them on the basis of their position on the COMPETITIVE POSITION – MARKET ATTRACTIVENESS MATRIX. Each SBU was assigned a specific set of strategic objectives and investment policy. A high-growth SBU would therefore perhaps be expected to increase market share when competitively weak, with cashflow profits being deferred. By contrast a strong, low growth business might be expected to keep investment to the minimum and to operate to maximize cashflow, which could be deployed elsewhere. While maintaining a multi-SBU set of divisions, GE was able to operate a variety of investment strategies within a division. In this case the division had its own small corporate staff which monitored and potentially adjusted the SBU's performance measures and rewards.

The SBU structure was introduced widely throughout the world in the 1980s. With a change in leadership at GE, the incoming regime under Dr. Jack Welch maintained the structure and extended it further. In the late 1980s, delayering was introduced within GE to eliminate corporate staff at every level, leaving business unit/corporate center strategy negotiations essentially between Dr. Welch and a very thin general management team, including himself and the SBU management.

As it did at GE, the SBU concept can allow highly diversified corporations to integrate their organizations so as to optimize the STRATEGIC FIT between related businesses and to reduce the complexity of the strategic planning process. The structure also helps to integrate the process of strategy formulation, at both the corporate and business levels, in a form of cascade. It also permits a hands-on approach by the CEO, which often proves increasingly impossible when the corporation is managed with a departmental structure, as the span of control increases with growing diversity. The SBU form of organization is illustrated in figure 1.

Unfortunately, many companies introducing an SBU structure have failed to achieve the "hands-on" approach found at GE and, as a consequence, few have actually achieved the relative success found there. The cause of this failure has often been the inability to recognize that each SBU should have an appropriate set of objectives and action plans that are consistent with the strategic position of the business.

Bibliography

Anonymous (1978). SBUs: hot new topic in the management of diversification. *Business Horizons*, **21** (1), 19.

Bettis, R. A. & Hall, W. K. (1983). The business portfolio approach – where it falls down in practice. *Long Range Planning*, **16** (2), 95–104.

Hale, W. K. (1978). General Electric. Reprinted in Thompson, A. A. & Strickland, A. J. (1993). *Strategic management*. Homewood, IL: Irwin. See pp. 228–31.

DEREK F. CHANNON

Scanlon plan   The Scanlon plan is a GAINSHARING plan that uses a BONUS formula based on improvements in historical production. The ratio used is the cost of labor to some measure of productivity (revenue, sales value of production, or net sales). Assuming a stable historical ratio, a bonus is realized when the ratio improves. The amount of savings creates a bonus pool that is shared between the employer and employees (often a 50 : 50 split). The employee share is then distributed among all employees in the work group (usually as a percentage of basic pay). The Scanlon plan recommends suggestion committees.

THERESA M. WELBOURNE

scenario planning   This technique has become relatively widespread as a way of visualizing alternative futures, and thus of designing flexible strategies that can be developed to cope with these visions of the future. The success of the method owes much to Royal Dutch Shell's use of scenarios, one of which successfully predicted the first oil-price shock in 1973. Other organizations which make use of future scenarios include the White House, the Pentagon, the Economic Planning Agency, Volvo, and Inland Steel. One definition of a scenario is "a tool for ordering one's perceptions about alternative future environments in which one's decisions might be played out."

Key characteristics of scenarios are that they implicitly incorporate the subjective assessments of individuals or groups, and that they recognize that decision makers have some influence on future development. Scenarios tend to be constructed upon facts and proven assumptions that have been accurate in the past. These positions are then extrapolated to create a series of alternate futures which, in themselves, are mutually consistent.

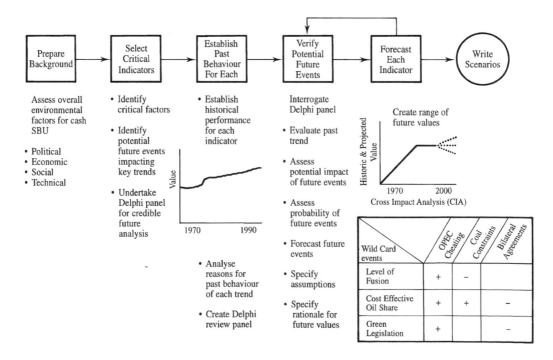

Figure 1 The process of scenario creation.

Within Royal Dutch Shell, every two to three years a series of usually three scenarios about the future are prepared, against which line managers are required to test their own business unit strategic plans. Historically, these scenarios have tended to predict optimistic, most likely, and pessimistic futures. Most recently, the most optimistic scenario has tended to be dropped, as this has never actually come to pass. Indeed, even the most pessimistic scenario has usually tended to be more optimistic than actual reality.

Most scenarios begin in the present and make assumptions about the future. The process of scenario development is illustrated in figure 1. It commences with a PEST ANALYSIS, which identifies the critical Political, Economic, Social and Technological factors which influence both the present and the future.

From this analysis, the critical indicators of the future environment are selected and any potential future events are impacted against these key trends. The use of a Delphi analysis, and consultations with relative experts, may well be a useful process through which to gain enlightened opinion on likely futures.

For each historical performance indicator, past trends are examined and analyzed to identify the reasons for the past behavior. The future is then assessed and tested against the opinions of the Delphi review panel. As a result, future events may be forecast subject to clearly defined assumptions and an established rationale for the prediction of forward values.

A series of usually no more than three scenarios can then be developed on the basis of alternate predictions. Cross-impact analysis should also be undertaken to examine the effect of contrary variables on alternate futures. At the end of this process, a series of scenarios can be established for issue to line business units, as a background against which they can develop alternate strategic plans for their operations.

To ensure that these scenarios will be useful in strategy formulation, it is important that the following criteria are applied:

- The scenarios must be internally consistent. Any internal contradiction may negate any SWOT ANALYSIS undertaken.
- The scenario must be possible. Any scenario which is seen as highly implausible will tend to be ignored by line business units.

Bibliography

Anonymous (1980). Shell's multiple scenario planning: a realistic alternative to the crystal ball. *World Business Weekly*, April 7.
Schwartz, P. (1991). *The art of the long view*. New York: Doubleday.
Wack, P. (1985). Scenarios: uncharted waters ahead. *Harvard Business Review*, 63, 72–89.

DEREK F. CHANNON

scientific management This term refers to the theory and practice of management originated by Frederick Winslow Taylor (1856–1915), an American engineer best known for his development of time and motion study. Taylor became concerned about the collective controls over output levels exercised by skilled workers and reinforced by strong social norms. He attributed management's inability to tackle these problems to its lack of scientific knowledge of the production process and therefore proposed to measure the time required for each element of a job in order to establish the "one best way" of performing that job, and the level of output that was possible. Management would then be able to reassert its control over production and prescribe work methods and output goals. Taylor also believed that jobs should be divided up into small units; workers should be motivated with financial incentives linked to performance (*see* MOTIVATION); they should be allocated a daily work quota (*see* GOAL SETTING); they should be subject to close supervision; and factory departments should be reorganized to permit the most efficient flow of work and materials (Kelly, 1982; Littler, 1982; Rose, 1988).

Underlying Taylor's ideas was a set of assumptions now referred to as THEORY X (*see* THEORY X AND Y): workers are alienated from their work, wish to avoid high levels of effort, are motivated solely or largely by pay, and distrust management. The worker–management relationship is therefore based on low TRUST, although Taylor believed co-operation was possible given high wages, high productivity, and positive attitudes by both parties.

Taylor and his associates measured a wide range of jobs in a range of industries – engineering, construction, transportation and often raised labor productivity, although the more spectacular claims – 100 percent productivity increases for instance – were probably exaggerated. At the same time, Taylor's practices and his authoritarian way of implementing them produced intense hostility from unionized workers, and the use of time and motion study became the focus of bitter conflict until well into the 1960s. Trade unions objected to the deskilling of work, to increased managerial CONTROL and to the "speed up" or intensification of effort levels.

Many of Taylor's principles were still popular in post-war American industry, where jobs were designed to minimize skill, costs, and training time, and subject to close supervision. Henry Ford combined these ideas with a moving assembly line to establish even tighter control of work levels. Even today many scientific management principles and practices are still widespread: work measurement, individual performance-related pay, performance targets and close supervision. Despite their progressive reputation many Japanese manufacturing plants display similar features (Fucini & Fucini, 1990).

Some of his ideas and practices have been questioned. There is a growing trend toward multiskilling of work since it became clear from the 1950s that assembly-line work was not always efficient and produced strong dissatisfaction amongst its workers. Moreover, a growing number of companies have sought to acquire the production knowledge of their workers in a co-operative way, through means such as quality circles. Taylor's ideas belief that workers hold antagonistic attitudes toward management are unfashionable but valid insights that should not be lost sight of.

see also Flexibility

Bibliography

Fucini, J. & Fucini, S. (1990). Working for the Japanese: Inside Mazda's American auto plant. New York: Free Press.
Kelly, J. E. (1982). Scientific management, job redesign and work performance. London: Academic Press.

Littler, C. (1982). The development of the labour process in capitalist societies. London: Heinemann.

Rose, M. (1988). Industrial behaviour: Theoretical development since Taylor, (3rd edn) Harmondsworth, UK: Penguin.

JOHN KELLY

secondary boycotts Secondary boycotts are union efforts, usually involving PICKETING, to force a second employer to "refrain from doing business with" an employer with whom the union has a labor dispute (Gould, 1986, p. 53). The term "boycott," which has the same meaning in several languages, derives from the name of an infamous 1879 Irish estate manager whose tenants isolated him (Funk, 1972). Such actions are illegal for most workers under American labor law (Section 8 (b) (4) (B), National Labor Relations Act), and give rise to swift legal penalties. However, the variation aimed at consumers is a technique used to good effect in the USA by farm workers, who are not covered by the National Labor Relations Act.

Bibliography

Cihon, P. J. & Castagnera, J. O. (1993). *Labor and Employment Law*, **2nd edn**, Belmont, CA: Wadsworth.

Funk, C. E. (1972). *Thereby Hangs a Tale*, New York: Warner.

Gould, W. B. IV (1986). *A Primer on American Labor Law*, **2nd edn**, Cambridge, MA: MIT Press.

HOYT N. WHEELER

secondary data Secondary data are data that are collected for some purpose other than the problem at hand. The development of commercially available databases and the use of computers has seen a large increase in the use of secondary data. While secondary data are used in all stages of the MARKETING RESEARCH process, they are mainly used in the initial exploratory stages.

Secondary data come from sources internal to the company such as accounting and sales records, and from external sources such as government, industry, and marketing research sources. In addition, libraries have access to books, reports, and articles on a wide range of topics.

The advantage of secondary data is that they can be obtained quickly and, usually, inexpensively. However, secondary data on the required topic may not be available. Secondary data that are available in the general area under study may not fit precisely the requirements of a particular problem. For instance, the geographic area for which the data are available may not coincide with the area for which the data are required. The definitions of the variables may differ; e.g., secondary data on unemployment may be of the numbers of people claiming unemployment benefit which may be different from the numbers available for work. Government data based on the governmental administration process may contain unquantifiable biases, e.g., national income data based on tax returns will be affected by tax evasion. Definitions used in the collection of secondary data may change over time. Secondary data may be published annually when quarterly or monthly data are required. Secondary data may be out of date by the time they are published, e.g., input–output tables.

Internal sources of secondary data include accounting records and sales reports. Sales invoices form the bases of internal accounting records of much of the internal secondary data of interest to marketers. These data when reanalyzed can give a picture of sales over time by product, by customer, by sales territory. Marketing expenditures on such variables as the sales force, advertising, promotion, distribution, new product development, and marketing research can also be determined from internal accounting records. Reports by salespersons on customers and market potential are another internal source of marketing data. The trend toward developing MARKETING INFORMATION SYSTEMS means that a coordinated effort is taking place to collect internal information and make it available on a regular basis to marketing decision-makers.

External sources of information include the growing services from computerized commercial database providers who gather together data from a wide variety of secondary sources. The majority of these provide numerical data but bibliographical databases provide references to articles, reports, and books based upon abstracts and key words. The best-known bibliographical database for marketers is ABI/Inform.

The government and its agencies and associates collect and make available data on a wide range of business and economic topics of interest to marketers. Topics include national income data, production, imports and exports, price data, agriculture, travel and tourism, consumer confidence, etc. UK government publications include the *Annual Abstract of Statistics*, the *Monthly Digest*, *Economic Trends*, the *National Income Blue Book*, the *Business Monitor Series* which give production systems for many different products, the *Family Expenditure Survey*: some of these data are available from the ESRC archives.

Many trade associations collect data about their industries, including size of markets, and distribute this information to members.

Marketing research organizations collect information for sale to customers or on behalf of syndicates of clients. Examples of surveys of the flow of products at the retail level in the UK are Nielsen's Retail Audits which measure sales of a large number of brands through retailers which in turn allows trends in brand shares in total or through different types of outlets or in different regions to be observed and reported to clients. Electronic point of sale scanner equipment which is improving the amount of such data and the speed with which they can be gathered is revolutionizing the provision and use of this kind of data. An example of a survey of consumers in the UK is the Target Group Index (TGI), a large annual survey based on diaries kept by a panel which provides information on who buys what product and prefers which brand. One example of a survey of interest to advertisers in the UK is the National Readership Survey which measures the readership of 200 leading newspapers and magazines, together with a lot of classification information, and is used by media owners to sell, and advertisers and advertising agencies to buy, press advertising. A survey for the UK Broadcasters Audience Research Board (BARB) provides data on TV audiences for the BBC and ITV companies and for advertisers and their agents.

A number of marketing research companies collect data on specific products, industries, or markets in order to sell to many clients. In the UK, Market Intelligence (Mintel), Retail Business, and Keynotes publish monthly reports on different markets.

The amount of secondary data available is great. The examples mentioned above are just a few of the sources of secondary data. The problem is to track down what is available on the topic of interest.

Bibliography

Moutinho, L. & Evans, M. (1992). *Applied marketing research.* Wokingham: Addison Wesley, pp. 12–14.

MIKE GREATOREX

securitization   Securitization is a process through which illiquid claims such as loans can be converted into liquid claims that can be sold and traded among third parties. The term is associated with two different but related phenomena: (1) disintermediation processes that allow for direct access to the security markets by companies that traditionally relied on bank funding (reflected, for instance, in the growth of the junk bond and commercial paper markets during the 1980s); and (2) the processes of off-balance sheet securitization (OBS), that enable banks to transfer part of their assets to third parties, retaining their monitoring and management functions and some exposure to credit risk, but avoiding their traditional role as direct providers of the funds. The process of OBS is simplified where the assets to be securitized are standardized (or standardizable) and can be bundled into well-diversified portfolios. Many of the traditional assets held by banks (home mortgage loans, credit card receivables, lease contract receivables) meet these requirements and are routinely transferred to non-bank institutions or into securities markets in the form of tradable securities.

Securitized assets of this kind have been common, especially in the USA, since the mid-1960s. However, a major surge in securitization deals occurred in the 1980s, influenced by the results of and the experience acquired with the US government mortgage-backed securities program. Home mortgages are still by far the biggest asset type in securitization deals, but a whole range of different assets – automobile receivables, commercial loans, commercial mortgages, consumer loans, lease receivables, interbank loans, and local authority loans, etc. – are suitable for securitization. The success experienced in the US market has stimulated comparable activity in most leading international financial centers. Despite the difficulties created by the idiosyncrasies of different regulatory and legal systems, the beginning of the 1990s saw the securitization procedures widely used in Canada and Australia as well as in several European financial markets.

Disintermediation-type securitization by-passes financial intermediaries with direct access to the financial markets changing the nature of the initial asset originated by the credit process but not involving any innovation by intermediaries or any real novelty in the nature of the securities available. OBS in contrast, tends to split up the customary intermediation components of the bank lending function. Traditionally, banks were largely self-funding and dealt simultaneously with the origination, funding, monitoring, and service of their loans. This demanded substantial resources to acquire the necessary expertise and scale in each area. With the development of securitization, banks no longer need to balance deposits with loans and can concentrate resources on only part of the process.

The literature on securitization has focused on two main topics: the reasons for the development of the process, and the expected consequences for the banking industry. The success of the securitization, as with all financial innovation, depends on creating more value for the economic agents involved, than the available alternatives. Securitization must provide securities whose after tax cash-flow structure could not be replicated by any of the securities (or combinations of securities) previously available.

The literature suggests several reasons why securitization processes add value in relation to the classic intermediation processes. OBS was stimulated by changes in regulatory requirements and tax laws during the 1980s, which effectively increased the cost of the reserves absorbed by assets on banks' balance-sheet (Benston, 1992; Kim and Santomero, 1988). Securitization allowed intermediaries to obtain origination fees but to remove assets from their balance sheets. Another advantage arises from improved risk management, because securitization allows intermediaries to buy or sell assets to create an efficient portfolio irrespective of any industry or sector bias in their loan origination, giving banks the freedom to specialize and exploit available scale economies. The transaction costs of securitization have also fallen sharply as technology has improved. Finally, securitization creates assets which have substantial liquidity advantages over the traditional lending instruments and this is reflected in more competitive funding costs.

But intermediaries are not the only beneficiaries from securitization. Non-financial companies are attracted by the low funding costs and high liquidity of securities markets and so have a strong incentive to approach the market directly. They may also perceive the agency relationship inherent in the classic bank lending process as more difficult to manage than the more transparent procedures involved in traded securities. The availability of external ratings from specialists such as Dun and Bradstreet enables industrial companies to bypass the monitoring function in the traditional bank lending system and to access markets on the basis of their own reputation. This option is generally attractive where a company has a lower risk rating than its potential financial intermediaries.

There are two competing views on the future impact of securitization in banking industry. Some authors argue that securitization will continue to generate new products capable of transferring an increasing portion of the banks' assets to the financial markets (Ocampo and Rosenthal, 1988; Bryan, 1988). Others argue that it will be very difficult for this growth to be sustainable in the long term (Benston, 1992; Sinkey, 1992), with securitization likely only for assets amenable to formal actuarial analysis. Variable rate securities or securities with early retirement, call, conversion, or other contingent features are much harder to value. As a result, banks still have a comparative advantage in the evaluation and control of credit risk which offers flexibility to borrowers that is difficult to obtain in the securities market.

Although some effort has gone into empirical analysis of the securitization process, a number of key issues are still a matter of debate:

1. How significant are standard regulations and fiscal rules in the success of securitization?

2. In what circumstances is securitization able to create value? Are the gains obtained by more creditworthy borrowers at the expense of weaker borrowers?
3. Will banks increase the use of securitization to achieve a fundamental change in their funding structure?
4. What impact will the trend to securitization have on the stability and soundness of the banking system? What plausible implications will the securitization have for the development of monetary and financial policies?
5. Will securitization lead to a major reversal in the trend towards universal banking?

Bibliography

Benston, G. J. (1992). The future of asset securitization: the benefits and costs of breaking up the bank. *Journal of Applied Corporate Finance*, 5, 71–82.

Benveniste, L. M. & Berger, A. N. (1987). Securitization with recourse: an instrument that offers uninsured bank depositors sequential claims. *Journal of Banking and Finance*, 11, 403–24.

Berger, A. N. & Udell, G. F. (1992). Securitization, risk, and the liquidity problem in banking. *Structural change in banking*. Klausner, M. & White, L. J. Homewood, IL: Irwin Publishing.

Bryan, L. L. (1988). Structured securitized credit: a superior technology for lending. *Journal of Applied Corporate Finance*, 1, 6–19.

Greenbaum, S. I. & Thakor, A. V. (1987). Bank funding modes: securitization versus deposits. *Journal of Banking and Finance*, 11, 379–401.

Kareken, J. H. (1987). The emergence and regulation of contingent commitment banking. *Journal of Banking and Finance*, 11, 359–77.

Kim, D. & Santomero, A. M. (1988). Risk in banking and capital regulation. *Journal of Finance*, 43, 1219–33.

Ocampo, J. M. & Rosenthal, J. A. (1988). The future of credit securitization and the financial services industry. *Journal of Applied Corporate Finance*, 1, 90–100.

Pavel, C. A. (1989). *Securitization: The analysis and development of loan based asset-backed securities markets*. Chicago, IL: Probus.

Sinkey, J., Jr. (1992). *Commercial bank financial management in the financial services industry*. 4th edn, New York: Macmillan.

Stone, C., Zissu, A. & Lederman, J. (1993). *The global asset backed securities market: Structuring, managing and allocating risk*. Chicago, IL: Probus.

J. AZEVEDO PEREIRA

security of information systems   The objective of information systems security (computer security, data security) efforts is to protect the computer and its information from accident and disasters and intentional security breaches (abuse). Information system security in the 1970s and 1980s dealt with hardware, programs, data, and computer service abuse. PCs introduced a concern about securing system assets against viruses. Computer communications networks, the Internet, and the World Wide Web have added authentication and encryption issues.

Information Security Policies

Policies serve to set the tone for how security is viewed within an organization. Useful security policies have widespread management support and are detailed enough to give an organization a clear sense of direction. Good policies also include guidelines for implementing disaster recovery plans, designing security controls into applications, establishing system-user access capabilities, carrying out investigations of computer crimes, and disciplining employees for security breaches.

In creating information security policies, it is critical that policies are well matched to the corporate culture. Consciously or unconsciously, employees will resist policies that conflict with the corporate mores or "ways of doing things." Moreover, policies that conflict with basic, underlying beliefs, attitudes, and values of the organization are likewise unlikely to be effective. Ultimately, mismatches result in policies that are either completely ignored or suboptimal in their impact.

There are at least four attitudes that can be adopted with respect to creating organizational security policies. Adapted from Bryan (1995), they are:

1 *Secretive*. This attitude, internalized by military organizations, can be simply stated as "you know only what you must." Organizations adopting this stance would seldom be inclined to connect to the Internet, for example.
2 *Prudent*. This method specifies that only connections and operations explicitly granted are permissible.
3 *Permissive*. This lenient approach allows everything that is not explicitly forbidden.
4 *Laissez-faire*. Organizations either explicitly or implicitly adopt the policy that "anything goes."

Extent of Security Losses from Intentional Abuse

The extent of losses due to computer system abuse is uncertain, but is estimated to be substantial. It has been reported that between 25 and 50 percent of US firms discover at least one serious abuse a year. It is possible that 50–90 percent have lost money through breaches in security (Hoffer & Straub, 1989). In 1994, Ernst and Young reported that over half of surveyed firms reported losses in the past two years due to computer abuse (Bryan, 1995). Given that possibly only 5–10 percent of computer abuse cases are actually reported to the authorities (Straub & Nance, 1990), the extent of abuse is very likely to be much greater. The magnitude of the problem is such that British banks reportedly fire 1 percent of their employees each year for computer fraud (Anderson, 1994).

Intentional Security Violations

Traditionally, computer abuse has been characterized as: (a) unauthorized use; (b) abuse of data; (c) abuse of programs; and (d) abuse of hardware (Straub, 1986; Hoffer & Straub, 1989). Unauthorized use, usually by employees, has been reported to be the most common form of abuse. This category, which includes activities such as exploiting organizational resources by playing computer games or creating and running personal databases, may account for about 40 percent of reported cases. Abuse of data, for example, the actual stealing of funds or data, may amount to about 20 percent of reported cases, while abuse of programs, such as theft or unauthorized copying of copyright routines, may explain 25 percent of reported cases. Hardware abuse, such as stealing the hardware, accounts for only about 5 percent of the total.

Abusers are overwhelmingly insiders: programmers, clerical personnel, users, students, and managers. Only about 2 percent were outsiders (most often hackers). In spite of belief that a large number of users, or a large number of privileged users, will result in vulnerable systems, there is no empirical evidence that this is the case (Straub, 1986; Hoffer & Straub, 1989). The reasons why people abuse computers are: personal gain (25 percent), ignorance of proper conduct (27 percent), revenge (22 percent), and misguided playfulness (26 percent).

PCs added a new security problem of protecting against viruses. Viruses (and so-called worms) are computer programs that invade a system and have the capability of damaging the host computer system either by changing and deleting data or by wasting computer resources. Viruses usually are introduced into computer systems through contaminated diskettes that contain the virus. When such a diskette is accessed, the virus attaches itself to the host computer and, depending on the type of virus, begins to multiply and disseminate itself. In this privileged position within the host computer, it has the ability to virtually destroy its host. Some viruses begin to activate themselves immediately, while others lie in wait for special dates. The origin of many viruses is uncertain, but hackers are suspected of much of this antisocial activity. Commercial software packages have been written to locate and protect systems from virus. Anti-virus packages are currently in use by 91 percent of organizations surveyed by Ernst and Young (Bryan, 1995).

Inadequate security is thought to be the main hindrance to the Internet becoming a viable commercial marketplace. Network information security has four main issues:

1 *Access control and authorization.* This area of security deals with questions of who is allowed into a network and for what purposes. However, the interdependence of authorization processes among networks and among host nodes complicates control and authorization.

2 *Information authenticity.* This area deals with identifying the source of information, i.e. the originator of the message. When an organization's network is connected to many others, it is impossible to identify network users with the traditional login and location method used in mainframes. Eavesdroppers can copy these and impersonate legitimate users. One of the proposed methods of overcoming this problem is the use of digital signatures.

3 *Information integrity.* Ensuring the integrity of information means ensuring that the data have not been altered. When information enters the organization's network from other networks, it is much harder to ensure that information has not been lost. Special protocols have been created for this purpose.

4 *Information privacy.* Privacy in networks generally means that personal and confidential information is not subject to eavesdropping. Privacy is often achieved using cryptography or cryptosystems.

Information Security and Accidents/Disasters

Information is also exposed to damage from events other than computer abuse. Accidents and disasters, such as damage due to human error or natural acts like hurricanes, are often dealt with through well-defined and tested contingency plans. These plans include automatic and manual database backups, uninterrupted power supply (UPS) systems, and offsite computer backups. In addition, many current hardware components like routers (telecommunications switches) are designed with redundancy so that if any one element fails, the system can continue to operate. Such characteristics are essential for many communication-intensive systems, such as teller machines and bank transaction processing systems.

Contingency plans include backup and recovery in the event of the computer-processing site being destroyed by fire, natural disaster, or other event. Site backup provisions may include:

1 *Hot backup.* This method ensures that a fully operational redundant site is ready to take over immediately a disaster occurs at a primary site.

2 *Warm backup.* This method is similar to hot backup, except that the auxiliary site becomes operational within a matter of hours.

3 *Split site.* In this method, organizational computing is performed at two sites so that when one site is disrupted, the other can take over critical applications.

4 *Cold backup.* In this method, a facility equipped with cabling and network connections is ready for rapid installation of new hardware and software and databases from backups.

Security Techniques

The effectiveness of security techniques depends upon the deterrent effect of having administrative policies in place, management commitment to good security, and user security awareness. To prevent losses from insecure systems, security software can also be used. Methods to detect abusive activities involve monitoring system use, suspicious systems activity, and security violations. Through use of these kinds of methods, management delivers the message that security is important to the firm and that there are penalties for violating security.

Methods that deal with specific aspects of security include:

1 *Physical security.* These measures are primarily aimed at protecting system assets from theft. They include locks, alarms, and embedding the company logo in hardware. In addition, restricted entrance to sensitive departments is often used and combined with automatically monitored entrance and departure recordings. Other useful measures include administrative regulations ensuring that removable disks with secured data be locked up and that sensitive data be kept only on secure disks.

2 *Backup.* Disk and tape backups are used to deal with data loss due to faulty devices and human errors. It is often suggested that companies utilize backups to assure their chances of survival in the event of data loss.

3 *Redundancy.* Redundant data, input–output devices, and processors ("shadowed," "mirrored," or synchronized machines) can be used as a method of fault management in crucial network management systems. These mechanisms provide fault-free operations by detecting, isolating, and resolving faults. Built-in redundancy methods often use EXPERT SYSTEMS.

4 *Passwords.* The first line of defense in maintaining data security is enforcing a sign-in and password verification procedure (login). This procedure can be augmented by administrative policies that require that power be turned off whenever a PC is not in active use. An extended defense can be achieved by using available security software that forces a login and automatically

encrypts protected subdirectories so that, if the login is bypassed, the files are not available.

5 *Authorizing access.* Once a user has entered the system using a password, many database management systems come with built-in authorization mechanisms that enable the systems administrators to authorize different types and locations of access to data according to user identification or group. Authorization control and security policy enforcement are also available as stand-alone software security tools.

6 *Encryption.* Even when a user has access to certain data, encryption can be used to ensure that the authorization process in a DBMS or a network is not circumvented. This method is often used to secure both data and communications. There are two types of cryptographic methods: those applying common keys and those applying private keys. The common key methods apply the same key for both encryption and decryption. These methods are faster and are often used for bulk data. A method frequently employed in this situation is the DES algorithm. The private key method allocates two keys to each user: a public key used for encrypting and a private one for decrypting. One of the commonly used algorithms for this type is RSA. Encryption algorithms are mostly only computationally secure, i.e. breaking the code is possible, but requires an unfeasible amount of computational time and resources. These protocols, including TMN and DSA, can be broken if the random number at the core of the method is shared; for example, if an eavesdropper follows the establishment of a communication protocol between two legitimate subscribers and uses a variation of their key to establish a session with an accomplice.

7 *Firewalls.* Firewalls are a computerized barrier that controls and prevents illicit messages and users from entering the network or parts of it. This feature is essential when companies let their customers and suppliers access their internal network. Firewalls protect resources by securing servers and sites as well as transactions. This is done by controlling authentication, message integrity, and unauthorized listening. The two currently available methods are *channel-based security* and *document-based security*. A channel-based security standard, such as SSL (secure socket layer), secures the entire channel; while a document-based standard, such as SHTTP (secure hypertext transport protocol), only guarantees that specific documents broadcast will be secure. World Wide Web commerce already exists for users with SSL servers.

The most common types of firewalls are (Bryan, 1995):

1 *Router-based filters.* These control the traffic at the IP level of TCP/IP (level 3 of the ISO OSI model) by controlling the packets allowed into the network. This method is probably the most commonly used at present. However, it does not work well with non-packet protocols.

2 *Gateways (alias bastions).* These firewalls reside on host computers and use the host computer to log activities via security software.

3 *Isolated networks.* This method is similar to gateways, with the exception that it creates an isolated internal network that connects to the outside networks through a gateway.

4 *Electronic signatures.* The digital signature algorithm (DSA) is a digital signature and verification mechanism used for digital, rather than written, signatures. DSA enables verification of signature, message origin, and message integrity without giving away information that would make signature forgery possible. DSA achieves this by allotting two different digital keys to each signature bearer: a secret private key for encrypting the message and a public key used for decrypting it. The private key is known only to the signature bearer, while the public key is known to all the network users.

Future Security Problems

Coming advances in computation will, no doubt, produce new security problems. Free agents, for example, are software programs that travel the Internet and run independently on host computers. While providing new and powerful communication tools, they also create security hazards and viruses. One of the proposed methods for controlling security with free agents is the creation of firewalls using object-oriented encapsulation which permits each free agent access only to its own and explicitly shared data. This method can be augmented with cryptographic agent authentication (Wayner, 1995).

Although advances in technology may change some features of security, it will continue to be true that information security must be seen as a human problem as much as a technology problem. Management must be involved. Without higher-level management support, there will be insufficient budgets for and insufficient attention paid to information security. Without sufficient budgets, necessary control changes will not be made. Without sufficient management attention, control decisions that need to be made will be ignored.

Bibliography

Anderson, R. J. (1994). Why cryptosystems fail. *Communications of the ACM*, **37** (11), 32–40.

Bryan, J. (1995). Build a firewall. *Byte*, **20** (4), 91–96.

Hoffer, J. A. & Straub, D. W. (1989). The 9 to 5 underground: are you policing computer crimes? *Sloan Management Review*, **31** (2), 35–43.

Straub, D. W. (1986). Computer abuse and computer security: update on an empirical study. *Security, Audit and Control Review*, **4** (2), 21–31.

Straub, D. W. & Nance, W. D. (1990). Discovering and disciplining computer abuse in organizations: a field study. *MIS Quarterly*, **14** (1), 45–52.

Wayner, P. (1995). Free agents. *Byte*, **20** (3), 105–14.

DAVID GEFEN and DETMAR W. STRAUB

segment   *see* MARKET SEGMENTATION

segmentation   The choice of which markets to address is a critical strategic decision for the firm. Therefore, the served market is some combination of customers, products, and geography. This choice is based on the segmentation of markets into smaller groupings. Moreover, the development of relational databases and data mining technologies allows firms to define their markets even more tightly. Successful segmentation of markets has proven to be a key source of strategic advantage, especially where this might involve reconfiguration of the value chain (*see* VALUE CHAIN ANALYSIS).

Bases for Market Segmentation

A range of variables can be used for segmenting both consumer and business markets. Typically these involve geographic, demographic, and psychographic factors. Normally more than one variable is used to try to identify a served market segment. Some researchers use consumer response variables such as quality, usage patterns, usage time, and branding. The main variables are described briefly below.

Geographic segmentation. In geographic segmentation, the market is broken down into different geographic units, such as nations, regions, countries, cities, and neighborhoods. The company may decide to operate in many or few areas, or to differentiate between regions or districts. For example, the insurance industry may operate differential pricing policies based on the demographics of different neighborhoods, crime rates, property values, and the like. Some food retailers may divide cities into different areas on the basis of age and/or ethnic mix.

Demographic segmentation. In demographic segmentation, markets are subdivided into groups on the basis of demographic variables such as age, sex, life cycle, education, income, ethnic background, and the like. Historically, demographic variables have been most widely used in consumer marketing segmentation. They are also used in business market segmentation to determine, for example, the size of company that should be attacked, the industry mix to be achieved, and the location areas to be selected. Demographic variables are also amongst the easiest to measure.

- *Age and life cycle stage.* Consumer needs and wealth change with age and position in the life cycle. Historically, this was relatively predictable, but is becoming more difficult to use as a variable. For example, historically, family life cycle could be assessed using the following sequence: single; married with no children; married with young children; married with children up to 18; married, children departed; retired married; retired single. Presently, marriage is a poor predictor due to the high rate of divorce, the growing preponderance of single-person households, and the growing number of working professional women. Nevertheless, age and life cycle still are important variables for segmentation and the mix of individuals is shifting, particularly toward ageing populations in the developed economies.
- *Gender.* Segmentation by gender has long been an important variable in areas such as cosmetics, magazines, and clothing. It has also been applied in areas not normally associated with gender, such as cigarettes, do-it-yourself materials, automobiles, and liquor.
- *Income.* Income segmentation has always been an important variable for many industries, such as automobiles, clothing, cosmetics, travel, and banking. It is not, however, necessarily a good predictor of profitability or of volume markets. For example, compact disks were originally sold to the market of audio *aficionados* or status seekers, but the market turned out to be driven by young people interested in listening to pop music.
- *Multiple attribute segmentation.* For most companies, markets are segmented by combinations of more than one demographic variable, such as age, income, and education. Thus in banking the young professional has a high income but also a high borrowing requirement in order to establish a professional practice, a mortgage, and the like. Such grouping can be further subdivided by ethnic, locational, and other variables. It is therefore important to attempt to combine variables in a way that clearly identifies an attractive target group profitable for the corporation to service.

Psychographic segmentation. In this form of segmentation, which has become increasingly widely used in recent times, buyers are divided upon the basis of social class, lifestyle, and personality. This form of segmentation has to a degree been used to replace demographic segmentation, as market researchers have discovered wide variations in behavior between subgroups within demographic profiling.

Behavioral segmentation. In this form of segmentation, which is widely used, purchasing behavior may vary significantly according to knowledge, attitude, usage rate, time of use, and attitude to the product.

Requirements for Effective Segmentation

To be useful, market segments should:

- be measurable
- be sufficiently large for products or services to be marketed profitably
- be accessible – distribution/delivery system channels should be open
- be differentiable – segments must be distinguishable from other elements of the market
- be actionable – it must be possible to design strategic marketing programs that permit the segmentation strategy to be implemented

see also **Geodemographics; Market segmentation; Organizational segmentation; Positioning; Psychographics; Segmentation variables**

Bibliography

Kotler, P. & Armstrong, G. (1989). *Principles of Marketing* (4th edn). New Jersey: Prentice-Hall.
Kotler, P. (1994). *Marketing management*, 8th edn. Englewood Cliffs, NJ: Prentice-Hall.
Roberts, A. A. (1961). Applying the strategy of market segmentation. *Business Horizons* (May), 65–72.
Robertson, T. S. & Barish, H. (1992). A successful approach to segmenting industrial markets. *Planning Forum* 5–11.

DEREK F. CHANNON

segmentation variables The segmentation model requires a selection of a basis for segmentation (the dependent variables) as well as descriptors (the independent variables) of the various segments. Descriptor variables are used to understand more about identified market segments and include: reference group influences, where people live, where and when they shop, their media habits, what social backgrounds they come from, etc. One of the main reasons for using descriptor variables to profile segments is that readership and viewership data on newspapers, magazines, and television programs tend to be expressed in this way.

Segmentation variables fall into two broad groups: customer characteristics, which include geographic and demographic variables; and consumer responses to a particular product, such as benefits sought, usage occasions, brand loyalties (Kotler, 1991).

Customer Characteristics

These include demographic and geographic variables. Demographic variables are most prevalent because consumers can be placed into categories which are easily understood, easily interpreted, relatively easily gathered, widely available from government sources, and easily transferable from one study to another. Demographics are often the best descriptors of identified segments. They include: age; sex; family size; type of residence, whether it be a flat or semi-detached house; income; occupation; education, e.g., secondary, graduate, postgraduate; religion; ethnic origin, e.g., African, Asian, Caribbean, European; nationality; and socioeconomic grouping (SEG). In the UK, one SEG which is commonly used is the A,B,C1, C2,D,E categorization, where A refers to those at the top of their professions such as judges, directors, etc. and E to those on a subsistence level, e.g., state pensioners.

Some markets can easily be segmented by age, e.g., the holiday market has 18–30 holidays and holidays for the over-fifties. However, it is important for marketers to realize that their target can be psychologically, rather than chronologically, young. Age stereotype needs to be guarded against. One can have a 70-year-old who is house bound and another who still actively engages in voluntary work.

Wells & Gubar (1966) identified nine life cycle stages, from a bachelor stage to a retired solitary survivor. The problems with their classification are that it takes no account of the number of single-parent families within many countries, or the increasing number of childless and single sex couples. In addition, the cycles are distorted because more women are postponing having children until later in their lives and family size has declined. Murphy & Staples (1979) devised a more modern family life structure, as follows: (1) Young single. (2) Young married without children. (3a) Young divorced without children. (3b) Young married with children, infant, 4–12 years old, adolescent. (3c) Young divorced with children, infant, 4–12 years old, adolescent. (4a) Middle-aged married without children. (4b) Middle-aged divorced without children. (4c) Middle-aged married with children, young, adolescent. (4d) Middle-aged divorced with children, young, adolescent. (4e) Middle-aged married without dependent children. (4f) Middle-aged divorced without dependent children. (5a) Older married. (5b) Older unmarried, divorced, widowed. (6) Others.

Geographic segmentation is used when consumer patterns and preferences vary by geographical location. This can involve looking at the: postcode; city; town; village; coastal or inland; county; region, e.g., television region; country; continent; climate; or population density. For example, a franchise restaurant organization may only locate in cities with a population greater than 100,000 people, while other companies may choose to locate in cities with less than 100,000 people to avoid well-entrenched competitors. Unlike population density, market density refers to the number of potential customers within a unit of land (such as a square kilometer). Unfortunately, many of the measurable

geographic variables are not closely related to needs. Only those which are related to local climate or terrain and natural resources can truly be said to have a direct influence on consumers' needs. For example, the market for snow tires is greater in certain mountainous parts of the USA than in Florida; and differences in hobbies such as mountain climbing, surfing, and other recreational activities can clearly be seen to be related to geography.

One major advancement in segmentation in the last two decades has been geodemographics (*see* GEODEMO-GRAPHICS). These identify groups of consumers by combining a large number of demographic and geographic variables together. Their advantage is that they are able not only to characterize consumers, but also to identify (to postcode level) where consumers are located. This helps enormously in market measurement and market accessibility.

Customer Response Characteristics

These are the second major category of segmentation variables. Basic demographic variables such as age and sex can determine needs well in certain markets, e.g., denim jeans, perfume, and jewelry, but they can result in market segments within which there is considerable variation in consumers' needs and outlook. The use of any variable as a base for market segmentation is ultimately be correlated with product purchase or use. Therein lies the fundamental limitation of using customer demographic characteristics, since they are usually only indirectly related to behavior. Although highly reliable in measurement terms, there is evidence that demographic data have generally failed to explain consumption behavior (see Mitchman, 1991; Sheth, 1977). Much more important are customer response variables such as benefits sought, usage patterns, and price sensitivity.

Benefit segmentation is the division of a market according to the benefits consumers want from a product. For example, the benefits sought in the soft/drinks market may be: energy; vitamins; low in calories; or low cost. One of the earliest attempts at benefit segmentation was made by Yankelovich (1964) who identified three main benefit segments for watches. These were: a price-sensitive segment, a durability and general product-quality segment, and a segment buying watches as symbols or gifts for some important occasion. Problems are sometimes encountered with benefit segmentation in terms of determining the size of the resultant benefit group and differences in the semantic variations of the stated benefits. Nonetheless, it remains one of the most conceptually-valid approaches to take.

Volume of consumption can be one way of segmenting markets, e.g., into non-users, light users, and heavy users of a product. Each user category can have different informational needs. For example, an advertisement to a non-user might give more information about the product class in general, while a regular user might be told the merits of one product versus another. Research has found fewer than half of the consumers can account for between 70 percent and 80 percent of total consumption (Twedt, 1974; Cook & Mindak, 1984). Heavy users of products often have common demographics, PSYCHOGRAPHICS, and media habits as well as needs which make them suitable for targeting with tailored marketing activities.

Another response characteristic is loyalty status (*see also* BRAND LOYALTY). Brand-loyal consumers are of greater value to marketers since it is estimated to cost five times more to attract a new customer than to retain an existing one. Kotler (1991) identifies four categories of loyalty status: hardcore loyals, who buy one brand all the time; softcore loyals who buy two or three brands regularly; shifting loyals, who shift from favoring one brand to another; and switchers who show no loyalty to any brand. By studying softcore loyals a company can pinpoint which brands are most competitive with its own, and by analyzing motives of customers who are shifting away from its brands a company can learn about its marketing weaknesses. Sometimes what appears to be a brand-loyal purchase pattern may reflect habit, indifference, low price, or the non-availability of alternatives. Following this line of argument, Dickson (1994) describes several types of brand loyalty which relate to the reasons for being loyal. These include: emotional loyalty, e.g., to a hospital that saves a child's life; identity loyalty, which is an expression of the self that bolsters the self-esteem, e.g., Porsche cars; differentiated loyalty, which is based on the perceived superiority of features and attributes of a particular appliance; contract loyalty, when the consumer believes that continued loyalty will earn him or her special treatment and that a social contract exists, e.g., loyalty schemes in petrol and grocery retailing; switching–cost loyalty, when the effort involved in considering alternatives and adapting to new alternatives is not worth the expected return, e.g., loyalty to a particular computer system; familiarity loyalty, the result of top–of–the–mind brand awareness, e.g., Coca Cola; and convenience loyalty, which is based on buying convenience, e.g., the most convenient snack at a counter.

Image segmentation involves the consumer's self-image or self-concept and its relationship to the image of the product, e.g., perfumes which try to differentiate themselves from each other by having their own distinctive image. While image-oriented features can be difficult to create in new brands, once established in the consumer's mind they can generate many years of consumer loyalty. Landon (1974) discusses two forms of self-concept: one is the regular concept, i.e., how we see ourselves; the other is the ideal concept, i.e., how we would like ourselves to be seen. One criticism of the use of self-image research is the difficulty in identifying cause and effect. If one considers self-image in relation to a product already purchased by the consumer, the consumer's self-image may have already been altered by the purchase of the product. In addition, there is the problem of the non-availability of products which exactly match a person's self-image (*see also* PSYCHOGRAPHICS).

Purchase occasion can influence the needs for a particular product. For example, products may be bought as gifts or as self-purchases. In purchase–occasion segmentation, consumers are grouped based on the reasons or times they purchase products. Consumers can also be divided by their *attitudes toward risk* (see PERCEIVED RISK) or their *willingness to purchase new products*. Dickson (1994) examines how *time pressure* can affect the purchase of new products and, therefore, be used as a possible segmentation variable. He argues that while the "wealthy" may have more money to buy innovative products, many

do not have the time to invest in learning how to use them. The real innovators, then, are likely to be consumers who have more leisure time to devote to their interests. One can observe an interesting role reversal where teenagers teach their parents how to use selected products, particularly electrical equipment. In addition, at any given time, people are at different stages of *readiness to purchase* a product: some are unaware of the product, some are aware, some are informed, some are interested, some have a desire to buy, and some have an intention. Consumers can also be categorized by their *degree of enthusiasm* for a product, e.g., enthusiastic, positive, indifferent, negative, or hostile, as well as by their *price sensitivity*, e.g., during economic recession segments tend to be more price sensitive.

Finally, buyers may differ in their *search behavior* and the way they can be "contacted" by marketers. They use different retail outlets, different shopping styles, are exposed to different media, and are sensitive to different creative advertisements. It is suggested that in mature markets it may be effective to segment by this *contact sensitivity* (Dickinson, 1994). Contact segmentation may also be less obvious to competitors and, therefore, more difficult to imitate.

see also **Market segmentation**

Bibliography

Cook, V. J. & Mindak, W. A. (1984). A search for constants: The "heavy user" revisited. *Journal of Marketing*, 48, (4), 79–81.
Dickson, P. R. (1994). *Marketing management*. Orlando, Fla: The Dryden Press international edn.
Kotler, P. (1991). *Marketing management: Analysis, planning, implementation and control*, 7th edn, Englewood Cliffs, NJ: Prentice-Hall.
Landon, E. L. (1974). Self concept, ideal self concept, and consumer purchase intentions. *Journal of Consumer Research*, 1, Sept., 44–51.
Mitchman, R. (1991). *Lifestyle market segmentation*. New York: Praeger.
Murphy, P. E. & Staples, W. A. (1979). A modernized family life cycle. *Journal of Consumer Research*, 6, June, 12–22.
Sheth, J. (1977). *What is multivariate analysis? Multivariate methods for market and survey research*. Chicago: American Marketing Association.
Twedt, D. W. (1974). How important to marketing strategy is the "Heavy User?" *Journal of Marketing*, 38, Jan., 70–76.
Wells, W. C. & Gubar, G. (1966). Life cycle concept in marketing research. *Journal of Marketing Research*, 3, Nov., 355–363.
Yankelovich, D. (1964). New criteria for market segmentation. *Harvard Business Review*, 42, Mar.–Apr., 83–90.

VINCE MITCHELL

selection models Selection models are descriptions of the ways in which organizations collect and use information to make decisions about the assignment of people to various treatments (e.g. hire, reject, promote, train). Decision-makers must first collect data using psychological tests or other assessment procedures that yield information relevant to the examinees' abilities to perform relevant job tasks. Decision-makers then need to combine that information in a way that provides correct predictions about the examinees' subsequent job performance.

Mechanical versus Judgmental Data Collection

Through JOB ANALYSIS, an organization identifies the type of knowledge, skills, abilities, and other characteristics (*see* KSAOs) required to perform the tasks that comprise a job.

Human resource specialists have developed a wide variety of techniques to assess the degree to which individuals possess these critical KSAOs. These data collection procedures include mechanical procedures such as psychological tests (or documentation of experience and education requirements), which are relatively easily and objectively scored. In contrast, other data collection procedures involve subjective judgments on the part of an evaluator as to whether an examinee possesses or lacks the required KSAOs. The most common judgmental approach to data collection is the EMPLOYMENT INTERVIEW, though there are certainly subjective elements in other data collection procedures, such as various work simulations, or even the evaluation of the degree to which particular credentials indicate the possession of a desired job-relevant attribute.

Actuarial versus Clinical Decision-making
Once relevant KSAO data are collected, the organizational decision-maker must determine *how* to combine that information to predict each applicant's expected job success. If the organization uses an *actuarial* approach to the use of information, it combines the information using a statistical formula that is based on the statistical relationship between KSAOs and subsequent job success as established in previous research studies. This procedure assumes that the KSAO–job performance relationship is the same in the current group of examinees as it was in those samples in which the research was conducted. Decision quality is dependent solely on the adequate identification of KSAO–job performance relationships.

In *clinical* decision-making, a person considers the entire array of information regarding an applicant's KSAOs. This information is compared to his or her own experience with the job and organization, and prior experience evaluating previous candidates (and those candidates' subsequent job performance). This approach to decision-making is much more individualistic and subjective; the skill of the decision-maker in integrating this array of information is a critical determinant of decision quality.

Non-compensatory and Compensatory Models
One other concern that is important when information is combined to make selection decisions is whether to use that information in a compensatory or non-compensatory fashion. A *compensatory* combination rule is one in which low levels on one ability can be compensated for by high levels on other abilities. For example, an applicant whose computer keyboarding skills are not great would be able to perform a job requiring such skills if he or she was motivated to attain the required level of skill. In effect, superior motivation would compensate for a current lack of keyboarding skills. Occasionally, a *non-compensatory* rule is appropriate. For example, one's technical competence in operating some piece of machinery would not compensate for a lack of color vision if the machine controls were color coded. In this case, no amount of technical competence could compensate for a lack of color vision. Both compensatory and non-compensatory approaches to combining information are possible with either clinical or actuarial decision-making.

Bibliography
Cascio, W. F. (1987). *Applied Psychology in Management*, Englewood Cliffs, NJ: Prentice-Hall.
Schneider, B. & Schmitt, N. (1986). *Staffing Organizations*, Prospect Heights, IL: Waveland Press.

NEAL SCHMITT

selection of expatriates   One of the most important tasks associated with managing an international firm is the selection of employees to represent the firm overseas. Expatriate selection is the process used to select employees who will have the best chances of success. Although many companies stress the importance of technical competence, many other factors should also enter into the selection equation. Improperly selected or improperly trained employees can do irreparable harm to an organization's overseas operations and image in a surprisingly short period of time.

The following discussion reviews a number of factors which must be addressed during the expatriate selection process. Failure to address even one of the factors may result in sending an unprepared or unsuitable employee overseas.

1 The task to be completed – Probably the most common concern of employers is whether the employee has the capability of carrying out the work in a foreign country. That is, is the employee well trained and qualified in the job? Is the employee technically prepared to accomplish what the employer expects? This must be judged not only from the actual tasks but also the ability to manage others to carry out the tasks. Someone who has never managed people should not be sent overseas for their first management position.

2 The country setting – Sending expatriates to a country which is similar to the home country (Canadians to the United States, for example) is a much simpler task than sending them to a country which is much different (US citizen to China). When the assignment country is very different from the home country extensive training should be undertaken to prepare the expatriate (and family members if accompanied) for not only business but daily life. Questions which require answers: "Is the employee a good student?;" "Does he or she enjoy learning and facing challenges?;" "Are the skills too different from existing skills for training to be effective?;" and "Does the company have the ability to train the employee in the appropriate skills needed for personal and business life while on assignment?" Many times employees are prepared for the business side of the assignment, but poorly prepared for dealing with personal or family problems which may arise.

3 Adaptability of expatriate – People being considered for expatriate positions must be flexible in their thinking, willing to learn new things, be able to get along with others well, and be adaptable to whatever situation arises. The inconveniences and surprises associated with overseas life also demand a good sense of humor and an understanding that the assignment is also an experience to be enjoyed. The employee must learn that differences exist and to not be judgmental. Categorizing different customs as wrong or right or good or bad places the expatriate in a precarious position especially when living and working in a culture that expresses the opposite values.

4 Language facility – The ability to converse in the native language of the host country is a positive factor in terms

of expatriate success. Although it is true that business is often carried out in English or some language other than the host country's, it is also true that it is easier to get along if the host country language is spoken by the expatriate. People are generally more accepting of someone from a foreign country if that person knows or at least attempts to learn and use the language. Although fluency is preferred, a good try is also respected in most countries. Not knowing the language also places a manager in a position of having to rely too heavily on others to accomplish even the simplest of tasks. This does not speak well of the manager's ability to take command of a situation when that becomes necessary.

5 Family considerations – If the expatriate has a family all of the items just reviewed also apply to "each" family member (except infants), except that the context is changed from business life to family life. Does the spouse expect to work? Will the spouse be allowed to work under the laws of the host country? Education for the children is also a major consideration. Many foreign assignment locations do not have educational facilities comparable to the home country. Provision of health-care may be through a completely different system than in the home country. This is also a major consideration especially if children are accompanying the expatriate.

Bibliography

Bird, A. & Dunbar, R. (1991). Getting the job done over there: Improving expatriate productivity. *National Productivity Review*, Spring, 145–56.

Black, J. S. (1988). Work role transitions: A study of American expatriate managers in Japan. *Journal of International Business Studies*, 19 (2), 277–94.

Black, J. S. & Stephens, G. K. (1989). The influence of the spouse on American expatriate adjustment and intent to stay in Pacific Rim overseas assignments. *Journal of Management*, 15 (4), 529–44.

Brown, R. (1987). How to choose the best expatriates. *Personnel Management*, June, 67.

Feldman, D. C. & Thomas, D. C. (1992). Career management issues facing expatriates. *Journal of International Business Studies*, 23 (2), 271–94.

Golding, J. (1993). *Working abroad: Essential financial planning for expatriates and their employers*. Plymouth: International Venture Handbooks.

Harris, J. E. (1989). Moving managers internationally: The care and feeding of expatriates. *Human Resources Planning*, 12, 49–53.

Harvey, M. (1985). The executive family: An overlooked variable in international assignments. *Journal of International Business Studies*. Columbia Journal of World Business, 785–800.

Hays, R. D. (1974). Expatriate selection: Insuring success and avoiding failure. *Journal of International Business Studies*, 5, 25–37.

Mendenhall, M. E., Dunbar, E. & Oddou, Gary (1987) Expatriate selection, training, and career pathing: A review and critique. *Human Resource Management*, 26, 331–45.

Napier, N. K. & Peterson, R. B. (1990). Expatriate reentry: What do repatriates have to say? *Human Resource Planning*, 14, 19–28.

Naumann, E. (1993). Organizational predictors of expatriate job satisfaction. *Journal of International Business Studies* 61–4.

Nicholson, W. (1989). On the far side: Stories about expatriate life. *The Expatriate Observer*, January, 26–7.

Ronen, S. & Tung, R. L. (1981). Selection and training of personnel for overseas assignments. *Columbia Journal of World Business*, Spring, 68–78.

Shahzad, N. (1984). The American expatriate manager: Present and future roles. *Personnel Administrator*, 29, 23–5.

JOHN O'CONNELL

selection utility models A selection utility model is a theoretical equation for translating the results of a criterion-related validity study into terms that are meaningful to organizational decision-makers, such as dollar-valued increases in job performance, percent increases in output, and reduction in the number of employees needed. The most frequently applied selection utility models provide decision-makers with a framework for systematically considering the benefits and costs of alternative personnel selection procedures or decisions.

Brogden's Selection Utility Model
Brogden's (1949) contributions are still the basis for much of the utility analysis work done by human resource researchers and practitioners today. Brogden demonstrated that an estimate of the dollar value, or utility, of a selection program is a function of the number of individuals hired, the correlation between the selection procedure scores and job performance scores, the standard deviation of job performance in dollar terms (SD_y), the mean selection procedure score (expressed in a standard score form, with mean and standard deviation equal to 0 and 1, respectively) of the newly hired employees, and the total cost of the selection program. As noted by several authors, a slightly modified version of Brogden's model can be used for examining the gain in utility of a new selection program over an existing one.

One of the most difficult quantities to estimate when applying Brogden's model is SD_y. Strictly speaking, one would need information about the dollar value of the performance of each employee to compute SD_y. Given the difficulties in obtaining such individual level data, several simpler methods for estimating SD_y have been proposed.

Global SD_y estimation procedures. Schmidt et al.'s (1979) procedure has subject matter experts (e.g. supervisors) estimate the dollar value, to the organization, of the goods and services produced by the average employee as well as by employees at the 15th and 85th percentiles. Under the assumption that the dollar value of employee performance is normally distributed, the differences between the values associated with the 50th and 15th percentiles and the 85th and 15th percentiles each represent estimation of SD_y. These separate estimates are then averaged to obtain a final estimate of SD_y. Alternative global SD_y estimation procedures, which employ consensus seeking processes or anchoring (feedback) and adjustment processes, have been evaluated (Burke and Frederick, 1984).

Cascio–Ramos estimate of performance in dollars (CREPID). Cascio and Ramos (1986) proposed an SD_y estimation procedure which relies on JOB ANALYSIS information, performance ratings, and labor costs. Essentially, the CREPID procedure produces a dollar value for each employee based on multiplying mean salary for the employee's job times the employee's weighted overall performance rating. The standard deviation of these employee dollar values is assumed to be equal to SD_y. Modifications to CREPID which rely on existing job analysis and employee PERFORMANCE APPRAISAL information have been proposed. Other types of SD_y estimates, which rely on rules of thumb (such as 40 percent of mean salary) or which have relevance to particular settings (e.g. military), have also been suggested. A number of studies (see Boudreau, 1991, for a review) have assisted us in gaining a better understanding of the relationships between alternative SD_y estimation procedures. A typical finding is that SD_y estimates based on the CREPID procedure and 40 percent of mean salary are somewhat consistent; whereas global estimates tend to be greater. These results are understandable given how utility is defined for each procedure as well as our knowledge of the mathematical relationships between the various SD_y estimation procedures.

Extensions and Modifications to Brogden's Selection Utility Model

The significant work of Cronbach and Gleser (1965) addressed the utility of classification, placement, and sequential selection. Boudreau (1991) and his colleagues' work more directly focused on extending Brogden's utility model to incorporate economic concepts (variable costs, taxes, and discounting), the effects of recruitment activities, and the flow of employees into and out of the organization. In addition, Cronshaw and Alexander (1985) incorporated capital budgeting techniques into Brogden's model and subsequently argued that dollar utility can be defined in terms of costs, revenues, and investments. Finally, regression-based utility equations which do not require correcting validity coefficients for range restriction (typically considered in VALIDITY GENERALIZATION analyses) have been presented (Raju et al., 1995).

The above adjustments to Brogden's utility model have given researchers and practitioners a better understanding of the complexities involved in estimating selection program utility. In addition, discussions in the literature concerning changes in performance levels over time, possible decays in the predictive effectiveness of selection procedures over time, and the assumed effects of labor market conditions on selection utility have advanced our understanding of the factors impacting selection utility estimates. Overall, this line of research has assisted organizations in gaining a better sense for the economic value of validated personnel selection programs.

Notwithstanding the complexities of estimating selection utility, researchers have discussed how one can deal with the uncertainty of these utility estimates in decision contexts. Among several approaches, focusing on break-even values (minimum values necessary for utility gain to meet the costs associated with a personnel selection program) offers a practical means for decision-making.

Raju, Burke, and Normand's Selection Utility Model

Based on a different set of assumptions than Brogden about the relationship between behavioral performance and the dollar value of job performance, Raju et al. (1990) presented another regression-based utility model and set of equations for estimating selection utility. Whereas Brogden's model requires an estimate of SD_y to compute selection utility in dollar terms, the Raju et al. model requires an estimate of the economic value of the job (the constant "A" in their equations) to express selection in dollars. Recently, researchers have debated the promise of this model for overcoming problems in the estimation of selection program utility.

It should also be noted that the criterion variable in both Brogden's and Raju et al.'s models (typically job performance expressed in dollars) is assumed to be continuous. Several researchers have proposed utility models for evaluating selection procedures based on a dichotomized criterion (i.e. when all individuals in the "unsuccessful group" are assigned the same low value on the criterion and all of those in the "successful group" are assigned the same high value on the criterion).

Jarrett's Selection Utility Model for Estimating Percentage Increase in Output

Jarrett (1948) presented a general formula for estimating the percentage increase in *output* for a validated personnel selection program. He showed that an estimate of the percentage increase in output was a direct function of the validity coefficient, the coefficient of variation (the ratio of the standard deviation of output to mean output), and the mean standard score on the selection procedure of the selected group. In recent years, researchers have examined the extent to which the coefficient of variation (sometimes referred to as SD_p) varies as a function of job complexity. Jarrett's utility model and subsequent research related to estimating the coefficient of variation has increased our understanding of the percentage increase in output resulting from the use of validated selection programs, especially for jobs where performance is quantifiable.

Bibliography

Boudreau, J. W. (1991). Utility analysis for decisions in human resource management. *Handbook of Industrial and Organizational Psychology*, 2, Eds. Dunnette, M. D. & Hough, L. M. Palo Alto, CA: Consulting Psychologists Press.

Brogden, H. E. (1949). When testing pays off. *Personnel Psychology*, 2, 171–83.

Burke, M. J. & Frederick, J. T. (1984). Two modified procedures for estimating standard deviations in utility analyses. *Journal of Applied Psychology*, 69, 482–9.

Cascio, W. F. & Ramos, R. A. (1986). Development and application of a new method for assessing job performance in behavioral/economic terms. *Journal of Applied Psychology*, 71, 20–8.

Cronbach, L. J. & Gleser, G. C. (1965). *Psychological Tests and Personnel Decisions*, Urbana, IL: University of Illinois Press.

Cronshaw, S. F. & Alexander, R. A. (1985). One answer to the demand for accountability: selection utility as an investment decision. *Organizational Behavior and Human Decision Processes*, 40, 270–86.

Jarrett, R. F. (1948). Per cent increase in output of selected personnel as an index of test efficiency. *Journal of Applied Psychology*, 32, 135–45.

Raju, N. S., Burke, M. J. & Maurer, T. (1995). A note on direct range restriction corrections in utility analyses. *Personnel Psychology*, 48, 143–9.

Raju, N. S., Burke, M. J. & Normand, J. (1990). A new approach for utility analysis. *Journal of Applied Psychology*, 75, 3–12.

Schmidt, F. L., Hunter, J. E., McKenzie, R. C. & Muldrow, T. (1979). The impact of valid selection procedures on work force productivity. *Journal of Applied Psychology*, 64, 609–24.

MICHAEL J. BURKE

self-awareness training   Students of human behavior have long suggested that knowledge of oneself (self-awareness) is essential to productive personal and interpersonal functioning. Dimensions of self-awareness include personal values, cognitive style, interpersonal orientation, personality and interests. Self-awareness training typically consists of the trainee completing and interpreting one or more self-assessment instruments (e.g. Myers–Briggs type indicator) and then receiving feedback from others, sometimes in an unstructured format known as sensitivity training. An increasingly popular form of self-awareness training involves "360 degree feedback" (Van Velsor and Leslie, 1991), which refers to feedback collected from all those within a trainee's sphere of influence (e.g. superiors, subordinates, peers and customers) (*see* 360 DEGREE APPRAISALS).

Bibliography

Van Velsor, E. & Leslie, J. B. (1991). *Feedback to Managers: a Review and Comparison of Sixteen Multi-rater Feedback Instruments (Technical Report No. 150)*, 2, Greensboro, NC: Center for Creative Leadership.

TIMOTHY T. BALDWIN

self-management   When work is done in an organization, four functions must be fulfilled. One, someone must actually *execute* the work – applying personal energy (physical or mental) to accomplish tasks. Two, someone must *monitor* and manage the work process – collecting and interpreting data about how the work is proceeding and initiating corrective action as needed. Three, someone must *design* the performing unit and arrange for needed organizational supports for the work – structuring tasks, deciding who will perform them, establishing core norms of conduct in the work setting, and making sure people have the resources and supports they need to carry out the work. Four, someone must set direction for the organizational unit, determining the collective objectives and aspirations that spawn the myriad of smaller tasks that pervade any organization.

Four types of performing units can be distinguished in terms how authority for these four functions are distributed. (The term *performing unit* refers to the people who have been assigned responsibility for accomplishing some specified task. A performing unit can be a single individual, a team (*see* SELF-MANAGING TEAMS), or an entire organizational unit whose members share responsibility for a major piece of organizational work.)

Manager-led units: Members have authority only for actually executing the task; managers monitor and manage performance processes, structure the unit and its context, and set overall directions. This type of unit has been common in US industry since the "scientific management" ideas of Taylor (1911) took hold early in the century (*see* SCIENTIFIC MANAGEMENT). In this view, managers manage, workers work, and the two functions are kept distinct.

Self-managing units: Members have responsibility not only for executing the task but also for monitoring and managing their own performance. This type of unit is often seen in new plants designed in accord with what has been termed the "COMMITMENT model" of management (Walton, 1985). Self-managing units are commonplace in managerial and professional work (e.g., a team of research assistants who share responsibility for collecting a set of data) (*see* MANAGERIAL BEHAVIOR).

Self-designing units: Members have the authority to modify the design of the unit itself or aspects of the organizational context in which the unit operates. Managers set the direction for such units but assign to members full authority to do what needs to be done to get the work accomplished. Top management task forces often are self-designing units (e.g., a team created to develop a new program and given free reign in determining how the work will be structured, supported, and carried out).

Self-governing units: Members have responsibility for all four of the major functions listed above: They decide what is to be done, structure the unit and its context, manage their own performance, and actually carry out the work. Examples of self-governing units include certain legislative bodies, some corporate boards of directors, advisory councils of community service agencies, worker cooperatives, and sole proprietorships.

Although the four types of units are described above as if they are distinct, that is merely a convenience. In practice, units often fall on the boundaries of the self-management categories.

see also **Employee involvement; Empowerment**

Bibliography

Hackman, J. R. (1986). The psychology of self-management in organizations. In M. S. Pallack & R. O. Perloff (Eds), Psychology and work: Productivity, change, and employment. Washington, DC: American Psychological Association.

Manz, C. E. & Sims, H. P. Jr. (1989). Superleadership: Leading others to lead themselves. Englewood Cliffs, NJ: Prentice-Hall.

Taylor, F. W. (1911). The principles of scientific management. New York: Harper.

Walton, R. E. (1985). From control to commitment: Transformation of workforce management strategies in the United States. In K. B. Clark, R. H. Hayes & C. Lorenz (Eds), The uneasy alliance: Managing the productivity-technology dilemma. Boston: Harvard Business School Press.

J. RICHARD HACKMAN

self-managing teams   Self-managing teams are groups of people who (a) perform interdependent work, (b) are collectively responsible for the accomplishment of a product or service, and (c) self-regulate their work. They are also referred to as semi-autonomous or autonomous work teams and self-regulating teams. Although they vary in their authority limits and amount of autonomy, they are all characterized by increased internal control that results when management tasks such as planning, scheduling and staffing, organizing, and monitoring work are made a team responsibility. By one typology (Hackman, 1982), a self-designing team also controls its team's design, including its goals and composition. Self-managing teams are a form of horizontal management.

Self-managing teams extend the principles of motivating job design, or job enrichment, to the team level (Hackman and Oldham, 1980). Teams are appropriate when an individual cannot perform a whole task, so whole product identification is only possible at the group level. Work technology also determines the appropriateness of teams. Self-managing teams are appropriate when work is interdependent and uncertain, requiring a great deal of on-line interaction and mutual adjustment. The determination of the appropriateness of the use of self-managing teams is often accomplished through a socio-technical analysis aimed at jointly optimizing the technical and social design of the work system (Pasmore, 1988).

Three conditions are especially important for successful application of self-managing teams (Cummings, 1978). First, the task of the team must be differentiated and self-contained. Second, the team must have boundary control over its inputs and outputs. These first two conditions exist when the team contains the necessary resources and skills to perform its production tasks and to do its own support tasks and quality control. It also interfaces directly with its suppliers and customers. The third condition is task control, the ability to self-regulate team behavior in converting inputs into products or services. These factors enable the team to be held accountable for its performance.

Implementation of self-managing teams requires the redesign of many aspects of the organizational system. Team members are generally cross-trained (see CROSS-TRAINING) to facilitate mutual coordination, provide flexibility in task assignment, and enable the team to perform expanded functions. Salary is often based, in part, on the skills that have been mastered by each individual. In addition, team bonuses are sometimes used to reward team performance. Personnel and performance management functions such as goal-setting, feedback, appraisal, interviewing and hiring, disciplining, and firing may all be team responsibilities. In some cases these are joint responsibilities with management.

Management structures and roles change significantly to provide a context suitable for self-managing teams. Supervisors may be responsible for several teams. Their role changes from day-to-day direction to helping to develop the team to manage itself (Manz and Sims, 1989). In some instances, the supervisory level may be eliminated altogether, as team leaders perform management tasks or leadership roles are dispersed among team members. Support functions such as maintenance or quality may be radically reduced in size, and remaining functional experts may be used in a consulting role to the teams.

The historical roots of self-managing teams lie in the socio-technical tradition and originated in Europe (e.g. Trist and Bamforth, 1951). Early applications focused on the shop floor, largely in production settings characterized by continuous process technology. Recently, use has spread to KNOWLEDGE WORK settings. Supporting design changes include flattening the organization, distributing performance-related information to employees, extensive training and development, eliminating status differences, rewarding for performance and skills, and creating conditions for employee empowerment.

Research on self-managing teams finds modest evidence of positive impact on attitudinal and organizational performance results (Cohen, 1994). Results are believed to be best when they are used in a supportive context and when adequate attention is given to examining and co-optimizing the technical system. Although dissemination of this approach has been slow, data show that the application of self-managing teams is steadily increasing. For example, over 60 percent of the largest US firms now employ self-managing teams in some operations (Lawler et al., 1995).

Bibliography

Cohen, S. G. (1994). Designing effective self-managing work teams. *Advances in Interdisciplinary Studies of Work Teams*, 1, Beyerlein, M., Greenwich, CT: JAI Press.

Cummings, T. G. (1978). Self-regulating work groups: a socio-technical synthesis. *Academy of Management Review*, 3, 625–34.

Hackman, J. R. (1982). The design of work teams. *The Handbook of Organizational Behavior*, Lorsch, J. W. Englewood Cliffs, NJ: Prentice-Hall.

Hackman, J. R. & Oldham, G. R. (1984). *Work Redesign*, Reading, MA: Addison-Wesley.

Lawler, E. E. III (1986). *High Involvement Management*, San Francisco: Jossey-Bass.

Lawler, E. E. III, Mohrman, S. A. & Ledford, G. E. Jr (1995). *Creating High Performance Organizations*, San Francisco: Jossey-Bass.

Manz, C. M. & Sims, H. P. (1989). *Super-leadership: Leading Others to Lead Themselves*, Englewood Cliffs, NJ: Prentice-Hall.

Pasmore, W. A. (1988). *Designing Effective Organizations: the Sociotechnical Systems Perspective*, New York: John Wiley & Sons.

Trist, E. L. & Bamforth, K. W. (1951). Some social psychological consequences of the longwall method of coal-getting. *Human Relations*, 338.

SUSAN ALBERS MOHRMAN

self-ratings   Self-ratings in an organizational setting involve asking organization members to evaluate themselves on overall performance, or, more often, on several individual dimensions of performance (e.g. job knowledge, planning, and organizing). Self-evaluations are used most often for developmental purposes, and often are used in conjunction with SUPERVISORY RATINGS or subordinates' ratings (see also 360 DEGREE APPRAISALS). Employees are then given these other ratings so that they can judge how they may have under- or overestimated their performance in each area. In addition, self-ratings are occasionally used as criterion scores for selection or other kinds of research when ratings from other sources are not available.

An obvious advantage of self-ratings is that the "rater" has a lot of knowledge about "ratee" performance. A disadvantage is that self-ratings may often overestimate actual performance levels. In fact, research shows that self-ratings are typically more lenient than PEER RATINGS or supervisor ratings (Borman, 1991). Further, a meta-analysis (Harris and Schaubroeck, 1988) found that inter-rater agreement between self-ratings and either peer ratings or supervisor ratings was low ($r = 0.35$ and 0.36, respectively) compared to the agreement between peers and supervisors ($r = 0.62$).

Finally, the issue of self-rating validity was explored by Mabe and West (1982). They conducted a meta-analysis of correlations between self-ratings of abilities and criterion scores (mostly test scores or supervisory ratings). The mean validity coefficient was 0.29, but these validities varied considerably. Relatively high validity coefficients were obtained when raters (a) made relative rather than absolute judgments, (b) had comparatively more experience providing ratings, (c) were told that their ratings were anonymous, (d) rated past rather than future performance, and (e) were told that their ratings would be compared to criterion scores.

Bibliography

Borman, W. C. (1991). Job behavior, performance, and effectiveness. *The Handbook of Industrial and Organizational Psychology*, 2, Eds. Dunnette, M. D. & Hough, L. M. Palo Alto, CA: Consulting Psychologists Press.

Harris, M. M. & Schaubroeck, J. (1988). A meta-analysis of self–supervisor, self–peer, and peer–supervisor ratings. *Personnel Psychology*, 41, 43–62.

Mabe, P. A. & West, S. G. (1982). Validity of self-evaluation of ability: a review and meta-analysis. *Journal of Applied Psychology*, **67**, 280–96.

WALTER C. BORMAN

service characteristics A number of generic characteristics of services distinguish them from products, namely, intangibility, inseparability, heterogeneity, and perishability (see Lovelock, 1983 & 1991 (Chapter 2); Gronroos, 1990).

Intangibility
Services are generally characterized as intangible although tangible elements may prevail (*see* SERVICE PRODUCT). Services may be seen as "performances" rather than products (e.g., entertainment, professional services, education), and are consumed rather than possessed (e.g., legal, hairdressing). They cannot be seen, touched, or used prior to use and often the results of use cannot be seen (e.g., medical treatment, insurance policies, education). This leads to problems for both service providers, e.g., patenting is not possible, promotion is difficult, and quality standards (*see* SERVICE QUALITY) are difficult to set and adhere to; and for the consumer, e.g., testing prior to purchase is not available (see Flipo, 1988).

Inseparability of Production and Consumption
For most services, creating or performing the service (production) may occur at the same time as partial or full consumption of it (e.g., entertainment, hairdressing). Further, services may be sold before they are produced and consumed (travel services, private and university education). In addition, many services cannot be separated from the person of the service provider (e.g., lawyer, real estate agent), and the service provider is often present when consumption takes place (e.g., hairdresser, advice services). In general the role of service providers' personnel (both customer-contact and "back-room" employees) has implications for human resource management issues. And customers may be involved in the production of a service (e.g., dentist, hairdresser, meal in a restaurant) and affect the service process (*see* SERVICE PROCESS) and the consumers' perceptions of service quality (*see* SERVICE QUALITY). In many instances, inseparability of production and consumption implies that direct sale is the only channel of distribution (*see* SERVICE DISTRIBUTION).

Heterogeneity
Heterogeneity of services refers to the variability or lack of standardization or uniformity in the "assembly," "production," and delivery of services. Service standards may not be precise due to a lack of mass production (in most services), i.e., the characteristics of the service product (*see* SERVICE PRODUCT) – e.g., haircuts, football team performance, professional services. There will also be variability with respect to the service environment, i.e., the mix of physical facilities involved, and the involvement of people (both service personnel and customers) in the production and delivery process.

Lovelock (1983 & 1991) also refers to variation with respect to customization and judgement in service delivery, i.e., the extent to which the service is customized to meet consumer needs (high for professional services, health care, education, restaurants), and the extent to which customer-contact personnel exercise judgement in meeting individual customers' demands.

Perishability
Services are perishable and so cannot be stored. Perishability is manifested in various ways: e.g., if theater seats and hotel rooms are not sold and occupied then their capacity is wasted; "no-shows" and vacant appointments with dentists and other service professionals represent an element of lost capacity although the provider may be able to use the time for some other, more peripheral, purpose; under-enrollment in a class is also wasted capacity and revenue – although it might improve the quality of service provided to those in the class. Potential perishability is exacerbated by fluctuating demand which service providers may be able to manage (e.g., with respect to utilities) or which may present problems (e.g., with respect to transport, accommodation, theater seats). Excess demand may lead to delays, unmet demand, and dissatisfied customers.

Service providers manage their supply and demand in a number of ways (see Sasser, 1976; Maister, 1985; Lovelock, 1991 (Chapter 6); Mudie & Cottam, 1993; Palmer, 1994). Demand may be managed by:

- differential pricing and price incentives at non-peak times
- developing and promoting non-peak demand
- developing complementary services for consumers while they are waiting
- creating reservation systems to reduce waiting
- using technology/computers in service delivery.

Alternatively, service companies aim to manage supply through a combination of:
- part-time employees
- increased customer participation (to reduce labor input)
- shared capacity and services
- multiple jobs for employees
- a substitution of machines for labor
- attempts to maximize efficiency.

Bibliography

Flipo, J. P. (1988). On the intangibility of services. *The Service Industries Journal*, 8, (3), 286–298.
Gronroos, C. (1990). *Service management and marketing*. Chapter 2 Lexington, MA: Lexington Books.
Lovelock, C. H. (1983). Classifying services to gain strategic marketing insights. *Journal of Marketing*, 47, Summer 9–20.
Lovelock, C. H. (1991). *Services marketing*, 2nd edn, Prentice-Hall. Chapters 2 & 6.
Maister, D. H. (1985). The psychology of waiting lines. In J. A. Czepiel, M. R. Solomon, C. F. Surprenant (Eds), *The service encounter* Lexington, MA: Lexington Books.
Mudie, P. & Cottam, A. (1993). *The management and marketing of services*. Oxford: Butterworth-Heinemann. Chapter 8.
Palmer, A. (1994). *Principles of marketing*. Maidenhead: McGraw-Hill. Chapter 7.
Sasser, W. E. (1976). Match supply and demand in service industries. *Harvard Business Review*, 48, Nov.–Dec., 133–140.

BARBARA LEWIS

service delivery The consumer may be actively involved in the production and delivery process, e.g., in applying for a loan, providing information for tax returns, using salad bars in restaurants, and explaining symptoms to a health care professional. The organization may have to "manage" the customer input; e.g., to tell him/her how to use equipment in a gym, to clear the table in McDonalds, and "how to behave" in DisneyWorld. This will facilitate and enhance the service encounter. Customers' participation in service delivery may provide them with some control in the service delivery process, allow more customization, and a faster service, and may lead to lower prices.

Technology is typically central to service delivery, and also integral to the SERVICE PRODUCT, service process, and service environment, and technological advances have made major contributions to facilitating customer–company exchanges and to increasing levels of service. For example, mechanization and computerization can increase speed, efficiency, and accuracy of service (e.g., in stocktaking, ordering and distribution, operations, reservations systems, management and marketing information systems, and security systems), but can also depersonalize service. Depersonalized service can free employees for other activities which may detract from customer contact and lead to less customer loyalty; or it may allow employees time to concentrate on developing interactions and relationships to maintain customer loyalty. Ultimately, technology will not replace people in the provision of service(s), and "high-tech" and "high-touch" go hand in hand – better personal service with enhanced technological efficiency.

see also **Service distribution**

Bibliography

Kelley, S. W., Donnelly, J. H. & Skinner, S. J. (1990). Customer participation in service production and delivery. *Journal of Retailing*, **66**, (3), Fall 315–335.

BARBARA LEWIS

service distribution   Service distribution channels comprise service firms, their intermediaries, and their customers. Typically, there are high levels of direct sale due to the inseparability of services and the provider organizations, e.g., business and professional services, utilities, personal services; together with the existence of intermediaries, e.g., agents for tourism, insurance, employment, and retailers. Quasi-retail outlets are also used to sell services: e.g., banks, building societies, launderettes, hotels, real estate agents.

In addition, one needs to consider the ways in which the customer is involved in service distribution (*see also* SERVICE DELIVERY). Sometimes the customer travels to the service-providing organization, e.g., theater, airplane, hotel; and at other times the provider comes to the customer, e.g., business and household cleaning services. Various services may have both types of distribution, e.g., taxi services, hairdressing, beauty services, professional business services. A third scenario may involve no direct personal interaction, e.g., TV and radio services, and other remote service operations.

A recent trend in service distribution is the growth of franchising; this happens when standardization is possible and includes industries such as fast food, hotel chains, car rental, dry cleaning, and employment services. Technology also has increasing impact on services distribution, e.g., in: financial services with delivery from remote locations; the use of software packages to facilitate "best deals" for buying insurance and mortgages; and reservation systems for tourism and hospitality organizations, professional services, health care, etc.

Bibliography

Cowell, D. W. (1984). *The marketing of services*. London: Heinemann. Chapter 10.
Palmer, A. (1994). *Principles of marketing*. Maidenhead: McGraw-Hill. Chapter 10.

BARBARA LEWIS

service product   A service or service product may be defined as "an activity(s) of more or less intangible nature that normally, but not necessarily, takes place in inter-action between the customer and service employees and/or physical resources or goods and/or systems of the service provider, which are provided as solutions to customer problems" (Shostack, 1984). Shostack highlights the fact that the distinction between services and products is not clear-cut, that there are few pure services and products. For example, a car is a physical object and an airline provides a service, but transport is common to both. Shostack (1977 & 1982) provides molecular models which combine product and service elements, and she also offers a continuum of market offerings of products and services with respect to their tangibility (*see* SERVICE CHARACTERISTICS), i.e., tangible elements (see figure 1).

A further view of the service product is provided by Gronroos (1987 & 1990) who develops a concept of the service product – the service offering – which is geared to the concept of perceived service quality (*see* SERVICE QUALITY). First, there is the basic or core service package, e.g., a hotel, with facilitating services which are required to facilitate consumption of the service (e.g., reception) together with supporting services which are not required but which enhance the service and differentiate it from competition (e.g., restaurants and bars, leisure and conference facilities). All this is what the customer receives. In addition, one needs to consider how the service is delivered or received which is dependent on the augmented service offering. This includes the accessibility of the service; the extent of customer participation; and interactions/communications between the service provider (its personnel, systems, technology, and environment) and the consumer.

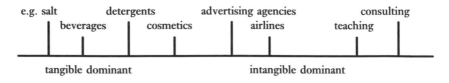

Figure 1: The Service Product
Source: Shostack, 1977 & 1982

Further aspects of the service product – i.e., service product planning and development – are discussed by Cowell (1984) and Palmer (1994).

Bibliography

Cowell, D. W. (1984). *The marketing of services.* London: Heinemann. Chapter 7.

Gronroos, C. (1987). Developing the service offering: A source of competitive advantage. Sept., Helsinki: Swedish School of Economics and Business Administration.

Gronroos, C. (1990). *Service management and marketing.* Lexington, MA: Lexington Books. Chapter 4.

Palmer, A. (1994). *Principles of services marketing.* Maidenhead: McGraw-Hill. Chapter 6.

Rathmell, J. (1966). What is meant by services. *Journal of Marketing,* **30**, Oct., 32–36.

Shostack, G. L. (1977). Breaking free from product marketing. *Journal of Marketing* Apr., 73–80.

Shostack, G. L. (1982). How to design a service. *European Journal of Marketing,* **16**, (1), 49–63.

Shostack, G. L. (1984). Designing services that deliver. *Harvard Business Review,* **62**, Jan.–Feb., 133–139.

Barbara Lewis

service quality dimensions The dimensions of service quality relate to the products/services being offered, delivery systems, delivery environment, technology, and employees (*see* SERVICE QUALITY), and have been widely conceptualized and researched. Lehtinen & Lehtinen (1982) refer to process quality, as judged by consumers during a service, and output quality judged after a service is performed. They also make a distinction between physical quality (products or support), interactive quality (where the dimensions of quality originate in the interaction between the customer and the service organization), and corporate quality (Lehtinen & Lehtinen, 1991).

Gronroos (1984) discussed the technical (outcome) quality of service encounters, i.e., what is received by the customer, and the functional quality of the process, i.e., the way in which the service is delivered. Functional aspects include the attitudes, behavior, appearance and personality, service-mindedness, accessibility, and approachability of customer-contact personnel. In addition, there exists the "corporate image" dimension of quality which is the result of how customers perceive an organization and is built up by the technical and functional quality of its services. This model was later incorporated with one from manufacturing which incorporates design, production, delivery, and relational dimensions (Gummesson & Gronroos, 1987).

LeBlanc & Nguyen (1988) suggested that corporate image, internal organization, physical support of the service product, systems, staff–customer interaction, and degree of customer satisfaction all contribute to service quality. Further, Edvardsson et al. (1989) present four aspects of quality which affect customers' perceptions:

- Technical quality – to include skills of service personnel and the design of the service system.
- Integrative quality – the ease with which different portions of the service delivery system work together.
- Functional quality – to include all aspects of the manner in which the service is delivered to the customer, to include style, environment, and availability.
- Outcome quality – whether or not the actual service product meets both service standards or specifications.

However, the most widely reported set of service quality determinants is that proposed by Parasuraman et al. (1985 & 1988). They suggest that the criteria used by consumers that are important in molding their expectations and perceptions of service fit ten dimensions:

- Tangibles: physical evidence.
- Reliability: getting it right the first time, honoring promises.
- Responsiveness: willingness, readiness to provide service.
- Communication: keeping customers informed in a language they can understand.
- Credibility: honesty, trustworthiness.
- Security: physical, financial, and confidentiality.
- Competence: possession of required skills and knowledge of all employees, e.g., to carry out instructions.
- Courtesy: politeness, respect, friendliness.
- Understanding/knowing the customer, e.g., his or her needs and requirements.
- Access: ease of approach and contact, e.g., opening hours, queues, phones.

Subsequent factor analysis and testing by Parasuraman et al. (1990) condensed these ten determinants into five categories (tangibles, reliability, responsiveness, assurance, and empathy) to which Gronroos (1988) added a sixth dimension – recovery (*see* SERVICE RECOVERY).

In addition, there is the contribution of Johnston et al. (1990) and Silvestro & Johnston (1990), investigating quality in UK organizations. They identified 15 dimensions of service quality which they categorized as: hygiene factors – expected by the customer and where failure to deliver will cause dissatisfaction (e.g., cleanliness in restaurant, train arrival on time); enhancing factors – which lead to customer satisfaction but where failure to deliver will not necessarily cause dissatisfaction (e.g., bank clerk addressing one by name); and dual threshold factors – where failure to deliver will cause dissatisfaction, and delivery above a certain level will enhance customers' perceptions of service and lead to satisfaction (e.g., a full explanation of a mortgage service).

Bibliography

Edvardsson, B., Gustavsson, B. O. & Riddle, D. I. (1989). An expanded model of the service encounter with emphasis on cultural context. Research Report 89: 4. University of Karlstad, Sweden: CTF Research Centre.

Gronroos, C. (1984). *Strategic management and marketing in the service sector.* Bromley, UK: Chartwell-Bratt.

Gronroos, C. (1988). Service quality: The six criteria of good perceived service quality. *Review of Business,* **9**, (3), Winter, 10–13.

Gummesson, E. & Gronroos, C. (1987). *Quality of products and services: A tentative synthesis between two models.* Research Report 87: 3. University of Karlstad, Sweden: Services Research Centre.

Johnston, R., Silvestro, R., Fitzgerald, L. & Voss, C. (1990). Developing the determinants of service quality. In E. Langeard & P. Eiglier (Eds), *Marketing, operations and human resources insights into service* (pp. 373–400). First International Research Seminar on Services Management. Aix-en-Provence, France: IAE.

LeBlanc, G. & Nguyen, N. (1988). Customers' perceptions of service quality in financial institutions. *International Journal of Bank Marketing*, 6, (4), 7–18.

Lehtinen, U. & Lehtinen, J. R. (1982). *Service quality: A study of quality dimensions.* Working paper. Helsinki: Service Management Institute.

Lehtinen, U. & Lehtinen, J. R. (1991). Two approaches to service quality dimensions. *The Service Industries Journal*, 11, (3), 287–303.

Parasuraman, A., Zeithaml, V. A. & Berry, L. L. (1985). A conceptual model of service quality and its implications for future research. *Journal of Marketing*, 49, Fall, 41–50.

Parasuraman, A., Zeithaml, V. A. & Berry, L. L. (1988). SERVQUAL: A multiple item scale for measuring consumer perceptions of service quality. *Journal of Retailing*, 64, (1), Spring, 14–40.

Parasuraman, A., Berry, L. L. & Zeithaml, V. A. (1990). Guidelines for conducting service quality research. *Marketing Research* Dec., 34–44.

Silvestro, R. & Johnston, R. (1990). *The determinants of service quality – hygiene and enhancing factors.* Warwick Business School, UK.

BARBARA LEWIS

services marketing Services marketing has evolved as a discipline for a number of reasons, in particular, an increasing acknowledgement that all organizations participate in marketing management (*see* MARKETING MANAGEMENT), and with the growth of service industries in developed economies.

The MARKETING CONCEPT is based on market exchange (*see* EXCHANGE) between buyers and sellers. All organizations have "products" and "markets" and are involved in market exchange and so need to be marketing oriented and to adopt the marketing concept. This includes public and private sector organizations, and profit and not-for-profit organizations – where business objectives may relate to social or community orientation. Further, organizations may have more than one market, e.g., charities and hospitals (see figure 1).

Charities are involved in exchanges with "donors" who contribute money, material goods, or their time/commit-

ment in return, typically, for "intangible" personal rewards; and also with "clients" who are recipients of help and benefits and who may, for example, be producing products which the charity can sell. Similarly, hospitals which are in the "business" of providing health care to patients are involved in numerous marketing exchanges with patients, employees, trustees, government, suppliers, etc. The concept of multiple customer markets is developed by Payne (1993) and by Christopher et al. (1991).

Charities and hospitals are examples of organizations/ businesses which comprise the services sector of an economy. As services have become increasingly critical within developed economies, so has the attention to MARKETING MANAGEMENT within the sector due, largely, to the characteristics of services (*see* SERVICE CHARACTERISTICS), and the ensuing implications for managing the marketing mix (*see* MARKETING MIX).

Services are typically seen to be characterized by intangibility, heterogeneity, inseparability, and perishability (*see* SERVICE CHARACTERISTICS). Further, the notion of service encounter is particular to the services sector and is concerned with interactions between services and their providing organizations and their personnel, and consumers. Service characteristics and service encounters are critical to understanding marketing management in the service sector, and have implications for the MARKETING MIX which includes product, price, place, and promotion (*see* SERVICE PRODUCT; SERVICE DISTRIBUTION). In addition, Booms & Bitner (1981) talk about an extended marketing mix for the services sector to include physical evidence, process, and people.

Bibliography
Bateson, J. E. G. (1992). *Managing services marketing*, 2nd edn, Chicago: The Dryden Press.

Blois, K. J. (1983). The structure of service firms and their marketing policies. *Strategic Management Journal*, 4, 251–261.

Booms, B. H. & Bitner, M. J. (1981). Marketing strategies and organization structures for service firms. In J. H. Donnelly & W. R. George (Eds), *Marketing of services* (pp. 47–51). Chicago: American Marketing Association.

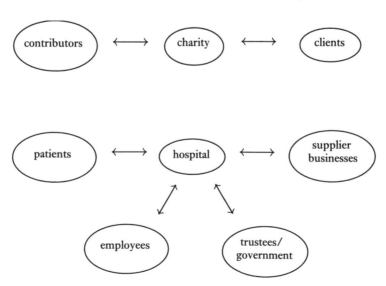

Figure 1   Services Marketing

Christopher, M., Payne, A. F. T. & Ballantyne, D. (1991). *Relationship marketing: Bringing quality, customer service and marketing together*. Oxford: Butterworth-Heinemann.

Cowell, D. W. (1984). *The marketing of services*. London: Heinemann. Chapter 2.

Kotler, P. (1979). Strategies for introducing marketing into non-profit organisations. *Journal of Marketing*, 43, Jan., 37–44.

Lovelock, C. H. (1991). *Services marketing*, 2nd edn, Prentice-Hall.

Mudie, P. & Cottam, A. (1993). *The management and marketing of services*. Oxford: Butterworth-Heinemann. Chapter 1.

Payne, A. (1993). *The essence of services marketing*. Prentice-Hall. Chapter 2.

BARBARA LEWIS

short run cost curves   The short run is defined as that period of time during which at least one input in production is fixed and cannot be changed. Frequently capital, such as plant and equipment, is treated as fixed in the short run while labor and materials are considered to be variable, but long-term labor contracts or unions may make some labor costs fixed as well. Given that at least one input is fixed in the short run, diminishing returns will apply to production.

Following convention and to simplify the discussion, consider a firm using only two inputs in production where capital will be treated as the fixed factor of production and labor will be considered variable. This means that, in the short run, the amount of capital the firm has available cannot be altered from its fixed level K_0 and the short run production function for the firm is then:

$$q = F(L, K_0) \qquad (1)$$

where q is the quantity of output produced and L is the quantity of labor employed. Total production costs for the firm will be equal to the wage rate (w) times the amount of labor employed (assuming labor can be hired at a constant wage) plus the fixed amount of capital times the economic cost of capital (r). Total costs are then:

$$TC = w \times L + r \times K_0 \qquad (2)$$

The first term on the right-hand side of equation (2) is the total labor cost for the firm and these are the firm's total variable costs in this example (*see* TOTAL VARIABLE COST). The second term on the right is the firm's economic cost of capital which is a fixed cost and does not vary with output. The firm's short run cost curves can then be derived by observing the changes in total costs (or the changes in total variable costs) as output changes. Since capital inputs are fixed in the short run, the firm must adjust labor inputs to change output, and the output which will be produced is determined by the production function in equation (1). In this example, total variable costs are just the labor costs in equation (2), so marginal costs are then equal to

$$MC = \frac{\Delta TVC}{\Delta q} = \frac{w \times \Delta L}{\Delta q}$$

$$= w \times \left\{ \frac{\Delta L}{\Delta q} \right\} = \frac{w}{MPL} \qquad (3)$$

where ΔTVC is the change in total variable costs, Δq is the change in output, and the term in braces on the right is the

inverse of the MARGINAL PRODUCT of labor (MP_L). The marginal cost curve is the slope of the total variable cost curve at different output levels and since the wage rate is assumed to be constant, marginal costs will vary with changes in the marginal product of labor. Variable and marginal costs will be zero if no labor is hired and no output is produced. If one worker were hired, the variable and marginal costs of producing the first few units of output would be high (because the marginal product of a single worker would be low), but as additional workers are hired, the marginal product of labor increases which causes marginal costs to decrease. Eventually, the marginal product of labor will reach a maximum value which, in this example, corresponds to the minimum value of the marginal cost curve. After this (point A in figure 1), the marginal product of labor decreases and the marginal cost of production increases.

The corresponding short run average cost curves can also be derived from the underlying production function and prices of inputs (see equations (1) and (2)). There are three short run average cost curves: average total costs (SRATC), average variable costs (SRAVC), and average fixed costs (SRAFC). These average cost curves are given by:

$$SRATC = \frac{TC}{q} = \frac{(w \times L + r \times K_0)}{q} \qquad (4)$$

$$SRAVC = \frac{TVC}{q} = \frac{w \times L}{q} \qquad (5)$$

$$SRAFC = \frac{TFC}{q} = \frac{r \times K_0}{q} \qquad (6)$$

where TC is the firm's total costs in equation (1) (including the opportunity costs of capital), TVC the firm's total variable costs and TFC the total fixed costs of the firm. Of these average cost curves, average fixed cost is the least important in economics because fixed costs do not affect short run decisions. The short run marginal, average and average variable cost curves are depicted in figure 1.

The marginal cost curve intersects both average cost curves at their respective minimum points (B and C), and as marginal costs continue to increase, the average cost curves rise but at a slower rate. As long as the marginal cost curve lies below the average variable and average total cost curves, the average cost curves must be falling because the cost of producing the last unit (the marginal cost) is less than the average cost of all the preceding units produced, and this pulls the average cost curves down. Similarly, when the marginal cost curve lies above the average variable and average total cost curves, it pulls them up since the cost of the last unit exceeds the average of the previous units produced and adding any number to an average which exceeds the average must force the average value to rise.

The average variable cost curve plays a role in short run decisions because the firm does not have to incur these costs and can choose to produce no output. Therefore, if the price the firm will receive for its output is too low, the revenues earned will not cover the firm's variable costs and the firm should shut down and produce nothing. Since

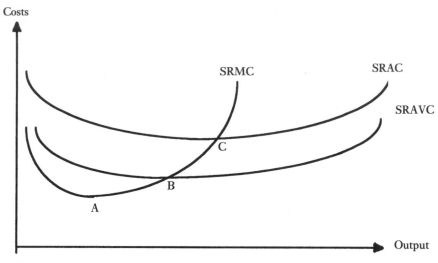

Figure 1   Short run cost curves

fixed costs must be paid whether or not the firm produces output, these costs should have no effect on a manager's decision to produce in the current period. But the firm must pay variable costs only when output is produced, and if those variable costs cannot be paid from the revenues generated from production, there is no reason to incur them. If the revenues can cover variable costs, then any additional earnings can be applied to fixed costs and reduce the firm's short run losses. A perfectly competitive firm will maximize profits by producing output where price equals marginal cost for those points where marginal cost lies above the short run average variable cost curve (the marginal cost curve above point B in figure 1).

Theoretically, the short run average total cost curve, ATC, serves as a benchmark to predict industry trends. As mentioned above, the ATC curve includes the opportunity cost of capital, which is the normal, risk-adjusted rate of return which could be earned if the firm's capital were employed in its next best use. When the firm's total revenues exceed its total costs (which include the normal return on capital), the firm is earning an ECONOMIC PROFIT. This occurs when the price of the product (which is average revenue) lies above the ATC curve at the firm's profit-maximizing output level. Therefore, when the product's price lies above the ATC curve, firms can earn higher returns in this industry than elsewhere and, if there are no barriers to entry, entry should occur in the long run. Similarly, if the price is below the firm's ATC curve, firms in this industry are earning less than they could earn elsewhere and there should be exit from this industry in the long run.

Unfortunately, as Stigler (1966) and Friedman (1976) have observed, average total costs (which include the opportunity cost of capital) will change as industry demand changes. For example, an increase demand will cause profits to rise and increases the value of the firm's assets. Or a firm might have access to better resources or a better location which lower its costs of production and allow the firm to enjoy a return apparently above the normal, competitive rate. However, in both cases, these resources could be sold for a capital gain and this is an opportunity cost to the firm. Therefore, if the firm valued its assets at this higher (market) value, its true long run average costs would be higher and its rate of return would be lower. What appears to be above normal profits may occur because of the failure to properly capitalize the value of the firm's assets.

Bibliography

Douglas, E. J. (1992). *Managerial Economics*. 4th edn, Englewood Cliffs, NJ: Prentice-Hall.
Friedman, M. (1976). *Price Theory*. 2nd edn, Chicago: Aldine.
Stigler, G. J. (1966). *The Theory of Price*. 3rd edn, New York: Macmillan.
Shughart, W. F., Chappell, W. F. Cottle, R. L. (1994). *Modern Managerial Economics*. Cincinatti, OH: South-Western Publishing.

ROBERT E. McAULIFFE

signaling   When information is not readily available, individuals can take the initiative to produce signals that reveal their attributes. Spence (1974) provided a systematic explanation of investment in education as a means of signaling productivity to the market. Suppose there are two types of workers: those with high ability whose marginal product of labor is 2 and those with low ability whose marginal product of labor is 1. Workers may invest in education or a degree at positive cost but by assumption, education does not increase on-the-job productivity. If information about each individual's productivity were available to the employer, workers would be paid their respective marginal product. When there is asymmetric information, where employers do not know their prospective workers' marginal products and workers do, the employer pays everyone the same wage. That wage would be equal to the expected productivity of a randomly chosen worker. High-ability workers in pursuit of higher wages would want to signal employers about their greater productivity. Also, employers would benefit from such a signal by selecting more productive workers and avoiding the cost of hiring and training workers that may potentially be fired. Education might be a credible signal if high ability workers can complete education with less effort (lower cost) than low ability workers. If education is used as a signal of differentiating high ability workers from low ability workers, employers and employees benefit from this information; however, in this model there is no other benefit from public spending on education. Even when there is a positive relationship between workers' productivity and spending on education, we find some overinvestment in education (Milgrom and Roberts, 1992).

Signaling has been used to explain a variety of other strategic decisions. The quality of the product that is known to the producer but not to the potential customer can be signaled by using price, advertising, guaranties or warranties, and so on. For example, a high quality producer may use a low price or uninformative advertising to signal high quality if his cost of using this signal is lower than that of a low quality producer (Nelson, 1974). Milgrom and Roberts (1982) show that when a firm that is entering the market does not know the costs of the established firm in the market, the established firm may be able to deter entry by charging a lower price because the reduced price signals to potential entrants that the costs of the established firm are so low that as entry occurs the entrant will experience a loss limit pricing. Milgrom and Roberts (1986) show that for goods which are purchased often, both price and advertising could be employed to provide signals to customers. For these goods, high quality firms have an incentive to set a low price expecting to earn profits on future purchases. On the other hand, durable goods should enter the market at a high price and as Bagwell and Riordan (1991) show, the price should decrease with time as information about the quality of the good spreads. In financial markets, managers have significantly more information about their company's performance and prospects than their investors. Signaling has been employed to analyze financial decisions which have the ability to influence what investors believe about the firm's prospects. For example, Ross (1977) showed that a choice of a company to increase its debt–equity ratio provided a signal for investors that its equity shares were more valuable.

Bibliography

Bagwell, K. Riordan, M. K. (1991). High and declining prices signal product quality. *American Economic Review*, 81, 224–39.

Milgrom, P. Roberts, J. (1982). Limit pricing and entry under incomplete information: an equilibrium analysis. *Econometrica*, 50, 443–59.

Milgrom, P. Roberts, J. (1986). Price and advertising signals of product quality. *Journal of Political Economy*, 94, 796–821.

Milgrom, P. Roberts, J. (1992). *Economics, Organization and Management*. Englewood Cliffs, NJ: Prentice-Hall.

Nelson, P. (1974). Advertising as information. *Journal of Political Economy*, 84, 729–54.

Ross, S. (1977). The determination of financial structure: the incentive signaling approach. *Bell Journal of Economics*, 8, 23–40.

Spence, A. M. (1974). *Market Signaling: Informational Transfer in Hiring and Related Screening Processes*. Cambridge, MA: Harvard University Press.

LIDIJA POLUTNIK

situational interview   The situational interview is a type of highly structured procedure used in EMPLOYMENT INTERVIEWS and first introduced by Latham et al. (1980). The basic assumption underlying this approach is that the future performance of applicants can be best predicted by finding out their goals and intentions for dealing with the dilemmas that they might encounter in specific job situations. The first step in developing a situational interview is to analyze the job using the CRITICAL INCIDENTS TECHNIQUE. From the incidents generated in this step, performance dimensions are identified that are then evaluated in the interview. Those incidents that best represent each of the dimensions are turned into interview questions by asking the applicant to consider "what they would do if" they were confronted with the situations described in the incidents. Interviewers ask the same questions of all applicants in exactly the same way, with no opportunity provided for follow-up questions or other conversation with the applicant. Also, interviewers are not given access to applications, test scores, or other ancillary data on the applicant until after they have finished evaluating the applicant. Interviewers evaluate the applicants on BEHAVIORALLY ANCHORED RATING SCALES, in which possible examples of good, average, or poor answers are used to anchor the points on the rating scale. After the applicant is asked each of the questions and rated on the performance dimensions, the ratings on the dimensions are then averaged to form a composite evaluation of the applicant.

The research has provided impressive support for the validity and reliability of the situational interview (McDaniel et al., 1994). Moreover, the job-relatedness of the situational interview makes it more defensible against charges of discrimination than the typical unstructured interview.

Bibliography

Latham, G. P., Saari, L. M., Pursell, E. D. & Campion, M. A. (1980). The situational interview. *Journal of Applied Psychology*, 65, 422–7.

McDaniel, M. A., Whetzel, D. L., Schmidt, F. L.& Maurer, S. (1994). The validity of employment interviews: a comprehensive review and meta-analysis. *Journal of Applied Psychology*, 79, 599–616.

ROBERT L. DIPBOYE

skill-based pay design   Three sets of issues are important in a skill-based pay design (Ledford, 1991). First, the plan must be tailored to its context – the business strategy, organizational structure, and organizational culture. Second, pay plan mechanics must be developed, including definition of compensable units of skill and creation of relevant training and assessment materials. Third, a plan for transition from the existing pay system is needed. Of these factors, the fit of the design with its context is probably the most important in determining effectiveness (Jenkins et al., 1992). Plans for knowledge workers are relatively new and present many special design challenges (Ledford, 1995).

Bibliography

Jenkins, G. D. Jr, Ledford, G. E. Jr, Gupta, N. & Doty, D. H. (1992). *Skill-based Pay: Practices, Payoffs, Pitfalls, and Prospects*, Scottsdale, AZ: American Compensation Association.

Ledford, G. E. Jr (1991). The design of skill-based pay plans. *The Compensation Handbook*, **3rd edn**, Eds. Rock, M. L. & Berger, L. New York: McGraw-Hill.

Ledford, G. E. Jr (1995). Paying for the skills, knowledge, and competencies of knowledge workers. *Compensation and Benefits Review*, 27, 55–62.

GERALD LEDFORD

skimming pricing   Skimming pricing is the use of high prices (often reflecting large profit margins) for the initial marketing of new products. Such new products will be adopted initially by the least price-sensitive parts of the market. Once demand in these niches falls off, subsequent incremental price reductions may be used to devolve the product to increasingly price-sensitive market areas until demand is replete. Thus, the objective of skimming is to maximize short-term profitability. Skimming pricing contrasts with PENETRATION PRICING in that it adopts a relatively high price compared to the relatively low price of penetration policies.

Skimming policies might be adopted where there is little prospect of a long-term market for offerings (e.g., novelty items), or where organizations perceive only a short-term sustainable differentiation in their offerings (e.g., fashion markets), or where premium pricing is based on strong brands and consumer loyalty (e.g., luxury goods), or by organizations placing a high priority on short payback periods as a key corporate measure (e.g., where capital costs are high), or by organizations simply seeking to capitalize on the unique benefits of their product (e.g., the sale of distinctive vehicle registrations). The advantages of successful skimming pricing include rapid cost recovery (thereby reducing investment risk), and less commitment to long-term policies to ensure break-even (thereby allowing a more flexible response to market developments and some insurance against forecasting errors). However, skimming strategies can be difficult to manage since an organization may have to defend its offering (e.g., by patent or branding) from any credible imitators that might be attracted by the high profits associated with skimming, but it must also ensure that the corporate image is not tarnished, nor potential demand alienated, by any appearance of profiteering.

Bibliography
Dean, J. (1950). Pricing policies for new products. *Harvard Business Review*, **28**, (6), Nov–Dec., 45–53.

DOMINIC WILSON

social class   Social class refers to the stratification of members of a society into a hierarchy. Every known human society is stratified, i.e., the hierarchical evaluation of people in different social positions is inherent in human social organizations. Within societies, different occupations, trades, and professions have a more immediate impact on a community and may attract social prestige and authority. Early definitions of social class focused on reputation. For example, Warner et al. (1949) defined social class in terms of how people in a community view one another and place their associates in the social structure, placing an emphasis on status/reputation and participation in the community.

More recently, various "objective" criteria have been used to define and measure social class: e.g., occupation, income level and source, wealth, house-type, area of residence, and educational level. Consequently, various categorizations of social class have been developed: e.g. those referring to typologies such as upper-middle-lower class, and the ABC1 C2DE system developed in the UK by the Joint Industry Committee for National Readership Surveys – based on the occupation of the head of the household. Current typologies are, however, specifically related to lifestyles, e.g., Acorn-types (*see* LIFESTYLES).

Levy (1964 & 1966) discussed social class in terms of variations which are a combination of a consumer's values, interpersonal attitudes, self-perceptions, and daily life. Such differences find expression in consumer behavior in a number of ways: (1) products and services bought: accumulation of certain products and services can serve as a symbol of class position; (2) use of and reaction to the media, e.g., critical or accepting response to advertisements, questioning of claims; (3) spending, saving, and investment, researched by Martineau (1958a); (4) stores used, again researched by Martineau (1958b); (5) reaction to innovation; (6) entertainment and leisure; (7) consumerism; and (8) use of credit cards and facilities: Mathews & Slocum (1969) considered instalment versus convenience usage of credit cards, and products and services which are acceptable to charge.

Social classes are considered to be relatively permanent and homogeneous. However, the concept of a hierarchy of social class suggests vertical mobility, both upward and downward. This may be a function of: educational mobility, witness the emergence of a "meritocracy" – professional and business leaders who have achieved prominence through intelligence and hard work; and changes in employment and income, witness the disappearing divisions between white and blue collar consumption habits as economic income levels. However, fundamental social values and attitudes may not change as suddenly as behavior, with increased spending power.

Further, one needs to be aware of the concept of "over/under privilege" within social classes (see Coleman, 1960 & 1983). This is the notion of looking at discretionary income within social class groups, such that certain luxury products and services are targeted at the "over-privileged" across all social classes.

Bibliography
Coleman, R. (1960). The significance of social stratification in selling. In M. L. Bell (Ed.), *Marketing: A maturing discipline*, (pp. 171–184). Chicago: American Marketing Association.

Coleman, R. P. (1983). The continuing significance of social class to marketing. *Journal of Consumer Research*, **10**, Dec. 265–280. Cited in H. H. Kassarjian & T. S. Robertson (1991). *Perspectives in consumer behavior*, 4th edn, (pp. 487–510). Prentice Hall.

Engel, J. F., Blackwell, R. D. & Miniard, P. W. (1990). *Consumer behavior*. 6th edn, Orlando, Fla: The Dryden Press. Chapter 4.

Hawkins, D. I., Best, R. J. & Coney, K. A. (1992). *Consumer behavior: Implications for marketing strategy*, 5th edn, Homewood, IL: Irwin. Chapter 4.

Levy, S. J. (1964). Symbolism and lifestyle. In S. A. Greyser (Ed.), *Towards scientific marketing* (pp. 140–150). Chicago: American Marketing Association.

Levy, S. J. (1966). In J. W. Newman (Ed.), Social class and consumer behavior. *On knowing the consumer* (pp. 146–160). New York: John Wiley.

Martineau, P. (1958a). Social classes and spending behavior. *Journal of Marketing*, **23**, Oct., 121–130.

Martineau, P. (1958b). The personality of the retail store. *Harvard Business Review*, 36, Jan.–Feb., 47–55.

Mathews, H. L. & Slocum, J. W. (1969). Social class and commercial bank credit card usage. *Journal of Marketing*, 33, Jan., 71–78.

Rich, S. U. & Jain, S. C. (1968). Social class and life cycle as predictors of shopping behavior. *Journal of Marketing Research*, 5, Feb., 41–49.

Schiffman, L. G. & Kanuk, L. Z. (1991). *Consumer behavior*. 4th edn, Prentice-Hall. Chapter 13.

Solomon, M. R. (1992). *Consumer behavior*. Needham Heights, MA: Allyn & Bacon. Chapter 12.

Warner, W. L., Meeker, M. & Eells, K. (1949). *Social class in America*. Chicago: Scientific Research Associates.

BARBARA LEWIS

social contract theory In business ethics social contract theory involves the use of hypothetical implied contracts to establish ethical rights and obligations for business firms, professionals, and managers. The legitimacy of these ethical rights and obligations is based upon the assumed consent of the group members to the terms of the social contract. Social contract theory focuses on a community or group of rational, self-interested individuals who are presumed to consent to the terms of a hypothetical agreement because it is in their rational interest to do so. Specific ethical obligations and rights are then deduced from this contract. Social contract theory may therefore be thought of as a communitarian, norm-based approach to ethics. The device of a social contract has been used in business ethics since the early 1980s.

I. A Brief History

The concept of a social contract or covenant goes back to Socrates and the Greek Sophists and even earlier. The Old Testament refers to a covenant between God and every living thing for all generations (Genesis 9). Social contract is associated with political theory as a device for understanding the role of government within a society. The use of social contract in political theory reached its apex in the Enlightenment writings of John Locke, Thomas Hobbes, and Jean-Jacques Rousseau. Their ideas about the relationship between government and the governed were very influential in the American and French revolutions and in the establishment of a constitutional form of government in the United States. Hobbes envisioned a social contract in which citizens gave over their liberty to an absolute sovereign as the only solution to the "warre" of man against man in Hobbes' imagined state of nature, where life was "solitary, poor, nasty, brutish and short." In Hobbes' social contract citizens have no right to resist the sovereign; because if there were such a right, society would quickly disintegrate into the feared state of nature.

Locke, who had great influence on the founders of the US government, assumed that humans have natural rights to life and property. Unfortunately, in a state of nature, these rights may go unprotected. Locke's solution is a social contract in which citizens form a civil government for the purpose of securing these natural rights. Locke's civil government has a defined responsibility and its subjects have a right to resist if the government interferes with their natural rights.

Rousseau envisions a moral community in which natural freedom and equality are transferred to civil society, based

upon the consent of the governed reflected in the "general will" of the people. More recently, in 1971, John Rawls uses the idea of social contract as the foundation for his influential book, *A Theory of Justice*. In 1986, David Gauthier, in *Morals by Agreement*, develops a rational-choice argument that self-interested parties will want to participate in a social contract recognizing certain principles of cooperation. Although business is not his primary focus, Gauthier recognizes the implications of his work for economic life: "Market interactions are a network of contractual arrangements, and this network is itself founded on an overall social contract, expressive of the two-sided instrumentality that constitutes society from the standpoint of economic man" (1986, p. 318).

II. Core Issues in Social Contract Theory

To be fully satisfying, social contract approaches must resolve certain core issues including: (1) explaining why it would be rational for everyone to agree to the terms of the social contract, (2) justifying the use of devices outside of the social contract itself as part of the theory, (3) explaining why individuals, in fact, would be willing to act consistently with the terms of the social contract, and (4) demonstrating that the espoused social contract is realistic and is based upon an accurate understanding of the nature of humanity.

Most of the issues result from the attempt to derive real world standards from a hypothetical or imaginary agreement. As a starting-point, a social contract theory must offer a plausible explanation as to why rational humans would agree to the terms of the proposed agreement. One approach, similar to that used by Rawls, is to rely upon critical extra-contractual assumptions that the contracting parties come together to set up the contract under very special conditions. Rawls (1971) and Donaldson (1982) both use such devices. Rawls' contract is made by people who act behind a veil of ignorance in which they do not know their particular endowments or preferences. In Donaldson's application of the social contract idea to business ethics, the original contractors are imagined as existing in a state of prehistory in which they know the characteristics of the organizations they wish to create, but they have control in the sense that they have complete flexibility in designing the surrounding legal and social environment. The devices of a veil of ignorance and a prescribed condition in prehistory come from outside the social contract itself and therefore require some type of independent justification. Some critics of social contract theory note this problem and conclude that the social contract approach is incapable of providing a satisfactory moral theory on its own.

A more common approach to answering the question of why self-interested individuals would agree to a particular social contract is to demonstrate that the contract is the only plausible solution to an acknowledged problem. This approach is used by Hobbes, Locke, and Donaldson/Dunfee. Each theorist starts with a definition of the problem (e.g. Hobbes: without society life is nasty, brutish, and short) and makes certain assumptions about the nature of humanity (people are self-interested egoists). Then, a particular vision of a social contract is proffered as a realistic solution to the problem.

After offering a plausible argument why the original contracting parties would agree to a particular set of social contract terms, the theorists then must suggest reasons why individuals within the contracting communities would continue to comply with the terms of the agreement. After all, once they actually face a conflict between their self-interests and the terms of the social contract, they may wish to deviate from the agreement. Various explanations have been offered by theorists, for example, that self-interested community members will nonetheless continue to comply with the contract in the reciprocal expectation that others will similarly comply. Other theorists argue that humans possess an intuitive moral sense that promises should be honored.

Many contractarians, particularly Hobbes and Gauthier, assume that humans are egoists acting purely in their own self-interest. Others, including some business ethicists, assume that humans may be naturally altruistic. The choice of these assumptions will, of course, influence whether the derived social contract terms appear to be realistic.

The concept of an informal agreement setting standards for society appears to be intuitive to many people. References to specific, existing social contracts are commonplace in the general business literature. For example, the term is frequently found in the human resource management literature in references to a social contract between employers and employees. Social contract terminology is also found in the public utility regulation, accounting, and capital gain taxation literature. Writers often refer to "the social contract" of a particular nation state. (See generally Dunfee, 1991.)

III. Social Contract Theory and Business Ethics

Social contract theory can be used to identify rights and obligations pertaining to business ethics. Thomas Donaldson develops a special social contract theory for issues of business ethics in Chapter 3 of his book, *Corporations and Morality* (1982). In this seminal effort, Donaldson focuses on the issue of corporate rights and obligations. Following the classical social contract tradition of using a hypothetical agreement as a device for parsing specific rights and obligations, Donaldson imagines the terms of an agreement that could be rationally entered into between all productive cooperative enterprises (firms) and the individual members of a given society in the aggregate prior to the beginnings of their economic system. He assumes that the parties would want the benefits of specialization of labor, output and distribution, increased wages, and the ability to pay for harms that would result from having corporations. On the other hand, the parties to the agreement would also want to limit pollution, depletion of natural resources, destruction of personal accountability, and worker alienation. Representatives of productive organizations want the members of society to agree to provide them with an environment conducive for them to provide needed goods and services, resulting, in turn, in reasonable profits. The terms of the resulting social contract require that the harms be minimized and that when the inevitable trade-offs are made, they be made consistently with "the general canons of justice" (1982, p. 53).

Donaldson broadens his theory (1989), and considers all economic actors, not just corporations, employees, and consumers. He also extends his focus beyond a single society to explicitly consider issues of cultural relativism. Donaldson envisions a global social contract setting a minimal floor of responsibility for all business firms. Specifically, global firms have an obligation to enhance the long-term welfare of employees and consumers, minimize the drawbacks of large productive organizations, and refrain from violating minimal standards of justice and human rights. These obligations are defined in terms of ten fundamental rights (e.g. freedom of physical movement, property ownership, minimal education, political participation, subsistence) which global firms should avoid depriving others of; and in some very limited circumstances, should protect against deprivation by others.

Others followed Donaldson in using the social contract device in the context of business responsibility. Keeley (1988) employs social contract as a metaphor to describe business firms as a series of contract-like agreements about social rules. Emphasizing the voluntary nature of agreements, Keeley relies upon a rights-based approach (personal claims based on a system of rules, such as rights to equal concern and respect, or to avoid personal harms). His approach is contrasted with an "organismic" model of the firm, which subordinates the welfare of individuals to the welfare of the organization.

In two joint articles, Donaldson and Dunfee (e.g. 1994) have set forth a social contract theory called Integrative Social Contracts Theory (ISCT) which is specifically applicable to business ethics. The term "integrative" is used to illustrate that ISCT is based upon a hypothetical social contract whose terms allow for the generation of binding ethical obligations through the recognition of actual norms created in real social and economic communities. A hypothetical social contract is thereby integrated with real or extant social contracts. The plural "contracts" is used to emphasize the fact that ISCT envisions literally millions of local community-based social contracts establishing ethical norms for those local groups.

The hypothetical social contract is derived from an imagined attempt by all humanity to design a global agreement concerning business ethics. The terms of the contract are based upon the contractors' recognition of two factors. First, they realize that significant bounded moral rationality exists for economic actors. That is, they would recognize the limits of their own ability to comprehend, interpret, and apply moral concepts. Similarly, they do not expect that a formal moral calculus can be designed in advance for all of the contexts in which diverse humanity faces ethical choices. Second, they recognize the need for a community-based moral fabric to enable them to satisfy their individual economic and social interests.

In response to these assumptions, Donaldson and Dunfee hypothesize that global-level contractors would design a universal or macrosocial contract with the following terms

1. Local communities may specify ethical norms for their members through microsocial contracts (called moral free space).
2. Norm-generating microsocial contracts must be grounded in informed consent buttressed by a right of community members to exit and to exercise voice within their communities.
3. In order to be obligatory, a microsocial contract norm must be compatible with hypernorms.

4. In case of conflicts among norms satisfying principles 1–3, priority must be established through the application of rules consistent with the spirit and letter of the macrosocial contract.

Hypernorms entail principles so fundamental that they should be reflected in a convergence of religious, philosophical, and cultural beliefs. The priority rules are derived from conflicts of laws principles found in international and US law. Through the application of ISCT it is possible to identify authentic ethical norms within communities (that bribes should not be paid), to test these under hypernorms, and against conflicting norms from other communities (that bribes of a certain character are acceptable), and to then determine which norms should be given priority.

Social contract approaches have been applied to specific issues in business ethics. A prime example is found in Scheppele's (1993) advocacy of restrictions on insider trading based upon a claim that there is a social-contract-based justification for providing equal access to financial markets. Other efforts include the application of Donaldson's original social contract to the agribusiness industry and the evaluation of the exportation of hazardous products under an unwritten social contract (see Dunfee, 1991, p. 31).

IV. Limitations and Advantages of a Social Contract Approach

Critics of social contract argue that it fails to provide an independent basis for moral obligation. They reason that many of the results of contractarian approaches can be achieved through the use of other ethical theories. Others are concerned about coercion, particularly in the case of use of actual consent as occurs with the microsocial contracts under ISCT. They worry that organizations will be able to impose group values upon individuals which will then be sanctioned by social contract theory. Another set of criticisms, particularly directed at ISCT, reflects concern that social contract theory cannot adequately protect important rights, such as freedom from gender-based discrimination.

Social contract theorists are refining their approaches in response to these criticisms. They note that social contract theory has great potential as a realistic, contextual basis for making normative judgments in business ethics. The realism must come from consistency of the contractarian assumptions with the empirical literature in the social sciences and moral psychology. The social contract approach is contextual by its very nature due to the emphasis on specific agreements. It explicitly recognizes the role of professional ethical norms and the understandings of right behavior that permeate business interactions. Ultimately, the distinguishing feature of social contract theory is its emphasis on the uncoerced, informed consent of those who will be bound by the ethical norms thereby established.

Bibliography

Business Ethics Quarterly. (1995). Special issue on social contracts and business ethics:, 5 (2).

Donaldson, T. (1982). *Corporations and Morality*. Englewood Cliffs, NJ: Prentice-Hall.

Donaldson, T. (1989). *The Ethics of International Business*. New York: Oxford University Press.

Donaldson, T. & Dunfee, T. W. (1994). Toward a unified conception of business ethics: Integrative social contracts theory. *Academy of Management Review*, **19**, (2), 252–84.

Dunfee, T. W. (1991). Business ethics and extant social contracts. *Business Ethics Quarterly*, **1**, (1), 23–51.

Gauthier, D. (1986). *Morals by Agreement*. New York: Oxford University Press.

Gough, J. W. (1957). *The Social Contract* 2nd edn, New York: Oxford University Press. (Historical summary of the use of social contract).

Keeley, M. (1988). *A Social-Contract Theory of Organizations*. Notre Dame, Ind.: University of Notre Dame Press.

Rawls, J. (1971). *A Theory of Justice*. Cambridge, Mass.: Harvard University Press.

Scheppele, K. L. (1993). "It's just not right": The ethics of insider trading. *Law and Contemporary Problems*, **56**, (3), 123–73.

THOMAS W. DUNFEE

social marketing Social marketing is part of "non-business" marketing (together with NOT-FOR-PROFIT marketing) which relates to marketing activities conducted by individuals and organizations to achieve some goal other than ordinary business goals of profit, market share, and return on investment.

Social marketing is concerned with the development of programs designed to influence the acceptability of social ideas, and may be defined to be a set of activities to create, maintain, and/or alter attitudes and/or behavior toward a social idea or cause, independently of a sponsoring organization or person. The purpose may be: to trigger one-time behavior from people (e.g., contribute to a foundation for AIDS research); to change behavior (e.g., to discourage cigarette smoking, drug abuse or drink abuse, unsafe sexual practice, to recycle more newspapers, plastics etc.); or to change attitudes and beliefs (e.g., toward birth control and family planning or toward pollution control).

Bibliography

Christy, R. (1995). The broader application of marketing. In G. Oliver (Ed.), *Marketing today*, 4th edn, (pp. 500–527). Hemel Hempstead, UK: Prentice-Hall. Chapter 24.

Dibb, S., Simkin, L., Pride, W. M. & Ferrell, O. C. (1991). *Marketing*. European edn, (pp. 693–694). Boston, MA: Houghton Mifflin Co.

Kotler, P. (1994). *Marketing management: Analysis, planning, implementation and control*, 8th edn, Englewood Cliffs, NJ: Prentice-Hall, p.155.

BARBARA LEWIS

social responsibility The term "social responsibility" most usually refers to an organization's obligation to maximize its long-term positive impact and minimize its negative impact on society. While it is sometimes used interchangeably with the concept of ethics (*see* MARKETING ETHICS), the distinction is generally made that social responsibility is an organizational concern whereas ethics are the concern of the individual manager or business decision-maker (see Carroll, 1981). However, this distinction is by no means universally accepted and debate continues as to whether organizations, given that they are artificial creations, can be said to have social responsibilities at all, or whether the term is only applicable to individuals within the organization. The difference between social responsibility and ethics is further highlighted by Robin & Reidenbach (1987), who define social responsibility as the social contract between business and the society in which it operates, stating that actionwith business may be found by moral philosophers as ethically unsound (see also Steiner, 1972).

Carroll (1981) has identified four specific areas of corporate social responsibility as economic, legal, ethical, and discretionary responsibility – in that order of priority. Davis et al. (1980) similarly represented social responsibility as three concentric circles, again indicating priority: the inner circle referred to the social responsibility aspects of the traditional economic role of business, such as social and ethical issues arising from the performance by business of basic functions; the middle circle contained issues such as ecology, environmental quality, and consumerism; and the outer circle, general social problems that business can help to alleviate.

It has been suggested that what becomes generally accepted as socially responsible will vary in different societies and will also change within society over time. However, a variety of specific social responsibility issues have been recently discussed in marketing literature, including consumer issues; issues of employee welfare; support for minorities; issues of community relations, such as the contribution made by business to the satisfaction and growth of communities by contributing resources to causes such as education, the arts, recreation, or disadvantaged members of the community; and green marketing.

While it has been proposed that the long-term value of conducting business in a socially responsible manner far outweighs short-term costs (see Stroup et al., 1987), there is some debate as to whether business, on the whole, is becoming more socially responsible in its actions. Robin & Reidenbach (1987) note a trend towards increased social involvement by business; however, Glueck (1980) found little evidence that social responsibility is a significant objective of most businesses, in spite of a good deal of pressure from some societal groups.

see also **Marketing concept**

Bibliography

Carroll, A. B. (1981). *Business and society*. Boston, MA: Little, Brown & Co.

Davis, K., Frederick, W. C. & Blomstrom, R. L. (1980). *Business and society*. New York: McGraw-Hill.

Glueck, W. F. (1980). *Business policy and strategic management*, 3rd edn, New York: McGraw-Hill.

Robin, D. P. & Reidenbach, R. E. (1987). Social responsibility, ethics and marketing strategy: Closing the gap between concept and application. *Journal of Marketing*, **51**, (1), Jan., 44–58.

Steiner, C. A. (1972). Social policies for business. *California Management Review*, Winter, 17–24.

Stroup, M. A., Newbert, R. L. & Anderson, J. W. Jr (1987). Doing good doing better: Two views of social responsibility. *Business Horizons*, Mar.–Apr., 23.

FIONA LEVERICK

socialization This is a process of ROLE taking frequently referred to as "learning the ropes." It has been applied in several different OB contexts, such as career entry, the joining-up process, entering work groups, and the entry/re-entry of EXPATRIATES. As discussed here, however, socialization will refer to new organization members, i.e., organizational socialization.

While almost all scholars agree that socialization is "learning the ropes," there is less agreement as to what this actually means. Van Maanen and Schein (1979, pp. 226–227) say that it involves three elements:

(1) learning new knowledge important for both one's own job performance and for general functioning in the organization;
(2) acquiring a strategic base, which is a set of decision rules for solving problems/making decisions; and
(3) learning the organization's mission, purpose, or mandate.

These three areas of learning are acknowledged to be closely related to each other. Other students of socialization go even further to include changes in newcomer attitudes and VALUES. These are different from the acquisition of knowledge, a strategic base, or organizational mission. When attitudes and values are changed, the newcomer as a person is also changed, and a deeper attachment to the organization is achieved.

Organizational socialization is a process not a specific event, in contrast to job interviews or psychological testing, for example. This is probably the main reason why experts have had difficulty specifying both the content and process of socialization. One popular view is that socialization is directly associated with boundary transitions, such as crossing from outside to inside, moving functionally within the organization, and moving up in the hierarchy (Van Maanen & Schein, 1979, pp. 217–226). According to this view, socialization efforts by members of the organization peak just prior to an individual's movement across one of these boundaries.

Organizational socialization refers to the changes in newcomers, rather than changes in the organization itself – a process sometimes referred to as "personalization." As such socialization is a specific example of general psychological processes as attitude change, compliance, conformity, INFLUENCE, RECIPROCITY, and the development of both loyalty and COMMITMENT. Clarifying the PSYCHOLOGICAL CONTRACT and mentoring are components of socialization. Because socialization is primarily accomplished via social learning, the newcomer's peers, co-workers, and boss all provide elements of that which is learned, as well as different types of conformity pressure. For example, one's boss is a source of authority, as well as both reward and punishment. Peers can influence newcomers by being desirable as friends, as well as through their informal ability to reward and punish (see Hackman, 1992, for a review of group influences on individuals; *see* GROUP DEVELOPMENT).

Most of the efforts at a theory of socialization has been paid to developing "stage models," which purport to describe the typical experiences of newcomers as they make the transition to "insider" status (see Wanous, 1992, pp. 200–214, for a review and comparison among these models). Most of the models that have been suggested have some or all of these stages:

(1) confronting and accepting organizational reality (which also includes anticipatory socialization);
(2) achieving role clarity;
(3) locating oneself in the organizational context; and
(4) detecting signposts of successful socialization.

In contrast, relatively little attention has been paid to the actual psychological processes of both the newcomer and the socializing agents. One noteworthy exception is the articulation of how newcomers can be "seduced" by an organization (Lewicki, 1981), although this is just one facet of socialization in general. The central tenet of organizational seduction is the assumption that newcomers are motivated by reciprocity, so that their loyalty results from the various rewards that are provided by the organization.

Rather than specifying the exact psychology of socialization, some have taken instead to describing the "tactics" that can be used on newcomers. These tactics have been divided into six dimensions:

(1) collective versus individual;
(2) formal versus informal;
(3) sequential versus random;
(4) fixed versus variable;
(5) serial versus disjunctive; and
(6) investiture versus divestiture (Van Maanen & Schein, 1979, pp. 230–254).

Early research on the effects of these six tactics indicates that newcomers are more likely to conform to the organization when their socializing experiences are like the first half of each pair (i.e., collective, formal, sequential, etc.), rather than the latter half of the pair (i.e., individual, informal, random, etc.).

Research on socialization has been plagued by a number of problems. As a result, what is actually known from empirical research is much less than one might suppose from reading all of the writings on socialization. The most difficult problem facing the researcher is designing and executing a study that will lead to valid conclusions (see VALIDITY). Because organizational socialization unfolds over a period of time with many possible socializing agents and a variety of specific foci, it is virtually impossible for any single study to address more than just one facet of this process. It is frequently the case that researchers will rely on cross-sectional data, rather than using a longitudinal design. This leads to problems of data interpretation, because cross-sectional designs do not include those individuals who left the organization – a group of important "socialization failures."

The two most common research designs, individual case study and survey research, both have important flaws that make their conclusions somewhat suspect (see SURVEY RESEARCH). Those who conduct a case study in a particular organization often generate interesting, "rich" accounts of a newcomer's experiences. However, the extent to which these accounts apply to other contexts is questionable. On the other hand, those who survey newcomers across a broad range of organizations only have the perceptions of the newcomers as data; they have no data from the socializing agents in each of the organizations that could be compared to what is reported by the newcomers themselves.

One review concluded that research has not yet supported the popular idea that socialization can be represented as a set of common stages. This is important because stage models are at the heart of most writing on socialization. Furthermore, the same review found that one of the most frequently cited research results about

socialization has never been replicated, i.e., that newcomers should be given as much job challenge as possible (Wanous & Colella, 1989). The belief that job challenge is an effective socialization tactic is based on one sample of AT&T employees (all men) hired in the early 1960s.

Future research and thinking about socialization should proceed in two directions. First, the role of cognitive processes should be given more attention. Although Louis (1980) called attention to this some time ago, little or no research has been produced. Second, Schneider (1987) has suggested that socialization has been dominated by a search for situational influences, rather than PERSONALITY traits. He has called for a more balanced view, i.e., interactionism.

see also **Learning organization; Career stages**

Bibliography

Hackman, J. R. (1992). Group influences on individuals in organizations. In M. D. Dunnette & L. M. Hough (Eds), Handbook of industrial & organizational psychology, (vol. 3, pp. 199–267). Palo Alto, CA: Consulting Psychologists Press.
Lewicki, R. J. (1981). Organizational seduction: Building commitment to organizations. Organizational Dynamics, Autumn, 5–21.
Louis, M. R. (1980). Surprise and sense-making: What newcomers experience in entering unfamiliar organizational settings. Administrative Science Quarterly, 25, 226–251.
Schneider, B. (1987). The people make the place. Personnel Psychology, 40, 437–453
Van Maanen, J. & Schein, E. H. (1979). Toward a theory of organizational socialization. In B. Staw (Ed.), Research in organizational behavior, (vol. 1, pp. 209–266). Greenwich, CT: JAI Press.
Wanous, J. P. (1992). Organizational entry: Recruitment, selection, orientation, and socialization of newcomers. Reading, MA: Addison-Wesley.
Wanous, J. P. & Colella, A. (1989). Organizational entry research: Current status and future directions. In G. Ferris & K. Rowland (Eds), Research in personnel and human resources management, (vol. 7, pp. 59–120). Greenwich, CT: JAI Press.

JOHN P. WANOUS

societal marketing A major development in the interpretation of the scope of marketing, societal marketing refers to the extension of marketing along its substantive dimension, i.e., the widening of the areas of concern of marketing to focus on the long-term interests of consumers and society. Although the two are often used interchangeably, societal marketing differs from social marketing, the latter referring to the further application of marketing techniques to not-for-profit organizations, such as charities (see Abratt & Sacks, 1989).

see also **Consumerism; Marketing; Marketing concept; Social responsibility**

Bibliography

Abratt, R. & Sacks, D. (1989). Perceptions of the societal marketing concept. European Journal of Marketing, 23, (6), 25–33.

FIONA LEVERICK

sourcing Sourcing is the securing of parts, supplies, materials, labor, and other items necessary to produce merchandise or other items for sale. Domestic companies often purchase resources locally even though the cost may be greater than the same resources (labor, for example) purchased in a foreign country. Global companies may purchase resources wherever the cost is lowest with respect to the overall cost of the finished product. It is common for a multinational company to use foreign sourcing whenever it is cost effective to do so.

JOHN O'CONNELL

sovereign risk Strictly speaking, sovereign risk arises when a sovereign government fails to honor its foreign debt obligations. Sovereign risk is unique because, unlike a private loan where there are well established legal proceedings to handle default and bankruptcy, there is no international court with the jurisdiction to deal with the defaults of sovereign governments.

However, when a government cannot or will not service its foreign debt for financial reasons, e.g. it does not possess sufficient foreign exchange reserves, it will in all likelihood forbid its private sector borrowers to remit foreign exchange to their international lenders as well. Therefore, both sectors will fail to honor the debt, even if the private borrower is creditworthy in terms of its current assets in domestic currency. In practice, therefore, the term sovereign risk has a broader meaning and is not limited to a sovereign loan. It is the risk that the actions of a government may affect the ability of that government, or government-affiliated corporations, or private borrowers residing in the country, to honor foreign debt obligations.

It is for this reason that the terms "sovereign risk" and "country risk" are often used interchangeably. It is this broader definition of sovereign risk which is implied in the following discussion.

Before the World War II, most foreign debts were in the form of bonds held by numerous bondholders all over the world. When a country encountered difficulties in servicing foreign debts, a common practice was repudiation, i.e. a simple cancelation of all its debt obligations. In the postwar period, most of the international loans are from a smaller number of banks, and the most common form of sovereign risk is rescheduling, i.e. announcing a delay in payment and renegotiating the terms of the loan (Saunders, 1994). The most notable event that taught the international banking community an unforgettable lesson about the importance of sovereign risk is the debt moratorium declared by the Mexican government in 1982, and which triggered the subsequent international debt crisis.

Analysis of Sovereign Risk
When making an international loan, a lender must assess two types of risk. The first is the creditworthiness of the borrower itself. This analysis is the same as a credit analysis of any domestic borrower. The second risk to assess is the sovereign risk of the country. In principle, a lender should not extend credit to a foreign borrower if the sovereign risk is unacceptable, notwithstanding that the borrower may have good credit quality. This second type of risk, or sovereign risk, should be the predominant consideration in international lending decisions.

The analysis of sovereign risk involves both economic and political analysis. Economic analysis should be primarily concerned with the capability of an economy to generate foreign exchange reserves. The foreign exchange reserves are the common pool of resources that both the private

sector and the government rely upon when servicing foreign debt. These reserves are the cumulative international balance of payments of a country which, in turn, depends upon its current account balance, or its foreign trade performance measured by exports minus imports. Macroeconomic theory reveals that a trade deficit (surplus) is the result of aggregate demand (aggregate consumption plus investments plus government spending), being greater (smaller) than aggregate production of a country. Therefore, all factors that influence the aggregate demand and aggregate production of an economy should be analyzed in order to understand the economics of sovereign risk.

In terms of political analysis, the focus is on the political decision-making process through which debt repudiation and rescheduling decisions are made. Also of importance is the capability of the political system to support the economic system and to maintain the credit quality of the country. By undertaking a dual analysis of both the economic and political systems of a country, an analyst can come to a comprehensive understanding of the sovereign risk.

Comparable international financial data can be found in the publications of supranational organizations such as the World Bank and the International Monetary Fund. It might also be helpful for analysts to take advantage of the cross-country credit ranking provided by such credit rating agencies as Moody's and Standard and Poor's, and financial publishers such as *Euromoney* and *Institutional Investor*.

Forecasting Sovereign Risk
In addition to a complete macroeconomic analysis, analysts can also study a number of financial ratios indicative of the financial soundness of a country. Examples of these ratios and their relationship with sovereign risk exposure include: debt ratio (foreign currency debt/GDP; foreign currency debt/exports), positive; import ratio (imports/foreign exchange reserves), positive; trade surplus ratio (trade surplus/GDP), negative; budget balance ratio (government budget deficit/GDP), positive; investment ratio (aggregate investment/GDP), negative; and inflation rate, positive. Based on selected ratios and the history of sovereign risk events across countries, a discriminant analysis model can be built to predict sovereign risks.

An alternative way to forecast sovereign risk is to utilize information in the secondary market for developing country debt, a market developed by major banks in the mid 1980s. The prices of these loans reflect the market's collective assessment about the sovereign risk of the indebted countries. Regression analysis can be performed to determine what variables (similar to those discussed above) are significantly associated with the prices of these loans and to estimate the extent of the association. Based on the projected values of the variables, this model can then be used to predict loan prices. Changes in loan prices are indicative of possible changes of sovereign risk (see Boehmer and Megginson, 1990).

Political Risk
Political risk arises when actions of a government or other groups in the political process adversely interfere with the operation of business. These actions may include expropriation, confiscation, foreign exchange control, kidnapping, civil unrest, *coup d'état*, and war. While both economics and politics should be considered in the analysis

of sovereign as well as political risks, the emphasis of sovereign risk is on economics and the focus of political risk is on the political process. Since sovereign risk events are the result of governmental actions, it can be viewed as part of political risk. Organizations such as Economist Intelligence Unit and Business International conduct extensive political risk analysis. Their publications are useful resources for international business executives.

Bibliography

Boehmer, E. & Megginson, W. L. (1990). Determinants of secondary market prices for developing country syndicated loans. *Journal of Finance*, **45**, 1517-40.

Saunders, A. (1986). *The international debt problem: Studies in banking and finance*. Amsterdam: North Holland.

Saunders, A. (1994). Sovereign risk. *Financial institutions management: A modern perspective*. Saunders, A., Boston, MA: Irwin. 261-92.

Shapiro, H. D. (1994). Country credit: accentuate the positive. *Institutional Investor*, **94**, 93-9.

van Duyn, A. (1994). Country risk: where in the world is Japan? *Euromoney*, 177-80.

PHILIP CHANG

span of control   This is defined as the number of persons reporting directly to an individual supervisor, who is responsible for their direction. A "wide" span of control is a large number of persons who would be less closely supervised than the smaller number of direct reports in a "narrow" span of control, with whom the supervisor could interact more closely. Classical management theory, emphasizing structure in a hierarchy of authority, advised that the span of control be limited (one authority, Graicunas (1937), suggested a limit of six direct reports) to insure adequate oversight. Span of control is a central feature of the hierarchical supervision deemed essential to maintain good organizational order and insure that tasks are properly performed. This assumption made more sense in the context of mass manufacturing operations with numerous identical or highly similar tasks that might be grouped together under a single supervisor.

The spans of control of supervisors at any level were structured to include all organization members the next level down; each supervisor fell in turn within the span of control of a single superior. All organization members would thus be ultimately linked beneath the command of the most senior officer of the organization. Such inclusive, rigid hierarchies assume clear distinctions between levels and between tasks, as well as static organizational needs – assumptions that have become increasingly questionable.

While hierarchy and direct supervision remain important, especially in more traditionally organized firms, contemporary trends in management have increasingly tended toward much broader spans of control, with far less direct supervision. Indeed, the term span of control is less used as emphasis has shifted away from direct supervision. In place of direct supervision of functionally similar workers who know only a small segment of the overall task, employees are now often organized into cross-functional teams responsible for substantial fractions of activity (design of a new product, for instance). Such teams often manage themselves (*see* SELF-MANAGING TEAMS).

see also **Managerial behavior; Organizational design; Communications**

Bibliography

Urwick, L. F. (1974). V. A. Graicunas and the span of control. *Academy of Management Journal*, **17**, June, 349-354.

MARIANN JELINEK

sponsorship   Sponsorship is an element of the marketing COMMUNICATIONS MIX and is considered to be the provision of assistance, financial or in kind, to an activity by a commercial organization, for the purpose of achieving commercial objectives.

Reasons for, or objectives of, sponsorship are interrelated and include: keeping the company name before the public; building or altering perceptions of the organization and, therefore, goodwill; portraying a socially concerned and community-involved company; identifying with a target market and, therefore, promoting products and brands; countering adverse PUBLICITY; aiding with recruitment; and helping sales forces with prospects.

Typically, sponsorship is associated with the arts, sports, and community activities, and so companies are seen to be supporting these "events" and would, therefore, claim such support to be an objective of their sponsorship.

Sponsorship monies might finance part of the cost of a community or cultural or sporting event; or assume responsibility for the production of a television or radio program. Thus, the sponsoring organization aims to establish high visibility and the credibility of being associated with the development and success of the venture.

A recent development with sponsorship is corporate hospitality, in particular at sporting and cultural events.

A major problem with sponsorship is measurement of its cost-effectiveness.

Bibliography

Dibb, S., Simkin, L., Pride, W. M. & Ferrell, O. C. (1994). *Marketing: Concepts and strategies*. European edn, Boston, MA: Houghton Mifflin Co. Chapter 15.

Meenaghan, T. (1991). The role of sponsorship in the marketing communications mix. *International Journal of Advertising*, **10**, (1).

DAVID YORKE

staffing   One of the most important international management functions is the selection and hiring of employees to staff positions domestically and overseas. International businesses have a large number of employee sources: their own operations throughout the world; employees from similar operations in other companies; and training new employees from countries in which operations are undertaken. Even though potential employees seem to be almost unlimited, companies tend to select on the basis of top management's feelings which may favor certain geographic regions. Hiring practices usually follow one of four strategies: polycentric approach, ethnocentric approach, regiocentric approach, or geocentric approach. The characteristics of each approach are reviewed below.

1 Polycentric approach to hiring – Polycentrism is the belief that managers and employees in a foreign operation should be from the host country. The feeling is that people native to the host country will not have problems with: culture shock, knowing the language, realizing and adhering to the local customs, values and

attitudes, and being effective immediately instead of after a learning process has taken place. Key positions in the foreign operation are filled with host country nationals (HCNs). This saves money associated with recruiting, training, and transferring expatriates from other countries in which the company also has operations. There are, however, possible negative aspects of a polycentric approach to hiring. One of the biggest problems relates to parent company control over the foreign subsidiary. The question arises: "Will host country managers be loyal to the parent or to the local operation?" A potential problem arises with coordination of activities, goals, and objectives between parent and subsidiary. The fact remains, though, that polycentric staffing and operation of foreign subsidiaries is successfully being applied by organizations. The parent company must be aware of potential problems and introduce control systems to uncover these problems before they are allowed to get out of hand.

2 Ethnocentric approach to hiring – If one is ethnocentric in hiring practices, employees of a multinational company who are from the home country will be given preference. This could be because of lack of knowledge of foreign employee's qualifications for positions or due to bias against workers from outside the home country. Ethnocentric hiring fills all important positions with employees from the home country. This reduces potential for advancement for all other employees. This method of staffing foreign operations is extremely expensive. It also disregards the need to develop management talent in host countries. Ethnocentric hiring may lead to host countries instituting regulations to restrict the number of expatriates coming to the country.

3 Regiocentric approach to hiring – A regiocentric approach to hiring selects management personnel from within a region of the world which most closely resembles that of the host country. The company has expanded its search beyond the borders of the host country, but has stopped short of seeking management personnel from its operations throughout the world. The theory behind this selection process is that nationals of the region in which operations actually take place are better able to deal with language and cultural problems than are managers from outside the region. The logic behind this hiring approach is probably sound, but it ignores the potential growth a manager goes through when forced to deal with different situations than those in which he/she is comfortable.

4 Geocentric approach to hiring – Under this approach to hiring, people are viewed in the context of how well they can accomplish a particular job or task rather than on the basis of their home country, religion, culture, or other factors. Employees are selected from throughout the organization without regard to nationality with a resulting workforce that is quite diverse. This approach to hiring is truly global in nature.

Bibliography

Deresky, Helen (1994). *International management.* 1st edn, New York: HarperCollins.
Dowling, P. J. & Schuler, R. S. (1990). *International dimensions of human resource management.* Boston, MA: PWS-Kent.
Edstron, A. & Lorange, P. (1984). Matching strategy and human resources in multinational corporations. *Journal of International Business Studies,* **15** (2), 125–37.
Heller, J. E. (1980). Criteria for selecting an international manager. *Personnel* May–June, 47–55.
Ishidi, H. (1986). Transferability of Japanese human resource management abroad. *Human Resource Management,* **259** (1), 103–20.
Martinez, Z. L. & Ricks, D. A. (1989). Multinational parent companies' influence over human resource decisions of affiliates: U.S. forms in Mexico. *Journal of International Business Studies,* **20** (3), 465–87.
Mendenhall, M., Punnett, B. & Ricks, D. (1995). *Global management.* Cambridge, MA: Blackwell Publishers.
Schuler, R. S. (1993). World class HR departments: Six crucial issues. *The Singapore Accounting and Business Review,* Inaugural Issue, September.

JOHN O'CONNELL

stakeholder analysis Stakeholders are all the people (and organizations) that have an interest in a company, and that may influence the company or be influenced by its activities.

Stakeholders may be internal (such as employees) or external (such as suppliers or pressure groups). Most can be identified within the ranks of owners and stockholders, bankers and other creditors, suppliers, buyers and customers, advertisers, management, employees, their unions, competitors, local and state government, regulators, the media, public interest groups, the arts, political and religious groups, and the military. Others may also be identifiable, and their numbers and complexity of interdependence are likely to increase over the life span of the organization.

However, these groups are rarely sufficient to categorize stakeholders themselves, and stakeholders typically form groupings which are subsets of the above (such as secretarial personnel), or even cut across them (such as the group against the introduction of new plant automation technology, which may include some suppliers, some management, and many employees). In general, the population of stakeholder groups is unstable, with new groups tending to emerge and influence strategy as a result of specific current or expected events, while redundant groups disappear or, in some cases, the members of certain stakeholder groups diverge to such an extent in their views and opinions that the corresponding groups divide and split. It is important to recognize here that while some of the groups are explicitly formed, and may even have their own administrative organization, others may have no such organization, and their members may not even consciously view themselves as part of such a group. Most individuals are likely to belong to more than one stakeholder group at the same time.

The Role of Stakeholders

Stakeholders are important to the organization by virtue of their ability to influence it. As a result, their views must be a component of decision making. It is rare, however, that all stakeholders agree on all issues, and some are more powerful than others, so the task of management is also a balancing act.

Given that management hold much of the decision making power, that they need some approval from some stakeholders to retain their power, but also that it is

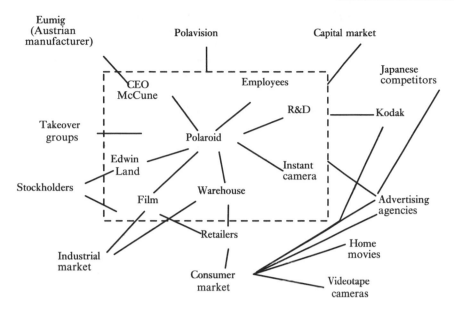

Figure 1 A map of the Polaroid Corporation's stakeholders in 1980.
Source: Rowe et al. (1994).

impossible for them to please all, management have a variety of balancing methods from which to choose. In principle, they can attempt to balance all interests equally; or according to their weight and importance; or they can focus on just one group of interests, satisfying all others only to the extent that they permit them to continue in office. This leading stakeholder group could be the organization's owners and shareholders, or it could well be the managers themselves, as they also are a major stakeholder.

In addition to strategy formulation, an analysis of an organization's stakeholders is also a powerful tool for evaluating strategies, by ascertaining the existence of objecting stakeholders and the extent of their power on any issue in question. In addition, a stakeholder analysis can form the basis, if it is so desired, for greater participation in decision making and better communication with stakeholders.

Stakeholder Mapping

Having established the importance of stakeholders, it is now necessary to find methods of obtaining an accurate picture of what the stakeholder groups are, which interests they represent in relation to the adoption of new strategies, whether they are likely to facilitate or inhibit change, how powerful these groups are, and how they should be dealt with (e.g., by means of side payments, the provision of information, and the like, to insure that they are sufficiently content so as not to take any action that could compromise the established strategies).

A typical stakeholder analysis would involve the identification of all stakeholders, a mapping of the significant relationships between them, an examination of this map for opportunities and threats, and the identification of the likely impact on the map of any proposed or likely change, so that the ground for this can be prepared. Figure 1 represents a typical stakcholder map.

Having identified who the most significant stakeholders are, a number of methods exist to decide how these should be dealt with. For example, the power/dynamism matrix, shown in figure 2, can be used to ascertain where political efforts should be channelled during the development of new strategies.

In this map, the most difficult group to deal with are those in segment D, since they are in a powerful position, and their stance is difficult to predict. In some cases, they can be dealt with by testing out new strategies with them before an irrevocable decision is made. Stakeholders in segment C are also important, although their stance is

Power \ Predictability	Low	High
Low	**A** **Fewer problems**	**B** **Unpredictable but manageable**
High	**C** **Powerful but predictable**	**D** **Greatest danger or opportunities**

Figure 2 Stakeholder mapping: the power/dynamism matrix.
Source: Johnson & Scholes (1993)

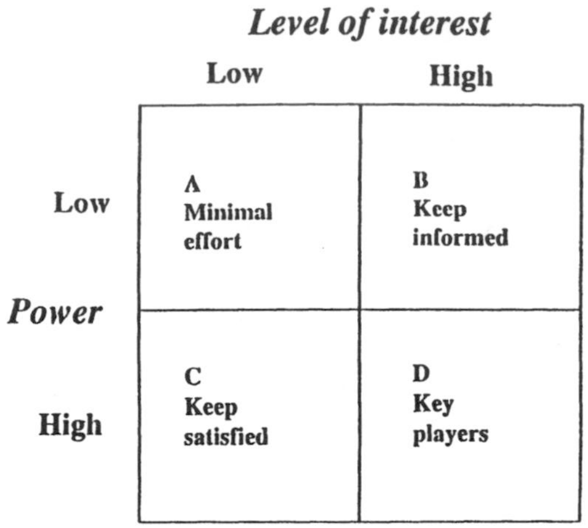

Level of interest

Figure 3   Stakeholder mapping: the power/interest matrix.
Source: Johnson & Scholes (1993)

predictable and so their expectations can often be met. Groups A and B are reasonably easy to deal with, although their power may increase if it is aggregated on any particular issue.

Similarly, the power/interest matrix, shown in figure 3, classifies stakeholderwhich they are likely to show interest in the organization's strategies, indicating the type of relationship that the organization will have to establish with each of them.

The acceptability of strategies to the key players D should be an important consideration in the evaluation of new strategies. Stakeholders in segment C are also very important as, although they are relatively passive in general, they may well emerge suddenly as a result of any specific event and become a very interested and significant party, moving to segment D on that particular issue. Similarly, the needs of stakeholders in segment B need to be addressed, largely through the provision of information, as these can influence the more powerful stakeholders.

The author would like to acknowledge the assistance of Diana Winstanley, The Management School, Imperial College for helpful comments on an earlier draft.

Bibliography

Donaldson, T. & Preston, L. G. (1995). The stakeholder theory of the corporation: concepts, evidence and implications. *Academy of Management Review*, **20** (2), 65–91.

Freeman, R. E. (1984). *Strategic management: a stakeholder approach*. London: Pitman.

Johnson and Scholes (1993). Exploring Corporate Strategy: text & cases. New York: Prentice Hall.

Mendelow, A. L. (1981). Environmental Scanning, *Proceedings of the 2nd International Conference on Information Systems*, Cambridge, MA.

Roberts, N. C. & King, P. J. (1989). The stakeholder audit goes public. *Organisational Dynamics* (Winter), 63–79.

Rowe, A. J., Mason, R. O., Dickel, K. E., Mann, R. B. & Mockler, R. J. (1994). *Strategic management: a methodological approach*, 4th edn, Reading, MA: Addison-Wesley. See pp. 134–44.

STEPHANOS AVGEROPOULOS

stakeholder theory   A *stakeholder*: any group or individual which can affect or is affected by an organization. This wide sense of the term includes suppliers, customers, stockholders, employees, communities, political groups, governments, media, etc. A more narrow definition is that the stakeholders in a firm are designated as suppliers, customers, employees, financiers, and communities.

Stakeholder theory: a set of propositions that suggest that managers of firms have obligations to some group of stakeholders. Stakeholder theory is usually juxtaposed with stockholder theory: the view that managers have a FIDUCIARY DUTY to act in the interests of stockholders. "Stakeholder" is an ironic twist of "stockholder" to signal that firms may well have broader obligations than the traditional economic theory has assumed.

The recent history of stakeholder theory has been well documented by Donaldson & Preston (1995). One can find vestiges of the concept in many areas of business from finance, strategic management (cf. Mason & Mitroff, 1982); organization theory (cf. Thompson, 1967; and Dill, 1958); and ethics (cf. Freeman, 1994). The actual word "stakeholder" first appeared in the management literature in an internal memorandum at the Stanford Research Institute (now SRI International, Inc.) in 1963. The term was meant to generalize the notion of stockholder as the only group to whom management need be responsive. Thus, the stakeholder concept was originally defined as "those groups without whose support the organization would cease to exist." Stemming from the work of Igor Ansoff and Robert Stewart in the planning department at Lockheed, and later Marion Doscher and Stewart at SRI, the original approach served an important information function in the SRI corporate planning process. The Swedish management theorist Eric Rhenman, who is perhaps the originator of the term, was instrumental in the development of stakeholder thinking in Scandinavia, where the concept became one of the cornerstones of industrial democracy. (See Nasi (1995) for the history of the concept in Scandinavia.)

Donaldson & Preston suggest the research on stakeholders has proceeded along three often confused lines. First, there is instrumental stakeholder theory, which assumes that if managers want to maximize the objective function of their firms, then they must take stakeholder interests into account. Second, there is the descriptive research about how managers, firms, and stakeholders in fact interact. Third, there is a normative sense of stakeholder theory that prescribes what managers ought to do, *vis à vis* the stakeholder. To this framework we can add a fourth dimension, the metaphorical use of "stakeholder" which depicts the idea as a figure in a broader narrative about corporate life. We shall combine the first two senses of stakeholders and call that "the analytical approach to stakeholder theory," while the second two senses can be called "the narrative approach to stakeholder theory."

The Analytical Approach to Stakeholder Theory

Any business needs to be understood at three levels of analysis. The first concerns how the business as a whole fits into its larger environment, or the *rational* level. The second concerns how the business relates to its environment as a matter of standard operating procedures and routine management processes, or the *process* level. The

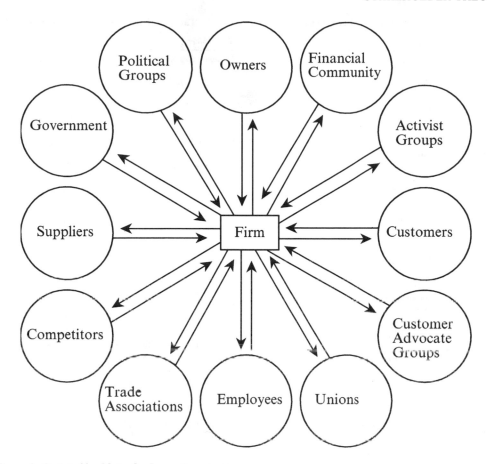

Figure 1: Stakeholder Map of a Large Organization

third concerns how the business executes actual *transactions*, or deals or contracts with those individuals who have a stake.

An example of the rational level is to think of business strategy as a game played, for example, between IBM and AT&T. IBM does action X and AT&T responds with action Y. An example of what we mean by the process level would be to look internally and see how the performance and reward procedures work at both AT&T and IBM. An example of the transactions level would be to closely examine the behavior of IBM and AT&T salespersons to see how each treats customers, and to examine the terms of various contracts, deals, promises, and individual motivations of each player. Obviously these three levels of analysis are connected. In fact, we argue that in successful businesses they fit together in a coherent pattern.

The rational level. The rational level of the stakeholder framework must give an accurate picture of the place of a business in its larger environment. It must identify those groups who have a stake, and it must depict the nature of the relationship between stakeholder and firm.

Stakeholder identification: Who are those groups and individuals who can affect and are affected by the achievement of an organization's purpose? How can we construct a stakeholder map of an organization? What are the problems in constructing such a map? Ideally, the starting-point for constructing a map for a particular business is a historical analysis of the environment of that particular firm. In the absence of such a historical document, figure 1 can serve as a checkpoint for an initial generic stakeholder map.

Figure 1 depicts a stakeholder map around one major strategic issue for one very large organization, the *XYZ* Company, based primarily in the United States. Unfortunately, most attempts at stakeholder analysis end with the construction of figure 1. The primary use of the stakeholder concept has been as a tool for gathering information about generic stakeholders. Table 1 is a chart of specific stakeholders to accompany figure 1 for the *XYZ* Company. Even in table 1 some groups are aggregated, in order to disguise the identity of the company. Thus, "Investment Banks" would be replaced by the names of those investment banks actually used by *XYZ*. Table 2 is an analysis of the stakes of some of those specific stakeholder groups listed in table 1. Thus, the stake of Political Parties no. 1 and no. 2 is as a heavy user of *XYZ*'s operations, and as being able to elevate *XYZ* to national attention via the political process. Customer Segment no. 1 used a lot of *XYZ*'s product and was interested in how the producer could be improved over time for a small incremental cost. Customer Segment no. 2 used only a small amount of *XYZ*'s product, but that small amount

Table 1 Specific Stakeholders in a Large Operation

General	Specific
Owners	Shareowners
	Bondholders
	Employees
Financial Community	Analysts
	Investment banks
	Commercial banks
	Federal Reserve
Activist Groups	Safety and health groups
	Environmental groups
	"Big business" groups
	Single-issue groups
Suppliers	Firm no. 1
	Firm no. 2
	Firm no. 3
	etc.
Government	Congress
	Courts
	Cabinet departments
	Agency no. 1
	Agency no. 2
Political Groups	Political part no. 1
	Political party no. 2
	national League of Cities
	National Council of Mayors
	etc.
Customers	Customer no. 1
	Customer no. 2
	etc.
Customer Advocate Groups	Consumer Federation of America
	Consumers' Union
	Council of Consumers
	etc.
Unions	Union of workers no. 1
	Union of Workers no. 2
	etc.
	Political action committees of unions
Employees	Employee segment no. 1
	Employment segment no. 2
	etc.
Trade Associations	Business Roundtable
	NAM
	Customer trade organization no. 1
	Customer trade organization no. 2
	etc.
Competitors	Domestic competitor no. 1
	Domestic competitor no. 2
	Foreign competitor no. 1
	etc.

was a critical ingredient for Customer Segment no. 2, and there were no readily available substitutes. As shown in figure 1 and tables 1 and 2, the construction of a rational stakeholder map is not an easy task in terms of identifying specific groups and the stakes of each. The figure and tables are enormously oversimplified, for they depict the stakeholders of XYZ as static, whereas in reality, they change over time, and their stakes change depending on the strategic issue under consideration.

Table 2 Stakes of Some Special Stakeholders

Stakeholder	Stake
Customer Segment no. 1	High users of produce
	Improvement of product
Political Parties nos. 1 and 2	High users of product
	Able to influence regulatory process
	Able to get media attention on a national scale
Customer Segment no. 2	Low users of product
	No available substitute
Consumer Advocate no. 1	Effects of XYZ on the elderly
Employees	Jobs and job security
	Pension benefits
Consumer Advocate no. 2	Safety of XYZ's products
Owners	Growth and income
	Stability of stock price and dividend

The process level. Large, complex organizations have many processes for accomplishing tasks. From routine applications of procedures and policies to the use of more sophisticated analytical tools, managers invent processes to accomplish routine tasks and to make complex tasks routine. To understand organizations and how they manage stakeholder relationships, it is necessary to look at the standard operating procedures – the organizational processes that are used to achieve some kind of fit with the external environment.

Organizational processes serve multiple purposes. One purpose is as a vehicle for communication and as symbols for what the corporation represents. Standard operating procedures depict what activities are necessary for success in the organization. And, the activities necessary for success inside the organization must bear some relationship to the tasks that the external environment requires of the organization if it is to be a successful and ongoing concern. Therefore, if the external environment is a rich multi-stakeholder, the strategic processes of the organization must reflect this complexity. These processes need not be rigid analytical devices, but rather existing strategic processes that work reasonably well with a concern for multiple stakeholders.

The transactional level. The bottom line for stakeholder management has to be the set of transactions that managers in organization have with stakeholders. How do the organization and its managers interact with stakeholders? What resources are allocated to interact with which groups? There has been a lot of research in social psychology about the so-called transactional environment of individuals and organizations, and we shall not attempt to recapitulate that research here. Suffice it to say that the nature of the behavior of organizational members and the nature of the goods and services being exchanged are key ingredients in successful organizational transactions with stakeholders.

Corporations have many daily transactions with stakeholder groups such as selling things to customers and buying things from suppliers. Other transactions are also fairly ordinary and unexciting, such as paying dividends to stockholders and negotiating a new contract with the union. Yet when we move from this relatively comfortable zone of

	A. Corporations ought to be governed . . .	B. Managers ought to act . . .	C. The background disciplines of "value creation" are . . .
Doctrine of Fair Contracts	. . . in accordance with the six principles. (Freeman, 1994)	. . . in the interests of stakeholders	– business theories – theories that explain stakeholder behaviour
Feminist Standpoint Theory	. . . in accordance with the principles of caring/ connection and relationships (Freeman, 1994)	. . . to maintain and care for relationships and networks of stakeholders	– business theories – feminist theory – social science understanding of networks
Ecological Principles	. . . in accordance with the principle of caring for the earth. (Freeman, 1994)	. . . to care for the earth.	– business theories – ecology – other

Figure 2: Stakeholder theory

transactions to dealing with some of the changes that have occurred in traditional marketplace stakeholders and the emergence of new stakeholder groups, there is little wonder that transactions with the corporation's stakeholder map become a real source of discontent.

If corporate managers ignore certain stakeholder groups at the rational and process level, then there is little to be done at the transactional level. Encounters between corporation and stakeholder will be, on the one hand, brief, episodic, and hostile, and on the other hand, nonexistent if another firm can supply stakeholders' needs. Successful transactions with stakeholders are built on understanding the legitimacy of the stakeholder and having processes to routinely surface their concerns. However, the transactions themselves must be executed by managers who understand the currencies in which the stakeholders are paid. There is simply no substitute for thinking through how a particular individual can win and how the organization can win at the same time.

The Narrative Approach to Stakeholder Theory

"The stakeholder theory" can be unpacked into a number of stakeholder theories, each of which has a "normative core," inextricably linked to the way that corporations should be governed and the way that managers should act. On the narrative approach, "stakeholder theory" is thus a genre of stories about how we could live. A "normative core" of a theory is a set of sentences that includes, among others:

(1) Corporations ought to be governed . .
(2) Managers ought to act to . .

where we need arguments or further narratives which include business and moral terms to fill in the blanks. This normative core is not always reducible to a fundamental ground like the theory of property, but certain normative cores are consistent with modern understandings of property. Certain elaborations of the theory of private property plus the other institutions of political liberalism give rise to particular normative cores. But there are other institutions and other political conceptions of how society ought to be structured so that there are different possible normative cores. Such a "reasonable pluralism" is what is meant by the idea of "enterprise strategy," but even that concept is too much in the instrumental/descriptive mode.

One normative core of a stakeholder theory might be the doctrine of Fair Contracts. Another might be Feminist Standpoint Theory, rethinking how we would restructure "value-creating activity" along principles of caring and connection. A third would be an Ecological (or several ecological) Normative Principles. Figure 2 is suggestive of how these theories could be developed.

Any normative core must address the questions in columns A or B, or explain why these questions may be irrelevant, as in the ecological view. In addition each narrative must place the normative core within a more full-fledged account of how we could understand value-creating activity differently (column C).

Research is proceeding along both the analytical and narrative lines. The rich panoply of concepts that is stakeholder theory threatens to replace, once and for all, the old way of thinking about the publicly held business as the sole property of stockholders, and offers the opportunity to build a wider shared vision of business into the twenty-first century.

Bibliography

Dill, William. (1958). Environment as an influence on managerial autonomy. *Administrative Science Quarterly*, 2 (4), 409–43.

Donaldson, T. J. and Preston, L. E. (1995). The stakeholder theory of the corporation: Concepts, evidence, and implications. *Academy of Management Review*, 20 (1), 65–91.

Freeman, R. E. (1984). *Strategic Management: A Stakeholder Approach*. Boston: Pitman.

Freeman, R. E. (1994). The politics of stakeholder theory: Some future directions. *Business Ethics Quarterly*, 4 (4), 409–21.

Mason, R. & Mitroff, I. (1982). *Challenging Strategic Planning Assumptions*. New York: John Wiley and Sons.

Nasi, J. (1995). *Understanding Stakeholder Thinking*. Helsinki: LSR-Julkaisut Oy.

Thompson, J.. (1967). *Organizations in Action*. New York: McGraw-Hill.

R. EDWARD FREEMAN

standard deviation The standard deviation of a random variable is the square root of its variance and it measures dispersion around the EXPECTED VALUE, or mean of that random variable. For a discrete random variable, X, which has specific outcomes denoted by X_i and where the probability distribution of the values of X is given by $f(x)$, then the standard deviation of X, σ, is calculated as

$$\sigma = \sqrt{\sum f(x) \times (X_i - E(X))^2}$$

where $E(X)$ is the expected value of the random variable, X, and denotes the summation over all possible values of X. Each squared deviation of the outcome, X, from the expected value, $E(X)$, is weighted by its probability, $f(x)$.

A manager who wishes to calculate the standard deviation for a sample of T observations would estimate the standard deviation using

$$s = \sqrt{\sum \frac{1}{T-1} \times (X_i - \overline{X})^2}$$

where $\overline{X}$ is the sample mean. Note that the squared deviations are divided by $T - 1$ and not by T because a *degree of freedom* has been lost. Some of the sample information has already been used to calculate the sample mean, and given this calculation only $T - 1$ of the observations are independent; see Maddala (1992) or Greene (1993). Most numerical software programs and spreadsheets will calculate the sample standard deviation for a set of observations.

Since more risk is associated with greater dispersion in the possible outcomes, the standard deviation can be used as a measure of risk. The coefficient of variation, one measure of risk per dollar of expected return, uses the standard deviation as a measure of risk. The standard error of an estimated coefficient can be used for hypothesis testing to determine if an explanatory variable in a linear regression has a significant effect on the dependent variable. Such a test would be useful to managers who may wish to determine if a recent change in policy (advertising, pricing, etc.) had significant effects on sales, profits, or some other variable of interest.

Bibliography

Douglas, E. J. (1992). *Managerial Economics*. 4th edn, Englewood Cliffs, NJ: Prentice-Hall.
Greene, W. H. (1993). *Econometric Analysis*. 2nd edn, New York: Macmillan.
Maddala, G. S. (1992). *Introduction to Econometrics*. 2nd edn, New York: Macmillan.

ROBERT E. MCAULIFFE

statistical sampling in auditing

Professional Standards

The American Institute of Certified Public Accountants (AICPA) has promulgated two Statements on Auditing Standards (SASs) that apply to the use of statistical sampling in auditing. These are SAS No. 39, "Audit Sampling," issued in June 1981 and SAS No. 47, "Audit Risk and Materiality in Conducting an Audit," issued in December 1983.

SAS 39 describes the use of sampling in auditing and the role of uncertainty and its relationship to risk. Sampling risk associated with incorrect decisions is described, as is the disaggregation of risk into four categories that pertain to auditors: inherent risk, control risk, analytical procedures risk, and tests of details risk. Two types of sampling applications, account balances tests and internal controls tests, are also described.

In SAS 47, audit risk and materiality and their impact on planning and implementing audit procedures are described. SAS 47 complements SAS 39 by more fully defining and describing inputs required to conduct audit sampling applications.

Research Summary

The earliest discussions of applications of audit sampling occurred in the 1940s (Editorial, "Testing 'very small' percentages," *Journal of Accountancy*, 72, 2–3, (1942)) when it was suggested that consideration of a small portion of a population might be an acceptable way of learning about the entire population. In the 1950s and 1960s most applications were in the compliance area with accounts receivable and inventories soon added to the list of audit sampling objects. Emphasis then was on *estimating* dollar balances rather than *testing* hypotheses about the balances. Elliott & Rogers (1972) criticized the continuing emphasis on estimation in audit sampling applications and went on to present a hypothesis–testing model that controlled the two primary risks an auditor must face when deciding whether or not to accept a client's book value balance. These risks are the risk of incorrect acceptance when a balance is materially misstated and the risk of incorrect rejection when a balance is not materially misstated. They used large sample normal distribution theory to calculate the necessary sample sizes to achieve the desired risk levels.

Throughout this period classical statistical procedures were introduced for use in auditing and they included simple random and stratified sampling, and the mean-per-unit estimator and a set of auxiliary information estimators. The estimators' expected uses were all based on large sample normal distribution theory. However, extensive research revealed that none of the estimators consistently achieved the nominal reliability levels (Kaplan, 1973; Neter & Loebbecke, 1975; Beck, 1980). The unreliability of the classical estimators and large sample theory in auditing applications prompted a need to know more about accounting populations so that the problems could be explained and possibly overcome. In the late 1970s and mid-1980s two major auditing firms made actual audit sampling databases available for study. These databases included both book and audit values so that error rates and error amounts could be studied. Analyses of these databases were conducted by Ramage, Krieger & Spero (1979); Johnson, Leitch & Neter (1981); Neter, Johnson & Leitch (1985); and Ham, Losell & Smieliauskas (1985).

The results of these analyses were consistent. Accounts receivable tended to have very low error rates with the preponderance of errors being overstatements. Inventory accounts tended to have larger error rates than accounts receivable with errors split approximately evenly between overstatements and understatements. While these databases were not selected randomly and could not be claimed to be representative of all accounting populations, the analyses provided support for the problems that had been reported in simulation studies.

In view of the problems with classical sampling theory and accounting populations, there has been a large volume of research into methods not requiring classical theory. One such development in sample selection methods is dollar unit sampling (DUS). When using DUS the probability of selecting an account is proportional to the number of dollars in the account, while in random sampling of individual accounts, the probability of selection is the same for all accounts. Auditors are naturally inclined to prefer DUS since larger individual accounts have a larger exposure to potential error amounts and also have a larger probability of selection.

Along with the attraction to DUS sampling, an attraction to a new estimator for audit sampling applications took place in the early 1970s. The Stringer bound, named for the person who developed it, was based on DUS. It became the subject of many simulation studies designed to test its reliability (Anderson & Teitlebaum, 1973; Goodfellow, Loebbecke & Neter, 1974a and b) since there was no underlying theory by which to demonstrate its reliability. The Stringer bound was constructed for use in a hypothesis testing context and is a "one-tail test" designed to provide protection against the most serious of the two possible decision errors, i.e., the probability of incorrect acceptance of a materially misstated balance. Without exception the reliability level achieved in all simulation studies exceeded the planned nominal level.

However, while these studies revealed conservatism in providing protection against the worst decision error, they prompted questions concerning how well the other decision error was controlled, i.e., the probability of incorrect rejection. Subsequently, simulation studies revealed that in most cases, the probability of making this error was surprisingly large. Despite this, the Stringer bound has become the most widely used of all the methods discussed here.

During the 1970s and 1980s many other bounds based on DUS were proposed. The general objective of bound construction was reliability, at least at the nominal level, and less conservative than the Stringer bound.

All of the DUS-based research reviewed above involved bounds designed for overstatement errors only. While auditors do not have the same aversion to understatements as they do for overstatements, not explicitly including understatements in the sampling design can help lead to the conservatism found in the Stringer and other bounds.

In the mid-1980s Dworin & Grimlund (1984) introduced the moment bound which accommodated both overstatements and understatements. It was based on a three-moment representation of the sampling distribution of the mean error in an accounting population. It used DUS and, similar to the Stringer bound, simulation was required to evaluate its potential usefulness. Many simulation studies have been conducted since the moment bound's introduction. These studies have shown it to be generally reliable and much less conservative than the Stringer bound with significant reductions in the probability of incorrect rejection. In the early 1990s one of the largest US Big Six auditing firms adopted it for use in its ongoing audit engagements.

In 1993 the augmented variance bound (AVE) was introduced by Rohrbach (1993) and was based on probability proportional to size (PPS) sampling without replacement. This is similar to DUS sampling except that once selected, an account is removed from the population

and further sampling is conducted from the remaining population items. AVE accommodated both overstatements and understatements and it also had to be studied by simulation. In the single published study of AVE so far (Rohrbach, 1993), it was shown that AVE achieves nominal reliability and also tends to be less conservative than the moment bound. In a working paper, Wurst, Neter & Godfrey (1994) also found that AVE generally had a smaller probability of incorrect rejection than the moment bound which supports the "less conservative" claim made in the Rohrbach study.

Current Status of Research

The use of statistical sampling by auditors has varied greatly over the past thirty years. Some audit firms have used it extensively, e.g., at one point one of the US largest firms required justification for not using statistical sampling on practically every audit engagement. Other firms have not insisted on its use, leaving it up to the auditors at the local operating level. It appears that in recent years overall use has diminished, although in the early 1990s, one of the largest US audit firms formally adopted the moment bound for use throughout the firm.

Statistical sampling in auditing has reached a stage where further improvements through research will be difficult. All recent advancements, beginning with the Stringer bound, have been based on DUS and their performance determined by simulation studies. The ideal research discovery would be a closed form model that guarantees control over the two primary decision risks and requires sample sizes small enough to be cost-effective for auditors. However, based on the progression of past research, attaining this ideal does not appear likely in the near term.

Finally, auditors have been extensively investigating other approaches to assessing and controlling audit risk and from a cost/benefit standpoint this may reduce the need to search for new developments in sampling.

Bibliography

Anderson, R. & Teitlebaum, A. D. (1973). Dollar-unit sampling. *Canadian Chartered Accountant*, 102, 4, 30–9.

Beck, P. J. (1980). A critical analysis of the regression estimator in audit sampling. *Journal of Accounting Research*, 18, 16–37.

Dworin, L. & Grimlund, R. A. (1984). Dollar-unit sampling for accounts receivable and inventory. *The Accounting Review*, 59, 218–41.

Elliott, R. K. & Rogers, J. R. (1972). Relating statistical sampling to audit objectives. *Journal of Accountancy*, 134, 46–55.

Goodfellow, J., Loebbecke, J. & Neter, J. (1974a). Some perspectives on CAV sampling plans, Part I. *CA Magazine*, 105, 4, 23–30.

Goodfellow, J., Loebbecke, J. & Neter, J. (1974b). Some perspectives on CAV sampling plans, Part II. *CA Magazine*, 105, 5, 47–53.

Ham, J., Losell, D. & Smieliauskas, W. (1985). An empirical study of error characteristics in accounting populations. *The Accounting Review*, 60, 387–406.

Johnson, J. R., Leitch, R. A. & Neter, J. (1981). Characteristics of errors in accounts receivable and inventory audits. *The Accounting Review*, 56, 270–93.

Kaplan, R. S. (1973). Statistical sampling in auditing with auxiliary information estimators. *Journal of Accounting Research*, 11, 238–58.

Neter, J. & Godfrey, J. T. (1988). Statistical sampling in auditing: A review. *Essays in honor of Franklin A. Graybill* J. N. Srivastava, (Ed.), Netherlands: Elsevier Science Publishers BV.

Neter, J., Johnson, J. & Leitch, R. A. (1985). Characteristics of dollar-unit taints and error rates in accounts receivable and inventory. *The Accounting Review*, **60**, 488–99.

Neter, J. & Loebbecke, J. K. (1975). *Behavior of major statistical estimators in sampling accounting applications – An empirical study*. New York: AICPA.

Ramage, J. K., Krieger, A. M. & Spero, L. L. (1979). An empirical study of error characteristics in audit populations. *Journal of Accounting Research*, **17**, supplement, 72–102.

Rohrbach, K. J. (1993). Variance augmentation to achieve nominal coverage probability in sampling from audit populations. *Auditing, A Journal of Practice and Theory*, **12**, 79–97.

Wurst, J. C., Neter, J. & Godfrey, J. T. (1994). Additional findings on effectiveness of rectification in audit sampling. Unpublished working paper.

JAMES GODFREY

status   This is a concept with descriptive and evaluative connotations. Descriptively, status is the position of a social entity in a social system based on a set of relevant dimensions (*see* SYSTEMS THEORY). For instance, a person may be the president of an organization. Associated with statuses are ROLES. Evaluatively, status refers to a ranking of a social entity in terms of the values of a social system. These judgments often are formed without conscious deliberation. For instance, the president of an organization is deemed important in both the organization and society. Status evaluations help determine hierarchy and maintain the LEGITIMACY of authority. Together, descriptive and evaluative status enhance the predictability of social interaction.

The general term status can be separated into three types (Mitchell, 1982). Social status is the standing of a person in general society. Occupational prestige is the importance of an occupation to society. Organizational status is the position one holds in an organizational setting.

For descriptive and analytic purposes, status dimensions can be partitioned. One partition is based on the amount of control the social actor has over them. Ascriptive dimensions are those which the social actor cannot control; for individuals, these include age and race. Achieved dimensions are those a social actor partially can control, such as educational attainment or job performance. A useful application of this division occurs in employment law; discrimination by a number of ascriptive dimensions is prohibited in some countries.

Evaluations of status require either global judgments or the evaluation of each of the descriptive dimensions of status. In the former case, status can be determined by asking organizational members to state the status of others. This reputational measure is similar to that used for prestige (see Wegener, 1992) and risks confounding the two. Alternatively, a dimensionalized approach requires the weighing of dimensions from the perspective of either organizational members (a realist strategy) or researchers (a nominalist strategy). Theoretically, evaluative status is multidimensional, not equivalent with a single status dimension such as prestige or economic position. For instance, a young engineer may have higher status than an older, more highly paid accountant.

In task groups, the formation of status hierarchies and its effects have been examined in depth, especially in laboratory studies. A well-established theory in this area involves a social psychological process which Webster and Foschi (1988) called status generalization. Group members form cognitive performance expectations based on status characteristics, including those called diffuse status characteristics which exist outside setting the group setting, such as gender and age. The performance expectations then lead to differences in behaviors, such as deference, LEADERSHIP, and effort. The status characteristics on which performance expectations are formed may be irrelevant to actual task performance, however.

Recently, researchers examining organizational status tended to focus on specific dimensions in their studies. Ibarra (1993, p. 474) acknowledged that she was using status dimensions such as experience and education as indicators of POWER in an examination of INNOVATION involvement. Messé, Kerr, and Sattler (1992) focused on formal authority in a study of supervisory privileges.

Bibliography

Ibarra, H. (1993). Network centrality, power, and innovation involvement: Determinants of technical and administrative roles. Academy of Management Journal, **36**, 471–501.

Messé, L. A., Kerr, N. L. & Sattler, D. N. (1992). But some animals are more equal than others: The supervisor as a privileged status in group contexts. In S. Worchel, W. Wood & J. A. Simpson (Eds), Group process and productivity, (pp. 203–223). Newbury Park, CA: Sage.

Mitchell, T. R. (1982). People in organizations. (2nd edn) New York: McGraw-Hill.

Webster, M. Jr. & Foschi, M. (1988). Status generalization: New theory and research. Stanford, CA: Stanford University Press.

Wegener, B. (1992). Concepts and measurement of prestige. In J. Blake & J. Hagan (Eds), Annual review of sociology, (vol. 18, pp. 253–280.)

DAVID L. DEEPHOUSE

stock market indices   Stock market indices measure the value of a portfolio of average of stock prices. Stock market indices as aggregate measures are an instrument to meet the information requirements of investors by characterizing the development of global markets and specific market segments (descriptive function). In their function as a basis of derivative instruments stock market indices facilitate the application of certain portfolio strategies such as hedging and arbitrage (operative function).

In order to perform these functions, a stock market index should fulfill statistical as well as economic requirements. The statistical requirements for indices in general were summarized by Fisher (1922), Eichhorn (1976), and Diewert (1986). Crucial for stock market indices are: (1) invariance to changes in scale; (2) symmetric treatment of components; (3) time reversal, that is, the index between any two dates will not be changed if the base period of the index is changed from one date to another; and (4) indifference to the incorporation of new stocks, that is, *ceteris paribus*, the inclusion or removal of a stock will not change the index compared to its previous value. As a representative stock market index only contains a selection of stocks, index construction involves a sampling problem.

The commonly used stock indices belong to one of the following three categories: averages, capitalization-weighted indices, and performance indices. The most prominent representative of the class of averages is the Dow Jones Industrial Average (DJIA). The DJIA is a price-weighted average of thirty blue chip stocks traded at the New York Stock Exchange (NYSE). The DJIA, comprising twelve stocks, first appeared in 1896 with a value of 40.94. In its present form with thirty common stocks the DJIA was first published in 1928. For the purpose of futures trading the Chicago Board of Trade formed the Major Market Index which comprises twenty shares of which sixteen are also included in the DJIA. Since 1975 the Nikkei 225 Stock Average has been calculated on the basis of stocks traded in the first section of the Tokyo Stock Exchange. In the case of all these indices, reductions of stock prices due to stock splits, as opposed to dividend payments, are accounted for in order to leave the average unaffected. The main disadvantage associated with the calculation method of these averages is the fact that a given percentage price change of a high-priced stock induces a larger change of the average than an identical percentage change of a low-priced stock.

The majority of stock indices belong to the category of capitalization-weighted indices using the Laspeyres, Paasche, or Fisher formula. The most prominent indices are the Standard and Poor's 500 (NYSE/AMEX/OTC market), the TOPIX (Tokyo Stock Exchange, first section), the FT-SE 100 (London Stock Exchange), the CAC 40 (Paris Stock Exchange), the SMI (twenty-four Swiss stocks), and the FAZ-Index (100 German stocks). Due to its breadth, the S&P 500 is widely used by portfolio managers as benchmark for the performance of their portfolios (Berlin, 1990). Empirical studies show that the average pre-tax return of the S&P 500 portfolio between 1925 and 1986 reached 12.1 percent per annum, while a portfolio of government bonds yielded 4.7 percent per annum on average. Since 1982 the S&P 500 has served as the basis for cash-settled stock index futures contracts. Some of the above indices contain an additional adjustment factor to allow for the case when the outstanding capital significantly exceeds the free floating capital.

The increasing use of stock market indices as a basis for derivative products called for provisions to allow a balanced reflection of the descriptive and the operative function. In response to this requirement the DAX (thirty shares listed at the Frankfurt Stock Exchange), introduced in 1988, was constructed as performance index (Janssen and Rudolph, 1992). The Swiss Performance Index and the FAZ Performance Index followed afterwards. These indices measure the total return of a portfolio under the following assumption: dividend payments and the hypothetical money value of share warrants from rights offers are immediately reinvested in the respective stock to obtain the change of the overall value of a particular portfolio compared to the value at a given base period.

For specific purposes, a variety of other indices has been developed. In order to provide a benchmark needed for international asset allocation, Morgan Stanley Capital International developed the MSCI World Index which is based on 1609 securities listed on the stock exchanges of twenty-two countries (as of January 1995). In contrast to all indices mentioned above, the value line arithmetic index assigns the same weight to each stock. It represents approximately 95 percent of the market values of all US securities. On the basis of portfolios which comprise stocks from a specific industry, a large variety of branch indices such as the Dow Jones Transportation Average, the AMEX

Oil Index, or the NYSE Utility Index have been constructed. In order to study the performance of initial public offerings, for each major European stock exchange the Institute for Advanced Studies established an initial public offerings index (IPOX) which is isomorphic to the respective stock market index (Haefke and Helmenstein, 1995). When IPOX futures become available, investors will have an instrument at hand to fully participate in promising initial public offerings without being rationed. Due to the increasing interest in derivatives, Trinkaus and Burkhardt designed the TUBOS as real-time index to measure the performance of German warrants *vis-à-vis* the DAX.

Bibliography

Berlin, H. M. (1990). *The handbook of financial market indexes, averages, and indicators.* Homewood, IL: Dow Jones-Irwin.

Diewert, W. E. (1986). Microeconomic approaches to the theory of international comparisons. Technical Working Paper No 53, Cambridge, MA: NBER.

Eichhorn, W. (1976). Fisher's tests revisited. *Econometrica,* **44,** 247–56.

Fisher, I. (1922). *The making of index numbers: A study of their varieties, tests, and reliability.* Publications of the Pollak Foundation for Economic Research, No. 1, Boston/New York: Houghton Mifflin.

Haefke, C. & Helmenstein, C. (1995). Neural networks in the capital markets: an application to index forecasting. *Computational methods in economics and finance.* Gllll, M. Dordrecht/Boston/London: Kluwer Academic Publishers.

Janssen, B. & Rudolph, B. (1992). *Der Deutsche Aktienindex DAX.* Frankfurt: Knapp.

CHRISTIAN HELMENSTEIN and
CHRISTIAN HAEFKE

stockholders' equity   The stockholders' equity section of the balance sheet (also referred to as shareholders' equity) represents the book value of the ownership interest in the assets of a business entity. Ownership interest is normally increased by issuing shares of stock and by earned income; ownership interest is decreased by net losses of the entity and by distributions of assets to owners. The ownership claim on the assets is secondary to claims by creditors, but the residual interest that accrues to owners encompasses all remaining assets after creditor claims are satisfied. Ownership bears the maximum risk of loss associated with the enterprise, but is also entitled to all of the residual rewards. Organization of the stockholders' equity section is by sources of capital formation. The primary sources of capital are contributed capital and earned capital.

Contributed Capital

Contributed capital refers to investment by owners in the capital stock of the corporation. Amounts paid in for capital stock are usually accounted for in two parts: par or stated value, and additional paid-in capital. The par or stated value of stock is a designated dollar amount (in the USA) per share and is set by the corporation. In the USA, the par value or stated value per share times the number of shares issued usually comprises legal capital. If there is no par or stated value, the entire investment may be defined as legal capital. Restrictions may exist on the ability of the corporation to make distributions to owners that would reduce stockholders' equity below what is considered legal capital.

Additional paid-in capital, or share premium, occurs if the investment per share exceeds the par or stated value per share of stock. Other sources of additional paid-in capital include the sale of treasury stock (i.e., shares temporarily reacquired by the issuing firm) or transfers from retained earnings through certain stock dividends. Accounting Principles Board (APB) Opinion No. 14 (March, 1969) states that the portion of the proceeds of debt securities issued with detachable stock purchase warrants that is allocable to the warrants shall be accounted for as additional paid-in capital.

The segregation of additional paid-in capital by source is recommended by Accounting Research Bulletin (ARB) No. 43 (June, 1953) and APB Opinion No. 5 (September, 1964). However, APB Opinion No. 5 also acknowledges that state corporation laws may specify treatments other than those preferred by generally accepted accounting principles and that these should be deemed acceptable. Since state corporation laws generally do not require segregation, many corporations do not maintain sufficiently detailed records to identify additional paid-in capital by source.

Earned Capital

The second primary source of corporate capital is earned capital, which is accounted for in the retained earnings account. Retained earnings represents the accumulation of undistributed earnings over the life of the corporation. A negative balance in retained earnings, or deficit, indicates the corporation currently has a cumulative net loss.

The most common event to affect the balance in retained earnings is the declaration of a dividend. According to the "Framework for the Preparation of Financial Statements" [International Accounting Standards Committee (IASC), 1989] and consistent with Statement of Financial Accounting Concepts (SFAC) No. 6 (December, 1985), distributions to owners decrease ownership interests in an enterprise; the declaration and payment of dividends do not lead to the recognition of an expense. Dividends become an obligation of the corporation only when they are declared by the board of directors; at declaration, the aggregate amount of the dividend is subtracted from retained earnings. Most dividends are paid in cash. Dividends can also be paid in kind; i.e., noncash assets such as inventory are distributed to the stockholders. APB No. 29 (May, 1973) mandates that dividends in kind be recorded at the fair value of the assets transferred.

Protection of creditors has high importance. Under the European Community (EC), Fourth Directive, recognition is given to the need for a company to establish a minimum share capital and to ensure that it is maintained. In the UK, there is no requirement to recover past losses of capital before a dividend is paid out of current profits. In general, however, the EC view is that a company should not be permitted to pay a dividend unless all prior losses, revenue and capital, have been recovered.

A second form of dividend is the stock dividend, which is a corporate distribution on a pro rata basis of additional shares of its own common stock to its common stockholders without payment of additional consideration. Accounting techniques for stock dividends are stated in ARB No. 43 (June, 1953). Stock distributions of additional shares totaling less than 20 to 25 percent of the previously outstanding shares are considered "small" stock dividends; for these distributors distributions, the fair market value of the shares distributed should be transferred from retained earnings to the common stock (for par or stated value of the shares issued) and additional paid-in capital (for amounts above par value) accounts.

Stock distributions involving issuance of additional shares totalling more than 25 percent of the number previously outstanding may be accounted for as a "large" stock dividend or as a stock split. If it is considered a stock dividend, the par value of the issued shares is transferred from retained earnings to the common stock account. If the distribution is considered a stock split, the par or stated value per share is adjusted so that legal capital remains unchanged. When a stock split is clearly for the purpose of effecting a reduction in the unit market price of the shares, no transfer from retained earnings is called for unless required by local law.

Certain conditions require a restatement of the beginning balance of the retained earnings account. In July 1990, the IASC issued "Statement of Intent: Comparability of Financial Statements," which proposes that the preferred accounting treatment for correction of fundamental errors and omissions, and variation resulting from accounting policy changes should be a restatement of the beginning balance in retained earnings. Alternatively, income effects of changes in accounting policy could be included in the determination of net income. The alternative treatment is consistent with accounting practice in the USA. According to APB No. 20 (July 1971), errors in financial statements are defined as errors resulting from mathematical mistakes, mistakes in the application of accounting principles, or oversight or misuses of facts that existed at the time the financial statements were prepared. SFAS No. 16 (June, 1977), as amended by SFAS No. 109 (February, 1992), states that only corrections of errors are properly recorded as prior period adjustments. SFAS No. 109 states that any item of profit and loss related to the correction of an error in the financial statements of a prior period shall be accounted for and reported as a prior period adjustment and excluded from the determination of net income for the current period. According to SFAS No. 15 (June, 1977), those items that are reported as a prior period adjustment shall, in single period statements, be reflected as adjustments of the opening balance of retained earnings. APB Opinion No. 9 (December, 1966) mandates that for comparative statements, corresponding adjustments shall be made of the amounts of net income, its components, retained earnings balances, and other affected balances from all of the years presented to reflect the retroactive application of the prior period adjustment.

Normally, a change in accounting principle is accounted for prospectively. However, certain items specifically identified in the standards are given retroactive treatment. A retroactive adjustment is made by recasting the statements of prior years on a basis consistent with the newly adopted principle. Any part of the cumulative effect attributable to years prior to those presented is treated as an adjustment of beginning retained earnings of the earliest year presented.

Treasury Stock

When a corporation acquires its own shares, these shares must either be retired or be placed in treasury. When shares are retired, they reassume the status of authorized, but unissued, shares. When shares are placed in treasury, they are considered issued, but not outstanding, shares. Some state corporation laws do distinguish between treasury shares and unissued stock on some dimensions. Treasury shares may be exempt from certain legal limitations on the issuance of authorized, but previously unissued, common shares. In the USA, in jurisdictions that have adopted the Model Business Corporation Act (MBCA), there are virtually no legal differences between treasury shares and retired shares. However, even in these states, many corporations retain the designation of treasury shares for financial reporting purposes.

Shares held in treasury are not assets of the corporation because these shares do not provide a future benefit that will result in revenues or income. Consistent with SFAC No. 6 (December, 1985) definitions, these distributions to owners decrease ownership interests and do not lead to recognition of revenue or expense.

Treasury stock is most commonly shown at cost, and it is a contra-equity account. The most common method of presentation is to deduct the aggregate cost of treasury shares from the total of all other equity accounts. GAAP also permits valuation of treasury shares at par value.

Donated Capital

Some corporations show a donated capital account in their stockholders' equity section. Donated capital arises from the contribution of assets to corporations without a commensurate issuance of equity claims. The donated assets are recorded at their fair market values as increases to the related asset accounts, and the credit is to an additional paid-in capital account. SFAS No. 116 (June, 1993), effective for reporting years beginning after December 15, 1994, mandates new accounting techniques to account for donations. Under this Statement, contributions received will be recorded as an increase in the related asset accounts, but the credit will be made to a revenue or gain account instead of being made directly to a capital account. Rather than a direct effect on stockholders' equity, the donation will indirectly increase stockholders' equity when the revenue and gain accounts are closed to retained earnings.

Other Adjustments to Stockholders' Equity

Quasi-reorganizations. Some US state laws permit a quasi-reorganization. This procedure eliminates an accumulated deficit in retained earnings and may be appropriate if new products or new management have substantially improved the economic conditions and operating results of a company. Some state laws prohibit declaring or paying dividends until a deficit has been replaced by earnings which could hinder a company's ability to obtain new capital. A quasi-reorganization eliminates the deficit in retained earnings through a reclassification of the stockholders' equity accounts but does not require intervention of the courts in a formal reorganization. To accomplish a quasi-reorganization, an amount equal to the cumulative deficit is removed from the additional paid-in capital accounts, resulting in a zero balance in the retained earnings account. In subsequent financial reports, the retained earnings must be dated for a period of five to ten years to show the fact and the date of the quasi-reorganization.

Foreign currency translation. In 1981, the US Financial Accounting Standards Board (FASB) issued SFAS No. 52 (December 1981), which calls for postponing the recognition of unrealized exchange rate gains and losses on foreign currency until the foreign operation is substantially liquidated. This postponement is accomplished by creating a stockholders' equity account to carry the unrealized amounts.

Marketable securities adjustments. Certain readily marketable debt and equity securities, not actively traded but available for sale, are valued at fair value at the end of the accounting period. According to SFAS No. 115 (May, 1993), the unrealized gain or loss associated with the change in asset value is captured in a stockholders' equity account.

Presentation of Contributed Capital According to the Fourth Directive

The Fourth Directive, which prescribes formats for financial statements, was issued by the European Community (EC) in 1978. With respect to contributed capital, subscribed capital is the first item disclosed in the equity section. If national law provides for called-up capital to be shown under this heading, the amounts of subscribed capital and paid-up capital must be separately disclosed. The share premium account immediately follows subscribed capital.

Classifications of Stock. All corporations have at least one class of capital stock identified as common stock; in addition, some corporations issue one or more classes of preferred stock. Common stock is the basic ownership equity of a company. Four rights normally accrue to each share of common stock: voting rights, dividend rights, liquidation rights, and preemptive rights. Each share of common stock is entitled to one vote; common stockholders elect the board of directors. When dividends are declared and paid, each share of common stock is entitled to receive a pro rata distribution. In liquidation, the residual assets of the company (assets remaining after the claims of all creditors and stockholders with preferred claims are satisfied) are distributed on a pro rata basis to each share of common stock. The preemptive right entitles stockholders to purchase a percentage share of any new stock offering equal to their current ownership percentage. Occasionally, there is more than one class of common stock with differences in the rights associated with each stock issue or class.

Preferred stock usually is entitled to senior claims on the net assets of the corporation relative to the common shares. Preferences usually relate to dividend and liquidation rights. Preferred stock has the right to receive a predetermined dividend each year before any dividends can be paid to common stock. The dividend may be expressed as a percentage of par or stated value, or as a cash amount per share. The preferred dividend may also be cumulative, which means that any dividend preferences not paid in previous years must be paid in full before common stockholders may receive a dividend. Unpaid cumulative dividends relating to prior years are referred to as "dividends in arrears." If the dividends are not cumulative, a dividend missed in prior years need not be paid. While the right to dividends is normally fixed on a per share basis, preferred stock may also be participating, which means that preferred stockholders may be entitled to additional dividends under contractual conditions. Claims of preferred stockholders in liquidation are senior to the claims of common stockholders, and are predetermined on a per share basis. Preferred stock normally does not have a right to vote.

Convertible preferred stock may be converted into another security, normally common shares, at a predetermined ratio. Callable preferred stock can be redeemed at a fixed per-share price at the option of the company. Normally, missed cumulative dividends must also be paid when the preferred stock is called. The preferred features, particularly the fixed dividend rate and the fixed liquidation value, give preferred stock some of the characteristics of debt. Important differences are that the preferred stockholders are not entitled to demand either the redemption of their shares or the declaration and subsequent payment of dividends. There may be multiple classes of preferred stock, each with different priorities and preferences relative to dividend and/or liquidation rights.

Fourth Directive Requirements

The Fourth Directive allows considerable flexibility in financial statement presentation. The overriding reporting standard is a "true and fair view," and this consideration overrides specific reporting requirements. If required disclosure is not sufficient to provide a true and fair view any necessary additional information must be provided in the financial statements or in the notes. Relative to stockholders' equity, notes to the financial statements should disclose: (1) the number and nominal value (or accounting par value) of shares subscribed during the year; (2) the number and nominal value (or accounting par value) of each class of share in issue; and (3) a description of any participation certificates, convertible debentures, or similar securities or rights, with an indication of their number and the rights they convey.

Disclosure Requirements in the USA

According to Accounting Principles Board (APB) Opinion No. 12 (December), 1967, proper disclosure requires an analysis and explanation of changes in the number of shares of stock issued and/or outstanding during the period. Disclosure may be included on the face of the financial statement or in the footnotes. Increases in capital stock may result from sale of additional shares of stock, conversion of preferred stock or debentures, issuance of stock through stock dividends or stock splits, issuance of stock in acquisitions or mergers, or issuance of stock pursuant to the exercise of stock options or stock warrants. Decreases may result from the purchase and retirement of stock, purchase of treasury stock, or reverse stock splits.

The need for disclosure in connection with complex capital structures is stated in APB No. 15 (May, 1969). Financial statements should include a summary description sufficient to explain the pertinent rights and privileges of the various securities outstanding. Disclosure requirements for capital stock include contractual obligations to potentially increase the number of shares outstanding of a given class of stock. Such obligations include: (1) conversion rights of debentures or preferred stock into common shares; (2) warrants outstanding entitling the holder to exchange them for shares; (3) stock options under compensation and bonus plans that call for the issuance of capital stock over a period of time at prices fixed in advance; and (4) commitments to issue capital stock under certain merger agreements. These disclosures are necessary to alert investors to potential increases in the number of shares outstanding and the related potential for dilution of earnings per share and book value per share.

Disclosures specific to preferred stock include the terms to which preferred stock may be subject. In particular, dividend rights, including participating and cumulative features, and liquidation rights must be disclosed. APB No. 10 (Dec. 1966) encourages disclosure of the aggregate liquidation value of preferred stock parenthetically rather than on a per-share basis or by disclosure in the footnotes.

The Use of Reserves in the Financial Statements

Restrictions on the availability of retained earnings to support distributions to owners may be accomplished by an appropriation of retained earnings, which is accomplished in some countries by legal provisions. Generally a reserve is created by a specific act of the board of directors, and it is recorded by crediting a special equity account called appropriated retained earnings or a specific purpose reserve account, and by debiting retained earnings. Appropriations of retained earnings can be reversed by a vote of the board. This appropriation has sometimes been called a reserve, and this is the only acceptable use of the term "reserve" under US generally accepted accounting principles.

In some countries outside of the USA however, the term reserve is used more broadly. Under the Fourth Directive, revaluation reserves and other legal reserves are to be disclosed on the balance sheet immediately after the share premium accounts. These reserves may be used for certain income items that do not flow through the income statement but instead increase or decrease stockholders' equity directly. In addition, common practice in certain countries permits shifting of income between accounting periods to either minimize income taxes or smooth earnings. The accounting mechanism used to accomplish this reporting result is also called a "reserve." Reserve accounts may appear on the balance sheet as a component of stockholders' equity. This use of reserves does not misstate total stockholders' equity, however. Instead of recognizing an item on the income statement and closing the item through retained earnings, thereby indirectly adjusting stockholders' equity, the use of the reserve allows a direct adjustment to the value of stockholders' equity. A company's ability to pay dividends may be limited by the existence of these reserves.

In countries other than the USA, firms may use reserves to revalue assets without showing an income effect for the current period. Accounting principles in the UK permit periodic revaluations of fixed assets and intangible assets to their current market value. The increased valuation of assets that usually occurs leads to an increase in a revaluation reserve account included in stockholders' equity.

Accounting principles in some countries (e.g., Japan, Germany, and France) require the establishment of reserves through appropriations of retained earnings.

Annual appropriations of earnings are accumulated until the balance in the reserve account equals a percentage of outstanding share capital. The purpose of this reserve is for the protection of creditors since assets of equal amounts would not be available for distribution to owners.

CYNTHIA JEFFREY

strategic alliances   Strategic alliances represent transitional mechanisms that enable firms to manage highly complex or fast-changing environments and to restructure their competitive STRATEGY. Alliances are linkages between firms to achieve economic benefits not available through arms-length market transactions, internal development or acquisition (Slocum and Lei, 1993). Firms can design strategic alliances as platforms to accelerate organizational learning of new skills and capabilities (Hamel, 1991; Lei and Slocum, 1992).

Factors Promoting the Rise of Alliances
All alliances are motivated by the need for risk reduction. Several environmental forces have accelerated alliance formation, including (a) sharing costs of commercializing cutting edge technologies in research and development intensive industries, (b) shaping or transforming standards in fast-changing industries, (b) pooling resources for global economies of scale in value-adding activities, (d) speeding entry into new markets, and (e) learning skills and technologies from partners.

Forms of Alliances
Alliances consist of long-term supply contracts, licensing agreements, technology development pacts, joint ventures, equity ownership stakes, and cross-holding relationships (Osborn and Baughn, 1990). Regardless of the specific organization design, each alliance entails sharing knowledge among partners (Hamel, 1991). The type of knowledge shared among partners is more important in determining the alliance's role in building competitive advantage than the specific alliance design used.

Shared knowledge may be broadly categorized as migratory and embedded; hence, its form fosters alliances classified as product links and knowledge links, respectively (Badaracco, 1991). Product links share knowledge that is easily understood, highly transparent, mobile, and embodied in specific product technologies or designs (thus the term migratory). Partners cooperate to lower product development, production and distribution costs or obstacles. Product links govern a division of labor among partners across value-adding activities. Many alliances involve STRATEGIC OUTSOURCING of different functions.

Knowledge links share highly tacit, organization-embedded skills deeply rooted in the firm's core competencies. Embedded knowledge is tightly interwoven within the organization's distinctive culture, communication paths, and operating practices. Alliances predicated on learning seek to develop new capabilities that are future sources of competitive advantage, spanning multiple products and technologies. Organizational learning and knowledge flows are more complex and difficult to manage in knowledge links than in product links.

Organizational Characteristics
Alliances reduce the boundaries between firms, thereby facilitating speedier product and technology development. Alliances are organization designs between markets and hierarchies; they evolve with firm strategy (Thorelli, 1988; Osborn and Baughn, 1990). Rate of organizational learning determines competitive advantage and bargaining power within the alliance (Hamel, 1991). Firms can structure alliances to create transitional, modular networks of relationships to specialized activities; knowledge transmission becomes highly permeable across boundaries, thus amplifying high levels of external interdependence.

Cooperation, Competition and Future Growth
Alliances compel firms to balance cooperation with competition. Knowledge flows (particularly tacit skills) can unintentionally strengthen future competitors, particularly if underlying technologies are applicable across numerous products (Lei and Slocum, 1992). Carefully managed alliances enable firms to learn new skills from multiple sources, thereby strengthening their core competencies and strategic flexibility. From a corporate strategy perspective, alliances represent strategic options for future expansion; they leverage firm-specific capabilities with managed growth. Excessive dependence on alliances can "hollow out" the firm's core competencies and skills.

Bibliography
Badaracco, J. L. (1991). *The Knowledge Link: How Firms Compete through Strategic Alliances*, Boston: Harvard Business School Press.

Bleeke, J. & Ernst, D. (1993). *Collaborating to Compete*, New York: John Wiley & Sons.

Borys, B. & Jemison, D. (1989). Hybrid arrangements as strategic alliances: theoretical issues in organizational combinations. *Academy of Management Review*, 14, 234–49.

Hamel, G. (1991). Competition for competence and interpartner learning within international alliances. *Strategic Management Journal*, 12, 83–103.

Harrigan, K. R. (1988). Joint ventures and competitive strategy. *Strategic Management Journal*, 9, 141–58.

Kanter, R. M. (1994). Collaborative advantage: the art of alliances. *Harvard Business Review*, 72, 96–108.

Lei, D. & Slocum, J. W. Jr (1992). Global strategy, competence building and strategic alliances. *California Management Review*, 35, 81–97.

Osborn, R. N. & Baughn, C. C. (1990). Forms of interorganizational governance for multinational strategic alliances. *Academy of Management Journal*, 33, 78–86.

Ring, P. S. & Van de Ven, A. (1992). Structuring cooperative relationships between organizations. *Strategic Management Journal*, 12, 483–98.

Slocum, J. W. Jr & Lei, D. (1993). Designing global strategic alliances: integrating cultural and economic factors. *Organizational Change for Improving Performance*, Eds. Huber, G. P. & Glick, W. M. New York: Oxford University Press.

Thorelli, H. (1988). Networks: between markets and hierarchies. *Strategic Management Journal*, 7, 37–51.

DAVID LEI

strategic behavior   Firms behave strategically when they engage in activities intended to change their rivals' expectations. A firm may reduce prices or significantly increase ADVERTISING expenditures when threatened by entry in an attempt to prevent entry. If these are credible strategies, then entry may be deterred. In addition, the firm may establish a reputation for aggressive behavior to send a signal to other potential entrants.

A variety of strategic options are available to firms, such as investing in excess capacity, engaging in research and development, pricing decisions, PRODUCT DIFFERENTIATION, quality choice and product proliferation. When the US Federal Trade Commission charged the ready-to-eat breakfast cereals firms of antitrust violations, one of the allegations made was that the existing firms introduced new brands to prevent entry. By saturating the market with new brands, there was no room left for new entry despite the high profits earned by the existing firms; see Schmalensee (1978).

Bibliography

Carlton, D. W. Perloff, J. M. (1994). *Modern Industrial Organization*. 2nd edn, New York: HarperCollins.

Schmalensee, R. (1978). Entry deterrence in the ready-to-eat breakfast cereal industry. *Bell Journal of Economics*, 9, 305–27.

ROBERT E. MCAULIFFE

strategic core competences "Core speak" has arrived. Hardly a business publication can be read today without finding references to companies focusing on, or retreating to, their core businesses, core activities, core processes – or core competences.

Why should this be so? Is it just a catch phrase? Is it a symptom of the recession? What exactly is meant by "core competences"? What are the ramifications for financial results? Is it easy or difficult? Here, an attempt is made to answer some of these questions.

Over recent years, the pressures of recession have been felt, to varying degrees, by all markets and industries; some companies have triumphed, while others have failed. A large number of those who have succeeded to the greatest extent have done so not by finding market niches but by understanding the roots of their competitive position and exploiting them. Imaginative companies are also seeking ways in which to grow and diversify successfully as they move out of recession without making the mistakes that they, or others, made so spectacularly in the last boom.

It is not an essentially difficult task for senior executives to shrink an organization in response to recessionary pressures, although clearly it can be painful – especially so if the same executives were responsible for the original expansion. What is fundamentally much more difficult is to develop and implement a successful growth strategy; one that will shape the future competitiveness and form of an organization while fighting off the near-term pressures of shrinking markets. It is the understanding of a companies' competitive roots and how these must be strengthened or replaced in the future – the notion of strategic core competences – that will be explored in what follows.

Background

The term "core competences" first became prevalent following award-winning articles published in the *Harvard Business Review* in 1989 and 1990 by C. K. Prahalad (University of Michigan) and Gary Hamel (London Business School) (Hamel et al., 1989; Prahalad & Hamel, 1990). They have since spoken on and published further developments of the concept, as well as producing a video, which has brought the subject to a wider audience.

Our definition of core competence is a distinctive combination of applied technologies, skill-sets, and/or business processes, which have evolved and been learned over a period of time in response to satisfying customer needs. We have also coined the term "strategic core competences" to describe the combination of competences required by an organization in the future to dominate its existing markets or create new ones – this may require some existing core competences to be abandoned, others strengthened, and some created. It is the interaction of these strategic core competences and their interrelation with an organization's strategic intent to deliver a competitive but affordable strategy that differentiates this approach from previous strategy models not based on the competence perspective.

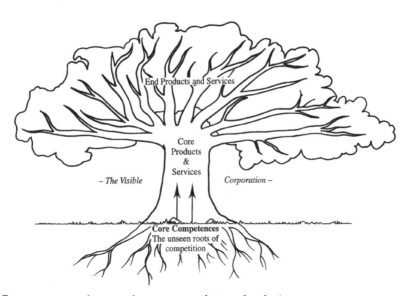

Figure 1 Competences are the roots that support and strengthen business.

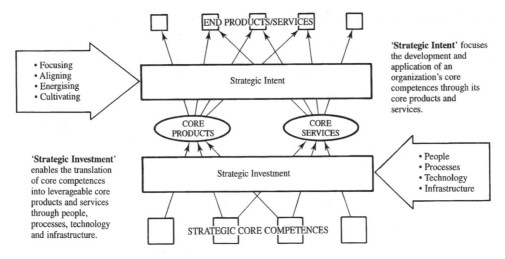

Figure 2 Competence-based strategies are catalysed by strategic investment and strategic intent.

This approach, when exploited to its full potential, enables a company to compete in a highly differentiated way that may then allow it to dominate a wide variety of markets through its competence-based strategy.

As Prahalad and Hamel point out, however, "There are major companies which have had the potential to build core competences but have failed to do so because their top management was unable to conceive of the company as anything other than a collection of discrete businesses."

Applying Competence-based Strategies

It is very unlikely that an organization will possess more than a handful of core competences, although it may well own a considerable list of component capabilities. Competences are the roots which give an organization its competitive strengths and which provide the nutrients for future business development through intermediate core products and/or services (see figure 1).

Unfortunately, organizations often think of competences only as technologies or skills that a firm has developed over time; this misses processes or business practices and totally avoids the link with market wants, and whether these will be needed in future end products or services. These issues and emotional ties to the past mean core competences are buried deep within the organization and may be deceptively difficult to identify (and, therefore, to cultivate and exploit) without a strong methodological approach. Once recognized, however, it is the cultivation and exploitation processes that are critical to the organization's success.

Once the strategic core competences have been found, they must be nurtured at board level by strategic investments in people, technology, processes, and infrastructure (such as alliances and facilities). These investments are needed in order to leverage the long-term benefits of a competence-based strategy through its

CONVENTIONAL MIND-SET	→	CORE COMPETENCE MIND-SET
• Strategic Business Units Framework • Narrow definition of market sectors • Serve specific end-use markets • Compete through head on rivalry	MARKETS	• Strategic Core Competences Framework • Broad understanding of industry factors • Explore new competitive space • Pursue different rules of engagement
• Discrete end product/service portfolios • Aim to dominate brand market share only • Innovation constrained by product applications • Offset development costs through JVs	PRODUCTS	• Flexible core product/service portfolios • Aim to dominate component market share first • Innovation liberated by competence applications • Leverage learning through strategic alliances
• 'Rightsize' by market conditions • Make v Buy decisions on costs • SBU confined resource allocation • Permanent functional organisation structures	RESOURCES	• 'Rightsize' by strategic direction • Make v Buy decisions on competences • Skill-set combination resource allocation • Temporary cross-functional team structures
• Succession of fashionable initiatives • 'Big Bang' change programmes • Take few high risks/executive decisions • Financial target performance measures	CULTURES	• Persistent strategic intent challenges • Build layers of empiric advantage • Take many low risks/encourage experimentation • Strategic intent progress measures

Figure 3 A wholly different strategic mind-set.

"strategic intent," a congruent concept also developed by Prahalad and Hamel (see figure 2).

"Strategic intent" focuses and stretches the organization toward mobilizing the core competences that it owns, or needs to own, to achieve its strategic objectives, and to liberate it into "new competitive spaces." This means adopting a wholly different strategic mind-set (see figure 3).

Bibliography

Hamel, G. & Prahalad, C. K. (1994). *Competing for the future.* Cambridge, MA: Harvard Business School Press.

Hamel, G., Doz, Y. & Prahalad, C. K. (1989). Collaborate with your competitors – and win. *Harvard Business Review*, **67**, 133–9.

Prahalad, C. K. & Hamel, G. (1990). The core competence of the corporation. *Harvard Business Review*, **68**, 79–81.

CHRIS ADAMS and DAVID JOHNSTON

strategic development   Strategic development is one approach to STRATEGIC STAFFING where management development programs are designed and implemented to be aligned with the strategic direction of the organization. Strategic development implies that management development activities should be responsive to strategic business needs, consistent with strategy formulation, and serve a role in strategy implementation (Schuler, 1992).

Strategic development is congruent with a fluid, organic view of organizations where both the manager's value to the organization (in terms of behaviors, skills, knowledge, attitudes, and motives) and strategic demands are viewed as evolving over time. In such situations, management development should influence at least three essential components of the strategic implementation process: (a) flexibility to take advantage of unanticipated events; (b) ongoing communications downward, upward and across the organization to shape and reshape strategy; and (c) cohesiveness among managers to coalesce around an emerging strategic vision. Strategic development is critical when implementation consists of the processes through which the organization comes to understand, accept, and commit to an evolving strategy. It is also critical to organizations that seek growth either by extension of their current businesses or by internally based diversification into very similar product lines or services (steady-state organizations). This is in contrast to organizations that seek growth by acquisition or mergers (evolutionary organizations), in which external selection plays a more important role in managerial alignments (Kerr and Jackofsky, 1989).

Bibliography

Kerr, J. L. & Jackofsky, E. F. (1989). Aligning managers with strategies: management development versus selection. *Strategic Management Journal*, **10**, 157–70.

Schuler, R. S. (1992). Strategic human resource management: linking the people with the strategic needs of the business. *Organizational Dynamics*, **21**, 18–31.

ELLEN F. JACKOFSKY

strategic fit   Strategic fit occurs usually in related diversified concerns (*see* RELATED DIVERSIFIED STRATEGY) as a result of superior competitive position arising from overall lower cost and the successful transfer of core skills, technology, and managerial know-how between businesses. The earlier concepts of SYNERGY and shared experience have similar meanings.

Strategic fit, however, may apply in apparently unrelated businesses where financial synergy may be found. For example, a high cashflow business may financially complement a business that is a high capital user. Examples of this phenomenon include Reo Stakis – a combination of casinos and hotels – the Ladbroke Group, and Donald Trump's empire, all of which are engaged in similar sets of activities.

Diversification into businesses in which shared technology, marketing, and production skills are required can lead to ECONOMIES OF SCOPE when the costs of operating two or more businesses together are less than operating each individually. The key to such cost reductions is therefore diversification into businesses with strategic fit.

Market-related fit occurs when the activity cost chains of different businesses overlap such that they attempt to reach the same consumers via similar distribution channels, or are marketed and promoted in similar ways. In addition to such economies of scope, it may also be possible to transfer selling skills, promotion and advertising skills, and product positioning/differentiation skills across businesses. Care must, however, be taken to insure that market-related fit is possible. Successful examples include Canon's strategic position in cameras and photographic equipment being logically extended into copying and imaging equipment, and Honda's position in motorcycles being extended into other activities using engines, including automobiles and lawnmowers. However, not all such moves are successful. Thus BAT found that selling branded cosmetics was different than selling branded tobacco items.

Operating fit is achieved where the potential for cost sharing or skills transfer can occur in procurement, R&D, production, assembly, and/or administration. Cost sharing amongst these activities can lead to ECONOMIES OF SCALE. Again, successes such as the sale of life insurance policies by retail banking branches can be identified. Similarly, failures are frequently due to inabilities to insure integration between activities from different businesses brought together by acquisition.

Management fit occurs when different business units enjoy comparable types of entrepreneurial, administrative or operating problems. This type of gain is very difficult to achieve due to differences in corporate culture. Classic failures in achieving such fit gains occurred in the attempted diversification moves by the oil industry majors after the first oil-price shock in 1973. Redefinitions of their businesses into "energy" and "raw materials" encouraged moves into minerals, coal, and gas. Most of these moves were serious failures, or the expected strategic fit did not materialize.

Ironically, the only strategic fit which is almost certain to be achieved is the financial one. The operational strategic fits have lower probabilities of success, that for marketing being higher than that for production which, in turn, is higher than that for R&D.

The strategic fit concept has also been criticized as being too static and limiting, focusing as it does on existing resources and the existing environment rather than seeking out the future opportunities and threats which are the focus of firms with strategic intent.

Bibliography

Ansoff, I. (1965). *Corporate strategy.* New York: McGraw-Hill. See chapter 7.

Kitching, J. (1967). Why do mergers miscarry? *Harvard Business Review*, November–December, 84–101.

Ohmae, K. (1983). *The mind of the strategist.* New York: Penguin. See pp. 121–4.

Porter, M.E. (1985). *Competitive advantage: creating and sustaining superior performance.* New York: The Free Press. See pp. 318–19 and 337–53.

DEREK F. CHANNON

strategic groups A strategic group consists of those rival firms with similar competitive approaches and positions in the market. The identification of strategic groups within an industry enables the competitive structure of the industry to be redefined to compare strategies of various competitors for similarities and differences. Thus some firms may have comparable product lines, be similarly vertically integrated, focus on similar customer segments, use the same distribution channels, sell with the same product positioning, and the like. If all competitors within an industry have similar strategic characteristics, then there will be only one strategic group. However, in most industries with a significant number of competitors it is common for more than one cluster of competitors to emerge. This is illustrated in the strategic group map of the US brewing industry, shown in figure 1, which positions the major competitors along the two dimensions of price/perceived quality and image and geographic coverage.

To construct such a strategic group map it is necessary to follow the procedure set out below:

1. Identify the key strategic characteristics which differentiate competitors, such as served market, product range, distribution channels used, price, and quality.
2. Plot firms on a two-dimensional map, using selected pairs of differentiating variables.
3. Cluster firms that fall in a similar strategic space into strategic groups.
4. Map the groups in terms of importance, by indicating the level of group total sales by the area of the circle surrounding clustered competitors.
5. If more than two significant strategic variables can be used for axes, draw a number of maps to identify alternate positions of competitive relationships.

This form of analysis helps to improve understanding of the degree and nature of competitive rivalry. As a generalization, the closer that strategic groups are to one another, the greater is the likelihood of competitive rivalry between the firms within the group. Firms that are strategically distant from the main groups may be subject to much less competitive pressure. As a result, the profit potentials of different competitors may be radically different and not necessarily correlated with size. Thus, a large competitor, despite enjoying the advantage of a high market share, may operate within a group in which competitive rivalry is intense, thus leading to profit erosion. By contrast, a number of competitors operating in a smaller market or strategic space may enjoy superior margins due to the lack of

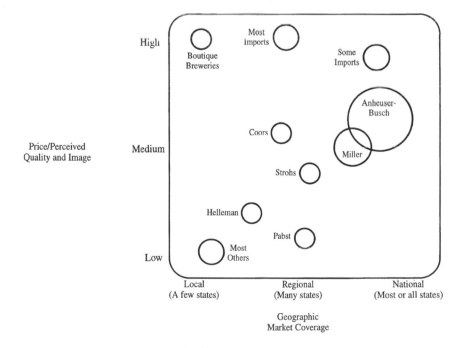

Figure 1 A strategic group map of the US brewing industry.
Source: Thompson & Strickland (1993, p. 77).

other competitors. Thus competitive pressures will tend to significantly favor some groups over others.

Bibliography

McGee, J. & Thomas, H. (1986). Strategic groups: theory, research and taxonomy. *Strategic Management Journal*, 7 (2), 141–60.

Porter, M. J. (1980). *Competitive strategy*. New York: The Free Press. See chapter 7.

Thompson, A. & Strickland A. J. (1993). *Strategic management*, 7th edn, New York: Irwin.

DEREK F. CHANNON

strategic human resource planning processes The term strategic human resource planning processes refers to the efforts of firms to identify the human resource implications of organizational changes and of key business issues, in order to align their human resources with needs resulting from those changes and issues (Schuler and Jackson, 1996). Earlier, in times of environmental stability, strategic human resource planning focused on matching human resource demand with human resource supply (Milkovich et al., 1983). At that time, forecasting human resource needs and planning the steps necessary to meet these needs was largely a numbers game. This process typically consisted of developing and implementing plans and programs to ensure that the right number and type of people were available at the right time and place to serve relatively predictable business needs. For example, if a business were growing at 10 percent per year, top management would continue to add to the workforce by 10 percent; it worked before, it "should" work again.

From Numbers to Issues
Today, because the environment is changing organizations so dramatically, human resources planning has become more of a dynamic, volatile issues game (Schuler and Walker, 1990), and the processes have changed. The question is, "What are the issues of most importance to the business?" Increasingly, the key business issues flow from dynamic organizational changes, but they can also result from situations associated with greater unpredictability. Then the question is, "What are the human resource implications?" Yes, strategic human resource planning still involves numbers, but its processes often involve much more: (a) crafting mission and value statements consistent with the business; (b) ensuring that employees understand and buy into the process of change; (c) systematically aligning the appropriate human resource activities based upon an explicit understanding of the business; and (d) creating a dynamic human resources planning process that mirrors the business planning process and that identifies key changes and implications for managing human resources.

Strategic human resource planning processes must consider both the long-term and short-term human resource implications of organizational changes. In fact, firms might typically go out five years in their planning and then work back to the present. Using strategic human resource planning helps to ensure that the human resource implications of organizational changes and key business issues are dealt with systematically and thoroughly. Regardless of the time horizon or the issues, strategic human resource planning processes involve five phases (Smith et al., 1992).

Phase 1: Identify the Key Business Issues
The first phase of strategic human resource planning involves gathering data to learn about and understand all aspects of the organization's environment. This helps the organization to anticipate and plan for issues arising from both stable and dynamic conditions. For example, planning for increased global competition based on cost could involve assessing current labor productivity and probable future productivity. If a company is going to expand its revenue by 10 percent over each of the next five years, it *may* need more employees. Or perhaps improved technologies will mean a need for fewer employees. Human resource planners and line managers together figure out just what the staffing implications are. To do this, they might use their HUMAN RESOURCE INFORMATION SYSTEMS (HRIS) to measure performance levels in specific divisions, offices, occupational groups, or positions.

Phase 2: Analysis to Determine Human Resource Implications
The objectives of the analysis phase are (a) to develop a clear understanding of how the information generated during phase 1 impacts the future *demands* of the organization, and (b) to develop an accurate picture of the current *supply* available internally.

Forecasting human resource demands. A variety of forecasting methods – some simple, some complex – can be used to determine an organization's demand for human resources. The type of forecast used depends on the time frame and the type of organization, the organization's size and dispersion, and the accuracy and certainty of available information. The time frame used in forecasting the organization's demand for human resources frequently parallels that used in forecasting the potential supply of human resources and the needs of the business. Comparing the demand and supply forecasts then determines the firm's short-, intermediate-, and long-term needs.

Forecasting human resource supplies. Forecasted supply can be derived from both internal and external sources of information. Internal sources of supply are generally the focus at this stage of planning. External sources are considered in later phases, as part of the process of designing the practices needed to prepare for the future.

Phase 3: Establishing Human Resources Objectives
After phase 2 is completed, a great deal of descriptive information about current and future conditions is available. The next phase involves interpreting this information and using it to establish priorities and set objectives and goals.

With a short time horizon, which is often the time frame adopted for downsizing efforts, objectives are often easy to state in quantifiable terms. Examples of short-term human resource objectives include: increasing the number of people who are attracted to the organization and apply for jobs (the applicant pool); attracting a different mix of applicants (with different skills, in different locations, and so forth); improving the qualifications of new hires; increasing the length of time that desirable employees stay with the organization; and helping current and newly hired employees to quickly develop the skills needed by the organization. Such objectives can generally be achieved in a straightforward way by applying state-of-the-art human resource management techniques and working with line managers to ensure agreement with and understanding of the program objectives.

Phase 4: Design and Implement Human Resource Policies, Programs and Practices

Whereas the focus of phase 3 was establishing *what* to accomplish, phase 4 addresses *how* to accomplish it. What specific human resource policies, programs and practices will help the organization achieve its stated objectives? A great variety of programs occur during this phase. These include: diversity programs to make organizations more attractive to a broader array of applicants; programs to improve the socialization efforts so that good employees want to remain with the organization; programs to downsize or rightsize the organization, such as early retirement incentives and generous severance packages to complement the normal attrition process; and programs to empower employees and increase participation in order to ensure success in a change to total quality management.

Phase 5: Evaluate, Revise, and Refocus

In this phase, the objectives set during phase 3 again come into play, for these define the criteria to be used in evaluating whether a program or initiative is successful or is in need of revision. For example, if personal self-development is the only objective one hopes to achieve from holding diversity awareness workshops, then asking employees whether the workshop experience was valuable may collect the only data needed. However, when large investments are made for the purposes of reducing turnover, attracting new or different employees to the firm, improving team functioning, or all three, then data relevant to these objectives should be examined.

Bibliography

Burack, E. H (1988). A strategic planning operational agenda for human resources. *Human Resource Planning*, 11, 63–8.

Caudron, S. (1994). Contingent work force spurs HR planning. *Personnel Journal*, July, 52–5.

Dyer, L. (1984). Studying human resource strategy: an approach and an agenda. *Industrial and Labor Relations Review*, 23, 156–69.

McKinlay, K. S. & McKinlay, A. (1993). *Strategy and the Human Resource*, Oxford: Blackwell Publishers.

Milkovich, G., Dyer, L. & Mahoney, T. (1983). The state of practice and research in human resource planning. *Human Resource Management in the 1980s*, Eds. Carroll, S. J. & Schuler, R. S. Washington, DC: Bureau of National Affairs.

Schuler, R. S. & Jackson, S. E. (1990). Human resource planning: challenges for industrial/organizational psychologists. *American Psychologist*, **February**,

Schuler, R. S. & Jackson, S. E. (1996). *Human Resource Management: Positioning for the 21st Century*, St Paul, MN: West Publishing.

Schuler, R. S. & Walker, J. W. (1990). Human resources strategy: focusing on issues and actions. *Organizational Dynamics*, **Summer**, 4–19.

Smith, B. J., Boroski, J. W. & Davis, G. E. (1992). Human resource planning. *Human Resource Management*, **Spring/Summer**, 81–93.

Walker, J. W. (1995). The ultimate human resource planning: integrating the human resource function with the business. *Handbook of Human Resources Management*, Ferris, G. R. Oxford: Blackwell Publishers.

RANDALL S. SCHULER

strategic issues in diversity   Before one can determine the strategic importance of managing work force diversity (*see* DIVERSITY), one needs to understand (a) what STRATEGY is (i.e. a plan for achieving competitive advantage) and (b) the factors (e.g. environment, mission, vision, culture, and key success variables) that influence effective STRATEGIC MANAGEMENT. In this context, the strategic importance of work force diversity is a function of its relevance to the enterprise's strategy, and the management of diversity becomes strategic itself when it is critical to successful strategy implementation.

Below, we list factors that some organizations consider strategic and then examine their relationship with work force diversity. In doing so we will demonstrate how the management of workforce diversity can be strategic.

Employer of Choice

Many organizations aspire to attract the "cream of the crop" and consider this capability to be a potential source of competitive advantage. When recruiting for the best talent available, managers in some organizations have come to recognize that the pool from which they are drawing is diverse. Further, they believe that effective *management* of this diverse "cream" will give them a competitive edge in becoming the employer of choice (Thomas, 1993).

Empowerment

To gain a competitive advantage, some managers have identified empowerment of employees as strategic. If the workforce is diverse, empowerment cannot be done to an optimal degree without an ability to effectively manage diversity.

Teaming

An increasing number of managers are contending that cross-functional teams and self-directed teams will be sources of competitive advantage. To the extent that team membership reflects diversity in significant aspects, the management of that diversity will be a critical determinant of the manager's ability to tap teaming as a strategic source. The challenge will be to meld team members into an effective unit without unnecessarily compromising the diversity they bring.

Right-sizing

Operating with the optimal number of human resources has been seen for many years as a basic strategic requirement. However, right-sizing places a premium on tapping the full potential of the remaining human resources. If the remaining participants are diverse, diversity management becomes a requirement for realizing the full benefit of right-sizing.

Customer-focused

With a rise in competitive pressures, many managers are stressing being customer-focused as a potential source of competitive advantage. The customer base, however, like workforce participants, is becoming increasingly more diverse. The ability to deal with this external diversity is enhanced by an ability to deal with internal work force diversity (Cox and Blake, 1991).

Enhance Creativity

Influenced by research (Cox and Blake, 1991) and/or anecdotal experiences, more managers are becoming convinced that a diverse workforce is more creative than one comprised of homogeneous participants. These managers see this enhanced creativity and innovation as a potential source of competitive advantage. An international corporation, for example, with a worldwide research operation will need to manage its global diversity as a means of enhancing creativity. Thus, in general, moving beyond simply creating diversity to harnessing it for enhanced innovation requires diversity management.

Total Quality

This approach to management has gained in popularity as a potential source of competitive advantage. One of its basic premises is the engagement of the workforce. If the workforce is diverse, diversity management becomes a prerequisite for engaging organizational participants and realizing the strategic importance of total quality (Thomas, 1991).

The management of workforce diversity is clearly strategic for many organizations. Managers need to determine the strategic significance of diversity management by relating it to the organization's strategic factors. In this context, the management of workforce diversity is no longer solely a legal, moral, or social responsibility issue, but a strategic force as well.

Bibliography

Cox, T. H. Jr & Blake, S. (1991). Managing cultural diversity: Implications for organizational competitiveness. *Academy of Management Executive*, 5, 345–56.
Morrison, A. M. (1992). *The New Leaders: Guidelines on Leadership Diversity in America*, San Francisco: Jossey-Bass.
Ohmae, K. (1982). *The Mind of the Strategist: Business Planning for Competitive Advantage*, New York: McGraw-Hill.
Schein, E. H. (1985). *Organizational Culture and Leadership*, San Francisco: Jossey-Bass.
Thomas, R. R. Jr (1991). *Beyond Race and Gender: Unleashing the Power of Your Total Workforce by Managing Diversity*, New York: AMACOM.
Thomas, R. R. Jr (1993). Managing diversity: utilizing the talents of the new work force. *The Portable MBA in Management*, Cohen, A. R. New York: Wiley.

R. ROOSEVELT THOMAS JR
AND CATHERINE OUELLETTE

strategic management   This concept consists of that set of decisions and actions which result in formulating a strategy, and its implementation to achieve the objectives of the corporation. The process of strategic decision making is illustrated in figure 1 and consists of a number of specific steps:

1. Determination of the MISSION of the corporation, including statements about purpose, philosophy, and objectives.
2. An assessment of the internal environment of the corporation, including an assessment of its culture, history, and informal as well as formal organization.
3. An assessment of its external environment by PEST ANALYSIS.
4. The matching of external opportunities and threats with internal strengths and weaknesses via SWOT ANALYSIS.
5. The identification of desired options from this analysis in the light of the corporate mission.
6. Strategic choice of a relevant set of long-term strategies and policies required to successfully achieve the chosen options.
7. The development of short- and medium-term strategies and action programs that are consistent with the long-term strategies and policies.
8. Implementation programs based on budgets, and action plans based on budgeted resource allocations and monitored via appropriate management information, planning and control systems, and reward and sanction systems.
9. Review and evaluation systems to monitor the strategy process and to provide an input for future decision making.

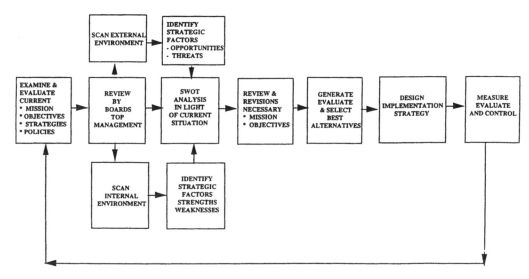

Figure 1   The strategic decision making process.

The process may or may not be articulated formally via a STRATEGIC PLANNING system. In addition, strategic management occurs at a number of hierarchical levels within the firm, dependent upon the complexity of the corporations – this usually involves three levels. At the top is the corporate level, at which decisions are taken by the senior executive officers and, in particular, the CEO in conjunction with the board of directors. This group is responsible for providing the vision of deciding where the company wants to and does go. They are also responsible for financial performance, legal structure, and for establishing overall corporate image and social responsibility, which reflect the views of the various stakeholders of the firm, including employees, shareholders, and society as a whole.

The corporate level also establishes an overall strategic perspective across the business activities of the firm. For multibusiness firms – which includes most large corporations – the corporate level determines: the portfolio balance and the position of each business within it; sets performance objectives; allocates resources; makes key appointments and sets human resources policies; creates the formal organizational structure (and influences the informal structure); sets the management information, planning, and control systems; and creates the reward and sanction systems. The corporate level is also usually responsible for the identification and implementation of any major acquisitions, although some companies delegate "fill in" acquisition strategy to the business unit level. Any new fields of activity, however, are normally determined at the corporate level.

The second main tier of strategic management occurs at the level of the business unit, although an intermediate division level may exist in some organizations, comprising a cluster of business units. At this level managers translate the general direction and thrust of the corporation into specific strategies relevant to their businesses and consistent with the overall portfolio investment strategy determined for them. At this level multifunctional strategies are formulated and implemented for the specific product market area in which the business operates. Such strategies might vary greatly in terms of commitment to growth. While some businesses may be expected to strive for growth, others may be expected to release resources by adopting harvesting or divestment strategies. A number of portfolio models to position businesses, including the ADVANTAGE MATRIX, COMPETITIVE POSITION – MARKET ATTRACTIVENESS MATRIX, directional policy matrix, GROWTH SHARE MATRIX, LIFE CYCLE STRATEGY, and VALUE-BASED PLANNING, are discussed elsewhere. All these models have been designed to aid the corporate center in identifying the appropriate position of each business within the corporate portfolio, and the development of appropriate strategies is discussed throughout many of the other entries in this volume.

The third tier of strategic management applies at the functional level of each business, at which managers from the principal functions of the business, such as marketing, production, operations, R&D, information technology, accounting, and human relations, develop operational strategies and tactics to implement the selected business level strategy. The overall process thus represents a cascade approach.

The characteristics of strategic management decisions vary with the hierarchical level of activity. Corporate level decisions tend to be value oriented, conceptual, and less precise than those at lower levels. In particular, the CEO's vision about how the corporation should develop is exceptionally important. This is especially true in large corporations which attempt to change direction, and in which overcoming the effect of historically established corporate inertia is perhaps the most challenging managerial task – unless the corporation is in crisis and a TURNAROUND STRATEGY is called for. Corporate level decisions are also characterized by greater risk and determine future profitability and the ability of the corporation to survive and prevail. Such decisions also cover all aspects of financial strategy, including capital structure, dividend policy, growth priorities, and selection of the business portfolio.

By contrast, functional decisions are effectively made up of action programs which, hopefully, support the overall corporate position. However, this is not always so, and in conditions of corporate level led radical change, serious dysfunctional behavior may be experienced, especially when shifts in the existing power structure may be experienced during programs such as re-engineering (see VALUE-DRIVEN RE-ENGINEERING). Functional level decisions are, however, normally concerned with relatively short-term, lower-risk, moderate-cost activities. They do not usually cut across businesses within the corporation unless interdependencies exist, and therefore tend to be confined to the individual business.

Decisions at the business level bridge those at corporate and functional levels. They are more risky and costly than those at the functional level and may involve significant changes in existing behavior, including factors such as plant location, segmentation strategy, geographic coverage, and the choice of distribution channel.

Evolution Toward Strategic Management

Relatively few companies can be said to have developed a full strategic management perspective, in which the whole corporation thinks strategically and has a clear vision of where it wants to go – and knows how to get there. Rather, companies evolve toward this position, as shown in figure 2.

McKinsey and Company believe that companies proceed through four stages of development. They start with simple financial planning (stage I); move through forecast-based planning (stage II); then externally oriented or strategic planning (stage III); and finally arrive at stage IV, strategic management.

In stage I, budgets and financial objectives dominate the planning process, and managers and planners are pre occupied with setting an accurate budget and achieving it. In such companies, senior management assumes that the status quo will continue, that industry change will not affect the way things are done, and that industry boundaries are clear and will not be breached by new competitors or technologies. The question of change of corporate direction is seldom raised and the firm's approach is inward-looking and execution-oriented. The process of planning is dominated by financial numbers rather than strategic variables and the development of

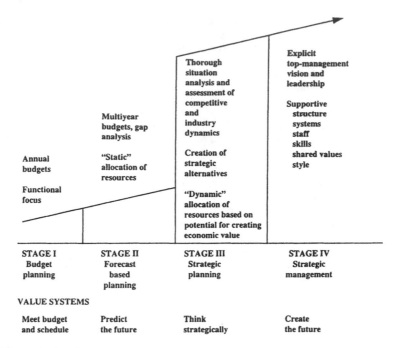

Figure 2 The evolution of strategic management.
Source: Gluck, F. W., Kauffman, S. P. & Wallek, A. S. (1980, p. 4).

budgets is usually undertaken by the finance and accounting function.

Movement of the company from stage I to stage II is an indication that management recognizes the need to extend the time horizon of the corporation beyond the single financial year and to think about the future. Usually, future forecasts extend for three years. In the 1970s and early 1980s such forward extrapolations often extended for longer periods, but the rapid growth of environmental turbulence, coupled with a recognition that future financial forecasts were relatively meaningless projections of the present position, has caused most managements to cut back to three-year projections. Even so, most such plans remain dominated by financial projections rather than strategic considerations. In many companies some managers also believe that senior management is mainly concerned with the first year of such a projection, and therefore tend to consider that extrapolations beyond this point are relatively meaningless. Again, the exercise tends to be dominated by the finance and accounting staff, with line management rarely participating in strategic decisions regarding operations, focusing instead on how to avoid or fill any profit gap.

A quantum leap in the effectiveness of strategic planning and decision making usually occurs with the transition of the corporation from stage II to stage III. At this point the corporation becomes more focused on the external environment in which it operates, and the focus switches from the forecasting of volume and revenues toward obtaining a better understanding of customer needs, competitive position, technological developments, and market characteristics. At this stage, line management become significantly involved in the development of strategy, professional corporate planning staff are introduced, and the system of developing strategy tends to become formalized with the introduction of detailed procedures and timetables.

The stage III company thus adds conceptual and analytic skills which theoretically enable it to develop strategies for sustainable competitive advantage. Many new variables are considered other than financial. Plans are sophisticated and resource allocations may be determined on the rational basis of the strategic positions of individual businesses. Despite these efforts, however, many such strategies fail to achieve necessary strategic changes in the corporation. This is due, in large part, to the fact that many line managers do not regard themselves as the owners of the plans and, as a result, fail to implement them. Moreover, many do not wish to change their perspective and in particular to accept the organizational, cultural, and power relationship changes which may be necessary to transform the corporation when faced with major shifts in the external environment.

In examining the reasons why companies in leadership positions went into decline, McKinsey and Company concluded that such firms fell into one or more of three major traps. First, they used unrealistic or obsolete criteria to assess company strengths and/or weaknesses. Second, they became complacent about their leadership position – and as such became inflexible and assumed that the status quo would go on indefinitely. Third, they failed to recognize industry change and take action to respond to it.

Companies making the transition from stage III to stage IV did recognize these traps. They understood that change was continuous and permanent, and that unwillingness to meet the challenge would ultimately result in failure. Moreover, change within the corporation might be radical. Within corporations such as IBM, Citicorp, and GE, this acceptance has been clearly led from the office of the CEO.

In stage IV companies therefore, strategic management is inculcated throughout the corporation. The corporation is continually adjusting its competitive strategy in response to the market and competition. Such firms are also constantly changing the rules in the markets in which they compete, in order to win. They are also low on bureaucracy, with strategic responsibility passing throughout the corporation. Planning becomes a line rather than staff function and line managers own the plans.

Strategically managed companies are also experts in self-renewal. They do not, however, simply establish systems and procedures and then retreat into them. Rather, they constantly reevaluate and reassess the requirements for success, as in GE's work out method. They use BENCH-MARKING to test themselves against the best, borrowing opportunistically the BEST PRACTICES of competitors and well managed noncompetitors wherever and whenever possible. They carefully blend strategic decision making with operational execution. They are uncompromising in their commitment to competitive success and develop a management style and system to support this commitment. They are also able to both institute continuous incremental change and make that quantum leap when considered necessary. As such, their leaders are prepared to make big and bold decisions, while planners are expected to provide insights for adapting the vision rather than mere descriptions.

Bibliography

Gluck, F. W. (1986). Strategic management: an overview. In J. R. Gardner, R. Rachlin, & H. W. A. Sweeny (eds), *Handbook of strategic planning*. New York: John Wiley.

Gluck, F. W., Kaufman, S. P. & Wallek, A. S. (1980). Strategic management for competitive advantage. *The McKinsey Quarterly*, Autumn, 2–16.

Hofer, C. W. & Schendel, D. (1978). *Strategy formulation: analytical concepts*. St. Paul, MN: West.

Hunsicker, J. Q. (1980). Can top managers be strategists? *Strategic Management Journal*, 1, 77–83.

DEREK F. CHANNON

strategic management (economics) The management of the organization with respect to how it fits into its environment, what its objectives are in that environment, and how the organization expects to achieve its goals and objectives. Strategic management is a process and as such can be broken into steps necessary to complete that process. The steps usually associated with strategic planning are:

1 Mission statement development – A mission statement is an expression of an organization's "reason for being" or a description of why the organization exists in the first place. A mission statement is extremely important because it is upon the mission statement that all corporate goals and objectives are based and evaluated as to their successful attainment. Virtually all actions that take place in an organization should in some way contribute to supporting the basic mission statement of that organization.

2 SWOT analysis – A SWOT analysis develops information on the organizations internal Strengths (core competencies, what the organization does best) and Weaknesses (potential problem areas with supply, management, internal expertise) as well as external Opportunities (new markets, new countries, new products) and Threats (competition, government regulation, trade barriers). The key is to concentrate on an organization's areas of competence to overcome problems and threats.

3 Develop strategic objectives – What exactly do we want to do, when, and how do we measure success. Objectives should be formulated to support the organization's mission statement. The goal is to conduct a concerted effort to plan for successful achievement of objectives which allow the organization to carry out its mission.

4 Develop a strategic plan – In order to achieve objectives a plan has to be developed. The plan includes specific areas that need attention in order to meet the objectives. It is not an operating plan (a detailed plan of how to carry out the everyday activities of the organization), but a plan at a higher level. The strategic plan delineates the overall actions necessary to achieve goals, but not the individual steps to implement the plan.

5 Monitoring phase – Once the strategic plan is placed into action, management must then measure attainment of objectives, monitor the performance of organizational units to determine if control mechanisms must be in place to "guide" certain departments toward organizational objectives, and generally fine tune the plan.

Bibliography

David, F. (1991). *Strategic management*. New York: Macmillan.

Hamel, G. & Prahalad, G. K. (1985). Do you really have a global strategy. *Harvard Business Review*, 63 (4), 139–48.

Herbert, T. T. (1984). Strategy and multinational organization structure: An interorganizational relationships perspective. *Academy of Management Review*, 19 (2), 259–71.

Higgins, J. M. & Vincze, J. W. (1993). *Strategic management and organizational policy*. New York: CBS College Publishing.

Huo, H. P. & McKinley, W. (1992). Nation as a context for strategy: The effects of national characteristics on business-level strategies. *Management International Review*, 32 (2), 103–13.

Huynh, B. S. (1993). Strategy in the open door era. *Columbia Journal of Business* Fall, 6–8.13–9.

Majaro, S. (1977). *Marketing: A strategic approach to world markets*. London: George Allen and Unwin.

Prahalad, C. K. & Hamel, G. (1990). The core competence of the corporation. *Harvard Business Review*, May–June, 79–91.

Roth, K. & Ricks, D. (1990). Objective setting in international business: An empirical analysis. *International Journal of Management*, March.

Rugman, A. M. & Hodgetts, R. M. (1995). *International management: A strategic management approach*. New York: McGraw-Hill Inc.

JOHN O'CONNELL

strategic marketing The essence of strategic marketing is to ensure that the organization's marketing adapts to changes in the external environment (*see* MARKETING ENVIRONMENT) and that it has the marketing resources to do so effectively. This may be achieved by using STRATEGIC PLANNING, although it may also embrace more opportunistic or entrepreneurial organizational behavior.

DALE LITTLER

strategic negotiations The term strategic negotiations joins two concepts, each with ancient roots. Negotiation implies two or more interacting parties with a mixture of common and competing interests; STRATEGY extends that interdependence by introducing a time horizon – where present actions by one party anticipate future actions by other parties. Combined, these concepts define the modern paradigm of bargaining in such varied contexts as international diplomacy, labor relations, and managerial decision-making.

In the modern literature, Schelling (1960) was the first to trace systematically the strategic implications of tactical actions in negotiations, exploring the various uses and limitations of threats, commitments, delegation, mediation, and information. Strategy subsequently became an integral part of the emerging negotiation literature, whether the focus was on the bargaining process (Walton and McKersie, 1965; Lax and Sebenius, 1986), the structure of negotiations (Strauss, 1978; Bacharach and Lawler, 1984), the psychology of negotiations (Pruitt, 1981; Bazerman and Neale, 1991), or general negotiations theory (Walton and McKersie, 1965; Breslin and Rubin, 1991; Walton et al., 1994). The book *Getting to YES* by Roger Fisher and William Ury (1981) is notable in the negotiations literature for elevating a set of integrative tactics into a normative strategy that has achieved broad acceptance.

Among frameworks for analyzing strategic choices, Pruitt (1983) identifies four strategies available to negotiators: problem-solving, contending, yielding, and inaction. He points out that choices among the strategies can be explained both through the use of Blake and Mouton's dual concerns model (1964) and a feasibility analysis. More recently, Walton et al. (1994) identified two concurrent outcomes of negotiations: substantive agreements and social contracts. Changes in social contracts are particularly likely to take on strategic significance. They then identify three strategies for negotiated change: forcing, fostering, and escape from the relationship. These strategies can be pursued separately, sequentially, or in combination. In addition, they interact with structural constraints and the dynamics of the negotiations process. Across all efforts to link the concepts of strategy and negotiations lie two core principles: (a) the identification and utilization of strategy serves both to enable and to constrain bargaining tactics; and (b) the dynamics of negotiation provide similar constraints and opportunities for change strategies. Thus, bringing together the ancient concepts of strategy and negotiations reveals the many ways in which they are intertwined.

Bibliography

Bacharach, S. B. & Lawler, E. (1984). *Bargaining: Power, Tactics, and Outcomes*, San Francisco: Jossey-Bass.
Bazerman, M. & Neale M. (1991). *Negotiating Rationally*, New York: The Free Press.
Blake, R. R. & Mouton, J. A. (1964). *The Managerial Grid*, Houston: Gulf.
Breslin, J. W. & Rubin, J. Z. (Eds) (1991). *Negotiation Theory and Practice*, Cambridge, MA: The Program on Negotiation at Harvard Law School.
Fisher, R. & Ury, W. (1981). *Getting to YES: Negotiating Agreement without Giving in*, Boston: Houghton Mifflin.
Lax, D. A. & Sebenius, J. K. (1986). *The Manager as Negotiator: Bargaining for Cooperation and Competitive Gain*, New York: The Free Press.
Pruitt, D. B. (1981). *Negotiation Behavior*, New York: Academic Press.
Pruitt, D. B. (1983). Strategic choice in negotiation. *American Behavioral Scientist*, 27, 167–83.
Rubin, J, Z,, Pruitt, D. G. & Kim, S. H. (1994). *Social Conflict: Escalation, Stalemate, and Settlement*, 2nd edn, New York: McGraw-Hill.
Schelling, T. C. (1960). *The Strategy of Conflict*, Cambridge, MA: Harvard University Press.
Strauss, A. (1978). *Negotiations: Varieties, Contexts, Processes, and Social Order*, San Francisco: Jossey-Bass.
Walton, R. E., Cutcher-Gershenfeld, J. E. & McKersie, R. B. (1994). *Strategic Negotiations: a Theory of Change in Labor–Management Relations*, Boston, MA: Harvard Business School Press.
Walton, R. E. & McKersie, R. B. (1965). *A Behavioral Theory of Labor Negotiations*, New York: McGraw-Hill.

JOEL E. CUTCHER-GERSHENFELD
and J. WILLIAM BRESLIN

strategic outsourcing Strategic outsourcing is a particular form of subcontracting for services or components. Outsourcing and insourcing can be seen as reflections of the classic make or buy decision. The outsourcing (or contracting) of certain services, such as security, catering, office cleaning, and information technology, has been a traditional, long-standing practice. However, outsourcing is now recognized as far more widespread and part of an ever-increasing trend. The increase is seen both in terms of the number of companies which now practice outsourcing and in terms of the wider span of activities which are now outsourced.

Outsourcing becomes strategic when the decisions do not rest on short-term cost-cutting but are part of a long-term plan which reappraises the core competencies of the organization and perceives enduring and emerging competitive advantage through a partnership alliance with vendors who bring special expertise to the organization.

Rationales and Drivers

One major driver is to reduce headcount and direct labor costs. (This sometimes, though not always, has involved subcontractors using nonunion labor in order to pay lower hourly rates; trade unions have therefore often viewed outsourcing as a union-busting device.)

It has also been facilitated by developments in information technology: companies can, for example, now outsource routine customer billing to remote stations in low labor cost parts of the world. The other main reasons for its growth include the following: (a) flexibility, i.e. the level of service provision can be increased or decreased to meet market circumstances without laying off core staff; (b) scrap levels can, in theory, be eliminated as defective parts can be rejected; and (c) outsourcing is a device to access specialist expertise which would be too expensive or even too difficult to accumulate in-house.

The more strategic reasons relate to the association with re-engineering and root and branch decisions about core functions and sources of competitive advantage. Strategic outsourcing thus ideally results from a rational and far-reaching competitive analysis process, one which seeks world class standards on an activity-by-activity basis. The device may also be used to gain close-up access to the latest technology and expertise.

The Case Against
There are several dangers associated with outsourcing.

(1) One danger is losing control of the service. This may antagonize customers or employees who cannot get timely access to information and who may blame the main company, not the contractor. Legal and tax complications are associated factors, especially in the United States.
(2) Contract workers may have lower commitment.
(3) The costs may in fact turn out to be higher rather than lower. This concern was given credence as a result of a survey of 100 firms by the Boston Consulting Group (*The Economist*, 1991).
(4) Companies may lose expertise in the outsourced functions, which may be impossible to regain.
(5) Hollowing of the organization may result in long-term decline if the choice of core competencies has been unwise.
(6) There are transaction costs in researching, negotiating, administering, and controlling numerous contractors.

Techniques for Successful Outsourcing
Guidelines from consultants emphasize several cautions regarding outsourcing, including: the importance of clarifying very carefully the objectives desired from each outsourcing decision; the need to expect and specify in the service contract high levels of quality, reliability, and other standards; and the need to avoid arbitrary contracting of all support services (the rationale will vary from company to company depending on its own strategy and sustainable competitive advantages) (Jacobs, 1994).

Bibliography
The Economist (1991). The ins and outs of outsourcing. *The Economist*, **August 31**, 65–6.
Jacobs, R. A. (1994). The invisible workforce: how to align contract and temporary workers with core organizational goals. *National Productivity Review*, 169–83.
Kochan, T. A., Wells, J. C. & Smith, M. (1992). Consequences of a failed IR system: contract workers in the petrochemical industry. *Sloan Management Review*, 79–89.
Minoli, D. (1995). *Analysing Outsourcing: Reengineering Information and Communication Systems*, New York: McGraw-Hill.
Quinn, J. B. & Hilmer, F. (1994). Strategic outsourcing. *Sloan Management Review*, **4**, 43–55.
Tully, S. (1993). The modular corporation. *Fortune*, **February 8**, 106.

JOHN STOREY

strategic planning Most corporations today have some form of corporate plan. However, very few are successfully implemented. In theory, strategic planning is the mechanism whereby the corporation organizes its resources and actions to achieve its objectives. It is a formal rather than an informal process, the usual contents of which are illustrated in table 1, while the process of strategic planning is illustrated in figure 1.

Planning will be conducted at hierarchical levels within the corporation, dependent upon its complexity. For the multibusiness firm, plans will be established at the corporate, business unit, and departmental or market segment levels.

Table 1 Strategic plan components.

Mission	Defines the present and desired position of the corporation. Similarly, a mission will apply at the business unit level.
Objectives	Qualitative and quantitative statements of what the corporation wishes to achieve over a measurable future. These should be internally consistent and fit the mission.
Goals	Specific short- and long-term quantitative results which directly support the objectives measured as key performance indicators. They should also reflect the critical successful factors for each business within the corporation.
Strategies	These will apply at both the corporate and business unit levels.

Strategic planning

• Corporate level – establishes strategy for the total corporation

• Business unit – applies in three phases, as follows:

  1. Formulating strategy
  What are the critical factors for success?
  What are the external opportunities and threats?
  What are the relative strengths and weaknesses?
  What strategic alternatives are available?
  What assumptions have been made?
  What sensitivities need to be tested?

  2. Detailed strategic programs
  What specific programs achieve objectives?
  What resources will these require?
  What are the risks/rewards of each program?
  How will these programs be managed?

  3. Strategy implementation
  What organization/human resources will be adopted?
  What milestones will be used to monitor progress?
  Is the MIS system appropriate?
  Is the reward and sanction system appropriate?

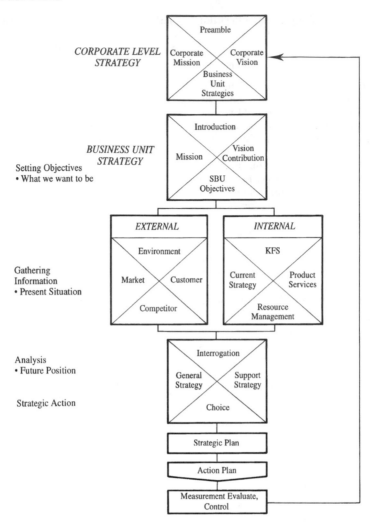

Figure 1 A Strategic plan flowchart.
Source: Channon (1994).

At the corporate level, for example, the overall MISSION is established consistent with internal resources and external opportunities and threats. The direction in which the corporation will go is determined in large part by a corporate vision of where it would like to be. The CEO plays a disproportionate role in the establishment of such a vision.

At the business unit level the concept of mission translates into the markets and activities that the business unit would like to address, subject to corporate level constraints such as resource allocation. At the market segment level, mission is less ambitious and more constrained, being based on the scope of activities assigned to that segment. Similar cascades apply to the other elements of a plan, as shown in table 2. The system is an iterative process, involving a repetitious sequence of strategic developments, strategic planning, plan implementation, and strategic performance measurement. The cycle is normally repeated on an annual basis, with plan horizons presently tending to be around three years in Western

companies. Normally, the procedures are standardized with schedules also phased throughout the planning cycle. A typical cycle is illustrated in figure 2.

The main steps often consist of the following elements, although the precise timing and content vary from company to company:

Executive briefing. The starting point of the plan commences with a senior management review which includes:

- assumptions about the external environment
- changes from previous assumptions
- alternate futures/scenarios – (*see* SCENARIO PLANNING)
- a review of progress against the existing plan and an update of performance against goals
- a possible theme for the forthcoming plan cycle

General management meeting. This establishes the mission, goals, and objectives of the corporation, and decisions reached are then broadly communicated to

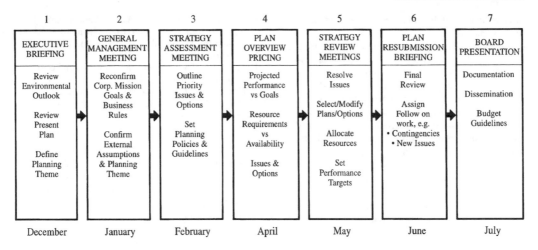

Figure 2 An annual planning cycle.
Source: King (1986).

Table 2 Hierarchical plan requirements.

	Corporate level	Business unit	Market segment level
Mission	Corporate mission	Markets, activities assigned to divisional constraints	Scope of activities assigned to develop market segment
Objectives	Corporate objectives	SBU objectives supporting corporate objective	Segment objective
Assumptions	Specific to corporation capabilities, opportunities, threats	Specific to scope of divisional activities	Specific to market: demand, competition, service
Competitive strength	Corporate strength, weakness	SBU strength, weakness	Specific share, strength, weakness
Assessment of market opportunity		As evaluated and reviewed at all levels	
Market portfolio strategy	Overall corporate mix and priority, including new areas of interest	Mix for markets assigned to SBU	Specific investment priority for this segment
Changes desired in controllable variables	Attack plans for change in corporate capabilities	Attack plan for change in SBU capabilities	Attack plans to change factors
Programs to implement change, specific to corporation	Specific to corporation	Specific to SBU capabilities	Specific to segment
Expected financial results	Corporate financial measures	SBU financial measures	Segment financial measures

operating managers at business unit level and to other operating managers.

Strategy assessment meeting. Follow-up meetings are held between corporate and SBU executives to discuss issues and options, and policies and guidelines.

Plan overview. Plan submissions from SBUs are consolidated and reviewed with corporate management.

Strategy review meetings. The corporate center and SBU management negotiate to develop shared views on SBU plans by selecting strategic options, plan modifications, resource allocations, and performance targets.

Plan resubmission. Resubmitted plans by SBUs are then consolidated with any corporate level adjustments and given a final review by corporate incentive management.

Board presentation. The final plan is then summarized in strategic terms, formally submitted to the board of directors for discussion, and usually approved.

The plan and planning cycle are never fully finalized in the sense that both internal and external events may cause them to change. Nevertheless, the plan should provide a blueprint for the development of the corporation over the next period of time.

One major consideration is the relationship between the plan and the budget. Theoretically, the two systems should coincide. However, many line executives tend to focus their attention more on the budget than the longer-term plan, and as a consequence there is often some cynicism about the plan unless it is clearly taken seriously by top management.

Interestingly, perhaps, the literature on strategic management in the 1990s pays little attention to the practicalities of the mechanics of strategic planning; unlike in the 1970s, when formal systems were emphasized. Moreover, while during the 1980s many corporations built up substantial central planning units, these have lost considerable credibility, since line management believes that they are the operational component of the corporation needed to implement plans. In addition, many line managers believe that top management in the West has become relatively obsessed with short-term rather than long-term performance.

Interestingly, Japanese corporations have built significant planning departments. Employees in these departments, however, have rarely been trained as specialist planners; rather, they are assigned to planning departments as a regular element in their development, based on job rotation, and many come to such departments from anywhere in the company. While plans themselves tend to have a three-year time horizon, they are not seriously changed each year. Furthermore, such plans, all of which have a formal name, usually form elements in much longer-term "visions" established by the president of the corporation. These visions may have time horizons spanning 20 years or more, and rather than being driven by financial objectives, have broader technical and social goals.

Bibliography

Channon, D. F. (1986). *Bank strategic planning and marketing.* Chichester: John Wiley.

Channon, D. F. (1994). Strategic management workbook. Working paper, Imperial College.

Chinn, W. D., Yoshihisa, M. & Vanderbrink, J. D. (1986). Strategic planning: a view from Japan. In J. R. Gardner, R. Rachlin & H. W. A. Sweeny (eds), *Handbook of strategic planning.* New York: John Wiley.

King, W. C. (1986). Formulating strategies and contingency plans. In J. R. Gardner, R. Rachlin & H. W. A. Sweeny (eds), *Handbook of strategic planning.* New York: John Wiley.

Toyohiro, K. (1992). *Long range planning in Japanese corporations.* Berlin: De Gruyter.

DEREK F. CHANNON

strategic recruiting   Strategic recruiting is the process of identifying, and attempting to attract, applicants in the external labor market who possess the characteristics or aptitudes that will enable the organization to achieve its strategic objectives. RECRUITING typically results from needs identified in the employment planning process, and is presumed to be driven by the need to fulfill immediate operational objectives. Strategic recruiting, on the other hand, derives from systematic assessment of the organization's mission and strategic objectives, and is undertaken to facilitate long-term organizational success.

Rynes and Barber (1990) have suggested that organizations facing a current or anticipated labor shortage could employ strategic recruiting as a means of attracting applicants, or could address the shortage through other strategies that do not involve applicant attraction. Olian and Rynes (1984) have indicated how organizational strategy might affect recruitment practices. More recently, Bretz and Judge (1994) have suggested that an organization's strategic objectives drive the choice of human resource systems that are implemented, and in doing so reveal to job applicants important contextual information that would otherwise be unknown. The use of REALISTIC JOB PREVIEWS to deliver accurate contextual information is critical if an organization wishes to use recruiting strategically, because the applicants' perceptions of good organizational fit affect their JOB SEARCH behaviors and their willingness to join the organization.

Bibliography

Bretz, R. D. & Judge, T. A. (1994). The role of human resource systems in job applicant decision processes. *Journal of Management*, **20**, 531–51.

Olian, J. D. & Rynes, S. L. (1984). Organizational staffing: Integrating practice with strategy. *Industrial Relations*, **23**, 170–83.

Rynes, S. L. & Barber, A. E. (1990). Applicant attraction strategies: an organizational perspective. *Academy of Management Review*, **15**, 286–310.

ROBERT D. BRUNER

strategic staffing   Strategic staffing is a process for identifying and filling future staffing needs to meet long-term business requirements. It has its roots in strategic human resource management and is viewed as a part of HUMAN RESOURCE STRATEGY implementation. Staffing is a crucial tool because it affects an organization's ability to successfully execute a particular competitive strategy (Miller, 1984). Strategic staffing begins with identifying the staffing implications of proposed business strategies. By developing and implementing strategic staffing plans, organizations can ensure the right mix of talent to meet changing business objectives and strategies.

Strategic staffing process involves the design of strategies for four broad clusters of activities: (a) the identification of talent through JOB ANALYSIS, skills inventories, and RECRUITING needed to enhance strategy; (b) the acquisition of the talent through recruitment and selection; (c) the orientation and socialization of employees; and (d) the movement of employees to appropriate positions within the organization through promotion, transfer, and demotion (Butler et al., 1991, p. 83). Much of the emphasis in strategic staffing focuses on managerial staffing (*see* SUCCESSION PLANNING). Researchers have developed models for aligning managerial staffing with business strategy (Kerr and Jackofsky, 1989; Bechet and Walker, 1993). Alignment involves matching managers with the appropriate skill mix and characteristics to an organization's strategic direction.

Bibliography

Bechet, T. P. & Walker, J. (1993). Aligning staffing with business strategy. *Human Resource Planning*, 16, 1–16.

Butler, J. E., Ferris, G. R. & Napier, N. K. (1991). *Strategy and Human Resource Management*, Cincinnati, OH: South-Western.

Kerr, J. & Jackofsky, E. (1989). Aligning managers with strategic management development versus selection. *Strategic Management Journal*, 10, 157–70.

Miller, E. L. (1984). Strategic staffing. *Strategic Human Resource Management*, Eds. Fombrun, C. J., Tichy, N. M. & Devanna, M. A. New York: John Wiley & Sons.

STELLA M. NKOMO

strategic use of information technology The first commercial uses of information technology (IT) often involved automating existing manual systems. Early "era 1" systems were often justified by anticipated reductions in clerical labor previously required to process business transactions. Starting in the early 1970s, firms began to make major investments in systems designed to improve both the efficiency and effectiveness of managers and other professionals. These "era 2" systems employed DECISION SUPPORT SYSTEMS, DATABASE MANAGEMENT SYSTEMS and EXECUTIVE INFORMATION SYSTEMS to improve decision-making. Simultaneous investments in office automation, including local area networks, wide area networks, and voice and electronic mail, were the hoped-for means to quickly implement decisions and to track decision effectiveness.

Organizations continued to pursue automation and decision support, but in the mid-1980s began to invest in a third era of IT. This third era represented the strategic use of IT, in which applications were intended to provide their owners with a distinct competitive advantage over competitors. Often the justification for such systems was a hoped-for increase in sales or market share. In other cases, a competitor's strategic application of technology might motivate investment in similar systems to help recover from a strategic disadvantage.

Today, we are entering a fourth era in which a new type of strategic system is emerging. Era 3 strategic systems were typically designed to align information technology investments with the strategic objectives of the firm and they were often based on proprietary communications networks. Era 4 systems, by contrast, are often at the very heart of completely new business opportunities in which the technology impacts strategy rather than being aligned

to it. Such systems will provide new marketing or distribution channels. They will largely rely on nonproprietary communications networks to reach directly to the final consumer. These new applications and businesses seem likely, over the next several years, to dramatically reshape commerce and industry as well as many other economic and social institutions.

Types of Strategic Use

In era 3, firms sometimes gained a competitive advantage by the development of a new *IT-based product or service*. For instance, Merrill Lynch, a large brokerage house, developed their Cash Management Account which allowed investors to earn a higher rate of return on cash than was possible in a bank's savings account. An era 4 strategic application, by contrast, is the attempt by Intuit to develop and sell a personal finance system, Quicken, that empowers consumers to manage their investments, bill paying, and day-to-day expenses. Quicken also provides links for home banking. A proposed merger between Intuit and Microsoft was recently denied by the US government, partly because of concerns that the combined company would be a major threat to the banking industry.

The denied merger of Intuit and Microsoft illustrates a second major opportunity to use information for strategic advantage: *control of a distribution channel*. Era 3 examples include the computer reservation systems developed by United and American Airlines, among others. Until forced to stop by legal action, the owners of the reservation systems were able to bias travel agents and passengers toward their own flights rather than those of competitors who did not have their own reservation systems. We are now witnessing the emergence of new marketing and distribution systems targeted directly at the consumer. For instance, NetScape Communications has in a very short period of time captured much of the market for the easy-to-use browser software people use to access the Internet's World Wide Web (WWW). As this browser is the first thing a user sees each time they use the WWW, it provides an excellent showcase for Netscape to highlight new products of their own or to favor those of their various business partners.

Interorganizational systems are another way to use IT strategically. Federal Express, for instance, provides corporate customers with software for preparing mailing labels for packages and summoning delivery vehicles. Such desktop applications are also being used for ordering office supplies, air travel, and so on. In the case of office supplies, such systems can provide the corporate customer with both convenience and a powerful tool for control. For instance, the prices displayed on an employee's screen can reflect discounts the firm has negotiated with the office supply distribution, constrain the amount purchased in any given month by a particular employee, or automatically inform internal auditors or management when unusual purchase behavior is detected.

Firms have also gained strategic advantage through systems linking them with suppliers, dealers, or government agencies. Large retailers, for instance, are using their influence to require suppliers to interface with them using electronic data interchange. In some cases they are even providing those suppliers with a direct look into information from point-of-sale terminals and then requiring the supplier to manage store inventories based on actual sales. Strategically advantageous interorganizational linkages often represent extensions of systems developed initially for the firm's own internal use. For instance, Federal Express has now made their package tracking systems accessible to customers via the World Wide Web.

Strategic advantage can also be achieved by *personalizing the service or product* to meet the unique needs of a specific customer. An illustration of a typical era 3 application is a paint manufacturer which provided its customers, the managers of large fleets of ocean-going vessels, with information on the painting requirements for each ship within the customer's fleet. The information was captured by the firm's worldwide network of dealers as ships tied up at port and was then made available for use by sales, marketing, and product development personnel. Era 4 systems will carry this personalization much further. They will permit online newspaper publishers to personalize your daily "paper", retailers to provide an electronic catalog reflecting your sizes and personal requirements, or perhaps even allow you to participate in the design of your own car, clothes, and so on.

Often, significant cost advantages can be achieved by *leveraging scarce expertise*. High-technology manufacturers, such as Apple Computer, are beginning to make databases previously used by their support personnel directly accessible by customers. Consulting firms are developing worldwide skills databases that permit them to quickly identify individuals meeting the requirements of a particular job. Firms are also reducing costs by electronically *moving* KNOWLEDGE WORK to sources of low-cost labor. The Internet, an early version of a global data highway, provides a relatively low-cost means to partition knowledge work across country boundaries. Software developers, for instance, can significantly reduce their labor costs by using programmers in India rather than California.

Sustaining Competitive Advantage

Era 1 and 2 applications tended to be justified on the basis of hard cost savings or soft expectations of increased professional productivity or higher-quality decisions. Strategic uses often draw their justifications instead from anticipated increases in revenues and market share. Assessing these benefits requires management to carefully consider the likely sustainability of the proposed application; that is, for how long can the firm expect to achieve unusually high returns before one or more competitors effectively responds? Sustainability depends on the three questions discussed below.

How long to copy?

Some strategic applications can be quickly copied by competitors. The technology may be available for purchase, customers or others may have a good understanding of how the system operates, or the firm's own personnel may be hired away by a competitor to produce a similar system. On the other hand, some systems may be protected by patents, copyright protection, secrecy, the inherent complexity of the application, or the unwillingness of a competitor to quickly respond.

Who can copy?

Firms competing in the same industry often may use quite different strategies and technologies. If a strategic applica-

tion of information technology builds on such a competitive asymmetry it may prove impossible for a competitor to duplicate. For instance, Wingtip Courier, a Dallas-based local package delivery service, installed radio communicating computer terminals in all its delivery vehicles. The despatch system they developed for the terminals permitted Wingtip to provide higher-quality service to the professional firms they served. It was an advantage that Wingtip's competitors found difficult to match. Wingtip owned its own vehicles and paid its drivers a wage, but most competitors contracted with independent drivers who worked for commission. Placing expensive computer systems in these vehicles and training the drivers was a nearly insurmountable barrier to competitive response.

Will it help to copy?

Once a competitor has duplicated a strategic system, they may discover that the "first-mover" has somehow pre-empted the challenger's response. For instance, airline frequent-flyer programs keep customers coming back because of the bank of miles they have accumulated in the past.

The answers to these three questions provide the basis for evaluating candidate strategic uses of information technology. They also can be useful starting points in seeking to identify uses of information technology that can provide competitive advantage.

BLAKE IVES

---

strategy (human resource management)   A strategy is a *pattern* of decisions and actions evident in an organization over time. An effective strategy may be deliberately planned by its managers, or it may emerge as a *post hoc* observation of a related group of decisions and actions. A distinctive characteristic of an organizational strategy is its comprehensiveness. That is, it includes and affects most parts of an organization. Mintzberg (1987) has noted that the word strategy is actually used in several different senses: a formal plan, a competitive ploy, a position in the mind of customers, a perspective in the mind of employees, and several others. In all cases, however, a pattern of organizational decisions and actions is observable.

There are three levels of strategy (*see* STRATEGIC MANAGEMENT). Corporate level strategy concerns the identification of the businesses in which the corporation will compete and the allocation of resources to those businesses. Business level strategy involves how businesses compete in their industries. Functional level strategy focuses on the integration of disparate parts of a business so that they are consistent with and supportive of the business strategy.

Generic Strategies

Much research has gone into discerning a limited number of generic strategies that are used across many different industries. Porter (1980, 1985) defined three generic business level strategies of differentiation (unique market-wide customer value), cost leadership (lowest costs among all competitors in a market), and focus (marketing to a limited, well defined group of buyers, sometimes divided into cost focus and differentiation focus). His concepts have been empirically explored by several scholars in various industry contexts.

Miles and Snow (1978) inductively developed four generic strategies of: defender (narrow product line, concentrates on efficient operations), prospector (innovator always looking for new opportunities), analyzer (operating in both stable and turbulent domains with corresponding foci on efficiency and innovation), and reactor (no consistent strategy, changes when forced to by the environment). These strategies cover both the corporate and the business level.

Miller and Friesen (1984) inductively developed several configurations or archetypes of organizational characteristics by studying a collection of business cases. These may also be seen as generic strategies. Six successful and four unsuccessful organizational configurations were found. In addition, they found nine configurations associated with organizational change. The configurations cover both corporate and business level strategy.

These are probably the best known, but other typologies and taxonomies of generic strategy exist. Unfortunately, the cumulative empirical evidence indicates that none of them holds across all or even most industries. Thus, the development of effective organizational strategies still requires a large dose of situational art. Of course, it cannot be otherwise in competitive economies because successful strategies are often imitated, thereby eliminating the competitive advantage.

Bibliography

Miles, R. E. & Snow, C. C. (1978). *Organizational Strategy, Structure, and Process*, New York: McGraw-Hill.

Miller, D. & Friesen, P. H. (1984). *Organizations: a Quantum View*, Englewood Cliffs, NJ: Prentice-Hall.

Mintzberg, H. (1987). Five Ps for strategy. *California Management Review*, 30, 11–24.

Porter, M. E. (1980). *Competitive Strategy: Techniques for Analyzing Industries and Competitors*, New York: Free Press.

Porter, M. E. (1985). *Competitive Advantage: Creating and Sustaining Superior Performance*, New York: Free Press.

BENJAMIN M. OVIATT

strategy (marketing) Strategy is derived from the Greek "strategia" meaning generalship. Von Clausewitz (1976) wrote the classic military strategy. The widespread use of the term in business occurred after the Second World War although businesses, in particular the Pennsylvania railroad, employed strategy in the 19th century. Zinkham & Pereira (1994) suggest that the notion of strategy was first introduced to the management literature in 1944 by Von Neumann & Morgenstern in their classic work on the theory of games which essentially focused on situations of conflict. Following on from this, there was a series of major contributions on strategy such as those of Selznick (1957), and Chandler (1962). Ansoff's comprehensive text *Corporate Strategy*, published in 1965, firmly established strategy in the management lexicon. The military connotations of strategy undoubtedly appeared apt given the traditional perspectives of competition in which firms were seen as "fighting for market share," engaging in "price wars" and embarking on advertising "campaigns." The military analogy was extended to MARKETING (James, 1985; Kotler & Singh, 1980). However, Liddell-Hart (1967) was critical of the view, put forward by Von Clausewitz, that: "The destruction of the enemy's main forces on the battlefield constitutes the only true aim in war." He suggested that:

"The 'object' in war is a better state of peace, even if only from your own point of view." Contemporary management theory is much more likely to identify a spectrum of strategies, ranging from the extreme competitive (*see* COMPETITIVE STRATEGY) through to various forms of cooperation. Indeed, many companies now regard strategic alliances, which may be formed for some markets with firms that are competitors in others, as strengthening their competitive position.

There are many definitions of strategy, but in general it is regarded as embodying the joint selection of the product market arenas in which the firm is or will compete and the key policies defining how it will compete (Rumelt et al., 1991). The Walker et al. definition (1992) suggested that an effective strategy would embrace: what is to be attained; which product markets should be the focus; and how resources and activities will be allocated to each product market to meet environmental opportunities and threats. Johnson & Scholes (1993) define strategy as: "the direction and scope of an organisation over the long term: ideally, which matches its resources to its changing environment, and in particular its markets, customers or clients so as to meet stakeholder expectations" (p. 10).

In general, a strategy encompasses the goals, regarded as a general statement of aim or purpose, and objectives, and the means by which these are to be achieved. It can apply at several levels: the organizational or corporate; the business and the product. Strategy may also be associated with certain activities. Thus, for example, there is reference to PRICING strategies and NEW PRODUCT DEVELOPMENT strategies. There is much debate about whether or not strategy can be clearly formulated in advance of being applied. However, as Mintzberg (1990) argues, managers may often define strategy in terms of past actions, rather than in terms of intentions. Moreover, a consciously conceived strategy may not be easily realized because of the intervention of, inter alia, UNCERTAINTY.

see also **Strategic planning**

Bibliography

Ansoff, H. I. (1965). *Corporate strategy: An analytical approach to business policy for growth and expansion*. New York: McGraw-Hill.

Chandler, A. D. Jr (1962). *Strategy and structure*. Cambridge, MA: The MIT Press.

James, B. G. (1985). *Business wargames*. Harmondsworth: Penguin.

Johnson, G. & Scholes, K. (1993). *Exploring corporate strategy*, 3rd edn, Prentice-Hall.

Kotler, P. & Singh, R. (1980). Marketing warfare in the 1980s. *Journal of Business Strategy*, 1, (3), 30–41.

Liddell-Hart, B. H. (1967). *Strategy*. New York: Praeger.

Mintzberg, H. (1990). The design school: Reconsidering the basic premises of strategic management. *Strategic Management Journal*, 11, (3), 171–195.

Rumelt, R., Schendel, D. & Tece, D. (1991). Strategic management and economics. *Strategic Management Journal*, (12), 5–29.

Selznick, P. (1957). *Leadership in administration*. New York: Harper & Row.

Von Clausewitz, C. (1976). *On war* (translated by M. Howard & P. Paret). Princeton University Press.

Von Neumann, J. & Morgenstern, O. (1994). *Theory of games and economic behavior*. Princeton University Press.

Walker, O. C., Boyd, H. & Larreche, J. (1992). *Marketing strategy: Planning and implementation*. Homewood, IL: Irwin.

Zinkham, G. M. & Pereira, A. (1994). An overview of marketing strategy and planning. *International Journal of Research in Marketing*, (11), 185–218.

DALE LITTLER

stress There are at least three uses of the word "stress" in OB. It is used as a *cause* (my job is inherently stressful); as a *consequence* (I feel stressed when I'm at work); as a *process* (this is happening when I am under stress). In its broadest sense "stress" has come to refer to a field of study which encompasses all the above meanings, and in OB to be concerned with organizational or occupational stress, though this has also come to include stress arising from UNEMPLOYMENT.

In keeping with this broad usage, the word is probably most usefully applied to stress as a process because the major organizational and personal consequences of stress occur over time. The process approach fits most closely with the definition of stress provided by Selye (1951). Selye was one of the founders of stress research and his medical training led him to an interest in the physiological, and disease consequences of exposure to physical and emotional stresses. Selye concluded that when faced with demands our psycho-physiological systems respond with a non-specific, uniform response which he labeled the General Adaptation Syndrome (GAS). The main components of this response are that digestion slows to release blood for muscles, breathing increases for extra oxygen supply to muscles, heart rate accelerates, blood pressure rises, perspiration increases to cool the body, muscles tense for action. All of these effects are under the influence of the hormonal system with cortisol, adrenaline, and nonadrenaline being the main biochemical agents.

According to Selye these nonspecific responses vary in intensity over time but if stress continues they produce the following pattern:

Alarm (in preparation for flight or fight); *Resistance* (sustained psycho-physiological mobilization at a lower level of intensity); *Exhaustion* (resulting from depletion of the body's stores of vitamins, sugars, proteins, and immune defenses). It is clear that this process can encompass all three uses of the word stress.

Cox and Ferguson (1991) claim that different approaches to stress have focused on different parts of the process corresponding to the main uses identified above. The causal approach is described by them as the "engineering" approach. Stress here defines the cause which produces the reaction strain. Many writers use the word strain to describe the psycho-physiological response to stress and it can include two of the uses described above (the current state of feeling strain and the more enduring state which occurs in Selye's Resistance phase). Following the medical literature these two states of strain can be acute or chronic. This is also true of the exposure to stress and the terms acute stress and chronic stress make the same distinction.

The engineering or stimulus oriented approach has led to a search for the causes of occupational stress and a well-known classification is:

- Factors intrinsic to the job (tasks, working conditions, shift work, dangers, etc.).
- ROLE factors (ROLE OVER/UNDERLOAD, ROLE AMBIGUITY, CONFLICT, etc.).
- Relationships at work (support from boss, colleagues, subordinates, etc.).
- CAREER (success, failure, JOB SECURITY, REWARDS, etc.).
- ORGANIZATIONAL DESIGN and climate (control versus discretion, openness, hierarchy, etc.).
- Home-work interface (effects of travel, work-family conflicts, women's roles) (*see* NON-WORK/WORK).

Recent studies of many of these variables and their relationship to measures of psychological and physiological strain can be found in Quick, Murphy, and Hurrell (1992). Any one of these variables has relatively small correlations (0.1–0.3) with measures of strain, though in combination they may account for 25 percent of the variance.

Cox and Ferguson describe a second theoretical stress focus as the medico-physiological or response approach. This approach has led to techniques for measuring both physiological and psychological reactions to stressful stimuli/situations. Many of these are self-report questionnaires and include symptoms from categories such as the following:

- Affect (anxiety, worry, panic, depressed mood).
- Cognition (failures, errors, inability to think logically, forgetting).
- Behavior (ABSENTEEISM; aggression; sabotage; alcohol and substance abuse).
- Symptoms (sleep loss, headaches, vomiting, sweating, impotence).

It is perhaps worth noting about the above four categories of strain that only the person themselves has privileged access to information/experience about them all. The outsider (manager or supervisor) only has access to observable behavior (unless the person confides in them). Since the mere presence of many of these symptoms does not necessarily indicate the presence of stress and strain (e.g., heavy smoking and drinking are ways of life for many people), the manager needs to be sensitive to *changes* in behavior as much as anything else. Not surprisingly, there are moderate correlations amongst the different symptom groups (e.g., psychological strain correlates about 0.45 with measures of physical ill health).

These studies have their difficulties and the association between self-report measures of strain and physiological evidence of strain is by no means compelling. The difficulties of conclusive research in organizations are described in Fried (1988).

Although the use of physiological markers of strain provide more objectives indices, a more fundamental question is how chronic stress might link to disease. Stress is hypothesized to be linked to hypertension, coronary heart disease (CHD), skin and other disorders though causal proof is surprisingly difficult to demonstrate. The link to CHD in particular has been associated with Type A Behaviour Pattern (TABP).

The third approach to modeling stress, and the most effective according to Cox and Ferguson, is the transactional approach. It is a processual approach as it assumes that a person is strained only if he/she appraises a situation to be a threat (Primary Appraisal), and resources, capacities, knowledge, etc., are unable to cope with the threat successfully (Secondary Appraisal). This model has been much influenced by the work of Folkman and Lazarus (1986). This model brings the person much more into the process so individual differences become important determinants of whether situations are stressful or not, though the outcome is always a function of the interaction of the person and the environment. Person-Environment fit models of stress have many similarities to the Folkman and Lazarus approach.

Individual differences are important here because they can influence all stages of the process. At the primary appraisal stage the neurotic PERSONALITY is more likely to see threat than the person high in hardiness. At the secondary appraisal stage, more intelligent, problem-solving, self-confident people are less likely to see their resources as unable to cope, even if there is threat. This concern with coping capacities has led to another active area of stress research: the measurement of coping or coping styles. Lazarus and his coworkers have been at the center of this development. Several authors have produced measures of coping, with similar dimensions. The three major ones are: Problem Focused coping (getting information, looking for solutions, trying out solutions, etc.); Emotion Focused coping (denial, wishful thinking, pretending it will go away); Appraisal Focused coping (redefining the situation, comparing self with others). Problem-focused styles seem more effective in work settings.

Programmes to help people improve their coping have grown in the last 30 years. Many of them are outside the work context, but organizations have also developed stress management programmes for their employees. As well as providing information and advice about coping strategies, programmes also include advice about diet, physical fitness, alcohol and substance abuse, health practices, counseling techniques including self-help groups, and techniques such as relaxation and meditation. Charlesworth and Nathan (1988) provide an excellent guide to stress management and Theorell (1993) has provided an evaluative review of stress management programmes in the workplace.

The literature also contains research on improving/changing the workplace to reduce stress through job redesign, organizational restructuring, and culture management. Karasek's (1979) highly influential paper on the causes of work stress demonstrated that the most stressful jobs were those combining high demands (workload, difficult tasks) with low discretion or autonomy. Low discretion is often associated with low levels of participation in decision making and this condition has been shown to be associated with higher levels of strain. An associated literature has grown up around the concept of social support and its role in helping to protect people from the effects of stress (Payne & Jones, 1987). Leaders and managers are, therefore, potential sources of stress, as well as sources of support, and responsibility for people has itself been shown to be a principal managerial stressor.

Although the popular literature emphasizes the stress of the modern executive, Karasek's model implies that their level of strain is buffered by their high levels of discretion. The epidemiological literature on work stress supports this analysis. Fletcher (1988) has shown that elevated levels of strain and poor health are more prevalent in lower level jobs. He also shows that at any one time about 15 percent of the workforce report levels of strain high enough to affect their attendance at work and their performance at work if they do attend. Whilst it is difficult to calculate the costs of stress at work, it has been estimated that stress may account for half of absenteeism, and that the total stress bill might be as much as 6 percent of sales in a company with an average absenteeism rate of 4 percent. Practically, theoretically, and methodologically stress continues to present a major challenge.

see also **Job design; Emotions in organizations**

Bibliography

Charlesworth, E. A. & Nathan (1988). Stress management: A comprehensive guide to your well-being. Guernsey, Channel Islands: Guernsey Press.

Cox, T. & Ferguson, E. (1991). Individual differences, stress and coping. In C. L. Cooper & R. Payne (Eds), Personality and stress: Individual differences in the stress process. Chichester, UK: Wiley.

Fletcher, B. C. (1988). The epidemiology of occupational stress. In C. L. Cooper & R. Payne (Eds), Causes, coping and consequences of stress at work. Chichester, UK: Wiley.

Folkman, S. & Lazarus, R. (1986). Stress process and depressive symptomology. Journal of Abnormal Psychology, 95, 107–13.

Fried, Y. (1988). The future of physiological assessments in work situations. In C. L. Cooper & R. Payne (Eds), Causes, coping and consequences of stress at work. Chichester, UK: Wiley.

Karasek, R. A. (1979). Job demands, job decision latitude, and mental strain: implications for job redesign. Administrative Science Quarterly, 24, 285–308.

Payne, R. L. & Jones, J. G. (1987). Measurement and methodological issues in social support. In S. Kasl & C. L. Cooper (Eds), Stress and health. Chichester, UK: Wiley.

Quick, J., Murphy, L. & Hurrell, J. (Eds), (1992). Work and well-being: Assessments and interventions for occupational mental health. Washington, DC: American Psychological Association.

Selye, H. (1951). The general adaptation syndrome and the gastrointestinal diseases of adaptation. American Journal of Proctology, 2, 167.

Theorell, T. (1993). Medical and physiological aspects of job interventions. In C. L. Cooper & I. T. Robertson (Eds), International review of industrial and organisational psychology, (Vol. 8, pp. 173–192). Chichester, UK: Wiley.

ROY L. PAYNE

strike Broadly defined, the strike is a collective abstention from work for the purposes of self-protection (Liso and Pisani, 1992). In American labor law, a strike is defined as a concerted stoppage of work, slowdown or interruption of operations (Section 501(2), Labor–Management Relations Act of 1947). In order to be protected under American law, it must be part of a controversy over terms and conditions of employment or about who represents the employees.

The strike comes in many types and varieties. In the USA there is the important distinction between the unfair labor practice strike (prompted by an employer's violation of labor laws), where the employer may only temporarily replace strikers, and the economic strike (any other lawful strike), where strikers can be permanently replaced. There are also: (a) the wildcat strike, which is not authorized by a union; (b) the National Emergency Strike, which affects an entire industry or a substantial part of it; (c) the recognition strike, where a union is seeking recognition as the representative of a group of employees; and (d) the jurisdictional strike, where a union is striking to claim work as against another union. There are also political strikes in which workers withdraw their labor as an act of political or social protest.

The possibility of a strike is what moves management to agree to union COLLECTIVE BARGAINING demands, so "the strike, however its shapes and forms change, is . . . integral to collective bargaining" (Barbash, 1984, p. 65). Nevertheless, its use has declined to historic lows in the United States in the past decade, leading to doubts of its continued viability.

Bibliography

Barbash, J. (1984). *The Elements of Industrial Relations*, Madison, WI: University of Wisconsin Press.

Bureau of National Affairs (1988). Strikes, picketing, and boycotts. *Labor Relations Expediter*, Washington, DC: Bureau of National Affairs.

Liso, F. & Pisani, E. (1992). Italy. *Workplace Justice: Employment Obligations in International Perspective*, Eds. Wheeler, H. N. & Rojot, J. Columbia, SC: University of South Carolina Press.

Wheeler, H. N. (1985). *Industrial Conflict: an Integrative Theory*, Columbia, SC: University of South Carolina Press.

HOYT N. WHEELER

structuring organizations Mintzberg has suggested n consists of five basic components that differ in size and importance. These components are illustrated in figure 1.

The first component, the *operating core*, consists of those personnel who undertake the basic work of the organization which is related directly to operations or the production of products/services. This component conducts four key functions:

- securing inputs
- transforming inputs into outputs
- distributing outputs
- providing direct support to the production process

The second main component is the *strategic apex*. This consists of managers responsible for the overall direction of the corporation. They manage the organization to achieve the objectives of those who own or control it. Their primary functions are as follows:

- direct supervision, resource allocation, structure planning and control system design, conflict resolution, and strategic decision making
- managing and monitoring relations with the external environment
- formulating organizational strategy

The third component is the *middle line*. This comprises the chain of managers with formal authority and connects the apex with the operating core. Historically it was seen as essential, because the apex could not directly supervise all the line operators. In addition, the middle line:

- provides feedback to the hierarchy about performance in the operating core
- makes some, basically operational, decisions and allocates some resources
- manages the relations of business units or functions with the external environment

As a result of re-engineering (*see* VALUE-DRIVEN RE-ENGINEERING) and the adoption of the HORIZONTAL STRUCTURE, the role of the middle line has come under

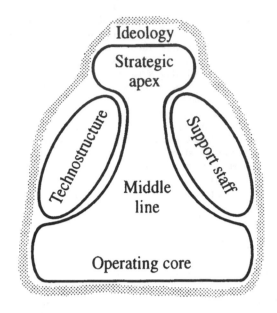

Figure 1   Five basic parts of the organization
Source: Mintzberg (1989)

serious threat, as the span of control of the apex has been considerably enlarged as a result of improved information technology systems. Moreover, there is some feeling amongst senior management in firms with operating horizontal structures that middle line managers act as an often undesirable block on the information flow between the apex and operations.

The fourth organizational component, *support staff*, provide support for line operations and include functions such as property, social affairs, legal industrial relations, payroll management, accounting, and the like. Historically, support staff were added to enable the firm to gain greater control over boundary activities in order to reduce perceived risk and uncertainty. These activities were usually loosely coupled to core processes and could be located at various levels in the hierarchy.

In recent years the size and scope of support staff numbers and duties have come under serious scrutiny in many corporations as part of re-engineering projects and cost reduction drives. As a result many concerns are turning to OUTSOURCING as an alternative to operating their own support functions. While this poses no serious threat in nontechnical areas, a number of strategic and/or specialized functions have been outsourced, including computer systems.

The final component is the *technostructure*. This consists of analysts who evaluate and influence the work of others. Many technostructure personnel are control specialists who attempt to increase the level of operational standardization, so reducing the level of skill required in the operating core. Three types of analysts are identified:

- work study analysts, whose task is to standardize work processes
- planning and control analysts, who attempt to standardize outputs such as planning, budgeting, quality systems, and the like

- personnel analysts, who seek to standardize organizational skills via training and recruitment

In order to accomplish the total task of the organization, it is also necessary to integrate the activities of the key components. Mintzberg identifies five specific coordinating mechanisms which help to achieve this:

- mutual adjustment – whereby work is coordinated through direct informal communication between related personnel
- direct supervision – a formal mechanism whereby an individual or manager is given authority over and takes responsibility for the work of others and for monitoring their activities
- standardization of work processes – whereby the content of work is specified or programmed
- standardization of outputs – which insures that the results of work conforms to predetermined standards and specifications
- standardization of skills – which is accomplished via appropriate training and recruitment

Bibliography

Galbraith, J. K. & Nathanson, D. A. (1980). *Strategy implementation*. St Paul, MN: West.

Mintzberg, H. (1979). *The structuring of organisations* Englewood Cliffs, NJ: Prentice-Hall.

Mintzberg, H. (1989). *Mintzberg on management*. New York: The Free Press.

DEREK F. CHANNON

succession planning Succession planning refers to the process and actions that aim at identifying and developing a pool of potential successors for senior or key jobs in the future. Unlike replacement planning, succession planning is more strategic, proactive, long-term oriented, and development-focused. It ensures the continual supply of qualified executive talent to lead and support business growth.

Such planning is of strategic importance to many corporations like GE (Friedman and LeVino, 1984). By adopting a fair and systematic succession planning process, companies are able to reap the following benefits: early identification of management talent, retention of high-potential employees, enhancement of managers' readiness for future roles and challenges, and, as a result, the building up of human capital for business continuity and stability. However, where companies require major shifts in strategic direction that call for external recruitment, succession planning through internal resourcing becomes less important.

Succession planning is vulnerable to corporate politics and personal bias that may be counterproductive to business success and realization of individuals' potential. For instance, businesses may be reluctant to release good people to other businesses and different businesses or functional units may wish to advance their candidates for senior management positions. Hence, to maximize the usefulness of succession planning, corporations need to pay attention to the following processes (Nowack, 1994).

Identify Leadership Competencies

Leadership competencies should be based on business strategies, customer requirements, and business cultures. These required competencies should reflect and profile the successful leaders of the corporation in the coming decade. To facilitate assessment, development, and evaluation, the competencies need to be defined and operationalized in observable behaviors and outcomes.

Develop a Comprehensive Database

A comprehensive and current database should be developed for the target population. Once the leadership competencies are identified, appropriate assessment methods can be used to measure the candidates along those competencies. To ensure objectivity, multiple sources of information need to be collected on a periodical basis, including in-depth interviews with high potential candidates, 360 DEGREE APPRAISALS, PERFORMANCE APPRAISALS, and ASSESSMENT CENTERS ratings. Ideally, the assessments should be conducted by special human resource staff members who have high personal integrity and are able to assess people accurately through multiple methods. To facilitate the organization and retrieval of information, many companies are using computer databases to store candidate information.

Conduct Executive Management Review Sessions

The purposes of executive management review sessions are to review the strengths and weaknesses of the candidates, to determine their promotability, and to recommend developmental plans for the candidates. The sessions are usually attended by incumbent executives and related human resource staff. Evaluation of candidates by potential, not by personal relationship, is the key success factor of these sessions. Therefore, it is important to create an open atmosphere to address the concerns of the candidates and to resolve conflicting interests among business units. Built-in check and balance mechanisms are also required to ensure the integrity and fairness of the process. For instance, a consensus among attending executives, rather than the recommendation of incumbent executives, may be required to determine the promotability and possible career plans of the candidates. Based on the information collected, human resource staff can also contribute to the fairness of the process by advocating or questioning the view of incumbent executives regarding specific candidates.

Provide Feedback and Implement Plans

While succession planning used to be secretive in order to minimize inflated expectations of the candidates and the effects of the self-fulfilling prophecy of the candidates' superiors (Schein, 1987), companies are realizing the importance of providing feedback to the potential candidates because it is important to match the company's succession plans with the candidates' career aspirations. Once the candidates are committed to the plans, development plans with both systematic on-the-job assignments and external training opportunities should be prepared and implemented.

Measure Developmental Progress

The candidates should be carefully reviewed by senior management regarding their career progress and accomplishment. Data should be periodically updated and the promotability and developmental plans of the candidates should be revised as time evolves.

In a nutshell, succession planning has to be managed carefully and systematically. It should be conceived as a strategic planning process from which companies cultivate their most critical resources: high quality executive talent.

Bibliography

Friedman, S. D. & LeVino, T. P. (1984). Strategic appraisal and development at General Electric Company. *Strategic Human Resource Management*, Eds. Fombrun, C., Tichy, N. M. &. Devanna, M. A. New York: John Wiley & Sons.

Nowack, K. M. (1994). The secrets of succession. *Training and Development*, **November**, 49–54.

Schein, E. H. (1987). Individuals and careers. *Handbook of Organizational Behavior*, Lorsch, J. Englewood Cliffs, NJ: Prentice-Hall.

ARTHUR K. YEUNG

sunk costs   Sunk costs are those costs which cannot be recovered by the firm. As with fixed costs, these costs do not vary with output produced and, as Tirole (1988) suggests, the differences between the two are matters of degree. Consider a firm which rents a machine for $100,000 per month which has an economic life of two years and costs $2 million to purchase. The $100,000 monthly rental fee is a fixed cost each month to the firm. Suppose instead that the firm decided to purchase the machine and, once purchased, the resale value of the machine was zero. Now the $2 million purchase price is a sunk cost to the firm because the asset has no alternative uses – its opportunity cost is zero (*see* OPPORTUNITY COSTS). If the firm could sell the machine for $1 million, then the sunk cost would be only $1 million, that portion of the original price which is not recoverable. The portion of any asset's purchase cost which is sunk will depend upon the resale market for that asset. Assets which are very specialized and unique to an industry or for which resale markets do not exist or are "thin" will have a greater percentage of their purchase cost "sunk".

Sunk costs play an important role in determining MARKET STRUCTURE because they represent a barrier to entry to new firms. Once incurred, sunk costs should have no effect on the pricing and output decisions of established firms and, if necessary, established firms would produce output as long as average variable costs were covered. This is not the case for a potential entrant who must pay these costs to enter the industry and must expect to cover them if entry is to succeed. An asymmetry is thus created between the established firms, for whom these costs are irrelevant, and potential entrants who must include them in the entry decision. Sunk costs act as a barrier to EXIT once firms are in an industry and may affect the intensity of competition between established firms, particularly if the industry is declining (*see* DECLINING INDUSTRY).

Baumol, Panzar and Willig (1982) argued that when entry and exit were absolutely free and costless the market was perfectly contestable (*see* CONTESTABLE MARKETS). Free, costless entry and exit require that entrants have no sunk costs (even if there are fixed costs), enabling them to quickly enter the industry, undercut the established firms, and exit before the incumbents could retaliate. In these markets, the threat of entry would discipline established firms (even a natural monopolist) to the point where they earned no ECONOMIC PROFIT. But Weitzman (1983) argued that there are no purely fixed costs and theoretically, economies of scale cannot exist without sunk costs. Both fixed costs and sunk costs imply some commitment by the firm for some period of time. For fixed costs, the commitment lasts for the duration of the short run, while sunk costs commit the firm for a longer period of time; see Tirole (1988). In replying to their critics, Baumol, Panzar and Willig usefully distinguished economic sunk costs from technological sunk costs. Although a firm might need a period of time to physically produce the goods or services for the market, an entrant could enter into conditional contracts with buyers and sell its output before actually producing the product. In such a case, the entrant would not incur the sunk costs of production unless enough contracts were sold and, once sold, the existing firm(s) would be subject to hit-and-run entry.

Sutton (1991) extended the notion of sunk costs by suggesting that there may be endogenous sunk costs in an industry in addition to exogenous sunk costs. He developed a two-stage model where in the first stage, if a firm chose to enter the industry, it would incur fixed setup costs to produce output, such as acquiring a MINIMUM EFFICIENT SCALE (MES) (MES) plant and incurring advertising and research and development expenses to establish the product(s). In the second stage, those firms in the industry would compete for profits through price or quantity competition. Sutton considered the fixed costs of acquiring an MES plant as exogenous sunk costs while the advertising and research and development expenditures were endogenous sunk costs because firms could adjust these costs in stage 1 to improve their competitive position in stage 2. In industries where exogenous sunk costs were most significant, the industry structure would become less concentrated as the market grew, but in those industries where endogenous sunk costs were more important, a concentrated industry structure arose even as market size increased. He found that industries with high concentration and high advertising and research and development expenditures in one country were also highly concentrated in other countries. He attributed this result to a competitive escalation of these endogenous sunk expenditures which kept industry concentration levels high and prevented entry from having a significant effect on industry structure.

Bibliography

Baumol, W. J., Panzar, J. C. & Willig, R. D. (1982). *Contestable Markets and the Theory of Industry Structure*. San Diego: Harcourt Brace Jovanovich.

Baumol, W. J., Panzar, J. C. & Willig, R. D. (1983). Contestable markets: an uprising in the theory of industry structure: reply. *American Economic Review*, 73, 491–6.

Schwartz, M. & Reynolds, R. J. (1983). Contestable markets: an uprising in the theory of industry structure: comment. *American Economic Review*, 73, 488–90.

Shepherd, W. G. (1984). 'Contestability' vs. competition. *American Economic Review*, 74, 572–87.

Sutton, J. (1991). *Sunk Costs and Market Structure*. Cambridge, MA: MIT.

Tirole, J. (1988). *The Theory of Industrial Organization*. Cambridge, MA: MIT.

Weitzman, M. L. (1983). Contestable markets: an uprising in the theory of industry structure: comment. *American Economic Review*, 73, 486–7.

ROBERT E. McAULIFFE

supervisory ratings   Supervisors are often asked to evaluate the performance of their subordinates. This is done either for administrative purposes, such as to aid in making pay or promotion decisions, or for research purposes, to help, for example, to validate new personnel selection procedures. The main advantage of supervisor ratings (as compared to PEER RATINGS or subordinate ratings) is that supervisors will typically have worked with many different subordinates and are, thus, well calibrated to make reasonably accurate ratings.

Recent research on supervisor ratings focuses on the cognitive processes associated with how supervisors arrive at judgments about their subordinates' performance (e.g. Borman, 1991; Murphy and Cleveland, 1991) (*see also* PERFORMANCE APPRAISAL, PEER RATINGS, SELF-RAT-INGS, and RATING ACCURACY).

Bibliography

Borman, W. C. (1991). Job behavior, performance, and effectiveness. *The Handbook of Industrial and Organizational Psychology*, 2, Eds. Dunnette, M. D. & Hough, L. M. Palo Alto, CA: Consulting Psychologists Press.

Murphy, K. R. & Cleveland, J. (1991). *Performance Appraisal: an Organizational Perspective*, Boston: Allyn & Bacon.

WALTER C. BORMAN

survey research

Introduction

Survey research is one of the four main sources of PRIMARY DATA, the others being OBSERVATION, QUALI-TATIVE RESEARCH, and experimental research. Surveys can provide information on past and intended behavior, attitudes, beliefs, opinions, and personal characteristics. While the data provided by surveys are basically descrip-tive, appropriate analysis of the survey data can provide evidence of association between variables.

Surveys involve asking people (respondents) questions, either verbal or written. The term sample survey indicates that survey data have been collected from a sample of a population. Data are collected with the aid of questionnaires through the mail or by means of computers or administered to individuals or groups in face-to-face interviews in the home or in the street or using the telephone.

In cross-sectional studies, data are collected at a single point in time from a cross-section of the population. Typical analysis of cross-sectional surveys involves attempting to measure characteristics of the population as a whole and/or breaking down the sample into subgroups and seeing if behavior, opinions, etc. vary between the groups.

In longitudinal studies, respondents are studied at different moments in time in order to examine trends and changes, if any, over time.

Types of Surveys

Surveys usually involve the use of structured interviews with the interviewer or respondent following the wording and order provided on a questionnaire. Survey methods are usually classified by mode of administration, the three main modes being personal, telephone, and postal interviewing.

Personal interviews. Personal interviews usually take place either in the home of the respondent or in a public place such as the street or a shopping mall.

In face-to-face interviews in the home, it is the interviewer's job to contact the respondent, often selected by the research director using some form of probability sampling, pose the questions, and record the answers. Lengthy interviews are possible and the interviewer can use physical stimuli as part of the interviewing process. The respondent is able to seek clarification of confusing questions or terms and the interviewer is able to observe the respondent, for instance, to see if the questions have been understood. In-home, or door-to-door, interviewing is expensive and its use is declining.

Street or shopping mall intercept interviews are the commonest type of personal interview. Interviewers inter-cept passers-by and either question them on the spot or take them to a nearby facility to conduct the interview. It is possible to get a random sample of passers-by by selecting every nth passer-by. However, it is unlikely that the population of interest will pass by the places where interviewers are located. For this reason mall intercept surveys are rarely statistically representative of the required populations and rely on quota sampling procedures to ensure some amount of representativeness. They are cheaper than door-to-door interviews and it takes less time to complete an intercept survey.

In direct computer interviewing, the computer presents the questions to a respondent on a screen and the respondent uses a keyboard or a mouse to answer. These are often used in shopping malls or at conferences and trade shows. For some surveys, respondents are selected by interviewers as in other types of personal interviewing research; in other surveys the computer is placed in a prominent place and interested passers-by select them-selves as respondents. As well as freeing the interviewer from posing the questions and recording the answers and reducing data inputting time and expenses, this method has an extra advantage in that interviewer bias is low.

Telephone interviews. Telephone interviewers, stationed at a central location, present their questions using the telephone to interviewees over a wide area. Computer-assisted telephone interviewing (CATI) is growing quickly. As in other computer assisted interviewing methods the questionnaire is programed into the computer. The interviewer reads the questions from the screen and records the answers directly into the computer. The computer can be programed to make the calls, for instance using random digit dialing, and subsequent recalls can be made when initial calls are unanswered.

Flexibility is the main advantage of computer-presented questionnaires. The questions can be varied according to earlier answers, e.g., buyers of a brand may be asked one set of questions and non-buyers a different set. Also, order problems caused in some closed questions where possible answers are presented to respondents can be averted by the computer varying the answers from respondent to respondent.

Low cost and the speed with which a survey can be carried out are two other advantages of telephone inter-views. Interim results and updates are easy to obtain as the data are recorded immediately. Interviewer bias is low, respondents can feel that their anonymity has been maintained, and sensitive questions can be posed with less embarrassment than in face-to-face interviews. On the other hand, it is difficult to use physical stimuli as part of the interview although the use of fax machines can ease this problem. The fact that not every household has a telephone, that some numbers are ex-directory, and that an individual member of a large household has a smaller chance of being chosen than a member of a small household, means that a sample may not be truly representative of a specified population.

Postal surveys. Questionnaires are delivered to the respondents who return completed questionnaires by post to the researcher. Postal interviews are widely used. They allow a large sample to be contacted very cheaply and the absence of an interviewer cuts out interviewer bias. On the other hand, complex questionnaires are unsuitable and the questionnaire has to be carefully constructed. The major disadvantages of postal surveys are the high level of non-response and the length of time allowed for respondents to reply.

Non-response is a problem for all types of surveys but especially so for postal surveys. Non-response can be reduced in the first place through pre-notification, by offering monetary inducements including a free entry to a prize draw, by use of reply-paid envelopes, by making the questionnaire interesting, etc. Follow-up contacts can be used to increase the overall response rate.

The critical issue concerning non-response is the extent to which the respondents and non-respondents are alike on the important variables. Among the ways of assessing this is to make comparisons of successive waves of respondents and to subsample intensively non-respondents for comparison with the original respondents. Unless care is taken to assess the effects of non-response on representativeness of the sample obtained, results from postal surveys should be treated cautiously.

Conclusion

Two problems of interviewing include the responses to sensitive questions and biases caused by interviewer effects. Since face-to-face interviews and, to a lesser extent, telephone interviews involve social interaction between interviewer and respondent, it is possible that respondents will answer sensitive questions with socially acceptable, rather than truthful, answers. Postal and computer surveys, which do not suffer from this social interaction, may yield more accurate answers to sensitive questions.

Interviewers may vary the way that they pose the questions, by changing the wording or simply altering their tone of voice or body language, from interview to interview, with the result that each respondent has a slightly different interview, a disadvantage in survey research. The interviewer's age, sex, appearance, social class, etc. may affect the answers as respondents seek to give answers that they believe will be acceptable to the interviewer. The recording of answers to open-ended questions may be biased by the interviewer's opinions. These interviewer effects will be most pronounced in personal interviews, least pronounced in computer and postal interviews, with telephone interviews somewhere in between.

Bibliography

Malhotra, N. K. (1993). *Marketing research: An applied orientation.* Englewood Cliffs, NJ: Prentice-Hall. Chapter 7.
Tull, D. S. & Hawkins, D. I. (1987). *Marketing research: Measurement and methods,* 4th edn, New York: Macmillan. Chapter 4.

MICHAEL GREATOREX

sustainable growth rate A company's sustainable rate of growth depends in part on, and is limited by, the rate at which it can generate funds that can be invested to achieve growth targets while at the same time paying interest and dividends, accounting for depreciated assets and inflation. The sources of these funds are generally retained earnings, debt, and new equity capital. Improved efficiency, which reduces capital intensity by superior asset turnover and greater productivity, can also enable a higher sustainable growth rate.

Debt, risk, dividend, and return policies and intentions should therefore be determined before overall corporate goals are established. These factors will essentially determine the limits to growth. The sustainable growth rate of the firm can then be calculated as follows.

The rate of growth is equal to the firm's return on equity if no dividends are paid. This is the rate of return (profit) less interest on debt, as follows:

$$\text{profit} = r(TA) - iD$$

where r is the rate of return, TA is the total assets, i is the interest rate, and D is debt. Since total assets are equal to the sum of debt and equity (E), their expression may be rewritten as:

$$\text{profit} = r(D + E) - iD$$

or

$$\text{profit} = rD + rE - iD$$

Dividing through by E, this becomes:

$$\text{profit/equity} = \left(\tfrac{D}{E}\right)(r - i) + r$$

or

$$\text{growth rate } (g) = \left(\tfrac{D}{E}\right)(r - i) + r.$$

However, the payment of dividends reduces this rate of growth due to the disbursement of funds. The effect of dividend payout can be accounted for by multiplying the expression by the percentage of earnings retained by p, the dividend payout ratio. The growth formula thus becomes:

$$g = \left(\tfrac{D}{E}\right)(r - i)p + rp.$$

Each of the financial variables in the growth formula can be used strategically to influence the growth rate of the firm. The sensitivity of the growth rate to the key variables of rate of return, interest rate paid, the debt : equity ratio, and the dividend payout ratio is demonstrated in table 1. In the table each of these variables has been changed in turn by 10 per cent with other variables remaining constant.

As expected, the most sensitive variable is return on assets. Most surprising for most observers is that the dividend payout ratio is the second most powerful variable, and not the debt : equity ratio. Interest rates tend to be relatively inconsequential. As a result, a significant increase in the debt : equity ratio may be a viable strategic alternative, even if higher interest rates are incurred as lenders perceive the firm as becoming more risky. Interestingly, perhaps, high leverage has been a significant reason behind the success of Japanese corporations, where the strength of the yen has also provided low rates of interest. Similarly, reduced dividend payment ratios help to accelerate corporate growth – again a characteristic of Japanese concerns. Indeed, by operating with a high debt : equity, a low dividend payout ratio, and constant attention to improved asset turnover – the inverse of lower capital intensity.

Table 1   Sensitivity analysis of four variables influencing corporate growth rate.

Variable	Growth rate	Growth rate in response to 10% change in variable
Earning power		
6.3%	4.8%	
7.0%	5.5%	12.7%
7.7%	6.2%	
Interest rate		
3.3%	5.35%	
3.0%	5.50%	2.7%
2.7%	5.65%	
Debt : Equity ratio		
0.9 : 1	5.30%	
1.0 : 1	5.50%	3.6%
1.1 : 1	5.70%	
Dividend payout		
45%	4.95%	
50%	5.50%	10.0%
55%	6.05%	

Source: Boston Consulting Group (1971)

As expected, the most sensitive variable is return on assets. Most surprising for most observers is that the dividend payout ratio is the second most powerful variable, and not the debt : equity ratio. Interest rates tend to be relatively inconsequential. As a result, a significant increase in the debt : equity ratio may be a viable strategic alternative, even if higher interest rates are incurred as lenders perceive the firm as becoming more risky. Interestingly, perhaps, high leverage has been a significant reason behind the success of Japanese corporations, where the strength of the yen has also provided low rates of interest. Similarly, reduced dividend payment ratios help to accelerate corporate growth – again a characteristic of Japanese concerns. Indeed, by operating with a high debt : equity, a low dividend payout ratio, and constant attention to improved asset turnover – the inverse of lower capital intensity – Japanese companies have been able to achieve superior investment performance compared to their nearest US counterparts during the past two decades.

The relationship between financial strategy and market share growth suggests several important conclusions: high margins do not necessarily indicate an attractive business, while reported earnings are not always meaningful. However, since most managers perceive margins as an indication of market attractiveness, the aggressive growth firm might seek to keep margins down in order to discourage competitive market entry.

Firms using debt aggressively and reducing dividend payouts can both cut price relative to competitors and finance an increase in market share. Provided that such growth achieves a satisfactory return, greater than the cost of equity, such a policy also builds shareholder value.

Bibliography

Boston Consulting Group (1971). *Growth and financial strategies.* Boston, MA: Boston Consulting Group.

Rowe, A. J., Mason, R. O., Dickel, K. E., Mann, R. B. & Mockler, R. J. (1994). *Strategic management*, 4th edn. Reading, MA: Addison-Wesley. See pp. 375–6.

DEREK F. CHANNON

SWOT analysis   An acronym of Strengths, Weaknesses, Opportunities, and Threats, SWOT analysis provides a simple but powerful tool for evaluating the strategic position of the firm. It is especially useful for senior executives undertaking a fundamental reappraisal of a business, in that it permits a free-thinking environment, unencumbered by

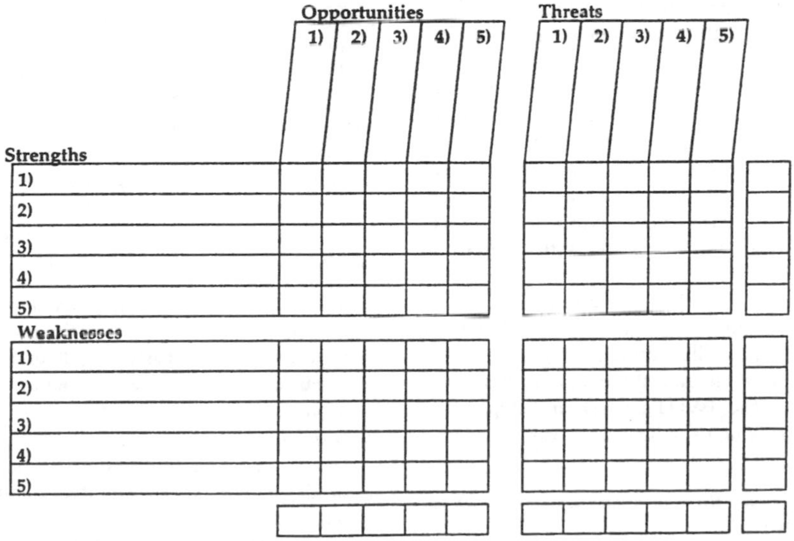

Figure 1 SWOT analysis.

SWOT analysis – potential key factors.

Potential strengths	Potential weaknesses
Core skills	Lack of strategic direction
Adequate finances	Obsolete plant
Good customer perception	Weak IT systems
High market share	Weak control systems
High productivity	Lack of finance
High product/service quality	Lack of management skills
Low production costs	Internal power struggle
Superior R&D	Weak marketing skills
High innovation record	Lack of raw material access
Good top management	Poor access to distribution
Proprietary technology	High cost structure
Access to distribution	Poor product quality
Political protection	Poor record on innovation
Well established strategy	Others?
Others?	
Potential opportunities	Potential threats
Entry to new markets/segments	New low cost competitors
Diversification to related activities	Technological substitutes
Vertical integration (forward or backward)	Slow growth
High growth prospects	New regulatory requirements
Export markets	Foreign exchange rates
Weak competitors	Bargaining power of customers/suppliers
Government contracts	Adverse demographic shift
Deregulation	Vulnerability to recession
Others?	Changing consumer needs
	Others?

the constraints often imposed by a finance-driven budgetary planning system. It also allows a test of perceived common purpose within an organization when carried out at various levels within the firm. The requirements for undertaking such an analysis are relatively simple and, at the end of the exercise, key information needs can usually be identified which might prove to be the subject of further research.

A list of common strengths, weaknesses, opportunities, and threats is shown in table 1. This list is not comprehensive and other critical factors may be identified. In terms of usage, executives may be divided into groups to initially identify – first as individuals and second as groups – their views as to the firm's SWOT. It may well be useful to focus on only a prioritized list of these and also to assess the cross-impacts of strengths and weaknesses on threats and opportunities, utilizing a form such as that shown in figure 1.

For strategy formulation, the firm attempts to build upon its strengths and eliminate its weaknesses. When the firm does not possess the skills required to take advantage of opportunities or avoid threats, the necessary resources may be identified from the SWOT analysis and steps taken to procure the strengths or to reduce any weaknesses.

Bibliography

Channon, D. F. (1986). *Bank strategic management and marketing.* Chichester: John Wiley.

Channon, D. F. (1994). *Strategic management workbook.* Imperial College, London. See pp. 87–9.

Thompson, A. & Strickland A. J. (1993). *Strategic management,* 7th edn, New York: Irwin.

DEREK F. CHANNON

synergy As originally conceived by Ansoff, synergy was seen as one of the major components in a firm's product market strategy. It was the extra value added achieved when two businesses were integrated together such that the sum of the whole was greater than that of the constituent parts. It was popularly described as "2 + 2 = 5." The concept lost some credibility when expected synergistic effects were found to be elusive, and it became said that in many situations "2 + 2 = 3." More recently, the term has tended to be less widely used, its nearest modern equivalent being STRATEGIC FIT. Ansoff classified synergy in terms of the components of the formula for return on investment:

- *Sales synergy.* This could occur when products used common distribution channels, sales administration, or warehousing. Similarly, a full line of related products enhanced sales force efficiency, while advertising, promotion, and reputation were also enhanced.

- *Operating synergy.* This occurred as a result of higher facilities and staff utilization rates, spreading of over-heads, shared experience effects, and greater purchasing power.

- *Investment synergy.* This could result from joint use of plant, common raw materials stocks, R&D transfers, a common technology base, and common plant and equipment.

- *Management synergy*. Less apparent than the other forms of synergy, management synergy was seen as an important element in the total synergy effect. This could come about when entry into a new industry allowed managers to transfer their skills into industry structures and problems similar to those experienced in the firm's original areas of business expertise.

Bibliography

Ansoff, I. (1987). *Corporate strategy*. Harmondsworth, UK: Penguin. See chapter 5.

Kitching, J. (1967). Why do mergers miscarry? *Harvard Business Review*, **45** (November–December), 84–101.

DEREK F. CHANNON

systems marketing   Especially in organizational markets (*see* ORGANIZATIONAL MARKETING), businesses have developed the capability to provide what might be termed "total solutions" to customer "problems" or requirements. Thus, suppliers of computerized businesses systems will design, develop, and implement, including the training of users, a management information system to meet the information requirements of customers; or process plant contractors might be involved in the design, construction, and commissioning of chemical plant. These suppliers may have all the resources in house to provide the total "package" or they may, as appropriate, subcontract to others. In some cases, there are firms, such as consultant engineers, which act as coordinators based on their skills in planning and managing the various activities required.

In many MARKETS, such as defence or where complex plant and equipment is required, there is a tradition of providing "systems." The purchaser often solicits tenders from what are termed prime contractors which are responsible for bidding and assembling the different activities necessary to supply what the customer wants. These prime contractors provide a "turn-key" operation, so called because the customer simply turns one key to obtain what is sought.

DALE LITTLER

systems theory   This denotes broad meta-theory for describing the structure and behavior of complex wholes called systems. Drawn from diverse work in the physical, biological, and social sciences, systems theory seeks to discover laws and principals which apply to all levels of systems from single cells to societies. Organizational behavior scholars use this cross-level perspective to describe the general properties of organizational systems, such as groups and organizations. These characteristics have a profound impact on how we view modern organizations.

One key feature has to do with the notion of system itself and how it forms an organized whole. A system is composed of parts and relationships among them. The system provides the framework or organizing principal for structuring the parts and relationships into an organized whole capable of behaving in a way that is greater than merely the sum of the behaviors of its parts.

In organizational systems, this draws attention to identifying the constituent members or subunits of the system and examining relationships among them. Equally important, it forces us to go beyond members... to assess the organizing principal through w... arranged into a coherent whole. Group dynam... for example, have spent considerable time addre... of group membership and member interaction. ... discovered different ways of organizing men... relations for performing tasks that members could not achieve working alone, such as SELF-MANAGING TEAMS and quality circles. Similarly, organization theorists have expended effort identifying the different components of organizations and examining relations among them. They have found different ways to organize the components and relationships for competitive advantage, such as the M-form organization, the BUREAUCRACY, and the MATRIX ORGANIZATION.

A second important feature of systems has to do with whether they are relatively closed or open to their environment. Closed systems do not interact with the environment, and consequently their behavior depends largely on the internal dynamics of their parts. OPEN SYSTEMS, on the other hand, exchange with the environment, and thus their behavior is influenced by external forces (*see* ORGANIZATION AND ENVIRONMENT).

Early conceptions of organizational systems tended to employ a closed-system perspective. Attention was directed mainly at the internal dynamics of groups and organizations, for example, and at how their behaviors could be controlled internally. This led to knowledge of a variety of internal control mechanisms, such as hierarchy, rules/procedures, and functional design. In the late 1960s, OB scholars began to broaden their focus to external forces affecting organizational systems. This open systems view was fueled by growing applications of it to the social sciences, and by realization that the behavior of organizational systems could not be adequately explained without examining environmental relationships and their effects on the system. It has led to considerable research and theory about organizational environments, their dynamics and effects, and how organizational systems interact with them. Moreover, open systems theory has provided a number of powerful concepts for understanding how organizations maintain themselves while adapting to external forces.

A third characteristic of systems has to do with their viability. In order to survive and prosper, open systems need to perform at least four critical functions:

(1) transformation of inputs of energy and information to produce useful outputs;
(2) transaction with the environment to gain needed inputs and to dispose of outputs;
(3) regulation of system behavior to achieve stable performance; and
(4) adaptation to changing conditions.

Because these different functions often place conflicting demands and tension on the system, system viability depends on maintaining a dynamic balance among them.

In organizational systems, considerable research is devoted to identifying and explaining how these four functions operate and contribute to ORGANIZATIONAL EFFECTIVENESS and survival. This has led to knowledge about how organizations and groups produce products and services through acquiring, operating, and developing ifferent technologies; how they protect their technologies from external disruptions while acquiring raw materials and marketing finished products; how they regulate themselves for stable performance while initiating and implementing innovation and change (*see* INNOVATION; ORGANIZATIONAL CHANGE; ORGANIZATION DEVELOPMENT). This research defines a key role of management in organizational systems as sustaining a dynamic balance among these functions; one that allows the organization or group sufficient stability to operate rationally yet requisite flexibility to adapt to changing conditions (*see* POPULATION ECOLOGY).

A fourth key feature of systems that has influenced our conceptions of organizational systems has to do with their multilevel nature. Systems exist at different levels. The levels display a hierarchical ordering, with each higher level of system being composed of systems at lower levels. For example, societies are composed of organizations; organizations are composed of groups; groups are composed of individuals; and so on. Because systems are embedded in other systems, it is necessary to look both upward and downward when describing a system and explaining its behavior. Higher-level systems provide constraints and opportunities for how a system organizes its parts, and the nature of those parts affects the system's organizing possibilities.

This multilevel perspective has led OB scholars to identify different levels of organizational systems, and to focus on understanding them and how they interact with each other. Considerable attention is directed at specifying appropriate levels of analysis, both for conceptualizing about organizational systems and for aggregating and disaggregating data that apply to different levels. As researchers have developed more extensive theories and more powerful analytical methods, they have made finer distinctions among levels of organizational systems, particularly above the organization level. Today scholars focus on at least six levels of organizational systems:

(1) individual member;
(2) group (*see* WORK GROUPS);
(3) organization (*see* ORGANIZATIONAL DESIGN);
(4) population of organizations and/or alliance among organizations (*see* INTERORGANIZATIONAL RELATIONS;
(5) community of populations and/or community of alliances; and
(6) nation (*see* NATIONAL CULTURE).

Bibliography

Buckley, W. (1968). Modern systems research for the behavioral scientist. Chicago: Aldine.
Cummings, T. (1980). Systems theory for organization development. Chichester, UK: Wiley.
Sutherland, J. (1973). A general systems philosophy for the social and behavioral sciences. New York: Braziller.

THOMAS G. CUMMINGS

T

target market This is a group of potential users or consumers which is the focus of the business's marketing effort for a particular product or service, usually identified by means of MARKET SEGMENTATION.

FIONA LEVERICK

targeting *see* MARKET SEGMENTATION; POSITIONING

task and maintenance behavior The distinction is widely used to differentiate behaviors in small groups and organizations which focus on getting the work done, from those which concentrate on building and sustaining the team or organization. Task behaviors include: initiating activity, seeking and giving information and opinions, elaborating, summarizing, testing for feasibility, evaluating, and diagnosis. Maintenance behaviors include: encouraging, gatekeeping, standard setting, expressing feelings, consensus-testing, harmonizing, and reducing tensions (Benne & Sheats, 1948). An integration of adequate frequencies of task and maintenance behavior are required if the team or organization is to become and remain effective. With shared LEADERSHIP, all members need to see themselves displaying both kinds of behavior when both are needed by the team or organization. Where responsibility and authority for leadership is lodged in an appointee or electee, he or she must exhibit both kinds of behavior, as needed by those being led. The two-fold classification is replicated in many theories of organization behavior. Misumi's Performance (P) & Maintenance (M) is illustrative (Misumi & Peterson, 1985).

see also **Team building; Group decision making**

Bibliography

Benne, K. D. & Sheats, P. (1948). Functional roles of group members. Journal of Social Issues, 4, 41–49.
Misumi, J. & Peterson, M. F. (1985). The performance–maintenance (PM) theory of leadership. Review of a Japanese research program. Administrative Science Quarterly, 30, 198–223.

BERNARD M. BASS

team-based incentives Team-based incentives consist of financial rewards provided to employees based on the performance of their group. Individuals are expected to have common goals and objectives, work in close collaboration with each other, and be dependent on each other for the performance of the team. The team incentives can be provided based on outcomes that are objectively measured (e.g. cost savings, number of units produced, revenues from a patent) or subjectively assessed (e.g. judgments made by a panel of executives). The goals, measurement criteria, and payment amount may be specified in advance or management may distribute the team rewards on an *ad hoc* basis (e.g. upon completion of a product design). Payments can be provided in cash, as company stock, or in the form of special non-monetary awards, such as time off, a trip, a dinner, and the like. Many team-based plans differentially allocate rewards within the team based on individual contributions to the team effort and the extent to which the employee cooperates with other team members and is able to work effectively with others in problem-solving assignments. In general, team-based incentives work better when teams are relatively permanent in their composition and have relatively impermeable boundaries between them, and intragroup interdependencies exceed intergroup interdependencies.

Bibliography

Welbourne, T. M., Balkin, D. G. & Gomez-Mejia, L. R. (1996). Mutual monitoring and gainsharing plans. *Academy of Management Journal*.
Welbourne, T. M. & Gomez-Mejia, L. R. (1991). Team incentives in the work place. *Handbook of Wage and Salary Administration*, Berger, L. New York: McGraw-Hill.

LUIS R. GOMEZ MEJIA

team building In the general field of ORGANIZATION DEVELOPMENT (OD), the title given to the grandfather process of intervening in organizations to improve productivity and morale has been called team building. It was probably the first innovation historically in the OD movement, advancing the basic premise, that before any group of people can begin to improve their performance, group members must be able to work together effectively and collaboratively. Team building, then, is a planned, systematic process designed to improve the collaborative efforts of people who must work together to achieve goals.

Team building methods grew out of an earlier invention called the Training Group (or T group). This learning process, developed in the late 1940s and 1950s, featured an unstructured group, usually for a collection of strangers, for the purpose of allowing interaction to occur without predetermined directions. Out of this interaction participants were trained to observe the dynamics and structure of a group emerge, and to gain insights into their own and other members' interaction style. Emphasis was also placed on giving personal feedback to all group members, and as the T group movement developed this latter emphasis began to predominate, subordinating group dynamics analysis to the detriment of team building activities.

Participants in early T groups were captivated by the impact the group had on the members in terms of increased TRUST, openness, and cohesiveness. In an attempt to transfer these same conditions back to their organizational settings, T group trainers we asked to come and conduct the T group for working staff. These early practitioners used the T group methodology at first but soon found that the method, appropriate for a focus on how a group forms and giving feedback with stranger groups, was less suited to groups of employees with specific assignments, common work goals, and longstanding knowledge of each other. The T group methodology had to be altered to take into account the conditions found in work groups of common goals, specific assignments, deadlines, allocation of important rewards such as salary and advancements, and often high task interdependence within an organization context where there was a given structure and on-going culture.

In his early analysis of organizations, Likert (1961) clearly pointed out that despite most organization charts showing individuals reporting to other individuals, the true nature of organization structure is a set of interlocking groups or teams variously called departments, divisions, sections, councils, or committees (*see* ORGANIZATIONAL DESIGN). Managers are not only reponsible for individual performance, but must be able to coordinate the efforts of these several individuals where cooperation and interdependence of effort is necessary. The modified T group approach, now called Team Building, became the new tool for building collaboration into a work unit.

The goals of almost all team building efforts were to help group members develop a sense of trust among themselves, open up channels of COMMUNICATION so all relevant issues could be discussed, make sure everyone understood the goals and the interlocking of assignments, make decisions with the real commitment of all members, prevent the leader from dominating the group, openly examine and resolve conflicts, carry out assignments and regularly review and critique work activities to improve processes.

While it was recognized early on that groups differed along a series of important dimensions: size, composition, length of life, nature of the task, degree of interconnectedness of individual tasks or assignments, sophistication of members in group performance, time frames and deadlines, management patterns, and organization culture, there has been a tendency to consider all groups (or teams) as being similar and team building methods were commonly applied to all types of groups. Practitioners began to consider that different actions needed to be taken if one was working with a new team, a team rife with CONFLICT, an apathetic team, a team dominated by a boss, or split into cliques. An expanded set of actions and skills were developed to meet these various conditions and a repertoire of team building models emerged.

In recent years, the most dramatic difference in team building methods has been between decision teams and work teams. A decision team such as a management executive committee or a university academic department, or a collection of doctors or lawyers in a clinic or firm, must function as a team primarily to make decisions. These team members do not have to coordinate their daily tasks to accomplish a goal. They do have to made decisions which people can accept and implement with real commitment. In contrast, a work team (a hospital operating unit, a police SWAT team, a NASA space crew and some production units, must coordinate their efforts constantly every day). This has led to a new set of methodologies around building the autonomous or semiautonomous work team (*see* AUTONOMOUS WORK GROUPS). It is apparent that work teams must also make a range of decisions, so effective decision making is a central activity.

Dyer (1994) found that many companies said they believed in team building but few (only 22 percent) actually engaged in any on-going team building.

When asked why team building programs were not being used, the companies listed the following:

(1) Managers did not know how to do team building.
(2) They did not understand the payoff or rewards for spending the time.
(3) They thought it would take too much time.
(4) Team building efforts were not really rewarded in the company.
(5) People felt their teams were all right – they did not need team building.
(6) People felt it was not supported by their superiors.

The simple designs for team building ask team members to come and be prepared to talk about the following kinds of matters:

(1) What keeps our work group from being an effective team?
(2) What changes would help us become a better team?
(3) What are we currently doing that helps us work together as a team?

All group members share their responses to the above questions, a list of issues is developed specifying changes needed and change actions are agreed on and taken.

Another common design (Role Clarification Model) asks each person in the work group to describe his/her work or job assignment, obtain clarification from others and then agreements from every other person about what is needed from them in order for the person in question to get the job accomplished. This is especially useful when work roles are not clear.

A fundamental principle of team building is that it is a process, not an event. Too many companies have a one-time team building event and then wonder why the organization's teams do not improve.

see also **Group decision making; Group development**

Bibliography

Dyer, W. (1994). Team building: Issues and alternatives. Reading, MA: Addison-Wesley.
Fisher, K. (1993). Leading self-directed work teams. New York: McGraw-Hill.
Likert, R. (1961). New patterns of management. New York: McGraw-Hill.
Zenger, J. H., Musselwhite, E. & Hurson, K. (1994). Leading teams. Homewood, IL: Business One Irwin.

WILLIAM G. DYER

technology assessment In many industries, technology drives strategic decision making, with new products, and new production systems, distribution channels, and markets, often stemming from technological advances. Today, increasingly, industries may be transformed by the impact of information technology, provided that it is not merely used to automate the business practices of the past. The monitoring of technological development can therefore be a critical factor, and many companies have woken up too late to recognize that their development has been eliminated by a technological bypass. For example, the camcorder eliminated amateur cine film in about three years, xerography eliminated diazo copying in a similar period, and automated teller machines now process over 90 per cent of cash withdrawals and some 65 per cent of deposits in Japan.

There are two basic components to technology. The first of these is tangible in the form of machines, tools, and materials. Second, which is more important, is the intangible component of technological knowledge. This factor drives skills and techniques which need to be learned and adopted by employees; plant layouts; machine operating procedures, computer software; and the like. It also forms the basis for achieving competitive advantage via patents and distribution know-how.

Assessing technological capability involves collecting data on the firm's relative technological position (technology scanning) and analyzing this position (technology evaluation). The outcome of this analysis is shown in figure 1.

To undertake technology scanning:

- Divide the corporation into SBUs
- For each SBU, determine (i) the technology currently in use and (ii) the technology used by key competitors.
- Determine potential new technologies. A widespread scan is important at this point, and is where many companies succumb to blind spots.
- Investigate sources of new technologies and their effects on all stakeholders.

To undertake technology evaluation, check the following:

- Is the technology important to the success of the business unit? Does it add value? Is it changing? Will it open new markets? Does it threaten existing markets? Does it significantly change cost structures?
- How strong is the company presently and in future with respect to the technology? This can be assessed by consideration of R&D expenditure, patents, R&D personnel employed, and adaptability to change. The company's relative position as a technological leader or follower should be evaluated.

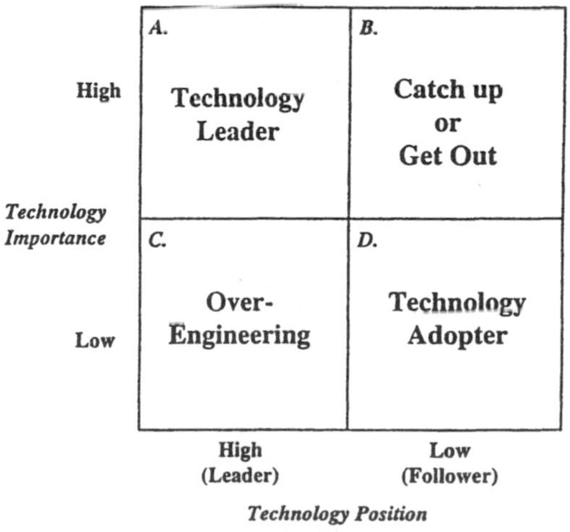

From this analysis the SBU's position is mapped on the technology evaluation matrix (see figure 1). Businesses which, in general, are high in both technology importance and technology position represent a strong position, which should be pursued aggressively in order to maintain competitive advantage. Businesses in which technology is important but the firm is in a follower position have several strategic alternatives. First, resources can be committed to strengthen the firm's technology position and attempt to gain competitive advantage. Second, the firm can exit and deploy released R&D resources to other businesses. Third, enough resources can be committed to maintain an adequate follower strategy position while monitoring opportunities for potential future technology shifts.

Businesses in quadrant C are probably guilty of over-engineering. The resource commitment is probably too high for the needs of the business, and consideration should be given to redeploying such resources to improve their effectiveness.

Businesses in quadrant D have a weak position in an important technology. Involvement in such an area should be reconsidered, and any technical requirements might be outsourced (see OUTSOURCING).

While technology alone usually does not sustain long-term competitive advantage, it can be a vital ingredient, especially during the early stages of the business life cycle. It may also be important in industries with short product life cycles. The role of technology at maturity might be one of transforming industry cost structure via substitution, rejuvenation by opening new market segments, and by product development to stimulate replacement demand.

Bibliography

Birnbaum, P. H. & Weiss, A. R. (1974). Competitive advantage and the basis for competition. Strategic Management Society Seventh Annual Meeting, Boston, MA.
Gould, J. M. (1983). Technology change and competition. *Journal of Business Strategy*, 4 (2), 62–73.
Rowe, A. J., Mason, R. O., Dickel, K. E., Mann, R. B. & Mockler, R. J. (1994). *Strategic management*, 4th edn, Reading. MA: Addison-Wesley. See pp. 116–21.

DEREK F. CHANNON

technology fusion This involves the combination and transformation of a number of different core technologies in order to create new product markets. The term was popularized by Fumio Kodama of Japan's Science and Technology Agency (STA) in the 1980s: "The fusion of technologies goes beyond mere combination. Fusion is more than complementaries, because it creates a new market and new growth opportunities for each participant in the innovation... it blends incremental improvements from several (often previously separate) fields to create a product."

The key elements of technology fusion are that it is both complementary and cooperative. Typically, it is the result of reciprocal and substantial R&D expenditure by companies from a range of industries and with different technological competences. For example, in the 1970s, the fusion of research by companies from the mechanical and electronic engineering sectors created what the Japanese call "mechatronics." A group of Japanese companies from a wide range of industries combined efforts. Fanuc, a spin-off from the computer company Fujitsu, led the group with

	A.	B.
High	Technology Leader	Catch up or Get Out
Low	C. Over-Engineering	D. Technology Adopter

High (Leader) — Low (Follower)

Technology Position

Figure 1 The technology evaluation matrix.
Source: Rowe et al. (1994).

the development of an electrohydraulic servomotor and a new controler; Nippon Seiko (NSK), Japan's leading bearing manufacturer, developed a new type of ballscrew; and material suppliers developed a new low-friction coating. This spawned the Japanese robotics and numerically controled machine tool industries, which now dominate world markets.

Technology fusion is of increasing importance in a wide range of industries in which American and European companies are currently strong. In the telecommunications sector the fusion of optics and electronics technologies has been critical. In the automotive industry the integration of electronic and mechanical systems has become a major locus of innovation, particularly in engine, transmission, and braking systems. In aerospace the development of fly-by-wire systems demands the fusion of electronics and hydraulics technologies – and the next generation of fly-by-light systems will also require expertise in optics technologies.

Significantly, Japanese companies have considerable expertise in electronics, opto–electronics, and hydraulics technologies and appear to be able to recognize and exploit the potential of technology fusion. Japanese companies are reflecting the importance of technology fusion in their slogans and company missions. For example, NEC uses "computers and communication," whereas Toshiba uses "energy and electronics." This is more than marketing alliteration, and reflects an explicit strategy of related diversification.

However, there are a number of potential problems with the concept of technology fusion, which must be resolved: the measurement of technology fusion; the level of analysis; and the organizational constraints. The first two issues are closely related. Most of the current analysis of technology fusion has been undertaken at the level of the industry or sector, and has been based on levels of R&D expenditure. In Japan, companies are required to report their R&D expenditure to the government, disaggregated into 31 different product fields. Studies suggest a that growing proportion of R&D expenditure lies outside the traditional core business. Two ratios are of particular significance:

$$\frac{\text{RD expenditure by industry A in other industries}}{\text{RD expenditure by industry A in itself}}$$

and

$$\frac{\text{RD expenditure by other industries in industry A}}{\text{RD expenditure by industry A in itself}}$$

The ratio of R&D in outside industries to that in the core business can be used as an indicator of technology fusion. Similarly, the R&D from outside industries into an industry as a ratio of the R&D within that industry can be calculated. However, strictly speaking, these ratios may simply indicate diversification; but, by definition, technology fusion involves reciprocal investment by companies in the respective industries.

Combining the two ratios for specific pairs of industries provides a better measure of reciprocal investment. For example, a coefficient of technology fusion (CTF) can be defined as follows:

$$CTF = \sqrt{(R_A R_B)},$$

where

$$R_A = \frac{\text{Total outside RD by A}}{\text{RD in B by A}}$$

and

$$R_B = \frac{\text{Total outside RD by B}}{\text{RD in A by B}}$$

Defined in this way, the closer the CTF is to unity (one), the greater the level of mutual R&D investment. Therefore one can construct year-by-year fusion maps based on the level of reciprocal R&D investment. Kodama has done this for several periods, and claims to have identified the emergence of mechatronics and biotechnology in the mid-1970s.

In Japan, the MITI now conducts fusion surveys on a periodic basis. However, there are several problems in applying this analysis. First, the standard industrial classification adopted may obscure occurrences of technology fusion. Second, the reliability of data on R&D is uncertain; for example, numerous studies suggest that the definition of R&D is variable, despite the OECD "Frascati" guidelines. Moreover, the precision of allocation into the different product groups is unknown. Third, only aggregate R&D expenditure by principal industries is published outside of Japan. Any attempt to allocate to different product groups would have to be based on primary data collection from companies, or estimates from annual reports and other sources.

For these reasons, other measures of technological capability and activity may be more appropriate at the level of the firm. Of the techniques available, patent analysis and bibliometric measurements based on publications are the most promising. Patent analysis will typically involve detailed study of between 1,000 and 10,000 patent applications, depending on the company and field of technology. For example, in the US 1,000 new patents are issued every day. A leading high-tech company, such as Hitachi, will be issued almost 2,000 patents each year. Patent data can be used in a number of ways, the most common being to measure changes in the number of patents granted in specific fields. In addition, maps of techfusion and the associated organizational linkages can be generated by examining the cross-citation of related patents.

Finally, there may be significant organizational barriers to technology fusion at the level of the firm. Past strategic choices clearly shape existing organizational structures and processes, and these structures and processes may constrain future strategic options. For example, most large firms are organized into strategic business units (SBUs), based on past product market linkages, but these linkages may no longer be relevant, and may prevent technological synergies across SBUs. This suggests a potential barrier to the recognition and exploitation of technology fusion. Independent strategies to optimize the performance of each division may not necessarily produce optimum corporate performance.

Bibliography

Kodama, F. (1991). *Analyzing Japanese high technologies*. London: Pinter.

JOE TIDD

telecommuting Telecommuting refers to the substitution of computer and telecommunication technologies for physical travel to a central work location. This term, commonly used in the USA, emphasizes the substitution of "telecommunication" for "physical commuting". In Europe, the term "telework" is more popular. The main notion of telework is on "work", made possible through the use of information technology, covering a range of new ways of working outside the traditional office environment. Other terms relating to similar concepts include remote work, distance working, flexiplace, virtual office and electronic cottage. Telecommuting or telework is often associated with home-based work, but the workplace of a telecommuter can also be a satellite office, a neighborhood work center, a hotel room, or even client premises. Telecommuting offers flexibility in both the workplace and in working time.

Not all office tasks lend themselves to telecommuting. Jobs that are good candidates for telecommuting include those that can be done with relatively little face-to-face contact with other people, those that require concentration, those that can be performed without close supervision, and those with defined milestones. The business sectors most involved with telecommuting are those with a high information content such as research, software development, financial services, insurance, journalism, publishing, customer services, and sales support. Experts estimate that about 10 percent of the workforce in the USA and Europe are potential telecommuters.

The initial interest in telecommuting started in the mid-1970s when the focus was on energy conservation. Today, telecommuting is seen as an option for work with benefits for individuals, employers, society, and the environment. Telecommuting can cut business costs by making better use of available skills and eliminating the need for large central offices. Telecommuting has been shown to lead to productivity gains of between 15 and 20 percent. The telecommuter enjoys more flexible working hours and avoids the struggle of daily commuting. Telecommuting increases the quality of life and gives individuals greater responsibility and flexibility by allowing work and other commitments to be better matched. In addition, telecommuting saves energy and reduces pollution by cutting down on commuter travel and easing traffic congestion in cities. Telecommuting also boosts local employment and regional development and provides employment opportunities to those who previously found it difficult to work outside the home, such as the elderly, handicapped, and parents with childcare responsibilities.

For the telecommuter, the potential disadvantages include role conflict stemming from the merging of home and office, feelings of isolation arising from lack of social interaction, and negative implications for career advancement. For the employer, the main concerns are the start-up and running costs, data security, difficulty in supervising and evaluating the performance of telecommuters, and the loss of face-to-face communication.

Telecommuting is enabled by advances in computer and telecommunications technologies. Telecommuters make use of a range of equipment and services to perform their work, including personal computers with modems, access to the Internet, electronic mail, telephones, mobile phones, voice mail, facsimile machines and audio- and video-conferencing. Telecommuters can work on a "dumb" terminal or a personal computer and transmit (upload) the completed task to the company's computer facilities via telephone lines or wireless means. With advanced information technology, it is possible for the telecommuter to maintain contact with and control over projects elsewhere, to communicate with colleagues in other time zones, and to gain access to resources on the Internet regardless of the time of day, the day of the week, or the weather conditions. As technologies improve and become more affordable, more organizations and individuals are likely to adopt telecommuting as a new form of work arrangement.

CHEE SING YAP

test marketing Test marketing involves the marketing of the product using the proposed marketing policy in a limited area that is representative of the total market. The ratio of the marketing effort for the test region to that agreed for the total market must be approximately the same as the ratio of the size of the test market to the total market.

Test marketing will generally be employed to predict the results of a full national launch. It is also a means of testing the implementation and management of the launch.

Although test marketing may be expensive, it will incur a lower cost than a full national launch, while information received during the test may be used to modify or even significantly alter the marketing program before a full national launch. It is an attempt to reduce risk.

There are a number of advantages of test marketing, such as the detection of possible weaknesses with the marketing mix and the experimentation of alternative marketing mixes in different test areas to assess brand awareness, brand loyalty, and repeat purchases that may result from variations in the marketing mix.

However, test marketing can alert competitors of an impending product launch. They may decide to develop a rival product which benefits from observations made of the test marketing exercise. Test marketing in any case gives competitors time to develop and launch their own product. In addition to competition, other conditions may also change, resulting in, for example, lost opportunities flowing from the decision not to market fully earlier.

Another risk is that other companies marketing products, which in some way compete with the new product, may take actions to disrupt the test market. They may increase advertising and promotion, introduce special offers, or temporarily cut prices. Meaningful conclusions on the performance of the new product will consequently be difficult to make.

The decision to test market is then a result of a careful balancing of the opportunity costs against the benefits of lowering risk and possibly improving the full market launch.

Stages in Planning a Test Market

There are several stages involved in planning a test market exercise:

Establish aims. In general, the aim will be to predict the sales that are likely to be obtained if the product was marketed in the total market. Moreover, since it is in effect a rehearsal of the national launch, the company will also be interested in evaluating the operation of the test marketing exercise.

Select of a test market representative of the total market. For many products, the area selected should be a microcosm of the national market in terms of demographic structure, number and size of retailing outlets, employment and socio–economic factors. This may be difficult to guarantee, and some approximations will have to be made. Where specialized market segments form the target, and/or where television advertising is not a component of the marketing program, more limited areas, including towns or areas of cities, may be selected.

Decide on the duration of the test. In general, companies will strive to obtain an indication of the "equilibrium" market share, while at the same time having as short a test market period as possible so as not to give competitors time to develop and market competitive products before the test marketer decides to go national. In order to gain a realistic insight into the acceptability of the product, marketers may wish to observe at least one repeat purchase cycle – particularly in the case of convenience products where it is the extent to which customers will purchase the product again (and again!) that is relevant. In deciding on the duration of the test, the following should be borne in mind: initial demand for a new product will inevitably involve much trial and experimentation; many of the initial users will, for various reasons, often not repurchase; and eventually sales will fall to some reasonably stable level that reflects the degree of repeat purchasing behavior.

Decide on the marketing research to be undertaken. Careful consideration should be paid to the sorts of information that need to be collected before, during, and after the test marketing *prior to* the start of the test. Companies may decide to measure retail sales achieved during the test marketing, the awareness of an attitude towards the advertising, the level of distribution, the sales per outlet, and so on.

The test market data may not, however, be a true indicator of the results to be obtained from a full national launch. There are a number of reasons why this might be the case:

- The test market may not be fully representative of the national market.
- There may be "learning effects" as a result of experience gained from the test market.
- The environment may change between the test marketing and the full launch; e.g., new competition may emerge, and economic conditions may alter.
- Competition may have disrupted the test marketing by engaging in exceptional marketing activity (such as severe price cutting, and dramatic promotional offers).

Bibliography

Dibb, S., Simkin, L., Pride, W. & Ferrell, O. C. (1994). *Marketing: concepts and strategies* 2nd European edn, Boston, MA: Houghton Mifflin Co.

Kotler, P. (1984). *Marketing management: Analysis, planning and control* 5th edn, Englewood Cliffs, NJ: Prentice-Hall.

Littler, D. A. (1984). *Marketing and product development.* Oxford: Philip Allan.

Urban, G. L. & Hauser, J. R. (1993). *Design and marketing of new products*, 2nd edn, Englewood Cliffs, NJ: Prentice-Hall.

MARGARET BRUCE

Theory x & y According to McGregor (1960), traditional management believed implicitly in Theory X, which postulates that employees are inherently lazy, indifferent to the needs of the organization, and uninterested in doing a good job. Employees should not be expected to do any more than absolutely necessary. As a consequence, management has to direct, motivate, and control the workforces, as if they were immature children. Control systems are essential, and assignments must be specific. Close monitoring and correction of performance by supervisors is essential. Thinking should be left to superiors. Discipline and fear of punishment should be used to maintain standards of performance. Employees should be motivated primarily by "carrots" for good performance and "sticks" for poor performance. Opposite to belief in Theory X is Theory Y, which postulates that employees essentially want to do a good job. They have ego needs as well as needs for material benefits. They respond positively to being treated like adults and given responsibilities commensurate with their capabilities. Their involvement, loyalty, and COMMITMENT to the organization are important motivators of their performance. Wherever possible, they should be able to participate in decisions affecting their performance.

The two theories are predicated on distinctive assumptions about human behavior. Theory X assumes workers must be persuaded, rewarded, punished, controlled, and directed if the coordination of effort is to be achieved. In fact, no work at all will get done unless there is active intervention by management. This is because employees are naturally lazy and will work as little as possible. They lack ambition, dislike accepting responsibility, and prefer to be led. They are only concerned with their own needs and not with the goals of their organization. They resist change (*see* RESISTANCE TO CHANGE). They are not good decision makers. As much as possible, all decisions within the organization should be routinized so that under all circumstances, the individual will require a minimum of thought without alternatives. Indeed, they must be told in detail what to do or they will not be able to do their job. They must be prodded with external incentives and close surveillance. While management is responsible for organizing the elements of productive enterprise – money, materials, equipment, people – in the interest of economic ends, employees develop passivity and resistance to organizational needs as a result of their experience in organizations (*see* RESISTANCE TO CHANGE).

Theory Y says that workers have the potential for development, the capacity for assuming responsibility, and the readiness to work for organizational goals. Management makes it possible for workers to recognize and develop these traits. Therefore, management is responsible for arranging organizational processes and conditions so that employees can achieve their own goals by directing their efforts toward organizational objectives. Management creates opportunities, releases potential, removes obstacles, encourages growth and provides guidance. Belief in Theory Y promotes decentralization, delegation, job enlargement, empowerment, participation, and self-management.

see also **Values; Employee involvement, Theory Z; Scientific management; Managerial behavior**

Bibliography

McGregor, D. M. (1960). The human side of enterprise. New York: McGraw-Hill.

BERNARD M. BASS

Theory z   Ouchi (1981) introduced the idea of Theory Z, to represent the beliefs underlying Japanese management, in contrast to THEORY X & THEORY Y. The management of Theory Z firms is characterized by long-term employment and intensive SOCIALIZATION of their workforce. Objectives and VALUES emphasize cooperation and teamwork. There is slow promotion from within the firm and jobs are rotated. Employees are expected to be generalists rather than specialists. PERFORMANCE APPRAISAL systems are complex. Emphasis is on WORK GROUPS rather than individuals, open COMMUNICATION, consultative DECISION MAKING, and a relations-oriented concern for employees. In comparison to Theory X organizations, Theory Z organizations are more decentralized and have fewer levels of management. Subordinates exercise more upward influence in dealing with their bosses in the Type Z than in the Type X organizations.

see also **Organizational culture; International management**

Bibliography

Ouchi, W. G. (1981). Theory Z: How American business can meet the Japanese challenge. Reading, MA: Addison-Wesley.

BERNARD M. BASS

third-party netting   Netting is a cash management technique in which cash flows, to and from operating units within a company, are forwarded to a netting center. Here inflows and outflows of each unit are netted out with just the balance either being deposited to the unit's account or being taken out of the account to pay other units. Third-party netting takes place when not only the owned units of a company use the netting center but also nonowned entities. If a company has both cash flows to and from another organization, those transactions could be handled more efficiently through a netting center.

see also **Multilateral netting**

JOHN O'CONNELL

time and motion study   A time and motion study is a very detailed analysis of the specific body movements and/or procedural steps that are used to perform a particular task. Typically, data for a time and motion study are collected by observing employees on the job and/or video taping employees as they work. The job analyst records the actions taken to complete the task and also the exact amount of time that each action takes. Descriptions of employee behaviors are recorded by using a standard list of basic body motions. These basic motions include actions such as grasping, searching, selecting, transporting, and assembling. (McCormick, 1979). Typically, the analyst develops a chart to show the actions associated with performing a task and the time required for each action. This chart typically uses symbols to represent workers' specific actions and the sequence in which they occur.

Time and motion studies provide detailed information about jobs. These studies concentrate on tasks that require relatively standard, repetitive actions to be completed. The methods are objective. They result in data that are particularly useful for the design of equipment to be used on the job and for setting PERFORMANCE STANDARDS for those operating the equipment. By observation of several individuals doing the tasks, a normal or standard time-to-complete can be established and used to evaluate the performance of employees. However, time and motion studies provide little information about the broader context in which the job is performed.

Bibliography

McCormick, E. J. (1979). *Job Analysis: Methods and Applications*, New York: AMACOM.

JAMES B. SHAW

time orientation   Time orientation can be interpreted in two different ways when applied to international business. (1) A culture's orientation to yesterday, today, and tomorrow. Some cultures place a great deal of emphasis on the past and the traditional ways of doing things. Things that are old are revered and respected. Other cultures seem to live for now and place little stock in tradition. Things that are old are discarded and looked upon as less useful. This form of time orientation impacts the workplace as well. Japan, well known for respect of tradition, also has widespread life time employment practices. The United States, on the other hand, views work as short term. Employees expect to move several times between employers and few expect a guarantee of lifetime employment. (2) Time orientation with respect to a culture's priorities toward punctuality. Although this may seem like a minor potential problem, there are very real and dramatic cultural differences with respect to punctuality and inferences related to not being on time. In the United States people are very aware of time, especially when concerning business meetings. To be late is considered poor business practice and rude. To be early in the United States may be taken in almost the same manner. Latin Americans view time in relative terms. Families are a priority in Latin America, thus if extra time is spent with family and business appointments are late, it is not considered rude nor out of character. Business can wait.

Problems with time orientation between cultures become evident when persons from two or more cultures must work together. Both cultures may read the other's lateness in different ways (one inferring rudeness and the other merely different priorities). Business meeting times may have to allow for leeway at the beginning and the end even though in an employee's home country, it seems like wasted time. Persons dealing with or living within cultures other than their own must be made aware of cultural differences and time orientation is certainly an important difference.

Bibliography

Deresky, Helen (1994). *International management*. 1st edn, New York: HarperCollins.

Doktor, R. H. (1990). Asian and American CEOs: A comparative study. *Organizational Dynamics* Winter, 49.

Landis, D. & Brislin, R. (1983). *Handbook on intercultural training*. New York: Pergamon Press.

Mead, Richard (1994). *International management: Cross cultural dimensions*. Cambridge, MA: Blackwell Publishers.

Mendenhall, M., Punnett, B. & Ricks, D. (1995). *Global management*. Cambridge, MA: Blackwell Publishers.

JOHN O'CONNELL

time series analysis A series of measurements made in chronological order is a time series. Finance research has concentrated on series of prices and returns to investors, although there has also been interest in series of earnings and dividends. Time-series analysis is a collection of statistical methods that is used to understand the dynamic behavior of the measured quantity, and to make forecasts about future values.

The earliest important insights into financial time series may be attributed to Holbrook Working and Maurice Kendall. The first detailed analysis of investment returns using time series methods is Fama (1965). Fama studied long time series of returns from US stocks and made three observations that have been corroborated in numerous subsequent studies. First, the sample correlation between the return during some period and the return during any subsequent period is close to zero. Prices follow a random walk when the theoretical correlations are zero for any pair of returns during different periods and expected returns are constant. Second, large positive and large negative returns are more likely than other returns to be followed by large returns. This phenomenon, known as volatility clustering or conditional heteroskedasticity, can be detected by measuring correlations between squared returns. Third, the distribution of returns is fat-tailed compared with the normal distribution because extreme returns are far more frequent than predicted by normal theory.

Methods for testing the random walk hypothesis usually rely on some alternative description of price behavior to motivate the tests. Trends in prices are one alternative, differences between fundamental values and market prices are another, and both alternatives motivate the variance-ratio test of Lo and MacKinlay (1988). The most recent alternative to attract interest is the idea that prices are chaotic. Empirical studies show that the random walk hypothesis is at least a good approximation. There is little evidence to support the ideas of chaotic dynamics. There is some evidence for trends in exchange rates and the prices of some firms, particularly small firms, but the evidence remains controversial. Trading rules based upon price forecasts obtained from time-series models are of little value after transactions costs and do not contradict the idea of market efficiency, except for forex markets where time-series rules obtain profits similar to those provided by some forms of technical analysis.

Time-series models for price volatility have attracted enormous interest in recent years because they can be used to forecast volatility and hence value derivatives. Engle (1982) developed the ARCH (autoregressive conditional heteroskedasticity) class of models that provide successful descriptions of future volatility conditioned on a set of recent observations. These models are very flexible and many new specifications have been developed. The GARCH model of Bollerslev et al. (1992) has become a popular choice.

Bibliography

Bollerslev, T., Chou, R. Y. & Kroner, K. F. (1992). ARCH modelling in finance: a review of the theory and empirical evidence. *Journal of Econometrics*, 52, 5–59.

Engle, R. F. (1982). Autoregressive conditional heteroscedasticity with estimates of the variance of United Kingdom inflation. *Econometrica*, 50, 987–1007.

Fama, E. F. (1965). The behaviour of stock market prices. Eds Lo, A. W. & MacKinlay, A. C. (1988). Stock market prices do not follow random walks: evidence from a simple specification test. *Review of Financial Studies*, 1, 41–66.

Taylor, S. J. (1996). *Modelling financial time series*. 2nd edn, Chichester: Wiley.

STEPHEN J. TAYLOR

top management teams The term "top management team" (TMT) has been adopted by organization and strategy theorists to refer to the relatively small group of most influential executives at the apex of an organization – usually the general manager and his or her direct reports. The term does not necessarily imply a formalized management-by-committee arrangement, but rather simply the constellation of, say, the top three to ten executives. As such, many top management "teams" may have few genuine team properties (interaction, shared purpose, collaboration) and might more accurately be referred to merely as top management groups.

A scholarly interest in top management teams emerged in the early 1980s and has been pervasive ever since. Realizing that top management typically is a shared activity, researchers have moved beyond an examination of singular leaders, to a wider focus on the top LEADERSHIP group.

The underlying assumption is that the collective dispositions and interactions of top managers affect the choices they make. The limited empirical evidence as to whether the characteristics of the top executive or of the entire top team are better predictors of organizational outcomes clearly supports the conclusion that the top team has greater effect. For example, the VALUES of top teams have been found to be more strongly related to INNOVATION strategies than are the values of chief executives alone. Similarly, major strategic change is more likely to occur following major changes in the composition of the TMT than when only the CEO changes (*see* ORGANIZATIONAL CHANGE).

The vast majority of research on TMTs has focused primarily on the composition of teams as predictors of organizational outcomes. Unfortunately, other team characteristics have not received as much attention, probably because they are more difficult for researchers to observe and measure. A complete portrayal of a TMT would include not only composition, but also team structure (e.g., group size and roles), incentives (e.g., financial and succession prospects) (*see* SUCCESSION PLANNING), processes (e.g., COMMUNICATION flows and socio-political dynamics), as well as the characteristics and behaviors of the group leader.

Complementing the larger body of work on the effects of TMTs, some research has examined the determinants of TMT characteristics. In this vein, both external factors (such as industry age, growth rate, and munificence) and organizational characteristics (including strategic profile, size, and financial resources) have been found to explain in part the characteristics of TMTs. One of the major limitations of many studies on TMTs is that the direction of causality has been imputed but not verified. It is most plausible to believe that firms select and promote executives who fit certain critical contingencies and, in turn, those executives make choices in line with their particular predispositions and COMPETENCIES. Over time, a reinforcing spiral probably occurs; hence establishing definitive causality will be difficult.

Available research does allow us to conclude that the biases, blind spots, experiences, and interactions of top executives greatly affect what happens to companies. Thus, CEOs or general managers who wish to improve the performance and fitness of their organizations are well advised to focus attention on the characteristics and qualities of their top teams.

see also **Culture; Team building; Group decision making; Organizational effectiveness**

Bibliography

Hambrick, D. C. (1994). Top management groups: A conceptual integration and reconsideration of the team label. In B. M. Staw & L. L. Cummings (Eds), Research in organizational behavior, (vol. 16) Greenwich, CT: JAI Press.

Hambrick, D. C. & Mason, P. A. (1984). Upper echelons: The organization as a reflection of its top managers. Academy of Management Review, 9, 195–206.

Jackson, S. E. (1991). Consequences of group processing for the interpersonal dynamics of strategic issue processing. In P. Shrivastava, A. Hugg & J. Dutton (Eds), Advances in strategic management, (vol. 8, pp. 345–382). Greenwich, CT: JAI Press.

Katzenbach, J. R. & Smith, D. K. (1991). The wisdom of teams. Boston: Harvard Business School.

DONALD C. HAMBRICK

total variable cost   Measures the total variable costs of production in the short run. Total variable costs are those costs which vary with the output level produced such as workers' wages, material inputs, etc. Total variable cost depends on the quantity of output produced and is equal to zero when no output is produced. In addition to the per unit input cost, the MARGINAL PRODUCT of inputs and the technology employed by the company influence the level of total variable cost (*see* SHORT RUN COST CURVES).

The curvature of a total variable cost curve is determined by the impact of successive increases in output on total variable cost. Typically, total variable costs will increase initially at a decreasing rate but will eventually increase at an increasing rate because of DIMINISHING RETURNS in production (*see* MARGINAL PRODUCT).

Labor costs are usually considered as variable in nature, i.e. they can be reduced if the worker works fewer hours and vice versa. However, there are many examples of labor costs which are not strictly related to the number of hours of work and can be defined as quasi-fixed. Examples are employee benefits such as health insurance, pension plans, costs of hiring and training new employees, and the costs of legally required social insurance programs. The company pays for these costs on a per worker rather than per labor hour worked basis. A company's decision about the optimal combination of inputs in its production process will be influenced by the amount of these quasi-fixed costs per worker. For example, part-time employees are less likely to be covered by the company's health insurance policy and are usually given fewer fringe benefits in general making them a relatively cheaper input in production than a full-time worker (Ehrenberg and Smith, 1994).

Bibliography

Carlton, D. W. & Perloff, J. M. (1994). Modern Industrial Organization. 2nd edn, New York: HarperCollins.

Douglas, E. J. (1992). Managerial Economics. 4th edn, Englewood Cliffs, NJ: Prentice-Hall.

Ehrenberg, R. G. & Smith, R. S. (1994). Modern Labor Economics. 5th edn, New York: HarperCollins.

LIDIJA POLUTNIK

trade financing   The majority of goods traded across borders are financed in one way or another. Most importers of goods will not release funds until they are certain the goods are delivered in good condition. This requires a system of financing to be in place to handle the enormous demand for what are normally short-term funds. Financing is conducted by the exporters themselves, export development banks and agencies in various countries, and by governments, individual investors, and commercial banks throughout the world.

JOHN O'CONNELL

trading area   A company's trading area is merely the geographic area in which the company has decided to pursue trade activities. Usually a company begins with a local trading area. As the company grows and products are accepted the trade area expands until it begins to cross international boundaries. Trading areas may be limited by a company's financial condition, laws associated with trade, management's knowledge of the market, or the creativity of the firm's owners/managers.

JOHN O'CONNELL

trading bloc   Trading blocs are a very important development in international trade. Although agreements between groups of countries have existed for decades, it has been only in the 1990s that trading blocs have gained recognition as potentially being able to control large amounts of trade not only within a specific trading bloc but throughout the entire world. Instead of a single country buying and selling goods, virtually all of western Europe (the European Community) or North America (the North American Free Trade Agreement – Nafta) has become a single market for imports and exports. Trading blocs exert a great deal of economic power. They can control the trade within member countries to make freedom of trade a reality. They can also make demands on other trading nations because of their tremendous purchasing power.

Bibliography

Bartlett, Christopher, A. & Ghoshal, Sumantra (1992). Transnational management. 2nd edn, Chicago: Irwin.

Daniels, J. D. & Radebaugh, L. E. (1994). International business: Environments and operations. 7th edn, Reading, MA: Addison-Wesley Publishing.

Grosse, R. & Kujawa, D. (1995). International business: Theory and managerial applications. 3rd edn, Boston, MA: Richard D. Irwin Inc.

JOHN O'CONNELL

training evaluation   Training evaluation is a formal attempt to determine the individual and organizational impact of attempts to make people or organizations more effective. In measuring the outcomes of training and development efforts, two important concerns must be addressed. First, the intended outcomes of the training must be specified in ways that allow for their measurement. Traditionally, trainee reactions, learning, behavior, and performance outcomes have all been considered in rigorous evaluation attempts (Kirkpatrick, 1967). In addition, system functioning, or the interrelationship between these outcomes and other organizational variables, should be considered (Schmitt and Klimoski, 1991, chapter 11). Kraiger et al. (1993) have asserted that the potential affective, behavioral, and cognitive outcomes of training should also be specified and measured.

The second major concern is the degree to which a research design with good internal and external validity (Cook and Campbell, 1979) can be implemented. Internal validity refers to the extent to which we can draw the inference that training has caused the desired outcome within the context of our evaluation study. Various types of research designs provide differing degrees of confidence in this regard (see Cook and Campbell, 1979, for a discussion of the strengths and liabilities of various research designs) and vary in the degree to which they may be practically feasible. External validity refers to the extent to which the effects of training, as measured in a training evaluation study, generalize to ongoing practice within an organization.

Training evaluation research should also include consideration of the theoretical and practical significance of the results, and an analysis of the process and content of training.

Bibliography

Cook, T. D. & Campbell, D. T. (1979). *Quasi-experimentation: Design and Analysis Issues for Field Settings*, Boston: Houghton-Mifflin.

Kraiger, K. J., Ford, J. K. & Salas, E. (1993). Application of cognitive, skill-based, and affective theories of learning outcomes to new methods of training evaluation. *Journal of Applied Psychology*, 78, 311–28.

Kirkpatrick, D. L. (1967). Evaluation of training. *Training and Development Handbook*, Eds. Craig, R. L. & Bittel, L. R. New York: McGraw-Hill.

Schmitt, N. & Klimoski, R. J. (1991). *Research Methods in Human Resources Management*, Cincinnati, OH: South-Western.

NEAL SCHMITT

training expatriate, *see* **expatriate training**

transaction costs The buyers and sellers of virtually any asset incur costs in attempting to trade the asset in a public domain. Transaction costs are directly or indirectly associated with efforts to assess the fair value of the asset and to search for a trading counterparty. The size and nature of transaction costs ultimately depends on various characteristics of the asset. In particular, assets whose values can be readily ascertained in relation to other similar assets can be traded with lower costs than assets that have unique characteristics. The size of the trade, as well as the total size of the market (and thus the potential trading volume), also affect transaction costs, due to often tremendous economies of scale in search costs. These characteristics will also determine the type of market structure that will exist to facilitate trading in the asset, or indeed whether a formal market structure for the asset will exist.

Most assets trade in one of four market structures – direct search, broker, dealer or auction markets. In a direct search market, buyers and sellers conduct their own search effort to find a trading counterparty. Cost and effort incurred by the seller may include placing advertisements in newspapers, placing the asset in a conspicuous public place with a "for sale" sign attached, or other means of drawing the attention of the public. For buyers, efforts may center on locating such advertisements or placing ads indicating an interest in purchasing the asset. Examples of assets commonly traded in direct search markets are real estate, collectables and used automobiles, though in none of these cases is direct search the predominant market structure.

In brokered markets, either the buyer or seller, or both, hire a broker to conduct a search for a counterparty. For this service, the trader pays the brokers a fee, or commission. The amount of the fee in relation to the value of the asset depends largely on the costs normally incurred by the broker. The broker incurs fixed costs for equipment and training (used to monitor the status of potential counterparties and the overall state of the market) that must be allocated to each trade, as well as variable costs specifically associated with a given trade. Examples of assets traded in brokered markets are real estate and fine art, as well as some financial assets such as municipal bonds and large blocks of common stocks.

In a dealer market, the dealer holds an inventory of the asset and stands ready to buy or sell directly against this inventory. Thus the dealer effectively eliminates search costs and trading delays for both buyers and sellers. In exchange for providing this immediacy of trade, the dealer receives compensation in the form of a spread between the price at which the dealer will purchase the asset, called the bid price, and a higher price at which the dealer will sell the asset, called the ask (or offer) price. Examples of assets that trade in dealer markets are new and used automobiles and financial assets such as secondary markets for US Treasury securities, corporate bonds, foreign exchange, and common stocks traded on the Nasdaq Stock Market and the London Stock Exchange. The difference between the ask and bid prices, expressed as a percentage of the average of these prices, is commonly used as a measure of transaction costs in a dealer market.

Auction markets are characterized by the simultaneous presence of many buyers and sellers in a given location, each monitoring counterparty bids and offers in an active attempt to trade at the best possible price. The auction market structure is best suited for assets with large trading volume. Examples of assets traded in auction markets include fine art and, among financial assets, new-issue US Treasury securities and common stocks traded on the New York Stock Exchange, the Paris Bourse and the Tokyo Stock Exchange. Trading on the NYSE actually reflects aspects of the broker, dealer and auction structures. Buyers and sellers submit their trade requests to a broker that is a member of the NYSE and is therefore allowed to trade on the floor of the exchange. On the floor, the broker engages in the auction process known as open-outcry, attempting to obtain the best price for the customer. Occasionally, however, there is an imbalance of purchase or sale orders for a given stock, and orders may languish. To avoid this problem, the NYSE assigns to each stock a specialist, a member firm who acts as an exclusive dealer in the stock. The specialist posts bid and ask prices and has a general fiduciary responsibility to facilitate trading in the stock. Brokerage fees paid by customers to the member firms reflect the high fixed cost, and relatively low variable cost, associated with the auction market structure. In addition, when trades are consummated between the customer and the specialist, rather than between two customers, the customer also implicitly pays the specialist for their service as a dealer. For this reason, researchers often estimate transaction costs on the NYSE as the sum of a representative brokerage commission plus the specialists' proportional bid–ask spread.

Bibliography

Garbade, K. (1982). *Securities markets.* New York: McGraw-Hill.

JOSEPH OGDEN

transaction exposure This exposure arises when a business enters into transactions in which foreign currency payments are expected to be made "to" the business in the future or in which foreign currency payments are to be made "by" the business in the future. As time passes currency values may change. If foreign currency values fall, the business will be paid in the lower value currency. If foreign currency values increase, the company will have to use more of its domestic currency to purchase foreign currency with which to pay future debt.

see also **Exchange exposures**

Bibliography

Eiteman, D. K., Stonehill, A. J. & Moffett, M. H. (1992). *Multinational business finance.* 6th edn, Reading, MA: Addison-Wesley Publishing.
Miletello, F. C. & Davis, H. A. (1994). *Foreign exchange management.* Morristown, NJ: Financial Executives Research Foundation.

JOHN O'CONNELL

transfer price The transfer price is the price paid for a good or service between members of the same corporate family. That is, the price charged by a subsidiary to a parent company for goods exported to the parent. Alterations of the transfer price may be used to move excessive amounts of money from a parent company to a subsidiary. This is especially useful if the parent is located in a high tax country and the subsidiary in a low tax country.

see also **Reinvoicing**

Bibliography

Celi, L. J. & Rutizer, B. (1991). *Global cash management.* 1st edn, New York: Harper Business (HarperCollins).

JOHN O'CONNELL

transfer pricing Transfer prices are the prices of goods sold by one division (or other responsibility center) to another within the firm. The prices of such internal sales do not directly affect the profits of the firm as a whole, since the selling division's revenue is offset by the buying division's expense. Transfer prices affect the firm indirectly, however, through their effect on manager's decisions. A well-designed transfer pricing system provides top management with meaningful information on individual responsibility centers' performance and provides responsibility center managers with both the incentive and the information needed to make the decisions that are best for the firm as a whole.

Surveys of practice (Tang, 1992; Price Waterhouse, 1984; earlier studies summarized in Grabski, 1985) have shown that market prices and full cost (actual or standard, with or without a markup to provide profit to the selling division) are the most common bases for transfer pricing. In the case of either market-based or cost-based prices, two alternative procedures for price-setting are available. A general rule may be established which defines "cost" or "market price" (e.g., standard full cost plus 10 percent or the average price offered by the three principal suppliers, updated at the end of each month), and the rule is thereafter followed mechanically. Alternatively, buyer and seller may negotiate transfer prices periodically, using market or cost data as a basis for the negotiation.

The appropriate basis and procedure for transfer pricing depend on characteristics of the firm and its environment. Market-based pricing is impossible in some settings because the goods to be transferred are not available in the market. In other cases, goods traded on the market may be similar to those produced in the firm but not identical in terms of quality, timeliness of delivery, etc. Adjustments to market prices may be necessary to allow for these factors, or for the reduction in the selling division's marketing and collection expenses that occurs when it sells internally instead of in the open market. When comparable market prices are available, however, and adjustments are trivial or easily agreed on, market-based transfer prices provide an objective measure of performance for both buying and selling divisions and provide an incentive to the selling division to control production costs.

Transfer prices based on actual cost may remove the incentive for cost control and provide an incentive for the selling division to distort reported costs for products transferred internally (e.g., by allocating more indirect costs to products sold internally). The use of standard rather than actual costs may reduce the magnitude of these problems, if the method of setting standards is sufficiently objective; other measures to encourage cost reduction and accurate costing can also help to make cost-based transfer prices effective.

If the selling division is a profit center rather than a cost center, transfer prices are often set at full cost plus a profit margin comparable to that which the division would earn on outside sales. Without such a profit margin, the selling division will prefer to sell to outsiders rather than sister divisions whenever possible, in order to maximize its own profits; and this may be disadvantageous to the firm as a whole. The potential difficulty with adding a profit allowance to cost, however, is that it can lead the buying division to price the final product too high, if the buyer adds its usual profit margin on top of costs that already include the seller's usual profit margin.

A general rule (either market-based or cost-based) which automatically adjusts transfer prices with every change of market prices or production costs saves the time and effort managers spend when price changes must be negotiated. The portion of this time and effort which managers spend in trying to get the larger share of the firm's profits for their own division does not benefit the firm; however, the negotiation process also includes exchanges of information that may lead to decisions increasing the size of the firm's overall profits. Experimental studies (De Jong et al., 1989; Chalos & Haka, 1990) have shown that transfer price negotiations grow more efficient (less likely to end in impasse, and more likely to increase total profits) when the negotiating parties gain more experience with the process and each other.

Theoretical economic studies (e.g., Hirshliefer, 1956; Banker & Datar, 1992) have suggested marginal cost as the optimal basis for transfer pricing. Although variable cost may appear as an appropriate surrogate, it is rarely used (Grabski, 1985; Tang, 1992). Recent studies suggests that in a multi-product firm, full cost is a reasonable proxy for long-run marginal cost. For a firm that maximizes profit in a competitive market, market price should be equivalent to marginal cost.

Mathematical programing approaches to transfer pricing have also been developed (see, e.g., Abdel-Khalik & Lusk, 1974; Kanodia, 1979; Harris et al., 1982), but are mainly useful as a way for top management to learn more about the characteristics of production in the divisions. While mathematical programing techniques allow top management to set transfer prices and quantities at (theoretically) profit-maximizing amounts, this procedure reduces the autonomy of divisional managers, thus undercutting one of the principal goals of transfer pricing systems. Such techniques could also generate divisional profit figures that fluctuated widely in response to small changes in conditions and would not be informative about divisional managers' performance.

In multinational firms, transfer prices play an important role in allocating costs and profits to national sub-units of the firm. High transfer prices to subsidiaries in high-tax jurisdictions and low transfer prices to low-tax jurisdictions may arouse suspicions of tax evasion. Local tax codes must be consulted for acceptable transfer price methods for tax purposes.

Bibliography

Abdel-khalik, A. R. & Lusk, E. J. (1974). Transfer pricing – a synthesis. *The Accounting Review*, **49**, Jan., 8–23.

Banker, R. D. & Datar, S. M. (1992). Optimal transfer pricing under postcontract information. *Contemporary Accounting Research*, Spring, 329–52.

Chalos, P. & Haka, S. (1990). Transfer pricing under bilateral bargaining. *The Accounting Review*, **65**, July, 624–41.

DeJong, D., Forsythe, R., Kim, J.-O. & Uecker, W. (1989). A laboratory investigation of alternative transfer pricing mechanisms. *Accounting, Organizations and Society*, **14**, Jan., 41–64.

Grabski, S. V. (1985). Transfer pricing in complex organizations: A review and integration of recent empirical and analytical research. *Journal of Accounting Literature*, **4**, 33–75.

Harris, M., Kriebel, C. H. & Raviv, A. (1982). Asymmetric information, incentives and intrafirm resource allocation. *Management Science*, June, 604–20.

Hirshleifer, J. (1956). On the economics of transfer pricing. *Journal of Business*, **29**.

Kanodia, C. (1979). Risk sharing and transfer price systems under uncertainty. *Journal of Accounting Research*, Spring, 74–98.

Price-Waterhouse (1984). *Transfer pricing practices of American industry*.

Tang, R. Y. W. (1992). Transfer pricing in the 1980s. *Management Accounting*, **70**, Feb., 22–6.

SEVERIN V. GRABSKI and JOAN LUFT

translation exposure Translation exposure is an accounting measure. If an organization has assets valued in a foreign currency, it faces the possibility that the foreign currency will fall in value. If this occurs, the decrease in value "translates" into reduced value of business assets.

see also **Exchange exposures**

Bibliography

Eiteman, D. K., Stonehill, A. J. & Moffett, M. H. (1992). *Multinational business finance*. 6th edn, Reading, MA: Addison-Wesley Publishing.

JOHN O'CONNELL

trends in unionism The term trends in unionism means the direction over time of the membership of unions, and/or of union penetration of the labor market. The latter is often referred to as union density, or extent of organization. Union density is analogous to the concept of real wages: just as nominal wages are adjusted to determine real wages, or the buying power of wages, so union membership is adjusted by employment to get a measure of real membership. Density is expressed as a percentage.

Trends in membership may be up, down, or unchanged, but in themselves are insufficient for understanding how well unions are succeeding in organizing; they do not account for changes compared to the labor market. Union density itself is a subtle index. It can rise even is membership is stable, as long as employment falls. Likewise, density can fall even if membership increases, but employment rises more quickly. Historically, density usually falls as a result of a decline in union membership relative to a rise in employment.

Economy-wide measures of unions' density are membership figures compared to nonfarm employment, or the civilian labor force. Similarly, density can be calculated relative to employment by industry, occupation, geography, gender, race and age, and cross-classifications of these variables. One of the most significant measures of trends in density compares the public with the private sectors of the labor market. Density can also be compared across countries, but problems of comparability in the statistics of union membership and employment figures may affect levels. Nevertheless, international trends in density are clearly discernible.

LEO TROY

trust When trust is used in the organizational literature, two significantly different definitions are usually found. The first defines trust between parties to a transaction or exchange as an expression of confidence or predictability in their expectations that they will not be harmed, or put at risk, by the actions of the other party (Zucker, 1986). In the second definition, the confidence of the parties rests in the other's goodwill (Ring & Van de Ven, 1992). Dealing with the concept of trust now appears to be essential in efforts to define the nature of relationships among individuals and between organizations. There is substantial evidence to support the inclusion of trust as a critical factor in the design and management of business organizations. Indeed, the philosopher Sissela Bok views trust as something that needs protection "just as much as the air we breathe or the water we drink. When [trust is] damaged, the community as a whole suffers; . . . when . . . destroyed, societies falter and collapse." The evidence of the importance of trust in economic (as well as social) exchange comes from economists, lawyers, sociologists, psychologists, ethicists, management, and organization scholars. In general, trust is a situational feature: reliance on trust, or trustworthy behavior by economic actors, is only necessary under conditions involving inter-dependence, UNCERTAINTY (where the actors on one economic actor hinge on choices made by others) and consequentiality, i.e., if an economic actor relies on trust, and it is not reciprocated, she will suffer substantial harm (*see* RECIPROCITY). In short, where one acts on faith alone, trust is not necessary. The same appears to be the case in situations involving perfect information. Thus, the conditions under which trust seems most likely to be a factor in organizational behaviors where alternative choices involve "exit, betrayal, defection," and "bad outcomes would make you regret your actions."

In the first definition above, trust is frequently equated with risk, or the predictability that future outcomes will be successful. TRANSACTION COST theory and AGENCY THEORY discuss how this risk-view of trust can be secured through a variety of impersonal institutional means, such as guarantees, insurance mechanisms, hostages, laws, and organizational hierarchy. These exogenous safeguards are needed because, standing alone, trust is not a sufficient condition for the effective social control of business behavior. The prevailing view of economic theory is that economic actors are self-interested and will pursue their interests opportunistically (with guile) if conditions under which exchange is to take place are right: frequent transactions, uncertainty, transaction specific assets, and small numbers of parties. This definition focuses, however, on outcomes and is principally relevant to analysis of the *ex post contract* stages of a business relationship.

In the second definition, connoting goodwill, trust is viewed as necessary for stable social relationships, and functions to reduce complexity in social worlds. It is a "lubricant" facilitating exchange on a continuing basis (Barber, 1983). Research flowing from the sociological literature provides organizational scholars with insights into the role that institutions play in creating trust, or dealing with its absence. The results of this research suggest that when trust is low, other control mechanisms are employed (Shapiro, 1987). Typically, legalistic remedies (e.g., accrediting organizations, insurance, bonds, guarantees, etc.) are used either to compensate for the lack of trust in exchange, restore trust, or to create conditions under which trust might be restored. However, the results of research investigating the effectiveness of these kinds of mechanisms also suggest that they can lead to higher levels of mistrust.

Effective or not, these remedies are costly and one consequence of the absence of trust in economic relationships is higher cost. When trust is present within organizations, or in relationships between economic actors, the cost of transacting appears to be lower. Fewer controls are needed to measure and monitor performance. Forecasts of future events are more realistic, as are budget projections. Cooperation improves along the value chain, productivity improves, and profitability is enhanced, all other things remaining equal.

When economic actors perceive that those with whom they are dealing are trustworthy, they tend to reciprocate that trust. The effectiveness of COMMUNICATION between economic actors is frequently a factor in determining the level of trust that exists between them. Another factor associated with the existence of, or reliance on, trust between economic actors is cooperation. The results of research exploring associations between trust and cooperation suggest that preexisting cooperation may be required if trust is to develop; other findings suggest that cooperation is an outcome of preexisting trust between economic actors (Gambetta, 1988).

Trust appears to flow from a variety of sources. When economic actors share important VALUES and norms trust seems more likely. Trust may also result from, or be supported by, institutional sources such as law (Luhmann, 1979). Finally, the processes that economic actors employ in their dealings can be a source of trust (Ring & Van de Ven, 1992).

Results of research suggest that trust evolves slowly, from on-going social or economic exchanges between parties. Two possible explanations for the emergence of trust can be found in the ORGANIZATIONAL BEHAVIOR literature. The first is based on the norms of equity which define the degree to which one party judges that another party will fulfill its commitments and that the relationship is equitable (*see* EQUITY THEORY). The concept of equity is developed in exchange theory, which argues that participants in a relationship desire:

(1) reciprocity, by which one is morally obligated to give something in return for something received;
(2) fair rates of exchange between utilitarian costs and benefits; and
(3) distributive justice, through which all parties receive benefits that are proportional to their investments (*see* DISTRIBUTIVE JUSTICE).

Alternatively, the emergence of trust can be based on more direct utilitarian reasoning. First, there are many nonlegal sanctions which make it expedient for individuals and organizations to fulfill commitments. Repeated personal interactions across firms encourages some minimum level of courtesy and consideration, and the prospect of ostracism among peers attenuate individual opportunism. At the organizational level, the prospect of repeat business discourages attempts to seek a narrow, short-term advantage.

Trust is also an individual attribute. Here the focus of the research is on individual characteristics associated with being perceived as trustworthy. Among those characteristics employed most frequently in survey instruments are items measuring the COMPETENCIES of the individual (technical SKILLS, levels of knowledge); the ability to keep confidences; fairness; integrity (honesty, moral character); loyalty; sincerity; openness; reliability; empathy; patience; stamina; self-assurance; and ingenuity (Sitkin & Roth, 1993).

Individuals evidencing high levels of trust seem less likely to lie, cheat, or steal. It also appears that they are more inclined to give others a second chance and to generally respect the rights of others. In so doing, they do not appear to be any more gullible than individuals who are classified as low trusters. Low trusters in situations involving economic exchange can be characterized as having a short-term focus, seek monetarized returns, and require a great deal of specificity in defining the terms of exchange. When "problems" arise, low trusters will attribute them to the bad faith of their partners, or to negligence. They will seek to resolve these "problems" by resort to coerced bargaining. Low trusters tend to play a "zero-sum" game (*see* GAME THEORY). High trusters, on the other hand, engage in economic exchange that is interwoven with social exchange. Their perspectives are longer term in nature, they accept "problems" are part of economic life, and they seek integrative solutions: those involving so-called "win–win" outcomes. These kinds of relational trust behaviors tend to spiral upward if reciprocated; downward if not (Husted, 1989).

see also **Interorganizational relations; Industrial relations; Negotiation; Conflict; Business ethics**

Bibliography

Anderson, E. & Weitz, B. (1989). Determinants of continuity in conventional industrial channel dyads. Marketing Science, 8, 310–323.

Baier, A. (1986). Trust and antitrust Ethics, 96, 231–260.

Barber, B. (1983). The logic and limits of trust. New Brunswick: NJ: Rutgers University.

Bhide, A. & Stevenson, H. (1992). Trust, uncertainty, and profits. Journal of Socio-Economics, 21, 91–208.

Butler, J. K. (1991). Toward understanding and measuring conditions of trust: Evolution of a conditions of trust inventory. Journal of Management, 17, 643–663.

Fox, A. (1974). Beyond contract: Work, power and trust relations. London: Faber & Faber.

Gambetta, D. (Ed.), (1988). Trust: Making and breaking cooperative relations. London: Basil Blackwell.

Husted, B. W. (1989). Trust in business relations: Directions for empirical research. Business and Professional Ethics Journal, 8, 23–40.

Luhmann, N. (1979). Trust and power. New York: Wiley.

Moorman, C., Zaltman, G. & Deshpande, R. (1992). Relationships between providers and users of market research: The dynamics of trust within and between organizations. Journal of Marketing Research, 29, 314–328.

Ring, P. S. & Van de Ven (1992). Structuring cooperative relationships between organizations. Strategies Management Journal, 3, 483–498.

Shapiro, S. P. (1987). The social control of interpersonal trust. American Journal of Sociology, 93, 623–658.

Sitkin, S. & Roth, N. L. (1993). Explaining the limited effectiveness of legalistic remedies for trust/distrust. Organization Science, 4, 367–392.

Zucker, L. G. (1986). Production of trust: Institutional sources of economic structure, 1984–1990. In B. M. Staw & L. L. Cummings (Eds), Research in organizational behavior, (vol. 8, pp. 53–122). Greenwich, CT: JAI Press.

PETER SMITH RING

turnaround strategy Turnaround strategies can be applied when a business is in decline but is worth saving. It is important to recognize the conditions under which an otherwise successful business may go into decline. Such recognition can suggest the appropriate solutions which might aid recovery.

Causative Factors

A number of factors have been identified as leading to decline.

1. Poor management. The personal characteristics of the chief executive and key management play a major role in causing decline. Apart from incompetence, the principal factors identified as poor management reasons for decline include the following:

- *One man rule*. This is acceptable while the company is successful, but rapid decline ensues when the leadership is seen to fail.
- *Combined chairman and chief executive role*. In this case there is no counterbalance over the activities of the CEO.
- *Ineffective boards of directors*. The board constitution is important. All too often, nonexecutive directors do not know enough about a business and/or do not participate. In addition, executive directors may be ineffective or only participate when topics specifically affect their area of interest.
- *Management neglect of core businesses*. This occurs especially when the core business matures and top management time becomes diverted by attempts at diversification.
- *Lack of management depth*. This may well occur in newly diversifying concerns, where traditional skills have tended to be functional and the firm lacks general management or succession skills.

2. Inadequate financial control. Apart from poor management, lack of adequate financial control is the most common characteristic of declining firms. Such a lack of control comes about because the control systems lack one or more of adequate cashflow forecasts, costing systems, and budgetary controls. In smaller firms all three items may be missing and only statutory financial information is prepared. In larger firms the problem is more likely to be due to inadequate systems. Four common problems have been identified:

- *Many management accounting systems have been poorly designed*. Often, control systems are too complex, produce poorly presented information, and may even produce the wrong information. The blame for this lies with top management but, regrettably, many may not understand the information that they really need, nor what can be provided by the information systems in place.
- *Management accounting information is poorly used*. Many senior managers do not understand how to use accounting information, actually running the business on heuristics or "rules of thumb."
- *The organizational structure hinders effective control*. In many corporations, centralization has been identified as a causal factor in decline and, in addition, the hierarchical level at which control is located may well be too high.
- *Methods of overhead allocation distort the costs*. Correct overhead cost allocation is not undertaken by many companies. Activity-based costing is a modern tool which tries to improve this problem.

3. Competition. Both price and product competition are seen as common causes of corporate decline: usually they occur together.

- *Product competition*. Firms which fail to revitalize their product offerings in response to changing market needs and competition ultimately end up in decline. Other problems are due to poor product introduction strategies; to mistaken beliefs about the viability of the old product; to a lack of financial and technological resources to pursue the introduction of new products; and to a failure to develop new product ideas.

- *Price competition.* Severe price competition is a common cause of decline in Western corporations, especially in those sectors targeted by Japanese and other Asian competitors. While the problem is especially acute in undifferentiated product markets, it has also occurred in areas in which product differentiation is important, such as automobiles and consumer electronics.

4. High cost structure. Firms with a substantially higher cost structure than major competitors usually experience a seriously competitive disadvantage. Six major sources of cost disadvantage have been identified. These are as follows:

- *Relative cost disadvantages.* There are two such disadvantages. First, there are those associated with experience effects (*see* EXPERIENCE AND LEARNING EFFECTS), while the second is due to ECONOMIES OF SCALE.
- *Absolute cost disadvantages.* These may be due to a number of factors, such as competitive cost disadvantage due to ownership or control of critical raw materials or components by competitors; access to cheaper labor; proprietary production know-how; and favorable site location.
- *Cost disadvantages due to diversification strategy.* Diversified firms may experience a cost disadvantage due to the allocation of corporate overheads. This can occur especially in industries with shared costs, where overheads are allocated in an arbitrary fashion without an activity-based costing system.
- *Cost disadvantage due to management style and organizational structure.* Some organizations deliberately lower costs by improving productivity, reducing labor costs via OUTSOURCING, reducing central staff overheads, and the like. Those concerns that do not so reduce overheads may suffer serious cost disadvantages.
- *Operating inefficiencies.* Such inefficiencies are usually the result of poor management and can occur in any function of the business.
- *Unfavorable government policies.* Some businesses may be placed at a disadvantage as a result of direct and/or indirect government policies, such as subsidies, tax differentials, exchange rates, preferential procurement, environmental controls, social policies, and the like.

5. Changes in market demand. An important causal factor in decline can be a reduction in demand or a change in the pattern of demand, to which the firm fails to respond or simply cannot respond. A drop in demand can be due to market obsolescence, such as buggy whips and gas lamps; cyclical demand, such as recession, which may cause serious but probably temporary decline; and seasonal decline, such as for ice cream in winter. This is not usually fatal unless the firm is in a weak financial condition. Failures to monitor secular decline trends regrettably often occur because the firm does not really want to see and acknowledge that this is happening, because of the resulting change in strategic behavior and the adjustment it may

entail. Cyclical decline failures are often the result of price wars in which competitors attempt to grow or maintain market share. Insurance is a classic example of an industry with such a pattern.

6. Adverse movements in commodity prices. Major changes in commodity prices which can occur suddenly have been responsible for many business failures. Examples include changes in the price of oil, as in the case of the first and second oil-price shocks; rapid changes in the prices of metals such as copper, aluminum, and steel; and significant movements in exchange rates, as with the rapid appreciation of the yen in the late 1980s, and again in the mid-1990s.

7. Lack of marketing effort. While most firms suffering serious decline have managerial problems throughout their organizations, the problem is often especially acute in the sales and marketing functions. Such problems occur as a result of:

- a poorly motivated sales force and weak sales force management
- ineffective and wasted advertising
- efforts not targeted on key customers and products
- poor after-sales service
- poor product quality
- lack of research/knowledge of customer buying habits
- loss of access to distribution channels
- weak or nonexistent new product development
- lack of marketing orientation

8. Large projects. Large projects that go wrong because costs were underestimated and/or revenues overestimated are a common cause of failure. There are a number of ways in which such projects can go wrong:

- *Underestimates of capital requirements.* These may arise because of: poor cost estimates at the project planning stage; poor project control; late design changes; and external factors such as strikes, bad weather, technical delays, and late delivery of equipment. Civil engineering and defense projects, such as the Channel Tunnel and the Eurofighter, regularly seem to be examples of such failures. However, the real losers may be banks, shareholders, and taxpayers.
- *Start-up difficulties.* Even after completion, projects may experience a variety of start-up problems which increase expense above forecasted levels. Technical problems with plant and equipment can lead to high wastage, significant downtime and losses in customer confidence and volume. For example, introductory problems with Eurostar trains thus compounded the problems of the Eurotunnel.
- *Capacity expansion.* This problem occurs especially in process industries such as oil and chemicals, when competitors all add capacity at the same time, resulting in overcapacity, price wars, and losses when each endeavors to maximize capacity utilization.
- *Market entry costs.* Problems may occur with the entry of new products, both to existing markets and, especially, to new markets. Each results in different risks, but DIVERSIFICATION carries particular risk.

- *Major contracts*. Poor cost estimating and pricing on major contracts are also a common cause of failure, especially in the construction and capital goods industries.

9. Acquisitions. Acquisitions play a major role in corporate strategy, especially for firms attempting to diversify. However, most acquisitions are considered to be failures. Three aspects of ACQUISITION STRATEGY have been identified as causes of decline for the acquiring company:

- the acquisition of losers – firms with weak competitive positions in their own markets
- paying an unjustifiably high purchase price for the acquired firm
- poor post-acquisition management and control

10. Financial policy. There are at least three direct causes of failure due to financial policy:

- *High debt : equity ratio*. Financial structures which contain moderate debt are perfectly rational, although the level of debt depends to some extent on the industry structure. In acquisition situations in recent years, high debt levels have often been incurred by the use of junk bonds and mezzanine subordinated debt, which has proved a serious problem for companies using these instruments during recession and periods of rising interest rates.
- *Conservative financial policies*. When a firm is characterized by a lack of reinvestment, a high dividend payout ratio, high liquidity, and low gearing, this conservative financial strategy effectively ends up by liquidating the firm and turning it into an acquisition target.
- *Inappropriate financing sources*. While some borrowing term mismatches are acceptable, this can be taken too far, as with the secondary banking crises of the 1970s and over-investment in commercial property in the late 1980s and early 1990s.

11. Overtrading. Overtrading occurs when a company's sales grow too rapidly, such that cashflow becomes inadequate to finance operations. The phenomenon can occur quickly when financial controls are inadequate to accurately identify the possibility of a decline situation. The problem is an important cause of failure in very high growth firms, in which the increased scale and complexity of such a business can rapidly outstrip its control systems.

The Symptoms of Decline

The symptoms of decline are often easier to identify than the causes. The most common symptoms include the following:

- decreasing profitability, as measured by declining profits before tax and interest, and reduced ROI, ROE, and ROS
- declining sales volumes, and in particular sales per employee, sales per square foot, and the like at constant prices
- increased debt
- declining liquidity, measured by falls in current test and acid test ratios, plus rising stocks and debtors as a percentage of sales
- reduced dividends and dividend cover

- accounting practices which delay publishing accounts and auditors' qualification of accounts
- rapid turnover of management
- a decline in market share
- a lack of strategic thinking by top management
- an unsatisfactory Z-score and trend

Successful Recovery Strategies

A number of generic successful turnaround strategies have been identified. It is common that a number of these will be deployed at the same time. They include the following:

- *Change of management*. This usually involves a change of CEO or chairman, or both, to provide a new vision for the corporation and to inspire confidence in shareholders and bankers.
- *Strong financial control*. This is essential for successful turnaround. All cash needs to be centralized initially, and every effort should be made to improve cashflow to reduce debt, including possible asset disposals.
- *Organizational change and decentralization*. This is not a short-term turnaround policy, but might be expected once new top management has been installed and often involves DOWNSIZING. Decentralization should also not occur until adequate financial controls are in place.
- *New product market focus*. This may well include: addition or deletion of product lines; addition or deletion of customers according to profitability potential; changes in the sales mix by focusing on specific products and customers; complete withdrawal from unattractive segments; and entry into new product market segments.
- *Improved marketing*. This is usually essential, as declining businesses tend to be weak in marketing.
- *Growth via acquisition*. This does not necessarily mean diversification, but the purchase of firms in the same industry, or in closely related industries. This alternative may not be open to firms in serious financial crisis.
- *Asset reduction*. This is usually an integral part of any turnaround strategy. In the short term, strict cash control and reduction in working capital assets are priorities, and in the medium term fixed asset disposals and sales of whole businesses may well be necessary.
- *Cost reduction strategies*. These are designed to increase product profitability and cashflow.
- *Investment strategies*. These should involve moves to reduce costs by asset reduction or by promoting growth.
- *Debt restructuring*. Frequently, financial problems may require restructuring any outstanding debt and reaching acceptable revised terms with lenders, or raising additional equity.

The precise management actions required for a successful turnaround will depend on the position of the firm. The combination of the above generic strategies will therefore be a function of the following factors:

- the causes of decline
- the severity of the crisis
- the attitudes of the stakeholders involved in the turnaround process
- the firm's historic strategy
- the characteristics of the industry or industries in which the firm competes

● the firm's cost–price structure

Bibliography

Argenti, J. (1976). *Corporate collapse: the causes and symptoms*. New York: McGraw-Hill.

Grinyer, P. & Spender, J. C. (1979). *Turnaround: managerial recipes for strategic success*. London: Associated Business Publications.

Hofer, C. W. & Schendel, D. (1978). *Strategy formulation: analytical concepts*. St. Paul, MN: West Publishing. See pp. 172–4.

Slatter, S. (1984). *Corporate recovery*. Harmondsworth, UK: Penguin. Very good: this entry was heavily influenced by this work.

DEREK F. CHANNON

two step flow model   The two step flow model is concerned with the flow of MARKETING COMMUNICATIONS from the MASS MEDIA, in particular ADVERTISING, via OPINION LEADERS to customers, or opinion "followers." Opinion leaders are portrayed as direct receivers of information from impersonal mass media sources, and they interpret, legitimize, and transmit this information to customers, i.e., they are middlemen.

This theory assumes that mass media influence on mass opinion is not direct, i.e., that the mass media alone cannot influence the sales of products; that mass media communications are mediated by opinion leaders; that opinion leaders are more exposed to mass media than those they influence; and that opinion leaders may alter communications messages (i.e., they are GATEKEEPERS).

However, this is not an accurate portrayal of the flow of information and influence. Modifications to the theory accept that: mass media and interpersonal channels of communications are complementary not competitive, i.e., that mass media may inform both opinion leaders and followers; and opinion leadership is not a dichotomous trait, i.e., that INTERPERSONAL COMMUNICATIONS can be initiated by both leaders and followers, e.g., receivers are not passive and may request information/advice from opinion leaders, or seek it directly from the mass media.

see also **Interpersonal communications; Opinion leaders**

Bibliography

Lazarsfeld, P. F., Berelson, B. & Goudet, H. (1948). *The people's choice*, 2nd edn, New York: Columbia Press.

Schiffman, L. G. & Kanuk, L. L. (1991). *Consumer behavior*, 4th edn, Prentice-Hall, p. 502.

BARBARA LEWIS

two-tiered pay structures   Under two-tiered pay structures, employees hired after a specified date, usually the effective date of the collective bargaining contract when tiers were first negotiated, are placed on lower pay scales than those hired previously. Tiers can be either *temporary*, where the pay of the low-tier employees gradually increases until it equals that of the higher tier, or *permanent*, where low-tier employees never reach the high-tier pay scales unless the contract is changed. Equity theory predictions that low-tier employees will exhibit poorer job attitudes than high-tier employees have been supported for permanent tiers (McFarlin and Frone, 1990; Martin, 1990), but not temporary tiers (Cappelli and Sherer, 1990).

Bibliography

Cappelli, P. & Sherer, P. D. (1990). Assessing worker attitudes under a two-tier wage plan. *Industrial and Labor Relations Review*, 43, 225–44.

McFarlin, D. B. & Frone, M. R. (1990). A two-tier wage structure in a nonunion firm. *Industrial Relations*, 29, 145–54

Martin, J. E. (1990). *Two-tier Compensation Structures*, Kalamazoo, MI: W E Upjohn Institute for Employment Research.

JAMES E. MARTIN

U

uncertainty This is a key concept in relation to a number of organizational areas. From an OPEN SYSTEM perspective, the environment is a key source of uncertainty since all organizations need to interact with, and are in some measure dependent on, their environments (*see* ORGANIZATION AND ENVIRONMENT). The more turbulent and complex the environment, the more difficult it is for organizations to control and predict events.

Thompson (1967) has suggested that the technical core of an organization (the transformational or production process) needs to be "buffered" from uncertainty. "Boundary-spanning" departments can perform this function, helping to shield the heart of the organization from damaging shocks and providing a measure of stability and continuity. In recent years, the trend has been for some companies to adopt just-in-time techniques and flexible working practices as alternative ways of coping with the uncertainty of the competitive environment.

Contingency theory suggests a number of ways in which the organization can cope with environmental uncertainty, particularly by altering its structural arrangements. To be successful, firms need to adapt to uncertainty by adopting appropriate mechanisms of differentiation and integration.

Technology also plays a part in influencing how uncertainty can be managed. The more uncertainty there is in the nature of the work (task uncertainty), the better information-processing must be.

Control over uncertainty can be a source of POWER. Hickson, Hinings, Lee, Schneck & Pennings (1971) put forward their "strategic contingencies theory," suggesting that *coping* with uncertainty is an important way of securing power for subunits in the organization, especially if the uncertainty affects a critical and central part of the organization's functioning.

Uncertainty is a key problem in DECISION MAKING as assumptions have to be made about the future, which is inherently uncertain. This is one reason why bounded rationality often prevails. "Uncertainty absorption" is also a factor. This is where information loses its uncertainty as it is passed through the organization – gradually appearing to be more precise and reliable than it actually is.

"Uncertainty avoidance" is one of the concepts used by Hofstede (1980) in his examination of national cultures (*see* NATIONAL CULTURE). It is used to denote the degree to which different cultures cope with novelty, either accepting the attendant uncertainty or seeking to reduce it.

The concept of uncertainty has a long history in the study of organizations as well as a number of particular meanings in specialist areas. Given that most organizations and individuals are faced with uncertainty, the pressure to understand its nature and origins, and the need to develop coping mechanisms is still of great current interest.

see also **Organizational effectiveness**

Bibliography

Hickson, D. J., Hinings, C. R., Lee, C. A., Schneck R. E. & Pennings, J. M. (1971). A strategic contingencies theory of intraorganizational power. Administrative Science Quarterly, **16**, (2), 216–229.
Hofstede, G. (1980). Culture's consequences: International differences in work-related values. Beverly Hills, CA: Sage.
Thompson, J. D. (1967). Organizations in action. New York: McGraw-Hill.

SUSAN MILLER

uncertainty (economics) Frank Knight (1971) emphasized the distinction between risk and uncertainty. He defined risk as measurable or quantifiable, such as when a life assurance firm calculates the probabilities of paying benefits to survivors. The term "risk" applies to known probabilities and outcomes. However, in many business situations, managers cannot reasonably calculate probabilities and may not know the possible outcomes in the future. In these cases, where risk cannot be quantified, Knight argued there is uncertainty. Situations involving uncertainty as defined by Knight are much more difficult for decision making and this is why profits are awarded to business people: as a reward and a return for significant risk bearing.

Bibliography

Douglas, E. J. (1992). *Managerial Economics*. 4th edn, Englewood Cliffs, NJ: Prentice-Hall.
Knight, F. H. (1971). *Risk, Uncertainty and Profit*. Chicago: The University of Chicago Press.

ROBERT E. MCAULIFFE

unfair trade This term describes transactions which involve goods being "dumped" on foreign markets, black-market goods, copied or otherwise counterfeited goods, or goods that are subsidized beyond normally acceptable levels. Countries that participate in unfair trade practices are subject to retaliatory measures by those countries which are treated unfairly.

see also **Intellectual property**

Bibliography

Viner, J. (1991). *Dumping: A problem in international trade*. Caldwell, NJ: Augustus M. Kelley Publishers.

JOHN O'CONNELL

union avoidance It is a well observed and recorded fact that managers generally prefer to work without the presence of unions in the workplace. Explanations offered for such managerial preference range from ideological opposition to managerial need for control for reasons of efficiency (Kochan et al., 1986). Bendix (1956, p. 444), in his seminal work on ideology in the workplace, argued that "ideologies of management can be explained only in part as rationalizations of self-interest; they also result from the legacy of institutions and ideas."

Thus, managers generally avoid unions to the best of their ability within the constraints of legal and political institutions. Three forms of union avoidance can be articulated based on historical experience.

Direct Opposition

For many organizations, the best way to avoid unions is to ensure that one is never formed. In the first half of the twentieth century, such avoidance frequently meant intimidation, coercion, dismissal, and on occasion, the use and/or threat of violence to deter employees from joining unions (Rayback, 1959).

Although many of those tactics are illegal in most countries, including Canada and the USA, the incidence of dismissal of union activists remains high (Freeman and Medoff, 1984; Cooke, 1985; ICFTU, 1994). In many parts of the USA and Canada, employers can also oppose union drives during a campaign that precedes the vote by employees. Some forms of employer intervention (such as free speech) during a campaign are legal in the USA. Although there is always a chance that employer opposition could backfire, i.e. workers alienated by employer behavior could punish the employer by voting for the union, there is considerable evidence that employer opposition is effective in preventing employees from voting for a union (Lawler and West, 1985; Lawler, 1990). A substantial consulting industry specializing in union avoidance know-how has taken root in the USA (Kilgur, 1978; Sullivan, 1978; Hughes, 1990; Bureau of National Affairs, 1995).

Union Substitution

Another union avoidance response is for managers to offer employees all those services that a union would normally provide: protection from arbitrary treatment, access to a grievance process, more say in workplace decisions, better communication, good wages and benefits, and so forth. Though nonunion companies did not provide these benefits to their employees traditionally, by the 1960s a growing number of firms began to adopt such policies and thus were able to sustain their nonunion status despite attempts to organize them (Foulkes, 1980). Notable among these firms were IBM, Polaroid, Eastman Kodak, and Hewlett-Packard. Empirical evidence supports the notion that such policies reduce the chances of unionization (Fiorito et al., 1987).

Disinvestment in Unionized Operations

Yet another route to union avoidance for unionized firms is to disinvest in unionized operations and to channel new investments into new plants that are nonunion. The disinvestment may be gradual over several years, or it may be sudden in the form of relocation, closure, or sale of a unionized facility. It is generally very difficult to find direct empirical evidence for such actions because investment decisions are made for many reasons. Compounded within each investment decision are reasons (proximity to markets, technology, labor costs, raw materials, and so forth) which are difficult to separate from the desire to avoid unions. A few studies have provided limited evidence of such disinvestment behavior (Verma, 1985; Kochan et al., 1986).

Union avoidance strategies of employers have been successful in the USA, where managers enjoy greater freedom to oppose unions than in most other industrialized nations. While union densities have fallen in most industrialized nations since 1980 (Galenson, 1994), the drop in the USA from 30 percent in 1965 to 15.5 percent in 1994 is one the most precipitous (Troy and Sheflin, 1985; Hirsch and Macpherson, 1995). It has been argued that union avoidance has played a major role in this decline (Freeman and Medoff, 1984; Presidential Commission on the Future of Labor–Management Relations, 1995).

A key related issue is the role of public policy, given what we know about union avoidance. Workers in most countries of the world today enjoy the legal right of association. If the employer's instincts are to oppose collective activity by employees, what role can public policy play to ensure that workers are able to exercise their legal right to join a union of their choice?

Bibliography

Bendix, R. (1956). *Work and Authority in Industry*, Berkeley, CA: University of California Press.

Bureau of National Affairs (1995). *Labor Relations Consultants: Issues, Trends and Controversies*, Washington, DC: Bureau of National Affairs Special Reports.

Cooke, W. N. (1985). The rising tool of discrimination against union activities. *Industrial Relations*, 24, 421–42.

Fiorito, J., Lowman, C. & Nelson, F. D. (1987). The impact of human resource policies on union organizing. *Industrial Relations*, 26, 113–26.

Foulkes, F. K. (1980). *Personnel Policies in Large Nonunion Companies*, Englewood Cliffs, NJ: Prentice-Hall.

Freeman, R. B. & Medoff, J. L. (1984). *What Do Unions Do?*, New York: Basic Books.

Galenson, W. (1994). *Trade Union Growth and Decline: an International Study*, Westport, CN: Praeger.

Hirsch B. T. & Macpherson, D. A. (1995). *Union Membership and Earnings Databook*, Washington, DC: Bureau of National Affairs.

Hughes, C. L. (1990). *Making Unions Unnecessary*, New York: Executive Enterprises.

ICFTU (International Confederation of Free Trade Unions) (1994). *Annual Survey of Violations of Trade Union Rights*, Brussels: ICFTU.

Kilgur, J. G. (1978). Before the union knocks. *Personnel Journal*, 57, 186–92.

Kochan, T. A., Katz, H. C. & McKerzie, R. B. (1986). *The Transformation of American Industrial Relations*, New York: Basic Books.

Lawler, J. J. (1990). *Unionization and Deunionization: Strategy, Tactics and Outcomes*, Columbia, SC: University of South Carolina Press.

Lawler, J. J. & West, R. (1985). Impact of union avoidance: strategies on representation elections. *Industrial Relations*, 24, 406–20.

Presidential Commission on the Future of Labor–Management Relations (1995). *Report and Recommendations*, Washington, DC: US Department of Labor.

Rayback, J. G. (1959). A History of American Labor. New York: Free Press.

Sullivan, F. L. (1978). Limiting union organizing activity through supervisors. *Personnel*, 55, 55–64.

Troy, L. & Sheflin, L. (1985). *US Union Sourcebook: Membership, Finances, Structure Directory*, West Orange, NJ: Industrial Relations Data and Information Sources.

Verma, A. (1985). Relative flow of capital to union and nonunion plants within a firm. *Industrial Relations*, 24, 395–405.

ANIL VERMA

union commitment   Union commitment can be generally defined as an attitudinal concept reflecting the extent to which workers identify with, or are attached to, the goals and values of the union in which they are a member.

Union commitment represents the application of more general organizational commitment concepts to specific situations involving labor unions. The dimensionality and measurement of union commitment has been subject to considerable debate. However, Gordon et al. (1980) have suggested that union commitment is composed of four underlying factors: (a) loyalty to the union, representing a sense of pride in union membership and a desire to remain a member; (b) responsibility to the union, focusing upon the member's willingness to fulfill obligations pertaining to the protection of union interests; (c) willingness to work for the union, reflecting a readiness to do special work on behalf of the union; and (d) belief in unionism, showing the member's ideological belief in the concept of unionism. Alternative definitions or measures suggest that union commitment represents both pro-union attitudes and the intent to engage in activities to support the union.

Union commitment has been identified by many researchers as an important predictor of actual membership participation in union activities (meeting attendance, political action, PICKETING, and so forth). In addition, considerable evidence suggests that union commitment is influenced by a worker's background experiences (e.g. parents' attitudes toward unions) and the degree to which a worker views the union as providing favorable treatment and outcomes for the union membership.

Bibliography
Barling, J., Fullagar, C. & Kelloway, E. K. (1992). *The Union and Its Members: a Psychological Approach*, Oxford: Oxford University Press.
Gallagher, D. G. & Clark, P. F. (1989). Research on union commitment: implications for labor. *Labor Studies Journal*, **14**, 52–71.
Gordon. M. E., Philpot, J. W., Burt, R. E., Thompson, C. A. & Spiller, W. E. (1980). Commitment to the union: development of a measure and examination of its correlates. *Journal of Applied Psychology*, **65**, 479–99.

DANIEL G. GALLAGHER

union effects on pay   The primary question addressed in union pay research is the degree to which a union worker earns more than he or she would earn in a nonunion environment. Researchers examine this question through studies of union and nonunion workers with similar demographic characteristics, similar union and nonunion establishments, and workers who move in and out of union membership across time. Lewis (1963, 1986) carefully analyzed over one hundred union wage studies and estimated that the union wage gap approximately ranged from 10 to 15 percent. Others have drawn similar conclusions (Hirsch and Addison, 1986). These estimates vary across time and labor market conditions. For example, Lewis (1986) found that union gap estimates had reached as high as 19 to 20 percent in the late 1970s and as low as 12 percent in the late 1960s.

The wage gap estimate also varies by demographic group because unions negotiate standard rate policies that do not allow management to pay workers on an individual basis (Freeman and Medoff, 1984). Standard rate pay results in raising the pay of workers who would otherwise receive lower pay. Thus, unions tend to increase younger workers' pay relative to older workers and blue-collar relative to white-collar workers' pay. However, analysis of numerous studies indicates ambiguous wage gap findings by race and sex (Lewis, 1986).

In summary, union pay research clearly shows that unions raise wages, but the amount they raise wages varies across time. This research also indicates that unions raise wages more for groups of workers who would otherwise receive lower pay.

Bibliography
Freeman, R. B. & Medoff, J. L. (1984). *What Do Unions Do?*, New York: Basic Books.
Hirsch, B. T. & Addison, J. T. (1986). *The Economic Analysis of Unions: New Approaches and Evidence*, London: Allen & Unwin.
Lewis, H. G. (1963). *Unionism and Relative Wages in the United States*, Chicago: University of Chicago Press.
Lewis, H. G. (1986). *Union Relative Wage Effects*, Chicago: University of Chicago Press.

NANCY BROWN JOHNSON

union representation procedures   Representation procedures are defined as those procedures used by the NATIONAL LABOR RELATIONS BOARD (NLRB) in the United States to determine the interest of employees in being represented by a union or employee association for the purpose of collective bargaining with their employer over wages, hours, and working conditions. These procedures are used as part of the representation election process. Many state labor relations agencies use a similar process for determining the interest of public and private sector employees in having union representation.

There are three ways in which employee representation may be determined. First, the NLRB may issue a directive where there is a deadlock between the union and employer. Second, the employer may voluntarily recognize the union or employee association based on evidence that the majority of employees in a defined BARGAINING UNIT wish union representation. This determination may be based on valid signed authorization cards. Finally, the NLRB may run a secret ballot election where the parties agree to: the proposed bargaining unit jurisdiction; eligibility to vote; and time, place, and rules for voting. This is called a consent election (Feldacker, 1990; Holley and Jennings, 1994).

In order for an election to take place, the union must show the local NLRB staff that at least 30 percent of the employees who would fall under the bargaining unit jurisdiction have signed a petition for such an election. In reality, few unions will request an election unless they have signatures from 50 to 70 percent of those employees who would fall into the proposed bargaining unit.

Bibliography
Feldacker, B. (1990). *Labor Guide to Labor Law*, 3rd edn, Englewood Cliffs, NJ: Prentice-Hall.
Holley, W. H. Jr & Jennings, K. M. (1994). *The Labor Relations Process*, 5th edn, Fort Worth, TX: Dryden Press.

RICHARD B. PETERSON

union shop   A union shop is a negotiated union security clause of a labor agreement, which is legal in states not covered by RIGHT TO WORK state laws. A negotiated union shop provision requires that all new employees become union members (or, at least, pay union dues) after at least 30 days after being employed (as provided by the Labor Management Relations Act of 1947). Under most union shop agreements employees may not later rescind their dues obligation.

JOHN C. SHEARER

union unfair labor practices Sections 8(b)(1) through 8(b)(7) of the National Labor Relations Act (Taft–Hartley Act of 1947) contain a number of complex union unfair labor practices. Section 8(b)(1) makes it illegal for a labor organization (union) to restrain or coerce employees and employers with regard to their selection or recognition of a bargaining representative. Section 8(b)(2) prevents a union from forcing an employer to discriminate against an employee in order to influence the employee's union membership. Section 8(b)(3) requires a union to bargain in good faith with an employer. The most complex set of union unfair labor practices are contained in section 8(b)(4). This section places restrictions on hot-cargo agreements (a firm agrees not to handle products produced by another firm), SECONDARY BOYCOTTS (forcing a neutral or secondary employer to become involved in a strike or other labor dispute), union organizing efforts in situations where another union has already been recognized as the employees' exclusive bargaining representative, and strikes over jurisdictional disputes (e.g. disputes in the construction industry over which union is entitled to perform specific work). Section 8(b)(5) forbids unions from charging excessive or discriminatory fees and dues to its members. Section 8(b)(6) prohibits the practice of featherbedding (a union forces an employer to pay workers for work that they did not perform). Section 8(b)(7) regulates organizational and recognition picketing by unions. Unions cannot, for example, engage in organizational picketing to encourage a group of employees to sign authorization cards within 12 months after these employees have been subjected to a valid NATIONAL LABOR RELATIONS BOARD representation election (Norris and Shershin, 1992; Mann, 1994).

Bibliography
Leap, T. L. (1995). *Collective Bargaining and Labor Relations*, **2nd edn**, Englewood Cliffs, NJ: Prentice-Hall.
Norris, J. A. & Shershin, M. J. Jr (1992). *How to Take a Case Before the NLRB*, **6th edn**, Washington, DC: Bureau of National Affairs.

TERRY L. LEAP

union voice Union voice refers to the mechanisms through which unions provide members with opportunities to communicate their collective concerns to management. Union voice mechanisms include COLLECTIVE BARGAINING and contract administration, particularly GRIEVANCE PROCEDURES.

How Voice Differs from Exit
Workers have two basic options for expressing dissatisfaction. First, employees may leave the firm. Exit provides employers with information about the preferences of marginal employees – those most willing and able to leave the organization. If enough workers quit, employers will alter their policies in an effort to reduce turnover. Second, employees may communicate their concerns

directly to management. Voice may be expressed on an individual or collective basis. Individual voice tends to be idiosyncratic, but through collective voice employers can learn about the preferences of their average employee. Research suggests that there are differences in the terms and conditions of employment offered by firms that rely on union (i.e. collective) voice and those that rely on exit as the principal means for learning about worker preferences.

Views on Union Voice
The literature offers two views on union voice. One view holds that union voice can reduce turnover, facilitate worker acquisition of firm-specific skills, and provide a source of productivity-enhancing suggestions. The other view argues that employers have other mechanisms to systematically learn about worker preferences and that any advantages are more than offset by the greater labor–management conflict and stifling of individual initiative that accompany union voice. Evidence exists to support both views (*see* UNIONISM EFFECTS).

Bibliography
Freeman, R. B. & Medoff, J. L. (1984). *What Do Unions Do?*, New York: Basic Books.
Hirsch, B. T. & Addison, J. T. (1986). *The Economic Analysis of Unions: New Approaches and Evidence*, Boston: Allen & Irwin.

PAUL JARLEY

unionism effects Unionism effects describe the changes that workers, employers, and society experience resulting from labor unions negotiating collective bargaining agreements as opposed to employers unilaterally determining the terms and conditions of employment.

Union Effects on Workers
Historically, business unions have primarily focused on improving the wages, hours, and working conditions of their members through COLLECTIVE BARGAINING. Thus, traditional union effect research has focused on whether unions have achieved these goals. Studies of UNION EFFECTS ON PAY have found that unions raise the wages of their members around 10 to 15 percent. Additionally, research indicates that unions increase their members' fringe benefit levels over nonunion members by even more than their wage effect (Freeman and Medoff, 1984). Thus, most evidence strongly suggests that unions successfully achieve their objective of increasing their members' compensation.

Despite the evidence that unions increase members' pay, a number of studies find that union coverage correlates with *decreased* job satisfaction and turnover. Because a large body of research typically finds that job satisfaction and turnover relate inversely, this research has attracted attention. Exit-voice theory (Hirschman, 1970) provides one explanation of this apparent contradiction by arguing that union grievance systems protect employees who voice discontent, and therefore serve to mobilize coworkers' discontent (Freeman and Medoff, 1984). A second theory argues that because unions affect job outcomes they also affect the importance of outcomes to the union members. Research drawing on this theoretical perspective has found that unions increase satisfaction with pay and this increased satisfaction offsets the decreased satisfaction with supervision and work itself (Berger et al., 1983). However, a recent study used a different sample than prior research and did not find evidence of decreased job satisfaction among union members. These researchers argue that the positive relationship between job satisfaction and turnover in union settings does not exist and the results of prior research resulted from statistical artefacts (Gordon and DeNisi, 1995).

Union Effects on Firms

Although unions affect firms in various ways, their productivity and profitability effects have received a great deal of attention. Controversy surrounds the union effect on productivity, in part because a number of offsetting influences exist. First, unions negotiate higher wages, potentially reducing employment. To enhance employment opportunities and to protect their members, unions negotiate work-rule provisions such as rigid job descriptions and job requirements that hinder productivity. However, unions also enhance productivity by changing managerial practices and reducing turnover through enhanced employee voice and seniority provisions. In more recent years, some unions have begun working jointly with management to enhance productivity. Because of the offsetting influences, however, researchers can make no definitive productivity predictions. As a result, there is considerable debate on interpretation of the empirical literature. For example, in separate literature reviews, Freeman and Medoff (1984) concluded that unions raise productivity and Addison and Hirsch (1989) found no compelling evidence of positive or negative productivity effects.

The union effect on firm profitability raises much less disagreement than the effect on productivity. Consistently, studies have found that unionized firms have significantly lower profitability than nonunion firms, regardless of the profit measure, unit of analysis, time period, or methods used (Hirsch, 1991).

Union Effects on Society

Economists examine the union effect on society by viewing unions as monopolies that raise wages above competitive levels, crowd the unorganized sector, and depress wages (Freeman and Medoff, 1984; Rees, 1989). Others have raised additional concerns regarding union effects on society as transmitted through their excessive political power and corruption. While acknowledging that unionization can contribute to these problems, others believe that unionization benefits outweigh these costs. They argue that unions through collective voice provide workplace and compensation practices more amenable to employees, improvements in productivity, and a reduction in wage inequality (Freeman and Medoff, 1984). Others also contend that worker protection from managerial authority and the representation of the general interests of workers serve to aid society (Rees, 1989).

Summary

The above discussion has only highlighted key union effects. Clearly, many other important union effects exist, such as STRIKES and their effects on nonunion organizations, public sector outcomes, politics, inflation, and job security.

There is also a question of whether the union effects described here will continue into the future. Kochan et al. (1986) have argued that industrial relations systems have

undergone a fundamental transformation, which suggests that future union effects may differ from those of the past. However, Dunlop (1993) states that although the environment has undergone modifications, the underlying elements of the US industrial relations system have remained essentially stable. This scenario suggests that union effects will remain largely unchanged.

Bibliography

Addison, J. T. & Hirsch, B. T. (1989). Union effects on productivity, profits and growth: has the long run arrived? *Journal of Labor Economics*, 7, 72–101.

Berger, C. J., Olson, C. A. & Boudreau, J. W. (1983). Effects of unions on job satisfaction: the role of work-related values and perceived rewards. *Organizational Behavior and Human Performance*, **32**, 289–324.

Dunlop, J. T. (1993). *Industrial Relations Systems*, Boston: Harvard Business School Press.

Freeman, R. B. & Medoff, J. L. (1984). *What Do Unions Do?*, New York: Basic Books.

Gordon, M. E. & DeNisi, A. S. (1995). A re-examination of the relationship between union membership and job satisfaction. *Industrial and Labor Relations Review*, 48, 222–36.

Hirsch, B. T. (1991). Union coverage and profitability among US firms. *Review of Economics and Statistics*, 73, 69–77.

Hirschman, A. O. (1970). *Exit, Voice, and Loyalty: Responses to Decline in Firms, Organizations, and States*, Cambridge, MA: Harvard University Press.

Kochan, T. A., Katz, H. C. & McKersie, R. (1986). *The Transformation of American Industrial Relations*, New York: Basic Books.

Rees, A. (1989). *The Economics of Trade Unions*, **3rd edn**, Chicago: University of Chicago Press.

NANCY BROWN JOHNSON

unionization determinants Unionization determinants are the factors that cause workers to form, support, or join unions or employee associations (*see* CRAFT UNIONS, INDUSTRIAL UNIONS). In the USA, workers unionize primarily for the purpose of engaging in COLLECTIVE BARGAINING. Workers may unionize to engage in collective political activities and to provide mutual assistance as well.

Theories of Unionization

Theories of unionization generally can be classified as to whether they view unions as revolutionary change agents in an inevitable class struggle between workers and capitalists (a Marxian perspective) or as a means for workers to improve their well-being within the existing socio-economic order (pure and simple unionism or business unionism, a perspective favored by US scholars). The latter perspective encompasses various narrower theories, but common among them is the notion that workers form, support, or join unions out of the belief that unions are an effective means to address workplace (primarily) and/or societal problems.

Forms of Unionization and Levels of Analysis

Hundreds of studies have examined the determinants of unionization. Unionization determinants can be conceptualized for various forms of unionization and at varying levels of analysis. In a narrow sense, unionization refers to whether a particular individual is a union member or the proportion of workers who are members in some aggregate unit (e.g. the USA), which is also referred to as union density. In a broad sense, unionization ranges from values, beliefs, attitudes, and behaviors concerning unions to actual membership and labor contract coverage. To illustrate the breadth of meaning intended here, attitudes toward unions may include those of the general public or nonunion workers, but also attitudes of unionized workers, such as UNION COMMITMENT.

Aggregate-level studies examine unionization and its causes across very broad units, such as industries, states, or nations, change within such units over time, or both. Individual-level studies examine membership, attitudes, and behaviors across individual workers or changes in individual attitudes, and so forth. Unionization also may be analyzed at various intermediate levels, such as a company or election unit.

Unionization determinants vary with the form of unionization in question and the level of analysis. Aggregate-level studies tend to focus on economic influences (such as inflation and unemployment) and public policies (such as RIGHT TO WORK laws and the National Labor Relations Act). Individual-level analyses stress psychological variables such as attitudes toward jobs and unions. Intermediate-level studies such as those of representation elections often include economic and psychological variables as well as measures of employer and union characteristics and tactics used to persuade workers to support or oppose unionization.

To some extent, the form of unionization examined and the level of analysis dictate the unionization determinants considered, in terms of either measure availability or relevance. An attitudinal measure may not be available for an aggregate unit or may be relatively constant across aggregate units. Conversely, a macroeconomic variable may not make sense at an individual level or may be essentially constant for all individuals in a given employing unit at one point in time. Similar or overlapping constructs may be represented by different measures at different levels of analysis. For example, in an aggregate study, one might specify past wage changes as an indication of union effectiveness; in an individual-level cross-section one might specify a scale of perceived union effectiveness. In both instances the underlying hypothesis is that workers support unions because they believe unions will improve their economic well-being.

To some extent the determinants considered also reflect the disciplinary orientation of researchers. Economists naturally tend to stress economic influences and objective measures, such as wage rates and unemployment rates. Psychologists note that persons act on their perceptions, and stress perceptual variables such as job satisfaction and perceptions of union effectiveness. Industrial relations scholars stress an interdisciplinary approach, recognizing that these and other disciplines can contribute collectively to a fuller understanding than is possible through any single discipline.

Aggregate-level Findings

In recent years, many studies have attempted to account for the fact that US unionization has dropped from roughly one-third of the workforce in the 1950s to about one-sixth in the 1990s. Studies suggest that unionization tends to be pro-cyclical, with unions expanding in prosperous times and declining in hard times, although these results tend to find less support in recent decades. Research also indicates

that unionization may be affected by "structural" factors, including occupational, industrial, and regional employment shifts, and changes in work force demographics, as well as public policies and the behavior of unions and employers within a given policy context. On the latter, several studies have cited a large or even dominant role for employer opposition to unions, in both legal and illegal forms (*see* UNION AVOIDANCE). In addition, some suggest that governments' labor market policies have reduced the need for unions, that worker values have become more individualistic, that job satisfaction has risen, or that unions have failed to respond effectively to these and other changes in their environments.

Individual-level Findings

Studies of individual decisions to form, support, or join unions stress psychological variables, as noted above. These studies consistently show that perceptions of union effectiveness, job dissatisfaction, and favorable general attitudes toward unions increase workers' unionization tendencies. Variants of these measures are often used, with similar findings. Additional measures for worker, employer, and union characteristics or organizing campaign tactics have been found influential in some studies. To an extent, however, the latter are simply acting as proxies for worker psychological states they may influence. For example, employer counter-organizing tactics and progressive human resource policies are often aimed at reducing perceptions of union effectiveness or increasing job satisfaction. Similarly, worker-demographic effects may simply reflect shared dissatisfactions among particular demographic groups. This does not necessarily imply that such proxies are unimportant. One often cannot observe worker psychological states, and the role of influences such as employer and union tactics are often intrinsically interwoven.

Bibliography

Fiorito, J., Gallagher, D. G. & Greer, C. R. (1986). Determinants of unionism: a review of the literature. *Research in Personnel and Human Resources Management*, Eds. Rowland, K. M. & Ferris, G. R., 4, Greenwich, CT: JAI Press.

Fiorito, J. & Maranto, C. L. (1987). The contemporary decline of union strength. *Contemporary Policy Issues*, 5, 12–27.

Freeman, R. B. & Rogers, J. (1993). Who speaks for us? Employee representation in a nonunion labor market. *Employee Representation: Alternatives and Future Directions*, Eds. Kaufman, B. E. & Kleiner, M. M. Madison, WI: Industrial Relations Research Association.

Freeman, R. B. & Rogers, J. (1994). Worker representation and participation survey: first report of findings (unpublished paper).

Hirsch, B. T. & Macpherson, D. A. (1995). *Union Membership and Earnings Data Book 1994: Compilations from the Current Population Survey*, Washington, DC: Bureau of National Affairs.

Jarley, P. & Fiorito, J. (1990). Associate membership: unionism or consumerism? *Industrial and Labor Relations Review*, 43, 209–24.

Lawler, J. J. (1990). *Unionization and Deunionization: Strategy, Tactics, and Outcomes*, Columbia, SC: University of South Carolina Press.

Perlman, S. (1928). *A Theory of the Labor Movement*, New York: Macmillan.

Strauss, G., Gallagher, D. G. & Fiorito, J. (1991). *The State of the Unions*, Madison, WI: Industrial Relations Research Association.

JACK FIORITO

universal copyright convention An international agreement which protects the authors of written works from unauthorized use of those works. The agreement calls for protection during the author's life plus an additional 50 years. Under this agreement written work is "automatically" protected if information related to publication (author's name, publication date, or completion date if unpublished), and the copyright symbol are made a part of the work. The agreement applies only to signatory countries.

see also **Intellectual property**

JOHN O'CONNELL

upward communication COMMUNICATION upward conveys important information regarding work and personnel-related problems, feedback, suggestions for work and quality improvements, and subordinate attitudes (*see* CONTINUOUS IMPROVEMENT). It also enables subordinates to INFLUENCE their task effectiveness, working conditions, and CAREER advancement. Evidence suggests that most organizations have difficulty encouraging upward communication. Superiors and subordinates typically demonstrate significant information gaps, and the gaps grow larger as messages are filtered and distorted by intervening hierarchical levels. Several factors increase the likelihood of distortion or miscommunication. There is a general tendency for communicators to exaggerate information favorable to themselves and to minimize or not pass on unfavorable information. This is stronger if the superior has influence over subordinate promotion or REWARDS, if the subordinate does not TRUST the superior, if the subordinate knows the superior withholds information, and if the subordinate has mobility aspirations. Whether subordinates communicate upward is strongly dependent on their perceptions of superior openness. Openness is signaled by the superior's willingness to listen, exhibited trust in the subordinate, willingness to approach the subordinate, warmth, and question asking. Introduction of information technologies such as electronic mail generally also result in increases in upward communication.

see also **Employee involvement; Decision making**

Bibliography

Jablin, F. M., Putnam, L. L., Roberts, K. H. & Porter, L. W. (1987). Handbook of organizational communication. Newbury Park, CA: Sage.

MARSHALL SCOTT POOLE

V

validity generalization   Validity generalization refers to the demonstration that the validities of abilities, aptitude tests, and other selection devices generalize across new settings, organizations, and geographical areas. The most important implication of this finding is that it is not necessary to conduct new validity studies in each setting.

Starting early in this century, selection psychologists observed considerable variability in validity findings from study to study even when the jobs and tests studied appeared to be similar or essentially identical. This variability showed itself both in statistical significance levels and in actual values of the observed validity coefficients. These findings led personnel psychologists to adopt the theory of situationally specific validity. This theory held that the nature of job performance differs from setting to setting and that the human observer or job analyst is too poor an information receiver and processor to detect these subtle but important differences. The conclusion was that validity is specific to each situation and must be estimated by a local validity study conducted in each situation or setting. This meant that validities were not generalizable. This led to the belief that a test that was shown to be valid for a job in Company A might well be completely invalid for an apparently identical job in Company B.

The methods used to test for validity generalization are the meta-analysis methods developed by John Hunter and Frank Schmidt (see Schmidt and Hunter, 1977). These methods have since been applied to many other research literatures in different social sciences, in medical research, in finance, in marketing, and in other areas (Hunter and Schmidt, 1990). John Callender, Hobart Osburn, Nambury Raju, and others have also made contributions to the development of validity generalization methods.

A validity generalization study is conducted in the following manner. First, all available validity studies (published and unpublished) are gathered and coded. The dependent variable is typically a measure of either overall job performance or performance in training. The *variance* of these observed validity estimates is then corrected for variability due to various statistical and measurement artefacts, the most important of which is usually sampling error. The mean of the observed validity coefficients is also corrected for downward biases created by measurement error in the performance measure and by range restriction. If 90 percent or more of the values in this corrected validity distribution are in the positive range, it is concluded that validity generalizes. Because not all artefacts that create variability across studies in validity estimates can be corrected for, these methods yield conservative estimates of the generalizability of validity.

Validity generalization studies have been conducted for over 500 research literatures in personnel selection. Predictors studied include cognitive ability tests, evaluations of education and experience, the EMPLOYMENT INTERVIEW, biographical history inventories, personality tests, and INTEGRITY TESTING. In many cases, artefacts accounted for all variance across studies. For cognitive tests, the average amount of variance accounted for has been about 80 percent. In most cases, it has been found that validities generalize across settings, and that mean validity is higher than has typically been believed. However, in some cases (such as the point method of evaluating education and experience) it has been found that mean validity is quite low and does not generalize.

These methods have been used to determine whether validities generalize across different jobs, as well as across settings for the same job. Validities of cognitive ability tests, employment interviews, and integrity tests, for example, have been found to generalize across widely varying jobs.

The purpose of the research program in validity generalization was to empirically test the theory of situational validity. This research program showed that theory to be false. In retrospect, it is clear that acceptance of the theory of situational validity was based on an inadequate understanding of the extent to which statistical and measurement artefacts cause apparent but false variability in findings across small sample validity studies. The ability of validity generalization and meta-analysis methods to quantify and remove such artefactual variation has made these methods useful in many research areas beyond personnel selection.

Bibliography

Hunter, J. E. & Schmidt, F. L. (1990). *Methods of Meta-analysis: Correcting Error and Bias in Research Findings*, Newbury Park, CA: Sage Publishing.

Schmidt, F. L. & Hunter, J. E. (1977). Development of a general solution to the problem of validity generalization. *Journal of Applied Psychology*, 62, 529–40.

FRANK SCHMIDT

value-based planning   Since the early 1980s, an increasing number of corporations have adopted the concept of value planning. An alternate model to other portfolio systems, value-based planning seeks to maximize the value of the corporation for shareholders. By examining the corporate portfolio with this objective, individual businesses may be seen as creating, sustaining, or destroying shareholder value. Those businesses which create value should be invested in, those sustaining value should be supported, and those destroying value should either be divested or closed.

The Concept of Value Planning

The fundamental economic relationship underlying value-based management is that shareholder value in developed economies with established stock markets is determined by the net present value of the future cashflow streams that can be expected from the corporation. At the same time, the value of the equity of the firm is given by the market value of the common stock. This assumes that the market is efficient, and that the market value represents a consensus of the expected present value of future cashflow streams based on the portfolio of existing assets and the returns that can be expected from future investments. Over the long term, and despite short-term market fluctuations, there is strong evidence to support this view. This market value can be contrasted to the book value of the corporation, which is based on the accountant's view of the value of historic contributions by shareholders. The market to book model has been derived from the comparison between these two values of the firm. The market/book (M/B) ratio is calculated as follows:

$$\frac{\text{market value}}{\text{book value}} = \frac{\text{expected future payments}}{\text{past capital invested}}$$

From the calculation the basic message is as follows:

- If M/B = 1, all future payments are yielding the expected rate of return required by the market, and the firm is neither creating nor losing value.
- If M/B > 1, the rate of return is greater than that expected by the market, and the firm is creating value.
- If M/B < 1, the rate of return is less than that required by the market, and the firm is destroying shareholder value.

Utilizing this basic principle, a number of portfolio models have been developed which compare market to book with the cost of equity. This latter factor is calculated roughly by the risk-free bond rate of return and adding a premium for equity risk. This in turn is finalized by multiplying by a beta value risk factor, which is based on the industry and the individual company. The precise calculation of the cost of equity varies slightly between consultancy company models. Comparing this calculated cost of equity with the full return on equity provides a term against which to compare M/B. Marakon Associates thus calculate the "spread," which is the actual return on equity minus the calculated return on equity. The combination of M/B versus spread is illustrated in figure 1, which indicates a positive association between the two. This model provides the basis for a useful comparison between competitors.

By contrast, McKinsey and Company use a different way of comparing the economic performance of a group of firms. In this method M/B is plotted against an indicator called the economic-to-book value ratio (see figure 2). This is calculated on the basis of historic performance projected into the future but, again, the measure is based on future cashflow streams discounted plus a residual term.

Strategic Planning Associates, a pioneer of the technique but subsequently acquired and now Mercer Management Consultants, used a term called the Value Leverage Index (VLI) and by comparing this with the M/B one can construct the value curve illustrated in figure 3. The VLI is estimated by dividing the actual to expected return on equity. The implications of the value curve are similar to those from the Marakon calculations. Only when the actual to expected ratios of return are equal will the market value of the corporation be equivalent to the book value. When the VLI is less than one, the curve flattens out, which is assessed as an underlying value and thus a potential acquisition premium, while a VLI greater than one indicates a growth in shareholder value and the market essentially rewarding the performance with a share premium. As shown, these models are all static.

Using Value Planning at the SBU Value Level

When growth is added, it can have a positive, negative, or neutral effect on the market/book ratio. Corporations adding shareholder value enhance M/B, those sustaining it remain on the curve in the case of SPA, while those producing negative value have a reduced level of M/B. Growth itself, therefore, is not necessarily seen as attractive, except when it leads to increased shareholder value.

When applied within the multibusiness firm, these methodologies attempt to evaluate the contribution of each business unit to the overall value of the firm. When SBUs

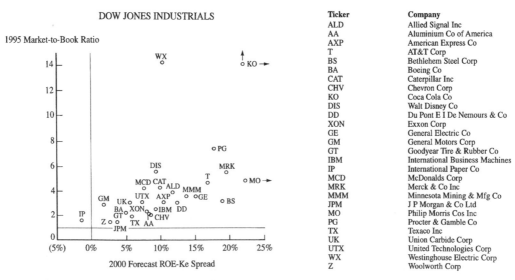

Figure 1 Market-to-book versus forecasted spread (note that Ke = Tech Ke).
Source: Value Line Investment Survey, Marakon Associates (1995).

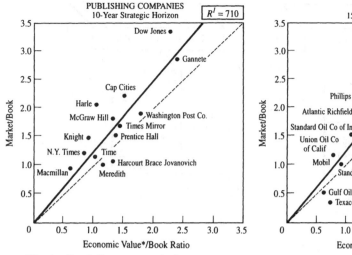
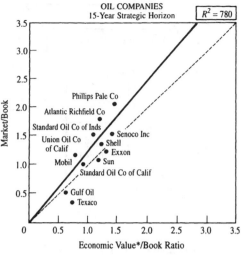

*Based on historic (five year average) values.

Figure 2 McKinsey's (M/B) versus (E/B) graph
Source: Lai (1983)

are free-standing and independent, the value of the firm is equal to the sum of the units.

The evaluation of the contribution of each business unit is critical to assessing the desired strategy at the SBU level. In particular, the impact of growth is critical. SBUs with a positive value contribution are candidates for investment, while those that destroy value should not be invested in, as further growth will accelerate this trend. However, the calculation of positive or negative value is complex, and may be subject to interpretation depending upon how return on equity at the business unit level is calculated. Thus, if the capital structure of each business unit is seen as proportional to that of the parent, return on equity may be substantially affected by the allocation of debt, equity, and risk. However, if each SBU is treated as if it were a microfirm, its capital structure might reflect the nature of

the industry in which it operates rather than that of the firm as a whole.

For example, as shown in figure 4, for two businesses with the same asset size and profitability, the return on assets value may be the same, while the return on equity value may be dramatically different, due to different capacities to generate free debt and apply leverage. Moreover, relative risk values may be quite different, and the future prospects of the business units may also vary widely. Similarly, risk, while a function of industry, will also vary according to the competitive position of both the corporation and the business unit itself. For example, selective segmentation in insurance may result in reduced risk, which is unrecognized by industry regulators.

In assessing the portfolio position of each business, Marakon notes that its capability to generate value is

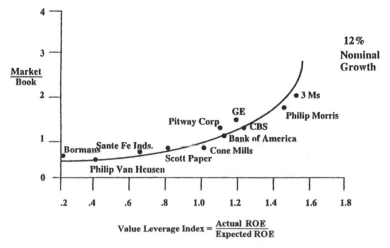

Figure 3 Across industries the higher the VLI the higher the market/book.
Source: Mercer Management Consultants.

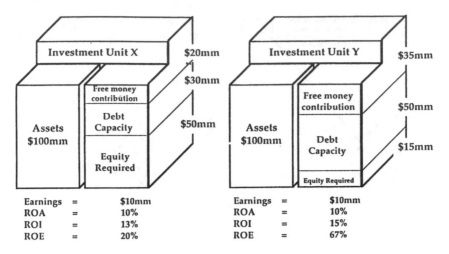

Figure 4 The capital structure effect on ROE.

determined by a combination of market economics and competitive position (see figure 5). Market economics are determined by competitors, that determine the average equity spread and growth rate over time for all competitors in its product market. Competitive position is based on factor 3, or on forces that jointly determine a specific competitor's equity spread and growth rate over time relative to the average competitor in its product market, where competitive position is defined in terms of a combination of product differentiation and economic cost position.

These two key variables can be used to assess the SBU's current and expected profitability of the business, as shown in figure 6. Business units with sustainable competitive advantages in attractive markets will always be substantially profitable: ROE will always exceed the cost of equity capital and M/B will always be greater than one.

SBUs with weak competitive positions in unattractive markets will always be unprofitable: they will produce economic losses and they will destroy existing shareholder value.

In the remaining two cases the linkage is less clear, although competitive position tends to have a greater influence on profitability than market economics. Marakon notes that when a business enjoys substantial competitive advantage but participates in unattractive markets, it still tends to generate value over time, although long-term profitability tends to be a function of size and the sustainability of its competitive advantage. Those businesses with a competitive disadvantage in attractive markets are usually unprofitable.

From this form of financial and strategic analysis combination, value planning advocates that business units should be assigned one of four strategies – grow, hold, invest, or divest. Ironically, by eliminating portfolio losers, divestiture results in an increase in market capitalization despite a reduction in corporate assets, as future expected cashflows increase long-term shareholder value.

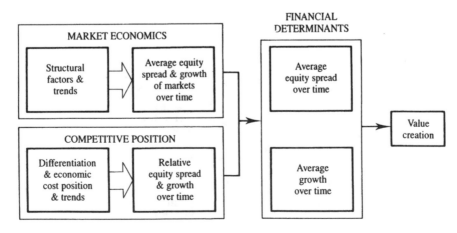

Figure 5   Strategic determinants of value creation
Source: Marakon Associates

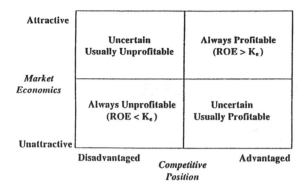

	Disadvantaged	Advantaged
Attractive	Uncertain Usually Unprofitable	Always Profitable (ROE > K_e)
Unattractive	Always Unprofitable (ROE < K_e)	Uncertain Usually Profitable

Figure 6 Linking strategic position to value creation.
Source: Marakon Associates.

Bibliography

Anonymous (1981). *Strategic and shareholders' value: the value curve.* Washington, DC: Strategic Planning Associates.

Copeland, T., Koller, J. & Murri, J. (1990). *Valuation.* New York: John Wiley.

Day, G. S. & Fahey, L. (1990). Putting strategy into shareholder value analysis. *Harvard Business Review,* 68, 156–62.

Hax, A. C. & Majluf, N. S. (1991). *The strategy concept and process.* Englewood Cliffs, NJ: Prentice-Hall.

McTaggart, J. M., Kontes, P. W. & Mankins, C. M. (1994). *The value imperative.* New York: The Free Press.

Rappaport, A. (1986). *Creating shareholder value.* New York: The Free Press.

DEREK F. CHANNON

value chain analysis   The activities that a firm performs become part of the value added produced from a raw material to its ultimate consumption. Individual actors may operate over a greater or lesser extent of the total value generated within an industry. The value chain for the firm is shown in figure 1, in which are also illustrated many of the key issues associated with each of the main functions within the value chain. At the same time, the firm does not exist in isolation but merely forms part of the industry chain. Thus

suppliers have value streams, as do customers and the channels that supply them. Moreover, in multibusiness firms there may well be a variety of value chains with different dimensions in which the firm is involved. The value system for single business and multibusiness firms is illustrated in figure 2.

The value chain concept allows the firm to be disaggregated into a variety of strategically relevant activities. In particular, it is important to identify those which have different economic characteristics; those which have a high potential for creating differentiation; and those which are most important in developing cost structure (Pareto analysis may be a useful tool for this purpose). The value chain concept thus helps to identify cost behavior in detail. As such, a number of the Japanese cost analysis techniques are useful in gaining this information. From this analysis, different strategic courses of action should be identifiable in order to develop differentiation and less price sensitive strategies. Competitive advantage is then achieved by performing strategic activities better or cheaper than competitors.

Value is the amount that buyers are willing to pay for the product or service that a firm provides. Profits alter when the value created by the firm exceeds the cost of providing it. This is the goal of strategy, and therefore value creation becomes a critical ingredient in competitive analysis. Every value activity incurs costs such as for raw materials, and other purchased goods and services for "purchased inputs," human resources (direct and indirect labor), and technology to transform raw materials into finished goods. Each value activity also creates information that is needed to establish what is going on in the business. Similarly, value is created by producing stocks, accounts receivable, and the like; while value is lost via raw material purchases and other liabilities. Most organizations thus engage in many activities in the process of creating value. These activities can generally be classified into either primary or support activities. These are illustrated in figure 3, which details the view of Michael Porter, who states that there are five generic categories of primary activities involved in competing in any industry. Each of these is divisible into a number of specific activities that vary according to the

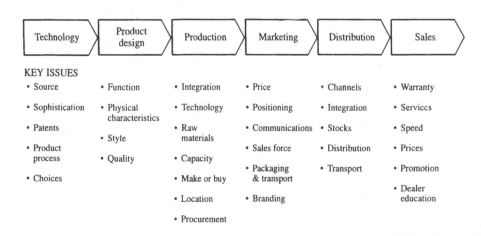

KEY ISSUES

Technology	Product design	Production	Marketing	Distribution	Sales
• Source	• Function	• Integration	• Price	• Channels	• Warranty
• Sophistication	• Physical characteristics	• Technology	• Positioning	• Integration	• Services
• Patents		• Raw materials	• Communications	• Stocks	• Speed
	• Style		• Sales force	• Distribution	• Prices
• Product process	• Quality	• Capacity		• Transport	• Promotion
		• Make or buy	• Packaging & transport		
• Choices					• Dealer education
		• Location	• Branding		
		• Procurement			

Figure 1   The business value chain

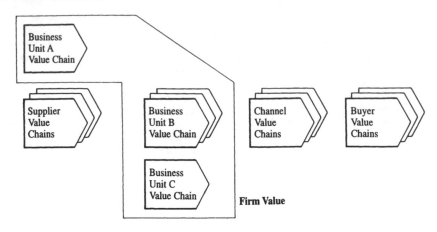

Figure 2   Competitive advantage value system for a diversified firm
Source: Porter (1985)

industry and chosen strategy of the firm. These categories are as follows:

- *Inbound logistics.* Activities associated with receiving, storing, and disseminating rights to the product, such as material handling, warehousing, stock management, and the like.
- *Operations.* All of the activities required to transform inputs into outputs and the critical functions which add value, such as machining, packaging, assembly, service, testing, and the like.
- *Outbound logistics.* All of the activities required to collect, store, and physically distribute the output. This activity can prove to be extremely important both in generating value and in improving differentiation, as in many industries control over distribution strategies is proving to be a major source of competitive advantage – especially as it is realized that up to 50 per cent of the value created in many industry chains occurs close to the ultimate buyer.
- *Marketing and sales.* Activities associated with informing potential buyers about the firm's products and services,

and inducing them to buy by personal selling, advertising and promotion, and the like.
- *Service.* The means of enhancing the physical product features through after-sales service, installation, repair, and the like.

While each firm provides these activities to a greater or lesser degree, they do not all do so to the same extent; nor is each function as important to all competitors, even within the same industry. This is illustrated in figure 4, in which is shown the value chain positioning of a variety of competitors in the consumer electronics industry is shown. The chart is meant to be illustrative rather than definitive.

Porter has also identified four generic support strategies. These are broad concepts which support the primary activities of the firm:

1. *Procurement.* This concerns the acquisition of inputs or resources. Although technically the responsibility of the purchasing department, almost everyone in the firm is responsible for purchasing something. While

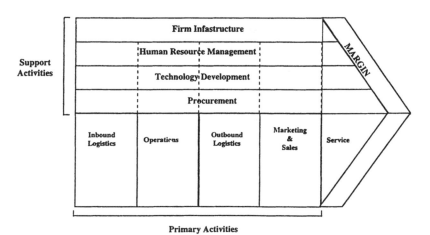

Figure 3 The generic value chain.
Source: Porter (1985).

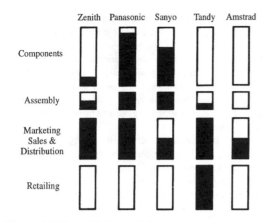

Figure 4 Value added activity structure.

the cost of procurement itself is relatively low, the impact can be very high.

2. *Human resource management.* This consists of all activities involved in recruiting, hiring, training, developing, rewarding, and sanctioning the people in the organization.

3. *Technology development.* This is concerned with the equipment, hardware, software, technical skills, and the like used by the firm in transforming inputs to outputs. Some such skills can be classified as scientific, while others – such as food preparation in a restaurant – are "artistic". Such skills are not always recognized. They may also support limited activities of the business, such as accounting, order procurement, and the like, and in this sense may be likened to the value added component of the experience effect (*see* EXPERIENCE AND LEARNING EFFECTS).

4. *Firm infrastructure.* This consists of the many activities, including general management, planning, finance, legal, external affairs, and the like, which support the operational aspect of the value chain. This may be self-contained in the case of an undiversified firm or divided between the parent and the firm's constituent business units.

Within each category of primary and support activities, Porter identifies three types of activity which play different roles in achieving competitive advantage:

- *Direct.* These are activities directly involved in creating value for buyers, such as assembly, sales, and advertising.
- *Indirect.* These are activities that facilitate the performance of the direct activities on a continuing basis, such as maintenance, scheduling, and administration.
- *Quality assurance.* These are activities that insure the quality of other activities, such as monitoring, inspecting, testing, and checking.

To diagnose competitive advantage, it is necessary to define the firm's value chain for operating in a particular industry and compare this with those of key competitors. A comparison of the value chains of different competitors often identifies ways of achieving strategic advantage by reconfiguring the value chain of the individual firm. In

assigning costs and assets it is important that the analysis be done strategically rather than seeking accounting precision. This should be accomplished using the following principles:

- operating costs should be assigned to activities where incurred
- assets should be assigned to activities where employed, controled, or influencing usage
- accounting systems should be adjusted to fit value analysis
- asset valuation may be difficult, but should recognize industry norms – particular care should be taken in evaluating property assets

The reconfiguration of the value chain has often been used by successful competitors in achieving competitive advantage. When seeking to reconfigure the value chain in an industry, the following questions need to be asked:

- How can an activity be done differently or even eliminated?
- How can linked value activities be reordered or regrouped?
- How could coalitions with other firms reduce or eliminate costs?

Successful reconfiguration strategies usually occur with one or more of the following moves:

- a new production process
- automation differences
- direct versus indirect sales strategy
- the opening of new distribution channels
- new raw materials used
- differences in forward and/or backward integration
- a relative location shift
- new advertising media

Bibliography

Porter, M. E. (1979). How competitive forces shape strategy. *Harvard Business Review*, 57, 137–45.

Porter, M. E. (1985). *Competitive advantage; creating and sustaining superior performance.* New York: The Free Press.

DEREK F. CHANNON

value-driven re-engineering   Much has been written and said about Business Process Re-engineering (BPR) since Michael Hammer's paper in the *Harvard Business Review* in 1990. He defined the term as a "fundamental rethink and radical re-design of business processes to achieve dramatic improvements in critical contemporary measures of performance, such as cost, quality, service and speed." He does not claim to have invented the concept, but merely to have discovered it.

Value Driven Re-engineering was pioneered by Andersen Consulting and is by necessity a broad, sweeping approach to strategic change, but it is based on practical, workable principles. It focuses on integrated processes, not piecemeal results. It combines innovation, creativity, and strikingly new perspectives with guiding principles, best practices, and a pragmatic appreciation of how customers, employees, and organizations really behave (see figure 1).

Compared to conventional quality improvement programs, it blends the best of two worlds; comprehensive change throughout the core processes of a business, and a profound respect for the smallest but most important details that make a company successful in the eyes of customers.

When do our customers feel they really get "value" from us? Why? How do we keep making that happen?

By focusing on end-to-end business processes rather than narrowly defined functions, re-engineering concentrates all of a company's resources on insuring that the costs of delivering excellent products and services are in complete harmony with the value that they provide to customers. In the early stages of a re-engineering effort, a company may be surprised to learn, for instance, that the "premium" service that it provides is costing far more than it is actually worth to certain customer segments.

While most businesses can be described in terms of 20–50 separate processes, re-engineering focuses on the five to ten that are critical to the company's ability to balance cost/value trade-offs. Instead of becoming trapped in one or more of the "functional silos" of sales, marketing, manufacturing, and distribution, re-engineering reveals a broad view of how all of these together, as integrated processes, affect a firm's management of those trade-offs.

As a result, Value-Driven Re-engineering becomes a powerful methodology for exploiting change rather than being overwhelmed by it.

Re-engineering considers the entire business enterprise, including the company's suppliers and customers. It is constant and relentless in its focus on integrating four key

drivers – people, processes, technology, and infrastructure – to create and sustain value for customers while managing costs.

There are normally three specific steps in a re-engineering program. They all relate to managing change and are targeted to balance the goal of long-term change with the need for practical, quick payback opportunities. These steps start with creating an environment to enable change to occur.

Typically, this involves formulating a shared vision for the enterprise that links the business strategy to operational realities. This vision becomes the foundation for defining and managing cost/value trade-offs. It is necessary to design the new processes and define the people skills, organizations, technology, and infrastructure needed to turn the vision into a reality. The first step concludes with a well-structured plan for implementing these changes.

The second step is to achieve change. The use of innovative change management techniques is important to help a company navigate from today to tomorrow. As appropriate, this involves the design and conduct of pilot programs. Most importantly, it involves implementing the comprehensive transformation of the organization and its skills, core processes, mission-critical systems, and infrastructure.

As this 12–36 month transformation is implemented, it is important to integrate the re-engineering effort with the company's culture and competitive strategy. To sustain the change – which is the third step – it is vital to complete the necessary changes in organization, processes, technology, and infrastructure. It is also necessary to establish measures

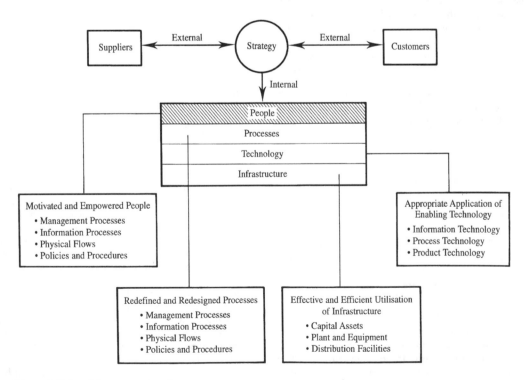

Figure 1 Value-driven re-engineering.
Source: Andersen Consulting.

for monitoring performance to insure continuous cost control and consistently high levels of customer satisfaction for many years beyond the re-engineering project itself.

To sustain change it is also necessary continuously to question how further improvement can be achieved. For example, when he successfully re-engineered Woolworths in the UK, Sir Geoffrey Mulcahy, CEO of Kingfisher, said that – even now – if ever a day passed when he did not imagine that company still to be in a turnaround situation, he would be failing his shareholders.

The guiding principles throughout all these steps are clear.

Guiding Principles of Value-Driven Re-engineering

- maintain a customer orientation
- think outside the box
- focus on outcomes and results
- challenge the rules
- empower people
- build in quality at the source
- define end-to-end solutions
- set stretch targets and goals
- eliminate non-value-added activities
- compress time
- communicate, communicate, communicate

Source: Andersen Consulting.

Why do BPR Initiatives Fail?

In reviewing some of the many re-engineering programs that have been undertaken, it is evident that the most common cause of failure or slowdown in the process is through failure properly to manage the "people" aspects, to demonstrate organizational commitment and build shared visions. A company must have a view of its longer-term strategy and its core skills. Without that focus, the substantial effort and resources dedicated to BPR are likely to be wasted on areas of the business which are not critical to success. Another cause of failure is "analysis paralysis" – companies over-analyze situations and attempt to quantify costs and benefits to an unnecessary degree.

Will BPR Fizzle out or Flourish by the Millennium?

BPR will continue to evolve during the 1990s until the majority of companies have incorporated new modes of operation that are consistent with today's environment. Successful BPR is an ongoing rather than one-off project, as well-managed BPR programs encourage organizations to see beyond their current mental models and continually challenge themselves to learn and generate new processes that support continual improvement.

In conclusion, to meet the competitive challenges of the 1990s and beyond, most companies need far more than steady, incremental improvements. They require, in fact, nothing less than strategic change.

Streamlining and automation used to be enough. A company could rely on reorganized operations, new or upgraded information systems, or more efficient production or distribution techniques. Taking comfort in the cliche, "If it ain't broke, don't fix it," many companies thought that they could keep their businesses competitive just by "tweaking things here and there."

Unfortunately, that relatively stable world is no more. Today, unless a firm is a notable exception, success is impossible without an order-of-magnitude improvement in all measures of performance – especially in the way in which the company balances the competing demands for added value to customers on the one hand and cost efficiency on the other.

Achieving such a goal requires a fundamental re-evaluation of the company's basic purpose. The question is not just "How do we cut costs without losing business?" but "Why are we in business? What do our customers really expect from us? How do we meet those expectations at a reasonable cost?"

Over many programs, Andersen Consulting has found that Value-Driven Re-engineering is the best methodology for performing such a sweeping re-evaluation. It has proven itself as the most efficient and reliable means of implementing strategic, sustainable change in today's fast-moving, highly competitive marketplace.

Bibliography

Hammer, M. (1990). Reengineering work: don't automate – obliterate. *Harvard Business Review*, **68**, 104–12.

Hammer, M. & Champy, J. (1993). *Reengineering the corporation*. New York: Harper Business.

Johansson, H. J., McHugh, P., Pendebery, A. J. & Wheeler, W. A. III (1993). *Business process reengineering*. Chichester: John Wiley.

PETER DEMPSEY and BILL LATTIMER

values These are a set of core beliefs held by individuals concerning how they should or ought to behave over broad ranges of situations. These values are generalized beliefs about modes of conduct (Rokeach, 1972) that form a primary component of the self-schema, the "ought" self (as compared to the "actual" or "desired" self). Because beliefs about the self tend to be the most deeply held and influential of cognitions, values are stable and central, and are pervasive in their influence on other cognitions, perception, and behavior.

This conceptualization differs from the interpretation of values as preferences for objects, which in turn affect responses to those objects (Locke, 1976). Values, as generalized, core beliefs, provide the standard that individuals use to determine whether an object has value or is to be preferred. Values as defined here act as a primary organizing structure for much of the rest of our belief system, including cognitions commonly perceived to be "facts," rather than simply acting as evaluative responses.

Values also act as motivational elements (*see* MOTIVATION) in that they indicate which behaviors are more desirable to perform than others from an ideal perspective, all other things (such as instrumentality) being equal. Acting on values may fulfill innate needs, however, there is no necessary correspondence between the two.

People typically will endorse value-oriented statements; therefore, individual differences in values lie not so much in the specific values that individuals hold, but in their order of importance. Thus values are hierarchical in nature. Because of this systemic quality, and because of their high social desirability, values are difficult to measure adequately outside of a forced choice or ranking format (Ravlin & Meglino, 1987).

Values are acquired from societal institutions (family, economic, and political systems) and their cultural context. They are initially learned in isolation, in an absolute fashion. As an individual matures, he/she integrates them into a hierarchical system, also based in part on PERSONALITY factors (Rokeach, 1973). A relatively small number of value dimensions seems to generalize across NATIONAL CULTURES (Hofstede, 1980); thus the role of values is pivotal in understanding cultural differences in ORGANIZATIONAL BEHAVIOR.

Because values are learned early in life, and occupy a central position in cognitive structure, they are difficult to change during adulthood in the self-schema and the network of beliefs, attitudes, and perceptions that the individual acquires over a lifetime. Pitting two conflicting values against one another may produce change. It is also possible that having violated a value once, individuals find it progressively easier to violate that value until it has lost its level of priority. Finally, repeated functional failure of value-related behavior may produce change. These latter propositions seem more likely to explain long-term, cross-situational change in the values of adults.

Organizational SOCIALIZATION is one avenue by which values are conveyed to adults. Myths, stories, repetition, and formal socialization processes are often cited as sources of work values. Organizational leaders may set the values of the organization and propagate them among employees. To be acquired, however, a value must serve some sort of function for the individual, or be presented as the only possible interpretation of the situation. Values may also eventually lose their priority if organizational reward systems facilitate their frequent violation (see REWARDS). Employees bring values to the organization with them, so under some circumstances, their values may influence those of the organization rather than the reverse.

Values act as a perceptual screening device to influence what we see in our environment, and as a channel to influence behavioral decisions (England, 1967). Goals may mediate the relationship between values and behavior, and potential moderators, such as personal discretion and the labeling of a behavior as value-relevant, may act to determine when values will be predictive of behavior. Specific values play important roles in influencing certain behaviors. In the context of ethics, a dominant honesty value produces more ethical decisions (see BUSINESS ETHICS). Altruism facilitates personal adjustment because it predisposes individuals to respond to information from their environments, and to adapt to it (Simon, 1993). These relationships between specific values and behavior typically are expected to be small at any one point in time, but stronger over time, as with other individual differences.

In some instances, individuals use value statements (espoused values) to provide some justification for behavior that has already occurred (see LEGITIMACY). However, empirical evidence shows that these justification effects are not the only process underlying values–behavior relationships.

Shared value systems (value congruence) also have been shown to have important effects. The sharing of values within an organization may positively influence internal processes (integration; Schein, 1985) such that common cognitive processing leads to less CONFLICT, less UNCERTAINTY, shared goals, and more predictability, interpersonal TRUST, and satisfaction (see JOB SATISFACTION). This view is consistent with the Attraction–Selection–Attrition (ASA) framework of Schneider (1987), which holds that organizations tend to attract and retain people with similar views, and thus become more homogeneous over time.

Alternative views of ORGANIZATIONAL CULTURE and value sharing within organizations include differentiation perspectives, which focus on the differences in beliefs that exist between groups within organizations, and fragmentation perspectives, which note that shared beliefs are temporary because of a multiplicity of societal beliefs and the innate ambiguity of complex systems (Martin, 1992) (see SYSTEMS THEORY). Each of these views is probably descriptive of part of the organization's value system at any given time. These differing perspectives have important implications for how and what research is conducted. Thus far, value congruence has been explored at multiple levels (individual–organization, supervisor–subordinate, between coworkers) in studies which primarily reflect either integration or differentiation perspectives.

Although evidence shows that value congruence does result in more positive attitudes, the relationship between the sharing of values and performance is unclear. The integration perspective tends to suggest that the existence of value congruence will lead to higher performance. Other points of view, in particular, the GROUP DECISION MAKING and ASA literatures, suggest that too much homogeneity of belief systems should hinder performance in nonroutine, changing situations. Recent research suggests that while routine task performance may be facilitated by value congruence, performance on nonroutine tasks is not. Clearly, many issues regarding this relationship are left unresolved.

see also **Motivation**

Bibliography

England, G. W. (1967). Organizational goals and expected behavior of American managers. Academy of Management Journal, **10**, 107–117.

Hofstede, G. (1980). Culture's consequences: International differences in work related values. Beverly Hills, CA: Sage.

Locke, E. A. (1976). The nature and consequences of job satisfaction. In M. D. Dunnette (Ed.), Handbook of industrial psychology, (pp. 1297–1349). Chicago: Rand-McNally.

Martin, J. (1992). Cultures in organizations. New York: Oxford University Press.

Ravlin, E. C. & Meglino, B. M. (1987). Effect of values on perception and decision making: A study of alternative work values measures. Journal of Applied Psychology, **72**, 666–673.

Rokeach, M. (1973). The nature of human values. New York: Free Press.

Schein, E. H. (1985). Organizational culture and leadership. San Francisco: Jossey-Bass.

Schneider, B. (1987). The people make the place. Personnel Psychology, **40**, 437–453.

Simon, H. (1993). Altruism and economics. American Economic Review, **83**, 156–161.

ELIZABETH C. RAVLIN

variable compensation Variable compensation refers to forms of pay that vary according to specified criteria and are not fixed in base pay. This contrasts with MERIT PAY, which usually becomes part of the employee's salary. Variable compensation may take many diverse forms, each with its own purposes.

Different forms of variable pay are associated with different organizational levels. Variable compensation for individual performance can include commission-based pay and manufacturing piecework. Variable pay for small group performance is team-based pay. Variable pay at the organizational unit level (for example, a manufacturing plant) usually takes the form of GAINSHARING. Finally, pay for corporate performance usually takes the form of PROFIT SHARING, or, in the case of EXECUTIVE COMPENSATION, stock grants or options. This variety makes it difficult to generalize about characteristics of variable pay plans and organizational conditions affecting their consequences for employees and organizations. Clearly, however, many forms of variable pay are widely used by corporations in the USA (Lawler et al., 1995) and elsewhere.

Variable pay usually is delivered in cash BONUSES. However, there are other options. The organization may vary benefits, such as contributions to employee retirement accounts or profit sharing plans. Stock options can be a lucrative reward for performance if the stock performs well during the option period.

Most variable pay plans are intended to achieve at least one of two key goals: increasing employee motivation and linking wages to the organization's ability to pay. Variable pay can motivate employees by varying employee wages with the performance of the employee or the organizational unit. To the extent that employees can affect the level of performance measured through the plan, and to the extent that increased performance is tied to rewards that employees value, employees will be motivated to increase their performance (Lawler, 1990). If the plan's metrics are built on financial returns or metrics that covary with financial returns, payments will reflect the organization's ability to pay (Schuster and Zingheim, 1992). This latter goal is often related to employment security, because it permits the organization to vary wages without layoffs. Japanese firms, for example, typically tie 30 to 40 percent of employee compensation to corporate profits.

Motivation and cost control goals often conflict. Unit performance, as measured by productivity or quality, often changes independently of financial performance, which is largely dependent on market conditions. However, a profitability metric may not have any motivational value, because employees in large firms cannot influence profits significantly.

In general, the more closely variable pay is tied to individual performance, the greater is its motivational effect. This is the "line of sight" between employee behavior and monetary return. However, plans at the team and unit levels can also be motivational and can increase cooperation in interdependent work systems. Organizations often attempt to combine the advantages of local line of sight and ability to pay by complex formulas that, for example, pay out based on unit productivity if the company or business unit earns a profit (McAdams and Hawk, 1994).

Bibliography

Lawler, E. E. III (1990). *Strategic Pay: Aligning Organizational Strategies and Pay Systems*, San Francisco: Jossey-Bass.

Lawler, E. E. III, Mohrman, S. A. & Ledford, G. E. Jr (1995). *Creating High Performance Organizations: Practices and Results of Employee Involvement and Total Quality Management in Fortune 1000 Companies*, San Francisco: Jossey-Bass.

McAdams, J. L. & Hawk, E. J. (1994). *Organization Performance and Rewards: 665 Experiences in Making the Link*, Scottsdale, AZ: American Compensation Association.

Schuster, J. R. & Zingheim, P. K. (1992). *The New Pay: Linking Employee and Organizational Performance*, New York: Lexington Books/MacMillan.

GERALD E. LEDFORD JR

volatility Volatility is the term used in finance to denote the standard deviation of returns on an asset. It is therefore the square root of the variance of asset returns. Given a sequence of n weekly returns, an equally weighted estimate of the weekly variance (volatility squared) would be $\sigma_w^2 = [1/(n-1)]\sum_i (r_i - R)^2$, where σ_w denotes weekly volatility, σ_w^2 is the weekly variance, r_i is an individual return and R is the mean of all returns.

It is customary to express volatility on an annual basis. If an asset price follows a random walk, then its variance grows linearly with time. Hence the annual volatility is 52 times the weekly variance and the annual volatility may be expressed as $\sigma = \sqrt{52} \times \sigma_w$. σ will be used henceforth to denote the annual volatility.

A rather simple example of estimating a volatility is given in table 1. Note that more than the ten prices given here would be required to obtain a reliable estimate and the table gives calculations which have been rounded to two decimal places.

Table 1. Estimating Volatility

Week	Price	r_i (%)	$(r_i - R)^2$
1	100		
2	110	9.53	56.33
3	115	4.45	19.76
4	110	−4.45	19.76
5	115	4.45	19.76
6	105	−9.10	82.76
7	110	4.65	21.64
8	120	8.70	75.71
9	125	4.08	16.66
10	120	−4.08	16.66
Sum =		18.23	329.05
Average (R) =		2.03	

Using the table, the weekly variance is then, $\sigma_w^2 = (1/8) \times 329.05 = 41.13$ and the weekly volatility is $\sqrt{41.13} = 6.41$ percent. The annual volatility is then, $\sigma = 6.41 \times \sqrt{52} = 46.25$ percent.

In the example, percentage returns were calculated as $r_t = \log(P_t/P_{t-1}) \times 100$. The reason for using (natural) logs in this calculation is that it is consistent with an asset which has a lognormally distributed price and this leads to returns which are normally distributed. Using such geometric returns has the commonsense feature that an increase in price followed by an equal fall in price gives returns which are equal and opposite, as in the sequence over weeks 2 to 3 (+4.45 percent) and 3 to 4 (−4.45 percent) in the example. Had arithmetic returns been used, the sequence would have given +4.54 percent and −4.35 percent, resulting in a positive average return when the price had not risen.

This simple example of estimating volatility assumed that all observations on returns were equally important. However, it is possible to weight recent returns more heavily than earlier ones, a typical arrangement being an exponential weighting scheme. Yet another approach is to take account of intra-day price movements, by using the day's high and low prices as well as the closing price (see Garman and Klass, 1980).

It is useful to know what levels of volatility typically arise in financial markets. Customary levels would be: shares 25 percent, commodities 25 percent, share indices 17 percent, bonds 14 percent and exchange rates 12 percent. From a few weeks of observations, it would not be unusual to find a share with a volatility as high as 70 percent or as low as 10 percent. After the stockmarket crash of 1987, estimated volatilities for shares exceeded 100 percent in some cases. Volatility for London's FTSE100 Index (estimated from 30-day data), was in the range 8 percent to 70 percent over the 1984–94 period. Extreme values do not persist, there being a tendency for volatility to revert towards its long-term mean.

Forecasting Volatility

The only unknown in the Black–Scholes options-pricing model is the volatility, so that trading in options is effectively trading in volatility. It is possible to solve the model iteratively in order to find that volatility which equates model and market prices, the so-called "implied volatility." This reveals the market consensus for the period to maturity of the chosen option. An interesting feature of implied volatilities is that they tend to be larger for options which are at very low or very high exercise prices, leading to "volatility with a smile." Observed smiles also tend to be skewed to the left, which is consistent with the evidence for some financial assets that volatility rises as the price falls. In principle the implied volatility might be expected to provide a better forecast than an estimate of volatility based upon past returns. Most empirical studies confirm this hypothesis, but not all (see Canina and Figlewski, 1993).

Although an asset may be weak-form efficient in terms of prices, with the direction of the next move not predictable from past moves, it is possible to predict whether the next move is likely to be larger or smaller than previous moves. In other words, there are systematic changes in volatility. Time-series models for the variance have been developed, known as ARCH models, which exploit this dependence (see Engle and Rothschild, 1992). There is a whole family of such models, some of which allow the distribution of returns to have fat tails and others of which incorporate skewness of the distribution. Despite a large volume of research, the ability of these models to forecast volatility is only marginally better than that of a simple, equally weighted, model as given in the example above. Nevertheless, they do confirm that good forecasts require skewness, fat tails, and mean reversion to be taken into account.

Volatility Spillovers

After the stockmarket crash of 1987, it became apparent that a large price movement in one time zone could spill over into another time zone. Not surprisingly, there is also evidence that an increase in volatility of the US stockmarket spills over into the European and Japanese markets (Hamao et al., 1990). A slightly different kind of volatility spillover is sometimes claimed to occur from futures and options markets to the stockmarket, to which the response in the United States has been to introduce "circuit breakers:" these prohibit further arbitrage between the stock and derivative markets until conditions are quieter.

Excess Volatility

A contentious aspect of volatility in finance is whether it can be "excessive." A share's price is fundamentally the present value of the stream of future dividends. Shiller (1981) argued that changes in share prices were larger than could be justified by subsequent changes in dividend payments and he called this "excess volatility." Later papers showed that Shiller's argument was not statistically significant and pointed to the potential error which can be made in forecasting dividends. There is also the question of whether investors require a larger risk premium in periods when the volatility is higher, thus affecting share prices.

Volatility of a Bond

In the analysis of bonds, volatility is defined in a rather different way: it is the percentage change in the price of a bond for a 1 percent change in its yield. For example, if the yield rose from 8 percent to 9 percent and the price of a bond fell from 100 to 95, then the bond's volatility would be equal to 5 percent/1 percent = 5. This measure of volatility is related to a bond's duration, as volatility = duration/(1 + yield).

Bibliography

Canina, L. & Figlewski, S. (1993). The informational content of implied volatility. *Review of Financial Studies*, **6**, 659–82.

Engle, R. & Rothschild, M. (eds) (1992). ARCH models in Finance. *Journal of Econometrics*, **52**, (supplement), 1–311.

Garman, M. & Klass, M. (1980). On the estimation of security price volatilities from historical data. *Journal of Business*, **53**, 67–78.

Hamao, Y., Masulis, R. & Ng, V. (1990). Correlations in price changes and volatility across international stock markets. *Review of Financial Studies*, **3**, 280–307.

Shiller, R. (1981). Do stock prices move too much to be justified by subsequent changes in dividends? *American Economic Review*, **71**, 421–36.

GORDON GEMMILL

W

wage and salary surveys   A wage and salary survey is a systematic way to collect information about the compensation systems of other employers (Milkovich and Newman, 1993, p. 223). This information can be collected using a variety of means, ranging from telephone interviews to mail survey instruments. The goal of such a survey is to generate estimates of the market wage for positions that tend to be common across a variety of employers (Rynes and Milkovich, 1986). These data are used to make decisions related to the EXTERNAL EQUITY/EXTERNAL COMPETITIVENESS of a company's salary structure.

Conducting such a survey requires a sequence of decisions that can have critical consequences for the results of the survey and the interpretability of the incoming data (Rynes and Milkovich, 1986). These decisions relate to such things as (a) defining the relevant labor market; (b) choosing benchmark jobs; (c) considering how to gather and interpret information about indirect forms of compensation and other attributes about the total pay system; and (d) making regional or international adjustments based upon the cost of living and/or currency exchange rates.

Incoming survey data from multiple organizations are typically combined in such a way that estimates can be made about the midpoints and pay RATE RANGES associated with a KEY JOB/BENCHMARK JOB. These estimates about direct pay must be interpreted in relation to other compensation-related employer costs (particularly expenditures associated with employee benefits).

Bibliography

Milkovich, G. T. & Newman, J. M. (1993). *Compensation*, Homewood, IL: Richard D. Irwin.

Rynes, S. L. & Milkovich, G. T. (1986). Wage surveys: dispelling some myths about the "Market Wage." *Personnel Psychology*, 39, 571–95.

GEORGE F. DREHER

wage/pay/salary structure   A wage structure represents a series of pay grades that order jobs on the basis of worth. As such, it reflects the entire spectrum, from low wage jobs to high wage jobs. Organizations with rapid promotion policies, but little pay advance for any given promotion, have relatively flat structures: the wage progression from grade to grade is small. Conversely, organizations with few promotion opportunities and sizable increases for any given promotion have steep structures.

JERRY M. NEWMAN

wheel of retailing   This is a theory suggesting that entrants to a new retail market will begin trading as cut-price, low overhead, low margin, and low status operations (McNair, 1958). Over time, these traders will increase their overheads by offering additional services and product lines, perhaps in better locations, smarter premises and with more sophisticated marketing communications. These retailers are then more vulnerable to new low cost entrants to the market who may be able to undercut the original retailer's prices. The retail cycle will then have come full circle.

The wheel theory is a generalization that may not hold true in all cases. Retailers entering new markets may be tempted to copy the trading format of established retailers which may require sophisticated trading patterns from the start. In other cases, such as times of recession, retailers may attempt to cut costs and even reduce some services, thus moving in the opposite direction to that which is suggested by the wheel theory.

Bibliography

McNair, M. P. (1958). Significant trends and developments in the post war period. In A. B. Smith (Ed.), *Competitive distribution in a free high level economy and its implications for the university* (pp. 1–25). University of Pittsburgh Press.

STEVE WORRALL

whistleblowing   A practice in which employees who know that their company is engaged in activities that (a) cause unnecessary harm, (b) are in violation of human rights, (c) are illegal, (d) run counter to the defined purpose of the institution, or (e) are otherwise immoral, inform the public or some governmental agency of those activities. The ethical problem is whether and under what conditions whistleblowing is acceptable behavior and/or morally required behavior. Whistleblowing, if required, would involve a conflict between the obligation of loyalty the individual is presumed to have to the company and the obligation to prevent harm the individual is presumed to have to the public. But the exact nature and demands of these conflicting obligations to the company and the public are disputed.

Most business ethicists claim that employees have some obligation to the company or employer, which is usually characterized as an obligation of loyalty. Whistleblowing violates that obligation. In that context the company is viewed as analogous to a sports team. In sports whistleblowing is the function of neutral, detached referees who are supposed to detect and penalize illicit behavior of opposing teams. It is neither acceptable nor a responsibility of a player to call a foul on one's teammates. If the analogy holds, what is unacceptable in sports is also unacceptable in business. From this perspective whistleblowing is viewed as an act of disloyalty ("finking," "tattle tale") and there is a presumption against it. Consequently, a countervailing obligation to the public would be the only justification for overriding the obligation to the team or company. There is a wide range of views on the issue ranging from the position that whistleblowing as an act of disloyalty is never justified to the opposite position that employees owe no loyalty to a company and given their right to freedom of expression they can ethically disclose whatever they wish about a company, except where their work contract expressly or at least implicitly prohibits it.

Most business ethicists writing on whistleblowing maintain a fiduciary obligation of loyalty that whistleblowing violates, so the burden of proof or justification falls to the whistleblower. However, defenders of whistleblowing maintain that in conditions where companies violate ethical and/or legal constraints, whatever obligation of loyalty an employee has is abrogated, and whistleblowing is not only permissible but may also be morally required, on the grounds that individuals have a responsibility to the general public to prevent harm or illegal activity. Hence the conflict of obligations we mentioned. However, it is possible to argue that even if the illegal or immoral behavior of the company abrogates the responsibility of loyalty, there is no consequent good samaritan obligation to the general public to "blow the whistle."

So two arguments are needed. One to show whistleblowing is permissible, a second to show it is required. This latter argument is quite important, since blowing the whistle can lead to harm to the whistleblower. Under what conditions is one required to do what would likely harm oneself?

The argument for the permissibility of whistleblowing sets down a set of conditions to be met before a whistleblower can justifiably inform on her company.

1. The whistleblowing should be done for the purpose of exposing unnecessary harm, violation of human rights, illegal activity, or conduct counter to the defined purpose of the corporation, and should be done from the appropriate moral motive, that is, not from a desire to get ahead, or out of spite or some such motive. Nevertheless, whether the act of whistleblowing is called for is not determined by the motive of the whistleblower but by the company acting either immorally or illegally.

2. The whistleblower should make certain that his or her belief that inappropriate actions are ordered or have occurred is based on evidence that would persuade a reasonable person.

3. The whistleblower should have acted only after a careful analysis of the danger: (a) how serious is the moral violation? (minor moral matters need not be reported); (b) how immediate is the moral violation? (the greater time before the violation occurs the greater chances that internal mechanisms will prevent the anticipated violation); (c) is the moral violation one that can be specified? (general claims about a rapacious company, obscene profits, and actions contrary to public interest simply will not do).

4. Except in special circumstances, the whistleblower should have exhausted all internal channels for dissent before informing the public. The whistleblower's action should be commensurate with one's responsibility for avoiding and/or exposing moral violations. If there are personnel in the company whose obligation it is to monitor and respond to immoral and/or illegal activities, it would be their responsibility to address those issues. Thus, the first obligation of the would-be whistleblower, would be to report the unethical activities to those persons, and only if they do not act, to inform the general public.

5. The whistleblower should have some chance of success. Ought implies can, so if there is no hope in arousing societal or government pressure, then one needlessly exposes oneself and one's loved ones to hardship for no conceivable moral gain.

But these conditions speak mainly to the *permissibility* of blowing the whistle. A further, often overlooked question is under what conditions is it morally required (*obligatory*), if ever, for an employee to blow the whistle? The literature on this subject is sparse, except that there seems to be a good deal of tacit agreement that some sort of good samaritan principle is operative here. Hence if there is an obligation to prevent harm, under conditions where there is a need and the person is capable of preventing the harm without sacrificing something of comparable moral worth, and if the person is the last resort, then that obligation would operate in the case of whistleblowing. Conditions 4 and 5 may be read as assuming that there is a responsibility to blow the whistle. But to show that obligation requires showing there is an obligation to the general public to prevent harm (Simon et al., 1972).

In the corporate context, the company is seen as a team and expects loyalty. Forsaking the team to function as a detached referee to blow the whistle is seen as disloyal and cause for punitive action. In such a culture, to blow the whistle requires a certain moral heroism. Given the fact that society depends on whistleblowers to protect it from unscrupulous operators, justified whistleblowers need some protection. To assure the existence of necessary whistleblowers (somebody's got to do it), sound legislation is needed to protect the whistleblower.

Finally, whistleblowing is not restricted to the area of business. It occurs in all walks of life. Professionals may be held to the standards of their profession, that sometimes require blowing a whistle. For example, accountants and engineers have a dual obligation to their clients and to the public. Hence, they have a fiduciary responsibility to report certain illegal or potentially harmful activities if they encounter them in the course of their auditing or accounting or constructing. These obligations come from the professional status of the accountants and engineers, just as such obligations extend to all professionals, such as doctors and lawyers, who have obligations to their profession and the public to blow the whistle on colleagues who violate certain canons of appropriate behavior. But beyond the professions, whistleblowing is required in other walks of life: for example, the participants in an honor code have a responsibility to report violations. While such whistleblowing activity is viewed unfavorably, it is a necessary part of human activity.

Enlightened companies, aware that harmful, immoral, or illegal behavior that needs to be reported is likely to occur from time to time, have begun to make provisions for regularizing the monitoring of behavior, with ombudspersons or corporate responsibility officers. Such offices provide an outlet for those who feel obliged to report the unseemly behavior of their companies, without the need to go public. These provisions are desirable because they will alleviate the necessity of going public and blowing the whistle on harmful or illegal behavior.

Bibliography

Bok, S. (1980). Whistleblowing and professional responsibility. *New York University Professional Quarterly*, **11** (summer), 2–7.
De George, R. (1986). *Business Ethics*, 2nd edn. New York: Macmillan.

Duska, R. F. (1985). Whistleblowing and employee loyalty. In J. R. Desjardins & J. J. McCall, (eds), *Contemporary Issues in Business Ethics*. Belmont, Calif.: Wadsworth, 295–300.

Glazer, M. P. & Glazer, P. M. (1989). *The Whistleblowers: Exposing Corruption in Government and Industry*. New York: Basic Books.

Larmer, R. A. (1992). Whistleblowing and employee loyalty. *Journal of Business Ethics*, 11, 125–8.

Nader, R., Petkas, P., & Blackwell, K. (1972). *Whistleblowing*. New York: Bantam Books.

Simon, J. G., Powers, C., & Gunneman, J. P. (1972). *The Ethical Investor*. New Haven: Yale University Press.

Westin, A. F. (1981). *Whistle Blowing: Loyalty and Dissent in the Corporation*. New York: McGraw-Hill.

RONALD F. DUSKA

wholesalers   Wholesalers form the part of the marketing channel between producers/manufacturers and the retailer. Wholesalers buy and sell in large quantities direct to the retailer and generally do not sell goods direct to the public.

see also **Retail distribution channels**

Bibliography
Lewison, D. (1994). *Retailing*. New York: Macmillan.

STEVE GREENLAND

wholly owned subsidiary   This form of market entry provides a company full control over its foreign operations. This method of market entry requires large capital investment, commitment of time and effort, and normally a willingness of some employees/management to travel to and live in a foreign country. Owned subsidiaries may be existing businesses which are acquired by the company. If this is so the investment in management and expatriate time and effort may not be as significant as a start-up operation.

see also **Market entry strategies**

Bibliography
Cateora, P. R. (1993). *International marketing*. 5th edn, Homewood, IL: Irwin.

JOHN O'CONNELL

WIPO   *see* WORLD INTELLECTUAL PROPERTY ORGANISATION

women at work   Most women have always worked, of course, but traditionally, fewer women than men have engaged in *paid* work. In 1890, for example, women made up only 17 percent of the US labor force; by 1980, women were 44 percent of the US labor force. In 1985, 54.5 percent of the US women 16 years of age an older and 64.7 percent of the women between the ages of 25 and 64 were employed (Statistical Abstract of the United States, 1988, Table No. 627). In the Scandinavian countries, typically 75 percent or more of adult women are in the labor force. The same was true in many countries of the former Soviet Union, but the current situation is unstable, changing rapidly, and unemployment among women is high in many of these countries. During the 1970s and 1980s in particular, women increased their share of the labor force in almost every country of the world (United Nations, 1991). Furthermore, in all areas of the world today, women in the prime child-bearing years (25–44) are more likely to be employed than women either younger or older in age (United Nations, 1991, Table 6.8).

The topic of "women at work" as a coherent subfield is less than 20 years old (e.g., Nieva & Gutek, 1981), and it tends to be interdisciplinary, involving researchers from many fields, e.g., management, psychology, sociology, economics, anthropology. While the field is not bereft of theory, so far, much of the research has been descriptive, a necessary step because the topic is fraught with misperceptions and misinformation. In all of the research, gender figures prominently, and women and their experiences are either overtly or covertly compared with men: Jobs are "sex-segregated" and in the job choice literature, women choose and work in either "male-dominated" or "female-dominated jobs." "Sex differences" is a common theme in the research and encompasses both differences between men and women and differences in treatment of men and women.

Women tend to work in "women's jobs," jobs defined in a particular time and place as appropriate for women. Although there are some consistencies across countries, cultures, and organizations (e.g., jobs involving children tend to be labeled women's jobs), there are also many examples of one job being a "man's job" in one country, culture, or organization, and a "woman's job" in another (e.g., medicine, sales, clerical work).

Women's work is characterized by horizontal and vertical segregation. Horizontal segregation means that women tend to have different occupations and career choices than men and they tend to work with other women. In 1970 in the United States about 55 percent of women were in female-dominated occupations (Jacobs, 1989, Table 2.4). Sex-segregation is measured by several statistics (see Jacobs, 1989), notably the index of segregation (also known as the index of dissimilarity, D) which tells the percentage of one sex who would have to change jobs so that they would be distributed across jobs the same as the other sex. In the United States, sex-segregation has declined from about 76 in 1910 to 62 in 1981 (Jacobs, 1989), and it has done so, not because more men are working in jobs traditionally held by women (they are not), but because women have moved into traditionally male jobs, especially professional and managerial jobs such as law, medicine, management, and the professorate. During the 1970s, in the United States a number of jobs that were male-dominated prior to the 1970s became sex-integrated or female-dominated between 1970 and 1980, including bartending, residential real estate, baking, accounting, editing, public relations, and pharmacy (Reskin & Roos, 1990). Reskin and Roos (1990) concluded that women made inroads into these male-dominated fields because either the jobs were rapidly growing so that not enough men were available to fill them and/or these jobs tended to have fewer attractions to men (e.g., declining pay, fewer fringe benefits, fewer opportunities for autonomy or entrepreneurial activity) who shifted their career attention to more attractive alternatives. Jacobs (1989) concluded that for every 11 women who enter a nontraditional job, 10 leave, yielding a net decrease in sex-segregation of jobs, but not as much change as might be expected given women's interest in the jobs. An extensive literature on women's career aspirations, CAREER CHOICES, and career development document the processes by which work maintains a sex-segregated character and the experiences of individual women (see, e.g., Betz & Fitzgerald, 1987; Gutek & Larwood, 1987).

Vertical segregation means that men and women are located at different places in the hierarchy in their work. Women tend to be located in lower level positions in their occupations and in their organizations whereas men are found in jobs throughout the hierarchy. Women are said to face a "glass ceiling" in that they are rarely found above certain hierarchical levels. Like horizontal segregation, vertical segregation is also decreasing, although women have made little headway at the top (see WOMEN MANAGERS).

It is worth noting that the research tends to focus disproportionately on women in nontraditional jobs (i.e., management and the male-dominated professions) and women at higher organizational ranks (managers and executives). Likewise, the research focuses disproportionately on white women and middle and upper class women. These features are characteristic of ORGANIZATIONAL BEHAVIOR as a whole, not just women at work.

In general, the research on women at work fits into one of three categories: sex-differences, problem-focused, and changes initiated to alleviate problems (e.g., Firth-Cozens & West, 1991).

One type of research focuses on differences and similarities between the sexes. Among the topics covered, and some of the researchers exploring each topic, are the following: differences in masculinity and femininity and their implications (Powell); differences or similarities in LEADERSHIP or managerial style or leadership style (Eagly; Dobbins); sex differences in CAREER CHOICES and career interests (Betz; Astin); and differences and similarities in achieving (Tangri; Lipman-Blumen). Early research focused on traits or characteristics believed to be associated with women more than men such as fear of success (Horner). A few areas are notable for the lack of expected sex differences. For example, while there is an active debate about whether men and women exhibit different leadership styles, the extant research suggests that men and women in leadership positions exhibit few differences (Eagly; Dobbins). And despite the fact that women's and men's job experiences tend to differ, they tend to report similar levels of JOB SATISFACTION, and in recent years, job COMMITMENT.

A large body of research on women at work focuses on problems faced by women. These topics include the following, listed with some researchers and theorists in each field: biases in selection, placement, PERFORMANCE APPRAISAL, and promotion (Nieva & Gutek; Swim et al.); sexual harassment (Fitzgerald; Gutek; Powell; Pryor; Terpstra & Baker); obstacles to achievement, advancement, and attainment of positions of leadership (Larwood; Morrison); lack of mentoring (Ragins; Fagenson); sex discrimination (Heilman; Crosby; Larwood); the pay gap (England; Olson; Konrad; Langton); stereotyping (Fiske); lack of job mobility (Brett); conflict between work and family responsibilities (Pleck; Brett; Burke; Davidson; Cooper); reproductive hazards at work; conflict between work role and gender role (Nieva & Gutek). Other researchers have noted the problems faced by tokens (women who are numerically rare) (Kanter; Laws), the "double whammy" of being minority and female in nontraditional jobs (Nkomo), and the problems faced by

women when there are few women in top management positions in the organization (Ely).

A third type of research focuses on the success or failure of attempts to alleviate problems faced by working women (see e.g., Sekaran, 1992), including the impacts of laws and other programs aimed at providing equal opportunity, addressing affirmative action, establishing the comparable worth of jobs, and eliminating sexual harassment. But laws are not the only approach to alleviating problems faced by working women. In general, the type of solution sought depends on the way the problem is defined. Nieva and Gutek (1981; see also Gutek, 1993) listed four models of problem definition and some problem-solving strategies that follow from them. They are: the individual deficit model, i.e., the problem is defined as problem people; the structural model, i.e., organizational structures and policies hamper women (see Kanter, 1977); the sex-role model, i.e., social roles and ROLE expectations and role stereotypes hamper women; and the intergroup model wherein men and women are viewed as opposing groups fighting over a limited amount of desirable jobs, POWER, and INFLUENCE. They conclude that the most commonly proposed solutions fit the individual-deficit model. Women are given training and opportunities to overcome their "deficits" through courses and self-help materials targeted at them. Examples include dressing for success, assertiveness training, how to write a business plan or obtain venture capital. Increasingly, men too are targets of training aimed at sensitizing them to issues like sexual harassment and sex discrimination.

Bibliography

Betz, N. & Fitzgerald, L. (1987). The career psychology of women. New York: Academic Press.

Firth-Cozens, J. & West, M. (Eds), (1991). Women at work; Psychological and organizational perspectives. Buckingham, UK: Open University Press.

Gutek, B. A. (1993). Changing the status of women in management. Applied Psychology: An International Review, 43, (4), 301–311.

Gutek, B. A. & Larwood, L. (Eds), (1987). Women's career development. Newbury Park, CA: Sage.

Jacobs, J. (1989). Revolving doors; Sex segregation and women's careers. Stanford, CA: Stanford University Press.

Kanter, R. M. (1977). Men and women of the corporation. New York: Basic Books.

Nieva, V. F. & Gutek, B. A. (1981). Women and work: Praeger.

Reskin, B. & Roos, P. A. (1990). Job queues, gender queues. Philadelphia, PA: Temple University Press.

Sekaran, U. (Ed.), (1992). Womanpower. Newbury Park, CA: Sage.

Statistical Abstract of the United States (1988). Washington, DC: U.S. Government Printing Office.

United Nations (1991). The world's women: Trends and statistics, 1970–1990. Social Statistics and Indicators, Series K, No. 8 New York: The United Nations.

BARBARA A. GUTEK

women managers Today women hold a larger share of managerial positions than ever and the subfield of women in management, though only about 20 years old (see Larwood & Wood, 1977), has grown as well (see Powell, 1993; Fagenson, 1993). Women have made the greatest inroads into management in those countries in which an academic degree (MBA, bachelor's degree in commerce) is used as criterion for obtaining the position of manager. The United States, where about 12 percent of all employees hold the position of manager, leads in moving women into management. In 1900, women were 4.4 percent of all US managers; in 1950, 13.6 percent; in 1980, 26.1 percent, and by 1992, women constituted 42 percent of all US managers (Fagenson, 1993). About 34.5 percent of Canadian managers are women, compared to 20 percent in (the former West) Germany, 23 percent in and Ireland, and 7.5 percent in Japan (Antal & Izraeli in Fagenson, 1993). In countries that do not rely much on formal educational programs to prepare people for management, the percentage of women is lower.

Although the numbers of women managers have increased, women are virtually unrepresented in the highest ranking DECISION MAKING positions in business and government in almost every country in the world. Women occupy less than 5 percent of high ranking positions in the United States and only one woman heads a *Fortune* 500 corporation. A study of the 1000 most valuable publicly held companies in the United States in 1989 showed only two women among CEOS (up from one in 1988). The $3.3 trillion in annual sales of these companies underscores the minuscule influence of women in big business in the United States. Over the past 10 years, the number of women at the senior management level of the United States' top corporations has increased by less than 2 percent. Currently, there is a lively debate over whether the gender gap between the lower and higher ranks of management is a temporary or more-or-less permanent phenomenon. Some scholars believe that insufficient time has passed for women to move into the top ranks whereas others disagree (see Gutek, 1993; Northcraft & Gutek in Fagenson, 1993); both sides are able to marshall some evidence for their position.

Another lively debate in the field addresses the issue of managerial style: do women have a unique management style or a style that differs from that typically used by men? Although those who argue that they do rely on people's experiences and "common sense" observations (Rosener, 1990), the bulk of the research evidence suggests that men and women who are in management do not differ in management style (Powell, 1993; *see* VALIDITY GENERALIZATION) on leadership style by Eagly and Johnson, 1990). There is more intra- than between-sex variation in management style.

Management represents a "nontraditional" job choice for women and has traditionally been viewed as more appropriate for men than women (*see* WOMEN AT WORK). A series of studies by V. Schein and colleagues (Brenner, Tomkiewicz, & Schein, 1989) showed that in the mid-1970s both sexes associated the traits of successful managers with stereotypically male traits but they were independent of stereotypes of female traits. Recent research by Schein suggests that this finding is generalizable to many different countries, although by the late 1980s in the United States, women but not men, were somewhat more likely to associate the traits of successful managers with traits associated with both men and women (*see* PERSONALITY).

see also **Women at work**

Bibliography

Brenner, O. C., Tomkiewicz, J. & Schein, V. E. (1989). The relationship between sex role stereotype and requisite management characteristics revisited. Academy of Management Journal, 32, 662–669.

Fagenson, E. A. (ed.) (1993). Women in management: Trends, issues, and challenges in managerial diversity, (vol. 4 in the Women and Work series) Newbury Park, CA: Sage.

Gutek, B. A. (1993). Changing the status of women in management. In E. Greenglass & J. Marshall (Editors of a special issue: Women in management) Applied Psychology: An International Review, 43, (4) 301–311.

Larwood, L. & Wood, M. (1977). Women in management. Lexington, MA: Lexington Books.

Powell, G. (1993). Women in management, (2nd edn) Newbury Park, CA: Sage.

Rosener, J. B. (1990). Ways women lead. Harvard Business Review, 68, (6) 119–125.

BARBARA A. GUTEK

women's career issues Women's career issues are defined as those issues that affect the progress of women in organizations, such as barriers to entry, sex segregation of occupational CAREER PATHING, the CAREER STAGES experienced by women, how women cope with WORK-FAMILY CONFLICT, and the factors affecting women's ability to break through the upper executive level (Powell and Mainiero, 1993). This discussion will focus on the organizational issues that affect the promotion of women as a group.

Initial Staffing and Promotion Decisions

Women often are hired into staff rather than line positions and subsequently find it hard to move into a line or field capacity. When women are stuck in career paths that preclude line experiences, their prospects for career advancement are limited. Larwood and Gattiker (1987) initially confirmed this notion in a study that tracked older and younger women's career paths. Overall, they found that men had greater professional standing, held line positions more often, and achieved higher positions in their departments than did women. Bureau of Labor statistics further confirm that even in the 1990s, fewer than 10 percent of women held positions at the upper executive level in Fortune 500 corporations. Although women are being promoted, their promotions do not seem to be as vital and may lead to early CAREER PLATEAU. What may be taking place is a pacification by promotion, so that women may be given promotions to create the appearance of increasing responsibility and opportunity, but such promotions may be essentially hollow (see Powell and Mainiero, 1993).

Career Progress Issues

Among those women who have broken through the GLASS CEILING to the upper executive level, defined as the vice president level or higher, studies of their career histories show five factors that affect their ability to become fast-tracked in their early career: (a) Getting assigned to a high-visibility project; (b) demonstrating critical skills for effective job performance; (c) attracting top level support; (d) displaying entrepreneurial initiative; and (e) accurately identifying what the company values (Mainiero, 1994). In summary, substantial groups of women have not sufficiently progressed to the upper levels to permit tracking of their career progress in a coherent manner. Most women who have made it to the upper levels, or even middle levels, have experienced a variety of career issues along the way, such as difficulties in obtaining mentors, coping with corporate politics, and work–family conflicts that may impede their career progress.

Bibliography

Larwood, L. & Gattiker, U. (1987). A comparison of the career paths used by successful women. *Women's Career Development*, Eds. Gutek, B. A. & Larwood, L. Beverly Hills, CA: Sage Publications.

Mainiero, L. A. (1994). Getting anointed for advancement: the case of executive women. *Academy of Management Executive*, 8, 53–67.

Powell, G. N. & Mainiero, L. A. (1993). Crosscurrents in the river of time: conceptualizing the complexities of women's careers. *Journal of Management*, 18, 215–38.

LISA MAINIERO

word-of-mouth communications Word-of-mouth communication is a non-commercial form of marketing communication where the sender of the message is assisted by intermediaries in attempting to reach the target buyer/customer/consumer. Opinion leaders (*see* OPINION LEADER) may benefit an organization with positive word-of-mouth communications but there is a danger that word of mouth may be detrimental to the organization and its products or services as a result of poor experiences of the intermediary.

see also **Interpersonal communications; Marketing communications**

DAVID YORKE

work constraints Work constraints refer to a variety of situational factors that interfere with the translation of task-relevant individual differences into corresponding differences in performance. Although situational factors had long been recognized as potentially important determinants of performance, research and understanding of work constraints was hampered by the absence of a formal conceptual framework to organize work in the area. Systematic efforts to study work constraints in their own right only recently appeared in the early 1980s (see Peters and O'Connor, 1980). Peters and O'Connor conceptualized situational constraints as factors beyond the control of the individual that are part of the immediate work environment, and that prevent people from fully utilizing their capabilities.

Peters and O'Connor (1980) used the critical incidents method to develop a fairly generalizable taxonomy of work constraints, and they provided a conceptual framework with testable propositions about the constraint construct. There are three hypotheses central to the Peters and O'Connor situational constraint framework. First, situational constraints were hypothesized to have direct negative effects on JOB PERFORMANCE and work attitudes (e.g. JOB SATISFACTION). Second, situational constraints were predicted to moderate the relationship between task-relevant individual differences and performance – individual differences would be expected to produce a stronger relationship with performance in low constraint as opposed to high constraint conditions. Finally, the observed variability in performance was expected to be greater in low constraint as opposed to high constraint conditions. In effect, constraints were hypothesized to impose an artificial ceiling on potential performance and thereby impede the translation of task-relevant attributes into corresponding performance differences.

Research on Work Constraints
Empirical support for these three predictions is mixed and largely inconclusive. One explanation for these mixed results, as Peters et al. (1985) noted, may be that few work settings have very severe work constraints. They characterized these low levels of constraints as resembling "nuisances" rather than obstacles. More significantly, they offered a set of boundary conditions to explain when constraints would be expected to influence performance, including: (a) the assignment of persons to tasks that demand the use of their abilities; (b) the maintenance of sufficiently demanding performance standards; (c) raters who do not somehow compensate for the presence of constraints in their ratings; and (d) that resources vary in their availability across individuals. Each of these is considered a necessary but not sufficient condition to sustain the hypothesized constraint–performance relationship. Information about these boundary conditions seems necessary to formulate confident conclusions.

Problems and Prospects
The consistent finding of small and seemingly negligible effects of constraints on performance (e.g. Olson and Borman, 1989) has stimulated interest in alternative conceptualizations of constraints and models of the constraint–performance relationship (Villanova and Roman, 1993). As one example, Schoorman and Schneider (1988) applied an open systems perspective to the study of constraints in group work settings. The current popularity of total quality management (and the emphasis it places on work system factors) and the potential practical significance promised from better understanding of constraints are likely to result in additional efforts to investigate this long-overlooked performance determinant.

Bibliography

Olson, D. M. & Borman, W. C. (1989). More evidence on relationships between the work environment and job performance. *Human Performance*, 2, 113–30.

Peters, L. H. & O'Connor, E. J. (1980). Situational constraints and work outcomes: the influences of a frequently overlooked construct. *Academy of Management Review*, 5, 391–7.

Peters, L. H., O'Connor, E. J. & Eulberg, J. R. (1985). Situational constraints: sources, consequences, and future considerations. *Research in Personnel and Human Resources Management*, Eds. Rowland, K. & Ferris, G. Greenwich, CT: JAI Press.

Schoorman, F. D. & Schneider, B. (1988). *Facilitating Work Effectiveness*, Lexington, MA: Lexington.

Villanova, P. & Roman, M. A. (1993). A meta-analytic review of situational constraints and work-related outcomes: alternative approaches to conceptualization. *Human Resource Management Review*, 3, 147–75.

PETER VILLANOVA

work values Values represent a social system's effort to encourage its members to behave in ways that foster the system's welfare. As such, values are enduring beliefs about how an individual *ought* to behave (Rokeach, 1973). The type of values and their specificity depend on the particular social system (e.g. society, a formal organization, one's group). The subset of values that are relevant to the workplace are called work values. This definition differs from the "value" one places on objects (Locke, 1991), although one's work values are important standards for making such evaluations.

Values found to be important in the workplace include achievement, concern for others, honesty, working hard, positive outlook, helping others, and fairness (Ravlin and Meglino, 1987), although certain organizations may endorse more specific values (e.g. customer service). Because values describe socially desirable behavior, one's choice of behavior depends on the centrality (i.e. relative importance) of his or her specific values. Values are, therefore, held in hierarchical form (Rokeach, 1973).

Values can characterize individuals as well as social systems such as organizations. An organization's system of values is said to underlie its organizational culture. Organizations impart their values on individuals through avenues that include ORGANIZATIONAL SOCIALIZATION. Value similarity among organizational members is also enhanced through a process that reflects the attraction–selection–attrition model. Work values are also assessed as part of personnel selection and promotion processes.

Work values affect one's perception and interpretation of environmental stimuli and encourage individuals to behave in accordance with their more dominant values (Ravlin and Meglino, 1987). Values also affect relationships through the process of value congruence. The more an individual's value system is similar or congruent with that of another person or work system, the more his or her interactions with that person and within that work system are likely to be positive (Meglino et al., 1989).

Bibliography
Locke, E. A. (1991). The motivation sequence, the motivation hub, and the motivation core. *Organizational Behavior and Human Decision Processes*, 50, 288–9.
Meglino, B. M., Ravlin, E. C. & Adkins, C. L. (1989). A work values approach to corporate culture: a field test of the value congruence process and its relationship to individual outcomes. *Journal of Applied Psychology*, 74, 424–32.
Ravlin, E. C. & Meglino, B. M. (1987). Issues in work values measurement. *Research in Corporate Social Performance and Policy*, 9, Frederick, W. C. Greenwich, CT: JAI Press.
Rokeach, M. (1973). *The Nature of Human Values*, New York: Free Press.

BRUCE M. MEGLINO

work–family conflict Work–family conflict is commonly understood to be a specific form of interrole conflict in which role pressures from the work and family life domains are mutually incompatible. Several models (e.g. spillover, compensation, segmentation) have been developed to describe and explain the relationship between work and the family (Zedeck and Mosier, 1990). Work–family conflict may be categorized by three dimensions (Greenhaus and Beutell, 1985). *Time-based* conflict is a consequence of competition for an individual's time from multiple role demands. *Strain-based* conflict results when role stressors in one domain induce physical or psychological strain in the individual, hampering fulfillment of role expectations in the other domain. *Behavior-based* conflict results when patterns of behavior that are appropriate in one domain are inappropriately practiced in the other domain.

Most commonly, work–family conflict is modeled as having both antecedent causes (e.g. social support, work setting characteristics) and outcome effects (e.g. job satisfaction, burnout, organizational commitment). Initially, research on work–family conflict primarily addressed WOMEN'S CAREER ISSUES and DUAL-CAREER COUPLES, but with recent demographic changes, research has broadened to incorporate other perspectives. Past investigations have also tended to center on objective, sent role conflict, neglecting the more subjective, personally experienced aspects of work–family conflict (Greenhaus, 1988). However, recent research addressing subjective perceptions has begun to enhance understanding of work–family conflict, addressing, for example, mood (Williams and Alliger, 1994), values discrepancies (Lobel, 1993), and individual motivations for choices regarding the relative balance between work and family (Stephens and Feldman, 1997).

Bibliography
Greenhaus, J. H. (1988). The intersection of work and family roles: individual, interpersonal, and organizational issues. *Journal of Social Behavior and Personality*, 3, 23–44.
Greenhaus, J. H. & Beutell, N. J. (1985). Sources of conflict between work and family roles. *Academy of Management Review*, 10, 76–88.
Lobel, S. A. (1993). A value-laden approach to integrating work and family life. *Human Resource Management*, 31, 249–65.
Stephens, G. K. & Feldman, D. C. (1997). A motivational approach for understanding career versus personal life investments. *Research in Personnel and Human Resources Management*, 15, Ferris, G. R. Greenwich, CT: JAI Press.
Williams, K. J. & Alliger, G. M. (1994). Role stressors, mood spillover, and perceptions of work–family conflict in employed parents. *Academy of Management Journal*, 37, 837–68.
Zedeck, S. & Mosier, K. L. (1990). Work in the family and employing organization. *American Psychologist*, 45, 240–51.

GREGORY K. STEPHENS

workforce diversity When an organization hires employees from different countries, or even different parts of the same country, workforce diversity occurs. As organizations grow, their workforce normally is comprised of persons of all races, religions, political beliefs, economic status, and geographic regions. Understanding and developing plans to deal with workforce diversity are essential steps to promoting goodwill among employees and fostering productivity in the workplace. Many of management's most difficult challenges arise because of diversity in the workplace. The major challenge is to motivate all employees toward organizational goals while at the same time allowing diversity to exist.

see also **Cultural diversity**

JOHN O'CONNELL

workforce flexibility Workforce flexibility is a term describing the extent to which an organization can adapt its human resources to new skills, functions, and structures in order to accommodate changing environmental conditions. Workforce flexibility suggests that workers are multiskilled, and have the foundation for continued training, so that the organization can benefit from their talents on an "as needed" basis. It also suggests that the employees have the capacity to adapt to organizational changes with little direct managerial supervision, instead of relying on self-managing mechanisms (*see* SELF-MANAGING TEAMS). We first examine the transformation of organizational contexts which creates the need for workforce flexibility, and then we review some of the human resources systems that need to be put in place or modified in order to support a flexible workforce.

Transformation of Organizational Contexts

Realizing that traditional organizational structures may not be efficient for global market competition, many organizations have taken on considerable changes in size, structure and designs of organizations and work systems.

Downsizing. A common strategy of American businesses during the late 1980s and early 1990s was reducing the size of an organization's workforce, more commonly known as downsizing. Two predominant reasons explain this: (a) to lower overhead costs by eliminating unnecessary positions; and (b) to increase the organization's ability to react quickly to environmental conditions. Combined, lower overhead and quicker responsiveness allow the organization better competitive positioning. Yet the actual task of reducing workforces proved to be a daunting challenge, as evidenced by the disappointing results found by many firms pursuing this strategy (Lalli, 1992). Too often the results of a downsizing initiative didn't lead to a smaller organization doing things more efficiently, but instead the downsized organization was merely the same organization doing things the same way, only with fewer workers ill-equipped to handle the transition.

Restructuring, redesigning and re-engineering. Organizational change can include restructuring communication channels of the organization, redesigning the hierarchical chains of command, or changing the technologies so that work itself is performed differently. Definitions of what constitutes organizational restructuring are plentiful and varied, but a helpful approach for understanding it is to ask the question, "If we were to build the organization from the ground up, how would we do it?" It requires abandoning the status quo altogether to design a way of doing things that would not be hindered by existing practices, individuals, or other sacred cows.

As evidence of the popularity of restructuring, several new organizational forms with names such as "Shamrock," "Starburst," and "Pizza" (Byrne, 1993) have been proposed as alternatives to the traditional pyramid structure. Characteristics of redesigned companies emphasize greater horizontal management, having fewer organizational levels, more direct interaction between organizational members (thereby de-emphasizing formal chains of command), and more boundary personnel (i.e. greater direct contact with parties outside of the organization, specifically customers and suppliers). In turn, this increased interaction will mean the organization will have a better sense of what customers want and an improved awareness of environmental conditions. Re-engineering jobs go hand in hand with technological change, most notably computers. As improved automation changes how the work is performed, so too does it change how work is organized. Different technologies allow for changes in the work sequence and who performs the work.

Creation of a Flexible Workforce

As organizations change so too must their work forces so that they can respond more quickly to variations in the external environment. Organizations will be forced to make do with fewer employees, who in turn will have greater responsibility for productivity, quality and customer service. Furthermore, the organizational context changes will also bring about a need for employees to be multi-skilled, to be more internally controlled and self-managed, and for work to be more team or group-based rather than individual-based. Fortunately, these changes can contribute to even greater levels of performance and more favorable employee reactions (e.g. Pfeffer, 1994). This change in organizational form prompted Daft and Lewin (1993) to suggest that we need to revise and update our theories of organizations.

Organizational Culture

Changing organizational structures and the roles of its members has a profound effect on the organization's culture. Organizational cultures are meant to provide an anchor for molding members' opinions and actions. In a rapidly changing environment, the organization is faced with a paradoxical dilemma of trying to achieve high levels of flexibility while simultaneously maintaining a stable culture. To reconcile, firms must embrace cultures which value change and innovation. Under Jack Welch, for example, General Electric (GE) restructured itself while implementing "Workout Program," leading to a cultural transformation in which speed, simplicity, and self-confidence were the guiding values (Ulrich and LaFasto, 1995). As with GE, other organizations' cultures must change to emphasize the dynamic potential of their employees. This means identifying an environment that encourages contribution and change.

Human Resources Systems to Support Workforce Flexibility

The success or failure of organizational context changes depends immeasurably on the efforts of a firm's workforce. As Pfeffer (1994) argues, in a rapidly changing business environment, it makes sense to invest in an organization's human capital since technical obsolescence occurs sooner and more frequently. In a rapidly changing environment, the human resources function must be "ahead of the curve" so that it can assist the rest of the organization through its transition. In the following sections, we identify several human resources functions, and discuss how current trends of organizational change are likely to affect the services offered by these functions.

Performance evaluation and promotion. Perhaps the most dramatic change to careers in the changing environment is that vertical mobility will no longer be the standard reward for job success. Flatter organizations have fewer opportunities for advancement, and recent downsizing initiatives have eliminated layers of middle management. However, this does not suggest a diminished need for performance appraisal. Instead, the dizzying pace of change makes it necessary that all workers be at their required skill levels, which places greater importance on evaluations. To complicate matters, the increasing use of teams changes how work is evaluated, since distinguishing between individual and group contributions becomes unclear. As a result, flexible organizations must implement PERFOR-

MANCE APPRAISAL procedures that identify job-related skills and individuals' competence levels in them. Supervisor ratings will be less common for two reasons: (a) managerial spans of control are broader in horizontal organizations, making individual managers less able to observe the behaviors of their workers, and (b) as mentioned earlier, jobs organized within team structures make identifying individual contributions difficult for outsiders. To compensate, performance appraisals will rely increasingly on PEER RATINGS, in which workers appraise their coworkers or team members. Additionally, the greater focus on customer service provides an opportunity for customers to rate workers (see 360 DEGREE APPRAISALS). Not only will this provide more accurate information regarding service, but it will also alleviate the burden put upon managers.

Promotions, although more rare, will still occur and it is important to note that firms must be cautious in their selections for advancement. In fact, some might argue that organizations would profit from moving away from a "fast track" system (with respect to mobility) toward a slower evaluation and promotion system, with longer time spent in positions before eligibility for promotion is achieved. This slower movement accomplishes at least two objectives of the organization. First, with people spending a longer time period in a job, organizations can gain a more accurate and informed assessment of their performance. Second, because skill acquisition and development are objectives of moving people through different jobs, it makes sense that longer time in grade will contribute to better skill acquisition, development, and learning than is often the case in fast track systems (Ferris and King, 1991).

Compensation. We have already established that if an organization expects to successfully turn into a flexible organization, it must rely on its human resources to carry out the transition. For this reason, there should be a premium on the caliber of employees, and their compensation should reflect this. In matters of compensation, conventional wisdom is correct when it suggests, "you get what you pay for." So companies should be willing be to pay at least the market value to recruit and maintain a qualified workforce. Not only do premium wages send a positive signal of worth to the employees, from a more pragmatic perspective, they discourage other companies from recruiting that firm's workers.

As alluded to above, the nature of work in a flexible organization is vastly different from that in traditional workplaces. As a result, typical organizational pay schemes such as salaries or hourly wages may be inappropriate for flexible organizations. To reward a flexible workforce, SKILL-BASED PAY DESIGN systems may be a preferred option, since they reflect what is important to the reorganizing efforts.

Much of the focus on flexible organizations pertains to team work and group processes. If reorganized companies pursue this structure, their compensation administration should reflect it as well. Team-based pay motivates the team to excel, and when properly administered, is fair to each of the members. Moreover, proper team-based compensation plans should minimize individual interests over those of the group and discourage detrimental individual behaviors such as grandstanding or free-riding.

Lastly, organizations seek flexibility for the simple reason of being more competitive and more profitable. As a result, tying organizational performance to the salary structure is a logical means to instill the purpose of the reorganization (see PAY FOR PERFORMANCE).

Training and development. Of the responsibilities added to the human resources function, perhaps none is more prevalent than the specialty of training and development. Restructuring and re-engineering demand sophisticated new skills to accommodate new technologies. And because flexible workforces require higher overall skill levels of their workers, training becomes especially vital. Realistically, the human resources function will not be able to keep up with the multitude of technological advancements to provide training from within the human resource function. Instead, organizations will rely on vendors or third party trainers to provide this service. However, it is necessary that the human resources function be actively involved with these transactions to identify training needs and monitor training effectiveness (see TRAINING EVALUATION).

Beyond the basic skill requirements of new technologies, flexible workforces require additional capabilities which are less obvious. While individuals can readily learn how to perform their jobs, they will simultaneously have to learn how to continuously improve their jobs. This is the type of "second-level thinking" that will become an integral component of organizational training programs.

Implications and Conclusion

Flexible organizations have yet to replace traditional structures in the commercial environment, but increasingly we are seeing more firms adopt the characteristics of those presented here. Unfortunately, while attempting to make an organization more flexible is generally desirable, the actual implementation is proving very difficult, as evidenced by disappointing results (Lalli, 1992). For this reason, we see the human resources function as a vital linchpin between the strategy formulation and the implementation. This will require the human resources function to change in concert with the rest of the organization (Whetten et al., 1995), and in the spirit of flexible workforces, it will have to continue adapting to accommodate the changing nature of organizations and business.

Bibliography

Byrne, J. (1993). The horizontal corporation. *Business Week*, **February 8**, 98–102.

Daft, R. L. & Lewin, A. Y. (1993). Where are the theories for the "new" organizational forms: an editorial essay. *Organization Science*, **4**, i–vi.

Ferris, G. R. & King, T. R. (1991) Politics in human resources decisions: a walk on the dark side. *Organizational Dynamics*, **20**, 59–71.

Lalli, F. (1992). Learn from my mistake. *Money*, **February 5**,

Pfeffer, J. (1994). *Competitive Advantage through People*, Boston: Harvard Business School Press.

Ulrich, D. O. & LaFasto, F. (1995). Organizational culture and human resource management. *Handbook of Human Resource Management*, Eds. Ferris, G. R., Rosen, S. D. & Barnum, D. T. Oxford: Blackwell Publishers.

Whetten, D. A., Keiser, J. D. & Urban, T. F. (1995). Implications of organizational downsizing for the human resource management function. *Handbook of Human Resource Management*, Eds.

Ferris, G. R., Rosen, S. D. & Barnum, D. T. Oxford: Blackwell Publishers.

JOHN D. KEISER and GERALD R. FERRIS

workplace security   Workplace security is a programmatic effort by an organization to protect itself, its property (both tangible and intangible), and its members from various unlawful threats such as theft, fraud, sabotage, industrial espionage, terrorism, and WORKPLACE VIOLENCE. Theft (or stealing) is the unauthorized use and/or consumption of organizational resources by employees and/or non-employees. Fraud refers to deceptions deliberately undertaken to secure unfair or illegal gain. Industrial espionage is unethical and/or illegal efforts to learn about another organization's confidential or proprietary plans, procedures, and practices. Terrorism is the unlawful use of force or violence to intimidate or to coerce the organization to respond or react in a certain way. Finally, workplace violence involves significant negative effects on persons or property that occur as a result of aggressive behavior.

Most workplace security programs focus on risk prevention, detection, and intervention. Risk prevention involves the initial planning, design, and implementation of various security systems. Some security systems are highly visible and represent tangible, hardware-based mechanisms. For example, some organizations require visitors to pass through metal detection devices before entering the offices of certain top managers. Traditional burglar alarm systems and video monitoring systems would also fit into this category.

Other systems are more administrative in nature. For example, most larger businesses require that all visitors sign in at a reception desk and secure an identification badge before entering other parts of the organization. Finally, other systems are more indirect in nature. For example, many work settings require that employees enter and leave the organization through one or a few doors. Among other things, this makes it more difficult for employees to steal resources.

Detection refers to mechanisms put into place to alert the organization to a security breach of some form or another. A wide array of detection mechanisms are used. In the case of a hardware-based system, for example, detection results in the activation of an alarm. Administrative control systems provide various channels for detection. For example, if all visitors are required to wear name badges, an individual seen on company premises without such a badge represents a security breach. Observation and other control devices are used to detect security problems in various other contexts.

Intervention refers to what steps, if any, the organization takes if a security problem is detected. In general, the intervention will be closely integrated with the nature and severity of the problem itself. A burglary alarm being set off in the middle of the night, for example, will likely prompt a police investigation. Alternatively, someone on company premises without a name badge might be handled simply by directing the individual back to the reception desk to secure a badge.

Bibliography

Crino, M. D. (1994). Employee sabotage: a random or preventable phenomenon? *Journal of Managerial Issues*, **6**, 311–30.

Gardiner, R. A. & Grassie, R. P. (1994). A comprehensive approach to workplace security. *Security Management*, **38**, 97–102.

Kandel, W. L. (1990). Employee dishonesty and workplace security: precautions about prevention. *Employee Relations Law Journal*, **16**, 217–31.

RICKY W. GRIFFIN

workplace violence   Workplace violence involves significant negative effects on persons or property as a result of organization-motivated aggression. Workplace violence can stem from a variety of sources. In many cases, workplace violence results from the efforts of external individuals or groups attempting to steal organizational resources. The commission of violence in conjunction with an armed robbery attempt would be a common example. Workplace violence is also frequently perpetrated by current or former employees. A former employee who feels unjustly terminated and who returns to the workplace to extract revenge would be an example. Occasionally, workplace violence is committed by an individual who is a personal acquaintance of an organizational member but who himself or herself is not a member of the organization. For example, an estranged spouse might come to the workplace of his or her spouse with the possible consequence of violence. Finally, there are relatively infrequent situations in which the occurrence of workplace violence is a random event. For example, a deranged individual might enter an organization at random and enact violent behavior.

Workplace violence may be targeted in a number of different ways. In some situations, perpetrators wish to do harm to the organization itself, in an abstract manner, and the victims of that harm either are symbols of the organization (e.g. the chief executive officer) or simply happen to have been in the wrong place at the wrong time. In other situations, the target may be a specific individual. For example, an individual who was fired may attempt to do harm to the supervisor or human resource manager whom the aggressor perceives to be the cause of the termination.

Workplace violence is triggered by a number of factors. In most cases, the individual who commits violence has been in a dysfunctional work setting for some time. He or she may have been passed over for promotion, may be experiencing personal difficulties, or may be overly anxious and/or under excessive stress. Specific triggers might be a termination notice, a work-related setback, a disagreement with someone else, or a similar event.

Workplace violence takes a number of forms. The most tragic and public form of violence is murder in the workplace. Assaults, fights, and other physical attacks are also clear examples of workplace violence. In addition, violence can take the form of verbal threats, invasion of personal space, sexual harassment, rape, and other forms of sexual assault, and any other stimulus that results in a threatening work environment.

Organizations that seek to control or minimize the potential for workplace violence have relatively few alternatives. One step they can take is to conduct thorough background checks of new employees. Another step is to closely monitor the processes used to terminate employees and/or provide other forms of negative feedback. Developing and maintaining an adequate WORKPLACE SECURITY system is another method that can be used to decrease the incidence of violence. Finally, organizations can also develop, communicate, and enforce policies and procedures consistent with the prevention of workplace violence. For example, an organization can maintain a policy that striking someone else in the workplace is grounds for immediate dismissal, and can then strictly enforce this policy.

Bibliography

Bandura, A. (1973). *Aggression: a Social Learning Analysis*, Englewood Cliffs, NJ: Prentice-Hall.

Berkowitz, L. (1993). *Aggression: Its Causes, Consequences, and Control*, New York: McGraw-Hill.

O'Leary-Kelly, A. M., Griffin, R. W. & Glew, D. J. (1996). Organization-motivated aggression: a research framework. *Academy of Management Review*.

RICKY W. GRIFFIN

World Intellectual Property Organization (WIPO)   The World Intellectual Property Organization was created in an attempt to coordinate and enforce intellectual property rights agreements between countries. WIPO has been charged with coordination of the following international agreements concerning intellectual property rights: The Berne Convention for the Protection of Literary and Artistic Works of 1866; the Patent Cooperation Treaty of 1970; and the Paris Convention for the Protection of Industrial Property of 1883. WIPO has also coordination

authority for almost twenty other programs or multilateral agreements associated with intellectual property rights protection. WIPO is a special agency of the United Nations.

see also **Berne Convention for the Protection of Literary and Artistic Works; Intellectual Property**

JOHN O'CONNELL

wrongful calling of guarantees   The unfair collection of a letter of credit, on-demand bond, or other guarantee of performance established by a company on behalf of a government. Companies are often required to put up a good faith guarantee of their performance before being allowed to begin work on a contract for a foreign government. For example, a road contractor may be required to provide 10% of the bid amount to a government before the government will agree to the contract. The guarantee is supposed to provide the government with leverage to force the contract to be accomplished on time and in a workman-like manner. Wrongful calling occurs when the government causes non-performance to occur. Cancellation of the contractor's permit to work in a country or restrictions on working hours could result in non-performance, thereby making the guarantee collectible by the government. Such collection is an example of a wrongful calling of a guarantee.

see also **Political risk; Political risk insurance**

JOHN O'CONNELL

zaibatsu structure These concerns formed the basis for the foundation of Japanese industrialization. They developed from a variety of sources, but emerged as highly diversified, family-dominated concerns from the late nineteenth century. Today they would be defined as conglomerates although at the time diversification moves tended to be seen as related, albeit opportunistic in some cases. The businesses within a zaibatsu were not necessarily legally independent concerns, but were sometimes organized as internal divisions (indeed, the Mitsubishi zaibatsu seems to have been the first recorded corporation to adopt a multidivisional structure in 1908, some 15 years before this structure developed in the USA). Nor necessarily were zaibatsu large, although the largest formed the core of Japanese industry. Moreover, not all large Japanese corporations were zaibatsu, with joint stock companies also being relatively undiversified in industries such as power generation and textiles. All of the large concerns were located in one of the major central cities – Tokyo, Osaka, Kobe, and Yokohama – with location being a subsequent influence on corporate evolution.

After the Meiji Restoration in Japan in 1868 eight major zaibatsu groups – Mitsui, Mitsubishi, Sumitomo, Yasuda, Furakawa, Okura, Asamo, and Fujita – had begun to develop. Two further groups, Kuhara and Suzuki, emerged around 1910. These ten concerns exerted substantial influence over the Japanese economy both qualitatively and quantitatively and in the industries in which they operated (and frequently dominated).

The rise of the zaibatsu was based around the concept of the family firm, despite the fact that the joint stock company concept was introduced early in the Meiji period. The main sources of wealth for the founding families which enabled them to embark on their diversification strategies came from profits generated as a result of government patronage and mining. The families invested their fortunes in new activities because of strong internal pressures, in part from family members, such as in the case of the Iwasaki family in Mitsubishi, but mainly from professional managers employed by the concerns.

By the early 1920s all the major zaibatsu had a multisubsidiary form of organization. In this structure, each of the businesses into which the zaibatsu diversified took the form not of a division but of a subsidiary company and, as in a multidivisional structure, each subsidiary functioned autonomously within the framework of the zaibatsu overall policy. This was established by the central office, which controlled the subsidiaries via share ownership. Although historically family businesses, the leading zaibatsu were also progressive in employing more educated managers who guided the affairs of the organization.

The four leading prewar zaibatsu, Mitsubishi, Mitsui, Sumitomo, and Yasuda, accounted for around 24 per cent of all Japanese industry. Created by Iwasaki Yatoro, a low-order samurai, the Mitsubishi zaibatsu was born out of shipping operations and diversified into trading, shipbuild-ing and heavy engineering, and banking and insurance. By 1945, Mitsubishi was engaged in virtually all sectors of manufacturing industry. The Iwasaki family still owned 55.5 per cent of the Mitsubishi Holding Company, which in turn owned more than 52 per cent of the subsidiary and affiliated companies. The Iwasaki family, however, owned directly only 0.4 per cent of subsidiary and affiliated companies. Under Iwasaki, management control was strongly centralized and this tradition continued with his sons. Professional managers were, however, given a great deal of power over operations.

Mitsui was initially concerned with the textile industry and money exchange, and dated back to the late seventeenth century. Following the Meiji Restoration, Mitsui developed with government encouragement as a bank, spinning off its dry goods retail business into a new family branch, Mitsukoshi, which – while outside the Mitsui clan – developed properly as a major retailing organization. Mitsui itself diversified by adding a trading company, which in turn diversified into mining and traded in a wide range of products. By the end of World War II, Mitsui had diversified substantially and consisted of some 22 subsidiary and affiliated companies. The Mitsui family owned some 67 per cent of the group holding company and over 50 per cent of the stocks of all subsidiaries and affiliates. As the group expanded and diversified away from its money exchange activities to become a major zaibatsu, management was passed to professional managers. Indeed, the family imposed a strict rule against the participation of family managers in company management.

The Sumitomo zaibatsu had its roots in copper mining and smelting, but after the Meiji Restoration diversification occurred into metal and commodities trading, shipping, warehousing, and financial services, and other areas of metal processing and timber. By 1946 the Sumitomo family held 29 per cent of the group's holding company and 13 per cent of the subsidiary and affiliated companies. However, the family had gradually dissociated itself from direct management of the businesses, and by the end of World War II Sumitomo was essentially managed by professionals.

The Yasuda zaibatsu, like Mitsui, had its origins as a privileged provider of fiscal services to the government. Founded by a low-rank samurai, Yasuda Zawjuro, at the end of the Tokugawa period, the organization began as a money changing concern before becoming a political merchant. After the Meiji Restoration, Yasuda cooperated with the new government in introducing unconvertible paper money. In 1876, Yasuda created a bank, which became the foundation of the group. Nonfinancial businesses were less significant than in the other three major zaibatsu.

After World War II, the zaibatsu became a target for the occupying powers. Eighty-three zaibatsu holding companies were initially identified for dissolution. This focused on breaking their ownership of banks, subsidiaries, and affiliates, freezing their assets and imposing a capital levy on their wealth. Where family interests remained, these linkages were also broken. The four largest zaibatsu, Mitsubishi, Mitsui, Sumitomo, and Yasuda, voluntarily made dissolution proposals and, to prevent the groups from reforming, US-style anti-monopoly laws were introduced. The deconcentration of 1,200 companies was planned at the end of 1947, but this policy had to be abandoned in the face of Japan's critical economic condition.

In 1957 a final treaty was signed which restored Japan's independence. The post-occupation government, anxious to restore the economy, allowed the former zaibatsu to re-establish links with banks of their former groups; defensive cross-shareholdings began to be established as a protection against acquisition, and soon the former Mitsubishi, Mitsui, and Sumitomo zaibatsu began to come together in the late 1950s. Unlike the prewar zaibatsu, however, these newly emerging groups had no family ownership and no overall holding companies. These new groups were the first of the postwar horizontal keiretsu groups (*see* KEIRETSU STRUCTURE).

Not all of the prewar zaibatsu re-established connections with former related companies. Partially in response to the emergence of the three leading former zaibatsu groups, other keiretsu groups formed around the major city banks, who were key providers of funds for redevelopment. The Yasuda zaibatsu thus reformed in part, to become a key element within the Fuyo group, centered on the Fuji Bank. The other leading keiretsu groups developed around the Sanwa and Dai Ichi Kangyo banks. By the mid-1960s the zaibatsu conglomerates had been superseded by keiretsu groups. The historic family structures of these groups, however, can be seen today to some extent in the evolution of chaebol groups in Korea (*see* CHAEBOL STRUCTURE) and the Chinese family business elsewhere in Asia. By contrast, the concept of family- or clan-based industrial conglomerates has not developed in the West, and an understanding of these two alternate structural modes helps to explain major differences in strategic evolution.

Bibliography

Bisson, T. A. (1954). *Zaibatsu dissolution in Japan*. Berkeley, CA: University of California Press.

Hattori, T. (1989). Japanese zaibatsu and Korean chaebol. In K. H. Chung & H. C. Lee (eds), *Korean managerial dynamics*. New York: Praeger. See pp. 79–88.

Min Chen (1995). *Asian management systems*. London: Routledge.

Morikawa, H. (1992). *Zaibatsu: the rise and fall of family enterprise groups in Japan*. Tokyo: University of Tokyo Press.

DEREK F. CHANNON